Webster's
New Explorer
Student's
Quick Reference

Webster's
New Explorer
Student's
Quick Reference

Created in Cooperation with the Editors of
MERRIAM-WEBSTER

FEDERAL
STREET
PRESS

A Division of Merriam-Webster, Incorporated
Springfield, Massachusetts

This edition published by
Federal Street Press
A Division of Merriam-Webster, Incorporated
P.O. Box 281
Springfield, MA 01102

Federal Street Press books are available for bulk purchase for sales promotion
and premium use. For details write the manager of special sales,
Federal Street Press, P.O. Box 281, Springfield, MA 01102.

Library of Congress Catalog Card Number 99-67809

ISBN 1-892859-14-9

Printed in the United States of America

00 01 02 03 04   5 4 3 2

Contents

Webster's Dictionary

Preface

Webster's Dictionary is a reference to those words that form the very core of the English vocabulary. This dictionary is one of the smallest of the family of dictionaries published by Merriam-Webster. It is intended to serve as a quick reference, especially for questions of spelling, pronunciation, and hyphenation of the most common words in everyday use.

This dictionary shares many details of presentation with the more comprehensive members of the Merriam-Webster family, such as *Merriam-Webster's Collegiate Dictionary, Tenth Edition*. However, conciseness of presentation necessarily requires special treatment of entries, and this book has a number of special features uniquely its own. Users need to be familiar with the following major features of this dictionary.

Main entries follow one another in alphabetical order. Centered periods within the entries show points at which a hyphen may be put when the word is broken at the end of a line.

Homographs (words spelled the same but having different meanings) are run in to a single main entry when they are closely related. Second and succeeding homographs are represented by a swung dash. Homographs of distinctly different origin are given separate entries with preceding raised numerals.

Variant spellings that are quite common appear at the main entry following a comma (as **judg•ment, judge•ment**) and following other boldface entry words, such as inflected forms and run-entries.

Inflected forms of nouns, verbs, adjectives, and adverbs are shown when they are irregular as when requiring the dropping of a final *e* or changing a final *y* to *i* before the suffix (as **waged; waging** at **wage**) or when the form of the base word itself changes (as **rode . . .; rid•den** at **ride**)—or when there might be doubt about their spellings (as pl. **egos** at **ego**). They are given either in full (as **bet•ter; best** at **good**) or cut back to a convenient point of division (as **-ut•ed; -ut•ing** at **dis•tri•bute**). Common variants of inflected forms are shown even if they are regular (as **burst** or **burst•ed** at **burst**). When the inflected forms of a verb involve no irregularity except the coupling of a

final consonant, the double consonant is shown instead of full or cutback inflected forms (as *vb* **-gg-** at **lug**). A variant or inflected form whose alphabetical place is distant from the main entry is entered at its own place with a cross-reference in small capital letters to the main entry (as **hung** *past of* HANG).

Several other kinds of entries are also found in this dictionary. A **run-in entry** is a term related to a main entry that appears within a definition (as **small intestine** at **in•tes•tine**). It is set off by parentheses. Derivative words, made up usually of the main entry and a common word element, such as a suffix, are shown as **undefined run-on entries** following all definitions of a main entry. These are set off by a dash (as—**gar•den•er** at **gar•den**). The meaning of an undefined run-on entry can be inferred from the meaning of the main entry where it appears and that of the added word element, shown elsewhere in the book. A **run-on phrase** is a group of two or more words having the main entry as a major element and having a special meaning of its own (as **in force** at **force** or **look after** at **look**). Run-on phrases are always defined.

Lists of undefined words formed by the addition of a common English prefix to a word entered in the dictionary and having meanings that can be inferred from the meaning of the root word and that of the prefix will be found at entries for the following prefixes: *anti-, bi-, co-, counter-, extra-, hyper-, in-, inter-, mini-, multi-, non-, over-, post-, pre-, re-, self-, sub-, super-, un-,* and *vice-*.

Pronunciation information is either given explicitly or implied for every entry in the dictionary. Where the pronunciation is not indicated at a particular entry, or is indicated in a cutback form, the full pronunciation is to be inferred from an earlier indicated pronunciation.

The grammatical function of entry words is indicated by an italic **functional label** (as *vb, n,* or *prefix*).

Hyphens that are a fixed part of hyphenated compounds such as *self-conscious* are converted to a special "double hyphen" when the compound appears in lightface type and that hyphen comes at the end of a line in this dictionary. This indicates to you that the hyphen is to be retained when the word is not at the end of a line. Fixed hyphens in boldface entry words are shown as short boldface dashes, which are a bit larger than ordinary hyphens. These short dashes or long hyphens in boldface words are retained at the end of a line in this dictionary.

Guide words are used at the tops of pages to indicate the range of entries on those pages. In choosing guide words for a page, we select the alphabetically first and last spelled-out boldface words or phrases on that page. This means that any boldface entry—main entry, variant spelling, inflected form, run-in or run-on entry—can be used as a guide word. Please keep this in mind if the word used as a guide word does not happen to be the first or last main entry on the page. The guide words themselves are in alphabetical order throughout the book, so occasionally it has been necessary to modify this rule. When the alphabetically last entry on one page would come later than the alphabetically first entry on the following page, a different word is chosen as a guide word. On pages that contain a substantial number of undefined words following a prefix entry, that prefix may be used as the first or last guide word.

All **abbreviations** that are used in this book are listed, along with a number of other common abbreviations, in a special section immediately following the dictionary proper.

A

¹a \'ā\ *n, pl* **a's** *or* **as** \'āz\ : 1st letter of the alphabet

²a \ə, 'ā\ *indefinite article* : one or some—used to indicate an unspecified or unidentified individual

aard·vark \'ärd,värk\ *n* : ant-eating African mammal

aback \ə'bak\ *adv* : by surprise

aba·cus \'abəkəs\ *n, pl* **aba·ci** \'abə,sī, -,kē\ *or* **aba·cus·es** : calculating instrument using rows of beads

abaft \ə'baft\ *adv* : toward or at the stern

ab·a·lo·ne \,abə'lōnē\ *n* : large edible shellfish

¹aban·don \ə'bandən\ *vb* : give up without intent to reclaim —**aban·don·ment** *n*

²abandon *n* : thorough yielding to impulses

aban·doned \ə'bandənd\ *adj* : morally unrestrained

abase \ə'bās\ *vb* **abased; abas·ing** : lower in dignity —**abase·ment** *n*

abash \ə'bash\ *vb* : embarrass —**abash·ment** *n*

abate \ə'bāt\ *vb* **abat·ed; abat·ing** : decrease or lessen

abate·ment \ə'bātmənt\ *n* : tax reduction

ab·at·toir \'abə,twär\ *n* : slaughterhouse

ab·bess \'abəs\ *n* : head of a convent

ab·bey \'abē\ *n, pl* **-beys** : monastery or convent

ab·bot \'abət\ *n* : head of a monastery

ab·bre·vi·ate \ə'brēvē,āt\ *vb* **-at·ed; -at·ing** : shorten —**ab·bre·vi·a·tion** \ə,brēvē-'āshən\ *n*

ab·di·cate \'abdi,kāt\ *vb* **-cat·ed; -cating** : renounce —**ab·di·ca·tion** \,abdi-'kāshən\ *n*

ab·do·men \'abdəmən, ab'dōmən\ *n* **1** : body area between chest and pelvis **2** : hindmost part of an insect —**ab·dom·i·nal** \ab'dämən³l\ *adj* —**ab·dom·i·nal·ly** *adv*

ab·duct \ab'dəkt\ *vb* : kidnap —**ab·duc·tion** \-'dəkshən\ *n* —**ab·duc·tor** \-tər\ *n*

abed \ə'bed\ *adv or adj* : in bed

ab·er·ra·tion \,abə'rāshən\ *n* : deviation or distortion —**ab·er·rant** \a'berənt\ *adj*

abet \ə'bet\ *vb* **-tt-** : incite or encourage —**abet·tor, abet·ter** \-ər\ *n*

abey·ance \ə'bāəns\ *n* : state of inactivity

ab·hor \əb'hor, ab-\ *vb* **-rr-** : hate —**ab·hor·rence** \-əns\ *n* —**ab·hor·rent** \-ənt\ *adj*

abide \ə'bīd\ *vb* **abode** \-'bōd\ *or* **abid·ed; abid·ing 1** : endure **2** : remain, last, or reside

ab·ject \'ab,jekt, ab'-\ *adj* : low in spirit or hope —**ab·jec·tion** \ab'jekshən\ *n* —**ab·ject·ly** *adv* —**ab·ject·ness** *n*

ab·jure \ab'júr\ *vb* **1** : renounce **2** : abstain from —**ab·ju·ra·tion** \,abjə'rāshən\ *n*

ablaze \ə'blāz\ *adj or adv* : on fire

able \'ābəl\ *adj* **abler** \-blər\; **ablest** \-bləst\ **1** : having sufficient power, skill, or resources **2** : skilled or efficient —**abil·i·ty** \ə'bilətē\ *n* —**ably** \'āblē\ *adv*

-able, -ible \əbəl\ *adj suffix* **1** : capable of, fit for, or worthy of **2** : tending, given, or liable to

ab·lu·tion \ə'blüshən, a'blü-\ *n* : washing of one's body

ab·ne·gate \'abni,gāt\ *vb* **-gat·ed; -gating 1** : relinquish **2** : renounce —**ab·ne·ga·tion** \,abni'gāshən\ *n*

ab·nor·mal \ab'nórməl\ *adj* : deviating from the normal or average —**ab·nor·mal·i·ty** \,abnər'malətē, -,nór-\ *n* —**ab·nor·mal·ly** *adv*

aboard \ə'bōrd\ *adv* : on, onto, or within a car, ship, or aircraft ~ *prep* : on or within a

abode \ə'bōd\ *n* : residence

abol·ish \ə'bälish\ *vb* : do away with —**ab·o·li·tion** \,abə'lishən\ *n*

abom·i·na·ble \ə'bämənəbəl\ *adj* : thoroughly unpleasant or revolting

abom·i·nate \ə'bämə,nāt\ *vb* **-nat·ed; -nating** : hate —**abom·i·na·tion** \ə,bämə-'nāshən\ *n*

---

ab·orig·i·nal \,abə'rijənəl\ *adj* **1** : original **2** : primitive

ab·orig·i·ne \-'rijənē\ *n* : original inhabitant

abort \ə'bórt\ *vb* : terminate prematurely —**abor·tive** \-'bórtiv\ *adj*

abor·tion \ə'bórshən\ *n* : spontaneous or induced termination of pregnancy

abound \ə'baúnd\ *vb* : be plentiful

about \ə'baút\ *adv* : around ~ *prep* **1** : on every side of **2** : on the verge of **3** : having as a subject

above \ə'bəv\ *adv* : in or to a higher place ~ *prep* **1** : in or to a higher place than **2** : more than

above·board *adv or adj* : without deception

abrade \ə'brād\ *vb* **abrad·ed; abrading** : wear away by rubbing —**abrasion** \-'brāzhən\ *n*

abra·sive \ə'brāsiv\ *n* : substance for grinding, smoothing, or polishing ~ *adj* **1** : tending to abrade **2** : causing irritation —**abra·sive·ly** *adv* —**abra·sive·ness** *n*

abreast \ə'brest\ *adv or adj* **1** : side by side **2** : up to a standard or level

abridge \ə'brij\ *vb* **abridged; abridging** : shorten or condense —**abridgment, abridge·ment** *n*

abroad \ə'bród\ *adv or adj* **1** : over a wide area **2** : outside one's country

ab·ro·gate \'abrə,gāt\ *vb* **-gat·ed; -gating** : annul or revoke —**ab·ro·ga·tion** \,abrə'gāshən\ *n*

abrupt \ə'brəpt\ *adj* **1** : sudden **2** : so quick as to seem rude —**abrupt·ly** *adv*

ab·scess \'ab,ses\ *n* : collection of pus surrounded by inflamed tissue —**abscessed** \-,sest\ *adj*

ab·scond \ab'skänd\ *vb* : run away and hide

ab·sent \'absənt\ *adj* : not present ~ **absent** \ab'sent\ *vb* : keep oneself away —**absence** \'absəns\ *n* —**absen·tee** \,absən'tē\ *n*

ab·sent·mind·ed \,absənt'mīndəd\ *adj* : unaware of one's surroundings or action —**ab·sent·mind·ed·ly** *adv* —**ab·sent·mind·ed·ness** *n*

ab·so·lute \'absə,lüt, ,absə'-\ *adj* **1** : pure **2** : free from restriction **3** : definite —**ab·so·lute·ly** *adv*

ab·so·lu·tion \,absə'lüshən\ *n* : remission of sins

ab·solve \əb'zälv, -'sälv\ *vb* **-solved; -solving** : set free of the consequences of guilt

ab·sorb \əb'sórb, -'zórb\ *vb* **1** : suck up or take in as a sponge does **2** : engage (one's attention) —**ab·sor·ben·cy** \-'sórbənsē, -'zór-\ *n* —**ab·sor·bent** \-bənt\ *adj or n* —**ab·sorb·ing** *adj* —**ab·sorb·ing·ly** *adv*

ab·sorp·tion \əb'sórpshən, -'zórp-\ *n* : process of absorbing —**ab·sorp·tive** \-tiv\ *adj*

ab·stain \əb'stān\ *vb* : refrain from doing something —**ab·stain·er** *n* —**ab·sten·tion** \-'stenchən\ *n* —**ab·sti·nence** \'abstə-nəns\ *n*

ab·ste·mi·ous \ab'stēmēəs\ *adj* : sparing in use of food or drink —**ab·ste·mi·ous·ly** *adv* —**ab·ste·mi·ous·ness** *n*

ab·stract \ab'strakt, 'ab,-\ *adj* **1** : expressing a quality apart from an object **2** : not representing something specific ~ \'ab,-\ *n* : summary ~ \ab'-, 'ab,-\ *vb* **1** : remove or separate **2** : make an abstract of —**ab·stract·ly** *adv* —**ab·stract·ness** *n*

ab·strac·tion \ab'strakshən\ *n* **1** : act of abstracting **2** : abstract idea or work of art

ab·struse \əb'strüs, ab-\ *adj* : hard to understand —**ab·struse·ly** *adv* —**ab·struse·ness** *n*

ab·surd \əb'sərd, -'zərd\ *adj* : ridiculous or unreasonable —**ab·sur·di·ty** \-ətē\ *n* —**ab·surd·ly** *adv*

abun·dant \ə'bəndənt\ *adj* : more than enough —**abun·dance** \-dəns\ *n* —**abun·dant·ly** *adv*

abuse \ə'byüz\ *vb* **abused; abus·ing 1** : misuse **2** : mistreat **3** : attack with words ~ \-'byüs\ *n* **1** : corrupt practice **2**

: improper use **3** : mistreatment **4** : coarse and insulting speech —**abus·er** *n* —**abu·sive** \-'byüsiv\ *adj* —**abu·sive·ly** *adv* —**abu·sive·ness** *n*

abut \ə'bət\ *vb* **-tt-** : touch along a border —**abut·ter** *n*

abut·ment \ə'bətmənt\ *n* : part of a bridge that supports weight

abys·mal \ə'bizməl\ *adj* **1** : immeasurably deep **2** : wretched —**abys·mal·ly** *adv*

abyss \ə'bis\ *n* : immeasurably deep gulf

-ac \,ak\ *n suffix* : one affected with

aca·cia \ə'kāshə\ *n* : leguminous tree or shrub

ac·a·dem·ic \,akə'demik\ *adj* **1** : relating to schools or colleges **2** : theoretical —**academic** *n* —**ac·a·dem·i·cal·ly** \-iklē\ *adv*

acad·e·my \ə'kadəmē\ *n, pl* **-mies 1** : private high school **2** : society of scholars or artists

acan·thus \ə'kanthəs\ *n, pl* **acanthus 1** : prickly Mediterranean herb **2** : ornament representing acanthus leaves

ac·cede \ak'sēd\ *vb* **-ced·ed; -ced·ing 1** : become a party to an agreement **2** : express approval **3** : enter upon an office

ac·cel·er·ate \ik'selə,rāt, ak-\ *vb* **-at·ed; -ating 1** : bring about earlier **2** : speed up —**ac·cel·er·a·tion** \-,selə'rāshən\ *n*

ac·cel·er·a·tor \ik'selə,rātər, ak-\ *n* : pedal for controlling the speed of a motor vehicle

ac·cent \'ak,sent\ *n* **1** : distinctive manner of pronunciation **2** : prominence given to one syllable of a word **3** : mark (as ´, `, ˆ) over a vowel in writing or printing to indicate pronunciation ~ \'ak,-, ak'-\ *vb* : emphasize —**ac·cen·tu·al** \ak'senchə-wəl\ *adj*

ac·cen·tu·ate \ak'senchə,wāt\ *vb* **-at·ed; -ating** : stress or show off by a contrast —**ac·cen·tu·a·tion** \-,senchə'wāshən\ *n*

ac·cept \ik'sept, ak-\ *vb* **1** : receive willingly **2** : agree to —**ac·cept·abil·i·ty** \ik-,septə'bilətē, ak-\ *n* —**ac·cept·able** \-'septəbəl\ *adj* —**ac·cep·tance** \-'septəns\ *n*

ac·cess \'ak,ses\ *n* : capability or way of approaching —**ac·ces·si·bil·i·ty** \ik,sesə-'bilətē, ak-\ *n* —**ac·ces·si·ble** \-'sesə-bəl\ *adj*

ac·ces·sion \ik'seshən, ak-\ *n* **1** : something added **2** : act of taking office

ac·ces·so·ry \ik'sesərē, ak-\ *n, pl* **-ries 1** : nonessential addition **2** : one guilty of aiding a criminal —**accessory** *adj*

ac·ci·dent \'aksədənt\ *n* **1** : event occurring by chance or unintentionally **2** : chance —**ac·ci·den·tal** \,aksə'dent³l\ *adj* —**ac·ci·den·tal·ly** *adv*

ac·claim \ə'klām\ *vb or n* : praise

ac·cla·ma·tion \,aklə'māshən\ *n* **1** : eager applause **2** : unanimous vote

ac·cli·mate \'aklə,māt, ə'klīmət\ *vb* **-mat·ed; -mat·ing** : acclimatize —**ac·cli·ma·tion** \,aklə'māshən, -,klī-\ *n*

ac·cli·ma·tize \ə'klīmə,tīz\ *vb* **-tized; -tizing** : accustom to a new climate or situation —**ac·cli·ma·ti·za·tion** \-,klīmətə'zāshən\ *n*

ac·co·lade \,akə,lād\ *n* : expression of praise

ac·com·mo·date \ə'kämə,dāt\ *vb* **-dat·ed; -dat·ing 1** : adapt **2** : provide with something needed **3** : hold without crowding

ac·com·mo·da·tion \ə,kämə'dāshən\ *n* **1** : quarters—usu. pl. **2** : act of accommodating

ac·com·pa·ny \ə'kəmpənē\ *vb* **-nied; -nying 1** : go or occur with **2** : play supporting music —**ac·com·pa·ni·ment** \-nəmənt\ *n* —**ac·com·pa·nist** \-nist\ *n*

ac·com·plice \ə'kämpləs, -'kəm-\ *n* : associate in crime

ac·com·plish \ə'kämplish, -'kəm-\ *vb* : do, fulfill, or bring about —**ac·com·plished** *adj* —**ac·com·plish·er** *n* —**ac·com·plish·ment** *n*

ac·cord \ə'kórd\ *vb* **1** : grant **2** : agree ~ *n*

---

1 : agreement **2** : willingness to act —**ac·cor·dance** \-'kórd³ns\ *n* —**ac·cor·dant** \-³nt\ *adj*

ac·cord·ing·ly \ə'kórdiŋlē\ *adv* : consequently

according to *prep* **1** : in conformity with **2** : as stated by

ac·cor·di·on \ə'kórdēən\ *n* : keyboard instrument with a bellows and reeds ~ *adj* : folding like an accordion bellows —**ac·cor·di·on·ist** \-nist\ *n*

ac·cost \ə'kóst\ *vb* : approach and speak to esp. aggressively

ac·count \ə'kaúnt\ *n* **1** : statement of business transactions **2** : credit arrangement with a vendor **3** : report **4** : worth **5** : sum deposited in a bank ~ *vb* : give an explanation

ac·count·able \ə'kaúntəbəl\ *adj* : responsible —**ac·count·abil·i·ty** \-,kaúntə'bil-ətē\ *n*

ac·coun·tant \ə'kaúnt³nt\ *n* : one skilled in accounting —**ac·coun·tan·cy** \-³nsē\ *n*

ac·count·ing \ə'kaúntiŋ\ *n* : financial record keeping

ac·cou·tre, ac·cou·ter \ə'kütər\ *vb* **-tred** *or* **-tered; -tring** *or* **-ter·ing** \-'kütəriŋ, -'kütriŋ\ : equip

ac·cou·tre·ment, ac·cou·ter·ment \ə'kütrə-mənt, -'kütər-\ *n* **1** : accessory item—usu. pl. **2** : identifying characteristic

ac·cred·it \ə'kredət\ *vb* **1** : approve officially **2** : attribute —**ac·cred·i·ta·tion** \-,kredə'tāshən\ *n*

ac·crue \ə'krü\ *vb* **-crued; -cru·ing** : be added by periodic growth —**ac·cru·al** \-əl\ *n*

ac·cu·mu·late \ə'kyümyə,lāt\ *vb* **-lat·ed; -lat·ing** : collect or pile up —**ac·cu·mu·la·tion** \-,kyümyə'lāshən\ *n* —**ac·cu·mu·la·tor** \-'kyümyə,lātər\ *n*

ac·cu·rate \'akyərət\ *adj* : free from error —**ac·cu·ra·cy** \-rəsē\ *n* —**ac·cu·rate·ly** *adv* —**ac·cu·rate·ness** *n*

ac·cursed \ə'kərst, -'kərsəd\, **ac·curst** \ə'kərst\ *adj* **1** : being under a curse **2** : damnable

ac·cuse \ə'kyüz\ *vb* **-cused; -cus·ing** : charge with an offense —**ac·cu·sa·tion** \,akyə'zāshən\ *n* —**ac·cus·er** *n*

ac·cused \ə'kyüzd\ *n, pl* **-cused** : defendant in a criminal case

ac·cus·tom \ə'kəstəm\ *vb* : make familiar through use or experience

ace \'ās\ *n* : one that excels

acer·bic \ə'sərbik, a-\ *adj* : sour or biting in temper, mood, or tone

acet·amin·o·phen \ə,sētə'minəfən\ *n* : pain reliever

ac·e·tate \'asə,tāt\ *n* : fabric or plastic derived from acetic acid

ace·tic acid \ə'sētik-\ *n* : acid found in vinegar

acet·y·lene \ə'set³l,ən, -³l,ēn\ *n* : colorless gas used as a fuel in welding

ache \'āk\ *vb* **ached; ach·ing 1** : suffer a dull persistent pain **2** : yearn —**ache** *n*

achieve \ə'chēv\ *vb* **achieved; achieving** : gain by work or effort —**achieve·ment** *n* —**achiev·er** *n*

ac·id \'asəd\ *adj* **1** : sour or biting to the taste **2** : sharp in manner **3** : of or relating to an acid ~ *n* : sour water-soluble chemical compound that reacts with a base to form a salt —**ac·id·ic** \ə'sidik\ *adj* —**acid·i·fy** \ə'sidə,fī\ *vb* —**acid·i·ty** \-ətē\ *n* —**ac·id·ly** *adv*

ac·knowl·edge \ik'nälij, ak-\ *vb* **-edged; -edg·ing 1** : admit as true **2** : admit the authority of **3** : express thanks for —**ac·knowl·edg·ment** *n*

ac·me \'akmē\ *n* : highest point

ac·ne \'aknē\ *n* : skin disorder marked esp. by pimples

ac·o·lyte \'akə,līt\ *n* : assistant to a member of clergy in a religious service

acorn \'ā,kórn, -kərn\ *n* : nut of the oak

acous·tic \ə'küstik\ *adj* : relating to hearing

or sound —**acous·ti·cal** \-stikəl\ *adj* —
acous·ti·cal·ly \-klē\ *adv*
acous·tics \ə'küstiks\ *n sing or pl* **1** : science of sound **2** : qualities in a room that affect how sound is heard
ac·quaint \ə'kwānt\ *vb* **1** : inform **2** : make familiar
ac·quain·tance \ə'kwānt³ns\ *n* **1** : personal knowledge **2** : person with whom one is acquainted —**ac·quain·tance·ship** *n*
ac·qui·esce \,akwē'es\ *vb* **-esced; -esc·ing** : consent or submit —**ac·qui·es·cence** \-'es³ns\ *n* —**ac·qui·es·cent** \-³nt\ *adj or n* —**ac·qui·es·cent·ly** *adv*
ac·quire \ə'kwīr\ *vb* **-quired; -quir·ing** : gain
ac·qui·si·tion \,akwə'zishən\ *n* : a gaining or something gained —**acqui·si·tive** \ə'kwizətiv\ *adj*
ac·quit \ə'kwit\ *vb* **-tt-** **1** : pronounce not guilty **2** : conduct (oneself) usu. well —**ac·quit·tal** \-³l\ *n*
acre \'ākər\ *n* **1** *pl* : lands **2** : 4840 square yards
acre·age \'ākərij\ *n* : area in acres
ac·rid \'akrəd\ *adj* : sharp and biting —**ac·rid·i·ty** \a'kridətē, ə-\ *n* —**ac·rid·ly** *adv* —**ac·rid·ness** *n*
ac·ri·mo·ny \'akrə,mōnē\ *n, pl* **-nies** : harshness of language or feeling —**ac·ri·mo·ni·ous** \,akrə'mōnēəs\ *adj* —**ac·ri·mo·ni·ous·ly** *adv*
ac·ro·bat \'akrə,bat\ *n* : performer of tumbling feats —**ac·ro·bat·ic** \,akrə'batik\ *adj*
across \ə'kròs\ *adv* : to or on the opposite side ~ *prep* **1** : to or on the opposite side of **2** : so as to cross
acryl·ic \ə'krilik\ *n* **1** : plastic used for molded parts or in paints **2** : synthetic textile fiber
act \'akt\ *n* **1** : thing done **2** : law **3** : main division of a play ~ *vb* **1** : perform in a play **2** : conduct oneself **3** : operate **4** : produce an effect
ac·tion \'akshən\ *n* **1** : legal proceeding **2** : manner or method of performing **3** : activity **4** : thing done over a period of time or in stages **5** : combat **6** : events of a literary plot **7** : operating mechanism
ac·ti·vate \'aktə,vāt\ *vb* **-vat·ed; -vat·ing** : make active or reactive —**ac·ti·va·tion** \,aktə'vāshən\ *n*
ac·tive \'aktiv\ *adj* **1** : causing action or change **2** : lively, vigorous, or energetic **3** : erupting or likely to erupt **4** : now in operation —**active** *n* —**ac·tive·ly** *adv*
ac·tiv·i·ty \ak'tivətē\ *n, pl* **-ties** **1** : quality or state of being active **2** : what one is actively doing
ac·tor \'aktər\ *n* : one that acts
ac·tress \'aktrəs\ *n* : woman who acts in plays
ac·tu·al \'akchəwəl\ *adj* : really existing —**ac·tu·al·i·ty** \,akchə'walətē\ *n* —**ac·tu·al·iza·tion** \,akchəwələ'zāshən\ *n* —**ac·tu·al·ize** \'akchəwə,līz\ *vb* —**ac·tu·al·ly** *adv*
ac·tu·ary \'akchə,werē\ *n, pl* **-ar·ies** : one who calculates insurance risks and premiums —**ac·tu·ar·i·al** \,akchə'werēəl\ *adj*
ac·tu·ate \'akchə,wāt\ *vb* **-at·ed; -at·ing** : put into action —**ac·tu·a·tor** \-,wātər\ *n*
acu·men \ə'kyümən\ *n* : mental keenness
acu·punc·ture \'akyu,pəŋkchər\ *n* : treatment by puncturing the body with needles —**acu·punc·tur·ist** \,akyu'pəŋkchərist\ *n*
acute \ə'kyüt\ *adj* **acut·er; acut·est** **1** : sharp **2** : containing less than 90 degrees **3** : mentally alert **4** : severe —**acute·ly** *adv* —**acute·ness** *n*
ad \'ad\ *n* : advertisement
ad·age \'adij\ *n* : old familiar saying
ad·a·mant \'adəmənt, -,mant\ *adj* : insistent —**ad·a·mant·ly** *adv*
adapt \ə'dapt\ *vb* : adjust to be suitable for a new use or condition —**adapt·abil·i·ty** \ə,daptə'bilatē\ *n* —**adapt·able** *adj* —**ad·ap·ta·tion** \,ad,ap'tāshən, -əp-\ *n* —**adapt·er** *n* —**adap·tive** \'daptiv\ *adj*
add \'ad\ *vb* **1** : join to something else so as to increase in amount **2** : say further **3** : find a sum —**ad·di·tion** \ə'dishən\ *n*
ad·der \'adər\ *n* **1** : poisonous European snake **2** : No. American snake
ad·dict \'adikt\ *n* : one who is psychologically or physiologically dependent (as on a drug) ~ \ə'dikt\ *vb* : cause to become an addict —**ad·dic·tion** \ə'dikshən\ *n* —**ad·dic·tive** \-'diktiv\ *adj*
ad·di·tion·al \ə'dishənəl\ *adj* : existing as a result of adding —**ad·di·tion·al·ly** *adv*
ad·di·tive \'adətiv\ *n* : substance added to another
ad·dle \'ad³l\ *vb* **-dled; -dling** : confuse
ad·dress \ə'dres\ *vb* **1** : direct one's remarks to **2** : mark an address on ~ \ə'dres, 'ad,res\ *n* **1** : formal speech **2** : place where a person may be reached or mail may be delivered
ad·duce \ə'düs, -'dyüs\ *vb* **-duced; -duc·ing** : offer as proof
ad·e·noid \'ad,nòid, -³nòid\ *n* : enlarged tis-

sue near the opening of the nose into the throat —usu. pl. —**adenoid, ad·e·noi·dal** \-³l\ *adj*
adept \ə'dept\ *adj* : highly skilled —**adept·ly** *adv* —**adept·ness** *n*
ad·e·quate \'adikwət\ *adj* : good or plentiful enough —**ad·e·qua·cy** \-kwəsē\ *n* —**ad·e·quate·ly** *adv*
ad·here \ad'hir, əd-\ *vb* **-hered; -her·ing** **1** : remain loyal **2** : stick fast —**ad·her·ence** \-'hirəns\ *n* —**ad·her·ent** \-ənt\ *adj or n*
ad·he·sion \ad'hēzhən, əd-\ *n* : act or state of adhering
ad·he·sive \-'hēsiv, -ziv\ *adj* : tending to adhere ~ *n* : adhesive substance
adieu \ə'dü, -'dyü\ *n, pl* **adieus** *or* **adieux** \-'düz,-'dyüz\ : farewell
ad·ja·cent \ə'jās³nt\ *adj* : situated near or next
ad·jec·tive \'ajiktiv\ *n* : word that serves as a modifier of a noun —**ad·jec·ti·val** \,ajik'tīvəl\ *adj* —**ad·jec·ti·val·ly** *adv*
ad·join \ə'jòin\ *vb* : be next to
ad·journ \ə'jərn\ *vb* : end a meeting —**ad·journ·ment** *n*
ad·judge \ə'jəj\ *vb* **-judged; -judg·ing** **1** : think or pronounce to be **2** : award by judicial decision
ad·ju·di·cate \ə'jüdi,kāt\ *vb* **-cat·ed; -cat·ing** : settle judicially —**ad·ju·di·ca·tion** \ə,jüdi'kāshən\ *n*
ad·junct \'aj,əŋkt\ *n* : something joined or added but not essential
ad·just \ə'jəst\ *vb* : fix, adapt, or set right —**ad·just·able** *adj* —**ad·just·er, ad·jus·tor** \ə'jəstər\ *n* —**ad·just·ment** \-mənt\ *n*
ad·ju·tant \'ajətənt\ *n* : aide esp. to a commanding officer
ad-lib \'ad'lib\ *vb* **-bb-** : speak without preparation —**ad-lib** *n or adj*
ad·min·is·ter \ad'minəstər\ *vb* **1** : manage **2** : give out esp. in doses —**ad·min·is·tra·ble** \-strəbəl\ *adj* —**ad·min·is·trant** \-strənt\ *n*
ad·min·is·tra·tion \ad,minə'strāshən, ad-\ *n* **1** : process of managing **2** : persons responsible for managing —**ad·min·is·tra·tive** \əd'minə,strātiv\ *adj* —**ad·min·is·tra·tive·ly** *adv*
ad·min·is·tra·tor \əd'minə,strātər\ *n* : one that manages
ad·mi·ra·ble \'admərəbəl\ *adj* : worthy of admiration —**ad·mi·ra·bly** \-blē\ *adv*
ad·mi·ral \'admərəl\ *n* : commissioned officer in the navy ranking next below a fleet admiral
ad·mire \əd'mīr\ *vb* **-mired; -mir·ing** : have high regard for —**ad·mi·ra·tion** \,admə'rāshən\ *n* —**ad·mir·er** *n* —**ad·mir·ing·ly** *adv*
ad·mis·si·ble \əd'misəbəl\ *adj* : that can be permitted —**ad·mis·si·bil·i·ty** \-,misə'bilətē\ *n*
ad·mis·sion \əd'mishən\ *n* **1** : act of admitting **2** : admittance or a fee paid for this **3** : acknowledgment of a fact
ad·mit \əd'mit\ *vb* **-tt-** **1** : allow to enter **2** : permit **3** : recognize as genuine —**ad·mit·ted·ly** *adv*
ad·mit·tance \əd'mit³ns\ *n* : permission to enter
ad·mix·ture \ad'mikschər\ *n* **1** : thing added in mixing **2** : mixture
ad·mon·ish \ad'mänish\ *vb* : rebuke —**ad·mon·ish·ment** \-mənt\ *n* —**ad·mo·ni·tion** \,admə'nishən\ *n* —**ad·mon·i·to·ry** \ad'mänə,tōrē\ *adj*
ado \ə'dü\ *n* **1** : fuss **2** : trouble
ado·be \ə'dōbē\ *n* : sun-dried building brick
ad·o·les·cence \,ad³l'es³ns\ *n* : period of growth between childhood and maturity —**ad·o·les·cent** \-³nt\ *adj or n*
adopt \ə'däpt\ *vb* **1** : take (a child of other parents) as one's own child **2** : take up and practice as one's own —**adop·tion** \-'däpshən\ *n*
adore \ə'dōr\ *vb* **adored; ador·ing** **1** : worship **2** : be extremely fond of —**ador·able** *adj* —**ador·ably** *adv* —**ad·o·ra·tion** \,adə'rāshən\ *n*
adorn \ə'dòrn\ *vb* : decorate with ornaments —**adorn·ment** *n*
adrift \ə'drift\ *adv or adj* **1** : afloat without motive power or moorings **2** : without guidance or purpose
adroit \ə'dròit\ *adj* : dexterous or shrewd —**adroit·ly** *adv* —**adroit·ness** *n*
adult \ə'dəlt, 'ad,əlt\ *adj* : fully developed and mature ~ *n* : grown-up person —**adult·hood** *n*
adul·ter·ate \ə'dəltə,rāt\ *vb* **-at·ed; -ating** : make impure by mixture —**adul·ter·a·tion** \-,dəltə'rāshən\ *n*
adul·tery \ə'dəltərē\ *n, pl* **-ter·ies** : sexual unfaithfulness of a married person —**adul·ter·er** \-tərər\ *n* —**adul·ter·ess** \-tərəs\ *n* —**adul·ter·ous** \-tərəs\ *adj*
ad·vance \əd'vans\ *vb* **-vanced; -vancing** **1** : bring or move forward **2** : promote **3** : lend ~ *n* **1** : forward movement **2** : improvement **3** : offer ~ *adj* : being ahead of time —**advance·ment** *n*

position **2** : benefit or gain —**ad·van·ta·geous** \,ad,van'tājəs, -vən-\ *adj* —**ad·van·ta·geous·ly** *adv*
ad·vent \'ad,vent\ *n* **1** *cap* : period before Christmas **2** : a coming into being or use
ad·ven·ti·tious \,advən'tishəs\ *adj* : accidental —**ad·ven·ti·tious·ly** *adv*
ad·ven·ture \əd'venchər\ *n* **1** : risky undertaking **2** : exciting experience —**ad·ven·tur·er** \-chərər\ *n* —**ad·ven·ture·some** \-chərsəm\ *adj* —**ad·ven·tur·ous** \-chərəs\ *adj*
ad·verb \'ad,vərb\ *n* : word that modifies a verb, an adjective, or another adverb —**ad·ver·bi·al** \ad'vərbēəl\ *adj* —**ad·ver·bi·al·ly** *adv*
ad·ver·sary \'advər,serē\ *n, pl* **-sar·ies** : enemy or rival —**adversary** *adj*
ad·verse \ad'vərs, 'ad-,\ *adj* : opposing or unfavorable —**ad·verse·ly** *adv*
ad·ver·si·ty \ad'vərsətē\ *n, pl* **-ties** : hard times
ad·vert \ad'vərt\ *vb* : refer
ad·ver·tise \'advər,tīz\ *vb* **-tised; -tis·ing** : call public attention to —**ad·ver·tise·ment** \,advər'tīzmənt, əd'vərtəzmənt\ *n* —**ad·ver·tis·er** *n*
ad·ver·tis·ing \'advər,tīziŋ\ *n* : business of preparing advertisements
ad·vice \əd'vīs\ *n* : recommendation with regard to a course of action
ad·vis·able \əd'vīzəbəl\ *adj* : wise or prudent —**ad·vis·abil·i·ty** \-,vīzə'bilətē\ *n*
ad·vise \əd'vīz\ *vb* **-vised; -vis·ing** : give advice to —**ad·vis·er, ad·vis·or** \-'vīzər\ *n*
ad·vise·ment \əd'vīzmənt\ *n* : careful consideration
ad·vi·so·ry \əd'vīzərē\ *adj* : having power to advise
ad·vo·cate \'advəkət, -,kāt\ *n* : one who argues or pleads for a cause or proposal ~ \-,kāt\ *vb* **-cat·ed; -cat·ing** : recommend —**ad·vo·ca·cy** \-vəkəsē\ *n*
adze \'adz\ *n* : tool for shaping wood
ae·gis \'ējəs\ *n* **1** : protection or sponsorship
ae·on \'ēən, 'ē,än\ *n* : indefinitely long time
aer·ate \'ar,āt\ *vb* **-at·ed; -at·ing** : supply or impregnate with air —**aer·a·tion** \ar'āshən\ *n* —**aer·a·tor** \'ar,ātər\ *n*
ae·ri·al \'arēəl\ *adj* : inhabiting, occurring in, or done in the air ~ *n* : antenna
ae·rie \'irē, 'erē\ *n* : eagle's nest
aer·o·bic \ar'ōbik\ *adj* : using or needing oxygen
aer·o·bics \-biks\ *n sing or pl* : exercises that produce a marked increase in respiration and heart rate
aero·dy·nam·ics \,arōdī'namiks\ *n* : science of bodies in motion in a gas —**aero·dy·nam·ic** \-ik\ *adj* —**aero·dy·nam·i·cal·ly** \-iklē\ *adv*
aero·nau·tics \,arə'nòtiks\ *n* : science dealing with aircraft —**aero·nau·ti·cal** \-ikəl\ *adj*
aero·sol \'arə,säl, -,sòl\ *n* **1** : liquid or solid particles suspended in a gas **2** : substance sprayed as an aerosol
aero·space \'arō,spās\ *n* : earth's atmosphere and the space beyond —**aero·space** *adj*
aes·thet·ic \es'thetik\ *adj* : relating to beauty —**aes·thet·i·cal·ly** \-iklē\ *adv*
aes·thet·ics \-'thetiks\ *n* : branch of philosophy dealing with beauty
afar \ə'fär\ *adv* : from, at, or to a great distance —**afar** *n*
af·fa·ble \'afəbəl\ *adj* : easy to talk to —**af·fa·bil·i·ty** \,afə'bilətē\ *n* —**af·fa·bly** \'afəblē\ *adv*
af·fair \ə'far\ *n* : something that relates to or involves one
[1]**af·fect** \ə'fekt, a-\ *vb* : assume for effect —**af·fec·ta·tion** \,af,ek'tāshən\ *n*
[2]**affect** *vb* : produce an effect on
af·fect·ed \ə'fektəd, a-\ *adj* **1** : pretending to some trait **2** : artificially assumed to impress —**af·fect·ed·ly** *adv*
af·fect·ing \ə'fektiŋ, a-\ *adj* : arousing pity or sorrow —**af·fect·ing·ly** *adv*
af·fec·tion \ə'fekshən\ *n* : kind or loving feeling —**af·fec·tion·ate** \-shənət\ *adj* —**af·fec·tion·ate·ly** *adv*
af·fi·da·vit \,afə'dāvət\ *n* : sworn statement
af·fil·i·ate \ə'filē,āt\ *vb* **-at·ed; -at·ing** : become a member or branch —**af·fil·i·ate** \-ēət\ *n* —**af·fil·i·a·tion** \-,filē'āshən\ *n*
af·fin·i·ty \ə'finətē\ *n, pl* **-ties** : close attraction or relationship
af·firm \ə'fərm\ *vb* : assert positively —**af·fir·ma·tion** \,afər'māshən\ *n*
af·fir·ma·tive \ə'fərmətiv\ *adj* : asserting the truth or existence of something ~ *n* : statement of affirmation or agreement
af·fix \ə'fiks\ *vb* : attach
af·flict \ə'flikt\ *vb* : cause pain and distress to —**af·flic·tion** \-'flikshən\ *n*
af·flu·ence \'af,lüəns, ə'flü-, ə-\ *n* : wealth —**af·flu·ent** \-ənt\ *adj*
af·ford \ə'fōrd\ *vb* **1** : manage to bear the cost of **2** : provide
af·fray \ə'frā\ *n* : fight
af·front \ə'frənt\ *vb or n* : insult

af·ghan \'af,gan, -gən\ *n* : crocheted or knitted blanket
afire \ə'fīr\ *adj or adv* : being on fire
aflame \ə'flām\ *adj or adv* : flaming
afloat \ə'flōt\ *adj or adv* : floating
afoot \ə'fůt\ *adv or adj* **1** : on foot **2** : in progress
afore·said \ə'fōr,sed\ *adj* : said or named before
afraid \ə'frād, South also ə'fred\ *adj* : filled with fear
afresh \ə'fresh\ *adv* : anew
aft \'aft\ *adv* : to or toward the stern or tail
af·ter \'aftər\ *adv* : at a later time ~ *prep* **1** : behind in place or time **2** : in pursuit of ~ *conj* : following the time when ~ *adj* **1** : later **2** : located toward the back
af·ter·life \'aftər,līf\ *n* : existence after death
af·ter·math \-,math\ *n* : results
af·ter·noon \,aftər'nün\ *n* : time between noon and evening
af·ter·thought *n* : later thought
af·ter·ward \'aftərwərd\, **af·ter·wards** \-wərdz\ *adv* : at a later time
again \ə'gen, -'gin\ *adv* **1** : once more **2** : on the other hand **3** : in addition
against \ə'genst\ *prep* **1** : directly opposite to **2** : in opposition to **3** : so as to touch or strike
agape \ə'gāp, -'gap\ *adj or adv* : having the mouth open in astonishment
ag·ate \'agət\ *n* : quartz with bands or masses of various colors
age \'āj\ *n* **1** : length of time of life or existence **2** : particular time in life (as majority or the latter part) **3** : quality of being old **4** : long time **5** : period in history ~ *vb* : become old or mature
-age \ij\ *n suffix* **1** : aggregate **2** : action or process **3** : result of **4** : rate of **5** : place of **6** : state or rank **7** : fee
aged \'ājəd\ *adj* : old **2** \'ājd\ : allowed to mature
age·less \'ājləs\ *adj* : eternal
agen·cy \'ājənsē\ *n, pl* **-cies** **1** : one through which something is accomplished **2** : office or function of an agent **3** : government administrative division
agen·da \ə'jendə\ *n* : list of things to be done
agent \'ājənt\ *n* **1** : means **2** : person acting or doing business for another
ag·gran·dize \ə'gran,dīz, 'agrən-\ *vb* **-dized; -diz·ing** : make great or greater —**ag·gran·dize·ment** \ə'grandəzmənt, -,dīz-, ,agrən'dīz-\ *n*
ag·gra·vate \'agrə,vāt\ *vb* **-vat·ed; -vating** **1** : make more severe **2** : irritate —**ag·gra·va·tion** \,agrə'vāshən\ *n*
ag·gre·gate \'agrigət\ *adj* : formed into a mass ~ \-,gāt\ *vb* **-gat·ed; -gat·ing** : collect into a mass ~ \-gət\ *n* **1** : mass **2** : whole amount
ag·gres·sion \ə'greshən\ *n* **1** : unprovoked attack **2** : hostile behavior —**ag·gres·sor** \-'gresər\ *n*
ag·gres·sive \ə'gresiv\ *adj* **1** : easily provoked to fight **2** : hard working and enterprising —**ag·gres·sive·ly** *adv* —**ag·gres·sive·ness** *n*
ag·grieve \ə'grēv\ *vb* **-grieved; -grieving** **1** : cause grief to **2** : inflict injury on
aghast \ə'gast\ *adj* : struck with amazement or horror
ag·ile \'ajəl\ *adj* : able to move quickly and easily —**agil·i·ty** \ə'jilətē\ *n*
ag·i·tate \'ajə,tāt\ *vb* **-tat·ed; -tat·ing** **1** : shake or stir back and forth **2** : excite or trouble the mind of **3** : try to arouse public feeling —**ag·i·ta·tion** \,ajə'tāshən\ *n* —**ag·i·ta·tor** \'ajə,tātər\ *n*
ag·nos·tic \ag'nästik, əg-\ *n* : one who doubts the existence of God
ago \ə'gō\ *adj or adv* : earlier than the present
agog \ə'gäg\ *adj* : full of excitement
ag·o·nize \'agə,nīz\ *vb* **-nized; -niz·ing** : suffer mental agony —**ag·o·niz·ing·ly** *adv*
ag·o·ny \'agənē\ *n, pl* **-nies** : extreme pain or mental distress
agrar·i·an \ə'grerēən\ *adj* : relating to land ownership or farming interests —**agrarian** *n* —**agrar·i·an·ism** *n*
agree \ə'grē\ *vb* **agreed; agree·ing** **1** : be of the same opinion **2** : express willingness **3** : get along together **4** : be similar **5** : be appropriate, suitable, or healthful
agree·able \-əbəl\ *adj* **1** : pleasing **2** : willing to give approval —**agreeable·ness** *n* —**agree·ably** *adv*
agree·ment \-mənt\ *n* **1** : harmony of opinion or purpose **2** : mutual understanding or arrangement
ag·ri·cul·ture \'agri,kəlchər\ *n* : farming —**ag·ri·cul·tur·al** \,agri'kəlchərəl\ *adj* —**ag·ri·cul·tur·ist** \-rist\, **ag·ri·cul·tur·al·ist** \-rəlist\ *n*
aground \ə'graůnd\ *adv or adj* : on or onto the bottom or shore
ague \'āgyü\ *n* **1** : fever with recurrent chills and sweating **2** : malaria
ahead \ə'hed\ *adv or adj* **1** : in or toward

the front **2** : into or for the future **3** : in a more advantageous position

ahead of prep **1** : in front or advance of **2** : in excess of

ahoy \ə'hȯi\ interj —used in hailing

aid \'ād\ vb : provide help or support ~ n : help

aide \'ād\ n : helper

AIDS \'ādz\ n : serious disease of the human immune system

ail \'āl\ vb **1** : trouble **2** : be ill

ai•le•ron \'ālə,rän\ n : movable part of an airplane wing

ail•ment \'ālmənt\ n : bodily disorder

aim \'ām\ vb **1** : point or direct (as a weapon) **2** : direct one's efforts ~ n **1** : an aiming or the direction of aiming **2** : object or purpose —**aim•less** adj —**aim•less•ly** adv —**aim•less•ness** n

air \'ar\ n **1** : mixture of gases surrounding the earth **2** : melody **3** : outward appearance **4** : artificial manner **5** : compressed air **6** : travel by or use of aircraft **7** : medium of transmission of radio waves ~ vb **1** : expose to the air **2** : broadcast —**air•borne** \-,bōrn\ adj

air–condition vb : equip with an apparatus (**air conditioner**) for filtering and cooling the air

air•craft n, pl aircraft : craft that flies

Aire•dale terrier \'ar,dāl-\ n : large terrier with a hard wiry coat

air•field n : airport or its landing field

air force n : military organization for conducting warfare by air

air•lift n : a transporting of esp. emergency supplies by aircraft —**airlift** vb

air•line n : air transportation system —**air•lin•er** n

air•mail n : system of transporting mail by airplane —**airmail** vb

air•man \-mən\ n **1** : aviator **2** : enlisted man in the air force in one of the 3 ranks below sergeant **3** : enlisted man in the air force ranking just below airman first class

airman basic n : enlisted man of the lowest rank in the air force

airman first class n : enlisted man in the air force ranking just below sergeant

air•plane n : fixed-wing aircraft heavier than air

air•port n : place for landing aircraft and usu. for receiving passengers

air•ship n : powered lighter-than-air aircraft

air•strip n : airfield runway

air•tight adj : tightly sealed to prevent flow of air

air•waves \'ar,wāvz\ n pl : medium of transmission of radio waves

airy \'arē\ adj **air•i•er; -est** **1** : delicate **2** : breezy

aisle \'īl\ n : passage between sections of seats

ajar \ə'jär\ adj or adv : partly open

akim•bo \ə'kimbō\ adj or adv : having the hand on the hip and the elbow turned outward

akin \ə'kin\ adj **1** : related by blood **2** : similar in kind

-al \əl\ adj suffix : of, relating to, or characterized by

al•a•bas•ter \'alə,bastər\ n : white or translucent mineral

alac•ri•ty \ə'lakrətē\ n : cheerful readiness

alarm \ə'lärm\ n **1** : warning signal or device **2** : fear at sudden danger ~ vb **1** : warn **2** : frighten

alas \ə'las\ interj —used to express unhappiness, pity, or concern

al•ba•tross \'albə,trȯs, -,träs\ n, pl -tross or -trosses : large seabird

al•be•it \ȯl'bēət, al-\ conj : even though

al•bi•no \al'bīnō\ n, pl -nos : person or animal with abnormally white skin —**al•bi•nism** \'albə,nizəm\ n

al•bum \'albəm\ n **1** : book for displaying a collection (as of photographs) **2** : collection of recordings

al•bu•men \al'byümən\ n **1** : white of an egg **2** : albumin

al•bu•min \-mən\ n : protein found in blood, milk, egg white, and tissues

al•che•my \'alkəmē\ n : medieval chemistry —**al•che•mist** \'alkəmist\ n

al•co•hol \'alkə,hȯl\ n **1** : intoxicating agent in liquor **2** : liquor —**alcoholic** adj

al•co•hol•ic \,alkə'hȯlik, -'häl-\ n : person affected with alcoholism

al•co•hol•ism \'alkə,hȯl,izəm\ n : addiction to alcoholic beverages

al•cove \'al,kōv\ n : recess in a room or wall

al•der•man \'ȯldərmən\ n : city official

ale \'āl\ n : beerlike beverage —**alehouse** n

alert \ə'lərt\ adj **1** : watchful **2** : quick to perceive and act ~ n : alarm ~ vb : warn —**alert•ly** adv —**alert•ness** n

ale•wife n : fish of the herring family

al•fal•fa \al'falfə\ n : cloverlike forage plant

al•ga \'algə\ n, pl -gae \-gē\ : any of a group of lower plants that includes seaweed —**al•gal** \-gəl\ adj

al•ge•bra \'aljəbrə\ n : branch of mathematics using symbols —**al•ge•bra•ic** \,aljə'brāik\ adj —**al•ge•bra•i•cal•ly** \-'brāəklē\ adv

alias \'ālēəs, 'ālyəs\ adv : otherwise called ~ n : assumed name

al•i•bi \'alə,bī\ n **1** : defense of having been elsewhere when a crime was committed **2** : justification ~ vb -bied; -bi•ing : offer an excuse

alien \'ālēən, 'ālyən\ adj : foreign ~ n **1** : foreign-born resident **2** : extraterrestrial

alien•ate \'ālēə,nāt, 'ālyə-\ vb -at•ed; -at•ing : cause to be no longer friendly —**alien•ation** \,ālēə'nāshən, ,ālyə-\ n

alight \ə'līt\ vb : dismount

align \ə'līn\ vb : bring into line —**align•er** n —**align•ment** n

alike \ə'līk\ adj : identical or very similar ~ adv : equally

al•i•men•ta•ry \,alə'mentərē\ adj : relating to or functioning in nutrition

al•i•mo•ny \'alə,mōnē\ n, pl -nies : money paid to a separated or divorced spouse

alive \ə'līv\ adj **1** : having life **2** : lively or animated

al•ka•li \'alkə,lī\ n, pl -lies or -lis : strong chemical base —**al•ka•line** \-kələn, -,līn\ adj —**al•ka•lin•i•ty** \,alkə'linətē\ n

all \'ȯl\ adj **1** : the whole of **2** : greatest possible **3** : every one of ~ adv **1** : wholly **2** : so much **3** : for each side ~ pron **1** : whole number or amount **2** : everything or everyone

Al•lah \'älə, 'al-\ n : God of Islam

all–around adj : versatile

al•lay \ə'lā\ vb **1** : alleviate **2** : calm

al•lege \ə'lej\ vb -leged; -leg•ing : assert without proof —**al•le•ga•tion** \,ali-'gāshən\ n —**al•leg•ed•ly** \ə'lejədlē\ adv

al•le•giance \ə'lējəns\ n : loyalty

al•le•go•ry \'alə,gōrē\ n, pl -ries : story in which figures and actions are symbols of general truths —**al•le•gor•i•cal** \,alə'gōri-kəl\ adj

al•le•lu•ia \,alə'lüyə\ interj : hallelujah

al•ler•gen \'alərjən\ n : something that causes allergy —**al•ler•gen•ic** \,alər'je-nik\ adj

al•ler•gy \'alərjē\ n, pl -gies : abnormal reaction to a substance —**al•ler•gic** \ə'lərjik\ adj —**al•ler•gist** \'alərjist\ n

al•le•vi•ate \ə'lēvē,āt\ vb -at•ed; -at•ing : relieve or lessen —**al•le•vi•a•tion** \ə,lēvē'āshən\ n

al•ley \'alē\ n, pl -leys **1** : place for bowling **2** : narrow passage between buildings

al•li•ance \ə'līəns\ n : association

al•li•ga•tor \'alə,gātər\ n : large aquatic reptile related to the crocodiles

al•lit•er•a•tion \ə,litə'rāshən\ n : repetition of initial sounds of words —**al•lit•er•a•tive** \-'litə,rātiv\ adj

al•lo•cate \'alə,kāt\ vb -cat•ed; -cat•ing : assign —**al•lo•ca•tion** \,alə'kāshən\ n

al•lot \ə'lät\ vb -tt- : distribute as a share —**al•lot•ment** n

al•low \ə'laů\ vb **1** : admit or concede **2** : permit —**al•low•able** adj

al•low•ance \-əns\ n **1** : allotted share **2** : money given regularly for expenses

al•loy \'al,ȯi\ n : metals melted together —**al•loy** \ə'lȯi\ vb

all right adv or adj **1** : satisfactorily **2** : yes **3** : certainly

all•spice \'ȯl,spīs\ n : berry of a West Indian tree made into a spice

al•lude \ə'lüd\ vb -lud•ed; -lud•ing : refer indirectly —**al•lu•sion** \-'lüzhən\ n —**al•lu•sive** \-'lüsiv\ adj —**al•lu•sive•ly** adv —**al•lu•sive•ness** n

al•lure \ə'lůr\ vb -lured; -lur•ing : entice ~ n : attractive power

al•ly \ə'lī, 'al,ī\ vb -lied; -ly•ing : enter into an alliance —**al•ly** \'al,ī, ə'lī\ n

-al•ly \əlē\ adv suffix : -ly

al•ma•nac \'ȯlmə,nak, 'al-\ n : annual information book

al•mighty \ȯl'mītē\ adj : having absolute power

al•mond \'ämənd, 'am-, 'alm-, 'älm-\ n : tree with nutlike fruit kernels

al•most \'ȯl,mōst, ȯl-\ adv : very nearly

alms \'ämz, 'älmz, 'almz\ n, pl alms : charitable gift

aloft \ə'lȯft\ adv : high in the air

alo•ha \ä'lōhä\ interj —used to greet or bid farewell

alone \ə'lōn\ adj **1** : separated from others **2** : not including anyone or anything else —**alone** adv

along \ə'lȯŋ\ prep **1** : in line with the direction of **2** : at a point on or during ~ adv **1** : forward **2** : as a companion **3** : all the time

along•side adv or prep : along or by the side

alongside of prep : alongside

aloof \ə'lüf\ adj : indifferent and reserved —**aloof•ness** n

aloud \ə'laůd\ adv : so as to be heard

al•paca \al'pakə\ n **1** : So. American mammal related to the llama **2** : alpaca wool or cloth made of this

al•pha•bet \'alfə,bet, -bət\ n : ordered set of letters of a language —**al•pha•bet•i•cal** \,alfə'betikəl\, **al•pha•bet•ic** \-'betik\ adj —**al•pha•bet•i•cal•ly** \-'betikəlē\ adv

al•pha•bet•ize \'alfəbə,tīz\ vb -ized; -izing : arrange in alphabetical order —**al•pha•bet•iz•er** n

al•ready \ȯl'redē\ adv : by a given time

al•so \'ȯlsō\ adv : in addition

al•tar \'ȯltər\ n : structure for rituals

al•ter•ca•tion \,ȯltər'kāshən\ n : dispute

al•ter•nate \'ȯltərnət, 'al-\ adj **1** : arranged or succeeding by turns **2** : every other ~ \-,nāt\ vb -nat•ed; -nat•ing : occur or cause to occur by turns ~ \-nət\ n : substitute —**al•ter•nate•ly** adv —**al•ter•na•tion** \,ȯltər'nāshən, ,al-\ n

alternating current n : electric current that regularly reverses direction

al•ter•na•tive \ȯl'tərnətiv, al-\ adj : offering a choice —**alternative** n

al•ter•na•tor \'ȯltər,nātər, 'al-\ n : alternating-current generator

al•though \ȯl'thō\ conj : even though

al•tim•e•ter \al'timətər, 'altə,mētər\ n : instrument for measuring altitude

al•ti•tude \'altə,tüd, -,tyüd\ n **1** : distance up from the ground **2** : angular distance above the horizon

al•to \'altō\ n, pl -tos : lower female choral voice

al•to•geth•er \,ȯltə'gethər\ adv **1** : wholly **2** : on the whole

al•tru•ism \'altrú,izəm\ n : concern for others —**al•tru•ist** \-ist\ n —**al•tru•is•tic** \,altrú'istik\ adj —**al•tru•is•ti•cal•ly** \-tiklē\ adv

al•um \'aləm\ n : crystalline compound containing aluminum

alu•mi•num \ə'lümənəm\ n : silver-white malleable ductile light metallic element

alum•na \ə'ləmnə\ n, pl -nae \-,nē\ : woman graduate

alum•nus \ə'ləmnəs\ n, pl -ni \-,nī\ : graduate

al•ways \'ȯlwēz, -wəz\ adv **1** : at all times **2** : forever

am pres 1st sing of BE

amal•gam \ə'malgəm\ n **1** : mercury alloy **2** : mixture

amal•gam•ate \ə'malgə,māt\ vb -at•ed; -at•ing : unite —**amal•ga•ma•tion** \-,malgə'māshən\ n

am•a•ryl•lis \,amə'riləs\ n : bulbous herb with clusters of large colored flowers like lilies

amass \ə'mas\ vb : gather

am•a•teur \'amə,tər, -,tůr, -,tyůr, -,chůr, -chər\ n **1** : person who does something for pleasure rather than for pay **2** : person who is not expert —**am•a•teurish** \,amə'tərish, -'tůr-, -'tyůr-\ adj —**am•a•teur•ism** \'amə,tər,izəm, -,tůr-, -,tyůr-, -,chůr-, -chər-\ n

am•a•to•ry \'amə,tōrē\ adj : of or expressing sexual love

amaze \ə'māz\ vb amazed; amaz•ing : fill with wonder —**amaze•ment** n —**amaz•ing•ly** adv

am•a•zon \'amə,zän, -zən\ n : tall strong woman —**am•a•zo•ni•an** \,amə'zōnēən\ adj

am•bas•sa•dor \am'basədər\ n : representative esp. of a government —**am•bas•sa•do•ri•al** \-,basə'dōrēəl\ adj —**am•bas•sa•dor•ship** n

am•ber \'ambər\ n : yellowish fossil resin or its color

am•ber•gris \'ambər,gris, -,grēs\ n : waxy substance from certain whales used in making perfumes

am•bi•dex•trous \,ambi'dekstrəs\ adj : equally skilled with both hands —**am•bi•dex•trous•ly** adv

am•bi•ence, am•bi•ance \'ambēəns, 'ämbē,äns\ n : pervading atmosphere

am•big•u•ous \am'bigyəwəs\ adj : having more than one interpretation —**am•bi•gu•i•ty** \,ambə'gyüətē\ n

am•bi•tion \am'bishən\ n : eager desire for success or power —**am•bi•tious** \-shəs\ adj —**am•bi•tious•ly** adv

am•biv•a•lence \am'bivələns\ n : simultaneous attraction and repulsion —**am•biv•a•lent** \-lənt\ adj

am•ble \'ambəl\ vb -bled; -bling : go at a leisurely gait —**amble** n

am•bu•lance \'ambyələns\ n : vehicle for carrying injured or sick persons

am•bu•la•to•ry \'ambyələ,tōrē\ adj **1** : relating to or adapted to walking **2** : able to walk about

am•bush \'am,bůsh\ n : trap by which a surprise attack is made from a place of hiding —**ambush** vb

ame•lio•rate \ə'mēlyə,rāt\ vb -rat•ed; -rat•ing : make or grow better —**ame•lio•ra•tion** \-,mēlyə'rāshən\ n

amen \'ā'men, 'ä-\ interj —used for affirmation esp. at the end of prayers

ame•na•ble \ə'mēnəbəl, -'men-\ adj : ready to yield or be influenced

amend \ə'mend\ vb **1** : improve **2** : alter in writing

amend•ment \-mənt\ n : change made in a formal document (as a law)

amends \ə'mendz\ n sing or pl : compensation for injury or loss

ame•ni•ty \ə'menətē, -'mē-\ n, pl -ties **1** : agreeableness **2** pl : social conventions **3** : something serving to comfort or accommodate

am•e•thyst \'aməthəst\ n : purple gemstone

ami•a•ble \'āmēəbəl\ adj : easy to get along with —**ami•a•bil•i•ty** \,āmēə'bilətē\ n —**ami•a•bly** \'āmēəblē\ adv

am•i•ca•ble \'amikəbəl\ adj : friendly —**am•i•ca•bly** \-blē\ adv

amid \ə'mid\, **amidst** \-'midst\ prep : in or into the middle of

amino acid \ə'mēnō-\ n : nitrogen-containing acid

amiss \ə'mis\ adv : in the wrong way ~ adj : wrong

am•me•ter \'am,ētər\ n : instrument for measuring electric current

am•mo•nia \ə'mōnyə\ n **1** : colorless gaseous compound of nitrogen and hydrogen **2** : solution of ammonia in water

am•mu•ni•tion \,amyə'nishən\ n **1** : projectiles fired from guns **2** : explosive items used in war

am•ne•sia \am'nēzhə\ n : sudden loss of memory —**am•ne•si•ac** \-zē,ak, -zhē-\, **am•ne•sic** \-zik, -sik\ adj or n

am•nes•ty \'amnəstē\ n, pl -ties : a pardon for a group —**amnesty** vb

amoe•ba \ə'mēbə\ n, pl -bas or -bae \-,bē\ : tiny one-celled animal that occurs esp. in water —**amoe•bic** \-bik\ adj

amok \ə'mək, -'mäk\ adv : in a violent or uncontrolled way

among \ə'məŋ\ prep **1** : in or through **2** : in the number or class of **3** : in shares to each of

am•o•rous \'amərəs\ adj **1** : inclined to love **2** : being in love **3** : indicative of love —**am•o•rous•ly** adv —**am•o•rous•ness** n

amor•phous \ə'mȯrfəs\ adj : shapeless

amor•tize \'amər,tīz, ə'mȯr-\ vb -tized; -tiz•ing : get rid of (as a debt) gradually with periodic payments —**amor•ti•za•tion** \,amərtə'zāshən, ə,mȯrt-\ n

amount \ə'maůnt\ vb **1** : be equivalent **2** : reach a total ~ n : total number or quantity

amour \ə'můr, ä-, a-\ n **1** : love affair **2** : lover

am•pere \'am,pir\ n : unit of electric current

am•per•sand \'ampər,sand\ n : character & used for the word and

am•phib•i•ous \am'fibēəs\ adj **1** : able to live both on land and in water **2** : adapted for both land and water —**am•phib•i•an** \-ən\ n

am•phi•the•ater \'amfə,thēətər\ n : oval or circular structure with rising tiers of seats around an arena

am•ple \'ampəl\ adj -pler \-plər\; -plest \-pləst\ **1** : large **2** : sufficient —**amply** \-plē\ adv

am•pli•fy \'amplə,fī\ vb -fied; -fy•ing : make louder, stronger, or more thorough —**am•pli•fi•ca•tion** \,ampləfə'kāshən\ n —**am•pli•fi•er** \'amplə,fīər\ n

am•pli•tude \-,tüd, -,tyüd\ n **1** : fullness **2** : extent of a vibratory movement

am•pu•tate \'ampyə,tāt\ vb -tat•ed; -tating : cut off (a body part) —**am•pu•ta•tion** \,ampyə'tāshən\ n —**am•pu•tee** \,ampyə'tē\ n

amuck \ə'mək\ var of AMOK

am•u•let \'amyələt\ n : ornament worn as a charm against evil

amuse \ə'myüz\ vb amused; amus•ing **1** : engage the attention of in an interesting and pleasant way **2** : make laugh —**amuse•ment** n

an \ən, 'an\ indefinite article : a —used before words beginning with a vowel sound

-an \ən\, **-ian** \ēən\, **-ean** \ēən\ n suffix **1** : one that belongs to **2** : one skilled in ~ adj suffix **1** : of or belonging to **2** : characteristic of or resembling

anach•ro•nism \ə'nakrə,nizəm\ n : one that is chronologically out of place —**anach•ro•nis•tic** \ə,nakrə'nistik\ adj

an•a•con•da \,anə'kändə\ n : large So. American snake

ana•gram \'anə,gram\ n : word or phrase made by transposing the letters of another word or phrase

anal \'ānəl\ adj : relating to the anus

an•al•ge•sic \,anəl'jēzik, -sik\ n : pain reliever

anal•o•gy \ə'naləjē\ n, pl -gies **1** : similarity between unlike things **2** : example of something similar —**ana•log•i•cal** \,anə'läjikəl\ adj —**ana•log•i•cal•ly** \-iklē\ adv —**anal•o•gous** \ə'naləgəs\ adj

anal•y•sis \ə'naləsəs\ n, pl -y•ses \-,sēz\ **1** : examination of a thing to determine its parts **2** : psychoanalysis —**an•a•lyst** \'an³list\ n —**an•a•lyt•ic** \,an³l'itik\, **an•a•lyt•i•cal** \-ikəl\ adj —**an•a•lyt•i•cal•ly** \-iklē\ adv

an•a•lyze \'an³l,īz\ vb -lyzed; -lyz•ing : make an analysis of

an·ar·chism \'anər,kizəm, -,när-\ n : theory that all government is undesirable —**an·ar·chist** \-kist\ n or adj —**an·ar·chis·tic** \anər'kistik\ adj

an·ar·chy \'anərkē, -,när-\ n : lack of government or order —**an·ar·chic** \a'närkik\ adj —**an·ar·chi·cal·ly** \-iklē\ adv

anath·e·ma \ə'nathəmə\ n 1 : solemn curse 2 : person or thing accursed or intensely disliked

anat·o·my \ə'natəmē\ n, pl -mies : science dealing with the structure of organisms —**an·a·tom·ic** \anə'tämik\, **an·a·tom·i·cal** \-ikəl\ adj —**an·a·tom·i·cal·ly** adv —**anat·o·mist** \ə'natəmist\ n

-ance \əns\ n suffix 1 : action or process 2 : quality or state 3 : amount or degree

an·ces·tor \'an,sestər\ n : one from whom an individual is descended

an·ces·tress \-trəs\ n : female ancestor

an·ces·try \-trē\ n 1 : line of descent 2 : ancestors —**an·ces·tral** \an'sestrəl\ adj

an·chor \'aŋkər\ n : heavy device that catches in the sea bottom to hold a ship in place ~ vb : hold or become held in place by or as if by an anchor —**an·chor·age** \-kərij\ n

an·chor·man \'aŋkər,man\ n : news broadcast coordinator

an·cho·vy \'an,chōvē, an'chō-\ n, pl -vies or -vy : small herringlike fish

an·cient \'änshənt\ adj 1 : having existed for many years 2 : belonging to times long past —**ancient** n

-ancy \ənsē\ n suffix : quality or state

and \ənd, 'and\ conj —used to indicate connection or addition

and·iron \'an,dīərn\ n : one of 2 metal supports for wood in a fireplace

an·drog·y·nous \an'dräjənəs\ adj 1 : having characteristics of both male and female 2 : suitable for either sex

an·ec·dote \'anik,dōt\ n : brief story —**an·ec·dot·al** \anik'dōt°l\ adj

ane·mia \ə'nēmēə\ n : blood deficiency —**ane·mic** \ə'nēmik\ adj

anem·o·ne \ə'nemənē\ n : small herb with showy usu. white flowers

an·es·the·sia \anəs'thēzhə\ n : loss of bodily sensation

an·es·thet·ic \anəs'thetik\ n : agent that produces anesthesia —**anesthetic** adj —**anes·the·tist** \ə'nesthətist\ n —**anes·the·tize** \-thə,tīz\ vb

anew \ə'nü, -'nyü\ adv : over again

an·gel \'ānjəl\ n : spiritual being superior to humans —**an·gel·ic** \an'jelik\, **an·gel·i·cal** \-ikəl\ adj —**an·gel·i·cal·ly** adv

an·ger \'aŋgər\ n : strong feeling of displeasure ~ vb : make angry

an·gi·na \an'jīnə\ n : painful disorder of heart muscles —**an·gi·nal** \an'jīn°l\ adj

¹an·gle \'aŋgəl\ n 1 : figure formed by the meeting of 2 lines in a point 2 : sharp corner 3 : point of view ~ vb -gled; -gling : turn or direct at an angle

²angle vb an·gled; an·gling : fish with a hook and line —**an·gler** \-glər\ n —**an·gle·worm** n —**angling** n

an·go·ra \aŋ'gōrə, an-\ n : yarn or cloth made from the hair of an Angora goat or rabbit

an·gry \'aŋgrē\ adj -gri·er; -est : feeling or showing anger —**an·gri·ly** \-grəlē\ adv

an·guish \'aŋgwish\ n : extreme pain or distress of mind —**an·guished** \-gwisht\ adj

an·gu·lar \'aŋgyələr\ adj 1 : having many or sharp angles 2 : thin and bony —**an·gu·lar·i·ty** \aŋgyə'larətē\ n

an·i·mal \'anəməl\ n 1 : living being capable of feeling and voluntary motion 2 : lower animal as distinguished from humans

an·i·mate \'anəmət\ adj : having life ~ \-,māt\ vb -mat·ed; -mat·ing 1 : give life or vigor to 2 : make appear to move —**an·i·mat·ed** adj

an·i·ma·tion \anə'māshən\ n 1 : liveliness 2 : animated cartoon

an·i·mos·i·ty \anə'mäsətē\ n, pl -ties : resentment

an·i·mus \'anəməs\ n : deep-seated hostility

an·ise \'anəs\ n : herb related to the carrot with aromatic seeds (**an·iseed** \-,sēd\) used in flavoring

an·kle \'aŋkəl\ n : joint or region between the foot and the leg —**an·kle·bone** n

an·nals \'an°lz\ n pl : chronological record of history —**an·nal·ist** \-°list\ n

an·neal \ə'nēl\ vb 1 : make less brittle by heating and then cooling 2 : strengthen or toughen

an·nex \ə'neks, 'an,eks\ vb : assume political control over (a territory) ~ \'an,eks, -iks\ n : added building —**an·nex·a·tion** \an,ek'sāshən\ n

an·ni·hi·late \ə'nīə,lāt\ vb -lat·ed; -lating : destroy —**an·ni·hi·la·tion** \-,nīə'lāshən\ n

an·ni·ver·sa·ry \anə'vərsərē\ n, pl -ries : annual return of the date of a notable event or its celebration

an·no·tate \'anə,tāt\ vb -tat·ed; -tat·ing : furnish with notes —**an·no·ta·tion**

\anə'tāshən\ n —**an·no·ta·tor** \'anə,tā-tər\ n

an·nounce \ə'nauns\ vb -nounced; -nouncing : make known publicly —**an·nounce·ment** n —**an·nounc·er** n

an·noy \ə'nói\ vb : disturb or irritate —**an·noy·ance** \-əns\ n —**an·noy·ing·ly** \-'nóiŋlē\ adv

an·nu·al \'anyəwəl\ adj 1 : occurring once a year 2 : living only one year —**annual** n —**an·nu·al·ly** adv

an·nu·ity \ə'nüətē, -'nyü-\ n, pl -ties : amount payable annually or the right to such a payment

an·nul \ə'nəl\ vb -ll- : make legally void —**an·nul·ment** n

an·ode \'an,ōd\ n 1 : positive electrode 2 : negative battery terminal —**an·od·ic** \a'nädik\ adj

anoint \ə'nóint\ vb : apply oil to as a rite —**anoint·ment** n

anom·a·ly \ə'näməlē\ n, pl -lies : something abnormal or unusual —**anom·a·lous** \ə'nämələs\ adj

anon·y·mous \ə'nänəməs\ adj : of unknown origin —**an·o·nym·i·ty** \anə'nimətē\ n —**anon·y·mous·ly** adv

an·oth·er \ə'nəthər\ adj 1 : any or some other 2 : one more ~ pron 1 : one more 2 : one different

an·swer \'ansər\ n 1 : something spoken or written in reply to a question 2 : solution to a problem ~ vb 1 : reply to 2 : be responsible 3 : be adequate —**an·swer·er** n

an·swer·able \-rəbəl\ adj : responsible

ant \'ant\ n : small social insect —**anthill** n

-ant \ənt\ n suffix 1 : one that performs or causes an action 2 : thing that is acted upon — adj suffix 1 : performing an action or being in a condition 2 : causing an action or process

an·tag·o·nism \an'tagə,nizəm\ n : active opposition or hostility —**an·tag·o·nist** \-ənist\ n —**an·tag·o·nis·tic** \-,tagə'nis-tik\ adj

an·tag·o·nize \an'tagə,nīz\ vb -nized; -nizing : cause to be hostile

ant·arc·tic \ant'ärktik, -'ärtik\ adj : relating to the region near the south pole

antarctic circle n : circle parallel to the equator approximately 23°27′ from the south pole

an·te·bel·lum \anti'beləm\ adj : existing before the U.S. Civil War

an·te·ced·ent \antə'sēd°nt\ n : one that comes before —**antecedent** adj

an·te·lope \'ant°l,ōp\ n, pl -lope or -lopes : deerlike mammal related to the ox

an·ten·na \an'tenə\ n, pl -nae \-,nē\ or -nas 1 : one of the long slender paired sensory organs on the head of an arthropod 2 pl -nas : metallic device for sending or receiving radio waves

an·te·ri·or \an'tirēər\ adj : located before in place or time

an·them \'anthəm\ n : song or hymn of praise or gladness

an·ther \'anthər\ n : part of a seed plant that contains pollen

an·thol·o·gy \an'thäləjē\ n, pl -gies : literary collection

an·thra·cite \'anthrə,sīt\ n : hard coal

an·thro·poid \'anthrə,póid\ n : large ape —**anthropoid** adj

an·thro·pol·o·gy \anthrə'päləjē\ n : science dealing with humans —**an·thro·po·log·i·cal** \-pə'läjikəl\ adj —**an·thro·pol·o·gist** \-'päləjist\ n

anti- \antē, -,tī\, **ant-**, **anth-** prefix 1 : opposite in kind, position, or action 2 : opposing or hostile toward 3 : defending against 4 : curing or treating

antiabortion	anticlerical
antiacademic	anticollision
antiadministra- tion	anticolonial anticommunism
antiaggression	anticommunist
antiaircraft	anticonservation
antialien	anticonserva- tionist
antiapartheid	anticonsumer
antiaristocratic	anticonventional
antiart	anticorrosion
antiauthoritarian	anticorrosive
antiauthority	anticorruption
antibacterial	anticrime
antibias	anticruelty
antiblack	anticult
antibourgeois	anticultural
antiboycott	antidandruff
antibureaucratic	antidemocratic
antiburglar	antidiscrimina- tion
antiburglary	antidrug
antibusiness	
anticancer	antidumping
anticapitalism	antiestablishment
anticapitalist	antievolution
anti-Catholic	antievolutionary
anticensorship	antievolutionary
anti-Christian	antifamily
anti-Christianity	antifascism
antichurch	antifascist
anticigarette	antifatigue

antifemale	antiprogressive
antifeminine	antiprostitution
antifeminism	antirabies
antifeminist	antiracketeering
antifertility	antiradical
antiforeign	antirape
antiforeigner	antirealism
antifraud	antirecession
antigambling	antireform
antiglare	antireligious
antigovernment	antirevolutionary
antiguerrilla	antiriot
antigun	antiromantic
antihijack	antirust
antihomosexual	antisegregation
antihuman	antisex
antihumanism	antisexist
antihumanistic	antisexual
antihunting	antishoplifting
anti-imperialism	antislavery
anti-imperialist	antismoking
anti-inflation	antismuggling
anti-inflationary	antismut
anti-institutional	antispending
anti-integration	antistrike
anti-intellectual	antistudent
anti-intellectual- ism	antisubmarine antisubversion
antijamming	antisubversive
anti-Jewish	antisuicide
antilabor	antitank
antiliberal	antitax
antiliberalism	antitechnological
antilitter	antitechnology
antilittering	antiterrorism
antilynching	antiterrorist
antimale	antitheft
antimanagement	antitobacco
antimaterialism	antitotalitarian
antimaterialist	antitoxin
antimicrobial	antitraditional
antimilitarism	antitrust
antimilitarist	antituberculosis
antimilitary	antitumor
antimiscegenation	antityphoid
antimonopolist	antiulcer
antimonopoly	antiunemploy- ment
antimosquito	
antinoise	antiunion
antiobesity	antiurban
antiobscenity	antiviolence
antipapal	antiviral
antipersonnel	antivivisection
antipolice	antiwar
antipollution	anti-West
antipornographic	anti-Western
antipornography	antiwhite
antipoverty	antiwoman
antiprofiteering	

an·ti·bi·ot·ic \antēbī'ätik, -bē-\ n : substance that inhibits harmful microorganisms —**antibiotic** adj

an·ti·body \'anti,bädē\ n : bodily substance that counteracts the effects of a foreign substance or organism

an·tic \'antik\ n : playful act ~ adj : playful

an·tic·i·pate \an'tisə,pāt\ vb -pat·ed; -pating 1 : be prepared for 2 : look forward to —**an·tic·i·pa·tion** \-,tisə'pāshən\ n —**an·tic·i·pa·to·ry** \-'tisəpə,tōrē\ adj

an·ti·cli·max \antē'klī,maks\ n : something strikingly less important than what has preceded it —**an·ti·cli·mac·tic** \-klī-maktik\ adj

an·ti·dote \'anti,dōt\ n : remedy for poison

an·ti·freeze \'anti,frēz\ n : substance to prevent a liquid from freezing

an·ti·mo·ny \'antə,mōnē\ n : brittle white metallic chemical element

an·ti·quar·i·an \antə'kwerēən\ adj : relating to antiquities or old books —**antiquarian** n —**an·ti·quar·i·an·ism** n

an·ti·quary \'antə,kwerē\ n, pl -quaries : one who collects or studies antiquities

an·ti·quat·ed \'antə,kwātəd\ adj : out-of-date

an·tique \an'tēk\ adj : very old or out-of-date —**antique** n

an·tiq·ui·ty \an'tikwətē\ n, pl -ties 1 : ancient times 2 pl : relics of ancient times

an·ti·sep·tic \antə'septik\ adj : killing or checking the growth of germs —**antiseptic** n —**an·ti·sep·ti·cal·ly** \-tiklē\ adv

an·tith·e·sis \an'tithəsəs\ n, pl -eses \-,sēz\ : direct opposite

ant·ler \'antlər\ n : solid branched horn of a deer —**ant·lered** \-lərd\ adj

ant·onym \'antə,nim\ n : word of opposite meaning

anus \'ānəs\ n : the rear opening of the alimentary canal

an·vil \'anvəl\ n : heavy iron block on which metal is shaped

anx·i·ety \aŋ'zīətē\ n, pl -eties : uneasiness usu. over an expected misfortune

anx·ious \'aŋkshəs\ adj 1 : uneasy 2 : earnestly wishing —**anx·ious·ly** adv

any \'enē\ adj 1 : one chosen at random 2 : of whatever number or quantity ~ pron

1 : any one or ones 2 : any amount ~ adv : to any extent or degree

any·body \-,bädē, -,bäd-\ pron : anyone

any·how \-,hau\ adv 1 : in any way 2 : nevertheless

any·more \-enē'mōr\ adv : at the present time

any·one \-'enē,wən\ pron : any person

any·place adv : anywhere

any·thing pron : any thing whatever

any·time adv : at any time whatever

any·way adv : anyhow

any·where adv : in or to any place

aor·ta \ā'órtə\ n, pl -tas or -tae \-ē\ : main artery from the heart —**aor·tic** \ā'órtik\ adj

apart \ə'pärt\ adv 1 : separately in place or time 2 : aside 3 : to pieces

apart·heid \ə'pär,tāt, -,tīt\ n : racial segregation

apart·ment \ə'pärtmənt\ n : set of usu. rented rooms

ap·a·thy \'apəthē\ n : lack of emotion or interest —**ap·a·thet·ic** \apə'thetik\ adj —**ap·a·thet·i·cal·ly** \-iklē\ adv

ape \'āp\ n : large tailless primate ~ vb aped; ap·ing : imitate

ap·er·ture \'apər,chúr, -chər\ n : opening

apex \'ā,peks\ n, pl apex·es or api·ces \'āpə,sēz, 'apə-\ : highest point

aphid \'āfid, 'a-\ n : small insect that sucks plant juices

aph·o·rism \'afə,rizəm\ n : short saying stating a general truth —**aph·o·ris·tic** \afə'ristik\ adj

aph·ro·di·si·ac \afrə'dēzē,ak, -'diz-\ n : substance that excites sexual desire

api·a·rist \'āpēərist\ n : beekeeper —**api·ary** \-pē,erē\ n

apiece \ə'pēs\ adv : for each one

aplen·ty \ə'plentē\ adj : plentiful or abundant

aplomb \ə'pläm, -'pləm\ n : complete calmness or self-assurance

apoc·a·lypse \ə'päkə,lips\ n : writing prophesying a cataclysm in which evil forces are destroyed —**apoc·a·lyp·tic** \-,päkə'liptik\ adj

apoc·ry·pha \ə'päkrəfə\ n : writings of dubious authenticity —**apoc·ry·phal** \-fəl\ adj

apol·o·get·ic \ə,pälə'jetik\ adj : expressing apology —**apol·o·get·i·cal·ly** \-iklē\ adv

apol·o·gize \ə'pälə,jīz\ vb -gized; -gizing : make an apology —**apol·o·gist** \-jist\ n

apol·o·gy \ə'päləjē\ n, pl -gies 1 : formal justification 2 : expression of regret for a wrong

ap·o·plexy \'apə,pleksē\ n : sudden loss of consciousness caused by rupture or obstruction of an artery of the brain —**ap·o·plec·tic** \apə'plektik\ adj

apos·ta·sy \ə'pästəsē\ n, pl -sies : abandonment of a former loyalty —**apos·tate** \ə'päs,tāt, -tət\ adj

apos·tle \ə'päsəl\ n : disciple or advocate —**apos·tle·ship** n —**ap·os·tol·ic** \apə'stälik\ adj

apos·tro·phe \ə'pästrə,fē\ n : punctuation mark ' to indicate the possessive case or the omission of a letter or figure

apoth·e·cary \ə'päthə,kerē\ n, pl -caries : druggist

ap·pall \ə'pól\ vb : fill with horror or dismay

ap·pa·ra·tus \apə'ratəs, -'rät-\ n, pl -tus·es or -tus 1 : equipment 2 : complex machine or device

ap·par·el \ə'parəl\ n : clothing

ap·par·ent \ə'parənt\ adj 1 : visible 2 : obvious 3 : seeming —**ap·par·ent·ly** adv

ap·pa·ri·tion \apə'rishən\ n : ghost

ap·peal \ə'pēl\ vb 1 : try to have a court case reheard 2 : ask earnestly 3 : have an attraction —**appeal** n

ap·pear \ə'pir\ vb 1 : become visible or evident 2 : come into the presence of someone 3 : seem

ap·pear·ance \ə'pirəns\ n 1 : act of appearing 2 : outward aspect

ap·pease \ə'pēz\ vb -peased; -peas·ing : pacify with concessions —**ap·pease·ment** n

ap·pel·late \ə'pelət\ adj : having power to review decisions

ap·pend \ə'pend\ vb : attach

ap·pend·age \ə'pendij\ n : something attached

ap·pen·dec·to·my \apən'dektəmē\ n, pl -mies : surgical removal of the appendix

ap·pen·di·ci·tis \ə,pendə'sītəs\ n : inflammation of the appendix

ap·pen·dix \ə'pendiks\ n, pl -dix·es or -di·ces \-də,sēz\ 1 : supplementary matter 2 : narrow closed tube extending from lower right intestine

ap·pe·tite \'apə,tīt\ n 1 : natural desire esp. for food 2 : preference

ap·pe·tiz·er \'apə,tīzər\ n : food or drink to stimulate the appetite

ap·pe·tiz·ing \-ziŋ\ adj : tempting to the appetite —**ap·pe·tiz·ing·ly** adv

ap•plaud \ə'plȯd\ vb : show approval esp. by clapping

ap•plause \ə'plȯz\ n : a clapping in approval

ap•ple \'apəl\ n : rounded fruit with firm white flesh

ap•ple•jack \-,jak\ n : brandy made from cider

ap•pli•ance \ə'plīəns\ n : household machine or device

ap•pli•ca•ble \'aplikəbəl, ə'plika-\ adj : capable of being applied —**ap•pli•ca•bil•i•ty** \,aplikə'bilətē, ə,plikə-\ n

ap•pli•cant \'aplikənt\ n : one who applies

ap•pli•ca•tion \,aplə'kāshən\ n 1 : act of applying or thing applied 2 : constant attention 3 : request

ap•pli•ca•tor \'aplə,kātər\ n : device for applying a substance

ap•pli•qué \,aplə'kā\ n : cut-out fabric decoration —**appliqué** vb

ap•ply \ə'plī\ vb -**plied; -ply•ing** 1 : place in contact 2 : put to practical use 3 : devote (one's) attention or efforts to something 4 : submit a request 5 : have reference or a connection

ap•point \ə'pȯint\ vb 1 : set or assign officially 2 : equip or furnish —**ap•poin•tee** \ə,pȯin'tē, ,a-\ n

ap•point•ment \ə'pȯintmənt\ n 1 : act of appointing 2 : nonelective political job 3 : arrangement for a meeting

ap•por•tion \ə'pȯrshən\ vb : distribute proportionately —**ap•por•tion•ment** n

ap•po•site \'apəzət\ adj : suitable —**ap•po•site•ly** adv —**ap•po•site•ness** n

ap•praise \ə'prāz\ vb -**praised; -praising** : set value on —**ap•prais•al** \-'prāzəl\ n —**ap•prais•er** n

ap•pre•cia•ble \ə'prēshəbəl\ adj : considerable —**ap•pre•cia•bly** \-blē\ adv

ap•pre•ci•ate \ə'prēshē,āt\ vb -**ated; -ating** 1 : value justly 2 : be grateful for 3 : increase in value —**ap•pre•ci•a•tion** \-,prēshē'āshən\ n

ap•pre•cia•tive \ə'prēshətiv, -shē,āt-\ adj : showing appreciation

ap•pre•hend \,apri'hend\ vb 1 : arrest 2 : look forward to in dread 3 : understand —**ap•pre•hen•sion** \-'henchən\ n

ap•pre•hen•sive \-'hensiv\ adj : fearful —**ap•pre•hen•sive•ly** adv —**ap•pre•hen•sive•ness** n

ap•pren•tice \ə'prentəs\ n : person learning a craft ~ vb -**ticed; -tic•ing** : employ or work as an apprentice —**ap•pren•tice•ship** n

ap•prise \ə'prīz\ vb -**prised; -pris•ing** : inform

ap•proach \ə'prōch\ vb 1 : move nearer or be close to 2 : make initial advances or efforts toward —**approach** n —**approach•able** adj

ap•pro•ba•tion \,aprə'bāshən\ n : approval

ap•pro•pri•ate \ə'prōprē,āt\ vb -**ated; -ating** 1 : take possession of 2 : set apart for a particular use ~ \-'prēat\ adj : suitable —**ap•pro•pri•ate•ly** adv —**ap•pro•pri•ate•ness** n —**ap•pro•pri•a•tion** \ə,prōprē•'āshən\ n

ap•prov•al \ə'prüvəl\ n : act of approving

ap•prove \ə'prüv\ vb -**proved; -proving** : accept as satisfactory

ap•prox•i•mate \ə'präksəmət\ adj : nearly correct or exact ~ \-,māt\ vb -**mat•ed; -mat•ing** : come near —**ap•prox•i•mate•ly** adv —**ap•prox•i•ma•tion** \ə,präksə'māshən\ n

ap•pur•te•nance \ə'pərtᵊnəns\ n : accessory —**ap•pur•te•nant** \-pərt-ᵊnənt\ adj

apri•cot \'aprə,kät, 'ā-\ n : peachlike fruit

April \'āprəl\ n : 4th month of the year having 30 days

apron \'āprən\ n : protective garment

ap•ro•pos \,aprə'pō, 'aprə,pō\ adv : suitably ~ adj : being to the point

apropos of prep : with regard to

apt \'apt\ adj 1 : suitable 2 : likely 3 : quick to learn —**apt•ly** adv —**apt•ness** n

ap•ti•tude \'aptə,tüd, -tyüd\ n 1 : capacity for learning 2 : natural ability

aqua \'akwə, 'äk-\ n : light greenish blue color

aquar•i•um \ə'kwareəm\ n, pl -**i•ums** or -**ia** \-ēə\ : glass container for aquatic animals and plants

aquat•ic \ə'kwätik, -'kwat-\ adj : of or relating to water —**aquatic** n

aq•ue•duct \'akwə,dəkt\ n : conduit for carrying running water

aq•ui•line \'akwə,līn, -lən\ adj : curved like an eagle's beak

-ar \ər\ adj suffix 1 : of, relating to, or being 2 : resembling

ar•a•besque \,arə'besk\ n : intricate design

ar•a•ble \'arəbəl\ adj : fit for crops

ar•bi•ter \'ärbətər\ n : final authority

ar•bi•trary \'ärbə,trerē\ adj 1 : selected at random 2 : autocratic —**ar•bi•trari•ly** \,ärbə'trerəlē\ adv —**ar•bi•trari•ness** \'ärbə,trerənəs\ n

ar•bi•trate \'ärbə,trāt\ vb -**trat•ed; -trat•ing** : settle a dispute as arbitrator —**ar•bi•tra•tion** \,ärbə'trāshən\ n

ar•bi•tra•tor \'ärbə,trātər\ n : one chosen to settle a dispute

ar•bor \'ärbər\ n : shelter under branches or vines

ar•bo•re•al \är'bōrēəl\ adj : living in trees

arc \'ärk\ n 1 : part of a circle 2 : bright sustained electrical discharge ~ vb **arced** \'ärkt\; **arc•ing** \'ärkiŋ\ : form an arc

ar•cade \är'kād\ n : arched passageway between shops

ar•cane \är'kān\ adj : mysterious or secret

¹arch \'ärch\ n : curved structure spanning an opening ~ vb : cover with or form into an arch

²arch adj 1 : chief —usu. in combination 2 : mischievous —**arch•ly** adv —**arch•ness** n

ar•chae•ol•o•gy, ar•che•ol•o•gy \,ärkē'äləjē\ n : study of past human life —**ar•chae•o•log•i•cal** \-kēə'läjikəl\ adj —**ar•chae•ol•o•gist** \-kē'äləjist\ n

ar•cha•ic \är'kāik\ adj : belonging to an earlier time —**ar•cha•i•cal•ly** \-iklē\ adv

arch•an•gel \'ärk,ānjəl\ n : angel of high rank

arch•bish•op \ärch'bishəp\ n : chief bishop —**arch•bish•op•ric** \-ə,prik\ n

arch•di•o•cese \-'dīəsəs, -,sēz, -,sēs\ n : diocese of an archbishop

ar•chery \'ärchərē\ n : shooting with bow and arrows —**ar•cher** \-chər\ n

ar•che•type \'ärki,tīp\ n : original pattern or model

ar•chi•pel•a•go \,ärkə'pelə,gō, ,ärchə-\ n, pl -**goes** or -**gos** : group of islands

ar•chi•tect \'ärkə,tekt\ n : building designer

ar•chi•tec•ture \'ärkə,tekchər\ n 1 : building design 2 : style of building 3 : manner of organizing elements —**ar•chi•tec•tur•al** \,ärkə'tekchərəl, -'tekshrəl\ adj —**ar•chi•tec•tur•al•ly** adv

ar•chives \'är,kīvz\ n pl : public records or their storage place —**archi•vist** \'ärkəvist, -,kī-\ n

arch•way n : passageway under an arch

arc•tic \'ärktik, 'ärt-\ adj 1 : relating to the region near the north pole 2 : frigid

arctic circle n : circle parallel to the equator approximately 23°27' from the north pole

-ard \ərd\ n suffix : one that is

ar•dent \'ärdᵊnt\ adj : characterized by warmth of feeling —**ar•dent•ly** adv

ar•dor \'ärdər\ n : warmth of feeling

ar•du•ous \'ärjəwəs\ adj : difficult —**ar•du•ous•ly** adv —**ar•du•ous•ness** n

are pres 2d sing or pres pl of BE

area \'areə\ n 1 : space for something 2 : amount of surface included 3 : region 4 : range covered by a thing or concept

area code n : 3-digit area-identifying telephone number

are•na \ə'rēnə\ n 1 : enclosed exhibition area 2 : sphere of activity

ar•gon \'är,gän\ n : colorless odorless gaseous chemical element

ar•got \'ärgət, -,gō\ n : special language (as of the underworld)

ar•gu•able \'ärgyəwəbəl\ adj : open to dispute

ar•gue \'ärgyü\ vb -**gued; -gu•ing** 1 : give reasons for or against something 2 : disagree in words

ar•gu•ment \'ärgyəmənt\ n 1 : reasons given to persuade 2 : dispute with words

ar•gu•men•ta•tive \,ärgyə'mentətiv\ adj : inclined to argue

ar•gyle \'är,gīl\ n : colorful diamond pattern in knitting

aria \'äreə\ n : opera solo

ar•id \'arəd\ adj : very dry —**arid•i•ty** \ə'ridətē\ n

arise \ə'rīz\ vb **arose** \-'rōz\; **aris•en** \-'rizᵊn\; **aris•ing** \-'rīziŋ\ 1 : get up 2 : originate

ar•is•toc•ra•cy \,arə'stäkrəsē\ n, pl -**cies** 1 : upper class 2 —**aris•to•crat** \ə'ristə,krat\ n —**ar•is•to•crat•ic** \ə,ristə'kratik\ adj

arith•me•tic \ə'rithmə,tik\ n : mathematics that deals with numbers —**ar•ith•met•ic** \,arith'metik\, **ar•ith•met•i•cal** \-ikəl\ adj

ark \'ärk\ n : big boat

¹arm \'ärm\ n 1 : upper limb 2 : branch —**armed** \'ärmd\ adj —**arm•less** adj

²arm vb : furnish with weapons ~ n 1 : weapon 2 : branch of the military forces 3 pl : family's heraldic designs

ar•ma•da \är'mädə, -'mäd-\ n : naval fleet

ar•ma•dil•lo \,ärmə'dilō\ n, pl -**los** : burrowing mammal covered with bony plates

ar•ma•ment \'ärməmənt\ n : military arms and equipment

ar•ma•ture \'ärmə,chùr, -chər\ n : rotating part of an electric generator or motor

armed forces n pl : military

ar•mi•stice \'ärməstəs\ n : truce

ar•mor \'ärmər\ n : protective covering —**ar•mored** \-mərd\ adj

ar•mory \'ärmərē\ n, pl -**mor•ies** : factory or storehouse for arms

arm•pit n : hollow under the junction of the arm and shoulder

ar•my \'ärmē\ n, pl -**mies** 1 : body of men organized for war esp. on land 2 : great number

aro•ma \ə'rōmə\ n : usu. pleasing odor —**ar•o•mat•ic** \,arə'matik\ adj

around \ə'raùnd\ adv 1 : in or along a circuit 2 : on all sides 3 : near 4 : in an opposite direction ~ prep 1 : surrounding 2 : along the circuit of 3 : to or on the other side of 4 : near

arouse \ə'raùz\ vb **aroused; arous•ing** 1 : awaken from sleep 2 : stir up —**arous•al** \-'raùzəl\ n

ar•raign \ə'rān\ vb 1 : call before a court to answer to an indictment 2 : accuse —**ar•raign•ment** n

ar•range \ə'rānj\ vb -**ranged; -rang•ing** 1 : put in order 2 : settle or agree on 3 : adapt (a musical composition) for voices or instruments —**ar•range•ment** n —**ar•rang•er** n

ar•ray \ə'rā\ vb 1 : arrange in order 2 : dress esp. splendidly ~ n 1 : arrangement 2 : rich clothing 3 : imposing group

ar•rears \ə'rirz\ n pl : state of being behind in paying debts

ar•rest \ə'rest\ vb 1 : stop 2 : take into legal custody —**arrest** n

ar•rive \ə'rīv\ vb -**rived; -riv•ing** 1 : reach a destination, point, or stage 2 : come near in time —**ar•riv•al** \-əl\ n

ar•ro•gant \'arəgənt\ adj : showing an offensive sense of superiority —**ar•ro•gance** \-gəns\ n —**ar•ro•gant•ly** adv

ar•ro•gate \-,gāt\ vb -**gat•ed; -gat•ing** : to claim without justification

ar•row \'arō\ n : slender missile shot from a bow —**ar•row•head** n

ar•royo \ə'rȯiō, -ə\ n, pl -**royos** 1 : watercourse 2 : gully

ar•se•nal \'ärsᵊnəl\ n 1 : place where arms are made or stored 2 : store

ar•se•nic \'ärsᵊnik\ n : solid grayish poisonous chemical element

ar•son \'ärsᵊn\ n : willful or malicious burning of property —**ar•son•ist** \-ist\ n

art \'ärt\ n 1 : skill 2 : branch of learning 3 : creation of things of beauty or works so produced 4 : ingenuity

ar•te•rio•scle•ro•sis \är,tirēōsklə'rōsəs\ n : hardening of the arteries —**ar•te•rio•scle•rot•ic** \-'rätik\ adj or n

ar•tery \'ärtərē\ n, pl -**ter•ies** 1 : tubular vessel carrying blood from the heart 2 : thoroughfare —**ar•te•ri•al** \är'tirēəl\ adj

art•ful \'ärtfəl\ adj 1 : ingenious 2 : crafty —**art•ful•ly** adv —**art•ful•ness** n

ar•thri•tis \är'thrītəs\ n, pl -**ti•des** \-'thritə,dēz\ : inflammation of the joints —**ar•thrit•ic** \-'thritik\ adj or n

ar•thro•pod \'ärthrə,päd\ n : invertebrate animal (as an insect or crab) with segmented body and jointed limbs —**arthro•pod** adj

ar•ti•choke \'ärtə,chōk\ n : tall thistlelike herb or its edible flower head

ar•ti•cle \'ärtikəl\ n 1 : distinct part of a written document 2 : nonfictional published piece of writing 3 : word (as an, the) used to limit a noun 4 : item or piece

ar•tic•u•late \är'tikyələt\ adj : able to speak effectively ~ \-,lāt\ vb -**lat•ed; -lat•ing** 1 : utter distinctly 2 : unite by joints —**ar•tic•u•late•ly** adv —**ar•tic•u•late•ness** n —**ar•tic•u•la•tion** \-,tikyə'lāshən\ n

ar•ti•fact \'ärtə,fakt\ n : object of esp. prehistoric human workmanship

ar•ti•fice \'ärtəfəs\ n 1 : trick or trickery 2 : ingenious device or ingenuity

ar•ti•fi•cial \,ärtə'fishəl\ adj 1 : man-made 2 : not genuine —**ar•ti•fi•ci•al•i•ty** \-,fishē'alətē\ n —**ar•ti•fi•cial•ly** adv —**ar•ti•fi•cial•ness** n

ar•til•lery \är'tilərē\ n, pl -**ler•ies** : large caliber firearms

ar•ti•san \'ärtəzən, -sən\ n : skilled craftsman

art•ist \'ärtist\ n : one who creates art —**ar•tis•tic** \är'tistik\ adj —**ar•tis•ti•cal•ly** \-iklē\ adv —**ar•tis•try** \'ärtəstrē\ n

art•less \'ärtləs\ adj : sincere or natural —**art•less•ly** adv —**art•less•ness** n

arty \'ärtē\ adj **art•i•er; -est** : pretentiously artistic —**art•i•ly** \'ärtᵊlē\ adv —**art•i•ness** n

-ary \,erē\ adj suffix : of, relating to, or connected with

as \əz, ,az\ adv 1 : to the same degree 2 : for example ~ conj 1 : in the same way or degree as 2 : while 3 : because 4 : though ~ pron —used after same or such ~ prep : in the capacity of

as•bes•tos \as'bestəs, az-\ n : fibrous incombustible mineral

as•cend \ə'send\ vb : move upward —**as•cen•sion** \-'senchən\ n

as•cen•dan•cy \ə'sendənsē\ n : domination

as•cen•dant \ə'sendənt\ n : dominant position ~ adj 1 : moving upward 2 : dominant

as•cent \ə'sent\ n 1 : act of moving upward 2 : degree of upward slope

as•cer•tain \,asər'tān\ vb : determine —**as•cer•tain•able** adj

as•cet•ic \ə'setik\ adj : self-denying —**ascetic** n —**as•cet•i•cism** \-'setə,sizəm\ n

as•cribe \ə'skrīb\ vb -**cribed; -crib•ing** : attribute —**as•crib•able** adj —**ascrip•tion** \-'skripshən\ n

asep•tic \ā'septik\ adj : free of disease germs

¹ash \'ash\ n : tree related to the olives

²ash n : matter left when something is burned —**ash•tray** n

ashamed \ə'shāmd\ adj : feeling shame —**asham•ed•ly** \-'shāmədlē\ adv

ash•en \'ashən\ adj : deadly pale

ashore \ə'shōr\ adv : on or to the shore

aside \ə'sīd\ adv 1 : toward the side 2 : out of the way

aside from prep 1 : besides 2 : except for

as•i•nine \'asᵊn,īn\ adj : foolish —**asi•nin•i•ty** \,asᵊn'inətē\ n

ask \'ask\ vb 1 : call on for an answer or help 2 : utter (a question or request) 3 : invite

askance \ə'skans\ adv 1 : with a side glance 2 : with mistrust

askew \ə'skyü\ adv or adj : out of line

asleep \ə'slēp\ adv or adj 1 : sleeping 2 : numbed 3 : inactive

as long as conj 1 : on condition that 2 : because

as of prep : from the time of

as•par•a•gus \ə'sparəgəs\ n : tall herb related to the lilies or its edible stalks

as•pect \'as,pekt\ n 1 : way something looks to the eye or mind 2 : phase

as•pen \'aspən\ n : poplar

as•per•i•ty \a'sperətē, ə-\ n, pl -**ties** 1 : roughness 2 : harshness

as•per•sion \ə'spərzhən\ n : remark that hurts someone's reputation

as•phalt \'as,fȯlt\ n : dark tarlike substance used in paving

as•phyx•ia \as'fiksēə\ n : lack of oxygen causing unconsciousness

as•phyx•i•ate \-sē,āt\ vb -**at•ed; -at•ing** : suffocate —**as•phyx•i•a•tion** \-,fiksē'āshən\ n

as•pi•ra•tion \,aspə'rāshən\ n : strong desire to achieve a goal

as•pire \ə'spīr\ vb -**pired; -pir•ing** : have an ambition —**as•pir•ant** \'aspərənt, ə'spīrənt\ n

as•pi•rin \'asprən\ n, pl **aspirin** or **aspirins** : pain reliever

ass \'as\ n 1 : long-eared animal related to the horse 2 : stupid person

as•sail \ə'sāl\ vb : attack violently —**as•sail•able** adj —**as•sail•ant** n

as•sas•si•nate \ə'sasᵊn,āt\ vb -**nat•ed; -nat•ing** : murder esp. for political reasons —**as•sas•sin** \-'sasᵊn\ n —**as•sas•si•na•tion** \-,sasᵊn'āshən\ n

as•sault \ə'sȯlt\ n or vb : attack

as•say \'as,ā, a'sā\ n : analysis (as of an ore) to determine quality or properties —**assay** \a'sā, 'as,ā\ vb

as•sem•ble \ə'sembəl\ vb -**bled; -bling** 1 : collect into one place 2 : fit together the parts of

as•sem•bly \-blē\ n, pl -**blies** 1 : meeting 2 cap : legislative body 3 : a fitting together of parts

as•sem•bly•man \-mən\ n : member of a legislative assembly

as•sem•bly•wom•an \-,wu̇-mən\ n : woman who is a member of a legislative assembly

as•sent \ə'sent\ vb or n : consent

as•sert \ə'sərt\ vb 1 : declare 2 : defend —**as•ser•tion** \-'sərshən\ n —**as•ser•tive** \-'sərtiv\ adj —**as•sert•ive•ness** n

as•sess \ə'ses\ vb 1 : impose (as a tax) 2 : evaluate for taxation —**as•sess•ment** n —**as•ses•sor** \-ər\ n

as•set \'as,et\ n 1 pl : individually owned property 2 : advantage or resource

as•sid•u•ous \ə'sijəwəs\ adj : diligent —**as•si•du•i•ty** \,asə'düətē, -'dyü-\ n —**as•sid•u•ous•ly** adv —**as•sid•u•ous•ness** n

as•sign \ə'sīn\ vb 1 : transfer to another 2 : appoint to a duty 3 : designate as a task 4 : attribute —**as•sign•ment** n

as•sim•i•late \ə'simə,lāt\ vb -**lat•ed; -lat•ing** 1 : absorb as nourishment 2 : understand —**as•sim•i•la•tion** \ə,simə'lāshən\ n

as•sist \ə'sist\ vb : help —**assist** n —**as•sis•tance** \-'sistəns\ n —**as•sis•tant** \-tənt\ n

as•so•ci•ate \ə'sōshē,āt, -sē-\ vb -**at•ed; -at•ing** 1 : join in companionship or partnership 2 : connect in thought —**as•so•ci•ate** \-shēət, -sēət\ n —**as•so•ci•a•tion** \-,sōshē'āshən, -sē-\ n

as soon as conj : when

as•sort•ed \ə'sȯrtəd\ adj : consisting of various kinds

as•sort•ment \-mənt\ n : assorted collection

as•suage \ə'swāj\ vb -**suaged; -suag•ing** : ease or satisfy

as•sume \ə'süm\ vb -**sumed; -sum•ing** 1 : take upon oneself 2 : pretend to have or be 3 : take as true

as•sump•tion \ə'səmpshən\ n : something assumed

as•sure \ə'shu̇r\ vb -**sured; -sur•ing** 1 : give confidence or conviction to 2 : guarantee —**as•sur•ance** \-əns\ n

as•ter \'astər\ n : herb with daisylike flowers

as·ter·isk \'astə,risk\ *n* : a character * used as a reference mark or as an indication of omission of words

astern \ə'stərn\ *adv or adj* 1 : behind 2 : at or toward the stern

as·ter·oid \'astə,róid\ *n* : small planet between Mars and Jupiter

asth·ma \'azmə\ *n* : disorder marked by difficulty in breathing —**asth·mat·ic** \az'matik\ *adj or n*

astig·ma·tism \ə'stigmə,tizəm\ *n* : visual defect —**as·tig·mat·ic** \astig'matik\ *adj*

as to *prep* 1 : concerning 2 : according to

as·ton·ish \ə'stänish\ *vb* : amaze —**aston·ish·ing·ly** *adv* —**as·ton·ish·ment** *n*

as·tound \ə'staúnd\ *vb* : fill with confused wonder —**as·tound·ing·ly** *adv*

astrad·dle \ə'stradᵊl\ *adv or prep* : so as to straddle

as·tral \'astrəl\ *adj* : relating to or coming from the stars

astray \ə'strā\ *adv or adj* : off the right path

astride \ə'strīd\ *adv* : with legs apart or one on each side ~ *prep* : with one leg on each side of

as·trin·gent \ə'strinjənt\ *adj* : causing shrinking or puckering of tissues —**as·trin·gen·cy** \-jənsē\ *n* —**astringent** *n*

as·trol·o·gy \ə'sträləjē\ *n* : prediction of events by the stars —**as·trol·o·ger** \-əjər\ *n* —**as·tro·log·i·cal** \astrə'läjikəl\ *adj*

as·tro·naut \'astrə,nót\ *n* : space traveler

as·tro·nau·tics \astrə'nótiks\ *n* : construction and operation of spacecraft —**as·tro·nau·tic** \-ik\, **as·tro·nau·ti·cal** \-ikəl\ *adj*

as·tro·nom·i·cal \astrə'nämikəl\ *adj* 1 : relating to astronomy 2 : extremely large

as·tron·o·my \ə'stränəmē\ *n, pl* -**mies** : study of the celestial bodies —**astron·o·mer** \-əmər\ *n*

as·tute \ə'stüt, -'styüt\ *adj* : shrewd —**as·tute·ly** *adv* —**as·tute·ness** *n*

asun·der \ə'səndər\ *adv or adj* 1 : into separate pieces 2 : separated

asy·lum \ə'sīləm\ *n* 1 : refuge 2 : institution for care esp. of the insane

asym·met·ri·cal \asə'metrikəl\, **asym·met·ric** \-trik\ *adj* : not symmetrical —**asym·me·try** \ā'simətrē\ *n*

at \ət, 'at\ *prep* 1 —used to indicate a point in time or space 2 —used to indicate a goal 3 —used to indicate condition, means, cause, or manner

at all *adv* : without restriction or under any circumstances

ate *past of* EAT

-ate \ət, ,āt\ *n suffix* 1 : office or rank 2 : group of persons holding an office or rank ~ *adj suffix* 1 : brought into or being in a state 2 : marked by having

athe·ist \'āthēist\ *n* : one who denies the existence of God —**athe·ism** \-,izəm\ *n* —**athe·is·tic** \āthē'istik\ *adj*

ath·ero·scle·ro·sis \athərōsklə'rōsəs\ *n* : arteriosclerosis with deposition of fatty substances in the arteries —**ath·ero·scle·rot·ic** \-'rätik\ *adj*

ath·lete \'ath,lēt\ *n* : one trained to compete in athletics

ath·let·ics \ath'letiks\ *n sing or pl* : exercises and games requiring physical skill —**ath·let·ic** \-ik\ *adj*

-ation \'āshən\ *n suffix* : action or process

-ative \ātiv, ətiv\ *adj suffix* 1 : of, relating to, or connected with 2 : tending to

atlas \'atləs\ *n* : book of maps

at·mo·sphere \'atmə,sfir\ *n* 1 : mass of air surrounding the earth 2 : surrounding influence —**at·mo·spher·ic** \atmə'sfirik, -'sfer-\ *adj* —**at·mo·spher·i·cal·ly** \-iklē\ *adv*

atoll \'a,tól, 'ā-, -,täl\ *n* : ring-shaped coral island

at·om \'atəm\ *n* 1 : tiny bit 2 : smallest particle of a chemical element that can exist alone or in combination

atom·ic \ə'tämik\ *adj* 1 : relating to atoms 2 : nuclear

atomic bomb *n* : bomb utilizing the energy released by splitting the atom

at·om·iz·er \'atə,mīzər\ *n* : device for dispersing a liquid as a very fine spray

atone \ə'tōn\ *vb* **atoned; aton·ing** : make amends —**atone·ment** *n*

atop \ə'täp\ *prep* : on top of ~ *adv or adj* : on, to, or at the top

atri·um \'ātrēəm\ *n, pl* **atria** \-trēə\ *or* **atri·ums** 1 : open central room or court 2 : heart chamber that receives blood from the veins

atro·cious \ə'trōshəs\ *adj* : appalling or abominable —**atro·cious·ly** *adv* —**atro·cious·ness** *n*

atroc·i·ty \ə'träsətē\ *n, pl* -**ties** : savage act

at·ro·phy \'atrəfē\ *n, pl* -**phies** : wasting away of a bodily part or tissue —**atro·phy** *vb*

at·ro·pine \'atrə,pēn\ *n* : drug used esp. to relieve spasms

at·tach \ə'tach\ *vb* 1 : seize legally 2 : bind by personalities 3 : join —**attach·ment** *n*

at·ta·ché \atə'shā, ,a,ta-, ə,ta-\ *n* : technical expert on a diplomatic staff

at·tack \ə'tak\ *vb* 1 : try to hurt or destroy with violence or words 2 : set to work on ~ *n* 1 : act of attacking 2 : fit of sickness

at·tain \ə'tān\ *vb* 1 : achieve or accomplish 2 : reach —**at·tain·abil·i·ty** \ə,tānə'bilətē\ *n* —**at·tain·able** *adj* —**at·tain·ment** *n*

at·tempt \ə'tempt\ *vb* : make an effort toward —**attempt** *n*

at·tend \ə'tend\ *vb* 1 : handle or provide for the care of something 2 : accompany 3 : be present at 4 : pay attention —**at·ten·dance** \-'tendəns\ *n* —**at·ten·dant** \-dənt\ *adj or n*

at·ten·tion \ə'tenchən\ *n* 1 : concentration of the mind on something 2 : notice or awareness —**at·ten·tive** \-'tentiv\ *adj* —**at·ten·tive·ly** *adv* —**at·ten·tive·ness** *n*

at·ten·u·ate \ə'tenyə,wāt\ *vb* -**at·ed; -ating** 1 : make or become thin 2 : weaken —**at·ten·u·a·tion** \-,tenyə'wāshən\ *n*

at·test \ə'test\ *vb* : certify or bear witness —**at·tes·ta·tion** \a,tes'tāshən\ *n*

at·tic \'atik\ *n* : space just below the roof

at·tire \ə'tīr\ *vb* -**tired; -tir·ing** : dress —**attire** *n*

at·ti·tude \'atə,tüd, -,tyüd\ *n* 1 : posture or relative position 2 : feeling, opinion, or mood

at·tor·ney \ə'tərnē\ *n, pl* -**neys** : legal agent

at·tract \ə'trakt\ *vb* 1 : draw to oneself 2 : have emotional or aesthetic appeal for —**at·trac·tion** \-'trakshən\ *n* —**at·trac·tive** \-'traktiv\ *adj* —**at·trac·tive·ly** *adv* —**at·trac·tive·ness** *n*

at·tri·bute \'atrə,byüt\ *n* : inherent characteristic ~ \ə'tribyət\ *vb* -**trib·ut·ed; -trib·ut·ing** 1 : regard as having a specific cause or origin 2 : regard as a characteristic —**at·trib·ut·able** *adj* —**at·tri·bu·tion** \atrə'byüshən\ *n*

at·tune \ə'tün, -'tyün\ *vb* : bring into harmony

au·burn \'óbərn\ *adj* : reddish brown

auc·tion \'ókshən\ *n* : public sale of property to the highest bidder —**auction** *vb* —**auc·tion·eer** \ókshə'nir\ *n*

au·dac·i·ty \ó'dasətē\ *n* : boldness or insolence —**au·da·cious** \ó'dāshəs\ *adj*

au·di·ble \'ódəbəl\ *adj* : capable of being heard —**au·di·bly** \-blē\ *adv*

au·di·ence \'ódēəns\ *n* 1 : formal interview 2 : group of listeners or spectators

au·dio \'ódē,ō\ *adj* 1 : relating to sound or its reproduction ~ *n* : television sound

au·dio·vi·su·al \ódēō'vizhəwəl\ *adj* : relating to both hearing and sight

au·dit \'ódət\ *vb* : examine financial accounts —**audit** *n* —**au·di·tor** \'ódətər\ *n*

au·di·tion \ó'dishən\ *n* : tryout performance —**audition** *vb*

au·di·to·ri·um \ódə'tōrēəm\ *n, pl* -**riums** *or* -**ria** \-'rēə\ : room or building used for public performances

au·di·to·ry \'ódə,tōrē\ *adj* : relating to hearing

au·ger \'ógər\ *n* : tool for boring

aug·ment \óg'ment\ *vb* : enlarge or increase —**aug·men·ta·tion** \ógmən'tāshən\ *n*

au·gur \'ógər\ *n* : prophet ~ *vb* : predict —**au·gu·ry** \'ógyərē, -gər-\ *n*

au·gust \ó'gəst\ *adj* : majestic

Au·gust \'ó'gəst\ *n* : 8th month of the year having 31 days

auk \'ók\ *n* : stocky diving seabird

aunt \'ant, 'änt\ *n* 1 : sister of one's father or mother 2 : wife of one's uncle

au·ra \'órə\ *n* 1 : distinctive atmosphere 2 : luminous radiation

au·ral \'órəl\ *adj* : relating to the ear or to hearing

au·ri·cle \'órikəl\ *n* : atrium or ear-shaped pouch in the atrium of the heart

au·ro·ra bo·re·al·is \ə'rórə,bórē'aləs\ *n* : display of light in the night sky of northern latitudes

aus·pic·es \'óspəsəz, -,sēz\ *n pl* : patronage and protection

aus·pi·cious \ó'spishəs\ *adj* : favorable

aus·tere \ó'stir\ *adj* : severe —**aus·tere·ly** *adv* —**aus·ter·i·ty** \ó'sterətē\ *n*

au·then·tic \ə'thentik, ó-\ *adj* : genuine —**au·then·ti·cal·ly** \-iklē\ *adv* —**au·then·tic·i·ty** \ó,then'tisətē\ *n*

au·then·ti·cate \ə'thenti,kāt, ó-\ *vb* -**cated; -cat·ing** : prove genuine —**au·then·ti·ca·tion** \-,thenti'kāshən\ *n*

au·thor \'óthər\ *n* 1 : writer 2 : creator —**au·thor·ship** *n*

au·thor·i·tar·i·an \ə,thärə'terēən, ə-, -,thór-\ *adj* : marked by blind obedience to authority

au·thor·i·ta·tive \ə'thärə,tātiv, ó-, -'thór-\ *adj* : being an authority —**au·thor·i·ta·tive·ly** *adv* —**au·thor·i·ta·tive·ness** *n*

au·thor·i·ty \ə'thärətē, ó-, -'thór-\ *n, pl* -**ties** 1 : expert 2 : right, responsibility, or power to influence 3 *pl* : persons in official positions

au·tho·rize \'óthə,rīz\ *vb* -**rized; -riz·ing** : permit or give official approval for —**au·tho·ri·za·tion** \óthərə'zāshən\ *n*

au·to \'ótō\ *n, pl* **autos** : automobile

au·to·bi·og·ra·phy \,ótəbī'ägrəfē, -bē-\ *n* : writer's own life story —**au·to·bi·og·ra·pher** \-fər\ *n* —**au·to·bio·graph·i·cal** \-,bīə'grafikəl\ *adj*

au·toc·ra·cy \ó'täkrəsē\ *n, pl* -**cies** : government by one person having unlimited power —**au·to·crat** \'ótə,krat\ *n* —**au·to·crat·ic** \ótə'kratik\ *adj* —**au·to·crat·i·cal·ly** \-iklē\ *adv*

au·to·graph \'ótə,graf\ *n* : signature ~ *vb* : write one's name on

au·to·mate \'ótə,māt\ *vb* -**mat·ed; -mating** : make automatic —**au·to·ma·tion** \ótə'māshən\ *n*

au·to·mat·ic \ótə'matik\ *adj* 1 : involuntary 2 : designed to function without human intervention ~ *n* : automatic device (as a firearm) —**au·to·mat·i·cal·ly** \-iklē\ *adv*

au·tom·a·ton \ó'tämətən, -,tän\ *n, pl* -**a·tons** *or* -**a·ta** \-tə, -,tä\ : robot

au·to·mo·bile \ótəmō'bēl, -'mō,bēl\ *n* : 4-wheeled passenger vehicle with its own power source

au·to·mo·tive \ótə'mōtiv\ *adj* : relating to automobiles

au·ton·o·mous \ó'tänəməs\ *adj* : self-governing —**au·ton·o·mous·ly** *adv* —**au·ton·o·my** \-mē\ *n*

au·top·sy \'ó,täpsē, 'ótəp-\ *n, pl* -**sies** : medical examination of a corpse

au·tumn \'ótəm\ *n* : season between summer and winter —**au·tum·nal** \ó'təmnəl\ *adj*

aux·il·ia·ry \óg'zilyərē, -lərē\ *adj* 1 : being a supplement or reserve 2 : accompanying a main verb form to express person, number, mood, or tense —**auxiliary** *n*

avail \ə'vāl\ *vb* : be of use or make use ~ *n* : use

avail·able \ə'vāləbəl\ *adj* 1 : usable 2 : accessible —**avail·abil·i·ty** \-,vālə'bilətē\ *n*

av·a·lanche \'avə,lanch\ *n* : mass of sliding or falling snow or rock

av·a·rice \'avərəs\ *n* : greed —**av·a·ri·cious** \avə'rishəs\ *adj*

avenge \ə'venj\ *vb* **avenged; aveng·ing** : take vengeance for —**aveng·er** *n*

av·e·nue \'avə,nü, -,nyü\ *n* 1 : way of approach 2 : broad street

av·er·age \'avrij\ *adj* 1 : being about midway between extremes 2 : ordinary ~ *vb* 1 : be usually 2 : find the mean of ~ *n* : mean

averse \ə'vərs\ *adj* : feeling dislike or reluctance —**aver·sion** \-'vərzhən\ *n*

avert \ə'vərt\ *vb* : turn away

avi·ary \'āvē,erē\ *n, pl* -**ar·ies** : place where birds are kept

avi·a·tion \,āvē'āshən, ,av-\ *n* : operation or manufacture of airplanes —**avi·a·tor** \'āvē,ātər, 'av-\ *n*

av·id \'avəd\ *adj* 1 : greedy 2 : enthusiastic —**avid·i·ty** \ə'vidətē, a-\ *n* —**av·id·ly** *adv*

av·o·ca·do \avə'kädō, ,äv-\ *n, pl* -**dos** : tropical fruit with green pulp

av·o·ca·tion \avə'kāshən\ *n* : hobby

avoid \ə'vóid\ *vb* 1 : keep away from 2 : prevent the occurrence of 3 : refrain from —**avoid·able** *adj* —**avoidance** \-əns\ *n*

av·oir·du·pois \avərdə'póiz\ *n* : system of weight based on the pound of 16 ounces

avow \ə'vaú\ *vb* : declare openly —**avow·al** \-'vaúəl\ *n*

await \ə'wāt\ *vb* : wait for

awake \ə'wāk\ *vb* **awoke** \-'wōk\; **awok·en** \-'wōkən\ *or* **awaked; awak·ing** : wake up —**awake** *adj*

awak·en \ə'wākən\ *vb* -**ened; -en·ing** : wake up

award \ə'wórd\ *vb* : give (something won or deserved) ~ *n* 1 : judgment 2 : prize

aware \ə'war\ *adj* : having realization or consciousness —**aware·ness** *n*

awash \ə'wósh, -'wäsh\ *adv or adj* : flooded

away \ə'wā\ *adv* 1 : from this or that place or time 2 : out of the way 3 : in another direction 4 : from one's possession ~ *adj* 1 : absent 2 : distant

awe \'ó\ *n* : respectful fear or wonder ~ *vb* **awed; aw·ing** : fill with awe —**awe·some** \-səm\ *adj* —**awe·struck** *adj*

aw·ful \'ófəl\ *adj* 1 : inspiring awe 2 : extremely disagreeable 3 : very great —**aw·ful·ly** *adv*

awhile \ə'hwīl\ *adv* : for a while

awk·ward \'ókwərd\ *adj* 1 : clumsy 2 : embarrassing —**awk·ward·ly** *adv* —**awk·ward·ness** *n*

awl \'ól\ *n* : hole-making tool

aw·ning \'ónin\ *n* : window cover

awry \ə'rī\ *adv or adj* : wrong

ax, axe \'aks\ *n* : chopping tool

ax·i·om \'aksēəm\ *n* : generally accepted truth —**ax·i·om·at·ic** \aksēə'matik\ *adj*

ax·is \'aksəs\ *n, pl* **ax·es** \-,sēz\ : center of rotation —**ax·i·al** \-sēəl\ *adj* —**ax·i·al·ly** *adv*

ax·le \'aksəl\ *n* : shaft on which a wheel revolves

aye \'ī\ *adv* : yes ~ *n* : a vote of yes

aza·lea \ə'zālyə\ *n* : rhododendron with funnel-shaped blossoms

az·i·muth \'azəməth\ *n* : horizontal direction expressed as an angle

azure \'azhər\ *n* : blue of the sky —**azure** *adj*

B

b \'bē\ *n, pl* **b's** *or* **bs** \'bēz\ : 2d letter of the alphabet

bab·ble \'babəl\ *vb* -**bled; -bling** 1 : utter meaningless sounds 2 : talk foolishly or too much —**babble** *n* —**bab·bler** *n*

babe \'bāb\ *n* : baby

ba·bel \'bābəl, 'bab-\ *n* : noisy confusion

ba·boon \ba'bün\ *n* : large Asian or African ape with a doglike muzzle

ba·by \'bābē\ *n, pl* -**bies** : very young child ~ *vb* -**bied; -by·ing** : pamper —**baby** *adj* —**ba·by·hood** *n* —**ba·by·ish** *adj*

ba·by·sit *vb* -**sat; -sit·ting** : care for children while parents are away —**baby-sitter** *n*

bac·ca·lau·re·ate \bakə'lórēət\ *n* : bachelor's degree

bac·cha·na·lia \bakə'nālyə\ *n, pl* -**lia** : drunken orgy —**bac·cha·na·lian** \-yən\ *adj*

bach·e·lor \'bachələr\ *n* 1 : holder of lowest 4-year college degree 2 : unmarried man —**bach·e·lor·hood** *n*

ba·cil·lus \bə'siləs\ *n, pl* -**li** \-,lī\ : rod-shaped bacterium —**bac·il·lary** \'basə,lerē\ *adj*

back \'bak\ *n* 1 : part of a human or animal body nearest the spine 2 : part opposite the front 3 : player farthest from the opponent's goal ~ *adv* 1 : to or at the back 2 : ago 3 : to or in a former place or state 4 : in reply ~ *adj* 1 : located at the back 2 : not paid on time 3 : moving or working backward 4 : not current ~ *vb* 1 : support 2 : go or cause to go back 3 : form the back of —**back·ache** *n* —**backer** *n* —**back·ing** *n* —**back·less** *adj* —**back·rest** *n*

back·bite *vb* -**bit; -bit·ten; -bit·ing** : say spiteful things about someone absent —**back·bit·er** *n*

back·bone *n* 1 : bony column in the back that encloses the spinal cord 2 : firm character

back·drop *n* : painted cloth hung across the rear of a stage

back·fire *n* : loud noise from the wrongly timed explosion of fuel in an engine ~ *vb* 1 : make or undergo a backfire 2 : have a result opposite of that intended

back·gam·mon \'bak,gamən\ *n* : board game

back·ground *n* 1 : scenery behind something 2 : sum of a person's experience or training

back·hand *n* : stroke (as in tennis) made with the back of the hand turned forward —**backhand** *adj or vb* —**back·hand·ed** *adj*

back·lash *n* : adverse reaction

back·log *n* : accumulation of things to be done —**backlog** *vb*

back·pack *n* : camping pack carried on the back ~ *vb* : hike with a backpack —**back·pack·er** *n*

back·slide *vb* -**slid; -slid** *or* -**slid·den** \-,slidᵊn\ -**slid·ing** : lapse in morals or religious practice —**back·slid·er** *n*

back·stage *adv or adj* : in or to an area behind a stage

back·up *n* : substitute

back·ward \'bakwərd\, **back·wards** *adv* 1 : toward the back 2 : with the back foremost 3 : in a reverse direction 4 : toward an earlier or worse state ~ *adj* 1 : directed, turned, or done backward 2 : retarded in development —**back·ward·ness** *n*

back·woods *n pl* : remote or isolated place

ba·con \'bākən\ *n* : salted and smoked meat from a pig

bac·te·ri·um \bak'tirēəm\ *n, pl* -**ria** \-ēə\ : microscopic plant —**bac·te·ri·al** \-ēəl\ *adj* —**bac·te·rio·log·ic** \-,tirēə'läjik\, **bac·te·rio·log·i·cal** \-ikəl\ *adj* —**bac·te·ri·ol·o·gist** \-ē'äləjist\ *n* —**bac·te·ri·ol·o·gy** \-jē\ *n*

bad \'bad\ *adj* **worse** \'wərs\; **worst** \'wərst\ 1 : not good 2 : naughty 3 : faulty 4

: spoiled —**bad** *n or adv* —**bad•ly** *adv*
—**bad•ness** *n*
bade *past of* BID
badge \'baj\ *n* : symbol of status
bad•ger \'bajər\ *n* : burrowing mammal ~
vb : harass
bad•min•ton \'bad,mint³n\ *n* : tennis-like
game played with a shuttlecock
baf•fle \'bafəl\ *vb* -**fled; -fling** : perplex ~
n : device to alter flow (as of liquid or
sound) —**baf•fle•ment** *n*
bag \'bag\ *n* : flexible usu. closable container ~ *vb* -**gg- 1** : bulge out **2** : put in
a bag **3** : catch in hunting
bag•a•telle \,baga'tel\ *n* : trifle
ba•gel \'bāgəl\ *n* : hard doughnut-shaped
roll
bag•gage \'bagij\ *n* : traveler's bags and be-
longings
bag•gy \'bagē\ *adj* -**gi•er; -est** : puffed out
like a bag —**bag•gi•ly** *adv* —**bag•gi•ness**
n
bag•pipe *n* : musical instrument with a bag,
a tube with valves, and sounding pipes —
often pl.
¹bail \'bāl\ *n* : container for scooping water
out of a boat —**bail** *vb* —**bail•er** *n*
²bail *n* **1** : security given to guarantee a
prisoner's appearance in court **2** : release
secured by bail ~ *vb* **1** : bring about the
release of by giving bail
bai•liff \'bāləf\ *n* **1** : British sheriff's aide **2**
: minor officer of a U.S. court
bai•li•wick \'bāli,wik\ *n* : one's special field
or domain
bail•out \'bā,laút\ *n* : rescue from financial
distress
bait \'bāt\ *vb* **1** : harass with dogs usu. for
sport **2** : furnish (a hook or trap) with bait
~ *n* : lure esp. for catching animals
bake \'bāk\ *vb* **baked; bak•ing 1** : cook in dry
heat esp. in an oven ~ *n* : party featuring
baked food —**baker** *n* —**bak•ery**
\'bākərē\ *n* —**bake•shop** *n*
bal•ance \'baləns\ *n* **1** : weighing device **2**
: counteracting weight, force, or influence
3 : equilibrium **4** : that which remains ~
vb -**anced; -anc•ing 1** : compute the balance **2** : equalize **3** : bring into harmony
or proportion —**bal•anced** *adj*
bal•co•ny \'balkənē\ *n, pl* -**nies** : platform
projecting from a wall
bald \'bòld\ *adj* **1** : lacking a natural or usual
covering (as of hair) **2** : plain —**bald•ing**
adj —**bald•ly** *adv* —**bald•ness** *n*
bal•der•dash \'bòldər,dash\ *n* : nonsense
bale \'bāl\ *n* : large bundle ~ *vb* **baled; bal-
ing** : pack in a bale —**bal•er** *n*
bale•ful \'bālfəl\ *adj* **1** : deadly **2** : ominous
balk \'bòk\ *n* : hindrance ~ *vb* **1** : thwart **2**
: stop short and refuse to go on —**balky**
adj
¹ball \'bòl\ *n* **1** : rounded mass **2** : game
played with a ball ~ *vb* **1** : form into a ball
²ball *n* : large formal dance —**ballroom** *n*
bal•lad \'baləd\ *n* **1** : narrative poem **2**
: slow romantic song —**bal•lad•eer**
\,balə'diər\ *n*
bal•last \'baləst\ *n* : heavy material to steady
a ship or balloon ~ *vb* : provide with bal-
last
bal•le•ri•na \,balə'rēna\ *n* : female ballet
dancer
bal•let \'ba,lā, ba'lā\ *n* : theatrical dancing
bal•lis•tics \bə'listiks\ *n sing or pl* : science
of projectile motion —**ballistic** *adj*
bal•loon \bə'lün\ *n* : inflated bag ~ *vb* **1**
: travel in a balloon **2** : swell out —**bal-
loon•ist** *n*
bal•lot \'balət\ *n* **1** : paper used to cast a vote
2 : system of voting ~ *vb* : vote
bal•ly•hoo \'balē,hü\ *n* : publicity —**bally-
hoo** *vb*
balm \'bäm, 'bälm\ *n* **1** : fragrant healing or
soothing preparation **2** : spicy fragrant
herb
balmy \'bämē, 'bälmē\ *adj* **balm•i•er; -est**
: gently soothing —**balm•i•ness** *n*
bal•sa \'bólsə\ *n* : very light wood of a tropical tree
bal•sam \-səm\ *n* **1** : aromatic resinous plant
substance **2** : balsam-yielding plant —
bal•sam•ic \bòl'samik\ *adj*
bal•us•ter \'baləstər\ *n* : upright support for
a rail
bal•us•trade \-,strād\ *n* : row of balusters
topped by a rail
bam•boo \bam'bü\ *n* : tall tropical grass
with strong hollow stems
bam•boo•zle \bam'büzəl\ *vb* -**zled; -zling**
: deceive
ban \'ban\ *vb* -**nn-** : prohibit ~ *n* : legal
prohibition
ba•nal \bə'näl, -'nal; 'bān³l\ *adj* : ordinary
and uninteresting —**ba•nal•i•ty** \bə'nalə-
tē\ *n*
ba•nana \bə'nanə\ *n* : elongated fruit of a
treelike tropical plant
¹band \'band\ *n* **1** : something that ties or
binds **2** : strip or stripe different (as in
color) from nearby matter **3** : range of
radio wavelengths ~ *vb* **1** : enclose with

a band **2** : unite for a common end —
band•ed *adj* —**band•er** *n*
²band *n* **1** : group **2** : musicians playing
together
ban•dage \'bandij\ *n* : material used esp. in
dressing wounds ~ *vb* : dress or cover
with a bandage
ban•dan•na, ban•dana \ban'dana\ *n* : large
colored figured handkerchief
ban•dit \'bandət\ *n* : outlaw or robber —
ban•dit•ry \-dətrē\ *n*
band•stand *n* : stage for band concerts
band•wag•on *n* : candidate, side, or movement gaining support
¹ban•dy \'bandē\ *vb* -**died; -dy•ing** : exchange in rapid succession
²bandy *adj* : curved outward
bane \'bān\ *n* **1** : poison **2** : cause of woe
—**bane•ful** *adj*
¹bang \'bang\ *vb* : strike, thrust, or move usu.
with a loud noise ~ *n* **1** : blow **2** : sudden
loud noise ~ *adv* : directly
²bang *n* : fringe of short hair over the forehead —usu. pl. ~ *n* : cut in bangs
ban•gle \'bangɡəl\ *n* : bracelet
ban•ish \'banish\ *vb* **1** : force by authority
to leave a country **2** : expel —**ban•ish-
ment** *n*
ban•is•ter \-əstər\ *n* **1** : baluster **2** : handrail
ban•jo \'ban,jō\ *n, pl* -**jos** : stringed instrument with a drumlike body —**banjo•ist** *n*
¹bank \'bank\ *n* **1** : piled-up mass **2** : rising
ground along a body of water **3**
: sideways slope along a curve ~ *vb* **1**
: form a bank **2** : cover (as a fire) to keep
inactive **3** : incline (an airplane) laterally
²bank *n* : tier of objects
³bank *n* **1** : money institution **2** : reserve
supply ~ *vb* : conduct business in a bank
—**bank•book** *n* —**bank•er** *n* —**bank•ing**
n
bank•rupt \'ban,krəpt\ *n* : one required by
law to forfeit assets to pay off debts ~
adj **1** : legally a bankrupt **2** : lacking
something essential —**bankrupt** *vb* —
bank•rupt•cy \-,krəpsē\ *n*
ban•ner \'banər\ *n* : flag ~ *adj* : excellent
banns \'banz\ *n pl* : announcement in
church of a proposed marriage
ban•quet \'bankwət\ *n* : ceremonial dinner
—**banquet** *vb*
ban•shee \'banshē\ *n* : wailing female spirit
that foretells death
ban•tam \'bantəm\ *n* : miniature domestic
fowl
ban•ter \'bantər\ *n* : good-natured joking —
banter *vb*
ban•yan \'banyən\ *n* : large tree that grows
new trunks from the limbs
bap•tism \'bap,tizəm\ *n* : Christian rite signifying spiritual cleansing —**baptis•mal**
\bap'tizməl\ *adj*
bap•tize \bap'tīz, 'bap,tīz\ *vb* -**tized; -tiz•ing**
: administer baptism to
bar \'bär\ *n* **1** : long narrow object used esp.
as a lever, fastening, or support **2** : barrier
3 : body of practicing lawyers **4** : wide
stripe **5** : food counter **6** : place where
liquor is served **7** : vertical line across the
musical staff ~ *vb* -**rr- 1** : obstruct with
a bar **2** : shut out **3** : prohibit ~ *prep*
: excluding —**barred** *adj* —**barroom** *n*
—**bar•tend•er** *n*
barb \'bärb\ *n* : sharp projection pointing
backward —**barbed** *adj*
bar•bar•ian \bär'barēən\ *adj* **1** : relating to
people considered backward **2** : not refined —**barbarian** *n*
bar•bar•ic \-'barik\ *adj* : barbarian
bar•ba•rous \'bärbərəs\ *adj* **1** : lacking refinement **2** : mercilessly cruel —**bar•bar-
ism** \-bə,rizəm\ *n* —**bar•bar•i•ty** \bär-
'barətē\ *n* —**bar•ba•rous•ly** *adv*
bar•be•cue \'bärbi,kyü\ *n* : gathering at
which barbecued food is served ~ *vb*
-**cued; -cu•ing** : cook over hot coals or
on a spit often with a highly seasoned
sauce
bar•ber \'bärbər\ *n* : one who cuts hair
bar•bi•tu•rate \bär'bichərət\ *n* : sedative or
hypnotic drug
bard \'bärd\ *n* : poet
bare \'bar\ *adj* **bar•er; bar•est 1** : naked **2**
: not concealed **3** : empty **4** : leaving
nothing to spare **5** : plain ~ *vb* **bared;
bar•ing** : make or lay bare —**bare•foot,
bare•foot•ed** *adv or adj* —**bare–hand•ed**
adv or adj —**bare•head•ed** *adv or adj* —
bare•ly *adv* —**bare•ness** *n*
bare•back, bare•backed *adv or adj*
: without a saddle
bare•faced *adj* : open and esp. brazen
bar•gain \'bärgən\ *n* **1** : agreement **2**
: something bought for less than its value
~ *vb* **1** : negotiate **2** : barter
barge \'bärj\ *n* : broad flat-bottomed boat ~
vb **barged; barg•ing** : move rudely or
clumsily —**barge•man** *n*
bari•tone \'barə,tōn\ *n* : male voice between
bass and tenor
bar•i•um \'barēəm\ *n* : silver-white metallic
chemical element
¹bark \'bärk\ *vb* **1** : make the sound of a

dog **2** : speak in a loud curt tone ~ *n*
: sound of a barking dog
²bark *n* : tough corky outer covering of a
woody stem or root ~ *vb* : remove bark
or skin from
³bark *n* : sailing ship with a fore-and-aft
rear sail
bark•er \'bärkər\ *n* : one who calls out to
attract people to a show
bar•ley \'bärlē\ *n* : cereal grass or its seeds
barn \'bärn\ *n* : building for keeping hay or
livestock —**barn•yard** *n*
bar•na•cle \'bärnikəl\ *n* : marine crustacean
barn•storm *vb* : tour through rural districts
giving performances
ba•rom•e•ter \bə'rämətər\ *n* : instrument for
measuring atmospheric pressure —**baro-
met•ric** \,barə'metrik\ *adj*
bar•on \'barən\ *n* **1** : British peer —**baron-
age** \-ij\ *n* —**ba•ro•ni•al** \bə'rōnēəl\ *adj*
—**bar•ony** \barənē\ *n*
bar•on•ess \-ənəs\ *n* **1** : baron's wife **2**
: woman holding a baronial title
bar•on•et \-ənət\ *n* : man holding a rank between a baron and a knight —**bar•on•et-
cy** \-sē\ *n*
ba•roque \bə'rōk, -'räk\ *adj* : elaborately or-
namented
bar•racks \'barəks\ *n sing or pl* : soldiers'
housing
bar•ra•cu•da \,barə'küdə\ *n, pl* -**da** or -**das**
: large predatory sea fish
bar•rage \bə'räzh, -'räj\ *n* : heavy artillery
fire
bar•rel \'barəl\ *n* **1** : closed cylindrical container **2** : amount held by a barrel **3**
: cylindrical part ~ *vb* -**reled** or -**relled;
-rel•ing** or -**rel•ling 1** : pack in a barrel **2**
: move at high speed —**bar•reled** *adj*
bar•ren \'barən\ *adj* **1** : unproductive of life
2 : uninteresting —**bar•ren•ness** *n*
bar•rette \bä'ret, ba-\ *n* : clasp for a woman's hair
bar•ri•cade \'barə,kād, ,barə'-\ *n* : barrier
—**barricade** *vb*
bar•ri•er \'barēər\ *n* : something that separates or obstructs
bar•ring \'bäriŋ\ *prep* : omitting
bar•ris•ter \'barəstər\ *n* : British trial lawyer
bar•row \'barō\ *n* : wheelbarrow
bar•ter \'bärtər\ *vb* : trade by exchange of
goods —**barter** *n*
ba•salt \bə'sólt, 'bā,-\ *n* : dark fine-grained
igneous rock —**ba•sal•tic** \bə'sóltik\ *adj*
¹base \'bās\ *n, pl* **bas•es 1** : bottom **2**
: fundamental part **3** : beginning point **4**
: supply source of a force **5** : compound
that reacts with an acid to form a salt ~
vb **based; bas•ing** : establish —**base•less**
adj
²base *adj* **bas•er; bas•est 1** : inferior **2**
: contemptible —**base•ly** *adv* —**baseness**
n
base•ball *n* : game played with a bat and
ball by 2 teams
base•ment \-mənt\ *n* : part of a building below ground level
bash \'bash\ *vb* : strike violently ~ *n* : heavy
blow
bash•ful \-fəl\ *adj* : self-conscious —**bash-
ful•ness** *n*
ba•sic \'bāsik\ *adj* **1** : relating to or forming
the base or essence **2** : relating to a chemical base —**ba•si•cal•ly** *adv* —**ba•sic•i•ty**
\bā'sisətē\ *n*
ba•sil \'bazəl, 'bās-, 'bāz-\ *n* : aromatic mint
ba•sil•i•ca \bə'silikə\ *n* : important church
or cathedral
ba•sin \'bās³n\ *n* **1** : large bowl or pan **2**
: region drained by a river
ba•sis \'bāsəs\ *n, pl* **bases** \-,sēz\ **1**
: something that supports **2** : fundamental
principle
bask \'bask\ *vb* : enjoy pleasant warmth
bas•ket \'baskət\ *n* : woven container —
bas•ket•ful *n*
bas•ket•ball *n* : game played with a ball on
a court by 2 teams
bas–re•lief \,bäri'lēf\ *n* : flat sculpture with
slightly raised design
¹bass \'bas\ *n, pl* **bass** or **bass•es**
: spiny-finned sport and food fish
²bass \'bās\ *n* **1** : deep tone **2** : lowest choral
voice
bas•set \'basət-\ *n* : short-legged dog
with long ears
bas•si•net \,basə'net\ *n* : baby's bed
bas•soon \bə'sün, ba-\ *n* : low-pitched wind
instrument
bas•tard \'bastərd\ *n* **1** : illegitimate child **2**
: offensive person ~ *adj* **1** : illegitimate
2 : inferior —**bas•tard•ize** *vb* —**bas•tardy**
n
¹baste \'bāst\ *vb* **bast•ed; bast•ing** : sew
temporarily with long stitches
²baste *vb* **bast•ed; bast•ing** : moisten at intervals while cooking
bas•tion \'baschən\ *n* : fortified position
¹bat \'bat\ *n* **1** : stick or club **2** : sharp blow
~ *vb* -**tt- 1** : hit with a bat
²bat *n* : small flying mammal
³bat *vb* -**tt-** : wink or blink
batch \'bach\ *n* : quantity used or produced
at one time

bate \'bāt\ *vb* **bat•ed; bat•ing** : moderate or
reduce
bath \'bath, 'báth\ *n, pl* **baths** \'bathz,
'baths, 'báthz, 'báths\ **1** : a washing of the
body **2** : water for washing the body **3**
: liquid in which something is immersed
4 : bathroom **5** : large financial loss —
bath•tub *n*
bathe \'bāth\ *vb* **bathed; bath•ing 1** : wash
in liquid **2** : flow against so as to wet **3**
: shine light over **4** : take a bath or a swim
—**bath•er** *n*
bath•robe *n* : robe worn around the house
bath•room *n* : room with a bathtub or
shower and usu. a sink and toilet
ba•tiste \bə'tēst\ *n* : fine sheer fabric
ba•ton \bə'tän\ *n* : musical conductor's stick
bat•tal•ion \bə'talyən\ *n* : military unit composed of a headquarters and two or more
companies
bat•ten \'bat³n\ *n* : strip of wood used to
seal or reinforce ~ *vb* : furnish or fasten
with battens
¹bat•ter \'batər\ *vb* : beat or damage with
repeated blows
²batter *n* : mixture of flour and liquid
³batter *n* : player who bats
bat•tery \'batərē\ *n, pl* -**ter•ies 1** : illegal
beating of a person **2** : group of artillery
guns **3** : group of electric cells
bat•ting \'batiŋ\ *n* : layers of cotton or wool
for stuffing
bat•tle \'bat³l\ *n* : military fighting ~ *vb*
-**tled; -tling** : engage in battle —**battlefield** *n*
bat•tle–ax *n* : long-handled ax formerly
used as a weapon
bat•tle•ment \-mənt\ *n* : parapet on top of a
wall
bat•tle•ship *n* : heavily armed warship
bat•ty \'batē\ *adj* -**ti•er; -est** : crazy
bau•ble \'bòbəl\ *n* : trinket
bawdy \'bòdē\ *adj* **bawd•i•er; -est** : obscene
or lewd —**bawd•i•ly** *adv* —**bawd•i•ness**
n
bawl \'bòl\ *vb* : cry loudly ~ *n* : long loud
cry
¹bay \'bā\ *adj* : reddish brown ~ *n*
2 : bay-colored animal
³bay *n* : European laurel
³bay *n* **1** : compartment **2** : area projecting
out from a building and containing a win-
dow (**bay window**)
⁴bay *vb* : bark with deep long tones ~ *n* **1**
: position of one unable to escape danger
2 : baying of dogs
⁵bay *n* : body of water smaller than a gulf
and nearly surrounded by land
bay•ber•ry \-,berē\ *n* : shrub bearing small
waxy berries
bay•o•net \'bāənət, ,bāə'net\ *n* : dagger that
fits on the end of a rifle ~ *vb* -**net•ed;
-net•ing** : stab with a bayonet
bay•ou \'bīü, -ō\ *n* : creek flowing through
marshy land
ba•zaar \bə'zär\ *n* **1** : market **2** : fair for
charity
ba•zoo•ka \-'zükə\ *n* : weapon that shoots
armor-piercing rockets
BB *n* : small shot pellet
be \'bē\ *vb* **was** \'wäz, 'wäz\, **were** \'wər\;
been \'bin\; **be•ing** \'bēiŋ\; **am** \əm,
'am\, **is** \'iz, əz\, **are** \ər, 'är\ **1** : equal **2**
: exist **3** : occupy a certain place **4** : occur
~ *verbal auxiliary* —used to show continuous action or to form the passive
voice
beach \'bēch\ *n* : sandy shore of a sea, lake,
or river ~ *vb* : drive ashore
beach•comb•er \-,kōmər\ *n* : one who
searches the shore for useful objects
beach•head *n* : shore area held by an attacking force in an invasion
bea•con \'bēkən\ *n* : guiding or warning
light or signal
bead \'bēd\ *n* : small round body esp. strung
on a thread ~ *vb* : form into a bead —
bead•ing *n* —**beady** *adj*
bea•gle \'bēgəl\ *n* : small short-legged
hound
beak \'bēk\ *n* : bill of a bird —**beaked** *adj*
bea•ker \'bēkər\ *n* **1** : large drinking cup **2**
: laboratory vessel
beam \'bēm\ *n* **1** : large long piece of timber
or metal **2** : ray of light **3** : directed radio
signals for the guidance of pilots ~ *vb* **1**
: send out light **2** : smile **3** : aim a radio broadcast
bean \'bēn\ *n* : edible plant seed borne in
pods
¹bear \'bar\ *n, pl* **bears** or *pl* **bear** : large
heavy mammal with shaggy hair **2** : gruff
or sullen person —**bearish** *adj*
²bear *vb* **bore** \'bōr\, **borne** \'bōrn\; **bearing 1** : carry **2** : give birth to or produce
3 : endure **4** : press **5** : go in an indicated
direction —**bear•able** *adj* —**bearer** *n*
beard \'bird\ *n* **1** : facial hair on a man **2**
: tuft like a beard ~ *vb* : confront boldly
—**beard•ed** *adj* —**beard•less** *adj*
bear•ing *n* **1** : way of carrying oneself **2**
: supporting object or purpose **3** : significance **4** : machine part in which an-

other part turns **5** : direction with respect esp. to compass points

beast \'bēst\ *n* **1** : animal **2** : brutal person —**beast·li·ness** *n* —**beast·ly** *adj*

beat \'bēt\ *vb* **beat; beat·en** \'bēt³n\ *or* **beat; beat·ing 1** : strike repeatedly **2** : defeat **3** : act or arrive before **4** : throb ~ *n* **1** : single stroke or pulsation **2** : rhythmic stress in poetry or music ~ *adj* : exhausted —**beat·er** *n*

be·atif·ic \bēə'tifik\ *adj* : blissful

be·at·i·fy \bē'atə,fī\ *vb* **-fied; -fy·ing** : make happy or blessed —**be·at·i·fi·ca·tion** \-,atəfə'kāshən\ *n*

be·at·i·tude \-'atə,tüd, -,tyüd\ *n* : saying in the Sermon on the Mount (Matthew 5:3-12) beginning ''Blessed are''

beau \'bō\ *n, pl* **beaux** \'bōz\ *or* **beaus** : suitor

beau·ty \'byütē\ *n, pl* **-ties** : qualities that please the senses or mind —**beau·te·ous** \-ēəs\ *adj* —**beau·te·ous·ly** *adv* —**beau·ti·fi·ca·tion** \,byütəfə'kāshən\ *n* —**beau·ti·fi·er** \'byütə,fīər\ *n* —**beau·ti·ful** \-ifəl\ *adj* —**beau·ti·ful·ly** *adv* —**beau·ti·fy** \-ə,fī\ *vb*

bea·ver \'bēvər\ *n* : large fur-bearing rodent

be·cause \bi'kóz, -'kəz\ *conj* : for the reason that

because of *prep* : by reason of

beck \'bek\ *n* : summons

beck·on \'bekən\ *vb* : summon esp. by a nod or gesture

be·come \bi'kəm\ *vb* **-came** \-'kām\ **-come; -com·ing 1** : come to be **2** : be suitable —**be·com·ing·ly** *adv*

bed \'bed\ *n* **1** : piece of furniture to sleep on **2** : flat or level surface ~ *vb* **-dd-** : put or go to bed —**bed·spread** *n*

bed·bug *n* : wingless bloodsucking insect

bed·clothes *n pl* : bedding

bed·ding *n* **1** : sheets and blankets for a bed **2** : soft material (as hay) for an animal's bed

be·deck \bi'dek\ *vb* : adorn

be·dev·il \-'devəl\ *vb* : harass

bed·lam \'bedləm\ *n* : uproar and confusion

be·drag·gled \bi'dragəld\ *adj* : dirty and disordered

bed·rid·den \'bed,rid³n\ *adj* : kept in bed by illness

bed·rock *n* : solid subsurface rock —**bedrock** *adj*

¹bee \'bē\ *n* **1** : 4-winged honey-producing insect —**bee·hive** *n* —**bee·keep·er** *n* —**bees·wax** *n*

²bee *n* : neighborly work session

beech \'bēch\ *n, pl* **beech·es** *or* **beech** : tree with smooth gray bark and edible nuts (**beech·nuts**) —**beech·en** \-ən\ *adj*

beef \'bēf\ *n, pl* **beefs** \'bēfs\ *or* **beeves** \'bēvz\ : flesh of a steer, cow, or bull ~ *vb* : strengthen —used with *up* —**beefsteak** *n*

bee·line *n* : straight course

been *past part of* BE

beep \'bēp\ *n* : short usu. high-pitched warning sound —**beep** *vb* —**beep·er** *n*

beer \'bir\ *n* : alcoholic drink brewed from malt and hops —**beery** *adj*

beet \'bēt\ *n* : garden root vegetable

bee·tle \'bēt³l\ *n* : 4-winged insect

be·fall \bi'fól\ *vb* **-fell; -fall·en** : happen to

be·fit \bi'fit\ *vb* : be suitable to

be·fore \bi'fōr\ *adv* **1** : in front **2** : earlier ~ *prep* **1** : in front of **2** : earlier than ~ *conj* : earlier than

be·fore·hand *adv or adj* : in advance

be·friend \bi'frend\ *vb* : act as friend to

be·fud·dle \-'fəd³l\ *vb* : confuse

beg \'beg\ *vb* **-gg-** : ask earnestly

be·get \bi'get\ *vb* **-got; -got·ten** *or* **-got; -get·ting** : become the father of

beg·gar \'begər\ *n* : one that begs ~ *vb* : make poor —**beg·gar·ly** *adj* —**beg·gary** *n*

be·gin \bi'gin\ *vb* **-gan** \-'gan\ **-gun** \-'gən\ **-gin·ning 1** : start **2** : come into being —**be·gin·ner** *n*

be·gone \bi'gón\ *vb* : go away

be·go·nia \-'gōnyə\ *n* : tropical herb with waxy flowers

be·grudge \-'grəj\ *vb* **1** : concede reluctantly **2** : look upon disapprovingly

be·guile \-'gīl\ *vb* **-guiled; -guil·ing 1** : deceive **2** : amuse

be·half \-'haf, -'häf\ *n* : benefit

be·have \-'hāv\ *vb* **-haved; -hav·ing** : act in a certain way

be·hav·ior \-'hāvyər\ *n* : way of behaving —**be·hav·ior·al** \-əl\ *adj*

be·head \-'hed\ *vb* : cut off the head of

be·hest \-'hest\ *n* : command

be·hind \bi'hīnd\ *adv* : at the back ~ *prep* **1** : in back of **2** : less than **3** : supporting

be·hold \-'hōld\ *vb* **-held; -hold·ing** : see —**be·hold·er** *n*

be·hold·en \-'hōldən\ *adj* : indebted

be·hoove \-'hüv\ *vb* **-hooved; -hoov·ing** : be necessary for

beige \'bāzh\ *n* : yellowish brown —**beige** *adj*

be·ing \'bēiŋ\ *n* **1** : existence **2** : living thing

be·la·bor \bi'lābər\ *vb* : carry on to absurd lengths

be·lat·ed \-'lātəd\ *adj* : delayed

belch \'belch\ *vb* **1** : expel stomach gas orally **2** : emit forcefully —**belch** *n*

be·lea·guer \bi'lēgər\ *vb* **1** : besiege **2** : harass

bel·fry \belfrē\ *n, pl* **-fries** : bell tower

be·lie \bi'lī\ *vb* **-lied; -ly·ing 1** : misrepresent **2** : prove false

be·lief \bə'lēf\ *n* **1** : trust **2** : something believed

be·lieve \-'lēv\ *vb* **-lieved; -liev·ing 1** : trust in **2** : accept as true **3** : hold as an opinion —**be·liev·able** *adj* —**believ·ably** *adv* —**be·liev·er** *n*

be·lit·tle \bi'lit³l\ *vb* **-lit·tled; -lit·tling 1** : disparage **2** : make seem less

bell \'bel\ *n* : hollow metallic device that rings when struck ~ *vb* : provide with a bell

bel·la·don·na \belə'dänə\ *n* : poisonous herb yielding a drug

belle \'bel\ *n* : beautiful woman

bel·li·cose \beli,kōs\ *adj* : pugnacious —**bel·li·cos·i·ty** \beli'käsətē\ *n*

bel·lig·er·ent \bə'lijərənt\ *adj* **1** : waging war **2** : truculent —**bel·lig·er·ence** \-rəns\ *n* —**bel·lig·er·en·cy** \-rənsē\ *n* —**belligerent** *n*

bel·low \'belō\ *vb* : make a loud deep roar or shout —**bellow** *n*

bel·lows \-ōz, -əz\ *n sing or pl* : device with sides that can be compressed to expel air

bell·weth·er \'bel'wethər, -,weth-\ *n* : leader

bel·ly \belē\ *n, pl* **-lies** : abdomen ~ *vb* **-lied; -ly·ing** : bulge

be·long \bi'lóŋ\ *vb* **1** : be suitable **2** : be owned **3** : be a part of

be·long·ings \-iŋz\ *n pl* : possessions

be·loved \bi'ləvəd, -'ləvd\ *adj* : dearly loved —**beloved** *n*

be·low \-'lō\ *adv* : in or to a lower place ~ *prep* : lower than

belt \'belt\ *n* **1** : strip (as of leather) worn about the waist **2** : endless band to impart motion **3** : distinct region ~ *vb* **1** : put a belt around **2** : thrash

be·moan \bi'mōn\ *vb* : lament

be·muse \-'myüz\ *vb* : confuse

bench \'bench\ *n* **1** : long seat **2** : judge's seat **3** : court

bend \'bend\ *vb* **bent** \'bent\ **bending 1** : curve or cause a change of shape in **2** : turn in a certain direction ~ *n* **1** : act of bending **2** : curve

be·neath \bi'nēth\ *adv or prep* : below

bene·dic·tion \benə'dikshən\ *n* : closing blessing

bene·fac·tor \'benə,faktər\ *n* : one who gives esp. charitable aid

be·nef·i·cence \bə'nefəsəns\ *n* : quality of doing good —**be·nef·i·cent** \-sənt\ *adj*

ben·e·fi·cial \benə'fishəl\ *adj* : being of benefit —**ben·e·fi·cial·ly** *adv*

ben·e·fi·cia·ry \-'fishē,erē, -'fishərē\ *n, pl* **-ries** : one who receives benefits

ben·e·fit \'benə,fit\ *n* **1** : something that does good **2** : help **3** : fund-raising event —**benefit** *vb*

be·nev·o·lence \bə'nevələns\ *n* **1** : charitable nature **2** : act of kindness —**be·nev·o·lent** \-lənt\ *adj* —**be·nev·o·lent·ly** *adv*

be·night·ed \bi'nītəd\ *adj* : ignorant

be·nign \bi'nīn\ *adj* **1** : gentle or kindly **2** : not malignant —**be·nig·ni·ty** \-'nignətē\ *n*

be·nig·nant \-'nignənt\ *adj* : benign

bent \'bent\ *n* : aptitude or interest

be·numb \bi'nəm\ *vb* **1** : make numb esp. by cold

ben·zene \'ben,zēn\ *n* : colorless flammable liquid

be·queath \bi'kwēth, -'kwēth\ *vb* **1** : give by will **2** : hand down

be·quest \bi'kwest\ *n* : something bequeathed

be·rate \-'rāt\ *vb* : scold harshly

be·reaved \-'rēvd\ *adj* : suffering the death of a loved one ~ *n, pl* **bereaved** : one who is bereaved —**be·reave·ment** *n*

be·reft \-'reft\ *adj* : deprived of or lacking something

be·ret \bə'rā\ *n* : round soft visorless cap

beri·beri \,berē'berē\ *n* : thiamine-deficiency disease

berm \'bərm\ *n* : bank of earth

ber·ry \'berē\ *n, pl* **-ries** : small pulpy fruit

ber·serk \bər'sərk, -'zərk\ *adj* : crazed —**berserk** *adv*

berth \'bərth\ *n* **1** : place where a ship is anchored **2** : place to sit or sleep esp. on a ship **3** : job ~ *vb* : to bring or come into a berth

ber·yl \'berəl\ *n* : light-colored silicate mineral

be·seech \bi'sēch\ *vb* **-sought** \-'sót\ *or* **-seeched; -seech·ing** : entreat

be·set \-'set\ *vb* **1** : harass **2** : hem in

be·side \-'sīd\ *prep* **1** : by the side of **2** : besides

be·sides \-'sīdz\ *adv* **1** : in addition **2** : moreover ~ *prep* **1** : other than **2** : in addition to

be·siege \-'sēj\ *vb* : lay siege to —**besieg·er** *n*

be·smirch \-'smərch\ *vb* : soil

be·sot \-'sät\ *vb* **-tt-** : become drunk

be·speak \bi'spēk\ *vb* **-spoke; -spo·ken; -speak·ing 1** : address **2** : indicate

best \'best\ *adj, superlative of* GOOD **1** : excelling all others **2** : most productive **3** : largest ~ *adv, superlative of* WELL **1** : in the best way **2** : most ~ *n* : one that is best ~ *vb* : outdo

bes·tial \'beschəl, 'bēs-\ *adj* **1** : relating to beasts **2** : brutish —**bes·ti·al·i·ty** \,beschē'alətē, ,bēs-\ *n*

be·stir \bi'stər\ *vb* : rouse to action

best man *n* : chief male attendant at a wedding

be·stow \bi'stō\ *vb* : give —**be·stow·al** \-əl\ *n*

bet \'bet\ *n* **1** : something risked or pledged on the outcome of a contest **2** : the making of a bet ~ *vb* **bet; bet·ting 1** : risk (as money) on an outcome **2** : make a bet with

be·tide \bi'tīd\ *vb* : happen to

be·to·ken \bi'tōkən\ *vb* : give an indication of

be·tray \bi'trā\ *vb* **1** : seduce **2** : report or reveal to an enemy by treachery **3** : abandon **4** : prove unfaithful to **5** : reveal unintentionally —**be·tray·al** *n* —**be·tray·er** *n*

be·troth \-'träth, -'tróth, -'trōth, *or with* th\ *vb* : promise to marry —**be·troth·al** *n* —**be·trothed** *n*

bet·ter \'betər\ *adj, comparative of* GOOD **1** : more than half **2** : improved in health **3** : of higher quality ~ *adv, comparative of* WELL **1** : in a superior manner **2** : more ~ *n* **1** : one that is better **2** : advantage ~ *vb* **1** : improve **2** : surpass —**bet·ter·ment** \-mənt\ *n*

bet·tor, bet·ter \'betər\ *n* : one who bets

be·tween \bi'twēn\ *prep* **1** —used to show two things considered together **2** : in the space separating **3** —used to indicate a comparison or choice ~ *adv* : in an intervening space or interval

bev·el \'bevəl\ *n* **1** : slant on an edge ~ *vb* **-eled** *or* **-elled; -el·ing** *or* **-el·ling 1** : cut or shape to a bevel **2** : incline

bev·er·age \'bevrij\ *n* : drink

bevy \'bevē\ *n* : large group

be·wail \bi'wāl\ *vb* : lament

be·ware \-'war\ *vb* : be cautious

be·wil·der \-'wildər\ *vb* : confuse —**be·wil·der·ment** *n*

be·witch \-'wich\ *vb* **1** : affect by witchcraft **2** : charm —**be·witch·ment** *n*

be·yond \bē'yänd\ *adv* **1** : farther **2** : besides ~ *prep* **1** : on or to the farther side of **2** : out of the reach of **3** : besides

bi- \'bī, ,bī\ *prefix* **1** : two **2** : coming or occurring every two **3** : twice, doubly, or on both sides

bicolored	**bifunctional**
biconcave	**bimetal**
biconcavity	**bimetallic**
biconvex	**binational**
biconvexity	**biparental**
bicultural	**bipolar**
bidirectional	**biracial**

bi·an·nu·al \bī'anyəwəl\ *adj* : occurring twice a year —**bi·an·nu·al·ly** *adv*

bi·as \'bīəs\ *n* **1** : line diagonal to the grain of a fabric **2** : prejudice ~ *vb* **-ased** *or* **-assed; -as·ing** *or* **-as·sing** : prejudice

bib \'bib\ *n* : shield tied under the chin to protect the clothes while eating

Bi·ble \'bībəl\ *n* **1** : sacred scriptures of Christians **2** : sacred scriptures of Judaism or of some other religion —**bib·li·cal** \'biblikəl\

bib·li·og·ra·phy \,biblē'ägrəfē\ *n, pl* **-phies** : list of writings on a subject or of an author —**bib·li·og·ra·pher** \-fər\ *n* —**bib·lio·graph·ic** \-lēə'grafik\ *adj*

bi·cam·er·al \bī'kamərəl\ *adj* : having 2 legislative chambers

bi·car·bon·ate \-'kärbə,nāt, -nət\ *n* : acid carbonate

bi·cen·ten·ni·al \,bīsen'tenēəl\ *n* : 200th anniversary —**bicentennial** *adj*

bi·ceps \'bī,seps\ *n* : large muscle of the upper arm

bick·er \'bikər\ *vb or n* : squabble

bi·cus·pid \bī'kəspəd\ *n* : double-pointed tooth

bi·cy·cle \'bī,sikəl\ *n* : 2-wheeled vehicle moved by pedaling ~ *vb* **-cled; -cling** : ride a bicycle —**bi·cy·cler** \-klər\ *n* —**bi·cy·clist** \-list\ *n*

bid \'bid\ *vb* **bade** \'bad, 'bād\ *or* **bid; bid·den** \'bid³n\ *or* **bid; bid·ding 1** : order **2** : invite **3** : express **4** : make a bid ~ *n* **1** : act of bidding **2** : buyer's proposed price —**bid·da·ble** \-əbəl\ *adj* —**bid·der** *n*

bide \'bīd\ *vb* **bode** \'bōd\ *or* **bid·ed; bided; bid·ing 1** : wait **2** : dwell

bi·en·ni·al \bī'enēəl\ *adj* **1** : occurring once in 2 years **2** : lasting 2 years —**biennial** *n* —**bi·en·ni·al·ly** *adv*

bier \'bir\ *n* : stand for a coffin

bi·fo·cals \'bī,fōkəlz\ *n pl* : eyeglasses that correct for near and distant vision

big \'big\ *adj* **-gg-** : large in size, amount, or scope —**big·ness** *n*

big·a·my \'bigəmē\ *n* : marrying one person while still married to another —**big·a·mist** \-mist\ *n* —**big·a·mous** \-məs\ *adj*

big·horn *n, pl* **-horn** *or* **-horns** : wild mountain sheep

bight \'bīt\ *n* **1** : loop of a rope **2** : bay

big·ot \'bigət\ *n* : one who is intolerant of others —**big·ot·ed** \-ətəd\ *adj* —**big·ot·ry** \-ətrē\ *n*

big shot *n* : important person

big·wig *n* : big shot

bike \'bīk\ *n* : bicycle or motorcycle

bi·ki·ni \bə'kēnē\ *n* : woman's brief 2-piece bathing suit

bi·lat·er·al \bī'latərəl\ *adj* : involving 2 sides —**bi·lat·er·al·ly** *adv*

bile \'bīl\ *n* **1** : greenish liver secretion that aids digestion **2** : bad temper

bi·lin·gual \bī'liŋgwəl\ *adj* : using 2 languages

bil·ious \'bilyəs\ *adj* : irritable —**bilious·ness** *n*

bilk \'bilk\ *vb* : cheat

¹bill \'bil\ *n* : jaws of a bird together with their horny covering ~ *vb* : caress fondly —**billed** *adj*

²bill *n* **1** : draft of a law **2** : list of things to be paid for **3** : printed advertisement **4** : piece of paper money ~ *vb* : submit a bill or account to

bill·board *n* : surface for displaying advertising bills

bil·let \'bilət\ *n* : soldiers' quarters ~ *vb* : lodge in a billet

bill·fold *n* : wallet

bil·liards \'bilyərdz\ *n* : game of driving balls into one another or into pockets on a table

bil·lion \'bilyən\ *n, pl* **billions** *or* **billion** : 1000 millions —**billion** *adj* —**billionth** \-yənth\ *adj or n*

bil·low \'bilō\ *n* **1** : great wave **2** : rolling mass ~ *vb* : swell out —**bil·lowy** \'biləwē\ *adj*

billy goat *n* : male goat

bin \'bin\ *n* : storage box

bi·na·ry \'bīnərē\ *adj* : consisting of 2 things —**binary** *n*

bind \'bīnd\ *vb* **bound** \'baúnd\ **binding 1** : tie **2** : obligate **3** : unite into a mass **4** : bandage —**bind·er** *n* —**binding** *n*

binge \'binj\ *n* : spree

bin·go \'biŋgō\ *n, pl* **-gos** : game of covering numbers on a card

bin·oc·u·lar \bī'näkyələr, bə-\ *adj* : of or relating to both eyes ~ *n* : binocular optical instrument —usu. pl.

bio·chem·is·try \,bīō'keməstrē\ *n* : chemistry dealing with organisms —**bio·chem·i·cal** *adj* —**bio·chem·ist** *n*

bio·de·grad·able \,bīōdi'grādəbəl\ *adj* : able to be reduced to harmless products by organisms —**bio·de·grad·abil·i·ty** *n* —**bio·deg·ra·da·tion** *n* —**bio·de·grade** *vb*

bi·og·ra·phy \bī'ägrəfē, bē-\ *n, pl* **-phies** : written history of a person's life —**bi·og·ra·pher** \-fər\ *n* —**bio·graph·i·cal** \,bīə'grafikəl\ *adj*

bi·ol·o·gy \bī'äləjē\ *n* : science of living beings and life processes —**bio·log·ic** \,bīə'läjik\, **bio·log·i·cal** \-əl\ *adj* —**bi·ol·o·gist** \bī'äljist\ *n*

bio·phys·ics \,bīō'fiziks\ *n* : application of physics to biological problems —**bio·phys·i·cal** *adj* —**bio·phys·i·cist** *n*

bi·op·sy \'bī,äpsē\ *n, pl* **-sies** : removal of live bodily tissue for examination

bio·tech·nol·o·gy \,bīōtek'näləjē\ *n* : manufacture of products using techniques involving the manipulation of DNA

bi·par·ti·san \bī'pärtəzən, -sən\ *adj* : involving members of 2 parties

bi·ped \'bī,ped\ *n* : 2-footed animal

birch \'bərch\ *n* : deciduous tree with close-grained wood —**birch, birch·en** \-ən\ *adj*

bird \'bərd\ *n* : warm-blooded egg-laying vertebrate with wings and feathers —**bird·bath** *n* —**bird·house** *n* —**bird·seed** *n*

bird's-eye \'bərdz,ī\ *adj* **1** : seen from above **2** : cursory

birth \'bərth\ *n* **1** : act or fact of being born or of producing young **2** : origin —**birth·day** *n* —**birth·place** *n* —**birth·rate** *n*

birth·mark *n* : unusual blemish on the skin at birth

birth·right *n* : something one is entitled to by birth

bis·cuit \'biskət\ *n* : small bread made with leavening other than yeast

bi·sect \'bī,sekt\ *vb* : divide into 2 parts —**bi·sec·tion** \'bī,sekshən\ *n* —**bi·sec·tor** \-tər\ *n*

bish·op \'bishəp\ *n* : clergy member higher than a priest

bish·op·ric \-shə,prik\ n 1 : diocese 2 : office of bishop

bis·muth \'bizməth\ n : heavy brittle metallic chemical element

bi·son \'bīsᵊn, 'bīz-\ n, pl **-son** : large shaggy wild ox of central U.S.

bis·tro \'bēstrō, 'bis-\ n, pl **-tros** : small restaurant or bar

1bit \'bit\ n 1 : part of a bridle that goes in a horse's mouth 2 : drilling tool

2bit n 1 : small piece or quantity 2 : small degree

bitch \'bich\ n : female dog ~ vb : complain

bite \'bīt\ vb **bit** \'bit\ **bit·ten** \'bitᵊn\ **bit·ing** \'bītiŋ\ 1 : to grip or cut with teeth or jaws 2 : dig in or grab and hold 3 : sting 4 : take bait ~ n 1 : act of biting 2 : bit of food 3 : wound made by biting —**bit·ing** adj

bit·ter \'bitər\ adj 1 : having an acrid lingering taste 2 : intense or severe 3 : extremely harsh or resentful —**bit·ter·ly** adv —**bit·ter·ness** n

bit·tern \'bitərn\ n : small heron

bi·tu·mi·nous coal \bə'tümənəs-, -'tyü-\ n : coal that yields volatile waste matter when heated

bi·valve \'bī,valv\ n : animal (as a clam) with a shell of 2 parts —**bivalve** adj

biv·ouac \'bivə,wak\ n : temporary camp ~ vb **-ouacked; -ouack·ing** : camp

bi·zarre \bə'zär\ adj : very strange —**bi·zarre·ly** adv

blab \'blab\ vb **-bb-** : talk too much

black \'blak\ adj 1 : of the color black 2 : Negro 3 : soiled 4 : lacking light 5 : wicked or evil 6 : gloomy ~ n 1 : black pigment or dye 2 : something black 3 : color of least lightness 4 : person of a dark-skinned race ~ vb : blacken —**black·ing** n —**black·ish** adj —**black·ly** adv —**black·ness** n

black–and–blue adj : darkly discolored from bruising

black·ball \'blak,bȯl\ vb 1 : ostracize 2 : boycott —**blackball** n

black·ber·ry \'blak,berē\ n : black or purple fruit of a bramble

black·bird n : bird of which the male is largely or wholly black

black·board n : dark surface for writing on with chalk

black·en \'blakən\ vb 1 : make or become black 2 : defame

black·guard \'blagərd, -,ärd\ n : scoundrel

black·head n : small dark oily mass plugging the outlet of a skin gland

black hole n : invisible extremely massive celestial object

black·jack n 1 : flexible leather-covered club 2 : card game ~ vb : hit with a blackjack

black·list n : list of persons to be punished or boycotted —**blacklist** vb

black·mail n 1 : extortion by threat of exposure 2 : something extorted by blackmail —**blackmail** vb —**blackmail·er** n

black·out n 1 : darkness due to electrical failure 2 : brief fainting spell —**black out** vb

black·smith n : one who forges iron

black·top n : dark tarry material for surfacing roads —**blacktop** vb

blad·der \'bladər\ n : sac into which urine passes from the kidneys

blade \'blād\ n 1 : leaf esp. of grass 2 : something resembling the flat part of a leaf 3 : cutting part of an instrument or tool —**blad·ed** \'blādəd\ adj

blame \'blām\ vb **blamed; blam·ing** 1 : find fault with 2 : hold responsible or responsible for —**blam·able** adj —**blame** n —**blame·less** adj —**blame·less·ly** adv —**blame·wor·thi·ness** n —**blame·worthy** adj

blanch \'blanch\ vb : make or become white or pale

bland \'bland\ adj 1 : smooth in manner 2 : soothing 3 : tasteless —**bland·ly** adv —**bland·ness** n

blan·dish·ment \'blandishmənt\ n : flattering or coaxing speech or act

blank \'blaŋk\ adj 1 : showing or causing a dazed look 2 : lacking expression 3 : empty 4 : free from writing 5 : downright ~ n 1 : an empty space 2 : form with spaces to write in 3 : unfinished form (as of a key) 4 : cartridge with no bullet ~ vb : cover or close up —**blank·ly** adv —**blank·ness** n

blan·ket \'blaŋkət\ n 1 : heavy covering for a bed 2 : covering layer ~ vb : cover ~ adj : applying to a group

blare \'blar\ vb **blared; blar·ing** : make a loud harsh sound —**blare** n

blar·ney \'blärnē\ n : skillful flattery

bla·sé \blä'zā\ adj : indifferent to pleasure or excitement

blas·pheme \blas'fēm\ vb **-phemed; -phem·ing** : speak blasphemy —**blas·phem·er** n

blas·phe·my \'blasfəmē\ n, pl **-mies** : irreverence toward God or anything sacred —**blas·phe·mous** adj

blast \'blast\ n 1 : violent gust of wind 2 : explosion ~ vb : shatter by or as if by explosive —**blast off** vb : take off esp. in a rocket

bla·tant \'blātᵊnt\ adj : offensively showy —**bla·tan·cy** \-ᵊnsē\ n —**bla·tant·ly** adv

1blaze \'blāz\ n 1 : intense direct light 3 : strong display ~ vb **blazed; blaz·ing** : burn or shine brightly

2blaze n 1 : white stripe on an animal's face 2 : trail marker esp. on a tree ~ vb **blazed; blaz·ing** : mark with blazes

blaz·er \-ər\ n : sports jacket

bleach \'blēch\ vb : whiten —**bleach** n

bleach·ers \-ərz\ n sing or pl : uncovered stand for spectators

bleak \'blēk\ adj 1 : desolately barren 2 : lacking cheering qualities —**bleak·ish** adj —**bleak·ly** adv —**bleak·ness** n

blear \'blir\ adj : dim with water or tears

bleary \'blirē\ adj : dull or dimmed esp. from fatigue

bleat \'blēt\ n : cry of a sheep or goat or a sound like it —**bleat** vb

bleed \'blēd\ vb **bled** \'bled\ **bleed·ing** 1 : lose or shed blood 2 : feel distress 3 : flow from a wound 4 : draw fluid from 5 : extort money from —**bleed·er** n

blem·ish \'blemish\ vb : spoil by a flaw ~ n : noticeable flaw

1blench \'blench\ vb : flinch

2blench vb : grow or make pale

blend \'blend\ vb 1 : mix thoroughly 2 : combine into an integrated whole —**blend** n —**blend·er** n

bless \'bles\ vb **blessed** \'blest\ **bless·ing** 1 : consecrate by religious rite 2 : invoke divine care for 3 : make happy —**blessed** \'blesəd\ **blest** \'blest\ adj —**blessed·ly** \'blesədlē\ adv —**bless·ed·ness** \'blesədnəs\ n —**bless·ing** n

blew past of BLOW

blight \'blīt\ n 1 : plant disorder marked by withering or an organism causing it 2 : harmful influence 3 : deteriorated condition ~ vb : affect with or suffer from blight

blimp \'blimp\ n : airship holding form by pressure of contained gas

blind \'blīnd\ adj 1 : lacking or quite deficient in ability to see 2 : not intelligently controlled 3 : having no way out ~ vb 1 : to make blind 2 : dazzle ~ n 1 : something to conceal or darken 2 : place of concealment —**blind·ly** adv —**blind·ness** n

blind·fold vb : cover the eyes of —**blindfold** n

blink \'bliŋk\ vb 1 : wink 2 : shine intermittently ~ n : wink

blink·er n : a blinking light

bliss \'blis\ n 1 : complete happiness 2 : heaven or paradise —**bliss·ful** adj —**bliss·ful·ly** adv

blis·ter \'blistər\ n 1 : raised area of skin containing watery fluid 2 : raised or swollen spot ~ vb : develop or cause blisters

blithe \'blīth, 'blith\ adj **blith·er; blith·est** : cheerful —**blithe·ly** adv —**blithe·some** \-səm\ adj

blitz \'blits\ n 1 : series of air raids 2 : fast intensive campaign —**blitz** vb

bliz·zard \'blizərd\ n : severe snowstorm

bloat \'blōt\ vb : swell

blob \'bläb\ n : small lump or drop

bloc \'bläk\ n : group working together

block \'bläk\ n 1 : solid piece 2 : frame enclosing a pulley 3 : quantity considered together 4 : large building divided into separate units 5 : a city square or the distance along one of its sides 6 : obstruction 7 : interruption of a bodily or mental function ~ vb : obstruct or hinder

block·ade \blä'kād\ n : isolation of a place usu. by troops or ships —**blockade** vb —**block·ad·er** n

block·head n : stupid person

blond, blonde \'bländ\ adj 1 : fair in complexion 2 : of a light color —**blond, blonde** n

blood \'bləd\ n 1 : red liquid that circulates in the heart, arteries, and veins of animals 2 : lifeblood 3 : lineage —**blood·ed** adj —**blood·less** adj —**blood·stain** n —**blood·stained** adj —**blood·suck·er** n —**blood·suck·ing** n —**blood·y** adj

blood·cur·dling adj : terrifying

blood·hound n : large hound with a keen sense of smell

blood·mo·bile \-mō,bēl\ n : truck for collecting blood from donors

blood·shed n : slaughter

blood·shot adj : inflamed to redness

blood·stream n : blood in a circulatory system

blood·thirsty adj : eager to shed blood —**blood·thirst·i·ly** adv —**blood·thirst·i·ness** n

bloom \'blüm\ n 1 : flower 2 : period of flowering 3 : fresh or healthy look ~ vb 1 : yield flowers 2 : mature —**bloomy** adj

bloo·mers \'blümərz\ n pl : woman's underwear of short loose trousers

bloop·er \'blüpər\ n : public blunder

blos·som \'bläsəm\ n or vb : flower

blot \'blät\ n 1 : stain 2 : blemish ~ vb **-tt-** 1 : spot 2 : dry with absorbent paper —**blot·ter** n

blotch \'bläch\ n : large spot —**blotch** vb —**blotchy** adj

blouse \'blaus, 'blauz\ n : loose garment reaching from the neck to the waist

1blow \'blō\ vb **blew** \'blü\ **blown** \'blōn\ **blow·ing** 1 : move forcibly 2 : send forth a current of air 3 : sound 4 : shape by blowing 5 : explode 6 : bungle ~ n 1 : gale 2 : act of blowing —**blow·er** n —**blowy** adj

2blow n 1 : forcible stroke 2 pl : fighting 3 : calamity

blow·out n : bursting of a tire

blow·torch n : small torch that uses a blast of air

1blub·ber \'bləbər\ n : fat of whales

2blubber vb : cry noisily

blud·geon \'bləjən\ n : short club ~ vb : hit with a bludgeon

blue \'blü\ adj **blu·er; blu·est** 1 : of the color blue 2 : melancholy ~ n : color of the clear sky —**blu·ish** \-ish\ adj

blue·bell n : plant with blue bell-shaped flowers

blue·ber·ry \-,berē\ n : edible blue or blackish berry

blue·bird n : small bluish songbird

blue·fish n : bluish marine food fish

blue jay n : American crested jay

blue·print n 1 : photographic print in white on blue of a mechanical drawing 2 : plan of action —**blueprint** vb

blues \'blüz\ n pl 1 : depression 2 : music in a melancholy style

1bluff \'bləf\ adj 1 : rising steeply with a broad flat front 2 : frank ~ n : cliff

2bluff vb : deceive by pretense ~ n : act of bluffing —**bluff·er** n

blu·ing, blue·ing \'blüiŋ\ n : laundry preparation to keep fabrics white

blun·der \'bləndər\ vb 1 : move clumsily 2 : make a stupid mistake ~ n : bad mistake

blun·der·buss \-,bəs\ n : obsolete shortbarreled firearm

blunt \'blənt\ adj 1 : not sharp 2 : tactless ~ vb : make dull —**blunt·ly** adv —**blunt·ness** n

blur \'blər\ n 1 : smear 2 : something perceived indistinctly ~ vb **-rr-** : cloud or obscure —**blur·ry** \-ē\ adj

blurb \'blərb\ n : short publicity notice

blurt \'blərt\ vb : utter suddenly

blush \'bləsh\ n : reddening of the face —**blush** vb —**blush·ful** adj

blus·ter \'bləstər\ vb 1 : blow violently 2 : talk or act with boasts or threats —**bluster** n —**blus·tery** adj

boa \'bōə\ n 1 : a large snake (as the **boa con·stric·tor** \-kən'striktər\) that crushes its prey 2 : fluffy scarf

boar \'bōr\ n : male swine

board \'bōrd\ n 1 : long thin piece of sawed lumber 2 : flat thin sheet esp. for games 3 : daily meals furnished for pay 4 : official body ~ vb 1 : go aboard 2 : cover with boards 3 : supply meals to —**board·er** n

board·walk n : wooden walk along a beach

boast \'bōst\ vb : praise oneself or one's possessions —**boast** n —**boast·er** n —**boast·ful** adj —**boast·ful·ly** adv

boat \'bōt\ n : small vessel for traveling on water —**boat** vb —**boat·man** \-mən\ n

boat·swain \'bōsᵊn\ n : ship's officer in charge of the hull

1bob \'bäb\ vb **-bb-** 1 : move up and down 2 : appear suddenly

2bob n 1 : float 2 : woman's short haircut ~ vb : cut hair in a bob

bob·bin \'bäbən\ n : spindle for holding thread

bob·ble \'bäbəl\ vb **-bled; -bling** : fumble —**bobble** n

bob·cat n : small American lynx

bob·o·link \'bäbə,liŋk\ n : American songbird

bob·sled \'bäb,sled\ n : racing sled —**bobsled** vb

bob·white \'bäb'hwīt\ n : quail

bock \'bäk\ n : dark beer

1bode \'bōd\ vb **bod·ed; bod·ing** : indicate by signs

2bode past of BIDE

bod·ice \'bädəs\ n : close-fitting top of dress

bodi·ly \'bädᵊlē\ adj : relating to the body ~ adv 1 : in the flesh 2 : as a whole

body \'bädē\ n, pl **bod·ies** 1 : the physical whole of an organism 2 : human being 3 : main part 4 : mass of matter 5 : group —**bod·ied** adj —**bodi·less** \-ilas, -ᵊləs\ adj —**body·guard** n

bog \'bäg, 'bȯg\ n : swamp ~ vb **-gg-** : sink in or as if in a swamp —**bog·gy** adj

bo·gey \'bügē, 'bō-\ n, pl **-geys** : someone or something frightening

bog·gle \'bägəl\ vb **-gled; -gling** : overwhelm with amazement

bo·gus \'bōgəs\ adj : fake

bo·he·mi·an \bō'hēmēən\ n : one living unconventionally —**bohemian** adj

1boil \'bȯil\ n : inflamed swelling

2boil vb 1 : heat to a temperature (**boiling point**) at which vapor forms 2 : cook in boiling liquid 3 : be agitated —**boil** n

boil·er \'bȯilər\ n : tank holding hot water or steam

bois·ter·ous \'bȯistərəs\ adj : noisily turbulent —**bois·ter·ous·ly** adv

bold \'bōld\ adj 1 : courageous 2 : insolent 3 : daring —**bold·ly** adv —**bold·ness** n

bo·le·ro \bə'lerō\ n, pl **-ros** 1 : Spanish dance 2 : short open jacket

boll \'bōl\ n : seed pod

boll weevil n : small grayish weevil that infests the cotton plant

bo·lo·gna \bə'lōnē\ n : large smoked sausage

bol·ster \'bōlstər\ n : long pillow ~ vb **-stered; -ster·ing** : support

bolt \'bōlt\ n 1 : flash of lightning 2 : sliding bar used to fasten a door 3 : roll of cloth 4 : threaded pin used with a nut ~ vb 1 : move suddenly 2 : fasten with a bolt 3 : swallow hastily

bomb \'bäm\ n : explosive device ~ vb : attack with bombs —**bomb·proof** adj

bom·bard \bäm'bärd, bəm-\ vb : attack with or as if with artillery —**bom·bard·ment** n

bom·bar·dier \,bämbə'dir\ n : one who releases the bombs from a bomber

bom·bast \'bäm,bast\ n : pretentious language —**bom·bas·tic** \bäm'bastik\ adj

bomb·er n 1 : one that bombs 2 : airplane for dropping bombs

bomb·shell n 1 : bomb 2 : great surprise

bona fide \'bōnə,fīd, 'bän-; ,bōnə'fīdē\ adj 1 : made in good faith 2 : genuine

bo·nan·za \bə'nanzə\ n : something yielding a rich return

bon·bon \'bän,bän\ n : piece of candy

bond \'bänd\ n 1 pl : fetters 2 : uniting force 3 : obligation made binding by money 4 : interest-bearing certificate ~ vb 1 : insure 2 : cause to adhere —**bond·holder** n

bond·age \'bändij\ n : slavery —**bond·man** \-mən\ n —**bond·woman** n

1bonds·man \'bändzmən\ n : slave

2bondsman n : surety

bone \'bōn\ n : skeletal material ~ vb **boned; bon·ing** : to free from bones —**bone·less** adj —**bony** \'bōnē\ adj

bon·er \'bōnər\ n : blunder

bon·fire \'bän,fīr\ n : outdoor fire

bo·ni·to \bə'nētō\ n, pl **-tos** or **-to** : medium-sized tuna

bon·net \'bänət\ n : hat for a woman or infant

bo·nus \'bōnəs\ n : extra payment

boo \'bü\ n, pl **boos** : shout of disapproval —**boo** vb

boo·by \'bübē\ n, pl **-bies** : dunce

book \'buk\ n 1 : paper sheets bound into a volume 2 : long literary work or a subdivision of one ~ vb : reserve —**book·case** n —**book·let** \-lət\ n —**book·mark** n —**book·sell·er** n —**book·shelf** n

book·end n : support to hold up a row of books

book·ie \-ē\ n : bookmaker

book·ish \-ish\ adj : fond of books and reading

book·keep·er n : one who keeps business accounts —**book·keep·ing** n

book·mak·er n : one who takes bets —**book·mak·ing** n

book·worm n : one devoted to reading

1boom \'büm\ n 1 : long spar to extend the bottom of a sail 2 : beam projecting from the pole of a derrick

2boom vb 1 : make a deep hollow sound 2 : grow rapidly esp. in value ~ n 1 : booming sound 2 : rapid growth

boo·mer·ang \'bümə,raŋ\ n : angular club that returns to the thrower

1boon \'bün\ n : benefit

2boon adj : congenial

boon·docks \'bün,däks\ n pl : rural area

boor \'bur\ n : rude person —**boor·ish** adj

boost \'büst\ vb 1 : raise 2 : promote —**boost** n —**boost·er** n

boot \'büt\ n 1 : covering for the foot and leg 2 : kick ~ vb : kick

boo·tee, boo·tie \'bütē\ n : infant's knitted sock

booth \'büth\ n, pl **booths** \'büthz, 'büths\ : small enclosed stall or seating area

boot·leg \'büt,leg\ vb : make or sell liquor illegally —**bootleg** adj or n —**boot·leg·ger** n

boo·ty \'bütē\ n, pl **-ties** : plunder

booze \'büz\ vb **boozed; booz·ing** : drink liquor to excess ~ n : liquor —**booz·er** n —**boozy** adj

bo·rax \'bōr,aks\ n : crystalline compound of boron

bor·der \'bōrdər\ n 1 : edge 2 : boundary ~ vb 1 : put a border on 2 : be close

1bore \'bōr\ vb **bored; bor·ing** 1 : pierce 2 : make by piercing ~ n : cylindrical hole or its diameter —**bor·er** n

2bore past of BEAR

3bore n : one that is dull ~ vb **bored; bor-**

ing : tire with dullness —**bore·dom** \'bōrdəm\ *n*

born \'bȯrn\ *adj* **1** : brought into life **2** : being such by birth

borne *past part of* BEAR

bo·ron \'bȯr,än\ *n* : dark-colored chemical element

bor·ough \'bərō\ *n* : incorporated town or village

bor·row \'bärō\ *vb* **1** : take as a loan **2** : take into use

bo·som \'bùzəm, 'bü-\ *n* : breast ~ *adj* : intimate —**bo·somed** *adj*

boss \'bȯs\ *n* : employer or supervisor ~ *vb* : supervise —**bossy** *adj*

bot·a·ny \'bätᵊnē\ *n* : plant biology —**bo·tan·i·cal** \bə'tanikəl\ *adj* —**bot·a·nist** \'bätᵊnist\ *n* —**bot·a·nize** \-ᵊn,īz\ *vb*

botch \'bäch\ *vb* : do clumsily —**botch** *n*

both \'bōth\ *adj or pron* : the one and the other ~ *conj* —used to show each of two is included

both·er \'bäthər\ *vb* **1** : annoy or worry **2** : take the trouble —**bother** *n* —**both·er·some** \-səm\ *adj*

bot·tle \'bätᵊl\ *n* : container with a narrow neck and no handles ~ *vb* **bottled; bot·tling** : put into a bottle

bot·tle·neck *n* : place or cause of congestion

bot·tom \'bätəm\ *n* **1** : supporting surface **2** : lowest part or place —**bottom** *adj* —**bot·tomed** *adj* —**bot·tom·less** *adj*

bot·u·lism \'bächə,lizəm\ *n* : acute food poisoning

bou·doir \'bü,dwär, 'bù-, ,bü'-, ,bù'-\ *n* : woman's private room

bough \'bau̇\ *n* : large tree branch

bought *past of* BUY

bouil·lon \'bù,yän; 'bùl,yän, -yən\ *n* : clear soup

boul·der \'bōldər\ *n* : large rounded rock —**boul·dered** *adj*

bou·le·vard \'bùlə,värd, 'bü-\ *n* : broad thoroughfare

bounce \'bau̇ns\ *vb* **bounced; bounc·ing 1** : spring back **2** : make bounce —**bounce** *n* —**bouncy** \'bau̇nsē\ *adj*

¹**bound** \'bau̇nd\ *adj* : intending to go

²**bound** *n* : limit or boundary ~ *vb* : be a boundary of —**bound·less** *adj* —**bound·less·ness** *n*

³**bound** *adj* **1** : obliged **2** : having a binding **3** : determined **4** : incapable of failing

⁴**bound** *n* : leap ~ *vb* : move by springing

bound·ary \'bau̇ndrē\ *n, pl* **-aries** : line marking extent or separation

boun·ty \'bau̇ntē\ *n, pl* **-ties 1** : generosity **2** : reward —**boun·te·ous** \-ēəs\ *adj* —**boun·te·ous·ly** *adv* —**boun·ti·ful** \-ifəl\ *adj* —**boun·ti·ful·ly** *adv*

bou·quet \bō'kā, bü-\ *n* **1** : bunch of flowers **2** : fragrance

bour·bon \'bərbən\ *n* : corn whiskey

bour·geoi·sie \,bùrzh,wä'zē\ *n* : middle class of society —**bour·geois** \'bùrzh,wä, bùrzh'wä\ *n or adj*

bout \'bau̇t\ *n* **1** : contest **2** : outbreak

bou·tique \bü'tēk\ *n* : specialty shop

bo·vine \'bō,vīn, -,vēn\ *adj* : relating to cattle —**bovine** *n*

¹**bow** \'bau̇\ *vb* **1** : submit **2** : bend the head or body ~ *n* : act of bowing

²**bow** \'bō\ *n* **1** : bend or arch **2** : weapon for shooting arrows **3** : knot with loops **4** : rod with stretched horsehairs for playing a stringed instrument ~ *vb* : curve or bend —**bow·man** \-mən\ *n* —**bow·string** *n*

³**bow** \'bau̇\ *n* : forward part of a ship —**bow** *adj*

bow·els \'bau̇əls\ *n pl* **1** : intestines **2** : inmost parts

bow·er \'bau̇ər\ *n* : arbor

¹**bowl** \'bōl\ *n* : concave vessel or part —**bowl·ful** \-,fùl\ *n*

²**bowl** *n* : round ball for bowling ~ *vb* : roll a ball in bowling —**bowl·er** *n*

bowl·ing *n* : game in which balls are rolled to knock down pins

¹**box** \'bäks\ *n, pl* **box** *or* **box·es** : evergreen shrub —**box·wood** \-,wùd\ *n*

²**box** *n* **1** : container usu. with 4 sides and a cover **2** : small compartment ~ *vb* : put in a box

³**box** *n* : slap ~ *vb* **1** : slap **2** : fight with the fists —**box·er** *n* —**box·ing** *n*

box·car *n* : roofed freight car

box office *n* : theater ticket office

boy \'bȯi\ *n* : male child —**boy·hood** *n* —**boy·ish** *adj* —**boy·ish·ly** *adv* —**boy·ish·ness** *n*

boy·cott \-,kät\ *vb* : refrain from dealing with —**boycott** *n*

boy·friend \'bȯi,frend\ *n* **1** : male friend **2** : woman's regular male companion

brace \'brās\ *n* **1** : crank for turning a bit **2** : something that resists weight or supports **3** : punctuation mark {or} ~ *vb* **braced; brac·ing 1** : make taut or steady **2** : invigorate **3** : strengthen

brace·let \'brāslət\ *n* : ornamental band for the wrist or arm

brack·et \'brakət\ *n* **1** : projecting support **2** : punctuation mark [or] **3** : class ~ *vb*

1 : furnish or fasten with brackets **2** : place within brackets **3** : group

brack·ish \-ish\ *adj* : salty

brad \'brad\ *n* : nail with a small head

brag \'brag\ *vb* **-gg-** : boast —**brag** *n*

brag·gart \'bragərt\ *n* : boaster

braid \'brād\ *vb* : interweave ~ *n* : something braided

braille \'brāl\ *n* : system of writing for the blind using raised dots

brain \'brān\ *n* **1** : organ of thought and nervous coordination enclosed in the skull **2** : intelligence ~ *vb* : smash the skull of —**brained** *adj* —**brain·less** *adj* —**brainy** *adj*

braise \'brāz\ *vb* **braised; brais·ing** : cook (meat) slowly in a covered dish

brake \'brāk\ *n* : device for slowing or stopping ~ *vb* **braked; brak·ing** : slow or stop by a brake

bram·ble \'brambəl\ *n* : prickly shrub

bran \'bran\ *n* : edible cracked grain husks

branch \'branch\ *n* **1** : division of a plant stem **2** : part ~ *vb* **1** : develop branches **2** : diverge —**branched** *adj*

brand \'brand\ *n* **1** : identifying mark made by burning **2** : stigma **3** : distinctive kind (as of goods from one firm) ~ *vb* : mark with a brand

bran·dish \'brandish\ *vb* : wave

brand-new *adj* : unused

bran·dy \'brandē\ *n, pl* **-dies** : liquor distilled from wine

brash \'brash\ *adj* **1** : impulsive **2** : aggressively self-assertive

brass \'bras\ *n* **1** : alloy of copper and zinc **2** : brazen self-assurance **3** : high-ranking military officers —**brassy** *adj*

bras·siere \brə'zir\ *n* : woman's undergarment to support the breasts

brat \'brat\ *n* : ill-behaved child —**brat·ti·ness** *n* —**brat·ty** *adj*

bra·va·do \brə'vädō\ *n, pl* **-does** *or* **-dos** : false bravery

¹**brave** \'brāv\ *adj* **brav·er; brav·est** : showing courage ~ *vb* **braved; brav·ing** : face with courage —**brave·ly** *adv* —**brav·ery** \-ərē\ *n*

²**brave** *n* : American Indian warrior

bra·vo \'brävō\ *n, pl* **-vos** : shout of approval

brawl \'brȯl\ *n* : noisy quarrel or violent fight —**brawl** *vb* —**brawl·er** *n*

brawn \'brȯn\ *n* : muscular strength —**brawny** \-ē\ *adj* —**brawn·i·ness** *n*

bray \'brā\ *n* : harsh cry of a donkey —**bray** *vb*

bra·zen \'brāzᵊn\ *adj* **1** : made of brass **2** : bold —**bra·zen·ly** *adv* —**bra·zen·ness** *n*

bra·zier \'brāzhər\ *n* : charcoal grill

breach \'brēch\ *n* **1** : breaking of a law, obligation, or standard **2** : gap ~ *vb* : make a breach in

bread \'bred\ *n* : baked food made of flour ~ *vb* : cover with bread crumbs

breadth \'bredth\ *n* : width

bread·win·ner *n* : wage earner

break \'brāk\ *vb* **broke** \'brōk\; **bro·ken** \'brōkən\; **break·ing 1** : knock into pieces **2** : transgress **3** : force a way into or out of **4** : exceed **5** : interrupt **6** : fail ~ *n* **1** : act or result of breaking **2** : stroke of good luck —**break·able** *adj or n* —**break·age** \'brākij\ *n* —**break·er** *n* —**break in** *vb* **1** : enter by force **2** : interrupt **3** : train —**break out** *vb* **1** : erupt with force **2** : develop a rash

break·down *n* : physical or mental failure —**break down** *vb*

break·fast \'brekfəst\ *n* : first meal of the day —**breakfast** *vb*

breast \'brest\ *n* **1** : milk-producing gland esp. of a woman **2** : front part of the chest

breast·bone *n* : sternum

breath \'breth\ *n* **1** : slight breeze **2** : air breathed in or out —**breath·less** *adj* —**breath·less·ly** *adv* —**breath·less·ness** *n* —**breathy** \'brethē\ *adj*

breathe \'brēth\ *vb* **breathed; breathing 1** : draw air into the lungs and expel it **2** : live **3** : utter

breath·tak·ing *adj* : exciting

breech·es \'brichəz\ *n pl* : trousers ending near the knee

breed \'brēd\ *vb* **bred** \'bred\; **breed·ing 1** : give birth to **2** : propagate **3** : raise ~ *n* **1** : kind of plant or animal usu. developed by humans **2** : class —**breed·er** *n*

breeze \'brēz\ *n* : light wind ~ *vb* **breezed; breez·ing** : move fast —**breezy** *adj*

breth·ren \'brethrən, -ərn\ *pl of* BROTHER

bre·via·ry \'brēvərē, 'bre-, -vyərē, -vē,erē\ *n, pl* **-ries** : prayer book used by Roman Catholic priests

brev·i·ty \'brevətē\ *n, pl* **-ties** : shortness or conciseness

brew \'brü\ *vb* : make by fermenting or steeping —**brew** *n* —**brew·er** *n* —**brew·ery** \'brüərē, 'brùrē\ *n*

bri·ar *var of* BRIER

bribe \'brīb\ *vb* **bribed; brib·ing** : corrupt or influence by gifts ~ *n* : something offered or given in bribing —**brib·able** *adj* —**brib·ery** \-ərē\ *n*

bric-a-brac \'brikə,brak\ *n pl* : small ornamental articles

brick \'brik\ *n* : building block of baked clay —**brick** *vb* —**brick·lay·er** *n* —**brick·lay·ing** *n*

bride \'brīd\ *n* : woman just married or about to be married —**brid·al** \-ᵊl\ *adj*

bride·groom *n* : man just married or about to be married

brides·maid *n* : woman who attends a bride at her wedding

¹**bridge** \'brij\ *n* **1** : structure built for passage over a depression or obstacle **2** : upper part of the nose **3** : compartment from which a ship is navigated **4** : artificial replacement for missing teeth ~ *vb* : build a bridge over —**bridge·able** *adj*

²**bridge** *n* : card game for 4 players

bri·dle \'brīdᵊl\ *n* : headgear to control a horse ~ *vb* **-dled; -dling 1** : put a bridle on **2** : restrain **3** : show hostility or scorn

brief \'brēf\ *adj* : short or concise ~ *n* : concise summary (as of a legal case) ~ *vb* : give final instructions or essential information to —**brief·ly** *adv* —**brief·ness** *n*

brief·case *n* : case for papers

¹**bri·er** \'brīər\ *n* : thorny plant

²**brier** *n* : heath of southern Europe

¹**brig** \'brig\ *n* : 2-masted ship

²**brig** *n* : jail on a naval ship

bri·gade \brig'ād\ *n* **1** : large military unit **2** : group organized for a special activity

brig·a·dier general \,brigə'dir-\ *n* : officer ranking next below a major general

brig·and \'brigənd\ *n* : bandit —**brig·and·age** \-ij\ *n*

bright \'brīt\ *adj* **1** : radiating or reflecting light **2** : cheerful **3** : intelligent —**bright·en** \-ᵊn\ *vb* —**bright·en·er** \'brītᵊnər\ *n* —**bright·ly** *adv* —**bright·ness** *n*

bril·liant \'brilyənt\ *adj* **1** : very bright **2** : splendid **3** : very intelligent —**bril·liance** \-yəns\ *n* —**bril·lian·cy** \-yənsē\ *n* —**bril·liant·ly** *adv*

brim \'brim\ *n* : edge or rim ~ *vb* : be or become full —**brim·less** *adj* —**brimmed** *adj*

brim·ful \-'fùl\ *adj* : full to the brim

brim·stone *n* : sulfur

brin·dled \'brindᵊld\ *adj* : gray or tawny with dark streaks or flecks

brine \'brīn\ *n* **1** : salt water **2** : ocean —**brin·i·ness** *n* —**briny** *adj*

bring \'brin\ *vb* **brought** \'brȯt\; **bring·ing 1** : cause to come with one **2** : persuade **3** : produce **4** : sell for —**bring·er** *n* —**bring about** : make happen —**bring up 1** : care for and educate **2** : cause to be noticed

brink \'brink\ *n* : edge

bri·quette, bri·quet \bri'ket\ *n* : pressed mass (as of charcoal)

brisk \'brisk\ *adj* **1** : lively **2** : invigorating —**brisk·ly** *adv* —**brisk·ness** *n*

bris·ket \'briskət\ *n* : breast or lower chest of a quadruped

bris·tle \'brisᵊl\ *n* : short stiff hair ~ *vb* **-tled; -tling 1** : stand erect **2** : show angry defiance **3** : appear as if covered with bristles —**bris·tly** *adj*

brit·tle \'britᵊl\ *adj* **-tler; -tlest** : easily broken —**brit·tle·ness** *n*

broach \'brōch\ *n* : pointed tool (as for opening casks) ~ *vb* **1** : pierce (as a cask) to open **2** : introduce for discussion

broad \'brȯd\ *adj* **1** : wide **2** : spacious **3** : clear or open **4** : obvious **5** : tolerant in outlook **6** : widely applicable **7** : dealing with essential points —**broad·en** \-ᵊn\ *vb* —**broad·ly** *adv* —**broad·ness** *n*

broad·cast *n* **1** : transmission by radio waves **2** : radio or television program ~ *vb* **-cast; -cast·ing 1** : scatter or sow in all directions **2** : make widely known **3** : send out on a broadcast —**broad·cast·er** *n*

broad·cloth *n* : fine cloth

broad·loom *adj* : woven on a wide loom esp. in solid color

broad-mind·ed *adj* : tolerant of varied opinions —**broad-mind·ed·ly** *adv* —**broad-mind·ed·ness** *n*

broad·side *n* **1** : simultaneous firing of all guns on one side of a ship **2** : verbal attack

bro·cade \brō'kād\ *n* : usu. silk fabric with a raised design

broc·co·li \'bräkəlē\ *n* : green vegetable akin to cauliflower

bro·chure \brō'shùr\ *n* : pamphlet

brogue \'brōg\ *n* : Irish accent

broil \'brȯil\ *vb* : cook by radiant heat —**broil** *n*

broil·er *n* **1** : utensil for broiling **2** : chicken fit for broiling

¹**broke** \'brōk\ *past of* BREAK

²**broke** *adj* : out of money

bro·ken \'brōkən\ *adj* : imperfectly spoken —**bro·ken·ly** *adv*

bro·ken·heart·ed \-'härtəd\ *adj* : overcome by grief or despair

bro·ker \'brōkər\ *n* : agent who buys and sells for a fee —**broker** *vb* —**bro·ker·age** \-ərij\ *n*

bro·mine \'brō,mēn\ *n* : deep red liquid corrosive chemical element

bron·chi·tis \brän'kītəs, brän-\ *n* : inflammation of the bronchi

bron·chus \'bränkəs\ *n, pl* **-chi** \-,kī, -,kē\ : division of the windpipe leading to a lung —**bron·chi·al** \-kēəl\ *adj*

bronze \'bränz\ *vb* **bronzed; bronz·ing** : make bronze in color ~ *n* **1** : alloy of copper and tin **2** : yellowish brown —**bronzy** \-ē\ *adj*

brooch \'brōch, 'brüch\ *n* : ornamental clasp or pin

brood \'brüd\ *n* : family of young ~ *vb* **1** : sit on eggs to hatch them **2** : ponder ~ *adj* : kept for breeding —**brood·er** *n* —**brood·ing·ly** *adv*

¹**brook** \'brùk\ *vb* : tolerate

²**brook** *n* : small stream

broom \'brüm, 'brùm\ *n* **1** : flowering shrub **2** : implement for sweeping —**broom·stick** *n*

broth \'brȯth\ *n, pl* **broths** \'brȯths, 'brȯthz\ : liquid in which meat has been cooked

broth·el \'bräthəl, 'brȯth-\ *n* : house of prostitutes

broth·er \'brəthər\ *n, pl* **brothers** *also* **breth·ren** \'brethrən, -ərn\ **1** : male sharing one or both parents with another person **2** : kinsman —**broth·er·hood** *n* —**broth·er·li·ness** *n* —**broth·er·ly** *adj*

broth·er-in-law *n, pl* **brothers-in-law** : brother of one's spouse or husband of one's sister or of one's spouse's sister

brought *past of* BRING

brow \'brau̇\ *n* **1** : eyebrow **2** : forehead **3** : edge of a steep place

brow·beat *vb* **-beat; -beat·en** *or* **-beat; -beat·ing** : intimidate

brown \'brau̇n\ *adj* **1** : of the color brown **2** : of dark or tanned complexion ~ *n* : a color like that of coffee ~ *vb* : make or become brown —**brown·ish** *adj*

browse \'brau̇z\ *vb* **browsed; brows·ing 1** : graze **2** : look over casually —**brows·er** *n*

bru·in \'brüən\ *n* : bear

bruise \'brüz\ *vb* **bruised; bruis·ing 1** : make a bruise on **2** : become bruised ~ *n* : surface injury to flesh

brunch \'brənch\ *n* : late breakfast, early lunch, or combination of both

bru·net, bru·nette \brü'net\ *adj* : having dark hair and usu. dark skin —**brunet, brunette** *n*

brunt \'brənt\ *n* : main impact

¹**brush** \'brəsh\ *n* **1** : small cut branches **2** : coarse shrubby vegetation

²**brush** *n* **1** : bristles set in a handle used esp. for cleaning or painting **2** : light touch ~ *vb* **1** : apply a brush to **2** : remove with or as if with a brush **3** : dismiss in an offhand way **4** : touch lightly —**brush up** *vb* : renew one's skill

³**brush** *n* : skirmish

brush-off *n* : curt dismissal

brusque \'brəsk\ *adj* : curt or blunt in manner —**brusque·ly** *adv*

bru·tal \'brütᵊl\ *adj* : like a brute and esp. cruel —**bru·tal·i·ty** \brü'talətē\ *n* —**bru·tal·ize** \'brütᵊl,īz\ *vb* —**bru·tal·ly** \-ᵊlē\ *adv*

brute \'brüt\ *adj* **1** : relating to beasts **2** : unreasoning **3** : purely physical ~ *n* **1** : beast **2** : brutal person —**brut·ish** \-ish\ *adj*

bub·ble \'bəbəl\ *vb* **-bled; -bling** : form, rise in, or give off bubbles ~ *n* : globule of gas in or covered with a liquid —**bub·bly** \-əlē\ *adj*

bu·bo \'bübō, 'byü-\ *n, pl* **buboes** : inflammatory swelling of a lymph gland —**bu·bon·ic** \bü'bänik, byü-\ *adj*

buc·ca·neer \,bəkə'nir\ *n* : pirate

buck \'bək\ *n, pl* **buck** *or* **bucks 1** : male animal (as a deer) **2** : dollar ~ *vb* **1** : jerk forward **2** : oppose

buck·et \'bəkət\ *n* : pail —**buck·et·ful** *n*

buck·le \'bəkəl\ *n* **1** : clasp (as on a belt) for two loose ends **2** : bend or fold ~ *vb* **-led; -ling 1** : fasten with a buckle **2** : apply oneself **3** : bend or crumple

buck·ler \'bəklər\ *n* : shield

buck·shot *n* : coarse lead shot

buck·skin *n* : soft leather (as from the skin of a buck) —**buckskin** *adj*

buck·tooth *n* : large projecting front tooth —**buck-toothed** *adj*

buck·wheat *n* : herb whose seeds are used as a cereal grain or the seeds themselves

bu·col·ic \byü'kälik\ *adj* : pastoral

bud \'bəd\ *n* **1** : undeveloped plant shoot **2** : partly opened flower ~ *vb* **-dd- 1** : form or put forth buds **2** : be or develop like a bud

Bud·dhism \'bü,dizəm, 'bù-\ *n* : religion of eastern and central Asia —**Bud·dhist** \'büdist, 'bùd-\ *n or adj*

bud·dy \'bədē\ *n, pl* **-dies** : friend

budge \'bəj\ *vb* **budged; budg·ing** : move from a place

bud•get \'bəjət\ *n* **1** : estimate of income and expenses **2** : plan for coordinating income and expenses **3** : money available for a particular use —**budget** *vb or adj* —**budget•ary** \-ə,terē\ *adj*

buff \'bəf\ *n* **1** : yellow to orange yellow color **2** : enthusiast ~ *adj* : of the color buff ~ *vb* : polish

buf•fa•lo \'bəfə,lō\ *n, pl* **-lo** *or* **-loes** : wild ox (as a bison)

¹buff•er \'bəfər\ *n* : shield or protector

²buffer *n* : one that buffs

¹buf•fet \'bəfət\ *n* : blow or slap ~ *vb* : hit esp. repeatedly

²buf•fet \bə'fā, bü-\ *n* **1** : sideboard **2** : meal at which people serve themselves

buf•foon \bə'fün\ *n* : clown —**buf•foon•ery** \-ərē\ *n*

bug \'bəg\ *n* **1** : small usu. obnoxious crawling creature **2** : 4-winged sucking insect **3** : unexpected imperfection **4** : disease-producing germ **5** : hidden microphone ~ *vb* **-gg-** **1** : pester **2** : conceal a microphone in

bug•a•boo \'bəgə,bü\ *n, pl* **-boos** : bogey

bug•bear *n* : source of dread

bug•gy \'bəgē\ *n, pl* **-gies** : light carriage

bu•gle \'byügəl\ *n* : trumpetlike brass instrument —**bu•gler** \-glər\ *n*

build \'bild\ *vb* **built** \'bilt\ **build•ing** **1** : put together **2** : establish **3** : increase ~ *n* : physique —**build•er** *n*

build•ing \'bildiŋ\ *n* **1** : roofed and walled structure **2** : art or business of constructing buildings

bulb \'bəlb\ *n* **1** : large underground plant bud **2** : rounded or pear-shaped object —**bul•bous** \-əs\ *adj*

bulge \'bəlj\ *n* : swelling projecting part ~ *vb* **bulged; bulg•ing** : swell out

bulk \'bəlk\ *n* **1** : magnitude **2** : indigestible food material **3** : large mass **4** : major portion ~ *vb* : cause to swell or bulge —**bulky** \-ē\ *adj*

bulk•head *n* : ship's partition

¹bull \'bul\ *n* : large adult male animal (as of cattle) ~ *adj* : male

²bull *n* **1** : papal letter **2** : decree

bull•dog *n* : compact short-haired dog

bull•doze \-,dōz\ *vb* **1** : move or level with a tractor (**bull•doz•er**) having a broad blade **2** : force

bul•let \'bulət\ *n* : missile to be shot from a gun —**bul•let•proof** *adj*

bul•le•tin \'bulətən\ *n* **1** : brief public report **2** : periodical

bull•fight *n* : sport of taunting and killing bulls —**bull•fight•er** *n*

bull•frog *n* : large deep-voiced frog

bull•head•ed *adj* : stupidly stubborn

bul•lion \'bulyən\ *n* : gold or silver esp. in bars

bull•ock \'bulək\ *n* **1** : young bull **2** : steer

bull's-eye *n, pl* **bull's-eyes** : center of a target

bul•ly \'bulē\ *n, pl* **-lies** : one who hurts or intimidates others ~ *vb* **-lied; -lying** : act like a bully toward

bul•rush \'bul,rəsh\ *n* : tall coarse rush or sedge

bul•wark \'bul,wərk, -,wȯrk; 'bəl,wərk\ *n* **1** : wall-like defense **2** : strong support or protection

bum \'bəm\ *vb* **-mm-** **1** : wander as a tramp **2** : get by begging ~ *n* : idle worthless person ~ *adj* : bad

bum•ble•bee \'bəmbəl,bē\ *n* : large hairy bee

bump \'bəmp\ *vb* : strike or knock forcibly ~ *n* **1** : sudden blow **2** : small bulge or swelling —**bumpy** *adj*

¹bump•er \'bəmpər\ *adj* : unusually large

²bump•er \'bəmpər\ *n* : shock-absorbing bar at either end of a car

bump•kin \'bəmpkən\ *n* : awkward country person

bun \'bən\ *n* : sweet biscuit or roll

bunch \'bənch\ *n* : group ~ *vb* : form into a group —**bunchy** *adj*

bun•dle \'bəndəl\ *n* **1** : several things bunched together **2** : something wrapped for carrying **3** : large amount ~ *vb* **-dled; -dling** : gather into a bundle

bun•ga•low \'bəŋgə,lō\ *n* : one-story house

bun•gle \'bəŋgəl\ *vb* **-gled; -gling** : do badly —**bungle** *n* —**bun•gler** *n*

bun•ion \'bənyən\ *n* : inflamed swelling of the first joint of the big toe

¹bunk \'bəŋk\ *n* : built-in bed that is often one of a tier ~ *vb* : sleep

²bunk *n* : nonsense

bun•ker \-ər\ *n* **1** : storage compartment **2** : protective embankment

bun•kum, bun•combe \'bəŋkəm\ *n* : nonsense

bun•ny \'bənē\ *n, pl* **-nies** : rabbit

¹bun•ting \'bəntiŋ\ *n* : small finch

²bunting *n* : flag material

buoy \'büē, 'bȯi\ *n* : floating marker anchored in water ~ *vb* **1** : keep afloat **2** : raise the spirits of —**buoy•an•cy** \'bȯiənsē, 'büyən-\ *n* —**buoy•ant** \-yənt\ *adj*

bur, burr \'bər\ *n* : rough or prickly covering of a fruit —**bur•ry** *adj*

bur•den \'bərdᵊn\ *n* **1** : something carried **2** : something oppressive **3** : cargo ~ *vb* : load or oppress —**bur•den•some** \-səm\ *adj*

bur•dock \'bər,däk\ *n* : tall coarse herb with prickly flower heads

bu•reau \'byurō\ *n* **1** : chest of drawers **2** : administrative unit **3** : business office

bu•reau•cra•cy \byu'räkrəsē\ *n, pl* **-cies** **1** : body of government officials **2** : unwieldy administrative system —**bu•reau•crat** \'byurə,krat\ *n* —**bu•reau•crat•ic** \,byurə'kratik\ *adj*

bur•geon \'bərjən\ *vb* : grow

bur•glary \'bərglərē\ *n, pl* **-glar•ies** : forcible entry into a building to steal —**bur•glar** \-glər\ *n* —**bur•glar•ize** \'bərglə,rīz\ *vb*

bur•gle \'bərgəl\ *vb* **-gled; -gling** : commit burglary on or in

Bur•gun•dy \'bərgəndē\ *n, pl* **-dies** : kind of table wine

buri•al \'berēəl\ *n* : act of burying

bur•lap \'bər,lap\ *n* : coarse fabric usu. of jute or hemp

bur•lesque \bər'lesk\ *n* **1** : witty or derisive imitation **2** : broadly humorous variety show ~ *vb* **-lesqued; -lesqu•ing** : mock

bur•ly \'bərlē\ *adj* **-li•er; -est** : strongly and heavily built

burn \'bərn\ *vb* **burned** \'bərnd, 'bərnt\ *or* **burnt** \'bərnt\ **burn•ing** **1** : be on fire **2** : feel or look as if on fire **3** : alter or become altered by or as if by fire or heat **4** : cause or make by fire ~ *n* : injury or effect produced by burning —**burn•er** *n*

bur•nish \'bərnish\ *vb* : polish

burp \'bərp\ *n or vb* : belch

bur•ro \'bərō, 'bur-\ *n, pl* **-os** : small donkey

bur•row \'bərō\ *n* : hole in the ground made by an animal ~ *vb* : make a burrow —**bur•row•er** *n*

bur•sar \'bərsər\ *n* : treasurer esp. of a college

bur•si•tis \bər'sītəs\ *n* : inflammation of a sac (**bur•sa** \'bərsə\) in a joint

burst \'bərst\ *vb* **burst** *or* **burst•ed; burst•ing** **1** : fly apart or into pieces **2** : enter or emerge suddenly ~ *n* : sudden outbreak or effort

bury \'berē\ *vb* **buried; bury•ing** **1** : deposit in the earth **2** : hide

bus \'bəs\ *n, pl* **bus•es** *or* **bus•ses** : large motor-driven passenger vehicle ~ *vb* **bused** *or* **bussed; bus•ing** *or* **bus•sing** : travel or transport by bus

bus•boy *n* : waiter's helper

bush \'bush\ *n* **1** : shrub **2** : rough uncleared country **3** : a thick tuft or mat —**bushy** *adj*

bush•el \'bushəl\ *n* : 4 pecks

bush•ing \'bushiŋ\ *n* : metal lining used as a guide or bearing

busi•ness \'biznəs, -nəz\ *n* **1** : vocation **2** : commercial or industrial enterprise **3** : personal concerns —**busi•ness•man** \-,man\ *n* —**busi•ness•wom•an** \-,wu̇mən\ *n*

¹bust \'bəst\ *n* **1** : sculpture of the head and upper torso **2** : breasts of a woman

²bust *vb* **1** : burst or break **2** : tame ~ *n* **1** : punch **2** : failure

¹bus•tle \'bəsəl\ *vb* **-tled; -tling** : move or work briskly ~ *n* : energetic activity

²bustle *n* : pad or frame formerly worn under a woman's skirt

busy \'bizē\ *adj* **busi•er; -est** **1** : engaged in action **2** : being in use **3** : full of activity ~ *vb* **bus•ied; busying** : make or keep busy —**busi•ly** *adv*

busy•body *n* : meddler

but \'bət\ *conj* **1** : if not for the fact **2** : that **3** : without the certainty that **4** : rather **5** : yet ~ *prep* : other than

butch•er \'buchər\ *n* **1** : one who slaughters animals or dresses their flesh **2** : brutal killer **3** : bungler —**butcher** *vb* —**butch•ery** \-ərē\ *n*

but•ler \'bətlər\ *n* : chief male household servant

¹butt \'bət\ *vb* : strike with a butt ~ *n* : blow with the head or horns

²butt *n* **1** : target **2** : victim

³butt *vb* : join edge to edge

⁴butt *n* : large end or bottom

⁵butt *n* : large cask

butte \'byüt\ *n* : isolated steep hill

but•ter \'bətər\ *n* : solid edible fat churned from cream ~ *vb* : spread with butter —**but•tery** *adj*

but•ter•cup *n* : yellow-flowered herb

but•ter•fat *n* : natural fat of milk and of butter

but•ter•fly *n* : insect with 4 broad wings

but•ter•milk *n* : liquid remaining after butter is churned

but•ter•nut *n* : edible nut of a tree related to the walnut or this tree

but•ter•scotch \-,skäch\ *n* : candy made from sugar, corn syrup, and water

but•tocks \'bətəks\ *n pl* : rear part of the hips

but•ton \'bətᵊn\ *n* **1** : small knob for fastening clothing **2** : buttonlike object ~ *vb* : fasten with buttons

but•ton•hole *n* : hole or slit for a button ~ *vb* : hold in talk

but•tress \'bətrəs\ *n* **1** : projecting structure to support a wall **2** : support —**buttress** *vb*

bux•om \'bəksəm\ *adj* : full-bosomed

buy \'bī\ *vb* **bought** \'bȯt\ **buy•ing** : purchase ~ *n* : bargain —**buy•er** *n*

buzz \'bəz\ *vb* : make a low humming sound ~ *n* : act or sound of buzzing

buz•zard \'bəzərd\ *n* : large bird of prey

buzz•er *n* : signaling device that buzzes

buzz•word \'bəz,wərd\ *n* : word or phrase in vogue

by \'bī\ *prep* **1** : near **2** : through **3** : beyond **4** : throughout **5** : no later than ~ *adv* **1** : near **2** : farther

by•gone \'bī,gȯn\ *adj* : past —**bygone** *n*

by•law, bye•law \'bī-\ *n* : organization's rule

by•line *n* : writer's name on an article

by•pass *n* : alternate route ~ *vb* : go around

by-prod•uct *n* : product in addition to the main product

by•stand•er *n* : spectator

by•way \'bī,wā\ *n* : side road

by•word *n* : proverb

C

c \'sē\ *n, pl* **c's** *or* **cs** \'sēz\ : 3d letter of the alphabet

cab \'kab\ *n* **1** : light closed horse-drawn carriage **2** : taxicab **3** : compartment for a driver —**cab•bie, cabby** *n* —**cab•stand** *n*

ca•bal \kə'bal\ *n* : group of conspirators

ca•bana \kə'banə, -'nyä\ *n* : shelter at a beach or pool

cab•a•ret \,kabə'rā\ *n* : nightclub

cab•bage \'kabij\ *n* : vegetable with a dense head of leaves

cab•in \-ən\ *n* **1** : private room on a ship **2** : small house **3** : airplane compartment

cab•i•net \'kabnət\ *n* **1** : display case or cupboard **2** : advisory council of a head of state —**cab•i•net•mak•er** *n* —**cab•i•net•mak•ing** *n* —**cab•i•net•work** *n*

ca•ble \'kābəl\ *n* **1** : strong rope, wire, or chain **2** : cablegram **3** : bundle of electrical wires ~ *vb* **-bled; -bling** : send a cablegram to

ca•ble•gram \-,gram\ *n* : message sent by a submarine telegraph cable

ca•boose \kə'büs\ *n* : crew car on a train

ca•cao \kə'kau̇, -'kāō\ *n, pl* **cacaos** : So. American tree whose seeds (**cacao beans**) yield cocoa and chocolate

cache \'kash\ *n* **1** : hiding place **2** : something hidden —**cache** *vb*

ca•chet \ka'shā\ *n* : prestige or a feature conferring this

cack•le \'kakəl\ *vb* **-led; -ling** : make a cry or laugh like the sound of a hen —**cackle** *n* —**cack•ler** *n*

ca•coph•o•ny \ka'käfənē\ *n, pl* **-nies** : harsh noise —**ca•coph•o•nous** \-nəs\ *adj*

cac•tus \'kaktəs\ *n, pl* **cac•ti** \-,tī\ *or* **-tus•es** : drought-resistant flowering plant with scales or prickles

cad \'kad\ *n* : ungentlemanly person —**cad•dish** \-ish\ *adj* —**cad•dish•ly** *adv* —**cad•dish•ness** *n*

ca•dav•er \kə'davər\ *n* : dead body —**ca•dav•er•ous** \-ərəs\ *adj*

cad•die, cad•dy \'kadē\ *n, pl* **-dies** : golfer's helper —**caddie, caddy** *vb*

cad•dy \'kadē\ *n, pl* **-dies** : small tea chest

ca•dence \'kādᵊns\ *n* : measure of a rhythmical flow —**ca•denced** \-ᵊnst\ *adj*

ca•det \kə'det\ *n* : student in a military academy

cadge \'kaj\ *vb* **cadged; cadg•ing** : beg —**cadg•er** *n*

cad•mi•um \'kadmēəm\ *n* : grayish metallic chemical element

cad•re \'ka,frā, kə-\ *n* : nucleus of highly trained people

ca•fé \ka'fā, kə-\ *n* : restaurant

caf•e•te•ria \,kafə'tirēə\ *n* : self-service restaurant

caf•feine \ka'fēn, 'ka,fēn\ *n* : stimulating alkaloid in coffee and tea

cage \'kāj\ *n* : box of wire or bars for confining an animal ~ *vb* **caged; caging** : put or keep in a cage

ca•gey \-ē\ *adj* **-gi•er; -est** : shrewd —**ca•gi•ly** *adv* —**ca•gi•ness** *n*

cais•son \'kā,sän, -sən\ *n* **1** : ammunition carriage **2** : watertight chamber for underwater construction

ca•jole \kə'jōl\ *vb* **-joled; -jol•ing** : persuade or coax —**ca•jol•ery** \-ərē\ *n*

cake \'kāk\ *n* **1** : food of baked or fried usu. sweet batter **2** : compacted mass ~ *vb* **caked; cak•ing** **1** : form into a cake **2** : encrust

cal•a•bash \'kalə,bash\ *n* : gourd

cal•a•mine \'kalə,mīn\ *n* : lotion of oxides of zinc and iron

ca•lam•i•ty \kə'lamətē\ *n, pl* **-ties** : disaster —**ca•lam•i•tous** \-ətəs\ *adj* —**ca•lam•i•tous•ly** *adv* —**ca•lam•i•tous•ness** *n*

cal•ci•fy \'kalsə,fī\ *vb* **-fied; -fy•ing** : harden —**cal•ci•fi•ca•tion** \,kalsəfə'kāshən\ *n*

cal•ci•um \'kalsēəm\ *n* : silver-white soft metallic chemical element

cal•cu•late \'kalkyə,lāt\ *vb* **-lat•ed; -lating** **1** : determine by mathematical processes **2** : judge —**cal•cu•la•ble** \-ləbəl\ *adj* —**cal•cu•la•tion** \,kalkyə'lāshən\ *n* —**cal•cu•la•tor** \'kalkyə,lātər\ *n*

cal•cu•lat•ing *adj* : shrewd

cal•cu•lus \'kalkyələs\ *n, pl* **-li** \-,lī\ : higher mathematics dealing with rates of change

cal•dron *var of* CAULDRON

cal•en•dar \'kaləndər\ *n* : list of days, weeks, and months

¹calf \'kaf, 'kȧf\ *n, pl* **calves** \'kavz, 'kȧvz\ : young cow or related mammal —**calf•skin** *n*

²calf *n, pl* **calves** : back part of the leg below the knee

cal•i•ber, cal•i•bre \'kaləbər\ *n* **1** : diameter of a bullet or shell or of a gun bore **2** : degree of mental or moral excellence

cal•i•brate \'kalə,brāt\ *vb* **-brat•ed; -brating** : adjust precisely —**cal•i•bra•tion** \,kalə'brāshən\ *n*

cal•i•co \'kali,kō\ *n, pl* **-coes** *or* **-cos** **1** : printed cotton fabric **2** : animal with fur having patches of different colors

cal•i•pers \'kaləpərz\ *n* : measuring instrument with two adjustable legs

ca•liph \'kāləf, 'kal-\ *n* : title of head of Islam —**ca•liph•ate** \-,āt, -ət\ *n*

cal•is•then•ics \,kaləs'theniks\ *n sing or pl* : stretching and jumping exercises —**cal•is•then•ic** *adj*

calk \'kȯk\ *var of* CAULK

call \'kȯl\ *vb* **1** : shout **2** : summon **3** : demand **4** : telephone **5** : make a visit **6** : name —**call** *n* —**call•er** *n* —**call down** *vb* : reprimand —**call off** *vb* : cancel

call•ing *n* : vocation

cal•li•ope \kə'līə,pē, 'kalē,ōp\ *n* : musical instrument of steam whistles

cal•lous \'kaləs\ *adj* **1** : thickened and hardened **2** : unfeeling ~ *vb* : make callous —**cal•los•i•ty** \ka'läsətē\ *n* —**cal•lous•ly** *adv* —**cal•lous•ness** *n*

cal•low \'kalō\ *adj* : inexperienced or innocent —**cal•low•ness** *n*

cal•lus \'kaləs\ *n* : callous area on skin or bark ~ *vb* : form a callus

calm \'käm, 'kälm\ *n* **1** : period or condition of peacefulness or stillness ~ *adj* : still or tranquil ~ *vb* : make calm —**calm•ly** *adv* —**calm•ness** *n*

ca•lor•ic \kə'lȯrik\ *adj* : relating to heat or calories

cal•o•rie \'kalərē\ *n* : unit for measuring heat and energy value of food

ca•lum•ni•ate \kə'ləmnē,āt\ *vb* **-at•ed; -ating** : slander —**ca•lum•ni•a•tion** \-,ləmnē'āshən\ *n*

cal•um•ny \'kaləmnē\ *n, pl* **-nies** : false and malicious charge —**ca•lum•ni•ous** \kə'ləmnēəs\ *adj*

calve \'kav, 'kȧv\ *vb* **calved; calv•ing** : give birth to a calf

calves *pl of* CALF

ca•lyp•so \kə'lipsō\ *n, pl* **-sos** : West Indian style of music

ca•lyx \'kāliks, 'kal-\ *n, pl* **-lyx•es** *or* **-ly•ces** \-lə,sēz\ : sepals of a flower

cam \'kam\ *n* : machine part that slides or rotates irregularly to transmit linear motion

ca•ma•ra•de•rie \,käm'rädərē, ,kam-, -mə'-, -'rad-\ *n* : fellowship

cam•bric \'kāmbrik\ *n* : fine thin linen or cotton fabric

came *past of* COME

cam•el \'kaməl\ *n* : large hoofed mammal of desert areas

ca•mel•ia \kə'mēlyə\ *n* : shrub or tree grown for its showy roselike flowers or the flower itself

cam•eo \'kamē,ō\ *n, pl* **-eos** : gem carved in relief

cam•era \'kamrə\ *n* : box with a lens for taking pictures —**cam•era•man** \-,man, -mən\ *n*

cam•ou•flage \'kamə,fläzh, -,fläj\ *vb* : hide by disguising —**camouflage** *n*

camp \'kamp\ *n* **1** : place to stay temporarily esp. in a tent **2** : group living in a camp ~ *vb* : make or live in a camp —**camp•er** *n* —**camp•ground** *n* —**camp•site** *n*

cam·paign \kam'pān\ n : series of military operations or of activities meant to gain a result —**campaign** vb

cam·pa·ni·le \kampə'nēlē, -'nēl\ n, pl **-ni·les** or **-ni·li** \-'nēlē\ : bell tower

cam·phor \'kamfər\ n : gummy volatile aromatic compound from an evergreen tree (**cam·phor tree**)

cam·pus \'kampəs\ n : grounds and buildings of a college or school

1can \kən, 'kan\ vb, past **could** \kəd, 'kúd\; pres sing & pl **can 1** : be able to 2 : be permitted to by conscience or feeling 3 : have permission or liberty to

2can \'kan\ n : metal container ~ vb **-nn-** : preserve by sealing in airtight cans or jars —**can·ner** n —**can·nery** \-ərē\ n

ca·nal \kə'nal\ n 1 : tubular passage in the body 2 : channel filled with water

can·a·pé \'kanəpē, -,pā\ n : appetizer

ca·nard \kə'närd\ n : false report

ca·nary \-'nerē\ n, pl **-nar·ies** : yellow or greenish finch often kept as a pet

can·cel \'kansəl\ vb **-celed** or **-celled**; **-cel·ing** or **-cel·ling** 1 : cross out 2 : destroy, neutralize, or match the force or effect of —**cancel** n —**can·cel·la·tion** \kansə'lā-shən\ n —**cancel, can·cel·ler** n

can·cer \'kansər\ n 1 : malignant tumor that tends to spread 2 : slowly destructive evil —**can·cer·ous** \-ərəs\ adj —**can·cer·ous·ly** adv

can·de·la·bra \kandə'läbrə, -'lab-\ n : candelabrum

can·de·la·brum \-rəm\ n, pl **-bra** \-rə\ : ornamental branched candlestick

can·did \'kandəd\ adj 1 : frank 2 : unposed —**can·did·ly** adv —**can·did·ness** n

can·di·date \'kandə,dāt, -dət\ n : one who seeks an office or membership —**can·di·da·cy** \-dəsē\ n

can·dle \'kandᵊl\ n : tallow or wax molded around a wick and burned to give light —**can·dle·light** n —**can·dle·stick** n

can·dor \'kandər\ n : frankness

can·dy \-dē\ n, pl **-dies** : food made from sugar ~ vb **-died**; **-dy·ing** : encrust in sugar

cane \'kān\ n 1 : slender plant stem 2 : a tall woody grass or reed 3 : stick for walking or beating ~ vb **caned**; **can·ing** 1 : beat with a cane 2 : weave or make with cane —**can·er** n

ca·nine \'kā,nīn\ adj : relating to dogs ~ n 1 : pointed tooth next to the incisors 2 : dog

can·is·ter \'kanəstər\ n : cylindrical container

can·ker \'kaŋkər\ n : mouth ulcer —**can·ker·ous** \-kərəs\ adj

can·na·bis \'kanəbəs\ n : preparation derived from hemp

can·ni·bal \'kanəbəl\ n : human or animal that eats its own kind —**can·ni·bal·ism** \-bə,lizəm\ n —**can·ni·bal·is·tic** \kanəbə'listik\ adj

can·ni·bal·ize \'kanəbə,līz\ vb **-ized**; **-iz·ing** 1 : take usable parts from 2 : practice cannibalism

can·non \'kanən\ n, pl **-nons** or **-non** : large heavy gun —**can·non·ball** n —**can·non·eer** \kanə'nir\ n

can·non·ade \kanə'nād\ n : heavy artillery fire ~ vb **-ad·ed**; **-ad·ing** : bombard

can·not \'kan,ät; kə'nät\ : can not —**cannot but** : be bound to

can·ny \'kanē\ adj **-ni·er**; **-est** : shrewd —**can·ni·ly** adv —**can·ni·ness** n

ca·noe \kə'nü\ n : narrow sharp-ended boat propelled by paddles —**canoe** vb —**ca·noe·ist** n

1can·on \'kanən\ n 1 : regulation governing a church 2 : authoritative list 3 : an accepted principle

2canon n : clergy member in a cathedral

ca·non·i·cal \kə'nänikəl\ adj 1 : relating to or conforming to a canon 2 : orthodox —**ca·non·i·cal·ly** adv

can·on·ize \'kanə,nīz\ vb **-ized** or **-nizd**; **-iz·ing** : recognize as a saint —**can·on·iza·tion** \kanənə'zāshən\ n

can·o·py \'kanəpē\ n, pl **-pies** : overhanging cover —**canopy** vb

1cant \'kant\ n 1 : slanting surface 2 : slant ~ vb 1 : tip up 2 : lean to one side

2cant vb : talk hypocritically ~ n 1 : jargon 2 : insincere talk

can't \'kant, 'känt\ : can not

can·ta·loupe \'kantᵊl,ōp\ n : muskmelon with orange flesh

can·tan·ker·ous \kan'taŋkərəs\ adj : hard to deal with —**can·tan·ker·ous·ly** adv —**can·tan·ker·ous·ness** n

can·ta·ta \kən'tätə\ n : choral work

can·teen \kan'tēn\ n 1 : place of recreation for service personnel 2 : water container

can·ter \'kantər\ n : slow gallop —**canter** vb

can·ti·cle \'kantikəl\ n : liturgical song

can·ti·le·ver \'kantᵊl,ēvər, -,ev-\ n : beam or structure supported only at one end

can·to \'kan,tō\ n, pl **-tos** : major division of a long poem

can·tor \'kantər\ n : synagogue official who sings liturgical music

can·vas \'kanvəs\ n 1 : strong cloth orig. used for making tents and sails 2 : set of sails 3 : oil painting

can·vass \-vəs\ vb : solicit votes, orders, or opinions from ~ n : act of canvassing —**can·vass·er** n

can·yon \'kanyən\ n : deep valley with steep sides

1cap \'kap\ n 1 : covering for the head 2 : top or cover like a cap 3 : upper limit ~ vb **-pp-** 1 : provide or protect with a cap 2 : climax —**cap·ful** \-,fúl\ n

ca·pa·ble \'kāpəbəl\ adj : able to do something —**ca·pa·bil·i·ty** \kāpə'bilətē\ n —**ca·pa·bly** \'kāpəblē\ adv

ca·pa·cious \kə'pāshəs\ adj : able to contain much

ca·pac·i·tance \kə'pasətəns\ n : ability to store electrical energy

ca·pac·i·tor \-ətər\ n : device for storing electrical energy

ca·pac·i·ty \-ətē\ n, pl **-ties** 1 : ability to contain 2 : volume 3 : ability 4 : role or job ~ adj : equaling maximum capacity

1cape \'kāp\ n : point of land jutting out into water

2cape n : garment that drapes over the shoulders

1ca·per \'kāpər\ n : flower bud of a shrub pickled for use as a relish

2caper vb : leap or prance about ~ n 1 : frolicsome leap 2 : escapade

cap·il·lary \'kapə,lerē\ adj 1 : resembling a hair 2 : having a very small bore ~ n, pl **-lar·ies** : tiny thin-walled blood vessel

1cap·i·tal \'kapətᵊl\ adj 1 : punishable by death 2 : being in the series A, B, C rather than a, b, c 3 : relating to capital 4 : excellent ~ n 1 : capital letter 2 : seat of government 3 : wealth 4 : total face value of a company's stock 5 : investors as a group

2capital n : top part of a column

cap·i·tal·ism \-,izəm\ n : economic system of private ownership of capital

cap·i·tal·ist \-ist\ n 1 : person with capital invested in business 2 : believer in capitalism ~ adj 1 : owning capital 2 : practicing, advocating, or marked by capitalism —**cap·i·tal·is·tic** \kapətᵊl'is-tik\ adj —**cap·i·tal·is·ti·cal·ly** \-klē\ adv

cap·i·tal·ize \-,īz\ vb **-ized**; **-iz·ing** 1 : write or print with a capital letter 2 : use as capital 3 : supply capital for 4 : turn something to advantage —**cap·i·tal·iza·tion** \kapətᵊlə'zāshən\ n

cap·i·tol \'kapətᵊl\ n : building in which a legislature sits

ca·pit·u·late \kə'pichə,lāt\ vb **-lat·ed**; **-lat·ing** : surrender —**ca·pit·u·la·tion** \-,pichə'lāshən\ n

ca·pon \'kā,pän, -pən\ n : castrated male chicken

ca·price \kə'prēs\ n : whim —**ca·pri·cious** \-'prishəs\ adj —**ca·pri·cious·ly** adv —**ca·pri·cious·ness** n

cap·size \'kap,sīz, kap'sīz\ vb **-sized**; **-siz·ing** : overturn

cap·stan \-stən, -,stan\ n : upright winch

cap·sule \'kapsəl, -sül\ n 1 : enveloping cover (as for medicine) 2 : small pressurized compartment for astronauts ~ adj : very brief or compact —**cap·su·lar** \-sələr\ adj —**cap·su·lat·ed** \-sə,lātəd\ adj

cap·tain \'kaptən\ n 1 : commander of a body of troops 2 : officer in charge of a ship 3 : commissioned officer in the navy ranking next below a rear admiral or a commodore 4 : commissioned officer (as in the army) ranking next below a major 5 : leader ~ vb : be captain of —**captain·cy** n

cap·tion \'kapshən\ n 1 : title 2 : explanation with an illustration —**caption** vb

cap·tious \'kapshəs\ adj : tending to find fault —**cap·tious·ly** adv

cap·ti·vate \'kaptə,vāt\ vb **-vat·ed**; **-vat·ing** : attract and charm —**cap·ti·va·tion** \kaptə'vāshən\ n —**cap·ti·va·tor** \'kaptə,vātər\ n

cap·tive \-tiv\ adj 1 : made prisoner 2 : confined or under control —**captive** n —**cap·tiv·i·ty** \kap'tivətē\ n

cap·tor \'kaptər\ n : one that captures

cap·ture \'kapchər\ n : seizure by force or trickery ~ vb **-tured**; **-tur·ing** : take captive

car \'kär\ n 1 : vehicle moved on wheels 2 : cage of an elevator

ca·rafe \kə'raf, -'räf\ n : decanter

car·a·mel \'karəməl, 'kärməl\ n 1 : burnt sugar used for flavoring and coloring 2 : firm chewy candy

1car·at var of KARAT

2car·at \'karət\ n : unit of weight for precious stones

car·a·van \'karə,van\ n : travelers journeying together (as in a line)

car·a·way \'karə,wā\ n : aromatic herb with seeds used in seasoning

car·bine \'kär,bēn, -,bīn\ n : short-barreled rifle

car·bo·hy·drate \,kärbō'hī,drāt, -drət\ n : compound of carbon, hydrogen, and oxygen

car·bon \'kärbən\ n 1 : chemical element occurring in nature esp. as diamond and graphite 2 : piece of carbon paper or a copy made with it

1car·bon·ate \'kärbə,nāt, -nət\ n : salt or ester of a carbon-containing acid

2car·bon·ate \-,nāt\ vb **-at·ed**; **-at·ing** : impregnate with carbon dioxide —**car·bon·ation** \kärbə'nāshən\ n

carbon paper n : thin paper coated with a pigment for making copies

car·bun·cle \'kär,bəŋkəl\ n : painful inflammation of the skin and underlying tissue

car·bu·re·tor \'kärbə,rātər, -byə-\ n : device for mixing fuel and air

car·cass \'kärkəs\ n : dead body

car·cin·o·gen \kär'sinəjən\ n : agent causing cancer —**car·ci·no·gen·ic** \,kärsᵊnō'je-nik\ adj

car·ci·no·ma \,kärsᵊn'ōmə\ n, pl **-mas** or **-ma·ta** \-mətə\ : malignant tumor —**car·ci·no·ma·tous** \-mətəs\ adj

1card \'kärd\ vb : comb (fibers) before spinning ~ n : device for carding fibers —**card·er** n

2card n 1 : playing card 2 pl : game played with playing cards 3 : small flat piece of paper

card·board n : stiff material like paper

car·di·ac \'kärdē,ak\ adj : relating to the heart

car·di·gan \'kärdigən\ n : sweater with an opening in the front

1car·di·nal \'kärdᵊnᵊl\ n 1 : official of the Roman Catholic Church 2 : bright red songbird

2cardinal adj : of basic importance

cardinal number n : number (as 1, 82, 357) used in counting

car·di·ol·o·gy \,kärdē'äləjē\ n : study of the heart —**car·di·ol·o·gist** \-jist\ n

car·dio·vas·cu·lar \-ō'vaskyələr\ adj : relating to the heart and blood vessels

care \'ker\ n 1 : anxiety 2 : watchful attention 3 : supervision ~ vb **cared**; **car·ing** 1 : feel anxiety or concern 2 : like 3 : provide care —**care·free** adj —**care·ful** \-fəl\ adj —**care·ful·ly** adv —**care·ful·ness** n —**care·giv·er** \-,givər\ n —**care·less** adj —**care·less·ly** adv —**care·less·ness** n

ca·reen \kə'rēn\ vb 1 : sway from side to side 2 : career

ca·reer \kə'rir\ n : vocation ~ vb : go at top speed

ca·ress \kə'res\ n : tender touch ~ vb : touch lovingly or tenderly

car·et \'karət\ n : mark ‸ showing where something is to be inserted

care·tak·er n : one in charge for another or temporarily

car·go \'kärgō\ n, pl **-goes** or **-gos** : transported goods

car·i·bou \'karə,bü\ n, pl **-bou** or **-bous** : large No. American deer

car·i·ca·ture \'karika,chúr\ n : distorted representation for humor or ridicule —**caricature** vb —**car·i·ca·tur·ist** \-ist\ n

car·ies \'karēz\ n, pl **caries** : tooth decay

car·il·lon \'karə,län\ n : set of tuned bells

car·mine \'kärmən, -,mīn\ n : vivid red

car·nage \'kärnij\ n : slaughter

car·nal \'kärnᵊl\ adj : sensual —**car·nal·i·ty** \kär'nalətē\ n —**car·nal·ly** adv

car·na·tion \kär'nāshən\ n : showy flower

car·ni·val \'kärnəvəl\ n 1 : festival 2 : traveling enterprise offering amusements

car·ni·vore \-,vōr\ n : flesh-eating animal —**car·niv·o·rous** \kär'nivərəs\ adj —**car·niv·o·rous·ly** adv —**car·niv·o·rous·ness** n

car·ol \'karəl\ n : song of joy —**carol** vb —**car·ol·er, car·ol·ler** \-ər\ n

car·om \-əm\ n or vb : rebound

ca·rouse \kə'raúz\ vb **-roused**; **-rous·ing** : drink and be boisterous —**ca·rouse** n —**ca·rous·er** n

car·ou·sel, car·rou·sel \karə'sel, 'karə,-\ n : merry-go-round

1carp \'kärp\ vb : find fault

2carp n, pl **carp** or **carps** : freshwater fish

car·pel \'kärpəl\ n : modified leaf forming part of the ovary of a flower

car·pen·ter \'kärpəntər\ n : one who builds with wood —**carpenter** vb —**car·pen·try** \-trē\ n

car·pet \'kärpət\ n : fabric floor covering ~ vb : cover with a carpet —**car·pet·ing** \-iŋ\ n

car·port n : open-sided automobile shelter

car·riage \'karij\ n 1 : conveyance 2 : manner of holding oneself 3 : wheeled vehicle

car·ri·on \'karēən\ n : dead and decaying flesh

car·rot \'karət\ n : orange root vegetable

car·ry \'karē\ vb **-ried**; **-ry·ing** 1 : move

while supporting 2 : hold (oneself) in a specified way 3 : support 4 : keep in stock 5 : reach to a distance 6 : win —**car·ri·er** \-ēər\ n —**carry on** vb 1 : conduct 2 : behave excitedly —**carry out** vb : put into effect

cart \'kärt\ n : wheeled vehicle ~ vb : carry in a cart —**cart·age** \-ij\ n —**cart·er** n

car·tel \kär'tel\ n : business combination designed to limit competition

car·ti·lage \'kärtᵊlij\ n : elastic skeletal tissue —**car·ti·lag·i·nous** \,kärtᵊl'ajənəs\ adj

car·tog·ra·phy \kär'tägrəfē\ n : making of maps —**car·tog·ra·pher** \-fər\ n

car·ton \'kärtᵊn\ n : cardboard box

car·toon \kär'tün\ n 1 : humorous drawing 2 : comic strip —**cartoon** vb —**car·toon·ist** n

car·tridge \'kärtrij\ n 1 : tube containing powder and a bullet or shot for a firearm 2 : container of material for insertion into an apparatus

carve \'kärv\ vb **carved**; **carv·ing** 1 : cut with care 2 : cut into pieces or slices —**carv·er** n

cas·cade \kas'kād\ n : small steep waterfall ~ vb **-cad·ed**; **-cad·ing** : fall in a cascade

1case \'kās\ n 1 : particular instance 2 : convincing argument 3 : inflectional form esp. of a noun or pronoun 4 : fact 5 : lawsuit 6 : instance of disease —**in case** : as a precaution —**in case of** : in the event of

2case n 1 : box 2 : outer covering ~ vb **cased**; **cas·ing** 1 : enclose 2 : inspect

case·ment \-mənt\ n : window that opens like a door

cash \'kash\ n 1 : ready money 2 : money paid at the time of purchase ~ vb : give or get cash for

ca·shew \'kashü, kə'shü\ n : tropical American tree or its nut

1ca·shier \ka'shir\ vb : dismiss in disgrace

2cashier n : person who receives and records payments

cash·mere \'kazh,mir, 'kash-\ n : fine goat's wool or a fabric of this

ca·si·no \kə'sēnō\ n, pl **-nos** : place for gambling

cask \'kask\ n : barrel-shaped container for liquids

cas·ket \'kaskət\ n : coffin

cas·se·role \'kasə,rōl\ n : baking dish or the food cooked in this

cas·sette \ka'set, kə-\ n : case containing magnetic tape

cas·sock \'kasək\ n : long clerical garment

cast \'kast\ vb **cast**; **cast·ing** 1 : throw 2 : deposit (a ballot) 3 : assign parts in a play 4 : mold ~ n 1 : throw 2 : appearance 3 : rigid surgical dressing 4 : actors in a play

cas·ta·nets \,kastə'nets\ n pl : shells clicked together in the hand

cast·away \'kastə,wā\ n : survivor of a shipwreck —**castaway** adj

caste \'kast\ n : social class or rank

cast·er \'kastər\ n : small wheel on furniture

cas·ti·gate \'kastə,gāt\ vb **-gat·ed**; **-gat·ing** : chastise severely —**cas·ti·ga·tion** \,kastə'gāshən\ n —**cas·ti·ga·tor** \'kastə,gā-tər\ n

cast iron n : hard brittle alloy of iron

cas·tle \'kasəl\ n : fortified building

cast-off adj : thrown away —**cast-off** n

cas·trate \'kas,trāt\ vb **-trat·ed**; **-trat·ing** : remove the testes of —**cas·tra·tion** \ka'strāshən\ n

ca·su·al \'kazhəwəl\ adj 1 : happening by chance 2 : showing little concern 3 : informal —**ca·su·al·ly** \-ē\ adv —**ca·su·al·ness** n

ca·su·al·ty \-tē\ n, pl **-ties** 1 : serious or fatal accident 2 : one injured, lost, or destroyed

ca·su·ist·ry \'kazhəwəstrē\ n, pl **-ries** : rationalization —**ca·su·ist** \-wist\ n

cat \'kat\ n 1 : small domestic mammal 2 : related animal (as a lion) —**cat·like** adj

cat·a·clysm \'katə,klizəm\ n : violent change —**cat·a·clys·mal** \,katə'klizməl\, **cat·a·clys·mic** \-'klizmik\ adj

cat·a·comb \'katə,kōm\ n : underground burial place

cat·a·log, cat·a·logue \'katᵊl,óg\ n 1 : list 2 : book containing a description of items ~ vb **-loged** or **-logued**; **-log·ing** or **-logu·ing** 1 : make a catalog of 2 : enter in a catalog —**cat·a·log·er, cat·a·logu·er** n

ca·tal·pa \kə'talpə\ n : tree with broad leaves and long pods

ca·tal·y·sis \kə'taləsəs\ n, pl **-y·ses** \-,sēz\ : increase in the rate of chemical reaction caused by a substance (**cat·a·lyst** \'katᵊlist\) that is itself unchanged —**cat·a·lyt·ic** \,katᵊl'itik\ adj

cat·a·ma·ran \,katəmə'ran\ n : boat with twin hulls

cat·a·mount \'katə,maúnt\ n : cougar

cat·a·pult \'katə,pəlt, -,púlt\ n : device for hurling or launching —**catapult** vb

cat·a·ract \'katə,rakt\ n 1 : large waterfall 2 : cloudiness of the lens of the eye

ca·tarrh \kə'tär\ n : inflammation of the nose and throat ca•tas•tro•phe \kə'tastrə,fē\ n 1 : great disaster or misfortune 2 : utter failure —cat•a•stroph•ic \,katə'sträfik\ adj —cat•a•stroph•i•cal•ly \-iklē\ adv

cat•bird n : American songbird

cat•call n : noise of disapproval

catch \'kach, 'kech\ vb caught \'kȯt\; catching 1 : capture esp. after pursuit 2 : trap 3 : detect esp. by surprise 4 : grasp 5 : get entangled 6 : become affected with or by 7 : seize and hold firmly ~ n 1 : act of catching 2 : something caught 3 : something that fastens 4 : hidden difficulty —catch•er n

catch•ing \-iŋ\ adj : infectious

catch•up \'kechəp, 'kach-; 'katsəp\ var of KETCHUP

catch•word n : slogan

catchy \-ē\ adj catch•i•er; -est : likely to catch interest

cat•e•chism \'katə,kizəm\ n : set of questions and answers esp. to teach religious doctrine

cat•e•gor•i•cal \,katə'gȯrikəl\ adj : absolute —cat•e•gor•i•cal•ly \-klē\ adv

cat•e•go•ry \'katə,gȯrē\ n, pl -ries : group or class —cat•e•go•ri•za•tion \,katigərə'zāshən\ n —cat•e•go•rize \'katigə,rīz\ vb

ca•ter \'kātər\ vb 1 : provide food for 2 : supply what is wanted —ca•ter•er n

cat•er•cor•ner \'katē'kȯrnər, ,katə-, ,kitē-\, cat•er•cor•nered adv or adj : in a diagonal position

cat•er•pil•lar \'katər,pilər\ n : butterfly or moth larva

cat•er•waul \'katər,wȯl\ vb : make the harsh cry of a cat —caterwaul n

cat•fish n : big-headed fish with feelers about the mouth

cat•gut n : tough cord made usu. from sheep intestines

ca•thar•sis \kə'thärsəs\ n, pl ca•thar•ses \-,sēz\ : a purging —ca•thar•tic \kə'thärtik\ adj or n

ca•the•dral \-'thēdrəl\ n : principal church of a diocese

cath•e•ter \'kathətər\ n : tube for insertion into a body cavity

cath•ode \'kath,ōd\ n 1 : negative electrode 2 : positive battery terminal —ca•thod•ic \ka'thädik\ adj

cath•o•lic \'kathəlik\ adj 1 : universal 2 cap : relating to Roman Catholics

Cath•o•lic n : member of the Roman Catholic Church —Ca•thol•i•cism \kə'thälə,sizəm\ n

cat•kin \'katkən\ n : long dense flower cluster

cat•nap n : short light nap —catnap vb

cat•nip \-,nip\ n : aromatic mint relished by cats

cat's-paw n, pl cat's-paws : person used as if a tool

cat•sup \'kechəp, 'kach-; 'katsəp\ var of KETCHUP

cat•tail n : marsh herb with furry brown spikes

cat•tle \'katᵊl\ n pl : domestic bovines —cat•tle•man \-mən, -,man\ n

cat•ty \'katē\ adj -ti•er; -est : mean or spiteful —cat•ti•ly adv —cat•ti•ness n

cat•walk n : high narrow walk

Cau•ca•sian \kȯ'kāzhən\ adj : relating to the white race —Caucasian n

cau•cus \'kȯkəs\ n : political meeting —caucus vb

caught past of CATCH

caul•dron \'kȯldrən\ n : large kettle

cau•li•flow•er \'kȯli,flaůər, 'käl-\ n : vegetable having a compact head of usu. white undeveloped flowers

caulk \'kȯk\ vb : make seams watertight —caulk n —caulk•er n

caus•al \'kȯzəl\ adj : relating to or being a cause —cau•sal•i•ty \kȯ'zalətē\ n —caus•al•ly \-ē\ adv

cause \'kȯz\ n 1 : something that brings about a result 2 : reason 3 : lawsuit 4 : principle or movement to support ~ vb caused; caus•ing : be the cause of —cau•sa•tion \kȯ'zāshən\ n —caus•ative \'kȯzətiv\ adj —cause•less adj —caus•er n

cause•way n : raised road esp. over water

caus•tic \'kȯstik\ adj 1 : corrosive 2 : sharp or biting —caustic n

cau•ter•ize \'kȯtə,rīz\ vb -ized; -iz•ing : burn to prevent infection or bleeding —cau•ter•i•za•tion \,kȯtərə'zāshən\ n

cau•tion \'kȯshən\ n 1 : warning 2 : care or prudence ~ vb : warn —cau•tion•ary \-shə,nerē\ adj

cau•tious \'kȯshəs\ adj : taking caution —cau•tious•ly adv —cau•tious•ness n

cav•al•cade \,kavəl'kād, 'kavəl,-\ n 1 : procession on horseback 2 : series

cav•a•lier \,kavə'lir\ n : mounted soldier ~ adj : disdainful or arrogant —cav•a•lier•ly adv

cav•al•ry \'kavəlrē\ n, pl -ries : troops on horseback or in vehicles —cav•al•ry•man \-mən, -,man\ n

cave \'kāv\ n : natural underground chamber —cave in vb : collapse

cav•ern \'kavərn\ n : large cave —cav•ern•ous adj —cav•ern•ous•ly adv

cav•i•ar, cav•i•are \'kavē,är, 'käv-\ n : salted fish roe

cav•il \'kavəl\ vb -iled or -illed; -il•ing or -il•ling : raise trivial objections —cavil n —cav•il•er, cav•il•ler n

cav•i•ty \'kavətē\ n, pl -ties 1 : unfilled place within a mass 2 : decay in a tooth

ca•vort \kə'vȯrt\ vb : prance or caper

caw \'kȯ\ vb : utter the harsh call of the crow —caw n

cay•enne pepper \,kī'en-, ,kā-\ n : ground dried fruits of a hot pepper

CD \sē'dē\ n : compact disc

cease \'sēs\ vb ceased; ceas•ing : stop

cease•less \-ləs\ adj : continuous

ce•dar \'sēdər\ n : cone-bearing tree with fragrant durable wood

cede \'sēd\ vb ced•ed; ced•ing : surrender —ced•er n

ceil•ing \'sēliŋ\ n 1 : overhead surface of a room 2 : upper limit

cel•e•brate \'selə,brāt\ vb -brat•ed; -brat•ing 1 : perform with appropriate rites 2 : honor with ceremonies 3 : extol —cel•e•brant \-brənt\ n —cel•e•bra•tion \,selə'brāshən\ n —cel•e•bra•tor \'selə,brātər\ n

cel•e•brat•ed \-əd\ adj : renowned

ce•leb•ri•ty \sə'lebrətē\ n, pl -ties 1 : renown 2 : well-known person

ce•ler•i•ty \sə'lerətē\ n : speed

cel•ery \'selərē\ n, pl -er•ies : herb grown for crisp edible stalks

ce•les•ta \sə'lestə\, ce•leste \sə'lest\ n : keyboard musical instrument

ce•les•tial \sə'leschəl\ adj 1 : relating to the sky 2 : heavenly

cel•i•ba•cy \'seləbəsē\ n 1 : state of being unmarried 2 : abstention from sexual intercourse —cel•i•bate \'seləbət\ n or adj

cell \'sel\ n 1 : small room 2 : tiny mass of protoplasm that forms the fundamental unit of living matter 3 : container holding an electrolyte for generating electricity —celled adj

cel•lar \'selər\ n : room or area below ground

cel•lo \'chelō\ n, pl -los : bass member of the violin family —cel•list \-ist\ n

cel•lo•phane \'selə,fān\ n : thin transparent cellulose wrapping

cel•lu•lar \'selyələr\ adj : relating to or consisting of cells

cel•lu•lose \'selyə,lōs\ n : complex plant carbohydrate

Cel•si•us \'selsēəs\ adj : relating to a thermometer scale on which the freezing point of water is 0° and the boiling point is 100°

ce•ment \si'ment\ n 1 : powdery mixture of clay and limestone that hardens when wetted 2 : binding agent ~ vb : unite or cover with cement —ce•ment•er n

cem•e•tery \'semə,terē\ n, pl -ter•ies : burial ground

cen•ser \'sensər\ n : vessel for burning incense

cen•sor \'sensər\ n : one with power to suppress anything objectionable (as in printed matter) ~ vb : be a censor of —cen•so•ri•al \sen'sōrēəl\ adj —cen•sor•ship \-,ship\ n

cen•so•ri•ous \sen'sōrēəs\ adj : critical —cen•so•ri•ous•ly adv —cen•so•ri•ous•ness n

cen•sure \'senchər\ n : official reprimand ~ vb -sured; -sur•ing : find blameworthy —cen•sur•able adj

cen•sus \'sensəs\ n : periodic population count —census vb

cent \'sent\ n : monetary unit equal to 1/100 of a basic unit of value

cen•taur \'sen,tȯr\ n : mythological creature that is half man and half horse

cen•ten•ni•al \sen'tenēəl\ n : 100th anniversary —centennial adj

cen•ter \'sentər\ n 1 : middle point 2 : point of origin or greatest concentration 3 : region of concentrated population 4 : player near the middle of the team ~ vb 1 : place, fix, or concentrate at or around a center 2 : have a center —cen•ter•piece n

cen•ti•grade \'sentə,grād, 'sänt-\ adj : Celsius

cen•ti•me•ter \'sentə,mētər, 'sänt-\ n : 1/100 meter

cen•ti•pede \'sentə,pēd\ n : long flat many-legged arthropod

cen•tral \'sentrəl\ adj 1 : constituting or being near a center 2 : essential or principal —cen•tral•ly adv

cen•tral•ize \-trə,līz\ vb -ized; -iz•ing : bring to a central point or under central control —cen•tral•i•za•tion \,sentrələ'zāshən\ n —cen•tral•iz•er n

cen•tre chiefly Brit var of CENTER

cen•trif•u•gal \sen'trifyəgəl, -'trifigəl\ adj : acting in a direction away from a center or axis

cen•tri•fuge \'sentrə,fyüj\ n : machine that separates substances by spinning

cen•trip•e•tal \sen'tripətᵊl\ adj : acting in a direction toward a center or axis

cen•tu•ri•on \sen'chúrēən, -'túr-\ n : Roman military officer

cen•tu•ry \'senchərē\ n, pl -ries : 100 years

ce•ram•ic \sə'ramik\ n 1 pl : art or process of shaping and hardening articles from clay 2 : product of ceramics —ceramic adj

ce•re•al \'sirēəl\ adj : made of or relating to grain or to the plants that produce it ~ n 1 : grass yielding edible grain 2 : food prepared from a cereal grain

cer•e•bel•lum \,serə'beləm\ n, pl -bellums or -bel•la \-'belə\ : part of the brain controlling muscular coordination —cer•e•bel•lar \-ər\ adj

ce•re•bral \sə'rēbrəl, 'serə-\ adj 1 : relating to the brain, intellect, or cerebrum 2 : appealing to the intellect

cerebral palsy n : disorder caused by brain damage and marked esp. by defective muscle control

ce•re•brate \'serə,brāt\ vb -brat•ed; -brat•ing : think —ce•re•bra•tion \,serə'brāshən\ n

ce•re•brum \sə'rēbrəm, 'serə-\ n, pl -brums or -bra \-brə\ : part of the brain that contains the higher nervous centers

cer•e•mo•ny \'serə,mōnē\ n, pl -nies 1 : formal act prescribed by law, ritual, or convention 2 : prescribed procedures —cer•e•mo•ni•al \,serə'mōnēəl\ adj or n —cer•e•mo•ni•ous \-nēəs\ adj

ce•rise \sə'rēs\ n : moderate red

cer•tain \'sərtᵊn\ adj 1 : settled 2 : true 3 : specific but not named 4 : bound 5 : assured ~ pron : certain ones —cer•tain•ly adv —cer•tain•ty \-tē\ n

cer•tif•i•cate \sər'tifikət\ n : document establishing truth or fulfillment

cer•ti•fy \'sərtə,fī\ vb -fied; -fy•ing 1 : verify 2 : endorse —cer•ti•fi•able \-,fīəbəl\ adj —cer•ti•fi•ably \-blē\ adv —cer•ti•fi•ca•tion \,sərtəfə'kāshən\ n —cer•ti•fi•er n

cer•ti•tude \'sərtə,tüd, -,tyüd\ n : state of being certain

cer•vix \'sərviks\ n, pl -vi•ces \-və,sēz\ or -vix•es 1 : neck 2 : narrow end of the uterus —cer•vi•cal \-vikəl\ adj

ce•sar•e•an \si'zarēən\ n : surgical operation to deliver a baby —cesarean adj

ce•si•um \'sēzēəm\ n : silver-white soft ductile chemical element

ces•sa•tion \se'sāshən\ n : a halting

ces•sion \'seshən\ n : a yielding

cess•pool \'ses,pül\ n : underground sewage pit

Cha•blis \'shab,lē; sha'blē\ n, pl Chablis \-,lēz, -'blēz\ : dry white wine

chafe \'chāf\ vb chafed; chaf•ing 1 : fret 2 : make sore by rubbing

chaff \'chaf\ n 1 : debris separated from grain 2 : something worthless

chafing dish \'chāfiŋ-\ n : utensil for cooking at the table

cha•grin \shə'grin\ n : embarrassment or humiliation ~ vb : cause to feel chagrin

chain \'chān\ n 1 : flexible series of connected links 2 pl : fetters 3 : linked series ~ vb : bind or connect with a chain

chair \'cher\ n 1 : seat with a back 2 : position of authority or dignity 3 : chairman ~ vb : act as chairman of

chair•man \-mən\ n : presiding officer —chair•man•ship n

chair•wom•an \-,wůmən\ n : woman who acts as a presiding officer

chaise longue \'shāz'lȯŋ\ n, pl chaise longues \-'lȯŋ, -'lȯŋz\ : long chair for reclining

cha•let \sha'lā\ n : Swiss mountain cottage with overhanging roof

chal•ice \'chaləs\ n : eucharistic cup

chalk \'chȯk\ n 1 : soft limestone 2 : chalky material used as a crayon ~ vb : mark with chalk —chalky adj —chalk up vb 1 : credit 2 : achieve

chalk•board n : blackboard

chal•lenge \'chalənj\ vb -lenged; -leng•ing 1 : dispute 2 : invite or dare to act or compete —challenge n —chal•leng•er n

cham•ber \'chāmbər\ n 1 : room 2 : enclosed space 3 : legislative meeting place or body 4 pl : judge's consultation room —cham•bered adj

cham•ber•maid n : bedroom maid

chamber music n : music by a small group for a small audience

cha•me•leon \kə'mēlyən\ n : small lizard whose skin changes color

cham•ois \'shamē\ n, pl cham•ois \-ē, -ēz\ 1 : goatlike antelope 2 : soft leather

¹champ \'champ, 'chämp\ vb : chew noisily

²champ \'champ\ n : champion

cham•pagne \sham'pān\ n : sparkling white wine

cham•pi•on \'champēən\ n 1 : advocate or defender 2 : winning contestant ~ vb : protect or fight for

cham•pi•on•ship \-,ship\ n 1 : title of a champion 2 : contest to pick a champion

chance \'chans\ n 1 : unpredictable element of existence 2 : opportunity 3 : probability 4 : risk 5 : raffle ticket ~ vb chanced; chanc•ing 1 : happen 2 : encounter unexpectedly 3 : risk —chance adj

chan•cel \'chansəl\ n : part of a church around the altar

chan•cel•lery, chan•cel•lory \'chansələrē\ n, pl -ler•ies or -lor•ies 1 : position of a chancellor 2 : chancellor's office

chan•cel•lor \-sələr\ n 1 : chief or high state official 2 : head of a university —chan•cel•lor•ship n

chan•cre \'shaŋkər\ n : skin ulcer esp. from syphilis

chancy \'chansē\ adj chanc•i•er; -est : risky

chan•de•lier \,shandə'lir\ n : hanging lighting fixture

chan•dler \'chandlər\ n : provisions dealer —chan•dlery n

change \'chānj\ vb changed; chang•ing 1 : make or become different 2 : exchange 3 : give or receive change for ~ n 1 : a changing 2 : excess from a payment 3 : money in smaller denominations 4 : coins —change•able adj —change•less adj —chang•er n

chan•nel \'chanᵊl\ n 1 : deeper part of a waterway 2 : means of passage or communication 3 : strait 4 : broadcast frequency ~ vb -neled or -nelled; -nel•ing or -nel•ling : make or direct through a channel

chant \'chant\ vb : sing or speak in one tone —chant n —chant•er n

chan•tey, chan•ty \'shantē, 'chant-\ n, pl -teys or -ties : sailors' work song

Cha•nu•kah \'känəkə, 'hän-\ var of HANUKKAH

cha•os \'kā,äs\ n : complete disorder —cha•ot•ic \kā'ätik\ adj —cha•ot•i•cal•ly \-iklē\ adv

¹chap \'chap\ n : fellow

²chap vb -pp- : dry and crack open usu. from wind and cold

chap•el \'chapəl\ n : private or small place of worship

chap•er•on, chap•er•one \'shapə,rōn\ n : older person who accompanies young people at a social gathering ~ vb -oned; -on•ing : act as chaperon at or for —chap•er•on•age \-ij\ n

chap•lain \'chaplən\ n : clergy member in a military unit or a prison —chap•lain•cy \-sē\ n

chap•ter \'chaptər\ n 1 : main book division 2 : branch of a society

char \'chär\ vb -rr- 1 : burn to charcoal 2 : scorch

char•ac•ter \'kariktər\ n 1 : letter or graphic mark 2 : trait or distinctive combination of traits 3 : peculiar person 4 : fictional person —char•ac•ter•i•za•tion \,kariktərə'zāshən\ n —char•ac•ter•ize \'kariktə,rīz\ vb

char•ac•ter•is•tic \,kariktə'ristik\ adj : typical ~ n : distinguishing quality —char•ac•ter•is•ti•cal•ly \-tiklē\ adv

cha•rades \shə'rādz\ n sing or pl : pantomime guessing game

char•coal \'chär,kōl\ n : porous carbon prepared by partial combustion

chard \'chärd\ n : leafy vegetable

charge \'chärj\ vb charged; charg•ing 1 : give an electric charge to 2 : impose a task or responsibility on 3 : command 4 : accuse 5 : rush forward in assault 6 : assume a debt for 7 : fix as a price ~ n 1 : excess or deficiency of electrons in a body 2 : tax 3 : responsibility 4 : accusation 5 : cost 6 : attack —charge•able adj

charg•er \-ər\ n : horse ridden in battle

char•i•ot \'charēət\ n : ancient 2-wheeled vehicle —char•i•o•teer \,charēə'tir\ n

cha•ris•ma \kə'rizmə\ n : special ability to lead —char•is•mat•ic \,karəz'matik\ adj

char•i•ty \'charətē\ n, pl -ties 1 : love for mankind 2 : generosity or leniency 3 : alms 4 : institution for relief of the needy —char•i•ta•ble \-əbəl\ adj —char•i•ta•ble•ness n —char•i•ta•bly \-blē\ adv

char•la•tan \'shärlətən\ n : impostor

charm \'chärm\ n 1 : something with magic power 2 : appealing trait 3 : small ornament ~ vb : fascinate —charm•er n —charm•ing adj —charm•ing•ly adv

char•nel house \'chärnᵊl-\ n : place for dead bodies

chart \'chärt\ n 1 : map 2 : diagram ~ vb 1 : make a chart of 2 : plan

char•ter \-ər\ n 1 : document granting rights 2 : constitution ~ vb 1 : establish by charter 2 : rent —char•ter•er n

char•treuse \shär'trüz, -'trüs\ n : brilliant yellow green

char•wom•an \'chär,wůmən\ n : cleaning woman

chary \'charē\ adj chari•er; -est : cautious —char•i•ly \'charəlē\ adv

¹chase \'chās\ vb chased; chas•ing 1 : follow trying to catch 2 : drive away —chase n —chas•er n

²chase \vb\ **chased; chas•ing** : decorate (metal) by embossing or engraving

chasm \'kazəm\ n : gorge

chas•sis \'chasē, 'shasē\ n, pl **chas•sis** \-ēz\ : supporting structural frame

chaste \'chāst\ adj **chast•er; chast•est 1** : abstaining from all or unlawful sexual relations **2** : modest or decent **3** : severely simple —**chaste•ly** adv —**chaste•ness** n —**chas•ti•ty** \'chastətē\ n

chas•ten \'chāsən\ vb : discipline

chas•tise \chas'tīz\ vb **-tised; -tis•ing 1** : punish **2** : censure —**chas•tise•ment** \-mənt, 'chastəz-\ n

chat \'chat\ n : informal talk —**chat** vb —**chat•ty** \-ē\ adj

châ•teau \sha'tō\ n, pl **-teaus** \-'tōz\ or **-teaux** \-'tō, -'tōz\ **1** : large country house **2** : French vineyard estate

chat•tel \'chatʰl\ n : item of tangible property other than real estate

chat•ter \'chatər\ vb **1** : utter rapidly succeeding sounds **2** : talk fast or too much —**chatter** n —**chat•ter•er** n

chat•ter•box n : incessant talker

chauf•feur \'shōfər, shō'fər\ n : hired car driver ~ vb : work as a chauffeur

chau•vin•ism \'shōvə,nizəm\ n : excessive patriotism —**chau•vin•ist** \-vənist\ n —**chau•vin•is•tic** \,shōvə'nistik\ adj

cheap \'chēp\ adj **1** : inexpensive **2** : shoddy —**cheap** adv —**cheap•en** \'chēpən\ vb —**cheap•ly** adv —**cheap•ness** n

cheap•skate n : stingy person

cheat \'chēt\ n **1** : act of deceiving **2** : one that cheats ~ vb **1** : deprive through fraud or deceit **2** : violate rules dishonestly —**cheat•er** n

check \'chek\ n **1** : sudden stoppage **2** : restraint **3** : test or standard for testing **4** : written order to a bank to pay money **5** : ticket showing ownership **6** : slip showing an amount due **7** : pattern in squares or fabric in such a pattern **8** : mark placed beside an item noted ~ vb **1** : slow down or stop **2** : restrain **3** : compare or correspond with a source or original **4** : inspect or test for condition **5** : mark with a check **6** : leave or accept for safekeeping or shipment **7** : checker —**check in** vb : report one's arrival —**check out** vb : settle one's account and leave

¹check•er \-ər\ n : piece in checkers ~ vb : mark with different colors or into squares

²checker n : one that checks

check•er•board \-,bōrd\ n : board of 64 squares of alternate colors

check•ers \-ərz\ n : game for 2 played on a checkerboard

check•mate vb : thwart completely —**checkmate** n

check•point n : place where traffic is checked

check•up n : physical examination

ched•dar \'chedər\ n : hard smooth cheese

cheek \'chēk\ n **1** : fleshy side part of the face **2** : impudence —**cheeked** \'chēkt\ adj —**cheeky** adj

cheep \'chēp\ vb : utter faint shrill sounds —**cheep** n

cheer \'chir\ n **1** : good spirits **2** : food and drink for a feast **3** : shout of applause or encouragement ~ vb **1** : give hope or courage to **2** : make or become glad **3** : urge on or applaud with shouts —**cheer•er** n —**cheer•ful** \-fəl\ adj —**cheer•ful•ly** adv —**cheer•ful•ness** n —**cheer•lead•er** n —**cheer•less** adj —**cheer•less•ly** adv —**cheer•less•ness** n

cheery \'chirē\ adj **cheer•i•er; -est** : cheerful —**cheer•i•ly** adv —**cheer•i•ness** n

cheese \'chēz\ n : curd of milk usu. pressed and cured —**cheesy** adj

cheese•cloth n : lightweight coarse cotton gauze

chee•tah \'chētə\ n : spotted swift-moving African cat

chef \'shef\ n : chief cook

chem•i•cal \'kemikəl\ adj **1** : relating to chemistry **2** : working or produced by chemicals ~ n : substance obtained by chemistry —**chem•i•cal•ly** \-klē\ adv

che•mise \shə'mēz\ n **1** : woman's one-piece undergarment **2** : loose dress

chem•ist \'kemist\ n **1** : one trained in chemistry **2** Brit : pharmacist

chem•is•try \-istrē\ n, pl **-tries** : science that deals with the composition and properties of substances

che•mo•ther•a•py \,kēmō'therəpē, ,kemō-\ n : use of chemicals in the treatment of disease —**che•mo•ther•a•peu•tic** adj

che•nille \shə'nēl\ n : yarn with protruding pile or fabric of such yarn

cheque \'chek\ chiefly Brit var of CHECK 4

cher•ish \'cherish\ vb : hold dear

cher•ry \'cherē\ n, pl **-ries** : small fleshy fruit of a tree related to the roses or the tree or its wood

cher•ub \'cherəb\ n **1** pl **-u•bim** \-ə,bim, -yə-\ : angel **2** pl **-ubs** : chubby child —**che•ru•bic** \chə'rübik\ adj

chess \'ches\ n : game for 2 played on a checkerboard —**chess•board** n —**chess•man** n

chest \'chest\ n **1** : boxlike container **2** : part of the body enclosed by the ribs and breastbone —**chest•ed** adj

chest•nut \'ches,nət\ n : nut of a tree related to the beech or the tree

chev•i•ot \'shevēət\ n **1** : heavy rough wool fabric **2** : soft-finished cotton fabric

chev•ron \'shevrən\ n : V-shaped insignia

chew \'chü\ vb : crush or grind with the teeth ~ n : something to chew —**chew•able** adj —**chew•er** n —**chewy** adj

chic \'shēk\ n : smart elegance of dress or manner ~ adj **1** : stylish **2** : currently fashionable

chi•ca•nery \shik'ānərē\ n, pl **-ner•ies** : trickery

chick \'chik\ n : young chicken or bird

chick•a•dee \-ə,dē\ n : small grayish American bird

chick•en \'chikən\ n **1** : common domestic fowl or its flesh used as food **2** : coward

chicken pox n : acute contagious virus disease esp. of children

chi•cle \'chikəl\ n : gum from a tropical evergreen tree

chic•o•ry \'chikərē\ n, pl **-ries** : herb used in salad or its dried ground root used to adulterate coffee

chide \'chīd\ vb **chid** \'chid\ or **chid•ed** \'chīdəd\ **chid** or **chid•den** \'chidʰn\ or **chided; chid•ing** \'chīdiŋ\ : scold

chief \'chēf\ n : leader ~ adj **1** : highest in rank **2** : most important —**chiefdom** n —**chief•ly** adv

chief•tain \'chēftən\ n : chief

chif•fon \shif'än, 'shif,-\ n : sheer fabric

chig•ger \'chigər\ n : bloodsucking mite

chi•gnon \'shēn,yän\ n : knot of hair

chil•blain \'chil,blān\ n : sore or inflamed swelling caused by cold

child \'chīld\ n, pl **chil•dren** \'childrən\ **1** : unborn or recently born person **2** : son or daughter —**child•bear•ing** n or adj —**child•birth** n —**child•hood** n —**child•ish** adj —**child•ish•ly** adv —**child•ish•ness** n —**child•less** adj —**child•less•ness** n —**child•like** adj —**child•proof** \-,prüf\ adj

chili, chile, chil•li \'chilē\ n, pl **chil•ies** or **chil•es** or **chil•lies 1** : hot pepper **2** : spicy stew of ground beef, chilies, and beans

chill \'chil\ vb : make or become cold or chilly ~ adj : moderately cold ~ n **1** : feeling of coldness with shivering **2** : moderate coldness

chilly \-ē\ adj **chill•i•er; -est** : noticeably cold —**chill•i•ness** n

chime \'chīm\ n : set of tuned bells or their sound ~ vb : make bell-like sounds —**chime in** vb : break into or join in a conversation

chi•me•ra, chi•mae•ra \kī'mirə, kə-\ n **1** : imaginary monster **2** : illusion —**chi•me•ri•cal** \-'merikəl\ adj

chim•ney \'chimnē\ n, pl **-neys 1** : passage for smoke **2** : glass tube around a lamp flame

chimp \'chimp, 'shimp\ n : chimpanzee

chim•pan•zee \,chim,pan'zē, ,shim-; chim-'panzē, shim-\ n : small ape

chin \'chin\ n : part of the face below the mouth —**chin•less** adj

chi•na \'chīnə\ n **1** : porcelain ware **2** : domestic pottery

chin•chil•la \chin'chilə\ n : small So. American rodent with soft pearl-gray fur or this fur

chink \'chiŋk\ n : small crack ~ vb : fill chinks of

chintz \'chints\ n : printed cotton cloth

chip \'chip\ n **1** : small thin flat piece cut or broken off **2** : thin crisp morsel of food **3** : counter used in games **4** : flaw where a chip came off **5** : small slice of semiconductor containing electronic circuits ~ vb **-pp-** : cut or break chips from —**chip in** vb : contribute

chip•munk \-,məŋk\ n : small striped ground-dwelling rodent

chip•per \-ər\ adj : lively and cheerful

chi•rop•o•dy \kə'räpədē, shə-\ n : podiatry —**chi•rop•o•dist** \-dist\ n

chi•ro•prac•tic \'kīrə,praktik\ n : system of healing based esp. on manipulation of body structures —**chi•ro•prac•tor** \-tər\ n

chirp \'chərp\ n : short sharp sound like that of a bird or cricket —**chirp** vb

chis•el \'chizəl\ n : sharp-edged metal tool ~ vb **-eled** or **-elled; -el•ing** or **-el•ling 1** : work with a chisel **2** : cheat —**chis•el•er** n

chit \'chit\ n : signed voucher for a small debt

chit•chat \-,chat\ n : casual conversation —**chitchat** vb

chiv•al•rous \'shivəlrəs\ adj : relating to chivalry **1** : honest, courteous, or generous —**chiv•al•rous•ly** adv —**chiv•al•rous•ness** n

chiv•al•ry \-rē\ n, pl **-ries 1** : system or practices of knighthood **2** : spirit or character of the ideal knight —**chi•val•ric** \shə-'valrik\ adj

chive \'chīv\ n : herb related to the onion

chlo•ride \'klōr,īd\ n : compound of chlorine

chlo•ri•nate \-ə,nāt\ vb **-nat•ed; -nat•ing** : treat or combine with chlorine —**chlo•ri•na•tion** \,klōrə'nāshən\ n

chlo•rine \'klōr,ēn\ n : chemical element that is a heavy strong-smelling greenish yellow irritating gas

chlo•ro•form \'klōrə,fôrm\ n : etherlike colorless heavy fluid ~ vb : anesthetize or kill with chloroform

chlo•ro•phyll \'klōrə,fil\ n : green coloring matter of plants

chock \'chäk\ n : wedge for blocking the movement of a wheel —**chock** vb

chock–full \'chäk'ful, 'chäk-\ adj : full to the limit

choc•o•late \'chäkələt, 'chôk-\ n **1** : ground roasted cacao beans or a beverage made from them **2** : candy made of or with chocolate **3** : dark brown

choice \'chois\ n **1** : act or power of choosing **2** : one selected **3** : variety offered for selection ~ adj **choic•er; choic•est 1** : worthy of being chosen **2** : selected with care **3** : of high quality

choir \'kwīr\ n : group of singers esp. in church —**choir•boy** n —**choir•mas•ter** n

choke \'chōk\ vb **choked; chok•ing 1** : hinder breathing **2** : clog or obstruct ~ n **1** : a choking or sound of choking **2** : valve for controlling air intake in a gasoline engine

chok•er \-ər\ n : tight necklace

chol•er \'kälər, 'kō-\ n : bad temper —**chol•er•ic** \'kälərik, kə'ler-\ adj

chol•era \'kälərə\ n : disease marked by severe vomiting and dysentery

cho•les•ter•ol \kə'lestə,rôl, -,rōl\ n : waxy substance in animal tissues

choose \'chüz\ vb **chose** \'chōz\; **cho•sen** \'chōzʰn\ **choos•ing 1** : select after consideration **2** : decide **3** : prefer —**chooser** n

choosy, choos•ey \'chüzē\ adj **choos•i•er; -est** : fussy in making choices

chop \'chäp\ vb **-pp- 1** : cut by repeated blows **2** : cut into small pieces ~ n **1** : sharp downward blow **2** : small cut of meat often with part of a rib

chop•per \-ər\ n **1** : one that chops **2** : helicopter

chop•py \-ē\ adj **-pi•er; -est 1** : rough with small waves **2** : jerky or disconnected —**chop•pi•ly** adv —**chop•pi•ness** n

chops \'chäps\ n pl : fleshy covering of the jaws

chop•sticks n pl : pair of sticks used in eating in oriental countries

cho•ral \'kōrəl\ adj : relating to or sung by a choir or chorus or in chorus —**cho•ral•ly** adv

cho•rale \kə'ral, -'räl\ n **1** : hymn tune or harmonization of a traditional melody **2** : chorus or choir

¹chord \'kôrd\ n : harmonious tones sounded together

²chord n **1** : cordlike anatomical structure **2** : straight line joining 2 points on a curve

chore \'chōr\ n **1** pl : daily household or farm work **2** : routine or disagreeable task

cho•re•og•ra•phy \,kōrē'ägrəfē\ n, pl **-phies** : art of composing and arranging dances —**cho•reo•graph** \'kōrēə,graf\ vb —**cho•re•og•ra•pher** \,kōrē'ägrəfər\ n —**cho•reo•graph•ic** \-ēə'grafik\ adj

cho•ris•ter \'kōrəstər\ n : choir singer

chor•tle \'chôrtʰl\ vb **-tled; -tling** : laugh or chuckle —**chortle** n

cho•rus \'kōrəs\ n **1** : group of singers or dancers **2** : part of a song repeated at intervals **3** : composition for a chorus ~ vb : sing or utter together

chose past of CHOOSE

cho•sen \'chōzʰn\ adj : favored

¹chow \'chaù\ n : food

²chow n : thick-coated muscular dog

chow•der \'chaùdər\ n : thick soup usu. of seafood and milk

chow mein \'chaù'mān\ n : thick stew of shredded vegetables and meat

chris•ten \'krisʰn\ vb **1** : baptize **2** : name —**chris•ten•ing** n

Chris•ten•dom \-dəm\ n : areas where Christianity prevails

Chris•tian \'krischən\ n : adherent of Christianity ~ adj : relating to or professing a belief in Christianity or Jesus Christ —**Chris•tian•ize** \'krischə,nīz\ vb

Chris•ti•an•i•ty \,krischē'anətē\ n : religion derived from the teachings of Jesus Christ

Christian name n : first name

Christ•mas \'krisməs\ n : December 25 celebrated as the birthday of Christ

chro•mat•ic \krō'matik\ adj **1** : relating to color **2** : proceeding by half steps of the musical scale

chrome \'krōm\ n : chromium or something plated with it

chro•mi•um \-ēəm\ n : a bluish white metallic element used esp. in alloys

chro•mo•some \'krōmə,sōm, -,zōm\ n : part of a cell nucleus that contains the genes —**chro•mo•som•al** \,krōmə'sōməl, -'zō-\ adj

chron•ic \'kränik\ adj : frequent or persistent —**chron•i•cal•ly** \-iklē\ adv

chron•i•cle \'känikəl\ n : history ~ vb **-cled; -cling** : record —**chron•i•cler** \-iklər\ n

chro•nol•o•gy \krə'näləjē\ n, pl **-gies** : list of events in order of their occurrence —**chron•o•log•i•cal** \,kränʰl'äjikəl\ adj —**chron•o•log•i•cal•ly** \-iklē\ adv

chro•nom•e•ter \krə'nämətər\ n : very accurate timepiece

chrys•a•lis \'krisələs\ n, pl **chry•sal•i•des** \kris'alə,dēz\ or **chrys•a•lis•es** : insect pupa enclosed in a shell

chry•san•the•mum \kris'anthəməm\ n : plant with showy flowers

chub•by \'chəbē\ adj **-bi•er; -est** : fat —**chub•bi•ness** n

¹chuck \'chək\ vb **1** : tap **2** : toss ~ n **1** : light pat under the chin **2** : toss

²chuck n **1** : cut of beef **2** : machine part that holds work or another part

chuck•le \'chəkəl\ vb **-led; -ling** : laugh quietly —**chuckle** n

chug \'chəg\ n : sound of a laboring engine ~ vb **-gg-** : work or move with chugs

chum \'chəm\ n : close friend ~ vb **-mm-** : be chums —**chum•my** \-ē\ adj

chump \'chəmp\ n : fool

chunk \'chəŋk\ n **1** : short thick piece **2** : sizable amount

chunky \-ē\ adj **chunk•i•er; -est 1** : stocky **2** : containing chunks

church \'chərch\ n **1** : building esp. for Christian public worship **2** : whole body of Christians **3** : denomination **4** : congregation —**church•go•er** n —**church•go•ing** adj or n

church•yard n : cemetery beside a church

churl \'chərl\ n : rude ill-bred person —**churl•ish** adj

churn \'chərn\ n : container in which butter is made ~ vb **1** : agitate in a churn **2** : shake violently

chute \'shüt\ n : trough or passage

chut•ney \'chətnē\ n, pl **-neys** : sweet and sour relish

chutz•pah \'hùtspə, 'kùt-, -,spä\ n : nerve or insolence

ci•ca•da \sə'kādə\ n : stout-bodied insect with transparent wings

ci•der \'sīdər\ n : apple juice

ci•gar \sig'är\ n : roll of leaf tobacco for smoking

cig•a•rette \,sigə'ret, 'sigə,ret\ n : cut tobacco rolled in paper for smoking

cinch \'sinch\ n **1** : strap holding a saddle or pack in place **2** : sure thing —**cinch** vb

cin•cho•na \siŋ'kōnə\ n : So. American tree that yields quinine

cinc•ture \'siŋkchər\ n : belt or sash

cin•der \'sindər\ n **1** : ashes **2** : piece of partly burned wood or coal

cin•e•ma \'sinəmə\ n : movies or a movie theater —**cin•e•mat•ic** \,sinə'matik\ adj

cin•na•mon \'sinəmən\ n : spice from an aromatic tree bark

ci•pher \'sīfər\ n **1** : zero **2** : code

cir•ca \'sərkə\ prep : about

cir•cle \'sərkəl\ n **1** : closed symmetrical curve **2** : cycle **3** : group with a common tie ~ vb **-cled; -cling 1** : enclose in a circle **2** : move or revolve around

cir•cuit \'sərkət\ n **1** : boundary **2** : regular tour of a territory **3** : complete path of an electric current **4** : group of electronic components

cir•cu•itous \,sər'kyüətəs\ adj : circular or winding

cir•cuit•ry \'sərkətrē\ n, pl **-ries** : arrangement of an electric circuit

cir•cu•lar \'sərkyələr\ adj **1** : round **2** : moving in a circle ~ n : advertising leaflet —**cir•cu•lar•i•ty** \,sərkyə'larətē\ n

cir•cu•late \'sərkyə,lāt\ vb **-lat•ed; -lating** : move or cause to move in a circle or from place to place or person to person —**cir•cu•la•tion** \,sərkyə'lāshən\ n —**cir•cu•la•to•ry** \'sərkyələ,tōrē\ adj

cir•cum•cise \'sərkəm,sīz\ vb **-cised; -cising** : cut off the foreskin of —**cir•cum•ci•sion** \,sərkəm'sizhən\ n

cir•cum•fer•ence \sər'kəmfrəns\ n : perimeter of a circle

cir•cum•flex \'sərkəm,fleks\ n : phonetic mark (as ˆ)

cir•cum•lo•cu•tion \,sərkəmlō'kyüshən\ n : excessive use of words

cir•cum•nav•i•gate \,sərkəm'navə,gāt\ vb : sail completely around —**cir•cum•nav•i•ga•tion** n

cir•cum•scribe \'sərkəm,skrīb\ vb **1** : draw a line around **2** : limit

cir•cum•spect \'sərkəm,spekt\ adj : careful —**cir•cum•spec•tion** \,sərkəm'spekshən\ n

cir•cum•stance \'sərkəm,stans\ n **1** : fact or event **2** pl : surrounding conditions **3** pl : financial situation —**cir•cum•stan•tial** \,sərkəm'stanchəl\ adj

cir·cum·vent \sərkəm'vent\ vb : get around esp. by trickery —**cir·cum·ven·tion** \-'venchən\ n

cir·cus \'sərkəs\ n : show with feats of skill, animal acts, and clowns

cir·rho·sis \sə'rōsəs\ n, pl **-rho·ses** \-,sēz\ : fibrosis of the liver —**cir·rhot·ic** \-'rätik\ adj or n

cir·rus \'sirəs\ n, pl **-ri** \-,ī\ : wispy white cloud

cis·tern \'sistərn\ n : underground water tank

cit·a·del \'sitəd°l, -ə,del\ n : fortress

cite \'sīt\ vb **cit·ed; cit·ing** 1 : summon before a court 2 : quote 3 : refer to esp. in commendation —**ci·ta·tion** \sī'tāshən\ n

cit·i·zen \'sitəzən\ n : member of a country —**cit·i·zen·ry** \-rē\ n —**cit·i·zen·ship** n

cit·ron \'sitrən\ n : lemonlike fruit

cit·rus \'sitrəs\ n, pl **-rus** or **-rus·es** : evergreen tree or shrub grown for its fruit (as the orange or lemon)

city \'sitē\ n, pl **cit·ies** : place larger or more important than a town

civ·ic \'sivik\ adj : relating to citizenship or civil affairs

civ·ics \-iks\ n : study of citizenship

civ·il \'sivəl\ adj 1 : relating to citizens 2 : polite 3 : relating to or being a lawsuit —**civ·il·ly** adv

ci·vil·ian \sə'vilyən\ n : person not in a military, police, or fire-fighting force

ci·vil·i·ty \sə'vilətē\ n, pl **-ties** : courtesy

civ·i·li·za·tion \,sivələ'zāshən\ n 1 : high level of cultural development 2 : culture of a time or place

civ·i·lize \'sivə,līz\ vb **-lized; -liz·ing** : raise from a primitive stage of cultural development —**civ·i·lized** adj

civil liberty n : freedom from arbitrary governmental interference —usu. pl.

civil rights n pl : nonpolitical rights of a citizen

civil service n : government service

civil war n : war among citizens of one country

clack \'klak\ vb : make or cause a clatter —**clack** n

clad \'klad\ adj : covered

claim \'klām\ vb 1 : demand or take as the rightful owner 2 : maintain ~ n 1 : demand of right or ownership 2 : declaration 3 : something claimed —**claim·ant** \-ənt\ n

clair·voy·ant \klar'vóiənt\ adj : able to perceive things beyond the senses —**clair·voy·ance** \-əns\ n —**clairvoyant** n

clam \'klam\ n : bivalve mollusk

clam·ber \'klambər\ vb : climb awkwardly

clam·my \'klamē\ adj **-mi·er; -est** : being damp, soft, and usu. cool —**clam·mi·ness** n

clam·or \-ər\ n 1 : uproar 2 : protest —**clamor** vb —**clam·or·ous** adj

clamp \'klamp\ n : device for holding things together —**clamp** vb

clan \'klan\ n : group of related families —**clan·nish** adj —**clan·nish·ness** n

clan·des·tine \klan'destən\ adj : secret

clang \'klaŋ\ n : loud metallic ringing —**clang** vb

clan·gor \-ər, -gər\ n : jumble of clangs

clank \'klaŋk\ n : brief sound of struck metal —**clank** vb

clap \'klap\ vb **-pp-** 1 : strike noisily 2 : applaud ~ n 1 : loud crash 2 : noise made by clapping the hands

clap·board \'klabərd, 'klap-, -,bōrd\ n : narrow tapered board used for siding

clap·per \'klapər\ n : tongue of a bell

claque \'klak\ n 1 : group hired to applaud at a performance 2 : group of sycophants

clar·et \'klarət\ n : dry red wine

clar·i·fy \'klarə,fī\ vb **-fied; -fy·ing** : make or become clear —**clar·i·fi·ca·tion** \,klarəfə'kāshən\ n

clar·i·net \,klarə'net\ n : woodwind instrument shaped like a tube —**clar·i·net·ist, clar·i·net·tist** \-ist\ n

clar·i·on \'klarēən\ adj : loud and clear

clar·i·ty \'klarətē\ n : clearness

clash \'klash\ vb 1 : make or cause a clash 2 : be in opposition or disharmony ~ n 1 : crashing sound 2 : hostile encounter

clasp \'klasp\ n 1 : device for holding things together 2 : embrace or grasp ~ vb 1 : fasten 2 : embrace or grasp

class \'klas\ n 1 : group of the same status or nature 2 : social rank 3 : course of instruction 4 : group of students ~ vb : classify —**class·less** adj —**class·mate** n —**class·room** n

clas·sic \'klasik\ adj 1 : serving as a standard of excellence 2 : classical ~ n : work of enduring excellence and esp. of ancient Greece or Rome —**clas·si·cal** \-ikəl\ adj —**clas·si·cal·ly** \-klē\ adv —**clas·si·cism** \'klasə,sizəm\ n —**clas·si·cist** \-sist\ n

clas·si·fied \'klasə,fīd\ adj : restricted for security reasons

clas·si·fy \-,fī\ vb **-fied; -fy·ing** : arrange in or assign to classes —**clas·si·fi·ca·tion** \,klasəfə'kāshən\ n —**clas·si·fi·er** \'klasə,fīər\ n

clat·ter \'klatər\ n : rattling sound —**clatter** vb

clause \'klóz\ n 1 : separate part of a document 2 : part of a sentence with a subject and predicate

claus·tro·pho·bia \,klóstrə'fōbēə\ n : fear of closed or narrow spaces —**claus·tro·pho·bic** \-bik\ adj

clav·i·chord \'klavə,kȯrd\ n : early keyboard instrument

clav·i·cle \'klavikəl\ n : collarbone

claw \'klȯ\ n : sharp curved nail or process (as on the toe of an animal) ~ vb : scratch or dig —**clawed** adj

clay \'klā\ n : plastic earthy material —**clay·ey** \-ē\ adj

clean \'klēn\ adj 1 : free from dirt or disease 2 : pure or honorable 3 : thorough ~ vb : make or become clean —**clean** adv —**clean·er** n —**clean·ly** \-lē\ adv —**clean·ness** n

clean·ly \'klenlē\ adj **-li·er; -est** : clean —**clean·li·ness** n

cleanse \'klenz\ vb **cleansed; cleans·ing** : make clean —**cleans·er** n

clear \'klir\ adj 1 : bright 2 : free from clouds 3 : transparent 4 : easily heard, seen or understood 5 : free from doubt 6 : free from restriction or obstruction ~ vb 1 : make or become clear 2 : go away 3 : free from accusation or blame 4 : explain or settle 5 : net 6 : jump or pass without touching ~ n : clear space or part —**clear** adv —**clear·ance** \'klirəns\ n

clear·ing \'kliriŋ\ n : land cleared of wood

clear·ly adv 1 : in a clear manner 2 : it is obvious that

cleat \'klēt\ n : projection that strengthens or prevents slipping

cleav·age \'klēvij\ n 1 : a splitting apart 2 : depression between a woman's breasts

¹cleave \'klēv\ vb **cleaved** \'klēvd\ or **clove** \'klōv\ **cleav·ing** : adhere

²cleave vb **cleaved** \'klēvd\ **cleav·ing** : split apart

cleav·er \'klēvər\ n : heavy chopping knife

clef \'klef\ n : sign on the staff in music to show pitch

cleft \'kleft\ n : crack

clem·ent \'klemənt\ adj 1 : merciful 2 : temperate or mild —**clem·en·cy** \-ənsē\ n

clench \'klench\ vb 1 : hold fast 2 : close tightly

cler·gy \'klərjē\ n : body of religious officials —**cler·gy·man** \-jimən\ n

cler·ic \'klerik\ n : member of the clergy

cler·i·cal \-ikəl\ adj 1 : relating to the clergy 2 : relating to a clerk or office worker

clerk \'klərk, Brit 'klärk\ n 1 : official responsible for record-keeping 2 : person doing general office work 3 : salesperson in a store —**clerk** vb —**clerk·ship** n

clev·er \'klevər\ adj 1 : resourceful 2 : marked by wit or ingenuity —**clev·er·ly** adv —**clev·er·ness** n

clew var of CLUE

cli·ché \kliˈshā\ n : trite phrase —**clichéd** \-'shād\ adj

click \'klik\ n : slight sharp noise ~ vb : make or cause to make a click

cli·ent \'klīənt\ n 1 : person who engages professional services 2 : customer

cli·en·tele \,klīən'tel, ,klē-\ n : body of customers

cliff \'klif\ n : high steep face of rock

cli·mate \'klīmət\ n : average weather conditions over a period of years —**cli·mat·ic** \klī'matik\ adj

cli·max \'klī,maks\ n : the highest point ~ vb : come to a climax —**cli·mac·tic** \klī'maktik\ adj

climb \'klīm\ vb 1 : go up or down by use of hands and feet 2 : rise ~ n : a climbing —**climb·er** n

clinch \'klinch\ vb 1 : fasten securely 2 : settle 3 : hold fast or firmly —**clinch** n —**clinch·er** n

cling \'kliŋ\ vb **clung** \'kləŋ\ **cling·ing** 1 : adhere firmly 2 : hold on tightly

clin·ic \'klinik\ n : facility for diagnosis and treatment of outpatients —**clin·i·cal** \-əl\ adj —**clin·i·cal·ly** \-klē\ adv

clink \'kliŋk\ vb : make a slight metallic sound —**clink** n

clin·ker \'kliŋkər\ n : fused stony matter esp. in a furnace

¹clip \'klip\ vb **-pp-** : fasten with a clip ~ n : device to hold things together

²clip vb **-pp-** 1 : cut or cut off 2 : hit ~ n 1 : clippers 2 : sharp blow 3 : rapid pace

clip·per \'klipər\ n 1 pl : implement for clipping 2 : fast sailing ship

clique \'klēk, 'klik\ n : small exclusive group of people

cli·to·ris \'klitərəs, kli'tórəs\ n, pl **cli·to·ri·des** \-'tórə,dēz\ : small organ at the front of the vulva

cloak \'klōk\ n 1 : loose outer garment 2 : something that conceals ~ vb : cover or hide with a cloak

clob·ber \'kläbər\ vb : hit hard

clock \'kläk\ n : timepiece not carried on the person ~ vb : record the time of

clock·wise \-,wīz\ adv or adj : in the same direction as a clock's hands move

clod \'kläd\ n 1 : lump esp. of earth 2 : dull insensitive person

clog \'kläg\ n 1 : restraining weight 2 : thick-soled shoe ~ vb **-gg-** 1 : impede with a clog 2 : obstruct passage through 3 : become plugged up

clois·ter \'klȯistər\ n 1 : monastic establishment 2 : covered passage ~ vb : shut away from the world

clone \'klōn\ n 1 : offspring produced from a single organism 2 : copy

¹close \'klōz\ vb **closed; clos·ing** 1 : shut 2 : cease operation 3 : terminate 4 : bring or come together ~ n : conclusion or end

²close \'klōs\ adj **clos·er; clos·est** 1 : confining 2 : secretive 3 : strict 4 : stuffy 5 : having little space between items 6 : fitting tightly 7 : near 8 : intimate 9 : accurate 10 : nearly even —**close** adv —**close·ly** adv —**close·ness** n

clos·et \'kläzət, 'klȯz-\ n : small compartment for household utensils or clothing ~ vb : take into a private room for a talk

clo·sure \'klōzhər\ n 1 : act of closing 2 : something that closes

clot \'klät\ n : dried mass of a liquid —**clot** vb

cloth \'klȯth\ n, pl **cloths** \'klȯthz, 'klȯths\ 1 : fabric 2 : tablecloth

clothe \'klȯth\ vb **clothed** or **clad** \'klad\; **cloth·ing** : dress

clothes \'klōthz, 'klōz\ n pl 1 : clothing 2 : bedclothes

cloth·ier \'klōthyər, -thēər\ n : maker or seller of clothing

cloth·ing \'klōthiŋ\ n : covering for the human body

cloud \'klaud\ n 1 : visible mass of particles in the air 2 : something that darkens, hides, or threatens ~ vb 1 : darken or hide —**cloud·i·ness** n —**cloud·less** adj —**cloudy** adj

cloud·burst n : sudden heavy rain

clout \'klaut\ n 1 : blow 2 : influence ~ vb : hit forcefully

¹clove \'klōv\ n : section of a bulb

²clove past of CLEAVE

³clove n : dried flower bud of an East Indian tree used as a spice

clo·ver \'klōvər\ n : leguminous herb with usu. 3-part leaves

clo·ver·leaf n, pl **-leafs** or **-leaves** : highway interchange

clown \'klaun\ n : funny costumed entertainer esp. in a circus ~ vb : act like a clown —**clown·ish** adj —**clown·ish·ly** adv —**clown·ish·ness** n

cloy \'klȯi\ vb : disgust with excess **cloy·ing·ly** \-iŋlē\ adv

club \'kləb\ n 1 : heavy wooden stick 2 : playing card of a suit marked with a black figure like a clover leaf 3 : group associated for a common purpose ~ vb **-bb-** : hit with a club

club·foot n : misshapen foot twisted out of position from birth —**club·foot·ed** \-,fútəd\ adj

cluck \'klək\ n : sound made by a hen —**cluck** vb

clue \'klü\ n : piece of evidence that helps solve a problem ~ vb **clued; clue·ing** or **clu·ing** : provide with a clue

clump \'kləmp\ n 1 : cluster 2 : heavy tramping sound ~ vb : tread heavily

clum·sy \'kləmzē\ adj **-si·er; -est** 1 : lacking dexterity, nimbleness, or grace 2 : tactless —**clum·si·ly** adv —**clum·si·ness** n

clung past of CLING

clunk·er \'kləŋkər\ n : old automobile

clus·ter \'kləstər\ n : group ~ vb : grow or gather in a cluster

clutch \'kləch\ vb : grasp ~ n 1 : grasping hand or claws 2 : control or power 3 : coupling for connecting two working parts in machinery

clut·ter \'klətər\ vb : fill with things that get in the way —**clutter** n

co- prefix : with, together, joint, or jointly

coact	coexistence
coactor	coexistent
coauthor	cofeature
coauthorship	cofinance
cocaptain	cofound
cochairman	cofounder
cochampion	coheir
cocomposer	coheiress
coconspirator	cohost
cocreator	cohostess
codefendant	coinvent
codesign	coinventor
codevelop	coinvestigator
codeveloper	coleader
codirect	comanagement
codirector	comanager
codiscoverer	co-organizer
codrive	co-own
codriver	co-owner
coedit	copartner
coeditor	copartnership
coexecutor	copresident
coexist	coprincipal

coprisoner	coresident
coproduce	cosignatory
coproducer	cosigner
coproduction	cosponsor
copromoter	costar
coproprietor	cowinner
copublish	coworker
copublisher	cowrite
corecipient	

coach \'kōch\ n 1 : closed 2-door 4-wheeled carriage 2 : railroad passenger car 3 : bus 4 : 2d-class air travel 5 : one who instructs or trains performers ~ vb : instruct or direct as a coach

co·ag·u·late \kō'agyə,lāt\ vb **-lat·ed; -lat·ing** : clot —**co·ag·u·lant** \-lənt\ n —**co·ag·u·la·tion** \-,agyə'lāshən\ n

coal \'kōl\ n 1 : ember 2 : black solid mineral used as fuel —**coal·field** n

co·alesce \,kōə'les\ vb **-alesced; -alescing** : grow together —**co·ales·cence** \-'les°ns\ n

co·ali·tion \-'lishən\ n : temporary alliance

coarse \'kȯrs\ adj **coars·er; coars·est** 1 : composed of large particles 2 : rough or crude —**coarse·ly** adv —**coars·en** \-°n\ vb —**coarse·ness** n

coast \'kōst\ n : seashore ~ vb : move without effort —**coast·al** \-°l\ adj

coast·er \-ər\ n 1 : one that coasts 2 : plate or mat to protect a surface

coast guard n : military force that guards or patrols a coast —**coast·guards·man** \'kōst,gärdzmən\ n

coast·line n : shape of a coast

coat \'kōt\ n 1 : outer garment for the upper body 2 : external growth of fur or feathers 3 : covering layer ~ vb : cover with a coat —**coat·ed** adj —**coat·ing** n

coax \'kōks\ vb : move to action or achieve by gentle urging or flattery

cob \'käb\ n : corncob

co·balt \'kō,bȯlt\ n : shiny silver-white magnetic metallic chemical element

cob·ble \'käbəl\ vb **cob·bled; cob·bling** : make or put together hastily

cob·bler \'käblər\ n 1 : shoemaker 2 : deep-dish fruit pie

cob·ble·stone n : small round paving stone

co·bra \'kōbrə\ n : venomous snake

cob·web \'käb,web\ n : network spun by a spider or a similar filament

co·caine \kō'kān, 'kō,kān\ n : drug obtained from the leaves of a So. American shrub (**co·ca** \'kōkə\)

co·chlea \'kōklēə, 'käk-\ n, pl **-chle·as** or **-chle·ae** \-lē,ē, -,ī\ : the usu. spiral part of the inner ear —**coch·le·ar** \-lēər\ adj

cock \'käk\ n 1 : male fowl 2 : valve or faucet ~ vb 1 : draw back the hammer of a firearm 2 : tilt to one side —**cock·fight** n

cock·ade \kä'kād\ n : badge on a hat

cock·a·too \'käkə,tü\ n, pl **-toos** : large Australian crested parrot

cock·eyed \'käk'īd\ adj 1 : tilted to one side 2 : slightly crazy

cock·le \'käkəl\ n : edible shellfish

cock·pit \'käk,pit\ n : place for a pilot, driver, or helmsman

cock·roach n : nocturnal insect often infesting houses

cock·tail \'käk,tāl\ n 1 : iced drink of liquor and flavorings 2 : appetizer

cocky \'käkē\ adj **cock·i·er; -est** : overconfident —**cock·i·ly** \-əlē\ adv —**cock·i·ness** n

co·coa \'kōkō\ n 1 : cacao 2 : powdered chocolate or a drink made from this

co·co·nut \'kōkə,nət\ n : large nutlike fruit of a tropical palm (**coconut palm**)

co·coon \kə'kün\ n : case protecting an insect pupa

cod \'käd\ n, pl **cod** : food fish of the No. Atlantic

cod·dle \'käd°l\ vb **-dled; -dling** : pamper

code \'kōd\ n 1 : system of laws or rules 2 : system of signals

co·deine \'kō,dēn\ n : narcotic drug used in cough remedies

cod·ger \'käjər\ n : odd fellow

cod·i·cil \'kädəsəl, -,sil\ n : postscript to a will

cod·i·fy \'kädə,fī, 'kōd-\ vb **-fied; -fy·ing** : arrange systematically —**cod·i·fi·ca·tion** \,kädəfə'kāshən, ,kōd-\ n

co·ed \'kō,ed\ n : female student in a coeducational institution —**coed** adj

co·ed·u·ca·tion \,kō-\ n : education of the sexes together —**co·ed·u·ca·tion·al** adj

co·ef·fi·cient \,kōə'fishənt\ n 1 : number that is a multiplier of another 2 : number that serves as a measure of some property

co·erce \kō'ərs\ vb **-erced; -erc·ing** : force —**co·er·cion** \-'ərzhən, -shən\ n —**co·er·cive** \-'ərsiv\ adj

cof·fee \'kȯfē\ n : drink made from the roasted and ground seeds (**coffee beans**) of a tropical shrub —**cof·fee·house** n —**cof·fee·pot** n

cof·fer \'kȯfər\ n : box for valuables

cof·fin \-fən\ n : box for burial

cog \käg\ *n* : tooth on the rim of a gear — **cogged** \kägd\ *adj* —**cog·wheel** *n*

co·gent \kōjənt\ *adj* : compelling or convincing —**co·gen·cy** \-jənsē\ *n*

cog·i·tate \käjə,tāt\ *vb* -**tat·ed; -tat·ing** : think over —**cog·i·ta·tion** \käjə'tāshən\ *n* —**cog·i·ta·tive** \käjə,tātiv\ *adj*

co·gnac \kōn,yak\ *n* : French brandy

cog·nate \käg,nāt\ *adj* : related —**cognate** *n*

cog·ni·tion \käg'nishən\ *n* : act or process of knowing —**cog·ni·tive** \kägnətiv\ *adj*

cog·ni·zance \kägnəzəns\ *n* : notice or awareness —**cog·ni·zant** \kägnəzənt\ *adj*

co·hab·it \kō'habət\ *vb* : live together as husband and wife —**co·hab·i·ta·tion** \-,habə'tāshən\ *n*

co·here \kō'hir\ *vb* -**hered; -her·ing** : stick together

co·her·ent \-'hirənt\ *adj* 1 : able to stick together 2 : logically consistent —**co·her·ence** \-əns\ *n* —**co·her·ent·ly** *adv*

co·he·sion \-'hēzhən\ *n* : a sticking together —**co·he·sive** \-siv\ *adj* —**co·he·sive·ly** *adv* —**co·he·sive·ness** *n*

co·hort \kō,hȯrt\ *n* 1 : group of soldiers 2 : companion

coif·fure \kwä'fyu̇r\ *n* : hair style

coil \kȯil\ *vb* : wind in a spiral ~ *n* : series of loops (as of rope)

coin \kȯin\ *n* : piece of metal used as money ~ *vb* 1 : make (a coin) by stamping 2 : create —**coin·age** \-ij\ *n* —**coin·er** *n*

co·in·cide \kōən'sīd, 'kōən,sīd\ *vb* -**cid·ed; -cid·ing** 1 : be in the same place 2 : happen at the same time 3 : be alike —**co·in·ci·dence** \kō'insədəns\ *n* —**co·in·ci·dent** \-ənt\ *adj* —**co·in·ci·den·tal** \-,insə'dentᵊl\ *adj*

co·itus \kōətəs\ *n* : sexual intercourse —**co·ital** \-ətᵊl\ *adj*

coke \kōk\ *n* : fuel made by heating soft coal

co·la \kōlə\ *n* : carbonated soft drink

col·an·der \kələndər, käl-\ *n* : perforated utensil for draining food

cold \kōld\ *adj* 1 : having a low or below normal temperature 2 : lacking warmth of feeling 3 : suffering from lack of warmth ~ *n* 1 : low temperature 2 : minor respiratory illness —**cold·ly** *adv* —**cold·ness** *n* —**in cold blood** : with premeditation

cold–blood·ed *adj* 1 : cruel or merciless 2 : having a body temperature that varies with the temperature of the environment

cole·slaw \kōl,slȯ\ *n* : cabbage salad

col·ic \kälik\ *n* : sharp abdominal pain —**col·icky** *adj*

col·i·se·um \kälə'sēəm\ *n* : arena

col·lab·o·rate \kə'labə,rāt\ *vb* -**rat·ed; -rat·ing** 1 : work jointly with others 2 : help the enemy —**col·lab·o·ra·tion** \-,labə'rāshən\ *n* —**col·lab·o·ra·tor** \-'labə,rātər\ *n*

col·lapse \kə'laps\ *vb* -**lapsed; -laps·ing** 1 : fall in 2 : break down physically or mentally 3 : fold down ~ *n* : breakdown —**col·laps·ible** *adj*

col·lar \kälər\ *n* : part of a garment around the neck ~ *vb* 1 : seize by the collar 2 : grab —**col·lar·less** *adj*

col·lar·bone *n* : bone joining the breastbone and the shoulder blade

col·lards \kälərdz\ *n pl* : kale

col·late \kə'lāt, 'käl,āt, 'kōl-\ *vb* -**lat·ed; -lat·ing** 1 : compare carefully 2 : assemble in order

col·lat·er·al \kə'latərəl\ *adj* 1 : secondary 2 : descended from the same ancestors but not in the same line 3 : similar ~ *n* : property used as security for a loan

col·league \käl,ēg\ *n* : associate

col·lect \kə'lekt\ *vb* 1 : bring, come, or gather together 2 : receive payment of ~ *adv or adj* : to be paid for by the receiver —**col·lect·ible, col·lect·able** *adj* —**col·lec·tion** \-'lekshən\ *n* —**col·lec·tor** \-'lektər\ *n*

col·lec·tive \-tiv\ *adj* : denoting or shared by a group ~ *n* : a cooperative unit —**col·lec·tive·ly** *adv*

col·lege \kälij\ *n* : institution of higher learning granting a bachelor's degree —**col·le·gian** \kə'lējən\ *n* —**col·le·giate** \kə'lējət\ *adj*

col·lide \kə'līd\ *vb* -**lid·ed; -lid·ing** : strike together —**col·li·sion** \-'lizhən\ *n*

col·lie \kälē\ *n* : large long-haired dog

col·loid \käl,ȯid\ *n* : tiny particles in suspension in a fluid —**col·loi·dal** \kə'lȯidᵊl\ *adj*

col·lo·qui·al \kə'lōkwēəl\ *adj* : used in informal conversation —**col·lo·qui·al·ism** \-ə,lizəm\ *n*

col·lo·quy \käləkwē\ *n, pl* -**quies** : formal conversation or conference

col·lu·sion \kə'lüzhən\ *n* : secret cooperation for deceit —**col·lu·sive** \-'lüsiv\ *adj*

co·logne \kə'lōn\ *n* : perfumed liquid

¹co·lon \kōlən\ *n, pl* **colons** or **co·la** \-lə\ : lower part of the large intestine —**co·lon·ic** \kō'länik\ *adj*

²colon *n, pl* **colons** : punctuation mark : used esp. to direct attention to following matter

col·o·nel \kərnᵊl\ *n* : commissioned officer (as in the army) ranking next below a brigadier general

col·o·nize \kälə,nīz\ *vb* -**nized; -niz·ing** 1 : establish a colony in 2 : settle —**col·o·ni·za·tion** \,kälənə'zāshən\ *n* —**col·o·niz·er** *n*

col·on·nade \kälə'nād\ *n* : row of supporting columns

col·o·ny \kälənē\ *n, pl* -**nies** 1 : people who inhabit a new territory or the territory itself 2 : animals of one kind (as bees) living together —**co·lo·nial** \kə'lōnēəl\ *adj or n* —**col·o·nist** \kälənist\ *n*

col·or \kälər\ *n* 1 : quality of visible things distinct from shape that results from light reflection 2 *pl* : flag 3 : liveliness ~ *vb* 1 : give color to 2 : blush —**col·or·fast** *adj* —**col·or·ful** *adj* —**col·or·less** *adj*

col·or·blind *adj* : unable to distinguish colors —**color blindness** *n*

col·ored \kälərd\ *adj* 1 : having color 2 : of a race other than the white ~ *n, pl* **colored** or **coloreds** : colored person

co·los·sal \kə'läsəl\ *adj* : very large or great

co·los·sus \-əs\ *n, pl* -**si** \-,sī\ : something of great size or scope

colt \kōlt\ *n* : young male horse —**colt·ish** *adj*

col·umn \käləm\ *n* 1 : vertical section of a printed page 2 : regular feature article (as in a newspaper) 3 : pillar 4 : row (as of soldiers) —**co·lum·nar** \kə'ləmnər\ *adj* —**col·um·nist** \käləmnist\ *n*

co·ma \kōmə\ *n* : deep prolonged unconsciousness —**co·ma·tose** \-,tōs, kämə-\ *adj*

comb \kōm\ *n* 1 : toothed instrument for arranging the hair 2 : crest on a fowl's head —**comb** *vb* —**combed** \kōmd\ *adj*

com·bat \kəm'bat, 'käm,bat\ *vb* -**bat·ed** or -**bat·ted; -bat·ing** or -**bat·ting** : fight —**com·bat** \käm,bat\ *n* —**com·bat·ant** \kəm'batᵊnt\ *n* —**com·bat·ive** \kəm'bativ\ *adj*

com·bi·na·tion \kämbə'nāshən\ *n* 1 : process or result of combining 2 : code for opening a lock

com·bine \kəm'bīn\ *vb* -**bined; -bin·ing** : join together ~ \käm,bīn\ *n* 1 : association for business or political advantage 2 : harvesting machine

com·bus·ti·ble \kəm'bəstəbəl\ *adj* : apt to catch fire —**com·bus·ti·bil·i·ty** \-,bəstə'bilətē\ *n* —**combustible** *n*

com·bus·tion \-'bəschən\ *n* : process of burning

come \kəm\ *vb* **came** \käm\; **come; com·ing** 1 : move toward or arrive at something 2 : reach a state 3 : originate or exist 4 : amount —**come clean** *vb* : confess —**come into** *vb* : acquire, achieve —**come off** *vb* : succeed —**come to** *vb* : regain consciousness —**come to pass** : happen —**come to terms** : reach an agreement

come·back *n* 1 : retort 2 : return to a former position —**come back** *vb*

co·me·di·an \kə'mēdēən\ *n* 1 : comic actor 2 : funny person 3 : entertainer specializing in comedy

co·me·di·enne \-,mēdē'en\ *n* : a woman who is a comedian

com·e·dy \kämədē\ *n, pl* -**dies** 1 : an amusing play 2 : humorous entertainment

come·ly \kəmlē\ *adj* -**li·er; -est** : attractive —**come·li·ness** *n*

com·et \kämət\ *n* : small bright celestial body having a tail

com·fort \kəmfərt\ *n* 1 : consolation 2 : well-being or something that gives it ~ *vb* 1 : give hope to 2 : console —**com·fort·able** \kəmftəbəl, 'kəmfərt-\ *adj* —**com·fort·ably** \-blē\ *adv* —**com·fort·less** *adj*

com·fort·er \kəmfərtər\ *n* 1 : one that comforts 2 : quilt

com·ic \kämik\ *adj* 1 : relating to comedy 2 : funny ~ *n* 1 : comedian 2 : sequence of cartoons —**com·i·cal** *adj*

com·ing \kəmiŋ\ *adj* : next

com·ma \kämə\ *n* : punctuation mark , used esp. to separate sentence parts

com·mand \kə'mand\ *vb* 1 : order 2 : control ~ *n* 1 : act of commanding 2 : an order given 3 : mastery 4 : troops under a commander —**com·man·dant** \kämən,dant, -,dänt\ *n*

com·man·deer \kämən'dir\ *vb* : seize by force

com·mand·er \kə'mandər\ *n* 1 : officer commanding an army or subdivision of an army 2 : commissioned officer in the navy ranking next below a captain

com·mand·ment \-'mandmənt\ *n* : order

command sergeant major *n* : noncommissioned officer in the army ranking above a first sergeant

com·mem·o·rate \kə'memə,rāt\ *vb* -**rat·ed; -rat·ing** : celebrate or honor —**com·mem·o·ra·tion** \-,memə'rāshən\ *n* —**com·mem·o·ra·tive** \-'memrətiv, -'memə,rāt-\ *adj*

com·mence \kə'mens\ *vb* -**menced; -menc·ing** : start

com·mence·ment \-mənt\ *n* 1 : beginning 2 : graduation ceremony

com·mend \kə'mend\ *vb* 1 : entrust 2 : recommend 3 : praise —**com·mend·able** \-əbəl\ *adj* —**com·men·da·tion** \kämən'dāshən, -en-\ *n*

com·men·su·rate \kə'mensərət, -'mench-\ *adj* : equal in measure or extent

com·ment \käm,ent\ *n* : statement of opinion or remark —**comment** *vb*

com·men·tary \-ən,terē\ *n, pl* -**tar·ies** : series of comments

com·men·ta·tor \-ən,tātər\ *n* : one who discusses news

com·merce \kämərs\ *n* : business

com·mer·cial \kə'mərshəl\ *adj* : designed for profit or for mass appeal ~ *n* : broadcast advertisement —**com·mer·cial·ize** \-,īz\ *vb* —**com·mer·cial·ly** \-ē\ *adv*

com·min·gle \kə'miŋgəl\ *vb* : mix

com·mis·er·ate \kə'mizə,rāt\ *vb* -**at·ed; at·ing** : sympathize —**com·mis·er·a·tion** \-,mizə'rāshən\ *n*

com·mis·sary \kämə,serē\ *n, pl* -**sar·ies** : store esp. for military personnel

com·mis·sion \kə'mishən\ *n* 1 : order granting power or rank 2 : panel to judge, approve, or act 3 : the doing of an act 4 : agent's fee ~ *vb* 1 : confer rank or authority to or for 2 : request something be done

com·mis·sion·er \-shənər\ *n* 1 : member of a commission 2 : head of a government department

com·mit \kə'mit\ *vb* -**tt-** 1 : turn over to someone for safekeeping or confinement 2 : perform or do 3 : pledge —**com·mit·ment** *n*

com·mit·tee \kə'mitē\ *n* : panel that examines or acts on something

com·mo·di·ous \kə'mōdēəs\ *adj* : spacious

com·mod·i·ty \kə'mädətē\ *n, pl* -**ties** : article for sale

com·mo·dore \kämə,dōr\ *n* 1 : former commissioned officer in the navy ranking next below a rear admiral 2 : officer commanding a group of merchant ships

com·mon \kämən\ *adj* 1 : public 2 : shared by several 3 : widely known, found, or observed 4 : ordinary ~ *n* : community land —**com·mon·ly** *adv* —**in common** : shared together

com·mon·place \kämən,plās\ *n* : cliché ~ *adj* : ordinary

common sense *n* : good judgment

com·mon·weal \-,wēl\ *n* : general welfare

com·mon·wealth \-,welth\ *n* : state

¹com·mune \kə'myün\ *vb* -**muned; -mun·ing** : communicate intimately

²com·mune \käm,yün, kə'myün\ *n* : community that shares all ownership and duties —**com·mu·nal** \-ᵊl\ *adj*

com·mu·ni·cate \kə'myünə,kāt\ *vb* -**cat·ed; -cat·ing** 1 : make known 2 : transmit 3 : exchange information or opinions —**com·mu·ni·ca·ble** \-'myünikəbəl\ *adj* —**com·mu·ni·ca·tion** \-,myünə'kāshən\ *n* —**com·mu·ni·ca·tive** \-'myüni,kātiv, -kət-\ *adj*

Com·mu·nion \kə'myünyən\ *n* : Christian sacrament of partaking of bread and wine

com·mu·ni·qué \kə'myünə,kā, -,myünə'kā\ *n* : official bulletin

com·mu·nism \kämyə,nizəm\ *n* 1 : social organization in which goods are held in common 2 *cap* : political doctrine based on revolutionary Marxist socialism —**com·mu·nist** \-nist\ *n or adj, often cap* —**com·mu·nis·tic** \kämyə'nistik\ *adj, often cap*

com·mu·ni·ty \kə'myünətē\ *n, pl* -**ties** : body of people living in the same place under the same laws

com·mute \kə'myüt\ *vb* -**mut·ed; -mut·ing** 1 : reduce (a punishment) 2 : travel back and forth regularly ~ *n* : trip made in commuting —**com·mu·ta·tion** \kämyə'tāshən\ *n* —**com·mut·er** *n*

¹com·pact \kəm'pakt, 'käm,pakt\ *adj* 1 : hard 2 : small or brief ~ *vb* : pack together ~ \käm,pakt\ *n* 1 : cosmetics case 2 : small car —**com·pact·ly** *adv* —**com·pact·ness** *n*

²com·pact \käm,pakt\ *n* : agreement

compact disc *n* : plastic-coated disc with laser-readable recorded music

com·pan·ion \kəm'panyən\ *n* 1 : close friend 2 : one of a pair —**com·pan·ion·able** *adj* —**com·pan·ion·ship** *n*

com·pa·ny \kəmpənē\ *n, pl* -**nies** 1 : business organization 2 : group of performers 3 : guests 4 : infantry unit

com·par·a·tive \kəm'parətiv\ *adj* 1 : relating to or being an adjective or adverb form that denotes increase 2 : relative —**comparative** *n* —**com·par·a·tive·ly** *adv*

com·pare \kəm'par\ *vb* -**pared; -par·ing** 1 : represent as similar 2 : check for likenesses or differences ~ *n* : comparison —**com·pa·ra·ble** \kämprəbəl\ *adj*

com·par·i·son \kəm'parəsən\ *n* 1 : act of comparing 2 : change in the form and meaning of an adjective or adverb to show different levels of quality, quantity, or relation

com·part·ment \kəm'pärtmənt\ *n* : section or room

com·pass \kəmpəs, 'käm-\ *n* 1 : scope 2 : device for drawing circles 3 : device for determining direction

com·pas·sion \kəm'pashən\ *n* : pity —**com·pas·sion·ate** \-ənət\ *adj*

com·pat·i·ble \-'patəbəl\ *adj* : harmonious —**com·pat·i·bil·i·ty** \-,patə'bilətē\ *n*

com·pa·tri·ot \kəm'pātrēət, -,trē,ät\ *n* : fellow countryman

com·pel \kəm'pel\ *vb* -**ll-** : cause through necessity

com·pen·di·ous \kam'pendēəs\ *adj* 1 : concise and comprehensive 2 : comprehensive

com·pen·di·um \-'pendēəm\ *n, pl* -**di·ums** or -**dia** \-dēə\ : summary

com·pen·sate \kämpən,sāt\ *vb* -**sat·ed; -sat·ing** 1 : offset or balance 2 : repay —**com·pen·sa·tion** \kämpən'sāshən\ *n* —**com·pen·sa·to·ry** \kəm'pensə,tōrē\ *adj*

com·pete \kəm'pēt\ *vb* -**pet·ed; -pet·ing** : strive to win —**com·pe·ti·tion** \kämpə'tishən\ *n* —**com·pet·i·tive** \kəm'petətiv\ *adj* —**com·pet·i·tive·ness** *n* —**com·pet·i·tor** \kəm'petətər\ *n*

com·pe·tent \kämpətənt\ *adj* : capable —**com·pe·tence** \-əns\ *n* —**com·pe·ten·cy** \-ənsē\ *n*

com·pile \kəm'pīl\ *vb* -**piled; -pil·ing** : collect or compose from several sources —**com·pi·la·tion** \kämpə'lāshən\ *n* —**com·pil·er** \kəm'pīlər\ *n*

com·pla·cen·cy \kəm'plāsᵊnsē\ *n* : self-satisfaction —**com·pla·cent** \-ᵊnt\ *adj*

com·plain \kəm'plān\ *vb* 1 : express grief, pain, or discontent 2 : make an accusation —**com·plain·ant** *n* —**com·plain·er** *n*

com·plaint \-'plānt\ *n* 1 : expression of grief or discontent 2 : ailment 3 : formal accusation

com·ple·ment \kämpləmənt\ *n* 1 : something that completes 2 : full number or amount ~ \-,ment\ *vb* : complete —**com·ple·men·ta·ry** \kämplə'mentərē\ *adj*

com·plete \kəm'plēt\ *adj* -**plet·er; -est** 1 : having all parts 2 : finished 3 : total ~ *vb* -**plet·ed; -plet·ing** 1 : make whole 2 : finish —**com·plete·ly** *adv* —**com·plete·ness** *n* —**com·ple·tion** \-'plēshən\ *n*

com·plex \käm'pleks, kəm-; 'käm,pleks\ *adj* 1 : having many parts 2 : intricate ~ \'käm,pleks\ *n* : psychological problem —**com·plex·i·ty** \kəm'pleksətē, käm-\ *n*

com·plex·ion \kəm'plekshən\ *n* : hue or appearance of the skin esp. of the face —**com·plex·ioned** *adj*

com·pli·cate \kämplə,kāt\ *vb* -**cat·ed; -cat·ing** : make complex or hard to understand —**com·pli·cat·ed** \-əd\ *adj* —**com·pli·ca·tion** \kämplə'kāshən\ *n*

com·plic·i·ty \kəm'plisətē\ *n, pl* -**ties** : participation in guilt

com·pli·ment \kämpləmənt\ *n* 1 : flattering remark 2 *pl* : greeting ~ \-,ment\ *vb* : pay a compliment to

com·pli·men·ta·ry \kämplə'mentərē\ *adj* 1 : praising 2 : free

com·ply \kəm'plī\ *vb* -**plied; -ply·ing** : conform or yield —**com·pli·ance** \-əns\ *n* —**com·pli·ant** \-ənt\ *n*

com·po·nent \kəm'pōnənt, 'käm,pō-\ *n* : part of something larger ~ *adj* : serving as a component

com·port \kəm'pōrt\ *vb* 1 : agree 2 : behave —**com·port·ment** \-mənt\ *n*

com·pose \kəm'pōz\ *vb* -**posed; -pos·ing** 1 : create (as by writing) or put together 2 : calm 3 : set type —**com·pos·er** *n* —**com·po·si·tion** \kämpə'zishən\ *n*

com·pos·ite \käm'päzət, kəm-\ *adj* : made up of diverse parts —**composite** *n*

com·post \käm,pōst\ *n* : decayed organic fertilizing material

com·po·sure \kəm'pōzhər\ *n* : calmness

com·pote \käm,pōt\ *n* : fruits cooked in syrup

¹com·pound \käm,pau̇nd, kəm'pau̇nd\ *vb* 1 : combine or add 2 : pay (interest) on principal and accrued interest ~ \käm,pau̇nd\ *adj* : made up of 2 or more parts ~ \käm,pau̇nd\ *n* : something that is compound

²com·pound \käm,pau̇nd\ *n* : enclosure

com·pre·hend \kämpri'hend\ *vb* 1 : understand 2 : include —**com·pre·hen·si·ble** \-'hensəbəl\ *adj* —**com·pre·hen·sion** \-'henchən\ *n* —**com·pre·hen·sive** \-siv\ *adj*

com·press \kəm'pres\ *vb* : squeeze together ~ \käm,pres\ *n* : pad for pressing on a wound —**com·pres·sion** \-'preshən\ *n* —**com·pres·sor** \-'presər\ *n*

compressed air *n* : air under pressure greater than that of the atmosphere

com·prise \kəm'prīz\ vb **-prised; -prising 1** : contain or cover **2** : be made up of

com·pro·mise \'kämprə,mīz\ vb **-mised; -mis·ing** : settle differences by mutual concessions —**compromise** n

comp·trol·ler \kən'trōlər, 'kämp,trō-\ n : financial officer

com·pul·sion \kəm'pəlshən\ n **1** : coercion **2** : irresistible impulse —**com·pul·sive** \-siv\ adj —**com·pul·so·ry** \-'pəlsərē\ adj

com·punc·tion \-'pəŋkshən\ n : remorse

com·pute \-'pyüt\ vb **-put·ed; -put·ing** : calculate —**com·pu·ta·tion** \,kämpyü-'tāshən\ n

com·put·er \kəm'pyütər\ n : electronic data processing machine —**com·put·er·i·za·tion** \-,pyütərə'zāshən\ n —**com·put·er·ize** \-'pyütə,rīz\ vb

com·rade \'käm,rad, -rəd\ n : companion —**com·rade·ship** n

¹**con** \'kän\ adv : against ~ n : opposing side or person

²**con** vb **-nn-** : swindle

con·cave \kän'kāv, 'kän,kāv\ adj : curved like the inside of a sphere —**con·cav·i·ty** \kän'kavətē\ n

con·ceal \kən'sēl\ vb : hide —**con·ceal·ment** n

con·cede \-'sēd\ vb **-ced·ed; -ced·ing** : grant

con·ceit \-'sēt\ n : excessively high opinion of oneself —**con·ceit·ed** \-əd\ adj

con·ceive \-'sēv\ vb **-ceived; -ceiv·ing 1** : become pregnant **2** : think of —**con·ceiv·able** \-'sēvəbəl\ adj —**con·ceiv·ably** \-blē\ adv

con·cen·trate \'känsən,trāt\ vb **-trat·ed; -trat·ing 1** : gather together **2** : make stronger **3** : fix one's attention ~ n : something concentrated —**con·cen·tra·tion** \,känsən'trāshən\ n

con·cen·tric \kən'sentrik\ adj : having a common center

con·cept \'kän,sept\ n : thought or idea

con·cep·tion \kən'sepshən\ n **1** : act of conceiving **2** : idea

con·cern \kən'sərn\ vb **1** : relate to **2** : involve ~ n **1** : affair **2** : worry **3** : business —**con·cerned** \-'sərnd\ adj —**con·cern·ing** \-'sərniŋ\ prep

con·cert \'kän,sərt\ n **1** : agreement or joint action **2** : public performance of music —**con·cert·ed** \kən'sərtəd\ adj

con·cer·ti·na \,känsər'tēnə\ n : accordion-like instrument

con·cer·to \kən'chertō\ n, pl **-ti** \-tē\ or **-tos** : orchestral work with solo instruments

con·ces·sion \-'seshən\ n **1** : act of conceding **2** : something conceded **3** : right to do business on a property

conch \'käŋk, 'känch\ n, pl **conchs** \'käŋks\ or **conch·es** \'känchəz\ : large spiral-shelled marine mollusk

con·cil·ia·to·ry \kən'silēə,tōrē\ adj : mollifying

con·cise \kən'sīs\ adj : said in few words —**con·cise·ly** adv —**con·cise·ness** n —**con·ci·sion** \-'sizhən\ n

con·clave \'kän,klāv\ n : private meeting

con·clude \kən'klüd\ vb **-clud·ed; -clud·ing 1** : end **2** : decide —**con·clu·sion** \-'klüzhən\ n —**con·clu·sive** \-siv\ adj —**con·clu·sive·ly** adv

con·coct \kən'käkt, kän-\ vb : prepare or devise —**con·coc·tion** \-'käkshən\ n

con·com·i·tant \-'kämətənt\ adj : accompanying —**concomitant** n

con·cord \'kän,kord, 'käŋ-\ n : agreement

con·cor·dance \kən'kordᵊns\ n **1** : agreement **2** : index of words —**con·cor·dant** \-ᵊnt\ adj

con·course \'kän,kōrs\ n : open space where crowds gather

con·crete \kän'krēt, 'kän,krēt\ adj **1** : naming something real **2** : actual or substantial **3** : made of concrete ~ \'kän,krēt, kän'krēt\ n : hard building material made of cement, sand, gravel, and water

con·cre·tion \kän'krēshən\ n : hard mass

con·cu·bine \'käŋkyü,bīn\ n : mistress

con·cur \kən'kər\ vb **-rr-** : agree —**con·cur·rence** \-'kərəns\ n

con·cur·rent \-ənt\ adj : happening at the same time

con·cus·sion \kən'kəshən\ n **1** : shock **2** : brain injury from a blow

con·demn \-'dem\ vb **1** : declare to be wrong, guilty, or unfit for use **2** : sentence —**con·dem·na·tion** \,kän,dem'nāshən\ n

con·dense \kən'dens\ vb **-densed; -dens·ing 1** : make or become more compact **2** : change from vapor to liquid —**con·den·sa·tion** \,kän,den'sāshən, -dən-\ n —**con·dens·er** n

con·de·scend \,kändi'send\ vb **1** : lower oneself **2** : act haughtily —**con·de·scen·sion** \-'senchən\ n

con·di·ment \'kändəmənt\ n : pungent seasoning

con·di·tion \kən'dishən\ n **1** : necessary situation or stipulation **2** pl : state of affairs **3** : state of being ~ vb : put into proper condition —**con·di·tion·al** \kən'dishə-nəl\ adj —**con·di·tion·al·ly** \-ē\ adv

con·do·lence \kən'dōləns\ n : expression of sympathy—usu. pl.

con·do·min·i·um \,kändə'minēəm\ n, pl **-ums** : individually owned apartment

con·done \kən'dōn\ vb **-doned; -don·ing** : overlook or forgive

con·dor \'kändər, -,dōr\ n : large western American vulture

con·du·cive \kən'düsiv, -'dyü-\ adj : tending to help or promote

con·duct \'kän,dəkt\ n **1** : management **2** : behavior ~ \kən'dəkt\ vb **1** : guide **2** : manage or direct **3** : be a channel for **4** : behave —**con·duc·tion** \-'dəkshən\ n —**con·duc·tive** \-'dəktiv\ adj —**con·duc·tiv·i·ty** \,kän,dək'tivətē\ n —**con·duc·tor** \-'dəktər\ n

con·duit \'kän,düət, -,dyü-\ n : channel (as for conveying fluid)

cone \'kōn\ n **1** : scaly fruit of pine and related trees **2** : solid figure having a circular base and tapering sides

con·fec·tion \kən'fekshən\ n : sweet dish or candy —**con·fec·tion·er** \-shənər\ n

con·fed·er·a·cy \kən'fedərəsē\ n, pl **-cies 1** : league **2** cap : 11 southern states that seceded from the U.S. in 1860 and 1861

con·fed·er·ate \-rət\ adj **1** : united in a league **2** cap : relating to the Confederacy ~ n **1** : ally **2** cap : adherent of the Confederacy ~ \-'fedə,rāt\ vb **-at·ed; -at·ing** : unite —**con·fed·er·a·tion** \-,fedə'rā-shən\ n

con·fer \kən'fər\ vb **-rr- 1** : give **2** : meet to exchange views —**con·fer·ee** \,känfə-'rē\ n —**con·fer·ence** \'känfərəns\ n

con·fess \kən'fes\ vb **1** : acknowledge or disclose one's misdeed, fault, or sin **2** : declare faith in —**con·fes·sion** \-'feshən\ n —**con·fes·sion·al** \-'feshənəl\ n or adj

con·fes·sor \kən'fesər, 2 also 'kän,fes-\ n **1** : one who confesses **2** : priest who hears confessions

con·fet·ti \kən'fetē\ n : bits of paper or ribbon thrown in celebration

con·fi·dant \'känfə,dant, -,dänt\ n : one to whom secrets are confided

con·fide \kən'fīd\ vb **-fid·ed; -fid·ing 1** : share private thoughts **2** : reveal in confidence

con·fi·dence \'känfədəns\ n **1** : trust **2** : self-assurance **3** : something confided —**con·fi·dent** \-ənt\ adj —**con·fi·den·tial** \,känfə'denchəl\ adj —**con·fi·den·tial·ly** \-ē\ adv —**con·fi·dent·ly** adv

con·fig·u·ra·tion \kən,figyə'rāshən\ n : arrangement

con·fine \kən'fīn\ vb **-fined; -fin·ing 1** : restrain or restrict to a limited area **2** : imprison —**con·fine·ment** n —**con·fin·er** n

confines \'kän,fīnz\ n pl : bounds

con·firm \kən'fərm\ vb **1** : ratify **2** : verify **3** : admit as a full member of a church or synagogue —**con·fir·ma·tion** \,känfər-'māshən\ n

con·fis·cate \'känfə,skāt\ vb **-cat·ed; -cat·ing** : take by authority —**con·fis·ca·tion** \,känfə'skāshən\ n —**con·fis·ca·to·ry** \kən'fiskə,tōrē\ adj

con·fla·gra·tion \,känflə'grāshən\ n : great fire

con·flict \'kän,flikt\ n **1** : war **2** : clash of ideas ~ \kən'flikt\ vb : clash

con·form \kən'fōrm\ vb **1** : make or be like **2** : obey —**con·for·mi·ty** \kən'fōrmətē\ n

con·found \kən'faùnd, kän-\ vb : confuse

con·front \kən'frənt\ vb : oppose or face —**con·fron·ta·tion** \,känfrən'tāshən\ n

con·fuse \kən'fyüz\ vb **-fused; -fus·ing 1** : make mentally uncertain **2** : jumble —**con·fu·sion** \-'fyüzhən\ n

con·fute \-'fyüt\ vb **-fut·ed; -fut·ing** : overwhelm by argument

con·geal \kən'jēl\ vb **1** : freeze **2** : become thick and solid

con·ge·nial \kən'jēnēəl\ adj : kindred or agreeable —**con·ge·ni·al·i·ty** n

con·gen·i·tal \kən'jenətᵊl\ adj : existing from birth

con·gest \kən'jest\ vb : overcrowd or overfill —**con·ges·tion** \-'jeschən\ n —**con·ges·tive** \-'jestiv\ adj

con·glom·er·ate \kən'glämərət\ adj : made up of diverse parts ~ \-ə,rāt\ vb **-at·ed; -at·ing** : form into a mass ~ \-ərət\ n : diversified corporation —**con·glom·er·a·tion** \-,gläm-ə'rāshən\ n

con·grat·u·late \kən'gracha,lāt, -'graj-\ vb **-lat·ed; -lat·ing** : express pleasure to for good fortune —**con·grat·u·la·tion** \-,gracha'lāshən, -,graj-\ n —**con·grat·u·la·to·ry** \-'grachələ,tōrē, -'graj-\ adj

con·gre·gate \'käŋgri,gāt\ vb **-gat·ed; -gat·ing** : assemble

con·gre·ga·tion \,käŋgri'gāshən\ n **1** : assembly of people at worship **2** : religious group —**con·gre·ga·tion·al** \-shənəl\ adj

con·gress \'käŋgrəs\ n : assembly of delegates or of senators and representatives —**con·gres·sio·nal** \kən'greshənəl, kän-\ adj —**con·gress·man** \'käŋgrəsmən\ n —**con·gress·wom·an** n

con·gru·ence \kən'grüəns, 'käŋgrəwəns\ n : likeness —**con·gru·ent** \-ənt\ adj

con·gru·ity \kən'grüətē, kän-\ n : correspondence between things —**con·gru·ous** \'käŋgrəwəs\ adj

con·ic \'känik\ adj : relating to or like a cone —**con·i·cal** \-ikəl\ adj

co·ni·fer \'känəfər, 'kōn-\ n : cone-bearing tree —**co·nif·er·ous** \kō'nifərəs\ adj

con·jec·ture \kən'jekchər\ n or vb : guess —**con·jec·tur·al** \-əl\ adj

con·join \kən'jóin\ vb : join together —**con·joint** \-'jóint\ adj

con·ju·gal \'känjigəl, kən'jü-\ adj : relating to marriage

con·ju·gate \'känjə,gāt\ vb **-gat·ed; -gat·ing** : give the inflected forms of (a verb) —**con·ju·ga·tion** \,känjə'gāshən\ n

con·junc·tion \kən'jəŋkshən\ n **1** : combination **2** : occurrence at the same time **3** : a word that joins other words together —**con·junc·tive** \-tiv\ adj

con·jure \'känjər, 'kän-\ vb **-jured; -jur·ing 1** : summon by sorcery **2** : practice sleight of hand **3** : entreat —**con·jur·er, con·ju·ror** \-jərər, 'kän-\ n

con·nect \kə'nekt\ vb : join or associate —**con·nect·able** adj —**con·nec·tion** \-'nekshən\ n —**con·nec·tive** \-tiv\ n or adj —**con·nec·tor** n

con·nive \kə'nīv\ vb **-nived; -niv·ing 1** : pretend ignorance of wrongdoing **2** : cooperate secretly —**con·niv·ance** n

con·nois·seur \,känə'sər, -'sur\ n : expert judge esp. of art

con·note \kə'nōt\ vb **-not·ed; -not·ing** : suggest additional meaning —**con·no·ta·tion** \,känə'tāshən\ n

con·nu·bi·al \kə'nübēəl, -'nyü-\ adj : relating to marriage

con·quer \'käŋkər\ vb : defeat or overcome —**con·quer·or** \-kərər\ n

con·quest \'kän,kwest, 'käŋ-\ n **1** : act of conquering **2** : something conquered

con·science \'känchəns\ n : awareness of right and wrong

con·sci·en·tious \,känchē'enchəs\ adj : honest and hard-working —**con·sci·en·tious·ly** adv

con·scious \'känchəs\ adj **1** : aware **2** : mentally awake or alert **3** : intentional —**con·scious·ly** adv —**con·scious·ness** n

con·script \kən'skript\ vb : draft for military service —**con·script** \'kän,skript\ n —**con·scrip·tion** \kən'skripshən\ n

con·se·crate \'känsə,krāt\ vb **-crat·ed; -crat·ing 1** : declare sacred **2** : devote to a solemn purpose —**con·se·cra·tion** \,känsə'krāshən\ n

con·sec·u·tive \kən'sekyətiv\ adj : following in order —**con·sec·u·tive·ly** adv

con·sen·sus \kən'sensəs\ n **1** : agreement in opinion **2** : collective opinion

con·sent \-'sent\ vb : give permission or approval —**consent** n

con·se·quence \'känsə,kwens\ n **1** : result or effect **2** : importance —**con·se·quent** \-kwənt, -,kwent\ adj —**con·se·quent·ly** adv

con·se·quen·tial \,känsə'kwenchəl\ adj : important

con·ser·va·tion \,känsər'vāshən\ n : planned management of natural resources —**con·ser·va·tion·ist** \-shənist\ n

con·ser·va·tive \kən'sərvətiv\ adj **1** : disposed to maintain the status quo **2** : cautious —**con·ser·va·tism** \-və,tizəm\ n —**conservative** n —**con·ser·va·tive·ly** adv

con·ser·va·to·ry \kən'sərvə,tōrē\ n, pl **-ries** : school for art or music

con·serve \-'sərv\ vb **-served; -serv·ing** : keep from wasting ~ \'kän,sərv\ n : candied fruit or fruit preserves

con·sid·er \kən'sidər\ vb **1** : think about **2** : give thoughtful attention to **3** : think that —**con·sid·er·ate** \-'sidərət\ adj —**con·sid·er·a·tion** \-,sidə'rāshən\ n

con·sid·er·able \-'sidərəbəl\ adj **1** : significant **2** : noticeably large —**con·sid·er·a·bly** \-blē\ adv

con·sid·er·ing prep : taking notice of

con·sign \kən'sīn\ vb **1** : transfer **2** : send to an agent for sale —**con·sign·ee** \,känsə-'nē, -,sī-; kən,sī-\ n —**con·sign·ment** \kən'sīnmənt\ n —**con·sign·or** \,känsə'nór, -,sī-; kən,sī-\ n

con·sist \kən'sist\ vb **1** : be inherent —used with in **2** : be made up —used with of

con·sis·ten·cy \-'sistənsē\ n, pl **-cies 1** : degree of thickness or firmness **2** : quality of being consistent

con·sis·tent \-tənt\ adj : being steady and regular —**con·sis·tent·ly** adv

¹**con·sole** \kən'sōl\ vb **-soled; -sol·ing** : soothe the grief of —**con·so·la·tion** \,känsə'lāshən\ n

²**con·sole** \'kän,sōl\ n : cabinet or part with controls

con·sol·i·date \kən'sälə,dāt\ vb **-dat·ed; -dat·ing** : unite or compact —**con·sol·i·da·tion** \-,sälə'dāshən\ n

con·som·mé \,känsə'mā\ n : clear soup

con·so·nance \'känsənəns\ n : agreement or harmony —**con·so·nant** \-nənt\ adj —**con·so·nant·ly** adv

con·so·nant \-nənt\ n **1** : speech sound marked by constriction or closure in the breath channel **2** : letter other than a, e, i, o, and u —**con·so·nan·tal** \,känsə'nantᵊl\ adj

con·sort \'kän,sórt\ n : spouse ~ \kən'sórt\ vb : keep company

con·spic·u·ous \kən'spikyəwəs\ adj : very noticeable —**con·spic·u·ous·ly** adv

con·spire \kən'spīr\ vb **-spired; -spir·ing** : secretly plan an unlawful act —**con·spir·a·cy** \-'spirəsē\ n —**con·spir·a·tor** \-'spirətər\ n —**con·spir·a·to·ri·al** \-,spirə'tōrēəl\ adj

con·sta·ble \'känstəbəl, 'kän-\ n : police officer

con·stab·u·lary \kən'stabyə,lerē\ n, pl **-lar·ies** : police force

con·stant \'känstənt\ adj **1** : steadfast or faithful **2** : not varying **3** : continually recurring ~ n : something unchanging —**con·stan·cy** \-stənsē\ n —**con·stant·ly** adv

con·stel·la·tion \,känstə'lāshən\ n : group of stars

con·ster·na·tion \-stər'nāshən\ n : amazed dismay

con·sti·pa·tion \-stə'pāshən\ n : difficulty of defecation —**con·sti·pate** \'känstə,pāt\ vb

con·stit·u·ent \kən'stichəwənt\ adj **1** : component **2** : having power to elect ~ n **1** : component part **2** : one who may vote for a representative —**con·stit·u·en·cy** \-wənsē\ n

con·sti·tute \'känstə,tüt, -,tyüt\ vb **-tut·ed; -tut·ing 1** : establish **2** : be all or a basic part of

con·sti·tu·tion \,känstə'tüshən, -'tyü-\ n **1** : physical composition or structure **2** : the basic law of an organized body or the document containing it —**con·sti·tu·tion·al** \-əl\ adj —**con·sti·tu·tion·al·i·ty** \-,tüshə'nalətē, -,tyü-\ n

con·strain \kən'strān\ vb **1** : compel **2** : confine **3** : restrain —**con·straint** \-'strānt\ n

con·strict \-'strikt\ vb : draw or squeeze together —**con·stric·tion** \-'strikshən\ n —**con·stric·tive** \-'striktiv\ adj

con·struct \kən'strəkt\ vb : build or make —**con·struc·tion** \-'strəkshən\ n —**con·struc·tive** \-tiv\ adj

con·strue \kən'strü\ vb **-strued; -stru·ing** : explain or interpret

con·sul \'känsəl\ n **1** : Roman magistrate **2** : government commercial official in a foreign country —**con·sul·ar** \-sələr\ adj —**con·sul·ate** \-lət\ n

con·sult \kən'səlt\ vb : ask the advice or opinion of **2** : confer —**con·sul·tant** \-ᵊnt\ n —**con·sul·ta·tion** \,känsəl'tā-shən\ n

con·sume \kən'süm\ vb **-sumed; -sum·ing** : eat or use up —**con·sum·able** adj —**con·sum·er** n

con·sum·mate \kən'səmət\ adj : complete or perfect ~ \'känsə,māt\ vb **-mat·ed; -mat·ing** : make complete —**con·sum·ma·tion** \,känsə'māshən\ n

con·sump·tion \kən'səmpshən\ n **1** : act of consuming **2** : use of goods **3** : tuberculosis —**con·sump·tive** \-tiv\ adj or n

con·tact \'kän,takt\ n **1** : a touching **2** : association or relationship **3** : connection or communication ~ vb **1** : come or bring into contact **2** : communicate with

con·ta·gion \kən'tājən\ n **1** : spread of disease by contact **2** : disease spread by contact —**con·ta·gious** \-jəs\ adj

con·tain \-'tān\ vb **1** : enclose or include **2** : have or hold within **3** : restrain —**con·tain·er** n —**con·tain·ment** n

con·tam·i·nate \kən'tamə,nāt\ vb **-nat·ed; -nat·ing** : soil or infect by contact or association —**con·tam·i·na·tion** \-,tamə'nāshən\ n

con·tem·plate \'käntəm,plāt\ vb **-plat·ed; -plat·ing** : view or consider thoughtfully —**con·tem·pla·tion** \,käntəm'plāshən\ n —**con·tem·pla·tive** \kən'templətiv, 'kän-təm,plāt-\ adj

con·tem·po·ra·ne·ous \kən,tempə'rānēəs\ adj : contemporary

con·tem·po·rary \-'tempə,rerē\ adj **1** : occurring or existing at the same time **2** : of the same age —**contemporary** n

con·tempt \kən'tempt\ n **1** : feeling of scorn **2** : state of being despised **3** : disobedience to a court or legislature —**con·temp·ible** \-'temptəbəl\ adj

con·temp·tu·ous \-'tempchəwəs\ adj : feeling or expressing contempt —**con·temp·tu·ous·ly** adv

con·tend \-'tend\ vb **1** : strive against rivals or difficulties **2** : argue **3** : maintain or claim —**con·tend·er** n

¹**con·tent** \kən'tent\ adj : satisfied ~ vb : satisfy ~ n : ease of mind —**content-**

ed *adj* —con·tent·ed·ly *adv* —con·tent·ed·ness *n* —con·tent·ment *n*

²con·tent \'kän,tent\ *n* 1 *pl* : something contained 2 *pl* : subject matter (as of a book) 3 : essential meaning 4 : proportion contained

con·ten·tion \kən'tenchən\ *n* : state of contending —con·ten·tious \-chəs\ *adj* —con·ten·tious·ly *adv*

con·test \kən'test\ *vb* : dispute or challenge ~ \'kän,test\ *n* 1 : struggle 2 : game —con·test·able \kən'testəbəl\ *adj* —con·tes·tant \-'testənt\ *n*

con·text \'kän,tekst\ *n* : words surrounding a word or phrase

con·tig·u·ous \kən'tigyəwəs\ *adj* : connected to or adjoining —con·ti·gu·i·ty \,käntə'gyüətē\ *n*

con·ti·nence \'käntᵊnəns\ *n* : self-restraint —con·ti·nent \-nənt\ *adj*

con·ti·nent \'käntᵊnənt\ *n* : great division of land on the globe —con·ti·nen·tal \,käntᵊn'entᵊl\ *adj*

con·tin·gen·cy \kən'tinjənsē\ *n*, *pl* -cies : possible event

con·tin·gent \-jənt\ *adj* : dependent on something else ~ *n* : a quota from an area or group

con·tin·u·al \kən'tinyəwəl\ *adj* 1 : continuous 2 : steadily recurring —con·tin·u·al·ly \-ē\ *adv*

con·tin·ue \kən'tinyü\ *vb* -tin·ued; -tin·u·ing 1 : remain in a place or condition 2 : endure 3 : resume after an intermission 4 : extend —con·tin·u·ance \-yəwəns\ *n* —con·tin·u·a·tion \-,tinyə'wāshən\ *n*

con·tin·u·ous \-'tinyəwəs\ *adj* : continuing without interruption —con·ti·nu·ity \,käntᵊn'üətē, -'yü-\ *n* —con·tin·u·ous·ly *adv*

con·tort \kən'tórt\ *vb* : twist out of shape —con·tor·tion \-'tórshən\ *n*

con·tour \'kän,túr\ *n* 1 : outline 2 *pl* : shape

con·tra·band \'käntrə,band\ *n* : illegal goods

con·tra·cep·tion \,käntrə'sepshən\ *n* : prevention of conception —con·tra·cep·tive \-'septiv\ *adj or n*

con·tract \'kän,trakt\ *n* : binding agreement ~ \kən'trakt, *1 usu* 'kän,trakt\ *vb* 1 : establish or undertake by contract 2 : become ill with 3 : make shorter —con·trac·tion \kən'trakshən\ *n* —con·trac·tor \'kän,traktər, kən'trak-\ *n* —con·trac·tu·al \kən'trakchəwəl\ *adj* —con·trac·tu·al·ly *adv*

con·tra·dict \,käntrə'dikt\ *vb* : state the contrary of —con·tra·dic·tion \-'dikshən\ *n* —con·tra·dic·to·ry \-'diktərē\ *adj*

con·tral·to \kən'traltō\ *n*, *pl* -tos : lowest female singing voice

con·trap·tion \kən'trapshən\ *n* : device or contrivance

con·trary \'kän,trerē; *4 often* kən'trer\ *adj* 1 : opposite in character, nature, or position 2 : mutually opposed 3 : unfavorable 4 : uncooperative or stubborn —con·trari·ly \,trerəlē, -'trer-\ *adv* —con·trari·wise \-,wīz\ *adv* —contrary \kən-, 'kän-,trer\ *n*

con·trast \'kän,trast\ *n* 1 : unlikeness shown by comparing 2 : unlike color or tone of adjacent parts ~ \kən'trast\ *vb* 1 : show differences 2 : compare so as to show differences

con·tra·vene \,käntrə'vēn\ *vb* -vened; -ven·ing : go or act contrary to

con·trib·ute \kən'tribyət\ *vb* -ut·ed; -ut·ing : give or help along with others —con·tri·bu·tion \,käntrə'byüshən\ *n* —con·trib·u·tor \kən'tribyətər\ *n* —con·trib·u·to·ry \-yə,tōrē\ *adj*

con·trite \'kän,trīt, kən'trīt\ *adj* : repentant —con·tri·tion \kən'trishən\ *n*

con·trive \kən'trīv\ *vb* -trived; -triv·ing 1 : devise or make with ingenuity 2 : bring about —con·triv·ance \-'trīvəns\ *n* —con·triv·er *n*

con·trol \kən'trōl\ *vb* -ll- 1 : exercise power over 2 : dominate or rule ~ *n* 1 : power to direct or regulate 2 : restraint 3 : regulating device —con·trol·la·ble *adj* —con·trol·ler \-'trōlər, 'kän,-\ *n*

con·tro·ver·sy \'käntrə,vərsē\ *n*, *pl* -sies : clash of opposing views —con·tro·ver·sial \,käntrə'vərshəl, -sēəl\ *adj*

con·tro·vert \'käntrə,vərt, ,käntrə'-\ *vb* : contradict —con·tro·vert·ible *adj*

con·tu·ma·cious \,käntə'māshəs, -tyə-\ *adj* : rebellious

con·tu·me·ly \kən'tüməlē, 'käntü,mēlē, -tyü-\ *n* : rudeness

con·tu·sion \kən'tüzhən, -tyü-\ *n* : bruise —con·tuse \-'tüz, -'tyüz\ *vb*

co·nun·drum \kə'nəndrəm\ *n* : riddle

con·va·lesce \,känvə'les\ *vb* -lesced; -lesc·ing : gradually recover health —con·va·les·cence \-'esᵊns\ *n* —con·va·les·cent \-ᵊnt\ *adj or n*

con·vec·tion \kən'vekshən\ *n* : circulation in fluids due to warmer portions rising and colder ones sinking —con·vec·tion·al \-'vekshənəl\ *adj* —con·vec·tive \-'vektiv\ *adj*

con·vene \kən'vēn\ *vb* -vened; -ven·ing : assemble or meet

con·ve·nience \-'vēnyəns\ *n* 1 : personal comfort or ease 2 : device that saves work

con·ve·nient \-nyənt\ *adj* 1 : suited to one's convenience 2 : near at hand —con·ve·nient·ly *adv*

con·vent \'känvənt, -,vent\ *n* : community of nuns

con·ven·tion \kən'venchən\ *n* 1 : agreement esp. between nations 2 : large meeting 3 : body of delegates 4 : accepted usage or way of behaving —con·ven·tion·al \-'venchənəl\ *adj* —con·ven·tion·al·ly *adv*

con·verge \kən'vərj\ *vb* -verged; -verg·ing : approach a single point —con·ver·gence \-'vərjəns\ *n* —con·ver·gent \-jənt\ *adj*

con·ver·sant \-'vərsᵊnt\ *adj* : having knowledge and experience

con·ver·sa·tion \,känvər'sāshən\ *n* : an informal talking together —con·ver·sa·tion·al \-shənᵊl\ *adj*

¹con·verse \kən'vərs\ *vb* -versed; -vers·ing : engage in conversation —con·verse \'kän,vərs\ *n*

²con·verse \kən'vərs, 'kän,vərs\ *adj* : opposite —con·verse \'kän,vərs\ *n* —con·verse·ly *adv*

con·ver·sion \kən'vərzhən\ *n* 1 : change 2 : adoption of religion

con·vert \kən'vərt\ *vb* 1 : turn from one belief or party to another 2 : change ~ \'kän,vərt\ *n* : one who has undergone religious conversion —con·vert·er, con·ver·tor \-'vərtər\ *n* —con·vert·ible *adj*

con·vert·ible \kən'vərtəbəl\ *n* : automobile with a removable top

con·vex \kän'veks, 'kän,-, kən'-\ *adj* : curved or rounded like the outside of a sphere —con·vex·i·ty \kən'veksətē, kän-\ *n*

con·vey \kən'vā\ *vb* -veyed; -vey·ing : transport or transmit —con·vey·ance \-'vāəns\ *n* —con·vey·or \-ər\ *n*

con·vict \kən'vikt\ *vb* : find guilty ~ \'kän,vikt\ *n* : person in prison

con·vic·tion \kən'vikshən\ *n* 1 : act of convicting 2 : strong belief

con·vince \-'vins\ *vb* -vinced; -vinc·ing : cause to believe —con·vinc·ing·ly *adv*

con·viv·ial \-'vivyəl, -'vivēəl\ *adj* : cheerful or festive —con·viv·i·al·i·ty \-,vivē'alətē\ *n* —con·viv·ial·ly \-vivēə'alətē\ *adv*

con·voke \kən'vōk\ *vb* -voked; -vok·ing : call together to a meeting —con·vo·ca·tion \,känvə'kāshən\ *n*

con·vo·lut·ed \'känvə,lütəd\ *adj* 1 : intricately folded 2 : intricate

con·vo·lu·tion \,känvə'lüshən\ *n* : convoluted structure

con·voy \'kän,vói, kən'vói\ *vb* : accompany for protection ~ \'kän,vói\ *n* : group of vehicles or ships moving together

con·vul·sion \kən'vəlshən\ *n* : violent involuntary muscle contraction —con·vulse \-'vəls\ *vb* —con·vul·sive \-'vəlsiv\ *adj*

coo \'kü\ *n* : sound of a pigeon —coo *vb*

cook \'kük\ *n* : one who prepares food ~ *vb* : prepare food —cook·book *n* —cook·er *n* —cook·ery \-ərē\ *n* —cook·ware *n*

cook·ie, cooky \'kükē\ *n*, *pl* -ies : small sweet flat cake

cool \'kül\ *adj* 1 : moderately cold 2 : not excited 3 : unfriendly ~ *vb* : make or become cool ~ *n* 1 : cool time or place 2 : composure —cool·ant \-ənt\ *n* —cool·er *n* —cool·ly *adv* —cool·ness *n*

coo·lie \'külē\ *n* : unskilled Oriental laborer

coop \'küp, 'kúp\ *n* : enclosure usu. for poultry ~ *vb* : confine in or as if in a coop

co-op \'kō,äp\ *n* : cooperative

coo·per \'küpər, 'kúp-\ *n* : barrel maker —cooper *vb*

co·op·er·ate \kō'äpə,rāt\ *vb* : act jointly —co·op·er·a·tion \-,äpə'rāshən\ *n*

co·op·er·a·tive \kō'äpərətiv, -'äpə,rāt-\ *adj* : willing to work with others ~ *n* : enterprise owned and run by those using its services

co-opt \kō'äpt\ *vb* 1 : elect as a colleague 2 : take over

co·or·di·nate \-'órdᵊnət\ *adj* : equal esp. in rank ~ *n* : any of a set of numbers used in specifying the location of a point on a surface or in space ~ \-ᵊn,āt\ *vb* -nat·ed; -nat·ing 1 : make or become coordinate 2 : work or act together harmoniously —co·or·di·nate·ly *adv* —co·or·di·na·tion \-,órdᵊn'āshən\ *n* —co·or·di·na·tor \-ᵊn,ātər\ *n*

coot \'küt\ *n* 1 : dark-colored ducklike bird 2 : harmless simple person

cop \'käp\ *n* : police officer

¹cope \'kōp\ *n* : cloaklike ecclesiastical vestment

²cope *vb* coped; cop·ing : deal with difficulties

co·pi·lot \'kō,pīlət\ *n* : assistant airplane pilot

cop·ing \'kōpiŋ\ *n* : top layer of a wall

co·pi·ous \'kōpēəs\ *adj* : very abundant —co·pi·ous·ly *adv* —co·pi·ous·ness *n*

cop·per \'käpər\ *n* 1 : malleable reddish metallic chemical element 2 : penny —cop·pery *adj*

cop·per·head *n* : largely coppery brown venomous snake

co·pra \'kōprə\ *n* : dried coconut meat

copse \'käps\ *n* : thicket

cop·u·la \'käpyələ\ *n* : verb linking subject and predicate —cop·u·la·tive \-,lātiv\ *adj*

cop·u·late \'käpyə,lāt\ *vb* -lat·ed; -lat·ing : engage in sexual intercourse —cop·u·la·tion \,käpyə'lāshən\ *n*

copy \'käpē\ *n*, *pl* cop·ies 1 : imitation or reproduction of an original 2 : writing to be set for printing ~ *vb* cop·ied; copy·ing 1 : make a copy of 2 : imitate —copi·er \-ər\ *n* —copy·ist *n*

copy·right *n* : sole right to a literary or artistic work ~ *vb* : get a copyright on

co·quette \kō'ket\ *n* : flirt

cor·al \'kórəl\ *n* 1 : skeletal material of colonies of tiny sea polyps 2 : deep pink —coral *adj*

cord \'kórd\ *n* 1 : usu. heavy string 2 : long slender anatomical structure 3 : measure of firewood equal to 128 cu. ft. 4 : small electrical cable ~ *vb* 1 : tie or furnish with a cord 2 : pile (wood) in cords

cor·dial \'kórjəl\ *adj* : warmly welcoming ~ *n* : liqueur —cor·di·al·i·ty \,kórjē'alətē, kórd'yal-\ *n* —cor·dial·ly \'kórjəlē\ *adv*

cor·don \'kórdᵊn\ *n* : encircling line of troops or police —cordon *vb*

cor·do·van \'kórdəvən\ *n* : soft fine-grained leather

cor·du·roy \'kórdə,rói\ *n* 1 : heavy ribbed fabric 2 *pl* : trousers of corduroy

core \'kór\ *n* 1 : central part of some fruits 2 : inmost part ~ *vb* cored; cor·ing : take out the core of —cor·er *n*

cork \'kórk\ *n* 1 : tough elastic bark of a European oak (cork oak) 2 : stopper of cork ~ *vb* : stop up with a cork —corky *adj*

cork·screw *n* : device for drawing corks from bottles

cor·mo·rant \'kórmərənt, -,rant\ *n* : dark seabird

¹corn \'kórn\ *n* : cereal grass or its seeds ~ *vb* : cure or preserve in brine —corn·meal *n* —corn·stalk *n* —corn·starch *n*

²corn *n* : local hardening and thickening of skin

corn·cob *n* : axis on which the kernels of Indian corn are arranged

cor·nea \'kórnēə\ *n* : transparent part of the coat of the eyeball —cor·ne·al *adj*

cor·ner \'kórnər\ *n* 1 : point or angle formed by the meeting of lines or sides 2 : place where two streets meet 3 : inescapable position 4 : control of the supply of something ~ *vb* 1 : drive into a corner 2 : get a corner on 3 : turn a corner

cor·ner·stone *n* 1 : stone at a corner of a wall 2 : something basic

cor·net \'kór'net\ *n* : trumpetlike instrument

cor·nice \'kórnəs\ *n* : horizontal wall projection

cor·nu·co·pia \,kórnə'kōpēə, -nyə-\ *n* : goat's horn filled with fruits and grain emblematic of abundance

co·rol·la \kə'rälə\ *n* : petals of a flower

cor·ol·lary \'kórə,lerē\ *n*, *pl* -lar·ies 1 : logical deduction 2 : consequence or result

co·ro·na \kə'rōnə\ *n* : shining ring around the sun seen during eclipses

cor·o·nary \'kórə,nerē\ *adj* : relating to the heart or its blood vessels ~ *n* 1 : thrombosis of an artery supplying the heart 2 : heart attack

cor·o·na·tion \,kórə'nāshən\ *n* : crowning of a monarch

cor·o·ner \'kórənər\ *n* : public official who investigates causes of suspicious deaths

¹cor·po·ral \'kórpərəl\ *adj* : bodily

²corporal *n* : noncommissioned officer ranking next below a sergeant

cor·po·ra·tion \,kórpə'rāshən\ *n* : legal creation with the rights and liabilities of a person —cor·po·rate \'kórpərət\ *adj*

cor·po·re·al \kór'pōrēəl\ *adj* : physical or material —cor·po·re·al·ly *adv*

corps \'kór\ *n*, *pl* corps \'kórz\ 1 : subdivision of a military force 2 : working group

corpse \'kórps\ *n* : dead body

cor·pu·lence \'kórpyələns\ *n* : obesity —cor·pu·lent \-lənt\ *adj*

cor·pus \'kórpəs\ *n*, *pl* -po·ra \-pərə\ 1 : corpse 2 : body of writings

cor·pus·cle \'kór,pəsəl\ *n* : blood cell

cor·ral \kə'ral\ *n* : enclosure for animals —corral *vb*

cor·rect \kə'rekt\ *vb* 1 : make right 2 : chastise ~ *adj* 1 : true or factual 2 : conforming to a standard —cor·rec·tion \-'rekshən\ *n* —cor·rec·tive \-'rektiv\ *adj* —cor·rect·ly *adv* —cor·rect·ness *n*

cor·re·late \'kórə,lāt\ *vb* -lat·ed; -lat·ing : show a connection between —cor·re·late \-lət, -,lāt\ *n* —cor·re·la·tion \,kórə'lāshən\ *n*

cor·rel·a·tive \kə'relətiv\ *adj* : regularly used together —correlative *n*

cor·re·spond \,kórə'spänd\ *vb* 1 : match 2 : communicate by letter —cor·re·spon·dence \-'spändəns\ *n* —cor·re·spond·ing·ly \-'spändiŋlē\ *adv*

cor·re·spon·dent \-'spändənt\ *n* 1 : person one writes to 2 : reporter

cor·ri·dor \'kórədər, -,dór\ *n* : passageway connecting rooms

cor·rob·o·rate \kə'räbə,rāt\ *vb* -rat·ed; -rat·ing : support with evidence —cor·rob·o·ra·tion \-,räbə'rāshən\ *n*

cor·rode \kə'rōd\ *vb* -rod·ed; -rod·ing : wear away by chemical action —cor·ro·sion \-'rōzhən\ *n* —cor·ro·sive \-'rōsiv\ *adj or n*

cor·ru·gate \'kórə,gāt\ *vb* -gat·ed; -gat·ing : form into ridges and grooves —cor·ru·gat·ed *adj* —cor·ru·ga·tion \,kórə'gāshən\ *n*

cor·rupt \kə'rəpt\ *vb* 1 : change from good to bad 2 : bribe ~ *adj* : morally debased —cor·rupt·ible *adj* —cor·rup·tion \-'rəpshən\ *n*

cor·sage \kór'säzh, -'säj\ *n* : bouquet worn by a woman

cor·set \'kórsət\ *n* : woman's stiffened undergarment

cor·tege \kór'tezh, 'kór,-\ *n* : funeral procession

cor·tex \'kór,teks\ *n*, *pl* -ti·ces \'kórtə,sēz\ *or* -tex·es : outer or covering layer of an organism or part (as the brain) —cor·ti·cal \'kórtikəl\ *adj*

cor·ti·sone \'kórtə,sōn, -zōn\ *n* : adrenal hormone

cos·met·ic \käz'metik\ *n* : beautifying preparation ~ *adj* : relating to beautifying

cos·mic \'käzmik\ *adj* 1 : relating to the universe 2 : vast or grand

cos·mo·naut \'käzmə,nót\ *n* : Soviet or Russian astronaut

cos·mo·pol·i·tan \,käzmə'pälətᵊn\ *adj* : belonging to all the world —cosmopolitan *n*

cos·mos \'käzməs, -,mōs, -,mäs\ *n* : universe

cos·sack \'käs,ak, -ək\ *n* : Russian czarist cavalryman

cost \'kóst\ *n* 1 : amount paid for something 2 : loss or penalty ~ *vb* cost; cost·ing 1 : require so much in payment 2 : cause to pay, suffer, or lose —cost·li·ness \-lēnəs\ *n* —cost·ly \-lē\ *adj*

cos·tume \'käs,tüm, -,tyüm\ *n* : clothing

co·sy \'kōzē\ *var of* COZY

cot \'kät\ *n* : small bed

cote \'kōt, 'kät\ *n* : small shed or coop

co·te·rie \'kōtə,rē, ,kōtə'-\ *n* : exclusive group of persons

co·til·lion \kō'tilyən\ *n* : formal ball

cot·tage \'kätij\ *n* : small house

cot·ton \'kätᵊn\ *n* : soft fibrous plant substance or thread or cloth made of it —cot·ton·seed *n* —cot·tony *adj*

cot·ton·mouth *n* : poisonous snake

couch \'kauch\ *vb* 1 : lie or place on a couch 2 : phrase ~ *n* : bed or sofa

cou·gar \'kügər, -,gär\ *n* : large tawny wild American cat

cough \'kóf\ *vb* : force air from the lungs with short sharp noises —cough *n*

could \'kúd\ *past of* CAN

coun·cil \'kaunsəl\ *n* 1 : assembly or meeting 2 : body of lawmakers —coun·cil·lor, coun·cil·or \-sələr\ *n* —coun·cil·man \-mən\ *n* —coun·cil·wom·an *n*

coun·sel \'kaunsəl\ *n* 1 : advice 2 : deliberation together 3 *pl* -sel : lawyer ~ *vb* -seled *or* -selled; -sel·ing *or* -sel·ling 1 : advise 2 : consult together —coun·sel·or, coun·sel·lor \-sələr\ *n*

¹count \'kaunt\ *vb* 1 : name or indicate one by one to find the total number 2 : recite numbers in order 3 : rely 4 : be of value or account ~ *n* 1 : act of counting or the total obtained by counting 2 : charge in an indictment —count·able *adj*

²count *n* : European nobleman

coun·te·nance \'kauntᵊnəns\ *n* : face or facial expression ~ *vb* -nanced; -nanc·ing : allow or encourage

¹coun·ter \'kauntər\ *n* 1 : piece for reckoning or games 2 : surface over which business is transacted

²coun·ter *n* : one that counts

³coun·ter *vb* : oppose ~ *adv* : in an opposite direction ~ *n* : offsetting force or move ~ *adj* : contrary

counter- *prefix* 1 : contrary or opposite 2 : opposing 3 : retaliatory

counteraccusation	counterblow
counteraggression	countercampaign
counterargue	countercharge
counterassault	counterclaim
counterattack	countercomplaint
counterbid	countercoup
counterblockade	countercriticism

counterdemand
counterdemonstration
counterdemonstrator
countereffort
counterevidence
counterguerrilla
counterinflationary
counterinfluence
countermeasure
countermove
countermovement
counteroffer
counterpetition
counterploy
counterpower
counterpressure
counterpropaganda
counterproposal
counterprotest
counterquestion
counterraid
counterrally
counterreform
counterresponse
counterretaliation
counterrevolution
counterrevolutionary
counterstrategy
counterstyle
countersue
countersuggestion
countersuit
countertendency
counterterror
counterterrorism
counterterrorist
counterthreat
counterthrust
countertrend

coun•ter•act \vb\ : lessen the force of — **coun•ter•ac•tive** adj

coun•ter•bal•ance n : balancing influence or weight ~ vb : oppose or balance

coun•ter•clock•wise adv or adj : opposite to the way a clock's hands move

coun•ter•feit \'kaùntər,fit\ vb 1 : copy in order to deceive 2 : pretend ~ adj : spurious ~ n : fraudulent copy —**coun•ter•feit•er** n

coun•ter•mand \-,mand\ vb : supersede with a contrary order

coun•ter•pane \-,pān\ n : bedspread

coun•ter•part n : one that is similar or corresponds

coun•ter•point n : music with interwoven melodies

coun•ter•sign n : secret signal ~ vb : add a confirming signature to

count•ess \'kaùntəs\ n : wife or widow of a count or an earl or a woman holding that rank in her own right

count•less \-ləs\ adj : too many to be numbered

coun•try \'kəntrē\ n, pl -tries 1 : nation 2 : rural area ~ adj : rural —**coun•try•man** \-mən\ n

coun•try•side n : rural area or its people

coun•ty \'kaùntē\ n, pl -ties : local government division esp. of a state

coup \'kü\ n, pl **coups** \'küz\ 1 : brilliant sudden action or plan 2 : sudden overthrow of a government

coupe \'küp\ n : 2-door automobile with an enclosed body

cou•ple \'kəpəl\ vb -pled; -pling : link together ~ n 1 : pair 2 : two persons closely associated or married

cou•pling \'kəpliŋ\ n : connecting device

cou•pon \'kü,pän, 'kyü-\ n : certificate redeemable for goods or a cash discount

cour•age \'kərij\ n : ability to conquer fear or despair —**cou•ra•geous** \kə'rājəs\ adj

cou•ri•er \'kùrēər, 'kərē-\ n : messenger

course \'kōrs\ n 1 : progress 2 : ground over which something moves 3 : part of a meal served at one time 4 : method of procedure 5 : subject taught in a series of classes ~ vb **coursed; cours•ing** 1 : hunt with dogs 2 : run speedily —**of course** : as might be expected

court \'kōrt\ n 1 : residence of a sovereign 2 : sovereign or his or her officials and advisers 3 : area enclosed by a building 4 : space marked for playing a game 5 : place where justice is administered ~ vb : woo —**court•house** n —**court•room** n —**court•ship** \-,ship\ n

cour•te•ous \'kərtēəs\ adj : showing politeness and respect for others —**cour•te•ous•ly** adv

cour•te•san \'kōrtəzən, 'kərt-\ n : prostitute

cour•te•sy \'kərtəsē\ n, pl -sies : courteous behavior

court•ier \'kōrtēər, 'kōrtyər\ n : person in attendance at a royal court

court•ly \'kōrtlē\ adj -li•er; -est : polite or elegant —**court•li•ness** n

court–mar•tial n, pl **courts–martial** : military trial court —**court–martial** vb

court•yard n : enclosure open to the sky that is attached to a house

cous•in \'kəzən\ n : child of one's uncle or aunt

cove \'kōv\ n : sheltered inlet or bay

cov•en \'kəvən\ n : group of witches

cov•e•nant \'kəvənənt\ n : binding agreement —**cov•e•nant** \-nənt, -,nant\ vb

cov•er \'kəvər\ vb 1 : place something over or upon 2 : protect or hide 3 : include or deal with ~ n : something that covers —**cov•er•age** \-ərij\ n

cov•er•let \-lət\ n : bedspread

co•vert \'kō,vərt, 'kəvərt\ adj : secret ~ \'kəvərt, 'kō-\ n : thicket that shelters animals

cov•et \'kəvət\ vb : desire enviously —**cov•et•ous** adj

cov•ey \'kəvē\ n, pl -eys : bird with her young 2 : small flock (as of quail)

¹**cow** \'kaù\ n : large adult female animal (as of cattle) —**cow•hide** n

²**cow** vb : intimidate

cow•ard \'kaùərd\ n : one who lacks courage —**cow•ard•ice** \-əs\ n —**cow•ard•ly** adv or adj

cow•boy n : a mounted ranch hand who tends cattle

cow•er \'kaùər\ vb : shrink from fear or cold

cow•girl n : woman ranch hand who tends cattle

cowl \'kaùl\ n : monk's hood

cow•lick \'kaù,lik\ n : turned-up tuft of hair that resists control

cow•slip \-,slip\ n : yellow flower

cox•swain \'käksən, -,swān\ n : person who steers a boat

coy \'kòi\ adj : shy or pretending shyness

coy•ote \'kī,ōt, kī'ōtē\ n, pl **coy•otes** or **coy•ote** : small No. American wolf

coz•en \'kəzən\ vb : cheat

co•zy \'kōzē\ adj -zi•er; -est : snug

crab \'krab\ n : short broad shellfish with pincers

crab•by \'krabē\ adj -bi•er; -est : cross

¹**crack** \'krak\ vb 1 : break with a sharp sound 2 : fail in tone 3 : break without completely separating ~ n 1 : sudden sharp noise 2 : witty remark 3 : narrow break 4 : sharp blow 5 : try

²**crack** adj : extremely proficient

crack•down n : disciplinary action —**crack down** vb

crack•er \-ər\ n : thin crisp bakery product

crack•le \'krakəl\ vb -led; -ling 1 : make snapping noises 2 : develop fine cracks in a surface —**crackle** n

crack•pot \'krak,pät\ n : eccentric

crack–up n : crash

cra•dle \'krādəl\ n : baby's bed ~ vb -dled; -dling 1 : place in a cradle 2 : hold securely

craft \'kraft\ n 1 : occupation requiring special skill 2 : craftiness 3 pl usu **craft** : structure designed to provide transportation 4 pl usu **craft** : small boat —**crafts•man** \'kraftsmən\ n —**crafts•man•ship** \-,ship\ n

crafty \'kraftē\ adj **craft•i•er; -est** : sly —**craft•i•ness** n

crag \'krag\ n : steep cliff —**crag•gy** \-ē\ adj

cram \'kram\ vb -mm- 1 : eat greedily 2 : pack in tight 3 : study intensely for a test

cramp \'kramp\ n 1 : sudden painful contraction of muscle 2 pl : sharp abdominal pains ~ vb 1 : affect with cramp 2 : restrain

cran•ber•ry \'kran,berē\ n : red acid berry of a trailing plant

crane \'krān\ n 1 : tall wading bird 2 : machine for lifting heavy objects ~ vb : **craned; cran•ing** : stretch one's neck to see

cra•ni•um \'krānēəm\ n, pl -ni•ums or -nia \-nēə\ : skull —**cra•ni•al** \-əl\ adj

crank \'kraŋk\ n 1 : bent lever turned to operate a machine 2 : eccentric ~ vb : start or operate by turning a crank

cranky \'kraŋkē\ adj **crank•i•er; -est** : irritable

cran•ny \'kranē\ n, pl -nies : crevice

craps \'kraps\ n : dice game

crash \'krash\ vb 1 : break noisily 2 : fall and hit something with noise and damage ~ n 1 : loud sound 2 : action of crashing 3 : failure

crass \'kras\ adj : crude or unfeeling

crate \'krāt\ n : wooden shipping container —**crate** vb

cra•ter \'krātər\ n : volcanic depression

cra•vat \krə'vat\ n : necktie

crave \'krāv\ vb **craved; crav•ing** : long for —**crav•ing** n

cra•ven \'krāvən\ adj : cowardly —**craven** n

craw•fish \'krò,fish\ n : crayfish

crawl \'kròl\ vb 1 : move slowly (as by drawing the body along the ground) 2 : swarm with creeping things ~ n : very slow pace

cray•fish \'krā,fish\ n : lobsterlike freshwater crustacean

cray•on \'krā,än, -ən\ n : stick of chalk or wax used for drawing or coloring —**crayon** vb

craze \'krāz\ vb **crazed; craz•ing** : make or become insane ~ n : fad

cra•zy \'krāzē\ adj **cra•zi•er; -est** 1 : mentally disordered 2 : wildly impractical —**cra•zi•ly** adv —**cra•zi•ness** n

creak \'krēk\ vb or n : squeak —**creaky** adj

cream \'krēm\ n 1 : yellowish fat-rich part of milk 2 : thick smooth sauce, confection, or cosmetic 3 : choicest part ~ vb : beat into creamy consistency —**creamy** adj

cream•ery \-ərē\ n, pl -er•ies : place where butter and cheese are made

crease \'krēs\ n : line made by folding —**crease** vb

cre•ate \krē'āt\ vb -at•ed; -at•ing : bring into being —**cre•a•tion** \krē'āshən\ n —**cre•**

a•tive \-'ātiv\ adj —**cre•a•tiv•i•ty** \,krēā'tivətē\ n —**cre•a•tor** \krē'ātər\ n

crea•ture \'krēchər\ n : lower animal or human being

cre•dence \'krēdəns\ n : belief

cre•den•tials \kri'denchəlz\ n : evidence of qualifications or authority

cred•i•ble \'kredəbəl\ adj : believable —**cred•i•bil•i•ty** \,kredə'bilətē\ n

cred•it \'kredət\ n 1 : balance in a person's favor 2 : time given to pay for goods 3 : belief 4 : esteem 5 : source of honor ~ vb 1 : believe 2 : give credit to

cred•it•able \-əbəl\ adj : worthy of esteem or praise —**cred•it•ably** \-əblē\ adv

cred•i•tor \-ər\ n : person to whom money is owed

cred•u•lous \'krejələs\ adj : easily convinced —**cre•du•li•ty** \kri'dülətē, -'dyü-\ n

creed \'krēd\ n : statement of essential beliefs

creek \'krēk, 'krik\ n : small stream

creel \'krēl\ n : basket for carrying fish

creep \'krēp\ vb **crept** \'krept\; **creep•ing** 1 : crawl 2 : grow over a surface like ivy —**creep** n —**creep•er** n

cre•mate \'krē,māt\ vb -mat•ed; -mat•ing : burn up (a corpse) —**cre•ma•tion** \kri'māshən\ n —**cre•ma•to•ry** \'krēmə,tōrē, 'krem-\ n

cre•o•sote \'krēə,sōt\ n : oily wood preservative

crepe, crêpe \'krāp\ n : light crinkled fabric

cre•scen•do \krə'shendō\ adv or adj : growing louder —**crescendo** n

cres•cent \'kresənt\ n : shape of the moon between new moon and first quarter

crest \'krest\ n 1 : tuft on a bird's head 2 : top of a hill or wave 3 : part of a coat of arms ~ vb : rise to a crest —**crest•ed** \-əd\ adj

crest•fall•en adj : sad

cre•tin \'krētən\ n : stupid person

cre•vasse \kri'vas\ n : deep fissure esp. in a glacier

crev•ice \'krevəs\ n : narrow fissure

crew \'krü\ n : body of workers (as on a ship) —**crew•man** \-mən\ n

crib \'krib\ n 1 : manger 2 : grain storage bin 3 : baby's bed ~ vb -bb- : put in a crib

crib•bage \'kribij\ n : card game scored by moving pegs on a board (**cribbage board**)

crick \'krik\ n : muscle spasm

¹**crick•et** \'krikət\ n : insect noted for the chirping of the male

²**cricket** n : bat and ball game played on a field with wickets

cri•er \'krīər\ n : one who calls out announcements

crime \'krīm\ n : serious violation of law

crim•i•nal \'krimənəl\ adj : relating to or being a crime or its punishment ~ n : one who commits a crime

crimp \'krimp\ vb : cause to become crinkled, wavy, or bent —**crimp** n

crim•son \'krimzən\ n : deep red —**crimson** adj

cringe \'krinj\ vb **cringed; cring•ing** : shrink in fear

crin•kle \'kriŋkəl\ vb -kled; -kling : wrinkle —**crinkle** n —**crin•kly** \-klē\ adj

crin•o•line \'krinələn\ n 1 : stiff cloth 2 : full stiff skirt or petticoat

crip•ple \'kripəl\ n : disabled person ~ vb -pled; -pling : disable

cri•sis \'krīsəs\ n, pl -ses \-,sēz\ : decisive or critical moment

crisp \'krisp\ adj 1 : easily crumbled 2 : firm and fresh 3 : lively 4 : invigorating —**crisp** vb —**crisp•ly** adv —**crisp•ness** n —**crispy** adj

criss•cross \'kris,krós\ n : pattern of crossed lines ~ vb : mark with or follow a crisscross

cri•te•ri•on \krī'tirēən\ n, pl -ria \-ēə\ : standard

crit•ic \'kritik\ n : judge of literary or artistic works

crit•i•cal \-ikəl\ adj 1 : inclined to criticize 2 : being a crisis 3 : relating to criticism or critics —**crit•i•cal•ly** \-iklē\ adv

crit•i•cize \'kritə,sīz\ vb -cized; -ciz•ing 1 : judge as a critic 2 : find fault —**crit•i•cism** \-ə,sizəm\ n

cri•tique \krə'tēk\ n : critical estimate

croak \'krōk\ n : hoarse harsh cry (as of a frog) —**croak** vb

cro•chet \krō'shā\ n : needlework done with a hooked needle —**crochet** vb

crock \'kräk\ n : thick earthenware pot or jar —**crock•ery** \-ərē\ n

croc•o•dile \'kräkə,dīl\ n : large reptile of tropical waters

cro•cus \'krōkəs\ n, pl -cus•es : herb with spring flowers

crone \'krōn\ n : ugly old woman

cro•ny \'krōnē\ n, pl -nies : chum

crook \'krùk\ n 1 : bent or curved tool or part 2 : thief ~ vb : curve sharply

crook•ed \'krùkəd\ adj 1 : bent 2 : dishonest —**crook•ed•ness** n

croon \'krün\ vb : sing softly —**croon•er** n

crop \'kräp\ n 1 : pouch in the throat of a bird or insect 2 : short riding whip 3 : something that can be harvested ~ vb -pp- 1 : trim 2 : appear unexpectedly — used with up

cro•quet \krō'kā\ n : lawn game of driving balls through wickets

cro•quette \-'ket\ n : mass of minced food deep-fried

cro•sier \'krōzhər\ n : bishop's staff

cross \'krós\ n 1 : figure or structure consisting of an upright and a cross piece 2 : interbreeding of unlike strains ~ vb 1 : intersect 2 : cancel 3 : go or extend across 4 : interbreed ~ adj 1 : going across 2 : contrary 3 : marked by bad temper —**cross•ing** n —**cross•ly** adv

cross•bow \-,bō\ n : short bow mounted on a rifle stock

cross•breed vb -bred; -breed•ing : hybridize

cross–ex•am•ine vb : question about earlier testimony —**cross–ex•am•i•na•tion** n

cross–eyed adj : having the eye turned toward the nose

cross–re•fer vb : refer to another place (as in a book) —**cross–ref•er•ence** n

cross•roads n : place where 2 roads cross

cross section n : representative portion

cross•walk n : path for pedestrians crossing a street

cross•ways adv : crosswise

cross•wise \-,wīz\ adv : so as to cross something —**crosswise** adj

crotch \'kräch\ n : angle formed by the parting of 2 legs or branches

crotch•ety \'krächətē\ adj : cranky, ill-natured

crouch \'kraùch\ vb : stoop over —**crouch** n

croup \'krüp\ n : laryngitis of infants

crou•ton \'krü,tän\ n : bit of toast

¹**crow** \'krō\ n : large glossy black bird

²**crow** vb 1 : make the loud sound of the cock 2 : gloat ~ n : cry of the cock

crow•bar n : metal bar used as a pry or lever

crowd \'kraùd\ vb : collect or cram together ~ n : large number of people

crown \'kraùn\ n 1 : wreath of honor or victory 2 : royal headdress 3 : top or highest part ~ vb 1 : place a crown on 2 : honor —**crowned** \'kraùnd\ adj

cru•cial \'krüshəl\ adj : vitally important

cru•ci•ble \'krüsəbəl\ n : heat-resisting container

cru•ci•fix \'krüsə,fiks\ n : representation of Christ on the cross

cru•ci•fix•ion \,krüsə'fikshən\ n : act of crucifying

cru•ci•fy \'krüsə,fī\ vb -fied; -fy•ing 1 : put to death on a cross 2 : persecute

crude \'krüd\ adj **crud•er; -est** 1 : not refined 2 : lacking grace or elegance ~ n : unrefined petroleum —**crude•ly** adv —**cru•di•ty** \-ətē\ n

cru•el \'krüəl\ adj -el•er or -el•ler; -el•est or -el•lest : causing suffering to others —**cru•el•ly** \-ē\ adv —**cru•el•ty** \-tē\ n

cru•et \'krüət\ n : bottle for salad dressings

cruise \'krüz\ vb **cruised; cruis•ing** 1 : sail to several ports 2 : travel at the most efficient speed —**cruise** n

cruis•er \'krüzər\ n 1 : warship 2 : police car

crumb \'krəm\ n : small fragment

crum•ble \'krəmbəl\ vb -bled; -bling : break into small pieces —**crum•bly** \-blē\ adj

crum•ple \'krəmpəl\ vb -pled; -pling 1 : crush together 2 : collapse

crunch \'krənch\ vb : chew or press with a crushing noise ~ n : crunching sound —**crunchy** adj

cru•sade \krü'sād\ n 1 cap : medieval Christian expedition to the Holy Land 2 : reform movement —**crusade** vb —**crusad•er** n

crush \'krəsh\ vb 1 : squeeze out of shape 2 : grind or pound to bits 3 : suppress ~ n 1 : severe crowding 2 : infatuation

crust \'krəst\ n 1 : hard outer part of bread or a pie 2 : hard surface layer —**crust•al** adj —**crusty** adj

crus•ta•cean \,krəs'tāshən\ n : aquatic arthropod having a firm shell

crutch \'krəch\ n : support for use by the disabled in walking

crux \'krəks, 'krùks\ n, pl **crux•es** 1 : hard problem 2 : crucial point

cry \'krī\ vb **cried; cry•ing** 1 : call out 2 : weep ~ n, pl **cries** 1 : shout 2 : fit of weeping 3 : characteristic sound of an animal

crypt \'kript\ n : underground chamber

cryp•tic \'kriptik\ adj : enigmatic

cryp•tog•ra•phy \krip'tägrəfē\ n : coding and decoding of messages —**cryp•tog•ra•pher** \-fər\ n

crys•tal \'kristəl\ n 1 : transparent quartz 2 : something (as glass) like crystal 3 : body formed by solidification that has a regular repeating atomic arrangement —**crys•tal•line** \-tələn\ adj

crys·tal·ize \-tə,līz\ vb -lized; -liz·ing : form crystals or a definite shape —**crys·tal·li·za·tion** \,kristələ'zāshən\ n

cub \'kəb\ n : young animal

cub·by·hole \'kəbē,hōl\ n : small confined space

cube \'kyüb\ n 1 : solid having 6 equal square sides 2 : product obtained by taking a number 3 times as a factor ~ vb **cubed; cub·ing** 1 : raise to the 3d power 2 : form into a cube 3 : cut into cubes — **cu·bic** \'kyübik\ adj

cu·bi·cle \-bikəl\ n : small room

cu·bit \'kyübət\ n : ancient unit of length equal to about 18 inches

cuck·old \'kəkəld, 'kük-\ n : man whose wife is unfaithful —**cuckold** vb

cuck·oo \'kükü, 'kük-\ n, pl -oos : brown European bird ~ adj : silly

cu·cum·ber \'kyü,kəmbər\ n : fleshy fruit related to the gourds

cud \'kəd\ n : food chewed again by ruminating animals

cud·dle \'kədᵊl\ vb -dled; -dling : lie close

cud·gel \'kəjəl\ n or vb : club

¹**cue** \'kyü\ n : signal —**cue** vb

²**cue** n : stick used in pool

¹**cuff** \'kəf\ n 1 : part of a sleeve encircling the wrist 2 : folded trouser hem

²**cuff** vb or n : slap

cui·sine \kwi'zēn\ n : manner of cooking

cu·li·nary \'kələ,nerē, 'kyülə-\ adj : of or relating to cookery

cull \'kəl\ vb : select

cul·mi·nate \'kəlmə,nāt\ vb -nat·ed; -nat·ing : rise to the highest point —**cul·mi·na·tion** \,kəlmə'nāshən\ n

cul·pa·ble \'kəlpəbəl\ adj : deserving blame

cul·prit \'kəlprət\ n : guilty person

cult \'kəlt\ n 1 : religious system 2 : faddish devotion —**cult·ist** n

cul·ti·vate \'kəltə,vāt\ vb -vat·ed; -vat·ing 1 : prepare for crops 2 : foster the growth of 3 : refine —**cul·ti·va·tion** \,kəltə'vāshən\ n

cul·ture \'kəlchər\ n 1 : cultivation 2 : refinement of intellectual and artistic taste 3 : particular form or stage of civilization —**cul·tur·al** \'kəlchərəl\ adj —**cul·tured** \'kəlchərd\ adj

cul·vert \'kəlvərt\ n : drain crossing under a road or railroad

cum·ber·some \'kəmbərsəm\ adj : awkward to handle due to bulk

cu·mu·la·tive \'kyümyələtiv, -,lāt-\ adj : increasing by additions

cu·mu·lus \'kyümyələs\ n, pl -li \-,lī, -,lē\ : massive rounded cloud

cun·ning \'kəniŋ\ adj 1 : crafty 2 : clever 3 : appealing ~ n 1 : skill 2 : craftiness

cup \'kəp\ n 1 : small drinking vessel 2 : contents of a cup 3 : a half pint ~ vb -pp- : shape like a cup —**cup·ful** n

cup·board \'kəbərd\ n : small storage closet

cup·cake n : small cake

cu·pid·i·ty \kyü'pidətē\ n, pl -ties : excessive desire for money

cu·po·la \'kyüpələ, -,lō\ n : small rooftop structure

cur \'kər\ n : mongrel dog

cu·rate \'kyürət\ n 1 : member of the clergy —**cu·ra·cy** \-əsē\ n

cu·ra·tor \kyü'rātər\ n : one in charge of a museum or zoo

curb \'kərb\ n 1 : restraint 2 : raised edging along a street ~ vb : hold back

curd \'kərd\ n : coagulated milk

cur·dle \'kərdᵊl\ vb -dled; -dling 1 : form curds 2 : sour

cure \'kyür\ n 1 : recovery from disease 2 : remedy ~ vb **cured; cur·ing** 1 : restore to health 2 : process for storage or use — **cur·able** adj

cur·few \'kər,fyü\ n : requirement to be off the streets at a set hour

cu·rio \'kyürē,ō\ n, pl -ri·os : rare or unusual article

cu·ri·ous \'kyürēəs\ adj 1 : eager to learn 2 : strange —**cu·ri·os·i·ty** \,kyürē'äsətē\ n —**cu·ri·ous·ness** n

curl \'kərl\ vb 1 : form into ringlets 2 : curve ~ n 1 : ringlet of hair 2 : something with a spiral form —**curl·er** n —**curly** adj

cur·lew \'kərlü, -,lyü\ n, pl -lews or -lew : long-legged brownish bird

cur·li·cue \'kərli,kyü\ n : fanciful curve

cur·rant \'kərənt\ n 1 : small seedless raisin 2 : berry of a shrub

cur·ren·cy \'kərənsē\ n, pl -cies 1 : general use or acceptance 2 : money

cur·rent \'kərənt\ adj : occurring in or belonging to the present ~ n 1 : swiftest part of a stream 2 : flow of electricity

cur·ric·u·lum \kə'rikyələm\ n, pl -la \-lə\ : course of study

¹**cur·ry** \'kərē\ vb -ried; -ry·ing : brush (a horse) with a wire brush (**cur·ry·comb** \-,kōm\) —**curry favor** : seek favor by flattery

²**curry** n, pl -ries : blend of pungent spices or a food seasoned with this

curse \'kərs\ n 1 : a calling down of evil or harm upon 2 : affliction ~ vb **cursed;**

curs·ing 1 : call down injury upon 2 : swear at 3 : afflict

cur·sor \'kərsər\ n : indicator on a computer screen

cur·so·ry \'kərsərē\ adj : hastily done

curt \'kərt\ adj : rudely abrupt —**curt·ly** adv —**curt·ness** n

cur·tail \kər'tāl\ vb : shorten —**cur·tail·ment** n

cur·tain \'kərtᵊn\ n : hanging screen that can be drawn back or raised —**curtain** vb

curt·sy, curt·sey \'kərtsē\ n, pl -sies or -seys : courteous bow made by bending the knees —**curtsy, curtsey** vb

cur·va·ture \'kərvə,chúr\ n : amount or state of curving

curve \'kərv\ vb **curved; curv·ing** : bend from a straight line or course ~ n 1 : a bending without angles 2 : something curved

cush·ion \'kúshən\ n 1 : soft pillow 2 : something that eases or protects ~ vb 1 : provide with a cushion 2 : soften the force of

cusp \'kəsp\ n : pointed end

cus·pid \'kəspəd\ n : a canine tooth

cus·pi·dor \'kəspə,dór\ n : spittoon

cus·tard \'kəstərd\ n : sweetened cooked mixture of milk and eggs

cus·to·dy \'kəstədē\ n, pl -dies : immediate care or charge —**cus·to·di·al** \kəs'tō-dēəl\ adj —**cus·to·di·an** \-ēən\ n

cus·tom \'kəstəm\ n 1 : habitual course of action 2 pl : import taxes ~ adj : made to personal order —**cus·tom·ar·i·ly** \,kəstə'merəlē\ adv —**cus·tom·ary** \'kəstə,merē\ adj —**cus·tom-built** adj —**cus·tom-made** adj

cus·tom·er \'kəstəmər\ n : buyer

cut \'kət\ vb **cut; cut·ting** 1 : penetrate or divide with a sharp edge 2 : experience the growth of (a tooth) through the gum 3 : shorten 4 : remove by severing 5 : intersect ~ n 1 : something separated by cutting 2 : reduction —**cut in** vb : thrust oneself between others

cu·ta·ne·ous \kyü'tānēəs\ adj : relating to the skin

cute \'kyüt\ adj **cut·er; -est** : pretty

cu·ti·cle \'kyütikəl\ n : outer layer (as of skin)

cut·lass \'kətləs\ n : short heavy curved sword

cut·lery \-lərē\ n : cutting utensils

cut·let \-lət\ n : slice of meat

cut·ter \'kətər\ n 1 : tool or machine for cutting 2 : small armed motorboat 3 : light sleigh

cut·throat n : murderer ~ adj : ruthless

-cy \sē\ n suffix 1 : action or practice 2 : rank or office 3 : body 4 : state or quality

cy·a·nide \'sīə,nīd, -nəd\ n : poisonous chemical salt

cy·cle \'sīkəl, 4 also 'sikəl\ n 1 : period of time for a series of repeated events 2 : recurring round of events 3 : long period of time 4 : bicycle or motorcycle ~ vb -cled; -cling : ride a cycle —**cy·clic** \'sīklik, 'sik-\, **cy·cli·cal** \-əl\ adj —**cy·clist** \'sīklist, 'sik-\ n

cy·clone \'sī,klōn\ n : tornado —**cy·clon·ic** \sī'klänik\ adj

cy·clo·pe·dia, cy·clo·pae·dia \,sīklə'pēdēə\ n : encyclopedia

cyl·in·der \'siləndər\ n 1 : long round body or figure 2 : rotating chamber in a revolver 3 : piston chamber in an engine — **cy·lin·dri·cal** \sə'lindrikəl\ adj

cym·bal \'simbəl\ n : one of 2 concave brass plates clashed together

cyn·ic \'sinik\ n : one who attributes all actions to selfish motives —**cyn·i·cal** \-ikəl\ adj —**cyn·i·cism** \-ə,sizəm\ n

cy·no·sure \'sīnə,shúr, 'sin-\ n : center of attraction

cy·press \'sīprəs\ n : evergreen tree related to the pines

cyst \'sist\ n : abnormal bodily sac —**cys·tic** \'sistik\ adj

czar \'zär\ n : ruler of Russia until 1917 — **czar·ist** n or adj

D

d \'dē\ n, pl **d's** or **ds** \'dēz\ : 4th letter of the alphabet

¹**dab** \'dab\ n : gentle touch or stroke ~ vb -bb- : touch or apply lightly

²**dab** n : small amount

dab·ble \'dabəl\ vb -bled; -bling 1 : splash 2 : work without serious effort —**dab·bler** \-blər\ n

dachs·hund \'däks,húnt\ n : small dog with a long body and short legs

dad \'dad\ n : father

dad·dy \'dadē\ n, pl -dies : father

daf·fo·dil \'dafə,dil\ n : narcissus with trumpetlike flowers

daft \'daft\ adj : foolish —**daft·ness** n

dag·ger \'dagər\ n : knife for stabbing

dahl·ia \'dalyə, 'däl-\ n : tuberous herb with showy flowers

dai·ly \'dālē\ adj 1 : occurring, done, or used every day or every weekday 2 : computed in terms of one day ~ n, pl -lies : daily newspaper —**daily** adv

dain·ty \'dāntē\ n, pl -ties : something delicious ~ adj -ti·er; -est : delicately pretty —**dain·ti·ly** adv —**dain·ti·ness** n

dairy \'derē\ n, pl -ies : farm that produces or company that processes milk —**dairy·maid** n —**dairy·man** \-mən, -,man\ n

da·is \'dāəs\ n : raised platform (as for a speaker)

dai·sy \'dāzē\ n, pl -sies : tall leafy-stemmed plant bearing showy flowers

dale \'dāl\ n : valley

dal·ly \'dalē\ vb -lied; -ly·ing 1 : flirt 2 : dawdle —**dal·li·ance** \-əns\ n

dal·ma·tian \dal'māshən\ n : large dog having a spotted white coat

¹**dam** \'dam\ n : female parent of a domestic animal

²**dam** n : barrier to hold back water —**dam** vb

dam·age \'damij\ n 1 : loss or harm due to injury 2 pl : compensation for loss or injury ~ vb -aged; -ag·ing : do damage to

dam·ask \'daməsk\ n : firm lustrous figured fabric

dame \'dām\ n : woman of rank or authority

damn \'dam\ vb 1 : condemn to hell 2 : curse —**dam·na·ble** \-nəbəl\ adj — **dam·na·tion** \dam'nāshən\ n —**damned** adj

damp \'damp\ n : moisture ~ vb 1 : reduce the draft in 2 : restrain 3 : moisten ~ adj : moist —**damp·ness** n

damp·en \'dampən\ vb 1 : diminish in activity or vigor 2 : make or become damp

damp·er \'dampər\ n : movable plate to regulate a flue draft

dam·sel \'damzəl\ n : young woman

dance \'dans\ vb **danced; danc·ing** : move rhythmically to music ~ n : act of dancing or a gathering for dancing —**danc·er** n

dan·de·li·on \'dandᵊl,īən\ n : common yellow-flowered herb

dan·der \'dandər\ n : temper

dan·druff \'dandrəf\ n : whitish thin dry scales of skin on the scalp

dan·dy \'dandē\ n, pl -dies : man too concerned with clothes 2 : something excellent ~ adj -di·er; -est : very good

dan·ger \'dānjər\ n 1 : exposure to injury or evil 2 : something that may cause injury —**dan·ger·ous** \'dānjərəs\ adj

dan·gle \'daŋgəl\ vb -gled; -gling 1 : hang and swing freely 2 : be left without support or connection 3 : allow or cause to hang 4 : offer as an inducement

dank \'daŋk\ adj : unpleasantly damp

dap·per \'dapər\ adj : neat and stylishly dressed

dap·ple \'dapəl\ vb -pled; -pling : mark with colored spots

dare \'dar\ vb **dared; dar·ing** 1 : have sufficient courage 2 : urge or provoke to contend —**dare** n —**dar·ing** \'dariŋ\ n or adj

dare·dev·il n : recklessly bold person

dark \'därk\ adj 1 : having little or no light 2 : not light in color 3 : gloomy ~ n : absence of light —**dark·en** \-ən\ vb — **dark·ly** adv —**dark·ness** n

dar·ling \'därliŋ\ n 1 : beloved 2 : favorite ~ adj 1 : dearly loved 2 : very pleasing

darn \'därn\ vb : mend with interlacing stitches —**darn·er** n

dart \'därt\ n 1 : small pointed missile 2 pl : game of throwing darts at a target 3 : tapering fold in a garment 4 : quick movement ~ vb : move suddenly or rapidly

dash \'dash\ vb 1 : smash 2 : knock or hurl violently 3 : ruin 4 : perform or finish hastily 5 : move quickly ~ n 1 : sudden burst, splash, or stroke 2 : punctuation mark — 3 : tiny amount 4 : showiness or liveliness 5 : sudden rush 6 : short race 7 : dashboard

dash·board n : instrument panel

dash·ing \'dashiŋ\ adj : dapper and charming

das·tard \'dastərd\ n : one who sneakingly commits malicious acts

das·tard·ly \-lē\ adj : base or malicious

da·ta \'dātə, 'dat-, 'dät-\ n sing or pl : factual information

da·ta·base \-,bās\ n : data organized for computer search

¹**date** \'dāt\ n : edible fruit of a palm

²**date** n 1 : day, month, or year when something is done or made 2 : historical time period 3 : social engagement or the person one goes out with ~ vb **dat·ed; dat·ing** 1 : determine or record the date of 2 : have a date with 3 : originate.—**to date** : up to now

dat·ed \-əd\ adj : old-fashioned

da·tum \'dātəm, 'dat-, 'dät-\ n, pl -ta \-ə\ or -tums : piece of data

daub \'dób\ vb : smear ~ n : something daubed on —**daub·er** n

daugh·ter \'dótər\ n : human female offspring

daugh·ter-in-law n, pl **daughters-in-law** : wife of one's son

daunt \'dónt\ vb : lessen the courage of

daunt·less \-ləs\ adj : fearless

dav·en·port \'davən,pórt\ n : sofa

daw·dle \'dódᵊl\ vb -dled; -dling 1 : waste time 2 : loiter

dawn \'dón\ vb 1 : grow light as the sun rises 2 : begin to appear, develop, or be understood ~ n : first appearance (as of daylight)

day \'dā\ n 1 : period of light between one night and the next 2 : 24 hours 3 : specified date 4 : particular time or age 5 : period of work for a day —**day·light** n —**day·time** n

day·break n : dawn

day·dream n : fantasy of wish fulfillment —**daydream** vb

daylight saving time n : time one hour ahead of standard time

daze \'dāz\ vb **dazed; daz·ing** 1 : stun by a blow 2 : dazzle —**daze** n

daz·zle \'dazəl\ vb -zled; -zling 1 : overpower with light 2 : impress greatly — **dazzle** n

DDT \,dē,dē'tē\ n : long-lasting insecticide

dea·con \'dēkən\ n : subordinate church officer

dea·con·ess \'dēkənəs\ n : woman who assists in church ministry

dead \'ded\ adj 1 : lifeless 2 : unresponsive or inactive 3 : exhausted 4 : obsolete 5 : precise ~ n, pl **dead** 1 : one that is dead —usu. with **the** 2 : most lifeless time ~ adv 1 : completely 2 : directly —**dead·en** \'dedᵊn\ vb

dead-beat n : one who will not pay debts

dead end n : end of a street with no exit — **dead-end** adj

dead heat n : tie in a contest

dead·line n : time by which something must be finished

dead·lock n : struggle that neither side can win —**deadlock** vb

dead·ly \'dedlē\ adj -li·er; -est 1 : capable of causing death 2 : very accurate 3 : fatal to spiritual progress 4 : suggestive of death 5 : very great ~ adv : extremely — **dead·li·ness** n

dead·pan adj : expressionless —**deadpan** n or vb or adv

dead·wood n : something useless

deaf \'def\ adj : unable or unwilling to hear —**deaf·en** \-ən\ vb —**deaf·ness** n

deaf-mute n : deaf person unable to speak

deal \'dēl\ n 1 : indefinite quantity 2 : distribution of playing cards 3 : negotiation or agreement 4 : treatment received 5 : bargain ~ vb **dealt** \'delt\; **deal·ing** \'dēliŋ\ 1 : distribute playing cards 2 : be concerned with 3 : administer or deliver 4 : take action 5 : sell 6 : reach a state of acceptance —**deal·er** n —**deal·ing** n

dean \'dēn\ n 1 : head of a group of clergy members 2 : university or school administrator 3 : senior member

dear \'dir\ adj 1 : highly valued or loved 2 : expensive ~ n : loved one —**dear·ly** adv —**dear·ness** n

dearth \'dərth\ n : scarcity

death \'deth\ n 1 : end of life 2 : cause of loss of life 3 : state of being dead 4 : destruction or extinction —**death·less** adj —**death·ly** adj or adv

de·ba·cle \di'bäkəl, -'bakəl\ n : disaster or fiasco

de·bar \di'bär\ vb : bar from something

de·bark \-'bärk\ vb : disembark —**de·bar·ka·tion** \,dē,bär'kāshən\ n

de·base \di'bās\ vb : disparage —**de·base·ment** n

de·bate \-'bāt\ vb -bat·ed; -bat·ing : discuss a question by argument —**de·bat·able** adj —**debate** n —**de·bat·er** n

de·bauch \-'bóch\ vb : seduce or corrupt — **de·bauch·ery** n

de·bil·i·tate \-'bilə,tāt\ vb -tat·ed; -tat·ing : make ill or weak

de·bil·i·ty \-'bilətē\ n, pl -ties : physical weakness

deb·it \'debət\ n : account entry of a payment or debt ~ vb : record as a debit

deb·o·nair \,debə'nar\ adj : suave

de·bris \də'brē, dā-; 'dā,brē\ n, pl -bris \-'brēz, -,brēz\ : remains of something destroyed

debt \'det\ n 1 : sin 2 : something owed 3 : state of owing —**debt·or** \-ər\ n de·bunk \dē'bənk\ vb : expose as false

de·but \'dā,byü, dā'byü\ n 1 : first public appearance 2 : formal entrance into society —debut vb —deb·u·tante \'debyü-,tänt\ n

de·cade \'dek,ād, -əd; de'kād\ n : 10 years

dec·a·dence \'dekədəns, di'kād°ns\ n 1 : deterioration —dec·a·dent \-ənt, -°nt\ adj or n

de·cal \'dē,kal, di'kal, 'dekəl\ n : picture or design for transfer from prepared paper

de·camp \di'kamp\ vb : depart suddenly

de·cant \di'kant\ vb : pour gently

de·cant·er \-ər\ n : ornamental bottle

de·cap·i·tate \di'kapə,tāt\ vb -tat·ed; -tat·ing : behead —de·cap·i·ta·tion \-,kapə·'tāshən\ n

de·cay \di'kā\ vb 1 : decline in condition 2 : decompose —decay n

de·cease \di'sēs\ n : death —decease vb

de·ceit \di'sēt\ n 1 : deception 2 : dishonesty —de·ceit·ful \-fəl\ adj —de·ceit·ful·ly adv —de·ceit·ful·ness n

de·ceive \-'sēv\ vb -ceived; -ceiv·ing : trick or mislead —de·ceiv·er n

de·cel·er·ate \dē'selə,rāt\ vb -at·ed; -at·ing : slow down

De·cem·ber \di'sembər\ n : 12th month of the year having 31 days

de·cent \'dēs°nt\ adj 1 : good, right, or just 2 : clothed 3 : not obscene 4 : fairly good —de·cen·cy \-°nsē\ n —de·cent·ly adv

de·cep·tion \di'sepshən\ n 1 : act or fact of deceiving 2 : fraud —de·cep·tive \-'septiv\ adj —de·cep·tive·ly adv —de·cep·tive·ness n

de·cide \di'sīd\ vb -cid·ed; -cid·ing 1 : make a choice or judgment 2 : bring to a conclusion 3 : cause to decide

de·cid·ed adj 1 : unquestionable 2 : resolute —de·cid·ed·ly adv

de·cid·u·ous \di'sijəwəs\ adj : having leaves that fall annually

dec·i·mal \'desəməl\ n : fraction in which the denominator is a power of 10 expressed by a point (decimal point) placed at the left of the numerator —decimal adj

de·ci·pher \di'sīfər\ vb : make out the meaning of —de·ci·pher·able adj

de·ci·sion \-'sizhən\ n 1 : act or result of deciding 2 : determination

de·ci·sive \-'sīsiv\ adj 1 : having the power to decide 2 : conclusive 3 : showing determination —de·ci·sive·ly adv —de·ci·sive·ness n

deck \'dek\ n 1 : floor of a ship 2 : pack of playing cards ~ vb 1 : array or dress up 2 : knock down

de·claim \di'klām\ vb : speak loudly or impressively —dec·la·ma·tion \deklə'māshən\ n

de·clare \di'klar\ vb -clared; -clar·ing 1 : make known formally 2 : state emphatically —dec·la·ra·tion \deklə'rāshən\ n —de·clar·a·tive \di'klarətiv\ adj —de·clar·a·to·ry \di'klarə,tōrē\ adj —de·clar·er n

de·clen·sion \di'klenchən\ n : inflectional forms of a noun, pronoun, or adjective

de·cline \di'klīn\ vb -clined; -clin·ing 1 : turn or slope downward 2 : wane 3 : refuse to accept 4 : inflect ~ n 1 : gradual wasting away 2 : change to a lower state or level 3 : a descending slope —dec·li·na·tion \deklə'nāshən\ n

de·code \dē'kōd\ vb : decipher (a coded message) —de·cod·er n

de·com·mis·sion \dēkə'mishən\ vb : remove from service

de·com·pose \dēkəm'pōz\ vb 1 : separate into parts 2 : decay —de·com·po·si·tion \dē,kämpə'zishən\ n

de·con·ges·tant \dēkən'jestənt\ n : agent that relieves congestion

de·cor, dé·cor \dā'kòr, 'dā,kòr\ n : room design or decoration

dec·o·rate \'dekə,rāt\ vb -rat·ed; -rat·ing 1 : add something attractive to 2 : honor with a medal —dec·o·ra·tion \dekə'rā-shən\ n —dec·o·ra·tive \'dekərətiv\ adj —dec·o·ra·tor \'dekə,rātər\ n

de·co·rum \di'kōrəm\ n : proper behavior —dec·o·rous \'dekərəs, di'kōrəs\ adj

de·coy \'dē,kòi, di'-\ n : something that tempts or draws attention from another ~ vb : tempt

de·crease \di'krēs\ vb -creased; -creas·ing : grow or cause to grow less —decrease \'dē,krēs\ n

de·cree \di'krē\ n : official order —decree vb

de·crep·it \di'krepət\ adj : impaired by age

de·cre·scen·do \,dākrə'shendō\ adv or adj : with a decrease in volume

de·cry \di'krī\ vb : express strong disapproval of

ded·i·cate \'dedi,kāt\ vb -cat·ed; -cat·ing 1 : set apart for a purpose (as honor or worship) 2 : address to someone as a compliment —ded·i·ca·tion \dedi'kāshən\ n —ded·i·ca·to·ry \'dedikə,tōrē\ adj

de·duce \di'düs, -'dyüs\ vb -duced; -duc·ing : derive by reasoning —de·duc·ible adj

de·duct \-'dəkt\ vb : subtract —de·duct·ible adj

de·duc·tion \-'dəkshən\ n 1 : subtraction 2 : reasoned conclusion —de·duc·tive \-'dəktiv\ adj

deed \'dēd\ n 1 : exploit 2 : document showing ownership ~ vb : convey by deed

deem \'dēm\ vb : think

deep \'dēp\ adj 1 : extending far or a specified distance down, back, within, or outward 2 : occupied 3 : dark and rich in color 4 : low in tone ~ adv 1 : deeply 2 : far along in time ~ n : deep place —deep·en \'dēpən\ vb —deep·ly adv

deep-seat·ed \-'sētəd\ adj : firmly established

deer \'dir\ n, pl deer : ruminant mammal with antlers in the male —deer·skin n

de·face \di'fās\ vb : mar the surface of —de·face·ment n —de·fac·er n

de·fame \di'fām\ vb -famed; -fam·ing : injure the reputation of —def·a·mation \defə'māshən\ n —de·fam·a·to·ry \di·'famə,tōrē\ adj

de·fault \di'fòlt\ n : failure in a duty —default vb —de·fault·er n

de·feat \di'fēt\ vb 1 : frustrate 2 : win victory over ~ n : loss of a battle or contest

def·e·cate \'defi,kāt\ vb -cat·ed; -cat·ing : discharge feces from the bowels —def·e·ca·tion \defi'kāshən\ n

de·fect \'dē,fekt, di'fekt\ n : imperfection ~ \di'-\ vb : desert —de·fec·tion \-'fekshən\ n —de·fec·tor \-'fektər\ n

de·fec·tive \di'fektiv\ adj : faulty or deficient —defective n

de·fend \-'fend\ vb 1 : protect from danger or harm 2 : take the side of —de·fend·er n

de·fen·dant \-'fendənt\ n : person charged or sued in a court

de·fense \-'fens\ n 1 : act of defending 2 : something that defends 3 : party, group, or team that opposes another —de·fense·less adj —de·fen·si·ble adj —de·fen·sive adj

1de·fer \di'fər\ vb -rr- : postpone —de·fer·ment \-'fərmənt\ n —de·fer·ra·ble \-əbəl\ adj

2defer vb -rr- : yield to the opinion or wishes of another —def·er·ence \'defrəns\ n —def·er·en·tial \defə'renchəl\ adj

de·fi·ance \di'fīəns\ n : disposition to resist —de·fi·ant \-ē·ənt\ adj

de·fi·cient \di'fishənt\ adj 1 : lacking something necessary 2 : not up to standard —de·fi·cien·cy \-'fishənsē\ n

def·i·cit \'defəsət\ n : shortage esp. in money

de·file \di'fīl\ vb -filed; -fil·ing 1 : make filthy or corrupt 2 : profane or dishonor —de·file·ment n

de·fine \di'fīn\ vb -fined; -fin·ing 1 : fix or mark the limits of 2 : clarify in outline 3 : set forth the meaning of —de·fin·able adj —de·fin·ably adv —de·fin·er n —def·i·ni·tion \defə'nishən\ n

def·i·nite \'defənət\ adj 1 : having distinct limits 2 : clear in meaning, intent, or identity 3 : typically designating an identified or immediately identifiable person or thing —def·i·nite·ly adv

de·fin·i·tive \di'finətiv\ adj 1 : conclusive 2 : authoritative

de·flate \di'flāt\ vb -flat·ed; -flat·ing 1 : release air or gas from 2 : reduce —de·fla·tion \-'flāshən\ n

de·flect \di'flekt\ vb : turn aside —de·flec·tion \-'flekshən\ n

de·fog \-'fòg, -'fäg\ vb : remove condensed moisture from —de·fog·ger n

de·fo·li·ate \dē'fōlē,āt\ vb -at·ed; -at·ing : deprive of leaves esp. prematurely —de·fo·li·ant \-lēənt\ n —de·fo·li·a·tion \-,fōlē'āshən\ n

de·form \di'fòrm\ vb 1 : distort 2 : disfigure —de·for·ma·tion \dē,fòr'māshən, ,de-fər-\ n —de·for·mi·ty \di'fòrmətē\ n

de·fraud \di'fròd\ vb : cheat

de·fray \di'frā\ vb : pay

de·frost \di'fròst\ vb 1 : thaw out 2 : free from ice —de·frost·er n

deft \'deft\ adj : quick and skillful —deft·ly adv —deft·ness n

de·fy \di'fī\ vb -fied; -fy·ing 1 : challenge 2 : boldly refuse to obey

de·gen·er·ate \di'jenərət\ adj : degraded or corrupt ~ n : degenerate person ~ \-ə,rāt\ vb : become degenerate —de·gen·er·a·cy \-ərəsē\ n —de·gen·er·a·tion \-,jenə'rāshən\ n —de·gen·er·a·tive \-'jenə,rā-tiv\ adj

de·grade \di'grād\ vb 1 : reduce from a higher to a lower rank or degree 2 : debase 3 : decompose —de·grad·able \-əbəl\ adj —deg·ra·da·tion \degrə'dā-shən\ n

de·gree \di'grē\ n 1 : step in a series 2 : extent, intensity, or scope 3 : title given to a college graduate 4 : a 360th part of the circumference of a circle 5 : unit for measuring temperature

de·hy·drate \dē'hī,drāt\ vb 1 : remove water from 2 : lose liquid —de·hy·dra·tion \dēhī'drāshən\ n

de·i·fy \'dēə,fī, 'dā-\ vb -fied; -fy·ing : make a god of —de·i·fi·ca·tion \dēəfə'kāshən, ,dā-\ n

deign \'dān\ vb : condescend

de·i·ty \'dēətē, 'dā-\ n, pl -ties 1 cap : God 2 : a god or goddess

de·ject·ed \di'jektəd\ adj : sad —de·jec·tion \-shən\ n

de·lay \di'lā\ n : a putting off of something ~ vb 1 : postpone 2 : stop or hinder for a time

de·lec·ta·ble \di'lektəbəl\ adj : delicious

del·e·gate \'deligət, -,gāt\ n : representative ~ \-,gāt\ vb -gat·ed; -gat·ing 1 : entrust to another 2 : appoint as one's delegate —del·e·ga·tion \deli'gāshən\ n

de·lete \di'lēt\ vb -let·ed; -let·ing : eliminate something written —de·le·tion \-'lēshən\ n

del·e·te·ri·ous \delə'tirēəs\ adj : harmful

de·lib·er·ate \di'libərət\ adj 1 : determined after careful thought 2 : intentional 3 : not hurried ~ \-ə,rāt\ vb -at·ed; -at·ing : consider carefully —de·lib·er·ate·ly adv —de·lib·er·ate·ness n —de·lib·er·a·tion \-,libə'rāshən\ n —de·lib·er·a·tive \-'libə,rātiv, -rət-\ adj

del·i·ca·cy \'delikəsē\ n, pl -cies 1 : something special and pleasing to eat 2 : fineness 3 : frailty

del·i·cate \'delikət\ adj 1 : subtly pleasing to the senses 2 : dainty and charming 3 : sensitive or fragile 4 : requiring fine skill or tact —del·i·cate·ly adv

del·i·ca·tes·sen \delikə'tes°n\ n : store that sells ready-to-eat food

de·li·cious \di'lishəs\ adj : very pleasing esp. in taste or aroma —de·li·cious·ly adv —de·li·cious·ness n

de·light \di'līt\ n 1 : great pleasure 2 : source of great pleasure ~ vb 1 : take great pleasure 2 : satisfy greatly —de·light·ful \-fəl\ adj —de·light·ful·ly adv

de·lin·e·ate \di'linē,āt\ vb -at·ed; -at·ing : sketch or portray —de·lin·e·a·tion \-,linē'āshən\ n

de·lin·quent \-'liŋkwənt\ n : delinquent person ~ adj 1 : violating duty or law 2 : overdue in payment —de·lin·quen·cy \-kwənsē\ n

de·lir·i·um \di'lirēəm\ n : mental disturbance —de·lir·i·ous \-ēəs\ adj

de·liv·er \di'livər\ vb 1 : set free 2 : hand over 3 : assist in birth 4 : say or speak 5 : send to an intended destination —de·liv·er·ance \-ərəns\ n —de·liv·er·er n —de·liv·ery \-ərē\ n

dell \'del\ n : small secluded valley

del·ta \'deltə\ n : triangle of land at the mouth of a river

de·lude \di'lüd\ vb -lud·ed; -lud·ing : mislead or deceive

de·luge \'delyüj\ n 1 : flood 2 : drenching rain ~ vb -uged; -ug·ing 1 : flood 2 : overwhelm

de·lu·sion \di'lüzhən\ n : false belief

de·luxe \di'lüks, -'ləks, -'lüks\ adj : very luxurious or elegant

delve \'delv\ vb delved; delv·ing 1 : dig 2 : seek information in records

dem·a·gogue, dem·a·gog \'demə,gäg\ n : politician who appeals to emotion and prejudice —dem·a·gogu·ery \-,gägərē\ n —dem·a·gogy \-,gägē, -,gäjē\ n

de·mand \di'mand\ n 1 : act of demanding 2 : something claimed as due 3 : ability and desire to buy 4 : urgent need ~ vb 1 : ask for with authority 2 : require

de·mar·cate \di'mär,kāt, 'dē,mär-\ vb -cat·ed; -cat·ing : mark the limits of —de·mar·ca·tion \dē,mär'kāshən\ n

de·mean \di'mēn\ vb : degrade

de·mean·or \-'mēnər\ n : behavior

de·ment·ed \di'mentəd\ adj : crazy

de·mer·it \-'merət\ n : mark given an offender

demi·god \'demi,gäd\ n : mythological being less powerful than a god

de·mise \di'mīz\ n 1 : death 2 : loss of status

demi·tasse \'demi,tas\ n : small cup of coffee

de·mo·bi·lize \di'mōbə,līz, dē-\ vb : disband from military service —de·mo·bi·li·za·tion \-,mōbələ'zāshən\ n

de·moc·ra·cy \di'mäkrəsē\ n, pl -cies 1 : government in which the supreme power is held by the people 2 : political unit with democratic government

dem·o·crat \'demə,krat\ n : adherent of democracy

dem·o·crat·ic \,demə'kratik\ adj : relating to or favoring democracy —dem·o·crat·i·cal·ly \-tiklē\ adv —de·moc·ra·tize \di'mäkrə,tīz\ vb

de·mol·ish \di'mälish\ vb 1 : tear down or smash 2 : put an end to —de·mo·li·tion \,demə'lishən, ,dē-\ n

de·mon \'dēmən\ n : evil spirit —de·mon·ic \di'mänik\ adj

dem·on·strate \'demən,strāt\ vb -strat·ed; -strat·ing 1 : show clearly or publicly 2 : prove 3 : explain —de·mon·stra·ble \di'mänstrəbəl\ adj —de·mon·stra·bly \-blē\ adv —dem·on·stra·tion \,demən-'strāshən\ n —de·mon·stra·tive \di-'mänstrətiv\ adj or n —dem·on·stra·tor \'demən,strātər\ n

de·mor·al·ize \di'mòrə,līz\ vb : destroy the enthusiasm of

de·mote \di'mōt\ vb -mot·ed; -mot·ing : reduce to a lower rank —de·mo·tion \-'mōshən\ n

de·mur \di'mər\ vb -rr- : object —demur n

de·mure \di'myùr\ adj : modest —de·mure·ly adv

den \'den\ n 1 : animal's shelter 2 : hiding place 3 : cozy private little room

de·na·ture \dē'nāchər\ vb -tured; -tur·ing : make (alcohol) unfit for drinking

de·ni·al \di'nīəl\ n : rejection of a request or of the validity of a statement

den·i·grate \'deni,grāt\ vb -grat·ed; -grat·ing : speak ill of

den·im \'denəm\ n 1 : durable twilled cotton fabric 2 pl : pants of denim

den·i·zen \'denəzən\ n : inhabitant

de·nom·i·na·tion \di,nämə'nāshən\ n 1 : religious body 2 : value or size in a series —de·nom·i·na·tion·al \-shənəl\ adj

de·nom·i·na·tor \-'nämə,nātər\ n : part of a fraction below the line

de·note \di'nōt\ vb 1 : mark out plainly 2 : mean —de·no·ta·tion \dēnō'tāshən\ n —de·no·ta·tive \dēnō,tātiv, di'nōtətiv\ adj

de·noue·ment \dā,nü'mä°\ n : final outcome (as of a drama)

de·nounce \di'naùns\ vb -nounced; -nounc·ing 1 : pronounce blameworthy or evil 2 : inform against

dense \'dens\ adj dens·er; -est 1 : thick, compact, or crowded 2 : stupid —dense·ly adv —dense·ness n —den·si·ty \'densətē\ n

dent \'dent\ n : small depression —dent vb

den·tal \'dent°l\ adj : relating to teeth or dentistry

den·ti·frice \'dentəfrəs\ n : preparation for cleaning teeth

den·tin \'dent°n\, den·tine \'den,tēn, ,den'-\ n : bonelike component of teeth

den·tist \'dentist\ n : one who cares for and replaces teeth —den·tist·ry n

den·ture \'denchər\ n : artificial teeth

de·nude \di'nüd, -'nyüd\ vb -nud·ed; -nud·ing : strip of covering

de·nun·ci·a·tion \di,nənsē'āshən\ n : act of denouncing

de·ny \-'nī\ vb -nied; -ny·ing 1 : declare untrue 2 : disavow 3 : refuse to grant

de·odor·ant \dē'ōdərənt\ n : preparation to prevent unpleasant odors —de·odor·ize \-,rīz\ vb

de·part \di'pärt\ vb 1 : go away or away from 2 : die —de·par·ture \-'pärchər\ n

de·part·ment \di'pärtmənt\ n 1 : area of responsibility or interest 2 : functional division —de·part·men·tal \di,pärt-'ment°l, dē-\ adj

de·pend \di'pend\ vb 1 : rely for support 2 : be determined by or based on something else —de·pend·abil·i·ty \-,pendə'bilətē\ n —de·pend·able adj —de·pen·dence \di'pendəns\ n —de·pen·den·cy \-dənsē\ n —de·pen·dent \-ənt\ adj or n

de·pict \di'pikt\ vb : show by or as if by a picture —de·pic·tion \-'pikshən\ n

de·plete \di'plēt\ vb -plet·ed; -plet·ing : use up resources of —de·ple·tion \-'plēshən\ n

de·plore \di-'plòr\ vb -plored; -plor·ing : regret strongly —de·plor·able \-əbəl\ adj

de·ploy \di'plòi\ vb : spread out for battle —de·ploy·ment \-mənt\ n

de·port \di'pòrt\ vb 1 : behave 2 : send out of the country —de·por·ta·tion \dē-,pòr'tāshən\ n —de·port·ment \di-'pòrtmənt\ n

de·pose \-'pōz\ vb -posed; -pos·ing 1 : remove (a ruler) from office 2 : testify —de·po·si·tion \depə'zishən, ,dē-\ n

de·pos·it \di'päzət\ vb -it·ed; -it·ing : place esp. for safekeeping ~ n 1 : state of being deposited 2 : something deposited 3 : act of depositing 4 : natural accumulation —de·pos·i·tor \-'päzətər\ n

de·pos·i·to·ry \-'päzə,tōrē\ n, pl -ries : place for deposit

de·pot \1 usu 'depō, 2 usu 'dēp-\ n 1 : place for storage 2 : bus or railroad station

de·prave \di'prāv\ vb -praved; -prav·ing : corrupt morally —de·praved adj —de·prav·i·ty \-'pravətē\ n

dep·re·cate \'depri,kāt\ vb -cat·ed; -cat·ing 1 : express disapproval of 2 : belittle —dep·re·ca·tion \depri'kāshən\ n —dep·re·ca·to·ry \'deprikə,tōrē\ adj

de·pre·ci·ate \di'prēshē,āt\ vb -at·ed; -at·ing 1 : lessen in value 2 : belittle —de·pre·ci·a·tion \-,prēshē'āshən\ n

dep·re·da·tion \,deprə'dāshən\ n : a laying waste or plundering —dep·re·date \'deprə,dāt\ vb

de•press \di'pres\ *vb* **1** : press down **2** : lessen the activity or force of **3** : discourage **4** : decrease the market value of —**de•pres•sant** \-³nt\ *n or adj* —**de•pressed** *adj* —**de•pres•sive** \-iv\ *adj or n* —**de•pres•sor** \-ər\ *n*

de•pres•sion \di'preshan\ *n* **1** : act of depressing or state of being depressed **2** : depressed place **3** : period of low economic activity

de•prive \-'prīv\ *vb* -**prived; -priv•ing** : take or keep something away from —**de•pri•va•tion** \depra'vāshan\ *n*

depth \'depth\ *n, pl* **depths** **1** : something that is deep **2** : distance down from a surface **3** : distance from front to back **4** : quality of being deep

dep•u•ta•tion \depyə'tāshan\ *n* : delegation

dep•u•ty \'depyətē\ *n, pl* -**ties** : person appointed to act for another —**dep•u•tize** \-,tīz\ *vb*

de•rail \di'rāl\ *vb* : leave the rails —**de•rail•ment** *n*

de•range \-'rānj\ *vb* -**ranged; -rang•ing** **1** : disarrange or upset **2** : make insane —**de•range•ment** *n*

der•by \'dərbē, Brit 'där-\ *n, pl* -**bies** **1** : horse race **2** : stiff felt hat with dome-shaped crown

de•reg•u•late \dē'regyù,lāt\ *vb* : remove restrictions on —**de•reg•u•la•tion** \-,regyù'lāshan\ *n*

der•e•lict \'derə,likt\ *adj* **1** : abandoned **2** : negligent ~ *n* **1** : something abandoned **2** : bum —**der•e•lic•tion** \derə'likshan\ *n*

de•ride \di'rīd\ *vb* -**rid•ed; -rid•ing** : make fun of —**de•ri•sion** \-'rizhan\ *n* —**de•ri•sive** \-'rīsiv\ *adj* —**de•ri•sive•ly** *adv* —**de•ri•sive•ness** *n*

de•rive \di'rīv\ *vb* -**rived; -riv•ing** **1** : obtain from a source or parent **2** : come from a certain source **3** : infer or deduce —**der•i•va•tion** \derə'vāshan\ *n* —**de•riv•a•tive** \di'rivativ\ *adj or n*

der•ma•tol•o•gy \dərmə'täləjē\ *n* : study of the skin and its disorders —**der•ma•tol•o•gist** \-jist\ *n*

de•rog•a•tive \di'rägətiv\ *adj* : derogatory

de•rog•a•to•ry \di'rägə,tōrē\ *adj* : intended to lower the reputation

der•rick \'derik\ *n* **1** : hoisting apparatus **2** : framework over an oil well

de•scend \di'send\ *vb* **1** : move or climb down **2** : derive **3** : extend downward **4** : appear suddenly (as in an attack) —**de•scen•dant, de•scen•dent** \-³nt\ *adj or n* —**de•scent** \di'sent\ *n*

de•scribe \-'skrīb\ *vb* -**scribed; -scrib•ing** : represent in words —**de•scrib•able** *adj* —**de•scrip•tion** \-'skripshan\ *n* —**de•scrip•tive** \-'skriptiv\ *adj*

de•scry \di'skrī\ *vb* -**scried; -scry•ing** : catch sight of

des•e•crate \'desi,krāt\ *vb* -**crat•ed; -crat•ing** : treat (something sacred) with disrespect —**des•e•cra•tion** \desi'krāshan\ *n*

de•seg•re•gate \dē'segrə,gāt\ *vb* : eliminate esp. racial segregation in —**de•seg•re•ga•tion** *n*

¹des•ert \'dezərt\ *n* : dry barren region —**desert** *adj*

²de•sert \di'zərt\ *n* : what one deserves

³de•sert \di'zərt\ *vb* : abandon —**de•sert•er** *n* —**de•ser•tion** \-'zərshan\ *n*

de•serve \-'zərv\ *vb* -**served; -serv•ing** : be worthy of

des•ic•cate \'desi,kāt\ *vb* -**cat•ed; -cat•ing** : dehydrate —**des•ic•ca•tion** \desi'kāshan\ *n*

de•sign \di'zīn\ *vb* **1** : create and work out the details of **2** : make a pattern or sketch of ~ *n* **1** : mental project or plan **2** : purpose **3** : preliminary sketch **4** : underlying arrangement of elements **5** : decorative pattern —**de•sign•er** *n*

des•ig•nate \'dezig,nāt\ *vb* -**nat•ed; -nat•ing** **1** : indicate, specify, or name **2** : appoint —**des•ig•na•tion** \dezig'nāshan\ *n*

de•sire \di'zīr\ *vb* -**sired; -sir•ing** **1** : feel desire for **2** : request ~ *n* **1** : strong conscious impulse to have, be, or do something **2** : something desired —**de•sir•abil•i•ty** \-,zīrə'bilətē\ *n* —**de•sir•able** \-'zīrəbəl\ *adj* —**de•sir•able•ness** *n* —**de•sir•ous** \-'zīrəs\ *adj*

de•sist \di'zist, -'sist\ *vb* : stop

desk \'desk\ *n* : table esp. for writing and reading

des•o•late \'desələt, 'dez-\ *adj* **1** : lifeless **2** : disconsolate ~ \-,lāt\ *vb* **1** : lay waste —**des•o•la•tion** \desə'lāshan, dez-\ *n*

de•spair \di'spar\ *vb* : lose all hope ~ *n* : loss of hope

des•per•a•do \despə'rädō, -'rād-\ *n, pl* -**does** *or* -**dos** : desperate criminal

des•per•ate \'despərət\ *adj* **1** : hopeless **2** : rash **3** : extremely intense —**des•per•ate•ly** *adv* —**des•per•a•tion** \despə'rāshan\ *n*

de•spi•ca•ble \di'spikabəl, 'despik-\ *adj* : deserving scorn

de•spise \di'spīz\ *vb* -**spised; -spis•ing** : feel contempt for

de•spite \-'spīt\ *prep* : in spite of

de•spoil \-'spȯil\ *vb* : strip of possessions or value

de•spon•den•cy \-'spändənsē\ *n* : dejection —**de•spon•dent** \-dənt\ *adj*

des•pot \'despət, -,pät\ *n* : tyrant —**des•pot•ic** \des'pätik\ *adj* —**des•po•tism** \'despə,tizəm\ *n*

des•sert \di'zərt\ *n* : sweet food, fruit, or cheese ending a meal

des•ti•na•tion \destə'nāshan\ *n* : place where something or someone is going

des•tine \'destən\ *vb* -**tined; -tin•ing** **1** : designate, assign, or determine in advance **2** : direct

des•ti•ny \'destənē\ *n, pl* -**nies** : that which is to happen in the future

des•ti•tute \'destə,tüt, -,tyüt\ *adj* **1** : lacking something **2** : very poor —**des•ti•tu•tion** \destə'tüshan, -'tyü-\ *n*

de•stroy \di'strȯi\ *vb* : kill or put an end to

de•stroy•er \-'strȯiər\ *n* **1** : one that destroys **2** : small speedy warship

de•struc•tion \-'strakshan\ *n* **1** : action of destroying **2** : ruin —**de•struc•ti•bil•i•ty** \-,strakta'bilatē\ *n* —**de•struc•ti•ble** \-'straktabəl\ *adj* —**de•struc•tive** \-'straktiv\ *adj*

des•ul•to•ry \'desəl,tōrē\ *adj* : aimless

de•tach \di'tach\ *vb* : separate

de•tached \-'tacht\ *adj* **1** : separate **2** : aloof or impartial

de•tach•ment \-'tachmant\ *n* **1** : separation **2** : troops or ships on special service **3** : aloofness **4** : impartiality

de•tail \di'tāl, 'dē,tāl\ *n* : small item or part ~ *vb* : give details of

de•tain \di'tān\ *vb* **1** : hold in custody **2** : delay

de•tect \di'tekt\ *vb* : discover —**de•tect•able** *adj* —**de•tec•tion** \-'tekshan\ *n* —**de•tec•tor** \-tər\ *n*

de•tec•tive \-'tektiv\ *n* : one who investigates crime

dé•tente \dā'täⁿt\ *n* : relaxation of tensions between nations

de•ten•tion \di'tenchan\ *n* : confinement

de•ter \-'tər\ *vb* -**rr-** : discourage or prevent —**de•ter•rence** \-əns\ *n* —**de•ter•rent** \-ənt\ *adj or n*

de•ter•gent \di'tərjant\ *n* : cleansing agent

de•te•ri•o•rate \-'tirēə,rāt\ *vb* -**rat•ed; -rat•ing** : make or become worse —**de•te•ri•o•ra•tion** \-,tirēə'rāshan\ *n*

de•ter•mi•na•tion \di,tərmə'nāshan\ *n* **1** : act of deciding or fixing **2** : firm purpose

de•ter•mine \-'tərmən\ *vb* -**mined; -min•ing** **1** : decide on, establish, or settle **2** : find out **3** : bring about as a result

de•test \-'test\ *vb* : hate —**de•test•able** *adj* —**de•tes•ta•tion** \dē,tes'tāshan\ *n*

det•o•nate \'det³n,āt\ *vb* -**nat•ed; -nat•ing** : explode —**det•o•na•tion** \det³n'āshan\ *n* —**det•o•na•tor** \'det³n,ātər\ *n*

de•tour \'dē,tùr\ *n* : temporary indirect route —**detour** *vb*

de•tract \di'trakt\ *vb* : take away —**de•trac•tion** \-'trakshan\ *n* —**de•trac•tor** \-'traktər\ *n*

det•ri•ment \'detrəmənt\ *n* : damage —**det•ri•men•tal** \detrə'ment³l\ *adj* —**det•ri•men•tal•ly** *adv*

deuce \'düs, 'dyüs\ *n* **1** : 2 in cards or dice **2** : tie in tennis **3** : devil —used as an oath

deut•sche mark \'dȯicha-\ *n* : monetary unit of Germany

de•val•ue \dē'val,yü\ *vb* : reduce the value of —**de•val•u•a•tion** *n*

dev•as•tate \'devə,stāt\ *vb* -**tat•ed; -tat•ing** : ruin —**dev•as•ta•tion** \devə'stāshan\ *n*

de•vel•op \di'veləp\ *vb* **1** : grow, increase, or evolve gradually **2** : cause to grow, increase, or reach full potential —**de•vel•op•er** *n* —**de•vel•op•ment** *n* —**de•vel•op•men•tal** \-,veləp'ment³l\ *adj*

de•vi•ate \'dēvē,āt\ *vb* -**at•ed; -at•ing** : change esp. from a course or standard —**de•vi•ant** \-vēənt\ *adj or n* —**de•vi•ate** \-vēət, -vē,āt\ *n* —**de•vi•a•tion** \dēvē'āshan\ *n*

de•vice \di'vīs\ *n* **1** : specialized piece of equipment or tool **2** : design

dev•il \'devəl\ *n* **1** : personified supreme spirit of evil **2** : demon **3** : wicked person ~ *vb* -**iled** *or* -**illed; -il•ing** *or* -**il•ling 1** : season highly **2** : pester —**dev•il•ish** \'devəlish\ *adj* —**dev•il•ry** \'devəlrē\, **dev•il•try** \-trē\ *n*

de•vi•ous \'dēvēəs\ *adj* : tricky

de•vise \di'vīz\ *vb* -**vised; -vis•ing 1** : invent **2** : plot **3** : give by will

de•void \di'vȯid\ *adj* : entirely lacking

de•vote \di'vōt\ *vb* -**vot•ed; -vot•ing** : set apart for a special purpose

de•vot•ed *adj* : faithful

dev•o•tee \devə'tē, -'tā\ *n* : ardent follower

de•vo•tion \di'vōshan\ *n* **1** : prayer —usu. pl. **2** : loyalty and dedication —**de•vo•tion•al** \-shanal\ *adj*

de•vour \di'vaùr\ *vb* : consume ravenously —**de•vour•er** *n*

de•vout \di'vaùt\ *adj* **1** : devoted to religion **2** : serious —**de•vout•ly** *adv* —**de•vout•ness** *n*

dew \'dü, 'dyü\ *n* : moisture condensed at night —**dew•drop** *n* —**dewy** *adj*

dex•ter•ous \'dekstrəs\ *adj* : skillful with the hands —**dex•ter•i•ty** \dek'sterətē\ *n* —**dex•ter•ous•ly** *adv*

dex•trose \'dek,strōs\ *n* : plant or blood sugar

di•a•be•tes \,dīə'bētēz, -'bētəs\ *n* : disorder in which the body has too little insulin and too much sugar —**di•a•bet•ic** \-'betik\ *adj or n*

di•a•bol•ic \-'bälik\, **di•a•bol•i•cal** \-ikəl\ *adj* : fiendish

di•a•crit•ic \-'kritik\ *n* : mark accompanying a letter and indicating a specific sound value —**di•a•crit•i•cal** \-'kritikəl\ *adj*

di•ag•no•sis \,dīig'nōsəs, -əg-\ *n, pl* -**no•ses** \-,sēz\ : identifying of a disease from its symptoms —**di•ag•nose** \'dīig,nōs, -əg-\ *vb* —**di•ag•nos•tic** \,dīig'nästik, -əg-\ *adj*

di•ag•o•nal \dī'agənəl\ *adj* : extending from one corner to the opposite corner ~ *n* : diagonal line, direction, or arrangement —**di•ag•o•nal•ly** *adv*

di•a•gram \'dīə,gram\ *n* : explanatory drawing or plan ~ *vb* -**gramed** *or* -**grammed; -gram•ing** *or* -**gram•ming** : represent by a diagram —**di•a•gram•mat•ic** \,dīəgrə'matik\ *adj*

di•al \'dīəl\ *n* **1** : face of a clock, meter, or gauge **2** : control knob or wheel ~ *vb* -**aled** *or* -**alled; -al•ing** *or* -**al•ling 1** : turn a dial to call, operate, or select

di•a•lect \'dīə,lekt\ *n* : variety of language confined to a region or group

di•a•logue \-,lȯg\ *n* : conversation

di•am•e•ter \dī'amətər\ *n* **1** : straight line through the center of a circle **2** : thickness

di•a•met•ric \,dīə'metrik\, **di•a•met•ri•cal** \-trikəl\ *adj* : completely opposite —**di•a•met•ri•cal•ly** \-iklē\ *adv*

di•a•mond \'dīmənd, 'dīə-\ *n* **1** : hard brilliant mineral that consists of crystalline carbon **2** : flat figure having 4 equal sides, 2 acute angles, and 2 obtuse angles **3** : playing card of a suit marked with a red diamond **4** : baseball field

di•a•per \'dīpər\ *n* : baby's garment for receiving bodily wastes ~ *vb* : put a diaper on

di•a•phragm \'dīə,fram\ *n* **1** : sheet of muscle between the chest and abdominal cavity **2** : contraceptive device

di•ar•rhea \,dīə'rēə\ *n* : abnormally watery discharge from bowels

di•a•ry \'dīərē\ *n, pl* -**ries** : daily record of personal experiences —**di•a•rist** \'dīərist\ *n*

di•a•tribe \'dīə,trīb\ *n* : biting or abusive denunciation

dice \'dīs\ *n, pl* **dice** : die or a game played with dice ~ *vb* **diced; dic•ing** : cut into small cubes

dick•er \'dikər\ *vb* : bargain

dic•tate \'dik,tāt\ *vb* -**tat•ed; -tat•ing 1** : speak for a person or a machine to record **2** : command ~ *n* : order —**dic•ta•tion** \dik'tāshan\ *n*

dic•ta•tor \'dik,tātər\ *n* : person ruling absolutely and often brutally —**dic•ta•to•ri•al** \,diktə'tōrēəl\ *adj* —**dic•ta•tor•ship** \dik'tātər,ship, 'dik,-\ *n*

dic•tion \'dikshan\ *n* **1** : choice of the best word **2** : precise pronunciation

dic•tio•nary \-shə,nerē\ *n, pl* -**nar•ies** : reference book of words with information about their meanings

dic•tum \'diktəm\ *n, pl* -**ta** \-tə\ : authoritative or formal statement

did *past of* DO

di•dac•tic \dī'daktik\ *adj* : intended to teach a moral lesson

¹die \'dī\ *vb* **died; dy•ing** \'dīiŋ\ **1** : stop living **2** : pass out of existence **3** : stop or subside **4** : long

²die \'dī\ *n* **1** *pl* **dice** \'dīs\ : small marked cube used in gambling **2** *pl* **dies** \'dīz\ : form for stamping or cutting

die•sel \'dēzəl, -səl\ *n* : engine in which high compression causes ignition of the fuel

di•et \'dīət\ *n* : food and drink regularly consumed (as by a person) ~ *vb* : eat less or according to certain rules —**di•etary** \'dīə,terē\ *adj or n* —**di•et•er** *n*

di•e•tet•ics \,dīə'tetiks\ *n sing or pl* : science of nutrition —**di•e•tet•ic** *adj* —**di•e•ti•tian, di•e•ti•cian** \-'tishan\ *n*

dif•fer \'difər\ *vb* **1** : be unlike **2** : vary **3** : disagree —**dif•fer•ence** \'difrəns\ *n*

dif•fer•ent \-rənt\ *adj* : not the same —**dif•fer•ent•ly** *adv*

dif•fer•en•ti•ate \,difə'renchē,āt\ *vb* -**at•ed; -at•ing 1** : make or become different **2** : distinguish —**dif•fer•en•ti•a•tion** \-,renchē'āshan\ *n*

dif•fi•cult \'difi,kəlt\ *adj* : hard to do, understand, or deal with

dif•fi•cul•ty \-kəltē\ *n, pl* -**ties 1** : difficult nature **2** : great effort **3** : something hard to do, understand, or deal with

dif•fi•dent \'difədənt\ *adj* : reserved —**dif•fi•dence** \-əns\ *n*

dif•fuse \dif'yüs\ *adj* **1** : wordy **2** : not con-

de•cen•trated ~ \-'yüz\ *vb* -**fused; -fus•ing** : pour out or spread widely —**dif•fu•sion** \-'yüzhan\ *n*

dig \'dig\ *vb* **dug** \'dəg\; **dig•ging 1** : turn up soil **2** : hollow out or form by removing earth **3** : uncover by turning up earth ~ *n* **1** : thrust **2** : cutting remark —**dig in** *vb* **1** : establish a defensive position **2** : begin working or eating —**dig up** *vb* : discover

¹di•gest \'dī,jest\ *n* : body of information in shortened form

²di•gest \dī'jest, də-\ *vb* **1** : think over **2** : convert (food) into a form that can be absorbed **3** : summarize —**di•gest•ible** *adj* —**di•ges•tion** \-'jeschan\ *n* —**di•ges•tive** \-'jestiv\ *adj*

dig•it \'dijət\ *n* **1** : any of the figures 1 to 9 inclusive and usu. the symbol 0 **2** : finger or toe

dig•i•tal \-³l\ *adj* : providing information in numerical digits —**dig•i•tal•ly** *adv*

dig•ni•fy \'dignə,fī\ *vb* -**fied; -fy•ing** : give dignity or attention to

dig•ni•tary \-,terē\ *n, pl* -**taries** : person of high position

dig•ni•ty \'dignətē\ *n, pl* -**ties 1** : quality or state of being worthy or honored **2** : formal reserve (as of manner)

di•gress \dī'gres, də-\ *vb* : wander from the main subject —**di•gres•sion** \-'greshan\ *n*

dike \'dīk\ *n* : earth bank or dam

di•lap•i•dat•ed \də'lapə,dātəd\ *adj* : fallen into partial ruin —**di•lap•i•da•tion** \-,lapə'dāshan\ *n*

di•late \dī'lāt, 'dī,lāt\ *vb* -**lat•ed; -lat•ing** : swell or expand —**di•la•ta•tion** \,dilə'tāshan\ *n* —**di•la•tion** \dī'lāshan\ *n*

di•la•to•ry \'dilə,tōrē\ *adj* **1** : delaying **2** : tardy or slow

di•lem•ma \də'lemə\ *n* **1** : undesirable choice **2** : predicament

dil•et•tante \'dilə,tänt, -,tant; ,dilə'tänt, -'tant\ *n, pl* -**tantes** *or* -**tan•ti** \-'täntē, -'tantē\ : one who dabbles in a field of interest

dil•i•gent \'diləjənt\ *adj* : attentive and busy —**dil•i•gence** \-jəns\ *n* —**dil•i•gent•ly** *adv*

dill \'dil\ *n* : herb with aromatic leaves and seeds

dil•ly•dal•ly \'dilē,dalē\ *vb* : waste time by delay

di•lute \dī'lüt, də-\ *vb* -**lut•ed; -lut•ing** : lessen the consistency or strength of by mixing with something else ~ *adj* : weak —**di•lu•tion** \-'lüshan\ *n*

dim \'dim\ *adj* -**mm- 1** : not bright or distinct **2** : having no luster **3** : not seeing or understanding clearly —**dim** *vb* —**dim•ly** *adv* —**dim•mer** *n* —**dim•ness** *n*

dime \'dīm\ *n* : U.S. coin worth 1/10 dollar

di•men•sion \də'menchan, dī-\ *n* **1** : measurement of extension (as in length, height, or breadth) **2** : extent —**di•men•sion•al** \-'menchanal\ *adj*

di•min•ish \də'minish\ *vb* **1** : make less or cause to appear less **2** : dwindle

di•min•u•tive \də'minyətiv\ *adj* : extremely small

dim•ple \'dimpəl\ *n* : small depression esp. in the cheek or chin

din \'din\ *n* : loud noise

dine \'dīn\ *vb* **dined; din•ing** : eat dinner

din•er \'dīnər\ *n* **1** : person eating dinner **2** : railroad dining car or restaurant resembling one

din•ghy \'diŋē, -gē, -kē\ *n, pl* -**ghies** : small boat

din•gy \'dinjē\ *adj* -**gi•er; -est 1** : dirty **2** : shabby —**din•gi•ness** *n*

din•ner \'dinər\ *n* : main daily meal

di•no•saur \'dīnə,sȯr\ *n* : extinct often huge reptile

dint \'dint\ *n* : force—in the phrase *by dint of*

di•o•cese \'dīəsəs, -,sēz, -,sēs\ *n, pl* -**ces•es** \-əz; 'dīə,sēz\ : territorial jurisdiction of a bishop —**di•oc•e•san** \dī'äsəsən, ,dīə'sēz³n\ *adj or n*

dip \'dip\ *vb* -**pp- 1** : plunge into a liquid **2** : take out with a ladle **3** : lower and quickly raise again **4** : sink or slope downward suddenly ~ *n* **1** : plunge into water for sport **2** : sudden downward movement or incline —**dip•per** *n*

diph•the•ria \dif'thirēə\ *n* : acute contagious disease

diph•thong \'dif,thȯŋ\ *n* : two vowel sounds joined to form one speech sound (as *ou* in *out*)

di•plo•ma \də'plōmə\ *n, pl* -**mas** : record of graduation from a school

di•plo•ma•cy \-məsē\ *n* **1** : business of conducting negotiations between nations **2** : tact —**dip•lo•mat** \'diplə,mat\ *n* —**dip•lo•mat•ic** \,diplə'matik\ *adj*

dire \'dīr\ *adj* **dir•er; -est 1** : very horrible **2** : extreme

di•rect \də'rekt, dī-\ *vb* **1** : address **2** : cause to move or to follow a certain course **3** : show (someone) the way **4** : regulate the activities or course of **5** : request with authority ~ *adj* **1** : leading to or coming from a point without deviation or interruption 2 : frank —**direct** adv —**di•rect•ly** adv —**di•rect•ness** n —**di•rec•tor** \-tər\ n

direct current n : electric current flowing in one direction only

di•rec•tion \də'rekshən, dī-\ n 1 : supervision 2 : order 3 : course along which something moves —**di•rec•tion•al** \-shənəl\ adj

di•rec•tive \-tiv\ n : order

di•rec•to•ry \-tərē\ n, pl **-ries** : alphabetical list of names and addresses

dirge \'dərj\ n : funeral hymn

di•ri•gi•ble \'dirəjəbəl, də'rijə-\ n : airship

dirt \'dərt\ n 1 : mud, dust, or grime that makes something unclean 2 : soil

dirty \'dərtē\ adj **dirt•i•er; -est** 1 : not clean 2 : unfair 3 : indecent ~ vb **dirt•ied; dirty•ing** : make or become dirty —**dirt•i•ness** n

dis•able \dis'ābəl\ vb **-abled; -abling** : make unable to function —**dis•abil•i•ty** \,disə'bilətē\ n

dis•abuse \,disə'byüz\ vb : free from error or misconception

dis•ad•van•tage \,disəd'vantij\ n : something that hinders success —**dis•ad•van•ta•geous** adj

dis•af•fect \,disə'fekt\ vb : cause discontent in —**dis•af•fec•tion** n

dis•agree \,disə'grē\ vb 1 : fail to agree 2 : differ in opinion —**dis•agree•ment** n

dis•agree•able \-əbəl\ adj : unpleasant

dis•al•low \,disə'laú\ vb : refuse to admit or recognize

dis•ap•pear \,disə'pir\ vb 1 : pass out of sight 2 : cease to be —**dis•ap•pear•ance** n

dis•ap•point \,disə'póint\ vb : fail to fulfill the expectation or hope of —**dis•ap•point•ment** n

dis•ap•prove \-ə'prüv\ vb 1 : condemn or reject 2 : feel or express dislike or rejection —**dis•ap•prov•al** n —**dis•ap•prov•ing•ly** adv

dis•arm \dis'ärm\ vb 1 : take weapons from 2 : reduce armed forces 3 : make harmless or friendly —**dis•ar•ma•ment** \-'ärmə-mənt\ n

dis•ar•range \,disə'rānj\ vb : throw into disorder —**dis•ar•range•ment** n

dis•ar•ray \,disə'rā\ n : disorder

dis•as•ter \diz'astər, dis-\ n : sudden great misfortune —**dis•as•trous** \-'astrəs\ adj

dis•avow \,disə'vaú\ vb : deny responsibility for —**dis•avow•al** \-'vaúəl\ n

dis•band \dis'band\ vb : break up the organization of

dis•bar \dis'bär\ vb : expel from the legal profession —**dis•bar•ment** n

dis•be•lieve \,disbi'lēv\ vb : hold not worthy of belief —**dis•be•lief** n

dis•burse \dis'bərs\ vb **-bursed; -burs•ing** : pay out —**dis•burse•ment** n

disc var of DISK

dis•card \dis'kärd, 'dis,kärd\ vb : get rid of as unwanted —**dis•card** \'dis,kärd\ n

dis•cern \dis'ərn, diz-\ vb : discover with the eyes or the mind —**dis•cern•ible** adj —**dis•cern•ment** n

dis•charge \dis'chärj, 'dis,chärj\ vb 1 : unload 2 : shoot 3 : set free 4 : dismiss from service 5 : let go or let off 6 : give forth fluid ~ \'dis,-, dis'-\ n 1 : act of discharging 2 : a flowing out (as of blood) 3 : dismissal

dis•ci•ple \di'sīpəl\ n : one who helps spread another's teachings

dis•ci•pli•nar•i•an \,disəplə'nerēən\ n : one who enforces order

dis•ci•pline \'disəplən\ n 1 : field of study 2 : training that corrects, molds, or perfects 3 : punishment 4 : control gained by obedience or training ~ vb **-plined; -plin•ing** 1 : punish 2 : train in self-control —**dis•ci•plin•ary** \'disəplə,nerē\ adj

dis•claim \dis'klām\ vb : disavow

dis•close \-'klōz\ vb : reveal —**dis•clo•sure** \-'klōzhər\ n

dis•col•or \dis'kələr\ vb : change the color of esp. for the worse —**dis•col•or•ation** \dis,kələ'rāshən\ n

dis•com•fit \dis'kəmfət\ vb : upset —**dis•com•fi•ture** \dis'kəmfə,chúr\ n

dis•com•fort \dis'kəmfərt\ n : uneasiness

dis•con•cert \,diskən'sərt\ vb : upset

dis•con•nect \,diskə'nekt\ vb : undo the connection of

dis•con•so•late \dis'känsələt\ adj : hopelessly sad

dis•con•tent \,diskən'tent\ n : uneasiness of mind —**dis•con•tent•ed** adj

dis•con•tin•ue \,diskən'tinyü\ vb : end —**dis•con•tin•u•ance** n —**dis•con•ti•nu•i•ty** \dis,käntə'nüətē, -'nyü-\ n —**dis•con•tin•u•ous** \,diskən'tinyəwəs\ adj

dis•cord \'dis,kórd\ n : lack of harmony —**dis•cor•dant** \dis'kórdənt\ adj —**dis•cor•dant•ly** adv

dis•count \'dis,kaúnt\ n : reduction from a regular price ~ \'dis,-, dis'-\ vb 1 : reduce the amount of 2 : disregard —**discount** adj —**dis•count•er** n

dis•cour•age \dis'kərij\ vb **-aged; -ag•ing** 1 : deprive of courage, confidence, or enthusiasm 2 : dissuade —**dis•cour•age•ment** n

dis•course \'dis,kórs\ n 1 : conversation 2 : formal treatment of a subject ~ \dis'-\ vb **-coursed; -cours•ing** : talk at length

dis•cour•te•ous \dis'kərtēəs\ adj : lacking courtesy —**dis•cour•te•ous•ly** adv —**dis•cour•te•sy** n

dis•cov•er \dis'kəvər\ vb 1 : make known 2 : obtain the first sight or knowledge of 3 : find out —**dis•cov•er•er** n —**dis•cov•ery** \-ərē\ n

dis•cred•it \dis'kredət\ vb 1 : disbelieve 2 : destroy confidence in ~ n 1 : loss of reputation 2 : disbelief —**dis•cred•it•able** adj

dis•creet \dis'krēt\ adj : capable of keeping a secret —**dis•creet•ly** adv

dis•crep•an•cy \dis'krepənsē\ n, pl **-cies** : difference or disagreement

dis•crete \dis'krēt, 'dis,-\ adj : individually distinct

dis•cre•tion \dis'kreshən\ n 1 : discreet quality 2 : power of decision or choice —**dis•cre•tion•ary** adj

dis•crim•i•nate \dis'krimə,nāt\ vb **-nat•ed; -nat•ing** 1 : distinguish 2 : show favor or disfavor unjustly —**dis•crim•i•na•tion** \-,krimə'nāshən\ n —**dis•crim•i•na•to•ry** \-'krimənə,tōrē\ adj

dis•cur•sive \dis'kərsiv\ adj : passing from one topic to another —**dis•cur•sive•ly** adv —**dis•cur•sive•ness** n

dis•cus \'diskəs\ n, pl **-cus•es** : disk hurled for distance in a contest

dis•cuss \dis'kəs\ vb : talk about or present —**dis•cus•sion** \-'kəshən\ n

dis•dain \dis'dān\ n : feeling of contempt ~ vb : look upon or reject with disdain —**dis•dain•ful** \-fəl\ adj —**dis•dain•ful•ly** adv

dis•ease \di'zēz\ n : condition of a body that impairs its functioning —**dis•eased** \-'zēzd\ adj

dis•em•bark \,disəm'bärk\ vb : get off a ship —**dis•em•bar•ka•tion** \dis,em,bär'kāshən\ n

dis•em•bod•ied \,disəm'bädēd\ adj : having no substance or reality

dis•en•chant \,disən'chant\ vb : to free from illusion —**dis•en•chant•ment** n

dis•en•chant•ed \-'chantəd\ adj : disappointed

dis•en•gage \-ən'gāj\ vb : release —**dis•en•gage•ment** n

dis•en•tan•gle \-ən'taŋgəl\ vb : free from entanglement

dis•fa•vor \dis'fāvər\ n : disapproval

dis•fig•ure \dis'figyər\ vb : spoil the appearance of —**dis•fig•ure•ment** n

dis•fran•chise \dis'fran,chīz\ vb : deprive of the right to vote —**dis•fran•chise•ment** n

dis•gorge \dis'górj\ vb : spew forth

dis•grace \dis'grās\ vb : bring disgrace to ~ n 1 : shame 2 : cause of shame —**dis•grace•ful** \-fəl\ adj —**dis•grace•ful•ly** adv

dis•grun•tle \dis'grəntəl\ vb **-tled; -tling** : put in bad humor

dis•guise \dis'gīz\ vb **-guised; -guis•ing** : hide the true identity or nature of ~ n : something that conceals

dis•gust \dis'gəst\ n : strong aversion ~ vb : provoke disgust in —**dis•gust•ed•ly** adv —**dis•gust•ing•ly** adv

dish \'dish\ n 1 : vessel for serving food or the food it holds 2 : food prepared in a particular way ~ vb : put in a dish —**dish•cloth** n —**dish•rag** n —**dish•wash•er** n —**dish•wa•ter** n

dis•har•mo•ny \dis'härmənē\ n : lack of harmony —**dis•har•mo•ni•ous** \dishär-'mōnēəs\ adj

dis•heart•en \dis'härtən\ vb : discourage

di•shev•el \di'shevəl\ vb **-eled** or **-elled; -el•ing** or **-el•ling** : throw into disorder —**di•shev•eled, di•shev•elled** adj

dis•hon•est \dis'änəst\ adj : not honest —**dis•hon•est•ly** adv —**dis•hon•es•ty** n

dis•hon•or \dis'änər\ n or vb : disgrace —**dis•hon•or•able** adj —**dis•hon•or•ably** adv

dis•il•lu•sion \,disə'lüzhən\ vb : to free from illusion —**dis•il•lu•sion•ment** n

dis•in•cli•na•tion \,dis,inklə'nāshən\ n : slight aversion —**dis•in•cline** \,disən-'klīn\ vb

dis•in•fect \,disən'fekt\ vb : destroy disease germs in or on —**dis•in•fec•tant** \-'fektənt\ adj or n —**dis•in•fec•tion** \-'fekshən\ n

dis•in•gen•u•ous \,disən'jenyəwəs\ adj : lacking in candor

dis•in•her•it \,disən'herət\ vb : prevent from inheriting property

dis•in•te•grate \dis'intə,grāt\ vb : break into parts or small bits —**dis•in•te•gra•tion** \dis,intə'grāshən\ n

dis•in•ter•est•ed \dis'intərəstəd, -,res-\ adj 1 : not interested 2 : not prejudiced —**dis•in•ter•est•ed•ness** n

dis•joint•ed \dis'jóintəd\ adj 1 : separated at the joint 2 : incoherent

disk \'disk\ n : something round and flat

dis•like \dis'līk\ n : regard with dislike ~ n : feeling that something is unpleasant and to be avoided

dis•lo•cate \'dislō,kāt, dis'-\ vb : move out of the usual or proper place —**dis•lo•ca•tion** \dislō'kāshən\ n

dis•lodge \dis'läj\ vb : force out of a place

dis•loy•al \dis'lóiəl\ adj : not loyal —**dis•loy•al•ty** n

dis•mal \'dizməl\ adj : showing or causing gloom —**dis•mal•ly** adv

dis•man•tle \dis'mantəl\ vb **-tled; -tling** : take apart

dis•may \dis'mā\ n vb **-mayed; -may•ing** : discourage —**dismay** n

dis•mem•ber \dis'membər\ vb : cut into pieces —**dis•mem•ber•ment** n

dis•miss \dis'mis\ vb 1 : send away 2 : remove from service 3 : put aside or out of mind —**dis•miss•al** n

dis•mount \dis'maúnt\ vb 1 : get down from something 2 : take apart

dis•obey \,disə'bā\ vb : refuse to obey —**dis•obe•di•ence** \-'bēdēəns\ n —**dis•obe•di•ent** \-ənt\ adj

dis•or•der \dis'órdər\ n 1 : lack of order 2 : breach of public order 3 : abnormal state of body or mind —**disorder** vb —**dis•or•der•li•ness** n —**dis•or•der•ly** adj

dis•or•ga•nize \dis'órgə,nīz\ vb : throw into disorder —**dis•or•ga•ni•za•tion** n

dis•own \dis'ōn\ vb : repudiate

dis•par•age \dis'parij\ vb **-aged; -ag•ing** : say bad things about —**dis•par•age•ment** n

dis•pa•rate \dis'parət, 'dispərət\ adj : different in quality or character —**dis•par•i•ty** \dis'parətē\ n

dis•pas•sion•ate \dis'pashənət\ adj : not influenced by strong feeling —**dis•pas•sion•ate•ly** adv

dis•patch \dis'pach\ vb 1 : send 2 : kill 3 : attend to rapidly 4 : defeat ~ n 1 : message 2 : news item from a correspondent 3 : promptness and efficiency —**dis•patch•er** n

dis•pel \dis'pel\ vb **-ll-** : clear away

dis•pen•sa•ry \dis'pensərē\ n, pl **-ries** : place where medical or dental aid is provided

dis•pen•sa•tion \,dispən'sāshən\ n 1 : system of principles or rules 2 : exemption from a rule 3 : act of dispensing

dis•pense \dis'pens\ vb **-pensed; -pens•ing** 1 : portion out 2 : make up and give out (remedies) —**dis•pens•er** n —**dispense with** : do without

dis•perse \-'pərs\ vb **-persed; -pers•ing** : scatter —**dis•per•sal** \-'pərsəl\ n —**dis•per•sion** \-'perzhən\ n

dis•place \-'plās\ vb 1 : expel or force to flee from home or native land 2 : take the place of —**dis•place•ment** \-mənt\ n

dis•play \-'plā\ vb : present to view —**display** n

dis•please \-'plēz\ vb : arouse the dislike of —**dis•plea•sure** \-'plezhər\ n

dis•port \dis'pórt\ vb 1 : amuse 2 : frolic

dis•pose \dis'pōz\ vb **-posed; -pos•ing** 1 : give a tendency to 2 : settle —**dis•pos•able** \-'pōzəbəl\ adj —**dis•pos•al** \-'pōzəl\ n —**dis•pos•er** n —**dispose of** 1 : determine the fate, condition, or use of 2 : get rid of

dis•po•si•tion \,dispə'zishən\ n 1 : act or power of disposing of 2 : arrangement 3 : natural attitude

dis•pos•sess \,dispə'zes\ vb : deprive of possession or occupancy —**dis•pos•ses•sion** \-'zeshən\ n

dis•pro•por•tion \,disprə'pórshən\ n : lack of proportion —**dis•pro•por•tion•ate** \-shənət\ adj

dis•prove \dis'prüv\ vb : prove false —**dis•proof** n

dis•pute \dis'pyüt\ vb **-put•ed; -put•ing** 1 : argue 2 : deny the truth or rightness of 3 : struggle against or over ~ n : debate or quarrel —**dis•put•able** \-əbəl, dis'pyət-\ adj —**dis•pu•ta•tion** \dispyə'tā-shən\ n

dis•qual•i•fy \dis'kwälə,fī\ vb : make ineligible —**dis•qual•i•fi•ca•tion** n

dis•qui•et \dis'kwīət\ vb : make uneasy or restless ~ n : anxiety

dis•re•gard \disri'gärd\ vb : pay no attention to ~ n : neglect

dis•re•pair \disri'par\ n : need of repair

dis•rep•u•ta•ble \dis'repyətəbəl\ adj : having a bad reputation

dis•re•pute \disri'pyüt\ n : low regard

dis•re•spect \disri'spekt\ n : lack of respect —**dis•re•spect•ful** adj

dis•robe \dis'rōb\ vb : undress

dis•rupt \dis'rəpt\ vb : throw into disorder —**dis•rup•tion** \-'rəpshən\ n —**dis•rup•tive** \-'rəptiv\ adj

dis•sat•is•fac•tion \,dis,satəs'fakshən\ n : lack of satisfaction

dis•sat•is•fy \dis'satəs,fī\ vb : fail to satisfy

dis•sect \di'sekt\ vb 1 : cut into parts esp. to examine —**dis•sec•tion** n

dis•sem•ble \di'sembəl\ vb **-bled; -bling** : disguise feelings or intention —**dis•sem•bler** n

dis•sem•i•nate \di'semə,nāt\ vb **-nat•ed; -nat•ing** : spread around —**dis•sem•i•na•tion** \-,semə'nāshən\ n

dis•sen•sion \di'senchən\ n : discord

dis•sent \di'sent\ vb : object or disagree ~ n : difference of opinion —**dis•sent•er** n —**dis•sen•tient** \-'senchənt\ adj or n

dis•ser•ta•tion \,disər'tāshən\ n : long written study of a subject

dis•ser•vice \dis'sərvəs\ n : injury

dis•si•dent \'disədənt\ n : one who differs openly with an establishment —**dis•si•dence** \-əns\ n —**dissident** adj

dis•sim•i•lar \di'simələr\ adj : different —**dis•sim•i•lar•i•ty** \di,simə'larətē\ n

dis•si•pate \'disə,pāt\ vb **-pat•ed; -pat•ing** 1 : break up and drive off 2 : squander —**dis•si•pa•tion** \,disə'pāshən\ n

dis•so•ci•ate \di'ōsē,āt, -shē-\ vb **-at•ed; -at•ing** : separate from association —**dis•so•ci•a•tion** \dis,ōsē'āshən, -shē-\ n

dis•so•lute \'disə,lüt\ adj : loose in morals or conduct

dis•so•lu•tion \,disə'lüshən\ n : act or process of dissolving

dis•solve \di'zälv\ vb 1 : break up or bring to an end 2 : pass or cause to pass into solution

dis•so•nance \'disənəns\ n : discord —**dis•so•nant** \-nənt\ adj

dis•suade \di'swād\ vb **-suad•ed; -suad•ing** : persuade not to do something —**dis•sua•sion** \-'swāzhən\ n

dis•tance \'distəns\ n 1 : measure of separation in space or time 2 : reserve

dis•tant \-tənt\ adj 1 : separate in space 2 : remote in time, space, or relationship 3 : reserved —**dis•tant•ly** adv

dis•taste \dis'tāst\ n : dislike —**dis•taste•ful** adj

dis•tem•per \dis'tempər\ n : serious virus disease of dogs

dis•tend \dis'tend\ vb : swell out —**disten•sion, dis•ten•tion** \-'tenchən\ n

dis•till \di'stil\ vb : obtain by distillation —**dis•til•late** \'distə,lāt, -lət\ n —**dis•till•er** n —**dis•till•ery** \di'stilərē\ n

dis•til•la•tion \,distə'lāshən\ n : purification of liquid by evaporating then condensing

dis•tinct \dis'tiŋkt\ adj 1 : distinguishable from others 2 : readily discerned —**dis•tinc•tive** \-tiv\ adj —**dis•tinc•tive•ly** adv —**dis•tinc•tive•ness** n —**dis•tinct•ly** adv —**dis•tinct•ness** n

dis•tinc•tion \di'tiŋkshən\ n 1 : act of distinguishing 2 : difference 3 : special recognition

dis•tin•guish \-'tiŋgwish\ vb 1 : perceive as different 2 : set apart 3 : discern 4 : make outstanding —**dis•tin•guish•able** adj —**dis•tin•guished** \-gwisht\ adj

dis•tort \dis'tórt\ vb 1 : twist out of shape, condition, or true meaning —**dis•tor•tion** \-'tórshən\ n

dis•tract \di'strakt\ vb : divert the mind or attention of —**dis•trac•tion** \-'strakshən\ n

dis•traught \di'strót\ adj : agitated with mental conflict

dis•tress \-'tres\ n 1 : suffering 2 : misfortune 3 : state of danger or great need ~ vb : subject to strain or distress —**dis•tress•ful** adj

dis•trib•ute \-'tribyət\ vb **-ut•ed; -ut•ing** 1 : divide among many 2 : spread or hand out —**dis•tri•bu•tion** \distrə'byüshən\ n —**dis•trib•u•tive** \dis'tribyətiv\ adj —**dis•trib•u•tor** \-ər\ n

dis•trict \'dis,trikt\ n : territorial division

dis•trust \dis'trəst\ vb or n : mistrust —**dis•trust•ful** \-fəl\ adj

dis•turb \dis'tərb\ vb 1 : interfere with 2 : destroy the peace, composure, or order of —**dis•tur•bance** \-'tərbəns\ n —**dis•turb•er** n

dis•use \dis'yüs\ n : lack of use

ditch \'dich\ n : trench ~ vb 1 : dig a ditch in 2 : get rid of

dith•er \'dithər\ n : highly nervous or excited state

dit•to \'ditō\ n, pl **-tos** : more of the same

dit•ty \'ditē\ n, pl **-ties** : short simple song

di•uret•ic \,dīyü'retik\ adj : tending to increase urine flow —**diuretic** n

di•ur•nal \dī'ərnəl\ adj 1 : daily 2 : of or occurring in the daytime

di•van \dī,van, di'-\ n : couch

dive \'dīv\ vb **dived** or **dove** \'dōv\; **dived; div•ing** 1 : plunge into water headfirst 2 : submerge 3 : descend quickly ~ n 1 : act of diving 2 : sharp decline —**div•er** n

di•verge \də'vərj, dī-\ vb **-verged; -verg•ing** 1 : move in different directions 2 : differ —**di•ver•gence** \-'vərjəns\ n —**di•ver•gent** \-jənt\ adj

di•vers \'dīvərz\ adj : various

di•verse \dī'vərs, də-, 'dī,vərs\ adj : involving different forms —**di•ver•si•fi•ca•tion** \də,vərsəfə'kāshən, dī-\ n —**di•ver•si•fy** \-'vərsə,fī\ vb —**di•ver•si•ty** \-sətē\ n

di•vert \də'vərt, dī-\ vb 1 : turn from a

course or purpose 2 : distract 3 : amuse —di•ver•sion \-'vərzhən\ n

di•vest \dī'vest, də-\ vb : strip of clothing, possessions, or rights

di•vide \də'vīd\ vb -vid•ed; -vid•ing 1 : separate 2 : distribute 3 : share 4 : subject to mathematical division ~ n : watershed —di•vid•er n

div•i•dend \'divə,dend\ n 1 : individual share 2 : bonus 3 : number to be divided

div•i•na•tion \,divə'nāshən\ n : practice of trying to foretell future events

di•vine \də'vīn\ adj -vin•er; -est 1 : relating to or being God or a god 2 : supremely good ~ n : clergy member ~ vb -vined; -vin•ing 1 : infer 2 : prophesy —di•vine•ly adv —di•vin•er n —di•vin•i•ty \də'vinətē\ n

di•vis•i•ble \-'vizəbəl\ adj : capable of being divided —di•vis•i•bil•i•ty \-,vizə'bilatē\ n

di•vi•sion \-'vizhən\ n 1 : distribution 2 : part of a whole 3 : disagreement 4 : process of finding out how many times one number is contained in another

di•vi•sive \-'vīsiv, -'vi-, -ziv\ adj : creating dissension

di•vi•sor \-'vīzər\ n : number by which a dividend is divided

di•vorce \də'vōrs\ n : legal breaking up of a marriage —divorce vb

di•vor•cée \-,vōr'sā, -'sē\ n : divorced woman

di•vulge \də'vəlj, dī-\ vb -vulged; -vulg•ing : reveal

diz•zy \'dizē\ adj -zi•er; -est 1 : having a sensation of whirling 2 : causing or caused by giddiness —diz•zi•ly adv —diz•zi•ness n

DNA \,dē,en'ā\ n : compound in cell nuclei that is the basis of heredity

do \'dü\ vb did \'did\; done \'dən\ do•ing \'düiŋ\; does \'dəz\ 1 : work to accomplish (an action or task) 2 : behave 3 : prepare or fix up 4 : fare 5 : finish 6 : serve the needs or purpose of 7 —used as an auxiliary verb —do away with 1 : get rid of 2 : destroy —do by : deal with —do•er \'düər\ n —do in vb 1 : ruin 2 : kill

doc•ile \'däsəl\ adj : easily managed —do•cil•i•ty \dä'silətē\ n

1dock \'däk\ vb 1 : shorten 2 : reduce

2dock n 1 : berth between 2 piers to receive ships 2 : loading wharf or platform ~ vb : bring or come into dock —dock•work•er n

3dock n : place in a court for a prisoner

dock•et \'däkət\ n 1 : record of the proceedings in a legal action 2 : list of legal causes to be tried —docket vb

doc•tor \'däktər\ n 1 : person holding one of the highest academic degrees 2 : one (as a surgeon) skilled in healing arts ~ vb 1 : give medical treatment to 2 : repair or alter —doc•tor•al \-tərəl\ adj

doc•trine \'däktrən\ n : something taught —doc•tri•nal \-trənᵊl\ adj

doc•u•ment \'däkyəmənt\ n : paper that furnishes information or legal proof —doc•u•ment \-,ment\ vb —doc•u•men•ta•tion \,däkyəmən'tāshən\ n

doc•u•men•ta•ry \,däkyə'mentərē\ adj 1 : of or relating to documents 2 : giving a factual presentation —documentary n

dod•der \'dädər\ vb : become feeble usu. from age

dodge \'däj\ vb dodged; dodg•ing 1 : move quickly aside or out of the way of 2 : evade —dodge n

do•do \'dōdō\ n, pl -does or -dos 1 : heavy flightless extinct bird 2 : stupid person

doe \'dō\ n, pl does or doe : adult female deer —doe•skin \-,skin\ n

does pres 3d sing of DO

doff \'däf\ vb : remove

dog \'dog\ n : flesh-eating domestic mammal ~ vb 1 : hunt down or track like a hound 2 : harass —dog•catch•er n —dog•gy \-ē\ n —dog•house n

dog-ear \'dog,ir\ n : turned-down corner of a page —dog-ear vb —dog-eared \-,ird\ adj

dog•ged \'dogəd\ adj : stubbornly determined

dog•ma \'dogmə\ n : tenet or code of tenets

dog•ma•tism \-,tizəm\ n : unwarranted stubbornness of opinion —dog•mat•ic \dog'matik\ adj

dog•wood n : flowering tree

doi•ly \'doilē\ n, pl -lies : small decorative mat

do•ings \'düiŋz\ n pl : events

dol•drums \'dōldrəmz,'däl-\ n pl : spell of listlessness, despondency, or stagnation

dole \'dōl\ n : distribution esp. of money to the needy or unemployed —dole out 1 : give out esp. in small portions

dole•ful \'dōlfəl\ adj : sad —dole•ful•ly adv

doll \'däl, 'dol\ n : small figure of a person used esp. as a child's toy

dol•lar \'dälər\ n : any of various basic monetary units (as in the U.S. and Canada)

dol•ly \'dälē\ n, pl -lies : small cart or wheeled platform

dol•phin \'dälfən\ n 1 : sea mammal related to the whales 2 : saltwater food fish

dolt \'dōlt\ n : stupid person —dolt•ish adj

-dom \dəm\ n suffix 1 : office or realm 2 : state or fact of being 3 : those belonging to a group

do•main \dō'mān, də-\ n 1 : territory over which someone reigns 2 : sphere of activity or knowledge

dome \'dōm\ n 1 : large hemispherical roof 2 : roofed stadium

do•mes•tic \də'mestik\ adj 1 : relating to the household or family 2 : relating and limited to one's own country 3 : tame ~ n : household servant —do•mes•ti•cal•ly \-tiklē\ adv

do•mes•ti•cate \-ti,kāt\ vb -cat•ed; -cat•ing : tame —do•mes•ti•ca•tion \-,mesti-'kāshən\ n

dom•i•cile \'dämə,sīl, 'dō-; 'däməsəl\ n : home —domicile vb

dom•i•nance \'dämənəns\ n : control —dom•i•nant \-nənt\ adj

dom•i•nate \-,nāt\ vb -nat•ed; -nat•ing 1 : have control over 2 : rise high above —dom•i•na•tion \,dämə'nāshən\ n

dom•i•neer \,dämə'nir\ vb : exercise arbitrary control

do•min•ion \də'minyən\ n 1 : supreme authority 2 : governed territory

dom•i•no \'dämə,nō\ n, pl -noes or -nos : flat rectangular block used as a piece in a game (dominoes)

don \'dän\ vb -nn- : put on (clothes)

do•nate \'dō,nāt\ vb -nat•ed; -nat•ing : make a gift of —do•na•tion \dō'nāshən\ n

1done \'dən\ past part of DO

2done adj 1 : finished or ended 2 : cooked sufficiently

don•key \'däŋkē, 'dəŋ-\ n, pl -keys : sturdy domestic ass

do•nor \'dōnər\ n : one that gives

doo•dle \'düdᵊl\ vb -dled; -dling : draw or scribble aimlessly —doodle n

doom \'düm\ n 1 : judgment 2 : fate 3 : ruin —doom vb

door \'dōr\ n : passage for entrance or a movable barrier that can open or close such a passage —door•jamb n —door•knob n —door•mat n —door•step n —door•way n

dope \'dōp\ n 1 : narcotic preparation 2 : stupid person 3 : information ~ vb : doped; dop•ing : drug

dor•mant \'dormənt\ adj : not actively growing or functioning —dor•man•cy \-mənsē\ n

dor•mer \'dormər\ n : window built upright in a sloping roof

dor•mi•to•ry \'dormə,tōrē\ n, pl -ries : residence hall (as at a college)

dor•mouse \'dor,maus\ n : squirrellike rodent

dor•sal \'dorsəl\ adj : relating to or on the back —dor•sal•ly adv

do•ry \'dōrē\ n, pl -ries : flat-bottomed boat

dose \'dōs\ n : quantity (as of medicine) taken at one time ~ vb dosed; dosing : give medicine to —dos•age \'dōsij\ n

dot \'dät\ n 1 : small spot 2 : small round mark made with or as if with a pen ~ vb -tt- : mark with dots

dot•age \'dōtij\ n : senility

dote \'dōt\ vb dot•ed; dot•ing 1 : act feebleminded 2 : be foolishly fond

dou•ble \'dəbəl\ adj 1 : consisting of 2 members or parts 2 : being twice as great or as many 3 : folded in two ~ n 1 : something twice another 2 : one that resembles another ~ adv : doubly ~ vb -bled; -bling 1 : make or become twice as great 2 : fold or bend 3 : clench

dou•ble-cross vb : deceive by trickery —dou•ble-cross•er n

dou•bly \'dəblē\ adv : to twice the degree

doubt \'daut\ vb 1 : be uncertain about 2 : mistrust 3 : consider unlikely ~ n 1 : uncertainty 2 : mistrust 3 : inclination not to believe —doubt•ful \-fəl\ adj —doubt•ful•ly adv —doubt•less \-ləs\ adv

douche \'düsh\ n : jet of fluid for cleaning a body part

dough \'dō\ n : stiff mixture of flour and liquid —doughy \'dōē\ adj

dough•nut \-,nət\ n : small fried ring-shaped cake

dough•ty \'dautē\ adj -ti•er; -est : able, strong, or valiant

dour \'daur, 'dur\ adj 1 : severe 2 : gloomy or sullen —dour•ly adv

douse \'daus, 'dauz\ vb doused; dous•ing 1 : plunge into or drench with water 2 : extinguish

1dove \'dəv\ n : small wild pigeon

2dove \'dōv\ past of DIVE

dove•tail \'dəv,tāl\ vb : fit together neatly

dow•a•ger \'dauijər\ n 1 : widow with wealth or a title 2 : dignified elderly woman

dowdy \'daudē\ adj dowd•i•er; -est : lacking neatness and charm

dow•el \'dauəl\ n 1 : peg used for fastening two pieces 2 : wooden rod

dow•er \'dauər\ n : property given a widow for life ~ vb : supply with a dower

1down \'daun\ adv 1 : toward or in a lower position or state 2 : to a lying or sitting position 3 : as a cash deposit 4 : on paper ~ adj 1 : lying on the ground 2 : directed or going downward 3 : being at a low level~ prep : toward the bottom of ~ vb 1 : cause to go down 2 : defeat

2down n : fluffy feathers

down•cast adj 1 : sad 2 : directed down

down•fall n : ruin or cause of ruin

down•grade n : downward slope ~ vb : lower in grade or position

down•heart•ed adj : sad

down•pour n : heavy rain

down•right adv : thoroughly ~ adj : absolute or thorough

downs \'daunz\ n pl : rolling treeless uplands

down•size \'daun,sīz\ vb : reduce in size

down•stairs adv : on or to a lower floor and esp. the main floor —downstairs adj or n

down–to–earth adj : practical

down•town adv : to, toward, or in the business center of a town —downtown n or adj

down•trod•den \'daun,trädᵊn\ adj : suffering oppression

down•ward \'daunwərd\, down•wards \-wərdz\ adv : to a lower place or condition —downward adj

down•wind adv or adj : in the direction the wind is blowing

downy \'daunē\ adj -i•er; -est : resembling or covered with down

dow•ry \'daurē\ n, pl -ries : property a woman gives her husband in marriage

dox•ol•o•gy \däk'säləjē\ n, pl -gies : hymn of praise to God

doze \'dōz\ vb dozed; doz•ing : sleep lightly —doze n

doz•en \'dəzᵊn\ n, pl -ens or -en : group of 12 —doz•enth \-ᵊnth\ adj

drab \'drab\ adj -bb- : dull —drab•ly adv —drab•ness n

dra•co•ni•an \drā'kōnēən, dra-\ adj, often cap : harsh, cruel

draft \'draft, 'dráft\ n 1 : act of drawing or hauling 2 : act of drinking 3 : amount drunk at once 4 : preliminary outline or rough sketch 5 : selection from a pool or the selection process 6 : order for the payment of money 7 : air current ~ vb 1 : select usu. on a compulsory basis 2 : make a preliminary sketch, version, or plan of ~ adj : drawn from a container —draft•ee \draf'tē, dráf-\ n —drafty \'draftē\ adj

drafts•man \'draftsmən, 'dráft-\ : person who draws plans

drag \'drag\ n 1 : something dragged over a surface or through water 2 : something that hinders progress or is boring 3 : act or an instance of dragging ~ vb -gg- 1 : haul 2 : move or work with difficulty 3 : pass slowly 4 : search or fish with a drag —drag•ger n

drag•net \-,net\ n 1 : trawl 2 : planned actions for finding a criminal

drag•on \'dragən\ n : fabled winged serpent

drag•on•fly n : large 4-winged insect

drain \'drān\ vb 1 : draw off or flow off gradually or completely 2 : exhaust ~ n : means or act of draining —drain•age \-ij\ n —drain•er n —drain•pipe n

drake \'drāk\ n : male duck

dra•ma \'drämə, 'dram-\ n 1 : composition for theatrical presentation esp. on a serious subject 2 : series of events involving conflicting forces —dra•mat•ic \drə'matik\ adj —dra•mat•i•cal•ly \-iklē\ adv —dram•a•tist \'dramətist, 'dräm-\ n —dram•a•ti•za•tion \,dramətə'zāshən, ,dräm-\ n —dra•ma•tize \'dramə,tīz, 'dräm-\ vb

drank past of DRINK

drape \'drāp\ vb draped; drap•ing 1 : cover or adorn with folds of cloth 2 : cause to hang in flowing lines or folds ~ n : curtain

drap•ery \'drāpərē\ n, pl -er•ies : decorative fabric hung esp. as a heavy curtain

dras•tic \'drastik\ adj : extreme or harsh —dras•ti•cal•ly \-tiklē\ adv

draught \'draft\, draughty \'draftē\ chiefly Brit var of DRAFT, DRAFTY

draw \'dro\ vb drew \'drü\; drawn \'dron\; draw•ing 1 : move or cause to move (as by pulling) 2 : attract or provoke 3 : extract 4 : take or receive (as money) 5 : bend a bow in preparation for shooting 6 : leave a contest undecided 7 : sketch 8 : write out 9 : deduce ~ n 1 : act, process, or result of drawing 2 : tie —draw out 1 : cause to speak candidly —draw up 1 : write out 2 : pull oneself erect 3 : bring or come to a stop

draw•back n : disadvantage

draw•bridge n : bridge that can be raised

draw•er \'dror, 'dróər\ n 1 : one that draws 2 : sliding boxlike compartment 3 pl : underpants

draw•ing \'droiŋ\ n 1 : occasion of choosing by lot 2 : act or art of making a figure, plan, or sketch with lines 3 : something drawn

drawl \'drol\ vb : speak slowly —drawl n

dread \'dred\ vb : feel extreme fear or reluctance ~ n : great fear ~ adj : causing dread —dread•ful \-fəl\ adj —dread•ful•ly adv

dream \'drēm\ n 1 : series of thoughts or visions during sleep 2 : dreamlike vision 3 : something notable 4 : ideal ~ vb dreamed \'dremt, 'drēmd\ or dreamt \'dremt\ dream•ing 1 : have a dream 2 : imagine —dream•er n —dream•like adj —dreamy adj

drea•ry \'drirē\ adj -ri•er; -est : dismal —drea•ri•ly \'drirəlē\ adv

1dredge \'drej\ n : machine for removing earth esp. from under water ~ vb dredged; dredg•ing 1 : dig up or search with a dredge —dredg•er n

2dredge vb dredged; dredg•ing : coat (food) with flour

dregs \'dregz\ n pl 1 : sediment 2 : most worthless part

drench \'drench\ vb : wet thoroughly

dress \'dres\ vb 1 : put clothes on 2 : decorate 3 : prepare (as a carcass) for use 4 : apply dressings, remedies, or fertilizer to ~ n 1 : apparel 2 : single garment of bodice and skirt ~ adj : suitable for a formal event —dress•mak•er n —dress•mak•ing n

dress•er \'dresər\ n : bureau with a mirror

dress•ing n 1 : act or process of dressing 2 : sauce or a seasoned mixture 3 : material to cover an injury

dressy \'dresē\ adj dress•i•er; -est 1 : showy in dress 2 : stylish

drew past of DRAW

drib•ble \'dribəl\ vb -bled; -bling 1 : fall or flow in drops 2 : drool —dribble n

drier comparative of DRY

driest superlative of DRY

drift \'drift\ n 1 : motion or course of something drifting 2 : mass piled up by wind 3 : general intention or meaning ~ vb 1 : float or be driven along (as by a current) 2 : wander without purpose 3 : pile up under force —drift•er n —drift•wood n

1drill \'dril\ vb 1 : bore with a drill 2 : instruct by repetition ~ n 1 : tool for boring holes 2 : regularly practiced exercise —drill•er n

2drill n : seed-planting implement

3drill n : twill-weave cotton fabric

drily var of DRYLY

drink \'driŋk\ vb drank \'draŋk\; drunk \'drəŋk\ or drank; drink•ing 1 : swallow liquid 2 : absorb 3 : drink alcoholic beverages esp. to excess ~ n 1 : beverage 2 : alcoholic liquor —drink•able adj —drink•er n

drip \'drip\ vb -pp- : fall or let fall in drops ~ n 1 : a dripping 2 : sound of falling drops

drive \'drīv\ vb drove \'drōv\; driv•en \'drivən\; driv•ing 1 : urge or force onward 2 : direct the movement or course of 3 : compel 4 : cause to become 5 : propel forcefully ~ n 1 : trip in a vehicle 2 : intensive campaign 3 : aggressive or dynamic quality 4 : basic need —driv•er n

drive-in adj : accommodating patrons in cars —drive-in n

driv•el \'drivəl\ vb -eled or -elled; -el•ing or -el•ling 1 : drool 2 : talk stupidly ~ n : nonsense

drive•way n : usu. short private road from the street to a house

driz•zle \'drizəl\ n : fine misty rain —drizzle vb

droll \'drōl\ adj : humorous or whimsical —droll•ery \-ərē\ n

drom•e•dary \'drämə,derē\ n, pl -dar•ies : speedy one-humped camel

drone \'drōn\ n 1 : male honeybee 2 : deep hum or buzz ~ vb droned; dron•ing : make a dull monotonous sound

drool \'drül\ vb : let liquid run from the mouth

droop \'drüp\ vb 1 : hang or incline downward 2 : lose strength or spirit —droop n —droopy \-ē\ adj

drop \'dräp\ n 1 : quantity of fluid in one spherical mass 2 pl : medicine used by drops 3 : decline or fall 4 : distance something drops ~ vb -pp- 1 : fall in drops 2 : let fall 3 : convey 4 : go lower or become less strong or less active —drop•let \-lət\ n —drop back vb : move toward the rear —drop behind : fail to keep up —drop in vb : pay an unexpected visit

drop•per n : device that dispenses liquid by drops

drop•sy \'dräpsē\ n : edema

dross \'dräs\ n : waste matter

drought \'draut\ n : long dry spell

1drove \'drōv\ *n* : crowd of moving people or animals

2drove *past of* DRIVE

drown \'draùn\ *vb* 1 : suffocate in water 2 : overpower or become overpowered

drowse \'draùz\ *vb* **drowsed; drows•ing** : doze —**drowse** *n*

drowsy \'draùzē\ *adj* **drows•i•er; -est** : sleepy —**drows•i•ly** *adv* —**drows•i•ness** *n*

drub \'drəb\ *vb* **-bb-** : beat severely

drudge \'drəj\ *vb* **drudged; drudg•ing** : do hard or boring work —**drudge** *n* —**drudg•ery** \-ərē\ *n*

drug \'drəg\ *n* 1 : substance used as or in medicine 2 : narcotic ~ *vb* **-gg-** : affect with drugs —**drug•gist** \-ist\ *n* —**drug•store** *n*

dru•id \'drüəd\ *n* : ancient Celtic priest

drum \'drəm\ *n* 1 : musical instrument that is a skin-covered cylinder beaten usu. with sticks 2 : drum-shaped object (as a container) ~ *vb* **-mm-** 1 : beat a drum 2 : drive, force, or bring about by steady effort —**drum•beat** *n* —**drum•mer** *n*

drum•stick *n* 1 : stick for beating a drum 2 : lower part of a fowl's leg

drunk \'drəŋk\ *adj* : having the faculties impaired by alcohol ~ *n* : one who is drunk —**drunk•ard** \'drəŋkərd\ *n* —**drunk•en** \-kən\ *adj* —**drunk•en•ly** *adv* —**drunk•en•ness** *n*

dry \'drī\ *adj* **dri•er** \'drīər\; **dri•est** \'drīəst\ 1 : lacking water or moisture 2 : thirsty 3 : marked by the absence of alcoholic beverages 4 : uninteresting 5 : not sweet ~ *vb* **dried; dry•ing** : make or become dry —**dry•ly** *adv* —**dry•ness** *n*

dry–clean *vb* : clean (fabrics) chiefly with solvents other than water —**dry cleaning** *n*

dry•er \'drīər\ *n* : device for drying

dry goods *n pl* : textiles, clothing, and notions

dry ice *n* : solid carbon dioxide

du•al \'düəl, 'dyü-\ *adj* : twofold —**du•al•ism** \-ə,lizəm\ *n* —**du•al•i•ty** \dü'alətē, dyü-\ *n*

dub \'dəb\ *vb* **-bb-** : name

du•bi•ous \'dübēəs, 'dyü-\ *adj* 1 : uncertain 2 : questionable —**du•bi•ous•ly** *adv* —**du•bi•ous•ness** *n*

du•cal \'dükəl, 'dyü-\ *adj* : relating to a duke or dukedom

duch•ess \'dəchəs\ *n* 1 : wife of a duke 2 : woman holding a ducal title

duchy \-ē\ *n, pl* **-ies** : territory of a duke or duchess

1duck \'dək\ *n, pl* : swimming bird related to the goose and swan ~ *vb* 1 : thrust or plunge under water 2 : lower the head or body suddenly 3 : evade —**duck•ling** \-liŋ\ *n*

2duck *n* : cotton fabric

duct \'dəkt\ *n* : canal for conveying a fluid —**duct•less** \-ləs\ *adj*

duc•tile \'dəktəl\ *adj* : able to be drawn out or shaped —**duc•til•i•ty** \,dək'tilətē\ *n*

dude \'düd, 'dyüd\ *n* 1 : dandy 2 : guy

dud•geon \'dəjən\ *n* : ill humor

due \'dü, 'dyü\ *adj* 1 : owed 2 : appropriate 3 : attributable 4 : scheduled ~ *n* 1 : something due 2 *pl* : fee ~ *adv* : directly

du•el \'düəl\ *n* : combat between 2 persons —**duel** *vb* —**du•el•ist** *n*

du•et \dü'et, dyü-\ *n* : musical composition for 2 performers

due to *prep* : because of

dug *past of* DIG

dug•out \'dəg,aùt\ *n* 1 : boat made by hollowing out a log 2 : shelter made by digging

duke \'dük, 'dyük\ *n* : nobleman of the highest rank —**duke•dom** *n*

dull \'dəl\ *adj* 1 : mentally slow 2 : blunt 3 : not brilliant or interesting —**dull** *vb* —**dul•lard** \'dələrd\ *n* —**dull•ness** *n* —**dul•ly** *adv*

du•ly \'dülē, 'dyü-\ *adv* : in a due manner or time

dumb \'dəm\ *adj* 1 : mute 2 : stupid —**dumb•ly** *adv*

dumb•bell \'dəm,bel\ *n* 1 : short bar with weights on the ends used for exercise 2 : stupid person

dumb•found, dum•found \,dəm'faùnd\ *vb* : amaze

dum•my \'dəmē\ *n, pl* **-mies** 1 : stupid person 2 : imitative substitute

dump \'dəmp\ *vb* : let fall in a pile ~ *n* : place for dumping something (as refuse) —**in the dumps** : sad

dump•ling \'dəmpliŋ\ *n* : small mass of boiled or steamed dough

dumpy \'dəmpē\ *adj* **dump•i•er; -est** : short and thick in build

1dun \'dən\ *adj* : brownish gray

2dun *vb* **-nn-** : hound for payment of a debt

dunce \'dəns\ *n* : stupid person

dune \'dün, 'dyün\ *n* : hill of sand

dung \'dəŋ\ *n* : manure

dun•ga•ree \,dəŋgə'rē\ *n* 1 : blue denim 2 *pl* : work clothes made of dungaree

dun•geon \'dənjən\ *n* : underground prison

dunk \'dəŋk\ *vb* : dip or submerge temporarily in liquid

duo \'düō, 'dyüō\ *n, pl* **du•os** : pair

du•o•de•num \,düə'dēnəm, ,dyü-; dù'ädənəm, dyü-\ *n, pl* **-na** \-'dēnə, -ənə\ *or* **-nums** : part of the small intestine nearest the stomach —**du•o•de•nal** \-'dēnəl, -ənəl\ *adj*

dupe \'düp, dyüp\ *n* : one easily deceived or cheated —**dupe** *vb*

du•plex \'dü,pleks, 'dyü-\ *adj* : double ~ *n* : 2-family house

du•pli•cate \'düplikət, 'dyü-\ *adj* 1 : consisting of 2 identical items 2 : being just like another ~ *n* : exact copy ~ \-,kāt\ *vb* **-cat•ed; -cat•ing** 1 : make an exact copy of 2 : repeat or equal —**du•pli•ca•tion** \,düpli'kāshən, ,dyü-\ *n* —**du•pli•ca•tor** \'düpli,kātər, dyü-\ *n*

du•plic•i•ty \dù'plisətē, ,dyü-\ *n, pl* **-ties** : deception

du•ra•ble \'dùrəbəl, 'dyùr-\ *adj* : lasting a long time —**du•ra•bil•i•ty** \,dùrə'bilətē, ,dyùr-\ *n*

du•ra•tion \dù'rāshən, dyü-\ *n* : length of time something lasts

du•ress \dù'res, dyü-\ *n* : coercion

dur•ing \'dùriŋ, 'dyùr-\ *prep* 1 : throughout 2 : at some point in

dusk \'dəsk\ *n* : twilight —**dusky** *adj*

dust \'dəst\ *n* : powdered matter ~ *vb* 1 : remove dust from 2 : sprinkle with fine particles —**dust•er** *n* —**dust•pan** *n* —**dusty** *adj*

du•ty \'dütē, 'dyü-\ *n, pl* **-ties** 1 : action required by one's occupation or position 2 : moral or legal obligation 3 : tax —**du•te•ous** \-əs\ *adj* —**du•ti•able** \-əbəl\ *adj* —**du•ti•ful** \'dütifəl, 'dyü-\ *adj*

dwarf \'dwòrf\ *n, pl* **dwarfs** \'dwòrfs\ *or* **dwarves** \'dwòrvz\ : one that is much below normal size ~ *vb* 1 : stunt 2 : cause to seem smaller —**dwarf•ish** *adj*

dwell \'dwel\ *vb* **dwelt** \'dwelt\ *or* **dwelled** \'dweld, 'dwelt\ **dwell•ing** 1 : reside 2 : keep the attention directed —**dwell•er** *n* —**dwell•ing** *n*

dwin•dle \'dwindəl\ *vb* **-dled; -dling** : become steadily less

dye \'dī\ *n* : coloring material ~ *vb* **dyed; dye•ing** : give a new color to

dying *pres part of* DIE

dyke *var of* DIKE

dy•nam•ic \dī'namik\ *adj* 1 : relating to physical force producing motion 2 : energetic or forceful

dy•na•mite \'dīnə,mīt\ *n* : explosive made of nitroglycerin —**dynamite** *vb*

dy•na•mo \-,mō\ *n, pl* **-mos** : electrical generator

dy•nas•ty \'dīnəstē, -,nas-\ *n, pl* **-ties** : succession of rulers of the same family —**dy•nas•tic** \dī'nastik\ *adj*

dys•en•tery \'disən,terē\ *n, pl* **-ter•ies** : disease marked by diarrhea

dys•lex•ia \dis'leksēə\ *n* : disturbance of the ability to read —**dys•lex•ic** \-sik\ *adj*

dys•pep•sia \-'pepshə, -sēə\ *n* : indigestion —**dys•pep•tic** \-'peptik\ *adj or n*

dys•tro•phy \'distrəfē\ *n, pl* **-phies** : disorder involving nervous and muscular tissue

E

e \'ē\ *n, pl* **e's** *or* **es** \'ēz\ : 5th letter of the alphabet

each \'ēch\ *adj* : being one of the class named ~ *pron* : every individual one ~ *adv* : apiece

ea•ger \'ēgər\ *adj* : enthusiastic or anxious —**ea•ger•ly** *adv* —**ea•ger•ness** *n*

ea•gle \'ēgəl\ *n* : large bird of prey

-ean —see -AN

1ear \'ir\ *n* : organ of hearing or the outer part of this —**ear•ache** *n* —**eared** *adj* —**ear•lobe** \-,lōb\ *n*

2ear *n* : fruiting head of a cereal

ear•drum *n* : thin membrane that receives and transmits sound waves in the ear

earl \'ərl\ *n* : British nobleman —**earl•dom** \-dəm\ *n*

ear•ly \'ərlē\ *adj* **-li•er; -li•est** 1 : relating to or occurring near the beginning or before the usual time 2 : ancient —**early** *adv*

ear•mark *vb* : designate for a specific purpose

earn \'ərn\ *vb* 1 : receive as a return for service 2 : deserve

ear•nest \'ərnəst\ *n* : serious state of mind —**earnest** *adj* —**ear•nest•ly** *adv* —**ear•nest•ness** *n*

ear•phone *n* : device that reproduces sound and is worn over or in the ear

ear•ring *n* : earlobe ornament

ear•shot *n* : range of hearing

earth \'ərth\ *n* 1 : soil or land 2 : planet inhabited by man —**earth•li•ness** *n* —**earth•ly** *adj* —**earth•ward** \-wərd\ *adv*

earth•en \'ərthən\ *adj* : made of earth or baked clay —**earth•en•ware** \-,war\ *n*

earth•quake *n* : shaking or trembling of the earth

earth•worm *n* : long segmented worm

earthy \'ərthē\ *adj* **earth•i•er; -est** 1 : relating to or consisting of earth 2 : practical 3 : coarse —**earth•i•ness** *n*

ease \'ēz\ *n* 1 : comfort 2 : naturalness of manner 3 : freedom from difficulty ~ *vb* **eased; eas•ing** 1 : relieve from distress 2 : lessen the tension of 3 : make easier

ea•sel \'ēzəl\ *n* : frame to hold a painter's canvas

east \'ēst\ *adv* : to or toward the east ~ *adj* : situated toward or at or coming from the east ~ *n* 1 : direction of sunrise 2 *cap* : regions to the east —**east•er•ly** \'ēstərlē\ *adv or adj* —**east•ward** *adv or adj* —**east•wards** *adv*

Eas•ter \'ēstər\ *n* : church feast celebrating Christ's resurrection

east•ern \'ēstərn\ *adj* 1 *cap* : relating to a region designated East 2 : lying toward or coming from the east —**East•ern•er** *n*

easy \'ēzē\ *adj* **eas•i•er; -est** 1 : marked by ease 2 : lenient —**eas•i•ly** \'ēzəlē\ *adv* —**eas•i•ness** \-ēnəs\ *n*

easy•go•ing *adj* : relaxed and casual

eat \'ēt\ *vb* **ate** \'āt\; **eat•en** \'ētən\; **eat•ing** 1 : take in as food 2 : use up or corrode —**eat•able** *adj* —**eat•er** *n*

eaves \'ēvz\ *n pl* : overhanging edge of a roof

eaves•drop *vb* : listen secretly —**eaves•drop•per** *n*

ebb \'eb\ *n* 1 : outward flow of the tide 2 : decline ~ *vb* 1 : recede from the flood state 2 : wane

eb•o•ny \'ebənē\ *n, pl* **-nies** : hard heavy wood of tropical trees ~ *adj* 1 : made of ebony 2 : black

ebul•lient \i'bùlyənt, -'bəl-\ *adj* : exuberant —**ebul•lience** \-yəns\ *n*

ec•cen•tric \ik'sentrik\ *adj* 1 : odd in behavior 2 : being off center —**eccentric** *n* —**ec•cen•tri•cal•ly** \-triklē\ *adv* —**ec•cen•tric•i•ty** \,ek,sen'trisətē\ *n*

ec•cle•si•as•tic \ik,lēzē'astik\ *n* : clergyman

ec•cle•si•as•ti•cal \-tikəl\, **ecclesiastic** *adj* : relating to a church —**ec•cle•si•as•ti•cal•ly** \-tiklē\ *adv*

ech•e•lon \'eshə,län\ *n* 1 : steplike arrangement 2 : level of authority

echo \'ekō\ *n, pl* **ech•oes** : repetition of a sound caused by a reflection of the sound waves —**echo** *vb*

éclair \ā'klar\ *n* : custard-filled pastry

eclec•tic \e'klektik, i-\ *adj* : drawing or drawn from varied sources

eclipse \i'klips\ *n* : total or partial obscuring of one celestial body by another —**eclipse** *vb*

ecol•o•gy \i'käləjē, e-\ *n, pl* **-gies** : science concerned with the interaction of organisms and their environment —**eco•log•i•cal** \,ēkə'läjikəl, ,ek-\ *adj* —**eco•log•i•cal•ly** *adv* —**ecol•o•gist** \i'käləjist, e-\ *n*

eco•nom•ic \,ekə'nämik, ,ēkə-\ *adj* : relating to the producing and the buying and selling of goods and services

eco•nom•ics \-'nämiks\ *n* : branch of knowledge dealing with goods and services —**econ•o•mist** \i'känəmist\ *n*

econ•o•mize \i'känə,mīz\ *vb* **-mized; -mizing** : be thrifty —**econ•o•miz•er** *n*

econ•o•my \-ə,mē\ *n, pl* **-mies** 1 : thrifty use of resources 2 : economic system —**eco•nom•i•cal** \,ekə'nämikəl, ,ēkə-\ *adj* —**eco•nom•i•cal•ly** *adv* —**economy** *adj*

ecru \'ekrü, 'äkrü\ *n* : beige

ec•sta•sy \'ekstəsē\ *n, pl* **-sies** : extreme emotional excitement —**ec•stat•ic** \ek'statik, ik-\ *adj* —**ec•stat•i•cal•ly** \-iklē\ *adv*

ec•u•men•i•cal \,ekyə'menikəl\ *adj* : promoting worldwide Christian unity

ec•ze•ma \ig'zēmə, 'egzəmə, 'eksə-\ *n* : itching skin inflammation

1-ed \d *after a vowel or* b, g, j, l, m, n, ŋ, r, th, v, z, zh; əd *after* d, t; t *after other sounds*\ *vb suffix or adj suffix* 1 —used to form the past participle of regular verbs 2 : having or having the characteristics of

2-ed *vb suffix* —used to form the past tense of regular verbs

ed•dy \'edē\ *n, pl* **-dies** : whirlpool —**eddy** *vb*

ede•ma \i'dēmə\ *n* : abnormal accumulation of fluid in the body tissues —**edem•a•tous** \-'demətəs\ *adj*

Eden \'ēdən\ *n* : paradise

edge \'ej\ *n* 1 : cutting side of a blade 2 : line where something begins or ends ~ *vb* **edged; edg•ing** 1 : give or form an edge 2 : move gradually 3 : narrowly defeat —**edg•er** *n*

edge•wise \-,wīz\ *adv* : sideways

edgy \'ejē\ *adj* **edg•i•er; -est** : nervous —**edg•i•ness** *n*

ed•i•ble \'edəbəl\ *adj* : fit or safe to be eaten —**ed•i•bil•i•ty** \,edə'bilətē\ *n* —**edible** *n*

edict \'ē,dikt\ *n* : order or decree

ed•i•fi•ca•tion \,edəfə'kāshən\ *n* : instruction or information —**ed•i•fy** \'edə,fī\ *vb*

ed•i•fice \'edəfəs\ *n* : large building

ed•it \'edət\ *vb* 1 : revise and prepare for publication 2 : delete —**ed•i•tor** \-ər\ *n* —**ed•i•tor•ship** *n*

edi•tion \i'dishən\ *n* 1 : form in which a text is published 2 : total number published at one time

ed•i•to•ri•al \,edə'tōrēəl\ *adj* 1 : relating to an editor or editing 2 : expressing opinion ~ *n* : article (as in a newspaper) expressing the views of an editor —**ed•i•to•ri•al•ize** \-ēə,līz\ *vb* —**ed•i•to•ri•al•ly** *adv*

ed•u•cate \'ejə,kāt\ *vb* **-cat•ed; -cat•ing** 1 : give instruction to 2 : develop mentally and morally 3 : provide with information —**ed•u•ca•ble** \'ejəkəbəl\ *adj* —**ed•u•ca•tion** \,ejə'kāshən\ *n* —**ed•u•ca•tion•al** \-shənəl\ *adj* —**ed•u•ca•tor** \-ər\ *n*

eel \'ēl\ *n* : snakelike fish

ee•rie \'irē\ *adj* **-ri•er; -est** : weird —**ee•ri•ly** \'irəlē\ *adv*

ef•face \i'fās, e-\ *vb* **-faced; -fac•ing** : obliterate by rubbing out —**ef•face•ment** *n*

ef•fect \i'fekt\ *n* 1 : result 2 : meaning 3 : influence 4 *pl* : goods or possessions ~ *vb* : cause to happen —**in effect** : in substance

ef•fec•tive \i'fektiv\ *adj* 1 : producing a strong or desired effect 2 : being in operation —**ef•fec•tive•ly** *adv* —**ef•fec•tive•ness** *n*

ef•fec•tu•al \i'fekchəwəl\ *adj* : producing an intended effect —**ef•fec•tu•al•ly** *adv* —**ef•fec•tu•al•ness** *n*

ef•fem•i•nate \ə'femənət\ *adj* : unsuitably womanish —**ef•fem•i•na•cy** \-nəsē\ *n*

ef•fer•vesce \,efər'ves\ *vb* **-vesced; -vesc•ing** 1 : bubble and hiss as gas escapes 2 : show exhilaration —**ef•fer•ves•cence** \-'vesəns\ *n* —**ef•fer•ves•cent** \-ənt\ *adj* —**ef•fer•ves•cent•ly** *adv*

ef•fete \e'fēt\ *adj* 1 : worn out 2 : weak or decadent 3 : effeminate

ef•fi•ca•cious \,efə'kāshəs\ *adj* : effective —**ef•fi•ca•cy** \'efikəsē\ *n*

ef•fi•cient \i'fishənt\ *adj* : working well with little waste —**ef•fi•cien•cy** \-ənsē\ *n* —**ef•fi•cient•ly** *adv*

ef•fi•gy \'efəjē\ *n, pl* **-gies** : usu. crude image of a person

ef•flu•ent \'e,flüənt, e'flü-\ *n* : something that flows out —**effluent** *adj*

ef•fort \'efərt\ *n* 1 : a putting forth of strength 2 : use of resources toward a goal 3 : product of effort —**ef•fort•less** *adj* —**ef•fort•less•ly** *adv*

ef•fron•tery \i'frəntərē\ *n, pl* **-ter•ies** : insolence

ef•fu•sion \i'fyüzhən, e-\ *n* : a gushing forth —**ef•fu•sive** \-'fyüsiv\ *adj* —**ef•fu•sive•ly** *adv*

1egg \'eg, 'āg\ *vb* : urge to action

2egg *n* 1 : rounded usu. hard-shelled reproductive body esp. of birds and reptiles from which the young hatches 2 : ovum —**egg•shell** *n*

egg•nog \-,näg\ *n* : rich drink of eggs and cream

egg•plant *n* : edible purplish fruit of a plant related to the potato

ego \'ēgō\ *n, pl* **egos** : self-esteem

ego•cen•tric \,ēgō'sentrik\ *adj* : self-centered

ego•tism \'ēgə,tizəm\ *n* : exaggerated sense of self-importance —**ego•tist** \-tist\ *n* —**ego•tis•tic** \,ēgə'tistik\, **ego•tis•ti•cal** \-tikəl\ *adj* —**ego•tis•ti•cal•ly** *adv*

egre•gious \i'grējəs\ *adj* : notably bad —**egre•gious•ly** *adv*

egress \'ē,gres\ *n* : a way out

egret \'ēgrət, i'gret, 'egrət\ *n* : long-plumed heron

ei•der•down \'īdər,daùn\ *n* : soft down obtained from a northern sea duck (**eider**)

eight \'āt\ *n* 1 : one more than 7 2 : 8th in a set or series 3 : something having 8 units —**eight** *adj or pron* —**eighth** \'āth\ *adj or adv or n*

eigh•teen \(,)ā'tēn\ *n* : one more than 17 —**eighteen** *adj or pron* —**eigh•teenth** \-'tēnth\ *adj or n*

eighty \'ātē\ *n, pl* **eight•ies** : 8 times 10 —**eight•i•eth** \'ātēəth\ *adj or n* —**eighty** *adj or pron*

ei•ther \'ēthər, 'ī-\ *adj* 1 : both 2 : being the one or the other of two ~ *pron* : one of two or more ~ *conj* : one or the other

ejac·u·late \i'jakyə,lāt\ *vb* **-lat·ed; -lat·ing** **1** : say suddenly **2** : eject a fluid (as semen) —**ejac·u·la·tion** \-,jakyə'lāshən\ *n*

eject \i'jekt\ *vb* : drive or throw out —**ejec·tion** \-'jekshən\ *n*

eke \'ēk\ *vb* **eked; ek·ing** : barely gain with effort —usu. with *out*

elab·o·rate \i'labərət\ *adj* **1** : planned in detail **2** : complex and ornate ~ \-ə,rāt\ *vb* **-rat·ed; -rat·ing** : work out in detail —**elab·o·rate·ly** *adv* —**elab·o·rate·ness** *n* —**elab·o·ra·tion** \-,labə'rāshən\ *n*

elapse \i'laps\ *vb* **elapsed; elaps·ing** : slip by

elas·tic \i'lastik\ *adj* **1** : springy **2** : flexible ~ *n* **1** : elastic material **2** : rubber band —**elas·tic·i·ty** \i,las'tisətē, ,ē,las-\ *n*

elate \i'lāt\ *vb* **elat·ed; elat·ing** : fill with joy —**ela·tion** \-'lāshən\ *n*

el·bow \'el,bō\ *n* **1** : joint of the arm **2** : elbow-shaped bend or joint ~ *vb* : push aside with the elbow

el·der \'eldər\ *adj* : older ~ *n* **1** : one who is older **2** : church officer

el·der·ber·ry \'eldər,berē\ *n* : edible black or red fruit or a tree or shrub bearing these

el·der·ly \'eldərlē\ *adj* : past middle age

el·dest \'eldəst\ *adj* : oldest

elect \i'lekt\ *adj* : elected but not yet in office ~ *n* **elect** *pl* : exclusive group ~ *vb* : choose esp. by vote —**elec·tion** \i-'lekshən\ *n* —**elec·tive** \i'lektiv\ *n or adj* —**elec·tor** \i'lektər\ *n* —**elec·tor·al** \-tərəl\ *adj*

elec·tor·ate \i'lektərət\ *n* : body of persons entitled to vote

elec·tric \i'lektrik\ *adj* **1** *or* **elec·tri·cal** \-trikəl\ **1** : relating to or run by electricity **2** : thrilling —**elec·tri·cal·ly** *adv*

elec·tri·cian \i,lek'trishən\ *n* : person who installs or repairs electrical equipment

elec·tric·i·ty \-'trisətē\ *n, pl* **-ties 1** : fundamental form of energy occurring naturally (as in lightning) or produced artificially **2** : electric current

elec·tri·fy \i'lektrə,fī\ *vb* **-fied; -fy·ing 1** : charge with electricity **2** : equip for use of electric power **3** : thrill —**elec·tri·fi·ca·tion** \-,lektrəfə'kāshən\ *n*

elec·tro·car·dio·gram \i,lektrō'kärdēə,gram\ *n* : tracing made by an electrocardiograph

elec·tro·car·dio·graph \-,graf\ *n* : instrument for monitoring heart function

elec·tro·cute \i'lektrə,kyüt\ *vb* **-cut·ed; -cut·ing** : kill by an electric shock —**elec·tro·cu·tion** \-,lektrə'kyüshən\ *n*

elec·trode \i'lek,trōd\ *n* : conductor at a nonmetallic part of a circuit

elec·trol·y·sis \i,lek'träləsəs\ *n* **1** : production of chemical changes by passage of an electric current through a substance **2** : destruction of hair roots with an electric current —**elec·tro·lyt·ic** \-,trə'litik\ *adj*

elec·tro·lyte \i'lektrə,līt\ *n* : nonmetallic electric conductor

elec·tro·mag·net \i,lektrō'magnət\ *n* : magnet made using electric current

elec·tro·mag·ne·tism \-nə,tizəm\ *n* : natural force responsible for interactions between charged particles —**elec·tro·mag·net·ic** \-mag'netik\ *adj* —**elec·tro·mag·net·i·cal·ly** \-iklē\ *adv*

elec·tron \i'lek,trän\ *n* : negatively charged particle within the atom

elec·tron·ic \i,lek'tränik\ *adj* : relating to electrons or electronics —**elec·tron·i·cal·ly** \-iklē\ *adv*

elec·tron·ics \-iks\ *n* : physics of electrons and their use esp. in devices

elec·tro·plate \i'lektrə,plāt\ *vb* : coat (as with metal) by electrolysis

el·e·gance \'eligəns\ *n* : refined gracefulness —**el·e·gant** \-gənt\ *adj* —**el·e·gant·ly** *adv*

el·e·gy \'eləjē\ *n, pl* **-gies** : poem expressing grief for one who is dead —**ele·gi·ac** \,elə'jīak, -,ak\ *adj*

el·e·ment \'eləmənt\ *n* **1** *pl* : weather conditions **2** : natural environment **3** : constituent part **4** *pl* : simplest principles **5** : substance that has atoms of only one kind —**el·e·men·tal** \,elə'ment°l\ *adj*

el·e·men·ta·ry \,elə'mentrē\ *adj* **1** : simple **2** : relating to the basic subjects of education

el·e·phant \'eləfənt\ *n* : huge mammal with a trunk and 2 ivory tusks

el·e·vate \'elə,vāt\ *vb* **-vat·ed; -vat·ing 1** : lift up **2** : exalt

el·e·va·tion \,elə'vāshən\ *n* : height or a high place

el·e·va·tor \'elə,vātər\ *n* **1** : cage or platform for raising or lowering something **2** : grain storehouse

elev·en \i'levən\ *n* **1** : one more than 10 **2** : 11th in a set or series **3** : something having 11 units —**eleven** *adj or pron* —**elev·enth** \-ənth\ *adj or n*

elf \'elf\ *n, pl* **elves** \'elvz\ : mischievous fairy —**elf·in** \'elfən\ *adj* —**elf·ish** \'elfish\ *adj*

elic·it \i'lisət\ *vb* : draw forth

el·i·gi·ble \'eləjəbəl\ *adj* : qualified to participate or to be chosen —**el·i·gibil·i·ty** \,eləjə'bilətē\ *n* —**eligible** *n*

elim·i·nate \i'limə,nāt\ *vb* **-nat·ed; -nat·ing** : get rid of —**elim·i·na·tion** \i,limə'nāshən\ *n*

elite \ā'lēt\ *n* : choice or select group

elix·ir \i'liksər\ *n* : medicinal solution

elk \'elk\ *n* : large deer

el·lipse \i'lips, e-\ *n* : oval

el·lip·sis \-'lipsəs\ *n, pl* **-lip·ses** \-,sēz\ **1** : omission of a word **2** : marks (as . . .) to show omission

el·lip·ti·cal \-tikəl\, **el·lip·tic** \-tik\ *adj* **1** : relating to or shaped like an ellipse **2** : relating to or marked by ellipsis

elm \'elm\ *n* : tall shade tree

el·o·cu·tion \,elə'kyüshən\ *n* : art of public speaking

elon·gate \i'lòŋ,gāt\ *vb* **-gat·ed; -gat·ing** : make or grow longer —**elon·ga·tion** \,ē,lòŋ'gāshən\ *n*

elope \i'lōp\ *vb* **eloped; elop·ing** : run away esp. to be married —**elope·ment** *n* —**elop·er** *n*

el·o·quent \'eləkwənt\ *adj* : forceful and persuasive in speech —**el·o·quence** \-kwəns\ *n* —**el·o·quent·ly** *adv*

else \'els\ *adv* **1** : in a different way, time, or place **2** : otherwise ~ *adj* **1** : other **2** : more

else·where *adv* : in or to another place

elu·ci·date \i'lüsə,dāt\ *vb* **-dat·ed; -dat·ing** : explain —**elu·ci·da·tion** \i,lüsə'dāshən\ *n*

elude \ē'lüd\ *vb* **elud·ed; elud·ing** : evade —**elu·sive** \ē'lüsiv\ *adj* —**elu·sive·ly** *adv* —**elu·sive·ness** *n*

elves *pl of* ELF

ema·ci·ate \i'māshē,āt\ *vb* **-at·ed; -at·ing** : become or make very thin —**ema·cia·tion** \i,māsē'āshən, -shē-\ *n*

em·a·nate \'emə,nāt\ *vb* **-nat·ed; -nat·ing** : come forth —**em·a·na·tion** \,emə'nāshən\ *n*

eman·ci·pate \i'mansə,pāt\ *vb* **-pat·ed; -pat·ing** : set free —**eman·ci·pa·tion** \i,mansə'pāshən\ *n* —**eman·ci·pa·tor** \i-'mansə,pātər\ *n*

emas·cu·late \i'maskyə,lāt\ *vb* **-lat·ed; -lat·ing 1** : castrate **2** : weaken —**emas·cu·la·tion** \i,maskyə'lāshən\ *n*

em·balm \im'bäm, -'bälm\ *vb* : preserve (a corpse) —**em·balm·er** *n*

em·bank·ment \im'baŋkmənt\ *n* : protective barrier of earth

em·bar·go \im'bärgō\ *n, pl* **-goes** : ban on trade —**embargo** *vb*

em·bark \-'bärk\ *vb* **1** : go on board a ship or airplane **2** : make a start —**em·bar·ka·tion** \,em,bär'kāshən\ *n*

em·bar·rass \im'barəs\ *vb* : cause distress and self-consciousness —**em·bar·rass·ment** *n*

em·bas·sy \'embəsē\ *n, pl* **-sies** : residence and offices of an ambassador

em·bed \im'bed\ *vb* **-dd-** : fix firmly

em·bel·lish \-'belish\ *vb* : decorate —**em·bel·lish·ment** *n*

em·ber \'embər\ *n* : smoldering fragment from a fire

em·bez·zle \im'bezəl\ *vb* **-zled; -zling** : steal (money) by falsifying records —**em·bez·zle·ment** *n* —**em·bez·zler** \-ələr\ *n*

em·bit·ter \im'bitər\ *vb* : make bitter

em·bla·zon \-'blāz°n\ *vb* : display conspicuously

em·blem \'embləm\ *n* : symbol —**em·blem·at·ic** \,emblə'matik\ *adj*

em·body \im'bädē\ *vb* **-bod·ied; -body·ing** : give definite form or expression to —**em·bodi·ment** \-'bädimənt\ *n*

em·boss \-'bäs, -'bòs\ *vb* : ornament with raised work

em·brace \-'brās\ *vb* **-braced; -brac·ing 1** : clasp in the arms **2** : welcome **3** : include —**embrace** *n*

em·broi·der \-'bróidər\ *vb* : ornament with or do needlework —**em·broi·dery** \-ərē\ *n*

em·broil \im'bróil\ *vb* : involve in conflict or difficulties

em·bryo \'embrē,ō\ *n* : living being in its earliest stages of development —**em·bry·on·ic** \,embrē'änik\ *adj*

emend \ē'mend\ *vb* : correct —**emen·da·tion** \,ē,men'dāshən\ *n*

em·er·ald \'emrəld, 'emə-\ *n* : green gem ~ *adj* : bright green

emerge \i'mərj\ *vb* **emerged; emerg·ing** : rise, come forth, or appear —**emer·gence** \-'mərjəns\ *n* —**emer·gent** \-jənt\ *adj*

emer·gen·cy \i'mərjənsē\ *n, pl* **-cies** : condition requiring prompt action

em·ery \'emərē\ *n, pl* **-er·ies** : dark granular mineral used for grinding

emet·ic \i'metik\ *n* : agent that induces vomiting —**emetic** *adj*

em·i·grate \'emə,grāt\ *vb* **-grat·ed; -grat·ing** : leave a country to settle elsewhere —**em·i·grant** \-igrənt\ *n* —**em·i·gra·tion** \,emə'grāshən\ *n*

em·i·nence \'emənəns\ *n* **1** : prominence or superiority **2** : person of high rank

em·i·nent \-nənt\ *adj* : prominent —**em·i·nent·ly** *adv*

em·is·sary \'emə,serē\ *n, pl* **-sar·ies** : agent

emis·sion \ē'mishən\ *n* : substance discharged into the air

emit \ē'mit\ *vb* **-tt-** : give off or out

emol·u·ment \i'mälyəmənt\ *n* : salary or fee

emote \i'mōt\ *vb* **emot·ed; emot·ing** : express emotion

emo·tion \i'mōshən\ *n* : intense feeling —**emo·tion·al** \-shənəl\ *adj* —**emo·tion·al·ly** *adv*

em·per·or \'empərər\ *n* : ruler of an empire

em·pha·sis \'emfəsəs\ *n, pl* **-pha·ses** \-,sēz\ : stress

em·pha·size \-,sīz\ *vb* **-sized; -siz·ing** : stress

em·phat·ic \im'fatik, em-\ *adj* : uttered with emphasis —**em·phat·i·cal·ly** \-iklē\ *adv*

em·pire \'em,pīr\ *n* : large state or a group of states

em·pir·i·cal \im'pirikəl\ *adj* : based on observation —**em·pir·i·cal·ly** \-iklē\ *adv*

em·ploy \im'plói\ *vb* **1** : use **2** : occupy ~ *n* : paid occupation —**em·ploy·ee, em·ploye** \im,plói'ē, -'plói,ē\ *n* —**em·ploy·er** *n* —**em·ploy·ment** \-mənt\ *n*

em·pow·er \im'pauər\ *vb* : give power to —**em·pow·er·ment** *n*

em·press \'emprəs\ *n* **1** : wife of an emperor **2** : woman emperor

emp·ty \'emptē\ *adj* **1** : containing nothing **2** : not occupied **3** : lacking value, sense, or purpose ~ *vb* **-tied; -ty·ing** : make or become empty —**emp·ti·ness** \-tēnəs\ *n*

emu \'ēmyü\ *n* : Australian bird related to the ostrich

em·u·late \'emyə,lāt\ *vb* **-lat·ed; -lat·ing** : try to equal or excel —**em·u·la·tion** \,emyə'lāshən\ *n*

emul·si·fy \i'məlsə,fī\ *vb* **-fied; -fy·ing** : convert into an emulsion —**emul·si·fi·ca·tion** \i,məlsəfə'kāshən\ *n* —**emul·si·fi·er** \-'məlsə,fīər\ *n*

emul·sion \i'məlshən\ *n* **1** : mixture of mutually insoluble liquids **2** : light-sensitive coating on photographic film

-en \ən, °n\ *vb suffix* **1** : become or cause to be **2** : cause or come to have

en·able \in'ābəl\ *vb* **-abled; -abling** : give power, capacity, or ability to

en·act \in'akt\ *vb* **1** : make into law **2** : act out —**en·act·ment** *n*

enam·el \in'aməl\ *n* **1** : glasslike substance used to coat metal or pottery **2** : hard outer layer of a tooth **3** : glossy paint —**enamel** *vb*

en·am·or \in'amər\ *vb* : excite with love

en·camp \in'kamp\ *vb* : make camp —**en·camp·ment** *n*

en·case \in'kās\ *vb* : enclose in or as if in a case

-ence \əns, °ns\ *n suffix* **1** : action or process **2** : quality or state

en·ceph·a·li·tis \in,sefə'lītəs\ *n, pl* **-lit·i·des** \-'litə,dēz\ : inflammation of the brain

en·chant \in'chant\ *vb* **1** : bewitch **2** : fascinate —**en·chant·ing·ly** *adv* —**en·chant·ment** *n* —**en·chant·ress** \-'chantrəs\ *n*

en·cir·cle \in'sərkəl\ *vb* : surround

en·close \in'klōz\ *vb* **1** : shut up or surround **2** : include —**en·clo·sure** \in'klōzhər\ *n*

en·co·mi·um \in'kōmēəm\ *n, pl* **-mi·ums** *or* **-mia** \-mēə\ : high praise

en·com·pass \in'kəmpəs, -'käm-\ *vb* : surround or include

en·core \'än,kór\ *n* : further performance

en·coun·ter \in'kauntər\ *vb* **1** : fight **2** : meet unexpectedly —**encounter** *n*

en·cour·age \in'kərij\ *vb* **-aged; -ag·ing 1** : inspire with courage and hope **2** : foster —**en·cour·age·ment** *n*

en·croach \in'krōch\ *vb* : enter upon another's property or rights —**en·croach·ment** *n*

en·crust \in'krəst\ *vb* : form a crust on

en·cum·ber \in'kəmbər\ *vb* : burden —**en·cum·brance** \-brəns\ *n*

-en·cy \ənsē, °n-\ *n suffix* : -ence

en·cyc·li·cal \in'siklikəl, en-\ *n* : papal letter to bishops

en·cy·clo·pe·dia \in,sīklə'pēdēə\ *n* : reference work on many subjects —**en·cy·clo·pe·dic** \-'pēdik\ *adj*

end \'end\ *n* **1** : point at which something stops or no longer exists **2** : cessation **3** : purpose ~ *vb* **1** : stop or finish **2** : be at the end of —**end·ed** *adj* —**end·less** *adj* —**end·less·ly** *adv*

en·dan·ger \in'dānjər\ *vb* : bring into danger

en·dear \in'dir\ *vb* : make dear —**en·dear·ment** \-mənt\ *n*

en·deav·or \in'devər\ *vb or n* : attempt

end·ing \'endiŋ\ *n* : end

en·dive \'en,dīv\ *n* : salad plant

en·do·crine \'endəkrən, -,krīn, -,krēn\ *adj* : producing secretions distributed by the bloodstream

en·dorse \in'dórs\ *vb* **-dorsed; -dors·ing 1** : sign one's name to **2** : approve —**en·dorse·ment** *n*

en·dow \in'dau\ *vb* **1** : furnish with funds **2** : furnish naturally —**en·dow·ment** *n*

en·dure \in'dúr, -'dyúr\ *vb* **-dured; -dur·ing 1** : last **2** : suffer patiently **3** : tolerate —**en·dur·able** *adj* —**en·dur·ance** \-əns\ *n*

en·e·ma \'enəmə\ *n* : injection of liquid into the rectum

en·e·my \-mē\ *n, pl* **-mies** : one that attacks or tries to harm another

en·er·get·ic \,enər'jetik\ *adj* : full of energy or activity —**en·er·get·i·cal·ly** \-iklē\ *adv*

en·er·gize \'enər,jīz\ *vb* **-gized; -giz·ing** : give energy to

en·er·gy \'enərjē\ *n, pl* **-gies 1** : capacity for action **2** : vigorous action **3** : capacity for doing work

en·er·vate \'enər,vāt\ *vb* **-vat·ed; -vat·ing** : make weak or listless —**en·er·va·tion** \,enər'vāshən\ *n*

en·fold \in'fōld\ *vb* : surround or embrace

en·force \-'fórs\ *vb* **1** : compel **2** : carry out —**en·force·able** \-əbəl\ *adj* —**en·force·ment** *n*

en·fran·chise \-'fran,chīz\ *vb* **-chised; -chis·ing** : grant voting rights to —**en·fran·chise·ment** \-,chīzmənt, -chəz-\ *n*

en·gage \in'gāj\ *vb* **-gaged; -gag·ing 1** : participate or cause to participate **2** : bring or come into working contact **3** : bind by a pledge to marry **4** : hire **5** : bring or enter into conflict —**en·gage·ment** \-mənt\ *n*

en·gag·ing *adj* : attractive

en·gen·der \in'jendər\ *vb* **-dered; -der·ing** : create

en·gine \'enjən\ *n* **1** : machine that converts energy into mechanical motion **2** : locomotive

en·gi·neer \,enjə'nir\ *n* **1** : one trained in engineering **2** : engine operator ~ *vb* : lay out or manage as an engineer

en·gi·neer·ing \-iŋ\ *n* : practical application of science and mathematics

en·grave \in'grāv\ *vb* **-graved; -grav·ing** : cut into a surface —**en·grav·er** *n* —**en·grav·ing** *n*

en·gross \-'grōs\ *vb* : occupy fully

en·gulf \-'gəlf\ *vb* : swallow up

en·hance \-'hans\ *vb* **-hanced; -hanc·ing** : improve in value —**en·hance·ment** *n*

enig·ma \i'nigmə\ *n* : puzzle or mystery —**enig·mat·ic** \,enig'matik, ,ē-\ *adj* —**enig·mat·i·cal·ly** *adv*

en·join \in'jóin\ *vb* **1** : command **2** : forbid

en·joy \-'jói\ *vb* : take pleasure in —**en·joy·able** *adj* —**en·joy·ment** *n*

en·large \-'lärj\ *vb* **-larged; -larg·ing** : make or grow larger —**en·large·ment** *n* —**en·larg·er** *n*

en·light·en \-'līt°n\ *vb* : give knowledge or spiritual insight to —**en·light·en·ment** *n*

en·list \-'list\ *vb* **1** : join the armed forces **2** : get the aid of —**en·list·ee** \-,lis'tē\ *n* —**en·list·ment** \-'listmənt\ *n*

en·liven \in'līvən\ *vb* : give life or spirit to

en·mi·ty \'enmətē\ *n, pl* **-ties** : mutual hatred

en·no·ble \in'ōbəl\ *vb* **-bled; -bling** : make noble

en·nui \,än'wē\ *n* : boredom

enor·mi·ty \i'nórmətē\ *n, pl* **-ties 1** : great wickedness **2** : huge size

enor·mous \i'nórməs\ *adj* : great in size, number, or degree —**enor·mous·ly** *adv* —**enor·mous·ness** *n*

enough \i'nəf\ *adj* : adequate ~ *adv* **1** : in an adequate manner **2** : in a tolerable degree ~ *pron* : adequate number, quantity, or amount

en·quire \in'kwīr\, **en·qui·ry** \in,kwīrē, in'-; 'inkwərē, 'iŋ-\ *var of* INQUIRE, INQUIRY

en·rage \in'rāj\ *vb* : fill with rage

en·rich \-'rich\ *vb* : make rich —**en·rich·ment** *n*

en·roll, en·rol \-'rōl\ *vb* **-rolled; -roll·ing 1** : enter on a list **2** : become enrolled —**en·roll·ment** *n*

en route \än'rüt, en-, in-\ *adv or adj* : on or along the way

en·sconce \in'skäns\ *vb* **-sconced; -sconc·ing** : settle snugly

en·sem·ble \än'sämbəl\ *n* **1** : small group **2** : complete costume

en·shrine \in'shrīn\ *vb* **1** : put in a shrine **2** : cherish

en·sign \'ensən, *1 also* 'en,sīn\ *n* **1** : flag **2** : lowest ranking commissioned officer in the navy

en·slave \in'slāv\ *vb* : make a slave of —**en·slave·ment** *n*

en·snare \-'snar\ *vb* : trap

en·sue \-'sü\ *vb* **-sued; -su·ing** : follow as a consequence

en·sure \-'shúr\ *vb* **-sured; -sur·ing** : guarantee

en·tail \-'tāl\ *vb* : involve as a necessary result

en·tan·gle \-'taŋgəl\ *vb* : tangle —**entan·gle·ment** *n*

en·ter \'entər\ *vb* **1** : go or come in or into **2** : start **3** : set down (as in a list)

en·ter·prise \'entər,prīz\ *n* **1** : an undertaking **2** : business organization **3** : initiative

en·ter·pris·ing \-,prīziŋ\ adj : showing initiative

en·ter·tain \,entər'tān\ vb 1 : treat or receive as a guest 2 : hold in mind 3 : amuse — **en·ter·tain·er** n — **en·ter·tain·ment** n

en·thrall, en·thral \in'throl\ vb -thralled; -thrall·ing : hold spellbound

en·thu·si·asm \-'thüzē,azəm, -'thyü-\ n : strong excitement of feeling or its cause — **en·thu·si·ast** \-,ast, -əst\ n — **en·thu·si·as·tic** \-,thüzē'astik, -,thyü-\ adj — **en·thu·si·as·ti·cal·ly** \-tiklē\ adv

en·tice \-'tīs\ vb -ticed; -tic·ing : tempt — **en·tice·ment** n

en·tire \in'tīr\ adj : complete or whole — **en·tire·ly** adv — **en·tire·ty** \-'tīrətē, -'tīrtē\ n

en·ti·tle \-'tīt∂l\ vb -tled; -tling 1 : name 2 : give a right to

en·ti·ty \'entətē\ n, pl -ties : something with separate existence

en·to·mol·o·gy \,entə'mäləjē\ n : study of insects — **en·to·mo·log·i·cal** \-mə'läjikəl\ adj — **en·to·mol·o·gist** \-'mäləjist\ n

en·tou·rage \,äntü'räzh\ n : retinue

en·trails \'entrālz, -,trälz\ n pl : intestines

¹**en·trance** \'entrəns\ n 1 : act of entering 2 : means or place of entering — **en·trant** \'entrənt\ n

²**en·trance** \in'trans\ vb -tranced; -tranc·ing : fascinate or delight

en·trap \in'trap\ vb : trap — **en·trap·ment** n

en·treat \-'trēt\ vb : ask urgently — **en·treaty** \-'trētē\ n

en·trée, en·tree \'än,trā\ n : principal dish of the meal

en·trench \in'trench\ vb : establish in a strong position — **en·trench·ment** n

en·tre·pre·neur \,äntrəprə'nər\ n : organizer or promoter of an enterprise

en·trust \in'trəst\ vb : commit to another with confidence

en·try \'entrē\ n, pl -tries 1 : entrance 2 : an entering in a record or an item so entered

en·twine \in'twīn\ vb : twine together or around

enu·mer·ate \i'nümə,rāt, -'nyü-\ vb -at·ed; -at·ing 1 : count 2 : list — **enu·mer·a·tion** \i,nümə'rāshən, -,nyü-\ n

enun·ci·ate \ē'nənsē,āt\ vb -at·ed; -ating 1 : announce 2 : pronounce — **enun·ci·a·tion** \-,nənsē'āshən\ n

en·vel·op \in'veləp\ vb : surround — **en·vel·op·ment** n

en·ve·lope \'envə,lōp, 'än-\ n : paper container for a letter

en·vi·ron·ment \in'vīrənmənt\ n : surroundings — **en·vi·ron·men·tal** \-,vīrən'ment∂l\ adj

en·vi·ron·men·tal·ist \-∂list\ n : person concerned about the environment

en·vi·rons \in'vīrənz\ n pl : vicinity

en·vis·age \in'vizij\ vb -aged; -ag·ing : have a mental picture of

en·vi·sion \-'vizhən\ vb : picture to oneself

en·voy \'en,vȯi, 'än-\ n : diplomat

en·vy \'envē\ n 1 : resentful awareness of another's advantage 2 : object of envy ~ vb -vied; -vy·ing : feel envy toward or on account of — **en·vi·able** \-vēəbəl\ adj — **en·vi·ous** \-vēəs\ adj — **en·vi·ous·ly** adv

en·zyme \'en,zīm\ n : biological catalyst

eon \'ēən, ē,än\ var of AEON

ep·au·let \,epə'let\ n : shoulder ornament on a uniform

ephem·er·al \i'femərəl\ adj : short-lived

ep·ic \'epik\ n : long poem about a hero — **epic** adj

ep·i·cure \'epi,kyúr\ n : person with fastidious taste esp. in food and wine — **ep·i·cu·re·an** \,epikyú'rēən, -'kyúrē-\ adj

ep·i·dem·ic \,epə'demik\ adj : affecting many persons at one time — **epidemic** n

epi·der·mis \,epə'dərməs\ n : outer layer of skin

ep·i·gram \'epə,gram\ n : short witty poem or saying — **ep·i·gram·mat·ic** \,epəgrə'matik\ adj

ep·i·lep·sy \'epə,lepsē\ n, pl -sies : nervous disorder marked by convulsive attacks — **ep·i·lep·tic** \,epə'leptik\ adj or n

epis·co·pal \i'piskəpəl\ adj : governed by bishops

ep·i·sode \'epə,sōd, -,zōd\ n : occurrence — **ep·i·sod·ic** \,epə'sädik, -'zäd-\ adj

epis·tle \i'pisəl\ n : letter

ep·i·taph \'epə,taf\ n : inscription in memory of a dead person

ep·i·thet \'epə,thet, -thət\ n : characterizing often abusive word or phrase

epit·o·me \i'pitəmē\ n 1 : summary 2 : ideal example — **epit·o·mize** \-,mīz\ vb

ep·och \'epək, 'ep,äk\ n : extended period — **ep·och·al** \'epəkəl, 'ep,äkəl\ adj

ep·oxy \'ep,äksē, ep'äksē\ n : synthetic resin used esp. in adhesives ~ vb -ox·ied or -oxyed; -oxy·ing : glue with epoxy

equa·ble \'ekwəbəl, 'ēkwə-\ adj : free from unpleasant extremes — **equa·bil·i·ty** \,ekwə'bilətē, ,ē-\ n — **eq·ua·bly** \-blē\ adv

equal \'ēkwəl\ adj : of the same quantity, value, quality, number, or status as an-

other ~ n : one that is equal ~ vb equaled or equalled; equal·ing or equal·ling : be or become equal to — **equal·i·ty** \i'kwälətē\ n — **equal·ize** \'ēkwə,līz\ vb — **equal·ly** \'ēkwəlē\ adv

equa·nim·i·ty \,ēkwə'nimətē, ,ek-\ n, pl -ties : calmness

equate \i'kwāt\ vb equat·ed; equat·ing : treat or regard as equal

equa·tion \i'kwāzhən, -shən\ n : mathematical statement that two things are equal

equa·tor \i'kwātər\ n : imaginary circle that separates the northern and southern hemispheres — **equa·to·ri·al** \,ēkwə'tōrēəl, ,ek-\ adj

eques·tri·an \i'kwestrēən\ adj : relating to horseback riding ~ n : horseback rider

equi·lat·er·al \,ēkwə'latərəl\ adj : having equal sides

equi·lib·ri·um \-'librēəm\ n, pl -ri·ums or -ria \-rēə\ : state of balance

equine \'ē,kwīn, 'ek,wīn\ adj : relating to the horse — **equine** n

equi·nox \'ēkwə,näks, 'ek-\ n : time when day and night are everywhere of equal length

equip \i'kwip\ vb -pp- : furnish with needed resources — **equip·ment** \-mənt\ n

eq·ui·ta·ble \'ekwətəbəl\ adj : fair

eq·ui·ty \'ekwətē\ n, pl -ties 1 : justice 2 : value of a property less debt

equiv·a·lent \i'kwivələnt\ adj : equal — **equiv·a·lence** \-ləns\ n — **equivalent** n

equiv·o·cal \i'kwivəkəl\ adj : ambiguous or uncertain

equiv·o·cate \i'kwivə,kāt\ vb -cat·ed; -cat·ing 1 : use misleading language 2 : avoid answering definitely — **equiv·o·ca·tion** \-,kwivə'kāshən\ n

¹**-er** \ər\ adj suffix or adv suffix —used to form the comparative degree of adjectives and adverbs and esp. those of one or two syllables

²**-er** \ər\, **-ier** \ēər, yər\, **-yer** \yər\ n suffix 1 : one that is associated with 2 : one that performs or is the object of an action 3 : one that is

era \'irə, 'erə, 'ērə\ n : period of time associated with something

erad·i·cate \i'radə,kāt\ vb -cat·ed; -cat·ing : do away with

erase \i'rās\ vb erased; eras·ing : rub or scratch out — **eras·er** n — **era·sure** \i-'rāshər\ n

ere \'er\ prep or conj : before

erect \i'rekt\ adj : not leaning or lying down ~ vb 1 : build 2 : bring to an upright position — **erec·tion** \i'rekshən\ n

er·mine \'ərmən\ n : weasel with white winter fur or its fur

erode \i'rōd\ vb erod·ed; erod·ing : wear away gradually

ero·sion \i'rōzhən\ n : process of eroding

erot·ic \i'rätik\ adj : sexually arousing — **erot·i·cal·ly** \-iklē\ adv — **erot·i·cism** \i'rätə,sizəm\ n

err \'er, 'ər\ vb : be or do wrong

er·rand \'erənd\ n : short trip taken to do something often for another

er·rant \-ənt\ adj 1 : traveling about 2 : going astray

er·rat·ic \ir'atik\ adj 1 : eccentric 2 : inconsistent — **er·rat·i·cal·ly** \-iklē\ adv

er·ro·ne·ous \ir'ōnēəs, e'rō-\ adj : wrong — **er·ro·ne·ous·ly** adv

er·ror \'erər\ n 1 : something that is not accurate 2 : state of being wrong

er·satz \'er,säts\ adj : phony

erst·while \'ərst,hwīl\ adv : in the past ~ adj : former

er·u·di·tion \,erə'dishən, ,eryə-\ n : great learning — **er·u·dite** \'erə,dīt, 'eryə-\ adj

erupt \i'rəpt\ vb : burst forth esp. suddenly and violently — **erup·tion** \i'rəpshən\ n — **erup·tive** \-tiv\ adj

-ery \ərē\ n suffix 1 : character or condition 2 : practice 3 : place of doing

¹**-es** \əz, iz after s, z, sh, ch; z after v or a vowel\ n pl suffix —used to form the plural of some nouns

²**-es** vb suffix —used to form the 3d person singular present of some verbs

es·ca·late \'eskə,lāt\ vb -lat·ed; -lat·ing : become quickly larger or greater — **es·ca·la·tion** \,eskə'lāshən\ n

es·ca·la·tor \'eskə,lātər\ n : moving stairs

es·ca·pade \'eskə,pād\ n : mischievous adventure

es·cape \is'kāp\ vb -caped; -cap·ing : get away or get away from ~ n 1 : flight from or avoidance of something unpleasant 2 : leakage 3 : means of escape — adj : providing means of escape — **es·cap·ee** \is,kā'pē, ,es-\ n

es·ca·role \'eskə,rōl\ n : salad green

es·carp·ment \is'kärpmənt\ n : cliff

es·chew \is'chü\ vb : shun

es·cort \'es,kȯrt\ n : one accompanying another — **es·cort** \is'kȯrt\ vb

es·crow \'es,krō\ n : deposit to be delivered upon fulfillment of a condition

esoph·a·gus \i'säfəgəs\ n, pl -gi \-,gī, -,jī\ : muscular tube connecting the mouth and stomach

es·o·ter·ic \,esə'terik\ adj : mysterious or secret

es·pe·cial·ly \is'peshəlē\ adv : particularly or notably

es·pi·o·nage \'espēə,näzh, -nij\ n : practice of spying

es·pous·al \is'pauzəl\ n 1 : betrothal 2 : wedding 3 : a taking up as a supporter — **es·pouse** \-'paúz\ vb

es·pres·so \e'spresō\ n, pl -sos : strong steam-brewed coffee

es·py \is'pī\ vb -pied; -py·ing : catch sight of

es·quire \'es,kwīr\ n —used as a title of courtesy

-ess \əs, ,es\ n suffix : female

es·say \'es,ā\ n : literary composition ~ vb \e'sā, 'es,ā\ : attempt — **es·say·ist** \'es,āist\ n

es·sence \'es∂ns\ n 1 : fundamental nature or quality 2 : extract 3 : perfume

es·sen·tial \i'senchəl\ adj : basic or necessary — **essential** n — **es·sen·tial·ly** adv

-est \əst, ist\ adj suffix or adv suffix —used to form the superlative degree of adjectives and adverbs and esp. those of 1 or 2 syllables

es·tab·lish \is'tablish\ vb 1 : bring into existence 2 : put on a firm basis 3 : cause to be recognized

es·tab·lish·ment \-mənt\ n 1 : business or a place of business 2 : an establishing or being established 3 : controlling group

es·tate \is'tāt\ n 1 : one's possessions 2 : large piece of land with a house

es·teem \is'tēm\ n or vb : regard

es·ter \'estər\ n : organic chemical compound

esthetic var of AESTHETIC

es·ti·ma·ble \'estəməbəl\ adj : worthy of esteem

es·ti·mate \'estə,māt\ vb -mat·ed; -mat·ing : judge the approximate value, size, or cost ~ \-mət\ n 1 : rough or approximate calculation 2 : statement of the cost of a job — **es·ti·ma·tion** \,estə'māshən\ n — **es·ti·ma·tor** \'estə,mātər\ n

es·trange \is'trānj\ vb -tranged; -trang·ing : make hostile — **es·trange·ment** n

es·tro·gen \'estrəjən\ n : hormone that produces female characteristics

es·tu·ary \'eschə,werē\ n, pl -ar·ies : arm of the sea at a river's mouth

et cet·era \et'setərə, -'setrə\ : and others esp. of the same kind

etch \'ech\ vb : produce by corroding parts of a surface with acid — **etch·er** n — **etch·ing** n

eter·nal \i'tərn∂l\ adj : lasting forever — **eter·nal·ly** adv

eter·ni·ty \-nətē\ n, pl -ties : infinite duration

eth·ane \'eth,ān\ n : gaseous hydrocarbon

eth·a·nol \'ethə,nȯl, -,nōl\ n : alcohol

ether \'ēthər\ n : light flammable liquid used as an anesthetic

ethe·re·al \i'thirēəl\ adj 1 : celestial 2 : exceptionally delicate

eth·i·cal \'ethikəl\ adj 1 : relating to ethics 2 : honorable — **eth·i·cal·ly** adv

eth·ics \-iks\ n sing or pl 1 : study of good and evil and moral duty 2 : moral principles or practice

eth·nic \'ethnik\ adj : relating to races or groups of people with common customs ~ n : member of a minority ethnic group

eth·nol·o·gy \eth'näləjē\ n : study of the races of human beings — **eth·no·log·i·cal** \,ethnə'läjikəl\ adj — **eth·nol·o·gist** \eth-'näləjist\ n

et·i·quette \'etikət, -,ket\ n : good manners

et·y·mol·o·gy \,etə'mäləjē\ n, pl -gies 1 : history of a word 2 : study of etymologies — **et·y·mo·log·i·cal** \-mə'läjikəl\ adj — **et·y·mol·o·gist** \-'mäləjist\ n

eu·ca·lyp·tus \,yükə'liptəs\ n, pl -ti \-,tī\ or -tus·es : Australian evergreen tree

Eu·cha·rist \'yükərəst\ n : Communion — **eu·cha·ris·tic** \,yükə'ristik\ adj

eu·lo·gy \'yüləjē\ n, pl -gies : speech in praise — **eu·lo·gis·tic** \,yülə'jistik\ adj — **eu·lo·gize** \'yülə,jīz\ vb

eu·nuch \'yünək\ n : castrated man

eu·phe·mism \'yüfə,mizəm\ n : substitution of a pleasant expression for an unpleasant or offensive one — **euphe·mis·tic** \,yü-fə'mistik\ adj

eu·pho·ni·ous \yu'fōnēəs\ adj : pleasing to the ear — **eu·pho·ny** \'yüfənē\ n

eu·pho·ria \yu'fōrēə\ n : elation — **euphor·ic** \-'fȯrik\ adj

eu·tha·na·sia \,yüthə'nāzhə, -zhēə\ n : mercy killing

evac·u·ate \i'vakyə,wāt\ vb -at·ed; -at·ing 1 : discharge wastes from the body 2 : remove or withdraw from — **evac·u·a·tion** \i,vakyə'wāshən\ n

evade \i'vād\ vb evad·ed; evad·ing : manage to avoid

eval·u·ate \i'valyə,wāt\ vb -at·ed; -at·ing : appraise — **eval·u·a·tion** \i,valyə'wā-shən\ n

evan·gel·i·cal \,ē,van'jelikəl, ,evən-\ adj : relating to the Christian gospel

evan·ge·lism \i'vanjə,lizəm\ n : the winning or revival of personal commitments to Christ — **evan·ge·list** \i'vanjəlist\ n — **evan·ge·lis·tic** \i,vanjə'listik\ adj

evap·o·rate \i'vapə,rāt\ vb -rat·ed; -rat·ing 1 : pass off in or convert into vapor 2 : disappear quickly — **evap·o·ra·tion** \i-,vapə'rāshən\ n — **evap·o·ra·tor** \i-'vapə,rātər\ n

eva·sion \i'vāzhən\ n : act or instance of evading — **eva·sive** \i'vāsiv\ adj — **eva·sive·ness** n

eve \'ēv\ n : evening

even \'ēvən\ adj 1 : smooth 2 : equal or fair 3 : fully revenged 4 : divisible by 2 ~ adv 1 : already 2 —used for emphasis ~ vb : make or become even — **even·ly** adv — **even·ness** n

eve·ning \'ēvniŋ\ n : early part of the night

event \i'vent\ n 1 : occurrence 2 : noteworthy happening 3 : eventuality — **event·ful** adj

even·tu·al \i'venchəwəl\ adj : later — **even·tu·al·ly** adv

even·tu·al·i·ty \i,venchə'walətē\ n, pl -ties : possible occurrence or outcome

ev·er \'evər\ adv 1 : always 2 : at any time 3 : in any case

ev·er·green adj : having foliage that remains green — **evergreen** n

ev·er·last·ing \,evər'lastiŋ\ adj : lasting forever

ev·ery \'evrē\ adj : being each one of a group 2 : all possible

ev·ery·body \'evri,bädē, -bəd-\ pron : every person

ev·ery·day adj : ordinary

ev·ery·one \-,wən\ pron : every person

ev·ery·thing pron : all that exists

ev·ery·where adv : in every place or part

evict \i'vikt\ vb : force (a person) to move from a property — **evic·tion** \i'vikshən\ n

ev·i·dence \'evədəns\ n 1 : outward sign 2 : proof or testimony

ev·i·dent \-ənt\ adj : clear or obvious — **ev·i·dent·ly** \-ədəntlē, -ə,dent-\ adv

evil \'ēvəl\ adj evil·er or evil·ler; evil·est or evil·lest : wicked ~ n 1 : sin 2 : source of sorrow or distress — **evil·do·er** \,ēvəl'düər\ n — **evil·ly** adv

evince \i'vins\ vb evinced; evinc·ing : show

evis·cer·ate \i'visə,rāt\ vb -at·ed; -at·ing : remove the viscera of — **evis·cer·a·tion** \i,visə'rāshən\ n

evoke \i'vōk\ vb evoked; evok·ing : call forth or up — **evo·ca·tion** \,ēvō'kāshən, ,evə-\ n — **evoc·a·tive** \i'väkətiv\ adj

evo·lu·tion \,evə'lüshən\ n : process of change by degrees — **evo·lu·tion·ary** \-shə,nerē\ adj

evolve \i'välv\ vb evolved; evolv·ing : develop or change by degrees

ewe \'yü\ n : female sheep

ew·er \'yüər\ n : water pitcher

ex·act \ig'zakt\ vb : compel to furnish ~ adj : precisely correct — **ex·act·ing** adj — **ex·ac·tion** \-'zakshən\ n — **ex·ac·ti·tude** \-'zaktə,tüd, -,tyüd\ n — **ex·act·ly** adv — **ex·act·ness** n

ex·ag·ger·ate \ig'zajə,rāt\ vb -at·ed; -at·ing : say more than is true — **ex·ag·ger·at·ed·ly** adv — **ex·ag·ger·a·tion** \-,zajə'rāshən\ n — **ex·ag·ger·a·tor** \-'zajərātər\ n

ex·alt \ig'zȯlt\ vb : glorify — **ex·al·ta·tion** \,eg,zȯl'tāshən, ,ek,sȯl-\ n

ex·am \ig'zam\ n : examination

ex·am·ine \-ən\ vb -ined; -in·ing 1 : inspect closely 2 : test by questioning — **ex·am·i·na·tion** \-,zamə'nāshən\ n

ex·am·ple \ig'zampəl\ n 1 : representative sample 2 : model 3 : problem to be solved for teaching purposes

ex·as·per·ate \ig'zaspə,rāt\ vb -at·ed; -at·ing : thoroughly annoy — **ex·as·per·a·tion** \-,zaspə'rāshən\ n

ex·ca·vate \'ekskə,vāt\ vb -vat·ed; -vat·ing : dig or hollow out — **ex·ca·va·tion** \,ekskə'vāshən\ n — **ex·ca·va·tor** \'ekskə,vātər\ n

ex·ceed \ik'sēd\ vb 1 : go or be beyond the limit of 2 : do better than

ex·ceed·ing·ly adv : extremely

ex·cel \ik'sel\ vb -ll- : do extremely well or far better than

ex·cel·lence \'eksələns\ n : quality of being excellent

ex·cel·len·cy \-lənsē\ n, pl -cies —used as a title of honor

ex·cel·lent \'eksələnt\ adj : very good — **ex·cel·lent·ly** adv

ex·cept \ik'sept\ vb : omit ~ prep : excluding ~ conj : but — **ex·cep·tion** \-'sepshən\ n

ex·cep·tion·al \-'sepshənəl\ adj : superior — **ex·cep·tion·al·ly** adv

ex·cerpt \'ek,sərpt, 'eg,zərpt\ n : brief passage ~ \ek'-, eg'-, 'ek,-, 'eg,-\ vb : select an excerpt

ex·cess \ik'ses, 'ek,ses\ n : amount left over —**excess** adj —**ex·ces·sive** \-'sesiv\ adj —**ex·ces·sive·ly** adv

ex·change \iks'chānj, 'eks,chānj\ n 1 : the giving or taking of one thing in return for another 2 : marketplace esp. for securities ~ vb -changed; -chang·ing : transfer in return for some equivalent —**ex·change·able** \iks'chānjəbəl\ adj

¹**ex·cise** \ek,sīz, -,sīs\ n : tax

²**ex·cise** \ik'sīz\ vb -cised; -cis·ing : cut out —**ex·ci·sion** \-'sizhən\ n

ex·cite \ik'sīt\ vb -cit·ed; -cit·ing 1 : stir up 2 : kindle the emotions of —**ex·cit·abil·i·ty** \-,sītə'bilətē\ n —**ex·cit·able** \-'sītəbəl\ adj —**ex·ci·ta·tion** \ek,sī'tāshən, -sə-\ n —**ex·cit·ed·ly** adv —**ex·cite·ment** \ik'sītmənt\ n

ex·claim \iks'klām\ vb : cry out esp. in delight —**ex·cla·ma·tion** \eksklə'māshən\ n —**ex·clam·a·to·ry** \iks'klamə,tōrē\ adj

exclamation point n : punctuation mark ! used esp. after an interjection or exclamation

ex·clude \iks'klüd\ vb -clud·ed; -clud·ing : leave out —**ex·clu·sion** \-'klüzhən\ n

ex·clu·sive \-'klüsiv\ adj 1 : reserved for particular persons 2 : stylish 3 : sole —**exclusive** n —**ex·clu·sive·ly** adv —**ex·clu·sive·ness** n

ex·com·mu·ni·cate \ekskə'myünə,kāt\ vb : expel from a church —**excom·mu·ni·ca·tion** \-,myünə'kāshən\ n

ex·cre·ment \ekskrəmənt\ n : bodily waste —**ex·cre·men·tal** \ekskrə-'ment°l\ adj

ex·crete \ik'skrēt\ vb -cret·ed; -cret·ing : eliminate wastes from the body —**ex·cre·tion** \-'skrēshən\ n —**ex·cre·to·ry** \ekskrə,tōrē\ adj

ex·cru·ci·at·ing \ik'skrüshē,ātiŋ\ adj : intensely painful —**ex·cru·ci·at·ing·ly** adv

ex·cul·pate \ekskəl,pāt\ vb -pat·ed; -pat·ing : clear from alleged fault

ex·cur·sion \ik'skərzhən\ n : pleasure trip

ex·cuse \ik'skyüz\ vb -cused; -cus·ing 1 : pardon 2 : release from an obligation 3 : justify ~ \-'skyüs\ n 1 : justification 2 : apology

ex·e·cute \eksi,kyüt\ vb -cut·ed; -cut·ing 1 : carry out fully 2 : enforce 3 : put to death —**ex·e·cu·tion** \eksi'kyüshən\ n —**ex·e·cu·tion·er** \-shənər\ n

ex·ec·u·tive \ig'zekyətiv\ adj : relating to the carrying out of decisions, plans, or laws — n 1 : branch of government with executive duties 2 : administrator

ex·ec·u·tor \-yətər\ n : person named in a will to execute it

ex·ec·u·trix \ig'zekyə,triks\ n, pl **ex·ec·u·tri·ces** \-,zekyə'trī,sēz\ or **ex·ec·u·trix·es** : woman executor

ex·em·pla·ry \ig'zemplərē\ adj : so commendable as to serve as a model

ex·em·pli·fy \-plə,fī\ vb -fied; -fy·ing : serve as an example of —**ex·em·pli·fi·ca·tion** \-,zempləfə'kāshən\ n

ex·empt \ig'zempt\ adj : being free from some liability ~ vb : make exempt —**ex·emp·tion** \-'zempshən\ n

ex·er·cise \eksər,sīz\ n 1 : a putting into action 2 : exertion to develop endurance or a skill 3 pl : public ceremony ~ vb -cised; -cis·ing 1 : exert 2 : engage in exercise —**ex·er·cis·er** n

ex·ert \ig'zərt\ vb : put into action —**ex·er·tion** \-'zərshən\ n

ex·hale \eks'hāl\ vb -haled; -hal·ing : breathe out —**ex·ha·la·tion** \eksha'lāshən\ n

ex·haust \ig'zòst\ vb 1 : draw out or develop completely 2 : use up 3 : tire or wear out ~ n : waste steam or gas from an engine or a system for removing it —**ex·haus·tion** \-'zòschən\ n —**ex·haus·tive** \-'zòstiv\ adj

ex·hib·it \ig'zibət\ vb : display esp. publicly ~ n 1 : act of exhibiting 2 : something exhibited —**ex·hi·bi·tion** \eksə'bishən\ n —**ex·hib·i·tor** \ig'zibətər\ n

ex·hil·a·rate \ig'zilə,rāt\ vb -rat·ed; -rat·ing : thrill —**ex·hil·a·ra·tion** \-,zilə'rāshən\ n

ex·hort \ig'zòrt\ vb : urge earnestly —**ex·hor·ta·tion** \eks,òr'tāshən, egz-, -ər-\ n

ex·hume \igz'üm, -'yüm; iks'yüm, -'hyüm\ vb -humed; -hum·ing : dig up (a buried corpse) —**ex·hu·ma·tion** \eksyü'māshən, -hyü-; ,egzü-, -zyü-\ n

ex·i·gen·cies \eksəjənsēz, ig'zijən-\ n pl : requirements (as of a situation)

ex·ile \eg,zīl, 'ek,sīl\ n 1 : banishment 2 : person banished from his or her country —**exile** vb

ex·ist \ig'zist\ vb 1 : have real or actual being 2 : live —**ex·is·tence** \-əns\ n —**ex·is·tent** \-ənt\ adj

ex·it \egzət, 'eksət\ n 1 : departure 2 : way out of an enclosed space 3 : way off an expressway —**exit** vb

ex·o·dus \eksədəs\ n : mass departure

ex·on·er·ate \ig'zänə,rāt\ vb -at·ed; -at·ing

: free from blame —**ex·on·er·a·tion** \-,zänə'rāshən\ n

ex·or·bi·tant \ig'zòrbətənt\ adj : exceeding what is usual or proper

ex·or·cise \ek,sòr,sīz, -sər-\ vb -cised; -cis·ing : drive out (as an evil spirit) —**ex·or·cism** \-,sizəm\ n —**ex·or·cist** \-,sist\ n

ex·ot·ic \ig'zätik\ adj : foreign or strange —**exotic** n —**ex·ot·i·cal·ly** \-iklē\ adv

ex·pand \ik'spand\ vb : enlarge

ex·panse \-'spans\ n : very large area

ex·pan·sion \-'spanchən\ n 1 : act or process of expanding 2 : expanded part

ex·pan·sive \-'spansiv\ adj 1 : tending to expand 2 : warmly benevolent 3 : of large extent —**ex·pan·sive·ly** adv —**ex·pan·sive·ness** n

ex·pa·tri·ate \ek'spātrē,āt, -ət\ n : exile —**expatriate** \-,āt\ adj or vb

ex·pect \ik'spekt\ vb 1 : look forward to 2 : consider probable or one's due —**ex·pec·tan·cy** \-ənsē\ n —**ex·pec·tant** \-ənt\ adj —**ex·pec·tant·ly** adv —**ex·pec·ta·tion** \ek,spek'tāshən\ n

ex·pe·di·ent \ik'spēdēənt\ adj : convenient or advantageous rather than right or just ~ n : convenient often makeshift means to an end

ex·pe·dite \ekspə,dīt\ vb -dit·ed; -dit·ing : carry out or handle promptly —**ex·pe·dit·er** n

ex·pe·di·tion \ekspə'dishən\ n : long journey for work or research or the people making this

ex·pe·di·tious \-əs\ adj : prompt and efficient

ex·pel \ik'spel\ vb -ll- : force out

ex·pend \-'spend\ vb 1 : pay out 2 : use up —**ex·pend·able** adj

ex·pen·di·ture \-'spendichər, -də,chúr\ n : act of using or spending

ex·pense \ik'spens\ n : cost —**ex·pen·sive** \-'spensiv\ adj —**ex·pen·sive·ly** adv

ex·pe·ri·ence \ik'spirēəns\ n 1 : a participating in or living through an event 2 : an event that affects one 3 : knowledge from doing ~ vb -enced; -enc·ing : undergo

ex·per·i·ment \ik'sperəmənt\ n : test to discover something ~ vb : make experiments —**ex·per·i·men·tal** \-,sperə'ment°l\ adj —**ex·per·i·men·ta·tion** \-mən'tāshən\ n —**ex·per·i·men·ter** \-'sperə,mentər\ n

ex·pert \ek,spərt\ adj : thoroughly skilled ~ n : person with special skill —**ex·pert·ly** adv —**ex·pert·ness** n

ex·per·tise \ekspər'tēz\ n : skill

ex·pi·ate \ekspē,āt\ vb : make amends for —**ex·pi·a·tion** \ekspē'āshən\ n

ex·pire \ik'spīr, ek-\ vb -pired; -pir·ing 1 : breathe out 2 : die 3 : end —**ex·pi·ra·tion** \ekspə'rāshən\ n

ex·plain \ik'splān\ vb 1 : make clear 2 : give the reason for —**ex·plain·able** \-əbəl\ adj —**ex·pla·na·tion** \eksplə'nāshən\ n —**ex·plan·a·to·ry** \ik'splanə,tōrē\ adj

ex·ple·tive \ekspletiv\ n : usu. profane exclamation

ex·pli·ca·ble \ek'splikəbəl, 'eksplik-\ adj : capable of being explained

ex·plic·it \ik'splisət\ adj : absolutely clear or precise —**ex·plic·it·ly** adv —**ex·plic·it·ness** n

ex·plode \ik'splōd\ vb -plod·ed; -plod·ing 1 : discredit 2 : burst or cause to burst violently 3 : increase rapidly

ex·ploit \ek,sploit\ n : heroic act ~ \ik-'sploit\ vb 1 : utilize 2 : use unfairly —**ex·ploi·ta·tion** \eksploi'tāshən\ n

ex·plore \ik'splōr\ vb -plored; -plor·ing : examine or range over thoroughly —**ex·plo·ra·tion** \eksplə'rāshən\ n —**ex·plor·a·to·ry** \ik'splōrə,tōrē\ adj —**ex·plor·er** n

ex·plo·sion \ik'splōzhən\ n : process or instance of exploding

ex·plo·sive \-siv\ adj 1 : able to cause explosion 2 : likely to explode —**explosive** n —**ex·plo·sive·ly** adv

ex·po·nent \ik'spōnənt, 'ek,spō-\ n 1 : mathematical symbol showing how many times a number is to be repeated as a factor 2 : advocate —**ex·po·nen·tial** \ekspə'nenchəl\ adj —**ex·po·nen·tial·ly** adv

ex·port \ek'spōrt, 'ek,spōrt\ vb : send to foreign countries —**export** \ek,-\ n —**ex·por·ta·tion** \ek,spōr'tāshən, -pər-\ n —**ex·port·er** \ek'spōrtər, 'ek,spōrt-\ n

ex·pose \ik'spōz\ vb -posed; -pos·ing 1 : deprive of shelter or protection 2 : subject (film) to light 3 : make known —**ex·po·sure** \-'spōzhər\ n

ex·po·sé, ex·po·se \ekspō'zā\ n : exposure of something discreditable

ex·po·si·tion \ekspə'zishən\ n : public exhibition

ex·pound \ik'spaúnd\ vb : set forth or explain in detail

¹**ex·press** \ik'spres\ adj 1 : clear 2 : specific 3 : traveling at high speed with few stops —**express** adv or n —**ex·press·ly** adv

²**express** vb 1 : make known in words or appearance 2 : press out (as juice)

ex·pres·sion \-'spreshən\ n 1 : utterance 2

: mathematical symbol 3 : significant word or phrase 4 : look on one's face —**ex·pres·sion·less** adj —**ex·pres·sive** \-'spresiv\ adj —**ex·pres·sive·ness** n

ex·press·way \ik'spres,wā\ n : high-speed divided highway with limited access

ex·pul·sion \ik'spəlshən\ n : an expelling or being expelled

ex·pur·gate \ekspər,gāt\ vb -gat·ed; -gat·ing : censor —**ex·pur·ga·tion** \ekspər-'gāshən\ n

ex·qui·site \ek'skwizət, 'ekskwiz-\ adj 1 : flawlessly beautiful and delicate 2 : keenly discriminating

ex·tant \ekstənt, ek'stant\ adj : existing

ex·tem·po·ra·ne·ous \ek,stempə'rānēəs\ adj : impromptu —**ex·tem·po·ra·ne·ous·ly** adv

ex·tend \ik'stend\ vb 1 : stretch forth or out 2 : prolong 3 : enlarge —**ex·tend·able, ex·tend·ible** \-'stendəbəl\ adj

ex·ten·sion \-'stenchən\ n 1 : an extending or being extended 2 : additional part 3 : extra telephone line

ex·ten·sive \-'stensiv\ adj : of considerable extent —**ex·ten·sive·ly** adv

ex·tent \-'stent\ n : range, space, or degree to which something extends

ex·ten·u·ate \ik'stenyə,wāt\ vb -at·ed; -at·ing : lessen the seriousness of —**ex·ten·u·a·tion** \-,stenyə'wāshən\ n

ex·te·ri·or \ek'stirēər\ adj : external ~ n : external part or surface

ex·ter·mi·nate \ik'stərmə,nāt\ vb -nat·ed; -nat·ing : destroy utterly —**ex·ter·mi·na·tion** \-,stərmə'nāshən\ n —**ex·ter·mi·na·tor** \-'stərmə,nātər\ n

ex·ter·nal \ek'stərn°l\ adj : relating to or on the outside —**ex·ter·nal·ly** adv

ex·tinct \ik'stiŋkt\ adj : no longer existing —**ex·tinc·tion** \-'stiŋkshən\ n

ex·tin·guish \ik'stiŋgwish\ vb : cause to stop burning —**ex·tin·guish·able** adj —**ex·tin·guish·er** n

ex·tir·pate \ekstər,pāt\ vb -pat·ed; -pat·ing : destroy

ex·tol \ik'stōl\ vb -ll- : praise highly

ex·tort \-'stòrt\ vb : obtain by force or improper pressure —**ex·tor·tion** \-'stòrshən\ n —**ex·tor·tion·er** n —**ex·tor·tion·ist** n

ex·tra \ekstrə\ adj 1 : additional 2 : superior —**extra** n or adv

ex·tract \ik'strakt\ vb 1 : pull out forcibly 2 : withdraw (as a juice) ~ \ek,-\ n 1 : excerpt 2 : product (as a juice) obtained by extracting —**ex·tract·able** adj —**ex·trac·tion** \ik'strakshən\ n —**ex·trac·tor** \-tər\ n

ex·tra·cur·ric·u·lar \ekstrəkə'rikyələr\ adj : lying outside the regular curriculum

ex·tra·dite \ekstrə,dīt\ vb -dit·ed; -dit·ing : bring or deliver a suspect to a different jurisdiction for trial —**ex·tra·di·tion** \ekstrə'dishən\ n

ex·tra·mar·i·tal \ekstrə'marət°l\ adj : relating to sexual relations of a married person outside of the marriage

ex·tra·ne·ous \ek'strānēəs\ adj : not essential or relevant —**ex·tra·ne·ous·ly** adv

ex·traor·di·nary \ik'strórdən,erē, ,ekstrə-'órd-\ adj : notably unusual or exceptional —**ex·traor·di·nar·i·ly** \ik,strórdən'erəlē, ,ekstrə,órd-\ adv

ex·tra·sen·so·ry \ekstrə'sensərē\ adj : outside the ordinary senses

ex·tra·ter·res·tri·al \ekstrətə'restrēəl\ n : one existing or coming from outside the earth — adj : relating to an extraterrestrial

ex·trav·a·gant \ik'stravigənt\ adj : wildly excessive, lavish, or costly —**ex·trav·a·gance** \-gəns\ n —**ex·trav·a·gant·ly** adv

ex·trav·a·gan·za \-,stravə'ganzə\ n : spectacular event

ex·tra·ve·hic·u·lar \ekstrəvē'hikyələr\ adj : occurring outside a spacecraft

ex·treme \ik'strēm\ adj 1 : very great or intense 2 : very severe 3 : not moderate 4 : most remote ~ n 1 : extreme state 2 : something located at one end or the other of a range —**ex·treme·ly** adv

ex·trem·i·ty \-'stremətē\ n, pl -ties 1 : most remote part 2 : human hand or foot 3 : extreme degree or state (as of need)

ex·tri·cate \ekstrə,kāt\ vb -cat·ed; -cat·ing : set or get free from an entanglement or difficulty —**ex·tri·ca·ble** \ik'strikəbəl, ek-; 'ekstrik-\ adj —**ex·tri·ca·tion** \ekstrə-'kāshən\ n

ex·tro·vert \ekstrə,vərt\ n : gregarious person —**ex·tro·ver·sion** \ekstrə'vərzhən\ n —**ex·tro·vert·ed** \ekstrə,vərtəd\ adj

ex·trude \ik'strüd\ vb -trud·ed; -trud·ing : to force or push out

ex·u·ber·ant \ig'zübərənt\ adj : joyously unrestrained —**ex·u·ber·ance** \-rəns\ n —**ex·u·ber·ant·ly** adv

ex·ude \ig'züd\ vb -ud·ed; -ud·ing 1 : discharge slowly through pores 2 : display conspicuously

ex·ult \ig'zəlt\ vb : rejoice —**ex·ul·tant** \-'zəlt°nt\ adj —**ex·ul·tant·ly** adv —**ex·ul·ta·tion** \eksəl'tāshən, ,egzəl-\ n

-**ey** —see -Y

eye \'ī\ n 1 : organ of sight consisting of a globular structure (**eye·ball**) in a socket of the skull with thin movable covers (**eye·lids**) bordered with hairs (**eye·lash·es**) 2 : vision 3 : judgment 4 : something suggesting an eye ~ vb eyed; eye·ing or ey·ing : look at —**eye·brow** \-,braú\ n —**eyed** \'īd\ adj —**eye·strain** n

eye·drop·per n : dropper

eye·glass·es n pl : glasses

eye·let \'īlət\ n : hole (as in cloth) for a lacing or rope

eye·open·er n : something startling —**eye·open·ing** adj

eye·piece n : lens at the eye end of an optical instrument

eye·sight n : sight

eye·sore n : unpleasant sight

eye·tooth n : upper canine tooth

eye·wit·ness n : person who actually sees something happen

ey·rie \'īrē, or like AERIE\ var of AERIE

F

f \'ef\ n, pl **f's** or **fs** \'efs\ : 6th letter of the alphabet

fa·ble \'fābəl\ n 1 : legendary story 2 : story that teaches a lesson —**fa·bled** \-bəld\ adj

fab·ric \'fabrik\ n 1 : structure 2 : material made usu. by weaving or knitting fibers

fab·ri·cate \'fabri,kāt\ vb -cat·ed; -cat·ing 1 : construct 2 : invent —**fab·ri·ca·tion** \,fabri'kāshən\ n

fab·u·lous \'fabyələs\ adj 1 : like, told in, or based on fable 2 : incredible or marvelous —**fab·u·lous·ly** adv

fa·cade \fə'säd\ n 1 : principal face of a building 2 : false or superficial appearance

face \'fās\ n 1 : front or principal surface (as of the head) 2 : presence 3 : facial expression 4 : grimace 5 : outward appearance ~ vb faced; fac·ing 1 : challenge or resist firmly or brazenly 2 : cover with different material 3 : sit or stand with the face toward 4 : have the front oriented toward —**faced** \'fāst\ adj —**face·less** n —**fa·cial** \'fāshəl\ adj

face·down adv : with the face downward

face·lift \'fās,lift\ n 1 : cosmetic surgery on the face 2 : modernization

fac·et \'fasət\ n 1 : surface of a cut gem 2 : phase —**fac·et·ed** adj

fa·ce·tious \fə'sēshəs\ adj : jocular —**fa·ce·tious·ly** adv —**fa·ce·tious·ness** n

fac·ile \'fasəl\ adj 1 : easy 2 : fluent

fa·cil·i·tate \fə'silə,tāt\ vb -tat·ed; -tat·ing : make easier

fa·cil·i·ty \fə'silətē\ n, pl -ties 1 : ease in doing or using 2 : something built or installed to serve a purpose or facilitate an activity

fac·ing \'fāsiŋ\ n : lining or covering or material for this

fac·sim·i·le \fak'siməlē\ n : exact copy

fact \'fakt\ n 1 : act or action 2 : something that exists or is real 3 : piece of information —**fac·tu·al** \'fakchəwəl\ adj —**fac·tu·al·ly** adv

fac·tion \'fakshən\ n : part of a larger group —**fac·tion·al·ism** \-shənə,lizəm\ n

fac·tious \'fakshəs\ adj : causing discord

fac·ti·tious \fak'tishəs\ adj : artificial

fac·tor \'faktər\ n 1 : something that has an effect 2 : gene 3 : number used in multiplying

fac·to·ry \'faktərē\ n, pl -ries : place for manufacturing

fac·to·tum \fak'tōtəm\ n : person (as a servant) with varied duties

fac·ul·ty \'fakəltē\ n, pl -ties 1 : ability to act 2 : power of the mind or body 3 : body of teachers or department of instruction

fad \'fad\ n : briefly popular practice or interest —**fad·dish** adj —**fad·dist** n

fade \'fād\ vb fad·ed; fad·ing 1 : wither 2 : lose or cause to lose freshness or brilliance 3 : grow dim 4 : vanish

fag \'fag\ vb -gg- 1 : drudge 2 : tire or exhaust

fag·ot, fag·got \'fagət\ n : bundle of twigs

Fahr·en·heit \'farən,hīt\ adj : relating to a thermometer scale with the boiling point at 212 degrees and the freezing point at 32 degrees

fail \'fāl\ vb 1 : decline in health 2 : die away

3 : stop functioning 4 : be unsuccessful 5 : become bankrupt 6 : disappoint 7 : neglect — *prep* : in the absence or lack of
fail•ing *n* : slight defect in character or conduct
faille \'fīl\ *n* : closely woven ribbed fabric
fail•ure \'fālyər\ *n* 1 : absence of expected action or performance 2 : bankruptcy 3 : deficiency 4 : one that has failed
faint \'fānt\ *adj* 1 : cowardly or spiritless 2 : weak and dizzy 3 : lacking vigor 4 : indistinct ~ *vb* : lose consciousness ~ *n* : act or condition of fainting —**faint-heart•ed** *adj* —**faint•ly** *adv* —**faint•ness** *n*
¹**fair** \'far\ *adj* 1 : pleasing in appearance 2 : not stormy or cloudy 3 : just or honest 4 : conforming with the rules 5 : open to legitimate pursuit or attack 6 : light in color 7 : adequate —**fair•ness** *n*
²**fair** *adv, chiefly Brit* : FAIRLY
³**fair** *n* : exhibition for judging or selling —**fair•ground** *n*
fair•ly \'farlē\ *adv* 1 : in a manner of speaking 2 : without bias 3 : somewhat
fairy \'farē\ *n, pl* **fair•ies** : usu. small imaginary being —**fairy tale** *n*
fairy•land \-,land\ *n* 1 : land of fairies 2 : beautiful or charming place
faith \'fāth\ *n, pl* **faiths** \'fāths, 'fāthz\ 1 : allegiance 2 : belief and trust in God 3 : confidence 4 : system of religious beliefs —**faith•ful** \-fəl\ *adj* —**faith•ful•ly** *adv* —**faith•ful•ness** *n* —**faith•less** *adj* —**faith•less•ly** *adv* —**faith•less•ness** *n*
fake \'fāk\ *vb* **faked; fak•ing** 1 : falsify 2 : counterfeit ~ *n* : copy, fraud, or impostor ~ *adj* : not genuine —**fak•er** *n*
fa•kir \fə'kir\ *n* : wandering beggar of India
fal•con \'falkən, 'fol-\ *n* : small long-winged hawk used esp. for hunting —**fal•con•ry** \-rē\ *n*
fall \'fol\ *vb* **fell** \'fel\; **fall•en** \'folən\; **fall•ing** 1 : go down by gravity 2 : hang freely 3 : go lower 4 : be defeated or ruined 5 : commit a sin 6 : happen at a certain time 7 : become gradually ~ *n* 1 : act of falling 2 : autumn 3 : downfall 4 *pl* : waterfall 5 : distance something falls
fal•la•cy \'faləsē\ *n, pl* **-cies** 1 : false idea 2 : false reasoning —**fal•la•cious** \fə'lāshəs\ *adj*
fal•li•ble \'faləbəl\ *adj* : capable of making a mistake —**fal•li•bly** \-blē\ *adv*
fall•out *n* 1 : radioactive particles from a nuclear explosion 2 : secondary effects
fal•low \'falō\ *adj* 1 : plowed but not planted 2 : dormant —**fallow** *n or vb*
false \'fols\ *adj* **fals•er; fals•est** 1 : not genuine, true, faithful, or permanent 2 : misleading —**false•ly** *adv* —**false•ness** *n* —**fal•si•fi•ca•tion** \,folsəfə'kāshən\ *n* —**fal•si•fy** \'folsə,fī\ *vb* —**fal•si•ty** \'folsətē\ *n*
false•hood \'fols,hud\ *n* : lie
fal•set•to \fol'setō\ *n, pl* **-tos** : artificially high singing voice
fal•ter \'foltər\ *vb* **-tered; -ter•ing** 1 : move unsteadily 2 : hesitate —**fal•ter•ing•ly** *adv*
fame \'fām\ *n* : public reputation —**famed** \'fāmd\ *adj*
fa•mil•ial \fə'milyəl\ *adj* : relating to a family
¹**fa•mil•iar** \fə'milyər\ *n* 1 : companion 2 : guardian spirit
²**familiar** *adj* 1 : closely acquainted 2 : forward 3 : frequently seen or experienced —**fa•mil•iar•i•ty** \fə,mil'yarətē, -,milē'yar-\ *n* —**fa•mil•iar•ize** \fə'milyə,rīz\ *vb* —**fa•mil•iar•ly** *adv*
fam•i•ly \'famlē\ *n, pl* **-lies** 1 : persons of common ancestry 2 : group living together 3 : parents and children 4 : group of related individuals
fam•ine \'famən\ *n* : extreme scarcity of food
fam•ish \'famish\ *vb* : starve
fa•mous \'fāməs\ *adj* : widely known or celebrated
fa•mous•ly *adv* : very well
¹**fan** \'fan\ *n* : device for producing a current of air ~ *vb* **-nn-** 1 : move air with a fan 2 : direct a current of air upon 3 : stir to activity
²**fan** *n* : enthusiastic follower or admirer
fa•nat•ic \fə'natik\, **fa•nat•i•cal** \-ikəl\ *adj* : excessively enthusiastic or devoted —**fanatic** *n* —**fa•nat•i•cism** \-,natə,sizəm\ *n*
fan•ci•er \'fansēər\ *n* : one devoted to raising a particular plant or animal
fan•cy \'fansē\ *n, pl* **-cies** 1 : liking 2 : whim 3 : imagination ~ *vb* **-cied; -cy•ing** 1 : like 2 : imagine ~ *adj* **-cier; -est** 1 : not plain 2 : of superior quality —**fan•ci•ful** \-sifəl\ *adj* —**fan•ci•ful•ly** \-fəlē\ *adv* —**fan•ci•ly** *adv*
fan•dan•go \fan'dangō\ *n, pl* **-gos** : lively Spanish dance
fan•fare \'fan,far\ *n* : a sounding of trumpets 2 : showy display
fang \'fang\ *n* : long sharp tooth
fan•light *n* : semicircular window
fan•ta•sia \fan'tāzhə, -zēə, ,fantə'zēə\ *n*

: music written to fancy rather than to form
fan•tas•tic \fan'tastik\ *adj* 1 : imaginary or unrealistic 2 : exceedingly or unbelievably great —**fan•tas•ti•cal•ly** \-tiklē\ *adv*
fan•ta•sy \'fantəsē\ *n* 1 : imagination 2 : product (as a daydream) of the imagination 3 : fantasia —**fan•ta•size** \'fantə,sīz\ *vb*
far \'fär\ *adv* **far•ther** \-thər\ *or* **fur•ther** \'fər-\; **far•thest** *or* **fur•thest** \-thəst\ 1 : at or to a distance 2 : much 3 : to a degree 4 : to an advanced point or extent ~ *adj* **farther** *or* **further; farthest** *or* **furthest** 1 : remote 2 : long 3 : being more distant
far•away *adj* : distant
farce \'färs\ *n* 1 : satirical comedy with an improbable plot 2 : ridiculous display —**far•ci•cal** *adj*
¹**fare** \'far\ *vb* **fared; far•ing** : get along
²**fare** *n* 1 : price of transportation 2 : range of food
fare•well \far'wel\ *n* 1 : wish of welfare at parting 2 : departure —**farewell** *adj*
far-fetched \'fär'fecht\ *adj* : improbable
fa•ri•na \fə'rēnə\ *n* : fine meal made from cereal grains
farm \'färm\ *n* : place where something is raised for food ~ *vb* 1 : use (land) as a farm 2 : raise plants or animals for food —**farm•er** *n* —**farm•hand** \-,hand\ *n* —**farm•house** *n* —**farm•ing** *n* —**farm•land** \-,land\ *n* —**farm•yard** *n*
far-off *adj* : remote in time or space
far•ri•er \'farēər\ *n* : blacksmith who shoes horses
far•row \'farō\ *vb* : give birth to a litter of pigs —**farrow** *n*
far•sight•ed *adj* 1 : better able to see distant things than near 2 : judicious or shrewd —**far•sight•ed•ness** *n*
far•ther \'färthər\ *adv* 1 : at or to a greater distance or more advanced point 2 : to a greater degree or extent ~ *adj* : more distant
far•ther•most *adj* : most distant
far•thest \'färthəst\ *adj* : most distant ~ *adv* 1 : to or at the greatest distance 2 : to the most advanced point 3 : by the greatest extent
fas•ci•cle \'fasikəl\ *n* 1 : small bundle 2 : division of a book published in parts —**fas•ci•cled** \-kəld\ *adj*
fas•ci•nate \'fas°n,āt\ *vb* **-nat•ed; -nat•ing** : transfix and hold spellbound —**fas•ci•na•tion** \,fas°n'āshən\ *n*
fas•cism \'fash,izəm\ *n* : dictatorship that exalts nation and race —**fas•cist** \-ist\ *n or adj* —**fas•cis•tic** \fa'shistik\ *adj*
fash•ion \'fashən\ *n* 1 : manner 2 : prevailing custom or style ~ *vb* : form or construct —**fash•ion•able** \-ənəbəl\ *adj* —**fash•ion•ably** \-blē\ *adv*
¹**fast** \'fast\ *adj* 1 : firmly fixed, bound, or shut 2 : faithful 3 : moving or acting quickly 4 : indicating ahead of the correct time 5 : deep and undisturbed 6 : permanently dyed 7 : wild or promiscuous ~ *adv* 1 : so as to be secure or bound 2 : soundly or deeply 3 : swiftly
²**fast** *vb* : abstain from food or eat sparingly ~ *n* : act or time of fasting
fas•ten \'fas°n\ *vb* : attach esp. by pinning or tying —**fas•ten•er** *n* —**fas•ten•ing** *n*
fas•tid•i•ous \fas'tidēəs\ *adj* : hard to please —**fas•tid•i•ous•ly** *adv* —**fas•tid•i•ous•ness** *n*
fat \'fat\ *adj* **-tt-** 1 : having much fat 2 : thick ~ *n* : animal tissue rich in greasy or oily matter —**fat•ness** *n* —**fat•ten** \'fat°n\ *vb* —**fat•ty** *adj or n*
fa•tal \'fāt°l\ *adj* : causing death or ruin —**fa•tal•i•ty** \fā'talətē, fə-\ *n* —**fa•tal•ly** *adv*
fa•tal•ism \'fāt°l,izəm\ *n* : belief that fate determines events —**fa•tal•ist** \-ist\ *n* —**fa•tal•is•tic** \,fāt°l'istik\ *adj* —**fa•tal•is•ti•cal•ly** \-tiklē\ *adv*
fate \'fāt\ *n* 1 : principle, cause, or will held to determine events 2 : end or outcome —**fat•ed** *adj* —**fate•ful** \-fəl\ *adj* —**fate•ful•ly** *adv*
fa•ther \'fäthər, 'fath-\ *n* 1 : male parent 2 *cap* : God 3 : originator —**father** *vb* —**fa•ther•hood** \-,hud\ *n* —**fa•ther•land** \-,land\ *n* —**fa•ther•less** *adj* —**fa•ther•ly** *adj*
father-in-law *n, pl* **fathers-in-law** : father of one's spouse
fath•om \'fathəm\ *n* : nautical unit of length equal to 6 feet ~ *vb* : understand —**fath•om•able** *adj* —**fath•om•less** *adj*
fa•tigue \fə'tēg\ *n* 1 : weariness from labor or use 2 : tendency to break under repeated stress ~ *vb* **-tigued; -tigu•ing** : tire out
fat•u•ous \'fachəwəs\ *adj* : foolish or stupid —**fat•u•ous•ly** *adv* —**fat•u•ous•ness** *n*
fau•cet \'fosət, 'fäs-\ *n* : fixture for drawing off a liquid
fault \'folt\ *n* 1 : weakness in character 2 : something wrong or imperfect 3 : responsibility for something wrong 4 : fracture in the earth's crust ~ *vb* : find fault in or with —**fault•find•er** *n* —**fault-**

: find•ing *n* —**fault•i•ly** \'foltəlē\ *adv* —**fault•less** *adj* —**fault•less•ly** *adv* —**faulty** *adj*
fau•na \'fonə\ *n* : animals or animal life esp. of a region —**fau•nal** \-°l\ *adj*
faux pas \'fō'pä\ *n, pl* **faux pas** *same or* -'päz\ : social blunder
fa•vor \'fāvər\ *n* 1 : approval 2 : partiality 3 : act of kindness ~ *vb* : regard or treat with favor —**fa•vor•able** \'fāvərəbəl\ *adj* —**fa•vor•ably** \-blē\ *adv*
fa•vor•ite \'fāvərət\ *n* : one favored —**favorite** *adj* —**fa•vor•it•ism** \-,izəm\ *n*
¹**fawn** \'fon\ *vb* : seek favor by groveling
²**fawn** *n* : young deer
faze \'fāz\ *vb* **fazed; faz•ing** : disturb the composure of
fear \'fir\ *n* : unpleasant emotion caused by expectation or awareness of danger ~ *vb* : be afraid of —**fear•ful** \-fəl\ *adj* —**fear•ful•ly** *adv* —**fear•less** *adj* —**fear•less•ly** *adv* —**fear•less•ness** *n* —**fear•some** \-səm\ *adj*
fea•si•ble \'fēzəbəl\ *adj* : capable of being done —**fea•si•bil•i•ty** \,fēzə'bilətē\ *n* —**fea•si•bly** \'fēzə'bilətē\ *adv*
feast \'fēst\ *n* 1 : large or fancy meal 2 : religious festival ~ *vb* : eat plentifully
feat \'fēt\ *n* : notable deed
feath•er \'fethər\ *n* : one of the light horny outgrowths that form the external covering of a bird's body —**feather** *vb* —**feath•ered** \-ərd\ *adj* —**feath•er•less** *adj* —**feath•ery** *adj*
fea•ture \'fēchər\ *n* 1 : shape or appearance of the face 2 : part of the face 3 : prominent characteristic 4 : special attraction ~ *vb* : give prominence to —**fea•ture•less** *adj*
Feb•ru•ary \'febyə,werē, 'febə-, 'febrə-\ *n* : 2d month of the year having 28 and in leap years 29 days
fe•ces \'fēsēz\ *n pl* : intestinal body waste —**fe•cal** \-kəl\ *adj*
feck•less \'fekləs\ *adj* : irresponsible
fe•cund \'fekənd, 'fē-\ *adj* : prolific —**fe•cun•di•ty** \fi'kəndətē, fe-\ *n*
fed•er•al \'fedrəl, -dərəl\ *adj* : of or constituting a government with power distributed between a central authority and constituent units —**fed•er•al•ism** \-rə,lizəm\ *n* —**fed•er•al•ist** \-list\ *n or adj* —**fed•er•al•ly** *adv*
fed•er•ate \'fedə,rāt\ *vb* **-at•ed; -at•ing** : join in a federation
fed•er•a•tion \,fedə'rāshən\ *n* : union of organizations
fe•do•ra \fi'dōrə\ *n* : soft felt hat
fed up *adj* : out of patience
fee \'fē\ *n* : fixed charge
fee•ble \'fēbəl\ *adj* **-bler; -blest** : weak or ineffective —**fee•ble•mind•ed** \,fēbəl'mīndəd\ *adj* —**fee•ble•mind•ed•ness** *n* —**fee•ble•ness** *n* —**fee•bly** \-blē\ *adv*
feed \'fēd\ *vb* **fed** \'fed\; **feed•ing** 1 : give food to 2 : eat 3 : furnish ~ *n* : food for livestock —**feed•er** *n*
feel \'fēl\ *vb* **felt** \'felt\; **feel•ing** 1 : perceive or examine through physical contact 2 : think or believe 3 : be conscious of 4 : seem 5 : have sympathy ~ *n* 1 : sense of touch 2 : quality of a thing imparted through touch —**feel•er** *n*
feel•ing \'fēliŋ\ *n* 1 : sense of touch 2 : state of mind 3 *pl* : sensibilities 4 : opinion
feet *pl of* FOOT
feign \'fān\ *vb* : pretend
feint \'fānt\ *n* : mock attack intended to distract attention —**feint** *vb*
fe•lic•i•tate \fi'lisə,tāt\ *vb* **-tat•ed; -tat•ing** : congratulate —**fe•lic•i•ta•tion** \-,lisə'tāshən\ *n*
fe•lic•i•tous \fi'lisətəs\ *adj* : aptly expressed —**fe•lic•i•tous•ly** *adv*
fe•lic•i•ty \fi'lisətē\ *n, pl* **-ties** 1 : great happiness 2 : pleasing faculty esp. in art or language
fe•line \'fē,līn\ *adj* : relating to cats —**feline** *n*
¹**fell** \'fel\ *vb* : cut or knock down
²**fell** *past of* FALL
fel•low \'felō\ *n* 1 : companion or associate 2 : man or boy —**fel•low•ship** \-,ship\ *n*
fel•low•man \,felō'man\ *n* : kindred human being
fel•on \'felən\ *n* : one who has committed a felony
fel•o•ny \'felənē\ *n, pl* **-nies** : serious crime —**fe•lo•ni•ous** \fə'lōnēəs\ *adj*
¹**felt** \'felt\ *n* : cloth made of pressed wool and fur
²**felt** *past of* FEEL
fe•male \'fē,māl\ *adj* : relating to or being the sex that bears young —**female** *n*
fem•i•nine \'femənən\ *adj* : relating to the female sex —**fem•i•nin•i•ty** \,femə'ninətē\ *n*
fem•i•nism \'femə,nizəm\ *n* : organized activity on behalf of women's rights —**fem•i•nist** \-nist\ *n or adj*
fe•mur \'fēmər\ *n, pl* **fe•murs** *or* **fem•o•ra** \'femərə\ : long bone of the thigh —**fem•o•ral** \'femərəl\ *adj*
fence \'fens\ *n* : enclosing barrier esp. of

wood or wire ~ *vb* **fenced; fenc•ing** 1 : enclose with a fence 2 : practice fencing —**fenc•er** *n*
fenc•ing \'fensiŋ\ *n* 1 : combat with swords for sport 2 : material for building fences
fend \'fend\ *vb* : ward off
fend•er \'fendər\ *n* : guard over an automobile wheel
fen•nel \'fen°l\ *n* : herb related to the carrot
fer•ment \fər'ment\ *vb* : cause or undergo fermentation ~ \'fər,ment\ *n* : agitation
fer•men•ta•tion \,fərmən'tāshən, -,men-\ *n* : chemical decomposition of an organic substance in the absence of oxygen
fern \'fərn\ *n* : flowerless seedless green plant
fe•ro•cious \fə'rōshəs\ *adj* : fierce or savage —**fe•ro•cious•ly** *adv* —**fe•ro•cious•ness** *n* —**fe•roc•i•ty** \-'räsətē\ *n*
fer•ret \'ferət\ *n* : white European polecat ~ *vb* : find out by searching
fer•ric \'ferik\, **fer•rous** \'ferəs\ *adj* : relating to or containing iron
fer•rule \'ferəl\ *n* : metal band or ring
fer•ry \'ferē\ *vb* **-ried; -ry•ing** : carry by boat over water ~ *n, pl* **-ries** : boat used in ferrying —**fer•ry•boat** *n*
fer•tile \'fərt°l\ *adj* 1 : producing plentifully 2 : capable of developing or reproducing —**fer•til•i•ty** \fər'tilətē\ *n*
fer•til•ize \'fərt°l,īz\ *vb* **-ized; -iz•ing** : make fertile —**fer•til•iza•tion** \,fərt°lə'zāshən\ *n* —**fer•til•iz•er** *n*
fer•vid \'fərvəd\ *adj* : ardent or zealous —**fer•vid•ly** *adv*
fer•vor \'fərvər\ *n* : passion —**fer•ven•cy** \-vənsē\ *n* —**fer•vent** \-vənt\ *adj* —**fer•vent•ly** *adv*
fes•ter \'festər\ *vb* 1 : form pus 2 : become more bitter or malignant
fes•ti•val \'festəvəl\ *n* : time of celebration
fes•tive \-tiv\ *adj* : joyous or happy —**fes•tive•ly** *adv* —**fes•tiv•i•ty** \fe'stivətē\ *n*
fes•toon \fe'stün\ *n* : decorative chain or strip hanging in a curve —**festoon** *vb*
fe•tal \'fēt°l\ *adj* : of, relating to, or being a fetus
fetch \'fech\ *vb* 1 : go or come after and bring or take back 2 : sell for
fetch•ing \'fechiŋ\ *adj* : attractive —**fetch•ing•ly** *adv*
fête \'fāt, 'fet\ *n* : lavish party ~ *vb* **fêt•ed; fêt•ing** : honor or commemorate with a fête
fet•id \'fetəd\ *adj* : having an offensive smell
fe•tish \'fetish\ *n* 1 : object believed to have magical powers 2 : object of unreasoning devotion or concern
fet•lock \'fet,läk\ *n* : projection on the back of a horse's leg above the hoof
fet•ter \'fetər\ *n* : chain or shackle for the feet —**fetter** *vb*
fet•tle \'fet°l\ *n* : state of fitness
fe•tus \'fētəs\ *n* : vertebrate not yet born or hatched
feud \'fyüd\ *n* : prolonged quarrel —**feud** *vb*
feu•dal \'fyüd°l\ *adj* : of or relating to feudalism
feu•dal•ism \-,izəm\ *n* : medieval political order in which land is granted in return for service —**feu•dal•is•tic** \,fyüd°l'istik\ *adj*
fe•ver \'fēvər\ *n* 1 : abnormal rise in body temperature 2 : state of heightened emotion —**fe•ver•ish** *adj* —**fe•ver•ish•ly** *adv*
few \'fyü\ *pron* : not many ~ *adj* : some but not many —often with *a* ~ *n* : small number —often with *a*
few•er \-ər\ *pron* : smaller number of things
fez \'fez\ *n, pl* **fez•zes** : round flat-crowned hat
fi•an•cé \,fē,än'sā\ *n* : man one is engaged to
fi•an•cée \,fē,än'sā\ *n* : woman one is engaged to
fi•as•co \fē'askō\ *n, pl* **-coes** : ridiculous failure
fi•at \'fēət, -,at, -,ät; 'fīət, -,at\ *n* : decree
fib \'fib\ *n* : trivial lie —**fib** *vb* —**fib•ber** *n*
fi•ber, fi•bre \'fībər\ *n* 1 : threadlike substance or structure (as a muscle cell or fine root) 2 : indigestible material in food 3 : element that gives texture or substance —**fi•brous** \-brəs\ *adj*
fi•ber•board *n* : construction material made of compressed fibers
fi•ber•glass *n* : glass in fibrous form in various products (as insulation)
fi•bril•la•tion \,fibrə'lāshən, ,fīb-\ *n* : rapid irregular contractions of heart muscle —**fib•ril•late** \'fibrə,lāt, 'fīb-\ *vb*
fib•u•la \'fibyələ\ *n, pl* **-lae** \-lē, -lī\ *or* **-las** : outer of the two leg bones below the knee —**fib•u•lar** \-lər\ *adj*
fick•le \'fikəl\ *adj* : unpredictably changeable —**fick•le•ness** *n*
fic•tion \'fikshən\ *n* : a made-up story or literature consisting of these —**fic•tion•al** \-shənəl\ *adj*
fic•ti•tious \fik'tishəs\ *adj* : made up or pretended
fid•dle \'fid°l\ *n* : violin ~ *vb* **-dled; -dling**

1 : play on the fiddle 2 : move the hands restlessly —**fid•dler** \'fidlər, -ᵊlə\ n

fid•dle•sticks n : nonsense —used as an interjection

fi•del•i•ty \fə'delətē, fī-\ n, pl **-ties** 1 : quality or state of being faithful 2 : quality of reproduction

fidg•et \'fijət\ n 1 pl : restlessness 2 : one that fidgets ~ vb : move restlessly —**fidg•ety** adj

fi•du•cia•ry \fə'düshē,erē, -'dyü-, -shərē\ adj : held or holding in trust —**fiduciary** n

field \'fēld\ n 1 : open country 2 : cleared land 3 : land yielding some special product 4 : sphere of activity 5 : area for sports 6 : region or space in which a given effect (as magnetism) exists ~ vb : put into the field —**field** adj —**field•er** n

fiend \'fēnd\ n 1 : devil 2 : extremely wicked person —**fiend•ish** adj —**fiend•ish•ly** adv

fierce \'firs\ adj **fierc•er; -est** 1 : violently hostile or aggressive 2 : intense 3 : menacing looking —**fierce•ly** adv —**fierce•ness** n

fi•ery \'fīərē\ adj **fi•er•i•er; -est** 1 : burning 2 : hot or passionate —**fi•eri•ness** \'fīərēnəs\ n

fi•es•ta \fē'estə\ n : festival

fife \'fīf\ n : small flute

fif•teen \fif'tēn\ n : one more than 14 —**fifteen** adj or pron —**fif•teenth** \-'tēnth\ adj or n

fifth \'fifth\ n 1 : one that is number 5 in a countable series 2 : one of 5 equal parts of something —**fifth** adj or adv

fif•ty \'fiftē\ n, pl **-ties** : 5 times 10 —**fif•ti•eth** \-tēəth\ adj or n —**fifty** adj or pron

fif•ty-fif•ty adv or adj : shared equally

fig \'fig\ n : pear-shaped edible fruit

fight \'fīt\ vb **fought** \'fȯt\ **fight•ing** 1 : contend against another in battle 2 : box 3 : struggle ~ n 1 : hostile encounter 2 : boxing match 3 : verbal disagreement —**fight•er** n

fig•ment \'figmənt\ n : something imagined or made up

fig•u•ra•tive \'figyərətiv, -gə-\ adj : metaphorical —**fig•u•ra•tive•ly** adv

fig•ure \'figyər, -gər\ n 1 : symbol representing a number 2 pl : arithmetical calculations 3 : price 4 : shape or outline 5 : illustration 6 : pattern or design 7 : prominent person ~ vb **-ured; -ur•ing** 1 : be important 2 : calculate —**fig•ured** adj

fig•u•rine \figyə'rēn\ n : small statue

fil•a•ment \'filəmənt\ n : fine thread or threadlike part —**fil•a•men•tous** \filə'mentəs\ adj

fil•bert \'filbərt\ n : edible nut of a European hazel

filch \'filch\ vb : steal furtively

¹**file** \'fīl\ n : tool for smoothing or sharpening ~ vb **filed; fil•ing** : rub or smooth with a file

²**file** vb **filed; fil•ing** 1 : arrange in order 2 : enter or record officially ~ n : device for keeping papers in order

³**file** n : row of persons or things one behind the other ~ vb **filed; fil•ing** : march in file

fil•ial \'filēəl, 'filyəl\ adj : relating to a son or daughter

fil•i•bus•ter \'filə,bəstər\ n : long speeches to delay a legislative vote —**filibuster** vb —**fil•i•bus•ter•er** n

fil•i•gree \'filə,grē\ n : ornamental designs of fine wire —**fil•i•greed** \-,grēd\ adj

fill \'fil\ vb 1 : make or become full 2 : stop up 3 : feed 4 : satisfy 5 : occupy fully 6 : spread through ~ n 1 : full supply 2 : material for filling —**fill•er** n —**fill** vb 1 : provide information to or for 2 : substitute

fil•let \'filət, fi'lā, 'fil,ā\ n : piece of boneless meat or fish ~ vb : cut into fillets

fill•ing n : material used to fill something

fil•ly \'filē\ n, pl **-lies** : young female horse

film \'film\ n 1 : thin skin or membrane 2 : thin coating or layer 3 : strip of material used in taking pictures 4 : movie ~ vb : make a movie of —**filmy** adj

film•strip n : strip of film with photographs for still projection

fil•ter \'filtər\ n 1 : device for separating matter from a fluid 2 : device (as on a camera lens) that absorbs light ~ vb 1 : pass through a filter 2 : remove by means of a filter —**fil•ter•able** adj —**fil•tra•tion** \fil'trāshən\ n

filth \'filth\ n : repulsive dirt or refuse —**filth•i•ness** n —**filthy** \'filthē\ adj

fin \'fin\ n 1 : thin external process controlling movement in an aquatic animal 2 : fin-shaped part (as on an airplane) 3 : flipper —**finned** \'find\ adj

fi•na•gle \fə'nāgəl\ vb **-gled; -gling** : get by clever or tricky means —**fi•na•gler** n

fi•nal \'fīnᵊl\ adj 1 : not to be changed 2 : ultimate 3 : coming at the end —**final** n —**fi•nal•ist** \'fīnᵊlist\ n —**fi•nal•i•ty** \fī-

'naləte, fə-\ n —**fi•nal•ize** \-,īz\ vb —**fi•nal•ly** adv

fi•na•le \fə'nalē, fi'näl-\ n : last or climactic part

fi•nance \fə'nans, 'fī,nans\ n 1 pl : money resources 2 : management of money affairs ~ vb **-nanced; -nanc•ing** 1 : raise funds for 2 : give necessary funds to 3 : sell on credit

fi•nan•cial \fə'nanchəl, fī-\ adj : relating to finance —**fi•nan•cial•ly** adv

fi•nan•cier \finən'sir, ,fī,nan-\ n : person who invests large sums of money

finch \'finch\ n : songbird (as a sparrow or linnet) with a strong bill

find \'fīnd\ vb **found** \'faund\ **find•ing** 1 : discover or encounter 2 : obtain by effort 3 : experience or feel 4 : gain or regain the use of 5 : decide on (a verdict) ~ n 1 : act or instance of finding 2 : something found —**find•er** n —**find•ing** n —**find out** vb : learn, discover, or verify something

fine \'fīn\ n : money paid as a penalty ~ vb **fined; fin•ing** : impose a fine on ~ adj **fin•er; -est** 1 : free from impurity 2 : small or thin 3 : not coarse 4 : superior in quality or appearance ~ adv : finely —**fine•ly** adv —**fine•ness** n

fin•ery \'fīnərē\ n, pl **-er•ies** : showy clothing and jewels

fi•nesse \fə'nes\ n 1 : delicate skill 2 : craftiness —**finesse** vb

fin•ger \'fingər\ n 1 : one of the 5 divisions at the end of the hand and esp. one other than the thumb 2 : something like a finger 3 : part of a glove for a finger ~ vb 1 : touch with the fingers 2 : identify as if by pointing —**fin•gered** adj —**fin•ger•nail** n —**fin•ger•tip** n

fin•ger•ling \-gərlin\ n : small fish

fin•ger•print n : impression of the pattern of marks on the tip of a finger —**fingerprint** vb

fin•icky \'finikē\ adj : excessively particular in taste or standards

fin•ish \'finish\ vb 1 : come or bring to an end 2 : use or dispose of entirely 3 : put a final coat or surface on ~ n 1 : end 2 : final treatment given a surface —**fin•isher** n

fi•nite \'fī,nīt\ adj : having definite limits

fink \'fink\ n : contemptible person

fiord var of FJORD

fir \'fər\ n : erect evergreen tree or its wood

fire \'fīr\ n 1 : light or heat and esp. the flame of something burning 2 : destructive burning (as of a house) 3 : enthusiasm 4 : the shooting of weapons ~ vb **fired; fir•ing** 1 : kindle 2 : stir up or enliven 3 : dismiss from employment 4 : shoot 5 : bake —**fire•bomb** n or vb —**fire•fight•er** n —**fire•less** adj —**fire•proof** adj or vb —**fire•wood** n

fire•arm n : weapon (as a rifle) that works by an explosion of gunpowder

fire•ball n 1 : ball of fire 2 : brilliant meteor

fire•boat n : boat equipped for fighting fire

fire•box n 1 : chamber (as of a furnace) that contains a fire 2 : fire-alarm box

fire•break n : cleared land for checking a forest fire

fire•bug n : person who deliberately sets destructive fires

fire•crack•er n : small firework that makes noise

fire•fly n : night-flying beetle that produces a soft light

fire•man \'fīrmən\ n 1 : person trained to put out fires 2 : stoker

fire•place n : opening made in a chimney to hold an open fire

fire•plug n : hydrant

fire•side n 1 : place near the fire or hearth 2 : home ~ adj : having an informal quality

fire•trap n : place apt to catch on fire

fire•work n : device that explodes to produce noise or a display of light

¹**firm** \'fərm\ adj 1 : securely fixed in place 2 : strong or vigorous 3 : not subject to change 4 : resolute ~ vb : make or become firm —**firm•ly** adv —**firm•ness** n

²**firm** n : business enterprise

fir•ma•ment \'fərməmənt\ n : sky

first \'fərst\ adj 1 : being number one 2 : foremost ~ adv 1 : before any other 2 : for the first time ~ n 1 : number one 2 : one that is first —**first class** n —**first-class** adj or adv —**first•ly** adv —**first-rate** adj or adv

first aid n : emergency care

first lieutenant n : commissioned officer ranking next below a captain

first sergeant n 1 : noncommissioned officer serving as the chief assistant to the commander of a military unit 2 : rank in the army below a command sergeant major and in the marine corps below a sergeant major

firth \'fərth\ n : estuary

fis•cal \'fiskəl\ adj : relating to money —**fis•cal•ly** adv

fish \'fish\ n, pl **fish** or **fish•es** : water animal

with fins, gills, and usu. scales ~ vb 1 : try to catch fish 2 : grope —**fish•er** n —**fish•hook** n —**fish•ing** n

fish•er•man \-mən\ n : one who fishes

fish•ery \'fishərē\ n, pl **-er•ies** : fishing business or a place for this

fishy \'fishē\ adj **fish•i•er; -est** 1 : relating to or like fish 2 : questionable

fis•sion \'fishən, 'fizh-\ n : splitting of an atomic nucleus —**fis•sion•able** \-ənəbəl\ adj

fis•sure \'fishər\ n : crack

fist \'fist\ n : hand doubled up —**fist•ed** \'fistəd\ adj —**fist•ful** \-,fu̇l\ n

fist•i•cuffs \'fisti,kəfs\ n : fist fight

fit \'fit\ n : sudden attack of illness or emotion

²**fit** adj **-tt-** 1 : suitable 2 : qualified 3 : sound in body ~ vb **-tt-** 1 : be suitable to 2 : insert or adjust correctly 3 : make room for 4 : supply or equip 5 : belong ~ n : state of fitting or being fitted —**fit•ly** adv —**fit•ness** n —**fit•ter** n

fit•ful \'fitfəl\ adj : restless —**fit•ful•ly** adv

fit•ting adj : suitable ~ n : a small part

five \'fīv\ n 1 : one more than 4 2 : 5th in a set or series 3 : something having 5 units —**five** adj or pron

fix \'fiks\ vb 1 : attach 2 : establish 3 : make right 4 : prepare 5 : improperly influence ~ n 1 : predicament 2 : determination of location —**fix•er** n

fix•a•tion \fik'sāshən\ n : obsessive attachment —**fix•ate** \'fik,sāt\ vb

fixed \'fikst\ adj 1 : stationary 2 : settled —**fixed•ly** \'fiksədlē\ adv —**fixed•ness** \-nəs\ n

fix•ture \'fikschər\ n : permanent part of something

fizz \'fiz\ vb : make a hissing sound ~ n : effervescence

fiz•zle \'fizəl\ vb **-zled; -zling** 1 : fizz 2 : fail ~ n : failure

fjord \fē'ȯrd\ n : inlet of the sea between cliffs

flab \'flab\ n : flabby flesh

flab•ber•gast \'flabər,gast\ vb : astound

flab•by \'flabē\ adj **-bi•er; -est** : not firm —**flab•bi•ness** n

flac•cid \'flaksəd, 'flasəd\ adj : not firm

¹**flag** \'flag\ n : flat stone

²**flag** n 1 : fabric that is a symbol (as of a country) 2 : something used to signal ~ vb **-gg-** : signal with a flag —**flag•pole** n —**flag•staff** n

³**flag** vb **-gg-** : lose strength or spirit

flag•el•late \'flajə,lāt\ vb **-lat•ed; -lat•ing** : whip —**flag•el•la•tion** \,flajə'lāshən\ n

flag•on \'flagən\ n : container for liquids

fla•grant \'flāgrənt\ adj : conspicuously bad —**fla•grant•ly** adv

flag•ship n : ship carrying a commander

flag•stone n : flag

flail \'flāl\ n : tool for threshing grain ~ vb : beat with or as if with a flail

flair \'flar\ n : natural aptitude

flak \'flak\ n, pl **flak** 1 : antiaircraft fire 2 : criticism

flake \'flāk\ n : small flat piece ~ vb **flaked; flak•ing** : separate or form into flakes

flam•boy•ant \flam'bȯiənt\ adj : showy —**flam•boy•ance** \-əns\ n —**flam•boy•ant•ly** adv

flame \'flām\ n 1 : glowing part of a fire 2 : state of combustion 3 : burning passion —**flame** vb —**flam•ing** adj

fla•min•go \flə'miŋgō\ n, pl **-gos** : long-legged long-necked tropical water bird

flam•ma•ble \'flamabəl\ adj : easily ignited

flange \'flanj\ n : rim

flank \'flank\ n : side of something ~ vb 1 : attack or go around the side of 2 : be at the side of

flan•nel \'flanᵊl\ n : soft napped fabric

flap \'flap\ n 1 : slap 2 : something flat that hangs loose ~ vb **-pp-** 1 : move (wings) up and down 2 : swing back and forth noisily

flap•jack \-,jak\ n : pancake

flare \'flar\ vb **flared; flar•ing** : become suddenly bright or excited ~ n : blaze of light

flash \'flash\ vb 1 : give off a sudden flame or burst of light 2 : appear or pass suddenly ~ n 1 : sudden burst of light or inspiration 2 : instant ~ adj : coming suddenly

flash•light n : small battery-operated light

flashy \'flashē\ adj **flash•i•er; -est** : showy —**flash•i•ly** adv —**flash•i•ness** n

flask \'flask\ n : flattened bottle

flat \'flat\ adj **-tt-** 1 : smooth 2 : broad and thin 3 : definite 4 : uninteresting 5 : deflated 6 : below the true pitch ~ n 1 : level surface of land 2 : flat note in music 3 : apartment 4 : deflated tire ~ adv **-tt-** 1 : exactly 2 : below the true pitch ~ vb **-tt-** : make flat —**flat•ly** adv —**flat•ness** n —**flat•ten** \-ᵊn\ vb

flat•car n : railroad car without sides

flat•fish n : flattened fish with both eyes on the upper side

flat•foot n, pl **flat•feet** : foot condition in

which the arch is flattened —**flat-foot•ed** adj

flat-out adj 1 : being maximum effort or speed 2 : downright

flat•ter \'flatər\ vb 1 : praise insincerely 2 : judge or represent too favorably —**flat•ter•er** n —**flat•tery** \'flatərē\ n

flat•u•lent \'flachələnt\ adj : full of gas —**flat•u•lence** \-ləns\ n

flat•ware n : eating utensils

flaunt \'flȯnt\ vb : display ostentatiously —**flaunt** n

fla•vor \'flāvər\ n 1 : quality that affects the sense of taste 2 : something that adds flavor ~ vb : give flavor to —**fla•vor•ful** adj —**fla•vor•ing** n —**fla•vor•less** adj

flaw \'flȯ\ n : fault —**flaw•less** adj —**flaw•less•ly** adv —**flaw•less•ness** n

flax \'flaks\ n : plant from which linen is made

flax•en \'flaksən\ adj : made of or like flax

flay \'flā\ vb 1 : strip off the skin of 2 : criticize harshly

flea \'flē\ n : leaping bloodsucking insect

fleck \'flek\ vb or n : streak or spot

fledg•ling \'flejlin\ n : young bird

flee \'flē\ vb **fled** \'fled\ **flee•ing** : run away

fleece \'flēs\ n : sheep's wool ~ vb **fleeced; fleec•ing** 1 : shear 2 : get money from dishonestly —**fleecy** adj

¹**fleet** \'flēt\ vb : pass rapidly ~ adj : swift —**fleet•ing** adj —**fleet•ness** n

²**fleet** n : group of ships

fleet admiral n : commissioned officer of the highest rank in the navy

flesh \'flesh\ n 1 : soft parts of an animal's body 2 : soft plant tissue (as fruit pulp) —**fleshed** \'flesht\ adj —**flesh out** vb : make fuller —**fleshy** adj

flesh•ly \'fleshlē\ adj : sensual

flew past of FLY

flex \'fleks\ vb : bend

flex•i•ble \'fleksəbəl\ adj 1 : capable of being flexed 2 : adaptable —**flex•i•bil•i•ty** \,fleksə'bilətē\ n —**flex•i•bly** \-əblē\ adv

flick \'flik\ n : light jerky stroke ~ vb 1 : strike lightly 2 : flutter

flick•er \'flikər\ vb 1 : waver 2 : burn unsteadily ~ n 1 : sudden movement 2 : wavering light

fli•er \'flīər\ n 1 : aviator 2 : advertising circular

¹**flight** \'flīt\ n 1 : act or instance of flying 2 : ability to fly 3 : a passing through air or space 4 : series of stairs —**flight•less** adj

²**flight** n : act or instance of running away

flighty \'flītē\ adj **flight•i•er; -est** : capricious or silly —**flight•i•ness** n

flim•flam \'flim,flam\ n : trickery

flim•sy \'flimzē\ adj **-si•er; -est** 1 : not strong or well made 2 : not believable —**flim•si•ly** adv —**flim•si•ness** n

flinch \'flinch\ vb : shrink from pain

fling \'flin\ vb **flung** \'fləŋ\ **fling•ing** 1 : move brusquely 2 : throw ~ n 1 : act or instance of flinging 2 : attempt 3 : period of self-indulgence

flint \'flint\ n : hard quartz that gives off sparks when struck with steel —**flinty** adj

flip \'flip\ vb **-pp-** 1 : cause to turn over quickly or many times 2 : move with a quick push ~ adj : insolent —**flip** n

flip•pant \'flipənt\ adj : not serious enough —**flip•pan•cy** \-ənsē\ n

flip•per \'flipər\ n : paddlelike limb (as of a seal) for swimming

flirt \'flərt\ vb 1 : be playfully romantic 2 : show casual interest ~ n : one who flirts —**flir•ta•tion** \flər'tāshən\ n —**flir•ta•tious** \-shəs\ adj

flit \'flit\ vb **-tt-** : dart

float \'flōt\ n 1 : something that floats 2 : vehicle carrying an exhibit ~ vb 1 : rest on or in a fluid without sinking 2 : wander 3 : finance by issuing stock or bonds —**float•er** n

flock \'fläk\ n : group of animals (as birds) or people ~ vb : gather or move as a group

floe \'flō\ n : mass of floating ice

flog \'fläg\ vb **-gg-** : beat with a rod or whip —**flog•ger** n

flood \'fləd\ n 1 : great flow of water over the land 2 : overwhelming volume ~ vb : cover or fill esp. with water —**flood•wa•ter** n

floor \'flōr\ n 1 : bottom of a room on which one stands 2 : story of a building 3 : lower limit ~ vb 1 : furnish with a floor 2 : knock down 3 : amaze —**floor•board** n —**floor•ing** \-in\ n

floo•zy, floo•zie \'flüzē\ n, pl **-zies** : promiscuous young woman

flop \'fläp\ vb **-pp-** 1 : flap 2 : slump heavily 3 : fail —**flop** n

flop•py \'fläpē\ adj **-pi•er; -est** : soft and flexible

flo•ra \'flōrə\ n : plants or plant life of a region

flo•ral \'flōrəl\ adj : relating to flowers

flor•id \'flōrəd\ adj 1 : very flowery in style 2 : reddish

flo•rist \'flōrist\ n : flower dealer

floss \fläs\ *n* 1 : soft thread for embroidery 2 : thread used to clean between teeth — **floss** *vb*

flo•ta•tion \flō'tāshən\ *n* : process or instance of floating

flo•til•la \flō'tilə\ *n* : small fleet

flot•sam \flätsəm\ *n* : floating wreckage

1flounce \flaůns\ *vb* **flounced; flounc•ing** : move with exaggerated jerky motions —**flounce** *n*

2flounce *n* : fabric border or wide ruffle

1floun•der \'flaůndər\ *n, pl* **flounder** or **flounders** : flatfish

2flounder *vb* 1 : struggle for footing 2 : proceed clumsily

flour \'flaůər\ *n* 1 : finely ground meal ~ *vb* : coat with flour —**floury** *adj*

flour•ish \'flərish\ *vb* 1 : thrive 2 : wave threateningly ~ *n* 1 : embellishment 2 : fanfare 3 : wave 4 : showiness of action

flout \'flaůt\ *vb* : treat with disdain

flow \'flō\ *vb* 1 : move in a stream 2 : proceed smoothly and readily ~ *n* : uninterrupted stream

flow•er \'flaůər\ *n* 1 : showy plant shoot that bears seeds 2 : state of flourishing ~ *vb* 1 : produce flowers 2 : flourish —**flow•ered** *adj* —**flow•er•i•ness** *n* —**flow•er•less** *adj* —**flow•er•pot** *n* —**flow•ery** \-ē\ *adj*

flown *past part of* FLY

flu \'flü\ *n* 1 : influenza 2 : minor virus ailment

flub \'fləb\ *vb* **-bb-** : bungle —**flub** *n*

fluc•tu•ate \'fləkchə,wāt\ *vb* **-at•ed; -at•ing** : change rapidly esp. up and down —**fluc•tu•a•tion** \,fləkchə'wāshən\ *n*

flue \'flü\ *n* : smoke duct

flu•ent \'flüənt\ *adj* : speaking with ease —**flu•en•cy** \-ənsē\ *n* —**flu•ent•ly** *adv*

fluff \'fləf\ *n* 1 : something soft and light 2 : blunder ~ *vb* 1 : make fluffy 2 : make a mistake —**fluffy** \-ē\ *adj*

flu•id \'flüəd\ *adj* : flowing ~ *n* : substance that can flow —**flu•id•i•ty** \flü'idətē\ *n* —**flu•id•ly** *adv*

fluid ounce *n* : unit of liquid measure equal to 1/16 pint

fluke \'flük\ *n* : stroke of luck

flume \'flüm\ *n* : channel for water

flung *past of* FLING

flunk \'fləŋk\ *vb* : fail in school work

flun•ky, flun•key \'fləŋkē\ *n, pl* **-kies** or **keys** : lackey

flu•o•res•cence \,flůr'esᵊns, ,flôr-\ *n* : emission of light after initial absorption —**flu•o•resce** \-'es\ *vb* —**flu•o•res•cent** \-'esᵊnt\ *adj*

flu•o•ri•date \'flôrə,dāt, 'flůr-\ *vb* **-dat•ed; -dat•ing** : add fluoride to —**flu•o•ri•da•tion** \,flôrə'dāshən, ,flůr-\ *n*

flu•o•ride \'flôr,īd, 'flůr-\ *n* : compound of fluorine

flu•o•rine \'flůr,ēn, -ən\ *n* : toxic gaseous chemical element

flu•o•ro•car•bon \,flôrō'kärbən, ,flůr-\ *n* : compound containing fluorine and carbon

flu•o•ro•scope \'flůrə,skōp\ *n* : instrument for internal examination —**flu•o•ro•scop•ic** \,flůrə'skäpik\ *adj* —**flu•o•ros•co•py** \,flůr'äskəpē\ *n*

flur•ry \'flərē\ *n, pl* **-ries** 1 : light snowfall 2 : bustle 3 : brief burst of activity —**flurry** *vb*

1flush \'fləsh\ *vb* : cause (a bird) to fly from cover

2flush *n* 1 : sudden flow (as of water) 2 : surge of emotion 3 : blush ~ *vb* 1 : blush 2 : wash out with a rush of liquid ~ *adj* 1 : filled to overflowing 2 : reddish healthy color 3 : smooth or level 4 : abutting —**flush** *adv*

3flush *n* : cards of the same suit

flus•ter \'fləstər\ *vb* : upset —**fluster** *n*

flute \'flüt\ *n* 1 : pipelike musical instrument 2 : groove —**flut•ed** *adj* —**flut•ing** *n* —**flut•ist** \-ist\ *n*

flut•ter \'flətər\ *vb* 1 : flap the wings rapidly 2 : move with quick wavering or flapping motions 3 : behave in an agitated manner ~ *n* 1 : a fluttering 2 : state of confusion —**flut•tery** \-ərē\ *adj*

flux \'fləks\ *n* : state of continuous change

1fly \'flī\ *vb* **flew** \'flü\; **flown** \'flōn\; **fly•ing** 1 : move through the air with wings 2 : float or soar 3 : flee 4 : move or pass swiftly 5 : operate an airplane

2fly *n, pl* **flies** : garment closure

3fly *n, pl* **flies** : winged insect

fly•er *var of* FLIER

fly•pa•per *n* : sticky paper for catching flies

fly•speck *n* 1 : speck of fly dung 2 : something tiny

fly•wheel *n* : rotating wheel that regulates the speed of machinery

foal \'fōl\ *n* : young horse —**foal** *vb*

foam \'fōm\ *n* 1 : mass of bubbles on top of a liquid 2 : material of cellular form ~ *vb* : form foam —**foamy** *adj*

fob \'fäb\ *n* : short chain for a pocket watch

fo'c'sle *var of* FORECASTLE

fo•cus \'fōkəs\ *n, pl* **-ci** \-,sī\ 1 : point at which reflected or refracted rays meet 2

: adjustment (as of eyeglasses) for clear vision 3 : central point ~ *vb* : bring to a focus —**fo•cal** \-kəl\ *adj* —**fo•cal•ly** *adv*

fod•der \'fädər\ *n* : food for livestock

foe \'fō\ *n* : enemy

fog \'fóg, 'fäg\ *n* 1 : fine particles of water suspended near the ground 2 : mental confusion ~ *vb* **-gg-** : obscure or be obscured with fog —**fog•gy** *adj*

fog•horn *n* : warning horn sounded in a fog

fo•gy \'fōgē\ *n, pl* **-gies** : person with old-fashioned ideas

foi•ble \'fóibəl\ *n* : minor character fault

1foil \'fóil\ *vb* : defeat ~ *n* : light fencing sword

2foil *n* 1 : thin sheet of metal 2 : one that sets off another by contrast

foist \'fóist\ *vb* : force another to accept

1fold \'fōld\ *n* 1 : enclosure for sheep 2 : group with a common interest

2fold *vb* 1 : lay one part over another 2 : embrace ~ *n* : part folded

fold•er \'fōldər\ *n* 1 : one that folds 2 : circular 3 : folded cover or envelope for papers

fol•de•rol \'fäldə,räl\ *n* : nonsense

fo•liage \'fōlēij, -lij\ *n* : plant leaves

fo•lio \'fōlē,ō\ *n, pl* **-li•os** : sheet of paper folded once

folk \'fōk\ *n, pl* **folk** or **folks** 1 : people in general 2 **folks** *pl* : one's family ~ *adj* : relating to the common people

folk•lore *n* : customs and traditions of a people —**folk•lor•ist** *n*

folksy \'fōksē\ *adj* **folks•i•er; -est** : friendly and informal

fol•li•cle \'fälikəl\ *n* : small anatomical cavity or gland

fol•low \'fälō\ *vb* 1 : go or come after 2 : pursue 3 : obey 4 : proceed along 5 : keep one's attention fixed on 6 : result from —**fol•low•er** *n*

fol•low•ing \'fäləwiŋ\ *adj* : next ~ *n* : group of followers ~ *prep* : after

fol•ly \'fälē\ *n, pl* **-lies** : foolishness

fo•ment \fō'ment\ *vb* : incite

fond \'fänd\ *adj* 1 : strongly attracted 2 : affectionate 3 : dear —**fond•ly** *adv* —**fond•ness** *n*

fon•dle \'fändᵊl\ *vb* **-dled; -dling** : touch lovingly

fon•due \fän'dü, -'dyü\ *n* : preparation of melted cheese

font \'fänt\ *n* 1 : baptismal basin 2 : fountain

food \'füd\ *n* : material eaten to sustain life

fool \'fül\ *n* 1 : stupid person 2 : jester ~ *vb* 1 : waste time 2 : meddle 3 : deceive —**fool•ery** \'fülərē\ *n* —**fool•ish** \'fülish\ *adj* —**fool•ish•ly** *adv* —**fool•ish•ness** *n* —**fool•proof** *adj*

fool•har•dy \'fül,härdē\ *adj* : rash —**fool•har•di•ness** *n*

foot \'fůt\ *n, pl* **feet** \'fēt\ 1 : end part of a leg 2 : unit of length equal to 1/3 yard 3 : unit of verse meter 4 : bottom —**foot•age** \-ij\ *n* —**foot•ed** *adj* —**foot•path** *n* —**foot•print** *n* —**foot•race** *n* —**foot•rest** *n* —**foot•wear** *n*

foot•ball *n* : ball game played by 2 teams on a rectangular field

foot•bridge *n* : bridge for pedestrians

foot•hill *n* : hill at the foot of higher hills

foot•hold *n* : support for the feet

foot•ing *n* 1 : foothold 2 : basis

foot•lights *n pl* : stage lights along the floor

foot•lock•er *n* : small trunk

foot•loose *adj* : having no ties

foot•man \'fůtmən\ *n* : male servant

foot•note *n* : note at the bottom of a page

foot•step *n* 1 : step 2 : distance covered by a step 3 : footprint

foot•stool *n* : stool to support the feet

foot•work *n* : skillful movement of the feet (as in boxing)

fop \'fäp\ *n* : dandy —**fop•pery** \-ərē\ *n* —**fop•pish** *adj*

for \'fór\ *prep* 1 —used to show preparation or purpose 2 : because of 3 —used to show a recipient 4 : in support of 5 : so as to support or help cure 6 : so as to be equal to 7 : concerning 8 : through the period of ~ *conj* : because

for•age \'fórij\ *n* : food for animals ~ *vb* **-aged; -ag•ing** 1 : hunt food 2 : search for provisions

for•ay \'fór,ā\ *n or vb* : raid

1for•bear \fór'bar\ *vb* **-bore** \-'bōr\; **-borne** \-'bôrn\; **-bear•ing** 1 : refrain from 2 : be patient —**for•bear•ance** \-'barəns\ *n*

2forbear *var of* FOREBEAR

for•bid \fór'bid\ *vb* **-bade** \-'bad, -'bād\ or **-bad** \-'bad\; **-bid•den** \-'bidᵊn\; **-bid•ding** 1 : prohibit 2 : order not to do something

for•bid•ding *adj* : tending to discourage

force \'fórs\ *n* 1 : exceptional strength or energy 2 : military strength 3 : body (as of persons) available for a purpose 4 : violence 5 : influence (as a push or pull) that causes motion ~ *vb* **forced; forc•ing** 1 : compel 2 : gain against resistance 3 : break open —**force•ful** \-fəl\ *adj* —**force•ful•ly** *adv* —**in force** 1 : in great numbers 2 : valid

for•ceps \'fórsəps\ *n, pl* **forceps** : surgical instrument for grasping objects

for•ci•ble \'fórsəbəl\ *adj* 1 : done by force 2 : showing force —**forc•i•bly** \-blē\ *adv*

ford \'fórd\ *n* : place to wade across a stream ~ *vb* : wade across

fore \'fōr\ *adv* : in or toward the front ~ *adj* : being or coming before in time, place, or order ~ *n* : front

fore-and-aft *adj* : lengthwise

fore•arm \'fōr,ärm\ *n* : part of the arm between the elbow and the wrist

fore•bear \'fōr,bar\ *n* : ancestor

fore•bod•ing \fōr'bōdiŋ\ *n* : premonition of disaster —**fore•bod•ing** *adj*

fore•cast \'fōr,kast\ *vb* **-cast; -cast•ing** : predict —**forecast** *n* —**fore•cast•er** *n*

fore•cas•tle \'fōksəl\ *n* : forward part of a ship

fore•close \fōr'klōz\ *vb* : take legal measures to terminate a mortgage —**fore•clo•sure** \-'klōzhər\ *n*

fore•fa•ther \'fōr,fäthər\ *n* : ancestor

fore•fin•ger \'fōr,fiŋgər\ *n* : finger next to the thumb

fore•foot \'fōr,fůt\ *n* : front foot of a quadruped

fore•front \'fōr,frənt\ *n* : foremost position or place

1fore•go \fōr'gō\ *vb* **-went; -gone; -go•ing** : precede

2forego *var of* FORGO

fore•go•ing *adj* : preceding

fore•gone *adj* : determined in advance

fore•ground \'fōr,graůnd\ *n* : part of a scene nearest the viewer

fore•hand \'fōr,hand\ *n* : stroke (as in tennis) made with the palm of the hand turned forward —**forehand** *adj*

fore•head \'fórəd, 'fōr,hed\ *n* : part of the face above the eyes

for•eign \'fórən\ *adj* 1 : situated outside a place or country and esp. one's own country 2 : belonging to a different place or country 3 : not pertinent 4 : related to or dealing with other nations —**for•eign•er** \-ər\ *n*

fore•know \fōr'nō\ *vb* **-knew; -known; -know•ing** : know beforehand —**fore•knowl•edge** *n*

fore•leg \'fōr,leg\ *n* : front leg

fore•lock \'fōr,läk\ *n* : front lock of hair

fore•man \'fōrmən\ *n* 1 : spokesman of a jury 2 : workman in charge

fore•most \'fōr,mōst\ *adj* : first in time, place, or order —**foremost** *adv*

fore•noon \'fōr,nün\ *n* : morning

fo•ren•sic \fə'rensik\ *adj* : relating to courts or public speaking or debate

fo•ren•sics \-siks\ *n pl* : art or study of speaking or debating

fore•or•dain \fōrór'dān\ *vb* : decree beforehand

fore•quar•ter \'fōr,kwórtər\ *n* : front half on one side of the body of a quadruped

fore•run•ner \'fōr,rənər\ *n* : one that goes before

fore•see \fōr'sē\ *vb* **-saw; -seen; -see•ing** : see or realize beforehand —**fore•see•able** *adj*

fore•shad•ow \fōr'shadō\ *vb* : hint or suggest beforehand

fore•sight \'fōr,sīt\ *n* : care or provision for the future —**fore•sight•ed** *adj* —**fore•sight•ed•ness** *n*

for•est \'fórəst\ *n* : large thick growth of trees and underbrush —**for•est•ed** \'fórəstəd\ *adj* —**for•est•er** \-əstər\ *n* —**for•est•land** \-,land\ *n* —**for•est•ry** \-əstrē\ *n*

fore•stall \fōr'stól, fór-\ *vb* : prevent by acting in advance

foreswear *var of* FORSWEAR

fore•taste \'fōr,tāst\ *n* : advance indication or notion ~ *vb* : anticipate

fore•tell \fōr'tel\ *vb* **-told; -tell•ing** : predict

fore•thought \'fōr,thót\ *n* : foresight

for•ev•er \fór'evər\ *adv* 1 : for a limitless time 2 : always

for•ev•er•more \-,evər'mōr\ *adv* : forever

fore•warn \fōr'wórn\ *vb* : warn beforehand

fore•word \'fōrwərd\ *n* : preface

for•feit \'fórfət\ *n* : something forfeited ~ *vb* : lose or lose the right to by an error or crime —**for•fei•ture** \-fə,chůr\ *n*

1forge \'fórj\ *n* : smithy ~ *vb* **forged; forg•ing** 1 : form (metal) by heating and hammering 2 : imitate falsely esp. to def aud —**forg•er** *n* —**forg•ery** \-ərē\ *n*

2forge *vb* **forged; forg•ing** : move ahead steadily

for•get \fər'get\ *vb* **-got** \-'gät\; **-got•ten** \-'gätᵊn\ or **-got; -get•ting** 1 : be unable to think of or recall 2 : fail to think of at the proper time —**for•get•ta•ble** *adj* —**for•get•ful** \-fəl\ *adj* —**for•get•ful•ly** *adv*

forget-me-not *n* : small herb with blue or white flowers

for•give \fər'giv\ *vb* **-gave** \-'gāv\; **-giv•en** \-'givən\; **-giv•ing** : pardon —**for•giv•able** *adj* —**for•give•ness** *n*

for•giv•ing *adj* 1 : able to forgive 2 : allowing room for error or weakness

for•go, fore•go \fór'gō\ *vb* **-went; -gone; -go•ing** : do without

fork \'fórk\ *n* 1 : implement with prongs for lifting, holding, or digging 2 : forked part 3 : a dividing into branches or a place where something branches ~ *vb* 1 : divide into branches 2 : move with a fork —**forked** \'fórkt, 'fórkəd\ *adj*

fork•lift *n* : machine for lifting with steel fingers

for•lorn \fər'lórn\ *adj* 1 : deserted 2 : wretched —**for•lorn•ly** *adv*

form \'fórm\ *n* 1 : shape 2 : set way of doing or saying something 3 : document with blanks to be filled in 4 : manner of performing with respect to what is expected 5 : mold 6 : kind or variety 7 : one of the ways in which a word is changed to show difference in use ~ *vb* 1 : give form or shape to 2 : train 3 : develop 4 : constitute —**for•ma•tive** \'fórmətiv\ *adj* —**form•less** \-ləs\ *adj*

for•mal \'fórməl\ *adj* : following established custom ~ *n* : formal social event —**for•mal•i•ty** \fór'malətē\ *n* —**for•mal•ize** \'fórmə,līz\ *vb* —**for•mal•ly** *adv*

form•al•de•hyde \fór'maldə,hīd\ *n* : colorless pungent gas used as a preservative and disinfectant

for•mat \'fór,mat\ *n* : general style or arrangement of something —**format** *vb*

for•ma•tion \fór'māshən\ *n* 1 : a giving form to something 2 : something formed 3 : arrangement

for•mer \'fórmər\ *adj* : coming before in time —**for•mer•ly** *adv*

for•mi•da•ble \'fórmədəbəl, fór'mid-\ *adj* 1 : causing fear or dread 2 : very difficult —**for•mi•da•bly** \-blē\ *adv*

for•mu•la \'fórmyələ\ *n, pl* **-las** or **-lae** \-,lē, -lī\ 1 : set form of words for ceremonial use 2 : recipe 3 : milk mixture for a baby 4 : group of symbols or figures briefly expressing information 5 : set form or method

for•mu•late \-,lāt\ *vb* **-lat•ed; -lat•ing** : design, devise —**for•mu•la•tion** \,fórmyə'lāshən\ *n*

for•ni•ca•tion \,fórnə'kāshən\ *n* : illicit sexual intercourse —**for•ni•cate** \'fórnə,kāt\ *vb* —**for•ni•ca•tor** \-,kātər\ *n*

for•sake \fər'sāk\ *vb* **-sook** \-'sůk\; **-sak•en** \-'sākən\; **-sak•ing** : renounce completely

for•swear \fór'swar\ *vb* **-swore; -sworn; -swear•ing** 1 : renounce under oath 2 : perjure

for•syth•ia \fər'sithēə\ *n* : shrub grown for its yellow flowers

fort \'fórt\ *n* 1 : fortified place 2 : permanent army post

forte \'fōrt, 'fór,tā\ *n* : something at which a person excels

forth \'fōrth\ *adv* : forward

forth•com•ing *adj* 1 : coming or available soon 2 : open and direct

forth•right *adj* : direct —**forth•right•ly** *adv* —**forth•right•ness** *n*

forth•with *adv* : immediately

for•ti•fy \'fórtə,fī\ *vb* **-fied; -fy•ing** : make strong —**for•ti•fi•ca•tion** \,fórtəfə'kā•shən\ *n*

for•ti•tude \'fórt,nīt\ *adj or n* : 2 weeks —**fort•night•ly** *adj or adv*

for•ti•tude \'fórtə,tüd, -,tyüd\ *n* : ability to endure

fort•night \'fórt,nīt\ *n* : 2 weeks —**fort•night•ly** *adj or adv*

for•tress \'fórtrəs\ *n* : strong fort

for•tu•itous \fór'tüətəs, -'tyü-\ *adj* : accidental

for•tu•nate \'fórchənət\ *adj* 1 : coming by good luck 2 : lucky —**for•tu•nate•ly** *adv*

for•tune \'fórchən\ *n* 1 : prosperity attained partly through luck 2 : good or bad luck 3 : destiny 4 : wealth

for•tune-tell•er \-,telər\ *n* : one who foretells a person's future —**for•tune-tell•ing** \-iŋ\ *n or adj*

for•ty \'fórtē\ *n, pl* **forties** : 4 times 10 —**for•ti•eth** \-ēəth\ *adj or n* —**forty** *adj or pron*

fo•rum \'fōrəm\ *n, pl* **-rums** 1 : Roman marketplace 2 : medium for open discussion

for•ward \'fórwərd\ *adj* 1 : being near or at or belonging to the front 2 : brash ~ *adv* : toward what is in front ~ *n* : player near the front of his team ~ *vb* 1 : help onward 2 : send on —**for•ward•er** \-wərdər\ *n* —**for•ward•ness** *n*

for•wards \'fórwərdz\ *adv* : forward

fos•sil \'fäsəl\ *n* : preserved trace of an ancient plant or animal ~ *adj* : being or originating from a fossil —**fos•sil•ize** *vb*

fos•ter \'fóstər\ *adj* : being, having, or relating to substitute parents ~ *vb* : help to grow or develop

fought *past of* FIGHT

foul \'faůl\ *adj* 1 : offensive 2 : clogged with dirt 3 : abusive 4 : wet and stormy 5 : unfair ~ *n* : a breaking of the rules in a game ~ *adv* : fully ~ *vb* 1 : make or become foul or filthy 2 : tangle —**foul•ly** *adv* —**foul-mouthed** \'maůthd, -'maůtht\ *adj* —**foul•ness** *n*

fou•lard \fü'lärd\ *n* : lightweight silk

foul-up *n* : error or state of confusion —**foul up** *vb* : bungle

1found \'faůnd\ *past of* FIND

²found vb : establish —**found•er** n

foun•da•tion \faùn'dāshən\ n 1 : act of founding 2 : basis for something 3 : endowed institution 4 : supporting structure —**foun•da•tion•al** \-shənəl\ adj

found•er \'faùndər\ vb : sink

found•ling \'faùndliŋ\ n : abandoned infant that is found

found•ry \'faùndrē\ n, pl **-dries** : place where metal is cast

fount \'faùnt\ n : fountain

foun•tain \'faùnt³n\ n 1 : spring of water 2 : source 3 : artificial jet of water

four \'fōr\ n 1 : one more than 3 2 : 4th in a set or series 3 : something having 4 units —**four** adj or pron

four•fold adj : quadruple —**four•fold** adv

four•score adj : 80

four•some \'fōrsəm\ n : group of 4

four•teen \-'tēn\ n : one more than 13 —**fourteen** adj or pron —**four•teenth** \-'tēnth\ adj or n

fourth \'fōrth\ n 1 : one that is 4th 2 : one of 4 equal parts of something —**fourth** adj or adv

fowl \'faùl\ n, pl **fowl** or **fowls** n 1 : bird 2 : chicken

fox \'fäks\ n, pl **fox•es** 1 : small mammal related to wolves 2 : clever person ~ vb : trick —**foxy** \'fäksē\ adj

fox•glove n : flowering plant that provides digitalis

fox•hole \'fäks,hōl\ n : pit for protection against enemy fire

foy•er \'fòiər, 'fòi,yā\ n : entrance hallway

fra•cas \'frākəs, 'frak-\ n, pl **-cas•es** \-əsəz\ : brawl

frac•tion \'frakshən\ n 1 : number indicating one or more equal parts of a whole 2 : portion —**frac•tion•al** \-shənəl\ adj —**frac•tion•al•ly** adv

frac•tious \'frakshəs\ adj : hard to control

frac•ture \'frakchər\ n : a breaking of something —**fracture** vb

frag•ile \'frajəl, -,īl\ adj : easily broken —**fra•gil•i•ty** \frə'jilətē\ n

frag•ment \'fragmənt\ n : part broken off ~ \-,ment\ vb : break into parts —**frag•men•tary** \'fragmən,terē\ adj —**frag•men•ta•tion** \,fragmən'tāshən, -,men-\ n

fra•grant \'frāgrənt\ adj : sweet-smelling —**fra•grance** \-grəns\ n —**fra•grant•ly** adv

frail \'frāl\ adj : weak or delicate —**frail•ty** \-tē\ n

frame \'frām\ vb **framed; fram•ing** 1 : plan 2 : formulate 3 : construct or arrange 4 : enclose in a frame 5 : make appear guilty ~ n 1 : makeup of the body 2 : supporting or enclosing structure 3 : state or disposition (as of mind) —**frame•work** n

franc \'fraŋk\ n : monetary unit (as of France)

fran•chise \'fran,chīz\ n 1 : special privilege 2 : the right to vote —**fran•chi•see** \,fran,chī'zē, -chə-\ n

fran•gi•ble \'franjəbəl\ adj : breakable —**fran•gi•bil•i•ty** \,franjə'bilətē\ n

¹frank \'fraŋk\ adj : direct and sincere —**frank•ly** adv —**frank•ness** n

²frank vb : mark (mail) with a sign showing it can be mailed free ~ n : sign on franked mail

frank•furt•er \'fraŋkfərtər, -,fərt-\ **frank•furt** \-fərt\ n : cooked sausage

frank•in•cense \'fraŋkən,sens\ n : incense resin

fran•tic \'frantik\ adj : wildly excited —**fran•ti•cal•ly** \-ik lē\ adv

fra•ter•nal \frə'tərn³l\ adj 1 : brotherly 2 : of a fraternity —**fra•ter•nal•ly** adv

fra•ter•ni•ty \frə'tərnətē\ n, pl **-ties** : men's student social group

frat•er•nize \'fratər,nīz\ vb **-nized; -niz•ing** 1 : mingle as friends 2 : associate with members of a hostile group —**frat•er•ni•za•tion** \,fratərnə'zāshən\ n

frat•ri•cide \'fratrə,sīd\ n : killing of a sibling —**frat•ri•cid•al** \,fratrə'sīd³l\ adj

fraud \'fròd\ n : trickery —**fraud•u•lent** \'fròjələnt\ adj —**fraud•u•lent•ly** adv

fraught \'fròt\ adj : full of or accompanied by something specified

¹fray \'frā\ n : fight

²fray vb 1 : wear by rubbing 2 : separate the threads of 3 : irritate

fraz•zle \'frazəl\ vb **-zled; -zling** : wear out ~ n : exhaustion

freak \'frēk\ n 1 : something abnormal or unusual 2 : enthusiast —**freak•ish** adj —**freak out** vb 1 : experience nightmarish hallucinations from drugs 2 : distress or become distressed

freck•le \'frekəl\ n : brown spot on the skin —**freckle** vb

free \'frē\ adj **fre•er; fre•est** 1 : having liberty or independence 2 : not taxed 3 : given without charge 4 : voluntary 5 : not in use 6 : not fastened ~ adv : without charge ~ vb **freed; free•ing** : set free —**free•dom** \'frēdəm\ n —**free•ly** adv

free•boo•ter \-,bütər\ n : pirate

free-for-all n : fight with no rules

free•load vb : live off another's generosity —**free•load•er** n

free•stand•ing adj : standing without support

free•way \'frē,wā\ n : expressway

free will n : independent power to choose —**free•will** adj

freeze \'frēz\ vb **froze** \'frōz\; **fro•zen** \'frōz³n\; **freez•ing** 1 : harden into ice 2 : become chilled 3 : damage by frost 4 : stick fast 5 : become motionless 6 : fix at one stage or level ~ n 1 : very cold weather 2 : state of being frozen —**freez•er** n

freeze-dry vb : preserve by freezing then drying —**freeze-dried** adj

freight \'frāt\ n 1 : carrying of goods or payment for this 2 : shipped goods ~ vb : load or ship goods —**freight•er** n

french fry vb : fry in deep fat —**french fry** n

fre•net•ic \fri'netik\ adj : frantic —**fre•net•i•cal•ly** \-ik lē\ adv

fren•zy \'frenzē\ n, pl **-zies** : violent agitation —**fren•zied** \-zēd\ adj

fre•quen•cy \'frēkwənsē\ n, pl **-cies** 1 : frequent or regular occurrence 2 : number of cycles or sound waves per second

fre•quent \'frēkwənt\ adj : happening often ~ \frē'kwent, 'frēkwənt\ vb : go to habitually —**fre•quent•er** n —**fre•quent•ly** adv

fres•co \'freskō\ n, pl **-coes** : painting on fresh plaster

fresh \'fresh\ adj 1 : not salt 2 : pure 3 : not preserved 4 : not stale 5 : like new 6 : insolent —**fresh•en** \-ən\ vb —**fresh•ly** adv —**fresh•ness** n

fresh•et \-ət\ n : overflowing stream

fresh•man \-mən\ n : first-year student

fresh•wa•ter n : water that is not salty

fret \'fret\ vb **-tt-** 1 : worry or become irritated 2 : fray 3 : agitate ~ n 1 : worn spot 2 : irritation 3 : ridge on neck of a stringed instrument —**fret•ful** \-fəl\ adj —**fret•ful•ly** adv —**fret•ful•ness** n

fri•a•ble \'frīəbəl\ adj : easily pulverized

fri•ar \'frīər\ n : member of a religious order

fri•ary \-ē\ n, pl **-ar•ies** : monastery of friars

fric•as•see \'frikə,sē, ,frikə'-\ n : meat stewed in a gravy ~ vb **-seed; -see•ing** : stew in gravy

fric•tion \'frikshən\ n 1 : a rubbing between 2 surfaces 2 : clash of opinions —**fric•tion•al** adj

Fri•day \'frīdā\ n : 6th day of the week

friend \'frend\ n : person one likes —**friend•less** \-ləs\ adj —**friend•li•ness** \-lēnəs\ n —**friend•ly** adj —**friend•ship** \-,ship\ n

frieze \'frēz\ n : ornamental band around a room

frig•ate \'frigət\ n : warship smaller than a destroyer

fright \'frīt\ n : sudden fear —**frigh•ten** \-³n\ vb —**fright•ful** \-fəl\ adj —**fright•ful•ly** adv —**fright•ful•ness** n

frig•id \'frijəd\ adj : intensely cold —**fri•gid•i•ty** \frij'idətē\ n

frill \'fril\ n 1 : ruffle 2 : pleasing but nonessential addition —**frilly** adj

fringe \'frinj\ n 1 : ornamental border of short hanging threads or strips 2 : edge —**fringe** vb

frisk \'frisk\ vb 1 : leap about 2 : search (a person) esp. for weapons

frisky \'friskē\ adj **frisk•i•er; -est** : playful —**frisk•i•ly** adv —**frisk•i•ness** n

¹frit•ter \'fritər\ n : fried batter containing fruit or meat

²fritter vb : waste little by little

friv•o•lous \'frivələs\ adj : not important or serious —**fri•vol•i•ty** \friv'älətē\ n —**friv•o•lous•ly** adv

frizz \'friz\ vb : curl tightly —**frizz** n —**frizzy** adj

fro \'frō\ adv : away

frock \'fräk\ n 1 : loose outer garment 2 : dress

frog \'fròg, 'fräg\ n 1 : leaping amphibian 2 : hoarseness 3 : ornamental braid fastener 4 : small holder for flowers

frog•man \-,man, -mən\ n : underwater swimmer

frol•ic \'frälik\ vb **-icked; -ick•ing** : romp ~ n : fun —**frol•ic•some** \-səm\ adj

from \'frəm, 'främ\ prep —used to show a starting point

frond \'fränd\ n : fern or palm leaf

front \'frənt\ n 1 : face 2 : behavior 3 : main side of a building 4 : forward part 5 : boundary between air masses ~ vb 1 : have the main side adjacent to something 2 : serve as a front —**fron•tal** \-³l\ adj

front•age \'frəntij\ n : length of boundary line on a street

fron•tier \,frən'tir\ n : outer edge of settled territory —**fron•tiers•man** \-'tirzmən\ n

fron•tis•piece \'frəntə,spēs\ n : illustration facing a title page

frost \'fròst\ n 1 : freezing temperature 2 : ice crystals on a surface ~ vb 1 : cover with frost 2 : put icing on (a cake) —**frosty** adj

frost•bite \-,bīt\ n : partial freezing of part of the body —**frost•bit•ten** \-,bit³n\ adj

frost•ing n : icing

froth \'fròth\ n, pl **froths** \'fròths, 'fròthz\ : bubbles on a liquid —**frothy** adj

fro•ward \'frōwərd\ adj : willful

frown \'fraùn\ vb or n : scowl

froze past of FREEZE

frozen past part of FREEZE

fru•gal \'frügəl\ adj : thrifty —**fru•gal•i•ty** \frü'galətē\ n —**fru•gal•ly** adv

fruit \'früt\ n 1 : usu. edible and sweet part of a seed plant 2 : result ~ vb : bear fruit —**fruit•cake** n —**fruit•ed** \-əd\ adj —**fruit•less** adj —**fruit•less•ly** adv —**fruity** adj

fru•ition \frü'ishən\ n : completion

frumpy \'frəmpē\ adj **frump•i•er; -est** : dowdy

frus•trate \'frəs,trāt\ vb **-trat•ed; -trat•ing** 1 : block 2 : cause to fail —**frus•trat•ing•ly** adv —**frus•tra•tion** \,frəs'trāshən\ n

¹fry \'frī\ vb **fried; fry•ing** : cook esp. with fat or oil 2 : be cooked by frying ~ n, pl **fries** 1 : something fried 2 : social gathering with fried food

²fry n, pl **fry** : recently hatched fish

fud•dle \'fəd³l\ vb **-dled; -dling** : muddle

fud•dy–dud•dy \'fədē,dədē\ n, pl **-dies** : one who is old-fashioned or unimaginative

fudge \'fəj\ vb **fudged; fudg•ing** : cheat or exaggerate ~ n : creamy candy

fu•el \'fyüəl\ n : material burned to produce heat or power ~ vb **-eled** or **-elled; -el•ing** or **-el•ling** : provide with or take in fuel

fu•gi•tive \'fyüjətiv\ adj 1 : running away or trying to escape 2 : not lasting —**fugitive** n

-ful \fəl\ adj suffix 1 : full of 2 : having the qualities of 3 : -able ~ n suffix : quantity that fills

ful•crum \'fùlkrəm, 'fəl-\ n, pl **-crums** or **-cra** \-krə\ : support on which a lever turns

ful•fill, ful•fil \fùl'fil\ vb **-filled; -fill•ing** 1 : perform 2 : satisfy —**ful•fill•ment** n

¹full \'fùl\ adj 1 : filled 2 : complete 3 : rounded 4 : having an abundance of something ~ adv 1 : entirely ~ n : utmost degree —**full•ness** n —**ful•ly** adv

²full vb : shrink and thicken woolen cloth —**full•er** n

full-fledged \'fùl'flejd\ adj : fully developed

ful•some \'fùlsəm\ adj : copious verging on excessive

fum•ble \'fəmbəl\ vb **-bled; -bling** : fail to hold something properly —**fumble** n

fume \'fyüm\ n : irritating gas ~ vb **fumed; fum•ing** 1 : give off fumes 2 : show annoyance

fu•mi•gate \'fyümə,gāt\ vb **-gat•ed; -gat•ing** : treat with pest-killing fumes —**fu•mi•gant** \'fyümigənt\ n —**fu•mi•ga•tion** \,fyümə'gāshən\ n

fun \'fən\ n 1 : something providing amusement or enjoyment 2 : enjoyment ~ adj : full of fun

func•tion \'fəŋkshən\ n 1 : special purpose 2 : formal ceremony or social affair ~ vb : have or carry on a function —**func•tion•al** \-shənəl\ adj —**func•tion•al•ly** adv

func•tion•ary \-shə,nerē\ n, pl **-ar•ies** : official

fund \'fənd\ n 1 : store 2 : sum of money intended for a special purpose 3 pl : available money ~ vb : provide funds for

fun•da•men•tal \,fəndə'ment³l\ adj 1 : basic 2 : of central importance or necessity —**fundamental** n —**fun•da•men•tal•ly** adv

fu•ner•al \'fyünərəl\ n : ceremony for a dead person —**funeral** adj —**fu•ne•re•al** \fyü'nirēəl\ adj

fun•gi•cide \'fənjə,sīd, 'fəŋgə-\ n : agent that kills fungi —**fun•gi•cid•al** \,fənjə'sīd³l, ,fəŋgə-\ adj

fun•gus \'fəŋgəs\ n, pl **fun•gi** \'fən,jī, 'fəŋ,gī\ : lower plant that lacks chlorophyll —**fun•gal** \'fəŋgəl\ adj —**fun•gous** \-gəs\ adj

funk \'fəŋk\ n : state of depression

funky \'fəŋkē\ adj **funk•i•er; -est** : unconventional and unsophisticated

fun•nel \'fən³l\ n 1 : cone-shaped utensil with a tube for directing the flow of a liquid 2 : ship's smokestack ~ vb **-neled; -nel•ing** : move to a central point or into a central channel

fun•nies \'fənēz\ n pl : section of comic strips

fun•ny \'fənē\ adj **-ni•er; -est** 1 : amusing 2 : strange

fur \'fər\ n 1 : hairy coat of a mammal 2 : article of clothing made with fur —**fur** adj —**furred** \'fərd\ adj —**fur•ry** \-ē\ adj

fur•bish \'fərbish\ vb : make lustrous or new looking

fu•ri•ous \'fyùrēəs\ adj : fierce or angry —**fu•ri•ous•ly** adv

fur•long \'fər,lòŋ\ n : a unit of distance equal to 220 yards

fur•lough \'fərlō\ n : authorized absence from duty —**furlough** vb

fur•nace \'fərnəs\ n : enclosed structure in which heat is produced

fur•nish \'fərnish\ vb 1 : provide with what is needed 2 : make available for use

fur•nish•ings \-iŋs\ n pl 1 : articles or accessories of dress 2 : furniture

fur•ni•ture \'fərnichər\ n : movable articles for a room

fu•ror \'fyùr,òr\ n 1 : anger 2 : sensational craze

fur•ri•er \'fərēər\ n : dealer in furs

fur•row \'fərō\ n 1 : trench made by a plow 2 : wrinkle or groove —**furrow** vb

fur•ther \'fərthər\ adv 1 : at or to a more advanced point 2 : more ~ adj : additional ~ vb : promote —**fur•ther•ance** \-ərəns\ n

fur•ther•more \'fərthər,mōr\ adv : in addition

fur•ther•most \-,mōst\ adj : most distant

fur•thest \'fərthəst\ adv or adj : farthest

fur•tive \'fərtiv\ adj : slyly or secretly done —**fur•tive•ly** adv —**fur•tive•ness** n

fu•ry \'fyùrē\ n, pl **-ries** 1 : intense rage 2 : violence

¹fuse \'fyüz\ n 1 : cord lighted to transmit fire to an explosive 2 usu **fuze** : device for exploding a charge ~, **fuze** vb **fused** or **fuzed; fus•ing** or **fuz•ing** : equip with a fuse

²fuse vb **fused; fus•ing** 1 : melt and run together 2 : unite ~ n : electrical safety device —**fus•ible** adj

fu•se•lage \'fyüsə,läzh, -,lāzh, -zə-\ n : main body of an aircraft

fu•sil•lade \'fyüsə,läd, -,lād, ,fyüsə'-, -zə-\ n : volley of fire

fu•sion \'fyüzhən\ n 1 : process of merging by melting 2 : union of atomic nuclei

fuss \'fəs\ n 1 : needless bustle or excitement 2 : show of attention 3 : objection or protest ~ vb : make a fuss

fuss•bud•get \-,bəjət\ n : one who fusses or is fussy about trifles

fussy \'fəsē\ adj **fuss•i•er; -est** 1 : irritable 2 : paying very close attention to details —**fuss•i•ly** adv —**fuss•i•ness** n

fu•tile \'fyüt³l, 'fyü,tīl\ adj : useless or vain —**fu•til•i•ty** \fyü'tilətē\ n

fu•ture \'fyüchər\ adj : coming after the present ~ n 1 : time yet to come 2 : what will happen —**fu•tur•is•tic** \,fyüchə'ristik\ adj

fuze var of FUSE

fuzz \'fəz\ n : fine particles or fluff

fuzzy \-ē\ adj **fuzz•i•er; -est** 1 : covered with or like fuzz 2 : indistinct —**fuzz•i•ness** n

-fy \,fī\ vb suffix : make — **-fi•er** \,fīər\ n suffix

G

g \'jē\ n, pl **g's** or **gs** \'jēz\ 1 : 7th letter of the alphabet 2 : unit of gravitational force

gab \'gab\ vb **-bb-** : chatter —**gab** n —**gab•by** \'gabē\ adj

gab•ar•dine \'gabər,dēn\ n : durable twilled fabric

ga•ble \'gābəl\ n : triangular part of the end of a building —**ga•bled** \-bəld\ adj

gad \'gad\ vb **-dd-** : roam about —**gad•der** n

gad•fly n : persistently critical person

gad•get \'gajət\ n : device —**gad•get•ry** \'gajətrē\ n

gaff \'gaf\ n : metal hook for lifting fish —**gaff** vb

gaffe \'gaf\ n : social blunder

gag \'gag\ vb **-gg-** 1 : prevent from speaking or crying out by stopping up the mouth 2 : retch or cause to retch ~ n 1 : something that stops up the mouth 2 : laugh-provoking remark or act

gage var of GAUGE

gag•gle \'gagəl\ n : flock of geese

gai•ety \'gāətē\ n, pl **-eties** : high spirits

gai•ly \'gālē\ adv : in a gay manner

gain \'gān\ n 1 : profit 2 : obtaining of profit or possessions 3 : increase ~ vb 1 : get possession of 2 : win 3 : arrive at 4

: increase or increase in **5** : profit —**gain•er** n —**gain•ful** adj —**gain•ful•ly** adv

gain•say \gān'sā\ vb -**said** \-'sād, -'sed'; -**say•ing; -says** \-'sāz, -'sez\ : deny or dispute —**gain•say•er** n

gait \'gāt\ n : manner of walking or running —**gait•ed** adj

gal \'gal\ n : girl

ga•la \'gālə, 'galə, 'gälə\ n : festive celebration —**gala** adj

gal•axy \'galəksē\ n, pl -**ax•ies** : very large group of stars —**ga•lac•tic** \gə'laktik\ adj

gale \'gāl\ n **1** : strong wind **2** : outburst

¹gall \'gȯl\ n **1** : bile **2** : insolence

²gall n **1** : skin sore caused by chafing **2** : swelling of plant tissue caused by parasites ~ vb **1** : chafe **2** : irritate or vex

gal•lant \gə'lant, -'länt; 'galənt\ n : man very attentive to women ~ \'galənt; gə'lant, -'länt\ adj **1** : splendid **2** : brave **3** : polite and attentive to women —**gal•lant•ly** adv —**gal•lant•ry** \'galəntrē\ n

gall•blad•der n : pouch attached to the liver in which bile is stored

gal•le•on \galyən\ n : large sailing ship formerly used esp. by the Spanish

gal•lery \galərē\ n, pl -**ler•ies 1** : outdoor balcony **2** : long narrow passage or hall **3** : room or building for exhibiting art **4** : spectators —**gal•ler•ied** \-rēd\ adj

gal•ley \'galē\ n, pl -**leys 1** : old ship propelled esp. by oars **2** : kitchen of a ship or airplane

gal•li•um \galēəm\ n : bluish white metallic chemical element

gal•li•vant \'galə,vant\ vb : travel or roam about for pleasure

gal•lon \'galən\ n : unit of liquid measure equal to 4 quarts

gal•lop \'galəp\ n : fast 3-beat gait of a horse —**gallop** vb —**gal•lop•er** n

gal•lows \'galōz\ n, pl -**lows** or -**lows•es** : upright frame for hanging criminals

gall•stone n : abnormal concretion in the gallbladder or bile passages

ga•lore \gə'lōr\ adj : in abundance

ga•losh \gə'läsh\ n : overshoe —usu. pl.

gal•va•nize \'galvə,nīz\ vb -**nized; -niz•ing 1** : shock into action **2** : coat (iron or steel) with zinc —**gal•va•ni•za•tion** \galvənə'zāshən\ n —**gal•va•niz•er** n

gam•bit \'gambit\ n **1** : opening tactic in chess **2** : stratagem

gam•ble \'gambəl\ vb -**bled; -bling 1** : play a game for stakes **2** : bet **3** : take a chance ~ n : risky undertaking —**gam•bler** \-blər\ n

gam•bol \'gambəl\ vb -**boled** or -**bolled; -bol•ing** or -**bol•ling** : skip about in play —**gambol** n

game \'gām\ n **1** : playing activity **2** : competition according to rules **3** : animals hunted for sport or food ~ vb **gamed; gam•ing** : gamble ~ adj **1** : plucky **2** : lame —**game•ly** adv —**game•ness** n

game•cock n : fighting cock

game•keep•er n : person in charge of game animals or birds

gam•ete \gə'mēt, 'gam,ēt\ n : mature germ cell —**ga•met•ic** \gə'metik\ adj

ga•mine \ga'mēn\ n : charming tomboy

gam•ut \'gamət\ n : entire range or series

gamy or **gam•ey** \'gāmē\ adj **gam•i•er; -est** : having the flavor of game esp. when slightly tainted —**gam•i•ness** n

¹gan•der \'gandər\ n : male goose

²gander n : glance

gang \'gaŋ\ n **1** : group of persons working together **2** : group of criminals ~ vb : attack in a gang —with up

gan•gling \'gaŋgliŋ\ adj : lanky

gan•gli•on \'gaŋglēən\ n, pl -**glia** \-glēə\ : mass of nerve cells

gang•plank n : platform used in boarding or leaving a ship

gan•grene \'gaŋ,grēn, gaŋ'-; 'gan-, gan-\ n : local death of body tissue —**gangrene** vb —**gan•gre•nous** \'gaŋgrənəs\ adj

gang•ster \'gaŋstər\ n : member of criminal gang

gang•way \-,wā\ n : passage in or out

gan•net \'ganət\ n : large fish-eating marine bird

gan•try \'gantrē\ n, pl -**tries** : frame structure supported over or around something

gap \'gap\ n **1** : break in a barrier **2** : mountain pass **3** : empty space

gape \'gāp\ vb **gaped; gap•ing 1** : open widely **2** : stare with mouth open —**gape** n

ga•rage \gə'räzh, -'räj\ n : shelter or repair shop for automobiles ~ vb -**raged; -rag•ing** : put or keep in a garage

garb \'gärb\ n : clothing ~ vb : dress

gar•bage \'gärbij\ n **1** : food waste **2** : trash —**gar•bage•man** n

gar•ble \'gärbəl\ vb -**bled; -bling** : distort the meaning of

gar•den \'gärd∂n\ n **1** : plot for growing fruits, flowers, or vegetables **2** : public recreation area ~ vb : work in a garden —**gar•den•er** \'gärd∂nər\ n

gar•de•nia \gär'dēnyə\ n : tree or shrub with fragrant white or yellow flowers or the flower

gar•gan•tuan \gär'ganchəwən\ adj : having tremendous size or volume

gar•gle \'gärgəl\ vb -**gled; -gling** : rinse the throat with liquid —**gargle** n

gar•goyle \'gär,gȯil\ n : waterspout in the form of a grotesque human or animal

gar•ish \'garish\ adj : offensively bright or gaudy

gar•land \'gärlənd\ n : wreath ~ vb : form into or deck with a garland

gar•lic \'gärlik\ n : herb with pungent bulbs used in cooking —**gar•licky** \-likē\ adj

gar•ment \'gärmənt\ n : article of clothing

gar•ner \'gärnər\ n : acquire by effort

gar•net \'gärnət\ n : deep red mineral

gar•nish \'gärnish\ vb : add decoration to (as food) —**garnish** n

gar•nish•ee \gärnə'shē\ vb -**eed; -ee•ing** : take (as a debtor's wages) by legal authority

gar•nish•ment \'gärnishmənt\ n : attachment of property to satisfy a creditor

gar•ret \'garət\ n : attic

gar•ri•son \'garəsən\ n : military post or the troops stationed there —**garrison** vb

gar•ru•lous \'garələs\ adj : talkative —**gar•ru•li•ty** \gə'rülətē\ n —**gar•ru•lous•ly** adv —**gar•ru•lous•ness** n

gar•ter \'gärtər\ n : band to hold up a stocking or sock

gas \'gas\ n, pl **gas•es 1** : fluid (as hydrogen or air) that tends to expand indefinitely **2** : gasoline ~ vb **gassed; gas•sing 1** : treat with gas **2** : fill with gasoline —**gas•eous** \'gasēəs, 'gashəs\ adj

gash \'gash\ n : deep long cut —**gash** vb

gas•ket \'gaskət\ n : material or a part used to seal a joint

gas•light n : light of burning illuminating gas

gas•o•line \'gasə,lēn, ,gasə'-\ n : flammable liquid from petroleum

gasp \'gasp\ vb **1** : catch the breath audibly **2** : breathe laboriously —**gasp** n

gas•tric \'gastrik\ adj : relating to or located near the stomach

gas•tron•o•my \gas'tränəmē\ n : art of good eating —**gas•tro•nom•ic** \gastrə'nämik\ adj

gate \'gāt\ n : an opening for passage in a wall or fence —**gate•keep•er** n —**gate•post** n

gate•way n : way in or out

gath•er \'gathər\ vb **1** : bring or come together **2** : harvest **3** : pick up little by little **4** : deduce —**gath•er•er** n —**gath•er•ing** n

gauche \'gōsh\ adj : crude or tactless

gaudy \'gȯdē\ adj **gaud•i•er; -est** : tastelessly showy —**gaud•i•ly** \'gȯd∂lē\ adv —**gaud•i•ness** n

gauge \'gāj\ n : instrument for measuring ~ vb **gauged; gaug•ing** : measure

gaunt \'gȯnt\ adj : thin or emaciated —**gaunt•ness** n

¹gaunt•let \-lət\ n **1** : protective glove **2** : challenge to combat

²gauntlet : ordeal

gauze \'gȯz\ n : thin often transparent fabric —**gauzy** adj

gave past of GIVE

gav•el \'gavəl\ n : mallet of a presiding officer, auctioneer, or judge

gawk \'gȯk\ vb : stare stupidly

gawky \-ē\ adj **gawk•i•er; -est** : clumsy

gay \'gā\ adj **1** : merry **2** : bright and lively **3** : homosexual —**gay** n

gaze \'gāz\ vb **gazed; gaz•ing** : fix the eyes in a steady intent look —**gaze** n —**gaz•er** n

ga•zelle \gə'zel\ n : small swift antelope

ga•zette \-'zet\ n : newspaper

gaz•et•teer \gazə'tir\ n : geographical dictionary

gear \'gir\ n **1** : clothing **2** : equipment **3** : toothed wheel —**gear** vb

gear•shift n : mechanism by which automobile gears are shifted

geek \'gēk\ n : socially inept person

geese pl of GOOSE

gei•sha \'gāshə, 'gē-\ n, pl -**sha** or -**shas** : Japanese girl or woman trained to entertain men

gel•a•tin \'jelət∂n\ n : sticky substance obtained from animal tissues by boiling —**ge•lat•i•nous** \jə'lat∂nəs\ adj

geld \'geld\ vb : castrate

geld•ing \-iŋ\ n : castrated horse

gem \'jem\ n : cut and polished valuable stone —**gem•stone** n

gen•der \'jendər\ n **1** : sex **2** : division of a class of words (as nouns) that determines agreement of other words

gene \'jēn\ n : segment of DNA that controls inheritance of a trait

ge•ne•al•o•gy \jēnē'äləjē, jen-, -'al-\ n, pl -**gies** : study of family pedigrees —**ge•ne•a•log•i•cal** \-ēə'läjikəl\ adj —**ge•ne•a•log•i•cal•ly** adv —**ge•ne•al•o•gist** \-ē'äləjist, -'al-\ n

genera pl of GENUS

gen•er•al \'jenrəl, 'jenə-\ adj **1** : relating to the whole **2** : applicable to all of a group **3** : common or widespread ~ n **1** : something that involves or is applicable to the whole **2** : commissioned officer in the army, air force, or marine corps ranking above a lieutenant general —**gen•er•al•ly** adv —**in general** : for the most part

gen•er•al•i•ty \jenə'ralətē\ n, pl -**ties** : general statement

gen•er•al•ize \jenrə,līz, 'jenə-\ vb -**ized; -iz•ing** : reach a general conclusion esp. on the basis of particular instances —**gen•er•al•i•za•tion** \jenrələ'zāshən, jenə-\ n

general of the air force : commissioned officer of the highest rank in the air force

general of the army : commissioned officer of the highest rank in the army

gen•er•ate \'jenə,rāt\ vb -**at•ed; -at•ing** : create or produce

gen•er•a•tion \jenə'rāshən\ n **1** : living beings constituting a single step in a line of descent **2** : production —**gen•er•a•tive** \'jenə,rātiv, -rət-\ adj

gen•er•a•tor \'jenə,rātər\ n **1** : one that generates **2** : machine that turns mechanical into electrical energy

ge•ner•ic \jə'nerik\ adj **1** : general **2** : not protected by a trademark **3** : relating to a genus —**generic** n

gen•er•ous \'jenərəs\ adj : freely giving or sharing —**gen•er•os•i•ty** \jenə'räsətē\ n —**gen•er•ous•ly** adv —**gen•er•ous•ness** n

ge•net•ics \jə'netiks\ n : biology dealing with heredity and variation —**ge•net•ic** \-ik\ adj —**ge•net•i•cal•ly** adv —**ge•net•i•cist** \-'netəsist\ n

ge•nial \'jēnēəl\ adj : cheerful —**ge•nial•i•ty** \jēnē'alətē\ n —**ge•nial•ly** adv

ge•nie \'jēnē\ n : supernatural spirit that often takes human form

gen•i•tal \'jenət∂l\ adj : concerned with reproduction —**gen•i•tal•ly** \-t∂lē\ adv

gen•i•ta•lia \jenə'tālyə\ n pl : external genital organs

gen•i•tals \'jenət∂lz\ n pl : genitalia

ge•nius \'jēnyəs\ n **1** : single strongly marked capacity **2** : extraordinary intellectual power or a person having such power

geno•cide \'jenə,sīd\ n : systematic destruction of a racial or cultural group

genre \'zhänrə, 'zhä∂rə\ n : category esp. of literary composition

gen•teel \jen'tēl\ adj : polite or refined

gen•tile \'jen,tīl\ n : person who is not Jewish —**gentile** adj

gen•til•i•ty \jen'tilətē\ n, pl -**ties 1** : good birth and family **2** : good manners

gen•tle \'jent∂l\ adj -**tler; -tlest 1** : of a family of high social station **2** : not harsh, stern, or violent **3** : soft or delicate ~ vb -**tled; -tling** : make gentle —**gen•tle•ness** n —**gent•ly** adv

gen•tle•man \-mən\ n : man of good family or manners —**gen•tle•man•ly** adv

gen•tle•wom•an \-,wùmən\ n : woman of good family or breeding

gen•try \'jentrē\ n, pl -**tries** : people of good birth or breeding

gen•u•flect \'jenyə,flekt\ vb : bend the knee in worship —**gen•u•flec•tion** \jenyə-'flekshən\ n

gen•u•ine \'jenyəwən\ adj : being the same in fact as in appearance —**gen•u•ine•ly** adv —**gen•u•ine•ness** n

ge•nus \'jēnəs\ n, pl **gen•era** \'jenərə\ : category of biological classification

ge•ode \'jē,ōd\ n : stone having a mineral-lined cavity

geo•des•ic \jēə'desik, -'dēs-\ adj : made of a framework of linked polygons

ge•og•ra•phy \jē'ägrəfē\ n **1** : study of the earth and its climate, products, and inhabitants **2** : natural features of a region —**ge•og•ra•pher** \-fər\ n —**geo•graph•ic** \jēə'grafik, **geo•graph•i•cal** \-ikəl\ adj —**geo•graph•i•cal•ly** adv

ge•ol•o•gy \jē'äləjē\ n : study of the history of the earth and its life esp. as recorded in rocks —**geo•log•ic** \jēə'läjik\ **geo•log•i•cal** \-ikəl\ adj —**geo•log•i•cal•ly** adv —**ge•ol•o•gist** \jē'äləjist\ n

ge•om•e•try \jē'ämətrē\ n, pl -**tries** : mathematics of the relations, properties, and measurements of solids, surfaces, lines, and angles —**geo•met•ric** \jēə-'metrik\, **geo•met•ri•cal** \-rikəl\ adj

geo•ther•mal \jē'thərməl, -∂-\ adj : relating to or derived from the heat of the earth's interior

ge•ra•ni•um \jə'rānēəm\ n : garden plant with clusters of white, pink, or scarlet flowers

ger•bil \'jərbəl\ n : burrowing desert rodent

ge•ri•at•ric \jerē'atrik\ adj **1** : relating to aging or the aged **2** : old

ge•ri•at•rics \-triks\ n : medicine dealing with the aged and aging

germ \'jərm\ n **1** : microorganism **2** : source or rudiment

ger•mane \jər'mān\ adj : relevant

ger•ma•ni•um \-'mānēəm\ n : grayish white hard chemical element

ger•mi•cide \'jərmə,sīd\ n : agent that destroys germs —**ger•mi•cid•al** \jərmə'sī-d∂l\ adj

ger•mi•nate \'jərmə,nāt\ vb -**nat•ed; -nat•ing** : begin to develop —**ger•mi•na•tion** \jərmə'nāshən\ n

ger•ry•man•der \jerē'mandər, 'jerē,-, ,jerē'-, 'gerē,-\ vb : divide into election districts so as to give one political party an advantage —**gerrymander** n

ger•und \'jerənd\ n : word having the characteristics of both verb and noun

ge•sta•po \gə'stäpō\ n, pl -**pos** : secret police

ges•ta•tion \je'stāshən\ n : pregnancy or incubation —**ges•tate** \'je,stāt\ vb

ges•ture \'jeschər\ n **1** : movement of the body or limbs that expresses something **2** : something said or done for its effect on the attitudes of others —**ges•tur•al** \-chərəl\ adj —**gesture** vb

ge•sund•heit \gə'zùnt,hīt\ interj —used to wish good health to one who has just sneezed

get \'get\ vb **got** \'gät\; **got** or **got•ten** \'gät∂n\; **get•ting 1** : gain or be in possession of **2** : succeed in coming or going **3** : cause to come or go or to be in a certain condition or position **4** : become **5** : be subjected to **6** : understand **7** : be obliged —**get along 1** : get by **2** : be on friendly terms —**get by** : meet one's needs

get•away \'getə,wā\ n **1** : escape **2** : a starting or getting under way

gey•ser \'gīzər\ n : spring that intermittently shoots up hot water and steam

ghast•ly \'gastlē\ adj -**li•er; -est** : horrible or shocking

gher•kin \'gərkən\ n : small pickle

ghet•to \'getō\ n, pl -**tos** or -**toes** : part of a city in which members of a minority group live

ghost \'gōst\ n : disembodied soul —**ghost•ly** adv

ghost•write vb -**wrote; -writ•ten** : write for and in the name of another —**ghost•writ•er** n

ghoul \'gül\ n : legendary evil being that feeds on corpses —**ghoul•ish** adj

GI \jē'ī\ n, pl **GI's** or **GIs** : member of the U.S. armed forces

gi•ant \'jīənt\ n **1** : huge legendary being **2** : something very large or very powerful —**giant** adj

gib•ber \'jibər\ vb -**bered; -ber•ing** : speak rapidly and foolishly

gib•ber•ish \'jibərish\ n : unintelligible speech or language

gib•bon \'gibən\ n : manlike ape

gibe \'jīb\ vb **gibed; gib•ing** : jeer at —**gibe** n

gib•lets \'jibləts\ n pl : edible fowl viscera

gid•dy \'gidē\ adj -**di•er; -est 1** : silly **2** : dizzy —**gid•di•ness** n

gift \'gift\ n **1** : something given **2** : talent —**gift•ed** adj

gi•gan•tic \jī'gantik\ adj : very big

gig•gle \'gigəl\ vb -**gled; -gling** : laugh in a silly manner —**giggle** n —**gig•gly** \-∂lē\ adj

gig•o•lo \'jigə,lō\ n, pl -**los** : man living on the earnings of a woman

Gi•la monster \'hēlə-\ n : large venomous lizard

gild \'gild\ vb **gild•ed** \'gildəd\ or **gilt** \'gilt\; **gild•ing 1** : cover with or as if with gold

gill \'gil\ n : organ of a fish for obtaining oxygen from water

gilt \'gilt\ adj : gold-colored ~ n : gold or goldlike substance on the surface of an object

gim•bal \'gimbəl, 'jim-\ n : device that allows something to incline freely

gim•let \'gimlət\ n : small tool for boring holes

gim•mick \'gimik\ n : new and ingenious scheme, feature, or device —**gim•mick•ry** n —**gim•micky** \-ikē\ adj

gimpy \'gimpē\ adj : lame

¹gin \'jin\ n : machine to separate seeds from cotton —**gin** vb

²gin n : clear liquor flavored with juniper berries

gin•ger \'jinjər\ n : pungent aromatic spice from a tropical plant —**gin•ger•bread** n

gin•ger•ly adj : very cautious or careful —**gingerly** adv

ging•ham \'giŋəm\ n : cotton clothing fabric

gin•gi•vi•tis \jinjə'vītəs\ n : inflammation of the gums

gink•go \'giŋkō\ n, pl -**goes** or -**gos** : tree of eastern China

gin•seng \'jin,siŋ, -,seŋ, -saŋ\ n : aromatic root of a Chinese herb

gi•raffe \jə'raf\ n : African mammal with a very long neck

gird \'gərd\ vb **gird•ed** \'gərdəd\ or **girt** \'gərt\; **gird•ing 1** : encircle or fasten with or as if with a belt **2** : prepare

gird•er \'gərdər\ n : horizontal supporting beam

gir•dle \'gərd∂l\ n : woman's supporting undergarment ~ vb : surround

girl \'gərl\ n **1** : female child **2** : young

woman 3 : sweetheart —**girl·hood** \-ˌhu̇d\ *n* —**girl·ish** *adj*

girlfriend *n* : frequent or regular female companion of a boy or man

girth \ˈgərth\ *n* : measure around something

gist \ˈjist\ *n* : main point or part

give \ˈgiv\ *vb* **gave** \ˈgāv\; **giv·en** \ˈgivən\; **giv·ing** 1 : put into the possession or keeping of another 2 : pay 3 : perform 4 : contribute or donate 5 : produce 6 : utter 7 : yield to force, strain, or pressure ~ *n* : capacity or tendency to yield to force or strain —**give in** *vb* : surrender —**give out** *vb* : become used up or exhausted —**give up** *vb* 1 : let out of one's control 2 : cease from trying, doing, or hoping

give·away *n* 1 : unintentional betrayal 2 : something given free

giv·en \ˈgivən\ *adj* 1 : prone or disposed 2 : having been specified

giz·zard \ˈgizərd\ *n* : muscular usu. horny-lined enlargement following the crop of a bird

gla·cial \ˈglāshəl\ *adj* 1 : relating to glaciers 2 : very slow —**gla·cial·ly** *adv*

gla·cier \ˈglāshər\ *n* : large body of ice moving slowly

glad \ˈglad\ *adj* **-dd-** 1 : experiencing or causing pleasure, joy, or delight 2 : very willing —**glad·den** \-ᵊn\ *vb* —**glad·ly** *adv* —**glad·ness** *n*

glade \ˈglād\ *n* : grassy open space in a forest

glad·i·a·tor \ˈgladēˌātər\ *n* : one who fought to the death for the entertainment of ancient Romans —**glad·i·a·to·ri·al** \ˌgladēəˈtōrēəl\ *adj*

glad·i·o·lus \ˌgladēˈōləs\ *n, pl* **-li** \-ˌlē, -ˌlī\ : plant related to the irises

glam·our, glam·or \ˈglamər\ *n* : romantic or exciting attractiveness —**glam·or·ize** \-əˌrīz\ *vb* —**glam·or·ous** \-ərəs\ *adj*

glance \ˈglans\ *vb* **glanced; glanc·ing** 1 : strike and fly off to one side 2 : give a quick look ~ *n* : quick look

gland \ˈgland\ *n* : group of cells that secretes a substance —**glan·du·lar** \ˈglanjələr\ *adj*

glans \ˈglanz\ *n, pl* **glan·des** \ˈglanˌdēz\ : conical vascular body forming the end of the penis or clitoris

glare \ˈglar\ *vb* **glared; glar·ing** 1 : shine with a harsh dazzling light 2 : stare angrily ~ *n* 1 : harsh dazzling light 2 : angry stare

glar·ing \ˈglariŋ\ *adj* : painfully obvious —**glar·ing·ly** *adv*

glass \ˈglas\ *n* 1 : hard usu. transparent material made by melting sand and other materials 2 : something made of glass 3 *pl* : lenses used to correct defects of vision —**glass·ful** \-ˌful\ *n* —**glass·ware** \-ˌwar\ *n* —**glassy** *adj*

glass·blow·ing *n* : art of shaping a mass of molten glass by blowing air into it —**glass·blow·er** *n*

glau·co·ma \glau̇ˈkōmə, glȯ-\ *n* : state of increased pressure within the eyeball

glaze \ˈglāz\ *vb* **glazed; glaz·ing** 1 : furnish with glass 2 : apply glaze to ~ *n* : glassy surface or coating

gla·zier \ˈglāzhər\ *n* : one who sets glass in window frames

gleam \ˈglēm\ *n* 1 : transient or partly obscured light 2 : faint trace ~ *vb* : send out gleams

glean \ˈglēn\ *vb* : collect little by little —**glean·able** *adj* —**glean·er** *n*

glee \ˈglē\ *n* : joy —**glee·ful** *adj*

glen \ˈglen\ *n* : narrow hidden valley

glib \ˈglib\ *adj* **-bb-** : speaking or spoken with ease —**glib·ly** *adv*

glide \ˈglīd\ *vb* **glid·ed; glid·ing** : move or descend smoothly and effortlessly —**glide** *n*

glid·er \ˈglīdər\ *n* 1 : winged aircraft having no engine 2 : swinging porch seat

glim·mer \ˈglimər\ *vb* : shine faintly or unsteadily ~ *n* 1 : faint light 2 : small amount

glimpse \ˈglimps\ *vb* **glimpsed; glimps·ing** : take a brief look at —**glimpse** *n*

glint \ˈglint\ *vb* : gleam or sparkle —**glint** *n*

glis·ten \ˈglisᵊn\ *vb* : shine or sparkle by reflection —**glisten** *n*

glit·ter \ˈglitər\ *vb* : shine with brilliant or metallic luster ~ *n* : small glittering ornaments —**glit·tery** *adj*

gloat \ˈglōt\ *vb* : think of something with triumphant delight

glob \ˈgläb\ *n* : large rounded lump

glob·al \ˈglōbəl\ *adj* : worldwide —**glob·al·ly** *adv*

globe \ˈglōb\ *n* : sphere 2 : the earth or a model of it

glob·u·lar \ˈgläbyələr\ *adj* 1 : round 2 : made up of globules

glob·ule \ˈgläbyül\ *n* : tiny ball

glock·en·spiel \ˈgläkənˌshpēl\ *n* : portable musical instrument consisting of tuned metal bars

gloom \ˈglüm\ *n* 1 : darkness 2 : sadness —**gloom·i·ly** *adv* —**gloom·i·ness** *n* —**gloomy** *adj*

glop \ˈgläp\ *n* : messy mass or mixture

glo·ri·fy \ˈglōrəˌfī\ *vb* **-fied; -fy·ing** 1 : make to seem glorious 2 : worship —**glo·ri·fi·ca·tion** \ˌglōrəfəˈkāshən\ *n*

glo·ry \ˈglōrē\ *n, pl* **-ries** 1 : praise or honor offered in worship 2 : cause for praise or renown 3 : magnificence 4 : heavenly bliss ~ *vb* **-ried; -ry·ing** : rejoice proudly —**glo·ri·ous** \ˈglōrēəs\ *adj* —**glo·ri·ous·ly** *adv*

1gloss \ˈgläs, ˈglȯs\ *n* : luster —**gloss·i·ly** \-əlē\ *adv* —**gloss·i·ness** \-ēnəs\ *n* —**gloss over** *vb* 1 : mask the true nature of 2 : deal with only superficially —**glossy** \-ē\ *adj*

2gloss *n* : brief explanation or translation ~ *vb* : translate or explain

glos·sa·ry \ˈgläsərē, ˈglȯs-\ *n, pl* **-ries** : dictionary —**glos·sar·i·al** \glaˈsarēəl, glȯ-\ *adj*

glove \ˈgləv\ *n* : hand covering with sections for each finger

glow \ˈglō\ *vb* 1 : shine with or as if with intense heat 2 : show exuberance ~ *n* : brightness or warmth of color or feeling

glow·er \ˈglau̇ər\ *vb* : stare angrily —**glower** *n*

glow·worm *n* : insect or insect larva that emits light

glu·cose \ˈglüˌkōs\ *n* : sugar found esp. in blood, plant sap, and fruits

glue \ˈglü\ *n* : substance used for sticking things together —**glue** *vb* —**glu·ey** \ˈglüē\ *adj*

glum \ˈgləm\ *adj* **-mm-** 1 : sullen 2 : dismal

glut \ˈglət\ *vb* **-tt-** : fill to excess —**glut** *n*

glu·ten \ˈglütᵊn\ *n* : gluey protein substance in flour

glu·ti·nous \ˈglütᵊnəs\ *adj* : sticky

glut·ton \ˈglətᵊn\ *n* : one who eats to excess —**glut·ton·ous** \ˈglətᵊnəs\ *adj* —**glut·tony** \-ē\ *n*

gnarled \ˈnärld\ *adj* 1 : knotty 2 : gloomy or sullen

gnash \ˈnash\ *vb* : grind (as teeth) together

gnat \ˈnat\ *n* : small biting fly

gnaw \ˈnȯ\ *vb* : bite or chew on —**gnaw·er** *n*

gnome \ˈnōm\ *n* : dwarf of folklore —**gnom·ish** *adj*

gnu \ˈnü, ˈnyü\ *n, pl* **gnu** *or* **gnus** : large African antelope

go \ˈgō\ *vb* **went** \ˈwent\, **gone** \ˈgȯn, ˈgän\; **go·ing** \ˈgȯiŋ\; **goes** \ˈgōz\ 1 : move, proceed, run, or pass 2 : leave 3 : extend or lead 4 : sell or amount —**with** *for* 5 : happen 6 —used in present participle to show intent or imminent action 7 : become 8 : fit or harmonize 9 : belong ~ *n, pl* **goes** 1 : act or manner of going 2 : vigor 3 : attempt —**go back on** : betray —**go by the board** : be discarded —**go for** : favor —**go off** : explode —**go one better** : outdo —**go over** 1 : examine 2 : study —**go to town** : be very successful —**on the go** : constantly active

goad \ˈgōd\ *n* : something that urges —**goad** *vb*

goal \ˈgōl\ *n* 1 : mark to reach in a race 2 : purpose 3 : object in a game through which a ball is propelled

goal·ie \ˈgōlē\ *n* : player who defends the goal

goal·keep·er *n* : goalie

goat \ˈgōt\ *n* : horned ruminant mammal related to the sheep —**goat·skin** *n*

goa·tee \gōˈtē\ *n* : small pointed beard

gob \ˈgäb\ *n* : lump

1gob·ble \ˈgäbəl\ *vb* **-bled; -bling** : eat greedily

2gobble *vb* **-bled; -bling** : make the noise of a turkey (**gob·bler**)

gob·ble·dy·gook \ˈgäbəldē,gük, -ˌgük\ *n* : nonsense

gob·let \ˈgäblət\ *n* : large stemmed drinking glass

gob·lin \ˈgäblən\ *n* : ugly mischievous sprite

god \ˈgäd, ˈgȯd\ *n* 1 *cap* : supreme being 2 : being with supernatural powers —**god·like** *adj* —**god·ly** *adj*

god·child *n* : person one sponsors at baptism —**god·daugh·ter** *n* —**god·son** *n*

god·dess \ˈgädəs, ˈgȯd-\ *n* : female god

god·less \-ləs\ *adj* : not believing in God —**god·less·ness** *n*

god·par·ent *n* : sponsor at baptism —**god·fa·ther** *n* —**god·moth·er** *n*

god·send \-ˌsend\ *n* : something needed that comes unexpectedly

goes *pres 3d sing of* GO

go-get·ter \ˈgōˌgetər\ *n* : enterprising person —**go-get·ting** \-iŋ\ *adj or n*

gog·gle \ˈgägəl\ *vb* **-gled; -gling** : stare wide-eyed

gog·gles \-əlz\ *n pl* : protective glasses

go·ings-on \ˌgōiŋzˈȯn, -ˈän\ *n pl* : events

goi·ter \ˈgȯitər\ *n* : abnormally enlarged thyroid gland

gold \ˈgōld\ *n* : malleable yellow metallic chemical element —**gold·smith** \-ˌsmith\ *n*

gold·brick \-ˌbrik\ *n* : person who shirks duty —**goldbrick** *vb*

gold·en \ˈgōldən\ *adj* 1 : made of, containing, or relating to gold 2 : having the color of gold 3 : precious or favorable

gold·en·rod \ˈgōldənˌräd\ *n* : herb having tall stalks with tiny yellow flowers

gold·finch \ˈgōldˌfinch\ *n* : yellow American finch

gold·fish \-ˌfish\ *n* : small usu. orange or golden carp

golf \ˈgälf, ˈgȯlf\ *n* : game played by hitting a small ball (**golf ball**) with clubs (**golf clubs**) into holes placed in a field (**golf course**) —**golf** *vb* —**golf·er** *n*

go·nad \ˈgōˌnad\ *n* : sex gland

gon·do·la \ˈgändələ (*usual for 1*), gänˈdō-\ *n* 1 : long narrow boat used on the canals of Venice 2 : car suspended from a cable

gon·do·lier \ˌgändəˈlir\ *n* : person who propels a gondola

gone \ˈgȯn\ *adj* 1 : past 2 : involved

gon·er \ˈgȯnər\ *n* : hopeless case

gong \ˈgäŋ, ˈgȯŋ\ *n* : metallic disk that makes a deep sound when struck

gon·or·rhea \ˌgänəˈrēə\ *n* : bacterial inflammatory venereal disease of the genital tract —**gon·or·rhe·al** \-ˈrēəl\ *adj*

goo \ˈgü\ *n* : thick or sticky substance —**goo·ey** \-ē\ *adj*

good \ˈgu̇d\ *adj* **bet·ter** \ˈbetər\; **best** \ˈbest\ 1 : satisfactory 2 : salutary 3 : considerable 4 : desirable 5 : well-behaved, kind, or virtuous ~ *n* 1 : something good 2 : benefit 3 *pl* : personal property 4 *pl* : wares ~ *adv* : well —**good-heart·ed** \-ˈhärtəd\ *adj* —**good-look·ing** *adj* —**good-na·tured** *adj* —**good·ness** *n* —**good-tem·pered** \-ˈtempərd\ *adj* —**for good** : forever

good-bye, good-by \gu̇dˈbī\ *n* : parting remark

good-for-noth·ing *n* : idle worthless person

Good Friday *n* : Friday before Easter observed as the anniversary of the crucifixion of Christ

good·ly *adj* **-li·er; -est** : considerable

good·will *n* 1 : good intention 2 : kindly feeling

goody \ˈgu̇dē\ *n, pl* **good·ies** : something that is good esp. to eat

goody-goody *adj* : affectedly or annoyingly sweet or self-righteous —**goody-goody** *n*

goof \ˈgüf\ *vb* 1 : blunder 2 : waste time —usu. with *off* or *around* —**goof** *n* —**goof-off** *n*

goofy \ˈgüfē\ *adj* **goof·i·er; -est** : crazy —**goof·i·ness** *n*

goose \ˈgüs\ *n, pl* **geese** \ˈgēs\ : large bird with webbed feet

goose·ber·ry \ˈgüsˌberē, ˈgüz-\ *n* : berry of a shrub related to the currant

goose bumps *n pl* : roughening of the skin caused by fear, excitement, or cold

goose·flesh *n* : goose bumps

goose pimples *n pl* : goose bumps

go·pher \ˈgōfər\ *n* : burrowing rodent

1gore \ˈgōr\ *n* : blood

2gore *vb* **gored; gor·ing** : pierce or wound with a horn or tusk

1gorge \ˈgȯrj\ *n* : narrow ravine

2gorge *vb* **gorged; gorg·ing** : eat greedily

gor·geous \ˈgȯrjəs\ *adj* : supremely beautiful

go·ril·la \gəˈrilə\ *n* : African manlike ape

gory \ˈgōrē\ *adj* **gor·i·er; -est** : bloody

gos·hawk \ˈgäsˌhȯk\ *n* : long-tailed hawk with short rounded wings

gos·ling \ˈgäzliŋ, ˈgȯz-\ *n* : young goose

gos·pel \ˈgäspəl\ *n* 1 : teachings of Christ and the apostles 2 : something accepted as infallible truth —**gospel** *adj*

gos·sa·mer \ˈgäsəmər, ˈgäz-\ *n* 1 : film of cobweb 2 : light filmy substance

gos·sip \ˈgäsəp\ *n* 1 : person who reveals personal information 2 : rumor or report of an intimate nature ~ *vb* : spread gossip —**gos·sipy** \-ē\ *adj*

got *past of* GET

Goth·ic \ˈgäthik\ *adj* : relating to a medieval style of architecture

gotten *past part of* GET

gouge \ˈgau̇j\ *n* 1 : rounded chisel 2 : cavity or groove scooped out ~ *vb* **gouged; goug·ing** 1 : cut or scratch a groove in 2 : overcharge

gou·lash \ˈgüˌläsh, -ˌlash\ *n* : beef stew with vegetables and paprika

gourd \ˈgōrd, ˈgu̇rd\ *n* 1 : any of a group of vines including the cucumber, squash, and melon 2 : inedible hard-shelled fruit of a gourd

gour·mand \ˈgu̇rˌmänd\ *n* : person who loves good food and drink

gour·met \ˈgu̇rˌmā, gu̇rˈmā\ *n* : connoisseur of food and drink

gout \ˈgau̇t\ *n* : disease marked by painful inflammation and swelling of the joints —**gouty** *adj*

gov·ern \ˈgəvərn\ *vb* 1 : control and direct policy in 2 : guide or influence strongly 3 : restrain —**gov·ern·ment** \-ərmənt\ *n* —**gov·ern·men·tal** \ˌgəvərˈmentᵊl\ *adj*

gov·ern·ess \ˈgəvərnəs\ *n* : female teacher in a private home

gov·er·nor \ˈgəvənər, ˈgəvər-\ *n* : head of

a political unit 2 : automatic speed-control device —**gov·er·nor·ship** *n*

gown \ˈgau̇n\ *n* 1 : loose flowing outer garment 2 : woman's formal evening dress —**gown** *vb*

grab \ˈgrab\ *vb* **-bb-** : take by sudden grasp —**grab** *n*

grace \ˈgrās\ *n* 1 : unmerited divine assistance 2 : short prayer before or after a meal 3 : respite 4 : ease of movement or bearing ~ *vb* **graced; grac·ing** 1 : honor 2 : adorn —**grace·ful** \-fəl\ *adj* —**grace·ful·ly** *adv* —**grace·ful·ness** *n* —**grace·less** *adj*

gra·cious \ˈgrāshəs\ *adj* : marked by kindness and courtesy or charm and taste —**gra·cious·ly** *adv* —**gra·cious·ness** *n*

grack·le \ˈgrakəl\ *n* : American blackbird

gra·da·tion \grāˈdāshən, grə-\ *n* : step, degree, or stage in a series

grade \ˈgrād\ *n* 1 : stage in a series, order, or ranking 2 : division of school representing one year's work 3 : mark of accomplishment in school 4 : degree of slope ~ *vb* **grad·ed; grad·ing** 1 : arrange in grades 2 : make level or evenly sloping 3 : give a grade to —**grad·er** *n*

grade school *n* : school including the first 4 or 8 grades

gra·di·ent \ˈgrādēənt\ *n* : slope

grad·u·al \ˈgrajəwəl\ *adj* : going by steps or degrees —**grad·u·al·ly** *adv*

grad·u·ate \ˈgrajəwət\ *n* : holder of a diploma ~ *adj* : of or relating to studies beyond the bachelor's degree ~ \-ˌwāt\ *vb* **-at·ed; -at·ing** 1 : grant or receive a diploma 2 : mark with degrees of measurement —**grad·u·a·tion** \ˌgrajəˈwāshən\ *n*

graf·fi·to \grəˈfētō, grä-\ *n, pl* **-ti** \-ē\ : inscription on a wall

graft \ˈgraft\ *vb* : join one thing to another so that they grow together ~ *n* 1 : grafted plant 2 : the getting of money dishonestly or the money so gained —**graft·er** *n*

grain \ˈgrān\ *n* 1 : seeds or fruits of cereal grasses 2 : small hard particle 3 : arrangement of fibers in wood —**grained** \ˈgrānd\ *adj* —**grainy** *adj*

gram \ˈgram\ *n* : metric unit of weight equal to 1/1000 kilogram

gram·mar \ˈgramər\ *n* : study of words and their functions and relations in the sentence —**gram·mar·i·an** \grəˈmarēən\ *n* —**gram·mat·i·cal** \-ˈmatikəl\ *adj* —**gram·mat·i·cal·ly** *adv*

grammar school *n* : grade school

gra·na·ry \ˈgrānərē, ˈgran-\ *n, pl* **-ries** : storehouse for grain

grand \ˈgrand\ *adj* 1 : large or striking in size or scope 2 : fine and imposing 3 : very good —**grand·ly** *adv* —**grand·ness** *n*

grand·child \-ˌchīld\ *n* : child of one's son or daughter —**grand·daugh·ter** *n* —**grand·son** *n*

gran·deur \ˈgranjər\ *n* : quality or state of being grand

gran·dil·o·quence \granˈdiləkwəns\ *n* : pompous speaking —**gran·dil·o·quent** \-kwənt\ *adj*

gran·di·ose \ˈgrandēˌōs, ˌgrandēˈ-\ *adj* 1 : impressive 2 : affectedly splendid —**gran·di·ose·ly** *adv*

grand·par·ent \ˈgrandˌparənt\ *n* : parent of one's father or mother —**grand·father** \-ˌfäthər, -ˌfath-\ *n* —**grand·moth·er** \-ˌməthər\ *n*

grand·stand \-ˌstand\ *n* : usu. roofed stand for spectators

grange \ˈgrānj\ *n* : farmers association

gran·ite \ˈgranət\ *n* : hard igneous rock

grant \ˈgrant\ *vb* 1 : consent to 2 : give 3 : admit as true ~ *n* 1 : act of granting 2 : something granted —**grant·ee** \grantˈē\ *n* —**grant·er** \ˈgrantər\ *n* —**grant·or** \-ər, -ˌȯr\ *n*

gran·u·late \ˈgranyəˌlāt\ *vb* **-lat·ed; -lat·ing** : form into grains or crystals —**gran·u·la·tion** \ˌgranyəˈlāshən\ *n*

gran·ule \ˈgranyül\ *n* : small particle —**gran·u·lar** \-yələr\ *adj* —**gran·u·lar·i·ty** \ˌgranyəˈlarətē\ *n*

grape \ˈgrāp\ *n* : smooth juicy edible berry of a woody vine (**grape·vine**)

grape·fruit *n* : large edible yellow-skinned citrus fruit

graph \ˈgraf\ *n* : diagram that shows relationships between things —**graph** *vb*

graph·ic \ˈgrafik\ *adj* 1 : vividly described 2 : relating to the arts (**graphic arts**) of representation and printing on flat surfaces ~ *n* 1 : picture used for illustration 2 *pl* : computer screen display —**graph·i·cal·ly** \-iklē\ *adv*

graph·ite \ˈgrafˌīt\ *n* : soft carbon used for lead pencils and lubricants

grap·nel \ˈgrapnəl\ *n* : small anchor with several claws

grap·ple \ˈgrapəl\ *vb* **-pled; -pling** 1 : seize or hold with or as if with a hooked implement 2 : wrestle

grasp \'grasp\ vb 1 : take or seize firmly 2 : understand ~ n 1 : one's hold or control 2 : one's reach 3 : comprehension

grass \'gras\ n : plant with jointed stem and narrow leaves —**grassy** adj

grass•hop•per \-,häpər\ n : leaping plant-eating insect

grass•land n : land covered with grasses

¹**grate** \'grāt\ n 1 : grating 2 : frame of iron bars to hold burning fuel

²**grate** vb **grat•ed; -ing** 1 : pulverize by rubbing against something rough 2 : irritate —**grat•er** n —**grat•ing•ly** adv

grate•ful \'grātfəl\ adj : thankful or appreciative —**grate•ful•ly** adv —**grate•ful•ness** n

grat•i•fy \'grata,fī\ vb **-fied; -fy•ing** : give pleasure to —**grat•i•fi•ca•tion** \,gratəfə-'kāshən\ n

grat•ing \'grātiŋ\ n : framework with bars across it

gra•tis \'gratəs, 'grāt-\ adv or adj : free

grat•i•tude \'grata,tüd, -,tyüd\ n : state of being grateful

gra•tu•itous \gra'tüətəs, -'tyü-\ adj 1 : free 2 : uncalled-for

gra•tu•ity \-ətē\ n, pl **-ities** : tip

¹**grave** \'grāv\ n : place of burial —**grave-stone** n —**grave•yard** n

²**grave** adj **grav•er; grav•est** 1 : threatening great harm or danger 2 : solemn —**grave-ly** adv —**grave•ness** n

grav•el \'gravəl\ n : loose rounded fragments of rock —**grav•el•ly** adj

grav•i•tate \'grava,tāt\ vb **-tat•ed; -tat•ing** : move toward something

grav•i•ta•tion \,grava'tāshən\ n : natural force of attraction that tends to draw bodies together —**grav•i•ta•tion•al** \-shənəl\ adj —**grav•i•ta•tion•al•ly** adv

grav•i•ty \'gravətē\ n, pl **-ties** 1 : serious importance 2 : gravitation

gra•vy \'grāvē\ n, pl **-vies** : sauce made from thickened juices of cooked meat

gray \'grā\ adj 1 : of the color gray 2 : having gray hair ~ n : neutral color between black and white ~ vb : make or become gray —**gray•ish** \-ish\ adj —**gray•ness** n

¹**graze** \'grāz\ vb **grazed; graz•ing** : feed on herbage or pasture —**graz•er** n

²**graze** vb **grazed; graz•ing** : touch lightly in passing

grease \'grēs\ n : thick oily material or fat ~ \'grēs, 'grēz\ vb **greased; greas•ing** : smear or lubricate with grease —**greasy** \'grēsē, -zē\ adj

great \'grāt\ adj 1 : large in size or number 2 : larger than usual —**great•ly** adv —**great•ness** n

grebe \'grēb\ n : diving bird related to the loon

greed \'grēd\ n : selfish desire beyond reason —**greed•i•ly** \-əlē\ adv —**greed•i•ness** \-ēnəs\ n —**greedy** \'grēdē\ adj

green \'grēn\ adj 1 : of the color green 2 : unripe 3 : inexperienced ~ vb : become green ~ n 1 : color between blue and yellow 2 pl : leafy parts of plants —**green•ish** adj —**green•ness** n

green•ery \'grēnərē\ n, pl **-er•ies** : green foliage or plants

green•horn n : inexperienced person

green•house n : glass structure for the growing of plants

greet \'grēt\ vb 1 : address with expressions of kind wishes 2 : react to —**greet•er** n

greet•ing n 1 : friendly address on meeting 2 pl : best wishes

gre•gar•i•ous \gri'gareəs\ adj : social or companionable —**gre•gar•i•ous•ly** adv —**gre•gar•i•ous•ness** n

grem•lin \'gremlən\ n : small mischievous gnome

gre•nade \grə'nād\ n : small missile filled with explosive or chemicals

grew past of GROW

grey var of GRAY

grey•hound \'grā,haund\ n : tall slender dog noted for speed

grid \'grid\ n 1 : grating 2 : evenly spaced horizontal and vertical lines (as on a map)

grid•dle \'grid³l\ n : flat metal surface for cooking

grid•iron \'grid,īrn\ n 1 : grate for broiling 2 : football field

grief \'grēf\ n 1 : emotional suffering caused by or as if by bereavement 2 : disaster

griev•ance \'grēvəns\ n : complaint

grieve \'grēv\ vb **grieved; griev•ing** : feel or cause to feel grief or sorrow

griev•ous \'grēvəs\ adj 1 : oppressive 2 : causing grief or sorrow —**griev•ous•ly** adv

grill \'gril\ vb 1 : cook on a grill 2 : question intensely ~ n 1 : griddle 2 : informal restaurant

grille, grill \'gril\ n : grating forming a barrier or screen —**grill•work** n

grim \'grim\ adj **-mm-** 1 : harsh and forbidding in appearance 2 : relentless —**grim-ly** adv —**grim•ness** n

gri•mace \'griməs, grim'ās\ n : facial expression of disgust —**grimace** vb

grime \'grīm\ n : embedded or accumulated dirt —**grimy** adj

grin \'grin\ vb **-nn-** : smile so as to show the teeth —**grin** n

grind \'grīnd\ vb **ground** \'graund\; **grinding** 1 : reduce to powder 2 : wear down or sharpen by friction 3 : operate or produce by turning a crank ~ n : monotonous labor or routine —**grind•er** n —**grind•stone** \'grīn,stōn\ n

grip \'grip\ vb **-pp-** : seize or hold firmly ~ n 1 : grasp 2 : control 3 : device for holding

gripe \'grīp\ vb **griped; grip•ing** 1 : cause pains in the bowels 2 : complain —**gripe** n

grippe \'grip\ n : influenza

gris•ly \'grizlē\ adj **-li•er; -est** : horrible or gruesome

grist \'grist\ n : grain to be ground or already ground —**grist•mill** n

gris•tle \'grisəl\ n : cartilage —**gris•tly** \-lē\ adj

grit \'grit\ n 1 : hard sharp granule 2 : material composed of granules 3 : unyielding courage ~ vb **-tt-** : press with a grating noise —**grit•ty** adj

grits \'grits\ n pl : coarsely ground hulled grain

griz•zled \'grizəld\ adj : streaked with gray

groan \'grōn\ vb 1 : moan 2 : creak under a strain —**groan** n

gro•cer \'grōsər\ n : food dealer —**grocery** \'grōsrē, 'grōsh-, -ərē\ n

grog \'gräg\ n : rum diluted with water

grog•gy \-ē\ adj **-gi•er; -est** : dazed and unsteady on the feet —**grog•gi•ly** adv —**grog•gi•ness** n

groin \'grōin\ n : juncture of the lower abdomen and inner thigh

grom•met \'grämət, 'grəm-\ n : eyelet

groom \'grüm, 'grum\ n 1 : one who cares for horses 2 : bridegroom ~ vb 1 : clean and care for (as a horse) 2 : make neat or attractive 3 : prepare

groove \'grüv\ n 1 : long narrow channel 2 : fixed routine —**groove** vb

grope \'grōp\ vb **groped; grop•ing** : search for by feeling

gros•beak \'grōs,bēk\ n : finch with large conical bill

¹**gross** \'grōs\ adj 1 : glaringly noticeable 2 : bulky 3 : consisting of an overall total exclusive of deductions 4 : vulgar ~ n : the whole before any deductions ~ vb : earn as a total —**gross•ly** adv —**gross-ness** n

²**gross** n, pl **gross** : 12 dozen

gro•tesque \grō'tesk\ adj 1 : absurdly distorted or repulsive 2 : ridiculous —**gro-tesque•ly** adv

grot•to \'grätō\ n, pl **-toes** : cave

grouch \'grauch\ n : complaining person —**grouch** vb —**grouchy** adj

¹**ground** \'graund\ n 1 : bottom of a body of water 2 pl : sediment 3 : basis for something 4 : surface of the earth 5 : conductor that makes electrical connection with the earth or a framework ~ vb 1 : force or bring down to the ground 2 : give basic knowledge to 3 : connect with an electrical ground —**ground•less** adj

²**ground** past of GRIND

ground•hog n : woodchuck

ground•wa•ter n : underground water

ground•work n : foundation

group \'grüp\ n : small group of men ~ vb : gather or collect into groups

grou•per \'grüpər\ n : large fish of warm seas

grouse \'graus\ n, pl **grouse** or **grouses** : ground-dwelling game bird

grout \'graut\ n : mortar for filling cracks —**grout** vb

grove \'grōv\ n : small group of trees

grov•el \'grävəl, 'grəv-\ vb **-eled** or **-elled; -el•ing** or **-el•ling** : abase oneself

grow \'grō\ vb **grew** \'grü\; **grown** \'grōn\; **grow•ing** 1 : come into existence and develop to maturity 2 : be able to grow 3 : advance or increase 4 : become 5 : cultivate —**grow•er** n

growl \'graul\ vb : utter a deep threatening sound —**growl** n

grown-up \'grōn,əp\ n : adult —**grown-up** adj

growth \'grōth\ n 1 : stage in growing 2 : process of growing 3 : result of something growing

grub \'grəb\ vb **-bb-** 1 : root out by digging 2 : search about ~ n 1 : thick wormlike larva 2 : food

grub•by \'grəbē\ adj **-bi•er; -est** : dirty —**grub•bi•ness** n

grub•stake n : supplies for a prospector

grudge \'grəj\ vb **grudged; grudg•ing** : be reluctant to give ~ n : feeling of ill will

gru•el \'grüəl\ n : thin porridge

gru•el•ing, gru•el•ling \-əliŋ\ adj : requiring extreme effort

grue•some \'grüsəm\ adj : horribly repulsive

gruff \'grəf\ adj : rough in speech or manner —**gruff•ly** adv

grum•ble \'grəmbəl\ vb **-bled; -bling** : mutter in discontent —**grum•bler** \-blər\ n

grumpy \-pē\ adj **grump•i•er; -est** : cross —**grump•i•ly** adv —**grump•i•ness** n

grun•ion \'grənyən\ n : fish of the California coast

grunt \'grənt\ n : deep guttural sound —**grunt** vb

gua•no \'gwänō\ n : excrement of seabirds used as fertilizer

guar•an•tee \,garən'tē\ n 1 : assurance of the fulfillment of a condition 2 : something given or held as a security ~ vb **-teed; -tee•ing** 1 : promise to be responsible for 2 : state with certainty —**guar•an•tor** \,garən'tor\ n

guar•an•ty \'garəntē\ n, pl **-ties** 1 : promise to answer for another's failure to pay a debt 2 : guarantee 3 : pledge ~ vb **-tied; -ty•ing** : guarantee

guard \'gärd\ n 1 : defensive position 2 : act of protecting 3 : an individual or group that guards against danger 4 : protective or safety device ~ vb 1 : protect or watch over 2 : take precautions —**guard•house** n —**guard•room** n

guard•ian \'gärdēən\ n : one who has responsibility for the care of the person or property of another —**guard•ian•ship** n

gua•va \'gwävə\ n : shrubby tropical tree or its mildly acid fruit

gu•ber•na•to•ri•al \,gübənə'tōrēəl, ,gyü-\ adj : relating to a governor

guer•ril•la, gue•ril•la \gə'rilə\ n : soldier engaged in small-scale harassing tactics

guess \'ges\ vb 1 : form an opinion from little evidence 2 : state correctly solely by chance 3 : think or believe —**guess** n

guest \'gest\ n 1 : person to whom hospitality (as of a house) is extended 2 : patron of a commercial establishment (as a hotel) 3 : person not a regular cast member who appears on a program

guf•faw \gə'fò, 'gəf,ò\ n : loud burst of laughter —**guf•faw** \gə'fò\ vb

guide \'gīd\ n 1 : one that leads or gives direction to another 2 : device on a machine to direct motion ~ vb **guid•ed; guid•ing** 1 : show the way to 2 : direct —**guid•able** adj —**guid•ance** \'gīd³ns\ n —**guide•book** n

guide•line \-,līn\ n : summary of procedures regarding policy or conduct

guild \'gild\ n : association

guile \'gīl\ n : craftiness —**guile•ful** adj —**guile•less** adj —**guile•less•ness** n

guil•lo•tine \'gilə,tēn, ,gēyə'tēn, 'gēyə,-\ n : machine for beheading persons —**guil-lotine** vb

guilt \'gilt\ n 1 : fact of having committed an offense 2 : feeling of responsibility for offenses —**guilt•i•ly** adv —**guilt•i•ness** n —**guilty** \'giltē\ adj

guin•ea \'ginē\ n 1 : old gold coin of United Kingdom 2 : 21 shillings

guinea pig n : small So. American rodent

guise \'gīz\ n : external appearance

gui•tar \gə'tär, gi-\ n : 6-stringed musical instrument played by plucking

gulch \'gəlch\ n : ravine

gulf \'gəlf\ n 1 : extension of an ocean or a sea into the land 2 : wide gap

¹**gull** \'gəl\ n : seabird with webbed feet

²**gull** vb : make a dupe of ~ n : dupe —**gull•ible** adj

gul•let \'gələt\ n : throat

gul•ly \'gəlē\ n, pl **-lies** : trench worn by running water

gulp \'gəlp\ vb : swallow hurriedly or greedily —**gulp** n

¹**gum** \'gəm\ n : tissue along the jaw at the base of the teeth

²**gum** n 1 : sticky plant substance 2 : gum usu. of sweetened chicle prepared for chewing —**gum•my** adj

gum•bo \'gəmbō\ n : thick soup

gum•drop n : gumlike candy

gump•tion \'gəmpshən\ n : initiative

gun \'gən\ n 1 : cannon 2 : portable firearm 3 : discharge of a gun 4 : something like a gun ~ vb **-nn-** : hunt with a gun —**gun-fight** n —**gun•fight•er** n —**gun•fire** n —**gun•man** \-mən\ n —**gun•pow•der** n —**gun•shot** n —**gun•smith** n

gun•boat n : small armed ship

gun•ner \'gənər\ n : person who uses a gun

gun•nery sergeant \'gənərē-\ n : noncommissioned officer in the marine corps ranking next below a first sergeant

gun•ny•sack \'gənē,sak\ n : burlap sack

gun•sling•er \'gən,sliŋər\ n : skilled gunman in the old West

gun•wale \'gən³l\ n : upper edge of a boat's side

gup•py \'gəpē\ n, pl **-pies** : tiny tropical fish

gur•gle \'gərgəl\ vb **-gled; -gling** : make a sound like that of a flowing and gently splashing liquid —**gurgle** n

gu•ru \'gü,rü\ n, pl **-rus** 1 : personal religious teacher in Hinduism 2 : expert

gush \'gəsh\ vb : pour forth violently or enthusiastically —**gush•er** \'gəshər\ n

gushy \-ē\ adj **gush•i•er; -est** : effusively sentimental

gust \'gəst\ n 1 : sudden brief rush of wind 2 : sudden outburst —**gust** vb —**gusty** adj

gus•ta•to•ry \'gəstə,tōrē\ adj : relating to the sense of taste

gus•to \'gəstō\ n : zest

gut \'gət\ n 1 pl : intestines 2 : digestive canal 3 pl : courage ~ vb **-tt-** : eviscerate

gut•ter \'gətər\ n : channel for carrying off rainwater

gut•tur•al \'gətərəl\ adj : sounded in the throat —**guttural** n

¹**guy** \'gī\ n : rope, chain, or rod attached to something to steady it —**guy** vb

²**guy** n : person

guz•zle \'gəzəl\ vb **-zled; -zling** : drink greedily

gym \'jim\ n : gymnasium

gym•na•si•um \jim'nāzēəm, -zhəm\ n, pl **-si•ums** or **-sia** \-zēə, -zhə\ : place for indoor sports

gym•nas•tics \jim'nastiks\ n : physical exercises performed in a gymnasium —**gym-nast** \'jim,nast\ n —**gym•nas•tic** adj

gy•ne•col•o•gy \,gīnə'käləjē, ,jin-\ n : branch of medicine dealing with the diseases of women —**gy•ne•col•og•ic** \-ikə-'läjik\, **gy•ne•co•log•i•cal** \-ikəl\ adj —**gy•ne•col•o•gist** \-ə'käləjist\ n

gyp \'jip\ n 1 : cheat 2 : trickery —**gyp** vb

gyp•sum \'jipsəm\ n : calcium-containing mineral

gy•rate \'jī,rāt\ vb **-rat•ed; -rat•ing** : revolve around a center —**gy•ra•tion** \jī-'rāshən\ n

gy•ro•scope \'jīrə,skōp\ n : wheel mounted to spin rapidly about an axis that is free to turn in various directions

H

h \'āch\ n, pl **h's** or **hs** \'āchəz\ : 8th letter of the alphabet

hab•er•dash•er \'habər,dashər\ n : men's clothier —**hab•er•dash•ery** \-ərē\ n

hab•it \'habət\ n 1 : monk's or nun's clothing 2 : usual behavior 3 : addiction —**hab•it-form•ing** adj

hab•it•able \-əbəl\ adj : capable of being lived in

hab•i•tat \'habə,tat\ n : place where a plant or animal naturally occurs

hab•i•ta•tion \,habə'tāshən\ n 1 : occupancy 2 : dwelling place

ha•bit•u•al \hə'bichəwəl\ adj 1 : commonly practiced or observed 2 : doing, practicing, or acting by habit —**ha•bit•u•al•ly** adv —**ha•bit•u•al•ness** n

ha•bit•u•ate \hə'bichə,wāt\ vb **-at•ed; -at•ing** : accustom

ha•ci•en•da \,häsē'endə\ n : ranch house

¹**hack** \'hak\ vb 1 : cut with repeated irregular blows 2 : cough in a short dry manner 3 : manage successfully —**hack** n —**hack•er** n

²**hack** n 1 : horse or vehicle for hire 2 : saddle horse 3 : writer for hire —**hack** adj —**hack•man** \-mən\ n

hack•le \'hakəl\ n 1 : long feather on the neck or back of a bird 2 pl : hairs that can be erected 3 pl : temper

hack•ney \-nē\ n, pl **-neys** 1 : horse for riding or driving 2 : carriage for hire

hack•neyed \-nēd\ adj : trite

hack•saw n : saw for metal

had past of HAVE

had•dock \'hadək\ n, pl **haddock** : Atlantic food fish

Ha•des \'hādēz\ n 1 : mythological abode of the dead 2 : often not cap : hell

haft \'haft\ n : handle of a weapon or tool

hag \'hag\ n 1 : witch 2 : ugly old woman

hag•gard \'hagərd\ adj : worn or emaciated —**hag•gard•ly** adv

hag•gle \'hagəl\ vb **-gled; -gling** : argue in bargaining —**hag•gler** n

¹**hail** \'hāl\ n 1 : precipitation in small lumps of ice 2 : something like a rain of hail ~ vb : rain hail —**hail•stone** n —**hail•storm** n

²**hail** vb 1 : greet or salute 2 : summon ~ n : expression of greeting or praise —often used as an interjection

hair \'har\ n : threadlike growth from the

skin —**hair•brush** n —**hair•cut** n —**hair•dress•er** n —**haired** adj —**hair•i•ness** n —**hair•less** adj —**hairpin** n —**hair•style** n —**hair•styl•ing** n —**hair•styl•ist** n —**hairy** adj

hair•breadth \-ˌbredth, **hairs•breadth** \'harz-\ n : tiny distance or margin

hair•do \-ˌdü\ n, pl **-dos** : style of wearing hair

hair•line n 1 : thin line 2 : outline of the hair on the head

hair•piece n : toupee

hair–rais•ing adj : causing terror or astonishment

hake \'hāk\ n : marine food fish

hal•cy•on \'halsēən\ adj : prosperous or most pleasant

¹hale \'hāl\ adj : healthy or robust

²hale vb **haled; hal•ing** 1 : haul 2 : compel to go

half \'haf, 'háf\ n, pl **halves** \'havz, 'hávz\ : either of 2 equal parts — adj 1 : being a half or nearly a half 2 : partial —**half** adv

half brother n : brother related through one parent only

half•heart•ed \-'härtəd\ adj : without enthusiasm —**half•heart•ed•ly** adv —**half•heart•ed•ness** n

half–life n : time for half of something to undergo a process

half sister n : sister related through one parent only

half•way adj : midway between 2 points —**half•way** adv

half–wit \-ˌwit\ n : foolish person —**half•wit•ted** \-ˌwitəd\ adj

hal•i•but \'haləbət\ n, pl **halibut** : large edible marine flatfish

hal•i•to•sis \ˌhalə'tōsəs\ n : bad breath

hall \'hól\ n 1 : large public or college or university building 2 : lobby 3 : auditorium

hal•le•lu•jah \ˌhalə'lüyə\ interj —used to express praise, joy, or thanks

hall•mark \'hól,märk\ n : distinguishing characteristic

hal•low \'halō\ vb : consecrate —**hallowed** \-ōd, -əwəd\ adj

Hal•low•een \ˌhalə'wēn, ˌhäl-\ n : evening of October 31 observed esp. by children in merrymaking and masquerading

hal•lu•ci•na•tion \hə,lüs⁹n'āshən\ n : perception of objects that are not real —**hal•lu•ci•nate** \hə'lüs⁹n,āt\ vb —**hal•lu•ci•na•to•ry** \-'lüs⁹nə,tōrē\ adj

hal•lu•ci•no•gen \hə'lüs⁹nəjən\ n : substance that induces hallucinations —**hal•lu•ci•no•gen•ic** \-,lüs⁹nə'jenik\ adj

hall•way n : entrance hall

ha•lo \'hālō\ n, pl **-los** or **-loes** : circle of light appearing to surround a shining body

¹halt \'hólt\ adj : lame

²halt vb : stop or cause to stop —**halt** n

hal•ter \'hóltər\ n 1 : rope or strap for leading or tying an animal 2 : brief blouse held up by straps ~ vb : catch (an animal) with a halter

halt•ing \'hóltiŋ\ adj : uncertain —**halt•ing•ly** adv

halve \'hav, 'háv\ vb **halved; halv•ing** 1 : divide into halves 2 : reduce to half

halves pl of HALF

ham \'ham\ n 1 : thigh—usu. pl. 2 : cut esp. of pork from the thigh 3 : showy actor 4 : amateur radio operator ~ vb **-mm-** : overplay a part —**ham** adj

ham•let \'hamlət\ n : small village

ham•mer \'hamər\ n 1 : hand tool for pounding 2 : gun part whose striking explodes the charge ~ vb : beat, drive, or shape with a hammer —**hammer out** vb : produce with effort

ham•mer•head n 1 : striking part of a hammer 2 : shark with a hammerlike head

ham•mock \'hamək\ n : swinging bed hung by cords at each end

¹ham•per \'hampər\ vb : impede

²hamper n : large covered basket

ham•ster \'hamstər\ n : stocky shorttailed rodent

ham•string \'ham,striŋ\ vb **-strung** \-,strəŋ\ **-string•ing** \-,striŋiŋ\ 1 : cripple by cutting the leg tendons 2 : make ineffective or powerless

hand \'hand\ n 1 : end of a front limb adapted for grasping 2 : side 3 : promise of marriage 4 : handwriting 5 : assistance or participation 6 : applause 7 : cards held by a player 8 : worker ~ vb : lead, assist, give, or pass with the hand —**hand•clasp** n —**hand•craft** vb —**hand•ful** n —**hand•gun** n —**hand•less** adj —**hand•made** adj —**hand•rail** n —**hand•saw** n —**hand•wo•ven** adj —**hand•writ•ing** n —**hand•writ•ten** adj

hand•bag n : woman's purse

hand•ball n : game played by striking a ball with the hand

hand•bill n : printed advertisement or notice distributed by hand

hand•book n : concise reference book

hand•cuffs n pl : locking bracelets that bind the wrists together —**handcuff** vb

hand•i•cap \'handē,kap\ n 1 : advantage given or disadvantage imposed to equalize a competition 2 : disadvantage —**handicap** vb —**hand•i•capped** adj —**hand•i•cap•per** n

hand•i•craft \'handē,kraft\ n 1 : manual skill 2 : article made by hand —**hand•i•craft•er** n —**hand•i•crafts•man** \-,kraftsmən\ n

hand•i•work \-,wərk\ n : work done personally or by the hands

hand•ker•chief \'haŋkərchəf, -,chēf\ n, pl **-chiefs** \-chəfs, -,chēfs\ : small piece of cloth carried for personal use

han•dle \'hand⁹l\ n : part to be grasped ~ vb **-dled; -dling** 1 : touch, hold, or manage with the hands 2 : deal with 3 : deal or trade in —**han•dle•bar** n —**han•dled** \-d⁹ld\ adj —**han•dler** \handlər\ n

hand•maid•en n : female attendant

hand•out n : something given out

hand•pick vb : select personally

hand•shake n : clasping of hands (as in greeting)

hand•some \'hansəm\ adj **-som•er; -est** 1 : sizable 2 : generous 3 : nice-looking —**hand•some•ly** adv —**hand•some•ness** n

hand•spring n : somersault on the hands

hand•stand n : a balancing upside down on the hands

handy \'handē\ adj **hand•i•er; -est** 1 : conveniently near 2 : easily used 3 : dexterous —**hand•i•ly** adv —**hand•i•ness** n

handy•man \-,man\ n : one who does odd jobs

hang \'haŋ\ vb **hung** \'həŋ\ **hang•ing** 1 : fasten or remain fastened to an elevated point without support from below 2 : suspend by the neck until dead—past tense often hanged 3 : droop ~ n 1 : way a thing hangs 2 : an understanding of something —**hang•er** n —**hang•ing** n

han•gar \'haŋər\ n : airplane shelter

hang•dog \'haŋ,dóg\ adj : ashamed or guilty

hang•man \-mən\ n : public executioner

hang•nail n : loose skin near a fingernail

hang•out n : place where one likes to spend time

hang•over n : sick feeling following heavy drinking

hank \'haŋk\ n : coil or loop

han•ker \'haŋkər\ vb : desire strongly —**han•ker•ing** n

han•ky–pan•ky \ˌhaŋkē'paŋkē\ n : questionable or underhanded activity

han•som \'hansəm\ n : 2-wheeled covered carriage

Ha•nuk•kah \'känəkə, 'hän-\ n : 8-day Jewish holiday commemorating the rededication of the Temple of Jerusalem after its defilement by Antiochus of Syria

hap•haz•ard \hap'hazərd\ adj : having no plan or order —**hap•haz•ard•ly** adv

hap•less \'hapləs\ adj : unfortunate —**hap•less•ly** adv —**hap•less•ness** n

hap•pen \'hapən\ vb 1 : take place 2 : be fortunate to encounter something unexpectedly —often used with infinitive

hap•pen•ing \-iŋ\ n : occurrence

hap•py \'hapē\ adj **-pi•er; -est** 1 : fortunate 2 : content, pleased, or joyous —**hap•pi•ly** \'hapəlē\ adv —**hap•pi•ness** n

ha•rangue \hə'raŋ\ n : ranting or scolding speech —**harangue** vb —**ha•rangu•er** \-'raŋər\ n

ha•rass \hə'ras, 'harəs\ vb 1 : disturb and impede by repeated raids 2 : annoy continually —**ha•rass•ment** n

har•bin•ger \'härbənjər\ n : one that announces or foreshadows what is coming

har•bor \'härbər\ n : protected body of water suitable for anchorage ~ vb 1 : give refuge to 2 : hold as a thought or feeling

hard \'härd\ adj 1 : not easily penetrated 2 : firm or definite 3 : close or searching 4 : severe or unfeeling 5 : strenuous or difficult 6 : physically strong or intense —**hard** adv —**hard•ness** n

hard•en \'härd⁹n\ vb : make or become hard or harder —**hard•en•er** n

hard•head•ed \,härd'hedəd\ adj 1 : stubborn 2 : realistic —**hard•head•ed•ly** adv —**hard•head•ed•ness** n

hard•heart•ed \-'härtəd\ adj : lacking sympathy —**hard•heart•ed•ly** adv —**hard•heart•ed•ness** n

hard•ly \'härdlē\ adv : only just 2 : certainly not

hard–nosed \-,nōzd\ adj : tough or uncompromising

hard•ship \-,ship\ n : suffering or privation

hard•tack \-,tak\ n : hard biscuit

hard•ware n 1 : cutlery or tools made of metal 2 : physical components of a vehicle or apparatus

hard•wood n : wood of a broad-leaved usu. deciduous tree —**hardwood** adj

har•dy \'härdē\ adj **-di•er; -est** : able to withstand adverse conditions —**har•di•ly** adv —**har•di•ness** n

hare \'har\ n, pl **hare** or **hares** : long-eared mammal related to the rabbit

hare•brained \-,brānd\ adj : foolish

hare•lip n : deformity in which the upper lip is vertically split —**harelipped** \-,lipt\ adj

ha•rem \'harəm\ n : house or part of a house allotted to women in a Muslim household or the women and servants occupying it

hark \'härk\ vb : listen

har•le•quin \'härlikən, -kwən\ n : clown

har•lot \'härlət\ n : prostitute

harm \'härm\ n 1 : physical or mental damage 2 : mischief ~ vb : cause harm —**harm•ful** \-fəl\ adj —**harm•ful•ly** adv —**harm•ful•ness** n —**harm•less** adj —**harm•less•ly** adv —**harm•less•ness** n

har•mon•ic \här'mänik\ adj 1 : of or relating to musical harmony 2 : pleasing to hear —**har•mon•i•cal•ly** \-iklē\ adv

har•mon•i•ca \här'mänikə\ n : small wind instrument with metallic reeds

har•mo•ny \'härmənē\ n, pl **-nies** 1 : musical combination of sounds 2 : pleasing arrangement of parts 3 : lack of conflict 4 : internal calm —**har•mo•ni•ous** \här'mōnēəs\ adj —**har•mo•ni•ous•ly** adv —**har•mo•ni•ous•ness** n —**har•mo•ni•za•tion** \,härmənə'zäshən\ n —**har•mo•nize** \'härmə,nīz\ vb

har•ness \'härnəs\ n : gear of a draft animal ~ vb 1 : put a harness on 2 : put to use

harp \'härp\ n : musical instrument with many strings plucked by the fingers ~ vb 1 : play on a harp 2 : dwell on a subject tiresomely —**harp•er** n —**harp•ist** n

har•poon \här'pün\ n : barbed spear used in hunting whales —**harpoon** vb —**har•poon•er** n

harp•si•chord \'härpsi,kórd\ n : keyboard instrument with strings that are plucked

har•py \'härpē\ n, pl **-pies** : shrewish woman

har•row \'harō\ n : implement used to break up soil ~ vb 1 : cultivate with a harrow 2 : distress

har•ry \'harē\ vb **-ried; -ry•ing** : torment by or as if by constant attack

harsh \'härsh\ adj 1 : disagreeably rough 2 : severe —**harsh•ly** adv —**harsh•ness** n

har•um–scar•um \,harəm'skarəm\ adv : recklessly

har•vest \'härvəst\ n 1 : act or time of gathering in a crop 2 : mature crop —**harvest** vb —**har•vest•er** n

has pres 3d sing of HAVE

hash \'hash\ vb : chop into small pieces ~ n : chopped meat mixed with potatoes and browned

hasp \'hasp\ n : hinged strap fastener esp. for a door

has•sle \'hasəl\ n 1 : quarrel 2 : struggle 3 : cause of annoyance —**hassle** vb

has•sock \'hasək\ n : cushion used as a seat or leg rest

haste \'hāst\ n 1 : rapidity of motion 2 : rash action 3 : excessive eagerness —**hast•i•ly** \'hāstəlē\ adv —**hast•i•ness** \-stēnəs\ n —**hasty** \-stē\ adj

has•ten \'hās⁹n\ vb : hurry

hat \'hat\ n : covering for the head

¹hatch \'hach\ n : small door or opening —**hatch•way** n

²hatch vb : emerge from an egg —**hatch•ery** \-ərē\ n

hatch•et \'hachət\ n : short-handled ax

hate \'hāt\ n : intense hostility and aversion ~ vb **hat•ed; hat•ing** 1 : express or feel hate 2 : dislike —**hate•ful** \-fəl\ adj —**hate•ful•ly** adv —**hate•ful•ness** n —**hat•er** n

ha•tred \'hātrəd\ n : hate

hat•ter \'hatər\ n : one that makes or sells hats

haugh•ty \'hótē\ adj **-ti•er; -est** : disdainfully proud —**haugh•ti•ly** adv —**haugh•ti•ness** n

haul \'hól\ vb 1 : draw or pull 2 : transport or carry ~ n 1 : amount collected 2 : load or the distance it is transported —**haul•er** n

haunch \'hónch\ n : hip or hindquarter —usu. pl.

haunt \'hónt\ vb 1 : visit often 2 : visit or inhabit as a ghost ~ n : place frequented —**haunt•er** n —**haunt•ing•ly** adv

have \'hav, in sense 2 before "to" usu 'haf\ vb **had** \'had\, **hav•ing** \'haviŋ\, **has** \'haz, in sense 2 before "to" usu 'has\ 1 : hold in possession, service, or affection 2 : be compelled or forced to 3 —used as an auxiliary with the past participle to form the present perfect, past perfect, or future perfect 4 : obtain or receive 5 : undergo 6 : cause to 7 : bear —**have to do with** : have in the way of connection or relation with or effect on

ha•ven \'hāvən\ n : place of safety

hav•oc \'havək\ n 1 : wide destruction 2 : great confusion

¹hawk \'hók\ n : bird of prey with a strong hooked bill and sharp talons

²hawk vb : offer for sale by calling out in the street —**hawk•er** n

haw•ser \'hózər\ n : large rope

haw•thorn \'hó,thórn\ n : spiny shrub or tree with pink or white fragrant flowers

hay \'hā\ n : herbs (as grass) cut and dried for use as fodder —**hay** vb —**hay•loft** n —**hay•mow** \-,maü\ n —**hay•stack** n

hay•cock \'hā,käk\ n : small pile of hay

hay•rick \-,rik\ n : large outdoor stack of hay

hay•seed \'hā,sēd\ n : bumpkin

hay•wire adj : being out of order

haz•ard \'hazərd\ n 1 : source of danger 2 : chance ~ vb : venture or risk —**haz•ard•ous** adj

¹haze \'hāz\ n : fine dust, smoke, or light vapor in the air that reduces visibility

²haze vb **hazed; haz•ing** : harass by abusive and humiliating tricks

ha•zel \'hāzəl\ n 1 : shrub or small tree bearing edible nuts (**ha•zel•nuts**) 2 : light brown color

hazy \'hāzē\ adj **haz•i•er; -est** 1 : obscured by haze 2 : vague or indefinite —**haz•i•ly** adv —**haz•i•ness** n

he \'hē\ pron 1 : that male one 2 : a or the person

head \'hed\ n 1 : front or upper part of the body 2 : mind 3 : upper or higher end 4 : director or leader 5 : place of leadership or honor ~ adj : principal or chief ~ vb 1 : provide with or form a head 2 : put, stand, or be at the head 3 : point or proceed in a certain direction —**head•ache** n —**head•band** n —**head•dress** n —**head•ed** adj —**head•first** adv or adj —**head•gear** n —**head•less** adj —**head•rest** n —**head•ship** n —**head•wait•er** n

head•ing \-iŋ\ n 1 : direction in which a plane or ship heads 2 : something (as a title) standing at the top or beginning

head•land \'hedlənd, -,land\ n : promontory

head•light n : light on the front of a vehicle

head•line n : introductory line of a newspaper story printed in large type

head•long \-'lóŋ\ adv 1 : head foremost 2 : in a rash or reckless manner —**head•long** \-,lóŋ\ adj

head•mas•ter n : man who is head of a private school

head•mis•tress n : woman who is head of a private school

head–on adj : having the front facing in the direction of initial contact —**head–on** adv

head•phone n : an earphone held on by a band over the head—usu. pl.

head•quar•ters n sing or pl : command or administrative center

head•stone n : stone at the head of a grave

head•strong adj : stubborn or willful

head•wa•ters n pl : source of a stream

head•way n : forward motion

heady \'hedē\ adj **head•i•er; -est** 1 : intoxicating 2 : shrewd

heal \'hēl\ vb : make or become sound or whole —**heal•er** n

health \'helth\ n : sound physical or mental condition

health•ful \-fəl\ adj : beneficial to health —**health•ful•ly** adv —**health•ful•ness** n

healthy \'helthē\ adj **health•i•er; -est** : enjoying or typical of good health —**health•i•ly** adv —**health•i•ness** n

heap \'hēp\ n : pile ~ vb : throw or lay in a heap

hear \'hir\ vb **heard** \'hərd\ **hear•ing** \'hiriŋ\ 1 : perceive by the ear 2 : heed 3 : learn

hear•ing n 1 : process or power of perceiving sound 2 : earshot 3 : session in which witnesses are heard

hear•ken \'härkən\ vb : give attention

hear•say n : rumor

hearse \'hərs\ n : vehicle for carrying the dead to the grave

heart \'härt\ n 1 : hollow muscular organ that keeps up the circulation of the blood 2 : playing card of a suit marked with a red heart 3 : whole personality or the emotional or moral part of it 4 : courage 5 : essential part —**heart•beat** n —**heart•ed** adj

heart•ache n : anguish of mind

heart•break n : crushing grief —**heart•break•er** n —**heart•break•ing** adj —**heart•bro•ken** adj

heart•burn n : burning distress in the heart area after eating

heart•en \'härt⁹n\ vb : encourage

hearth \'härth\ n 1 : area in front of a fireplace 2 : home —**hearth•stone** n

heart•less \'härtləs\ adj : cruel

heart•rend•ing \-,rendiŋ\ adj : causing intense grief or anguish

heart•sick adj : very despondent —**heart•sick•ness** n

heart•strings n pl : deepest emotions

heart•throb n : sweetheart

heart•warm•ing adj : inspiring sympathetic feeling

heart•wood n : central portion of wood

hearty \'härtē\ *adj* **heart•i•er; -est 1** : vigorously healthy **2** : nourishing — **heart•i•ly** *adv* —**heart•i•ness** *n*

heat \'hēt\ *vb* : make or become warm or hot ~ *n* **1** : condition of being hot **2** : form of energy that causes a body to rise in temperature **3** : intensity of feeling — **heat•ed•ly** *adv* —**heat•er** *n*

heath \'hēth\ *n* **1** : often evergreen shrubby plant of wet acid soils **2** : tract of wasteland —**heathy** *adj*

hea•then \'hēthən\ *n, pl* **-thens** *or* **-then** : uncivilized or godless person —**heathen** *adj*

heath•er \'hethər\ *n* : evergreen heath with lavender flowers —**heathery** *adj*

heat•stroke *n* : disorder that follows prolonged exposure to excessive heat

heave \'hēv\ *vb* **heaved** *or* **hove** \'hōv\; **heav•ing 1** : rise or lift upward **2** : throw **3** : rise and fall ~ *n* **1** : an effort to lift or raise **2** : throw

heav•en \'hevən\ *n* **1** *pl* : sky **2** : abode of the Deity and of the blessed dead **3** : place of supreme happiness **heav•en•ly** *adj* — **heav•en•ward** *adv or adj*

heavy \'hevē\ *adj* **heavi•er; -est 1** : having great weight **2** : hard to bear **3** : greater than the average —**heavi•ly** *adv* — **heavi•ness** *n* —**heavy-weight** *n*

heavy-du•ty *adj* : able to withstand unusual strain

heavy-set *adj* : stocky and compact in build

heck•le \'hekəl\ *vb* **-led; -ling** : harass with gibes —**heck•ler** \-'heklər\ *n*

hec•tic \'hektik\ *adj* : filled with excitement, activity, or confusion —**hec•ti•cal•ly** \-ti-klē\ *adv*

hedge \'hej\ *n* **1** : fence or boundary of shrubs or small trees **2** : means of protection ~ *vb* **hedged; hedg•ing 1** : protect oneself against loss **2** : evade the risk of commitment —**hedg•er** *n*

hedge•hog *n* : spiny mammal (as a porcupine)

he•do•nism \'hēd²n,izəm\ *n* : way of life devoted to pleasure —**he•do•nist** \-²nist\ *n* —**he•do•nis•tic** \,hēd²n'istik\ *adj*

heed \'hēd\ *vb* : pay attention ~ *n* : attention —**heed•ful** \-fəl\ *adj* —**heed•ful•ly** *adv* —**heed•ful•ness** *n* —**heed•less** *adj* —**heed•less•ly** *adv* —**heed•less•ness** *n*

¹**heel** \'hēl\ *n* **1** : back of the foot **2** : crusty end of a loaf of bread **3** : solid piece forming the back of the sole of a shoe —**heel•less** \'hēlləs\ *adj*

²**heel** *vb* : tilt to one side

heft \'heft\ *n* : weight ~ *vb* : judge the weight of by lifting

hefty \'heftē\ *adj* **heft•i•er; -est** : big and bulky

he•ge•mo•ny \hi'jemənē\ *n* : preponderant influence over others

heif•er \'hefər\ *n* : young cow

height \'hīt, 'hītth\ *n* **1** : highest part or point **2** : distance from bottom to top **3** : altitude

height•en \'hīt²n\ *vb* : increase in amount or degree

hei•nous \'hānəs\ *adj* : shockingly evil — **hei•nous•ly** *adv* —**hei•nous•ness** *n*

heir \'ar\ *n* : one who inherits or is entitled to inherit property

heir•ess \'arəs\ *n* : female heir esp. to great wealth

heir•loom \'ar,lüm\ *n* : something handed on from one generation to another

held *past of* HOLD

he•li•cal \'helikəl, 'hē-\ *adj* : spiral

he•li•cop•ter \'helə,käptər, 'hē-\ *n* : aircraft supported in the air by rotors

he•lio•trope \'hēlyə,trōp\ *n* : garden herb with small fragrant white or purple flowers

he•li•um \'hēlēəm\ *n* : very light nonflammable gaseous chemical element

he•lix \'hēliks\ *n, pl* **-li•ces** \'helə,sēz, 'hē-\ : something spiral

hell \'hel\ *n* **1** : nether world in which the dead continue to exist **2** : realm of the devil **3** : place or state of torment or destruction —**hell•ish** *adj*

hell•gram•mite \'helgrə,mīt\ *n* : aquatic insect larva

hell•ion \'helyən\ *n* : troublesome person

hel•lo \hə'lō, he-\ *n, pl* **-los** : expression of greeting

helm \'helm\ *n* : lever or wheel for steering a ship —**helms•man** \'helmzmən\ *n*

hel•met \'helmət\ *n* : protective covering for the head

help \'help\ *vb* **1** : supply what is needed **2** : be of use **3** : refrain from or prevent ~ *n* **1** : something that helps or a source of help **2** : one who helps another —**help•er** *n* —**help•ful** \-fəl\ *adj* —**help•ful•ly** *adv* —**help•ful•ness** *n* —**help•less** *adj* —**help•less•ly** *adv* —**help•less•ness** *n*

help•ing \'helpiŋ\ *n* : portion of food

help•mate *n* **1** : helper **2** : wife

help•meet \-,mēt\ *n* : helpmate

hel•ter-skel•ter \,heltər'skeltər\ *adv* : in total disorder

hem \'hem\ *n* : border of an article of cloth doubled back and stitched down ~ *vb*

-mm- 1 : sew a hem **2** : surround restrictively —**hem•line** *n*

he•ma•tol•o•gy \,hēmə'täləjē\ *n* : study of the blood and blood-forming organs — **hema•to•log•ic** \-,mat²l'äjik\ *adj* —**hema•tol•o•gist** \-'täləjist\ *n*

hemi•sphere \'hemə,sfir\ *n* : one of the halves of the earth divided by the equator into northern and southern parts (**northern hemisphere, southern hemisphere**) or by a meridian into eastern and western parts (**eastern hemisphere, western hemisphere**) —**hemi•spher•ic** \,hemə-'sfirik, -'sfer-\, **hemi•spher•i•cal** \-'sfir-ikəl, -'sfer-\ *adj*

hem•lock \'hem,läk\ *n* **1** : poisonous herb related to the carrot **2** : evergreen tree related to the pines

he•mo•glo•bin \'hēmə,glōbən\ *n* : iron-containing compound found in red blood cells

he•mo•phil•ia \,hēmə'filēə\ *n* : hereditary tendency to severe prolonged bleeding — **he•mo•phil•i•ac** \-ē,ak\ *adj or n*

hem•or•rhage \'hemərij\ *n* : large discharge of blood —**hemorrhage** *vb* —**hem•or•rhag•ic** \,hemə'rajik\ *adj*

hem•or•rhoids \'hemə,roidz\ *n pl* : swollen mass of dilated veins at or just within the anus

hemp \'hemp\ *n* : tall Asian herb grown for its tough fiber —**hemp•en** \'hempən\ *adj*

hen \'hen\ *n* : female domestic fowl

hence \'hens\ *adv* **1** : away **2** : therefore **3** : from this source or origin

hence•forth *adv* : from this point on

hence•for•ward *adv* : henceforth

hench•man \'henchmən\ *n* : trusted follower

hen•na \'henə\ *n* : reddish brown dye from a tropical shrub used esp. on hair

hen•peck \'hen,pek\ *vb* : subject (one's husband) to persistent nagging

he•pat•ic \hi'patik\ *adj* : relating to or resembling the liver

hep•a•ti•tis \,hepə'tītəs\ *n, pl* **-tit•i•des** \-'titə,dēz\ : disease in which the liver becomes inflamed

her \'hər\ *adj* : of or relating to her or herself ~ \ər, (')hər\ *pron, objective case of* SHE

her•ald \'herəld\ *n* **1** : official crier or messenger **2** : harbinger ~ *vb* : give notice

her•ald•ry \'herəldrē\ *n, pl* **-ries** : practice of devising and granting stylized emblems (as for a family) —**he•ral•dic** \he-'raldik, hə-\ *adj*

herb \'ərb, 'hərb\ *n* **1** : seed plant that lacks woody tissue **2** : plant or plant part valued for medicinal or savory qualities —**her•ba•ceous** \,ər'bāshəs, ,hər-\ *adj* —**herb•age** \'ərbij, 'hər-\ *n* —**herb•al** \-bəl\ *n or adj* —**herb•al•ist** \-bəlist\ *n*

her•bi•cide \'ərbə,sīd, 'hər-\ *n* : agent that destroys plants —**her•bi•cid•al** \,ərbə-'sīd²l, ,hər-\ *adj*

her•biv•o•rous \,ər'bivərəs, ,hər-\ *adj* : feeding on plants —**her•bi•vore** \'ər-bə,vōr, 'hər-\ *n*

her•cu•le•an \,hərkyə'lēən, ,hər'kyülēən\ *adj* : of extraordinary power, size, or difficulty

herd \'hərd\ *n* : group of animals of one kind ~ *vb* : assemble or move in a herd —**herd•er** *n* —**herds•man** \'hərdzmən\ *n*

here \'hir\ *adv* **1** : in, at, or to this place **2** : now **3** : at or in this point or particular **4** : in the present life or state ~ *n* : this place —**here•abouts** \'hirə,bauts\, **here•about** \-,baut\ *adv*

here•af•ter *adv* : in some future time or state ~ *n* : existence beyond earthly life

here•by *adv* : by means of this

he•red•i•tary \hə'redə,terē\ *adj* **1** : genetically passed or passable from parent to offspring **2** : passing by inheritance

he•red•i•ty \-ətē\ *n* : the passing of characteristics from parent to offspring

here•in *adv* : in this

here•of *adv* : of this

here•on *adv* : on this

her•e•sy \'herəsē\ *n, pl* **-sies** : opinion or doctrine contrary to church dogma —**her•e•tic** \-,tik\ *n* —**he•ret•i•cal** \hə'retikəl\ *adj*

here•to *adv* : to this document

here•to•fore \'hirtü,fōr\ *adv* : up to this time

here•un•der *adv* : under this

here•un•to *adv* : to this

here•upon *adv* : on this

here•with *adv* **1** : with this **2** : hereby

her•i•tage \'herətij\ *n* **1** : inheritance **2** : birthright

her•maph•ro•dite \hər'mafrə,dīt\ *n* : animal or plant having both male and female reproductive organs —**hermaphrodite** *adj* —**her•maph•ro•dit•ic** \-,mafrə'ditik\ *adj*

her•met•ic \hər'metik\ *adj* : sealed airtight —**her•met•i•cal•ly** \-iklē\ *adv*

her•mit \'hərmət\ *n* : one who lives in solitude

her•nia \'hərnēə\ *n, pl* **-ni•as** *or* **-ni•ae** \-nē-,ē, -nē,ī\ : protrusion of a bodily part

through the weakened wall of its enclosure —**her•ni•ate** \-nē,āt\ *vb*

he•ro \'hērō, 'hirō\ *n, pl* **-roes** : one that is much admired or shows great courage — **he•ro•ic** \hi'rōik\ *adj* —**he•ro•i•cal•ly** \-iklē\ *adv* —**he•ro•ics** \-iks\ *n pl* —**her•o•ism** \'herə,wizəm\ *n*

her•o•in \'herəwən\ *n* : strongly addictive narcotic

her•o•ine \'herəwən\ *n* : woman of heroic achievements or qualities

her•on \'herən\ *n* : long-legged long-billed wading bird

her•pes \'hərpēz\ *n* : virus disease characterized by the formation of blisters

her•pe•tol•o•gy \,hərpə'täləjē\ *n* : study of reptiles and amphibians —**her•pe•tol•o•gist** \-pə'täləjist\ *n*

her•ring \'heriŋ\ *n, pl* **-ring** *or* **-rings** : narrow-bodied Atlantic food fish

hers \'hərz\ *pron* : one or the ones belonging to her

her•self \hər'self\ *pron* : she, her —used reflexively or for emphasis

hertz \'herts, 'hərts\ *n, pl* **hertz** : unit of frequency equal to one cycle per second

hes•i•tant \'hezətənt\ *adj* : tending to hesitate —**hes•i•tance** \-təns\ *n* —**hes•i•tan•cy** \-tənsē\ *n* —**hes•i•tant•ly** *adv*

hes•i•tate \'hezə,tāt\ *vb* **-tat•ed; -tat•ing 1** : hold back esp. in doubt **2** : pause —**hes•i•ta•tion** \,hezə'tāshən\ *n*

het•er•o•ge•neous \,hetərə'jēnēəs, -nyəs\ *adj* : consisting of dissimilar ingredients or constituents —**het•er•o•ge•ne•ity** \-jə'nēətē\ *n* —**het•er•o•ge•neous•ly** *adv*

het•ero•sex•u•al \,hetərō'sekshəwəl\ *adj* : oriented toward the opposite sex —**heterosexual** *n* —**het•ero•sex•u•al•i•ty** \-,seksh'walətē\ *n*

hew \'hyü\ *vb* **hewed; hewed** *or* **hewn** \'hyün\ **hew•ing 1** : cut or shape with or as if with an ax **2** : conform strictly — **hew•er** *n*

hex \'heks\ *vb* : put an evil spell on —**hex** *n*

hexa•gon \'heksə,gän\ *n* : 6-sided polygon —**hex•ag•o•nal** \hek'sagən²l\ *adj*

hey•day \'hā,dā\ *n* : time of flourishing

hi•a•tus \hī'ātəs\ *n* : lapse in continuity

hi•ba•chi \hi'bächē\ *n* : brazier

hi•ber•nate \'hībər,nāt\ *vb* **-nat•ed; -nat•ing** : pass the winter in a torpid or resting state —**hi•ber•na•tion** \,hībər'nāshən\ *n* —**hi•ber•na•tor** \'hībər,nātər\ *n*

hic•cup \'hikəp\ *vb* **-cuped; -cup•ing** : to inhale spasmodically and make a peculiar sound ~ *n pl* : attack of hiccuping

hick \'hik\ *n* : awkward provincial person —**hick** *adj*

hick•o•ry \'hikərē\ *n, pl* **-ries** : No. American hardwood tree —**hickory** *adj*

¹**hide** \'hīd\ *vb* **hid** \'hid\; **hid•den** \'hid²n\ *or* **hid; hid•ing** : put or remain out of sight —**hid•er** *n*

²**hide** *n* : animal skin

hide•bound \'hīd,baund\ *adj* : inflexible or conservative

hid•eous \'hidēəs\ *adj* : very ugly —**hid•eous•ly** *adv* —**hid•eous•ness** *n*

hie \'hī\ *vb* **hied; hy•ing** *or* **hie•ing** : hurry

hi•er•ar•chy \'hīə,rärkē\ *n, pl* **-chies** : persons or things arranged in a graded series —**hi•er•ar•chi•cal** \,hīə'rärkikəl\ *adj*

hi•ero•glyph•ic \,hīərə'glifik\ *n* : character in the picture writing of the ancient Egyptians

high \'hī\ *adj* **1** : having large extension upward **2** : elevated in pitch **3** : exalted in character **4** : of greater degree or amount than average **5** : expensive **6** : excited or stupefied by alcohol or a drug ~ *adv* : at or to a high place or degree ~ *n* **1** : elevated point or level **2** : automobile gear giving the highest speed —**high•ly** *adv*

high•boy *n* : high chest of drawers on legs

high•brow \-,braù\ *n* : person of superior learning or culture —**highbrow** *adj*

high-flown *adj* : pretentious

high-hand•ed *adj* : willful and arrogant — **high-hand•ed•ly** *adv* —**high-hand•ed•ness** *n*

high•land \'hīlənd\ *n* : hilly country — **high•land•er** \-ləndər\ *n*

high•light *n* : event or detail of major importance ~ *vb* **1** : emphasize **2** : be a highlight of

high•ness \-nəs\ *n* **1** : quality or degree of being high **2** —used as a title (as for kings)

high-rise *adj* : having several stories

high school *n* : school usu. including grades 9 to 12 or 10 to 12

high-spir•it•ed *adj* : lively

high-strung \'hī'strəŋ\ *adj* : very nervous or sensitive

high•way *n* : public road

high•way•man \-mən\ *n* : one who robs travelers on a road

hi•jack \'hī,jak\ *vb* : steal esp. by commandeering a vehicle —**hijack** *n* —**hi•jack•er** *n*

hike \'hīk\ *vb* **hiked; hik•ing 1** : raise quickly **2** : take a long walk ~ *n* **1** : long walk **2** : increase —**hik•er** *n*

hi•lar•i•ous \hi'larēəs, hī'-\ *adj* : extremely funny —**hi•lar•i•ous•ly** *adv* —**hi•lar•i•ty** \-ətē\ *n*

hill \'hil\ *n* : place where the land rises — **hill•side** *n* —**hill•top** *n* —**hilly** *adj*

hill•bil•ly \'hil,bilē\ *n, pl* **-lies** : person from a backwoods area

hill•ock \'hilək\ *n* : small hill

hilt \'hilt\ *n* : handle of a sword

him \'him\ *pron, objective case of* HE

him•self \him'self\ *pron* : he, him —used reflexively or for emphasis

¹**hind** \'hīnd\ *n* : female deer

²**hind** *adj* : back

hin•der \'hindər\ *vb* : obstruct or hold back

hind•most *adj* : farthest to the rear

hind•quar•ter *n* : back half of a complete side of a carcass

hin•drance \'hindrəns\ *n* : something that hinders

hind•sight *n* : understanding of an event after it has happened

Hin•du•ism \'hindü,izəm\ *n* : body of religious beliefs and practices native to India —**Hin•du** *n or adj*

hinge \'hinj\ *n* : jointed piece on which a swinging part (as a door) turns ~ *vb* **hinged; hing•ing 1** : attach by or furnish with hinges **2** : depend

hint \'hint\ *n* **1** : indirect suggestion **2** : clue **3** : very small amount —**hint** *vb*

hin•ter•land \'hintər,land\ *n* : remote region

hip \'hip\ *n* : part of the body on either side just below the waist —**hip•bone** *n*

hip•po•pot•a•mus \,hipə'pätəməs\ *n, pl* **-mus•es** *or* **-mi** \-,mī\ : large thick-skinned African river animal

hire \'hīr\ *n* **1** : payment for labor **2** : employment **3** : one who is hired ~ *vb* **hired; hir•ing** : employ for pay

hire•ling \-liŋ\ *n* : one who serves another only for gain

hir•sute \'hər,süt, 'hir-\ *adj* : hairy

his \'hiz\ *adj* : of or belonging to him ~ *pron* : ones belonging to him

hiss \'his\ *vb* **1** : make a sibilant sound **2** : show dislike by hissing —**hiss** *n*

his•to•ri•an \his'tōrēən\ *n* : writer of history

his•to•ry \'histərē\ *n, pl* **-ries 1** : chronological record of significant events **2** : study of past events **3** : an established record —**his•tor•ic** \his'tòrik\, **his•tor•i•cal** \-ikəl\ *adj* —**his•tor•i•cal•ly** \-klē\ *adv*

his•tri•on•ics \,histrē'äniks\ *n pl* : exaggerated display of emotion

hit \'hit\ *vb* **hit; hit•ting 1** : reach with a blow **2** : come or cause to come in contact **3** : affect detrimentally ~ *n* **1** : blow **2** : great success —**hit•ter** *n*

hitch \'hich\ *vb* **1** : move by jerks **2** : catch by a hook **3** : hitchhike ~ *n* **1** : jerk **2** : sudden halt

hitch•hike \'hich,hīk\ *vb* : travel by securing free rides from passing vehicles —**hitch•hik•er** *n*

hith•er \'hithər\ *adv* : to this place

hith•er•to \-,tü\ *adv* : up to this time

hive \'hīv\ *n* **1** : container housing honeybees **2** : colony of bees —**hive** *vb*

hives \'hīvz\ *n sing or pl* : allergic disorder with itchy skin patches

HMO \,āch,em'ō\ *n* : comprehensive health-care organization financed by clients

hoard \'hōrd\ *n* : hidden accumulation — **hoard** *vb* —**hoard•er** *n*

hoar•frost \'hōr,fròst\ *n* : frost

hoarse \'hōrs\ *adj* **hoars•er; -est 1** : harsh in sound **2** : speaking in a harsh strained voice —**hoarse•ly** *adv* —**hoarse•ness** *n*

hoary \'hōrē\ *adj* **hoar•i•er; -est** : gray or white with age —**hoar•i•ness** *n*

hoax \'hōks\ *n* : act intended to trick or dupe —**hoax** *vb* —**hoax•er** *n*

hob•ble \'häbəl\ *vb* **-bled; -bling** : limp along ~ *n* : hobbling movement

hob•by \'häbē\ *n, pl* **-bies** : interest engaged in for relaxation —**hob•by•ist** \-ēist\ *n*

hob•gob•lin \'häb,gäblən\ *n* **1** : mischievous goblin **2** : bogey

hob•nail \-,nāl\ *n* : short nail for studding shoe soles —**hob•nailed** \-,nāld\ *adj*

ho•bo \'hōbō\ *n, pl* **-boes** : tramp

¹**hock** \'häk\ *n* : joint or region in the hind limb of a quadruped corresponding to the human ankle

²**hock** *n or vb* : pawn

hock•ey \'häkē\ *n* : game played on ice or a field by 2 teams

hod \'häd\ *n* : carrier for bricks or mortar

hodge•podge \'häj,päj\ *n* : heterogeneous mixture

hoe \'hō\ *n* : long-handled tool for cultivating or weeding —**hoe** *vb*

hog \'hòg, 'häg\ *n* **1** : domestic adult swine **2** : glutton ~ *vb* : take selfishly —**hog•gish** *adj*

hogs•head \'hógz,hed, 'hägz-\ *n* : large cask or barrel

hog•wash *n* : nonsense

hoist \ˈhȯist\ vb : lift ~ n 1 : lift 2 : apparatus for hoisting

hok•ey \ˈhōkē\ adj **hok•i•er; -est 1** : tiresomely simple or sentimental **2** : phony

1hold \ˈhōld\ vb **held** \ˈheld\; **hold•ing 1** : possess **2** : restrain **3** : have a grasp on **4** : remain or keep in a particular situation or position **5** : contain **6** : regard **7** : cause to occur **8** : occupy esp. by appointment or election — n **1** : act or manner of holding **2** : restraining or controlling influence —**hold•er** n —**hold forth** : speak at length —**hold to** : adhere to —**hold with** : agree with

2hold n : cargo area of a ship

hold•ing \ˈhōldiŋ\ n : property owned — usu. pl.

hold•up n **1** : robbery at the point of a gun **2** : delay

hole \ˈhōl\ n **1** : opening into or through something **2** : hollow place (as a pit) **3** : den —**hole** vb

hol•i•day \ˈhälə‚dā\ n **1** : day of freedom from work **2** : vacation —**holiday** vb

ho•li•ness \ˈhōlēnəs\ n : quality or state of being holy—used as a title for a high religious official

ho•lis•tic \hō·listik\ adj : relating to a whole (as the body)

hol•ler \ˈhälər\ vb : cry out —**holler** n

hol•low \ˈhälō\ adj -**low•er** \-əwər\; -**est 1** : sunken **2** : having a cavity within **3** : sounding like a noise made in an empty place **4** : empty of value or meaning ~ vb : make or become hollow — n **1** : surface depression **2** : cavity —**hol•low•ness** n

hol•ly \ˈhälē\ n, pl **-lies** : evergreen tree or shrub with glossy leaves

hol•ly•hock \-‚häk, -‚hȯk\ n : tall perennial herb with showy flowers

ho•lo•caust \ˈhälə‚kȯst, ˈhō-, ˈhȯ-\ n : thorough destruction esp. by fire

hol•stein \ˈhōl‚stēn, -‚stīn\ n : large black-and-white dairy cow

hol•ster \ˈhōlstər\ n : case for a pistol

ho•ly \ˈhōlē\ adj -**li•er; -est 1** : sacred **2** : spiritually pure

hom•age \ˈämij, ˈhä-\ n : reverent regard

home \ˈhōm\ n **1** : residence **2** : congenial environment **3** : place of origin or refuge ~ vb **homed; hom•ing** : go or return home —**home•bred** adj —**home•coming** n —**home•grown** adj —**home•land** \-‚land\ n —**home•less** adj —**home•made** \-ˈmād\ adj

home•ly \-lē\ adj -**li•er; -est** : plain or unattractive —**home•li•ness** n

home•mak•er n : one who manages a household —**home•mak•ing** n

home•sick adj : longing for home —**home•sick•ness** n

home•spun \-‚spən\ adj : simple

home•stead \-‚sted\ n : home and land occupied and worked by a family —**home•stead•er** \-ər\ n

home•stretch n **1** : last part of a racetrack **2** : final stage

home•ward \-wərd\, **home•wards** \-wərdz\ adv : toward home —**homeward** adj

home•work n : school lessons to be done outside the classroom

hom•ey \ˈhōmē\ adj **hom•i•er; -est** : characteristic of home

ho•mi•cide \ˈhämə‚sīd, ˈhō-\ n : the killing of one human being by another —**hom•i•cid•al** \‚hämə'sīd⁹l, ‚hō-\ adj

hom•i•ly \ˈhäməlē\ n, pl **-lies** : sermon

hom•i•ny \ˈhämənē\ n : type of processed hulled corn

ho•mo•ge•neous \‚hōmə'jēnēəs, -nyəs\ adj : of the same or a similar kind —**ho•mo•ge•ne•i•ty** \-jə'nēətē\ n —**ho•mo•ge•neous•ly** adv

ho•mog•e•nize \hō'mäjə‚nīz, hə-\ vb -**nized; -niz•ing** : make the particles in (as milk) of uniform size and even distribution —**ho•mog•e•ni•za•tion** \-‚mäjənə'zāshən\ n —**ho•mog•e•niz•er** n

ho•mo•graph \ˈhämə‚graf, ˈhō-\ n : one of 2 or more words (as the noun conduct and the verb conduct) spelled alike but different in origin or meaning or pronunciation

hom•onym \ˈhämə‚nim, ˈhō-\ n **1** : homophone **2** : homograph **3** : one of 2 or more words (as pool of water and pool of the game) spelled and pronounced alike but different in meaning

ho•mo•phone \ˈhämə‚fōn, ˈhō-\ n : one of 2 or more words (as to, too, and two) pronounced alike but different in origin or meaning or spelling

Ho•mo sa•pi•ens \‚hōmō'sapēənz, -'sā-\ n : humankind

ho•mo•sex•u•al \‚hōmə'sekshəwəl\ adj : oriented toward one's own sex —**homosexual** n —**ho•mo•sex•u•al•i•ty** \-‚sekshə'walətē\ n

hone \ˈhōn\ vb : sharpen with or as if with an abrasive stone

hon•est \ˈänəst\ adj **1** : free from deception **2** : trustworthy **3** : frank —**hon•est•ly** adv —**hon•esty** \-əstē\ n

hon•ey \ˈhənē\ n, pl **-eys** : sweet sticky substance made by bees (**hon•ey•bees**) from the nectar of flowers

hon•ey•comb n : mass of 6-sided wax cells built by honeybees or something like it ~ vb : make or become full of holes like a honeycomb

hon•ey•moon n : holiday taken by a newly married couple —**honeymoon** vb

hon•ey•suck•le \-‚səkəl\ n : shrub or vine with flowers rich in nectar

honk \ˈhäŋk, ˈhȯŋk\ n : cry of a goose or a similar sound —**honk** vb —**honk•er** n

hon•or \ˈänər\ n **1** : good name **2** : outward respect or symbol of this **3** : privilege **4** : person of superior rank or position — used esp. as a title **5** : something or someone worthy of respect **6** : integrity ~ vb **1** : regard with honor **2** : confer honor on **3** : fulfill the terms of —**hon•or•able** \ˈänərəbəl\ adj —**hon•or•ably** \-blē\ adv —**hon•or•ari•ly** \‚änə'rerəlē\ adv —**hon•or•ary** \ˈänə‚rerē\ adj —**hon•or•ee** \‚änə'rē\ n

hood \ˈhud\ n **1** : part of a garment that covers the head **2** : covering over an automobile engine compartment —**hood•ed** adj

-hood \‚hud\ n suffix **1** : state, condition, or quality **2** : individuals sharing a state or character

hood•lum \ˈhudləm, ˈhud-\ n : thug

hood•wink \ˈhud‚wiŋk\ vb : deceive

hoof \ˈhuf, ˈhuf\ n, pl **hooves** \ˈhuvz, ˈhuvz\ or **hoofs** : horny covering of the toes of some mammals (as horses or cattle) —**hoofed** \ˈhuft, ˈhuft\ adj

hook \ˈhuk\ n **1** : curved or bent device for catching, holding, or pulling ~ vb : seize or make fast with a hook —**hook•er** n

hook•worm n : parasitic intestinal worm

hoo•li•gan \ˈhuligən\ n : thug

hoop \ˈhup\ n : circular strip, figure, or object

hoot \ˈhut\ vb **1** : shout in contempt **2** : make the cry of an owl —**hoot** n —**hoot•er** n

1hop \ˈhäp\ vb -**pp-** : move by quick springy leaps —**hop** n

2hop n : vine whose ripe dried flowers are used to flavor malt liquors

hope \ˈhōp\ vb **hoped; hop•ing** : desire with expectation of fulfillment ~ n **1** : act of hoping **2** : something hoped for —**hope•ful** \-fəl\ adj —**hope•ful•ly** adv —**hope•ful•ness** n —**hope•less** adj —**hope•less•ly** adv —**hope•less•ness** n

hop•per \ˈhäpər\ n : container that releases its contents through the bottom

horde \ˈhȯrd\ n : throng or swarm

ho•ri•zon \hə'rīz⁹n\ n : apparent junction of earth and sky

hor•i•zon•tal \‚hȯrə'zänt⁹l\ adj : parallel to the horizon —**hor•i•zon•tal•ly** adv

hor•mone \ˈhȯr‚mōn\ n : cell product in body fluids that has a specific effect on other cells —**hor•mon•al** \hȯr'mōn⁹l\ adj

horn \ˈhȯrn\ n **1** : hard bony projection on the head of a hoofed animal **2** : brass wind instrument —**horned** adj —**horn•less** adj

hor•net \ˈhȯrnət\ n : large social wasp

horny \ˈhȯrnē\ adj **horn•i•er; -est 1** : made of horn **2** : hard or callous **3** : sexually aroused

horo•scope \ˈhȯrə‚skōp\ n : astrological forecast

hor•ren•dous \hȯ'rendəs\ adj : horrible

hor•ri•ble \ˈhȯrəbəl\ adj **1** : having or causing horror **2** : highly disagreeable —**hor•ri•ble•ness** n —**hor•ri•bly** \-blē\ adv

hor•rid \ˈhȯrəd\ adj : horrible —**hor•rid•ly** adv

hor•ri•fy \ˈhȯrə‚fī\ vb -**fied; -fy•ing** : cause to feel horror

hor•ror \ˈhȯrər\ n **1** : intense fear, dread, or dismay **2** : intense repugnance **3** : something horrible

hors d'oeuvre \ȯr'dərv\ n, pl **hors d'oeuvres** \-'dərvz\ : appetizer

horse \ˈhȯrs\ n : large solid-hoofed domesticated mammal —**horse•back** n or adv —**horse•hair** n —**horse•hide** n —**horse•less** adj —**horse•man** \-mən\ n —**horse•man•ship** n —**horse•wom•an** n —**horsey, horsy** adj

horse•fly n : large fly with bloodsucking female

horse•play n : rough boisterous play

horse•pow•er n : unit of mechanical power

horse•rad•ish n : herb with a pungent root used as a condiment

horse•shoe n : U-shaped protective metal plate fitted to the rim of a horse's hoof

hor•ti•cul•ture \ˈhȯrtə‚kəlchər\ n : science of growing fruits, vegetables, and flowers —**hor•ti•cul•tur•al** \‚hȯrtə'kəlchərəl\ adj —**hor•ti•cul•tur•ist** \-rist\ n

ho•san•na \hō'zanə, -'zän-\ interj —used as a cry of acclamation and adoration —**hosanna** n

hose \ˈhōz\ n **1** pl **hose** : stocking or sock **2** pl **hos•es** : flexible tube for conveying fluids ~ vb **hosed; hos•ing** : spray, water, or wash with a hose

ho•siery \ˈhōzhərē, ˈhōzə-\ n : stockings or socks

hos•pice \ˈhäspəs\ n **1** : lodging (as for travelers) maintained by a religious order **2** : facility or program for caring for dying persons

hos•pi•ta•ble \hä'spitəbəl, 'häs‚pit-\ adj : given to generous and cordial reception of guests —**hos•pi•ta•bly** \-blē\ adv

hos•pi•tal \ˈhäs‚pit⁹l\ n : institution where the sick or injured receive medical care —**hos•pi•tal•iza•tion** \‚häs‚pit⁹lə'zāshən\ n —**hos•pi•tal•ize** \ˈhäs‚pit⁹l‚īz\ vb

hos•pi•tal•i•ty \‚häspə'talətē\ n, pl **-ties** : hospitable treatment, reception, or disposition

1host \ˈhōst\ n **1** : army **2** : multitude

2host n : one who receives or entertains guests —**host** vb

3host n : eucharistic bread

hos•tage \ˈhästij\ n : person held to guarantee that promises be kept or demands met

hos•tel \ˈhäst⁹l\ n : lodging for youth —**hos•tel•er** n

hos•tel•ry \-rē\ n, pl **-ries** : hotel

host•ess \ˈhōstəs\ n : woman who is host

hos•tile \ˈhäst⁹l, -‚tīl\ adj **1** : openly or actively unfriendly or opposed to someone or something —**hostile** n —**hos•tile•ly** adv —**hos•til•i•ty** \häs'tilətē\ n

hot \ˈhät\ adj -**tt- 1** : having a high temperature **2** : giving a sensation of heat or burning **3** : ardent **4** : pungent —**hot** adv —**hot•ly** adv —**hot•ness** n

hot•bed n : environment that favors rapid growth

hot dog n : frankfurter

ho•tel \hō'tel\ n : building where lodging and personal services are provided

hot•head•ed adj : impetuous —**hot•head** n —**hot•head•ed•ly** adv —**hot•head•ed•ness** n

hot•house n : greenhouse

hound \ˈhaund\ n : long-eared hunting dog ~ vb : pursue relentlessly

hour \ˈauər\ n **1** : 24th part of a day **2** : time of day —**hour•ly** adv or adj

hour•glass n : glass vessel for measuring time

house \ˈhaus\ n, pl **hous•es** \ˈhauzəz\ **1** : building to live in **2** : household **3** : legislative body **4** : business firm ~ \ˈhauz\ vb **housed; hous•ing** : provide with or take shelter —**house•boat** \ˈhaus‚bōt\ n —**house•clean** \ˈhaus‚klēn\ vb —**house•cleaning** n —**house•ful** \-ˌful\ n —**house•maid** n —**house•wares** n pl —**house•work** n

house•bro•ken \-‚brōkən\ adj : trained in excretory habits acceptable in indoor living

house•fly n : two-winged fly common about human habitations

house•hold \-‚hōld\ n : those who dwell as a family under the same roof ~ adj **1** : domestic **2** : common or familiar —**house•hold•er** n

house•keep•ing \-‚kēpiŋ\ n : care and management of a house or institution —**house•keep•er** n

house•warm•ing n : party to celebrate moving into a house

house•wife \ˈhaus‚wīf\ n : married woman in charge of a household —**house•wife•ly** adj —**house•wif•ery** \-‚wīfərē\ n

hous•ing \ˈhauziŋ\ n **1** : dwellings for people **2** : protective covering

hove past of HEAVE

hov•el \ˈhəvəl, ˈhäv-\ n : small wretched house

hov•er \ˈhəvər, ˈhäv-\ vb **1** : remain suspended in the air **2** : move about in the vicinity

how \ˈhau\ adv **1** : in what way or condition **2** : for what reason **3** : to what extent ~ conj : the way or manner in which

how•ev•er \hau'evər\ conj : in whatever manner ~ adv **1** : to whatever degree or in whatever manner **2** : in spite of that

how•it•zer \ˈhauətsər\ n : short cannon

howl \ˈhaul\ vb : emit a loud long doleful sound like a dog —**howl** n —**howl•er** n

hoy•den \ˈhȯid⁹n\ n : girl or woman of saucy or carefree behavior

hub \ˈhəb\ n : central part of a circular object (as of a wheel) —**hub•cap** n

hub•bub \ˈhəb‚əb\ n : uproar

hu•bris \ˈhyübrəs\ n : excessive pride

huck•le•ber•ry \ˈhəkəl‚berē\ n **1** : shrub related to the blueberry or its berry **2** : blueberry

huck•ster \ˈhəkstər\ n : peddler

hud•dle \ˈhəd⁹l\ vb -**dled; -dling 1** : crowd together **2** : confer —**huddle** n

hue \ˈhyü\ n : color or gradation of color —**hued** \ˈhyüd\ adj

huff \ˈhəf\ n : fit of pique —**huffy** adj

hug \ˈhəg\ vb -**gg- 1** : press tightly in the arms **2** : stay close to —**hug** n

huge \ˈhyüj\ adj **hug•er; hug•est** : very large or extensive —**huge•ly** adv —**huge•ness** n

hu•la \ˈhülə\ n : Polynesian dance

hulk \ˈhəlk\ n **1** : bulky or unwieldy person or thing **2** : old ship unfit for service —**hulk•ing** adj

hull \ˈhəl\ n **1** : outer covering of a fruit or seed **2** : frame or body of a ship or boat ~ vb : remove the hulls of —**hull•er** n

hul•la•ba•loo \ˈhələbə‚lü\ n, pl **-loos** : uproar

hum \ˈhəm\ vb -**mm- 1** : make a prolonged sound like that of the speech sound \m\ **2** : be busily active **3** : run smoothly **4** : sing with closed lips —**hum** n —**hum•mer** n

hu•man \ˈhyümən, ˈyü-\ adj **1** : of or relating to the species people belong to **2** : by, for, or like people —**human** n —**hu•man•kind** n —**hu•man•ly** adv —**hu•man•ness** n

hu•mane \hyü'mān, ‚yü-\ adj : showing compassion or consideration for others —**hu•mane•ly** adv —**hu•mane•ness** n

hu•man•ism \ˈhyümə‚nizəm, ˈyü-\ n : doctrine or way of life centered on human interests or values —**hu•man•ist** \-nist\ n or adj —**hu•man•is•tic** \‚hyümə'nistik, ‚yü-\ adj

hu•man•i•tar•i•an \hyü‚manə'terēən, ‚yü-\ n : person promoting human welfare —**humanitarian** adj —**hu•man•i•tar•i•an•ism** n

hu•man•i•ty \hyü'manətē, ‚yü-\ n, pl **-ties 1** : human or humane quality or state **2** : the human race

hu•man•ize \ˈhyümə‚nīz, ˈyü-\ vb -**ized; -iz•ing** : make human or humane —**hu•man•iza•tion** \‚hyümənə'zāshən, ‚yü-\ n —**hu•man•iz•er** n

hu•man•oid \ˈhyümə‚nȯid, ˈyü-\ adj : having human form —**humanoid** n

hum•ble \ˈhəmbəl\ adj -**bler; -blest 1** : not proud or haughty **2** : not pretentious ~ vb -**bled; -bling** : make humble —**hum•ble•ness** n —**hum•bler** n —**hum•bly** \-blē\ adv

hum•bug \ˈhəm‚bəg\ n : nonsense

hum•drum \-‚drəm\ adj : monotonous

hu•mid \ˈhyüməd, ˈyü-\ adj : containing or characterized by moisture —**hu•mid•i•fi•ca•tion** \hyü‚midəfə'kāshən\ n —**hu•mid•i•fi•er** \-'midə‚fīər\ n —**hu•mid•i•fy** \-‚fī\ vb —**hu•mid•ly** adv

hu•mid•i•ty \hyü'midətē, ‚yü-\ n, pl **-ties** : atmospheric moisture

hu•mi•dor \ˈhyümə‚dȯr, ˈyü-\ n : humidified storage case (as for cigars)

hu•mil•i•ate \hyü'milē‚āt, ‚yü-\ vb -**at•ed; -at•ing** : injure the self-respect of —**hu•mil•i•at•ing•ly** adv —**hu•mil•i•a•tion** \-‚milē'āshən\ n

hu•mil•i•ty \hyü'milətē, ‚yü-\ n : humble quality or state

hum•ming•bird \ˈhəmiŋ‚bərd\ n : tiny American bird that can hover

hum•mock \ˈhəmək\ n : mound or knoll —**hum•mocky** \-məkē\ adj

hu•mor \ˈhyümər, ˈyü-\ n **1** : mood **2** : quality of being laughably ludicrous or incongruous **3** : appreciation of what is ludicrous or incongruous **4** : something intended to be funny ~ vb : comply with the wishes or mood of —**hu•mor•ist** \-ərist\ n —**hu•mor•less** adj —**hu•mor•less•ly** adv —**hu•mor•less•ness** n —**hu•mor•ous** \ˈhyümərəs, ˈyü-\ adj —**hu•mor•ous•ly** adv

hump \ˈhəmp\ n : rounded protuberance —**humped** adj

hump•back n : hunchback —**humpbacked** adj

hu•mus \ˈhyüməs, ˈyü-\ n : dark organic part of soil

hunch \ˈhənch\ vb : assume or cause to assume a bent or crooked posture ~ n : strong intuitive feeling

hunch•back n **1** : back with a hump **2** : person with a crooked back —**hunchbacked** adj

hun•dred \ˈhəndrəd\ n, pl **-dreds** or **-dred** : 10 times 10 —**hundred** adj —**hun•dredth** \-drədth\ adj or n

1hung past of HANG

2hung adj : unable to reach a verdict

hun•ger \ˈhəŋgər\ n **1** : craving or urgent need for food **2** : strong desire —**hunger** vb —**hun•gri•ly** \-grəlē\ adv —**hun•gry** adj

hunk \ˈhəŋk\ n : large piece

hun•ker \ˈhəŋkər\ vb : settle in for a sustained period—used with down

hunt \ˈhənt\ vb **1** : pursue for food or sport **2** : try to find ~ n : act or instance of hunting —**hunt•er** n

hur•dle \ˈhərd⁹l\ n **1** : barrier to leap over in a race **2** : obstacle —**hurdle** vb —**hur•dler** n

hurl \ˈhərl\ vb : throw with violence —**hurl** n —**hurl•er** n

hur•rah \hu'rä, -'rȯ\ interj —used to express joy or approval

hur•ri•cane \ˈhərə‚kān\ n : tropical storm with winds of 74 miles per hour or greater

hur•ry \ˈhərē\ vb -**ried; -ry•ing** : go or cause to go with haste ~ n : extreme haste —**hur•ried•ly** adv —**hur•ried•ness** n

hurt \'hərt\ *vb* **hurt; hurt•ing 1** : feel or cause pain 2 : do harm to ~ *n* 1 : bodily injury 2 : harm —**hurt•ful** \-fəl\ *adj* —**hurt•ful•ness** *n*

hur•tle \'hərt^əl\ *vb* **-tled; -tling** : move rapidly or forcefully

hus•band \'həzbənd\ *n* : married man ~ *vb* : manage prudently

hus•band•ry \-bəndrē\ *n* 1 : careful use 2 : agriculture

hush \'həsh\ *vb* : make or become quiet ~ *n* : silence

husk \'həsk\ *n* : outer covering of a seed or fruit ~ *vb* : strip the husk from —**husk•er** *n*

¹hus•ky \'həskē\ *adj* **-ki•er; -est** : hoarse —**hus•ki•ly** *adv* —**hus•ki•ness** *n*

²husky *adj* **-ki•er; -est** : burly —**husk•i•ness** *n*

³husky *n, pl* **-kies** : working dog of the arctic

hus•sy \'həsē, -zē\ *n, pl* **-sies 1** : brazen woman 2 : mischievous girl

hus•tle \'həsəl\ *vb* **-tled; -tling 1** : hurry 2 : work energetically —**hustle** *n* —**hus•tler** \'həslər\ *n*

hut \'hət\ *n* : small often temporary dwelling

hutch \'həch\ *n* 1 : cupboard with open shelves 2 : pen for an animal

hy•a•cinth \'hīə,sinth\ *n* : bulbous herb grown for bell-shaped flowers

hy•brid \'hībrəd\ *n* : offspring of genetically differing parents —**hybrid** *adj* —**hy•brid•iza•tion** \,hībrədə'zāshən\ *n* —**hy•brid•ize** \'hībrəd,īz\ *vb* —**hy•brid•iz•er** *n*

hy•drant \'hīdrənt\ *n* : pipe from which water may be drawn to fight fires

hy•drau•lic \hī'drölik\ *adj* : operated by liquid forced through a small hole —**hy•drau•lics** \-liks\ *n*

hy•dro•car•bon \,hīdrə'kärbən\ *n* : organic compound of carbon and hydrogen

hy•dro•elec•tric \,hīdrōi'lektrik\ *adj* : producing electricity by waterpower —**hy•dro•elec•tric•i•ty** \-,lek'trisətē\ *n*

hy•dro•gen \'hīdrəjən\ *n* : very light gaseous colorless odorless flammable chemical element

hydrogen bomb *n* : powerful bomb that derives its energy from the union of atomic nuclei

hy•dro•pho•bia \,hīdrə'fōbēə\ *n* : rabies

hy•dro•plane \'hīdrə,plān\ *n* : speedboat that skims the water

hy•drous \'hīdrəs\ *adj* : containing water

hy•e•na \hī'ēnə\ *n* : nocturnal carnivorous mammal of Asia and Africa

hy•giene \'hī,jēn\ *n* : conditions or practices conducive to health —**hy•gien•ic** \hī'jenik, -'jēn-; ,hījē'enik\ *adj* —**hy•gien•i•cal•ly** \-iklē\ *adv* —**hy•gien•ist** \hī'jēnist, -'jen-; 'hī,jēn-\ *n*

hy•grom•e•ter \hī'grämətər\ *n* : instrument for measuring atmospheric humidity

hying *pres part of* HIE

hymn \'him\ *n* : song of praise esp. to God —**hymn** *vb*

hym•nal \'himnəl\ *n* : book of hymns

hype \'hīp\ *vb* **hyped; hyp•ing** : publicize extravagantly —**hype** *n*

hyper- *prefix* **1** : above or beyond 2 : excessively or excessive

hyperacid	hypermasculine
hyperacidity	hypernationalistic
hyperactive	hyperreactive
hyperacute	hyperrealistic
hyperaggressive	hyperromantic
hypercautious	hypersensitive
hypercorrect	hypersensitive-
hypercritical	ness
hyperemotional	hypersensitivity
hyperenergetic	hypersexual
hyperexcitable	hypersusceptible
hyperfastidious	hypertense
hyperintense	hypervigilant

hy•per•bo•le \hī'pərbəlē\ *n* : extravagant exaggeration

hy•per•ten•sion \'hīpər,tenchən\ *n* : high blood pressure —**hy•per•ten•sive** \,hīpər'tensiv\ *adj or n*

hy•phen \'hīfən\ *n* : punctuation mark - used to divide or compound words —**hyphen** *vb*

hy•phen•ate \'hīfə,nāt\ *vb* **-at•ed; -at•ing** : connect or divide with a hyphen —**hy•phen•ation** \,hīfə'nāshən\ *n*

hyp•no•sis \hip'nōsəs\ *n, pl* **-no•ses** \-,sēz\ : induced state like sleep in which the subject is responsive to suggestions of the inducer (**hyp•no•tist** \'hipnətist\) —**hyp•no•tism** \'hipnə,tizəm\ *n* —**hyp•no•tiz•able** \'hipnə'tīzəbəl\ *adj* —**hyp•no•tize** \'hipnə,tīz\ *vb*

hyp•not•ic \hip'nätik\ *adj* : relating to hypnosis —**hypnotic** *n* —**hyp•not•i•cal•ly** \-iklē\ *adv*

hy•po•chon•dria \,hīpə'kändrēə\ *n* : morbid concern for one's health —**hy•po•chon•dri•ac** \-drē,ak\ *adj or n*

hy•poc•ri•sy \hip'äkrəsē\ *n, pl* **-sies** : a feigning to be what one is not —**hypo•-**

crite \'hipə,krit\ *n* —**hyp•o•crit•i•cal** \,hipə'kritikəl\ *adj* —**hyp•o•crit•i•cal•ly** *adv*

hy•po•der•mic \,hīpə'dərmik\ *adj* : administered or used in making an injection beneath the skin ~ *n* : hypodermic syringe

hy•pot•e•nuse \hī'pätə,nüs, -,nüz, -,nyüs, -,nyüz\ *n* : side of a right-angled triangle opposite the right angle

hy•poth•e•sis \hī'päthəsəs\ *n, pl* **-e•ses** \-,sēz\ : assumption made in order to test its consequences —**hy•poth•e•size** \-,sīz\ *vb* —**hy•po•thet•i•cal** \,hīpə'thetikəl\ *adj* —**hy•po•thet•i•cal•ly** *adv*

hys•ter•ec•to•my \,histə'rektəmē\ *n, pl* **-mies** : surgical removal of the uterus

hys•te•ria \his'terēə, -tir-\ *n* : uncontrollable fear or outburst of emotion —**hys•ter•i•cal** \-'terikəl\ *adj* —**hys•ter•i•cal•ly** *adv*

hys•ter•ics \-'teriks\ *n pl* : uncontrollable laughter or crying

I

i \'ī\ *n, pl* **i's** *or* **is** \'īz\ : 9th letter of the alphabet

I \'ī\ *pron* : the speaker

-ial *adj suffix* : of, relating to, or characterized by

-ian —see -AN

ibis \'ībəs\ *n, pl* **ibis** *or* **ibis•es** : wading bird with a down-curved bill

-ible —see -ABLE

ibu•pro•fen \,ībyü'prōfən\ *n* : drug used to relieve inflammation, pain, and fever

-ic \ik\ *adj suffix* 1 : of, relating to, or being 2 : containing 3 : characteristic of 4 : marked by 5 : caused by

-i•cal \ikəl\ *adj suffix* : -ic —**-i•cal•ly** \iklē, -kəlē\ *adv suffix*

ice \'īs\ *n* 1 : frozen water 2 : flavored frozen dessert ~ *vb* **iced; ic•ing 1** : freeze 2 : chill 3 : cover with icing

ice•berg \'īs,bərg\ *n* : large floating mass of ice

ice•box *n* : refrigerator

ice•break•er *n* : ship equipped to cut through ice

ice cream *n* : sweet frozen food

ice-skate *vb* : skate on ice —**ice skat•er** *n*

ich•thy•ol•o•gy \,ikthē'äləjē\ *n* : study of fishes —**ich•thy•ol•o•gist** \-jist\ *n*

ici•cle \'ī,sikəl\ *n* : hanging mass of ice

ic•ing \'īsiŋ\ *n* : sweet usu. creamy coating for baked goods

icon \'ī,kän\ *n* 1 : religious image 2 : small picture on a computer screen identified with an available function

icon•o•clast \ī'känə,klast\ *n* : attacker of cherished beliefs or institutions —**icon•o•clasm** \-,klazəm\ *n*

icy \'īsē\ *adj* **ic•i•er; -est 1** : covered with or consisting of ice 2 : very cold —**ic•i•ly** *adv* —**ic•i•ness** *n*

id \'id\ *n* : unconscious instinctual part of the mind

idea \ī'dēə\ *n* 1 : something imagined in the mind 2 : purpose or plan

ide•al \ī'dēəl\ *adj* 1 : imaginary 2 : perfect ~ *n* 1 : standard of excellence 2 : model 3 : aim —**ide•al•ly** *adv*

ide•al•ism \ī'dēə,lizəm\ *n* : adherence to ideals —**ide•al•ist** \-list\ *n* —**ide•al•is•tic** \ī,dēə'listik\ *adj* —**ide•al•is•ti•cal•ly** \-ti•klē\ *adv*

ide•al•ize \ī'dēə,līz\ *vb* **-ized; -iz•ing** : think of or represent as ideal —**ide•al•i•za•tion** \-,dēələ'zāshən\ *n*

iden•ti•cal \ī'dentikəl\ *adj* 1 : being the same 2 : exactly or essentially alike

iden•ti•fi•ca•tion \ī,dentəfə'kāshən\ *n* 1 : act of identifying 2 : evidence of identity

iden•ti•fy \ī'dentə,fī\ *vb* **-fied; -fy•ing 1** : associate 2 : establish the identity of —**iden•ti•fi•able** \ī,dentə'fīəbəl\ *adj* —**iden•ti•fi•er** \ī'dentə,fīər\ *n*

iden•ti•ty \ī'dentətē\ *n, pl* **-ties 1** : sameness of essential character 2 : individuality 3 : fact of being what is supposed

ide•ol•o•gy \,īdē'äləjē, ,id-\ *n, pl* **-gies** : body of beliefs —**ide•o•log•i•cal** \,īdēə'läjikəl, ,id-\ *adj*

id•i•om \'idēəm\ *n* 1 : language peculiar to a person or group 2 : expression with a special meaning —**id•i•om•at•ic** \,idēə'matik\ *adj* —**id•i•om•at•i•cal•ly** \-iklē\ *adv*

id•io•syn•cra•sy \,idēō'siŋkrəsē\ *n, pl* **-sies** : personal peculiarity —**id•io•syn•crat•ic** \-sin'kratik\ *adj* —**id•io•syn•crat•i•cal•ly** \-'kratiklē\ *adv*

id•i•ot \'idēət\ *n* : mentally retarded or foolish person —**id•i•o•cy** \-əsē\ *n* —**id•i•ot•ic** \,idē'ätik\ *adj* —**id•i•ot•i•cal•ly** \-iklē\ *adv*

idle \'īd^əl\ *adj* **idler; idlest 1** : worthless 2 : inactive 3 : lazy ~ *vb* **idled; idling** : spend time doing nothing —**idle•ness** *n* —**idler** *n* —**idly** \'īdlē\ *adv*

idol \'īd^əl\ *n* 1 : image of a god 2 : object of devotion —**idol•iza•tion** \,īd^ələ'zāshən\ *n* —**idol•ize** \'īd^əl,īz\ *vb*

idol•a•ter, idol•a•tor \ī'dälətər\ *n* : worshiper of idols —**idol•a•trous** \-trəs\ *adj* —**idol•a•try** \-trē\ *n*

idyll \'īd^əl\ *n* : period of peace and contentment —**idyl•lic** \ī'dilik\ *adj*

-ier —see -ER

if \'if\ *conj* 1 : in the event that 2 : whether 3 : even though

-i•fy \ə,fī\ *vb suffix* : -fy

ig•loo \'iglü\ *n, pl* **-loos** : hut made of snow blocks

ig•nite \ig'nīt\ *vb* **-nit•ed; -nit•ing** : set afire or catch fire —**ig•nit•able** \-'nītəbəl\ *adj*

ig•ni•tion \ig'nishən\ *n* 1 : a setting on fire 2 : process or means of igniting fuel

ig•no•ble \ig'nōbəl\ *adj* : not honorable —**ig•no•bly** \-blē\ *adv*

ig•no•min•i•ous \,ignə'minēəs\ *adj* 1 : dishonorable 2 : humiliating —**ig•no•min•i•ous•ly** *adv* —**ig•no•mi•ny** \'ignə,minē, ig'nämənē\ *n*

ig•no•ra•mus \,ignə'rāməs\ *n* : ignorant person

ig•no•rant \'ignərənt\ *adj* 1 : lacking knowledge 2 : showing a lack of knowledge or intelligence 3 : unaware —**ig•no•rance** \-rəns\ *n* —**ig•no•rant•ly** *adv*

ig•nore \ig'nōr\ *vb* **-nored; -nor•ing** : refuse to notice

igua•na \i'gwänə\ *n* : large tropical American lizard

ilk \'ilk\ *n* : kind

ill \'il\ *adj* **worse** \'wərs\; **worst** \'wərst\ 1 : sick 2 : bad 3 : rude or unacceptable 4 : hostile ~ *adv* **worse; worst** 1 : with displeasure 2 : harshly 3 : scarcely 4 : badly ~ *n* 1 : evil 2 : misfortune 3 : sickness

il•le•gal \il'lēgəl\ *adj* : not lawful —**il•le•gal•i•ty** \ili'galətē\ *n* —**il•le•gal•ly** \il'lēgəlē\ *adv*

il•leg•i•ble \il'lejəbəl\ *adj* : not legible —**il•leg•i•bil•i•ty** \il,lejə'bilətē\ *n* —**il•leg•i•bly** \il'lejəblē\ *adv*

il•le•git•i•mate \ili'jitəmət\ *adj* 1 : born of unmarried parents 2 : illegal —**il•le•git•i•ma•cy** \-əməsē\ *n* —**il•le•git•i•mate•ly** *adv*

il•lic•it \il'lisət\ *adj* : not lawful —**il•lic•it•ly** *adv*

il•lim•it•able \il'limətəbəl\ *adj* : boundless —**il•lim•it•ably** \-blē\ *adv*

il•lit•er•ate \il'litərət\ *adj* : unable to read or write —**il•lit•er•a•cy** \-ərəsē\ *n* —**illiter•ate** *n*

ill-na•tured \-'nāchərd\ *adj* : cross —**ill-na•tured•ly** *adv*

ill•ness \'ilnəs\ *n* : sickness

il•log•i•cal \il'läjikəl\ *adj* : contrary to sound reasoning —**il•log•i•cal•ly** *adv*

ill-starred \il'stärd\ *adj* : unlucky

il•lu•mi•nate \il'ümə,nāt\ *vb* **-nat•ed; -nat•ing 1** : light up 2 : make clear —**il•lu•mi•nat•ing•ly** \-,nātiŋlē\ *adv* —**il•lu•mi•na•tion** \-,ümə'nāshən\ *n*

ill-use \-'yüz\ *vb* : abuse —**ill-use** \-'yüs\ *n*

il•lu•sion \il'üzhən\ *n* 1 : mistaken idea 2 : misleading visual image

il•lu•so•ry \il'üsərē, -'üz-\ *adj* : based on or producing illusion

il•lus•trate \'iləs,trāt\ *vb* **-trat•ed; -trat•ing 1** : explain by example 2 : provide with pictures or figures —**il•lus•tra•tor** \-ər\ *n*

il•lus•tra•tion \,iləs'trāshən\ *n* 1 : example that explains 2 : pictorial explanation

il•lus•tra•tive \il'əstrətiv\ *adj* : designed to illustrate —**il•lus•tra•tive•ly** *adv*

il•lus•tri•ous \-trēəs\ *adj* : notably or brilliantly outstanding —**il•lus•tri•ous•ness** *n*

ill will *n* : unfriendly feeling

im•age \'imij\ *n* 1 : likeness 2 : visual counterpart of an object formed by a lens or mirror 3 : mental picture ~ *vb* **-aged; -ag•ing** : create a representation of

im•ag•ery \'imijrē\ *n* 1 : images 2 : figurative language

imag•i•nary \im'ajə,nerē\ *adj* : existing only in the imagination

imag•i•na•tion \im,ajə'nāshən\ *n* 1 : act or power of forming a mental image 2 : creative ability —**imag•i•na•tive** \im'ajənətiv, -,nātiv\ *adj* —**imag•i•na•tive•ly** *adv*

imag•ine \im'ajən\ *vb* **-ined; -in•ing** : form a mental picture of something not present —**imag•in•able** \-'ajənəbəl\ *adj* —**imag•in•ably** \-blē\ *adv*

im•bal•ance \im'baləns\ *n* : lack of balance

im•be•cile \'imbəsəl, -,sil\ *n* : idiot —**im•-**

becile, im•be•cil•ic \imbə'silik\ *adj* —**im•be•cil•i•ty** \-'silətē\ *n*

im•bibe \im'bīb\ *vb* **-bibed; -bib•ing** : drink —**im•bib•er** *n*

im•bro•glio \im'brōlyō\ *n, pl* **-glios** : complicated situation

im•bue \-'byü\ *vb* **-bued; -bu•ing** : fill (as with color or a feeling)

im•i•tate \'imə,tāt\ *vb* **-tat•ed; -tat•ing 1** : follow as a model 2 : mimic —**im•i•ta•tive** \-,tātiv\ *adj* —**im•i•ta•tor** \-ər\ *n*

im•i•ta•tion \,imə'tāshən\ *n* 1 : act of imitating 2 : copy —**imitation** *adj*

im•mac•u•late \im'akyələt\ *adj* : without stain or blemish —**im•mac•u•late•ly** *adv*

im•ma•te•ri•al \,imə'tirēəl\ *adj* 1 : spiritual 2 : not relevant —**im•ma•te•ri•al•i•ty** \,tirē'alətē\ *n*

im•ma•ture \,imə'tùr, -'tyùr\ *adj* : not yet mature —**im•ma•tu•ri•ty** \-'tùrətē\ *n*

im•mea•sur•able \im'ezhərəbəl\ *adj* : indefinitely extensive —**im•mea•sur•ably** \-blē\ *adv*

im•me•di•a•cy \im'ēdēəsē\ *n, pl* **-cies** : quality or state of being urgent

im•me•di•ate \-ēət\ *adj* 1 : direct 2 : being next in line 3 : made or done at once 4 : not distant —**im•me•di•ate•ly** *adv*

im•me•mo•ri•al \,imə'mōrēəl\ *adj* : old beyond memory

im•mense \im'ens\ *adj* : vast —**im•mense•ly** *adv* —**im•men•si•ty** \-'ensətē\ *n*

im•merse \im'ərs\ *vb* **-mersed; -mers•ing 1** : plunge or dip esp. into liquid 2 : engross —**im•mer•sion** \-'ərzhən\ *n*

im•mi•grant \'imigrənt\ *n* : one that immigrates

im•mi•grate \'imə,grāt\ *vb* **-grat•ed; -grat•ing** : come into a place and take up residence —**im•mi•gra•tion** \,imə'grāshən\ *n*

im•mi•nent \'imənənt\ *adj* : ready to take place —**im•mi•nence** \-nəns\ *n* —**im•mi•nent•ly** *adv*

im•mo•bile \im'ōbəl\ *adj* : incapable of being moved —**im•mo•bil•i•ty** \imō'bilətē\ *n* —**im•mo•bi•lize** \im'ōbə,līz\ *vb*

im•mod•er•ate \im'ädərət\ *adj* : not moderate —**im•mod•er•a•cy** \-ərəsē\ *n* —**im•mod•er•ate•ly** *adv*

im•mod•est \im'ädəst\ *adj* : not modest —**im•mod•est•ly** *adv* —**im•mod•es•ty** \-əstē\ *n*

im•mo•late \'imə,lāt\ *vb* **-lat•ed; -lat•ing** : offer in sacrifice —**im•mo•la•tion** \,imə'lāshən\ *n*

im•mor•al \im'ōrəl\ *adj* : not moral —**im•mor•al•i•ty** \imō'ralətē, ,imə-\ *n* —**im•mor•al•ly** *adv*

im•mor•tal \im'ort^əl\ *adj* 1 : not mortal 2 : having lasting fame ~ *n* : one exempt from death or oblivion —**im•mor•tal•i•ty** \,imˌor'talətē\ *n* —**im•mor•tal•ize** \im'ort^əl,īz\ *vb*

im•mov•able \im'üvəbəl\ *adj* 1 : stationary 2 : unyielding —**im•mov•abil•i•ty** \imˌüvə'bilətē\ *n* —**im•mov•ably** \-blē\ *adv*

im•mune \im'yün\ *adj* : not liable esp. to disease —**im•mu•ni•ty** \im'yünətē\ *n* —**im•mu•ni•za•tion** \,imyənə'zāshən\ *n* —**im•mu•nize** \imyə,nīz\ *vb*

im•mu•nol•o•gy \,imyə'näləjē\ *n* : science of immunity to disease —**im•mu•no•log•ic** \-yənə^əl'äjik, **im•mu•no•log•i•cal** \-ikəl\ *adj* —**im•mu•nol•o•gist** \,imyə'näləjist\ *n*

im•mu•ta•ble \im'yütəbəl\ *adj* : unchangeable —**im•mu•ta•bil•i•ty** \im,yütə'bilətē\ *n* —**im•mu•ta•bly** *adv*

imp \'imp\ *n* 1 : demon 2 : mischievous child

im•pact \im'pakt\ *vb* 1 : press close 2 : have an effect on ~ \'im,pakt\ *n* 1 : forceful contact 2 : influence

im•pact•ed \im'paktəd\ *adj* : wedged between the jawbone and another tooth

im•pair \im'par\ *vb* : diminish in quantity, value, or ability —**im•pair•ment** *n*

im•pa•la \im'palə\ *n, pl* **impalas** *or* **impala** : large African antelope

im•pale \im'pāl\ *vb* **-paled; -pal•ing** : pierce with something pointed

im•pal•pa•ble \im'palpəbəl\ *adj* : incapable of being felt —**im•pal•pa•bly** *adv*

im•pan•el \im'pan^əl\ *vb* : enter in or on a panel

im•part \-'pärt\ *vb* : give from or as if from a store

im•par•tial \im'pärshəl\ *adj* : not partial —**im•par•tial•i•ty** \im,pärshē'alətē\ *n* —**im•par•tial•ly** *adv*

im•pass•able \im'pasəbəl\ *adj* : not passable —**im•pass•ably** \-'pasəblē\ *adv*

im•passe \'im,pas\ *n* : inescapable predicament

im•pas•sioned \im'pashənd\ *adj* : filled with passion

im•pas•sive \im'pasiv\ *adj* : showing no feeling or interest —**im•pas•sive•ly** *adv* —**im•pas•siv•i•ty** \,im,pa'sivətē\ *n*

im•pa•tiens \im'pāshənz, -shəns\ *n* : annual herb with showy flowers

im•pa•tient \im'pāshənt\ *adj* : not patient —**im•pa•tience** \-shəns\ *n* —**im•pa•tient•ly** *adv* im·peach \im'pēch\ vb 1 : charge (an official) with misconduct 2 : cast doubt on 3 : remove from office for misconduct — **im·peach·ment** n

im·pec·ca·ble \im'pekəbəl\ adj : faultless — **im·pec·ca·bly** adv

im·pe·cu·nious \impi'kyünēəs\ adj : broke — **im·pe·cu·nious·ness** n

im·pede \im'pēd\ vb -ped·ed; -ped·ing : interfere with

im·ped·i·ment \-'pedəmənt\ n 1 : hindrance 2 : speech defect

im·pel \-'pel\ vb -pelled; -pel·ling : urge forward

im·pend \-'pend\ vb : be about to occur

im·pen·e·tra·ble \im'penətrəbəl\ adj : incapable of being penetrated or understood — **im·pen·e·tra·bil·i·ty** \-,penətrə'bilətē\ n — **im·pen·e·tra·bly** adv

im·pen·i·tent \im'penətənt\ adj : not penitent — **im·pen·i·tence** \-təns\ n

im·per·a·tive \im'perətiv\ adj 1 : expressing a command 2 : urgent ~ n 1 : imperative mood or verb form 2 : unavoidable fact, need, or obligation — **im·per·a·tive·ly** adv

im·per·cep·ti·ble \impər'septəbəl\ adj : not perceptible — **im·per·cep·ti·bly** adv

im·per·fect \im'pərfikt\ adj : not perfect — **im·per·fec·tion** n — **im·per·fect·ly** adv

im·pe·ri·al \im'pirēəl\ adj 1 : relating to an empire or an emperor 2 : royal

im·pe·ri·al·ism \im'pirēə,lizəm\ n : policy of controlling other nations — **im·pe·ri·al·ist** \-list\ n or adj — **im·pe·ri·al·is·tic** \-,pirēə'listik\ adj — **im·pe·ri·al·is·ti·cal·ly** \-tiklē\ adv

im·per·il \im'perəl\ vb -iled or -illed; -il·ing or -il·ling : endanger

im·pe·ri·ous \im'pirēəs\ adj : arrogant or domineering — **im·pe·ri·ous·ly** adv

im·per·ish·able \im'perishəbəl\ adj : not perishable

im·per·ma·nent \-'pərmənənt\ adj : not permanent — **im·per·ma·nent·ly** adv

im·per·me·able \-'pərmēəbəl\ adj : not permeable

im·per·mis·si·ble \impər'misəbəl\ adj : not permissible

im·per·son·al \im'pərsənəl\ adj : not involving human personality or emotion — **im·per·son·al·i·ty** \im,pərsn'alətē\ n — **im·per·son·al·ly** adv

im·per·son·ate \im'pərsn,āt\ vb -at·ed; -at·ing : assume the character of — **im·per·son·ation** \-,pərsn'āshən\ n — **im·per·son·ator** \-'pərsn,ātər\ n

im·per·ti·nent \im'pərtənənt\ adj 1 : irrelevant 2 : insolent — **im·per·ti·nence** \-nəns\ n — **im·per·ti·nent·ly** adv

im·per·turb·able \impər'tərbəbəl\ adj : calm and steady

im·per·vi·ous \im'pərvēəs\ adj : incapable of being penetrated or affected

im·pet·u·ous \im'pechəwəs\ adj : impulsive — **im·pet·u·os·i·ty** \im,pechə'wäsətē\ n — **im·pet·u·ous·ly** adv

im·pe·tus \'impətəs\ n : driving force

im·pi·ety \im'pītē\ n : quality or state of being impious

im·pinge \im'pinj\ vb -pinged; -ping·ing : encroach — **im·pinge·ment** \-mənt\ n

im·pi·ous \'impēəs, im'pī-\ adj : not pious

imp·ish \'impish\ adj : mischievous — **imp·ish·ly** adv — **imp·ish·ness** n

im·pla·ca·ble \im'plakəbəl, -'plā-\ adj : not capable of being appeased or changed — **im·pla·ca·bil·i·ty** \im,plakə'bilətē, -,plā-\ n — **im·pla·ca·bly** \im'plakəblē\ adv

im·plant \im'plant\ vb 1 : set firmly or deeply 2 : fix in the mind or spirit ~ \'im,plant\ n : something implanted in tissue — **im·plan·ta·tion** \im,plan'tāshən\ n

im·plau·si·ble \im'plözəbəl\ adj : not plausible — **im·plau·si·bil·i·ty** \im,plözə'bilətē\ n

im·ple·ment \'impləmənt\ n : tool, utensil ~ \-,ment\ vb : put into practice — **im·ple·men·ta·tion** \impləmən'tāshən\ n

im·pli·cate \'implə,kāt\ vb -cat·ed; -cat·ing : involve

im·pli·ca·tion \implə'kāshən\ n 1 : an implying 2 : something implied

im·plic·it \im'plisət\ adj 1 : understood though only implied 2 : complete and unquestioning — **im·plic·it·ly** adv

im·plode \im'plōd\ vb -plod·ed; -plod·ing : burst inward — **im·plo·sion** \-'plōzhən\ n — **im·plo·sive** \-'plōsiv\ adj

im·plore \im'plōr\ vb -plored; -plor·ing : entreat

im·ply \-'plī\ vb -plied; -ply·ing : express indirectly

im·po·lite \impə'līt\ adj : not polite

im·pol·i·tic \im'pälə,tik\ adj : not politic

im·pon·der·a·ble \im'pändərəbəl\ adj : incapable of being precisely evaluated — **imponderable** n

im·port \im'pōrt\ vb 1 : mean 2 : bring in from an external source ~ \'im,pōrt\ n 1 : meaning 2 : importance 3 : something imported — **im·por·ta·tion** \im,pōr'tāshən\ n — **im·port·er** n

im·por·tant \im'pōrtənt\ adj : having great

worth, significance, or influence — **im·por·tance** \-∂ns\ n — **im·por·tant·ly** adv

im·por·tu·nate \im'pōrchənət\ adj : troublesomely persistent or urgent

im·por·tune \,impər'tün, -'tyün; im'pōrchən\ vb -tuned; -tun·ing : urge or beg persistently — **im·por·tu·ni·ty** \im-pər'tünətē, -'tyü-\ n

im·pose \im'pōz\ vb -posed; -pos·ing 1 : establish as compulsory 2 : take unwarranted advantage of — **im·po·si·tion** \impə'zishən\ n

im·pos·ing \im'pōziŋ\ adj : impressive — **im·pos·ing·ly** adv

im·pos·si·ble \im'päsəbəl\ adj 1 : incapable of occurring 2 : enormously difficult — **im·pos·si·bil·i·ty** \im,päsə'bilətē\ n — **im·pos·si·bly** \im'päsəblē\ adv

im·post \'im,pōst\ n : tax

im·pos·tor, im·pos·ter \im'pästər\ n : one who assumes an identity or title to deceive — **im·pos·ture** \-'päschər\ n

im·po·tent \'impətənt\ adj 1 : lacking power 2 : sterile — **im·po·tence** \-pətəns\ n — **im·po·ten·cy** \-ənsē\ n — **im·po·tent·ly** adv

im·pound \im'paund\ vb : seize and hold in legal custody — **im·pound·ment** n

im·pov·er·ish \im'pävərish\ vb : make poor — **im·pov·er·ish·ment** n

im·prac·ti·ca·ble \im'praktikəbəl\ adj : not practicable

im·prac·ti·cal \im'praktikəl\ adj : not practical

im·pre·cise \impri'sīs\ adj : not precise — **im·pre·cise·ly** adv — **im·pre·cise·ness** n — **im·pre·ci·sion** \-'sizhən\ n

im·preg·na·ble \im'pregnəbəl\ adj : able to resist attack — **im·preg·na·bil·i·ty** \im-,pregnə'bilətē\ n

im·preg·nate \im'preg,nāt\ vb -nat·ed; -nat·ing 1 : make pregnant 2 : cause to be filled, permeated, or saturated — **im·preg·na·tion** \im,preg'nāshən\ n

im·pre·sa·rio \imprə'särē,ō\ n, pl -ri·os : one who sponsors an entertainment

¹im·press \im'pres\ vb 1 : apply with or produce by pressure 2 : press, stamp, or print in or upon 3 : produce a vivid impression of 4 : affect (as the mind) forcibly

²im·press \im'pres\ vb : force into naval service — **im·press·ment** n

im·pres·sion \im'preshən\ n 1 : mark made by impressing 2 : marked influence or effect 3 : printed copy 4 : vague notion or recollection — **im·pres·sion·able** \-'preshənəbəl\ adj

im·pres·sive \im'presiv\ adj : making a marked impression — **im·pres·sive·ly** adv — **im·pres·sive·ness** n

im·pri·ma·tur \impra'mä,tür\ n : official approval (as of a publication by a censor)

im·print \im'print, 'im,-\ vb : stamp or mark by or as if by pressure ~ \'im,-\ n : something imprinted or printed

im·pris·on \im'prizn\ vb : put in prison — **im·pris·on·ment** \-mənt\ n

im·prob·a·ble \im'präbəbəl\ adj : unlikely to be true or to occur — **im·prob·a·bil·i·ty** \im,präbə'bilətē\ n — **im·prob·a·bly** adv

im·promp·tu \im'prämptü, -tyü\ adj : not planned beforehand — **impromptu** adv or n

im·prop·er \im'präpər\ adj : not proper — **im·prop·er·ly** adv

im·pro·pri·ety \impra'prīətē\ n, pl -eties : state or instance of being improper

im·prove \im'prüv\ vb -proved; -prov·ing : grow or make better — **im·prov·able** \-'prüvəbəl\ adj — **im·prove·ment** n

im·prov·i·dent \im'prävədənt\ adj : not providing for the future — **im·prov·i·dence** \-əns\ n

im·pro·vise \impra,vīz\ vb -vised; -vis·ing : make, invent, or arrange offhand — **im·pro·vi·sa·tion** \im,prävə'zāshən, ,imprə-və-\ n — **im·pro·vis·er, im·pro·vi·sor** \'impra,vīzər\ n

im·pru·dent \im'prüd∂nt\ adj : not prudent — **im·pru·dence** \-∂ns\ n

im·pu·dent \'impyədənt\ adj : insolent — **im·pu·dence** \-əns\ n — **im·pu·dent·ly** adv

im·pugn \im'pyün\ vb : attack as false

im·pulse \'im,pəls\ n 1 : moving force 2 : sudden inclination

im·pul·sive \im'pəlsiv\ adj : acting on impulse — **im·pul·sive·ly** adv — **im·pul·sive·ness** n

im·pu·ni·ty \im'pyünətē\ n : exemption from punishment or harm

im·pure \im'pyür\ adj : not pure — **im·pu·ri·ty** \-'pyürətē\ n

im·pute \im'pyüt\ vb -put·ed; -put·ing : credit to or blame on a person or cause — **im·pu·ta·tion** \impyə'tāshən\ n

in \'in\ prep 1 —used to indicate location, inclusion, situation, or manner 2 : into 3 : during ~ adv : to or toward the inside ~ adj : located inside

in- \in\ prefix 1 : not 2 : lack of

inability
inaccessibility
inaccessible
inaccuracy
inaccurate
inaction
inactive
inactivity
inadequacy
inadequate
inadequately
inadmissibility
inadmissible
inadvisability
inadvisable
inapparent
inapplicable
inapposite
inappositely
inappositeness
inappreciative
inapproachable
inappropriate
inappropriately
inappropriateness
inapt
inarguable
inartistic
inartistically
inattentive
inattentively
inattentiveness
inaudible
inaudibly
inauspicious
inauthentic
incapability
incapable
incautious
incoherence
incoherent
incoherently
incombustible
incommensurate
incommodious
incommunicable
incompatibility
incompatible
incomplete
incompletely
incompleteness
incomprehensible
inconclusive
incongruent
inconsecutive
inconsiderate
inconsiderately
inconsiderateness
inconsistency
inconsistent
inconsistently
inconspicuous
inconspicuously
inconstancy
inconstant
inconstantly
inconsumable
incontestable
incontestably
incorporeal
incorporeally
incorrect
incorrectly
incorrectness
incorruptible
inculpable
incurable
incurious
indecency
indecent
indecently
indecipherable
indecisive
indecisively
indecorous
indecorously
indecorousness
indefensible
indefinable
indefinably
indescribable
indescribably
indestructibility
indestructible
indigestible
indiscernible
indiscreet
indiscreetly

indiscretion
indisputable
indisputably
indistinct
indistinctly
indistinctness
indivisibility
indivisible
ineducable
ineffective
ineffectively
ineffectiveness
ineffectual
ineffectually
ineffectualness
inefficiency
inefficient
inefficiently
inelastic
inelasticity
inelegance
inelegant
ineligibility
ineligible
ineradicable
inessential
inexact
inexactly
inexpedient
inexpensive
inexperience
inexperienced
inexpert
inexpertly
inexpertness
inexplicable
inexplicably
inexplicit
inexpressible
inexpressibly
inextinguishable
inextricable
infeasibility
infeasible
infelicitous
infelicity
infertile
infertility
inflexibility
inflexible
inflexibly
infrequent
infrequently
inglorious
ingloriously
ingratitude
inhumane
inhumanely
inhumanity
injudicious
injudiciously
injudiciousness
inoffensive
inoperable
inoperative
insalubrious
insensitive
insensitivity
inseparable
insignificant
insincere
insincerely
insincerity
insolubility
insoluble
instability
insubstantial
insufficiency
insufficient
insufficiently
insupportable
intangibility
intangible
intangibly
intolerable
intolerably
intolerance
intolerant
intractable
invariable
invariably
inviable
invisibility
invisible
invisibly
involuntarily
involuntary
invulnerability
invulnerable
invulnerably

in·ad·ver·tent \,inad'vart∂nt\ adj : unintentional — **in·ad·ver·tence** \-∂ns\ n — **in·ad·ver·ten·cy** \-∂nsē\ n — **in·ad·ver·tent·ly** adv

in·alien·able \in'ālyənəbəl, -'ālēənə-\ adj : incapable of being transferred or given up — **in·alien·abil·i·ty** \in,ālyənə'bilətē, -'ālēənə-\ n — **in·alien·ably** adv

inane \in'ān\ adj inan·er; -est : silly or stupid — **inan·i·ty** \in'anətē\ n

in·an·i·mate \in'anəmət\ adj : not animate or animated — **in·an·i·mate·ly** adv — **in·an·i·mate·ness** n

in·ap·pre·cia·ble \inə'prēshəbəl\ adj : too

small to be perceived — **in·ap·pre·cia·bly** adv

in·ar·tic·u·late \inär'tikyələt\ adj : without the power of speech or effective expression — **in·ar·tic·u·late·ly** adv

in·as·much as \,inaz'məchaz\ conj : because

in·at·ten·tion \inə'tenchən\ n : failure to pay attention

in·au·gu·ral \in'ōgyərəl, -gərəl\ adj 1 : relating to an inauguration ~ n 1 : inaugural speech 2 : inauguration

in·au·gu·rate \in'ōgyə,rāt, -gərə-\ vb -rat·ed; -rat·ing 1 : install in office 2 : start — **in·au·gu·ra·tion** \-,ōgyə'rāshən, -gə-\ n

in·board \'in,bōrd\ adv : inside a vehicle or craft — **inboard** adj

in·born \'in'bōrn\ adj : present from birth

in·bred \'in,bred\ adj : deeply ingrained in one's nature

in·breed·ing \'in,brēdiŋ\ n : interbreeding of closely related individuals — **in·breed** \-,brēd\ vb

in·cal·cu·la·ble \in'kalkyələbəl\ adj : too large to be calculated — **in·cal·cu·la·bly** adv

in·can·des·cent \inkən'des∂nt\ adj 1 : glowing with heat 2 : brilliant — **in·can·des·cence** \-∂ns\ n

in·can·ta·tion \in,kan'tāshən\ n : use of spoken or sung charms or spells as a magic ritual

in·ca·pac·i·tate \inkə'pasə,tāt\ vb -tat·ed; -tat·ing : disable

in·ca·pac·i·ty \inkə'pasətē\ n, pl -ties : quality or state of being incapable

in·car·cer·ate \in'kärsə,rāt\ vb -at·ed; -at·ing : imprison — **in·car·cer·a·tion** \in,kärsə'rāshən\ n

in·car·nate \in'kärnət, -,nāt\ adj : having bodily form and substance — **in·car·nate** \-,nāt\ vb — **in·car·na·tion** \-,kär'nāshən\ n

in·cen·di·ary \in'sendē,erē\ adj 1 : pertaining to or used to ignite fire 2 : tending to excite — **incendiary** n

in·cense \'in,sens\ n : material burned to produce a fragrant odor or its smoke ~ \in'sens\ vb -censed; -cens·ing : make very angry

in·cen·tive \in'sentiv\ n : inducement to do something

in·cep·tion \in'sepshən\ n : beginning

in·ces·sant \in'ses∂nt\ adj : continuing without interruption — **in·ces·sant·ly** adv

in·cest \'in,sest\ n : sexual intercourse between close relatives — **in·ces·tu·ous** \in-'seschəwəs\ adj

inch \'inch\ n : unit of length equal to 1/12 foot ~ vb : move by small degrees

in·cho·ate \in'kōət, 'inkə,wāt\ adj : new and not fully formed or ordered

in·ci·dent \'insədənt\ n : occurrence — **in·ci·dence** \-∂ns\ n — **incident** adj

in·ci·den·tal \insə'dent∂l\ adj 1 : subordinate, nonessential, or attendant 2 : met by chance ~ n 1 : something incidental 2 pl : minor expenses that are not itemized — **in·ci·den·tal·ly** adv

in·cin·er·ate \in'sinə,rāt\ vb -at·ed; -at·ing : burn to ashes — **in·cin·er·a·tor** \-,rātər\ n

in·cip·i·ent \in'sipēənt\ adj : beginning to be or appear

in·cise \in'sīz\ vb -cised; -cis·ing : carve into

in·ci·sion \in'sizhən\ n : surgical cut

in·ci·sive \in'sīsiv\ adj : keen and discerning — **in·ci·sive·ly** adv

in·ci·sor \in'sīzər\ n : tooth for cutting

in·cite \in'sīt\ vb -cit·ed; -cit·ing : arouse to action — **in·cite·ment** n

in·ci·vil·i·ty \insə'vilətē\ n : rudeness

in·clem·ent \in'klemənt\ adj : stormy — **in·clem·en·cy** \-∂nsē\ n

in·cline \in'klīn\ vb -clined; -clin·ing 1 : bow 2 : tend toward an opinion 3 : slope ~ n : slope — **in·cli·na·tion** \inklə'nāshən\ n — **in·clin·er** n

inclose, inclosure var of ENCLOSE, ENCLOSURE

in·clude \in'klüd\ vb -clud·ed; -clud·ing : take in or comprise — **in·clu·sion** \in-'klüzhən\ n — **in·clu·sive** \-'klüsiv\ adj

in·cog·ni·to \,in,käg'nētō, in'kägnə,tō\ adv or adj : with one's identity concealed

in·come \'in,kəm\ n : money gained (as from work or investment)

in·com·ing \'in,kəmiŋ\ adj : coming in

in·com·mu·ni·ca·do \,inkə,myünə'kädō\ adv or adj : without means of communication

in·com·pa·ra·ble \in'kämpərəbəl\ adj : eminent beyond comparison

in·com·pe·tent \in'kämpətənt\ adj : lacking sufficient knowledge or skill — **in·com·pe·tence** \-pətəns\ n — **in·com·pe·ten·cy** \-ənsē\ n — **incompetent** n

in·con·ceiv·able \inkən'sēvəbəl\ adj 1 : impossible to comprehend 2 : unbelievable — **in·con·ceiv·ably** \-blē\ adv

in·con·gru·ous \in'käŋgrəwəs\ adj : inappropriate or out of place — **in·con·gru·i·ty** \inkən'grüətē, -kän-\ n — **in·con·gru·ous·ly** adv

in·con·se·quen·tial \in,känsə'kwenchəl\ *adj* : unimportant —**in·con·se·quence** \in'känsə,kwens\ *n* —**in·con·se·quen·tial·ly** *adv*

in·con·sid·er·able \inkən'sidərəbəl\ *adj* : trivial

in·con·sol·able \inkən'sōləbəl\ *adj* : incapable of being consoled —**in·con·sol·ably** *adv*

in·con·ve·nience \inkən'vēnyəns\ *n* 1 : discomfort 2 : something that causes trouble or annoyance ~ *vb* : cause inconvenience to —**in·con·ve·nient** \inkən-'vēnyənt\ *adj* —**in·con·ve·nient·ly** *adv*

in·cor·po·rate \in'kôrpə,rāt\ *vb* -**rat·ed;** -**rat·ing** 1 : blend 2 : form into a legal body —**in·cor·po·rat·ed** *adj* —**in·cor·po·ra·tion** \-,kôrpə'rāshən\ *n*

in·cor·ri·gi·ble \in'kôrəjəbəl\ *adj* : incapable of being corrected or reformed —**in·cor·ri·gi·bil·i·ty** \in,kôrəjə'bilətē\ *n*

in·crease \in'krēs, 'in,krēs\ *vb* -**creased;** -**creas·ing** : make or become greater ~ \'in,-, in'-\ *n* 1 : enlargement in size 2 : something added —**in·creas·ing·ly** \-'krēsiŋlē\ *adv*

in·cred·i·ble \in'kredəbəl\ *adj* : too extraordinary to be believed —**in·cred·i·bil·i·ty** \in,kredə'bilətē\ *n* —**in·cred·i·bly** \in-'kredəblē\ *adv*

in·cred·u·lous \in'krejələs\ *adj* : skeptical —**in·cre·du·li·ty** \inkri'dülətē, -'dyü-\ *n* —**in·cred·u·lous·ly** *adv*

in·cre·ment \'iŋkrəmənt, 'in-\ *n* : increase or amount of increase —**in·cre·men·tal** \iŋkrə'mentʰl, in-\ *adj*

in·crim·i·nate \in'krimə,nāt\ *vb* -**nat·ed;** -**nat·ing** : show to be guilty of a crime —**in·crim·i·na·tion** \-,krimə'nāshən\ *n* —**in·crim·i·na·to·ry** \-'krimənə,tōrē\ *adj*

in·cu·bate \'iŋkyə,bāt, 'in-\ *vb* -**bat·ed;** -**bat·ing** : keep (as eggs) under conditions favorable for development —**in·cu·ba·tion** \iŋkyə'bāshən, in-\ *n* —**in·cu·ba·tor** \'iŋkyə,bātər, 'in-\ *n*

in·cul·cate \in'kəl,kāt, 'in,kəl-\ *vb* -**cat·ed;** -**cat·ing** : instill by repeated teaching —**in·cul·ca·tion** \in,kəl'kāshən\ *n*

in·cum·bent \in'kəmbənt\ *n* : holder of an office ~ *adj* : obligatory —**in·cum·ben·cy** \-bənsē\ *n*

in·cur \in'kər\ *vb* -**rr-** : become liable or subject to

in·cur·sion \in'kərzhən\ *n* : invasion

in·debt·ed \in'detəd\ *adj* : owing something —**in·debt·ed·ness** *n*

in·de·ci·sion \indi'sizhən\ *n* : inability to decide

in·deed \in'dēd\ *adv* : without question

in·de·fat·i·ga·ble \indi'fatigəbəl\ *adj* : not tiring —**in·de·fat·i·ga·bly** \-blē\ *adv*

in·def·i·nite \in'defənət\ *adj* 1 : not defining or identifying 2 : not precise 3 : having no fixed limit —**in·def·i·nite·ly** *adv*

in·del·i·ble \in'deləbəl\ *adj* : not capable of being removed or erased —**in·del·i·bly** *adv*

in·del·i·cate \in'delikət\ *adj* : improper —**in·del·i·ca·cy** \in'delikəsē\ *n*

in·dem·ni·fy \in'demnə,fī\ *vb* -**fied;** -**fy·ing** : repay for a loss —**in·dem·ni·fi·ca·tion** \-,demnəfə'kāshən\ *n*

in·dem·ni·ty \in'demnətē\ *n, pl* -**ties** : security against loss or damage

¹**in·dent** \in'dent\ *vb* : leave a space at the beginning of a paragraph

²**indent** *vb* : force inward so as to form a depression or dent

in·den·ta·tion \in,den'tāshən\ *n* 1 : notch, recess, or dent 2 : action of indenting 3 : space at the beginning of a paragraph

in·den·ture \in'denchər\ *n* : contract binding one person to work for another for a given period —usu. in pl. ~ *vb* -**tured;** -**tur·ing** : bind by indentures

Independence Day *n* : July 4 observed as a legal holiday in commemoration of the adoption of the Declaration of Independence in 1776

in·de·pen·dent \ində'pendənt\ *adj* 1 : not governed by another 2 : not requiring or relying on something or somebody else 3 : not easily influenced —**in·de·pen·dence** \-dəns\ *n* —**independent** *n* —**in·de·pen·dent·ly** *adv*

in·de·ter·mi·nate \indi'tərmənət\ *adj* : not definitely determined —**in·de·ter·mi·na·cy** \-nəsē\ *n* —**in·de·ter·mi·nate·ly** *adv*

in·dex \'in,deks\ *n, pl* -**dex·es** *or* -**di·ces** \-də,sēz\ 1 : alphabetical list of items (as topics in a book) 2 : a number that serves as a measure or indicator of something ~ *vb* 1 : provide with an index 2 : serve as an index of

index finger *n* : forefinger

in·di·cate \'ində,kāt\ *vb* -**cat·ed;** -**cat·ing** 1 : point out or to 2 : show indirectly 3 : state briefly —**in·di·ca·tion** \ində'kā-shən\ *n* —**in·di·ca·tor** \'ində,kātər\ *n*

in·dic·a·tive \in'dikətiv\ *adj* : serving to indicate

in·dict \in'dīt\ *vb* : charge with a crime —**in·dict·able** *adj* —**in·dict·ment** *n*

in·dif·fer·ent \in'difrənt\ *adj* 1 : having no preference 2 : showing neither interest nor dislike 3 : mediocre —**in·dif·fer·ence** \-'difrəns\ *n* —**in·dif·fer·ent·ly** *adv*

in·dig·e·nous \in'dijənəs\ *adj* : native to a particular region

in·di·gent \'indijənt\ *adj* : needy —**in·di·gence** \-jəns\ *n*

in·di·ges·tion \indī'jeschən, -də-\ *n* : discomfort from inability to digest food

in·dig·na·tion \indig'nāshən\ *n* : anger aroused by something unjust or unworthy —**in·dig·nant** \in'dignənt\ *adj* —**in·dig·nant·ly** *adv*

in·dig·ni·ty \in'dignətē\ *n, pl* -**ties** 1 : offense against self-respect 2 : humiliating treatment

in·di·go \'indi,gō\ *n, pl* -**gos** *or* -**goes** 1 : blue dye 2 : deep reddish blue color

in·di·rect \ində'rekt, -dī-\ *adj* : not straight or straightforward —**in·di·rec·tion** \-'rekshən\ *n* —**in·di·rect·ly** *adv* —**in·di·rect·ness** *n*

in·dis·crim·i·nate \indis'krimənət\ *adj* 1 : not careful or discriminating 2 : haphazard —**in·dis·crim·i·nate·ly** *adv*

in·dis·pens·able \indis'pensəbəl\ *adj* : absolutely essential —**in·dis·pens·abil·i·ty** \-,pensə'bilətē\ *n* —**indispensable** *n* —**in·dis·pens·ably** \-'pensəblē\ *adv*

in·dis·posed \-'pōzd\ *adj* : slightly ill —**in·dis·po·si·tion** \in,dispə'zishən\ *n*

in·dis·sol·u·ble \indis'älyəbəl\ *adj* : not capable of being dissolved or broken

in·di·vid·u·al \ində'vijəwəl\ *n* 1 : single member of a category 2 : person —**individual** *adj* —**in·di·vid·u·al·ly** *adv*

in·di·vid·u·al·ist \-əwəlist\ *n* : person who is markedly independent in thought or action

in·di·vid·u·al·i·ty \-,vijə'walətē\ *n* : special quality that distinguishes an individual

in·di·vid·u·al·ize \-'vijəwə,līz\ *vb* -**ized;** -**iz·ing** 1 : make individual 2 : treat individually

in·doc·tri·nate \in'däktrə,nāt\ *vb* -**nat·ed;** -**nat·ing** : instruct in fundamentals (as of a doctrine) —**in·doc·tri·na·tion** \in-,däktrə'nāshən\ *n*

in·do·lent \'indələnt\ *adj* : lazy —**in·do·lence** \-ləns\ *n*

in·dom·i·ta·ble \in'dämətəbəl\ *adj* : invincible —**in·dom·i·ta·bly** \-blē\ *adv*

in·door \'in'dôr\ *adj* : relating to the inside of a building

in·doors \in'dôrz\ *adv* : in or into a building

in·du·bi·ta·ble \in'dübətəbəl, -'dyü-\ *adj* : being beyond question —**in·du·bi·ta·bly** \-blē\ *adv*

in·duce \in'düs, -'dyüs\ *vb* -**duced;** -**duc·ing** 1 : persuade 2 : bring about —**in·duce·ment** *n* —**in·duc·er** *n*

in·duct \in'dəkt\ *vb* 1 : put in office 2 : admit as a member 3 : enroll (as for military service) —**in·duct·ee** \in,dək'tē\ *n*

in·duc·tion \in'dəkshən\ *n* 1 : act or instance of inducting 2 : reasoning from particular instances to a general conclusion

in·duc·tive \in'dəktiv\ *adj* : reasoning by induction

in·dulge \in'dəlj\ *vb* -**dulged;** -**dulg·ing** : yield to the desire of or for —**indul·gence** \-'dəljəns\ *n* —**in·dul·gent** \-jənt\ *adj* —**in·dul·gent·ly** *adv*

in·dus·tri·al \in'dəstrēəl\ *adj* 1 : relating to industry 2 : heavy-duty —**in·dus·tri·al·ist** \-əlist\ *n* —**in·dus·tri·al·iza·tion** \-,dəstrēələ'zāshən\ *n* —**in·dus·tri·al·ize** \-'dəstrēə,līz\ *vb*

in·dus·tri·ous \in'dəstrēəs\ *adj* : diligent or busy —**in·dus·tri·ous·ly** *adv* —**in·dus·tri·ous·ness** *n*

in·dus·try \'indəstrē\ *n, pl* -**tries** 1 : diligence 2 : manufacturing enterprises or activity

in·e·bri·at·ed \in'ēbrē,ātəd\ *adj* : drunk —**in·e·bri·a·tion** \-,ēbrē'āshən\ *n*

in·ef·fa·ble \in'efəbəl\ *adj* : incapable of being expressed in words —**in·ef·fa·bly** \-blē\ *adv*

in·ept \in'ept\ *adj* 1 : inappropriate or foolish 2 : generally incompetent —**in·ep·ti·tude** \in'eptə,tüd, -,tyüd\ *n* —**in·ept·ly** *adv* —**in·ept·ness** *n*

in·equal·i·ty \ini'kwälətē\ *n* : quality of being unequal or uneven

in·ert \in'ərt\ *adj* 1 : powerless to move or act 2 : sluggish —**in·ert·ly** *adv* —**in·ert·ness** *n*

in·er·tia \in'ərshə\ *n* : tendency of matter to remain at rest or in motion —**in·er·tial** \-shəl\ *adj*

in·es·cap·able \inə'skāpəbəl\ *adj* : inevitable —**in·es·cap·ably** \-blē\ *adv*

in·es·ti·ma·ble \in'estəməbəl\ *adj* : incapable of being estimated —**in·es·ti·ma·bly** \-blē\ *adv*

in·ev·i·ta·ble \in'evətəbəl\ *adj* : incapable of being avoided or escaped —**in·ev·i·ta·bil·i·ty** \-,evətə'bilətē\ *n* —**in·ev·i·ta·bly** \in'evətəblē\ *adv*

without excuse or justification —**in·ex·cus·ably** \-blē\ *adv*

in·ex·haust·ible \inig'zòstəbəl\ *adj* : incapable of being used up or tired out —**in·ex·haust·ibly** \-blē\ *adv*

in·ex·o·ra·ble \in'eksərəbəl\ *adj* : unyielding or relentless —**in·ex·o·ra·bly** *adv*

in·fal·li·ble \in'faləbəl\ *adj* : incapable of error —**in·fal·li·bil·i·ty** \in,falə'bilətē\ *n* —**in·fal·li·bly** *adv*

in·fa·mous \'infəməs\ *adj* : having the worst kind of reputation —**in·fa·mous·ly** *adv*

in·fa·my \-mē\ *n, pl* -**mies** : evil reputation

in·fan·cy \'infənsē\ *n, pl* -**cies** 1 : early childhood 2 : early period of existence

in·fant \'infənt\ *n* : baby

in·fan·tile \'infən,tīl, -tʰl, -,tēl\ *adj* 1 : relating to infants 2 : childish

in·fan·try \'infəntrē\ *n, pl* -**tries** : soldiers that fight on foot

in·fat·u·ate \in'facha,wāt\ *vb* -**at·ed;** -**at·ing** : inspire with foolish love or admiration —**in·fat·u·a·tion** \-,facha'wāshən\ *n*

in·fect \in'fekt\ *vb* : contaminate with disease-producing matter —**in·fec·tion** \-'fekshən\ *n* —**in·fec·tious** \-shəs\ *adj* —**in·fec·tive** \-'fektiv\ *adj*

in·fer \in'fər\ *vb* -**rr-** : deduce —**in·fer·ence** \'infərəns\ *n* —**in·fer·en·tial** \infə'ren-chəl\ *adj*

in·fe·ri·or \in'firēər\ *adj* 1 : being lower in position, degree, rank, or merit 2 : of lesser quality —**inferior** *n* —**in·fe·ri·or·i·ty** \in,firē'orətē\ *n*

in·fer·nal \in'fərnʰl\ *adj* : of or like hell—often used as a general expression of disapproval —**in·fer·nal·ly** *adv*

in·fer·no \in'fərnō\ *n, pl* -**nos** : place or condition suggesting hell

in·fest \in'fest\ *vb* : swarm or grow in or over —**in·fes·ta·tion** \in,fes'tāshən\ *n*

in·fi·del \'infədʰl, -fə,del\ *n* : one who does not believe in a particular religion

in·fi·del·i·ty \infə'delətē, -fī-\ *n, pl* -**ties** : lack of faithfulness

in·field \'in,fēld\ *n* : baseball field inside the base lines —**in·field·er** *n*

in·fil·trate \in'fil,trāt, 'infil-\ *vb* -**trat·ed;** -**trat·ing** : enter or become established in without being noticed —**in·fil·tra·tion** \,infil'trāshən\ *n*

in·fi·nite \'infənət\ *adj* 1 : having no limit or extending indefinitely 2 : vast —**infinite** *n* —**in·fi·nite·ly** *adv* —**in·fi·ni·tude** \in'finə,tüd, -tyüd\ *n*

in·fin·i·tes·i·mal \in,finə'tesəməl\ *adj* : immeasurably small —**in·fin·i·tes·i·mal·ly** *adv*

in·fin·i·tive \in'finətiv\ *n* : verb form in English usu. used with *to*

in·fin·i·ty \in'finətē\ *n, pl* -**ties** 1 : quality or state of being infinite 2 : indefinitely great number or amount

in·firm \in'fərm\ *adj* : feeble from age —**in·fir·mi·ty** \-'fərmətē\ *n*

in·fir·ma·ry \in'fərmərē\ *n, pl* -**ries** : place for the care of the sick

in·flame \in'flām\ *vb* -**flamed;** -**flam·ing** 1 : excite to intense action or feeling 2 : affect or become affected with inflammation —**in·flam·ma·to·ry** \-'flamə,tōrē\ *adj*

in·flam·ma·ble \in'flaməbəl\ *adj* : flammable

in·flam·ma·tion \,inflə'māshən\ *n* : response to injury in which an affected area becomes red and painful and congested with blood

in·flate \in'flāt\ *vb* -**flat·ed;** -**flat·ing** 1 : swell or puff up (as with gas) 2 : expand or increase abnormally —**in·flat·able** *adj*

in·fla·tion \in'flāshən\ *n* 1 : act of inflating 2 : continual rise in prices —**in·fla·tion·ary** \-shə,nerē\ *adj*

in·flec·tion \in'flekshən\ *n* 1 : change in pitch or loudness of the voice 2 : change in form of a word —**in·flect** \-'flekt\ *vb* —**in·flec·tion·al** \-'flekshənəl\ *adj*

in·flict \in'flikt\ *vb* : give by or as if by hitting —**in·flic·tion** \-'flikshən\ *n*

in·flu·ence \'in,flüəns\ *n* 1 : power or capacity of causing an effect in indirect or intangible ways 2 : one that exerts influence ~ *vb* -**enced;** -**enc·ing** : affect or alter by influence —**in·flu·en·tial** \influ-'enchəl\ *adj*

in·flu·en·za \,inflü'enzə\ *n* : acute very contagious virus disease

in·flux \'in,fləks\ *n* : a flowing in

in·form \in'fôrm\ *vb* : give information or knowledge to —**in·for·mant** \-ənt\ *n* —**in·form·er** *n*

in·for·mal \in'fôrməl\ *adj* 1 : without formality or ceremony 2 : for ordinary or familiar use —**in·for·mal·i·ty** \infôr-'malətē, -fər-\ *n* —**in·for·mal·ly** *adv*

in·for·ma·tion \,infər'māshən\ *n* : knowledge obtained from investigation, study, or instruction —**in·for·ma·tion·al** \-shə-nəl\ *adj*

in·for·ma·tive \in'fôrmətiv\ *adj* : giving knowledge

in·frac·tion \in'frakshən\ *n* : violation

in·fra·red \infrə'red\ *adj* : being, relating to, or using radiation of wavelengths longer than those of red light —**infrared** *n*

in·fra·struc·ture \'infrə,strəkchər\ *n* : foundation of a system or organization

in·fringe \in'frinj\ *vb* -**fringed;** -**fring·ing** : violate another's right or privilege —**in·fringe·ment** *n*

in·fu·ri·ate \in'fyůrē,āt\ *vb* -**at·ed;** -**at·ing** : make furious —**in·fu·ri·at·ing·ly** \-,ātiŋlē\ *adv*

in·fuse \in'fyüz\ *vb* -**fused;** -**fus·ing** 1 : instill a principle or quality in 2 : steep in liquid without boiling —**in·fu·sion** \-'fyüzhən\ *n*

¹**-ing** \iŋ\ *vb suffix or adj suffix* —used to form the present participle and sometimes an adjective resembling a present participle

²**-ing** *n suffix* 1 : action or process 2 : something connected with or resulting from an action or process

in·ge·nious \in'jēnyəs\ *adj* : very clever —**in·ge·nious·ly** *adv* —**in·ge·nious·ness** *n*

in·ge·nue, in·gé·nue \'anjə,nü, 'än-; 'an, zhə-, 'änn-\ *n* : naive young woman

in·ge·nu·i·ty \injə'nüətē, -'nyü-\ *n, pl* -**ties** : skill or cleverness in planning or inventing

in·gen·u·ous \in'jenyəwəs\ *adj* : innocent and candid —**in·gen·u·ous·ly** *adv* —**in·gen·u·ous·ness** *n*

in·gest \in'jest\ *vb* : eat —**in·ges·tion** \-'jeschən\ *n*

in·gle·nook \'iŋgəl,nůk\ *n* : corner by the fireplace

in·got \'iŋgət\ *n* : block of metal

in·grained \in'grānd\ *adj* : deep-seated

in·grate \in,grāt\ *n* : ungrateful person

in·gra·ti·ate \in'grāshē,āt\ *vb* -**at·ed;** -**at·ing** : gain favor for (oneself) —**in·gra·ti·at·ing** *adj*

in·gre·di·ent \in'grēdēənt\ *n* : one of the substances that make up a mixture

in·grown \'in,grōn\ *adj* : grown in and esp. into the flesh

in·hab·it \in'habət\ *vb* : live or dwell in —**in·hab·it·able** *adj* —**in·hab·it·ant** \-ətənt\ *n*

in·hale \in'hāl\ *vb* -**haled;** -**hal·ing** : breathe in —**in·hal·ant** \-ənt\ *n* —**in·ha·la·tion** \inhə'lāshən, inə-\ *n* —**in·hal·er** *n*

in·here \in'hir\ *vb* -**hered;** -**her·ing** : be inherent

in·her·ent \in'hirənt, -'her-\ *adj* : being an essential part of something —**in·her·ent·ly** *adv*

in·her·it \in'herət\ *vb* : receive from one's ancestors —**in·her·it·able** \-əbəl\ *adj* —**in·her·i·tance** \-ətəns\ *n* —**in·her·i·tor** \-ətər\ *n*

in·hib·it \in'hibət\ *vb* : hold in check —**in·hi·bi·tion** \inhə'bishən, inə-\ *n*

in·hu·man \in'hyümən, -'yü-\ *adj* : cruel or impersonal —**in·hu·man·i·ty** \-hyü-'manətē, -yü-\ *n* —**in·hu·man·ly** *adv* —**in·hu·man·ness** *n*

in·im·i·cal \in'imikəl\ *adj* : hostile or harmful —**in·im·i·cal·ly** *adv*

in·im·i·ta·ble \in'imətəbəl\ *adj* : not capable of being imitated

in·iq·ui·ty \in'ikwətē\ *n, pl* -**ties** : wickedness —**in·iq·ui·tous** \-wətəs\ *adj*

ini·tial \in'ishəl\ *adj* 1 : of or relating to the beginning 2 : first ~ *n* : 1st letter of a word or name —**in·tialed** *or* -**tialled;** -**tial·ing** *or* -**tial·ling** : put initials on —**ini·tial·ly** *adv*

ini·ti·ate \in'ishē,āt\ *vb* -**at·ed;** -**at·ing** 1 : start 2 : induct into membership 3 : instruct in the rudiments of something —**initiate** \-'isheət\ *n* —**ini·ti·a·tion** \-,ishē'āshən\ *n* —**ini·tia·to·ry** \-'ishēə-,tōrē\ *adj*

ini·tia·tive \in'ishətiv\ *n* 1 : first step 2 : readiness to undertake something on one's own

in·ject \in'jekt\ *vb* : force or introduce into something —**in·jec·tion** \-'jekshən\ *n*

in·junc·tion \in'jəŋkshən\ *n* : court writ requiring one to do or to refrain from doing a specified act

in·jure \'injər\ *vb* -**jured;** -**jur·ing** : do damage, hurt, or a wrong to

in·ju·ry \'injərē\ *n, pl* -**ries** 1 : act that injures 2 : hurt, damage, or loss sustained —**in·ju·ri·ous** \in'jůrēəs\ *adj*

in·jus·tice \in'jəstəs\ *n* : unjust act

ink \'iŋk\ *n* : usu. liquid and colored material for writing and printing ~ *vb* : put ink on —**ink·well** \-,wel\ *n* —**inky** *adj*

in·kling \'iŋkliŋ\ *n* : hint or idea

in·land \'in,land, -lənd\ *n* : interior of a country —**inland** *adj or adv*

in–law \'in,lò\ *n* : relative by marriage

in·lay \in'lā, 'in,lā\ *vb* -**laid** \-'lād\ -**lay·ing** : set into a surface for decoration ~ \'in-,lā\ *n* 1 : inlaid work 2 : shaped filling cemented into a tooth

in·let \'in,let, -lət\ *n* : small bay

in·mate \'in,māt\ *n* : person confined to an asylum or prison

in me•mo•ri•am \inmə'mōrēəm\ *prep* : in memory of

in•most \'in,mōst\ *adj* : deepest within

inn \'in\ *n* : hotel

in•nards \'inərdz\ *n pl* : internal parts

in•nate \in'āt\ *adj* 1 : inborn 2 : inherent — **in•nate•ly** *adv*

in•ner \'inər\ *adj* : being on the inside

in•ner•most \'inər,mōst\ *adj* : farthest inward

in•ner•sole \inər'sōl\ *n* : insole

in•ning \'iniŋ\ *n* : baseball team's turn at bat

inn•keep•er \'in,kēpər\ *n* : owner of an inn

in•no•cent \'inəsənt\ *adj* 1 : free from guilt 2 : harmless 3 : not sophisticated — **in•no•cence** \-səns\ *n* —**innocent** *n* —**in•no•cent•ly** *adv*

in•noc•u•ous \in'äkyəwəs\ *adj* 1 : harmless 2 : inoffensive

in•no•va•tion \inə'vāshən\ *n* : new idea or method —**in•no•vate** \inə,vāt\ *vb* —**in•no•va•tive** \inə,vātiv\ *adj* —**in•no•va•tor** \-,vātər\ *n*

in•nu•en•do \inyə'wendō\ *n, pl* **-dos** *or* **-does** : insinuation

in•nu•mer•a•ble \in'ümərəbəl, -'yüm-\ *adj* : countless

in•oc•u•late \in'äkyə,lāt\ *vb* **-lat•ed; -lat•ing** : treat with something esp. to establish immunity —**in•oc•u•la•tion** \-,äkyə'lāshən\ *n*

in•op•por•tune \in,äpər'tün, -'tyün\ *adj* : inconvenient —**in•op•por•tune•ly** *adv*

in•or•di•nate \in'ȯrdənət\ *adj* : unusual or excessive —**in•or•di•nate•ly** *adv*

in•or•gan•ic \in,ȯr'ganik\ *adj* : made of mineral matter

in•pa•tient \'in,pāshənt\ *n* : patient who stays in a hospital

in•put \'in,pút\ *n* : something put in —**input** *vb*

in•quest \'in,kwest\ *n* : inquiry esp. before a jury

in•quire \in'kwīr\ *vb* **-quired; -quir•ing** 1 : ask 2 : investigate —**in•quir•er** *n* —**in•quir•ing•ly** *adv* —**in•qui•ry** \in,kwīrē, in'kwīrē; 'inkwərē, 'iŋ-\ *n*

in•qui•si•tion \inkwə'zishən, iŋ-\ *n* 1 : official inquiry 2 : severe questioning —**in•quis•i•tor** \in'kwizətər\ *n* —**in•quis•i•to•ri•al** \-,kwizə'tōrēəl\ *adj*

in•quis•i•tive \in'kwizətiv\ *adj* : curious —**in•quis•i•tive•ly** *adv* —**in•quis•i•tive•ness** *n*

in•road \'in,rōd\ *n* : encroachment

in•rush \'in,rəsh\ *n* : influx

in•sane \in'sān\ *adj* 1 : not sane 2 : absurd —**in•sane•ly** *adv* —**in•san•i•ty** \in'sanətē\ *n*

in•sa•tia•ble \in'sāshəbəl\ *adj* : incapable of being satisfied —**in•sa•tia•bil•i•ty** \in-,sāshə'bilətē\ *n* —**in•sa•tia•bly** *adv*

in•scribe \in'skrīb\ *vb* 1 : write 2 : engrave 3 : dedicate (a book) to someone —**in•scrip•tion** \-'skripshən\ *n*

in•scru•ta•ble \in'skrütəbəl\ *adj* : mysterious —**in•scru•ta•bly** *adv*

in•seam \'in,sēm\ *n* : inner seam (of a garment)

in•sect \'in,sekt\ *n* : small usu. winged animal with 6 legs

in•sec•ti•cide \in'sektə,sīd\ *n* : insect poison —**in•sec•ti•cid•al** \in,sektə'sīdəl\ *adj*

in•se•cure \insi'kyùr\ *adj* 1 : uncertain 2 : unsafe 3 : fearful —**in•se•cure•ly** *adv* —**in•se•cu•ri•ty** \-'kyùrətē\ *n*

in•sem•i•nate \in'semə,nāt\ *vb* **-nat•ed; -nat•ing** : introduce semen into —**in•sem•i•na•tion** \-,semə'nāshən\ *n*

in•sen•si•ble \in'sensəbəl\ *adj* 1 : unconscious 2 : unable to feel 3 : unaware —**in•sen•si•bil•i•ty** \in,sensə'bil-ətē\ *n* —**in•sen•si•bly** *adv*

in•sen•tient \in'senchənt\ *adj* : lacking feeling —**in•sen•tience** \-chəns\ *n*

in•sert \in'sərt\ *vb* : put in —**insert** \'in,sərt\ *n* —**in•ser•tion** \in'sərshən\ *n*

in•set \'in,set\ *vb* **inset** *or* **in•set•ted; in•set•ting** : set in —**inset** *n*

in•shore \in'shōr\ *adj* 1 : situated near shore 2 : moving toward shore ~ *adv* : toward shore

in•side \in'sīd, 'in,sīd\ *n* 1 : inner side 2 *pl* : innards ~ *prep* 1 : in or into the inside of 2 : within ~ *adv* 1 : on the inner side 2 : into the interior —**inside** *adj* —**in•sid•er** \in'sīdər\ *n*

inside of *prep* : inside

in•sid•i•ous \in'sidēəs\ *adj* 1 : treacherous 2 : seductive —**in•sid•i•ous•ly** *adv* —**in•sid•i•ous•ness** *n*

in•sight \'in,sīt\ *n* : understanding —**in•sight•ful** \in,sītfəl, in'sīt-\ *adj*

in•sig•nia \in'signēə\, **in•sig•ne** \-,nē\ *n, pl* **-nia** *or* **-ni•as** : badge of authority or office

in•sin•u•ate \in'sinyə,wāt\ *vb* **-at•ed; -at•ing** 1 : imply 2 : bring in artfully —**in•sin•u•a•tion** \in,sinyə'wāshən\ *n*

in•sip•id \in'sipəd\ *adj* 1 : tasteless 2 : not stimulating —**in•si•pid•i•ty** \,insə'pidətē\ *n*

in•sist \in'sist\ *vb* : be firmly demanding —

in•sis•tence \in'sistəns\ *n* —**in•sis•tent** \-tənt\ *adj* —**in•sis•tent•ly** *adv*

in•so•far as \insō'färəz\ *conj* : to the extent that

in•sole \'in,sōl\ *n* : inside sole of a shoe

in•so•lent \'insələnt\ *adj* : contemptuously rude —**in•so•lence** \-ləns\ *n*

in•sol•vent \in'sälvənt\ *adj* : unable or insufficient to pay debts —**in•sol•ven•cy** \-vənsē\ *n*

in•som•nia \in'sämnēə\ *n* : inability to sleep

in•so•much as \insō'məchaz\ *conj* : inasmuch as

insomuch that *conj* : to such a degree that

in•sou•ci•ance \in'süsēəns, aⁿsü'syäⁿs\ *n* : lighthearted indifference —**in•sou•ci•ant** \in'süsēənt, aⁿsü'syäⁿ\ *adj*

in•spect \in'spekt\ *vb* : view closely and critically —**in•spec•tion** \-'spekshən\ *n* —**in•spec•tor** \-tər\ *n*

in•spire \in'spīr\ *vb* **-spired; -spir•ing** 1 : inhale 2 : influence by example 3 : bring about 4 : stir to action —**in•spi•ra•tion** \inspə'rāshən\ *n* —**in•spi•ra•tion•al** \-'rāshənəl\ *adj* —**in•spir•er** *n*

in•stall, in•stal \in'stȯl\ *vb* **-stalled; -stall•ing** 1 : induct into office 2 : set up for use —**in•stal•la•tion** \instə'lāshən\ *n*

in•stall•ment \in'stȯlmənt\ *n* : partial payment

in•stance \'instəns\ *n* 1 : request or instigation 2 : example

in•stant \'instənt\ *n* : moment ~ *adj* 1 : immediate 2 : ready to mix —**in•stan•ta•neous** \instən'tānēəs\ *adj* —**in•stan•ta•neous•ly** *adv* —**in•stant•ly** *adv*

in•stead \in'sted\ *adv* : as a substitute or alternative

instead of *prep* : as a substitute for or alternative to

in•step \'in,step\ *n* : part of the foot in front of the ankle

in•sti•gate \'instə,gāt\ *vb* **-gat•ed; -gat•ing** : incite —**in•sti•ga•tion** \instə'gāshən\ *n* —**in•sti•ga•tor** \'instə,gātər\ *n*

in•still \in'stil\ *vb* **-stilled; -still•ing** : impart gradually

in•stinct \'in,stiŋkt\ *n* 1 : natural talent 2 : natural inherited or subconsciously motivated behavior —**in•stinc•tive** \in'stiŋktiv\ *adj* —**in•stinc•tive•ly** *adv* —**in•stinc•tu•al** \in'stiŋkchəwəl\ *adj*

in•sti•tute \'instə,tüt, -,tyüt\ *vb* **-tut•ed; -tut•ing** : establish, start, or organize ~ *n* 1 : organization promoting a cause 2 : school

in•sti•tu•tion \instə'tüshən, -'tyü-\ *n* 1 : act of instituting 2 : custom 3 : corporation or society of a public character —**in•sti•tu•tion•al** \-shənəl\ *adj* —**in•sti•tu•tion•al•ize** \-,īz\ *vb* —**in•sti•tu•tion•al•ly** *adv*

in•struct \in'strəkt\ *vb* 1 : teach 2 : give an order to —**in•struc•tion** \in'strəkshən\ *n* —**in•struc•tion•al** \-shənəl\ *adj* —**in•struc•tive** \in'strəktiv\ *adj* —**in•struc•tor** \in'strəktər\ *n* —**in•struc•tor•ship** *n*

in•stru•ment \'instrəmənt\ *n* 1 : something that produces music 2 : means 3 : device for doing work and esp. precision work 4 : legal document —**in•stru•men•tal** \instrə'mentᵊl\ *adj* —**in•stru•men•tal•ist** \-ist\ *n* —**in•stru•men•tal•i•ty** \instrə-mən'talətē, -,men-\ *n* —**in•stru•men•ta•tion** \instrəmən'tāshən, -,men-\ *n*

in•sub•or•di•nate \insə'bȯrdᵊnət\ *adj* : not obeying —**in•sub•or•di•na•tion** \-,bȯr-dᵊn'āshən\ *n*

in•suf•fer•able \in'səfərəbəl\ *adj* : unbearable —**in•suf•fer•ably** \-blē\ *adv*

in•su•lar \'insülər, -syü-\ *adj* 1 : relating to or residing on an island 2 : narrowminded —**in•su•lar•i•ty** \,insü'larətē, -syü-\ *n*

in•su•late \'insə,lāt\ *vb* **-lat•ed; -lat•ing** : protect from heat loss or electricity —**in•su•la•tion** \insə'lāshən\ *n* —**in•su•la•tor** \'insə,lātər\ *n*

in•su•lin \'insələn\ *n* : hormone used by diabetics

in•sult \in'səlt\ *vb* : treat with contempt ~ \'in,səlt\ *n* : insulting act or remark —**in•sult•ing•ly** \-iŋlē\ *adv*

in•su•per•a•ble \in'süpərəbəl\ *adj* : too difficult —**in•su•per•a•bly** \-blē\ *adv*

in•sure \in'shùr\ *vb* **-sured; -sur•ing** 1 : guarantee against loss 2 : make certain —**in•sur•able** \-əbəl\ *adj* —**in•sur•ance** \-əns\ *n* —**in•sured** \in'shùrd\ *n* —**in•sur•er** *n*

in•sur•gent \in'sərjənt\ *n* : rebel —**in•sur•gence** \-jəns\ *n* —**in•sur•gen•cy** \-jənsē\ *n* —**in•sur•gent** *adj*

in•sur•mount•able \insər'maùntəbəl\ *adj* : too great to be overcome —**in•sur•mount•ably** \-blē\ *adv*

in•sur•rec•tion \insə'rekshən\ *n* : revolution —**in•sur•rec•tion•ist** *n*

in•tact \in'takt\ *adj* : undamaged

in•take \'in,tāk\ *n* 1 : opening through which something enters 2 : act of taking in 3 : amount taken in

in•te•ger \'intijər\ *n* : number that is not a fraction and does not include a fraction

in•te•gral \'intigrəl\ *adj* : essential

in•te•grate \'intə,grāt\ *vb* **-grat•ed; -grat•ing** 1 : unite 2 : end segregation of or at —**in•te•gra•tion** \intə'grāshən\ *n*

in•teg•ri•ty \in'tegrətē\ *n* 1 : soundness 2 : adherence to a code of values 3 : completeness

in•tel•lect \'intᵊl,ekt\ *n* : power of knowing or thinking —**in•tel•lec•tu•al** \intᵊl'ek-chəwəl\ *adj or n* —**in•tel•lec•tu•al•ism** \-chəwə,lizəm\ *n* —**in•tel•lec•tu•al•ly** *adv*

in•tel•li•gence \in'teləjəns\ *n* 1 : ability to learn and understand 2 : mental acuteness 3 : information

in•tel•li•gent \in'teləjənt\ *adj* : having or showing intelligence —**in•tel•li•gent•ly** *adv*

in•tel•li•gi•ble \in'teləjəbəl\ *adj* : understandable —**in•tel•li•gi•bil•i•ty** \-,teləjə'bilətē\ *n* —**in•tel•li•gi•bly** *adv*

in•tem•per•ance \in'tempərəns\ *n* : lack of moderation —**in•tem•per•ate** \-pərət\ *adj* —**in•tem•per•ate•ness** *n*

in•tend \in'tend\ *vb* : have as a purpose

in•tend•ed \in'tendəd\ *n* : engaged person —**intended** *adj*

in•tense \in'tens\ *adj* 1 : extreme 2 : deeply felt —**in•tense•ly** *adv* —**inten•si•fi•ca•tion** \-,tensəfə'kāshən\ *n* —**in•ten•si•fy** \-'tensə,fī\ *vb* —**in•ten•si•ty** \in'tensətē\ *n* —**in•ten•sive** \in'tensiv\ *adj* —**in•ten•sive•ly** *adv*

¹in•tent \in'tent\ *n* : purpose —**in•ten•tion** \-'tenchən\ *n* —**in•ten•tion•al** \-'ten-chənəl\ *adj* —**in•ten•tion•al•ly** *adv*

²intent *adj* : concentrated —**in•tent•ly** *adv* —**in•tent•ness** *n*

in•ter \in'tər\ *vb* **-rr-** : bury

inter- *prefix* : between or among

interagency	interinstitutional
interatomic	interisland
interbank	interlibrary
interborough	intermolecular
intercampus	intermountain
interchurch	interoceanic
intercity	interoffice
interclass	interparticle
intercoastal	interparty
intercollegiate	interpersonal
intercolonial	interplanetary
intercommunal	interpopulation
intercommunity	interprovincial
intercompany	interracial
intercontinental	interregional
intercounty	interreligious
intercultural	interscholastic
interdenomina-tional	intersectional
	interstate
interdepartmental	interstellar
interdivisional	intersystem
interelectronic	interterm
interethnic	interterminal
interfaculty	intertribal
interfamily	intertroop
interfiber	intertropical
interfraternity	interuniversity
intergalactic	interurban
intergang	intervalley
intergovernmen-tal	intervillage
	interwar
intergroup	interzonal
interhemispheric	interzone
interindustry	

in•ter•ac•tion \intər'akshən\ *n* : mutual influence —**in•ter•act** \-'akt\ *vb* —**in•ter•ac•tive** *adj*

in•ter•breed \intər'brēd\ *vb* **-bred** \-'bred\; **-breed•ing** : breed together

in•ter•ca•late \in'tərkə,lāt\ *vb* **-lat•ed; -lat•ing** : insert —**in•ter•ca•la•tion** \-,tərkə'lāshən\ *n*

in•ter•cede \intər'sēd\ *vb* **-ced•ed; -ced•ing** : act to reconcile —**in•ter•ces•sion** \-'seshən\ *n* —**in•ter•ces•sor** \-'sesər\ *n*

in•ter•cept \intər'sept\ *vb* : interrupt the progress of —**intercept** \'intər,sept\ *n* —**in•ter•cep•tion** \intər'sepshən\ *n* —**in•ter•cep•tor** \-'septər\ *n*

in•ter•change \intər'chānj\ *vb* 1 : exchange 2 : change places ~ \'intər,chānj\ *n* 1 : exchange 2 : junction of highways —**in•ter•change•able** \intər'chānjəbəl\ *adj*

in•ter•course \'intər,kōrs\ *n* 1 : relations between persons or nations 2 : copulation

in•ter•de•pen•dent \intərdi'pendənt\ *adj* : mutually dependent —**in•ter•de•pen•dence** \-dəns\ *n*

in•ter•dict \intər'dikt\ *vb* 1 : prohibit 2 : destroy or cut (an enemy supply line) —**in•ter•dic•tion** \-'dikshən\ *n*

in•ter•est \'intrəst, -tə,rest\ *n* 1 : right 2 : benefit 3 : charge for borrowed money 4 : readiness to pay special attention 5 : quality that causes interest ~ *vb* 1 : concern 2 : get the attention of —**in•ter•est•ing** *adj* —**in•ter•est•ing•ly** *adv*

in•ter•face \'intər,fās\ *n* : common boundary —**in•ter•fa•cial** \,intər'fāshəl\ *adj*

in•ter•fere \intər'fir\ *vb* **-fered; -fer•ing** 1 : collide or be in opposition 2 : try to run

the affairs of others —**in•ter•fer•ence** \-'firəns\ *n*

in•ter•im \'intərəm\ *n* : time between —**interim** *adj*

in•te•ri•or \in'tirēər\ *adj* : being on the inside ~ *n* 1 : inside 2 : inland area

in•ter•ject \intər'jekt\ *vb* : stick in between

in•ter•jec•tion \-'jekshən\ *n* : an exclamatory word —**in•ter•jec•tion•al•ly** \-shənᵊlē\ *adv*

in•ter•lace \intər'lās\ *vb* : cross or cause to cross one over another

in•ter•lin•ear \intər'linēər\ *adj* : between written or printed lines

in•ter•lock \intər'läk\ *vb* 1 : interlace 2 : connect for mutual effect —**inter•lock** \'intər,läk\ *n*

in•ter•lop•er \intər'lōpər\ *n* : intruder or meddler

in•ter•lude \'intər,lüd\ *n* : intervening period

in•ter•mar•ry \intər'marē\ *vb* 1 : marry each other 2 : marry within a group —**in•ter•mar•riage** \-'marij\ *n*

in•ter•me•di•ary \intər'mēdē,erē\ *n, pl* **-ar•ies** : agent between individuals or groups —**intermediary** *adj*

in•ter•me•di•ate \intər'mēdēət\ *adj* : between extremes —**intermediate** *n*

in•ter•ment \in'tərmənt\ *n* : burial

in•ter•mi•na•ble \in'tərmənəbəl\ *adj* : endless —**in•ter•mi•na•bly** *adv*

in•ter•min•gle \intər'miŋgəl\ *vb* : mingle

in•ter•mis•sion \intər'mishən\ *n* : break in a performance

in•ter•mit•tent \-'mitᵊnt\ *adj* : coming at intervals —**in•ter•mit•tent•ly** *adv*

in•ter•mix \intər'miks\ *vb* : mix together —**in•ter•mix•ture** \-'mikschər\ *n*

¹in•tern \'in,tərn, in'tərn\ *vb* : confine esp. during a war —**in•tern•ee** \in,tər'nē\ *n* —**in•tern•ment** *n*

²in•tern \'in,tərn\ *n* : advanced student (as in medicine) gaining supervised experience ~ *vb* : act as an intern —**in•tern•ship** *n*

in•ter•nal \in'tərnᵊl\ *adj* 1 : inward 2 : inside of the body 3 : relating to or existing in the mind —**in•ter•nal•ly** *adv*

in•ter•na•tion•al \intər'nashənᵊl\ *adj* : affecting 2 or more nations ~ *n* : something having international scope —**in•ter•na•tion•al•ism** \-,izəm\ *n* —**in•ter•na•tion•al•ize** \-,īz\ *vb* —**in•ter•na•tion•al•ly** *adv*

in•ter•nist \'in,tərnist\ *n* : specialist in nonsurgical medicine

in•ter•play \'intər,plā\ *n* : interaction

in•ter•po•late \in'tərpə,lāt\ *vb* **-lat•ed; -lat•ing** : insert —**in•ter•po•la•tion** \-,tərpə'lāshən\ *n*

in•ter•pose \intər'pōz\ *vb* **-posed; -pos•ing** 1 : place between 2 : intrude —**in•ter•po•si•tion** \-pə'zishən\ *n*

in•ter•pret \in'tərprət\ *vb* : explain the meaning of —**in•ter•pre•ta•tion** \-,tərprə'tāshən\ *n* —**in•ter•pre•ta•tive** \-'tərprə,tātiv\ *adj* —**in•ter•pret•er** *n* —**in•ter•pre•tive** \-'tərprətiv\ *adj*

in•ter•re•late \intəri'lāt\ *vb* : have a mutual relationship —**in•ter•re•lat•ed•ness** \-'lātədnəs\ *n* —**in•ter•re•la•tion** \-'lā-shən\ *n* —**in•ter•re•la•tion•ship** *n*

in•ter•ro•gate \in'terə,gāt\ *vb* **-gat•ed; -gat•ing** : question —**in•ter•ro•ga•tion** \-,terə'gāshən\ *n* —**in•ter•rog•a•tive** \,intə'rägətiv\ *adj or n* —**in•ter•ro•ga•tor** \-'terə,gātər\ *n* —**in•ter•rog•a•to•ry** \,intə'rägə,tōrē\ *adj*

in•ter•rupt \intə'rəpt\ *vb* : intrude so as to hinder or end continuity —**in•ter•rupt•er** *n* —**in•ter•rup•tion** \-'rəpshən\ *n* —**in•ter•rup•tive** \-'rəptiv\ *adj*

in•ter•sect \intər'sekt\ *vb* 1 : cut across or divide 2 : cross —**in•ter•sec•tion** \-'sekshən\ *n*

in•ter•sperse \intər'spərs\ *vb* **-spersed; -spers•ing** : insert at intervals —**in•ter•sper•sion** \-'spərzhən\ *n*

in•ter•stice \in'tərstəs\ *n, pl* **-stic•es** \-stə,sēz, -stəsəz\ : space between —**in•ter•sti•tial** \intər'stishəl\ *adj*

in•ter•twine \intər'twīn\ *vb* : twist together —**in•ter•twine•ment** *n*

in•ter•val \'intərvəl\ *n* 1 : time between 2 : space between

in•ter•vene \intər'vēn\ *vb* **-vened; -ven•ing** 1 : happen between events 2 : intercede —**in•ter•ven•tion** \-'venchən\ *n*

in•ter•view \'intər,vyü\ *n* : a meeting to get information —**interview** *vb* —**in•ter•view•er** *n*

in•ter•weave \intər'wēv\ *vb* **-wove** \-'wōv\; **-wo•ven** \-'wōvən\; **-weav•ing** : weave together —**in•ter•wo•ven** \-'wōvən\ *adj*

in•tes•tate \in'tes,tāt, -tət\ *adj* : not leaving a will

in•tes•tine \in'testən\ *n* : tubular part of the digestive system after the stomach including a long narrow upper part (**small intestine**) followed by a broader shorter lower part (**large intestine**) —**in•tes•ti•nal** \-tənᵊl\ *adj*

in•ti•mate \'intə,māt\ *vb* **-mat•ed; -mat•ing** : hint ~ \'intəmət\ *adj* **1** : very friendly **2** : suggesting privacy **3** : very personal ~ *n* : close friend **—in•ti•ma•cy** \'intəməsē\ *n* **—in•ti•mate•ly** *adv* **—in•ti•ma•tion** \,intə'māshən\ *n*

in•tim•i•date \in'timə,dāt\ *vb* **-dat•ed; -dat•ing** : make fearful **—in•tim•i•da•tion** \-,timə'dāshən\ *n*

in•to \intü\ *prep* **1** : to the inside of **2** : to the condition of **3** : against

in•to•na•tion \,intō'nāshən\ *n* : way of singing or speaking

in•tone \in'tōn\ *vb* **-toned; -ton•ing** : chant

in•tox•i•cate \in'täksə,kāt\ *vb* **-cat•ed; -cat•ing** : make drunk **—in•tox•i•cant** \-sikənt\ *n or adj* **—in•tox•i•ca•tion** \-,täksə'kāshən\ *n*

in•tra•mu•ral \,intrə'myürəl\ *adj* : within a school

in•tran•si•gent \in'transəjənt\ *adj* : uncompromising **—in•tran•si•gence** \-jəns\ *n* **—intransigent** *n*

in•tra•ve•nous \,intrə'vēnəs\ *adj* : by way of the veins **—in•tra•ve•nous•ly** *adv*

in•trep•id \in'trepəd\ *adj* : fearless **—in•tre•pid•i•ty** \,intrə'pidətē\ *n*

in•tri•cate \'intrikət\ *adj* : very complex and delicate **—in•tri•ca•cy** \-trikəsē\ *n* **—in•tri•cate•ly** *adv*

in•trigue \in'trēg\ *vb* **-trigued; -trigu•ing 1** : scheme **2** : arouse curiosity of ~ *n* **1** : secret scheme **—in•trigu•ing•ly** \-iŋlē\ *adv*

in•trin•sic \in'trinzik, -sik\ *adj* : essential **—in•trin•si•cal•ly** \-ziklē, -si-\ *adv*

in•tro•duce \,intrə'düs, -'dyüs\ *vb* **-duced; -duc•ing 1** : bring in esp. for the 1st time **2** : cause to be acquainted **3** : bring to notice **4** : put in **—in•tro•duc•tion** \'dəkshən\ *n* **—in•tro•duc•to•ry** \-'dəktərē\ *adj*

in•tro•spec•tion \,intrə'spekshən\ *n* : examination of one's own thoughts or feelings **—in•tro•spec•tive** \-'spektiv\ *adj* **—in•tro•spec•tive•ly** *adv*

in•tro•vert \'intrə,vərt\ *n* : shy or reserved person **—in•tro•ver•sion** \,intrə'vərzhən\ *n* **—introvert** *adj* **—in•tro•vert•ed** \'intrə,vərtəd\ *adj*

in•trude \in'trüd\ *vb* **-trud•ed; -trud•ing 1** : thrust in **2** : encroach **—in•trud•er** *n* **—in•tru•sion** \-'trüzhən\ *n* **—in•tru•sive** \-'trüsiv\ *adj* **—in•tru•sive•ness** *n*

in•tu•ition \,intü'ishən, -tyü-\ *n* : quick and ready insight **—in•tu•it** \in'tüət, -'tyü-\ *vb* **—in•tu•i•tive** \-ətiv\ *adj* **—in•tu•i•tive•ly** *adv*

in•un•date \'inən,dāt\ *vb* **-dat•ed; -dat•ing** : flood **—in•un•da•tion** \inən'dāshən\ *n*

in•ure \in'ür, -'yür\ *vb* **-ured; -ur•ing** : accustom to accept something undesirable

in•vade \in'vād\ *vb* **-vad•ed; -vad•ing** : enter for conquest **—in•vad•er** *n* **—in•va•sion** \-'vāzhən\ *n*

¹in•val•id \'ärk\ *adj* : not true or legal **—in•va•lid•i•ty** \,invə'lidətē\ *n* **—in•val•id•ly** *adv*

²in•va•lid \'invələd\ *adj* : sickly ~ *n* : one chronically ill

in•val•i•date \in'valə,dāt\ *vb* : make invalid **—in•val•i•da•tion** \in,valə'dāshən\ *n*

in•valu•able \in'valyəwəbəl\ *adj* : extremely valuable

in•va•sive \in'vāsiv\ *adj* : involving entry into the body

in•vec•tive \in'vektiv\ *n* : abusive language **—invective** *adj*

in•veigh \in'vā\ *vb* : protest or complain forcefully

in•vei•gle \in'vāgəl, -'vē-\ *vb* **-gled; -gling** : win over or get by flattery

in•vent \in'vent\ *vb* **1** : think up **2** : create for the 1st time **—in•ven•tion** \-'venchən\ *n* **—in•ven•tive** \-'ventiv\ *adj* **—in•ven•tive•ness** *n* **—in•ven•tor** \-'ventər\ *n*

in•ven•to•ry \'invən,tōrē\ *n, pl* **-ries 1** : list of goods **2** : stock **—inventory** *vb*

in•verse \in'vərs, 'in,vərs\ *adj or n* : opposite **—in•verse•ly** *adv*

in•vert \in'vərt\ *vb* **1** : turn upside down or inside out **2** : reverse **—in•ver•sion** \-'vərzhən\ *n*

in•ver•te•brate \in'vərtəbrət, -,brāt\ *adj* : lacking a backbone ~ *n* : invertebrate animal

in•vest \in'vest\ *vb* **1** : give power or authority to **2** : endow with a quality **3** : commit money to someone else's use in hope of profit **—in•vest•ment** \-mənt\ *n* **—in•ves•tor** \-'vestər\ *n*

in•ves•ti•gate \in'vestə,gāt\ *vb* **-gat•ed; -gat•ing** : study closely and systematically **—in•ves•ti•ga•tion** \-,vestə'gāshən\ *n* **—in•ves•ti•ga•tive** \-'vestə,gātiv\ *adj* **—in•ves•ti•ga•tor** \-'vestə,gātər\ *n*

in•ves•ti•ture \in'vestə,chür, -chər\ *n* : act of establishing in office

in•vet•er•ate \in'vetərət\ *adj* : acting out of habit

in•vid•i•ous \in'vidēəs\ *adj* : harmful or obnoxious **—in•vid•i•ous•ly** *adv*

in•vig•o•rate \in'vigə,rāt\ *vb* **-rat•ed; -rat•ing** : give life and energy to **—in•vig•o•ra•tion** \-,vigə'rāshən\ *n*

in•vin•ci•ble \in'vinsəbəl\ *adj* : incapable of being conquered **—in•vin•ci•bil•i•ty** \-,vinsə'bilətē\ *n* **—in•vin•ci•bly** \in'vinsəblē\ *adv*

in•vi•o•la•ble \in'vīələbəl\ *adj* : safe from violation or desecration **—in•vi•o•la•bil•i•ty** \in,vīələ'bilətē\ *n*

in•vi•o•late \in'vīələt\ *adj* : not violated or profaned

in•vite \in'vīt\ *vb* **-vit•ed; -vit•ing 1** : entice **2** : increase the likelihood of **3** : request the presence or participation of **4** : encourage **—in•vi•ta•tion** \invə'tāshən\ *n* **—in•vit•ing** \in'vītiŋ\ *adj*

in•vo•ca•tion \,invə'kāshən\ *n* **1** : prayer **2** : incantation

in•voice \'in,vòis\ *n* **1** : itemized bill for goods shipped ~ *vb* **-voiced; -voic•ing** : bill

in•voke \in'vōk\ *vb* **-voked; -vok•ing 1** : call on for help **2** : cite as authority **3** : conjure **4** : carry out

in•volve \in'välv\ *vb* **-volved; -volv•ing 1** : draw in as a participant **2** : relate closely **3** : require as a necessary part **4** : occupy fully **—in•volve•ment** *n*

in•volved \-'välvd\ *adj* : intricate

¹in•ward \'inwərd\ *adj* : inside

²inward, in•wards \-wərdz\ *adv* : toward the inside, center, or inner being

in•ward•ly *adv* **1** : mentally or spiritually **2** : internally **3** : to oneself

io•dide \'ī,ə,dīd\ *n* : compound of iodine

io•dine \'ī,ə,dīn, -əd⁰n\ *n* **1** : nonmetallic chemical element **2** : solution of iodine used as an antiseptic

io•dize \'ī,ə,dīz\ *vb* **-dized; -diz•ing** : treat with iodine or an iodide

ion \'ī,ən, 'ī,än\ *n* : electrically charged particle **—ion•ic** \ī'änik\ *adj* **—ion•iz•able** \'ī,ə,nīzəbəl\ *adj* **—ion•iza•tion** \,ī,ə,nə-'zāshən\ *n* **—ion•ize** \'ī,ə,nīz\ *vb* **—ion•iz•er** \'ī,ə,nīzər\ *n*

-ion *n suffix* **1** : act or process **2** : state or condition

ion•o•sphere \ī'änə,sfir\ *n* : layer of the upper atmosphere containing ionized gases **—ion•o•spher•ic** \ī,änə'sfirik, -'sfer-\ *adj*

io•ta \ī'ōtə\ *n* : small quantity

IOU \,ī,ō'yü\ *n* : acknowledgment of a debt

iras•ci•ble \ir'asəbəl, ī'ras-\ *adj* : marked by hot temper **—iras•ci•bil•i•ty** \-,asə'bilətē, -,ras-\ *n*

irate \ī'rāt\ *adj* : roused to intense anger **—irate•ly** *adv*

ire \'īr\ *n* : anger

ir•i•des•cence \,irə'des⁰ns\ *n* : rainbowlike play of colors **—ir•i•des•cent** \-⁰nt\ *adj*

iris \'īrəs\ *n, pl* **iris•es** *or* **iri•des** \'īrə,dēz, 'ir-\ **1** : colored part around the pupil of the eye **2** : plant with long leaves and large showy flowers

irk \'ərk\ *vb* : annoy **—irk•some** \-səm\ *adj* **—irk•some•ly** *adv*

iron \'īərn\ *n* **1** : heavy metallic chemical element **2** : something made of iron **3** : heated device for pressing clothes **4** : hardness, determination ~ *vb* : press or smooth out with an iron **—iron•ware** *n* **—iron•work** *n* **—iron•work•er** *n* **—iron•works** *n pl*

iron•clad \-'klad\ *adj* **1** : sheathed in iron armor **2** : strict or exacting

iron•ing \'īərniŋ\ *n* : clothes to be ironed

iron•wood \-,wud\ *n* : tree or shrub with very hard wood or this wood

iro•ny \'īrənē\ *n, pl* **-nies 1** : use of words to express the opposite of the literal meaning **2** : incongruity between the actual and expected result of events **—iron•ic** \ī'ränik\, **iron•i•cal** \-ikəl\ *adj* **—iron•i•cal•ly** \-iklē\ *adv*

ir•ra•di•ate \ir'ādē,āt\ *vb* **-at•ed; -at•ing** : treat with radiation **—ir•ra•di•a•tion** \-,ādē'āshən\ *n*

ir•ra•tio•nal \ir'ashənəl\ *adj* **1** : incapable of reasoning **2** : not based on reason **—ir•ra•tio•nal•i•ty** \ir,ashə'nalətē\ *n* **—ir•ra•tio•nal•ly** *adv*

ir•rec•on•cil•able \ir,ekən'sīləbəl\ *adj* : impossible to reconcile **—irrec•on•cil•abil•i•ty** \-,sīlə'bilətē\ *n*

ir•re•cov•er•able \,iri'kəvərəbəl\ *adj* : not capable of being recovered **—ir•re•cov•er•ably** \-blē\ *adv*

ir•re•deem•able \,iri'dēməbəl\ *adj* : not redeemable

ir•re•duc•ible \,iri'düsəbəl, -'dyü-\ *adj* : not reducible **—ir•re•duc•ibly** \-blē\ *adv*

ir•ref•ut•able \,iri'fyütəbəl, ir'refyət-\ *adj* : impossible to refute

ir•reg•u•lar \ir'egyələr\ *adj* : not regular or normal **—irregular** *n* **—ir•reg•u•lar•i•ty** \ir,egyə'larətē\ *n* **—ir•reg•u•lar•ly** *adv*

ir•rel•e•vant \ir'eləvənt\ *adj* : not relevant **—ir•rel•e•vance** \-vəns\ *n*

ir•re•li•gious \,iri'lijəs\ *adj* : not following religious practices

ir•rep•a•ra•ble \ir'epərəbəl\ *adj* : impossible to make good, undo, or remedy

ir•re•place•able \,iri'plāsəbəl\ *adj* : not replaceable

ir•re•press•ible \-'presəbəl\ *adj* : impossible to repress or control

ir•re•proach•able \-'prōchəbəl\ *adj* : blameless

ir•re•sist•ible \-'zistəbəl\ *adj* : impossible to successfully resist **—ir•re•sist•ibly** \-blē\ *adv*

ir•res•o•lute \ir'ezəlüt\ *adj* : uncertain **—ir•res•o•lute•ly** *adv* **—ir•res•o•lu•tion** \-,ezə'lüshən\ *n*

ir•re•spec•tive of \,iri'spektiv-\ *prep* : without regard to

ir•re•spon•si•ble \,iri'spänsəbəl\ *adj* : not responsible **—ir•re•spon•si•bil•i•ty** \-,spänsə'bilətē\ *n* **—ir•re•spon•si•bly** *adv*

ir•re•triev•able \,iri'trēvəbəl\ *adj* : not retrievable

ir•rev•er•ence \ir'evərəns\ *n* **1** : lack of reverence **2** : irreverent act or utterance **—ir•rev•er•ent** \-rənt\ *adj*

ir•re•vers•ible \,iri'vərsəbəl\ *adj* : incapable of being reversed

ir•re•vo•ca•ble \ir'evəkəbəl\ *adj* : incapable of being revoked **—ir•rev•o•ca•bly** \-blē\ *adv*

ir•ri•gate \'irə,gāt\ *vb* **-gat•ed; -gat•ing** : supply with water by artificial means **—ir•ri•ga•tion** \,irə'gāshən\ *n*

ir•ri•tate \'irə,tāt\ *vb* **-tat•ed; -tat•ing 1** : excite to anger **2** : make sore or inflamed **—ir•ri•ta•bil•i•ty** \,irətə'bilətē\ *n* **—ir•ri•ta•ble** \'irətəbəl\ *adj* **—ir•ri•ta•bly** \'irətəblē\ *adv* **—ir•ri•tant** \'irətənt\ *adj or n* **—ir•ri•tat•ing•ly** *adv* **—ir•ri•ta•tion** \,irə'tāshən\ *n*

is *pres 3d sing of* BE

-ish \ish\ *adj suffix* **1** : characteristic of **2** : somewhat

Is•lam \is'läm, iz-, -'lam\ *n* : religious faith of Muslims **—Is•lam•ic** \-ik\ *adj*

is•land \'īlənd\ *n* : body of land surrounded by water **—is•land•er** \'īləndər\ *n*

isle \'īl\ *n* : small island

is•let \'īlət\ *n* : small island

-ism \izəm\ *n suffix* **1** : act or practice **2** : characteristic manner **3** : condition **4** : doctrine

iso•late \'īsə,lāt\ *vb* **-lat•ed; -lat•ing** : place or keep by itself **—iso•la•tion** \,īsə'lāshən\ *n*

iso•met•rics \,īsə'metriks\ *n sing or pl* : exercise against unmoving resistance **—isometric** *adj*

isos•ce•les \ī'säsə,lēz\ *adj* : having 2 equal sides

iso•tope \'īsə,tōp\ *n* : species of atom of a chemical element **—iso•to•pic** \,īsə'täpik, -'tō-\ *adj*

is•sue \'ishü\ *vb* **-sued; -su•ing 1** : go, come, or flow out **2** : descend from a specified ancestor **3** : emanate or result **4** : put forth or distribute officially ~ *n* **1** : action of issuing **2** : offspring **3** : result **4** : point of controversy **5** : act of giving out or printing **6** : quantity given out or printed **—is•su•ance** \'ishəwəns\ *n* **—is•su•er** *n*

-ist \ist\ *n suffix* **1** : one that does **2** : one that plays **3** : one that specializes in **4** : follower of a doctrine

isth•mus \'isməs\ *n* : narrow strip of land connecting 2 larger portions

it \'it\ *pron* **1** : that one —used of a lifeless thing or an abstract entity **2** —used as an anticipatory subject or object ~ *n* : player who tries to catch others (as in a game of tag)

ital•ic \ə'talik, i-, ī-\ *n* : style of type with slanting letters **—italic** *adj* **—ital•i•ciza•tion** \ə,taləsə'zāshən, i-, ī-\ *n* **—ital•i•cize** \ə'talə,sīz, i-, ī-\ *vb*

itch \'ich\ *n* **1** : uneasy irritating skin sensation **2** : skin disorder **3** : persistent desire **—itch** *vb* **—itchy** *adj*

item \'ītəm\ *n* **1** : particular in a list, account, or series **2** : piece of news **—item•iza•tion** \,ītəmə'zāshən\ *n* **—item•ize** \'ītə,mīz\ *vb*

itin•er•ant \ī'tinərənt, ə-\ *adj* : traveling from place to place

itin•er•ary \ī'tinə,rerē, ə-\ *n, pl* **-ar•ies** : route or outline of a journey

its \'its\ *adj* : relating to it

it•self \it'self\ *pron* : it—used reflexively or for emphasis

-ity \ətē\ *n suffix* : quality, state, or degree

-ive \iv\ *adj suffix* : that performs or tends toward an action

ivo•ry \'īvərē\ *n, pl* **-ries 1** : hard creamy-white material of elephants' tusks **2** : pale yellow color

ivy \'īvē\ *n, pl* **ivies** : trailing woody vine with evergreen leaves

-ize \īz\ *vb suffix* **1** : cause to be, become, or resemble **2** : subject to an action **3** : treat or combine with **4** : engage in an activity

J

j \'jā\ *n, pl* **j's** *or* **js** \'jāz\ : 10th letter of the alphabet

jab \'jab\ *vb* **-bb-** : thrust quickly or abruptly ~ *n* : short straight punch

jab•ber \'jabər\ *vb* : talk rapidly or unintelligibly **—jabber** *n*

jack \'jak\ *n* **1** : mechanical device to raise a heavy body **2** : small flag **3** : small 6-pointed metal object used in a game (**jacks**) **4** : electrical socket ~ *vb* **1** : raise with a jack **2** : increase

jack•al \'jakəl, -,ól\ *n* : wild dog

jack•ass *n* **1** : male ass **2** : stupid person

jack•et \'jakət\ *n* : garment for the upper body

jack•ham•mer \'jak,hamər\ *n* : pneumatic tool for drilling

jack•knife \'jak,nīf\ *n* : pocketknife ~ *vb* : fold like a jackknife

jack-o'-lan•tern \'jakə,lantərn\ *n* : lantern made of a carved pumpkin

jack•pot \'jak,pät\ *n* : sum of money won

jack•rab•bit \-,rabət\ *n* : large hare of western No. America

jade \'jād\ *n* : usu. green gemstone

jad•ed \'jādəd\ *adj* : dulled or bored by having too much

jag•ged \'jagəd\ *adj* : sharply notched

jag•uar \'jag,wär, 'jagyə-\ *n* : black-spotted tropical American cat

jai alai \'hī,lī\ *n* : game with a ball propelled by a basket on the hand

jail \'jāl\ *n* : prison **—jail** *vb* **—jail•break** *n* **—jail•er, jail•or** *n*

ja•la•pe•ño \,hälə'pān,yō, -,pēnō\ *n* : Mexican hot pepper

ja•lopy \jə'läpē\ *n, pl* **-lop•ies** : dilapidated vehicle

jal•ou•sie \'jaləsē\ *n* : door or window with louvers

jam \'jam\ *vb* **-mm- 1** : press into a tight position **2** : cause to become wedged and unworkable ~ *n* **1** : crowded mass that blocks or impedes **2** : difficult situation **3** : thick sweet food made of cooked fruit

jamb \'jam\ *n* : upright framing piece of a door

jam•bo•ree \,jambə'rē\ *n* : large festive gathering

jan•gle \'jaŋgəl\ *vb* **-gled; -gling** : make a harsh ringing sound **—jangle** *n*

jan•i•tor \'janətər\ *n* : person who has the care of a building **—jan•i•to•ri•al** \,janə'tōrēəl\ *adj*

Jan•u•ary \'janyə,werē\ *n* : 1st month of the year having 31 days

¹jar \'jär\ *vb* **-rr- 1** : have a harsh or disagreeable effect **2** : vibrate or shake ~ *n* **1** : jolt **2** : painful effect

²jar *n* : wide-mouthed container

jar•gon \'järgən, -,gän\ *n* : special vocabulary of a group

jas•mine \'jazmən\ *n* : climbing shrub with fragrant flowers

jas•per \'jaspər\ *n* : red, yellow, or brown opaque quartz

jaun•dice \'jóndəs\ *n* : yellowish discoloration of skin, tissues, and body fluids

jaun•diced \-dəst\ *adj* : exhibiting envy or hostility

jaunt \'jónt\ *n* : short pleasure trip

jaun•ty \'jóntē\ *adj* **-ti•er; -est** : lively in manner or appearance **—jaun•ti•ly** \'jónt⁰lē\ *adv* **—jaun•ti•ness** *n*

jave•lin \'javələn\ *n* : light spear

jaw \'jó\ *n* **1** : either of the bony or cartilaginous structures that support the mouth **2** : one of 2 movable parts for holding or crushing ~ *vb* : talk indignantly or at length **—jaw•bone** \-,bōn\ *n* **—jawed** \'jód\ *adj*

jay \'jā\ *n* : noisy brightly colored bird

jay•bird *n* : jay

jay•walk *vb* : cross a street carelessly **—jay•walk•er** *n*

jazz \'jaz\ *vb* : enliven ~ *n* **1** : kind of American music involving improvisation **2** : empty talk **—jazzy** *adj*

jeal•ous \'jeləs\ *adj* : suspicious of a rival or of one believed to enjoy an advantage **—jeal•ous•ly** *adv* **—jeal•ou•sy** \-sē\ *n*

jeans \'jēnz\ *n pl* : pants made of durable twilled cotton cloth

jeep \'jēp\ *n* : 4-wheel army vehicle

jeer \'jir\ *vb* **1** : speak or cry out in derision **2** : ridicule ~ *n* : taunt

Je•ho•vah \ji'hōvə\ *n* : God

je•june \ji'jün\ *adj* : dull or childish

jell \'jel\ *vb* **1** : come to the consistency of jelly **2** : take shape

jel•ly \'jelē\ *n, pl* **-lies** : a substance (as food) with a soft somewhat elastic consistency **—jelly** *vb*

jel•ly•fish *n* : sea animal with a saucer-shaped jellylike body

jen·ny \jenē\ n, pl **-nies** : female bird or donkey

jeop·ar·dy \jepərdē\ n : exposure to death, loss, or injury —**jeop·ar·dize** \-ər,dīz\ vb

jerk \jərk\ vb **1** : give a sharp quick push, pull, or twist **2** : move in short abrupt motions ~ n **1** : short quick pull or twist **2** : stupid or foolish person —**jerk·i·ly** adv —**jerky** adj

jer·kin \jərkən\ n : close-fitting sleeveless jacket

jer·ry-built \jerē,bilt\ adj : built cheaply and flimsily

jer·sey \jərzē\ n, pl **-seys** : plain knit fabric **2** : knitted shirt

jest \jest\ n : witty remark —**jest** vb

jest·er \jestər\ n : one employed to entertain a court

¹jet \jet\ n : velvet-black coal used for jewelry

²jet vb **-tt- 1** : spout or emit in a stream **2** : travel by jet ~ n **1** : forceful rush of fluid through a narrow opening **2** : jet-propelled airplane

jet-propelled adj : driven by an engine (**jet engine**) that produces propulsion (**jet propulsion**) by the rearward discharge of a jet of fluid

jet·sam \jetsəm\ n : jettisoned goods

jet·ti·son \jetəsən\ vb **1** : throw (goods) overboard **2** : discard —**jettison** n

jet·ty \jetē\ n, pl **-ties** : pier or wharf

Jew \jü\ n : one whose religion is Judaism —**Jew·ish** adj

jew·el \jüəl\ n **1** : ornament of precious metal **2** : gem ~ vb **-eled** or **-elled**; **-el·ing** or **-el·ling** : adorn with jewels —**jew·el·er, jew·el·ler** \-ər\ n —**jew·el·ry** \-rē\ n

jib \jib\ n : triangular sail

jibe \jīb\ vb **jibed**; **jib·ing** : be in agreement

jif·fy \jifē\ n, pl **-fies** : short time

jig \jig\ n : lively dance ~ vb **-gg-** : dance a jig

jig·ger \jigər\ n : measure used in mixing drinks

jig·gle \jigəl\ vb **-gled**; **-gling** : move with quick little jerks —**jiggle** n

jig·saw n : machine saw with a narrow blade that moves up and down

jilt \jilt\ vb : drop (a lover) unfeelingly

jim·my \jimē\ n, pl **-mies** : small crowbar ~ vb **-mied**; **-my·ing** : pry open

jim·son·weed \jimsən,wēd\ n : coarse poisonous weed

jin·gle \jiŋgəl\ vb **-gled**; **-gling** : make a light tinkling sound ~ n **1** : light tinkling sound **2** : short verse or song

jin·go·ism \jiŋgō,izəm\ n : extreme chauvinism or nationalism —**jin·go·ist** \-ist\ n —**jin·go·is·tic** \,jiŋgō'istik\ adj

jinx \jiŋks\ n : one that brings bad luck —**jinx** vb

jit·ney \jitnē\ n, pl **-neys** : small bus

jit·ters \jitərz\ n pl : extreme nervousness —**jit·tery** \-ərē\ adj

job \jäb\ n **1** : something that has to be done **2** : regular employment —**job·hold·er** n —**job·less** adj

job·ber \jäbər\ n : middleman

jock·ey \jäkē\ n, pl **-eys** : one who rides a horse in a race ~ vb **-eyed**; **-ey·ing** : manipulate or maneuver adroitly

jo·cose \jō'kōs\ adj : jocular

joc·u·lar \jäkyələr\ adj : marked by jesting —**joc·u·lar·i·ty** \,jäkyə'larətē\ n —**joc·u·lar·ly** adv

jo·cund \jäkənd\ adj : full of mirth or gaiety

jodh·purs \jädpərz\ n pl : riding breeches

¹jog \jäg\ vb **-gg- 1** : give a slight shake or push to **2** : run or ride at a slow pace ~ n **1** : slight shake **2** : slow pace —**jog·ger** n

²jog n : brief abrupt change in direction or line

join \join\ vb **1** : come or bring together **2** : become a member of —**join·er** n

joint \joint\ n **1** : point of contact between bones **2** : place where 2 parts connect **3** : often disreputable place ~ adj : common to 2 or more —**joint·ed** adj —**joint·ly** adv

joist \joist\ n : beam supporting a floor or ceiling

joke \jōk\ n : something said or done to provoke laughter ~ vb **joked**; **jok·ing** : make jokes —**jok·er** n —**jok·ing·ly** \jōkiŋlē\ adv

jol·li·ty \jälətē\ n, pl **-ties** : gaiety or merriment

jol·ly \jälē\ adj **-li·er**; **-est** : full of high spirits

jolt \jōlt\ vb **1** : move with a sudden jerky motion **2** : give a jolt to ~ n **1** : abrupt jerky blow or movement **2** : sudden shock —**jolt·er** n

jon·quil \jänkwəl\ n : narcissus with white or yellow flowers

josh \jäsh\ vb : tease or joke

jos·tle \jäsəl\ vb **-tled**; **-tling** : push or shove

jot \jät\ n : least bit ~ vb **-tt-** : write briefly and hurriedly

jounce \jauns\ vb **jounced**; **jounc·ing** : jolt —**jounce** n

jour·nal \jərnᵊl\ n **1** : brief account of daily events **2** : periodical (as a newspaper)

jour·nal·ism \jərnᵊl,izəm\ n : business of reporting or printing news —**jour·nal·ist** \-ist\ n —**jour·nal·is·tic** \,jərnᵊl'istik\ adj

jour·ney \jərnē\ n, pl **-neys** : a going from one place to another ~ vb **-neyed**; **-ney·ing** : make a journey

jour·ney·man \-mən\ n : worker who has learned a trade and works for another person

joust \jaust\ n : combat on horseback between 2 knights with lances —**joust** vb

jo·vial \jōvēəl\ adj : marked by good humor —**jo·vi·al·i·ty** \,jōvē'alətē\ n —**jo·vi·al·ly** \jōvēəlē\ adv

¹jowl \jaul\ n : loose flesh about the lower jaw or throat

²jowl n : lower jaw **2** : cheek

joy \joi\ n **1** : feeling of happiness **2** : source of happiness —**joy** vb —**joy·ful** adj —**joy·ful·ly** adv —**joy·less** adj —**joy·ous** \joiəs\ adj —**joy·ous·ly** adv —**joy·ous·ness** n

joy·ride n : reckless ride for pleasure —**joy·rid·er** n —**joy·rid·ing** n

ju·bi·lant \jübələnt\ adj : expressing great joy —**ju·bi·lant·ly** adv —**ju·bi·la·tion** \,jübə'lāshən\ n

ju·bi·lee \jübə,lē\ n **1** : 50th anniversary **2** : season or occasion of celebration

Ju·da·ism \jüdə,izəm\ n : religion developed among the ancient Hebrews —**Ju·da·ic** \jü'dāik\ adj

judge \jəj\ vb **judged**; **judg·ing 1** : form an opinion **2** : decide as a judge ~ n **1** : public official authorized to decide questions brought before a court **2** : one who gives an authoritative opinion —**judge·ship** n

judg·ment, judge·ment \jəjmənt\ n **1** : decision or opinion given after judging **2** : capacity for judging —**judg·men·tal** \,jəj'mentᵊl\ adj —**judg·men·tal·ly** adv

ju·di·ca·ture \jüdikə,chur\ n : administration of justice

ju·di·cial \jü'dishəl\ adj : relating to judicature or the judiciary —**ju·di·cial·ly** adv

ju·di·cia·ry \jü'dishē,erē, -'dishərē\ n : system of courts of law or the judges of them —**judiciary** adj

ju·di·cious \jü'dishəs\ adj : having or characterized by sound judgment —**ju·di·cious·ly** adv

ju·do \jüdō\ n : form of wrestling —**judo·ist** n

jug \jəg\ n : large deep container with a narrow mouth and a handle

jug·ger·naut \jəgər,not\ n : massive inexorable force or object

jug·gle \jəgəl\ vb **-gled**; **-gling 1** : keep several objects in motion in the air at the same time **2** : manipulate for an often tricky purpose —**jug·gler** \jəglər\ n

jug·u·lar \jəgyələr\ adj : in or on the throat or neck

juice \jüs\ n **1** : extractable fluid contents of cells or tissues **2** : electricity —**juic·er** n —**juic·i·ly** \jüsəlē\ adv —**juic·i·ness** \-sēnəs\ n —**juicy** \jüsē\ adj

ju·jube \jü,jüb, 'jüjü,bē\ n : gummy candy

juke·box \jük,bäks\ n : coin-operated machine for playing music recordings

ju·lep \jüləp\ n : mint-flavored bourbon drink

Ju·ly \jù'lī\ n : 7th month of the year having 31 days

jum·ble \jəmbəl\ vb **-bled**; **-bling** : mix in a confused mass —**jumble** n

jum·bo \jəmbō\ n, pl **-bos** : very large version —**jumbo** adj

jump \jəmp\ vb **1** : rise into or through the air esp. by muscular effort **2** : pass over **3** : give a start **4** : rise or increase sharply ~ n **1** : a jumping **2** : sharp sudden increase **3** : initial advantage

¹jump·er \jəmpər\ n : one that jumps

²jumper n : sleeveless one-piece dress

jumpy \jəmpē\ adj **jump·i·er**; **-est** : nervous or jittery

junc·tion \jəŋkshən\ n **1** : a joining **2** : place or point of meeting

junc·ture \jəŋkchər\ n **1** : joint or connection **2** : critical time or state of affairs

June \jün\ n : 6th month of the year having 30 days

jun·gle \jəŋgəl\ n : thick tangled mass of tropical vegetation

ju·nior \jünyər\ n **1** : person who is younger or of lower rank than another **2** : student in the next-to-last year ~ adj : younger or lower in rank

ju·ni·per \jünəpər\ n : evergreen shrub or tree

¹junk \jəŋk\ n **1** : discarded articles **2** : shoddy product ~ vb : discard or scrap —**junky** adj

²junk n : flat-bottomed ship of Chinese waters

jun·ket \jəŋkət\ n : trip made by an official at public expense

jun·ta \hùntə, 'jəntə, 'həntə\ n : group of persons controlling a government

ju·ris·dic·tion \,jùrəs'dikshən\ n **1** : right or authority to interpret and apply the law **2** : limits within which authority may be exercised —**ju·ris·dic·tion·al** \-shənəl\ adj

ju·ris·pru·dence \-'prüdᵊns\ n **1** : system of laws **2** : science or philosophy of law

ju·rist \jùrist\ n : judge

ju·ror \jùrər\ n : member of a jury

ju·ry \jùrē\ n, pl **-ries** : body of persons sworn to give a verdict on a matter

just \jəst\ adj **1** : reasonable **2** : correct or proper **3** : morally or legally right **4** : deserved ~ adv **1** : exactly **2** : very recently **3** : barely **4** : only **5** : quite **6** : possibly —**just·ly** adv —**just·ness** n

jus·tice \jəstəs\ n **1** : administration of what is just **2** : judge **3** : administration of law **4** : fairness

jus·ti·fy \jəstə,fī\ vb **-fied**; **-fy·ing** : prove to be just, right, or reasonable —**jus·ti·fi·able** adj —**jus·ti·fi·ca·tion** \,jəstəfə'kāshən\ n

jut \jət\ vb **-tt-** : stick out

jute \jüt\ n : strong glossy fiber from a tropical plant

ju·ve·nile \jüvə,nīl, -vənᵊl\ adj : relating to children or young people ~ n : young person

jux·ta·pose \jəkstə,pōz\ vb **-posed**; **-pos·ing** : place side by side —**jux·ta·po·si·tion** \,jəkstəpə'zishən\ n

K

k \kā\ n, pl **k's** or **ks** \kāz\ : 11th letter of the alphabet

kai·ser \kīzər\ n : German ruler

kale \kāl\ n : curly cabbage

ka·lei·do·scope \kə'līdə,skōp\ n : device containing loose bits of colored material reflecting in many patterns —**ka·lei·do·scop·ic** \-,līdə'skäpik\ adj —**ka·lei·do·scop·i·cal·ly** \-iklē\ adv

kan·ga·roo \,kaŋgə'rü\ n, pl **-roos** : large leaping Australian mammal

ka·o·lin \kāələn\ n : fine white clay

kar·at \karət\ n : unit of gold content

ka·ra·te \kə'rätē\ n : art of self-defense by crippling kicks and punches

ka·ty·did \kātē,did\ n : large American grasshopper

kay·ak \kī,ak\ n : Eskimo canoe

ka·zoo \kə'zü\ n, pl **-zoos** : toy musical instrument

keel \kēl\ n : central lengthwise strip on the bottom of a ship —**keeled** \kēld\ adj

keen \kēn\ adj **1** : sharp **2** : severe **3** : enthusiastic **4** : mentally alert —**keen·ly** adv —**keen·ness** n

keep \kēp\ vb **kept**; **keep·ing 1** : perform **2** : guard **3** : maintain **4** : retain in one's possession **5** : detain **6** : continue in good condition **7** : refrain ~ n **1** : fortress **2** : means by which one is kept —**keep·er** n

keep·ing \kēpiŋ\ n : conformity

keep·sake \kēp,sāk\ n : souvenir

keg \keg\ n : small cask or barrel

kelp \kelp\ n : coarse brown seaweed

ken \ken\ n : range of sight or understanding

ken·nel \kenᵊl\ n : dog shelter —**kennel** vb

ker·chief \kərchəf, -,chēf\ n : square of cloth worn as a head covering

ker·nel \kərnᵊl\ n **1** : inner softer part of a seed or nut **2** : whole seed of a cereal **3** : central part

ker·o·sene, ker·o·sine \kerə,sēn, ,kerə'-\ n : thin flammable oil from petroleum

ketch·up \kechəp, ka-\ n : spicy tomato sauce

ket·tle \ketᵊl\ n : vessel for boiling liquids

ket·tle·drum \-,drum\ n : brass or copper kettle-shaped drum

¹key \kē\ n **1** : usu. metal piece to open a lock **2** : explanation **3** : lever pressed by a finger in playing an instrument or operating a machine **4** : leading individual or principle **5** : system of musical tones or pitch ~ vb : attune ~ adj : basic —**key·hole** n —**key up** vb : make nervous

²key n : low island or reef

key·board n : arrangement of keys

key·note \-,nōt\ n **1** : 1st note of a scale **2** : central fact, idea, or mood ~ vb **1** : set the keynote of **2** : deliver the major speech

key·stone n : wedge-shaped piece at the crown of an arch

kha·ki \kakē, 'käk-\ n : light yellowish brown color

khan \kän, 'kan\ n : Mongol leader

kib·butz \kib'ùts, -'üts\ n, pl **-but·zim** \-,üt'sēm, -,üt-\ : Israeli communal farm or settlement

ki·bitz·er \kibətsər, kə'bit-\ n : one who offers unwanted advice —**kib·itz** \kibəts\ vb

kick \kik\ vb **1** : strike out or hit with the foot **2** : object strongly **3** : recoil ~ n **1** : thrust with the foot **2** : recoil of a gun **3** : stimulating effect —**kick·er** n

kid \kid\ n **1** : young goat **2** : child ~ vb **-dd- 1** : deceive as a joke **2** : tease —**kid·der** n —**kid·ding·ly** adv

kid·nap \kid,nap\ vb **-napped** or **-naped** \-,napt\, **-nap·ping** or **-nap·ing** : carry a person away by illegal force —**kid·nap·per, kid·nap·er** n

kid·ney \kidnē\ n, pl **-neys** : either of a pair of organs that excrete urine

kill \kil\ vb **1** : deprive of life **2** : finish **3** : use up (time) ~ n : act of killing —**kill·er** n

kiln \kil, 'kiln\ n : heated enclosure for burning, firing, or drying —**kiln** vb

ki·lo \kēlō\ n, pl **-los** : kilogram

ki·lo·cy·cle \kilə,sīkəl\ n : kilohertz

ki·lo·gram \kēlə,gram, 'kilə-\ n : basic metric mass unit nearly equal to the mass of 1000 cubic centimeters of water at its maximum density

ki·lo·hertz \kilə,hərts, 'kēlə-, -,herts\ n : 1000 hertz

ki·lo·me·ter \kil'ämətər, 'kilə,mēt-\ n : 1000 meters

ki·lo·volt \kilə,vōlt\ n : 1000 volts

ki·lo·watt \kilə,wät\ n : 1000 watts

kilt \kilt\ n : knee-length pleated skirt

kil·ter \kiltər\ n : proper condition

ki·mo·no \kə'mōnō\ n, pl **-nos** : loose robe

kin \kin\ n **1** : one's relatives **2** : kinsman

kind \kīnd\ n **1** : essential quality **2** : group with common traits **3** : variety ~ adj **1** : of a sympathetic nature **2** : arising from sympathy —**kind·heart·ed** adj —**kind·ness** n

kin·der·gar·ten \kindər,gärtᵊn\ n : class for young children —**kin·der·gart·ner** \-,gärtnər\ n

kin·dle \kindᵊl\ vb **-dled**; **-dling 1** : set on fire or start burning **2** : stir up

kin·dling \kindliŋ, 'kinᵊl-\ n : material for starting a fire

kind·ly \kīndlē\ adj **-li·er**; **-est** : of a sympathetic nature ~ adv **1** : sympathetically **2** : courteously —**kind·li·ness** n

kin·dred \kindrəd\ n **1** : related individuals **2** : kin ~ adj : of a like nature

kin·folk \kin,fōk\, **kinfolks** n pl : kin

king \kiŋ\ n : male sovereign —**king·dom** \-dəm\ n —**king·less** adj —**king·ly** adj —**king·ship** n

king·fish·er \-,fishər\ n : bright-colored crested bird

kink \kiŋk\ n **1** : short tight twist or curl **2** : cramp —**kinky** adj

kin·ship n : relationship

kins·man \kinzmən\ n : male relative

kins·wom·an \-,wùmən\ n : female relative

kip·per \kipər\ n : dried or smoked fish —**kipper** vb

kiss \kis\ vb : touch with the lips as a mark of affection —**kiss** n

kit \kit\ n : set of articles (as tools or parts)

kitch·en \kichən\ n : room with cooking facilities

kite \kīt\ n **1** : small hawk **2** : covered framework flown at the end of a string

kith \kith\ n : familiar friends

kit·ten \kitᵊn\ n : young cat —**kit·ten·ish** adj

¹kit·ty \kitē\ n, pl **-ties** : kitten

²kitty n, pl **-ties** : fund or pool (as in a card game)

kit·ty-cor·ner, kit·ty-cor·nered var of CATERCORNER

ki·wi \kē,wē\ n : small flightless New Zealand bird

klep·to·ma·nia \,kleptə'mānēə\ n : neurotic impulse to steal —**klep·to·ma·ni·ac** \-nē-,ak\ n

knack \nak\ n **1** : clever way of doing something **2** : natural aptitude

knap·sack \nap,sak\ n : bag for carrying supplies on one's back

knave \nāv\ n : rogue —**knav·ery** \nāvərē\ n —**knav·ish** \nāvish\ adj

knead \nēd\ vb **1** : work and press with the hands **2** : massage —**knead·er** n

knee \nē\ n : joint in the middle part of the leg —**kneed** \nēd\ adj

knee·cap \nē,kap\ n : bone forming the front of the knee

kneel \nēl\ vb **knelt** \nelt\ or **kneeled**; **kneel·ing** : rest on one's knees

knell \nel\ n : stroke of a bell

knew past of KNOW

knick•ers \\'nikərz\\ *n pl* : pants gathered at the knee

knick-knack \\'nik,nak\\ *n* : small decorative object

knife \\'nīf\\ *n, pl* **knives** \\'nīvz\\ : sharp blade with a handle ~ *vb* **knifed; knif•ing** : stab or cut with a knife

knight \\'nīt\\ *n* 1 : mounted warrior of feudal times 2 : man honored by a sovereign ~ *vb* : make a knight of —**knight•hood** *n* —**knight•ly** *adv*

knit \\'nit\\ *vb* **knit** *or* **knit•ted; knit•ting** 1 : link firmly or closely 2 : form a fabric by interlacing yarn or thread ~ *n* : knitted garment —**knit•ter** *n*

knob \\'näb\\ *n* : rounded protuberance or handle —**knobbed** \\'näbd\\ *adj* —**knob•by** \\'näbē\\ *adj*

knock \\'näk\\ *vb* 1 : strike with a sharp blow 2 : collide 3 : find fault with ~ *n* : sharp blow —**knock out** *vb* : make unconscious

knock•er *n* : device hinged to a door to knock with

knoll \\'nōl\\ *n* : small round hill

knot \\'nät\\ *n* 1 : interlacing (as of string) that forms a lump 2 : base of a woody branch in the stem 3 : group 4 : one nautical mile per hour ~ *vb* **-tt-** : tie in or with a knot —**knot•ty** *adj*

know \\'nō\\ *vb* **knew** \\'nü, 'nyü\\ **known** \\'nōn\\ **know•ing** 1 : perceive directly or understand 2 : be familiar with —**know•able** *adj* —**know•er** *n*

know•ing \\'nōiŋ\\ *adj* : shrewdly and keenly alert —**know•ing•ly** *adv*

knowl•edge \\'nälij\\ *n* 1 : understanding gained by experience 2 : range of information —**knowl•edge•able** *adj*

knuck•le \\'nəkəl\\ *n* : rounded knob at a finger joint

ko•ala \\kō'älə\\ *n* : gray furry Australian animal

kohl•ra•bi \\kōl'räbē, -'räb-\\ *n, pl* **-bies** : cabbage that forms no head

Ko•ran \\kə'ran, -'rän\\ *n* : book of Islam containing revelations made to Muhammad by Allah

ko•sher \\'kōshər\\ *adj* : ritually fit for use according to Jewish law

kow•tow \\kau'tau, 'kau,tau\\ *vb* : show excessive deference

kryp•ton \\'krip,tän\\ *n* : gaseous chemical element used in lamps

ku•dos \\'kyü,däs, 'kü-, -,dōz\\ *n* : fame and renown

kum•quat \\'kəm,kwät\\ *n* : small citrus fruit

L

l \\'el\\ *n, pl* **l's** *or* **ls** \\'elz\\ : 12th letter of the alphabet

lab \\'lab\\ *n* : laboratory

la•bel \\'lābəl\\ *n* 1 : identification slip 2 : identifying word or phrase ~ *vb* **-beled** *or* **-belled; -bel•ing** *or* **-bel•ling** : put a label on

la•bi•al \\'lābēəl\\ *adj* : of or relating to the lips

la•bor \\'lābər\\ *n* 1 : physical or mental effort 2 : physical efforts of childbirth 3 : task 4 : people who work manually ~ *vb* : work esp. with great effort —**la•bor•er** *n*

lab•o•ra•to•ry \\'labrə,tōrē\\ *n, pl* **-ries** : place for experimental testing

Labor Day *n* : 1st Monday in September observed as a legal holiday in recognition of working people

la•bo•ri•ous \\lə'bōrēəs\\ *adj* : requiring great effort —**la•bo•ri•ous•ly** *adv*

lab•y•rinth \\'labə,rinth\\ *n* : maze —**lab•y•rin•thine** \\,labə'rinthən\\ *adj*

lace \\'lās\\ *n* 1 : cord or string for tying 2 : fine net usu. figured fabric ~ *vb* **laced; lac•ing** 1 : tie 2 : adorn with lace —**lacy** \\'lāsē\\ *adj*

lac•er•ate \\'lasə,rāt\\ *vb* **-at•ed; -at•ing** : tear roughly —**lac•er•a•tion** \\,lasə'rāshən\\ *n*

lach•ry•mose \\'lakrə,mōs\\ *adj* : tearful

lack \\'lak\\ *vb* : be missing or deficient in ~ *n* : deficiency

lack•a•dai•si•cal \\,lakə'dāzikəl\\ *adj* : lacking spirit —**lack•a•dai•si•cal•ly** \\-klē\\ *adv*

lack•ey \\'lakē\\ *n, pl* **-eys** 1 : footman or servant 2 : toady

lack•lus•ter \\'lak,ləstər\\ *adj* : dull

la•con•ic \\lə'känik\\ *adj* : sparing of words —**la•con•i•cal•ly** \\-iklē\\ *adv*

lac•quer \\'lakər\\ *n* : glossy surface coating —**lacquer** *vb*

la•crosse \\lə'krós\\ *n* : ball game played with long-handled rackets

lac•tate \\'lak,tāt\\ *vb* **-tat•ed; -tat•ing** : secrete milk —**lac•ta•tion** \\lak'tāshən\\ *n*

lac•tic \\'laktik\\ *adj* : relating to milk

la•cu•na \\lə'künə, -'kyü-\\ *n, pl* **-nae** \\,nē\\ *or* **-nas** : blank space or missing part

lad \\'lad\\ *n* : boy

lad•der \\'ladər\\ *n* : device with steps or rungs for climbing

lad•en \\'lādʰn\\ *adj* : loaded

la•dle \\'lādʰl\\ *n* : spoon with a deep bowl —**ladle** *vb*

la•dy \\'lādē\\ *n, pl* **-dies** 1 : woman of rank or authority 2 : woman

la•dy•bird \\'lādē,bərd\\ *n* : ladybug

la•dy•bug \\-,bəg\\ *n* : brightly colored beetle

lag \\'lag\\ *vb* **-gg-** : fail to keep up ~ *n* 1 : a falling behind 2 : interval

la•ger \\'lägər\\ *n* : beer

lag•gard \\'lagərd\\ *adj* : slow ~ *n* : one that lags —**lag•gard•ly** *adv or adj* —**lag•gard•ness** *n*

la•gniappe \\lan,yap\\ *n* : bonus

la•goon \\lə'gün\\ *n* : shallow sound, channel, or pond near or connecting with a larger body of water

laid *past of* LAY

lain *past part of* LIE

lair \\'lar\\ *n* : den

lais•sez–faire \\,les,ā'far\\ *n* : doctrine opposing government interference in business

la•ity \\'lāətē\\ *n* 1 : people of a religious faith who are not clergy members

lake \\'lāk\\ *n* : inland body of water

la•ma \\'lämə\\ *n* : Buddhist monk

lamb \\'lam\\ *n* : young sheep or its flesh used as food

lam•baste, lam•bast \\lam'bāst, -'bast\\ *vb* 1 : beat 2 : censure

lam•bent \\'lambənt\\ *adj* : light or bright —**lam•ben•cy** \\-bənsē\\ *n* —**lam•bent•ly** *adv*

lame \\'lām\\ *adj* **lam•er; lam•est** 1 : having a limb disabled 2 : weak ~ *vb* **lamed; lam•ing** : make lame —**lame•ly** *adv* —**lame•ness** *n*

la•mé \\lä'mā, la-\\ *n* : cloth with tinsel threads

lame•brain \\'lām,brān\\ *n* : fool

la•ment \\lə'ment\\ *vb* 1 : mourn 2 : express sorrow for ~ *n* 1 : mourning 2 : complaint —**lam•en•ta•ble** \\'laməntə-bəl, lə'mentə-\\ *adj* —**lam•en•ta•bly** \\-blē\\ *adv* —**lam•en•ta•tion** \\,lamən'tāshən\\ *n*

lam•i•nat•ed \\'lamə,nātəd\\ *adj* : made of thin layers of material —**lam•i•nate** \\-,nāt\\ *vb* —**lam•i•nate** \\-nət\\ *n or adj* —**lam•i•na•tion** \\,lamə'nāshən\\ *n*

lamp \\'lamp\\ *n* : device for producing light or heat

lam•poon \\lam'pün\\ *n* : satire —**lampoon** *vb*

lam•prey \\'lamprē\\ *n, pl* **-preys** : sucking eellike fish

lance \\'lans\\ *n* : spear ~ *vb* **lanced; lanc•ing** : pierce or open with a lancet

lance corporal *n* : enlisted man in the marine corps ranking above a private first class and below a corporal

lan•cet \\'lansət\\ *n* : pointed surgical instrument

land \\'land\\ *n* 1 : solid part of the surface of the earth 2 : country ~ *vb* 1 : go ashore 2 : catch or gain 3 : touch the ground or a surface —**land•less** *adj* —**land•own•er** *n*

land•fill *n* : dump

land•ing \\'landiŋ\\ *n* 1 : action of one that lands 2 : place for loading passengers and cargo 3 : level part of a staircase

land•la•dy \\'land,lādē\\ *n* : woman landlord

land•locked *adj* : enclosed by land

land•lord *n* : owner of property

land•lub•ber \\-,ləbər\\ *n* : one with little sea experience

land•mark \\-,märk\\ *n* 1 : object that marks a boundary or serves as a guide 2 : event that marks a turning point

land•scape \\-,skāp\\ *n* : view of natural scenery ~ *vb* **-scaped; -scap•ing** : beautify a piece of land (as by decorative planting)

land•slide *n* 1 : slipping down of a mass of earth 2 : overwhelming victory

land•ward \\'landwərd\\ *adj* : toward the land —**landward** *adv*

lane \\'lān\\ *n* : narrow way

lan•guage \\'laŋgwij\\ *n* : words and the methods of combining them for communication

lan•guid \\'laŋgwəd\\ *adj* 1 : weak 2 : sluggish —**lan•guid•ly** *adv* —**lan•guid•ness** *n*

lan•guish \\'laŋgwish\\ *vb* : become languid or discouraged

lan•guor \\'laŋgər\\ *n* : listless indolence —**lan•guor•ous** *adj* —**lan•guor•ous•ly** *adv*

lank \\'laŋk\\ *adj* 1 : thin 2 : limp

lanky *adj* **lank•i•er; -est** : tall and thin

lan•o•lin \\'lanʰlən\\ *n* : fatty wax from sheep's wool used in ointments

lan•tern \\'lantərn\\ *n* : enclosed portable light

¹lap \\'lap\\ *n* 1 : front part of the lower trunk and thighs of a seated person 2 : overlapping part 3 : one complete circuit completing a course (as around a track or pool) ~ *vb* **-pp-** : fold over

²lap *vb* **-pp-** 1 : scoop up with the tongue 2 : splash gently

lap•dog *n* : small dog

la•pel \\lə'pel\\ *n* : fold of the front of a coat

lap•i•dary \\'lapə,derē\\ *n* : one who cuts and polishes gems ~ *adj* : relating to gems

lapse \\'laps\\ *n* 1 : slight error 2 : termination of a right or privilege 3 : interval ~ *vb* **lapsed; laps•ing** 1 : slip 2 : subside 3 : cease

lap•top \\'lap,täp\\ *adj* : of a size that may be used on one's lap

lar•board \\'lärbərd\\ *n* : port side

lar•ce•ny \\'lärsʰnē\\ *n, pl* **-nies** : theft —**lar•ce•nous** \\'lärsʰnəs\\ *adj*

larch \\'lärch\\ *n* : tree like a pine that loses its needles

lard \\'lärd\\ *n* : pork fat

lar•der \\'lärdər\\ *n* : pantry

large \\'lärj\\ *adj* **larg•er; larg•est** : greater than average —**large•ly** *adv* —**large•ness** *n*

lar•gesse, lar•gess \\lär'zhes, -'jes; 'lär,-\\ *n* : liberal giving

lar•i•at \\'larēət\\ *n* : lasso

¹lark \\'lärk\\ *n* : small songbird

²lark *vb or n* : romp

lar•va \\'lärvə\\ *n, pl* **-vae** \\-,vē\\ : wormlike form of an insect —**lar•val** \\-vəl\\ *adj*

lar•yn•gi•tis \\,larən'jītəs\\ *n* : inflammation of the larynx

lar•ynx \\'lariŋks\\ *n, pl* **-ryn•ges** \\lə'rin,jēz\\ *or* **-ynx•es** : upper part of the trachea —**la•ryn•ge•al** \\,larən'jēəl, lə'rinjēəl\\ *adj*

la•sa•gna \\lə'zänyə\\ *n* : flat noodles baked usu. with tomato sauce, meat, and cheese

las•civ•i•ous \\lə'sivēəs\\ *adj* : lewd —**las•civ•i•ous•ness** *n*

la•ser \\'lāzər\\ *n* : device that produces an intense light beam

¹lash \\'lash\\ *vb* ~ *n* 1 : stroke esp. of a whip 2 : eyelash

²lash *vb* : bind with a rope or cord

lass \\'las\\ *n* : girl

lass•ie \\'lasē\\ *n* : girl

las•si•tude \\'lasə,tüd, -,tyüd\\ *n* 1 : fatigue 2 : listlessness

las•so \\'lasō, la'sü\\ *n, pl* **-sos** *or* **-soes** : rope with a noose for catching livestock —**lasso** *vb*

¹last \\'last\\ *vb* : continue in existence or operation

²last *adj* 1 : final 2 : previous 3 : least likely ~ *adv* 1 : at the end 2 : most recently 3 : in conclusion ~ *n* : something that is last —**last•ly** *adv* —**at last** : finally

³last *n* : form on which a shoe is shaped

latch \\'lach\\ *vb* : catch or get hold ~ *n* : catch that holds a door closed

late \\'lāt\\ *adj* **lat•er; lat•est** 1 : coming or staying after the proper time 2 : advanced toward the end 3 : recently deceased 4 : recent —**late** *adv* —**late•com•er** \\-,kəmər\\ *n* —**late•ly** *adv* —**late•ness** *n*

la•tent \\'lātʰnt\\ *adj* : present but not visible or expressed —**la•ten•cy** \\-ʰnsē\\ *n*

lat•er•al \\'latərəl\\ *adj* : on or toward the side —**lat•er•al•ly** *adv*

la•tex \\'lā,teks\\ *n, pl* **-ti•ces** \\'lātə,sēz, 'lat-\\ *or* **-tex•es** : emulsion of synthetic rubber or plastic

lath \\'lath, 'lath\\ *n, pl* **laths** *or* **lath** : building material (as a thin strip of wood) used as a base for plaster —**lath** *vb* —**lath•ing** \\-iŋ\\ *n*

lathe \\'lāth\\ *n* : machine that rotates material for shaping

lath•er \\'lathər\\ *n* : foam ~ *vb* : form or spread lather

lat•i•tude \\'latə,tüd, -,tyüd\\ *n* 1 : distance north or south from the earth's equator 2 : freedom of action

la•trine \\lə'trēn\\ *n* : toilet

lat•ter \\'latər\\ *adj* 1 : more recent 2 : being the second of 2 —**lat•ter•ly** *adv*

lat•tice \\'latəs\\ *n* : framework of crossed strips

laud *vb or n* : praise —**laud•able** *adj* —**laud•ably** *adv*

laugh \\'laf, 'läf\\ *vb* : show mirth, joy, or scorn with a smile and explosive sound —**laugh** *n* —**laugh•able** *adj* —**laugh•ing•ly** \\-iŋlē\\ *adv*

laugh•ing•stock \\'lafiŋ,stäk, 'läf-\\ *n* : object of ridicule

laugh•ter \\'laftər, 'läf-\\ *n* : action or sound of laughing

¹launch \\'lónch\\ *vb* 1 : hurl or send off 2 : set afloat 3 : start —**launch** *n* —**launch•er** *n*

²launch *n* : small open boat

laun•der \\'lóndər\\ *vb* : wash or iron fabrics —**laun•der•er** *n* —**laun•dress** \\-drəs\\ *n* —**laun•dry** \\-drē\\ *n*

lau•re•ate \\'lórēət\\ *n* : recipient of honors —**laureate** *adj*

lau•rel \\'lórəl\\ *n* 1 : small evergreen tree 2 : honor

la•va \\'lävə, 'lav-\\ *n* : volcanic molten rock

lav•a•to•ry \\'lavə,tōrē\\ *n, pl* **-ries** : bathroom

lav•en•der \\'lavəndər\\ *n* 1 : aromatic plant used for perfume 2 : pale purple color

lav•ish \\'lavish\\ *adj* : expended profusely ~ *vb* : expend or give freely —**lav•ish•ly** *adv* —**lav•ish•ness** *n*

law \\'ló\\ *n* 1 : established rule of conduct 2 : body of such rules 3 : principle of construction or procedure 4 : rule stating uniform behavior under uniform conditions 5 : lawyer's profession —**law•break•er** *n* —**law•giv•er** *n* —**law•less** *adj* —**law•less•ly** *adv* —**law•less•ness** *n* —**law•mak•er** *n* —**law•man** \\-mən\\ *n* —**law•suit** *n*

law•ful \\'lófəl\\ *adj* : permitted by law —**law•ful•ly** *adv*

lawn \\'lón\\ *n* : grass-covered yard

law•yer \\'lóyər\\ *n* : legal practitioner

lax \\'laks\\ *adj* : not strict or tense —**lax•i•ty** \\'laksətē\\ *n* —**lax•ly** *adv*

lax•a•tive \\'laksətiv\\ *n* : drug relieving constipation

¹lay \\'lā\\ *vb* **laid** \\'lād\\ **lay•ing** 1 : put or set down 2 : produce eggs 3 : bet 4 : impose as a duty or burden 5 : put forward ~ *n* : way something lies or is laid

²lay *past of* LIE

³lay *n* : song

⁴lay *adj* : of the laity —**lay•man** \\-mən\\ *n* —**lay•wom•an** \\-,wúmən\\ *n*

lay•er \\'lāər\\ *n* 1 : one that lays 2 : one thickness over or under another

lay•off \\'lā,óf\\ *n* : temporary dismissal of a worker

lay•out \\'lā,aút\\ *n* : arrangement

la•zy \\'lāzē\\ *adj* **-zi•er; -est** : disliking activity or exertion —**la•zi•ly** \\'lāzəlē\\ *adv* —**la•zi•ness** *n*

lea \\'lē, 'lā\\ *n* : meadow

leach \\'lēch\\ *vb* : remove (a soluble part) with a solvent

¹lead \\'lēd\\ *vb* **led** \\'led\\; **lead•ing** 1 : guide on a way 2 : direct the activity of 3 : go at the head of 4 : tend to a definite result ~ *n* : position in front —**lead•er** *n* —**lead•er•less** *adj* —**lead•er•ship** *n*

²lead \\'led\\ *n* 1 : heavy bluish white chemical element 2 : marking substance in a pencil —**lead•en** \\'ledʰn\\ *adj*

leaf \\'lēf\\ *n, pl* **leaves** \\'lēvz\\ 1 : green outgrowth of a plant stem 2 : leaflike thing ~ *vb* 1 : produce leaves 2 : turn book pages —**leaf•age** \\'lēfij\\ *n* —**leafed** \\'lēft\\ *adj* —**leaf•less** *adj* —**leafy** —**leaved** \\'lēfd\\

leaf•let \\'lēflət\\ *n* : pamphlet

¹league \\'lēg\\ *n* : unit of distance equal to about 3 miles

²league *n* : association for a common purpose —**league** *vb* —**leagu•er** *n*

leak \\'lēk\\ *vb* 1 : enter or escape through a leak 2 : become or make known ~ *n* : opening that accidentally admits or lets out a substance —**leak•age** \\'lēkij\\ *n* —**leaky** *adj*

¹lean \\'lēn\\ *vb* 1 : bend from a vertical position 2 : rely on for support 3 : incline in opinion —**lean** *n*

²lean *adj* 1 : lacking in flesh 2 : lacking richness —**lean•ness** \\'lēnnəs\\ *n*

leap \\'lēp\\ *vb* **leapt** *or* **leaped** \\'lēpt, 'lept\\; **leap•ing** : jump —**leap** *n*

leap year *n* : 366-day year

learn \\'lərn\\ *vb* 1 : gain understanding or skill by study or experience 2 : memorize 3 : find out —**learn•er** *n*

learn•ed \\-əd\\ *adj* : having great learning —**learn•ed•ness** *n*

learn•ing \\-iŋ\\ *n* : knowledge

lease \\'lēs\\ *n* : contract transferring real estate for a term and usu. for rent ~ *vb* **leased; leas•ing** : grant by or hold under a lease

leash \\'lēsh\\ *n* : line to hold an animal —**leash** *vb*

least \\'lēst\\ *adj* 1 : lowest in importance or position 2 : smallest 3 : scantiest ~ *n* : one that is least ~ *adv* : in the smallest or lowest degree

leath•er \\'lethər\\ *n* : dressed animal skin —**leath•ern** \\-ərn\\ *adj* —**leath•ery** *adj*

¹leave \\'lēv\\ *vb* **left** \\'left\\; **leav•ing** 1 : bequeath 2 : allow or cause to remain 3 : have as a remainder 4 : go away ~ *n* 1 : permission 2 : authorized absence 3 : departure

²leave *vb* **leaved; leav•ing** : leaf

leav•en \\'levən\\ *n* : substance for producing fermentation ~ *vb* : raise dough with a leaven

leaves *pl of* LEAF

lech•ery \\'lechərē\\ *n* : inordinate indulgence in sex —**lech•er** \\'lechər\\ *n* —**lech•er•ous** \\-chərəs\\ *adj* —**lech•er•ous•ly** *adv*

lec•tern \\'lektərn\\ *n* : reading desk

lec•ture \\'lekchər\\ *n* 1 : instructive talk 2 : reprimand —**lecture** *vb* —**lec•tur•er** *n* —**lec•ture•ship** *n*

led *past of* LEAD

ledge \\'lej\\ *n* : shelflike projection

led•ger \'lejər\ *n* : account book
lee \'lē\ *n* : side sheltered from the wind — **lee** *adj*
leech \'lēch\ *n* : segmented freshwater worm that feeds on blood
leek \'lēk\ *n* : onionlike herb
leer \'lir\ *n* : suggestive or malicious look — **leer** *vb*
leery \'lirē\ *adj* : suspicious or wary
lees \'lēz\ *n pl* : dregs
lee•ward \'lēwərd, 'lüərd\ *adj* : situated away from the wind ~ *n* : the lee side
lee•way \'lē,wā\ *n* : allowable margin
1left \'left\ *adj* : on the same side of the body as the heart ~ *n* : left hand — **left** *adv*
2left *past of* LEAVE
leg \'leg\ *n* 1 : limb of an animal that supports the body 2 : something like a leg 3 : clothing to cover the leg ~ *vb* -**gg**- : walk or run — **legged** \'legəd\ *adj* — **leg•less** *adj*
leg•a•cy \'legəsē\ *n, pl* -**cies** : inheritance
le•gal \'lēgəl\ *adj* 1 : relating to law or lawyers 2 : lawful — **le•gal•is•tic** \,lēgə'listik\ *adj* — **le•gal•i•ty** \li'galətē\ *n* — **le•gal•ize** \'lēgə,līz\ *vb* — **le•gal•ly** \-gəlē\ *adv*
le•gate \'legət\ *n* : official representative
le•ga•tion \li'gāshən\ *n* 1 : diplomatic mission 2 : official residence and office of a diplomat
leg•end \'lejənd\ *n* 1 : story handed down from the past 2 : inscription 3 : explanation of map symbols — **leg•end•ary** \-ən,derē\ *adj*
leg•er•de•main \,lejərdə'mān\ *n* : sleight of hand
leg•ging, leg•gin \'legən, -in\ *n* : leg covering
leg•i•ble \'lejəbəl\ *adj* : capable of being read — **leg•i•bil•i•ty** \,lejə'bilətē\ *n* — **leg•i•bly** \'lejəblē\ *adv*
le•gion \'lējən\ *n* 1 : large army unit 2 : multitude 3 : association of former servicemen — **le•gion•ary** \-,erē\ *n* — **le•gion•naire** \,lējən'ar\ *n*
leg•is•late \'lejə,slāt\ *vb* -**lat•ed; -lat•ing** : enact or bring about with laws — **leg•is•la•tion** \,lejə'slāshən\ *n* — **leg•is•la•tive** \'lejə,slātiv\ *adj* — **leg•is•la•tor** \-,slātər\ *n*
leg•is•la•ture \'lejə,slāchər\ *n* : organization with authority to make laws
le•git•i•mate \li'jitəmət\ *adj* 1 : lawfully begotten 2 : genuine 3 : conforming with law or accepted standards — **le•git•i•ma•cy** \-məsē\ *n* — **le•git•i•mate•ly** *adv* — **le•git•i•mize** \-,mīz\ *vb*
le•gume \'leg,yüm, li'gyüm\ *n* : plant bearing pods — **le•gu•mi•nous** \li'gyümənəs\ *adj*
lei \'lā\ *n* : necklace of flowers
lei•sure \'lēzhər, 'lezh-, 'lāzh-\ *n* 1 : free time 2 : ease 3 : convenience — **lei•sure•ly** *adj or adv*
lem•ming \'lemin\ *n* : short-tailed rodent
lem•on \'lemən\ *n* : yellow citrus fruit — **lem•ony** *adj*
lem•on•ade \,lemə'nād\ *n* : sweetened lemon beverage
lend \'lend\ *vb* **lent** \'lent\; **lend•ing** 1 : give for temporary use 2 : furnish — **lend•er** *n*
length \'lenth\ *n* 1 : longest dimension 2 : duration in time 3 : piece to be joined to others — **length•en** \'lenthən\ *vb* — **length•wise** *adv or adj* — **lengthy** *adj*
le•nient \'lēnēənt, -nyənt\ *adj* : of mild and tolerant disposition or effect — **le•ni•en•cy** \'lēnēənsē -nyənsē\ *n* — **le•ni•ent•ly** *adv*
len•i•ty \'lenətē\ *n* : leniency
lens \'lenz\ *n* 1 : curved piece for forming an image in an optical instrument 2 : transparent body in the eye that focuses light rays
Lent \'lent\ *n* : 40-day period of penitence and fasting from Ash Wednesday to Easter — **Lent•en** \-ᵊn\ *adj*
len•til \'lentᵊl\ *n* : legume with flat edible seeds
le•o•nine \'lēə,nīn\ *adj* : like a lion
leop•ard \'lepərd\ *n* : large tawny black-spotted cat
le•o•tard \'lēə,tärd\ *n* : close-fitting garment
lep•er \'lepər\ *n* : person with leprosy
lep•re•chaun \'leprə,kän\ *n* : mischievous Irish elf
lep•ro•sy \'leprəsē\ *n* : chronic bacterial disease — **lep•rous** \-rəs\ *adj*
les•bi•an \'lezbēən\ *n* : female homosexual — **lesbian** *adj* — **les•bi•an•ism** \-,izəm\ *n*
le•sion \'lēzhən\ *n* : abnormal area in the body due to injury or disease
less \'les\ *adj* 1 : fewer 2 : of lower rank, degree, or importance 3 : smaller ~ *adv* : to a lesser degree ~ *n, pl* **less** : smaller portion ~ *prep* : minus — **less** *vb*
-less \ləs\ *adj suffix* 1 : not having 2 : unable to act or be acted on
less•ee \le'sē\ *n* : tenant under a lease
less•er \'lesər\ *adj* : of less size, quality, or significance
les•son \'lesᵊn\ *n* 1 : reading or exercise to be studied by a pupil 2 : something learned

les•sor \'les,or, le'sòr\ *n* : one who transfers property by a lease
lest \'lest\ *conj* : for fear that
2let *vb* **let; let•ting** 1 : cause to 2 : rent 3 : permit
-let \lət\ *n suffix* : small one
le•thal \'lēthəl\ *adj* : deadly — **le•thal•ly** *adv*
leth•ar•gy \'lethərjē\ *n* 1 : drowsiness 2 : state of being lazy or indifferent — **le•thar•gic** \li'thärjik\ *adj*
let•ter \'letər\ *n* 1 : unit of an alphabet 2 : written or printed communication 3 *pl* : literature or learning 4 : literal meaning ~ *vb* : mark with letters — **let•ter•er** *n*
let•tuce \'letəs\ *n* : garden plant with crisp leaves
leu•ke•mia \lü'kēmēə\ *n* : cancerous blood disease — **leu•ke•mic** \-mik\ *adj or n*
lev•ee \'levē\ *n* : embankment to prevent flooding
lev•el \'levəl\ *n* 1 : device for establishing a flat surface 2 : horizontal surface 3 : position in a scale ~ *vb* -**eled** or -**elled; -el•ing** or -**el•ling** 1 : make flat or level 2 : aim 3 : raze ~ *adj* 1 : having an even surface 2 : of the same height or rank — **lev•el•er** *n* — **lev•el•ly** *adv* — **lev•el•ness** *n*
le•ver \'levər, 'lē-\ *n* : bar for prying or dislodging something — **le•ver•age** \'levərij, 'lēv-\ *n*
le•vi•a•than \li'vīəthən\ *n* 1 : large sea animal 2 : enormous thing
lev•i•ty \'levətē\ *n* : unseemly frivolity
levy \'levē\ *n, pl* **lev•ies** : imposition or collection of a tax ~ *vb* **lev•ied; levy•ing** 1 : impose or collect legally 2 : enlist for military service 3 : wage
lewd \'lüd\ *adj* 1 : sexually unchaste 2 : vulgar — **lewd•ly** *adv* — **lewd•ness** *n*
lex•i•cog•ra•phy \,leksə'kägrəfē\ *n* : dictionary making — **lex•i•cog•ra•pher** \-fər\ *n* — **lex•i•co•graph•i•cal** \-,kō'grafikəl\ or **lex•i•co•graph•ic** \-ik\ *adj*
lex•i•con \'leksə,kän\ *n, pl* -**i•ca** \-sikə\ or -**icons** : dictionary
li•a•ble \'līəbəl\ *adj* 1 : legally obligated 2 : probable 3 : susceptible — **li•a•bil•i•ty** \,līə'bilətē\ *n*
li•ai•son \'lēə,zän, lē'ā-\ *n* 1 : close bond 2 : communication between groups
li•ar \'līər\ *n* : one who lies
li•bel \'lībəl\ *n* : action, crime, or an instance of injuring a person's reputation esp. by something written — **beled** or -**belled; -bel•ing** or **-bel•ling** : make or publish a libel — **li•bel•er** *n* — **li•bel•ist** *n* — **li•bel•ous, li•bel•lous** \-bələs\ *adj*
lib•er•al \'librəl, 'libə-\ *adj* 1 : not stingy, narrow, or conservative — **liberal** *n* — **lib•er•al•ism** \-,izəm\ *n* — **lib•er•al•i•ty** \,libə'ralətē\ *n* — **lib•er•al•ize** \'librə,līz, 'libə-\ *vb* — **lib•er•al•ly** \-rəlē\ *adv*
lib•er•ate \'libə,rāt\ *vb* -**at•ed; -at•ing** : set free — **lib•er•a•tion** \,libə'rāshən\ *n* — **lib•er•a•tor** \'libə,rātər\ *n*
lib•er•tine \'libər,tēn\ *n* : one who leads a dissolute life
lib•er•ty \'libərtē\ *n, pl* -**ties** 1 : quality or state of being free 2 : action going beyond normal limits
li•bi•do \lə'bēdō, -'bīd-\ *n, pl* -**dos** : sexual drive — **li•bid•i•nal** \lə'bidᵊnəl\ *adj* — **li•bid•i•nous** \-əs\ *adj*
li•brary \'lī,brerē\ *n, pl* -**brar•ies** 1 : place where books are kept for use 2 : collection of books — **li•brar•i•an** \lī-'brerēən\ *n*
li•bret•to \lə'bretō\ *n, pl* -**tos** or -**ti** \-ē\ : text of an opera — **li•bret•tist** \-ist\ *n*
lice *pl of* LOUSE
li•cense, li•cence \'līsᵊns\ *n* 1 : legal permission to engage in some activity 2 : document or tag providing proof of a license 3 : irresponsible use of freedom — **license** *vb* — **li•cens•ee** \līsᵊn'sē\ *n*
li•cen•tious \lī'senchəs\ *adj* : disregarding sexual restraints — **li•cen•tious•ly** *adv* — **li•cen•tious•ness** *n*
li•chen \'līkən\ *n* : complex lower plant made up of an alga and a fungus
lic•it \'lisət\ *adj* : lawful
lick \'lik\ *vb* 1 : draw the tongue over 2 : beat ~ *n* 1 : stroke of the tongue 2 : small amount
lic•o•rice \'likərish, -rəs\ *n* : dried root of a European legume or candy flavored by it
lid \'lid\ *n* 1 : movable cover 2 : eyelid
1lie \'lī\ *vb* **lay** \'lā\; **lain** \'lān\; **ly•ing** \'līin\ 1 : be in, rest in, or assume a horizontal position 2 : occupy a certain relative position ~ *n* : position in which something lies
2lie *vb* **lied; ly•ing** \'līin\ : tell a lie ~ *n* : untrue statement
liege \'lēj\ *n* : feudal superior or vassal
lien \'lēn, 'lēən\ *n* : legal claim on the property of another
lieu•ten•ant \lü'tenənt\ *n* 1 : representative 2 : first lieutenant or second lieutenant 3 : commissioned officer in the navy ranking next below a lieutenant commander — **lieu•ten•an•cy** \-ənsē\ *n*
lieutenant colonel *n* : commissioned officer (as in the army) ranking next below a colonel
lieutenant commander *n* : commissioned officer in the navy ranking next below a commander
lieutenant general *n* : commissioned officer (as in the army) ranking next below a general
lieutenant junior grade *n, pl* **lieutenants junior grade** : commissioned officer in the navy ranking next below a lieutenant
life \'līf\ *n, pl* **lives** \'līvz\ 1 : quality that distinguishes a vital and functional being from a dead body or inanimate matter 2 : physical and mental experiences of an individual 3 : biography 4 : period of existence 5 : way of living 6 : liveliness — **life•less** *adj* — **life•like** *adj*
life•blood *n* : basic source of strength and vitality
life•boat *n* : boat for saving lives at sea
life•guard *n* : one employed to safeguard bathers
life•long *adj* : continuing through life
life•sav•ing *n* : art or practice of saving lives — **life•sav•er** \-,sāvər\ *n*
life•style \'līf,stīl\ *n* : a way of life
life•time *n* : duration of an individual's existence
lift \'lift\ *vb* 1 : move upward or cause to move upward 2 : put an end to — **lift** *n* — **lift•er** *n*
lift-off \'lift,òf\ *n* : vertical takeoff by a rocket
lig•a•ment \'ligəmənt\ *n* : band of tough tissue that holds bones together
lig•a•ture \'ligə,chùr, -chər\ *n* : something that binds or ties
1light \'līt\ *n* 1 : radiation that makes vision possible 2 : daylight 3 : source of light 4 : public knowledge 5 : aspect 6 : celebrity 7 : flame for lighting ~ *adj* 1 : bright 2 : weak in color ~ *vb* **lit** \'lit\ or **light•ed; light•ing** 1 : make or become light 2 : cause to burn — **light•er** *n* — **light•ness** *n* — **light•proof** *adj*
2light *adj* : not heavy, serious, or abundant — **light** *adv* — **light•ly** *adv* — **light•ness** *n* — **light•weight** *adj*
3light *vb* **light•ed** or **lit** \'lit\; **light•ing** : settle or dismount
1light•en \'lītᵊn\ *vb* 1 : make light or bright 2 : give out flashes of lightning
2lighten *vb* 1 : relieve of a burden 2 : become lighter
light•heart•ed \-'härtəd\ *adj* : free from worry — **light•heart•ed•ly** *adv* — **light•heart•ed•ness** *n*
light•house *n* : structure with a powerful light for guiding sailors
light•ning \'lītnin\ *n* : flashing discharge of atmospheric electricity
light-year \'līt,yir\ *n* : distance traveled by light in one year equal to about 5.88 trillion miles
lig•nite \'lig,nīt\ *n* : brownish black soft coal
like \'līk\ *vb* **liked; lik•ing** 1 : enjoy 2 : desire ~ *n* : preference — **lik•able, like•able** \'līkəbəl\ *adj*
2like *adj* : similar ~ *prep* 1 : similar or similarly to 2 : typical of 3 : such as ~ *n* : counterpart ~ *conj* : as or as if — **like•ness** *n* — **like•wise** *adv*
-like \līk\ *adj comb form* : resembling or characteristic of
like•li•hood \'līklē,hùd\ *n* : probability
like•ly \'līklē\ *adj* **-li•er; -est** 1 : probable 2 : believable ~ *adv* : in all probability
lik•en \'līkən\ *vb* : compare
lik•ing \'līkin\ *n* : favorable regard
li•lac \'līlək, -,lak, -,läk\ *n* : shrub with clusters of fragrant pink, purple, or white flowers
lilt \'lilt\ *n* : rhythmical swing or flow
lily \'lilē\ *n, pl* **lil•ies** : tall bulbous herb with funnel-shaped flowers
lima bean \'līmə-\ *n* : flat edible seed of a plant or the plant itself
limb \'lim\ *n* 1 : projecting appendage used in moving or grasping 2 : tree branch — **limb•less** *adj*
lim•ber \'limbər\ *adj* : supple or agile ~ *vb* : make or become limber
lim•bo \'limbō\ *n, pl* -**bos** : place or state of confinement or oblivion
1lime \'līm\ *n* : caustic white oxide of calcium
2lime *n* : small green lemonlike citrus fruit — **lime•ade** *n*
lime•light *n* : center of public attention
lim•er•ick \'limərik\ *n* : light poem of 5 lines
lime•stone *n* : rock that yields lime when burned
lim•it \'limət\ *n* 1 : boundary 2 : something that restrains or confines ~ *vb* : set limits on — **lim•i•ta•tion** \,limə'tāshən\ *n* — **lim•it•less** *adj*
lim•ou•sine \'limə,zēn, ,limə'-\ *n* : large luxurious sedan
limp \'limp\ *vb* : walk lamely ~ *n* : limping movement or gait ~ *adj* : lacking firmness and body — **limp•ly** *adv* — **limp•ness** *n*

lim•pid \'limpəd\ *adj* : clear or transparent
lin•den \'lindən\ *n* : tree with large heart-shaped leaves
1line \'līn\ *vb* **lined; lin•ing** : cover the inner surface of — **lin•ing** *n*
2line *n* 1 : cord, rope, or wire 2 : row or something like a row 3 : note 4 : course of action or thought 5 : state of agreement 6 : occupation 7 : limit 8 : transportation system 9 : long narrow mark ~ *vb* **lined; lin•ing** 1 : mark with a line 2 : place in a line 3 : form a line
lin•eage \'linēij\ *n* : descent from a common ancestor
lin•eal \'linēəl\ *adj* 1 : linear 2 : in a direct line of ancestry
lin•ea•ments \'linēəmənts\ *n pl* : features or contours esp. of a face
lin•ear \'linēər\ *adj* 1 : straight 2 : long and narrow
lin•en \'linən\ *n* 1 : cloth or thread made of flax 2 : household articles made of linen cloth
lin•er \'līnər\ *n* 1 : one that lines 2 : ship or airplane belonging to a line
line•up \'līn,əp\ *n* 1 : line of persons for inspection or identification 2 : list of players in a game
-ling \lin\ *n suffix* 1 : one linked with 2 : young, small, or minor one
lin•ger \'lingər\ *vb* : be slow to leave or act — **lin•ger•er** *n*
lin•ge•rie \,länjə'rā, ,lanzhə-, -'rē\ *n* : women's underwear
lin•go \'lingō\ *n, pl* -**goes** : usu. strange language
lin•guist \'lingwist\ *n* 1 : person skilled in speech or languages 2 : student of language — **lin•guis•tic** \lin'gwistik\ *adj* — **lin•guis•tics** *n pl*
lin•i•ment \'linəmənt\ *n* : liquid medication rubbed on the skin
link \'link\ *n* 1 : connecting structure (as a ring of a chain) 2 : bond — **link** *vb* — **link•age** \-ij\ *n* — **link•er** *n*
li•no•leum \lə'nōlēəm\ *n* : floor covering with hard surface
lin•seed \'lin,sēd\ *n* : seeds of flax yielding an oil (**linseed oil**)
lint \'lint\ *n* : fine fluff or loose short fibers from fabric
lin•tel \'lintᵊl\ *n* : horizontal piece over a door or window
li•on \'līən\ *n* : large cat of Africa and Asia — **li•on•ess** \'līənəs\ *n*
li•on•ize \'līə,nīz\ *vb* -**ized; -iz•ing** : treat as very important — **li•on•iza•tion** \,līən-'zāshən\ *n*
lip \'lip\ *n* 1 : either of the 2 fleshy folds surrounding the mouth 2 : edge of something hollow — **lipped** \'lipt\ *adj* — **lip•read•ing** *n*
li•po•suc•tion \'lipə,səkshən, 'lī-\ *n* : surgical removal of fat deposits (as from the thighs)
lip•stick \'lip,stik\ *n* : stick of cosmetic to color lips
liq•ue•fy \'likwə,fī\ *vb* -**fied; -fy•ing** : make or become liquid — **liq•ue•fi•er** \'likwə-,fīər\ *n*
li•queur \li'kər\ *n* : sweet or aromatic alcoholic liquor
liq•uid \'likwəd\ *adj* 1 : flowing freely like water 2 : neither solid nor gaseous 3 : of or convertible to cash — **liquid** *n* — **li•quid•i•ty** \lik'widətē\ *n*
liq•ui•date \'likwə,dāt\ *vb* -**dat•ed; -dat•ing** 1 : pay off 2 : dispose of — **liq•ui•da•tion** \,likwə'dāshən\ *n*
li•quor \'likər\ *n* : liquid substance and esp. a distilled alcoholic beverage
lisp \'lisp\ *vb* : pronounce *s* and *z* imperfectly — **lisp** *n*
lis•some \'lisəm\ *adj* : supple or agile
1list \'list\ *n* 1 : series of names or items ~ *vb* 1 : make a list of 2 : put on a list
2list *vb* : tilt or lean over ~ *n* : slant
lis•ten \'lisᵊn\ *vb* 1 : pay attention in order to hear 2 : heed — **lis•ten•er** \'lisᵊnər\ *n*
list•less \'listləs\ *adj* : having no desire to act — **list•less•ly** *adv* — **list•less•ness** *n*
lit \'lit\ *past of* LIGHT
lit•a•ny \'litᵊnē\ *n, pl* -**nies** 1 : prayer said as a series of responses to a leader 2 : long recitation
li•ter \'lētər\ *n* : unit of liquid measure equal to about 1.06 quarts
lit•er•al \'litərəl\ *adj* : being exactly as stated — **lit•er•al•ly** *adv*
lit•er•ary \'litə,rerē\ *adj* : relating to literature
lit•er•ate \'litərət\ *adj* : able to read and write — **lit•er•a•cy** \'litərəsē\ *n*
lit•er•a•ture \'litərə,chùr, -chər\ *n* : writings of enduring interest
lithe \'līth, 'lith\ *adj* 1 : supple 2 : graceful — **lithe•some** \-səm\ *adj*
lith•o•graph \'lithə,graf\ *n* : print from a drawing on metal or stone — **li•thog•ra•pher** \lith'ägrəfər, 'lithə,grafər\ *n* — **lith•o•graph•ic** \,lithə'grafik\ *adj* — **li•thog•ra•phy** \lith'ägrəfē\ *n*

lit·i·gate \'litə,gāt\ vb **-gat·ed; -gat·ing** : carry on a lawsuit —**lit·i·gant** \'litigənt\ n —**lit·i·ga·tion** \,litə'gāshən\ n —**lit·i·gious** \lə'tijəs, li-\ adj —**li·ti·gious·ness** n

lit·mus \'litməs\ n : coloring matter that turns red in acid solutions and blue in alkaline

lit·ter \'litər\ n 1 : animal offspring of one birth 2 : stretcher 3 : rubbish 4 : material to absorb animal waste ~ vb 1 : give birth to young 2 : strew with litter

lit·tle \'litᵊl\ adj **lit·tler** or **less** \'les\ or **less·er** \'lesər\; **lit·tlest** or **least** \'lēst\ 1 : not big 2 : not much 3 : not important ~ adv **less** \'les\, **least** \'lēst\ 1 : slightly 2 : not often ~ n : small amount —**lit·tle·ness** n

lit·ur·gy \'litərjē\ n, pl **-gies** : rite of worship —**li·tur·gi·cal** \lə'tərjikəl\ adj —**li·tur·gi·cal·ly** \-klē\ adv —**lit·ur·gist** \'litərjist\ n

liv·able \'livəbəl\ adj : suitable for living in or with —**liv·a·bil·i·ty** \,livə'bilətē\ n

¹live \'liv\ vb **lived; liv·ing** 1 : be alive 2 : conduct one's life 3 : subsist 4 : reside

²live \'liv\ adj 1 : having life 2 : burning 3 : connected to electric power 4 : not exploded 5 : of continuing interest 6 : involving the actual presence of real people

live·li·hood \'livlē,hud\ n : means of subsistence

live·long \'liv'loŋ\ adj : whole

live·ly \'livlē\ adj **-li·er; -est** : full of life and vigor —**live·li·ness** n

liv·en \'livən\ vb : enliven

liv·er \'livər\ n : organ that secretes bile

liv·ery \'livərē\ n, pl **-er·ies** 1 : servant's uniform 2 : care of horses for pay —**liv·er·ied** \-ēd\ adj —**liv·ery·man** \-mən\ n

lives pl of LIFE

live·stock \'liv,stäk\ n : farm animals

liv·id \'livəd\ adj 1 : discolored by bruising 2 : pale 3 : enraged

liv·ing \'liviŋ\ adj : having life ~ n : livelihood

liz·ard \'lizərd\ n : reptile with 4 legs and a long tapering tail

lla·ma \'lämə\ n : So. American mammal related to the camel

load \'lōd\ n 1 : cargo 2 : supported weight 3 : burden 4 : a large quantity—usu. pl. ~ vb 1 : put a load on 2 : burden 3 : put ammunition in

¹loaf \'lōf\ n, pl **loaves** \'lōvz\ : mass of bread

²loaf vb : waste time —**loaf·er** n

loam \'lōm, 'lum\ n : soil —**loamy** adj

loan \'lōn\ n 1 : money borrowed at interest 2 : something lent temporarily 3 : grant of use ~ vb : lend

loath \'lōth, 'lōth\ adj : very reluctant

loathe \'lōth\ vb **loathed; loath·ing** : hate

loath·ing \'lōthiŋ\ n : extreme disgust

loath·some \'lōthsəm, 'lōth-\ adj : repulsive

lob \'läb\ vb **-bb-** : throw or hit in a high arc —**lob** n

lob·by \'läbē\ n, pl **-bies** 1 : public waiting room at the entrance of a building 2 : persons lobbying ~ vb **-bied; -by·ing** : try to influence legislators —**lob·by·ist** n

lobe \'lōb\ n : rounded part —**lo·bar** \'lōbər\ adj —**lobed** \'lōbd\ adj

lo·bot·o·my \lō'bätəmē\ n, pl **-mies** : surgical severance of nerve fibers in the brain

lob·ster \'läbstər\ n : marine crustacean with 2 large pincerlike claws

lo·cal \'lōkəl\ adj : confined to or serving a limited area —**local** n —**lo·cal·ly** adv

lo·cale \lō'kal\ n : setting for an event

lo·cal·i·ty \lō'kalətē\ n, pl **-ties** : particular place

lo·cal·ize \'lōkə,liz\ vb **-ized; -iz·ing** : confine to a definite place —**lo·cal·i·za·tion** \,lōkələ'zāshən\ n

lo·cate \'lō,kāt, lō'kāt\ vb **-cat·ed; -cat·ing** 1 : settle 2 : find a site for 3 : discover the place of —**lo·ca·tion** \lō'kāshən\ n

¹lock \'läk\ n : tuft or strand of hair

²lock n 1 : fastener using a bolt 2 : enclosure in a canal to raise or lower boats ~ vb 1 : make fast with a lock 2 : confine 3 : interlock

lock·er \'läkər\ n : storage compartment

lock·et \'läkət\ n : small case worn on a necklace

lock·jaw n : tetanus

lock·out n : closing of a plant by an employer during a labor dispute

lock·smith \-,smith\ n : one who makes or repairs locks

lo·co·mo·tion \,lōkə'mōshən\ n : power of moving —**lo·co·mo·tive** \-'mōtiv\ adj

lo·co·mo·tive \-'mōtiv\ n : vehicle that moves railroad cars

lo·co·weed \'lōkō,wēd\ n : western plant poisonous to livestock

lo·cust \'lōkəst\ n 1 : migratory grasshopper 2 : cicada 3 : tree with hard wood or this wood

lo·cu·tion \lō'kyüshən\ n : way of saying something

lode \'lōd\ n : ore deposit

lode·stone n : magnetic rock

lodge \'läj\ vb **lodged; lodg·ing** 1 : provide quarters for 2 : come to rest 3 : file ~ n 1 : special house (as for hunters) 2 : animal's den 3 : branch of a fraternal organization —**lodg·er** \'läjər\ n —**lodg·ing** n —**lodg·ment, lodge·ment** \-mənt\ n

loft \'loft\ n 1 : attic 2 : upper floor (as of a warehouse)

lofty \'loftē\ adj **loft·i·er; -est** 1 : noble 2 : proud 3 : tall or high —**loft·i·ly** adv —**loft·i·ness** n

log \'log, 'läg\ n 1 : unshaped timber 2 : daily record of a ship's or plane's progress ~ vb **-gg-** 1 : cut (trees) for lumber 2 : enter in a log —**log·ger** \-ər\ n

log·a·rithm \'logə,rithəm, 'läg-\ n : exponent to which a base number is raised to produce a given number

loge \'lōzh\ n : box in a theater

log·ger·head \'logər,hed, 'läg-\ n : large Atlantic sea turtle —**at loggerheads** : in disagreement

log·ic \'läjik\ n 1 : science of reasoning 2 : sound reasoning —**log·i·cal** \-ikəl\ adj —**log·i·cal·ly** adv —**lo·gi·cian** \lō'jishən\ n

lo·gis·tics \lō'jistiks\ n sing or pl : procurement and movement of people and supplies —**lo·gis·tic** adj

logo \'lōgō, 'log-, 'läg-\ n, pl **log·os** \-ōz\ : advertising symbol

loin \'loin\ n 1 : part of the body on each side of the spine between the hip and lower ribs 2 pl : pubic regions

loi·ter \'loitər\ vb : remain around a place idly —**loi·ter·er** n

loll \'läl\ vb : lounge

lol·li·pop, lol·ly·pop \'läli,päp\ n : hard candy on a stick

lone \'lōn\ adj 1 : alone or isolated 2 : only —**lone·li·ness** n —**lone·ly** adj —**lon·er** \'lōnər\ n

lone·some \-səm\ adj : sad from lack of company —**lone·some·ly** adv —**lone·some·ness** n

long \'loŋ\ adj **lon·ger** \'loŋgər\; **long·est** \'loŋgəst\ 1 : extending far or for a considerable time 2 : having a specified length 3 : tedious 4 : well supplied—used with on ~ adv : for a long time ~ n : long period ~ vb : feel a strong desire —**long·ing** \'loŋiŋ\ n —**long·ing·ly** adv

lon·gev·i·ty \län'jevətē\ n : long life

long·hand n : handwriting

long·horn n : cattle with long horns

lon·gi·tude \'länjə,tüd, -,tyüd\ n : angular distance east or west from a meridian

lon·gi·tu·di·nal \,länjə'tüdᵊnəl, -'tyüd-\ adj : lengthwise —**lon·gi·tu·di·nal·ly** adv

long·shore·man \'loŋ'shōrmən\ n : one who loads and unloads ships

¹look \'luk\ vb 1 : see 2 : seem 3 : direct one's attention 4 : face ~ n 1 : action of looking 2 : appearance of the face 3 : aspect —**look after** : take care of —**look for** 1 : expect 2 : search for

look·out n 1 : one who watches 2 : careful watch

¹loom \'lüm\ n : frame or machine for weaving

²loom vb : appear large and indistinct or impressive

loon \'lün\ n : black-and-white diving bird

loo·ny, loo·ney \'lünē\ adj **-ni·er; -est** : crazy

loop \'lüp\ n 1 : doubling of a line that leaves an opening 2 : something like a loop —**loop** vb

loop·hole \'lüp,hōl\ n : means of evading

loose \'lüs\ adj **loos·er; -est** 1 : not fixed tight 2 : not restrained 3 : not dense 4 : slack 5 : not exact ~ vb **loosed; loos·ing** 1 : release 2 : untie or relax —**loose** adv —**loose·ly** adv —**loos·en** \'lüsᵊn\ vb —**loose·ness** n

loot \'lüt\ n or vb : plunder —**loot·er** n

lop \'läp\ vb **-pp-** : cut off

lope \'lōp\ n : bounding gait —**lope** vb

lop·sid·ed \'läp'sidəd\ adj 1 : leaning to one side 2 : not symmetrical —**lop·sid·ed·ly** adv —**lop·sid·ed·ness** n

lo·qua·cious \lō'kwāshəs\ adj : very talkative —**lo·quac·i·ty** \-'kwasətē\ n

lord \'lord\ n 1 : one with authority over others 2 : British nobleman

lord·ly \-lē\ adj **-li·er; -est** : haughty

lord·ship \-,ship\ n : rank of a lord

Lord's Supper n : Communion

lore \'lōr\ n : traditional knowledge

lose \'lüz\ vb **lost** \'lost\; **los·ing** \'lüziŋ\ 1 : have pass from one's possession 2 : be deprived of 3 : waste 4 : be defeated in 5 : fail to keep to or hold 6 : get rid of —**los·er** n

loss \'los\ n 1 : something lost 2 pl : killed, wounded, or captured soldiers 3 : failure to win

lost \'lost\ adj 1 : not used, won, or claimed 2 : unable to find the way

lot \'lät\ n 1 : object used in deciding something by chance 2 : share 3 : fate 4 : plot of land 5 : much

loth \'lōth, 'lōth\ var of LOATH

lo·tion \'lōshən\ n : liquid to rub on the skin

lot·tery \'lätərē\ n, pl **-ter·ies** : drawing of lots with prizes going to winners

lo·tus \'lōtəs\ n 1 : legendary fruit that causes forgetfulness 2 : water lily

loud \'laud\ adj 1 : high in volume of sound 2 : noisy 3 : obtrusive in color or pattern —**loud** adv —**loud·ly** adv —**loud·ness** n

loud·speak·er n : device that amplifies sound

lounge \'launj\ vb **lounged; loung·ing** : act or move lazily ~ n : room with comfortable furniture

lour \'laur\ var of LOWER

louse \'laus\ n, pl **lice** \'līs\ : parasitic wingless usu. flat insect

lousy \'lauzē\ adj **lous·i·er; -est** 1 : infested with lice 2 : not good —**lous·i·ly** adv —**lous·i·ness** n

lout \'laut\ n : stupid awkward person —**lout·ish** adj —**lout·ish·ly** adv

lou·ver, lou·vre \'lüvər\ n : opening having parallel slanted slats for ventilation or such a slat

love \'ləv\ n 1 : strong affection 2 : warm attachment 3 : beloved person ~ vb **loved; lov·ing** 1 : feel affection for 2 : enjoy greatly —**lov·able** \-əbəl\ adj —**love·less** adj —**lov·er** n —**lov·ing·ly** adv

love·lorn \-,lorn\ adj : deprived of love or of a lover

love·ly \'ləvlē\ adj **-li·er; -est** : beautiful —**love·li·ness** n —**lovely** adv

¹low \'lō\ vb or n : moo

²low adj **low·er; low·est** 1 : not high or tall 2 : below normal level 3 : not loud 4 : humble 5 : sad 6 : less than usual 7 : falling short of a standard 8 : unfavorable ~ n : something low 2 : automobile gear giving the slowest speed —**low** adv —**low·ness** n

low·brow \'lō,brau\ n : person with little taste or intellectual interest

¹low·er \'lauər\ vb 1 : scowl 2 : become dark and threatening

²low·er \'lōər\ adj : relatively low (as in rank)

³low·er \'lōər\ vb 1 : drop 2 : let descend 3 : reduce in amount

low·land \'lōlənd, -,land\ n : low flat country

low·ly \'lōlē\ adj **-li·er; -est** 1 : humble 2 : low in rank —**low·li·ness** n

loy·al \'loiəl\ adj : faithful to a country, cause, or friend —**loy·al·ist** n —**loy·al·ly** adv —**loy·al·ty** \'loiəltē\ n

loz·enge \'läzᵊnj\ n : small medicated candy

lu·bri·cant \'lübrikənt\ n : material (as grease) to reduce friction

lu·bri·cate \-,kāt\ vb **-cat·ed; -cat·ing** : apply a lubricant to —**lu·bri·ca·tion** \,lübrə'kāshən\ n —**lu·bri·ca·tor** \'lübrə-,kātər\ n

lu·cid \'lüsəd\ adj 1 : mentally sound 2 : easily understood —**lu·cid·i·ty** \lü'sidətē\ n —**lu·cid·ly** adv —**lu·cid·ness** n

luck \'lək\ n 1 : chance 2 : good fortune —**luck·i·ly** adv —**luck·i·ness** n —**luck·less** adj —**lucky** adj

lu·cra·tive \'lükrətiv\ adj : profitable —**lu·cra·tive·ly** adv —**lu·cra·tive·ness** n

lu·di·crous \'lüdəkrəs\ adj : comically ridiculous —**lu·di·crous·ly** adv —**lu·di·crous·ness** n

lug \'ləg\ vb **-gg-** : drag or carry laboriously

lug·gage \'ləgij\ n : baggage

lu·gu·bri·ous \lu'gübrēəs\ adj : mournful often to an exaggerated degree —**lu·gu·bri·ous·ly** adv —**lu·gu·bri·ous·ness** n

luke·warm \'lük'worm\ adj 1 : moderately warm 2 : not enthusiastic

lull \'ləl\ vb : make or become quiet or relaxed ~ n : temporary calm

lul·la·by \'lələ,bī\ n, pl **-bies** : song to lull children to sleep

lum·ba·go \,ləm'bāgō\ n : rheumatic back pain

lum·ber \'ləmbər\ n : timber dressed for use ~ vb : cut logs —**lum·ber·man** n —**lum·ber·yard** n

lum·ber·jack \-,jak\ n : logger

lu·mi·nary \'lümə,nerē\ n, pl **-nar·ies** : very famous person

lu·mi·nes·cence \,lümə'nesᵊns\ n : low-temperature emission of light —**lu·mi·nes·cent** \-ᵊnt\ adj

lu·mi·nous \'lümənəs\ adj : emitting light —**lu·mi·nance** \-nəns\ n —**lu·mi·nos·i·ty** \,lümə'näsətē\ n —**lu·mi·nous·ly** adv

lump \'ləmp\ n 1 : mass of irregular shape 2 : abnormal swelling ~ vb : heap together —**lump·ish** adj —**lumpy** adj

lu·na·cy \'lünəsē\ n, pl **-cies** : state of insanity

lu·nar \'lünər\ adj : of the moon

lu·na·tic \'lünə,tik\ adj : insane —**lunatic** n

lunch \'lənch\ n : noon meal ~ vb : eat lunch

lun·cheon \'lənchən\ n : usu. formal lunch

lung \'ləŋ\ n : breathing organ in the chest —**lunged** \'ləŋd\ adj

lunge \'lənj\ n 1 : sudden thrust 2 : sudden move forward —**lunge** vb

lurch \'lərch\ n : sudden swaying —**lurch** vb

lure \'lur\ n 1 : something that attracts 2 : artificial fish bait ~ vb **lured; lur·ing** : attract

lu·rid \'lurəd\ adj 1 : gruesome 2 : sensational —**lu·rid·ly** adv

lurk \'lərk\ vb : lie in wait

lus·cious \'ləshəs\ adj 1 : pleasingly sweet in taste or smell 2 : sensually appealing —**lus·cious·ly** adv —**lus·cious·ness** n

lush \'ləsh\ adj : covered with abundant growth

lust \'ləst\ n 1 : intense sexual desire 2 : intense longing —**lust** vb —**lust·ful** adj

lus·ter, lus·tre \'ləstər\ n 1 : brightness from reflected light 2 : magnificence —**lus·ter·less** adj —**lus·trous** \-trəs\ adj

lusty \'ləstē\ adj **lust·i·er; -est** : full of vitality —**lust·i·ly** adv —**lust·i·ness** n

lute \'lüt\ n : pear-shaped stringed instrument —**lute·nist, lu·ta·nist** \'lütᵊnist\ n

lux·u·ri·ant \,ləg'zhurēənt, ,lək'shur-\ adj 1 : growing plentifully 2 : rich and varied —**lux·u·ri·ance** \-ēəns\ n —**lux·u·ri·ant·ly** adv

lux·u·ri·ate \-ē,āt\ vb **-at·ed; -at·ing** : revel

lux·u·ry \'ləkshərē, 'ləgzh-\ n, pl **-ries** 1 : great comfort 2 : something adding to pleasure or comfort —**lux·u·ri·ous** \,ləg'zhurēəs, ,lək'shur-\ adj —**lux·u·ri·ous·ly** adv

-ly adj suffix 1 : in a specified way 2 : from a specified point of view

ly·ce·um \lī'sēəm, 'līsē-\ n : hall for public lectures

lye \'lī\ n : caustic alkaline substance

lying pres part of LIE

lymph \'limf\ n : bodily liquid consisting chiefly of blood plasma and white blood cells —**lym·phat·ic** \lim'fatik\ adj

lynch \'linch\ vb : put to death by mob action —**lynch·er** n

lynx \'links\ n, pl **lynx·es** or **lynx** : wildcat

lyre \'līr\ n : ancient Greek stringed instrument

lyr·ic \'lirik\ adj 1 : suitable for singing 2 : expressing direct personal emotion ~ n 1 : lyric poem 2 pl : words of a song —**lyr·i·cal** \-ikəl\ adj

M

m \'em\ n, pl **m's** or **ms** \'emz\ : 13th letter of the alphabet

ma'am \'mam\ n : madam

ma·ca·bre \mə'käb, -'käbər, -'käbrə\ adj : gruesome

mac·ad·am \mə'kadəm\ n : pavement of cemented broken stone —**mac·ad·am·ize** \-,īz\ vb

mac·a·ro·ni \,makə'rōnē\ n : tube-shaped pasta

mac·a·roon \,makə'rün\ n : cookie of ground almonds or coconut

ma·caw \mə'ko\ n : large long-tailed parrot

¹mace \'mās\ n 1 : heavy spiked club 2 : ornamental staff as a symbol of authority

²mace n : spice from the fibrous coating of the nutmeg

ma·chete \mə'shetē\ n : large heavy knife

mach·i·na·tion \,makə'nāshən, ,mash-\ n : plot or scheme —**mach·i·nate** \'makə,nāt, 'mash-\ vb

ma·chine \mə'shēn\ n : combination of mechanical or electrical parts ~ vb **-chined; -chin·ing** : modify by machine-operated tools —**ma·chin·able** adj —**ma·chin·ery** \-ərē\ n —**ma·chin·ist** n

mack·er·el \'makərəl\ n, pl **-el** or **-els** : No. Atlantic food fish

mack·i·naw \'makə,no\ n : short heavy plaid coat

mac·ra·mé \,makrə'mā\ n : coarse lace or fringe made by knotting

mac·ro \'makrō\ adj : very large

mac·ro·cosm \'makrə,käzəm\ n : universe

mad \'mad\ adj **-dd-** 1 : insane or rabid 2 : rash and foolish 3 : angry 4 : carried away by enthusiasm —**mad·den** \'madᵊn\ vb —**mad·den·ing·ly** \'madᵊniŋlē\ adv —**mad·ly** adv —**mad·ness** n

mad·am \'madəm\ n, pl **mes·dames** \mā'däm\ —used in polite address to a woman

ma·dame \mə'dam, before a surname also 'madəm\ n, pl **mes·dames** \mā'däm\ —

used as a title for a woman not of English-speaking nationality

mad·cap \'mad,kap\ *adj* : wild or zany —**madcap** *n*

made *past of* MAKE

Ma·dei·ra \mə'dirə\ *n* : amber-colored dessert wine

ma·de·moi·selle \,madmwə'zel, -mə'zel\ *n, pl* **ma·de·moi·selles** \-'zelz\ *or* **mes·de·moi·selles** \,mādmwə'zel\ : an unmarried girl or woman —used as a title for a woman esp. of French nationality

mad·house *n* 1 : insane asylum 2 : place of great uproar or confusion

mad·man \-,man, -mən\ *n* : lunatic

mad·ri·gal \'madrigəl\ *n* : elaborate song for several voice parts

mad·wom·an \'mad,wumən\ *n* : woman who is insane

mael·strom \'mālstrəm\ *n* 1 : whirlpool 2 : tumult

mae·stro \'mīstrō\ *n, pl* **-stros** *or* **-stri** \-,strē\ : eminent composer or conductor

Ma·fia \'mäfēə\ *n* : secret criminal organization

ma·fi·o·so \,mäfē'ōsō\ *n, pl* **-si** \-sē\ : member of the Mafia

mag·a·zine \'magə,zēn\ *n* 1 : storehouse 2 : publication issued at regular intervals 3 : cartridge container in a gun

ma·gen·ta \mə'jentə\ *n* : deep purplish red color

mag·got \'magət\ *n* : wormlike fly larva —**mag·goty** *adj*

mag·ic \'majik\ *n* 1 : art of using supernatural powers 2 : extraordinary power or influence 3 : sleight of hand —**magic, mag·i·cal** \-ikəl\ *adj* —**mag·i·cal·ly** *adv* —**ma·gi·cian** \mə'jishən\ *n*

mag·is·te·ri·al \,majə'stirēəl\ *adj* 1 : authoritative 2 : relating to a magistrate

mag·is·trate \'majə,strāt\ *n* : judge —**mag·is·tra·cy** \-strəsē\ *n*

mag·ma \'magmə\ *n* : molten rock

mag·nan·i·mous \mag'nanəməs\ *adj* : noble or generous —**mag·na·nim·i·ty** \,magnə'nimətē\ *n* —**mag·nan·i·mous·ly** *adv* —**mag·nan·i·mous·ness** *n*

mag·ne·sia \mag'nēzhə, -shə\ *n* : oxide of magnesium used as a laxative

mag·ne·sium \mag'nēzēəm, -zhəm\ *n* : silver-white metallic chemical element

mag·net \'magnət\ *n* 1 : body that attracts iron 2 : something that attracts —**mag·net·ic** \mag'netik\ *adj* —**mag·net·i·cal·ly** \-iklē\ *adv* —**mag·ne·tism** \'magnə,tizəm\ *n*

mag·ne·tite \'magnə,tīt\ *n* : black iron ore

mag·ne·tize \'magnə,tīz\ *vb* **-tized; -tiz·ing** 1 : attract like a magnet 2 : give magnetic properties to —**mag·ne·tiz·able** *adj* —**mag·ne·ti·za·tion** \,magnətə'zāshən\ *n* —**mag·ne·tiz·er** *n*

mag·nif·i·cent \mag'nifəsənt\ *adj* : splendid —**mag·nif·i·cence** \-səns\ *n* —**mag·nif·i·cent·ly** *adv*

mag·ni·fy \'magnə,fī\ *vb* **-fied; -fy·ing** 1 : intensify 2 : enlarge —**mag·ni·fi·ca·tion** \,magnəfə'kāshən\ *n* —**mag·ni·fi·er** \'magnə,fīər\ *n*

mag·ni·tude \'magnə,tüd, -,tyüd\ *n* 1 : greatness of size or extent 2 : quantity

mag·no·lia \mag'nōlyə\ *n* : shrub with large fragrant flowers

mag·pie \'mag,pī\ *n* : long-tailed black-and-white bird

ma·hog·a·ny \mə'hägənē\ *n, pl* **-nies** : tropical evergreen tree or its reddish brown wood

maid \'mād\ *n* 1 : unmarried young woman 2 : female servant

maid·en \'mādᵊn\ *n* : unmarried young woman ~ *adj* : unmarried 2 : first —**maid·en·hood** \-,hud\ *n* —**maid·en·ly** *adj* **maid·en·hair** \-,har\ *n* : fern with delicate feathery fronds

¹**mail** \'māl\ *n* 1 : something sent or carried in the postal system 2 : postal system ~ *vb* : send by mail —**mail·box** *n* —**mail·man** \-,man, -mən\ *n*

²**mail** *n* : armor of metal links or plates

maim \'mām\ *vb* : seriously wound or disfigure

main \'mān\ *n* 1 : force 2 : ocean 3 : principal pipe, duct, or circuit of a utility system ~ *adj* : chief —**main·ly** *adv*

main·frame \'mān,frām\ *n* : large fast computer

main·land \'mān,land, -lənd\ *n* : part of a country on a continent

main·stay *n* : chief support

main·stream *n* : prevailing current or direction of activity or influence —**mainstream** *adj*

main·tain \mān'tān\ *vb* 1 : keep in an existing state (as of repair) 2 : sustain 3 : declare —**main·tain·abil·i·ty** \-,tānə'bilətē\ *n* —**main·tain·able** \-'tānəbəl\ *adj* —**main·te·nance** \'māntᵊnəns\ *n*

mai·tre d'hô·tel \,mātrəd'ōtel, ,me-\ *n* : head of a dining room staff

maize \'māz\ *n* : corn

maj·es·ty \'majəstē\ *n, pl* **-ties** 1 : sovereign power or dignity —used as a title 2

: grandeur or splendor —**ma·jes·tic** \mə'jestik\ *adj* —**ma·jes·ti·cal·ly** \-tiklē\ *adv*

ma·jor \'mājər\ *adj* 1 : larger or greater 2 : noteworthy or conspicuous ~ *n* 1 : commissioned officer (as in the army) ranking next below a lieutenant colonel 2 : main field of study ~ *vb* **-jored; -jor·ing** : pursue an academic major

ma·jor·do·mo \,mājər'dōmō\ *n, pl* **-mos** : head steward

major general *n* : commissioned officer (as in the army) ranking next below a lieutenant general

ma·jor·i·ty \mə'jorətē\ *n, pl* **-ties** 1 : age of full civil rights 2 : quantity more than half

make \'māk\ *vb* **made** \'mād\; **mak·ing** 1 : cause to exist, occur, or appear 2 : fashion or manufacture 3 : formulate in the mind 4 : constitute 5 : prepare 6 : cause to be or become 7 : carry out or perform 8 : compel 9 : gain 10 : have an effect —used with *for* ~ *n* : brand —**mak·er** *n* —**make do** *vb* : get along with what is available —**make good** *vb* 1 : repay 2 : succeed —**make out** *vb* 1 : draw up or write 2 : discern or understand 3 : fare —**make up** *vb* 1 : invent 2 : become reconciled 3 : compensate for

make–be·lieve *n* : a pretending to believe ~ *adj* : imagined or pretended

make·shift *n* : temporary substitute —**makeshift** *adj*

make·up \-,əp\ *n* 1 : way in which something is constituted 2 : cosmetics

mal·ad·just·ed \,malə'jəstəd\ *adj* : poorly adjusted (as to one's environment) —**mal·ad·just·ment** \-'jəstmənt\ *n*

mal·adroit \,malə'droit\ *adj* : clumsy or inept

mal·a·dy \'malədē\ *n, pl* **-dies** : disease or disorder

mal·aise \mə'lāz, ma-\ *n* : sense of being unwell

mal·a·mute \'malə,myüt\ *n* : powerful heavy-coated dog

mal·a·prop·ism \'malə,präp,izəm\ *n* : humorous misuse of a word

ma·lar·ia \mə'lerēə\ *n* : disease transmitted by a mosquito —**ma·lar·i·al** \-əl\ *adj*

ma·lar·key \mə'lärkē\ *n* : foolishness

mal·con·tent \malkən'tent\ *n* : discontented person —**malcontent** *adj*

male \'māl\ *adj* 1 : relating to the sex that performs a fertilizing function 2 : masculine ~ *n* : male individual —**male·ness** *n*

male·dic·tion \,malə'dikshən\ *n* : curse

male·fac·tor \'malə,faktər\ *n* : one who commits an offense esp. against the law

ma·lef·i·cent \mə'lefəsənt\ *adj* : harmful

ma·lev·o·lent \mə'levələnt\ *adj* : malicious or spiteful —**ma·lev·o·lence** \-ləns\ *n*

mal·fea·sance \mal'fēzᵊns\ *n* : misconduct by a public official

mal·for·ma·tion \malfor'māshən\ *n* : distortion or faulty formation —**malformed** \mal'formd\ *adj*

mal·func·tion \mal'fəŋkshən\ *vb* : fail to operate properly —**malfunction** *n*

mal·ice \'maləs\ *n* : desire to cause pain or injury to another —**ma·li·cious** \mə'lishəs\ *adj* —**ma·li·cious·ly** *adv*

ma·lign \mə'līn\ *adj* 1 : wicked 2 : malignant ~ *vb* : speak evil of

ma·lig·nant \mə'lignənt\ *adj* 1 : harmful 2 : likely to cause death —**ma·lig·nan·cy** \-nənsē\ *n* —**ma·lig·nant·ly** *adv* —**ma·lig·ni·ty** \-nətē\ *n*

ma·lin·ger \mə'liŋgər\ *vb* : pretend illness to avoid duty —**ma·lin·ger·er** *n*

mall \'mol\ *n* 1 : shaded promenade 2 : concourse providing access to rows of shops

mal·lard \'malərd\ *n, pl* **-lard** *or* **-lards** : common wild duck

mal·lea·ble \'malēəbəl\ *adj* 1 : easily shaped 2 : adaptable —**mal·le·a·bil·i·ty** \,malēə'bilətē\ *n*

mal·let \'malət\ *n* : hammerlike tool

mal·nour·ished \mal'nərisht\ *adj* : poorly nourished

mal·nu·tri·tion \malnü'trishən, -nyü-\ *n* : inadequate nutrition

mal·odor·ous \mal'ōdərəs\ *adj* : foul-smelling —**mal·odor·ous·ly** *adv* —**mal·odor·ous·ness** *n*

mal·prac·tice \-'praktəs\ *n* : failure of professional duty

malt \'molt\ *n* : sprouted grain used in brewing

mal·treat \mal'trēt\ *vb* : treat badly —**mal·treat·ment** *n*

ma·ma, mam·ma \'mämə\ *n* : mother

mam·mal \'maməl\ *n* : warm-blooded vertebrate animal that nourishes its young with milk —**mam·ma·li·an** \mə'mālēən, ma-\ *adj or n*

mam·ma·ry \'mamərē\ *adj* : relating to the milk-secreting glands (**mammary glands**) of mammals

mam·mo·gram \'mamə,gram\ *n* : X-ray photograph of the breasts

mam·moth \'maməth\ *n* : large hairy extinct elephant ~ *adj* : enormous

man \'man\ *n, pl* **men** \'men\ 1 : human being 2 : adult male 3 : mankind ~ *vb* **-nn-** : supply with people for working —**man·hood** *n* —**man·hunt** *n* —**man·li·ness** *n* —**man·ly** *adj or adv* —**man–made** *adj* —**man·nish** *adj* —**man·nish·ly** *adv* —**man·nish·ness** *n* —**man·size, man–sized** *adj*

man·a·cle \'manikəl\ *n* : shackle for the hands or wrists —**manacle** *vb*

man·age \'manij\ *vb* **-aged; -ag·ing** 1 : control 2 : direct or carry on business or affairs 3 : cope —**man·age·abil·i·ty** \,manijə'bilətē\ *n* —**man·age·able** \'manijəbəl\ *adj* —**man·age·able·ness** *n* —**man·age·ably** \-blē\ *adv* —**man·age·ment** \'manijmənt\ *n* —**man·ag·er** \'manijər\ *n* —**man·a·ge·ri·al** \,manə'jirēəl\ *adj*

man·da·rin \'mandərən\ *n* : Chinese imperial official

man·date \'man,dāt\ *n* : authoritative command

man·da·to·ry \'mandə,tōrē\ *adj* : obligatory

man·di·ble \'mandəbəl\ *n* : lower jaw —**man·dib·u·lar** \man'dibyələr\ *adj*

man·do·lin \,mandə'lin, 'mandᵊlən\ *n* : stringed musical instrument

man·drake \'man,drāk\ *n* : herb with a large forked root

mane \'mān\ *n* : animal's neck hair —**maned** \'mānd\ *adj*

ma·neu·ver \mə'nüvər, -'nyü-\ *n* 1 : planned movement of troops or ships 2 : military training exercise 3 : clever or skillful move or action —**maneuver** *vb* —**ma·neu·ver·abil·i·ty** \-,nüvərə'bilətē, -,nyü-\ *n*

man·ful \'manfəl\ *adj* : courageous —**man·ful·ly** *adv*

man·ga·nese \'maŋgə,nēz, -,nēs\ *n* : gray metallic chemical element

mange \'mānj\ *n* : skin disease of domestic animals —**mangy** \'mānjē\ *adj*

man·ger \'mānjər\ *n* : feeding trough for livestock

man·gle \'maŋgəl\ *vb* **-gled; -gling** 1 : mutilate 2 : bungle —**man·gler** *n*

man·go \'maŋgō\ *n, pl* **-goes** : juicy yellowish red tropical fruit

man·grove \'man,grōv, 'maŋ-\ *n* : tropical tree growing in salt water

man·han·dle \'man,han'dᵊl\ *vb* : handle roughly

man·hole *n* : entry to a sewer

ma·nia \'mānēə, -nyə\ *n* 1 : insanity marked by uncontrollable emotion or excitement 2 : excessive enthusiasm —**ma·ni·ac** \-nē,ak\ *n* —**ma·ni·a·cal** \mə'nīəkəl\ *adj* —**man·ic** \'manik\ *adj or n*

man·i·cure \'manə,kyur\ *n* : treatment for the fingernails ~ *vb* **-cured; -cur·ing** 1 : do manicure work on 2 : trim precisely —**man·i·cur·ist** \-,kyurist\ *n*

¹**man·i·fest** \'manə,fest\ *adj* : clear to the senses or to the mind ~ *vb* : make evident —**man·i·fes·ta·tion** \,manəfə'stāshən\ *n* —**man·i·fest·ly** *adv*

²**manifest** *n* : invoice of cargo or list of passengers

man·i·fes·to \,manə'festō\ *n, pl* **-tos** *or* **-toes** : public declaration of policy or views

man·i·fold \'manə,fōld\ *adj* : marked by diversity or variety ~ *n* : pipe fitting with several outlets for connections

ma·nila paper \mə'nilə-\ *n* : durable brownish paper

ma·nip·u·late \mə'nipyə,lāt\ *vb* **-lat·ed; -lat·ing** 1 : treat or operate manually or mechanically 2 : influence esp. by cunning —**ma·nip·u·la·tion** \mə,nipyə'lāshən\ *n* —**ma·nip·u·la·tive** \-'nipyə,lātiv, -,lətiv\ *adj* —**ma·nip·u·la·tor** \-'nipyə,lātər\ *n*

man·kind \'man'kīnd\ *n* : human race

man·na \'manə\ *n* : something valuable that comes unexpectedly

manned \'mand\ *adj* : carrying or performed by a man

man·ne·quin \'manikən\ *n* : dummy used to display clothes

man·ner \'manər\ *n* 1 : kind 2 : usual way of acting 3 : artistic method 4 *pl* : social conduct

man·nered \-ərd\ *adj* 1 : having manners of a specified kind 2 : artificial

man·ner·ism \'manə,rizəm\ *n* : individual peculiarity of action

man·ner·ly \-lē\ *adj* : polite —**man·ner·li·ness** *n* —**mannerly** *adv*

man-of-war \,manə'wor, -əv'wor\ *n, pl* **men-of-war** \,men-\ : warship

man·or \'manər\ *n* : country estate —**ma·no·ri·al** \mə'nórēəl\ *adj*

man·pow·er *n* : supply of people available for service

man·sard \'man,särd\ *n* : roof with two slopes on all sides and the lower slope the steeper

manse \'mans\ *n* : parsonage

man·ser·vant *n, pl* **men·ser·vants** : a male servant

man·sion \'manchən\ *n* : very big house

man·slaugh·ter *n* : unintentional killing of a person

man·tel \'mantᵊl\ *n* : shelf above a fireplace

man·tis \'mantəs\ *n, pl* **-tis·es** *or* **-tes** \'man,tēz\ : large green insect-eating insect with stout forelegs

man·tle \'mantᵊl\ *n* 1 : sleeveless cloak 2 : something that covers, enfolds, or envelops —**mantle** *vb*

man·tra \'mantrə\ *n* : mystical chant

man·u·al \'manyəwəl\ *adj* : involving the hands or physical force ~ *n* : handbook —**man·u·al·ly** *adv*

man·u·fac·ture \,manyə'fakchər, ,manə-\ *n* : process of making wares by hand or by machinery ~ *vb* **-tured; -tur·ing** : make from raw materials —**man·u·fac·tur·er** *n*

ma·nure \mə'nur, -'nyur\ *n* : animal excrement used as fertilizer

manu·script \'manyə,skript\ *n* 1 : something written or typed 2 : document submitted for publication

many \'menē\ *adj* **more** \'mōr\; **most** \'mōst\ : consisting of a large number —**many** *n or pron*

map \'map\ *n* : representation of a geographical area ~ *vb* **-pp-** 1 : make a map of 2 : plan in detail —**map·pa·ble** \-əbəl\ *adj* —**map·per** *n*

ma·ple \'māpəl\ *n* : tree with hard light-colored wood

mar \'mär\ *vb* **-rr-** : damage

mar·a·schi·no \,marə'skēnō, -'shē-\ *n, pl* **-nos** : preserved cherry

mar·a·thon \'marə,thän\ *n* 1 : long-distance race 2 : test of endurance —**mar·a·thon·er** \-,thänər\ *n*

ma·raud \mə'rod\ *vb* : roam about in search of plunder —**ma·raud·er** *n*

mar·ble \'märbəl\ *n* 1 : crystallized limestone 2 : small glass ball used in a children's game (**marbles**)

mar·bling \-bəliŋ\ *n* : intermixture of fat and lean in meat

march \'märch\ *vb* : move with regular steps or in a purposeful manner ~ *n* 1 : distance covered in a march 2 : measured stride 3 : forward movement 4 : music for marching —**march·er** *n*

March *n* : 3d month of the year having 31 days

mar·chio·ness \'märshənəs\ *n* : woman holding the rank of a marquess

Mar·di Gras \'märdē,grä\ *n* : Tuesday before the beginning of Lent often observed with parades and merrymaking

mare \'mar\ *n* : female horse

mar·ga·rine \'märjərən\ *n* : butter substitute made usu. from vegetable oils

mar·gin \'märjən\ *n* 1 : edge 2 : spare amount, measure, or degree

mar·gin·al \-jənᵊl\ *adj* 1 : relating to or situated at a border or margin 2 : close to the lower limit of acceptability —**mar·gin·al·ly** *adv*

mari·gold \'marə,gōld\ *n* : garden plant with showy flower heads

mar·i·jua·na \,marə'wänə, -'hwä-\ *n* : intoxicating drug obtained from the hemp plant

ma·ri·na \mə'rēnə\ *n* : place for mooring pleasure boats

mar·i·nate \'marə,nāt\ *vb* **-nat·ed; -nat·ing** : soak in a savory sauce

ma·rine \mə'rēn\ *adj* 1 : relating to the sea 2 : relating to marines ~ *n* : infantry soldier associated with a navy

mar·i·ner \'marənər\ *n* : sailor

mar·i·o·nette \,marēə'net\ *n* : puppet

mar·i·tal \'marətᵊl\ *adj* : relating to marriage

mar·i·time \'marə,tīm\ *adj* : relating to the sea or commerce on the sea

mar·jo·ram \'märjərəm\ *n* : aromatic mint used as a seasoning

mark \'märk\ *n* 1 : something aimed at 2 : something (as a line) designed to record position 3 : visible sign 4 : written symbol 5 : grade 6 : lasting impression 7 : blemish ~ *vb* 1 : designate or set apart by a mark or make a mark on 2 : characterize 3 : remark —**mark·er** *n*

marked \'märkt\ *adj* : noticeable —**mark·ed·ly** \'märkədlē\ *adv*

mar·ket \'märkət\ *n* 1 : buying and selling of goods or the place this happens 2 : demand for commodities 3 : store ~ *vb* : sell —**mar·ket·able** *adj*

mar·ket·place *n* 1 : market 2 : world of trade or economic activity

marks·man \'märksmən\ *n* : good shooter —**marks·man·ship** *n*

mar·lin \'märlən\ *n* : large oceanic fish

mar·ma·lade \'märmə,lād\ *n* : jam with pieces of fruit and rind

mar·mo·set \'märmə,set\ *n* : small bushy-tailed monkey

mar·mot \'märmət\ *n* : burrowing rodent

¹**ma·roon** \mə'rün\ *vb* : isolate without hope of escape

²**maroon** *n* : dark red color

mar·quee \mär'kē\ *n* : canopy over an entrance

mar·quess \'märkwəs\, **mar·quis** \'märk-**

wəs, mär'kē\ *n, pl* **-quess•es** or **-quis•es** or **-quis** : British noble ranking next below a duke

mar•quise \mär'kēz\ *n, pl* **mar•quises** \-'kēz, -'kēzəz\ : marchioness

mar•riage \marij\ *n* 1 : state of being married 2 : wedding ceremony —**mar•riage•able** *adj*

mar•row \marō\ *n* : soft tissue in the cavity of bone

mar•ry \marē\ *vb* **-ried; -ry•ing** 1 : join as husband and wife 2 : take or give in marriage —**mar•ried** *adj or n*

marsh \märsh\ *n* : soft wet land —**marshy** *adj*

mar•shal \märshəl\ *n* 1 : leader of ceremony 2 : usu. high military or administrative officer ~ *vb* **-shaled** or **-shalled; -shal•ing** or **-shal•ling** 1 : arrange in order, rank, or position 2 : lead with ceremony

marsh•mal•low \märsh,melō, -,malō\ *n* : spongy candy

mar•su•pi•al \mär'süpēəl\ *n* : mammal that nourishes young in an abdominal pouch —**marsupial** *adj*

mart \märt\ *n* : market

mar•ten \märt°n\ *n, pl* **-ten** or **-tens** : weasellike mammal with soft fur

mar•tial \märshəl\ *adj* 1 : relating to war or an army 2 : warlike

mar•tin \märt°n\ *n* : small swallow

mar•ti•net \märt°n'et\ *n* : strict disciplinarian

mar•tyr \märtər\ *n* : one who dies or makes a great sacrifice for a cause ~ *vb* : make a martyr of —**mar•tyr•dom** \-dəm\ *n*

mar•vel \märvəl\ *vb* **-veled** or **-velled; -vel•ing** or **-vel•ling** : feel surprise or wonder ~ *n* : something amazing —**mar•vel•ous, mar•vel•lous** \märvələs\ *adj* —**mar•vel•ous•ly** *adv* —**mar•vel•ous•ness** *n*

Marx•ism \märk,sizəm\ *n* : political and social principles of Karl Marx —**Marx•ist** \-sist\ *n or adj*

mas•cara \mas'karə\ *n* : eye cosmetic

mas•cot \mas,kät, -kət\ *n* : one believed to bring good luck

mas•cu•line \maskyələn\ *adj* : relating to the male sex —**mas•cu•lin•i•ty** \,maskyə'linətē\ *n*

mash \mash\ *n* 1 : crushed steeped grain for fermenting 2 : soft pulpy mass ~ *vb* 1 : reduce to a pulpy mass 2 : smash —**mash•er** *n*

mask \mask\ *n* : disguise for the face ~ *vb* 1 : disguise 2 : cover to protect —**mask•er** *n*

mas•och•ism \masə,kizəm, maz-\ *n* : pleasure in being abused —**mas•och•ist** \-kist\ *n* —**mas•och•is•tic** \masə'kistik, ,maz-\ *adj*

ma•son \mās°n\ *n* : workman who builds with stone or brick —**ma•son•ry** \-rē\ *n*

mas•quer•ade \maskə'rād\ *n* 1 : costume party 2 : disguise ~ *vb* **-ad•ed; -ad•ing** 1 : disguise oneself 2 : take part in a costume party —**mas•quer•ad•er** *n*

mass \mas\ *n* 1 : large amount of matter or number of things 2 : expanse or magnitude 3 : great body of people —usu. pl. ~ *vb* : form into a mass —**mass•less** \-ləs\ *adj* —**massy** *adj*

Mass *n* : worship service of the Roman Catholic Church

mas•sa•cre \masikər\ *n* : wholesale slaughter —**massacre** *vb*

mas•sage \mə'säzh, -'säj\ *n* : a rubbing of the body —**massage** *vb*

mas•seur \ma'sər\ *n* : man who massages

mas•seuse \-'sēz, -'süz\ *n* : woman who massages

mas•sive \masiv\ *adj* 1 : being a large mass 2 : large in scope —**mas•sive•ly** *adv* —**mas•sive•ness** *n*

mast \mast\ *n* : tall pole esp. for supporting sails —**mast•ed** *adj*

mas•ter \mastər\ *n* 1 : male teacher 2 : holder of an academic degree between a bachelor's and a doctor's 3 : one highly skilled 4 : one in authority ~ *vb* 1 : subdue 2 : become proficient in —**mas•ter•ful** \-fəl\ *adj* —**mas•ter•ful•ly** *adv* —**mas•ter•ly** *adj* —**mas•tery** \mastərē\ *n*

master chief petty officer *n* : petty officer of the highest rank in the navy

master gunnery sergeant *n* : noncommissioned officer in the marine corps ranking above a master sergeant

mas•ter•piece \mastər,pēs\ *n* : great piece of work

master sergeant *n* 1 : noncommissioned officer in the army ranking next below a sergeant major 2 : noncommissioned officer in the air force ranking next below a senior master sergeant 3 : noncommissioned officer in the marine corps ranking next below a master gunnery sergeant

mas•ter•work *n* : masterpiece

mas•tic \mastik\ *n* : pasty glue

mas•ti•cate \masti,kāt\ *vb* **-cat•ed; -cat•ing** : chew —**mas•ti•ca•tion** \masti'kāshən\ *n*

mas•tiff \mastəf\ *n* : large dog

mast•odon \mastə,dän\ *n* : extinct elephantlike animal

mas•toid \mas,toíd\ *n* : bone behind the ear —**mastoid** *adj*

mas•tur•ba•tion \,mastər'bāshən\ *n* : stimulation of sex organs by hand —**mas•tur•bate** \mastər,bāt\ *vb*

¹**mat** \mat\ *n* 1 : coarse woven or plaited fabric 2 : mass of tangled strands 3 : thick pad ~ *vb* **-tt-** : form into a mat

²**mat** *vb* **-tt-** 1 : make matte 2 : provide (a picture) with a mat ~ or **matt** or **matte** *n* : border around a picture

³**mat** *var of* MATTE

mat•a•dor \matə,dór\ *n* : bullfighter

¹**match** \mach\ *n* 1 : one equal to another 2 : one able to cope with another 3 : suitable pairing 4 : game 5 : marriage ~ *vb* 1 : set in competition 2 : marry 3 : be or provide the equal of 4 : fit or go together —**match•less** *adj* —**match•mak•er** *n*

²**match** *n* : piece of wood or paper material with a combustible tip

mate \māt\ *n* 1 : companion 2 : subordinate officer on a ship 3 : one of a pair ~ *vb* **mat•ed; mat•ing** 1 : fit together 2 : come together as a pair 3 : copulate

ma•te•ri•al \mə'tirēəl\ *adj* 1 : natural 2 : relating to matter 3 : important 4 : of a physical or worldly nature ~ *n* : stuff something is made of —**ma•te•ri•al•ly** *adv*

ma•te•ri•al•ism \mə'tirēə,lizəm\ *n* 1 : theory that matter is the only reality 2 : preoccupation with material and not spiritual things —**ma•te•ri•al•ist** \-list\ *n or adj* —**ma•te•ri•al•is•tic** \-,tirēə'listik\ *adj*

ma•te•ri•al•ize \mə'tirēə,līz\ *vb* **-ized; -iz•ing** : take or cause to take bodily form —**ma•te•ri•al•i•za•tion** \mə,tirēələ'zāshən\ *n*

ma•té•ri•el, ma•te•ri•el \mə,tirē'el\ *n* : military supplies

ma•ter•nal \mə'tərn°l\ *adj* : motherly —**ma•ter•nal•ly** *adv*

ma•ter•ni•ty \mə'tərnətē\ *n, pl* **-ties** 1 : state of being a mother 2 : hospital's childbirth facility ~ *adj* 1 : worn during pregnancy 2 : relating to the period close to childbirth

math \math\ *n* : mathematics

math•e•mat•ics \mathə'matiks\ *n pl* : science of numbers and of shapes in space —**math•e•mat•i•cal** \-ikəl\ *adj* —**math•e•mat•i•cal•ly** *adv* —**math•e•ma•ti•cian** \mathəmə'tishən\ *n*

mat•i•nee, mat•i•née \mat°n'ā\ *n* : afternoon performance

mat•ins \mat°nz\ *n* : morning prayers

ma•tri•arch \mātrē,ärk\ *n* : woman who rules a family —**ma•tri•ar•chal** \,mātrē-'ärkəl\ *adj* —**ma•tri•ar•chy** \mātrē,ärkē\ *n*

ma•tri•cide \matrə,sīd, mā-\ *n* : murder of one's mother —**ma•tri•cid•al** \,matrə-'sīd°l, ,mā-\ *adj*

ma•tric•u•late \mə'trikyə,lāt\ *vb* **-lat•ed; -lat•ing** : enroll in school —**ma•tric•u•la•tion** \-,trikyə'lāshən\ *n*

mat•ri•mo•ny \matrə,mōnē\ *n* : marriage —**mat•ri•mo•ni•al** \,matrə'mōnēəl\ *adj* —**mat•ri•mo•ni•al•ly** *adv*

ma•trix \mātriks\ *n, pl* **-tri•ces** \mātrə,sēz, 'ma-\ or **-trix•es** \mātriksəz\ : something (as a mold) that gives form, foundation, or origin to something else enclosed in it

ma•tron \mātrən\ *n* 1 : dignified mature woman 2 : woman supervisor —**ma•tron•ly** *adj*

matte \mat\ *adj* : not shiny

mat•ter \matər\ *n* 1 : subject of interest 2 *pl* : circumstances 3 : trouble 4 : physical substance ~ *vb* : be important

mat•tock \matək\ *n* : a digging tool

mat•tress \matrəs\ *n* : pad to sleep on

ma•ture \mə'túr, -'tyúr, -'chúr\ *adj* **-tur•er; -est** 1 : carefully considered 2 : fully grown or developed 3 : due for payment ~ *vb* **-tured; -tur•ing** : become mature —**mat•u•ra•tion** \,machə'rāshən\ *n* —**ma•ture•ly** *adv* —**ma•tu•ri•ty** \mə'túrətē\ *n*

maud•lin \módlən\ *adj* : excessively sentimental

maul \mól\ *n* : heavy hammer ~ *vb* 1 : beat 2 : handle roughly

mau•so•le•um \,mósə'lēəm, ,mózə-\ *n, pl* **-leums** or **-lea** \-'lēə\ : large aboveground tomb

mauve \mōv, móv\ *n* : lilac color

ma•ven, ma•vin \māvən\ *n* : expert

mav•er•ick \mavrik\ *n* 1 : unbranded range animal 2 : nonconformist

maw \mó\ *n* 1 : stomach 2 : throat, esophagus, or jaws

mawk•ish \mókish\ *adj* : sickly sentimental —**mawk•ish•ly** *adv* —**mawk•ish•ness** *n*

max•im \maksəm\ *n* : proverb

max•i•mum \maksəməm\ *n, pl* **-ma** \-səmə\ or **-mums** 1 : greatest quantity 2 : upper limit 3 : largest number —**max•imum** *adj* —**max•i•mize** \-sə-,mīz\ *vb*

may \mā\ *verbal auxiliary, past* **might** \mīt\ *pres sing & pl* **may** 1 : have permission 2 : be likely to 3 —used to express desire, purpose, or contingency

May \mā\ *n* : 5th month of the year having 31 days

may•ap•ple *n* : woodland herb having edible fruit

may•be \mābē\ *adv* : perhaps

may•flow•er *n* : spring-blooming herb

may•fly *n* : fly with an aquatic larva

may•hem \mā,hem, māəm\ *n* 1 : crippling or mutilation of a person 2 : needless damage

may•on•naise \māə,nāz\ *n* : creamy white sandwich spread

may•or \māər, 'mer\ *n* : chief city official —**may•or•al** \-əl\ *adj* —**may•or•al•ty** \-əltē\ *n*

maze \māz\ *n* : confusing network of passages —**mazy** *adj*

ma•zur•ka \mə'zərkə\ *n* : Polish dance

me \mē\ *pron, objective case of* I

mead \mēd\ *n* : alcoholic beverage brewed from honey

mead•ow \medō\ *n* : low-lying usu. level grassland —**mead•ow•land** \-,land\ *n*

mead•ow•lark *n* : songbird with a yellow breast

mea•ger, mea•gre \mēgər\ *adj* 1 : thin 2 : lacking richness or strength —**mea•ger•ly** *adv* —**mea•ger•ness** *n*

¹**meal** \mēl\ *n* 1 : food to be eaten at one time 2 : act of eating —**meal•time** *n*

²**meal** *n* : ground grain —**mealy** *adj*

¹**mean** \mēn\ *adj* 1 : humble 2 : worthy of or showing little regard 3 : stingy 4 : malicious —**mean•ly** *adv* —**mean•ness** *n*

²**mean** \mēn\ *vb* **meant** \ment\; **mean•ing** \mēniŋ\ 1 : intend 2 : serve to convey, show, or indicate 3 : be important

³**mean** *n* 1 : middle point 2 *pl* : something that helps gain an end 3 *pl* : material resources 4 : sum of several quantities divided by the number of quantities ~ *adj* : being a mean

me•an•der \mē'andər\ *vb* **-dered; -der•ing** 1 : follow a winding course 2 : wander aimlessly —**meander** *n*

mean•ing \mēniŋ\ *n* 1 : idea conveyed or intended to be conveyed 2 : aim —**mean•ing•ful** \-fəl\ *adj* —**mean•ing•ful•ly** *adv* —**mean•ing•less** *adj*

mean•time \mēn,tīm\ *n* : intervening time —**meantime** *adv*

mean•while \-,hwīl\ *n* : meantime ~ *adv* 1 : meantime 2 : at the same time

mea•sles \mēzəlz\ *n pl* : disease that is marked by red spots on the skin

mea•sly \mēzlē\ *adj* **-sli•er; -est** : contemptibly small in amount

mea•sure \mezhər, māzh-\ *n* 1 : moderate amount 2 : dimensions or amount 3 : something to show amount 4 : unit or system of measurement 5 : act of measuring 6 : means to an end ~ *vb* **-sured; -sur•ing** 1 : find out or mark off size or amount of 2 : have a specified measurement —**mea•sur•able** \mezhərəbəl, 'māzh-\ *adj* —**mea•sur•ably** \-blē\ *adv* —**mea•sure•less** *adj* —**mea•sure•ment** *n* —**mea•sur•er** *n*

meat \mēt\ *n* 1 : food 2 : animal flesh used as food —**meat•ball** *n* —**meaty** *adj*

me•chan•ic \mi'kanik\ *n* : worker who repairs cars

me•chan•i•cal \mi'kanikəl\ *adj* 1 : relating to machines or mechanics 2 : involuntary —**me•chan•i•cal•ly** *adv*

me•chan•ics \-iks\ *n sing or pl* 1 : branch of physics dealing with energy and forces in relation to bodies 2 : mechanical details

mech•a•nism \mekə,nizəm\ *n* 1 : piece of machinery 2 : technique for gaining a result 3 : basic processes producing a phenomenon —**mech•a•nis•tic** \,mekə'nistik\ *adj* —**mech•a•ni•za•tion** \mekənə'zāshən\ *n* —**mech•a•nize** \mekə,nīz\ *vb* —**mech•a•niz•er** *n*

med•al \med°l\ *n* 1 : religious pin or pendant 2 : coinlike commemorative metal piece

med•al•ist, med•al•list \med°list\ *n* : person awarded a medal

me•dal•lion \mə'dalyən\ *n* : large medal

med•dle \med°l\ *vb* **-dled; -dling** : interfere —**med•dler** \med°lər\ *n* —**med•dle•some** \med°lsəm\ *adj*

me•dia \mēdēə\ *n pl* : communications organizations

me•di•an \mēdēən\ *n* : middle value in a range —**median** *adj*

me•di•ate \mēdē,āt\ *vb* **-at•ed; -at•ing** : help settle a dispute —**me•di•a•tion** \,mēdē'āshən\ *n* —**me•di•a•tor** \mēdē-,ātər\ *n*

med•ic \medik\ *n* : medical worker esp. in the military

med•i•ca•ble \medikəbəl\ *adj* : curable

med•ic•aid \medi,kād\ *n* : government program of medical aid for the poor

med•i•cal \medikəl\ *adj* : relating to medicine —**med•i•cal•ly** \-klē\ *adv*

medi•care \medi,ker\ *n* : government program of medical care for the aged

med•i•cate \medə,kāt\ *vb* **-cat•ed; -cat•ing** : treat with medicine

med•i•ca•tion \,medə'kāshən\ *n* 1 : act of medicating 2 : medicine

med•i•cine \medəsən\ *n* 1 : preparation used to treat disease 2 : science dealing with the cure of disease —**me•dic•i•nal** \mə'dis°nəl\ *adj* —**me•dic•i•nal•ly** *adv*

me•di•e•val, me•di•ae•val \,mēdē'ēval, ,med-, ,mid-; ,mē'dē-, ,me-, ,mi-\ *adj* : of or relating to the Middle Ages —**me•di•eval•ist** \-ist\ *n*

me•di•o•cre \,mēdē'ōkər\ *adj* : not very good —**me•di•oc•ri•ty** \-'äkrətē\ *n*

med•i•tate \medə,tāt\ *vb* **-tat•ed; -tat•ing** : contemplate —**med•i•ta•tion** \,medə'tāshən\ *n* —**med•i•ta•tive** \medə,tātiv\ *adj* —**med•i•ta•tive•ly** *adv*

me•di•um \mēdēəm\ *n, pl* **-diums** or **-dia** \-ēə\ 1 : middle position or degree 2 : means of effecting or conveying something 3 : surrounding substance 4 : means of communication 5 : mode of artistic expression —**medium** *adj*

med•ley \medlē\ *n, pl* **-leys** : series of songs performed as one

meek \mēk\ *adj* 1 : mild-mannered 2 : lacking spirit —**meek•ly** *adv* —**meek•ness** *n*

meer•schaum \mirshəm, -,shóm\ *n* : claylike tobacco pipe

¹**meet** \mēt\ *vb* **met** \met\; **meet•ing** 1 : run into 2 : join 3 : oppose 4 : assemble 5 : satisfy 6 : be introduced to ~ *n* : sports team competition

²**meet** *adj* : proper

meet•ing \mētiŋ\ *n* : a getting together —**meet•ing•house** *n*

mega•byte \megə,bīt\ *n* : unit of computer storage capacity

mega•hertz \-,hərts, -,herts\ *n* : one million hertz

mega•phone \megə,fōn\ *n* : cone-shaped device to intensify or direct the voice

mel•an•choly \melən,kälē\ *n* : depression —**mel•an•chol•ic** \melən'kälik\ *adj* —**melancholy** *adj*

mel•a•no•ma \,melə'nōmə\ *n, pl* **-mas** : usu. malignant skin tumor

me•lee \mā,lā, mā'lā\ *n* : brawl

me•lio•rate \mēlyə,rāt, mēlēə-\ *vb* **-rat•ed; -rat•ing** : improve —**me•lio•ra•tion** \,mēlyə'rāshən, ,mēlēə-\ *n* —**me•lio•ra•tive** \mēlyə,rātiv, mēlēə-\ *adj*

mel•lif•lu•ous \me'liflawəs, mə-\ *adj* : sweetly flowing —**mel•lif•lu•ous•ly** *adv* —**mel•lif•lu•ous•ness** *n*

mel•low \melō\ *adj* 1 : grown gentle or mild 2 : rich and full —**mellow** *vb* —**mel•low•ness** *n*

melo•dra•ma \melə,drämə, -,dram-\ *n* : overly theatrical play —**melo•dra•mat•ic** \,melədrə'matik\ *adj* —**melo•dra•mat•i•cal•ly** \-tiklē\ *adv*

mel•o•dy \melədē\ *n, pl* **-dies** 1 : agreeable sound 2 : succession of musical notes —**me•lod•ic** \mə'lädik\ *adj* —**me•lod•i•cal•ly** \-iklē\ *adv* —**me•lo•di•ous** \mə'lōdēəs\ *adj* —**me•lo•di•ous•ly** *adv* —**me•lo•di•ous•ness** *n*

mel•on \melən\ *n* : gourdlike fruit

melt \melt\ *vb* 1 : change from solid to liquid usu. by heat 2 : dissolve or disappear gradually 3 : move or be moved emotionally

mem•ber \membər\ *n* 1 : part of a person, animal, or plant 2 : one of a group 3 : part of a whole —**mem•ber•ship** \-,ship\ *n*

mem•brane \mem,brān\ *n* : thin layer esp. in an organism —**mem•bra•nous** \-brənəs\ *adj*

me•men•to \mi'mentō\ *n, pl* **-tos** or **-toes** : souvenir

memo \memō\ *n, pl* **mem•os** : memorandum

mem•oirs \mem,wärz\ *n pl* : autobiography

mem•o•ra•bil•ia \,memərə'bilēə, -'bil-yə\ *n pl* 1 : memorable things or mementos

mem•o•ra•ble \memərəbəl\ *adj* : worth remembering —**mem•o•ra•bil•i•ty** \,memə-rə'bilətē\ *n* —**mem•o•ra•ble•ness** *n* —**mem•o•ra•bly** \-blē\ *adv*

mem•o•ran•dum \,memə'randəm\ *n, pl* **-dums** or **-da** \-də\ : informal note

me•mo•ri•al \mə'mōrēəl\ *n* : something (as a monument) meant to keep remembrance alive —**memorial** *adj* —**me•mo•ri•al•ize** *vb*

Memorial Day *n* : last Monday in May or formerly May 30 observed as a legal holiday in commemoration of dead servicemen

mem•o•ry \memrē, 'memə-\ *n, pl* **-ries** 1 : power of remembering 2 : something remembered 3 : commemoration 4 : time within which past events are remembered —**mem•o•ri•za•tion** \,memərə'zāshən\ *n* —**mem•o•rize** \memə,rīz\ *vb* —**mem•o•riz•er** *n*

men *pl of* MAN

men•ace \menəs\ *n* : threat of danger ~ *vb*

-aced; -ac•ing 1 : threaten 2 : endanger —men•ac•ing•ly adv

me•nag•er•ie \mə'najərē\ n : collection of wild animals

mend \'mend\ vb 1 : improve 2 : repair 3 : heal —mend n —mend•er n

men•da•cious \men'dāshəs\ adj : dishonest —men•da•cious•ly adv —men•dac•i•ty \-'dasətē\ n

men•di•cant \'mendikənt\ n : beggar — men•di•can•cy \-kənsē\ n —mendicant adj

men•ha•den \men'hādᵊn, mən-\ n, pl -den : fish related to the herring

me•nial \'mēnēəl, -nyəl\ adj 1 : relating to servants 2 : humble ~ n : domestic servant —me•ni•al•ly adv

men•in•gi•tis \menən'jītəs\ n, pl -git•i•des \-'jitə,dēz\ : disease of the brain and spinal cord

meno•pause \'menə,póz\ n : time when menstruation ends —meno•paus•al \menə'pózəl\ adj

me•no•rah \mə'nōrə\ n : candelabrum used in Jewish worship

men•stru•a•tion \menstrə'wāshən, men'strā-\ n : monthly discharge of blood from the uterus —men•stru•al \'menstrəwəl\ adj —men•stru•ate \menstrə,wāt, -,strāt\ vb

-ment \mənt\ n suffix 1 : result or means of an action 2 : action or process 3 : place of an action 4 : state or condition

men•tal \'mentᵊl\ adj : relating to the mind or its disorders —men•tal•i•ty \men'talətē\ n —men•tal•ly adv

men•thol \'men,thól, -,thōl\ n : soothing substance from oil of peppermint —men•tho•lat•ed \-thə,lātəd\ adj

men•tion \'menchən\ vb : refer to —mention n

men•tor \'men,tór, 'mentər\ n : instructor

menu \'menyü\ n 1 : restaurant's list of food 2 : list of offerings

me•ow \mē'aù\ n : characteristic cry of a cat —meow vb

mer•can•tile \'mərkən,tēl, -,tīl\ adj : relating to merchants or trade

mer•ce•nary \'mərsᵊn,erē\ n, pl -nar•ies : hired soldier ~ adj : serving only for money

mer•chan•dise \'mərchən,dīz, -,dīs\ n : goods bought and sold ~ vb -dised; -dis•ing : buy and sell — mer•chan•dis•er n

mer•chant \'mərchənt\ n : one who buys and sells

merchant marine n : commercial ships

mer•cu•ri•al \mər'kyùrēəl\ adj : unpredictable —mer•cu•ri•al•ly adv —mer•cu•ri•al•ness n

mer•cu•ry \'mərkyərē\ n : heavy liquid metallic chemical element

mer•cy \'mərsē\ n, pl -cies 1 : show of pity or leniency 2 : divine blessing —mer•ci•ful \-sifəl\ adj —mer•ci•ful•ly adv —mer•ci•less \-siləs\ adj —mer•ci•less•ly adv —mercy adj

mere \'mir\ adj, superlative mer•est : nothing more than —mere•ly adv

merge \'mərj\ vb merged; merg•ing 1 : unite 2 : blend —merg•er \'mərjər\ n

me•rid•i•an \mə'ridēən\ n : imaginary circle on the earth's surface passing through the poles —meridian adj

me•ringue \mə'raŋ\ n : baked dessert topping of beaten egg whites

me•ri•no \mə'rēnō\ n, pl -nos 1 : kind of sheep 2 : fine soft woolen yarn

mer•it \'merət\ n 1 : praiseworthy quality 2 pl : rights and wrongs of a legal case ~ vb : deserve —mer•i•to•ri•ous \merə'tōrēəs\ adj —mer•i•to•ri•ous•ly adv —mer•i•to•ri•ous•ness n

mer•maid \'mər,mād\ n : legendary female sea creature

mer•ry \'merē\ adj -ri•er; -est : full of high spirits —mer•ri•ly adv —mer•ri•ment \'merimənt\ n —mer•ry•mak•er \merē,mākər\ n —mer•ry•mak•ing \merē,mākiŋ\ n

merry-go-round n : revolving amusement ride

me•sa \'māsə\ n : steep flat-topped hill

mes•dames pl of MADAM or of MADAME or of MRS.

mes•de•moi•selles pl of MADEMOISELLE

mesh \'mesh\ n 1 : one of the openings in a net 2 : net fabric 3 : working contact ~ vb : fit together properly —meshed \'mesht\ adj

mes•mer•ize \'mezmə,rīz\ vb -ized; -iz•ing : hypnotize

mess \'mes\ n 1 : meal eaten by a group 2 : confused, dirty, or offensive state ~ vb 1 : make dirty or untidy 2 : putter 3 : interfere —messy adj

mes•sage \'mesij\ n : news, information, or a command sent by one person to another

mes•sen•ger \'mesᵊnjər\ n : one who carries a message or does an errand

Mes•si•ah \mə'sīə\ n 1 : expected deliverer of the Jews 2 : Jesus Christ not cap : great leader

messieurs pl of MONSIEUR

Messrs. pl of MR.

mes•ti•zo \me'stēzō\ n, pl -zos : person of mixed blood

met past of MEET

me•tab•o•lism \mə'tabə,lizəm\ n : biochemical processes necessary to life —met•a•bol•ic \metə'bälik\ adj —me•tab•o•lize \mə'tabə,līz\ vb

met•al \'metᵊl\ n : shiny substance that can be melted and shaped and conducts heat and electricity —me•tal•lic \mə'talik\ adj —met•al•ware n —met•al•work n —met•al•work•er n —met•al•work•ing n

met•al•lur•gy \'metᵊl,ərjē\ n : science of metals —met•al•lur•gi•cal \metᵊl'ərjikəl\ adj —met•al•lur•gist \metᵊl,ərjist\ n

meta•mor•pho•sis \metə'mórfəsəs\ n, pl -pho•ses \-,sēz\ : sudden and drastic change (as of form) —metamorphose \-,fōz, -,fōs\ vb

met•a•phor \'metə,fòr, -fər\ n : use of a word denoting one kind of object or idea in place of another to suggest a likeness between them —met•a•phor•i•cal \metə'fórikəl\ adj

meta•phys•ics \metə'fiziks\ n : study of the causes and nature of things —meta•phys•i•cal \-'fizikəl\ adj

mete \'mēt\ vb met•ed; met•ing : allot

me•te•or \'mētēər, -ē,ór\ n : small body that produces a streak of light as it burns up in the atmosphere

me•te•or•ic \mētē'órik\ adj 1 : relating to a meteor 2 : sudden and spectacular —me•te•or•i•cal•ly \-'iklē\ adv

me•te•or•ite \'mētēə,rīt\ n : meteor that reaches the earth

me•te•o•rol•o•gy \mētēə'räləjē\ n : science of weather —me•te•o•ro•log•ic \metē,órə'läjik\ —me•te•o•ro•log•i•cal \-'läjikəl\ adj —me•te•o•rol•o•gist \-ēə'räləjist\ n

¹me•ter \'mētər\ n : rhythm in verse or music

²meter n : unit of length equal to 39.37 inches

³meter n : measuring instrument

meth•a•done \'methə,dōn\ n : synthetic addictive narcotic

meth•ane \'meth,ān\ n : colorless odorless flammable gas

meth•a•nol \'methə,nól, -,nōl\ n : volatile flammable poisonous liquid

meth•od \'methəd\ n 1 : procedure for achieving an end 2 : orderly arrangement or plan —me•thod•i•cal \mə'thädikəl\ adj —me•thod•i•cal•ly \-klē\ adv —me•thod•i•cal•ness n

me•tic•u•lous \mə'tikyələs\ adj : extremely careful in attending to details —me•tic•u•lous•ly adv —me•tic•u•lous•ness n

met•ric \'metrik\ met•ri•cal \-trikəl\ adj : relating to meter or the metric system —met•ri•cal•ly adv

metric system n : system of weights and measures using the meter and kilogram

met•ro•nome \'metrə,nōm\ n : instrument that ticks regularly to mark a beat in music

me•trop•o•lis \mə'träpələs\ n : major city —met•ro•pol•i•tan \metrə'pälətᵊn\ adj

met•tle \'metᵊl\ n : spirit or courage —met•tle•some \-səm\ adj

mez•za•nine \'mezᵊn,ēn, ,mezᵊn'ēn\ n 1 : intermediate level between 2 main floors 2 : lowest balcony

mez•zo-so•pra•no \metsōsə'pranō, medz-\ n : voice between soprano and contralto

mi•as•ma \mī'azmə\ n 1 : noxious vapor 2 : harmful influence —mi•as•mic \-mik\ adj

mi•ca \'mīkə\ n : mineral separable into thin transparent sheets

mice pl of MOUSE

mi•cro \'mīkrō\ adj : very small

mi•crobe \'mī,krōb\ n : disease-causing microorganism —mi•cro•bi•al \mī'krōbēəl\ adj

mi•cro•bi•ol•o•gy \mīkrōbī'äləjē\ n : biology dealing with microscopic life —mi•cro•bi•o•log•i•cal \mīkrō,bīə'läjikəl\ adj —mi•cro•bi•ol•o•gist \mīkrōbī'äləjist\ n

mi•cro•com•put•er \'mīkrōkəm,pyütər\ n : small computer that uses a microprocessor

mi•cro•cosm \'mīkrə,käzəm\ n : one thought of as a miniature universe

mi•cro•film \-,film\ n : small film recording printed matter —microfilm vb

mi•crom•e•ter \mī'krämətər\ n : instrument for measuring minute distances

mi•cro•min•ia•tur•ized \mīkrō'minēəchə,rīzd, -'minichə-\ adj : reduced to a very small size —mi•cro•min•ia•tur•iza•tion \-,minēə,chùrə'zāshən, -,mini,chùr-, -chər-\ n

mi•cron \'mī,krän\ n : one millionth of a meter

mi•cro•or•gan•ism \mīkrō'órgə,nizəm\ n : very tiny living thing

mi•cro•phone \'mīkrə,fōn\ n : instrument for changing sound waves into variations of an electric current

mi•cro•pro•ces•sor \'mīkrō,präsesər\ n : miniaturized computer processing unit on a single chip

mi•cro•scope \-,skōp\ n : optical device for magnifying tiny objects —mi•cro•scop•ic \mīkrə'skäpik\ adj —mi•cro•scop•i•cal•ly adv —mi•cros•co•py \mī'kräskəpē\ n

mi•cro•wave \'mīkrə,wāv\ n 1 : short radio wave 2 : oven that cooks food using microwaves ~ vb : heat or cook in a microwave oven —mi•cro•wav•able, mi•cro•wave•able \mīkrə'wāvəbəl\ adj

mid \'mid\ adj : middle —mid•point n —mid•stream n —mid•sum•mer n —mid•town n or adj —mid•week n —mid•win•ter n —mid•year n

mid•air n : a point in the air well above the ground

mid•day n : noon

mid•dle \'midᵊl\ adj 1 : equally distant from the extremes 2 : being at neither extreme ~ n : middle part or point

Middle Ages n pl : period from about A.D. 500 to about 1500

mid•dle•man \-,man\ n : dealer or agent between the producer and consumer

mid•dling \'midliŋ, -lən\ adj 1 : of middle or medium size, degree, or quality 2 : mediocre

midge \'mij\ n : very tiny fly

midg•et \'mijət\ n : very small person or thing

mid•land \'midlənd, -,land\ n : interior of a country

mid•most adj : being nearest the middle —midmost adv

mid•night n : 12 o'clock at night

mid•riff \'mid,rif\ n : mid-region of the torso

mid•ship•man \'mid,shipmən, ,mid'ship-\ n : student naval officer

midst \'midst\ n : position close to or surrounded by others —midst prep

mid•way \'mid,wā\ n : concessions and amusements at a carnival ~ adv : in the middle

mid•wife \'mid,wīf\ n : person who aids at childbirth —mid•wife•ry \mid'wīfərē, -'wīf-\ n

mien \'mēn\ n : appearance

¹might \'mīt\ past of MAY —used to express permission or possibility or as a polite alternative to may

²might n : power or resources

mighty \'mītē\ adj might•i•er; -est 1 : very strong 2 : great —might•i•ly adv —might•i•ness n —mighty adv

mi•graine \'mī,grān\ n : severe headache often with nausea

mi•grant \'mīgrənt\ n : one who moves frequently to find work

mi•grate \'mī,grāt\ vb -grat•ed; -grat•ing 1 : move from one place to another 2 : pass periodically from one region or climate to another —mi•gra•tion \mī'grāshən\ n —mi•gra•to•ry \'mīgrə,tōrē\ adj

mild \'mīld\ adj 1 : gentle in nature or behavior 2 : moderate in action or effect —mild•ly adv —mild•ness n

mil•dew \'mil,dü, -,dyü\ n : whitish fungal growth —mildew vb

mile \'mīl\ n : unit of length equal to 5280 feet

mile•age \'mīlij\ n 1 : allowance per mile for traveling expenses 2 : amount or rate of use expressed in miles

mile•stone n : significant point in development

mi•lieu \mēl'yü, -'yœ\ n, pl -lieus or -lieux \-'yüz, -'yœ\ : surroundings or setting

mil•i•tant \'milətənt\ adj : aggressively active or hostile —mil•i•tan•cy \-tənsē\ n —militant n —mil•i•tant•ly adv

mil•i•ta•rism \'milətə,rizəm\ n : dominance of military ideals or of a policy of aggressive readiness for war —mil•i•ta•rist \-rist\ n —mil•i•ta•ris•tic \milətə'ristik\ adj

mil•i•tary \'milə,terē\ adj 1 : relating to soldiers, arms, or war 2 : relating to or performed by armed forces ~ n : armed forces or the people in them —mil•i•tar•i•ly \milə'terəlē\ adv

mil•i•tate \-,tāt\ vb -tat•ed; -tat•ing : have an effect

mi•li•tia \mə'lishə\ n : civilian soldiers —mi•li•tia•man \-mən\ n

milk \'milk\ n : white nutritive fluid secreted by female mammals for feeding their young ~ vb 1 : draw off the milk of 2 : draw something from as if by milking —milk•er n —milk•i•ness \-ēnəs\ n —milky adj

milk•man \-,man, -mən\ n : man who sells or delivers milk

milk•weed n : herb with milky juice

¹mill \'mil\ n 1 : building in which grain is ground into flour 2 : manufacturing plant 3 : machine used esp. for forming or processing ~ vb 1 : subject to a process in a mill 2 : move in a circle —mill•er n

²mill n : 1/10 cent

mil•len•ni•um \mə'lenēəm\ n, pl -nia \-ēə\ or -niums : a period of 1000 years

mil•let \'milət\ n : cereal and forage grass with small seeds

mil•li•gram \'milə,gram\ n : 1/1000 gram

mil•li•li•ter \-,lētər\ n : 1/1000 liter

mil•li•me•ter \-,mētər\ n : 1/1000 meter

mil•li•ner \'milənər\ n : person who makes or sells women's hats —mil•li•nery \milə,nerē\ n

mil•lion \'milyən\ n, pl millions or million : 1000 thousands —million adj —mil•lionth \-yənth\ adj or n

mil•lion•aire \milyə'nar, 'milyə,nar\ n : person worth a million or more (as of dollars)

mil•li•pede \'milə,pēd\ n : longbodied arthropod with 2 pairs of legs on most segments

mill•stone n : either of 2 round flat stones used for grinding grain

mime \'mīm\ n 1 : mimic 2 : pantomime —mime vb

mim•eo•graph \'mimēə,graf\ n : machine for making many stencil copies —mimeograph vb

mim•ic \'mimik\ n : one that mimics ~ vb -icked; -ick•ing 1 : imitate closely 2 : ridicule by imitation —mim•ic•ry \'mimikrē\ n

min•a•ret \minə'ret\ n : tower attached to a mosque

mince \'mins\ vb minced; minc•ing 1 : cut into small pieces 2 : choose (one's words) carefully 3 : walk in a prim affected manner

mind \'mīnd\ n 1 : the part of an individual that feels, perceives, and esp. reasons 3 : intention 4 : normal mental condition 5 : opinion 6 : intellectual ability ~ vb 1 : attend to 2 : obey 3 : be concerned about 4 : be careful —mind•ed adj —mind•less \'mīndləs\ adj —mind•less•ly adv —mind•less•ness n

mind•ful \-fəl\ adj : aware or attentive —mind•ful•ly adv —mind•ful•ness n

¹mine \'mīn\ pron : that which belongs to me

²mine \'mīn\ n 1 : excavation from which minerals are taken 2 : explosive device placed in the ground or water for destroying enemy vehicles or vessels that later pass ~ vb mined; min•ing 1 : get ore from 2 : place military mines in —mine•field n —min•er n

min•er•al \'minərəl\ n 1 : crystalline substance not of organic origin 2 : useful natural substance (as coal) obtained from the ground —mineral adj

min•er•al•o•gy \minə'räləjē, -'ral-\ n : science dealing with minerals —min•er•al•og•i•cal \minərə'läjikəl\ adj —min•er•al•o•gist \minə'räləjist, -'ral-\ n

min•gle \'miŋgəl\ vb -gled; -gling : bring together or mix

mini- comb form : miniature or of small dimensions

min•ia•ture \'minēə,chùr, 'mini,chùr, -chər\ n : tiny copy or very small version —miniature adj —min•ia•tur•ize \-ēəchə,rīz, -ichə-\ vb

mini•bike \'minē,bīk\ n : small motorcycle

mini•bus \-,bəs\ n : small bus

mini•com•put•er \-kəm,pyütər\ n : computer intermediate between a mainframe and a microcomputer in size and speed

mini•course \-,kōrs\ n : short course of study

min•i•mal \'minəməl\ adj : relating to or being a minimum —min•i•mal•ly adv

min•i•mize \'minə,mīz\ vb -mized; -miz•ing 1 : reduce to a minimum 2 : underestimate intentionally

min•i•mum \'minəməm\ n, pl -ma \-mə\ or -mums : lowest quantity or amount —minimum adj

min•ion \'minyən\ n 1 : servile dependent 2 : subordinate official

mini•se•ries \'minē,sirēz\ n : television story in several parts

mini•skirt \-,skərt\ n : very short skirt

min•is•ter \'minəstər\ n 1 : Protestant member of the clergy 2 : high officer of state 3 : diplomatic representative ~ vb : give aid or service —min•is•te•ri•al \minə'stirēəl\ adj —min•is•tra•tion n

min•is•try \'minəstrē\ n, pl -tries 1 : office or duties of a minister 2 : body of ministers 3 : government department headed by a minister

mini•van \'minē,van\ n : small van

mink \'miŋk\ n, pl mink or minks : weasellike mammal or its soft brown fur

min•now \'minō\ n, pl -nows : small freshwater fish

mi•nor \'mīnər\ adj 1 : less in size, importance, or value 2 : not serious ~ n 1 : person not yet of legal age 2 : secondary field of academic specialization

mi•nor•i•ty \mə'nórətē, mī-\ n, pl -ties 1 : time or state of being a minor 2 : smaller number (as of votes) 3 : part of a population differing from others (as in race or religion)

min·strel \\'minstrəl\\ n 1 : medieval singer of verses 2 : performer in a program usu. of black American songs and jokes —**min·strel·sy** \\-sē\\ n

1mint \\'mint\\ n 1 : fragrant herb that yields a flavoring oil 2 : mint-flavored piece of candy —**minty** adj

2mint n 1 : place where coins are made 2 : vast sum ~ adj : unused —**mint** vb —**mint·er** n

min·u·et \\,minyə'wet\\ n : slow graceful dance

mi·nus \\'mīnəs\\ prep 1 : diminished by 2 : lacking ~ n : negative quantity or quality

mi·nus·cule \\'minəs,kyül, min'əs-\\, **min·is·cule** \\'minis-\\ adj : very small

1min·ute \\'minət\\ n 1 : 60th part of an hour or of a degree 2 : short time 3 pl : official record of a meeting

2mi·nute \\mī'nüt, mə-, -'nyüt\\ adj **-nut·er; -est** 1 : very small 2 : marked by close attention to details —**mi·nute·ly** adv —**mi·nute·ness** n

mir·a·cle \\'mirikəl\\ n 1 : extraordinary event taken as a sign of divine intervention in human affairs 2 : marvel —**mi·rac·u·lous** \\mə'rakyələs\\ adj —**mi·rac·u·lous·ly** adv

mi·rage \\mə'räzh\\ n : distant illusion caused by atmospheric conditions (as in the desert)

mire \\'mīr\\ n : heavy deep mud ~ vb **mired; mir·ing** : stick or sink in mire —**miry** adj

mir·ror \\'mirər\\ n : smooth surface (as of glass) that reflects images ~ vb : reflect in or as if in a mirror

mirth \\'mərth\\ n : gladness and laughter —**mirth·ful** \\-fəl\\ adj —**mirth·ful·ly** adv —**mirth·ful·ness** n —**mirth·less** adj

mis·an·thrope \\'misⁿn,thrōp\\ n : one who hates mankind —**mis·an·throp·ic** \\misⁿn'thräpik\\ adj —**mis·an·thro·py** \\mis'anthrəpē\\ n

mis·ap·pre·hend \\,mis,aprə'hend\\ vb : misunderstand —**mis·ap·pre·hen·sion** n

mis·ap·pro·pri·ate \\,misə'prōprē,āt\\ vb : take dishonestly for one's own use —**mis·ap·pro·pri·a·tion** n

mis·be·got·ten \\-bi'gätⁿn\\ adj 1 : illegitimate 2 : ill-conceived

mis·be·have \\,misbi'hāv\\ vb : behave improperly —**mis·be·hav·er** n —**mis·be·hav·ior** n

mis·cal·cu·late \\mis'kalkyə,lāt\\ vb : calculate wrongly —**mis·cal·cu·la·tion** n

mis·car·ry \\mis'karē, 'mis,karē\\ vb 1 : give birth prematurely before the fetus can survive 2 : go wrong or be unsuccessful —**mis·car·riage** \\-rij\\ n

mis·ce·ge·na·tion \\mis,ejə'nāshən, ,misijə'nā-\\ n : marriage between persons of different races

mis·cel·la·neous \\,misə'lānēəs\\ adj : consisting of many things of different kinds —**mis·cel·la·neous·ly** adv —**mis·cel·la·neous·ness** n

mis·cel·la·ny \\'misə,lānē\\ n, pl **-nies** : collection of various things

mis·chance \\mis'chans\\ n : bad luck

mis·chief \\'mischəf\\ n : conduct esp. of a child that annoys or causes minor damage

mis·chie·vous \\'mischəvəs\\ adj 1 : causing annoyance or minor injury 2 : irresponsibly playful —**mis·chie·vous·ly** adv —**mis·chie·vous·ness** n

mis·con·ceive \\,miskən'sēv\\ vb : interpret incorrectly —**mis·con·cep·tion** n

mis·con·duct \\mis'kändəkt\\ n 1 : mismanagement 2 : bad behavior

mis·con·strue \\,miskən'strü\\ vb : misinterpret —**mis·con·struc·tion** n

mis·cre·ant \\'miskrēənt\\ n : one who behaves criminally or viciously —**miscreant** adj

mis·deed \\mis'dēd\\ n : wrong deed

mis·de·mean·or \\,misdi'mēnər\\ n : crime less serious than a felony

mi·ser \\'mīzər\\ n : person who hoards and is stingy with money —**mi·ser·li·ness** \\-lēnəs\\ n —**mi·ser·ly** adj

mis·er·a·ble \\'mizərəbəl\\ adj 1 : wretchedly deficient 2 : causing extreme discomfort 3 : shameful —**mis·er·a·ble·ness** n —**mis·er·a·bly** \\-blē\\ adv

mis·ery \\'mizərē\\ n, pl **-er·ies** : suffering and want caused by distress or poverty

mis·fire \\mis'fīr\\ vb 1 : fail to fire 2 : miss an intended effect —**mis·fire** \\'mis,fīr\\ n

mis·fit \\'mis,fit, mis'fit\\ n : person poorly adjusted to his environment

mis·for·tune \\mis'fōrchən\\ n 1 : bad luck 2 : unfortunate condition or event

mis·giv·ing \\mis'giviŋ\\ n : doubt or concern

mis·guid·ed \\mis'gīdəd\\ adj : mistaken, uninformed, or deceived

mis·hap \\'mis,hap\\ n : accident

mis·in·form \\,misⁿn'fōrm\\ vb : give wrong information to —**mis·in·for·ma·tion** \\,mis,infər'māshən\\ n

mis·in·ter·pret \\,misⁿn'tərprət\\ vb : under-

stand or explain wrongly —**mis·in·ter·pre·ta·tion** \\,tərprə'tāshən\\ n

mis·judge \\mis'jəj\\ vb : judge incorrectly or unjustly —**mis·judg·ment** n

mis·lay \\mis'lā\\ vb **-laid; -lay·ing** : misplace

mis·lead \\mis'lēd\\ vb **-led; -lead·ing** : lead in a wrong direction or into error —**mis·lead·ing·ly** adv

mis·man·age \\mis'manij\\ vb : manage badly —**mis·man·age·ment** n

mis·no·mer \\mis'nōmər\\ n : wrong name

mi·sog·y·nist \\mis'säjənist\\ n : one who hates or distrusts women —**mi·sog·y·nis·tic** \\mə,säjə'nistik\\ adj —**mi·sog·y·ny** \\-nē\\ n

mis·place \\mis'plās\\ vb : put in a wrong or unremembered place

mis·print \\'mis,print, mis'-\\ n : error in printed matter

mis·pro·nounce \\,misprə'naúns\\ vb : pronounce incorrectly —**mis·pro·nun·ci·a·tion** n

mis·quote \\mis'kwōt\\ vb : quote incorrectly —**mis·quo·ta·tion** \\,miskwō'tāshən\\ n

mis·read \\mis'rēd\\ vb **-read; -read·ing** : read or interpret incorrectly

mis·rep·re·sent \\,mis,repri'zent\\ vb : represent falsely or unfairly —**mis·rep·re·sen·ta·tion** n

mis·rule \\mis'rül\\ vb : govern badly ~ n 1 : bad or corrupt government 2 : disorder

1miss \\'mis\\ vb 1 : fail to hit, reach, or contact 2 : notice the absence of 3 : fail to obtain 4 : avoid 5 : omit —**miss** n

2miss n : young unmarried woman or girl —often used as a title

mis·sal \\'misəl\\ n : book containing what is said at mass during the year

mis·shap·en \\mis'shāpən\\ adj : distorted

mis·sile \\'misəl\\ n : object (as a stone or rocket) thrown or shot

miss·ing \\'misiŋ\\ adj : absent or lost

mis·sion \\'mishən\\ n 1 : ministry sent by a church to spread its teaching 2 : group of diplomats sent to a foreign country 3 : task

mis·sion·ary \\'mishə,nerē\\ adj : relating to religious missions ~ n, pl **-ar·ies** : person sent to spread religious faith

mis·sive \\'misiv\\ n : letter

mis·spell \\mis'spel\\ vb : spell incorrectly —**mis·spell·ing** n

mis·state \\mis'stāt\\ vb : state incorrectly —**mis·state·ment** n

mis·step \\'mis,step\\ n 1 : wrong step 2 : mistake

mist \\'mist\\ n : particles of water falling as fine rain

mis·take \\mə'stāk\\ n 1 : misunderstanding or wrong belief 2 : wrong action or statement —**mistake** vb

mis·tak·en \\-'stākən\\ adj : having a wrong opinion or incorrect information —**mis·tak·en·ly** adv

mis·ter \\'mistər\\ n : sir —used without a name in addressing a man

mis·tle·toe \\'misəl,tō\\ n : parasitic green shrub with waxy white berries

mis·treat \\mis'trēt\\ vb : treat badly —**mis·treat·ment** n

mis·tress \\'mistrəs\\ n 1 : woman in control 2 : a woman who has his wife with whom a married man has recurrent sexual relations

mis·tri·al \\mis'trīəl\\ n : trial that has no legal effect

mis·trust \\-'trəst\\ n : lack of confidence ~ vb : have no confidence in —**mis·trust·ful** \\-fəl\\ adj —**mis·trust·ful·ly** adv —**mis·trust·ful·ness** n

misty \\'mistē\\ adj **mist·i·er; -est** 1 : obscured by mist 2 : tearful —**mist·i·ly** adv —**mist·i·ness** n

mis·un·der·stand \\,misəndər'stand\\ vb 1 : fail to understand 2 : interpret incorrectly

mis·un·der·stand·ing \\-'standiŋ\\ n 1 : wrong interpretation 2 : disagreement

mis·use \\mis'yüz\\ vb 1 : use incorrectly 2 : mistreat —**mis·use** \\-'yüs\\ n

mite \\'mīt\\ n 1 : tiny spiderlike animal 2 : small amount

mi·ter, mi·tre \\'mītər\\ n 1 : bishop's headdress 2 : angular joint in wood ~ vb **-tered; -tred; -ter·ing** or **-tring** \\'mītəriŋ\\ : bevel the ends of for a miter joint

mit·i·gate \\'mitə,gāt\\ vb **-gat·ed; -gat·ing** : make less severe —**mit·i·ga·tion** \\,mitə'gāshən\\ n —**mit·i·ga·tive** \\'mitə,gātiv\\ adj

mi·to·sis \\mī'tōsəs\\ n, pl **-to·ses** \\-,sēz\\ : process of forming 2 cell nuclei from one —**mi·tot·ic** \\-'tätik\\ adj

mitt \\'mit\\ n : mittenlike baseball glove

mit·ten \\'mitⁿn\\ n : hand covering without finger sections

mix \\'miks\\ vb : combine or join into one mass or group ~ n : commercially prepared food mixture —**mix·able** adj —**mix·er** n —**mix up** : confuse

mix·ture \\'mikschər\\ n : act or product of mixing

mix–up n : instance of confusion

mne·mon·ic \\ni'mänik\\ adj : relating to or assisting memory

moan \\'mōn\\ n : low prolonged sound of pain or grief —**moan** vb

moat \\'mōt\\ n : deep wide trench around a castle

mob \\'mäb\\ n 1 : large disorderly crowd 2 : criminal gang ~ vb **-bb-** : crowd around and attack or annoy

mo·bile \\'mōbəl, -,bēl, -,bīl\\ adj : capable of moving or being moved ~ \\'mō,bēl\\ n : suspended art construction with freely moving parts —**mo·bil·i·ty** \\mō'bilətē\\ n

mo·bi·lize \\'mōbə,līz\\ vb **-lized; -liz·ing** : assemble and make ready for war duty —**mo·bi·li·za·tion** \\,mōbələ'zāshən\\ n

moc·ca·sin \\'mäkəsən\\ n 1 : heelless shoe 2 : venomous U.S. snake

mo·cha \\'mōkə\\ n 1 : mixture of coffee and chocolate 2 : dark brown color

mock \\'mäk, 'mȯk\\ vb 1 : ridicule 2 : mimic in derision ~ adj 1 : simulated 2 : phony —**mock·er** n —**mock·ery** \\-ərē\\ n —**mock·ing·ly** adv

mock·ing·bird \\'mäkiŋ,bərd, 'mȯk-\\ n : songbird that mimics other birds

mode \\'mōd\\ n 1 : particular form or variety 2 : style —**mod·al** \\-ᵊl\\ adj —**mod·ish** \\'mōdish\\ adj

mod·el \\'mädᵊl\\ n 1 : structural design 2 : miniature representation 3 : something worthy of copying 4 : one who poses for an artist or displays clothes 5 : type or design ~ vb **-eled** or **-elled; -el·ing** or **-el·ling** 1 : shape 2 : work as a model ~ adj 1 : serving as a pattern 2 : being a miniature representation of

mo·dem \\'mōdəm, -,dem\\ n : device by which a computer communicates with another computer over telephone lines

mod·er·ate \\'mädərət\\ adj : avoiding extremes ~ \\'mädə,rāt\\ vb **-at·ed; -at·ing** 1 : lessen the intensity of 2 : act as a moderator —**moderate** n —**mod·er·ate·ly** adv —**mod·er·ate·ness** n —**mod·er·a·tion** \\,mädə'rāshən\\ n

mod·er·a·tor \\'mädə,rātər\\ n : one who presides

mod·ern \\'mädərn\\ adj : relating to or characteristic of the present —**modern** n —**mo·der·ni·ty** \\mə'dərnətē\\ n —**mod·ern·iza·tion** \\,mädərnə'zāshən\\ n —**mod·ern·ize** \\'mädər,nīz\\ vb —**mod·ern·iz·er** \\'mädər,nīzər\\ n —**mod·ern·ly** adv —**mod·ern·ness** n

mod·est \\'mädəst\\ adj 1 : having a moderate estimate of oneself 2 : reserved or decent in thoughts or actions 3 : limited in size, amount, or aim —**mod·est·ly** adv —**mod·es·ty** \\-əstē\\ n

mod·i·cum \\'mädikəm\\ n : small amount

mod·i·fy \\'mädə,fī\\ vb **-fied; -fy·ing** 1 : limit the meaning of 2 : change —**mod·i·fi·ca·tion** \\,mädəfə'kāshən\\ n —**mod·i·fi·er** \\'mädə,fīər\\ n

mod·u·lar \\'mäjələr\\ adj : built with standardized units —**mod·u·lar·ized** \\-lə,rīzd\\ adj

mod·u·late \\'mäjə,lāt\\ vb **-lat·ed; -lat·ing** 1 : keep in proper measure or proportion 2 : vary a radio wave —**mod·u·la·tion** \\,mäjə'lāshən\\ n —**mod·u·la·tor** \\'mäjə,lātər\\ n —**mod·u·la·to·ry** \\-lə,tōrē\\ adj

mod·ule \\'mäjül\\ n : standardized unit

mo·gul \\'mōgəl\\ n : important person

mo·hair \\'mō,har\\ n : fabric made from the hair of the Angora goat

moist \\'mȯist\\ adj : slightly or moderately wet —**moist·en** \\'mȯisᵊn\\ vb —**moist·en·er** \\'mȯisᵊnər\\ n —**moist·ly** adv —**moist·ness** n

mois·ture \\'mȯischər\\ n : small amount of liquid that causes dampness —**mois·tur·ize** \\-chə,rīz\\ vb —**mois·tur·iz·er** n

mo·lar \\'mōlər\\ n : grinding tooth —**molar** adj

mo·las·ses \\mə'lasəz\\ n : thick brown syrup from raw sugar

1mold \\'mōld\\ n : crumbly organic soil

2mold n : frame or cavity for forming ~ vb : shape in or as if in a mold —**mold·er** n

3mold n : surface growth of fungus ~ vb : become moldy —**mold·i·ness** \\'mōldēnəs\\ n —**moldy** adj

mold·er \\'mōldər\\ vb : crumble

mold·ing \\'mōldiŋ\\ n : decorative surface, plane, or strip

1mole \\'mōl\\ n : spot on the skin

2mole n : small burrowing mammal —**mole·hill** n

mol·e·cule \\'mäli,kyül\\ n : small particle of matter —**mo·lec·u·lar** \\mə'lekyələr\\ adj

mole·skin \\-,skin\\ n : heavy cotton fabric

mo·lest \\mə'lest\\ vb 1 : annoy or disturb 2 : force physical and usu. sexual contact on —**mo·les·ta·tion** \\,mōl,es'tāshən, ,mäl-\\ n —**mo·lest·er** n

mol·li·fy \\'mälə,fī\\ vb **-fied; -fy·ing** : soothe in temper —**mol·li·fi·ca·tion** \\,mäləfə'kāshən\\ n

mol·lusk, mol·lusc \\'mäləsk\\ n : shelled aquatic invertebrate —**mol·lus·can** \\mə'ləskən\\ adj

mol·ly·cod·dle \\'mälē,kädᵊl\\ vb **-dled; -dling** : pamper

molt \\'mōlt\\ vb : shed hair, feathers, outer skin, or horns periodically —**molt** n —**molt·er** n

mol·ten \\'mōltᵊn\\ adj : fused or liquefied by heat

mom \\'mäm, 'mȯm\\ n : mother

mo·ment \\'mōmənt\\ n 1 : tiny portion of time 2 : time of excellence 3 : importance

mo·men·tari·ly \\'mōmən,terəlē\\ adv 1 : for a moment 2 : at any moment

mo·men·tary \\'mōmən,terē\\ adj : continuing only a moment —**mo·men·tari·ness** n

mo·men·tous \\mō'mentəs\\ adj : very important —**mo·men·tous·ly** adv —**mo·men·tous·ness** n

mo·men·tum \\-əm\\ n, pl **-ta** \\-ə\\ or **-tums** : force of a moving body

mon·arch \\'mänərk, -,ärk\\ n : ruler of a kingdom or empire —**mo·nar·chi·cal** \\mə'närkikəl\\ adj

mon·ar·chist \\'mänərkist\\ n : believer in monarchical government —**mon·ar·chism** \\-,kizəm\\ n

mon·ar·chy \\'mänərkē\\ n, pl **-chies** : realm of a monarch

mon·as·tery \\'mänə,sterē\\ n, pl **-ter·ies** : house for monks

mo·nas·tic \\mə'nastik\\ adj : relating to monasteries, monks, or nuns —**monastic** n —**mo·nas·ti·cal·ly** \\-tiklē\\ adv —**mo·nas·ti·cism** \\-tə,sizəm\\ n

Mon·day \\'məndā, -dē\\ n : 2d day of the week

mon·e·tary \\'mänə,terē, 'mən-\\ adj : relating to money

mon·ey \\'mənē\\ n, pl **-eys** or **-ies** \\'mənēz\\ 1 : something (as coins or paper currency) used in buying 2 : wealth —**mon·eyed** \\-ēd\\ adj —**mon·ey·lend·er** n

mon·ger \\'məŋgər, 'mäŋ-\\ n : dealer

mon·gol·ism \\'mäŋgə,lizəm\\ n : congenital mental retardation —**Mon·gol·oid** \\-gə,lȯid\\ adj or n

mon·goose \\'mäŋ,güs, 'mäŋ-\\ n, pl **-goos·es** : small agile mammal esp. of India

mon·grel \\'mäŋgrəl, 'məŋ-\\ n : offspring of mixed breed

mon·i·tor \\'mänətər\\ n 1 : student assistant 2 : television screen ~ vb : watch or observe esp. for quality

monk \\'məŋk\\ n : member of a religious order living in a monastery —**monk·ish** adj

mon·key \\'məŋkē\\ n, pl **-keys** : small longtailed arboreal primate ~ vb 1 : fool 2 : tamper

mon·key·shines \\-,shīnz\\ n pl : pranks

monks·hood \\'məŋks,hủd\\ n : poisonous herb with showy flowers

mon·o·cle \\'mänikəl\\ n : eyeglass for one eye

mo·nog·a·my \\mə'nägəmē\\ n 1 : marriage with one person at a time 2 : practice of having a single mate for a period of time —**mo·nog·a·mist** \\mə'nägəmist\\ n —**mo·nog·a·mous** \\-məs\\ adj

mono·gram \\'mänə,gram\\ n : sign of identity made of initials —**monogram** vb

mono·graph \\-,graf\\ n : learned treatise

mono·lin·gual \\,mänə'liŋgwəl\\ adj : using only one language

mono·lith \\'mänᵊl,ith\\ n 1 : single great stone 2 : single uniform massive whole —**mono·lith·ic** \\,mänᵊl'ithik\\ adj

mono·logue \\'mänᵊl,ȯg\\ n : long speech —**mono·logu·ist** \\-,ȯgist\\, **mo·nol·o·gist** \\mə'näləjist, 'mänᵊl,ȯgist\\ n

mono·nu·cle·o·sis \\,mänō,nüklē'ōsəs, -,nyü-\\ n : acute infectious disease

mo·nop·o·ly \\mə'näpəlē\\ n, pl **-lies** 1 : exclusive ownership or control of a commodity 2 : one controlling a monopoly —**mo·nop·o·list** \\-list\\ n —**mo·nop·o·lis·tic** \\mə,näpə'listik\\ adj —**mo·nop·o·li·za·tion** \\mə,näpələ'zāshən\\ n —**mo·nop·o·lize** \\mə'näpə,līz\\ vb

mono·rail \\'mänə,rāl\\ n : single rail for a vehicle or a vehicle or system using it

mono·syl·lab·ic \\,mänəsə'labik\\ adj : consisting of or using words of only one syllable —**mono·syl·la·ble** \\mänə,siləbəl\\ n

mono·the·ism \\'mänōthē,izəm\\ n : doctrine or belief that there is only one deity —**mono·the·ist** \\-,thēist\\ n —**mono·the·is·tic** \\mänōthē'istik\\ adj

mono·tone \\'mänə,tōn\\ n : succession of words in one unvarying tone

mo·not·o·nous \\mə'nätᵊnəs\\ adj 1 : sounded in one unvarying tone 2 : tediously uniform —**mo·not·o·nous·ly** adv —**mo·not·o·nous·ness** n —**mo·not·o·ny** \\-ᵊnē\\ n

mon·ox·ide \\mə'näk,sīd\\ n : oxide containing one atom of oxygen in a molecule

mon·sieur \\məs'yər, mäs-\\ n, pl **mes·sieurs** \\-yərz, mā'syərz\\ : man of high rank or station —used as a title for a man esp. of French nationality

mon·si·gnor \\män'sēnyər\\ n, pl **monsignors** or **mon·si·gno·ri** \\,män,sēn'yōrē\\ : Roman Catholic prelate —used as a title

mon•soon \män'sün\ *n* : periodic rainy season

mon•ster \'mänstər\ *n* **1** : abnormal or terrifying animal **2** : ugly, wicked, or cruel person —**mon•stros•i•ty** \män'sträsətē\ *n* —**mon•strous** \'mänstrəs\ *adj* —**mon•strous•ly** *adv*

mon•tage \mən'täzh\ *n* : artistic composition of several different elements

month \'mənth\ *n* : 12th part of a year —**month•ly** *adv or adj or n*

mon•u•ment \'mänyəmənt\ *n* : structure erected in remembrance

mon•u•men•tal \mänyə'mentᵊl\ *adj* **1** : serving as a monument **2** : outstanding **3** : very great —**mon•u•men•tal•ly** *adv*

moo \'mü\ *vb* : make the noise of a cow —**moo** *n*

mood \'müd\ *n* : state of mind or emotion

moody \'müdē\ *adj* **mood•i•er; -est 1** : sad **2** : subject to changing moods and esp. to bad moods —**mood•i•ly** \'müdᵊlē\ *adv* —**mood•i•ness** \-ēnəs\ *n*

moon \'mün\ *n* : natural satellite (as of earth) —**moon•beam** *n* —**moon•light** *n* —**moon•lit** *adj*

moon•light \-ˌlīt\ *vb* **-ed; -ing** : hold a 2d job —**moon•light•er** *n*

moon•shine *n* **1** : moonlight **2** : meaningless talk **3** : illegally distilled liquor

¹**moor** \'mu̇r\ *n* : open usu. swampy wasteland —**moor•land** \-lənd, -ˌland\ *n*

²**moor** *vb* : fasten with line or anchor

moor•ing \-iŋ\ *n* : place where boat can be moored

moose \'müs\ *n, pl* **moose** : large heavy-antlered deer

moot \'müt\ *adj* : open to question

mop \'mäp\ *n* : floor-cleaning implement ~ *vb* **-pp-** : use a mop on

mope \'mōp\ *vb* **moped; mop•ing** : be sad or listless

mo•ped \'mō,ped\ *n* : low-powered motorbike

mo•raine \mə'rān\ *n* : glacial deposit of earth and stones

mor•al \'mȯrəl\ *adj* **1** : relating to principles of right and wrong **2** : conforming to a standard of right behavior **3** : relating to or acting on the mind, character, or will ~ *n* **1** : point of a story **2** *pl* : moral practices or teachings —**mor•al•ist** \'mȯrəlist\ *n* —**mor•al•is•tic** \mȯrə'listik\ *adj* —**mor•al•i•ty** \mə'ralətē\ *n* —**mor•al•ize** \'mȯrə,līz\ *vb* —**mor•al•ly** *adv*

mo•rale \mə'ral\ *n* : emotional attitude

mo•rass \mə'ras\ *n* : swamp

mor•a•to•ri•um \mȯrə'tȯrēəm\ *n, pl* **-ri•ums** *or* **-ria** \-ēə\ : suspension of activity

mo•ray \'mȯr,ā, mə'rā\ *n* : savage eel

mor•bid \'mȯrbəd\ *adj* **1** : relating to disease **2** : gruesome —**mor•bid•i•ty** \mȯr'bidətē\ *n* —**mor•bid•ly** *adv* —**mor•bid•ness** *n*

mor•dant \'mȯrdᵊnt\ *adj* : sarcastic —**mor•dant•ly** *adv*

more \'mȯr\ *adj* **1** : greater **2** : additional ~ *adv* **1** : in addition **2** : to a greater degree ~ *n* **1** : greater quantity **2** : additional amount ~ *pron* : additional ones

mo•rel \mə'rel\ *n* : pitted edible mushroom

more•over \mȯr'ōvər\ *adv* : in addition

mo•res \'mȯr,āz, -ēz\ *n, pl* : customs

morgue \'mȯrg\ *n* : temporary holding place for dead bodies

mor•i•bund \'mȯrə,bənd\ *adj* : dying

morn \'mȯrn\ *n* : morning

morn•ing \'mȯrniŋ\ *n* : time from sunrise to noon

mo•ron \'mȯr,än\ *n* **1** : mentally retarded person **2** : very stupid person —**mo•ron•ic** \mə'ränik\ *adj* —**mo•ron•i•cal•ly** *adv*

mo•rose \mə'rōs\ *adj* : sullen —**mo•rose•ly** *adv* —**mo•rose•ness** *n*

mor•phine \'mȯr,fēn\ *n* : addictive painkilling drug

mor•row \'märō\ *n* : next day

Morse code \'mȯrs-\ *n* : code of dots and dashes or long and short sounds used for transmitting messages

mor•sel \'mȯrsəl\ *n* : small piece or quantity

mor•tal \'mȯrtᵊl\ *adj* **1** : causing or subject to death **2** : extreme —**mortal** *n* —**mor•tal•i•ty** \mȯr'talətē\ *n* —**mor•tal•ly** \'mȯrtᵊlē\ *adv*

mor•tar \'mȯrtər\ *n* **1** : strong bowl **2** : short-barreled cannon **3** : masonry material used to cement bricks or stones in place —**mortar** *vb*

mort•gage \'mȯrgij\ *n* : transfer of property rights as security for a loan —**mortgage** *vb* —**mort•gag•ee** \mȯrgi'jē\ *n* —**mort•ga•gor** \mȯrgi'jȯr\ *n*

mor•ti•fy \'mȯrtə,fī\ *vb* **-fied; -fy•ing 1** : subdue by abstinence or self-inflicted pain **2** : humiliate —**mor•ti•fi•ca•tion** \mȯrtəfə'kāshən\ *n*

mor•tu•ary \'mȯrchə,werē\ *n, pl* **-ar•ies** : place where dead bodies are kept until burial

mo•sa•ic \mō'zāik\ *n* : inlaid stone decoration —**mosaic** *adj*

Mos•lem \'mäzləm\ *var of* MUSLIM

mosque \'mäsk\ *n* : building where Muslims worship

mos•qui•to \mə'skētō\ *n, pl* **-toes** : biting bloodsucking insect

moss \'mȯs\ *n* : green seedless plant —**mossy** *adj*

most \'mōst\ *adj* **1** : majority of **2** : greatest ~ *adv* : to the greatest or a very great degree ~ *n* : greatest amount ~ *pron* : greatest number or part

-most \ˌmōst\ *adj suffix* : most : most toward

most•ly \'mōstlē\ *adv* : mainly

mote \'mōt\ *n* : small particle

mo•tel \mō'tel\ *n* : hotel with rooms accessible from the parking lot

moth \'mȯth\ *n* : small pale insect related to the butterflies

moth•er \'məthər\ *n* **1** : female parent **2** : source ~ *vb* **1** : give birth to **2** : cherish or protect —**moth•er•hood** \-,hu̇d\ *n* —**moth•er•land** \-,land\ *n* —**moth•er•less** *adj* —**moth•er•ly** *adj*

moth•er-in-law *n, pl* **mothers-in-law** : spouse's mother

mo•tif \mō'tēf\ *n* : dominant theme

mo•tion \'mōshən\ *n* **1** : act or instance of moving **2** : proposal for action ~ *vb* : direct by a movement —**mo•tion•less** *adj* —**mo•tion•less•ly** *adv* —**mo•tion•less•ness** *n*

motion picture *n* : movie

mo•ti•vate \'mōtə,vāt\ *vb* **-vat•ed; -vat•ing** : provide with a motive —**mo•ti•va•tion** \mōtə'vāshən\ *n* —**mo•ti•va•tor** \'mōtə,vātər\ *n*

mo•tive \'mōtiv\ *n* : cause of a person's action ~ *adj* **1** : moving to action **2** : relating to motion —**mo•tive•less** *adj*

mot•ley \'mätlē\ *adj* : of diverse colors or elements

mo•tor \'mōtər\ *n* : unit that supplies power or motion ~ *vb* : travel by automobile —**mo•tor•ist** \-ist\ *n* —**mo•tor•ize** \'mōtə,rīz\ *vb*

mo•tor•bike *n* : lightweight motorcycle

mo•tor•boat *n* : engine-driven boat

mo•tor•car *n* : automobile

mo•tor•cy•cle *n* : 2-wheeled automotive vehicle —**mo•tor•cy•clist** *n*

mo•tor•truck *n* : automotive truck

mot•tle \'mätᵊl\ *vb* **-tled; -tling** : mark with spots of different color

mot•to \'mätō\ *n, pl* **-toes** : brief guiding rule

mould \'mōld\ *var of* MOLD

¹**mound** \'maund\ *n* : pile (as of earth)

²**mount** \'maunt\ *n* : mountain

²**mount** *vb* **1** : increase in amount **2** : get up on **3** : put in position ~ *n* **1** : frame or support **2** : horse to ride —**mount•able** *adj* —**mount•er** *n*

moun•tain \'mauntᵊn\ *n* : elevated land higher than a hill —**moun•tain•ous** \'mauntᵊnəs\ *adj* —**moun•tain•top** *n*

moun•tain•eer \mauntᵊn'ir\ *n* : mountain resident or climber

moun•te•bank \'maunti,baŋk\ *n* : impostor

mourn \'mȯrn\ *vb* : feel or express grief —**mourn•er** *n* —**mourn•ful** \-fəl\ *adj* —**mourn•ful•ly** *adv* —**mourn•ful•ness** *n* —**mourn•ing** *n*

mouse \'maus\ *n, pl* **mice** \'mīs\ **1** : small rodent **2** : device for controlling cursor movement on a computer display —**mouse•trap** *n or vb* —**mousy, mous•ey** \'mausē, -zē\ *adj*

mousse \'müs\ *n* **1** : light chilled dessert **2** : foamy hair-styling preparation

mous•tache \'məs,tash, məs'tash\ *var of* MUSTACHE

mouth \'mauth\ *n* : opening through which an animal takes in food ~ \'mauth\ *vb* **1** : speak **2** : repeat without comprehension or sincerity **3** : form soundlessly with the lips —**mouthed** \'mauthd, 'mautht\ *adj* —**mouth•ful** \-,fu̇l\ *n*

mouth•piece *n* **1** : part (as of a musical instrument) held in or to the mouth **2** : spokesman

mou•ton \'mü,tän\ *n* : processed sheepskin

move \'müv\ *vb* **moved; mov•ing 1** : go or cause to go to another point **2** : change residence **3** : change or cause to change position **4** : take or cause to take action **5** : make a formal request **6** : stir the emotions ~ *n* **1** : act or instance of moving **2** : step taken to achieve a goal —**mov•able, move•able** \-əbəl\ *adj* —**move•ment** *n* —**mov•er** *n*

mov•ie \'müvē\ *n* : projected picture in which persons and objects seem to move

¹**mow** \'mau\ *n* : part of a barn where hay or straw is stored

²**mow** \'mō\ *vb* **mowed; mowed** *or* **mown** \'mōn\ **mow•ing** : cut with a machine —**mow•er** *n*

Mr. \'mistər\ *n, pl* **Messrs.** \'mesərz\—conventional title for a man

Mrs. \'misəz, *esp South* 'mizəz, -əs\ *n, pl* **Mes•dames** \mā'däm, -'dam\—conventional title for a married woman

Ms. \'miz\ *n* —conventional title for a woman

much \'məch\ *adj* **more** \'mȯr\; **most** \'mōst\ : great in quantity, extent, or de-

gree ~ *adv* **more; most** : to a great degree or extent ~ *n* : great quantity, extent, or degree

mu•ci•lage \'myüsəlij\ *n* : weak glue

muck \'mək\ *n* : manure, dirt, or mud —**mucky** *adj*

mu•cus \'myükəs\ *n* : slippery protective secretion of membranes (**mucous membranes**) lining body cavities —**mu•cous** \-kəs\ *adj*

mud \'məd\ *n* : soft wet earth —**mud•di•ly** \'mədᵊlē\ *adv* —**mud•di•ness** \-ēnəs\ *n* —**mud•dy** *adj or vb*

mud•dle \'mədᵊl\ *vb* **-dled; -dling 1** : make, be, or act confused **2** : make a mess of —**muddle** *n* —**mud•dle•head•ed** \mədᵊl'hedəd\ *adj*

mu•ez•zin \mü'ezᵊn, myü-\ *n* : Muslim who calls the hour of daily prayer

¹**muff** \'məf\ *n* : tubular hand covering

²**muff** *vb* : bungle —**muff** *n*

muf•fin \'məfən\ *n* : soft cake baked in a cup-shaped container

muf•fle \'məfəl\ *vb* **-fled; -fling 1** : wrap up **2** : dull the sound of —**muf•fler** \'məflər\ *n*

muf•ti \'məftē\ *n* : civilian clothes

¹**mug** \'məg\ *n* : drinking cup ~ *vb* **-gg-** : make faces

²**mug** *vb* **-gg-** : assault with intent to rob —**mug•ger** *n*

mug•gy \'məgē\ *adj* **-gi•er; -est** : hot and humid —**mug•gi•ness** *n*

Mu•ham•mad•an \mō'hamədən, -'häm-; mü-\ *n* : Muslim —**Mu•ham•mad•an•ism** \-,izəm\ *n*

mu•lat•to \mu̇'lätō, -'lat-\ *n, pl* **-toes** *or* **-tos** : person of mixed black and white ancestry

mul•ber•ry \'məl,berē\ *n* : tree with small edible fruit

mulch \'məlch\ *n* : protective ground covering —**mulch** *vb*

mulct \'məlkt\ *n or vb* : fine

¹**mule** \'myül\ *n* **1** : offspring of a male ass and a female horse **2** : stubborn person —**mul•ish** \'myülish\ *adj* —**mul•ish•ly** *adv* —**mu•lish•ness** *n*

²**mule** *n* : backless shoe

mull \'məl\ *vb* : ponder

mul•let \'mələt\ *n, pl* **-let** *or* **-lets** : marine food fish

multi- *comb form* **1** : many or multiple **2** : many times over

multiarmed	multimillion
multibarreled	multimillionaire
multibillion	multipart
multibranched	multipartite
multibuilding	multiparty
multicenter	multiplant
multichambered	multipolar
multichannel	multiproblem
multicolored	multiproduct
multicounty	multipurpose
multicultural	multiracial
multidimensional	multiroom
multidirectional	multisense
multidisciplinary	multiservice
multidiscipline	multisided
multidivisional	multispeed
multifaceted	multistage
multifamily	multistep
multifilament	multistory
multifunction	multisyllabic
multifunctional	multitalented
multigrade	multitrack
multiheaded	multiunion
multihospital	multiunit
multihued	multiuse
multilane	multivitamin
multilevel	multiwarhead
multimedia	multiyear
multimember	

mul•ti•far•i•ous \məltə'farēəs\ *adj* : diverse

mul•ti•lat•er•al \məlti'latərəl, -,tī-\ *adj* : having many sides or participants

mul•ti•lin•gual \-'liŋgwəl\ *adj* : knowing or using several languages —**mul•ti•lin•gual•ism** \-gwə,lizəm\ *n*

mul•ti•na•tion•al \-'nashənəl\ *adj* **1** : relating to several nations or nationalities **2** : having divisions in several countries —**multinational** *n*

mul•ti•ple \'məltəpəl\ *adj* **1** : several or many **2** : various ~ *n* : product of one number by another

multiple sclerosis \-sklə'rōsəs\ *n* : brain or spinal disease affecting muscle control

mul•ti•pli•ca•tion \məltəplə'kāshən\ *n* **1** : increase **2** : short method of repeated addition

mul•ti•plic•i•ty \məltə'plisətē\ *n, pl* **-ties** : great number or variety

mul•ti•ply \'məltə,plī\ *vb* **-plied; -ply•ing 1** : increase in number **2** : perform multiplication —**mul•ti•pli•er** \-,plīər\ *n*

mul•ti•tude \'məltə,tüd, -,tyüd\ *n* : great number —**mul•ti•tu•di•nous** \məltə'tüdᵊnəs, -'tyü-\ *adj*

¹**mum** \'məm\ *adj* : silent

²**mum** *n* : chrysanthemum

mum•ble \'məmbəl\ *vb* **-bled; -bling** : speak indistinctly —**mumble** *n* —**mum•bler** *n*

mum•mer \'məmər\ *n* **1** : actor esp. in a pantomime **2** : disguised merrymaker —**mum•mery** *n*

mum•my \'məmē\ *n, pl* **-mies** : embalmed body —**mum•mi•fi•ca•tion** \,məmifə'kāshən\ *n* —**mum•mi•fy** \'məmi,fī\ *vb*

mumps \'məmps\ *n sing or pl* : virus disease with swelling esp. of the salivary glands

munch \'mənch\ *vb* : chew

mun•dane \mən'dān, 'mən,-\ *adj* **1** : relating to the world **2** : lacking concern for the ideal or spiritual —**mun•dane•ly** *adv*

mu•nic•i•pal \myu̇'nisəpəl\ *adj* : of or relating to a town or city —**mu•nic•i•pal•i•ty** \myu̇,nisə'palətē\ *n*

mu•nif•i•cent \myu̇'nifəsənt\ *adj* : generous —**mu•nif•i•cence** \-səns\ *n*

mu•ni•tion \myu̇'nishən\ *n* : armaments

mu•ral \'myu̇rəl\ *adj* : relating to a wall ~ *n* : wall painting —**mu•ra•list** *n*

mur•der \'mərdər\ *n* : unlawful killing of a person ~ *vb* : commit a murder —**mur•der•er** *n* —**mur•der•ess** \-əs\ *n* —**mur•der•ous** \-əs\ *adj* —**mur•der•ous•ly** *adv*

murk \'mərk\ *n* : darkness —**murk•i•ly** \'mərkəlē\ *adv* —**murk•i•ness** \-kēnəs\ *n* —**murky** *adj*

mur•mur \'mərmər\ *n* **1** : muttered complaint **2** : low indistinct sound —**murmur** *vb* —**mur•mur•er** *n* —**mur•mur•ous** *adj*

mus•ca•tel \məskə'tel\ *n* : sweet wine

mus•cle \'məsəl\ *n* **1** : body tissue capable of contracting to produce motion **2** : strength ~ *vb* **-cled; -cling** : force one's way —**mus•cled** *adj* —**mus•cu•lar** \'məskyələr\ *adj* —**mus•cu•lar•i•ty** \məskyə'larətē\ *n*

muscular dystrophy *n* : disease marked by progressive wasting of muscles

mus•cu•la•ture \'məskyələ,chu̇r\ *n* : bodily muscles

¹**muse** \'myüz\ *vb* **mused; mus•ing** : ponder —**mus•ing•ly** *adv*

²**muse** *n* : source of inspiration

mu•se•um \myu̇'zēəm\ *n* : institution displaying objects of interest

mush \'məsh\ *n* **1** : corn meal boiled in water or something of similar consistency **2** : sentimental nonsense —**mushy** *adj*

mush•room \'məsh,rüm, -,ru̇m\ *n* : caplike organ of a fungus ~ *vb* : grow rapidly

mu•sic \'myüzik\ *n* : vocal or instrumental sounds —**mu•si•cal** \-zikəl\ *adj or n* —**mu•si•cal•ly** *adv*

mu•si•cian \myu̇'zishən\ *n* : composer or performer of music —**mu•si•cian•ly** *adj* —**mu•si•cian•ship** *n*

musk \'məsk\ *n* : strong-smelling substance from an Asiatic deer used in perfume —**musk•i•ness** \'məskēnəs\ *n* —**musky** *adj*

mus•kel•lunge \'məskə,lənj\ *n, pl* **-lunge** : large No. American pike

mus•ket \'məskət\ *n* : former shoulder firearm —**mus•ke•teer** \məskə'tir\ *n*

musk•mel•on \'məsk,melən\ *n* : small edible melon

musk-ox \'məsk,äks\ *n* : shaggy-coated wild ox of the arctic

musk•rat \-,rat\ *n, pl* **-rat** *or* **-rats** : No. American aquatic rodent

Mus•lim \'məzləm, 'mu̇s-, 'mu̇z-\ *n* : adherent of Islam —**Muslim** *adj*

mus•lin \'məzlən\ *n* : cotton fabric

muss \'məs\ *n* : untidy state ~ *vb* : disarrange —**muss•i•ly** \'məsəlē\ *adv* —**muss•i•ness** \-ēnəs\ *n* —**mussy** *adj*

mus•sel \'məsəl\ *n* : edible mollusk

must \'məst\ *vb* —used as an auxiliary esp. to express a command, obligation, or necessity ~ \'məst\ *n* : something necessary

mus•tache \'məs,tash, məs'-\ *n* : hair of the human upper lip

mus•tang \'məs,taŋ\ *n* : wild horse of Western America

mus•tard \'məstərd\ *n* : pungent yellow seasoning

mus•ter \'məstər\ *vb* **1** : assemble **2** : rouse ~ *n* : assembled group

musty \'məstē\ *adj* **mus•ti•er; -est** : stale —**must•i•ly** *adv* —**must•i•ness** *n*

mu•ta•ble \'myütəbəl\ *adj* : changeable —**mu•ta•bil•i•ty** \myütə'bilətē\ *n*

mu•tant \'myütᵊnt\ *adj* : relating to or produced by mutation —**mutant** *n*

mu•tate \'myü,tāt\ *vb* **-tat•ed; -tat•ing** : undergo mutation —**mu•ta•tive** \'myü,tātiv, 'myütət-\ *adj*

mu•ta•tion \myü'tāshən\ *n* : change in a hereditary character —**mu•ta•tion•al** *adj*

mute \'myüt\ *adj* **mut•er; mut•est 1** : unable to speak **2** : silent ~ *n* **1** : one who is mute **2** : muffling device ~ *vb* **mut•ed; mut•ing** : muffle —**mute•ly** *adv* —**mute•ness** *n*

mu•ti•late \'myütᵊl,āt\ *vb* **-lat•ed; -lat•ing** : damage seriously (as by cutting off or altering an essential part) —**mu•ti•la•tion** \myütᵊl'āshən\ *n* —**mu•ti•la•tor** \'myütᵊl,ātər\ *n* mu·ti·ny \'myütənē\ n, pl -nies : rebellion —mu·ti·neer \,myüt⁰n'ir\ n —mu·ti·nous \'myüt⁰nəs\ adj —mu·ti·nous·ly adv —mutiny vb

mutt \'mət\ n : mongrel

mut·ter \'mətər\ vb 1 : speak indistinctly or softly 2 : grumble —mutter n

mut·ton \'mət⁰n\ n : flesh of a mature sheep —mut·tony adj

mu·tu·al \'myüchəwəl\ adj 1 : given or felt by one another in equal amount 2 : common —mu·tu·al·ly adv

muz·zle \'məzəl\ n 1 : nose and jaws of an animal 2 : muzzle covering to immobilize an animal's jaws 3 : discharge end of a gun ~ vb -zled; -zling : restrain with or as if with a muzzle

my \'mī\ adj 1 : relating to me or myself 2 —used interjectionally esp. to express surprise

my·nah, my·na \'mīnə\ n : dark crested Asian bird

my·o·pia \mī'ōpēə\ n : nearsightedness —my·o·pic \-'ōpik, -'äpik\ adj —my·o·pi·cal·ly adv

myr·i·ad \'mirēəd\ n : indefinitely large number —myriad adj

myrrh \'mər\ n : aromatic plant gum

myr·tle \'mərt⁰l\ n : shiny evergreen

my·self \mī'self\ pron : I, me —used reflexively or for emphasis

mys·tery \'mistərē\ n, pl -ter·ies 1 : religious truth 2 : something not understood 3 : puzzling or secret quality or state —mys·te·ri·ous \mis'tirēəs\ adj —mys·te·ri·ous·ly adv —mys·te·ri·ous·ness n

mys·tic \'mistik\ adj : mystical or mysterious ~ n : one who has mystical experiences —mys·ti·cism \-tə,sizəm\ n

mys·ti·cal \'mistikəl\ adj 1 : spiritual 2 : relating to direct communion with God —mys·ti·cal·ly adv

mys·ti·fy \'mistə,fī\ vb -fied; -fy·ing : perplex —mys·ti·fi·ca·tion \,mis-təfə'kāshən\ n

mys·tique \mis'tēk\ n : aura of mystery surrounding something

myth \'mith\ n 1 : legendary narrative explaining a belief or phenomenon 2 : imaginary person or thing —myth·i·cal \-ikəl\ n

my·thol·o·gy \mith'äləjē\ n, pl -gies : body of myths —myth·o·log·i·cal \,mithə'läjikəl\ adj —my·thol·o·gist \mith'äləjist\ n

N

n \'en\ n, pl n's or ns \'enz\ : 14th letter of the alphabet

nab \'nab\ vb -bb- : seize or arrest

na·dir \'nā,dir, 'nādər\ n : lowest point

¹nag \'nag\ n : old or decrepit horse

²nag vb -gg- 1 : complain 2 : scold or urge continually 3 : be persistently annoying ~ n : one who nags habitually

na·iad \'nāəd, 'nī-, -,ad\ n, pl -iads or -ia·des \-ə,dēz\ : mythological water nymph

nail \'nāl\ n 1 : horny sheath at the end of each finger and toe 2 : pointed metal fastener ~ vb : fasten with a nail —nail·er n

na·ive, na·ïve \nä'ēv\ adj -iv·er; -est 1 : innocent and unsophisticated 2 : easily deceived —na·ive·ly adv —na·ive·ness n

na·ive·té \,nä,ēvə'tā, nä'ēvə,-\ n : quality or state of being naive

na·ked \'nākəd, 'nekəd\ adj 1 : having no clothes on 2 : uncovered 3 : plain or obvious 4 : unaided —na·ked·ly adv —na·ked·ness n

nam·by–pam·by \,nambē'pambē\ adj : weak or indecisive

name \'nām\ n 1 : word by which a person or thing is known 2 : disparaging word for someone 3 : distinguished reputation ~ vb named; nam·ing 1 : give a name to 2 : mention or identify by name 3 : nominate or appoint ~ adj 1 : relating to a name 2 : prominent —name·able adj —name·less adj —name·less·ly adv

name·ly \'nāmlē\ adv : that is to say

name·sake \-,sāk\ n : one named after another

¹nap \'nap\ vb -pp- 1 : sleep briefly 2 : be off guard ~ n : short sleep

²nap n : soft downy surface —nap·less adj —napped \'napt\ adj

na·palm \'nā,pälm, -,päm\ n : gasoline in the form of a jelly

nape \'nāp, 'nap\ n : back of the neck

naph·tha \'nafthə\ n : flammable solvent

nap·kin \'napkən\ n : small cloth for use at the table

nar·cis·sism \'närsə,sizəm\ n : self-love —nar·cis·sist \-sist\ n or adj —nar·cis·sis·tic \,närsə'sistik\ adj

nar·cis·sus \när'sisəs\ n, pl -cis·sus or -cis·sus·es or -cis·si \-'sis,ī, -,ē\ : plant with flowers usu. borne separately

nar·cot·ic \när'kätik\ n : painkilling addictive drug —narcotic adj

nar·rate \'nar,āt\ vb nar·rat·ed; nar·rat·ing : tell (a story) —nar·ra·tion \na-'rāshən\ n —nar·ra·tive \'narətiv\ n or adj —nar·ra·tor \'nar,ātər\ n

nar·row \'narō\ adj 1 : of less than standard width 2 : limited 3 : not liberal 4 : barely successful ~ vb : make narrow —nar·row·ly adv —nar·row·ness n

nar·row–mind·ed \,narō'mīndəd\ adj : shallow, provincial, or bigoted

nar·rows \'narōz\ n pl : narrow passage

nar·whal \'när,hwäl, 'närwəl\ n : sea mammal with a tusk

na·sal \'nāzəl\ adj : relating to or uttered through the nose —na·sal·ly adv

nas·tur·tium \nə'stərshəm, na-\ n : herb with showy flowers

nas·ty \'nastē\ adj nas·ti·er; -est 1 : filthy 2 : indecent 3 : malicious or spiteful 4 : difficult or disagreeable 5 : unfair —nas·ti·ly \'nastəlē\ adv —nas·ti·ness \-tēnəs\ n

na·tal \'nāt⁰l\ adj : relating to birth

na·tion \'nāshən\ n 1 : people of similar characteristics 2 : community with its own territory and government —na·tion·al \'nashənəl\ adj or n —na·tion·al·ly adv —na·tion·hood n —na·tion·wide adj

na·tion·al·ism \'nashənəl,izəm\ n : devotion to national interests, unity, and independence —na·tion·al·ist \-ist\ n or adj —na·tion·al·is·tic \,nashənəl'istik\ adj

na·tion·al·i·ty \,nashə'nalətē\ n, pl -ties 1 : national character 2 : membership in a nation 3 : political independence 4 : ethnic group

na·tion·al·ize \'nashənəl,īz\ vb -ized; -iz·ing 1 : make national 2 : place under government control —na·tion·al·i·za·tion \,nashənələ'zāshən\ n

na·tive \'nātiv\ adj 1 : belonging to a person at or by way of birth 2 : born or produced in a particular place ~ n : one who belongs to a country by birth

Na·tiv·i·ty \nə'tivətē, nā-\ n, pl -ties 1 : birth of Christ 2 not cap : birth

nat·ty \'natē\ adj -ti·er; -est : smartly dressed —nat·ti·ly \'nat⁰lē\ adv —nat·ti·ness \-ēnəs\ n

nat·u·ral \'nachərəl\ adj 1 : relating to or determined by nature 2 : not artificial 3 : simple and sincere 4 : lifelike ~ n : one having an innate talent —nat·u·ral·ness n

nat·u·ral·ism \'nachərə,lizəm\ n : realism in art and literature —nat·u·ral·is·tic \,nachərə'listik\ adj

nat·u·ral·ist \-list\ n 1 : one who practices naturalism 2 : student of animals or plants

nat·u·ral·ize \-,līz\ vb -ized; -iz·ing 1 : become or cause to become established 2 : confer citizenship on —nat·u·ral·i·za·tion \,nachərələ'zāshən\ n

nat·u·ral·ly \'nachərəlē\ adv 1 : in a natural way 2 : as might be expected

na·ture \'nāchər\ n 1 : basic quality of something 2 : kind 3 : disposition 4 : physical universe 5 : natural environment

naught \'nòt, 'nät\ n 1 : nothing 2 : zero

naugh·ty \'nótē, 'nät-\ adj -ti·er; -est 1 : disobedient or misbehaving 2 : improper —naught·i·ly \'nót⁰lē, 'nät-\ adv —naught·i·ness \-ēnəs\ n

nau·sea \'nòzēə, -shə\ n 1 : sickness of the stomach with a desire to vomit 2 : extreme disgust —nau·seous \-shəs, -zēəs\ adj

nau·se·ate \'nòzē,āt, -zhē-, -sē-, -shē-\ vb -at·ed; -at·ing : affect or become affected with nausea —nau·se·at·ing·ly \-,ātiŋlē\ adv

nau·ti·cal \'nòtikəl\ adj : relating to ships and sailing —nau·ti·cal·ly adv

nau·ti·lus \'nòt⁰ləs\ n, pl -lus·es or -li \-⁰l,ī, -,ē\ : sea mollusk with a spiral shell

na·val \'nāvəl\ adj : relating to a navy

nave \'nāv\ n : central part of a church

na·vel \'nāvəl\ n : depression in the abdomen

nav·i·ga·ble \'navigəbəl\ adj : capable of being navigated —nav·i·ga·bil·i·ty \,navigə'bilətē\ n

nav·i·gate \'navə,gāt\ vb -gat·ed; -gat·ing 1 : sail on or through 2 : direct the course of —nav·i·ga·tion \,navə'gāshən\ n —nav·i·ga·tor \'navə,gātər\ n

na·vy \'nāvē\ n, pl -vies 1 : fleet 2 : nation's organization for sea warfare

nay \'nā\ adv : no—used in oral voting ~ n : negative vote

Na·zi \'nätsē, 'nat-\ n : member of a German fascist party from 1933 to 1945 —Nazi adj —Na·zism \'nät,sizəm, 'nat-\, Na·zi·ism \-sē,izəm\ n

near \'nir\ adv : at or close to ~ prep : close to ~ adj 1 : not far away 2 : very much like ~ vb : approach —near·ly adv —near·ness n

near·by \nir'bī, 'nir,bī\ adv or adj : near

near·sight·ed \'nir'sītəd\ adj : seeing well at short distances only —near·sight·ed·ly adv —near·sight·ed·ness n

neat \'nēt\ adj 1 : not diluted 2 : tastefully simple 3 : orderly and clean —neat adv —neat·ly adv —neat·ness n

neb·u·la \'nebyələ\ n, pl -lae \-,lē, -,lī\ : large cloud of interstellar gas —neb·u·lar \-lər\ adj

neb·u·lous \-ləs\ adj : indistinct

nec·es·sary \'nesə,serē\ n, pl -saries : indispensable item ~ adj 1 : inevitable 2 : compulsory 3 : positively needed —nec·es·sar·i·ly \,nesə'serəlē\ adv

ne·ces·si·tate \ni'sesə,tāt\ vb -tat·ed; -tat·ing : make necessary

ne·ces·si·ty \ni'sesətē\ n, pl -ties 1 : very great need 2 : something that is necessary 3 : poverty 4 : circumstances that cannot be changed

neck \'nek\ n 1 : body part connecting the head and trunk 2 : part of a garment at the neck 3 : narrow part ~ vb : kiss and caress —necked \'nekt\ adj

neck·er·chief \'nekərchəf, -,chēf\ n, pl -chiefs \-chəfs, -,chēfs\ : cloth worn tied about the neck

neck·lace \'nekləs\ n : ornament worn around the neck

neck·tie n : ornamental cloth tied under a collar

nec·ro·man·cy \'nekrə,mansē\ n : art of conjuring up the spirits of the dead —nec·ro·man·cer \-sər\ n

ne·cro·sis \nə'krōsəs, ne-\ n, pl -cro·ses \-,sēz\ : death of body tissue

nec·tar \'nektər\ n : sweet plant secretion

nec·tar·ine \,nektə'rēn\ n : smooth-skinned peach

née, nee \'nā\ adj—used to identify a married woman by maiden name

need \'nēd\ n 1 : obligation 2 : lack of something or what is lacking 3 : poverty ~ vb 1 : be in want 2 : have cause for 3 : be under obligation —need·ful \-fəl\ adj —need·less adj —need·less·ly adv —needy adj

nee·dle \'nēd⁰l\ n 1 : pointed sewing implement or something like it 2 : movable bar in a compass 3 : hollow instrument for injecting or withdrawing material ~ vb -dled; -dling : incite to action by repeated gibes —nee·dle·work \-,wərk\ n

nee·dle·point \'nēd⁰l,pòint\ n 1 : lace fabric 2 : embroidery on canvas —needlepoint adj

ne·far·i·ous \ni'farēəs\ adj : very wicked —ne·far·i·ous·ly adv

ne·gate \ni'gāt\ vb -gat·ed; -gat·ing 1 : deny 2 : nullify —ne·ga·tion \-'gāshən\ n

neg·a·tive \'negətiv\ adj 1 : marked by denial or refusal 2 : showing a lack of something suspected or desirable 3 : less than zero 4 : having more electrons than protons 5 : having light and shadow images reversed ~ n 1 : negative word or vote 2 : a negative number 3 : negative photographic image —neg·a·tive·ly adv —neg·a·tive·ness n —neg·a·tiv·i·ty \,negə'tivətē\ n

ne·glect \ni'glekt\ vb 1 : disregard 2 : leave unattended to ~ n 1 : act of neglecting 2 : condition of being neglected —ne·glect·ful \-fəl\ adj

neg·li·gee \,neglə'zhā\ n : woman's loose robe

neg·li·gent \'neglijənt\ adj : marked by neglect —neg·li·gence \-jəns\ n —neg·li·gent·ly adv

neg·li·gi·ble \'neglijəbəl\ adj : insignificant

ne·go·ti·ate \ni'gōshē,āt\ vb -at·ed; -at·ing 1 : confer with another to settle a matter 2 : obtain cash for 3 : get through successfully —ne·go·tia·ble \-shəbəl, -shēə-\ adj —ne·go·ti·a·tion \-,gōshē-'āshən, -shē'ā-\ n —ne·go·ti·a·tor \-'gōshē,ātər\ n

Ne·gro \'nēgrō\ n, pl -groes : member of the black race —Negro adj —Ne·groid \'nē-,gròid\ n or adj, often not cap

neigh \'nā\ n : cry of a horse —neigh vb

neigh·bor \'nābər\ n 1 : one living nearby 2 : fellowman ~ vb : be near or next to —neigh·bor·hood \-,hùd\ n —neigh·bor·li·ness n —neigh·bor·ly adj

nei·ther \'nēthər, 'nī-\ pron or adj : not the one or the other ~ conj 1 : not either ~

nem·e·sis \'nemosəs\ n, pl -e·ses \-ə,sēz\ 1 : old and usu. frustrating rival 2 : retaliation

ne·ol·o·gism \nē'älə,jizəm\ n : new word

ne·on \'nē,än\ n : gaseous colorless chemical element that emits a reddish glow in electric lamps —neon adj

neo·phyte \'nēə,fīt\ n : beginner

neph·ew \'nefyü, chiefly Brit 'nev-\ n : a son of one's brother, sister, brother-in-law, or sister-in-law

nep·o·tism \'nepə,tizəm\ n : favoritism shown in hiring a relative

nerd \'nərd\ n : one who is not stylish or socially at ease —nerdy adj

nerve \'nərv\ n 1 : strand of body tissue that connects the brain with other parts of the body 2 : self-control 3 : daring 4 pl : nervousness —nerved \'nərvd\ adj —nerve·less adj

ner·vous \'nərvəs\ adj 1 : relating to or made up of nerves 2 : easily excited 3 : timid or fearful —ner·vous·ly adv —ner·vous·ness n

ner·vy \'nərvē\ adj nerv·i·er; -est : insolent or presumptuous

-ness \nəs\ n suffix : condition or quality

nest \'nest\ n 1 : shelter prepared by a bird for its eggs 2 : place where eggs (as of insects or fish) are laid and hatched 3 : snug retreat 4 : set of objects fitting one inside or another ~ vb : build or occupy a nest

nes·tle \'nesəl\ vb -tled; -tling : settle snugly (as in a nest)

¹net \'net\ n : fabric with spaces between strands or something made of this ~ vb -tt- : cover with or catch in a net

²net vb : remaining after deductions ~ vb -tt- : have as profit

neth·er \'nethər\ adj : situated below

net·tle \'net⁰l\ n : coarse herb with stinging hairs ~ vb -tled; -tling : provoke or vex —net·tle·some adj

net·work n : system of crossing or connected elements

neu·ral \'nùrəl, 'nyùr-\ adj : relating to a nerve

neu·ral·gia \nù'raljə, nyù-\ n : pain along a nerve —neu·ral·gic \-jik\ adj

neu·ri·tis \nù'rītəs, nyù-\ n, pl -rit·i·des \-'ritə,dēz\ or -ri·tis·es : inflammation of a nerve

neu·rol·o·gy \nù'räləjē, nyù-\ n : study of the nervous system —neu·ro·log·i·cal \,nùrə'läjikəl, ,nyùr-\, neu·ro·log·ic \-ik\ adj —neu·rol·o·gist \nù'räləjist, nyù-\ n

neu·ro·sis \nù'rōsəs, nyù-\ n, pl -ro·ses \-,sēz\ : nervous disorder

neu·rot·ic \nù'rätik, nyù-\ adj : relating to neurosis ~ n : unstable person —neu·rot·i·cal·ly adv

neu·ter \'nütər, 'nyü-\ adj : neither masculine nor feminine ~ vb : castrate or spay

neu·tral \-trəl\ adj 1 : not favoring either side 2 : being neither one thing nor the other 3 : not decided in color 4 : not electrically charged ~ n 1 : one that is neutral 2 : position of gears that are not engaged —neu·tral·i·za·tion \,nütrələ'zāshən, ,nyü-\ n —neu·tral·ize \'nütrə,līz, 'nyü-\ vb

neu·tral·i·ty \nü'tralətē, nyü-\ n : state of being neutral

neu·tron \'nü,trän, 'nyü-\ n : uncharged atomic particle

nev·er \'nevər\ adv 1 : not ever 2 : not in any degree, way, or condition

nev·er·more adv : never again

nev·er·the·less adv : in spite of that

new \'nü, 'nyü\ adj 1 : not old or familiar 2 : different from the former 3 : recently discovered or learned 4 : not accustomed 5 : refreshed or regenerated 6 : being such for the first time ~ adv : newly —new·ish adj —new·ness n

new·born adj 1 : recently born 2 : born anew ~ n, pl -born or -borns : newborn individual

new·ly \-lē\ adv : recently

news \'nüz, 'nyüz\ n : report of recent events —news·let·ter n —news·mag·a·zine n —news·man \-mən, -,man\ n —news·pa·per n —news·pa·per·man \-,man\ n —news·stand n —news·wom·an \-,wù-mən\ n —news·wor·thy adj

news·cast \-,kast\ n : broadcast of news —news·cast·er \-,kastər\ n

news·print n : paper made from wood pulp

newsy \'nüzē, 'nyü-\ adj news·i·er; -est : filled with news

newt \'nüt, 'nyüt\ n : small salamander

New Year n : New Year's Day

New Year's Day n : January 1 observed as a legal holiday

next \'nekst\ adj : immediately preceding or following ~ adv 1 : in the time or place nearest 2 : at the first time yet to come ~ prep : nearest to

nex·us \'neksəs\ n, pl -us·es \-səsəz\ or -us \-səs, -,süs\ : connection

nib \'nib\ n : pen point

nib·ble \'nibəl\ vb -bled; -bling : bite gently or bit by bit ~ n : small bite

nice \'nīs\ adj nic·er; nic·est 1 : fastidious 2 : very precise or delicate 3 : pleasing 4 : respectable —nice·ly adv —nice·ness n

nice•ty \'nīsətē\ n, pl **-ties 1** : dainty or elegant thing **2** : fine detail **3** : exactness

niche \'nich\ n **1** : recess in a wall **2** : fitting place, work, or use

nick \'nik\ n **1** : small broken area or chip **2** : critical moment ~ vb : make a nick in

nick•el \'nikəl\ n **1** : hard silver-white metallic chemical element used in alloys **2** : U.S. 5-cent piece

nick•name \'nik,nām\ n : informal substitute name —**nickname** vb

nic•o•tine \'nikə,tēn\ n : poisonous and addictive substance in tobacco

niece \'nēs\ n : a daughter of one's brother, sister, brother-in-law, or sister-in-law

nig•gard•ly \'nigərdlē\ adj : stingy —**niggard** n —**nig•gard•li•ness** n

nig•gling \'nigliŋ\ adj : petty and annoying

nigh \'nī\ adv or adj or prep : near

night \'nīt\ n **1** : period between dusk and dawn **2** : the coming of night —**night** adj —**night•ly** adj or adv —**night•time** n

night•clothes n pl : garments worn in bed

night•club \-,kləb\ n : place for drinking and entertainment open at night

night crawler n : earthworm

night•fall n : the coming of night

night•gown n : gown worn for sleeping

night•in•gale \'nīt°n,gāl, -iŋ-\ n : Old World thrush that sings at night

night•mare \'nīt,mar\ n : frightening dream —**nightmare** adj —**night•mar•ish** \-,marish\ adj

night•shade \'nīt,shād\ n : group of plants that include poisonous forms and food plants (as the potato and eggplant)

nil \'nil\ n : nothing

nim•ble \'nimbəl\ adj **-bler; -blest 1** : agile **2** : clever —**nim•ble•ness** n —**nim•bly** \-blē\ adv

nine \'nīn\ n **1** : one more than 8 **2** : 9th in a set or series —**nine** adj or pron —**ninth** \'nīnth\ adj or adv or n

nine•pins n : bowling game using 9 pins

nine•teen \nīn'tēn\ n : one more than 18 —**nineteen** adj or pron —**nine•teenth** \-'tēnth\ adj or n

nine•ty \'nīntē\ n, pl **-ties** : 9 times 10 —**nine•ti•eth** \-ēəth\ adj or n —**ninety** adj or pron

nin•ny \'ninē\ n, pl **nin•nies** : fool

¹nip \'nip\ vb **-pp- 1** : catch hold of and squeeze tightly **2** : pinch or bite off **3** : destroy the growth or fulfillment of ~ n **1** : biting cold **2** : tang **3** : pinch or bite

²nip n : small quantity of liquor ~ vb **-pp-** : take liquor in nips

nip•per \'nipər\ n **1** : one that nips **2** pl : pincers **3** : small boy

nip•ple \'nipəl\ n : tip of the breast or something resembling it

nip•py \'nipē\ adj **-pi•er; -est 1** : pungent **2** : chilly

nir•va•na \nir'vänə\ n : state of blissful oblivion

nit \'nit\ n : egg of a parasitic insect

ni•ter \'nītər\ n : potassium nitrate used in gunpowder or fertilizer or in curing meat

ni•trate \'nī,trāt, -trət\ n : chemical salt used esp. in curing meat

ni•tric acid \'nītrik-\ n : liquid acid used in making dyes, explosives, and fertilizers

ni•trite \-,trīt\ n : chemical salt used in curing meat

ni•tro•gen \'nītrəjən\ n : tasteless odorless gaseous chemical element

ni•tro•glyc•er•in, ni•tro•glyc•er•ine \,nītrō'glisərən\ n : heavy oily liquid used as an explosive and as a blood-vessel relaxer

nit•wit \'nit,wit\ n : stupid person

no \'nō\ adv **1** —used to express the negative **2** : in no respect or degree **3** : not so **4** —used as an interjection of surprise or doubt ~ adj **1** : not any **2** : not a ~ n, pl **noes** or **nos** \'nōz\ **1** : refusal **2** : negative vote

no•bil•i•ty \nō'bilətē\ n **1** : quality or state of being noble **2** : class of people of noble rank

no•ble \'nōbəl\ adj **-bler; -blest 1** : illustrious **2** : aristocratic **3** : stately **4** : of outstanding character ~ n : nobleman —**no•ble•ness** n —**no•bly** adv

no•ble•man \-mən\ n : member of the nobility

no•ble•wom•an \-,wumən\ n : a woman of noble rank

no•body \'nōbədē, -,bädē\ pron : no person ~ n, pl **-bod•ies** : person of no influence or importance

noc•tur•nal \näk'tərn°l\ adj : relating to, occurring at, or active at night

noc•turne \'näk,tərn\ n : dreamy musical composition

nod \'näd\ vb **-dd- 1** : bend the head downward or forward (as in bowing or going to sleep or as a sign of assent) **2** : move up and down **3** : show by a nod of the head —**nod** n

node \'nōd\ n : stem part from which a leaf arises —**nod•al** \-°l\ adj

nod•ule \'näjül\ n : small lump or swelling —**nod•u•lar** \'näjələr\ adj

no•el \nō'el\ n **1** : Christmas carol **2** cap : Christmas season

noes pl of NO

nog•gin \'nägən\ n **1** : small mug **2** : person's head

no•how \'nō,haù\ adv : in no manner

noise \'nóiz\ n **1** : loud or unpleasant sound ~ vb **noised; nois•ing** : spread by rumor —**noise•less** adj —**noise•less•ly** adv —**noise•mak•er** n —**nois•i•ly** \'nóizəlē\ adv —**nois•i•ness** \-zēnəs\ n —**noisy** \'nóizē\ adj

noi•some \'nóisəm\ adj : harmful or offensive

no•mad \'nō,mad\ n : one who has no permanent home —**nomad** adj —**no•mad•ic** \nō'madik\ adj

no•men•cla•ture \'nōmən,klāchər\ n : system of names

nom•i•nal \'nämən°l\ adj **1** : being something in name only **2** : small or negligible —**nom•i•nal•ly** adv

nom•i•nate \'nämə,nāt\ vb **-nat•ed; -nat•ing** : propose or choose as a candidate —**nom•i•na•tion** \,nämə'nāshən\ n

nom•i•na•tive \'nämənətiv\ adj : relating to or being a grammatical case marking typically the subject of a verb —**nominative** n

nom•i•nee \,nämə'nē\ n : person nominated

non- \,nän, ,nän\ prefix **1** : not, reverse of, or absence of **2** : not important

nonabrasive	noninfectious
nonabsorbent	noninflationary
nonacademic	nonintegrated
nonaccredited	nonintellectual
nonacid	noninterference
nonaddictive	nonintoxicating
nonadhesive	noninvasive
nonadjacent	non-Jewish
nonadjustable	nonlegal
nonaffiliated	nonlethal
nonaggression	nonliterary
nonalcoholic	nonliving
nonaligned	nonmagnetic
nonappearance	nonmalignant
nonautomatic	nonmedical
nonbeliever	nonmember
nonbinding	nonmetal
nonbreakable	nonmetallic
noncancerous	nonmilitary
noncandidate	nonmusical
non-Catholic	nonnative
non-Christian	nonnegotiable
nonchurchgoer	nonobjective
noncitizen	nonobservance
nonclassical	nonorthodox
nonclassified	nonparallel
noncombat	nonparticipant
noncombatant	nonparticipating
noncombustible	nonpaying
noncommercial	nonpayment
noncommunist	nonperformance
noncompliance	nonperishable
nonconflicting	nonphysical
nonconforming	nonpoisonous
nonconsecutive	nonpolitical
nonconstructive	nonpolluting
noncontagious	nonporous
noncontrollable	nonpregnant
noncontroversial	nonproductive
noncorrosive	nonprofessional
noncriminal	nonprofit
noncritical	nonracial
noncumulative	nonradioactive
noncurrent	nonrated
nondeductible	nonrealistic
nondeferrable	nonrecurring
nondegradable	nonrefillable
nondelivery	nonrefundable
nondemocratic	nonreligious
nondenominational	nonrenewable
	nonrepresentative
nondestructive	nonresident
nondiscrimination	nonresponsive
nondiscriminatory	nonrestricted
	nonreversible
noneducational	nonsalable
nonelastic	nonscientific
nonelected	nonscientist
nonelective	nonsegregated
nonelectric	non-self-governing
nonelectronic	
nonemotional	nonsexist
nonenforcement	nonsexual
nonessential	nonsignificant
nonexclusive	nonskier
nonexistence	nonsmoker
nonexistent	nonsmoking
nonexplosive	nonspeaking
nonfat	nonspecialist
nonfatal	nonspecific
nonfattening	nonstandard
nonfictional	nonstick
nonflammable	nonstop
nonflowering	nonstrategic
nonfunctional	nonstudent
nongovernmental	nonsugar
nongraded	nonsurgical
nonhazardous	nonswimmer
nonhereditary	nontaxable
nonindustrial	nonteaching
nonindustrialized	nontechnical

---

nontoxic | nonuser
nontraditional | nonvenomous
nontransferable | nonverbal
nontropical | nonvoter
nontypical | nonwhite
nonunion | nonworker

non•age \'nänij, 'nōnij\ n : period of youth and esp. legal minority

nonce \'näns\ n : present occasion ~ adj : occurring, used, or made only once

non•cha•lant \,nänshə'länt\ adj : showing indifference —**non•cha•lance** \-'läns\ n —**non•cha•lant•ly** adv

non•com•mis•sioned officer \,nänkə'mishənd-\ n : subordinate officer in the armed forces appointed from enlisted personnel

non•com•mit•tal \,nänkə'mit°l\ adj : indicating neither consent nor dissent

non•con•duc•tor n : substance that is a very poor conductor

non•con•form•ist n : one who does not conform to an established belief or mode of behavior —**non•con•for•mi•ty** n

non•de•script \,nändi'skript\ adj : lacking distinctive qualities

none \'nən\ pron : not any ~ adv : not at all

non•en•ti•ty n : one of no consequence

none•the•less \,nənthə'les\ adv : nevertheless

non•pa•reil \,nänpə'rel\ adj : having no equal ~ n **1** : one who has no equal **2** : chocolate candy disk

non•par•ti•san adj : not influenced by political party bias

non•per•son n : person without social or legal status

non•plus \,nän'pləs\ vb **-ss-** : perplex

non•pre•scrip•tion adj : available without a doctor's prescription

non•pro•lif•er•a•tion adj : aimed at ending increased use of nuclear arms

non•sched•uled adj : licensed to carry by air without a regular schedule

non•sense \'nän,sens, -səns\ n : foolish or meaningless words or actions —**non•sen•si•cal** \nän'sensikəl\ adj —**non•sen•si•cal•ly** adv

non•sup•port n : failure in a legal obligation to provide for someone's needs

non•vi•o•lence n : avoidance of violence esp. in political demonstrations —**non•vi•o•lent** adj

noo•dle \'nüd°l\ n : ribbon-shaped food paste

nook \'nuk\ n **1** : inside corner **2** : private place

noon \'nün\ n : middle of the day —**noon** adj

noon•day \-,dā\ n : noon

no one pron : no person

noon•time n : noon

noose \'nüs\ n : rope loop that slips down tight

nor \nör\ conj : and not—used esp. after neither to introduce and negate the 2d member of a series

norm \'nörm\ n **1** : standard usu. derived from an average **2** : typical widespread practice or custom

nor•mal \'nörməl\ adj : average, regular, or standard —**nor•mal•cy** \-sē\ n —**nor•mal•i•ty** \nör'malətē\ n —**nor•mal•i•za•tion** \,nörmələ'zāshən\ n —**nor•mal•ize** \'nörmə,līz\ vb —**nor•mal•ly** adv

north \'nörth\ adv : to or toward the north ~ adj : situated toward, at, or coming from the north ~ n **1** : direction to the left of one facing east **2** cap : regions to the north —**north•er•ly** \'nörthərlē\ adv or adj —**north•ern** \-ərn\ adj —**North•ern•er** n —**north•ern•most** \-,mōst\ adj —**north•ward** \-wərd\ adv or adj —**north•wards** \-wərdz\ adv

north•east \nörth'ēst\ n **1** : direction between north and east **2** cap : regions to the northeast —**northeast** adj or adv —**north•east•er•ly** \-ərlē\ adv or adj —**north•east•ern** \-ərn\ adj

northern lights n pl : aurora borealis

north pole n : northernmost point of the earth

north•west \-'west\ n **1** : direction between north and west **2** cap : regions to the northwest —**northwest** adj or adv —**north•west•er•ly** \-ərlē\ adv or adj —**north•west•ern** \-ərn\ adj

nose \'nōz\ n **1** : part of the face containing the nostrils **2** : sense of smell **3** : front part ~ vb **nosed; nos•ing 1** : detect by smell **2** : push aside with the nose **3** : pry **4** : inch ahead —**nose•bleed** n —**nosed** \'nōzd\ adj —**nose out** vb : narrowly defeat

nose•gay \-,gā\ n : small bunch of flowers

nos•tal•gia \nä'staljə, nə-\ n : wistful yearning for something past —**nos•tal•gic** \-jik\ adj

nos•tril \'nästrəl\ n : opening of the nose

nos•trum \-trəm\ n : questionable remedy

nosy, nos•ey \'nōzē\ adj **nos•i•er; -est** : tending to pry

---

not \'nät\ adv—used to make a statement negative

no•ta•ble \'nōtəbəl\ adj **1** : noteworthy **2** : distinguished ~ n : notable person —**no•ta•bil•i•ty** \,nōtə'bilətē\ n —**no•ta•bly** \'nōtəblē\ adv

no•ta•rize \'nōtə,rīz\ vb **-rized; -riz•ing** : attest as a notary public

no•ta•ry public \'nōtərē-\ n, pl **-ries public** or **-ry publics** : public official who attests writings to make them legally authentic

no•ta•tion \nō'tāshən\ n **1** : note **2** : act, process, or method of marking things down

notch \'näch\ n : V-shaped hollow —**notch** vb

note \'nōt\ vb **not•ed; not•ing 1** : notice **2** : write down ~ n **1** : musical tone **2** : written comment or record **3** : short informal letter **4** : notice or heed —**note•book** n

not•ed \'nōtəd\ adj : famous

note•wor•thy \-,wərthē\ adj : worthy of special mention

noth•ing \'nəthiŋ\ pron **1** : no thing **2** : no part **3** : one of no value or importance ~ adv : not at all ~ n **1** : something that does not exist **2** : zero **3** : one of little or no importance —**noth•ing•ness** n

no•tice \'nōtəs\ n **1** : warning or announcement **2** : attention ~ vb **-ticed; -tic•ing** : take notice of —**no•tice•able** adj —**no•tice•ably** adv

no•ti•fy \'nōtə,fī\ vb **-fied; -fy•ing** : give notice of or to —**no•ti•fi•ca•tion** \,nōtəfə'kāshən\ n

no•tion \'nōshən\ n **1** : idea or opinion **2** : whim

no•to•ri•ous \nō'tōrēəs\ adj : widely and unfavorably known —**no•to•ri•ety** \,nōtə'rīətē\ n —**no•to•ri•ous•ly** adv

not•with•stand•ing \,nätwith'standiŋ, -with-\ prep : in spite of ~ adv : nevertheless ~ conj : although

nou•gat \'nügət\ n : nuts or fruit pieces in a sugar paste

nought \'nöt, 'nät\ var of NAUGHT

noun \'naùn\ n : word that is the name of a person, place, or thing

nour•ish \'nərish\ vb : promote the growth of —**nour•ish•ing** adj —**nour•ish•ment** n

no•va \'nōvə\ n, pl **-vas** or **-vae** \-,vē, -,vī\ : star that suddenly brightens and then fades gradually

nov•el \'nävəl\ adj : new or strange ~ n : long invented prose story —**nov•el•ist** \-əlist\ n

nov•el•ty \'nävəltē\ n, pl **-ties 1** : something new or unusual **2** : newness **3** : small manufactured article—usu. pl.

No•vem•ber \nō'vembər\ n : 11th month of the year having 30 days

nov•ice \'nävəs\ n **1** : one preparing to take vows in a religious order **2** : one who is inexperienced or untrained

no•vi•tiate \nō'vishət, nə-\ n : period or state of being a novice

now \'naù\ adv **1** : at the present time or moment **2** : forthwith **3** : under these circumstances ~ conj : in view of the fact ~ n : present time

now•a•days \'naùə,dāz\ adv : now

no•where \-,hwer\ adv : not anywhere —**nowhere** n

nox•ious \'näkshəs\ adj : harmful

noz•zle \'näzəl\ n : device to direct or control a flow of fluid

nu•ance \'nü,äns, 'nyü-\ n : subtle distinction or variation

nub \'nəb\ n **1** : knob or lump **2** : gist

nu•bile \'nü,bīl, 'nyü-, -bəl\ adj **1** : of marriageable condition or age **2** : sexually attractive

nu•cle•ar \'nüklēər, 'nyü-\ adj **1** : relating to the atomic nucleus or atomic energy **2** : relating to a weapon whose power is from a nuclear reaction

nu•cle•us \'nükləs, 'nyü-\ n, pl **-clei** \-klē,ī\ : central mass or part (as of a cell or an atom)

nude \'nüd, 'nyüd\ adj **nud•er; nud•est** : naked ~ n : nude human figure —**nu•di•ty** \'nüdətē, 'nyü-\ n

nudge \'nəj\ vb **nudged; nudg•ing** : touch or push gently —**nudge** n

nud•ism \'nüd,izəm, 'nyü-\ n : practice of going nude —**nud•ist** \'nüdist, 'nyü-\ n

nug•get \'nəgət\ n : lump of gold

nui•sance \'nüs°ns, 'nyü-\ n : something annoying

null \'nəl\ adj : having no legal or binding force —**nul•li•ty** \'nälətē\ n

nul•li•fy \'nälə,fī\ vb **-fied; -fy•ing** : make null or valueless —**nul•li•fi•ca•tion** \,nələfə'kāshən\ n

numb \'nəm\ adj : lacking feeling —**numb** vb —**numb•ly** adv —**numb•ness** n

num•ber \'nəmbər\ n **1** : total of individuals taken together **2** : indefinite total **3** : unit of a mathematical system **4** : numeral **5** : one in a sequence ~ vb **1** : count **2** : assign a number to **3** : comprise in number —**num•ber•less** adj

nu•mer•al \'nümərəl, 'nyü-\ n : conventional symbol representing a number

nu·mer·a·tor \\ˈnüməˌrātər, ˈnyü-\\ *n* : part of a fraction above the line

nu·mer·i·cal \\nüˈmerikəl, nyü-\\, **nu·meric** \\-ˈmerik\\ *adj* 1 : relating to numbers 2 : expressed in or involving numbers —**nu·mer·i·cal·ly** *adv*

nu·mer·ol·o·gy \\ˌnüməˈräləjē, ˌnyü-\\ *n* : occult study of numbers —**nu·mer·ol·o·gist** \\-jist\\ *n*

nu·mer·ous \\ˈnümərəs, ˈnyü-\\ *adj* : consisting of a great number

nu·mis·mat·ics \\ˌnüməzˈmatiks, ˌnyü-\\ *n* : study or collection of monetary objects —**nu·mis·mat·ic** \\-ik\\ *adj* —**nu·mis·ma·tist** \\nüˈmizmətist, nyü-\\ *n*

num·skull \\ˈnəmˌskəl\\ *n* : stupid person

nun \\ˈnən\\ *n* 1 : woman belonging to a religious order —**nun·nery** \\-ərē\\ *n*

nup·tial \\ˈnəpshəl\\ *adj* : relating to marriage or a wedding ~ *n* : marriage or wedding—usu. pl.

nurse \\ˈnərs\\ *n* 1 : one hired to care for children 2 : person trained to care for sick people ~ *vb* **nursed; nurs·ing** 1 : suckle 2 : care for

nurs·ery \\ˈnərsərē\\ *n, pl* **-er·ies** 1 : place where children are cared for 2 : place where young plants are grown

nursing home *n* : private establishment providing care for persons who are unable to care for themselves

nur·ture \\ˈnərchər\\ *n* 1 : training or upbringing 2 : food or nourishment ~ *vb* **-tured; -tur·ing** 1 : care for or feed 2 : educate

nut \\ˈnət\\ *n* 1 : dry hard-shelled fruit or seed with a firm inner kernel 2 : metal block with a screw hole through it 3 : foolish, eccentric, or crazy person 4 : enthusiast —**nut·crack·er** *n* —**nut·shell** *n* —**nut·ty** *adj*

nut·hatch \\ˈnətˌhach\\ *n* : small bird

nut·meg \\ˈnətˌmeg, -ˌmāg\\ *n* : nutlike aromatic seed of a tropical tree

nu·tri·ent \\ˈnütrēənt, ˈnyü-\\ *n* : something giving nourishment —**nutrient** *adj*

nu·tri·ment \\-trəmənt\\ *n* : nutrient

nu·tri·tion \\nüˈtrishən, nyü-\\ *n* : act or process of nourishing esp. with food —**nu·tri·tion·al** \\-ˈtrishənəl\\ *adj* —**nu·tri·tious** \\-ˈtrishəs\\ *adj* —**nu·tri·tive** \\ˈnütrətiv, ˈnyü-\\ *adj*

nuts \\ˈnəts\\ *adj* 1 : enthusiastic 2 : crazy

nuz·zle \\ˈnəzəl\\ *vb* **-zled; -zling** 1 : touch with or as if with the nose 2 : snuggle

ny·lon \\ˈnīˌlän\\ *n* 1 : tough synthetic material used esp. in textiles 2 *pl* : stockings made of nylon

nymph \\ˈnimf\\ *n* 1 : lesser goddess in ancient mythology 2 : girl 3 : immature insect

O

o \\ˈō\\ *n, pl* **o's** *or* **os** \\ˈōz\\ 1 : 15th letter of the alphabet 2 : zero

O *var of* OH

oaf \\ˈōf\\ *n* : stupid or awkward person —**oaf·ish** \\ˈōfish\\ *adj*

oak \\ˈōk\\ *n, pl* **oaks** *or* **oak** : tree bearing a thin-shelled nut or its wood —**oak·en** \\ˈōkən\\ *adj*

oar \\ˈōr\\ *n* : pole with a blade at the end used to propel a boat

oar·lock \\-ˌläk\\ *n* : u-shaped device for holding an oar

oa·sis \\ōˈāsəs\\ *n, pl* **oa·ses** \\-ˌsēz\\ : fertile area in a desert

oat \\ˈōt\\ *n* : cereal grass or its edible seed —**oat·cake** *n* —**oat·en** \\-ən\\ *adj* —**oat·meal** *n*

oath \\ˈōth\\ *n, pl* **oaths** \\ˈōthz, ˈōths\\ 1 : solemn appeal to God as a pledge of sincerity 2 : profane utterance

ob·du·rate \\ˈäbdürət, -dyü-\\ *adj* : stubbornly resistant —**ob·du·ra·cy** \\-rəsē\\ *n*

obe·di·ent \\ōˈbēdēənt\\ *adj* : willing to obey —**obe·di·ence** \\-əns\\ *n* —**obe·di·ent·ly** *adv*

obei·sance \\ōˈbēsəns, -ˈbās-\\ *n* : bow of respect or submission

obe·lisk \\ˈäbəˌlisk\\ *n* : 4-sided tapering pillar

obese \\ōˈbēs\\ *adj* : extremely fat —**obe·si·ty** \\-ˈbēsətē\\ *n*

obey \\ōˈbā\\ *vb* **obeyed; obey·ing** : follow the commands or guidance of 2 : behave in accordance with

ob·fus·cate \\ˈäbfəˌskāt\\ *vb* **-cat·ed; -cat·ing** : confuse —**ob·fus·ca·tion** \\ˌäbfəsˈkāshən\\ *n*

obit·u·ary \\ōˈbichəˌwerē\\ *n, pl* **-ar·ies** : death notice

¹**ob·ject** \\ˈäbjikt\\ *n* 1 : something that may be seen or felt 2 : purpose 3 : noun or equivalent toward which the action of a verb is directed or which follows a preposition

²**ob·ject** \\əbˈjekt\\ *vb* : offer opposition or disapproval —**ob·jec·tion** \\-ˈjekshən\\ *n* —**ob·jec·tion·able** \\-shənəbəl\\ *adj* —**ob·jec·tion·ably** \\-blē\\ *adv* —**ob·jec·tor** \\-ˈjektər\\ *n*

ob·jec·tive \\əbˈjektiv\\ *adj* 1 : relating to an object or end 2 : existing outside an individual's thoughts or feelings 3 : treating facts without distortion 4 : relating to or being a grammatical case marking objects ~ *n* : aim or end of action —**ob·jec·tive·ly** *adv* —**ob·jec·tive·ness** *n* —**ob·jec·tiv·i·ty** \\ˌäbˌjekˈtivətē\\ *n*

ob·li·gate \\ˈäbləˌgāt\\ *vb* **-gat·ed; -gat·ing** : bind legally or morally —**ob·li·ga·tion** \\ˌäbləˈgāshən\\ *n* —**oblig·a·to·ry** \\əˈbligəˌtōrē, ˈäbligə-\\ *adj*

oblige \\əˈblīj\\ *vb* **obliged; oblig·ing** 1 : compel 2 : do a favor for —**oblig·ing·ly** *adv*

oblique \\ōˈblēk, -ˈblīk\\ *adj* 1 : lying at a slanting angle 2 : indirect —**oblique·ly** *adv* —**oblique·ness** *n* —**obliq·ui·ty** \\-ˈblikwətē\\ *n*

oblit·er·ate \\əˈblitəˌrāt\\ *vb* **-at·ed; -at·ing** : completely remove or destroy —**oblit·er·a·tion** \\-ˌblitəˈrāshən\\ *n*

obliv·i·on \\əˈblivēən\\ *n* 1 : state of having lost conscious awareness 2 : state of being forgotten

obliv·i·ous \\-ēəs\\ *adj* : not aware or mindful—with *to* or *of* —**obliv·i·ous·ly** *adv* —**obliv·i·ous·ness** *n*

ob·long \\ˈäbˌlȯŋ\\ *adj* : longer in one direction than in the other with opposite sides parallel —**oblong** *n*

ob·lo·quy \\ˈäbləkwē\\ *n, pl* **-quies** 1 : strongly condemning utterance 2 : bad repute

ob·nox·ious \\äbˈnäkshəs, əb-\\ *adj* : repugnant —**ob·nox·ious·ly** *adv* —**ob·nox·ious·ness** *n*

oboe \\ˈōbō\\ *n* : slender woodwind instrument with a reed mouthpiece —**obo·ist** \\ō,bōist\\ *n*

ob·scene \\äbˈsēn, əb-\\ *adj* : repugnantly indecent —**ob·scene·ly** *adv* —**ob·scen·i·ty** \\-ˈsenətē\\ *n*

ob·scure \\äbˈskyur, əb-\\ *adj* 1 : dim or hazy 2 : not well known 3 : vague ~ *vb* : make indistinct or unclear —**ob·scure·ly** *adv* —**ob·scu·ri·ty** \\-ˈskyurətē\\ *n*

ob·se·quies \\ˈäbsəkwēz\\ *n pl* : funeral or burial rite

ob·se·qui·ous \\əbˈsēkwēəs\\ *adj* : excessively attentive or flattering —**ob·se·qui·ous·ly** *adv* —**ob·se·qui·ous·ness** *n*

ob·ser·va·to·ry \\əbˈzərvəˌtōrē\\ *n, pl* **-ries** : place for observing astronomical phenomena

ob·serve \\əbˈzərv\\ *vb* **-served; -serv·ing** 1 : conform to 2 : celebrate 3 : see, watch, or notice 4 : remark —**ob·serv·able** *adj* —**ob·ser·vance** \\-ˈzərvəns\\ *n* —**ob·ser·vant** \\-vənt\\ *adj* —**ob·ser·va·tion** \\ˌäbsərˈvāshən, -zər-\\ *n*

ob·sess \\äbˈses\\ *vb* : preoccupy intensely or abnormally —**ob·ses·sion** \\äbˈseshən, əb-\\ *n* —**ob·ses·sive** \\-ˈsesiv\\ *adj* —**ob·ses·sive·ly** *adv*

ob·so·les·cent \\ˌäbsəˈlesᵊnt\\ *adj* : going out of use —**ob·so·les·cence** \\-ᵊns\\ *n*

ob·so·lete \\ˌäbsəˈlēt, ˈäbsə-\\ *adj* : no longer in use

ob·sta·cle \\ˈäbstikəl\\ *n* : something that stands in the way or opposes

ob·stet·rics \\əbˈstetriks\\ *n sing or pl* : branch of medicine that deals with childbirth —**ob·stet·ric** \\-rik\\, **ob·stet·ri·cal** \\-rikəl\\ *adj* —**ob·ste·tri·cian** \\ˌäbstəˈtrishən\\ *n*

ob·sti·nate \\ˈäbstənət\\ *adj* : stubborn —**ob·sti·na·cy** \\-nəsē\\ *n* —**ob·sti·nate·ly** *adv*

ob·strep·er·ous \\əbˈstrepərəs\\ *adj* : uncontrollably noisy or defiant —**ob·strep·er·ous·ness** *n*

ob·struct \\əbˈstrəkt\\ *vb* : block or impede —**ob·struc·tion** \\-ˈstrəkshən\\ *n* —**ob·struc·tive** \\-ˈstrəktiv\\ *adj* —**ob·struc·tor** \\-tər\\ *n*

ob·tain \\əbˈtān\\ *vb* 1 : gain by effort 2 : be generally recognized —**ob·tain·able** *adj*

ob·trude \\əbˈtrüd\\ *vb* **-trud·ed; -trud·ing** 1 : thrust out 2 : intrude —**ob·tru·sion** \\-ˈtrüzhən\\ *n* —**ob·tru·sive** \\-ˈtrüsiv\\ *adj* —**ob·tru·sive·ly** *adv* —**ob·tru·sive·ness** *n*

ob·tuse \\äbˈtüs, -ˈtyüs\\ *adj* 1 : slow-witted 2 : exceeding 90 but less than 180 degrees —**ob·tuse·ly** *adv* —**ob·tuse·ness** *n*

ob·verse \\ˈäbˌvərs, äbˈ-\\ *n* : principal side (as of a coin)

ob·vi·ate \\ˈäbvēˌāt\\ *vb* **-at·ed; -at·ing** : make

unnecessary —**ob·vi·a·tion** \\ˌäbvēˈāshən\\ *n*

ob·vi·ous \\ˈäbvēəs\\ *adj* : plain or unmistakable —**ob·vi·ous·ly** *adv* —**obvi·ous·ness** *n*

oc·ca·sion \\əˈkāzhən\\ *n* 1 : favorable opportunity 2 : cause 3 : time of an event 4 : special event ~ *vb* : cause —**oc·ca·sion·al** \\-ˈkäzhənəl\\ *adj* —**oc·ca·sion·al·ly** *adv*

oc·ci·den·tal \\ˌäksəˈdentᵊl\\ *adj* : western —**Occidental** *n*

oc·cult \\əˈkəlt, ˈäkˌəlt\\ *adj* : secret or mysterious 2 : relating to supernatural agencies —**oc·cult·ism** \\-ˈkəlˌtizəm\\ *n* —**oc·cult·ist** \\-tist\\ *n*

oc·cu·pan·cy \\ˈäkyəpənsē\\ *n, pl* **-cies** : an occupying

oc·cu·pant \\-pənt\\ *n* : one who occupies

oc·cu·pa·tion \\ˌäkyəˈpāshən\\ *n* 1 : vocation 2 : action or state of occupying —**oc·cu·pa·tion·al** \\-shənəl\\ *adj* —**oc·cu·pa·tion·al·ly** *adv*

oc·cu·py \\ˈäkyəˌpī\\ *vb* **-pied; -py·ing** 1 : engage the attention of 2 : fill up 3 : take or hold possession of 4 : reside in —**oc·cu·pi·er** \\-ˌpīər\\ *n*

oc·cur \\əˈkər\\ *vb* **-rr-** 1 : be found or met with 2 : take place 3 : come to mind

oc·cur·rence \\əˈkərəns\\ *n* : something that takes place

ocean \\ˈōshən\\ *n* 1 : whole body of salt water 2 : very large body of water —**ocean·front** *n* —**ocean·go·ing** *adj* —**oce·an·ic** \\ˌōshēˈanik\\ *adj*

ocean·og·ra·phy \\ˌōshəˈnägrəfē\\ *n* : science dealing with the ocean —**ocean·og·ra·pher** \\-fər\\ *n* —**ocean·o·graph·ic** \\-nəˈgrafik\\ *adj*

oce·lot \\ˈäsəˌlät, ˈōsə-\\ *n* : medium-sized American wildcat

ocher, ochre \\ˈōkər\\ *n* : red or yellow pigment

o'·clock \\əˈkläk\\ *adv* : according to the clock

oc·ta·gon \\ˈäktəˌgän\\ *n* : 8-sided polygon —**oc·tag·o·nal** \\äkˈtagənᵊl\\ *adj*

oc·tave \\ˈäktiv\\ *n* : musical interval of 8 steps or the notes within this interval

Oc·to·ber \\äkˈtōbər\\ *n* : 10th month of the year having 31 days

oc·to·pus \\ˈäktəpəs\\ *n, pl* **-pus·es** *or* **-pi** \\-ˌpī\\ : sea mollusk with 8 arms

oc·u·lar \\ˈäkyələr\\ *adj* : relating to the eye

oc·u·list \\ˈäkyəlist\\ *n* 1 : ophthalmologist 2 : optometrist

odd \\ˈäd\\ *adj* 1 : being only one of a pair or set 2 : not divisible by two without a remainder 3 : additional to what is usual or to the number mentioned 4 : queer —**odd·ly** *adv* —**odd·ness** *n*

odd·i·ty \\ˈädətē\\ *n, pl* **-ties** : something odd

odds \\ˈädz\\ *n pl* 1 : difference by which one thing is favored 2 : disagreement 3 : ratio between winnings and the amount of the bet

ode \\ˈōd\\ *n* : solemn lyric poem

odi·ous \\ˈōdēəs\\ *adj* : hated —**odi·ous·ly** *adv* —**odi·ous·ness** *n*

odi·um \\ˈōdēəm\\ *n* 1 : merited loathing 2 : disgrace

odor \\ˈōdər\\ *n* : quality that affects the sense of smell —**odor·less** *adj* —**odor·ous** *adj*

od·ys·sey \\ˈädəsē\\ *n, pl* **-seys** : long wandering

o'er \\ˈȯr\\ *adv or prep* : OVER

of \\ˈəv, ˈäv\\ *prep* 1 : from 2 : distinguished by 3 : because of 4 : made or written by 5 : made with, being, or containing 6 : belonging to or connected with 7 : about 8 : that is 9 : concerning 10 : before

off \\ˈȯf\\ *adv* 1 : from a place 2 : unattached or removed 3 : to a state of being no longer in use 4 : away from work 5 : at a distance in time or space ~ *prep* 1 : away from 2 : at the expense of 3 : not engaged in or abstaining from 4 : below the usual level of ~ *adj* 1 : not operating, up to standard, or correct 2 : remote 3 : provided for

of·fal \\ˈȯfəl\\ *n* 1 : waste 2 : viscera and trimmings of a butchered animal

of·fend \\əˈfend\\ *vb* 1 : sin or act in violation 2 : hurt, annoy, or insult —**of·fend·er** *n*

of·fense, of·fence \\əˈfens, ˈäfˌens\\ *n* : attack, misdeed, or insult

of·fen·sive \\əˈfensiv, ˈäfˌen-\\ *adj* : causing offense ~ *n* : attack —**offen·sive·ly** *adv* —**of·fen·sive·ness** *n*

of·fer \\ˈȯfər\\ *vb* 1 : present for acceptance 2 : propose 3 : put up (an effort) ~ *n* 1 : proposal 2 : bid —**of·fer·ing** *n*

of·fer·to·ry \\ˈȯfərˌtōrē\\ *n, pl* **-ries** : presentation of offerings or its musical accompaniment

off·hand *adv or adj* : without previous thought or preparation

of·fice \\ˈȯfəs\\ *n* 1 : position of authority (as in government) 2 : rite 3 : place where a business is transacted —**of·fice·hold·er** *n*

of·fi·cer \\ˈȯfəsər\\ *n* 1 : one charged with law enforcement 2 : one who holds an office of trust or authority 3 : one who holds a commission in the armed forces

of·fi·cial \\əˈfishəl\\ *n* : one in office ~ *adj* : authorized or authoritative —**of·fi·cial·dom** \\-dəm\\ *n* —**of·fi·cial·ly** *adv*

of·fi·ci·ant \\əˈfishēənt\\ *n* : clergy member who officiates at a religious rite

of·fi·ci·ate \\əˈfishēˌāt\\ *vb* **-at·ed; -at·ing** : perform a ceremony or function

of·fi·cious \\əˈfishəs\\ *adj* : volunteering one's services unnecessarily —**of·fi·cious·ly** *adv* —**of·fi·cious·ness** *n*

off·ing \\ˈȯfiŋ\\ *n* : future

off·set \\ˈȯfˌset\\ *vb* **-set; -set·ting** : provide an opposite or equaling effect to

off·shoot \\ˈȯfˌshüt\\ *n* : outgrowth

off·shore *adv* : at a distance from the shore ~ *adj* : moving away from or situated off the shore

off·spring \\ˈȯfˌspriŋ\\ *n, pl* **offspring** : one coming into being through animal or plant reproduction

of·ten \\ˈȯfən, ˈȯft-\\ *adv* : many times —**of·ten·times, oft·times** *adv*

ogle \\ˈōgəl\\ *vb* **ogled; ogling** : stare at lustily —**ogle** *n* —**ogler** \\-ələr\\ *n*

ogre \\ˈōgər\\ *n* 1 : monster 2 : dreaded person

oh \\ˈō\\ *interj* 1—used to express an emotion 2—used in direct address

ohm \\ˈōm\\ *n* : unit of electrical resistance —**ohm·ic** \\ˈōmik\\ *adj* —**ohm·me·ter** \\ˈōmˌmētər\\ *n*

oil \\ˈȯil\\ *n* 1 : greasy liquid substance 2 : petroleum ~ *vb* : put oil in or on —**oil·er** *n* —**oil·i·ness** \\ˈȯilēnəs\\ *n* —**oily** \\ˈȯilē\\ *adj*

oil·cloth *n* : cloth treated with oil or paint and used for coverings

oil·skin *n* : oiled waterproof cloth

oink \\ˈȯiŋk\\ *n* : natural noise of a hog —**oink** *vb*

oint·ment \\ˈȯintmənt\\ *n* : oily medicinal preparation

OK *or* **okay** \\ōˈkā\\ *adv or adj* : all right ~ *vb* **OK'd** *or* **okayed; OK'ing** *or* **okay·ing** : approve ~ *n* : approval

okra \\ˈōkrə, *South also* -krē\\ *n* : leafy vegetable with edible green pods

old \\ˈōld\\ *adj* 1 : of long standing 2 : of a specified age 3 : relating to a past era 4 : having existed a long time —**old·ish** \\ˈōldish\\ *adj*

old·en \\ˈōldən\\ *adj* : of or relating to a bygone era

old-fash·ioned \\-ˈfashənd\\ *adj* : out-of-date 2 : conservative

old maid *n* : spinster

old-tim·er \\ˈōldˈtīmər\\ *n* 1 : veteran 2 : one who is old

ole·an·der \\ˈōlēˌandər\\ *n* : poisonous evergreen shrub

oleo·mar·ga·rine \\ˌōlēōˈmärjərən\\ *n* : margarine

ol·fac·to·ry \\älˈfaktərē, ōl-\\ *adj* : relating to the sense of smell

oli·gar·chy \\ˈäləˌgärkē, ˈōlə-\\ *n, pl* **-chies** 1 : government by a few people 2 : those holding power in an oligarchy —**oli·garch** \\-ˌgärk\\ *n* —**oli·gar·chic** \\ˌäləˈgärkik, ˌōlə-\\, **oli·gar·chi·cal** \\-kikəl\\ *adj*

ol·ive \\ˈäliv, -əv\\ *n* 1 : evergreen tree bearing small edible fruit or the fruit 2 : dull yellowish green color

om·buds·man \\ˈämˌbudzmən, ämˈbudz-\\ *n, pl* **-men** \\-mən\\ : complaint investigator

om·e·let, om·e·lette \\ˈämələt\\ *n* : beaten eggs lightly fried and folded

omen \\ˈōmən\\ *n* : sign or warning of the future

om·i·nous \\ˈämənəs\\ *adj* : presaging evil —**om·i·nous·ly** *adv* —**om·i·nous·ness** *n*

omit \\ōˈmit\\ *vb* **-tt-** 1 : leave out 2 : fail to perform —**omis·si·ble** \\ōˈmisəbəl\\ *adj* —**omis·sion** \\-ˈmishən\\ *n*

om·nip·o·tent \\ämˈnipətənt\\ *adj* : almighty —**om·nip·o·tence** \\-əns\\ *n* —**om·nip·o·tent·ly** *adv*

om·ni·pres·ent \\ˌämniˈprezᵊnt\\ *adj* : everpresent —**om·ni·pres·ence** \\-ᵊns\\ *n*

om·ni·scient \\ämˈnishənt\\ *adj* : all-knowing —**om·ni·science** \\-əns\\ *n* —**om·ni·scient·ly** *adv*

om·niv·o·rous \\ämˈnivərəs\\ *adj* 1 : eating both meat and vegetables 2 : avid —**om·niv·o·rous·ly** *adv*

on \\ˈȯn, ˈän\\ *prep* 1 : in or to a position over and in contact with 2 : at or to 3 : about 4 : from 5 : with regard to 6 : in a state or process 7 : during the time of ~ *adv* 1 : in or into contact with 2 : forward 3 : into operation

once \\ˈwəns\\ *adv* 1 : one time only 2 : at any one time 3 : formerly ~ *n* : one time ~ *conj* : as soon as ~ *adj* : former —**at once** 1 : simultaneously 2 : immediately

once-over *n* : swift examination

on·com·ing *adj* : approaching

one \\ˈwən\\ *adj* 1 : being a single thing 2 : being one in particular 3 : being the same in kind ~ *pron* 1 : certain indefinitely indicated person or thing 2 : a person in general ~ *n* 1 : 1st in a series 2 : single person or thing —**one·ness** *n*

on·er·ous \\ˈänərəs, ˈōnə-\\ *adj* : imposing a burden

one·self \\ˌwənˈself\\ *pron* : one's own self—usu. used reflexively or for emphasis

one–sid·ed \-'sīdəd\ adj 1 : occurring on one side only 2 : partial

one·time n : former

one–way adj : made or for use in only one direction

on·go·ing adj : continuing

on·ion \'ənyən\ n : plant grown for its pungent edible bulb or this bulb

on·ly \'ōnlē\ adj : alone in its class ~ adv 1 : merely or exactly 2 : solely 3 : at the very least 4 : as a result ~ conj : but

on·set n : start

on·shore adj 1 : moving toward shore 2 : lying on or near the shore —**onshore** adv

on·slaught \'än,slót, 'ón-\ n : attack

on·to \'óntü, 'än-\ prep : to a position or point on

onus \'ōnəs\ n : burden (as of obligation or blame)

on·ward \'ónwərd, 'än-\ adv or adj : forward

on·yx \'äniks\ n : quartz used as a gem

ooze \'üz\ n : soft mud ~ vb **oozed; ooz·ing** : flow or leak out slowly —**oozy** \'üzē\ adj

opac·i·ty \ō'pasətē\ n : quality or state of being opaque or an opaque spot

opal \'ōpəl\ n : gem with delicate colors

opaque \ō'pāk\ adj 1 : blocking light 2 : not easily understood 3 : dull-witted —**opaque·ly** adv

open \'ōpən\ adj 1 : not shut or shut up 2 : not secret or hidden 3 : frank or generous 4 : extended 5 : free from controls 6 : not decided ~ vb 1 : make or become open 2 : make or become functional 3 : start ~ n : outdoors —**open·er** \-ər\ n —**open·ly** adv —**open·ness** n

open·hand·ed \-'handəd\ adj : generous —**open·hand·ed·ly** adv

open·ing \'ōpəniŋ\ n 1 : act or instance of making open 2 : something that is open 3 : opportunity

op·era \'äpərə, 'äprə\ n : drama set to music —**op·er·at·ic** \äpə'ratik\ adj

op·er·a·ble \'äpərəbəl\ adj 1 : usable or in working condition 2 : suitable for surgical treatment

op·er·ate \'äpə,rāt\ vb **-at·ed; -at·ing** 1 : perform work 2 : perform an operation 3 : manage —**op·er·a·tor** \-,rātər\ n

op·er·a·tion \,äpə'rāshən\ n 1 : act or process of operating 2 : surgical work on a living body 3 : military action or mission —**op·er·a·tion·al** \-shənəl\ adj

op·er·a·tive \'äpərətiv, -,rāt-\ adj : working or having an effect

op·er·et·ta \,äpə'retə\ n : light opera

oph·thal·mol·o·gy \,äf,thal'mäləjē\ n : branch of medicine dealing with the eye —**oph·thal·mol·o·gist** \-jist\ n

opi·ate \'ōpēət, -pē,āt\ n : preparation or derivative of opium

opine \ō'pīn\ vb **opined; opin·ing** : express an opinion

opin·ion \ō'pinyən\ n 1 : belief 2 : judgment 3 : formal statement by an expert

opin·ion·at·ed \-yə,nātəd\ adj : stubborn in one's opinions

opi·um \'ōpēəm\ n : addictive narcotic drug that is the dried juice of a poppy

opos·sum \ə'päsəm\ n : common tree-dwelling nocturnal mammal

op·po·nent \ə'pōnənt\ n : one that opposes

op·por·tune \,äpər'tün, -'tyün\ adj : suitable or timely —**op·por·tune·ly** adv

op·por·tun·ism \-'tü,nizəm, -'tyü-\ n : a taking advantage of opportunities —**op·por·tun·ist** \-nist\ n —**op·por·tu·nis·tic** \-tü-'nistik, -tyü-\ adj

op·por·tu·ni·ty \-'tünətē, -'tyü-\ n, pl **-ties** : favorable time

op·pose \ə'pōz\ vb **-posed; -pos·ing** 1 : place opposite or against something 2 : resist —**op·po·si·tion** \,äpə'zishən\ n

op·po·site \'äpəzət\ n : one that is opposed ~ adj 1 : set facing something else 2 : at the other side or end 2 : opposed or contrary ~ adv : on opposite sides ~ prep : across from —**op·po·site·ly** adv

op·press \ə'pres\ vb 1 : persecute 2 : weigh down —**op·pres·sion** \ə'preshən\ n —**op·pres·sive** \-siv\ adj —**op·pres·sive·ly** adv —**op·pres·sor** \-'presər\ n

op·pro·bri·ous \ə'prōbrēəs\ adj : expressing or deserving opprobrium —**op·pro·bri·ous·ly** adv

op·pro·bri·um \-brēəm\ n 1 : something that brings disgrace 2 : infamy

opt \'äpt\ vb : choose

op·tic \'äptik\ adj : relating to vision or the eye

op·ti·cal \'äptikəl\ adj : relating to optics, vision, or the eye

op·ti·cian \äp'tishən\ n : maker of or dealer in eyeglasses

op·tics \'äptiks\ n pl : science of light and vision

op·ti·mal \'äptəməl\ adj : most favorable —**op·ti·mal·ly** adv

op·ti·mism \'äptə,mizəm\ n : tendency to hope for the best —**op·ti·mist** \-mist\ n

—**op·ti·mis·tic** \,äptə'mistik\ adj —**op·ti·mis·ti·cal·ly** adv

op·ti·mum \'äptəməm\ n, pl **-ma** \-mə\ : amount or degree of something most favorable to an end —**optimum** adj

op·tion \'äpshən\ n 1 : ability to choose 2 : right to buy or sell a stock 3 : alternative —**op·tion·al** \-shənəl\ adj

op·tom·e·try \äp'tämətrē\ n : profession of examining the eyes —**op·tom·e·trist** \-trist\ n

op·u·lent \'äpyələnt\ adj : lavish —**op·u·lence** \-ləns\ n —**op·u·lent·ly** adv

opus \'ōpəs\ n, pl **opera** \'ōpərə, 'äpə-\ : work esp. of music

or \'ór\ conj —used to indicate an alternative

-or \ər\ n suffix : one that performs an action

or·a·cle \'órəkəl\ n 1 : one held to give divinely inspired answers or revelations 2 : wise person or an utterance of such a person —**orac·u·lar** \ó'rakyələr\ adj

oral \'órəl\ adj 1 : spoken 2 : relating to the mouth —**oral·ly** adv

or·ange \'órinj\ n 1 : reddish yellow citrus fruit 2 : color between red and yellow —**or·ange·ade** \,órinj'ād\ n

orang·u·tan \ə'raŋə,taŋ, -,tan\ n : large reddish brown ape

ora·tion \ō'rāshən\ n : elaborate formal speech

or·a·tor \'órətər\ n : one noted as a public speaker

or·a·to·rio \,órə'tōrē,ō\ n, pl **-ri·os** : major choral work

or·a·to·ry \'órə,tōrē\ n : art of public speaking —**or·a·tor·i·cal** \,órə'tórikəl\ adj

orb \'órb\ n : spherical body

or·bit \'órbət\ n : path made by one body revolving around another ~ vb : revolve around —**or·bit·al** \-əl\ adj —**or·bit·er** n

or·chard \'órchərd\ n : place where fruit or nut trees are grown —**or·chard·ist** \-ist\ n

or·ches·tra \'órkəstrə\ n 1 : group of musicians 2 : front seats of a theater's main floor —**or·ches·tral** \ór'kestrəl\ adj —**or·ches·tral·ly** adv

or·ches·trate \'órkə,strāt\ vb **-trat·ed; -trat·ing** 1 : compose or arrange for an orchestra 2 : arrange or combine for best effect —**or·ches·tra·tion** \,órkə'strāshən\ n

or·chid \'órkəd\ n : plant with showy 3-petal flowers or its flower

or·dain \ór'dān\ vb 1 : admit to the clergy 2 : decree

or·deal \ór'dēl, 'ór,dēl\ n : severely trying experience

or·der \'órdər\ n 1 : rank, class, or special group 2 : arrangement 3 : rule of law 4 : authoritative regulation or instruction 5 : working condition 6 : special request for a purchase or what is purchased ~ vb 1 : arrange 2 : give an order to 3 : place an order for

or·der·ly \-lē\ adj 1 : being in order or tidy 2 : well behaved ~ n, pl **-lies** 1 : officer's attendant 2 : hospital attendant —**or·der·li·ness** n

or·di·nal \'órdənəl\ n : number indicating order in a series

or·di·nance \-əns\ n : municipal law

or·di·nary \'órdən,erē\ adj 1 : of common occurrence, quality, or ability —**or·di·nar·i·ly** \,órdən'erəlē\ adv

or·di·na·tion \,órdən'āshən\ n : act of ordaining

ord·nance \'órdnəns\ n : military supplies

ore \'ór\ n : mineral containing a valuable constituent

oreg·a·no \ə'regə,nō\ n : mint used as a seasoning and source of oil

or·gan \'órgən\ n 1 : air-powered or electronic keyboard instrument 2 : animal or plant structure with special function 3 : periodical

or·gan·ic \ór'ganik\ adj 1 : relating to a bodily organ 2 : relating to living things 3 : relating to or containing carbon or its compounds 4 : relating to foods produced without the use of laboratory-made products —**or·gan·i·cal·ly** adv

or·gan·ism \'órgə,nizəm\ n : a living thing

or·gan·ist \'órgənist\ n : organ player

or·ga·nize \'órgə,nīz\ vb **-nized; -niz·ing** : form parts into a functioning whole —**or·ga·ni·za·tion** \,órgənə'zāshən\ n —**or·ga·ni·za·tion·al** \-shənəl\ adj —**or·ga·niz·er** n

or·gasm \'ór,gazəm\ n : climax of sexual excitement —**or·gas·mic** \ór'gazmik\ adj

or·gy \'órjē\ n : unrestrained indulgence (as in sexual activity)

ori·ent \'ōrē,ent\ vb 1 : set in a definite position 2 : acquaint with a situation —**ori·en·ta·tion** \,ōrēən'tāshən\ n

ori·en·tal \,ōrē'entəl\ adj : Eastern —**Oriental** n

or·i·fice \'órəfəs\ n : opening

or·i·gin \'órəjən\ n 1 : ancestry 2 : rise, beginning, or derivation from a source —**orig·i·nate** \ə'rijə,nāt\ vb —**orig·i·na·tor** \-ər\ n

orig·i·nal \ə'rijənəl\ n : something from

which a copy is made ~ adj 1 : first 2 : not copied from something else 3 : inventive —**orig·i·nal·i·ty** n —**orig·i·nal·ly** adv

ori·ole \'ōrē,ōl, -ēəl\ n : American songbird

or·na·ment \'órnəmənt\ n : something that adorns ~ vb : provide with ornament —**or·na·men·tal** \,órnə'mentəl\ adj —**or·na·men·ta·tion** \-mən'tāshən\ n

or·nate \ór'nāt\ adj : elaborately decorated —**or·nate·ly** adv —**or·nate·ness** n

or·nery \'órnərē, 'än-\ adj : irritable

or·ni·thol·o·gy \,órnə'thäləjē\ n, pl **-gies** : study of birds —**or·ni·tho·log·i·cal** \-thə'läjikəl\ adj —**or·ni·thol·o·gist** \-'thäləjist\ n

or·phan \'órfən\ n : child whose parents are dead —**orphan** vb —**or·phan·age** \-ənij\ n

or·tho·don·tics \,órthə'däntiks\ n : dentistry dealing with the straightening of teeth —**or·tho·don·tist** \-'däntist\ n

or·tho·dox \'órthə,däks\ adj 1 : conforming to established doctrine 2 cap : of or relating to a Christian church originating in the Eastern Roman Empire —**or·tho·doxy** \-,däksē\ n

or·thog·ra·phy \ór'thägrəfē\ n : spelling —**or·tho·graph·ic** \,órthə'grafik\ adj

or·tho·pe·dics \,órthə'pēdiks\ n sing or pl : correction or prevention of skeletal deformities —**or·tho·pe·dic** \-ik\ adj —**or·tho·pe·dist** \-'pēdist\ n

-o·ry \órē, órē, ərē\ adj suffix 1 : of, relating to, or characterized by 2 : serving for, producing, or maintaining

os·cil·late \'äsə,lāt\ vb **-lat·ed; -lat·ing** : swing back and forth —**os·cil·la·tion** \,äsə'lāshən\ n

os·mo·sis \äz'mōsəs, äs-\ n : diffusion esp. of water through a membrane —**os·mot·ic** \-'mätik\ adj

os·prey \'äsprē, -,prā\ n, pl **-preys** : large fish-eating hawk

os·si·fy \'äsə,fī\ vb **-fied; -fy·ing** : make or become hardened or set in one's ways

os·ten·si·ble \ä'stensəbəl\ adj : seeming —**os·ten·si·bly** \-blē\ adv

os·ten·ta·tion \,ästən'tāshən\ n : pretentious display —**os·ten·ta·tious** \-shəs\ adj —**os·ten·ta·tious·ly** adv

os·te·op·a·thy \,ästē'äpəthē\ n : system of healing that emphasizes manipulation (as of joints) —**os·te·o·path** \'ästēə,path\ n —**os·te·o·path·ic** \,ästēə'pathik\ adj

os·te·o·po·ro·sis \,ästēōpə'rōsəs\ n, pl **-ro·ses** \-,sēz\ : condition characterized by fragile and porous bones

os·tra·cize \'ästrə,sīz\ vb **-cized; -ciz·ing** : exclude by common consent —**os·tra·cism** \-,sizəm\ n

os·trich \'ästrich, 'ós-\ n : very large flightless bird

oth·er \'əthər\ adj 1 : being the one left 2 : alternate 3 : additional ~ pron 1 : remaining one 2 : different one

oth·er·wise adv 1 : in a different way 2 : in different circumstances 3 : in other respects —**otherwise** adj

ot·ter \'ätər\ n : fish-eating mammal with webbed feet

ot·to·man \'ätəmən\ n : upholstered footstool

ought \'ót\ verbal auxiliary —used to express obligation, advisability, or expectation

ounce \'aúns\ n 1 : unit of weight equal to about 28.3 grams 2 : unit of capacity equal to about 29.6 milliliters

our \'är, 'aúr\ adj : of or relating to us

ours \'aúrz, 'ärz\ pron : that which belongs to us

our·selves \är'selvz, aúr-\ pron : we, us —used reflexively or for emphasis

-ous \əs\ adj suffix : having or having the qualities of

oust \'aúst\ vb : expel or eject

oust·er \'aústər\ n : expulsion

out \'aút\ adv 1 : away from the inside or center 2 : beyond control 3 : to extinction, exhaustion, or completion 4 : in or into the open ~ vb : become known ~ adj 1 : situated outside 2 : absent ~ prep 1 : out through 2 : outward on or along —**out·bound** adj —**out·build·ing** n

out·age \'aútij\ n : period of no electricity

out·board \'aút,bórd\ n : outside a boat or ship —**outboard** adj

out·break \'aút,brāk\ n : sudden occurrence

out·burst \-,bərst\ n : violent expression of feeling

out·cast \-,kast\ n : person cast out by society

out·come \-,kəm\ n : result

out·crop \'aút,kräp\ n : part of a rock stratum that appears above the ground —**outcrop** vb

out·cry \-,krī\ n : loud cry

out·dat·ed \aút'dātəd\ adj : out-of-date

out·dis·tance vb : go far ahead of

out·do \aút'dü\ vb **-did** \-'did\; **-done** \-'dən\; **-do·ing** \-'düiŋ\; **-does** \-'dəz\ : do better than

out·doors \aút'dórz\ adv : in or into the open air ~ n : open air —**outdoor** adj

out·er \'aútər\ adj 1 : external 2 : farther out —**out·er·most** adj

out·field \'aút,fēld\ n : baseball field beyond the infield —**out·field·er** \-,fēldər\ n

out·fit \'aút,fit\ n 1 : equipment for a special purpose 2 : group ~ vb **-tt-** : equip —**out·fit·ter** n

out·go \'aút,gō\ n, pl **outgoes** : expenditure

out·go·ing \'aút,gōiŋ\ adj 1 : retiring from a position 2 : friendly

out·grow \aút'grō\ vb **-grew** \-'grü\; **-grown** \-'grōn\; **-grow·ing** 1 : grow faster than 2 : grow too large for

out·growth \'aút,grōth\ n 1 : product of growing out 2 : consequence

out·ing \'aútiŋ\ n : excursion

out·land·ish \aút'landish\ adj : very strange —**out·land·ish·ly** adv

outlast vb : last longer than

out·law \'aút,ló\ n : lawless person ~ vb : make illegal

out·lay \'aút,lā\ n : expenditure

out·let \'aút,let, -lət\ n 1 : exit 2 : means of release 3 : market for goods 4 : electrical device that gives access to wiring

out·line \'aút,līn\ n 1 : line marking the outer limits 2 : summary ~ vb 1 : draw the outline of 2 : indicate the chief parts of

out·live \aút'liv\ vb : live longer than

out·look \'aút,lúk\ n 1 : viewpoint 2 : prospect for the future

out·ly·ing \'aút,līiŋ\ adj : far from a central point

out·ma·neu·ver \,aútmə'nüvər, -'nyü-\ vb : defeat by more skillful maneuvering

out·mod·ed \aút'mōdəd\ adj : out-of-date

out·num·ber \-'nəmbər\ vb : exceed in number

out of prep 1 : out from within 2 : beyond the limits of 3 : among 4 —used to indicate absence or loss 5 : because of 6 : from or with

out–of–date adj : no longer in fashion or in use

out·pa·tient n : person treated at a hospital who does not stay overnight

out·post n : remote military post

out·put n : amount produced ~ vb **-put·ted** or **-put; -put·ting** : produce

out·rage \'aút,rāj\ n 1 : violent or shameful act 2 : injury or insult 3 : extreme anger ~ vb **-raged; -rag·ing** 1 : subject to violent injury 2 : make very angry

out·ra·geous \aút'rājəs\ adj : extremely offensive or shameful —**out·ra·geous·ly** adv —**out·ra·geous·ness** n

out·right adv 1 : completely 2 : instantly ~ adj 1 : complete 2 : given without reservation

out·set n : beginning

out·side \aút'sīd, 'aút,-\ n 1 : place beyond a boundary 2 : exterior 3 : utmost limit ~ adj 1 : outer 2 : coming from without 3 : remote ~ adv : on or to the outside ~ prep 1 : on or to the outside of 2 : beyond the limits of

outside of prep 1 : outside 2 : besides

out·sid·er \-'sīdər\ n : one who does not belong to a group

out·skirts \'aút,skərts\ n pl : outlying parts (as of a city)

out·smart \aút'smärt\ vb : outwit

out·spo·ken adj : direct and open in speech —**out·spo·ken·ness** n

out·stand·ing adj 1 : unpaid 2 : very good —**out·stand·ing·ly** adv

out·strip \aút'strip\ vb 1 : go faster than 2 : surpass

¹**out·ward** \'aútwərd\ adj 1 : being toward the outside 2 : showing outwardly

²**outward, out·wards** \-wərdz\ adv : toward the outside —**out·ward·ly** adv

out·wit \aút'wit\ vb : get the better of by superior cleverness

ova pl of OVUM

oval \'ōvəl\ adj : egg-shaped —**oval** n

ova·ry \'ōvərē\ n, pl **-ries** 1 : egg-producing organ 2 : seed-producing part of a flower —**ovar·i·an** \ō'varēən\ adj

ova·tion \ō'vāshən\ n : enthusiastic applause

ov·en \'əvən\ n : chamber (as in a stove) for baking

over \'ōvər\ adv 1 : across 2 : upside down 3 : in excess or addition 4 : above 5 : at an end 6 : again ~ prep 1 : above in position or authority 2 : more than 3 : along, through, or across 4 : because of ~ adj 1 : upper 2 : remaining 3 : ended

over- prefix 1 : so as to exceed or surpass 2 : excessive or excessively

overabundance	overassertive
overabundant	overbake
overachiever	overbid
overactive	overbill
overaggressive	overbold
overambitious	overborrow
overanalyze	overbright
overanxiety	overbroad
overanxious	overbuild
overarousal	overburden

overbusy
overbuy
overcapacity
overcapitalize
overcareful
overcautious
overcharge
overcivilized
overclean
overcommit
overcompensate
overcomplicate
overconcern
overconfidence
overconfident
overconscientious
overconsume
overconsumption
overcontrol
overcook
overcorrect
overcritical
overcrowd
overdecorate
overdependence
overdependent
overdevelop
overdose
overdramatic
overdramatize
overdress
overdrink
overdue
overeager
overeat
overeducated
overelaborate
overemotional
overemphasis
overemphasize
overenergetic
overenthusiastic
overestimate
overexaggerate
overexaggeration
overexcite
overexcited
overexercise
overexert
overexertion
overexpand
overexpansion
overexplain
overexploit
overexpose
overextend
overextension
overexuberant
overfamiliar
overfatigued
overfeed
overfertilize
overfill
overfond
overgeneraliza-
   tion
overgeneralize
overgenerous
overglamorize
overgraze
overharvest
overhasty
overheat
overidealize
overimaginative
overimpress
overindebtedness
overindulge

overindulgence
overindulgent
overinflate
overinsistent
overintense
overintensity
overinvestment
overladen
overlarge
overlend
overload
overlong
overloud
overmedicate
overmodest
overmuch
overobvious
overoptimistic
overorganize
overparticular
overpay
overpayment
overplay
overpopulated
overpraise
overprescribe
overpressure
overprice
overprivileged
overproduce
overproduction
overpromise
overprotect
overprotective
overqualified
overrate
overreact
overreaction
overrefined
overregulate
overregulation
overreliance
overrepresented
overrespond
overripe
oversaturate
oversell
oversensitive
overserious
oversexed
oversimple
oversimplify
oversolicitous
overspecialize
overspend
overstaff
overstimulation
overstock
overstrain
overstress
overstretch
oversubtle
oversupply
oversuspicious
oversweeten
overtax
overtighten
overtip
overtired
overtrain
overtreat
overuse
overutilize
overvalue
overweight
overwork
overzealous

over•age \ˈōvərˈāj\ *adj* : too old
[2]**over•age** \ˈōvərij\ *n* : surplus
over•all *adj* : including everything
over•alls \ˈōvərˌȯlz\ *n pl* : pants with an extra piece covering the chest
over•awe *vb* : subdue by awe
over•bear•ing \-ˈbariŋ\ *adj* : arrogant
over•blown \-ˈblōn\ *adj* : pretentious
over•board *adv* : over the side into the water
over•cast *adv* : clouded over ~ *n* : cloud covering
over•coat *n* : outer coat
over•come *vb* **-came** \-ˈkäm\; **-come; -coming** 1 : defeat 2 : make helpless or exhausted
over•do *vb* **-did; -done; -do•ing; -does** : do too much
over•draft *n* : overdrawn sum
over•draw *vb* **-drew; -drawn; -draw•ing** : write checks for more than one's bank balance
over•flow \ˌōvərˈflō\ *vb* 1 : flood 2 : flow over —**over•flow** \ˈōvərˌflō\ *n*
over•grow *vb* **-grew; -grown; -grow•ing** : grow over
over•hand *adj* : made with the hand brought down from above —**overhand** *adv* — **over•hand•ed** \-ˌhandəd\ *adv or adj*
over•hang *vb* **-hung; -hang•ing** : jut out over ~ *n* : something that overhangs
over•haul *vb* 1 : repair 2 : overtake
over•head \ˌōvərˈhed\ *adv* : aloft ~ \ˈōvərˌ-\

adj : situated above ~ \ˈōvərˌ-\ *n* : general business expenses
over•hear *vb* **-heard; -hear•ing** : hear without the speaker's knowledge
over•joyed *adj* : filled with joy
over•kill *n* : large excess
over•land \-ˌland, -lənd\ *adv or adj* : by, on, or across land
over•lap *vb* : lap over —**over•lap** \ˈōvərˌlap\ *n*
over•lay \ˌōvərˈlā\ *vb* **-laid; -lay•ing** : lay over or across —**over•lay** \ˈōvərˌlā\ *n*
over•look \ˌōvərˈlu̇k\ *vb* 1 : look down on 2 : fail to see 3 : ignore 4 : pardon 5 : supervise ~ \ˈōvərˌ-\ *n* : observation point
over•ly \ˈōvərlē\ *adv* : excessively
over•night *adv* 1 : through the night 2 : suddenly —**overnight** *adj*
over•pass *n* : bridge over a road
over•pow•er *vb* : conquer
over•reach \ˌōvərˈrēch\ *vb* : try or seek too much
over•ride *vb* **-rode; -rid•den; -rid•ing** : neutralize action of
over•rule *vb* : rule against or set aside
over•run *vb* **-ran; -run•ning** 1 : swarm or flow over 2 : go beyond ~ *n* : an exceeding of estimated costs
over•seas *adv or adj* : beyond or across the sea
over•see \ˌōvərˈsē\ *vb* **-saw; -seen; -see•ing** : supervise —**over•seer** \ˈōvərˌsiər\ *n*
over•shad•ow *vb* : exceed in importance
over•shoe *n* : protective outer shoe
over•shoot *vb* **-shot; -shoot•ing** : shoot or pass beyond
over•sight *n* : inadvertent omission or error
over•sleep *vb* **-slept; -sleep•ing** : sleep longer than intended
over•spread *vb* **-spread; -spread•ing** : spread over or above
over•state *vb* : exaggerate —**over•state•ment** *n*
over•stay *vb* : stay too long
over•step *vb* : exceed
overt \ō'vərt, ˈōˌvərt\ *adj* : not secret — **overt•ly** *adv*
over•take *vb* **-took; -tak•en; -tak•ing** : catch up with
over•throw \ˌōvərˈthrō\ *vb* **-threw; -thrown; -throw•ing** 1 : upset 2 : defeat —**over•throw** \ˈōvərˌ-\ *n*
over•time *n* : extra working time —**overtime** *adv*
over•tone *n* 1 : higher tone in a complex musical tone 2 : suggestion
over•ture \ˈōvərˌchu̇r, -chər\ *n* 1 : opening offer 2 : musical introduction
over•turn *vb* 1 : turn over 2 : nullify
over•view *n* : brief survey
over•ween•ing \ˌōvərˈwēniŋ\ *adj* 1 : arrogant 2 : excessive
over•whelm \ˌōvərˈhwelm\ *vb* : overcome completely —**over•whelm•ing•ly** \-ˈhwelmiŋlē\ *adv*
over•wrought \ˌōvərˈrȯt\ *adj* : extremely excited
ovoid \ˈōˌvȯid\, **ovoi•dal** \ōˈvȯidᵊl\ *adj* : egg-shaped
ovu•late \ˈävyəˌlāt, ˈōv-\ *vb* **-lat•ed; -lat•ing** : produce eggs from an ovary —**ovu•la•tion** \ˌävyəˈlāshən\ *n*
ovum \ˈōvəm\ *n, pl* **ova** \-və\ : female germ cell
owe \ˈō\ *vb* **owed; ow•ing** 1 : have an obligation to pay 2 : be indebted to or for
owing to *prep* : because of
owl \ˈau̇l\ *n* : nocturnal bird of prey —**owl•ish** *adj* —**owl•ish•ly** *adv*
own \ˈōn\ *adj* : belonging to oneself ~ *vb* 1 : have as property 2 : acknowledge ~ *pron* : one or ones belonging to oneself —**own•er** *n* —**own•er•ship** *n*
ox \ˈäks\ *n, pl* **ox•en** \ˈäksən\ : bovine mammal and esp. a castrated bull
ox•ide \ˈäkˌsīd\ *n* : compound of oxygen
oxi•dize \ˈäksəˌdīz\ *vb* **-dized; -diz•ing** : combine with oxygen —**ox•i•da•tion** \ˌäksəˈdāshən\ *n* —**ox•i•diz•er** *n*
ox•y•gen \ˈäksijən\ *n* : gaseous chemical element essential for life
oys•ter \ˈȯistər\ *n* : bivalve mollusk —**oys•ter•ing** \-riŋ\ *n*
ozone \ˈōˌzōn\ *n* : very reactive bluish form of oxygen

P

p \ˈpē\ *n, pl* **p's** *or* **ps** \ˈpēz\ : 16th letter of the alphabet
pace \ˈpās\ *n* 1 : walking step 2 : rate of progress ~ *vb* **paced; pac•ing** 1 : go at a pace 2 : cover with slow steps 3 : set the pace of

pace•mak•er *n* : electrical device to regulate heartbeat
pachy•derm \ˈpakiˌdərm\ *n* : elephant
pa•cif•ic \pəˈsifik\ *adj* : calm or peaceful
pac•i•fism \ˈpasəˌfizəm\ *n* : opposition to war or violence —**pac•i•fist** \-fist\ *n or adj* —**pac•i•fis•tic** \ˌpasəˈfistik\ *adj*
pac•i•fy \ˈpasəˌfī\ *vb* **-fied; -fy•ing** : make calm —**pac•i•fi•ca•tion** \ˌpasəfəˈkāshən\ *n* —**pac•i•fi•er** \ˈpasəˌfīər\ *n*
pack \ˈpak\ *n* 1 : compact bundle 2 : group of animals ~ *vb* 1 : put into a container 2 : fill tightly or completely 3 : send without ceremony —**pack•er** *n*
pack•age \ˈpakij\ *n* : items bundled together ~ *vb* **-aged; -ag•ing** : enclose in a package
pack•et \ˈpakət\ *n* : small package
pact \ˈpakt\ *n* : agreement
pad \ˈpad\ *n* 1 : cushioning part or thing 2 : floating leaf of a water plant 3 : tablet of paper ~ *vb* **-dd- 1** : furnish with a pad 2 : expand with needless matter —**padding** *n*
pad•dle \ˈpadᵊl\ *n* : implement with a flat blade ~ *vb* **-dled; -dling** : move, beat, or stir with a paddle
pad•dock \ˈpadək\ *n* : enclosed area for racehorses
pad•dy \ˈpadē\ *n, pl* **-dies** : wet land where rice is grown
pad•lock *n* : lock with a U-shaped catch — **padlock** *vb*
pae•an \ˈpēən\ *n* : song of praise
pa•gan \ˈpāgən\ *n or adj* : heathen —**pa•gan•ism** \-ˌizəm\ *n*
[1]**page** \ˈpāj\ *n* : messenger ~ *vb* **paged; pag•ing** : summon by repeated calls — **pag•er** *n*
[2]**page** *n* : single leaf (as of a book) or one side of the leaf
pag•eant \ˈpajənt\ *n* : elaborate spectacle or procession —**pag•eant•ry** \-əntrē\ *n*
pa•go•da \pəˈgōdə\ *n* : tower with roofs curving upward
paid *past of* PAY
pail \ˈpāl\ *n* : cylindrical container with a handle —**pail•ful** \-ˌfu̇l\ *n*
pain \ˈpān\ *n* 1 : punishment or penalty 2 : suffering of body or mind 3 *pl* : great care ~ *vb* : cause or experience pain — **pain•ful** \-fəl\ *adj* —**pain•ful•ly** *adv* — **pain•kill•er** *n* —**pain•kill•ing** *adj* — **pain•less** *adj* —**pain•less•ly** *adv*
pains•tak•ing \ˈpānˌstākiŋ\ *adj* : taking pains —**painstaking** *n* —**pains•tak•ing•ly** *adv*
paint \ˈpānt\ *vb* 1 : apply color or paint to 2 : portray esp. in color ~ *n* : mixture of pigment and liquid —**paint•brush** *n* — **paint•er** *n* —**paint•ing** *n*
pair \ˈpar\ *n* : a set of two ~ *vb* : put or go together as a pair
pa•ja•mas \pəˈjäməz, -ˈjam-\ *n pl* : loose suit for sleeping
pal \ˈpal\ *n* : close friend
pal•ace \ˈpaləs\ *n* 1 : residence of a chief of state 2 : mansion —**pa•la•tial** \pəˈlāshəl\ *adj*
pal•at•able \ˈpalətəbəl\ *adj* : agreeable to the taste
pal•ate \ˈpalət\ *n* 1 : roof of the mouth 2 : taste —**pa•la•tal** \-ᵊtᵊl\ *adj*
pa•la•ver \pəˈlavər, -ˈläv-\ *n* : talk —**palaver** *vb*
[1]**pale** \ˈpāl\ *adj* **pal•er; pal•est** 1 : lacking in color or brightness 2 : light in color or shade ~ *vb* **paled; pal•ing** : make or become pale —**pale•ness** *n*
[2]**pale** *n* 1 : fence stake 2 : enclosed place
pa•le•on•tol•o•gy \ˌpālē ˌänˈtäləjē\ *n* : branch of biology dealing with ancient forms of life known from fossils —**pa•le•on•tol•o•gist** \-ᵊnˈtäləjist, -ᵊn-\ *n*
pal•ette \ˈpalət\ *n* : board on which paints are laid and mixed
pal•i•sade \ˌpaləˈsād\ *n* 1 : high fence 2 : line of cliffs
[1]**pall** \ˈpȯl\ *n* 1 : cloth draped over a coffin 2 : something that produces gloom
[2]**pall** *vb* : lose in interest or attraction
pall•bear•er *n* : one who attends the coffin at a funeral
[1]**pal•let** \ˈpalət\ *n* : makeshift bed
[2]**pallet** *n* : portable storage platform
pal•li•ate \ˈpalēˌāt\ *vb* **-at•ed; -at•ing** 1 : ease without curing 2 : cover or conceal by excusing —**pal•li•a•tion** \ˌpalēˈāshən\ *n* —**pal•li•a•tive** \ˈpalēˌātiv\ *adj or n*
pal•lid \ˈpaləd\ *adj* : pale
pal•lor \ˈpalər\ *n* : paleness
[1]**palm** \ˈpäm, ˈpälm\ *n* 1 : tall tropical tree crowned with large leaves 2 : symbol of victory
[2]**palm** *n* : underside of the hand ~ *vb* 1 : conceal in the hand 2 : impose by fraud
palm•ist•ry \ˈpäməstrē, ˈpälmə-\ *n* : reading a person's character or future in his palms —**palm•ist** \ˈpämist, ˈpälm-\ *n*
palmy \ˈpämē, ˈpälmē\ *adj* **palm•i•er; -est** : flourishing
pal•o•mi•no \ˌpaləˈmēnō\ *n, pl* **-nos** : light-colored horse

pal•pa•ble \ˈpalpəbəl\ *adj* 1 : capable of being touched 2 : obvious —**pal•pa•bly** \-blē\ *adv*
pal•pi•tate \ˈpalpəˌtāt\ *vb* **-tat•ed; -tat•ing** : beat rapidly —**pal•pi•ta•tion** \ˌpalpə-ˈtāshən\ *n*
pal•sy \ˈpȯlzē\ *n, pl* **-sies** 1 : paralysis 2 : condition marked by tremor —**pal•sied** \-zēd\ *adj*
pal•try \ˈpȯltrē\ *adj* **-tri•er; -est** : trivial
pam•per \ˈpampər\ *vb* : spoil or indulge
pam•phlet \ˈpamflət\ *n* : unbound publication —**pam•phle•teer** \ˌpamfləˈtir\ *n*
pan \ˈpan\ *n* : broad, shallow, and open container ~ *vb* 1 : wash gravel in a pan to search for gold 2 : criticize severely
pan•a•cea \ˌpanəˈsēə\ *n* : remedy for all ills or difficulties
pan•cake *n* : fried flat cake
pan•cre•as \ˈpaŋkrēəs, ˈpan-\ *n* : gland that produces insulin —**pan•cre•at•ic** \ˌpaŋ-krēˈatik, ˌpan-\ *adj*
pan•da \ˈpandə\ *n* : black-and-white bear-like animal
pan•de•mo•ni•um \ˌpandəˈmōnēəm\ *n* : wild uproar
pan•der \ˈpandər\ *n* 1 : pimp 2 : one who caters to others' desires or weaknesses ~ *vb* : act as a pander
pane \ˈpān\ *n* : sheet of glass
pan•e•gyr•ic \ˌpanəˈjirik\ *n* : eulogistic oration —**pan•e•gyr•ist** \-ˈjirist\ *n*
pan•el \ˈpanᵊl\ *n* 1 : list of persons (as jurors) 2 : discussion group 3 : flat piece of construction material 4 : board with instruments or controls ~ *vb* **-eled** *or* **-elled; -el•ing** *or* **-el•ling** : decorate with panels —**pan•el•ing** *n* —**pan•el•ist** \-ist\ *n*
pang \ˈpaŋ\ *n* : sudden sharp pain
pan•han•dle \ˈpanˌhandᵊl\ *vb* **-dled; -dling** : ask for money on the street —**pan•han•dler** \-ər\ *n*
pan•ic \ˈpanik\ *n* : sudden overpowering fright ~ *vb* **-icked; -ick•ing** : affect or be affected with panic —**pan•icky** \-ikē\ *adj*
pan•o•ply \ˈpanəplē\ *n, pl* **-plies** 1 : full suit of armor 2 : impressive array
pan•o•ra•ma \ˌpanəˈramə, -ˈräm-\ *n* : view in every direction —**pan•o•ram•ic** \-ˈra-mik\ *adj*
pan•sy \ˈpanzē\ *n, pl* **-sies** : low-growing garden herb with showy flowers
pant \ˈpant\ *vb* 1 : breathe with great effort 2 : yearn ~ *n* : panting sound
pan•ta•loons \ˌpantᵊlˈünz\ *n pl* : pants
pan•the•on \ˈpanthēˌän, -ən\ *n* 1 : the gods of a people 2 : group of famous people
pan•ther \ˈpanthər\ *n* : large wild cat
pant•ies \ˈpantēz\ *n pl* : woman's or child's short underpants
pan•to•mime \ˈpantəˌmīm\ *n* 1 : play without words 2 : expression by bodily or facial movements ~ *vb* : represent by pantomime
pan•try \ˈpantrē\ *n, pl* **-tries** : storage room for food and dishes
pants \ˈpants\ *n pl* 1 : 2-legged outer garment 2 : panties
pap \ˈpap\ *n* : soft food
pa•pa•cy \ˈpāpəsē\ *n, pl* **-cies** 1 : office of pope 2 : reign of a pope
pa•pal \ˈpāpəl\ *adj* : relating to the pope
pa•pa•ya \pəˈpīə\ *n* : tropical tree with large yellow edible fruit
pa•per \ˈpāpər\ *n* 1 : pliable substance used to write or print on, to wrap things in, or to cover walls 2 : printed or written document 3 : newspaper —**paper** *adj* — **pa•per•hang•er** *n* —**pa•per•weight** *n* —**pa•pery** \ˈpāpərē\ *adj*
pa•per•board *n* : cardboard
pa•pier-mâ•ché \ˌpāpərməˈshā, ˌpap,yā-mə-, -ma-\ *n* : molding material of waste paper
pa•poose \paˈpüs, pə-\ *n* : young child of American Indian parents
pa•pri•ka \pəˈprēkə, pa-\ *n* : mild red spice from sweet peppers
pa•py•rus \pəˈpīrəs\ *n, pl* **-rus•es** *or* **-ri** \-ˌrē, -ˌrī\ 1 : tall grasslike plant 2 : paper from papyrus
par \ˈpär\ *n* 1 : stated value 2 : common level 3 : accepted standard or normal condition —**par** *adj*
par•a•ble \ˈparəbəl\ *n* : simple story illustrating a moral truth
para•chute \ˈparəˌshüt\ *n* : large umbrella-shaped device for making a descent through air —**parachute** *vb* —**para•chut•ist** \-ˌshütist\ *n*
pa•rade \pəˈrād\ *n* 1 : pompous display 2 : ceremonial formation and march ~ *vb* **-rad•ed; -rad•ing** 1 : march in a parade 2 : show off
par•a•digm \ˈparəˌdīm, -ˌdim\ *n* : model
par•a•dise \ˈparəˌdīs, -ˌdīz\ *n* : place of bliss
par•a•dox \ˈparəˌdäks\ *n* : statement that seems contrary to common sense yet is perhaps true —**par•a•dox•i•cal** \ˌparə-ˈdäksikəl\ *adj* —**par•a•dox•i•cal•ly** *adv*
par•af•fin \ˈparəfən\ *n* : white waxy substance used esp. for making candles and sealing foods

par·a·gon \'parə,gän, -gən\ *n* : model of perfection

para·graph \'parə,graf\ *n* : unified division of a piece of writing ~ *vb* : divide into paragraphs

par·a·keet \'parə,kēt\ *n* : small slender parrot

par·al·lel \'parə,lel\ *adj* 1 : lying or moving in the same direction but always the same distance apart 2 : similar ~ *n* 1 : parallel line, curve, or surface 2 : line of latitude 3 : similarity ~ *vb* 1 : compare 2 : correspond to —**par·al·lel·ism** \-,izəm\ *n*

par·al·lel·o·gram \,parə'lelə,gram\ *n* : 4-sided polygon with opposite sides equal and parallel

pa·ral·y·sis \pə'raləsəs\ *n, pl* **-y·ses** \-,sēz\ : loss of function and esp. of voluntary motion —**par·a·lyt·ic** \,parə'litik\ *adj or n*

par·a·lyze \'parə,līz\ *vb* **-lyzed; -lyz·ing** : affect with paralysis —**par·a·lyz·ing·ly** *adv*

para·med·ic \,parə'medik\ *n* : person trained to provide initial emergency medical treatment

pa·ram·e·ter \pə'ramətər\ *n* : characteristic element —**para·met·ric** \,parə'metrik\ *adj*

par·a·mount \'parə,maunt\ *adj* : superior to all others

par·amour \'parə,mùr\ *n* : illicit lover

para·noia \,parə'nóiə\ *n* : mental disorder marked by irrational suspicion —**paranoid** \'parə,nóid\ *adj or n*

par·a·pet \'parəpət, -,pet\ *n* : protecting rampart in a fort

par·a·pher·na·lia \,parəfə'nālyə, -fər-\ *n sing or pl* : equipment

para·phrase \'parə,frāz\ *n* : restatement of a text giving the meaning in different words —**paraphrase** *vb*

para·ple·gia \,parə'plējə, -jēə\ *n* : paralysis of the lower trunk and legs —**para·ple·gic** \-,jik\ *adj or n*

par·a·site \'parə,sīt\ *n* : organism living on another —**par·a·sit·ic** \,parə'sitik\ *adj*— **par·a·sit·ism** \'parəsə,tizəm, -,sīt,iz-\ *n*

para·sol \'parə,sól\ *n* : umbrella used to keep off the sun

para·troops \-,trüps\ *n pl* : troops trained to parachute from an airplane —**para·troop·er** \-,trüpər\ *n*

par·boil \'pär,bóil\ *vb* : boil briefly

par·cel \'pärsəl\ *n* 1 : lot 2 : package ~ *vb* **-celed** *or* **-celled; -cel·ing** *or* **-cel·ling** : divide into portions

parch \'pärch\ *vb* : toast or shrivel with dry heat

parch·ment \'pärchmənt\ *n* : animal skin prepared to write on

par·don \'pärdᵊn\ *n* : excusing of an offense ~ *vb* : free from penalty —**par·don·able** \'pärdᵊnəbəl\ *adj* —**par·don·er** \-ᵊnər\ *n*

pare \'par\ *vb* **pared; par·ing** 1 : trim off an outside part 2 : reduce as if by paring —**par·er** *n*

par·e·gor·ic \,parə'górik\ *n* : tincture of opium and camphor

par·ent \'parənt\ *n* : one that begets or brings up offspring —**par·ent·age** \-ij\ *n* —**pa·ren·tal** \pə'rentᵊl\ *adj* —**par·ent·hood** *n*

par·en·the·sis \pə'renthəsəs\ *n, pl* **-the·ses** \-,sēz\ 1 : word or phrase inserted in a passage 2 : one of a pair of punctuation marks ( ) —**par·en·thet·ic** \,parən'thetik\, **par·en·thet·i·cal** \-ikəl\ *adj* —**par·en·thet·i·cal·ly** *adv*

par·fait \pär'fā\ *n* : layered cold dessert

pa·ri·ah \pə'rīə\ *n* : outcast

par·ish \'parish\ *n* : local church community

pa·rish·io·ner \pə'rishənər\ *n* : member of a parish

par·i·ty \'parətē\ *n, pl* **-ties** : equality

park \'pärk\ *n* : land set aside for recreation or for its beauty ~ *vb* : leave a vehicle standing

par·ka \'pärkə\ *n* : usu. hooded heavy jacket

park·way \'pärk,wā\ *n* : broad landscaped thoroughfare

par·lance \'pärləns\ *n* : manner of speaking

par·lay \'pär,lā\ *n* : the risking of a stake plus its winnings —**parlay** *vb*

par·ley \'pärlē\ *n, pl* **-leys** : conference about a dispute —**parley** *vb*

par·lia·ment \'pärləmənt\ *n* : legislative assembly —**par·lia·men·tar·i·an** *n* —**par·lia·men·ta·ry** \,pärlə'mentərē\ *adj*

par·lor \'pärlər\ *n* 1 : reception room 2 : place of business

pa·ro·chi·al \pə'rōkēəl\ *adj* 1 : relating to a church parish 2 : provincial —**pa·ro·chi·al·ism** \-ə,lizəm\ *n*

par·o·dy \'parədē\ *n, pl* **-dies** : humorous or satirical imitation —**parody** *vb*

pa·role \pə'rōl\ *n* : conditional release of a prisoner —**parole** *vb* —**pa·rol·ee** \-,rō'lē, -'rō,lē\ *n*

par·ox·ysm \'parək,sizəm, pə'räk-\ *n* : convulsion

par·quet \'pär,kā, pär'kā\ *n* : flooring of patterned wood inlay

par·ra·keet *var of* PARAKEET

par·rot \'parət\ *n* : bright-colored tropical bird

par·ry \'parē\ *vb* **-ried; -ry·ing** 1 : ward off a blow 2 : evade adroitly —**parry** *n*

parse \'pärs\ *vb* **parsed; pars·ing** : analyze grammatically

par·si·mo·ny \'pärsə,mōnē\ *n* : extreme frugality —**par·si·mo·ni·ous** \,pärsə'mōnēəs\ *adj* —**par·si·mo·ni·ous·ly** *adv*

pars·ley \'pärslē\ *n* : garden plant used as a seasoning or garnish

pars·nip \'pärsnəp\ *n* : carrotlike vegetable with a white edible root

par·son \'pärsᵊn\ *n* : minister

par·son·age \'pärsᵊnij\ *n* : parson's house

part \'pärt\ *n* 1 : one of the units into which a larger whole is divided 2 : function or role ~ *vb* 1 : take leave 2 : separate 3 : go away 4 : give up

par·take \pär'tāk, pər-\ *vb* **-took; -tak·en; -tak·ing** : have or take a share —**par·tak·er** *n*

par·tial \'pärshəl\ *adj* 1 : favoring one over another 2 : affecting a part only —**par·tial·i·ty** \,pärshē'alətē\ *n* —**par·tial·ly** \'pärshəlē\ *adv*

par·tic·i·pate \pər'tisə,pāt, pär-\ *vb* **-pat·ed; -pat·ing** : take part in something —**par·tic·i·pant** \-pənt\ *adj or n* —**par·tic·i·pa·tion** \-,tisə'pāshən\ *n* —**par·tic·i·pa·to·ry** \-'tisəpə,tōrē\ *adj*

par·ti·ci·ple \'pärtə,sipəl\ *n* : verb form with functions of both verb and adjective —**par·ti·cip·i·al** \,pärtə'sipēəl\ *adj*

par·ti·cle \'pärtikəl\ *n* : small bit

par·tic·u·lar \pär'tikyələr\ *adj* 1 : relating to a specific person or thing 2 : individual 3 : hard to please ~ *n* : detail —**par·tic·u·lar·ly** *adv*

par·ti·san \'pärtəzen, -sən\ *n* 1 : adherent 2 : guerrilla —**partisan** *adj* —**par·ti·san·ship** *n*

par·tite \'pär,tīt\ *adj* : divided into parts

par·ti·tion \pər'tishən, pär-\ *n* 1 : distribution 2 : something that divides —**partition** *vb*

part·ly \'pärtlē\ *adv* : in some degree

part·ner \'pärtnər\ *n* 1 : associate 2 : companion 3 : business associate —**part·ner·ship** *n*

part of speech : class of words distinguished esp. according to function

par·tridge \'pärtrij\ *n, pl* **-tridge** *or* **-tridg·es** : stout-bodied game bird

par·ty \'pärtē\ *n, pl* **-ties** 1 : political organization 2 : participant 3 : company of persons esp. with a purpose 4 : social gathering

par·ve·nu \'pärvə,nü, -,nyü\ *n* : social upstart

pass \'pas\ *vb* 1 : move past, over, or through 2 : go away or die 3 : allow to elapse 4 : go unchallenged 5 : transfer or undergo transfer 6 : render a judgment 7 : occur 8 : enact 9 : undergo testing successfully 10 : be regarded 11 : decline ~ *n* 1 : low place in a mountain range 2 : act of passing 3 : accomplishment 4 : permission to leave, enter, or move about —**pass·able** *adj* —**pass·ably** *adv* —**pass·er** *n* —**pass·er·by** *n*

pas·sage \'pasij\ *n* 1 : process of passing 2 : means of passing 3 : voyage 4 : right to pass 5 : literary selection —**pas·sage·way** *n*

pass·book *n* : bankbook

pas·sé \pa'sā\ *adj* : out-of-date

pas·sen·ger \'pasᵊnjər\ *n* : traveler in a conveyance

pass·ing \'pasiŋ\ *n* : death

pas·sion \'pashən\ *n* 1 : strong feeling esp. of anger, love, or desire 2 : object of affection or enthusiasm —**pas·sion·ate** \'pashənət\ *adj* —**pas·sion·ate·ly** *adv* —**pas·sion·less** *adj*

pas·sive \'pasiv\ *adj* 1 : not active but acted upon 2 : submissive —**passive** *n* —**pas·sive·ly** *adv* —**pas·siv·i·ty** \pa'sivətē\ *n*

Pass·over \'pas,ōvər\ *n* : Jewish holiday celebrated in March or April in commemoration of the Hebrews' liberation from slavery in Egypt

pass·port \'pas,pōrt\ *n* : government document needed for travel abroad

pass·word \-,wərd\ *n* 1 : word or phrase spoken to pass a guard 2 : sequence of characters needed to get into a computer system

past \'past\ *adj* 1 : ago 2 : just gone by 3 : having existed before the present 4 : expressing past time ~ *prep or adv* : beyond ~ *n* 1 : time gone by 2 : past tense expressing time gone by 3 : past life

pas·ta \'pästə\ *n* : fresh or dried shaped dough

paste \'pāst\ *n* 1 : smooth ground food 2 : moist adhesive ~ *vb* **past·ed; past·ing** : attach with paste —**pasty** *adj*

paste·board *n* : cardboard

pas·tel \pas'tel\ *n* : light color —**pastel** *adj*

pas·teur·ize \'paschə,rīz, 'pastə-\ *vb* **-ized; -iz·ing** : heat (as milk) so as to kill germs —**pas·teur·i·za·tion** \,paschərə'zāshən, ,pastə-\ *n*

pas·time \'pas,tīm\ *n* : amusement

pas·tor \'pastər\ *n* : priest or minister serving a church or parish —**pas·tor·ate** \-tərət\ *n*

pas·to·ral \'pastərəl\ *adj* 1 : relating to rural life 2 : of or relating to spiritual guidance or a pastor ~ *n* : literary work dealing with rural life

pas·try \'pāstrē\ *n, pl* **-ries** : sweet baked goods

pas·ture \'paschər\ *n* : land used for grazing ~ *vb* **-tured; -tur·ing** : graze

pat \'pat\ *n* 1 : light tap 2 : small mass ~ *vb* **-tt-** : tap gently ~ *adj or adv* 1 : apt or glib 2 : unyielding

patch \'pach\ *n* 1 : piece used for mending 2 : small area distinct from surrounding area ~ *vb* 1 : mend with a patch 2 : make of fragments 3 : repair hastily —**patchy** \-ē\ *adj*

patch·work *n* : something made of pieces of different materials, shapes, or colors

pate \'pāt\ *n* : crown of the head

pas·tel \pə'telə\ *n, pl* **-lae** \-'tel,ē, -,ī\ *or* **-las** : kneecap

pa·tent *adj* 1 \'patᵊnt, 'pāt-\ : obvious 2 \'pat-\ : protected by a patent ~ \'pat-\ *n* : document conferring or securing a right ~ \'pat-\ *vb* : secure by patent —**pat·ent·ly** *adv*

pa·ter·nal \pə'tərnᵊl\ *adj* 1 : fatherly 2 : related through or inherited from a father —**pa·ter·nal·ly** *adv*

pa·ter·ni·ty \pə'tərnətē\ *n* : fatherhood

path \'path, 'päth\ *n* 1 : trodden way 2 : route or course —**path·find·er** *n* —**path·way** *n* —**path·less** *adj*

pa·thet·ic \pə'thetik\ *adj* : pitiful —**pa·thet·i·cal·ly** *adv*

pa·thol·o·gy \pə'thäləjē\ *n, pl* **-gies** 1 : study of disease 2 : physical abnormality —**path·o·log·i·cal** \,pathə'läjikəl\ *adj* —**pa·thol·o·gist** \pə'thäləjist\ *n*

pa·thos \'pā,thäs\ *n* : element evoking pity

pa·tience \'pāshəns\ *n* : habit or fact of being patient

pa·tient \'pāshənt\ *adj* : bearing pain or trials without complaint ~ *n* : one under medical care —**pa·tient·ly** *adv*

pa·ti·na \pə'tēnə, 'patᵊnə\ *n, pl* **-nas** \-nəz\ *or* **-nae** \-,nē, -,nī\ : green film formed on copper and bronze

pa·tio \'patē,ō, 'pät-\ *n, pl* **-ti·os** 1 : courtyard 2 : paved recreation area near a house

pa·tri·arch \'pātrē,ärk\ *n* 1 : man revered as father or founder 2 : venerable old man —**pa·tri·ar·chal** \,pātrē'ärkəl\ *adj* —**pa·tri·ar·chy** \-,ärkē\ *n*

pa·tri·cian \pə'trishən\ *n* : person of high birth —**patrician** *adj*

pat·ri·mo·ny \'patrə,mōnē\ *n* : something inherited —**pat·ri·mo·ni·al** \,patrə'mōnēəl\ *adj*

pa·tri·ot \'pātrēət, -,ät\ *n* : one who loves his or her country —**pa·tri·ot·ic** \,pātrē'ätik\ *adj* —**pa·tri·ot·i·cal·ly** *adv* —**pa·tri·o·tism** \'pātrēə,tizəm\ *n*

pa·trol \pə'trōl\ *n* 1 : a going around for observation or security 2 : group on patrol ~ *vb* **-ll-** : carry out a patrol

pa·trol·man \-mən\ *n* : police officer

pa·tron \'pātrən\ *n* 1 : special protector 2 : wealthy supporter 3 : customer

pa·tron·age \'patrənij, 'pā-\ *n* 1 : support or influence of a patron 2 : trade of customers 3 : control of government appointments

pa·tron·ess \'pātrənəs\ *n* : woman who is a patron

pa·tron·ize \'pātrə,nīz, 'pa-\ *vb* **-ized; -iz·ing** 1 : be a customer of 2 : treat with condescension

¹**pat·ter** \'patər\ *vb* : talk glibly or mechanically ~ *n* : rapid talk

²**patter** *vb* : pat or tap rapidly ~ *n* : quick succession of pats or taps

pat·tern \'patərn\ *n* 1 : model for imitation or for making things 2 : artistic design 3 : noticeable formation or set of characteristics ~ *vb* : form according to a pattern

pat·ty \'patē\ *n, pl* **-ties** : small flat cake

pau·ci·ty \'pósətē\ *n* : shortage

paunch \'pónch\ *n* : large belly —**paunchy** *adj*

pau·per \'pópər\ *n* : poor person —**pau·per·ism** \-pə,rizəm\ *n* —**pau·per·ize** \-pə,rīz\ *vb*

pause \'póz\ *n* : temporary stop ~ *vb* **paused; pausing** : stop briefly

pave \'pāv\ *vb* **paved; pav·ing** : cover to smooth or firm the surface —**pave·ment** \-mənt\ *n* —**pav·ing** *n*

pa·vil·ion \pə'vilyən\ *n* 1 : large tent 2 : light structure used for entertainment or shelter

paw \'pó\ *n* : foot of a 4-legged clawed animal ~ *vb* 1 : handle clumsily or rudely 2 : touch or strike with a paw

pawn \'pón\ *n* 1 : goods deposited as security for a loan 2 : state of being pledged ~ *vb* : deposit as a pledge —**pawn·bro·ker** *n* —**pawn·shop** *n*

pay \'pā\ *vb* **paid** \'pād\; **pay·ing** 1 : make due return for goods or services 2 : discharge indebtedness for 3 : requite 4 : give freely or as fitting 5 : be profitable ~ *n* 1 : status of being paid 2 : something paid —**pay·able** *adj* —**pay·check** *n* —**pay·ee** \pā'ē\ *n* —**pay·ment** *n*

PC \,pē'sē\ *n, pl* **PCs** *or* **PC's** : microcomputer

pea \'pē\ *n* : round edible seed of a leguminous vine

peace \'pēs\ *n* 1 : state of calm and quiet 2 : absence of war or strife —**peace·able** \-əbəl\ *adj* —**peace·ably** \-blē\ *adv* —**peace·ful** \-fəl\ *adj* —**peace·ful·ly** *adv* —**peace·keep·er** *n* —**peace·keep·ing** *n* —**peace·mak·er** *n* —**peace·time** *n*

peach \'pēch\ *n* : sweet juicy fruit of a flowering tree or this tree

pea·cock \'pē,käk\ *n* : brilliantly colored male pheasant

peak \'pēk\ *n* 1 : pointed or projecting part 2 : top of a hill 3 : highest level ~ *vb* : reach a maximum —**peak** *adj*

peak·ed \'pēkəd\ *adj* : sickly

peal \'pēl\ *n* : loud sound (as of ringing bells) ~ *vb* : give out peals

pea·nut \'pē,nət\ *n* : annual herb that bears underground pods or the pod or the edible seed inside

pear \'par\ *n* : fleshy fruit of a tree related to the apple

pearl \'pərl\ *n* : gem formed within an oyster —**pearly** \pərlē\ *adj*

peas·ant \'pezᵊnt\ *n* : tiller of the soil —**peas·ant·ry** \-ᵊntrē\ *n*

peat \'pēt\ *n* : decayed organic deposit often dried for fuel —**peaty** *adj*

peb·ble \'pebəl\ *n* : small stone —**pebbly** *adj*

pe·can \pi'kän, -'kan\ *n* : hickory tree bearing a smooth-shelled nut or the nut

pec·ca·dil·lo \,pekə'dilō\ *n, pl* **-loes** *or* **-los** : slight offense

¹**peck** \'pek\ *n* : unit of dry measure equal to 8 quarts

²**peck** *vb* : strike or pick up with the bill ~ *n* : quick sharp stroke

pec·tin \'pektən\ *n* : water-soluble plant substance that causes fruit jellies to set —**pec·tic** \-tik\ *adj*

pec·to·ral \'pektərəl\ *adj* : relating to the breast or chest

pe·cu·liar \pi'kyülyər\ *adj* 1 : characteristic of only one 2 : strange —**pe·cu·liar·i·ty** \-,kyül'yarətē, -ē-\ *n* —**pe·cu·liar·ly** *adv*

pe·cu·ni·ary \pi'kyünē,erē\ *adj* : relating to money

ped·a·go·gy \'pedə,gōjē, -,gäj-\ *n* : art or profession of teaching —**ped·a·gog·ic** \,pedə'gäjik, -'gōj-\, **ped·a·gog·i·cal** \-ikəl\ *adj* —**ped·a·gogue** \'pedə,gäg\ *n*

ped·al \'pedᵊl\ *n* : lever worked by the foot ~ *adj* : relating to the foot ~ *vb* : use a pedal

ped·ant \'pedᵊnt\ *n* : learned bore —**pe·dan·tic** \pi'dantik\ *adj* —**ped·ant·ry** \'pedᵊntrē\ *n*

ped·dle \'pedᵊl\ *vb* **-dled; -dling** : offer for sale —**ped·dler** \'pedlər\ *n*

ped·es·tal \'pedəst°l\ *n* : support or foot of something upright

pe·des·tri·an \pə'destrēən\ *adj* 1 : ordinary 2 : walking ~ *n* : person who walks

pe·di·at·rics \,pēdē'atriks\ *n* : branch of medicine dealing with children —**pe·di·at·ric** \-trik\ *adj* —**pe·di·a·tri·cian** \,pēdēə'trishən\ *n*

ped·i·gree \'pedə,grē\ *n* : line of ancestors or a record of it

ped·i·ment \'pedəmənt\ *n* : triangular gablelike decoration on a building

peek \'pēk\ *vb* 1 : look furtively 2 : glance —**peek** *n*

peel \'pēl\ *vb* 1 : strip the skin or rind from 2 : lose the outer layer ~ *n* : skin or rind —**peel·ing** *n*

¹**peep** \'pēp\ *vb or n* : cheep

²**peep** *vb* 1 : look slyly 2 : begin to emerge ~ *n* : brief look —**peep·er** *n* —**peep·hole** *n*

¹**peer** \'pir\ *n* 1 : one's equal 2 : nobleman —**peer·age** \-ij\ *n*

²**peer** *vb* : look intently or curiously

peer·less \-ləs\ *adj* : having no equal

peeve \'pēv\ *vb* **peeved; peev·ing** : make resentful ~ *n* : complaint —**peev·ish** \-ish\ *adj* —**peev·ish·ly** *adv* —**peev·ish·ness** *n*

peg \'peg\ *n* : small pinlike piece ~ *vb* **-gg-** 1 : put a peg into 2 : fix or mark with or as if with pegs

peignoir \pān'wär, pen-\ *n* : negligee

pe·jo·ra·tive \pi'jórativ\ *adj* : having a negative or degrading effect ~ *n* : a degrading word or phrase —**pe·jo·ra·tive·ly** *adv*

pel·i·can \'pelikən\ *n* : large-billed seabird

pel·la·gra \pə'lagrə, -'läg-\ *n* : protein-deficiency disease

pel·let \'pelət\ *n* : little ball —**pel·let·al** \-ᵊl\ *adj* —**pel·let·ize** \-,īz\ *vb*

pell–mell \'pel'mel\ *adv* : in confusion or haste

pel•lu•cid \pə'lüsəd\ *adj* : very clear

1pelt \'pelt\ *n* : skin of a fur-bearing animal

2pelt *vb* : strike with blows or missiles

pel•vis \'pelvəs\ *n, pl* **-vis•es** \-vəsəz\ *or* **-ves** \-,vēz\ : cavity formed by the hip bones —**pel•vic** \-vik\ *adj*

1pen \'pen\ *n* : enclosure for animals ~ *vb* **-nn-** : shut in a pen

2pen *n* : tool for writing with ink ~ *vb* **-nn-** : write

pe•nal \'pēnəl\ *adj* : relating to punishment

pe•nal•ize \'pēnəl,īz, 'pen-\ *vb* **-ized; -iz•ing** : put a penalty on

pen•al•ty \'penəltē\ *n, pl* **-ties** 1 : punishment for crime 2 : disadvantage, loss, or hardship due to an action

pen•ance \'penəns\ *n* : act performed to show repentance

pence \'pens\ *pl of* PENNY

pen•chant \'penchənt\ *n* : strong inclination

pen•cil \'pensəl\ *n* : writing or drawing tool with a solid marking substance (as graphite) as its core ~ *vb* **-ciled** *or* **-cilled; -cil•ing** *or* **-cil•ling** : draw or write with a pencil

pen•dant \'pendənt\ *n* : hanging ornament

pen•dent, pen•dant \'pendənt\ *adj* : hanging

pend•ing \'pendiŋ\ *prep* : while awaiting ~ *adj* : not yet decided

pen•du•lous \'penjələs, -dyùləs\ *adj* : hanging loosely

pen•du•lum \-ləm\ *n* : a hanging weight that is free to swing

pen•e•trate \'penə,trāt\ *vb* **-trat•ed; -trat•ing** 1 : enter into 2 : permeate 3 : see into —**pen•e•tra•ble** \-trəbəl\ *adj* —**pen•e•tra•tion** \,penə'trāshən\ *n* —**pen•e•tra•tive** \'penə,trātiv\ *adj*

pen•guin \'peŋgwən, 'pen-\ *n* : short-legged flightless seabird

pen•i•cil•lin \,penə'silən\ *n* : antibiotic usu. produced by a mold

pen•in•su•la \pə'ninsələ, -'nincha-\ *n* : land extending out into the water —**pen•in•su•lar** \-lər\ *adj*

pe•nis \'pēnəs\ *n, pl* **-nes** \-,nēz\ *or* **-nis•es** : male organ of copulation

pen•i•tent \'penətənt\ *adj* : feeling sorrow for sins or offenses ~ *n* : penitent person —**pen•i•tence** \-təns\ *n* —**pen•i•ten•tial** \,penə'tenchəl\ *adj*

pen•i•ten•tia•ry \,penə'tenchərē\ *n, pl* **-ries** : state or federal prison

pen•man•ship \'penmən,ship\ *n* : art or practice of writing

pen•nant \'penənt\ *n* : nautical or championship flag

pen•ny \'penē\ *n, pl* **-nies** \-ēz\ *or* **pence** \'pens\ 1 : monetary unit equal to 1/100 pound 2 *pl* **-nies** : cent —**pen•ni•less** \'peniləs\ *adj*

pen•sion \'penchən\ *n* : retirement income ~ *vb* : pay a pension to —**pen•sion•er** *n*

pen•sive \'pensiv\ *adj* : thoughtful —**pen•sive•ly** *adv*

pent \'pent\ *adj* : confined

pent•a•gon \'pentə,gän\ *n* : 5-sided polygon —**pen•tag•o•nal** \pen'tagənəl\ *adj*

pen•tam•e•ter \pen'tamətər\ *n* : line of verse containing 5 metrical feet

pent•house \'pent,haùs\ *n* : rooftop apartment

pen•u•ry \'penyərē\ *n* 1 : poverty 2 : thrifty or stingy manner —**pe•nu•ri•ous** \pə'nûrēəs, -'nyûr-\ *adj*

pe•on \'pē,än, -ən\ *n, pl* **-ons** *or* **-ones** \-'ōnēz\ : landless laborer in Spanish America —**pe•on•age** \-ənij\ *n*

pe•o•ny \'pēənē\ *n, pl* **-nies** : garden plant having large flowers

peo•ple \'pēpəl\ *n, pl* **people** 1 *pl* : human beings in general 2 *pl* : human beings in a certain group (as a family) or community 3 *pl* **peoples** : tribe, nation, or race ~ *vb* **-pled; -pling** : constitute the population of

pep \'pep\ *n* : brisk energy ~ *vb* **pepped; pep•ping** : put pep into —**pep•py** *adj*

pep•per \'pepər\ *n* 1 : pungent seasoning from the berry (**pep•per•corn**) of a shrub 2 : vegetable grown for its hot or sweet fruit ~ *vb* : season with pepper —**pep•pery** \-ərē\ *adj*

pep•per•mint \-,mint, -mənt\ *n* : pungent aromatic mint

pep•per•o•ni \,pepə'rōnē\ *n* : spicy beef and pork sausage

pep•tic \'peptik\ *adj* : relating to digestion or the effect of digestive juices

per \'pər\ *prep* 1 : by means of 2 : for each 3 : according to

per•am•bu•late \pə'rambyə,lāt\ *vb* **-lat•ed; -lat•ing** : walk —**per•am•bu•la•tion** \-,rambyə'lāshən\ *n*

per•cale \pər'kāl, 'pər-,; 'pər'kal\ *n* : fine woven cotton cloth

per•ceive \pər'sēv\ *vb* **-ceived; -ceiv•ing** 1 : realize 2 : become aware of through the senses —**per•ceiv•able** *adj*

per•cent \pər'sent\ *adv* : in each hundred ~ *n, pl* **-cent** *or* **-cents** 1 : one part in a hundred 2 : percentage

per•cent•age \pər'sentij\ *n* : part expressed in hundredths

per•cen•tile \pər'sen,tīl\ *n* : a standing on a scale of 0–100

per•cep•ti•ble \pər'septəbəl\ *adj* : capable of being perceived —**per•cep•ti•bly** \-blē\ *adv*

per•cep•tion \pər'sepshən\ *n* 1 : act or result of perceiving 2 : ability to understand

per•cep•tive \pər'septiv\ *adj* : showing keen perception —**per•cep•tive•ly** *adv*

1perch \'pərch\ *n* : roost for birds ~ *vb* : roost

2perch *n, pl* **perch** *or* **perch•es** : freshwater spiny-finned food fish

per•co•late \'pərkə,lāt\ *vb* **-lat•ed; -lat•ing** : trickle or filter down through a substance —**per•co•la•tor** \-,lātər\ *n*

per•cus•sion \pər'kəshən\ *n* 1 : sharp blow 2 : musical instrument sounded by striking

pe•remp•to•ry \pə'remptərē\ *adj* 1 : imperative 2 : domineering —**pe•remp•to•ri•ly** \-tərəlē\ *adv*

pe•ren•ni•al \pə'renēəl\ *adj* 1 : present at all seasons 2 : continuing from year to year 3 : recurring regularly ~ *n* : perennial plant —**pe•ren•ni•al•ly** *adv*

per•fect \'pərfikt\ *adj* 1 : being without fault or defect 2 : exact 3 : complete ~ \pər'fekt\ *vb* : make perfect —**per•fect•ibil•i•ty** \pər,fektə'bilətē\ *n* —**per•fect•ible** \pər'fektəbəl\ *adj* —**per•fect•ly** *adv* —**per•fect•ness** *n*

per•fec•tion \pər'fekshən\ *n* 1 : quality or state of being perfect 2 : highest degree of excellence —**per•fec•tion•ist** \-shənist\ *n*

per•fid•i•ous \pər'fidēəs\ *adj* : treacherous —**per•fid•i•ous•ly** *adv*

per•fo•rate \'pərfə,rāt\ *vb* **-rat•ed; -rat•ing** : make a hole in —**per•fo•ra•tion** \,pərfə'rāshən\ *n*

per•force \pər'fōrs\ *adv* : of necessity

per•form \pər'fôrm\ *vb* 1 : carry out 2 : do in a set manner 3 : give a performance —**per•form•er** *n*

per•for•mance \pər'fôr,məns\ *n* 1 : act or process of performing 2 : public presentation

per•fume \pər,fyüm, pər'-\ *n* 1 : pleasant odor 2 : something that gives a scent ~ \pər'-, 'pər,-\ *vb* **-fumed; -fum•ing** : add scent to

per•func•to•ry \pər'fəŋktərē\ *adj* : done merely as a duty —**per•func•to•ri•ly** \-tərəlē\ *adv*

per•haps \pər'haps\ *adv* : possibly but not certainly

per•il \'perəl\ *n* : danger —**per•il•ous** *adj* —**per•il•ous•ly** *adv*

pe•rim•e•ter \pə'rimətər\ *n* : outer boundary of a body or figure

pe•ri•od \'pirēəd\ *n* 1 : punctuation mark . used esp. to mark the end of a declarative sentence or an abbreviation 2 : division of time 3 : stage in a process or development

pe•ri•od•ic \,pirē'ädik\ *adj* : occurring at regular intervals —**pe•ri•od•i•cal•ly** *adv*

pe•ri•od•i•cal \,pirē'ädikəl\ *n* : newspaper or magazine

pe•riph•ery \pə'rifərē\ *n, pl* **-er•ies** : outer boundary —**pe•riph•er•al** \-ərəl\ *adj*

peri•scope \'perə,skōp\ *n* : optical instrument for viewing from a submarine

per•ish \'perish\ *vb* : die or spoil —**per•ish•able** \-əbəl\ *adj or n*

per•ju•ry \'pərjərē\ *n* : lying under oath —**per•jure** \'pərjər\ *vb* —**per•jur•er** *n*

1perk \'pərk\ *vb* 1 : thrust (as the head) up jauntily 2 : freshen 3 : gain vigor or spirit —**perky** *adj*

2perk *vb* : percolate

3perk *n* : privilege or benefit in addition to regular pay

per•ma•nent \'pərmənənt\ *adj* : lasting ~ *n* : hair wave —**per•ma•nence** \-nəns\ *n* —**per•ma•nent•ly** *adv*

per•me•able \'pərmēəbəl\ *adj* : permitting fluids to seep through —**per•me•a•bil•i•ty** \,pərmēə'bilətē\ *n*

per•me•ate \'pərmē,āt\ *vb* **-at•ed; -at•ing** 1 : seep through 2 : pervade —**per•me•ation** \,pərmē'āshən\ *n*

per•mis•si•ble \pər'misəbəl\ *adj* : that may be permitted

per•mis•sion \pər'mishən\ *n* : formal consent

per•mis•sive \pər'misiv\ *adj* : granting freedom esp. to excess —**per•mis•sive•ly** *adv* —**per•mis•sive•ness** *n*

per•mit \pər'mit\ *vb* **-tt-** 1 : approve 2 : make possible ~ \'pər,-, pər'-\ *n* : license

per•ni•cious \pər'nishəs\ *adj* : very harmful —**per•ni•cious•ly** *adv*

per•ox•ide \pə'räk,sīd\ *n* : compound (as hydrogen peroxide) in which oxygen is joined to oxygen

per•pen•dic•u•lar \,pərpən'dikyələr\ *adj* 1 : vertical 2 : meeting at a right angle —**perpendicular** *n* —**per•pen•dic•u•lar•i-**

ty \-,dikyə'larətē\ *n* —**per•pen•dic•u•lar•ly** *adv*

per•pe•trate \'pərpə,trāt\ *vb* **-trat•ed; -trat•ing** : be guilty of doing —**per•pe•tra•tion** \,pərpə'trāshən\ *n* —**per•pe•tra•tor** \'pərpə,trātər\ *n*

per•pet•u•al \pər'pechəwəl\ *adj* 1 : continuing forever 2 : occurring continually —**per•pet•u•al•ly** *adv* —**per•pe•tu•ity** \,pərpə'tüətē, -'tyü-\ *n*

per•pet•u•ate \pər'pechə,wāt\ *vb* **-at•ed; -at•ing** : make perpetual —**per•pet•u•a•tion** \-,pechə'wāshən\ *n*

per•plex \pər'pleks\ *vb* : confuse —**per•plex•i•ty** \-ətē\ *n*

per•se•cute \'pərsi,kyüt\ *vb* **-cut•ed; -cut•ing** : harass, afflict —**per•se•cu•tion** \,pərsi'kyüshən\ *n* —**per•se•cu•tor** \'pər,si,kyütər\ *n*

per•se•vere \,pərsə'vir\ *vb* **-vered; -ver•ing** : persist —**per•se•ver•ance** \-'virəns\ *n*

per•sist \pər'sist, -'zist\ *vb* 1 : go on resolutely in spite of difficulties 2 : continue to exist —**per•sis•tence** \-'sistəns, -'zis-\ *n* —**per•sis•ten•cy** \-tənsē\ *n* —**per•sis•tent** \-tənt\ *adj* —**per•sis•tent•ly** *adv*

per•son \'pərsən\ *n* 1 : human being 2 : human being's body or individuality 3 : reference to the speaker, one spoken to, or one spoken of

per•son•able \'pərsənəbəl\ *adj* : having a pleasing personality

per•son•age \'pərsənij\ *n* : person of rank or distinction

per•son•al \'pərsənəl\ *adj* 1 : relating to a particular person 2 : done in person 3 : affecting one's body 4 : offensive to a certain individual —**per•son•al•ly** *adv*

per•son•al•i•ty \,pərsən'alətē\ *n, pl* **-ties** 1 : manner and disposition of an individual 2 : distinctive or well-known person

per•son•al•ize \'pərsənə,līz\ *vb* **-ized; -iz•ing** : mark as belonging to a particular person

per•son•i•fy \pər'sänə,fī\ *vb* **-fied; -fy•ing** 1 : represent as a human being 2 : be the embodiment of —**per•son•i•fi•ca•tion** \-,sänəfə'kāshən\ *n*

per•son•nel \,pərs°n'el\ *n* : body of persons employed

per•spec•tive \pər'spektiv\ *n* 1 : apparent depth and distance in painting 2 : view of things in their true relationship or importance

per•spi•ca•cious \,pərspə'kāshəs\ *adj* : showing keen understanding or discernment —**per•spi•cac•i•ty** \-'kasətē\ *n*

per•spire \pər'spīr\ *vb* **-spired; -spir•ing** : sweat —**per•spi•ra•tion** \,pərspə'rāshən\ *n*

per•suade \pər'swād\ *vb* **-suad•ed; -suad•ing** : win over to a belief or course of action by argument or entreaty —**per•sua•sion** \pər'swāzhən\ *n* —**per•sua•sive** \-'swāsiv, -ziv\ *adj* —**per•sua•sive•ly** *adv* —**per•sua•sive•ness** *n*

pert \'pərt\ *adj* : flippant or irreverent

per•tain \pər'tān\ *vb* 1 : belong 2 : relate

per•ti•nent \'pərt°nənt\ *adj* : relevant —**per•ti•nence** \-əns\ *n*

per•turb \pər'tərb\ *vb* : make uneasy —**per•tur•ba•tion** \,pərtər'bāshən\ *n*

pe•ruse \pə'rüz\ *vb* **-rused; -rus•ing** : read attentively —**pe•rus•al** \-'rüzəl\ *n*

per•vade \pər'vād\ *vb* **-vad•ed; -vad•ing** : spread through every part of —**per•va•sive** \-'vāsiv, -ziv\ *adj*

per•verse \pər'vərs\ *adj* 1 : corrupt 2 : unreasonably contrary —**per•verse•ly** *adv* —**per•verse•ness** *n* —**per•ver•sion** \pər'vərzhən\ *n* —**per•ver•si•ty** \-'vərsətē\ *n*

per•vert \pər'vərt\ *vb* : corrupt or distort ~ \'pər,-\ *n* : one that is perverted

pe•so \'pāsō\ *n, pl* **-sos** : monetary unit (as of Mexico)

pes•si•mism \'pesə,mizəm\ *n* : inclination to expect the worst —**pes•si•mist** \-mist\ *n* —**pes•si•mis•tic** \,pesə'mistik\ *adj*

pest \'pest\ *n* 1 : nuisance 2 : plant or animal detrimental to humans or their crops —**pes•ti•cide** \'pestə,sīd\ *n*

pes•ter \'pestər\ *vb* **-tered; -ter•ing** : harass with petty matters

pes•ti•lence \'pestələns\ *n* : plague —**pes•ti•lent** \-lənt\ *adj*

pes•tle \'pesəl, 'pest°l\ *n* : implement for grinding substances in a mortar

pet \'pet\ *n* 1 : domesticated animal kept for pleasure 2 : favorite ~ *vb* **-tt-** : stroke gently or lovingly

pet•al \'pet°l\ *n* : modified leaf of a flower head

pe•tite \pə'tēt\ *adj* : having a small trim figure

pe•ti•tion \pə'tishən\ *n* : formal written request ~ *vb* : make a request —**pe•ti•tion•er** *n*

pet•ri•fy \'petrə,fī\ *vb* **-fied; -fy•ing** 1 : change into stony material 2 : make rigid or inactive (as from fear) —**pet•ri•fac•tion** \,petrə'fakshən\ *n*

pe•tro•leum \pə'trōlēəm\ *n* : raw oil obtained from the ground

pet•ti•coat \'petē,kōt\ *n* : skirt worn under a dress

pet•ty \'petē\ *adj* **-ti•er; -est** 1 : minor 2 : of no importance 3 : narrow-minded or mean —**pet•ti•ly** \'pet°lē\ *adv* —**pet•ti•ness** *n*

petty officer *n* : subordinate officer in the navy or coast guard

pet•u•lant \'pechələnt\ *adj* : irritable —**pet•u•lance** \-ləns\ *n* —**pet•u•lant•ly** *adv*

pe•tu•nia \pi'tünyə, -'tyü-\ *n* : tropical herb with bright flowers

pew \'pyü\ *n* : bench with a back used in a church

pew•ter \'pyütər\ *n* : alloy of tin used for household utensils

pH \pē'āch\ *n* : number expressing relative acidity and alkalinity

pha•lanx \'fā,laŋks\ *n, pl* **-lanx•es** *or* **-lan•ges** \fə'lan,jēz\ 1 : body (as of troops) in compact formation 2 *pl* **phalanges** : digital bone of the hand or foot

phal•lus \'faləs\ *n, pl* **-li** \'fal,ī\ *or* **-lus•es** : penis —**phal•lic** *adj*

phan•ta•sy *var of* FANTASY

phan•tom \'fantəm\ *n* : something that only appears to be real —**phantom** *adj*

pha•raoh \'ferō, 'farō\ *n* : ruler of ancient Egypt

phar•ma•ceu•ti•cal \,färmə'sütikəl\ *adj* : relating to pharmacy or the making and selling of medicinal drugs —**pharmaceutical** *n*

phar•ma•col•o•gy \,färmə'käləjē\ *n* : science of drugs esp. as related to medicinal uses —**phar•ma•co•log•i•cal** \-ikəl\ *adj* —**phar•ma•col•o•gist** \-'käləjist\ *n*

phar•ma•cy \'färməsē\ *n, pl* **-cies** 1 : art or practice of preparing and dispensing medical drugs 2 : drugstore —**phar•ma•cist** \-sist\ *n*

phar•ynx \'fariŋks\ *n, pl* **pha•ryn•ges** \fə'rin,jēz\ : space behind the mouth into which the nostrils, esophagus, and windpipe open —**pha•ryn•ge•al** \fə'rinjəl, ,farən'jēəl\ *adj*

phase \'fāz\ *n* 1 : particular appearance or stage in a recurring series of changes 2 : stage in a process —**phase in** *vb* : introduce in stages —**phase out** *vb* : discontinue gradually

pheas•ant \'fez°nt\ *n, pl* **-ant** *or* **-ants** : long-tailed brilliantly colored game bird

phe•nom•e•non \fi'nämə,nän, -nən\ *n, pl* **-na** \-nə\ *or* **-nons** 1 : observable fact or event 2 *pl* **-nons** : prodigy —**phe•nom•e•nal** \-'nämən°l\ *adj*

phi•lan•der•er \fə'landərər\ *n* : one who makes love without serious intent

phi•lan•thro•py \fə'lanthrəpē\ *n, pl* **-pies** : charitable act or gift or an organization that distributes such gifts —**phil•an•throp•ic** \,filən'thräpik\ *adj* —**phi•lan•thro•pist** \fə'lanthrəpist\ *n*

phi•lat•e•ly \fə'lat°lē\ *n* : collection and study of postage stamps —**phi•lat•e•list** \-°list\ *n*

phi•lis•tine \'filə,stēn, fə'listən\ *n* : one who is smugly indifferent to intellectual or artistic values —**philistine** *adj*

philo•den•dron \,filə'dendrən\ *n, pl* **-drons** *or* **-dra** \-drə\ : plant grown for its showy leaves

phi•los•o•pher \fə'läsəfər\ *n* 1 : reflective thinker 2 : student of philosophy

phi•los•o•phy \fə'läsəfē\ *n, pl* **-phies** 1 : critical study of fundamental beliefs 2 : sciences and liberal arts exclusive of medicine, law, and theology 3 : system of ideas 4 : sum of personal convictions —**phil•o•soph•ic** \,filə'säfik\, **phil•o•soph•i•cal** \-ikəl\ *adj* —**phil•o•soph•i•cal•ly** \-klē\ *adv* —**phi•los•o•phize** \fə'läsə,fīz\ *vb*

phle•bi•tis \fli'bītəs\ *n* : inflammation of a vein

phlegm \'flem\ *n* : thick mucus in the nose and throat

phlox \'fläks\ *n, pl* **phlox** *or* **phlox•es** : herb grown for its flower clusters

pho•bia \'fōbēə\ *n* : irrational persistent fear

phoe•nix \'fēniks\ *n* : legendary bird held to burn itself to death and rise fresh and young from its ashes

phone \'fōn\ *n* : telephone ~ *vb* **phoned; phon•ing** : call on a telephone

pho•neme \'fō,nēm\ *n* : basic distinguishable unit of speech —**pho•ne•mic** \fō'nēmik\ *adj*

pho•net•ics \fə'netiks\ *n* : study of speech sounds —**pho•net•ic** \-ik\ *adj* —**pho•ne•ti•cian** \,fōnə'tishən\ *n*

phon•ics \'fäniks\ *n* : method of teaching reading by stressing sound values of syllables and words

pho•no•graph \'fōnə,graf\ *n* : instrument that reproduces sounds from a grooved disc

pho•ny, pho•ney \'fōnē\ *adj* **-ni•er; -est** : not sincere or genuine —**phony** *n*

phos•phate \'fäs,fāt\ *n* : chemical salt used in fertilizers —**phos•phat•ic** \fäs'fatik\ *adj*

phos·phor \'fäsfər\ n : phosphorescent substance

phos·pho·res·cence \ˌfäsfə'resᵊns\ : luminescence from absorbed radiation —**phos·pho·res·cent** \-ᵊnt\ adj —**phos·pho·res·cent·ly** adv

phos·pho·rus \'fäsfərəs\ n : poisonous waxy chemical element —**phos·phor·ic** \fäs'förik, -'fär-\ adj —**phos·pho·rous** \'fäsfərəs, fäs'förəs\ adj

pho·to \'fōtō\ n, pl **-tos** : photograph —**photo** vb or adj

pho·to·copy \'fōtəˌkäpē\ n : photographic copy (as of a printed page) —**photocopy** vb

pho·to·elec·tric \ˌfōtōi'lektrik\ adj : relating to an electrical effect due to the interaction of light with matter

pho·to·gen·ic \ˌfōtə'jenik\ adj : suitable for being photographed

pho·to·graph \'fōtəˌgraf\ n : picture taken by photography —**photograph** vb —**pho·tog·ra·pher** \fə'tägrəfər\ n

pho·tog·ra·phy \fə'tägrəfē\ n : process of using light to produce images on a sensitized surface —**pho·to·graph·ic** \ˌfōtə'grafik\ adj —**pho·to·graph·i·cal·ly** adv

pho·to·syn·the·sis \ˌfōtō'sinthəsəs\ n : formation of carbohydrates by chlorophyll-containing plants exposed to sunlight —**pho·to·syn·the·size** \-ˌsīz\ vb —**pho·to·syn·thet·ic** \-sin'thetik\ adj

phrase \'frāz\ n 1 : brief expression 2 : group of related words that express a thought ~ vb **phrased; phras·ing** : express in a particular manner

phrase·ol·o·gy \ˌfrāzē'äləjē\ n, pl **-gies** : manner of phrasing

phy·lum \'fīləm\ n, pl **-la** \-lə\ : major division of the plant or animal kingdom

phys·i·cal \'fizikəl\ adj 1 : relating to nature 2 : material as opposed to mental or spiritual 3 : relating to the body ~ n : medical examination —**phys·i·cal·ly** \-klē\ adv

phy·si·cian \fə'zishən\ n : doctor of medicine

physician's assistant n : person certified to provide basic medical care under a physician's supervision

phys·i·cist \'fizəsist\ n : specialist in physics

phys·ics \'fiziks\ n : science that deals with matter and motion

phys·i·og·no·my \ˌfizē'ägnəmē\ n, pl **-mies** : facial appearance esp. as a reflection of inner character

phys·i·ol·o·gy \ˌfizē'äləjē\ n : functional processes in an organism —**phys·i·o·log·i·cal** \-ēə'läjikəl\, **phys·i·o·log·ic** \-ik\ adj —**phys·i·ol·o·gist** \-ē'äləjist\ n

phy·sique \fə'zēk\ n : build of a person's body

pi \'pī\ n, pl **pi** also **pis** \'pīz\ : symbol π denoting the ratio of the circumference of a circle to its diameter or the ratio itself

pi·a·nist \pē'anist, 'pēənist\ n : one who plays the piano

pi·ano \pē'anō\ n, pl **-anos** : musical instrument with strings sounded by hammers operated from a keyboard

pi·az·za \pē'azə, -'äz-, -tsə\ n, pl **-zas** or **-ze** \-tsä\ : public square in a town

pic·a·yune \ˌpikē'yün\ adj : trivial or petty

pic·co·lo \'pikəˌlō\ n, pl **-los** : small shrill flute

¹pick \'pik\ vb 1 : break up with a pointed instrument 2 : remove bit by bit 3 : gather by plucking 4 : select 5 : rob 6 : provoke 7 : unlock with a wire 8 : eat sparingly ~ n 1 : act of choosing 2 : choicest one —**pick·er** n —**pick up** vb 1 : improve 2 : put in order

²pick n : pointed digging tool

pick·ax n : pick

pick·er·el \'pikərəl\ n, pl **-el** or **-els** : small pike

pick·et \'pikət\ n 1 : pointed stake (as for a fence) 2 : worker demonstrating on strike ~ vb : demonstrate as a picket

pick·le \'pikəl\ n 1 : brine or vinegar solution for preserving foods or a food preserved in a pickle 2 : bad state —**pickle** vb

pick·pock·et \'pikˌpäkət\ n : one who steals from pockets

pick·up \'pikˌəp\ n 1 : revival or acceleration 2 : light truck with an open body

pic·nic \'pikˌnik\ n : outing with food usu. eaten in the open ~ vb **-nicked; -nick·ing** : go on a picnic

pic·to·ri·al \pik'tōrēəl\ adj : relating to pictures

pic·ture \'pikchər\ n 1 : representation by painting, drawing, or photography 2 : vivid description 3 : copy 4 : movie ~ vb **-tured; -tur·ing** : form a mental image of

pic·tur·esque \ˌpikchə'resk\ adj : attractive or charming enough for a picture —**pic·tur·esque·ness** n

pie \'pī\ n : pastry crust and a filling

pie·bald \'pīˌbȯld\ adj : blotched with white and black

piece \'pēs\ n 1 : part of a whole 2 : one of

a group or set 3 : single item 4 : product of creative work ~ vb **pieced; piec·ing** : join into a whole

piece·meal \'pēsˌmēl\ adv or adj : gradually

pied \'pīd\ adj : colored in blotches

pier \'pir\ n 1 : support for a bridge span 2 : deck or wharf built out over water 3 : pillar

pierce \'pirs\ vb **pierced; pierc·ing** 1 : enter or thrust into or through 2 : penetrate 3 : see through

pi·ety \'pīətē\ n, pl **-eties** : devotion to religion

pig \'pig\ n 1 : young swine 2 : dirty or greedy individual 3 : iron casting —**pig·gish** \-ish\ adj —**pig·let** \-lət\ n —**pig·pen** n —**pig·sty** n

pi·geon \'pijən\ n : stout-bodied short-legged bird

pi·geon·hole n : small open compartment for letters or documents ~ vb 1 : place in a pigeonhole 2 : classify

pig·gy·back \'pigēˌbak\ adv or adj : up on the back and shoulders

pig·head·ed \-'hedəd\ adj : stubborn

pig·ment \'pigmənt\ n : coloring matter —**pig·men·ta·tion** n

pig·my var of PYGMY

pig·tail n : tight braid of hair

¹pike \'pīk\ n, pl **pike** or **pikes** : large freshwater fish

²pike n : former weapon consisting of a long wooden staff with a steel point

³pike n : turnpike

pi·laf, pi·laff \pi'läf, 'pē,läf\, **pi·lau** \pi'lō, -'lò; pē'lō, -läü\ n : dish of seasoned rice

¹pile \'pīl\ n : supporting pillar driven into the ground

²pile n : quantity of things thrown on one another ~ vb **piled; pil·ing** : heap up, accumulate

³pile n : surface of fine hairs or threads —**piled** adj

piles \'pīls\ n pl : hemorrhoids

pil·fer \'pilfər\ vb : steal in small quantities

pil·grim \'pilgrəm\ n 1 : one who travels to a shrine or holy place in devotion 2 cap : one of the English settlers in America in 1620

pil·grim·age \-grəmij\ n : pilgrim's journey

pill \'pil\ n : small rounded mass of medicine —**pill·box** n

pil·lage \'pilij\ vb **-laged; -lag·ing** : loot and plunder —**pillage** n

pil·lar \'pilər\ n : upright usu. supporting column —**pil·lared** adj

pil·lo·ry \'pilərē\ n, pl **-ries** : wooden frame for public punishment with holes for the head and hands ~ vb **-ried; -ry·ing** 1 : set in a pillory 2 : expose to public scorn

pil·low \'pilō\ n : soft cushion for the head —**pil·low·case** n

pi·lot \'pīlət\ n 1 : helmsman 2 : person licensed to take ships into and out of a port 3 : guide 4 : one that flies an aircraft or spacecraft ~ vb : act as pilot of —**pi·lot·less** adj

pi·men·to \pə'mentō\ n, pl **-tos** or **-to** 1 : allspice 2 : pimiento

pi·mien·to \pə'mentō, -'myen-\ n, pl **-tos** : mild red sweet pepper

pimp \'pimp\ n : man who solicits clients for a prostitute —**pimp** vb

pim·ple \'pimpəl\ n : small inflamed swelling on the skin —**pim·ply** \-pəlē\ adj

pin \'pin\ n 1 : fastener made of a small pointed piece of wire 2 : ornament or emblem fastened to clothing with a pin 3 : wooden object used as a target in bowling ~ vb **-nn-** 1 : fasten with a pin 2 : hold fast or immobile —**pin·hole** n

pin·a·fore \'pinəˌfōr\ n : sleeveless dress or apron fastened at the back

pin·cer \'pinsər\ n 1 pl : gripping tool with 2 jaws 2 : pincerlike claw

pinch \'pinch\ vb 1 : squeeze between the finger and thumb or between the jaws of a tool 2 : compress painfully 3 : restrict 4 : steal ~ n 1 : emergency 2 : painful effect 3 : act of pinching 4 : very small quantity

pin·cush·ion n : cushion for storing pins

¹pine \'pīn\ n : evergreen cone-bearing tree or its wood

²pine vb **pined; pin·ing** 1 : lose health through distress 2 : yearn for intensely

pine·ap·ple n : tropical plant bearing an edible juicy fruit

pin·feath·er n : new feather just coming through the skin

¹pin·ion \'pinyən\ vb : restrain by binding the arms

²pinion n : small gear

¹pink \'piŋk\ n 1 : plant with narrow leaves and showy flowers 2 : highest degree

²pink n : light red color —**pink** adj —**pink·ish** adj

pink·eye n : contagious eye inflammation

pin·na·cle \'pinəkəl\ n : highest point

pi·noch·le \'pēˌnəkəl\ n : card game played with a 48-card deck

pin·point vb : locate, hit, or aim with great precision

pint \'pīnt\ n : 1/2 quart

pin·to \'pinˌtō\ n, pl **pintos** : spotted horse or pony

pin·worm n : small parasitic intestinal worm

pi·o·neer \ˌpīə'nir\ n 1 : one that originates or helps open up a new line of thought or activity 2 : early settler ~ vb : act as a pioneer

pi·ous \'pīəs\ adj 1 : conscientious in religious practices 2 : affectedly religious —**pi·ous·ly** adv

pipe \'pīp\ n 1 : tube that produces music when air is forced through 2 : bagpipe 3 : long tube for conducting a fluid 4 : smoking tool ~ vb **piped; pip·ing** 1 : play on a pipe 2 : speak in a high voice 3 : convey by pipes —**pip·er** n

pipe·line n 1 : line of pipe 2 : channel for information

pip·ing \'pīpiŋ\ n 1 : music of pipes 2 : narrow fold of material used to decorate edges or seams

pi·quant \'pēkənt\ adj 1 : tangy 2 : provocative or charming —**pi·quan·cy** \-kənsē\ n

pique \'pēk\ n : resentment ~ vb **piqued; piqu·ing** 1 : offend 2 : arouse by provocation

pi·qué, pi·que \pi'kā\ n : durable ribbed clothing fabric

pi·ra·cy \'pīrəsē\ n, pl **-cies** 1 : robbery on the seas 2 : unauthorized use of another's production or invention

pi·ra·nha \pə'ranyə, -'ränə\ n : small So. American fish with sharp teeth

pi·rate \'pīrət\ n : one who commits piracy —**pirate** vb —**pi·rat·i·cal** \pə'ratikəl, pī-\ adj

pir·ou·ette \ˌpirə'wet\ n : ballet turn on the toe or ball of one foot —**pirouette** vb

pis pl of PI

pis·ta·chio \pə'stashēˌō, -'stäsh-\ n, pl **-chios** : small tree bearing a greenish edible seed or its seed

pis·til \'pistᵊl\ n : female reproductive organ in a flower —**pis·til·late** \'pistəˌlāt\ adj

pis·tol \'pistᵊl\ n : firearm held with one hand

pis·ton \'pistən\ n 1 : sliding piece that receives and transmits motion usu. inside a cylinder

¹pit \'pit\ n 1 : hole or shaft in the ground 2 : sunken or enclosed place for a special purpose 3 : hell 4 : hollow or indentation ~ vb **-tt-** 1 : form pits in 2 : become marred with pits

²pit n : stony seed of some fruits ~ vb **-tt-** : remove the pit from

pit bull n : powerful compact dog bred for fighting

¹pitch \'pich\ n : resin from conifers —**pitchy** adj

²pitch vb 1 : erect and fix firmly in place 2 : throw 3 : set at a particular tone level 4 : fall headlong ~ n 1 : action or manner of pitching 2 : degree of slope 3 : relative highness of a tone 4 : sales talk —**pitched** adj

¹pitch·er \'pichər\ n : container for liquids

²pitcher n : one that pitches (as in baseball)

pitch·fork n : long-handled fork for pitching hay

pit·e·ous \'pitēəs\ adj : arousing pity —**pit·e·ous·ly** adv

pit·fall \'pit,fȯl\ n 1 : hidden danger

pith \'pith\ n 1 : spongy plant tissue 2 : essential or meaningful part —**pithy** adj

piti·able \'pitēəbəl\ adj : pitiful

piti·ful \'pitifəl\ adj 1 : arousing or deserving pity 2 : contemptible —**piti·ful·ly** adv

pit·tance \'pitᵊns\ n : small portion or amount

pi·tu·itary \pə'tüəˌterē, -'tyü-\ adj : relating to or being a small gland attached to the brain

pity \'pitē\ n, pl **pit·ies** 1 : sympathetic sorrow 2 : something to be regretted ~ vb **pit·ied; pity·ing** : feel pity for —**piti·less** adj —**piti·less·ly** adv

piv·ot \'pivət\ n : fixed pin on which something turns ~ vb : turn on or as if on a pivot —**piv·ot·al** adj

pix·ie, pixy \'piksē\ n, pl **pix·ies** : mischievous sprite

piz·za \'pētsə\ n : thin pie of bread dough spread with a spiced mixture (as of tomatoes, cheese, and meat)

piz·zazz, pi·zazz \pə'zaz\ n : glamour

piz·ze·ria \ˌpētsə'rēə\ n : pizza restaurant

plac·ard \'plakərd, -ˌärd\ n : poster ~ vb : display placards in or on

pla·cate \'plāˌkāt, 'plak,āt\ vb **-cat·ed; -cat·ing** : appease —**pla·ca·ble** \'plakəbəl, 'plākə-\ adj

place \'plās\ n 1 : space or room 2 : indefinite area 3 : a particular building, locality, area, or part 4 : relative position in a scale or sequence 5 : seat 6 : job ~ vb **placed; plac·ing** 1 : put in a place 2 : identify —**place·ment** n

pla·ce·bo \plə'sēbō\ n, pl **-bos** : something inactive prescribed as a remedy for its psychological effect

pla·cen·ta \plə'sentə\ n, pl **-tas** or **-tae** \-ˌē\ : structure in a uterus by which a fetus is nourished —**pla·cen·tal** \-'sentᵊl\ adj

plac·id \'plasəd\ adj : undisturbed or peaceful —**pla·cid·i·ty** \pla'sidətē\ n —**plac·id·ly** adv

pla·gia·rize \'plājəˌrīz\ vb **-rized; -riz·ing** : use (words or ideas) of another as if your own —**pla·gia·rism** \-ˌrizəm\ n —**pla·gia·rist** \-rist\ n

plague \'plāg\ n 1 : disastrous evil 2 : destructive contagious bacterial disease ~ vb **plagued; plagu·ing** 1 : afflict with disease or disaster 2 : harass

plaid \'plad\ n : woolen fabric with a pattern of crossing stripes or the pattern itself —**plaid** adj

plain \'plān\ n : expanse of relatively level treeless country ~ adj 1 : lacking ornament 2 : not concealed or disguised 3 : easily understood 4 : frank 5 : not fancy or pretty —**plain·ly** adv —**plain·ness** \'plānnəs\ n

plain·tiff \'plāntəf\ n : complaining party in a lawsuit

plain·tive \'plāntiv\ adj : expressive of suffering or woe —**plain·tive·ly** adv

plait \'plāt, 'plat\ n 1 : pleat 2 : braid of hair or straw —**plait** vb

plan \'plan\ n 1 : drawing or diagram 2 : method for accomplishing something ~ vb **-nn-** 1 : form a plan of 2 : intend —**plan·less** adj —**plan·ner** n

¹plane \'plān\ vb **planed; plan·ing** : smooth or level off with a plane ~ n : smoothing or shaping tool —**plan·er** n

²plane n 1 : level surface 2 : level of existence, consciousness, or development 3 : airplane ~ adj 1 : flat 2 : dealing with flat surfaces or figures

plan·et \'planət\ n : celestial body that revolves around the sun —**plan·e·tary** \-əˌterē\ adj

plan·e·tar·i·um \ˌplanə'terēəm\ n, pl **-iums** or **-ia** \-ēə\ : building or room housing a device to project images of celestial bodies

plank \'plaŋk\ n 1 : heavy thick board 2 : article in the platform of a political party —**plank·ing** n

plank·ton \'plaŋktən\ n : tiny aquatic animal and plant life —**plank·ton·ic** \plaŋk'tänik\ adj

plant \'plant\ vb 1 : set in the ground to grow 2 : place firmly or forcibly ~ n 1 : living thing without sense organs that cannot move about 2 : land, buildings, and machinery used esp. in manufacture

¹plan·tain \'plantᵊn\ n : short-stemmed herb with tiny greenish flowers

²plantain n : banana plant with starchy greenish fruit

plan·ta·tion \plan'tāshən\ n : agricultural estate usu. worked by resident laborers

plant·er \'plantər\ n 1 : plantation owner 2 : plant container

plaque \'plak\ n 1 : commemorative tablet 2 : film layer on a tooth

plas·ma \'plazmə\ n : watery part of blood —**plas·mat·ic** \plaz'matik\ adj

plas·ter \'plastər\ n 1 : medicated dressing 2 : hardening paste for coating walls and ceilings ~ vb : cover with plaster —**plas·ter·er** n

plas·tic \'plastik\ adj : capable of being molded ~ n : material that can be formed into rigid objects, films, or filaments —**plas·tic·i·ty** \plas'tisətē\ n

plate \'plāt\ n 1 : flat thin piece 2 : plated metalware 3 : shallow usu. circular dish 4 : denture or the part of it that fits to the mouth 5 : something printed from an engraving ~ vb **plat·ed; plat·ing** : overlay with metal —**plat·ing** n

pla·teau \pla'tō\ n, pl **-teaus** or **-teaux** \-'tōz\ : large level area of high land

plat·form \'plat,förm\ n 1 : raised flooring or stage 2 : declaration of principles for a political party

plat·i·num \'platᵊnəm\ n : heavy grayish-white metallic chemical element

plat·i·tude \'platəˌtüd, -ˌtyüd\ n : trite remark —**plat·i·tu·di·nous** \ˌplatə'tüdᵊnəs, -'tyüd-\ adj

pla·toon \plə'tün\ n : small military unit

platoon sergeant n : noncommissioned officer in the army ranking below a first sergeant

plat·ter \'platər\ n : large serving plate

platy·pus \'platipəs\ n : small aquatic egg-laying mammal

plau·dit \'plȯdət\ n : act of applause

plau·si·ble \'plȯzəbəl\ adj : reasonable or believeable —**plau·si·bil·i·ty** \ˌplȯzə'bilətē\ n —**plau·si·bly** \-blē\ adv

play \'plā\ n 1 : action in a game 2 : recreational activity 3 : light or fitful movement 4 : free movement 5 : stage representation of a drama ~ vb 1 : engage in recreation 2 : move or toy with aimlessly 3 : perform music 4 : act in a drama —**play·act·ing** n —**play·er** n —**play·ful** \-fəl\ adj —**play·ful·ly** adv —**play·ful-**

ness *n* —**play•pen** *n* — **play•suit** *n* — **play•thing** *n*

play•ground *n* : place for children to play

play•house *n* **1** : theater **2** : small house for children to play in

playing card *n* : one of a set of 24 to 78 cards marked to show its rank and suit and used to play a game of cards

play•mate *n* : companion in play

play–off *n* : contest or series of contests to determine a champion

play•wright \-,rīt\ *n* : writer of plays

pla•za \'plazə, 'pläz-\ *n* **1** : public square **2** : shopping mall

plea \'plē\ *n* **1** : defendant's answer to charges **2** : urgent request

plead \'plēd\ *vb* **plead•ed** \'plēdəd\ *or* **pled** \'pled\; **plead•ing 1** : argue for or against in court **2** : answer to a charge or indictment **3** : appeal earnestly —**plead•er** *n*

pleas•ant \'plez°nt\ *adj* **1** : giving pleasure **2** : marked by pleasing behavior or appearance —**pleas•ant•ly** *adv* —**pleas•ant•ness** *n*

pleas•ant•ries \-°ntrēz\ *n pl* : pleasant and casual conversation

please \'plēz\ *vb* **pleased; pleas•ing 1** : give pleasure or satisfaction to **2** : desire or intend

pleas•ing \'plēziŋ\ *adj* : giving pleasure —**pleas•ing•ly** *adv*

plea•sur•able \'plezhərəbəl\ *adj* : pleasant —**plea•sur•ably** \-blē\ *adv*

plea•sure \'plezhər\ *n* **1** : desire or inclination **2** : enjoyment **3** : source of delight

pleat \'plēt\ *vb* : arrange in pleats ~ *n* : fold in cloth

ple•be•ian \pli'bēən\ *n* : one of the common people ~ *adj* : ordinary

pledge \'plej\ *n* **1** : something given as security **2** : promise or vow ~ *vb* **pledged; pledg•ing 1** : offer as or bind by a pledge **2** : promise

ple•na•ry \'plēnərē, 'plen-\ *adj* : full

pleni•po•ten•tia•ry \,plenəpə'tenchərē, -'tenchē,erē\ *n* : diplomatic agent having full authority —**plenipotentiary** *adj*

plen•i•tude \'plenə,tüd, -,tyüd\ *n* **1** : completeness **2** : abundance

plen•te•ous \'plentēəs\ *adj* : existing in plenty

plen•ty \'plentē\ *n* : more than adequate number or amount —**plen•ti•ful** \'plentifəl\ *adj* —**plen•ti•ful•ly** *adv*

pleth•o•ra \'plethərə\ *n* : excess

pleu•ri•sy \'plurəsē\ *n* : inflammation of the chest membrane

pli•able \'plīəbəl\ *adj* : flexible

pli•ant \'plīənt\ *adj* : flexible —**pli•an•cy** \-ənsē\ *n*

pli•ers \'plīərz\ *n pl* : pinching or gripping tool

1plight \'plīt\ *vb* : pledge

2plight *n* : bad state

plod \'pläd\ *vb* **-dd- 1** : walk heavily or slowly **2** : work laboriously and monotonously —**plod•der** *n* —**plod•ding•ly** \-iŋlē\ *adv*

plot \'plät\ *n* **1** : small area of ground **2** : ground plan **3** : main story development (as of a book or movie) **4** : secret plan for doing something ~ *vb* **-tt- 1** : make a plot or plan of **2** : plan or contrive —**plot•ter** *n*

plo•ver \'pləvər, 'plōvər\ *n, pl* **-ver** *or* **-vers** : shorebird related to the sandpiper

plow, plough \'plau\ *n* **1** : tool used to turn soil **2** : device for pushing material aside ~ *vb* **1** : break up with a plow **2** : cleave or move through like a plow —**plow•man** \-mən, -,man\ *n*

plow•share \-,sher\ *n* : plow part that cuts the earth

ploy \'ploi\ *n* : clever maneuver

pluck \'plək\ *vb* **1** : pull off or out **2** : tug or twitch ~ *n* **1** : act or instance of plucking **2** : spirit or courage

plucky \'pləkē\ *adj* **pluck•i•er; -est** : courageous or spirited

plug \'pləg\ *n* **1** : something for sealing an opening **2** : electrical connector at the end of a cord **3** : piece of favorable publicity ~ *vb* **-gg- 1** : stop or make tight or secure by inserting a plug **2** : publicize

plum \'pləm\ *n* **1** : smooth-skinned juicy fruit **2** : fine reward

plum•age \'plümij\ *n* : feathers of a bird —**plum•aged** \-mijd\ *adj*

plumb \'pləm\ *n* : weight on the end of a line (**plumb line**) to show vertical direction ~ *adv* **1** : vertically **2** : completely ~ *vb* : sound or test with a plumb ~ *adj* : vertical

plumb•er \'pləmər\ *n* : one who repairs usu. water pipes and fixtures

plumb•ing \'pləmiŋ\ *n* : system of water pipes in a building

plume \'plüm\ *n* : large, conspicuous, or showy feather ~ *vb* **plumed; plum•ing 1** : provide or deck with feathers **2** : indulge in pride —**plumed** \'plümd\ *adj*

plum•met \'pləmət\ *vb* : drop straight down

1plump \'pləmp\ *vb* : drop suddenly or heavily ~ *adv* **1** : straight down **2** : in a direct manner

2plump *adj* : having a full rounded form —**plump•ness** *n*

plun•der \'pləndər\ *vb* : rob or take goods by force (as in war) ~ *n* : something taken in plundering —**plun•der•er** *n*

plunge \'plənj\ *vb* **plunged; plung•ing 1** : thrust or drive with force **2** : leap or dive into water **3** : begin an action suddenly **4** : dip or move suddenly forward or down ~ *n* : act or instance of plunging —**plung•er** *n*

plu•ral \'plúrəl\ *adj* : relating to a word form denoting more than one —**plural** *n*

plu•ral•i•ty \plu'ralətē\ *n, pl* **-ties** : greatest number of votes cast when not a majority

plu•ral•ize \'plúrə,līz\ *vb* **-ized; -iz•ing** : make plural —**plu•ral•i•za•tion** \,plúrələ'zāshən\ *n*

plus \'pləs\ *prep* : with the addition of ~ *n* **1** : sign + (**plus sign**) in mathematics to indicate addition **2** : added or positive quantity ~ *adj* : being more or in addition ~ *conj* : and

plush \'pləsh\ *n* : fabric with a long pile ~ *adj* : luxurious —**plush•ly** *adv* —**plushy** *adj* —**plush•ness** *n*

plu•toc•ra•cy \plü'täkrəsē\ *n, pl* **-cies 1** : government by the wealthy **2** : a controlling class of the wealthy —**plu•to•crat** \'plütə,krat\ *n* —**plu•to•crat•ic** \,plütə'kratik\ *adj*

plu•to•ni•um \plü'tōnēəm\ *n* : radioactive chemical element

1ply \'plī\ *n, pl* **plies** : fold, thickness, or strand of which something is made

2ply *vb* **plied; ply•ing 1** : use or work at **2** : keep supplying something to **3** : travel regularly usu. by sea

ply•wood *n* : sheets of wood glued and pressed together

pneu•mat•ic \nu'matik, nyü-\ *adj* **1** : moved by air pressure **2** : filled with compressed air —**pneu•mat•i•cal•ly** *adv*

pneu•mo•nia \nu'mōnyə, nyü-\ *n* : inflammatory lung disease

1poach \'pōch\ *vb* : cook in simmering liquid

2poach *vb* : hunt or fish illegally —**poach•er** *n*

pock \'päk\ *n* : small swelling on the skin or its scar —**pock•mark** *n* —**pock•marked** *adj*

pock•et \'päkət\ *n* **1** : small open bag sewn into a garment **2** : container or receptacle **3** : isolated area or group ~ *vb* : put in a pocket —**pock•et•ful** \-,fúl\ *n*

pock•et•book *n* **1** : purse **2** : financial resources

pock•et•knife *n* : knife with a folding blade carried in the pocket

pod \'päd\ *n* **1** : dry fruit that splits open when ripe **2** : compartment on a ship or craft

po•di•a•try \pə'dīətrē, pō-\ *n* : branch of medicine dealing with the foot —**po•di•a•trist** \pə'dīətrist, pō-\ *n*

po•di•um \'pōdēəm\ *n, pl* **-di•ums** *or* **-dia** \-ēə\ : dais

po•em \'pōəm\ *n* : composition in verse

po•et \'pōət\ *n* : writer of poetry

po•et•ry \'pōətrē\ *n* **1** : metrical writing **2** : poems —**po•et•ic** \pō'etik\, **po•et•i•cal** \-ikəl\ *adj*

po•grom \'pōgrəm, pə'gräm, 'pägrəm\ *n* : organized massacre

poi•gnant \'poinyənt\ *adj* **1** : emotionally painful **2** : deeply moving —**poi•gnan•cy** \-nyənsē\ *n*

poin•set•tia \poin'setēə, -'setə\ *n* : showy tropical American plant

point \'point\ *n* **1** : individual often essential detail **2** : purpose **3** : particular place, time, or stage **4** : sharp end **5** : projecting piece of land **6** : dot or period **7** : division of the compass **8** : unit of counting ~ *vb* **1** : sharpen **2** : indicate direction by extending a finger **3** : direct attention to **4** : aim —**point•ed•ly** \-ədlē\ *adv* —**point•less** *adj*

point–blank *adj* **1** : so close to a target that a missile fired goes straight to it **2** : direct —**point–blank** *adv*

point•er \'pointər\ *n* **1** : one that points out **2** : large short-haired hunting dog **3** : hint or tip

poise \'poiz\ *vb* **poised; pois•ing** : balance ~ *n* : self-possessed calmness

poi•son \'poiz°n\ *n* : chemical that can injure or kill ~ *vb* **1** : injure or kill with poison **2** : apply poison to **3** : affect destructively —**poi•son•er** *n* —**poi•son•ous** \'poiz°nəs\ *adj*

poke \'pōk\ *vb* **poked; pok•ing 1** : prod **2** : dawdle ~ *n* : quick thrust

1pok•er \'pōkər\ *n* : rod for stirring a fire

2po•ker *n* : card game for gambling

po•lar \'pōlər\ *adj* : relating to a geographic or magnetic pole

po•lar•ize \'pōlə,rīz\ *vb* **-ized; -iz•ing 1** : cause to have magnetic poles **2** : break

up into opposing groups —**po•lar•i•za•tion** \,pōlərə'zāshən\ *n*

1pole \'pōl\ *n* : long slender piece of wood or metal

2pole *n* **1** : either end of the earth's axis **2** : battery terminal **3** : either end of a magnet

pole•cat \'pōl,kat\ *n, pl* **polecats** *or* **polecat 1** : European carnivorous mammal **2** : skunk

po•lem•ics \pə'lemiks\ *n sing or pl* : practice of disputation —**po•lem•i•cal** \-ikəl\ *adj* —**po•lem•i•cist** \-əsist\ *n*

po•lice \pə'lēs\ *n, pl* **police 1** : department of government that keeps public order and enforces the laws **2** : members of the police ~ *vb* **-liced; -lic•ing** : regulate and keep in order —**po•lice•man** \-mən\ *n* —**po•lice•wom•an** *n*

police officer *n* : member of the police

pol•i•cy \'päləsē\ *n, pl* **-cies** : course of action selected to guide decisions

2policy *n, pl* **-cies** : insurance contract —**pol•i•cy•hold•er** *n*

po•lio \'pōlē,ō\ *n* : poliomyelitis —**polio** *adj*

po•lio•my•eli•tis \-,mīə'lītəs\ *n* : acute virus disease of the spinal cord

pol•ish \'pälish\ *vb* **1** : make smooth and glossy **2** : develop or refine ~ *n* **1** : shiny surface **2** : refinement

po•lite \pə'līt\ *adj* **-lit•er; -est** : marked by courteous social conduct —**po•lite•ly** *adv* —**po•lite•ness** *n*

pol•i•tic \'pälə,tik\ *adj* : shrewdly tactful

politically correct *adj* : seeking to avoid offending members of a different group

pol•i•tics \'pälə,tiks\ *n sing or pl* : practice of government and managing of public affairs —**po•lit•i•cal** \pə'litikəl\ *adj* —**po•lit•i•cal•ly** *adv* —**pol•i•ti•cian** \,pälə'tishən\ *n*

pol•ka \'pōlkə\ *n* : lively couple dance —**polka** *vb*

pol•ka dot \'pōkə,dät\ *n* : one of a series of regular dots in a pattern

poll \'pōl\ *n* **1** : head **2** : place where votes are cast—usu. pl. **3** : a sampling of opinion ~ *vb* **1** : cut off **2** : receive or record votes **3** : question in a poll —**poll•ster** \-stər\ *n*

pol•len \'pälən\ *n* : spores of a seed plant

pol•li•na•tion \,pälə'nāshən\ *n* : the carrying of pollen to fertilize the seed —**pol•li•nate** \'pälə,nāt\ *vb* —**pol•li•na•tor** \-ər\ *n*

pol•lute \pə'lüt\ *vb* **-lut•ed; -lut•ing** : contaminating with waste products —**pol•lut•ant** \-'lüt°nt\ *n* —**pol•lut•er** *n* —**pol•lu•tion** \-'lüshən\ *n*

pol•ly•wog, pol•li•wog \'pälē,wäg\ *n* : tadpole

po•lo \'pōlō\ *n* : game played by 2 teams on horseback using long-handled mallets to drive a wooden ball

pol•ter•geist \'pōltər,gīst\ *n* : mischievous ghost

pol•troon \päl'trün\ *n* : coward

poly•es•ter \'päle,estər\ *n* : synthetic fiber

po•lyg•a•my \pə'ligəmē\ *n* : marriage to several spouses at the same time —**po•lyg•a•mist** \-mist\ *n* —**po•lyg•a•mous** \-məs\ *adj*

poly•gon \'päli,gän\ *n* : closed plane figure with straight sides

poly•mer \'päləmər\ *n* : chemical compound of molecules joined in long strings —**po•lym•er•i•za•tion** \pə,limərə'zāshən\ *n* —**po•lym•er•ize** \pə'limə,rīz\ *vb*

poly•tech•nic \,päli'teknik\ *adj* : relating to many technical arts or applied sciences

poly•the•ism \'pälithē,izəm\ *n* : worship of many gods —**poly•the•ist** \-,thēist\ *adj or n*

poly•un•sat•u•rat•ed \,päle,ən'sacha,rātəd\ *adj* : having many double or triple bonds in a molecule

pome•gran•ate \'päm,granət, 'pämə-\ *n* : tropical reddish fruit with many seeds

pom•mel \'pəməl, 'päm-\ *n* **1** : knob on the hilt of a sword **2** : knob at the front of a saddle ~ \'pəməl\ *vb* **-meled** *or* **-melled; -mel•ing** *or* **-mel•ling** : pummel

pomp \'pämp\ *n* **1** : brilliant display **2** : ostentation

pomp•ous \'pämpəs\ *adj* : pretentiously dignified —**pom•pos•i•ty** \päm'päsətē\ *n* —**pomp•ous•ly** *adv*

pon•cho \'pänchō\ *n, pl* **-chos** : blanketlike cloak

pond \'pänd\ *n* : small body of water

pon•der \'pändər\ *vb* : consider

pon•der•ous \'pändərəs\ *adj* **1** : very heavy **2** : clumsy **3** : oppressively dull

pon•tiff \'päntəf\ *n* : pope —**pon•tif•i•cal** \pän'tifikəl\ *adj*

pon•tif•i•cate \pän'tifə,kāt\ *vb* **-cat•ed; -cat•ing** : talk pompously

pon•toon \pän'tün\ *n* : flat-bottomed boat or float

po•ny \'pōnē\ *n, pl* **-nies** : small horse

po•ny•tail \-,tāl\ *n* : hair arrangement like the tail of a pony

poo•dle \'püd°l\ *n* : dog with a curly coat

1pool \'pül\ *n* **1** : small body of water **2** : puddle

2pool *n* **1** : amount contributed by participants in a joint venture **2** : game of pocket billiards ~ *vb* : combine in a common fund

poor \'púr, 'pōr\ *adj* **1** : lacking material possessions **2** : less than adequate **3** : arousing pity **4** : unfavorable —**poor•ly** *adv*

1pop \'päp\ *vb* **-pp- 1** : move suddenly **2** : burst with or make a sharp sound **3** : protrude ~ *n* **1** : sharp explosive sound **2** : flavored soft drink

2pop *adj* : popular

pop•corn \'päp,kórn\ *n* : corn whose kernels burst open into a light mass when heated

pope \'pōp\ *n, often cap* : head of the Roman Catholic Church

pop•lar \'päplər\ *n* : slender quick-growing tree

pop•lin \'päplən\ *n* : strong plain-woven fabric with crosswise ribs

pop•over \'päp,ōvər\ *n* : hollow muffin made from egg-rich batter

pop•py \'päpē\ *n, pl* **-pies** : herb with showy flowers

pop•u•lace \'päpyələs\ *n* **1** : common people **2** : population

pop•u•lar \'päpyələr\ *adj* **1** : relating to the general public **2** : widely accepted **3** : commonly liked —**pop•u•lar•i•ty** \,päpyə'larətē\ *n* —**pop•u•lar•ize** \'päpyələ,rīz\ *vb* —**pop•u•lar•ly** \-lərlē\ *adv*

pop•u•late \'päpyə,lāt\ *vb* **-lat•ed; -lat•ing** : inhabit or occupy

pop•u•la•tion \,päpyə'lāshən\ *n* : people or number of people in an area

pop•u•list \'päpyəlist\ *n* : advocate of the rights of the common people —**pop•u•lism** \-,lizəm\ *n*

pop•u•lous \'päpyələs\ *adj* : densely populated —**pop•u•lous•ness** *n*

por•ce•lain \'pōrsələn\ *n* : fine-grained ceramic ware

porch \'pōrch\ *n* : covered entrance

por•cu•pine \'pōrkyə,pīn\ *n* : mammal with sharp quills

1pore \'pōr\ *vb* **pored; por•ing** : read attentively

2pore *n* : tiny hole (as in the skin) —**pored** *adj*

pork \'pōrk\ *n* : pig meat

pork barrel *n* : government projects benefiting political patrons

por•nog•ra•phy \pōr'nägrəfē\ *n* : depiction of erotic behavior intended to cause sexual excitement —**por•no•graph•ic** \,pōrnə'grafik\ *adj*

po•rous \'pōrəs\ *adj* : permeable to fluids —**po•ros•i•ty** \pə'räsətē\ *n*

por•poise \'pōrpəs\ *n* **1** : small whale with a blunt snout **2** : dolphin

por•ridge \'pōrij\ *n* : soft boiled cereal

por•rin•ger \'pōrənjər\ *n* : low one-handled metal bowl or cup

1port \'pōrt\ *n* **1** : harbor **2** : city with a harbor

2port *n* **1** : inlet or outlet (as in an engine) for a fluid **2** : porthole

3port *n* : left side of a ship or airplane looking forward —**port** *adj*

4port *n* : sweet wine

por•ta•ble \'pōrtəbəl\ *adj* : capable of being carried —**portable** *n*

por•tage \'pōrtij, pōr'täzh\ *n* : carrying of boats overland between navigable bodies of water or the route where this is done —**portage** *vb*

por•tal \'pōrt°l\ *n* : entrance

por•tend \pōr'tend\ *vb* : give a warning of beforehand

por•tent \'pōr,tent\ *n* : something that foreshadows a coming event —**por•ten•tous** \pōr'tentəs\ *adj*

por•ter \'pōrtər\ *n* : baggage carrier

por•ter•house \-,haús\ *n* : choice cut of steak

port•fo•lio \pōrt'fōlē,ō\ *n, pl* **-lios 1** : portable case for papers **2** : office or function of a diplomat **3** : investor's securities

port•hole \'pōrt,hōl\ *n* : window in the side of a ship or aircraft

por•ti•co \'pōrti,kō\ *n, pl* **-coes** *or* **-cos** : colonnade forming a porch

por•tion \'pōrshən\ *n* : part or share of a whole ~ *vb* : divide into or allot portions

port•ly \'pōrtlē\ *adj* **-li•er; -est** : somewhat stout

por•trait \'pōrtrət, -,trāt\ *n* : picture of a person —**por•trait•ist** \-ist\ *n* —**por•trai•ture** \'pōrtrə,chúr\ *n*

por•tray \pōr'trā\ *vb* **1** : make a picture of **2** : describe in words **3** : play the role of —**por•tray•al** *n*

por•tu•laca \,pōrchə'lakə\ *n* : tropical herb with showy flowers

pose \'pōz\ *vb* **posed; pos•ing 1** : assume a posture or attitude **2** : propose **3** : pretend to be what one is not ~ *n* **1** : sustained posture **2** : pretense —**pos•er** *n*

posh \'päsh\ *adj* : elegant

po•si•tion \pə'zishən\ *n* **1** : stand taken on a question **2** : place or location **3** : status **4** : job —**position** *vb*

pos·i·tive \'päzətiv\ *adj* **1** : definite **2** : confident **3** : relating to or being an adjective or adverb form that denotes no increase **4** : greater than zero **5** : having a deficiency of electrons **6** : affirmative — **pos·i·tive·ly** *adv* — **pos·i·tive·ness** *n*

pos·se \'päse\ *n* : emergency assistants of a sheriff

pos·sess \pə'zes\ *vb* **1** : have as property or as a quality **2** : control — **pos·ses·sion** \-'zeshən\ *n* — **pos·ses·sor** \-'zesər\ *n*

pos·ses·sive \pə'zesiv\ *adj* **1** : relating to a grammatical case denoting ownership **2** : jealous — **possessive** *n* — **pos·ses·sive·ness** *n*

pos·si·ble \'päsəbəl\ *adj* **1** : that can be done **2** : potential — **pos·si·bil·i·ty** \päsə'bilətē\ *n* — **pos·si·bly** *adv*

pos·sum \'päsəm\ *n* : opossum

1post \'pōst\ *n* : upright stake serving to support or mark ~ *vb* : put up or announce by a notice

2post \'pōst\ *vb* **1** : mail **2** : inform

3post *n* **1** : sentry's station **2** : assigned task **3** : army camp ~ *vb* : station

post- *prefix* : after or subsequent to

postadolescent	postinoculation
postattack	postmarital
postbaccalaureate	postmenopausal
postbiblical	postnatal
postcollege	postnuptial
postcolonial	postproduction
postelection	postpuberty
postexercise	postrecession
postflight	postretirement
postgame	postrevolutionary
postgraduate	postseason
postgraduation	postsecondary
postharvest	postsurgical
posthospital	posttreatment
postimperial	posttrial
postinaugural	postvaccination
postindustrial	postwar

post·age \'pōstij\ *n* : fee for mail

post·al \'pōstəl\ *adj* : relating to the mail

post·card *n* : card for mailing a message

post·date \'pōst'dāt\ *vb* : assign a date to that is later than the actual date of execution

post·er \'pōstər\ *n* : large usu. printed notice

pos·te·ri·or \pō'stirēər, pä-\ *adj* **1** : later **2** : situated behind ~ *n* : buttocks

pos·ter·i·ty \pä'sterətē\ *n* : all future generations

post·haste \'pōst'hāst\ *adv* : speedily

post·hu·mous \'päschəwəs\ *adj* : occurring after one's death — **post·hu·mous·ly** *adv*

post·man \'pōstmən, -,man\ *n* : mail carrier

post·mark *n* : official mark on mail — **post·mark** *vb*

post·mas·ter *n* : chief of a post office

post me·ri·di·em \'pōstmə'ridēəm, -ē,em\ *adj* : being after noon

post·mor·tem \'pōst'mōrtəm\ *adj* : occurring or done after death ~ *n* **1** : medical examination of a corpse **2** : analysis after an event

post office *n* : agency or building for mail service

post·op·er·a·tive \'pōst'äpərətiv, -'äpə,rāt-\ *adj* : following surgery

post·paid *adv* : with postage paid by the sender

post·par·tum \-'pärtəm\ *adj* : following childbirth — **postpartum** *adv*

post·pone \pōst'pōn\ *vb* **-poned; -pon·ing** : put off to a later time — **post·pone·ment** *n*

post·script \'pōst,skript\ *n* : added note

pos·tu·lant \'päschələnt\ *n* : candidate for a religious order

pos·tu·late \'päschə,lāt\ *vb* **-lat·ed; -lat·ing** : assume as true ~ *n* : assumption

pos·ture \'päschər\ *n* : bearing of the body ~ *vb* **-tured; -tur·ing** : strike a pose

po·sy \'pōzē\ *n, pl* **-sies** : flower or bunch of flowers

pot \'pät\ *n* : rounded container ~ *vb* **-tt-** : place in a pot — **pot·ful** *n*

po·ta·ble \'pōtəbəl\ *adj* : drinkable

pot·ash \'pät,ash\ *n* : white chemical salt of potassium used esp. in agriculture

po·tas·si·um \pə'tasēəm\ *n* : silver-white metallic chemical element

po·ta·to \pə'tātō\ *n, pl* **-toes** : edible plant tuber

pot·bel·ly *n* : paunch — **pot·bel·lied** *adj*

po·tent \'pōtənt\ *adj* : powerful or effective — **po·ten·cy** \-ənsē\ *n*

po·ten·tate \'pōtən,tāt\ *n* : powerful ruler

po·ten·tial \pə'tenchəl\ *adj* : capable of becoming actual ~ *n* **1** : something that can become actual **2** : degree of electrification with reference to a standard — **po·ten·ti·al·i·ty** \pə,tenchē'alətē\ *n* — **po·ten·tial·ly** *adv*

poth·er \'päthər\ *n* : fuss

pot·hole \'pät,hōl\ *n* : large hole in a road surface

po·tion \'pōshən\ *n* : liquid medicine or poison

pot·luck *n* : whatever food is available

pot·pour·ri \,pōpù'rē\ *n* **1** : mix of flowers, herbs, and spices used for scent **2** : miscellaneous collection

pot·shot *n* **1** : casual or easy shot **2** : random critical remark

pot·ter \'pätər\ *n* : pottery maker

pot·tery \'pätərē\ *n, pl* **-ter·ies** : objects (as dishes) made from clay

pouch \'paùch\ *n* **1** : small bag **2** : bodily sac

poul·tice \'pōltəs\ *n* : warm medicated dressing — **poultice** *vb*

poul·try \'pōltrē\ *n* : domesticated fowl

pounce \'paùns\ *vb* **pounced; pounc·ing** : spring or swoop upon and seize

1pound \'paùnd\ *n* **1** : unit of weight equal to 16 ounces **2** : monetary unit (as of the United Kingdom) — **pound·age** \-ij\ *n*

2pound *n* : shelter for stray animals

3pound *vb* **1** : crush by beating **2** : strike heavily **3** : drill **4** : move along heavily

pour \'pōr\ *vb* **1** : flow or supply esp. copiously **2** : rain hard

pout \'paùt\ *vb* : look sullen — **pout** *n*

pov·er·ty \'pävərtē\ *n* **1** : lack of money or possessions **2** : poor quality

pow·der \'paùdər\ *n* : dry material of fine particles ~ *vb* : sprinkle or cover with powder — **pow·dery** *adj*

pow·er \'paùər\ *n* **1** : position of authority **2** : ability to act **3** : one that has power **4** : physical might **5** : force or energy used to do work ~ *vb* : supply with power — **pow·er·ful** \-fəl\ *adj* — **pow·er·ful·ly** *adv* — **pow·er·less** *adj*

pow·er·house *n* : dynamic or energetic person

pow·wow \'paù,waù\ *n* : conference

pox \'päks\ *n, pl* **pox** *or* **pox·es** : disease marked by skin rash

prac·ti·ca·ble \'praktikəbəl\ *adj* : feasible — **prac·ti·ca·bil·i·ty** \,praktikə'bilətē\ *n*

prac·ti·cal \'praktikəl\ *adj* **1** : relating to practice **2** : virtual **3** : capable of being put to use **4** : inclined to action as opposed to speculation — **prac·ti·cal·i·ty** \,prakti'kalətē\ *n* — **prac·ti·cal·ly** \'praktiklē\ *adv*

prac·tice, prac·tise \'praktəs\ *vb* **-ticed** *or* **-tised; -tic·ing** *or* **-tis·ing** **1** : perform repeatedly to become proficient **2** : do or perform customarily **3** : be professionally engaged in ~ *n* **1** : actual performance **2** : habit **3** : exercise for proficiency **4** : exercise of a profession

prac·ti·tio·ner \prak'tishənər\ *n* : one who practices a profession

prag·ma·tism \'pragmə,tizəm\ *n* : practical approach to problems — **prag·mat·ic** \prag'matik\ *adj* — **prag·mat·i·cal·ly** *adv*

prai·rie \'prerē\ *n* : broad grassy rolling tract of land

praise \'prāz\ *vb* **praised; prais·ing** : express approval of **2** : glorify — **praise** *n* — **praise·wor·thy** *adj*

prance \'prans\ *vb* **pranced; pranc·ing** : spring from the hind legs **2** : swagger — **prance** *n* — **pranc·er** *n*

prank \'praŋk\ *n* : playful or mischievous act — **prank·ster** \-stər\ *n*

prate \'prāt\ *vb* **prat·ed; prat·ing** : talk long and foolishly

prat·fall \'prat,fol\ *n* : fall on the buttocks

prat·tle \'prat^ə l\ *vb* **-tled; -tling** : babble — **prattle** *n*

prawn \'prón\ *n* : shrimplike crustacean

pray \'prā\ *vb* **1** : entreat **2** : ask earnestly for something **3** : address God or a god

prayer \'prer\ *n* **1** : earnest request **2** : an addressing of God or a god **3** : words used in praying — **prayer·ful** *adj* — **prayer·ful·ly** *adv*

praying mantis *n* : mantis

pre- *prefix* : before, prior to, or in advance

preadmission	precut
preadolescence	predawn
preadolescent	predefine
preadult	predeparture
preanesthetic	predesignate
prearrange	predetermine
prearrangement	predischarge
preassembled	predrill
preassign	preelection
prebattle	preelectric
prebiblical	preemployment
prebreakfast	preestablish
precalculus	preexist
precancel	preexistence
precancellation	preexistent
preclear	prefight
preclearance	preform
precollege	pregame
precolonial	preheat
precombustion	preinaugural
precompute	preindustrial
preconceive	preinterview
preconception	prejudge
preconcert	prekindergarten
precondition	prelaunch
preconstructed	prelife
preconvention	premarital
precook	premenopausal
precool	premenstrual

premix	prerelease
premodern	preretirement
premodify	prerevolutionary
premoisten	prerinse
premold	presale
prenatal	preschool
prenotification	preseason
prenotify	preselect
prenuptial	preset
preopening	preshrink
preoperational	preshrunk
preoperative	presoak
preordain	presort
prepackage	prestamp
prepay	presterilize
preplan	prestrike
preprocess	presurgery
preproduction	presweeten
preprofessional	pretape
preprogram	pretelevision
prepubertal	pretournament
prepublication	pretreat
prepunch	pretreatment
prepurchase	pretrial
prerecorded	prewar
preregister	prewash
preregistration	prewrap
prerehearsal	

preach \'prēch\ *vb* **1** : deliver a sermon **2** : advocate earnestly — **preach·er** *n* — **preach·ment** *n*

pre·am·ble \'prē,ambəl\ *n* : introduction

pre·can·cer·ous \prē'kansərəs\ *adj* : likely to become cancerous

pre·car·i·ous \pri'karēəs\ *adj* : dangerously insecure — **pre·car·i·ous·ly** *adv* — **pre·car·i·ous·ness** *n*

pre·cau·tion \pri'kóshən\ *n* : care taken beforehand — **pre·cau·tion·ary** \-shə,nerē\ *adj*

pre·cede \pri'sēd\ *vb* **-ced·ed; -ced·ing** : be, go, or come ahead of — **pre·ce·dence** \'presədəns, pri'sēd^ə ns\ *n*

prec·e·dent \'presədənt\ *n* : something said or done earlier that serves as an example

pre·cept \'prē,sept\ *n* : rule of action or conduct

pre·cinct \'prē,siŋkt\ *n* **1** : district of a city **2** *pl* : vicinity

pre·cious \'preshəs\ *adj* **1** : of great value **2** : greatly cherished **3** : affected

prec·i·pice \'presəpəs\ *n* : steep cliff

pre·cip·i·tate \pri'sipə,tāt\ *vb* **-tat·ed; -tat·ing** **1** : cause to happen quickly or abruptly **2** : cause to separate out of a liquid **3** : fall as rain, snow, or hail ~ *n* : solid matter precipitated from a liquid ~ \-'sipətət, -ə,tāt\ *adj* : unduly hasty — **pre·cip·i·tate·ly** *adv* — **pre·cip·i·tate·ness** *n* — **pre·cip·i·tous** \pri'sipətəs\ *adj* — **pre·cip·i·tous·ly** *adv*

pre·cip·i·ta·tion \pri,sipə'tāshən\ *n* **1** : rash haste **2** : rain, snow, or hail

pré·cis \prā'sē\ *n, pl* **pré·cis** \-'sēz\ : concise summary of essentials

pre·cise \pri'sīs\ *adj* **1** : definite **2** : highly accurate — **pre·cise·ly** *adv* — **pre·cise·ness** *n*

pre·ci·sion \pri'sizhən\ *n* : quality or state of being precise

pre·clude \pri'klüd\ *vb* **-clud·ed; -clud·ing** : make impossible

pre·co·cious \pri'kōshəs\ *adj* : exceptionally advanced — **pre·co·cious·ly** *adv* — **pre·coc·i·ty** \pri'käsətē\ *n*

pre·cur·sor \pri'kərsər\ *n* : harbinger

pred·a·to·ry \'predə,tōrē\ *adj* : preying upon others — **pred·a·tor** \'predətər\ *n*

pre·de·ces·sor \'predə,sesər, 'prēd-\ *n* : a previous holder of a position

pre·des·tine \prē'destən\ *vb* : settle beforehand — **pre·des·ti·na·tion** \-,destə'nāshən\ *n*

pre·dic·a·ment \pri'dikəmənt\ *n* : difficult situation

pred·i·cate \'predikət\ *n* : part of a sentence that states something about the subject ~ \'predə,kāt\ *vb* **-cat·ed; -cat·ing** **1** : affirm **2** : establish — **pred·i·ca·tion** \,predə'kāshən\ *n*

pre·dict \pri'dikt\ *vb* : declare in advance — **pre·dict·abil·i·ty** \-,diktə'bilətē\ *n* — **pre·dict·able** \-'diktəbəl\ *adj* — **pre·dict·ably** \-blē\ *adv* — **pre·dic·tion** \-'dikshən\ *n*

pre·di·lec·tion \,pred^ə l'ekshən, ,prēd-\ *n* : established preference

pre·dis·pose \,prēdis'pōz\ *vb* : cause to be favorable or susceptible to something beforehand — **pre·dis·po·si·tion** \,prē,dis pə'zishən\ *n*

pre·dom·i·nate \pri'dämə,nāt\ *vb* : be superior — **pre·dom·i·nance** \-nəns\ *n* — **pre·dom·i·nant** \-nənt\ *adj* — **pre·dom·i·nant·ly** *adv*

pre·em·i·nent \prē'emənənt\ *adj* : having highest rank — **pre·em·i·nence** \-nəns\ *n* — **pre·em·i·nent·ly** *adv*

pre·empt \prē'empt\ *vb* **1** : seize for oneself **2** : take the place of — **pre·emp·tion** \-'empshən\ *n* — **pre·emp·tive** \-'emptiv\ *adj*

preen \'prēn\ *vb* : dress or smooth up (as feathers)

pre·fab·ri·cat·ed \'prē'fabrə,kātəd\ *adj* : manufactured for rapid assembly elsewhere — **pre·fab·ri·ca·tion** \,prē,fabri'kāshən\ *n*

pref·ace \'prefəs\ *n* : introductory comments ~ *vb* **-aced; -ac·ing** : introduce with a preface — **pref·a·to·ry** \'prefə,tōrē\ *adj*

pre·fect \'prē,fekt\ *n* : chief officer or judge — **pre·fec·ture** \-,fekchər\ *n*

pre·fer \pri'fər\ *vb* **-rr-** **1** : like better **2** : bring (as a charge) against a person — **pref·er·a·ble** \'prefərəbəl\ *adj* — **pref·er·a·bly** *adv* — **pref·er·ence** \-ərəns\ *n* — **pref·er·en·tial** \,prefə'renchəl\ *adj*

pre·fer·ment \pri'fərmənt\ *n* : promotion

pre·fig·ure \prē'figyər\ *vb* : foreshadow

1pre·fix \'prē,fiks, prē'fiks\ *vb* : place before

2pre·fix \'prē,fiks\ *n* : affix at the beginning of a word

preg·nant \'pregnənt\ *adj* **1** : containing unborn young **2** : meaningful — **preg·nan·cy** \-nənsē\ *n*

pre·hen·sile \prē'hensəl, -,sīl\ *adj* : adapted for grasping

pre·his·tor·ic \,prēhis'tórik\, **pre·his·tor·i·cal** \-ikəl\ *adj* : relating to the period before written history

prej·u·dice \'prejədəs\ *n* **1** : damage esp. to one's rights **2** : unreasonable attitude for or against something ~ *vb* **-diced; -dic·ing** **1** : damage **2** : cause to have prejudice — **prej·u·di·cial** \,prejə'dishəl\ *adj*

prel·ate \'prelət\ *n* : clergy member of high rank — **prel·a·cy** \-əsē\ *n*

pre·lim·i·nary \pri'limə,nerē\ *n, pl* **-nar·ies** : something that precedes or introduces — **preliminary** *adj*

pre·lude \'prel,üd, -,yüd; 'prā,lüd\ *n* : introductory performance, event, or musical piece

pre·ma·ture \,prēmə'tùər, -'tyùr, -'chùr\ *adj* : coming before the usual or proper time — **pre·ma·ture·ly** *adv*

pre·med·i·tate \pri'medə,tāt\ *vb* : plan beforehand — **pre·med·i·ta·tion** \-,medə'tāshən\ *n*

pre·mier \pri'mir, -'myir; 'prēmēər\ *adj* : first in rank or importance ~ *n* : prime minister — **pre·mier·ship** *n*

pre·miere \pri'myer, -'mir\ *n* : 1st performance ~ *vb* **-miered; -mier·ing** : give a 1st performance of

prem·ise \'preməs\ *n* **1** : statement made or implied as a basis of argument **2** *pl* : piece of land with the structures on it

pre·mi·um \'prēmēəm\ *n* **1** : bonus **2** : sum over the stated value **3** : sum paid for insurance **4** : high value

pre·mo·ni·tion \,prēmə'nishən, ,premə-\ *n* : feeling that something is about to happen — **pre·mon·i·to·ry** \pri'mänə,tōrē\ *adj*

pre·oc·cu·pied \prē'äkyə,pīd\ *adj* : lost in thought

pre·oc·cu·py \-,pī\ *vb* : occupy the attention of — **pre·oc·cu·pa·tion** \prē,äkyə'pā shən\ *n*

pre·pare \pri'par\ *vb* **-pared; -par·ing** **1** : make or get ready beforehand **2** : put together or compound — **prep·a·ra·tion** \,prepə'rāshən\ *n* — **pre·pa·ra·to·ry** \pri'parə,tōrē\ *adj* — **pre·pared·ness** \-'parədnəs\ *n*

pre·pon·der·ant \pri'pändərənt\ *adj* : having great weight, power, importance, or numbers — **pre·pon·der·ance** \-rəns\ *n* — **pre·pon·der·ant·ly** *adv*

prep·o·si·tion \,prepə'zishən\ *n* : word that combines with a noun or pronoun to form a phrase — **prep·o·si·tion·al** \-'zishənəl\ *adj*

pre·pos·sess·ing \,prēpə'zesiŋ\ *adj* : tending to create a favorable impression

pre·pos·ter·ous \pri'pästərəs\ *adj* : absurd

pre·req·ui·site \prē'rekwəzət\ *n* : something required beforehand — **prerequisite** *adj*

pre·rog·a·tive \pri'rägətiv\ *n* : special right or power

pre·sage \'presij, pri'sāj\ *vb* **-saged; -sag·ing** **1** : give a warning of **2** : predict — **pres·age** \'presij\ *n*

pres·by·ter \'prezbətər\ *n* : priest or minister

pre·science \'prēshəns, 'presh-\ *n* : foreknowledge of events — **pre·scient** \-ənt\ *adj*

pre·scribe \pri'skrīb\ *vb* **-scribed; -scrib·ing** **1** : lay down as a guide **2** : direct the use of as a remedy

pre·scrip·tion \pri'skripshən\ *n* : written direction for the preparation and use of a medicine or the medicine prescribed

pres·ence \'prez^ə ns\ *n* **1** : fact or condition of being present **2** : appearance or bearing

1pres·ent \'prez^ə nt\ *n* : gift

2pre·sent \pri'zent\ *vb* **1** : introduce **2** : bring before the public **3** : make a gift to or of **4** : bring before a court for inquiry — **pre·sent·able** *adj* — **pre·sen·ta·tion** \,prē,zen'tāshən, ,prez^ə n-\ *n* — **pre·sent·ment** \pri'zentmənt\ *n*

³pres•ent \'prezᵊnt\ adj : now existing, in progress, or attending ~ n : present time

pre•sen•ti•ment \pri'zentəmənt\ n : premonition

pres•ent•ly \'prezᵊntlē\ adv 1 : soon 2 : now

present participle n : participle that typically expresses present action

pre•serve \pri'zərv\ vb -served; -serv•ing 1 : keep safe from danger or spoilage 2 : maintain ~ n 1 : preserved fruit —often in pl. 2 : area for protection of natural resources —pres•er•va•tion \prezər'vā-shən\ n —pre•ser•va•tive \pri'zərvətiv\ adj or n —pre•serv•er \-'zərvər\ n

pre•side \pri'zīd\ vb -sid•ed; -sid•ing 1 : act as chairman 2 : exercise control

pres•i•dent \'prezədənt\ n 1 : one chosen to preside 2 : chief official (as of a company or nation) —pres•i•den•cy \-ənsē\ n —pres•i•den•tial \prezə'denchəl\ adj

press \'pres\ n 1 : crowded condition 2 : machine or device for exerting pressure and esp. for printing 3 : pressure 4 : printing or publishing establishment 5 : news media and esp. newspapers ~ vb 1 : lie against and exert pressure on 2 : smooth with an iron or squeeze with something heavy 3 : urge 4 : crowd 5 : force one's way —press•er n

press•ing adj : urgent

pres•sure \'preshər\ n 1 : burden of distress or urgent business 2 : direct application of force —pressure vb —pres•sur•i•za•tion \preshərə'zāshən\ n —pres•sur•ize \-,īz\ vb

pres•ti•dig•i•ta•tion \prestə,dijə'tāshən\ n : sleight of hand

pres•tige \pres'tēzh, -'tēj\ n : estimation in the eyes of people —pres•ti•gious \-'tijəs\ adj

pres•to \'prestō\ adv or adj : quickly

pre•sume \pri'züm\ vb -sumed; -sum•ing 1 : assume authority without right to do so 2 : take for granted —pre•sum•able \-'zümbəl\ adj —pre•sum•ably \-blē\ adv

pre•sump•tion \pri'zəmpshən\ n 1 : presumptuous attitude or conduct 2 : belief supported by probability —pre•sump•tive \-tiv\ adj

pre•sump•tu•ous \pri'zəmpchəwəs\ adj : too bold or forward —pre•sump•tu•ous•ly adv

pre•sup•pose \,prēsə'pōz\ vb : take for granted —pre•sup•po•si•tion \prē,səpə-'zishən\ n

pre•tend \pri'tend\ vb 1 : act as if something is real or true when it is not 2 : act in a way that is false 3 : lay claim —pre•tend•er n

pre•tense, pre•tence \'prē,tens, pri'tens\ n 1 : insincere effort 2 : deception —pre•ten•sion \pri'tenchən\ n

pre•ten•tious \pri'tenchəs\ adj : overly showy or self-important —pre•ten•tious•ly adv —pre•ten•tious•ness n

pre•ter•nat•u•ral \,prētər'nachərəl\ adj : exceeding what is natural 2 : inexplicable by ordinary means —pre•ter•nat•u•ral•ly adv

pre•text \'prē,tekst\ n : falsely stated purpose

pret•ty \'pritē, 'pùrt-\ adj -ti•er; -est : pleasing by delicacy or attractiveness ~ adv : in some degree ~ vb -tied; -ty•ing : make pretty —pret•ti•ly \'pritᵊlē\ adv —pret•ti•ness n

pret•zel \'pretsəl\ n : twisted thin bread that is glazed and salted

pre•vail \pri'vāl\ vb 1 : triumph 2 : urge successfully 3 : be frequent, widespread, or dominant

prev•a•lent \'prevələnt\ adj : widespread —prev•a•lence \-ləns\ n

pre•var•i•cate \pri'varə,kāt\ vb -cat•ed; -cat•ing : deviate from the truth —pre•var•i•ca•tion \-,varə'kāshən\ n —pre•var•i•ca•tor \-'varə,kātər\ n

pre•vent \pri'vent\ vb : keep from happening or acting —pre•vent•able adj —pre•ven•tion \-'venchən\ n —pre•ven•tive \-'ventiv\ adj or n —pre•ven•ta•tive \-'ventətiv\ adj or n

pre•view \'prē,vyü\ vb : view or show beforehand —preview n

pre•vi•ous \'prēvēəs\ adj : having gone, happened, or existed before —pre•vi•ous•ly adv

prey \'prā\ n, pl preys 1 : animal taken for food by another 2 : victim ~ vb 1 : seize and devour animals as prey 2 : have a harmful effect on

price \'prīs\ n : cost ~ vb priced; pric•ing : set a price on

price•less \-ləs\ adj : too precious to have a price

pric•ey \'prīsē\ adj pric•i•er; -est : expensive

prick \'prik\ n 1 : tear or small wound made by a point 2 : something sharp or pointed ~ vb : pierce slightly with a sharp point —prick•er n

prick•le \'prikəl\ n 1 : small sharp spine or

---

thorn 2 : slight stinging pain ~ vb -led; -ling : tingle —prick•ly \'priklē\ adj

pride \'prīd\ n : quality or state of being proud ~ vb prid•ed; prid•ing : indulge in pride —pride•ful adj

priest \'prēst\ n : person having authority to perform the sacred rites of a religion —priest•hood n —priest•li•ness \-lēnəs\ n —priest•ly adj

priest•ess \'prēstəs\ n : woman who is a priest

prig \'prig\ n : one who irritates by rigid or pointed observance of proprieties —prig•gish \-ish\ adj —prig•gish•ly adv

prim \'prim\ adj -mm- : stiffly formal and proper —prim•ly adv —prim•ness n

pri•mal \'prīməl\ adj 1 : original or primitive 2 : most important

pri•ma•ry \'prī,merē, 'prīmərē\ adj : first in order of time, rank, or importance ~ n, pl -ries : preliminary election —pri•mar•i•ly \prī'merəlē\ adv

primary school n : elementary school

pri•mate n 1 \'prī,māt, -mət\ : highest-ranking bishop 2 \-,māt\ : mammal of the group that includes humans and monkeys

prime \'prīm\ n : earliest or best part or period ~ adj : standing first (as in significance or quality) ~ vb primed; prim•ing 1 : fill or load 2 : lay a preparatory coating on

prime minister n : chief executive of a parliamentary government

¹prim•er \'primər\ n : small introductory book

²prim•er \'prīmər\ n 1 : device for igniting an explosive 2 : material for priming a surface

pri•me•val \prī'mēvəl\ adj : relating to the earliest ages

prim•i•tive \'primətiv\ adj 1 : relating to or characteristic of an early stage of development 2 : of or relating to a tribal people or culture ~ n : one that is primitive —prim•i•tive•ly adv —prim•i•tive•ness n

pri•mor•di•al \prī'mórdēəl\ adj : primeval

primp \'primp\ vb : dress or groom in a finicky manner

prim•rose \'prim,rōz\ n 1 : low herb with clusters of showy flowers

prince \'prins\ n 1 : ruler 2 : son of a king or queen —prince•ly adj

prin•cess \'prinsəs, -,ses\ n 1 : daughter of a king or queen 2 : wife of a prince

prin•ci•pal \'prinsəpəl\ adj : most important ~ n 1 : leading person 2 : head of a school 3 : sum lent at interest —prin•ci•pal•ly adv

prin•ci•pal•i•ty \,prinsə'palətē\ n, pl -ties : territory of a prince

prin•ci•ple \'prinsəpəl\ n 1 : general or fundamental law 2 : rule or code of conduct or devotion to such a code

print \'print\ n 1 : mark or impression made by pressure 2 : printed state or form 3 : printed matter 4 : copy made by printing 5 : cloth with a figure stamped on it ~ vb 1 : produce impressions of (as from type) 2 : write in letters like those of printer's type —print•able adj —print•er n

print•ing \'printiŋ\ n : art or business of a printer

print•out \'print,aùt\ n : printed output produced by a computer —print out vb

¹pri•or \'prīər\ n : head of a religious house —pri•o•ry \'prīərē\ n

²prior adj : coming before in time, order, or importance —pri•or•i•ty \prī'órətē\ n

pri•or•ess \'prīərəs\ n : nun who is head of a religious house

prism \'prizəm\ n : transparent 3-sided object that separates light into colors —pris•mat•ic \priz'matik\ adj

pris•on \'prizᵊn\ n : place where criminals are confined

pris•on•er \'prizᵊnər\ n : person on trial or in prison

pris•sy \'prisē\ adj -si•er; -est : overly prim —pris•si•ness n

pris•tine \'pris,tēn, pris'-\ adj : pure

pri•va•cy \'prīvəsē\ n, pl -cies : quality or state of being apart from others

pri•vate \'prīvət\ adj 1 : belonging to a particular individual or group 2 : carried on independently 3 : withdrawn from company or observation ~ n : enlisted person of the lowest rank in the marine corps or one of the two lowest ranks in the army —pri•vate•ly adv

pri•va•teer \,prīvə'tir\ n : private ship armed to attack enemy ships and commerce

private first class n : enlisted person ranking next below a corporal in the army and next below a lance corporal in the marine corps

pri•va•tion \prī'vāshən\ n : lack of what is needed for existence

priv•i•lege \'privəlij\ n : right granted as an advantage or favor —priv•i•leged adj

privy \'privē\ adj 1 : private or secret 2 : having access to private or secret information —n, pl priv•ies : outdoor toilet —priv•i•ly \'privəlē\ adv

---

¹prize \'prīz\ n 1 : something offered or striven for in competition or in contests of chance 2 : something very desirable —prize adj —prize•win•ner n —prize•win•ning adj

²prize vb prized; priz•ing : value highly

³prize vb prized; priz•ing : pry

prize•fight n : professional boxing match —prize•fight•er n —prize•fight•ing n

¹pro \'prō\ n 1 : favorable argument or person ~ adv 1 : in favor

²pro n or adj : professional

prob•a•ble \'präbəbəl\ adj : seeming true or real or to have a good chance of happening —prob•a•bil•i•ty \,präbə'bilətē\ n —prob•a•bly \'präbəblē\ adv

pro•bate \'prō,bāt\ n : judicial determination of the validity of a will ~ vb -bat•ed; -bat•ing : establish by probate

pro•ba•tion \prō'bāshən\ n 1 : period of testing and trial 2 : freedom for a convict during good behavior under supervision —pro•ba•tion•ary \-shə,nerē\ adj —pro•ba•tion•er n

probe \'prōb\ n 1 : slender instrument for examining a cavity 2 : investigation ~ vb probed; prob•ing 1 : examine with a probe 2 : investigate

pro•bi•ty \'prōbətē\ n : honest behavior

prob•lem \'präbləm\ n 1 : question to be solved 2 : source of perplexity or vexation —problem adj —prob•lem•at•ic \,präblə'matik\ adj —prob•lem•at•i•cal \-ikəl\ adj

pro•bos•cis \prə'bäsəs\ n, pl -cis•es also -ci•des \-ə,dēz\ : long flexible snout

pro•ce•dure \prə'sējər\ n 1 : way of doing something 2 : series of steps in regular order —pro•ce•dur•al \-'sējərəl\ adj

pro•ceed \prō'sēd\ vb 1 : come forth 2 : go on in an orderly way 3 : begin and carry on an action 4 : advance

pro•ceed•ing n 1 : procedure 2 pl : something said or done or its official record

pro•ceeds \'prō,sēdz\ n pl : total money taken in

pro•cess \'präs,es, 'prōs-\ n, pl -cess•es \-,esəz, -əsəz, -ə,sēz\ 1 : something going on 2 : natural phenomenon marked by gradual changes 3 : series of actions or operations directed toward a result 4 : summons 5 : projecting part ~ vb : subject to a process —pro•ces•sor \-ər\ n

pro•ces•sion \prə'seshən\ n : group moving along in an orderly way

pro•ces•sion•al \-'seshənəl\ n : music for a procession

pro•claim \prō'klām\ vb : announce publicly or with conviction —proc•la•ma•tion \,präklə'māshən\ n

pro•cliv•i•ty \prō'klivətē\ n, pl -ties : inclination

pro•cras•ti•nate \prə'krastə,nāt\ vb -nat•ed; -nat•ing : put something off until later —pro•cras•ti•na•tion \-,krastə'nāshən\ n —pro•cras•ti•na•tor \-'krastə,nātər\ n

pro•cre•ate \'prōkrē,āt\ vb -at•ed; -at•ing : produce offspring —pro•cre•ation \,prōkrē'āshən\ n —pro•cre•ative \'prō-krē,ātiv\ adj —pro•cre•ator \-,ātər\ n

proc•tor \'präktər\ n : supervisor of students (as at an examination) —proctor vb

pro•cure \prə'kyùr\ vb -cured; -cur•ing : get possession of —pro•cur•able \-'kyùrəbəl\ adj —pro•cure•ment n —pro•cur•er n

prod \'präd\ vb -dd- : push with or as if with a pointed instrument —prod n

prod•i•gal \'prädigəl\ adj : recklessly extravagant or wasteful —prodigal n —prod•i•gal•i•ty \,prädə'galətē\ n

pro•di•gious \prə'dijəs\ adj : extraordinary in size or degree —pro•di•gious•ly adv

prod•i•gy \'prädəjē\ n, pl -gies : extraordinary person or thing

pro•duce \prə'düs, -'dyüs\ vb -duced; -duc•ing 1 : present to view 2 : give birth to 3 : bring into existence ~ \'präd,üs, -prōd,-, -,yüs\ n 1 : product 2 : agricultural products —pro•duc•er \prə'düsər, -'dyü-\ n

prod•uct \'präd,əkt\ n 1 : number resulting from multiplication 2 : something produced

pro•duc•tion \prə'dəkshən\ n : act, process, or result of producing —pro•duc•tive \-'dəktiv\ adj —pro•duc•tive•ness n —pro•duc•tiv•i•ty \,prō,dək'tivətē, ,prä-\ n

pro•fane \prō'fān\ vb -faned; -fan•ing : treat with irreverence ~ adj 1 : not concerned with religion 2 : serving to debase what is holy —pro•fane•ly adv —pro•fane•ness n —pro•fan•i•ty \prō'fanətē\ n

pro•fess \prə'fes\ vb 1 : declare openly 2 : confess one's faith in —pro•fessed•ly \-ədlē\ adv

pro•fes•sion \prə'feshən\ n 1 : open declaration of belief 2 : occupation requiring specialized knowledge and academic training

pro•fes•sion•al \prə'feshənəl\ adj 1 : of, relating to, or engaged in a profession 2 : playing sport for pay —professional n

---

—pro•fes•sion•al•ism n —pro•fes•sion•al•ize vb —pro•fes•sion•al•ly adv

pro•fes•sor \prə'fesər\ n : university or college teacher —pro•fes•so•ri•al \,prōfə-'sōrēəl, ,präfə-\ adj —pro•fes•sor•ship n

prof•fer \'präfər\ vb -fered; -fer•ing : offer —proffer n

pro•fi•cient \prə'fishənt\ adj : very good at something —pro•fi•cien•cy \-ənsē\ n —proficient n —pro•fi•cient•ly adv

pro•file \'prō,fīl\ n : picture in outline —profile vb

prof•it \'präfət\ n 1 : valuable return 2 : excess of the selling price of goods over cost ~ vb : gain a profit —prof•it•able \'präfətəbəl\ adj —prof•it•ably adv —prof•it•less adj

prof•i•teer \,präfə'tir\ n : one who makes an unreasonable profit —profiteer vb

prof•li•gate \'präfligət, -lə,gāt\ adj 1 : shamelessly immoral 2 : wildly extravagant —prof•li•ga•cy \-gəsē\ n —profligate n —prof•li•gate•ly adv

pro•found \prə'faùnd\ adj 1 : marked by intellectual depth or insight 2 : deeply felt —pro•found•ly adv —pro•fun•di•ty \-'fəndətē\ n

pro•fuse \prə'fyüs\ adj : pouring forth liberally —pro•fuse•ly adv —pro•fu•sion \-'fyüzhən\ n

pro•gen•i•tor \prō'jenətər\ n : direct ancestor

prog•e•ny \'präjənē\ n, pl -nies : offspring

pro•ges•ter•one \prō'jestə,rōn\ n : female hormone

prog•no•sis \präg'nōsəs\ n, pl -no•ses \-,sēz\ : prospect of recovery from disease

prog•nos•ti•cate \präg'nästə,kāt\ vb -cat•ed; -cat•ing : predict from signs or symptoms —prog•nos•ti•ca•tion \-,nästə'kāshən\ n —prog•nos•ti•ca•tor \-'nästə,kātər\ n

pro•gram \'prō,gram, -grəm\ n 1 : outline of the order to be pursued or the subjects included (as in a performance) 2 : plan of procedure 3 : coded instructions for a computer ~ vb -grammed or -gramed; -gram•ming or -gram•ing 1 : enter in a program 2 : provide a computer with a program —pro•gram•ma•bil•i•ty \,prō,gramə'bilətē\ n —pro•gram•ma•ble \'prō,graməbəl\ adj —pro•gram•mer \'prō,gramər\ n

prog•ress \'prägrəs, -,res\ n : movement forward or to a better condition ~ \prə'gres\ vb 1 : move forward 2 : improve —pro•gres•sive \-'gresiv\ adj —pro•gres•sive•ly adv

pro•gres•sion \prə'greshən\ n 1 : act of progressing 2 : continuous connected series

pro•hib•it \prō'hibət\ vb : prevent by authority

pro•hi•bi•tion \,prōə'bishən\ n 1 : act of prohibiting 2 : legal restriction on sale or manufacture of alcoholic beverages —pro•hi•bi•tion•ist \-bishənist\ n —pro•hib•i•tive \prō'hibətiv\ adj —pro•hib•i•tive•ly adv —pro•hib•i•to•ry \-'hibə,tōrē\ adj

proj•ect \'präj,ekt, -ikt\ n : planned undertaking ~ \prə'jekt\ vb 1 : design or plan 2 : protrude 3 : throw forward —pro•jec•tion \-'jekshən\ n

pro•jec•tile \prə'jektᵊl\ n : missile hurled by external force

pro•jec•tor \-'jektər\ n : device for projecting pictures on a screen

pro•le•tar•i•an \,prōlə'terēən\ n : member of the proletariat —proletarian adj

pro•le•tar•i•at \-ēət\ n : laboring class

pro•lif•er•ate \prə'lifə,rāt\ vb -at•ed; -at•ing : grow or increase in number rapidly —pro•lif•er•a•tion \-,lifə'rāshən\ n

pro•lif•ic \prə'lifik\ adj : producing abundantly —pro•lif•i•cal•ly adv

pro•logue \'prō,lóg, -,läg\ n : preface

pro•long \prə'lóŋ\ vb : lengthen in time or extent —pro•lon•ga•tion \,prō,lóŋ'gā-shən\ n

prom \'präm\ n : formal school dance

prom•e•nade \,prämə'nād, -'näd\ n 1 : leisurely walk 2 : place for strolling —promenade vb

prom•i•nence \'prämənəns\ n 1 : quality, state, or fact of being readily noticeable or distinguished 2 : something that stands out —prom•i•nent \-nənt\ adj —prom•i•nent•ly adv

pro•mis•cu•ous \prə'miskyəwəs\ adj : having a number of sexual partners —prom•is•cu•i•ty \,prämis'kyüətē, ,prō-mis-\ n —pro•mis•cu•ous•ly adv —pro•mis•cu•ous•ness n

prom•ise \'präməs\ n 1 : statement that one will do or not do something 2 : basis for expectation —promise vb —prom•is•so•ry \-ə,sōrē\ adj

prom•is•ing adj : likely to succeed —prom•is•ing•ly adv

prom•on•to•ry \'prämən,tōrē\ n, pl -ries : point of land jutting into the sea

pro•mote \prə'mōt\ vb -mot•ed; -mot•ing 1 : advance in rank 2 : contribute to the growth, development, or prosperity of —

pro•mot•er *n* —**pro•motion** \-'mōshən\ *n*
—**pro•mo•tion•al** \-'mōshənəl\ *adj*

¹**prompt** \'prämpt\ *vb* **1** : incite **2** : give a cue to (an actor or singer) —**prompt•er** *n*

²**prompt** *adj* : ready and quick —**prompt•ly** *adv* —**prompt•ness** *n*

prone \'prōn\ *adj* **1** : having a tendency **2** : lying face downward —**prone•ness** \'prōnnəs\ *n*

prong \'prȯŋ\ *n* : sharp point of a fork —**pronged** \'prȯŋd\ *adj*

pro•noun \'prō,naün\ *n* : word used as a substitute for a noun

pro•nounce \prə'naüns\ *vb* —**nounced; -nounc•ing 1** : utter officially or as an opinion **2** : say or speak esp. correctly —**pro•nounce•able** *adj* —**pro•nounce•ment** *n* —**pro•nun•ci•a•tion** \-,nənsē'āshən\ *n*

pro•nounced \-'naünst\ *adj* : decided

¹**proof** \'prüf\ *n* **1** : evidence of a truth or fact **2** : trial impression or print

²**proof** *adj* : designed for or successful in resisting or repelling

proof•read *vb* : read and mark corrections in —**proof•read•er** *n*

prop \'präp\ *vb* **-pp- 1** : support **2** : sustain —**prop** *n*

pro•pa•gan•da \,präpə'gandə, ,prōpə-\ *n* : the spreading of ideas or information to further or damage a cause —**pro•pa•gan•dist** \-dist\ *n* —**pro•pa•gan•dize** \-,dīz\ *vb*

prop•a•gate \'präpə,gāt\ *vb* **-gat•ed; -gat•ing 1** : reproduce biologically **2** : cause to spread —**prop•a•ga•tion** \,präpə'gāshən\ *n*

pro•pane \'prō,pān\ *n* : heavy flammable gaseous fuel

pro•pel \prə'pel\ *vb* **-ll-** : drive forward —**pro•pel•lant, pro•pel•lent** *n or adj*

pro•pel•ler \prə'pelər\ *n* : hub with revolving blades that propels a craft

pro•pen•si•ty \prə'pensətē\ *n, pl* **-ties** : particular interest or inclination

prop•er \'präpər\ *adj* **1** : suitable or right **2** : limited to a specified thing **3** : correct **4** : strictly adhering to standards of social manners, dignity, or good taste —**prop•er•ly** *adv*

prop•er•ty \'präpərtē\ *n, pl* **-ties 1** : quality peculiar to an individual **2** : something owned **3** : piece of real estate **4** : ownership

proph•e•cy \'präfəsē\ *n, pl* **-cies** : prediction

proph•e•sy \-,sī\ *vb* **-sied; -sy•ing** : predict —**proph•e•si•er** \-,sīər\ *n*

proph•et \'präfət\ *n* : one who utters revelations or predicts events —**proph•et•ess** \-əs\ *n* —**pro•phet•ic** \prə'fetik\, **pro•phet•i•cal** \-ikəl\ *adj* —**pro•phet•i•cal•ly** *adv*

pro•pin•qui•ty \prə'piŋkwətē\ *n* : nearness

pro•pi•ti•ate \prō'pishē,āt\ *vb* **-at•ed; -at•ing** : gain or regain the favor of —**pro•pi•ti•a•tion** \-,pishē'āshən\ *n* —**pro•pi•tia•to•ry** \-'pishē,tōrē\ *adj*

pro•pi•tious \prə'pishəs\ *adj* : favorable

pro•po•nent \prə'pōnənt\ *n* : one who argues in favor of something

pro•por•tion \prə'pōrshən\ *n* **1** : relation of one part to another or to the whole with respect to magnitude, quantity, or degree **2** : symmetry **3** : share ~ *vb* : adjust in size in relation to others —**pro•por•tion•al** \-shənəl\ *adj* —**pro•por•tion•al•ly** *adv* —**pro•por•tion•ate** \-shənət\ *adj* —**pro•por•tion•ate•ly** *adv*

pro•pose \prə'pōz\ *vb* **-posed; -pos•ing 1** : plan or intend **2** : make an offer of marriage **3** : present for consideration —**pro•pos•al** \-'pōzəl\ *n*

prop•o•si•tion \,präpə'zishən\ *n* : something proposed ~ *vb* : suggest sexual intercourse to

pro•pound \prə'paünd\ *vb* : set forth for consideration

pro•pri•e•tor \prə'prīətər\ *n* : owner —**pro•pri•e•tary** \prə'prīə,terē\ *adj* —**pro•pri•e•tor•ship** *n* —**pro•pri•e•tress** \-'prīətrəs\ *n*

pro•pri•e•ty \prə'prīətē\ *n, pl* **-ties** : standard of acceptability in social conduct

pro•pul•sion \prə'pəlshən\ *n* **1** : action of propelling **2** : driving power —**pro•pul•sive** \-siv\ *adj*

pro•sa•ic \prō'zāik\ *adj* : dull

pro•scribe \prō'skrīb\ *vb* **-scribed; -scrib•ing** : prohibit —**pro•scrip•tion** \-'skripshən\ *n*

prose \'prōz\ *n* : ordinary language

pros•e•cute \'präsi,kyüt\ *vb* **-cut•ed; -cut•ing 1** : follow to the end **2** : seek legal punishment of —**pros•e•cu•tion** \,präsi'kyüshən\ *n* —**pros•e•cu•tor** \'präsi,kyütər\ *n*

pros•e•lyte \'präsə,līt\ *n* : new convert —**pros•e•ly•tize** \'präsələ,tīz\ *vb*

pros•pect \'präs,pekt\ *n* **1** : extensive view **2** : something awaited **3** : potential buyer ~ *vb* : look for mineral deposits —**pro•spec•tive** \prə'spektiv, 'präs,pek-\ *adj* —**pro•spec•tive•ly** *adv* —**pros•pec•tor** \-,pektər, -'pek-\ *n*

pro•spec•tus \prə'spektəs\ *n* : introductory description of an enterprise

pros•per \'präspər\ *vb* : thrive or succeed —**pros•per•ous** \-pərəs\ *adj*

pros•per•i•ty \präs'perətē\ *n* : economic well-being

pros•tate \'präs,tāt\ *n* : glandular body about the base of the male urethra —**prostate** *adj*

pros•the•sis \präs'thēsəs, 'prästhə-\ *n, pl* **-the•ses** \-,sēz\ : artificial replacement for a body part —**pros•thet•ic** \präs'thetik\ *adj*

pros•ti•tute \'prästə,tüt, -,tyüt\ *vb* **-tuted; -tut•ing 1** : offer sexual activity for money **2** : put to corrupt or unworthy purposes ~ *n* : one who engages in sexual activities for money —**pros•ti•tu•tion** \,prästə'tüshən, -'tyü-\ *n*

pros•trate \'präs,trāt\ *adj* : stretched out with face on the ground ~ *vb* **-trat•ed; -trat•ing 1** : fall or throw (oneself) into a prostrate position **2** : reduce to helplessness —**pros•tra•tion** \präs'trāshən\ *n*

pro•tag•o•nist \prō'tagənist\ *n* : main character in a drama or story

pro•tect \prə'tekt\ *vb* : shield from injury —**pro•tec•tor** \-tər\ *n*

pro•tec•tion \prə'tekshən\ *n* **1** : act of protecting **2** : one that protects —**pro•tec•tive** \-'tektiv\ *adj*

pro•tec•tor•ate \-tərət\ *n* : state dependent upon the authority of another state

pro•té•gé \'prōtə,zhā\ *n* : one under the care and protection of an influential person

pro•tein \'prō,tēn\ *n* : complex combination of amino acids present in living matter

pro•test \'prō,test\ *n* **1** : organized public demonstration of disapproval **2** : strong objection ~ \prə'test\ *vb* **1** : assert positively **2** : object strongly —**pro•tes•ta•tion** \,prätəs'tāshən\ *n* —**pro•test•er, pro•tes•tor** \'prō,testər\ *n*

Prot•es•tant \'prätəstənt\ *n* : Christian not of a Catholic or Orthodox church —**Prot•es•tant•ism** \'prätəstənt,izəm\ *n*

pro•to•col \'prōtə,kȯl\ *n* : diplomatic etiquette

pro•ton \'prō,tän\ *n* : positively charged atomic particle

pro•to•plasm \'prōtə,plazəm\ *n* : complex colloidal living substance of plant and animal cells —**pro•to•plas•mic** \,prōtə-'plazmik\ *adj*

pro•to•type \'prōtə,tīp\ *n* : original model

pro•to•zo•an \,prōtə'zōən\ *n* : single-celled lower invertebrate animal

pro•tract \prō'trakt\ *vb* : prolong

pro•trac•tor \-'traktər\ *n* : instrument for drawing and measuring angles

pro•trude \prō'trüd\ *vb* **-trud•ed; -trud•ing** : stick out or cause to stick out —**pro•tru•sion** \-'trüzhən\ *n*

pro•tu•ber•ance \prō'tübərəns, -'tyü-\ *n* : something that protrudes —**pro•tu•ber•ant** *adj*

proud \'praüd\ *adj* **1** : having or showing excessive self-esteem **2** : highly pleased **3** : having proper self-respect **4** : glorious —**proud•ly** *adv*

prove \'prüv\ *vb* **proved; proved** or **prov•en** \'prüvən\; **prov•ing 1** : test by experiment or by a standard **2** : establish the truth of by argument or evidence **3** : turn out esp. after trial or test —**prov•able** \'prüvəbəl\ *adj*

prov•en•der \'prävəndər\ *n* : dry food for domestic animals

prov•erb \'präv,ərb\ *n* : short meaningful popular saying —**pro•ver•bi•al** \prə-'vərbēəl\ *adj*

pro•vide \prə'vīd\ *vb* **-vid•ed; -vid•ing 1** : take measures beforehand **2** : make a stipulation **3** : supply what is needed —**pro•vid•er** *n*

pro•vid•ed *conj* : if

prov•i•dence \'prävədəns\ *n* **1** *often cap* : divine guidance **2** *cap* : God **3** : quality of being provident

prov•i•dent \-ədənt\ *adj* **1** : making provision for the future **2** : thrifty —**prov•i•dent•ly** *adv*

prov•i•den•tial \,prävə'denchəl\ *adj* **1** : relating to Providence **2** : opportune

pro•vid•ing *conj* : provided

prov•ince \'prävəns\ *n* **1** : administrative district **2** *pl* : all of a country outside the metropolis **3** : sphere

pro•vin•cial \prə'vinchəl\ *adj* **1** : relating to a province **2** : limited in outlook —**pro•vin•cial•ism** \-,izəm\ *n*

pro•vi•sion \prə'vizhən\ *n* **1** : act of providing **2** : stock of food —usu. in pl. **3** : stipulation ~ *vb* : supply with provisions

pro•vi•sion•al \-'vizhənəl\ *adj* : provided for a temporary need —**pro•vi•sion•al•ly** *adv*

pro•vi•so \prə'vīzō\ *n, pl* **-sos** or **-soes** : stipulation

pro•voke \prə'vōk\ *vb* **-voked; -vok•ing 1** : incite to anger **2** : stir up on purpose —**prov•o•ca•tion** \,prävə'kāshən\ *n* —**pro•voc•a•tive** \prə'väkətiv\ *adj*

prow \'praü\ *n* : bow of a ship

prow•ess \'praüəs\ *n* **1** : valor **2** : extraordinary ability

prowl \'praül\ *vb* : roam about stealthily —**prowl** *n* —**prowl•er** *n*

prox•i•mate \'präksəmət\ *adj* : very near

prox•im•i•ty \präk'simətē\ *n* : nearness

proxy \'präksē\ *n, pl* **prox•ies** : authority to act for another —**proxy** *adj*

prude \'prüd\ *n* : one who shows extreme modesty —**prud•ery** \'prüdərē\ *n* —**prud•ish** \'prüdish\ *adj*

pru•dent \'prüdᵊnt\ *adj* **1** : shrewd **2** : cautious **3** : thrifty —**pru•dence** \-ᵊns\ *n* —**pru•den•tial** \prü'denchəl\ *adj* —**pru•dent•ly** *adv*

¹**prune** \'prün\ *n* : dried plum

²**prune** *vb* **pruned; prun•ing** : cut off unwanted parts

pru•ri•ent \'prürēənt\ *adj* : lewd —**pru•ri•ence** \-ēəns\ *n*

¹**pry** \'prī\ *vb* **pried; pry•ing** : look closely or inquisitively

²**pry** *vb* **pried; pry•ing** : raise, move, or pull apart with a lever

psalm \'säm, 'sälm\ *n* : sacred song or poem —**psalm•ist** *n*

pseu•do•nym \'südᵊn,im\ *n* : fictitious name —**pseu•don•y•mous** \sü'dänəməs\ *adj*

pso•ri•a•sis \sə'rīəsəs\ *n* : chronic skin disease

psy•che \'sīkē\ *n* : soul or mind

psy•chi•a•try \sə'kīətrē, sī-\ *n* : branch of medicine dealing with mental, emotional, and behavioral disorders —**psy•chi•at•ric** \,sīkē'atrik\ *adj* —**psy•chi•a•trist** \sə'kīətrist, sī-\ *n*

psy•chic \'sīkik\ *adj* **1** : relating to the psyche **2** : sensitive to supernatural forces ~ *n* : person sensitive to supernatural forces —**psy•chi•cal•ly** *adv*

psy•cho•anal•y•sis \,sīkō'naləsəs\ *n* : study of the normally hidden content of the mind esp. to resolve conflicts —**psy•cho•an•a•lyst** \-'anᵊlist\ *n* —**psy•cho•an•a•lyt•ic** \-,anᵊl'itik\ *adj* —**psy•cho•an•a•lyze** \-'anᵊl,īz\ *vb*

psy•chol•o•gy \sī'käləjē\ *n, pl* **-gies 1** : science of mind and behavior **2** : mental and behavioral aspect (as of an individual) —**psy•cho•log•i•cal** \,sīkə'läjikəl\ *adj* —**psy•cho•log•i•cal•ly** *adv* —**psy•chol•o•gist** \sī'käləjist\ *n*

psy•cho•path \'sīkə,path\ *n* : mentally ill or unstable person —**psy•cho•path•ic** \,sīkə'pathik\ *adj*

psy•cho•sis \sī'kōsəs\ *n, pl* **-cho•ses** \-,sēz\ : mental derangement (as paranoia) —**psy•chot•ic** \-'kätik\ *adj or n*

psy•cho•so•mat•ic \,sīkəsə'matik\ *adj* : relating to bodily symptoms caused by mental or emotional disturbance

psy•cho•ther•a•py \,sīkō'therəpē\ *n* : treatment of mental disorder by psychological means —**psy•cho•ther•a•pist** \-pist\ *n*

pto•maine \'tō,mān\ *n* : bacterial decay product

pu•ber•ty \'pyübərtē\ *n* : time of sexual maturity

pu•bic \'pyübik\ *adj* : relating to the lower abdominal region

pub•lic \'pəblik\ *adj* **1** : relating to the people as a whole **2** : civic **3** : not private **4** : open to all **5** : well-known ~ *n* : people as a whole —**pub•lic•ly** *adv*

pub•li•ca•tion \,pəblə'kāshən\ *n* **1** : process of publishing **2** : published work

pub•lic•i•ty \,pə'blisətē\ *n* **1** : news information given out to gain public attention **2** : public attention

pub•li•cize \'pəblə,sīz\ *vb* **-cized; -ciz•ing** : bring to public attention —**pub•li•cist** \-sist\ *n*

pub•lish \'pəblish\ *vb* **1** : announce publicly **2** : reproduce for sale esp. by printing —**pub•lish•er** *n*

puck•er \'pəkər\ *vb* : pull together into folds or wrinkles ~ *n* : wrinkle

pud•ding \'pudiŋ\ *n* : creamy dessert

pud•dle \'pədᵊl\ *n* : very small pool of water

pudgy \'pəjē\ *adj* **pudg•i•er; -est** : short and plump

pu•er•ile \'pyürəl\ *adj* : childish

puff \'pəf\ *vb* **1** : blow in short gusts **2** : pant **3** : enlarge ~ *n* **1** : short discharge (as of air) **2** : slight swelling **3** : something light and fluffy —**puffy** *adj*

pug \'pəg\ *n* : small stocky dog

pu•gi•lism \'pyüjə,lizəm\ *n* : boxing —**pu•gi•list** \-list\ *n* —**pu•gi•lis•tic** \,pyüjə-'listik\ *adj*

pug•na•cious \,pəg'nāshəs\ *adj* : prone to fighting —**pug•nac•i•ty** \-'nasətē\ *n*

puke \'pyük\ *vb* **puked; puk•ing** : vomit —**puke** *n*

pul•chri•tude \'pəlkrə,tüd, -,tyüd\ *n* : beauty —**pul•chri•tu•di•nous** \,pəl-krə'tüdᵊnəs, -,tyüd-\ *adj*

pull \'pul\ *vb* **1** : exert force so as to draw (something) toward or out **2** : move **3** : stretch or tear ~ *n* **1** : act of pulling **2** : influence **3** : device for pulling something —**pull•er** *n*

pul•let \'pulət\ *n* : young hen

pul•ley \'pulē\ *n, pl* **-leys** : wheel with a grooved rim

Pull•man \'pulmən\ *n* : railroad car with berths

pull•over \'pul,ōvər\ *adj* : put on by being pulled over the head —**pullover** *n*

pul•mo•nary \'pulmə,nerē, 'pəl-\ *adj* : relating to the lungs

pulp \'pəlp\ *n* **1** : soft part of a fruit or vegetable **2** : soft moist mass (as of mashed wood) —**pulpy** *adj*

pul•pit \'pul,pit\ *n* : raised desk used in preaching

pul•sate \'pəl,sāt\ *vb* **-sat•ed; -sat•ing** : expand and contract rhythmically —**pul•sa•tion** \,pəl'sāshən\ *n*

pulse \'pəls\ *n* : arterial throbbing caused by heart contractions —**pulse** *vb*

pul•ver•ize \'pəlvə,rīz\ *vb* **-ized; -iz•ing** : beat or grind into a powder

pu•ma \'pümə, 'pyü-\ *n* : cougar

pum•ice \'pəməs\ *n* : light porous volcanic glass used in polishing

pum•mel \'pəməl\ *vb* **-meled; -mel•ing** : beat

¹**pump** \'pəmp\ *n* : device for moving or compressing fluids ~ *vb* **1** : raise (as water) with a pump **2** : fill by means of a pump —with *up* **3** : move like a pump —**pump•er** *n*

²**pump** *n* : woman's low shoe

pum•per•nick•el \'pəmpər,nikəl\ *n* : dark rye bread

pump•kin \'pəŋkən, 'pəmpkən\ *n* : large usu. orange fruit of a vine related to the gourd

pun \'pən\ *n* : humorous use of a word in a way that suggests two or more interpretations —**pun** *vb*

¹**punch** \'pənch\ *vb* **1** : strike with the fist **2** : perforate with a punch ~ *n* : quick blow with the fist —**punch•er** *n*

²**punch** *n* : tool for piercing or stamping

³**punch** *n* : mixed beverage often including fruit juice

punc•til•i•ous \,pəŋk'tilēəs\ *adj* : marked by precise accordance with conventions

punc•tu•al \'pəŋkchəwəl\ *adj* : prompt —**punc•tu•al•i•ty** \,pəŋkchə'walətē\ *n* —**punc•tu•al•ly** *adv*

punc•tu•ate \'pəŋkchə,wāt\ *vb* **-at•ed; -at•ing** : mark with punctuation

punc•tu•a•tion \,pəŋkchə'wāshən\ *n* : standardized marks in written matter to clarify the meaning and separate parts

punc•ture \'pəŋkchər\ *n* : act or result of puncturing ~ *vb* **-tured; -tur•ing** : make a hole in

pun•dit \'pəndət\ *n* **1** : learned person **2** : expert or critic

pun•gent \'pənjənt\ *adj* : having a sharp or stinging odor or taste —**pun•gen•cy** \-jənsē\ *n* —**pun•gent•ly** *adv*

pun•ish \'pənish\ *vb* : impose a penalty on or for —**pun•ish•able** *adj* —**pun•ish•ment** *n*

pu•ni•tive \'pyünətiv\ *adj* : inflicting punishment

pun•kin *var of* PUMPKIN

¹**punt** \'pənt\ *n* : long narrow flat-bottomed boat ~ *vb* : propel (a boat) by pushing with a pole

²**punt** *vb* : kick a ball dropped from the hands ~ *n* : act of punting a ball

pu•ny \'pyünē\ *adj* **-ni•er; -est** : slight in power or size

pup \'pəp\ *n* : young dog

pu•pa \'pyüpə\ *n, pl* **-pae** \-,pē, -,pī\ or **-pas** : insect (as a moth) when it is in a cocoon —**pu•pal** \-pəl\ *adj*

¹**pu•pil** \'pyüpəl\ *n* : young person in school

²**pupil** *n* : dark central opening of the iris of the eye

pup•pet \'pəpət\ *n* : small doll moved by hand or by strings —**pup•pe•teer** \,pəpə'tir\ *n*

pup•py \'pəpē\ *n, pl* **-pies** : young dog

pur•chase \'pərchəs\ *vb* **-chased; -chas•ing** : obtain in exchange for money ~ *n* **1** : act of purchasing **2** : something purchased **3** : secure grasp —**purchas•er** *n*

pure \'pyür\ *adj* **pur•er; pur•est** : free of foreign matter, contamination, or corruption —**pure•ly** *adv*

pu•ree \pyu'rā, -'rē\ *n* : thick liquid mass of food —**puree** *vb*

pur•ga•to•ry \'pərgə,tōrē\ *n, pl* **-ries** : intermediate state after death for purification by expiating sins —**pur•ga•to•ri•al** \,pərgə'tōrēəl\ *adj*

purge \'pərj\ *vb* **purged; purg•ing 1** : purify esp. from sin **2** : have or cause emptying of the bowels **3** : to get rid of ~ *n* **1** : act or result of purging **2** : something that purges —**pur•ga•tive** \'pərgətiv\ *adj or n*

pu•ri•fy \'pyürə,fī\ *vb* **-fied; -fy•ing** : make or become pure —**pu•ri•fi•ca•tion** \,pyürəfə'kāshən\ *n* —**pu•ri•fi•er** \-,fīər\ *n*

Pu•rim \'purim\ *n* : Jewish holiday celebrated in February or March in commemoration of the deliverance of the Jews from the massacre plotted by Haman

pu•ri•tan \'pyürət³n\ *n* : one who practices or preaches a very strict moral code —**pu•ri•tan•i•cal** \pyürə'tanikəl\ *adj* —**pu•ri•tan•i•cal•ly** *adv*

pu•ri•ty \'pyürətē\ *n* : quality or state of being pure

purl \'pərl\ *n* : stitch in knitting ~ *vb* : knit in purl stitch

pur•ple \'pərpəl\ *n* : bluish red color —**pur•plish** \'pərpəlish\ *adj*

pur•port \pər'pōrt\ *vb* : convey outwardly as the meaning ~ \'pər,pōrt\ *n* : meaning —**pur•port•ed•ly** \-ədlē\ *adv*

pur•pose \'pərpəs\ *n* 1 : something (as a result) aimed at 2 : resolution ~ *vb* -**posed; -pos•ing** : intend —**pur•pose•ful** \-fəl\ *adj* —**pur•pose•ful•ly** *adv* —**pur•pose•less** *adj* —**pur•pose•ly** *adv*

purr \'pər\ *n* : low murmur typical of a contented cat —**purr** *vb*

¹**purse** \'pərs\ *n* 1 : bag or pouch for money and small objects 2 : financial resource 3 : prize money

²**purse** *vb* **pursed; purs•ing** : pucker

pur•su•ance \pər'süəns\ *n* : act of carrying out or into effect

pursuant to \-'süənt\ *prep* : according to

pur•sue \pər'sü\ *vb* -**sued; -su•ing** 1 : follow in order to overtake 2 : seek to accomplish 3 : proceed along 4 : engage in —**pur•su•er** *n*

pur•suit \pər'süt\ *n* 1 : act of pursuing 2 : occupation

pur•vey \pər'vā\ *vb* -**veyed; -vey•ing** : supply (as provisions) usu. as a business —**pur•vey•or** \-ər\ *n*

pus \'pəs\ *n* : thick yellowish fluid (as in a boil)

push \'push\ *vb* 1 : press against to move forward 2 : urge on or provoke ~ *n* 1 : vigorous effort 2 : act of pushing —**push•cart** *n* —**push•er** \'pushər\ *n*

pushy \'pushē\ *adj* **push•i•er; -est** : objectionably aggressive

pu•sil•lan•i•mous \ˌpyüsə'lanəməs\ *adj* : cowardly

pussy \'pusē\ *n, pl* **puss•ies** : cat

pus•tule \'pəschül\ *n* : pus-filled pimple

put \'püt\ *vb* **put; put•ting** 1 : bring to a specified position or condition 2 : subject to pain, suffering, or death 3 : impose or cause to exist 4 : express 5 : cause to be used or employed —**put off** *vb* : postpone or delay —**put out** *vb* : bother or inconvenience —**put up** *vb* 1 : prepare for storage 2 : lodge 3 : contribute or pay —**put up with** : endure

pu•tre•fy \'pyütrə,fī\ *vb* -**fied; -fy•ing** : make or become putrid —**pu•tre•fac•tion** \pyütrə'fakshən\ *n*

pu•trid \'pyütrəd\ *adj* : rotten —**pu•trid•i•ty** \pyü'tridətē\ *n*

put•ty \'pətē\ *n, pl* -**ties** : doughlike cement —**putty** *vb*

puz•zle \'pəzəl\ *vb* -**zled; -zling** 1 : confuse 2 : attempt to solve —**with** *out* or *over* ~ *n* : something that confuses or tests ingenuity —**puz•zle•ment** *n* —**puz•zler** \-ələr\ *n*

pyg•my \'pigmē\ *n, pl* -**mies** : dwarf —**pygmy** *adj*

py•lon \'pī,län, -lən\ *n* : tower or tall post

pyr•a•mid \'pirə,mid\ *n* : structure with a square base and 4 triangular sides meeting at a point

pyre \'pīr\ *n* : material heaped for a funeral fire

py•ro•ma•nia \ˌpīrō'mānēə\ *n* : irresistible impulse to start fires —**py•ro•ma•ni•ac** \-nē,ak\ *n*

py•ro•tech•nics \ˌpīrə'tekniks\ *n pl* : spectacular display (as of fireworks) —**py•ro•tech•nic** \-nik\ *adj*

Pyr•rhic \'pirik\ *adj* : achieved at excessive cost

py•thon \'pī,thän, -thən\ *n* : very large constricting snake

Q

q \'kyü\ *n, pl* **q's** *or* **qs** \'kyüz\ : 17th letter of the alphabet

¹**quack** \'kwak\ *vb* : make a cry like that of a duck —**quack** *n*

²**quack** *n* : one who pretends to have medical or healing skill —**quack** *adj* —**quack•ery** \-ərē\ *n* —**quack•ish** *adj*

quad•ran•gle \'kwäd,raŋgəl\ *n* : rectangular courtyard

quad•rant \'kwädrənt\ *n* : 1/4 of a circle

quad•ri•lat•er•al \ˌkwädrə'latərəl\ *n* : 4-sided polygon

qua•drille \kwä'dril, kə-\ *n* : square dance for 4 couples

quad•ru•ped \'kwädrə,ped\ *n* : animal having 4 feet

qua•dru•ple \kwä'drüpəl, -'drəp-; 'kwä-drəp-\ *vb* -**pled; -pling** \-pliŋ\ : multiply by 4 ~ *adj* : being 4 times as great or as many

qua•dru•plet \kwä'drəplət, -'drüp-; 'kwä-drəp-\ *n* : one of 4 offspring born at one birth

quaff \'kwäf, 'kwaf\ *vb* : drink deeply or repeatedly —**quaff** *n*

quag•mire \'kwag,mīr, 'kwäg-\ *n* : soft land or bog

qua•hog \'kō,hóg, 'kwó-, 'kwō-, -,häg\ *n* : thick-shelled clam

¹**quail** \'kwāl\ *n, pl* **quail** *or* **quails** : short-winged plump game bird

²**quail** *vb* : cower in fear

quaint \'kwānt\ *adj* : pleasingly old-fashioned or odd —**quaint•ly** *adv* —**quaint•ness** *n*

quake \'kwāk\ *vb* **quaked; quak•ing** : shake or tremble ~ *n* : earthquake

qual•i•fi•ca•tion \ˌkwäləfə'kāshən\ *n* 1 : limitation or stipulation 2 : special skill or experience for a job

qual•i•fy \'kwälə,fī\ *vb* -**fied; -fy•ing** 1 : modify or limit 2 : fit by skill or training for some purpose 3 : become eligible —**qual•i•fied** *adj* —**qual•i•fi•er** \-,fīər\ *n*

qual•i•ty \'kwälətē\ *n, pl* -**ties** 1 : peculiar and essential character, nature, or feature 2 : excellence or distinction

qualm \'kwäm, 'kwälm, 'kwóm\ *n* : sudden feeling of doubt or uneasiness

quan•da•ry \'kwändrē\ *n, pl* -**ries** : state of perplexity or doubt

quan•ti•ty \'kwäntətē\ *n, pl* -**ties** 1 : something that can be measured or numbered 2 : considerable amount

quan•tum theory \'kwäntəm-\ *n* : theory in physics that radiant energy (as light) is composed of separate packets of energy

quar•an•tine \'kwórən,tēn\ *n* 1 : restraint on the movements of persons or goods to prevent the spread of pests or disease 2 : place or period of quarantine —**quarantine** *vb*

quar•rel \'kwórəl\ *n* : basis of conflict —**quarrel** *vb* —**quar•rel•some** \-səm\ *adj*

¹**quar•ry** \'kwórē\ *n, pl* **quarries** : prey

²**quarry** *n, pl* -**ries** : excavation for obtaining stone —**quarry** *vb*

quart \'kwórt\ *n* : unit of liquid measure equal to .95 liter or of dry measure equal to 1.10 liters

quar•ter \'kwórtər\ *n* 1 : 1/4 part 2 : 1/4 of a dollar 3 : city district 4 *pl* : place to live esp. for a time 5 : mercy ~ *vb* : divide into 4 equal parts

quar•ter•ly \'kwórtərlē\ *adv or adj* : at 3-month intervals ~ *n, pl* -**lies** : periodical published 4 times a year

quar•ter•mas•ter *n* 1 : ship's helmsman 2 : army supply officer

quar•tet \kwór'tet\ *n* 1 : music for 4 performers 2 : group of 4

quar•to \'kwórtō\ *n, pl* -**tos** : book printed on pages cut 4 from a sheet

quartz \'kwórts\ *n* : transparent crystalline mineral

quash \'kwash, 'kwósh\ *vb* 1 : set aside by judicial action 2 : suppress summarily and completely

qua•si \'kwä,zī, -sī; 'kwäzē, 'kwäs-; 'kwāzē\ *adj* : similar or nearly identical

qua•train \'kwä,trān\ *n* : unit of 4 lines of verse

qua•ver \'kwāvər\ *vb* : tremble or trill —**quaver** *n*

quay \'kē, 'kā, 'kwā\ *n* : wharf

quea•sy \'kwēzē\ *adj* -**si•er; -est** : nauseated —**quea•si•ly** \-zəlē\ *adv* —**quea•si•ness** \-zēnəs\ *n*

queen \'kwēn\ *n* 1 : wife or widow of a king 2 : female monarch 3 : woman of rank, power, or attractiveness 4 : fertile female of a social insect —**queen•ly** *adj*

queer \'kwir\ *adj* : differing from the usual or normal —**queer•ly** *adv* —**queer•ness** *n*

quell \'kwel\ *vb* : put down by force

quench \'kwench\ *vb* 1 : put out 2 : satisfy (a thirst) —**quench•able** *adj* —**quench•er** *n*

quer•u•lous \'kwerələs, -yələs\ *adj* : fretful or whining —**quer•u•lous•ly** *adv* —**quer•u•lous•ness** *n*

que•ry \'kwirē, 'kwer-\ *n, pl* -**ries** : question —**query** *vb*

quest \'kwest\ *n or vb* : search

ques•tion \'kweschən\ *n* 1 : something asked 2 : subject for debate 3 : dispute ~ *vb* 1 : ask questions 2 : doubt or dispute 3 : subject to analysis —**ques•tion•er** *n*

ques•tion•able \'kweschənəbəl\ *adj* 1 : not certain 2 : of doubtful truth or morality —**ques•tion•ably** \-blē\ *adv*

question mark *n* : a punctuation mark ? used esp. at the end of a sentence to indicate a direct question

ques•tion•naire \ˌkweschə'nar\ *n* : set of questions

queue \'kyü\ *n* 1 : braid of hair 2 : a waiting line ~ *vb* **queued; queu•ing** *or* **queue•ing** : line up

quib•ble \'kwibəl\ *n* : minor objection —**quibble** *vb* —**quib•bler** *n*

quick \'kwik\ *adj* 1 : rapid 2 : alert or perceptive ~ *n* : sensitive area of living flesh —**quick** *adv* —**quick•ly** *adv* —**quick•ness** *n*

quick•en \'kwikən\ *vb* 1 : come to life 2 : increase in speed

quick•sand *n* : deep mass of sand and water

quick•sil•ver *n* : mercury

qui•es•cent \kwī'es³nt\ *adj* : being at rest —**qui•es•cence** \-³ns\ *n*

qui•et \'kwīət\ *adj* 1 : marked by little motion or activity 2 : gentle 3 : free from noise 4 : not showy 5 : secluded ~ *vb* : pacify —**quiet** *adv or n* —**qui•et•ly** *adv* —**qui•et•ness** *n*

qui•etude \'kwīə,tüd, -,tyüd\ *n* : quietness or repose

quill \'kwil\ *n* 1 : a large stiff feather 2 : porcupine's spine

quilt \'kwilt\ *n* : padded bedspread ~ *vb* : stitch or sew in layers with padding in between

quince \'kwins\ *n* : hard yellow applelike fruit

qui•nine \'kwī,nīn\ *n* : bitter drug used against malaria

quin•tes•sence \kwin'tes³ns\ *n* 1 : purest essence of something 2 : most typical example —**quint•es•sen•tial** \ˌkwintə'senchəl\ *adj or n*

quin•tet \kwin'tet\ *n* 1 : music for 5 performers 2 : group of 5

quin•tu•ple \kwin'tüpəl, -'tyüp-, -'təp-; 'kwintəp-\ *adj* 1 : having 5 units or members 2 : being 5 times as great or as many —**quintuple** *n or vb*

quin•tu•plet \-plət\ *n* : one of 5 offspring at one birth

quip \'kwip\ *vb* -**pp-** : make a clever remark —**quip** *n*

quire \'kwīr\ *n* : 24 or 25 sheets of paper of the same size and quality

quirk \'kwərk\ *n* : peculiarity of action or behavior —**quirky** *adj*

quit \'kwit\ *vb* **quit; quit•ting** 1 : stop 2 : leave —**quit•ter** *n*

quite \'kwīt\ *adv* 1 : completely 2 : to a considerable extent

quits \'kwits\ *adj* : even or equal with another (as by repaying a debt)

¹**quiv•er** \'kwivər\ *n* : case for arrows

²**quiver** *vb* : shake or tremble —**quiver** *n*

quix•ot•ic \kwik'sätik\ *adj* : idealistic to an impractical degree —**quix•ot•i•cal•ly** \-ti-klē\ *adv*

quiz \'kwiz\ *n, pl* **quiz•zes** : short test ~ *vb* -**zz-** : question closely

quiz•zi•cal \'kwizikəl\ *adj* 1 : teasing 2 : curious

quoit \'kóit, 'kwóit, 'kwät\ *n* : ring thrown at a peg in a game (**quoits**)

quon•dam \'kwändəm, -,dam\ *adj* : former

quo•rum \'kwórəm\ *n* : required number of members present

quo•ta \'kwōtə\ *n* : proportional part or share

quotation mark *n* : one of a pair of punctuation marks " " or ' ' used esp. to indicate the beginning and the end of a quotation

quote \'kwōt\ *vb* **quot•ed; quot•ing** 1 : repeat (another's words) exactly 2 : state (a price) —**quot•able** *adj* —**quo•ta•tion** \kwō'tāshən\ *n* —**quote** *n*

quo•tient \'kwōshənt\ *n* : number obtained from division

R

r \'är\ *n, pl* **r's** *or* **rs** \'ärz\ : 18th letter of the alphabet

rab•bet \'rabət\ *n* : groove in a board

rab•bi \'rab,ī\ *n* : Jewish religious leader —**rab•bin•ic** \rə'binik\, **rab•bin•i•cal** \-ikəl\ *adj*

rab•bin•ate \'rabənət, -,nāt\ *n* : office of a rabbi

rab•bit \'rabət\ *n, pl* -**bit** *or* -**bits** : long-eared burrowing mammal

rab•ble \'rabəl\ *n* : mob

ra•bid \'rabəd\ *adj* 1 : violent 2 : fanatical 3 : affected with rabies

ra•bies \'rābēz\ *n, pl* **rabies** : acute deadly virus disease

rac•coon \ra'kün\ *n, pl* -**coon** *or* -**coons** : tree-dwelling mammal with a black mask and a bushy ringed tail

¹**race** \'rās\ *n* 1 : strong current of water 2 : contest of speed 3 : election campaign ~ *vb* **raced; rac•ing** 1 : run in a race 2 : rush —**race•course** *n* —**rac•er** *n* —**race•track** *n*

²**race** *n* 1 : family, tribe, people, or nation of the same stock 2 : division of mankind based on hereditary traits —**ra•cial** \'rāshəl\ *adj* —**ra•cial•ly** *adv*

race•horse *n* : horse used for racing

rac•ism \'rās,izəm\ *n* : discrimination based on the belief that some races are by nature superior —**rac•ist** \-ist\ *n*

rack \'rak\ *n* 1 : framework for display or storage 2 : instrument that stretches the body for torture ~ *vb* : torture with or as if with a rack

¹**rack•et** \'rakət\ *n* : bat with a tight netting across an open frame

²**racket** *n* 1 : confused noise 2 : fraudulent scheme —**rack•e•teer** \ˌrakə'tir\ *n* —**rack•e•teer•ing** *n*

ra•con•teur \ˌrak,än'tər\ *n* : storyteller

racy \'rāsē\ *adj* **rac•i•er; -est** : risqué —**rac•i•ly** *adv* —**rac•i•ness** *n*

ra•dar \'rā,där\ *n* : radio device for determining distance and direction of distant objects

ra•di•al \'rādēəl\ *adj* : having parts arranged like rays coming from a common center —**ra•di•al•ly** *adv*

ra•di•ant \'rādēənt\ *adj* 1 : glowing 2 : beaming with happiness 3 : transmitted by radiation —**ra•di•ance** \-əns\ *n* —**ra•di•ant•ly** *adv*

ra•di•ate \'rādē,āt\ *vb* -**at•ed; -at•ing** 1 : issue rays or in rays 2 : spread from a center —**ra•di•a•tion** \ˌrādē'āshən\ *n*

ra•di•a•tor \'rādē,ātər\ *n* : cooling or heating device

rad•i•cal \'radikəl\ *adj* 1 : fundamental 2 : extreme ~ *n* : person favoring extreme changes —**rad•i•cal•ism** \-,izəm\ *n* —**rad•i•cal•ly** *adv*

radii *pl of* RADIUS

ra•dio \'rādē,ō\ *n, pl* -**di•os** 1 : wireless transmission or reception of sound by means of electric waves 2 : radio receiving set ~ *vb* : send a message to by radio —**radio** *adj*

ra•dio•ac•tiv•i•ty \ˌrādēō,ak'tivətē\ *n* : property of an element that emits energy through nuclear disintegration —**ra•dio•ac•tive** \-'aktiv\ *adj*

ra•di•ol•o•gy \ˌrādē'äləjē\ *n* : medical use of radiation —**ra•di•ol•o•gist** \-jist\ *n*

rad•ish \'radish\ *n* : pungent fleshy root usu. eaten raw

ra•di•um \'rādēəm\ *n* : metallic radioactive chemical element

ra•di•us \'rādēəs\ *n, pl* -**dii** \-ē,ī\ 1 : line from the center of a circle or sphere to the circumference or surface 2 : area defined by a radius

ra•don \'rā,dän\ *n* : gaseous radioactive chemical element

raff•ish \'rafish\ *adj* : flashily vulgar —**raff•ish•ly** *adv* —**raff•ish•ness** *n*

raf•fle \'rafəl\ *n* : lottery among people who have bought tickets ~ *vb* -**fled; -fling** : offer in a raffle

¹**raft** \'raft\ *n* : flat floating platform ~ *vb* : travel or transport by raft

²**raft** *n* : large amount or number

raf•ter \'raftər\ *n* : beam supporting a roof

¹**rag** \'rag\ *n* : waste piece of cloth

²**rag** *n* : composition in ragtime

rag•a•muf•fin \'ragə,məfən\ *n* : ragged dirty person

rage \'rāj\ *n* 1 : violent anger 2 : vogue ~ *vb* **raged; rag•ing** 1 : be extremely angry or violent 2 : be out of control

rag•ged \'ragəd\ *adj* : torn —**rag•ged•ly** *adv* —**rag•ged•ness** *n*

ra•gout \ra'gü\ *n* : meat stew

rag•time *n* : syncopated music

rag•weed *n* : coarse weedy herb with allergenic pollen

raid \'rād\ *n* : sudden usu. surprise attack —**raid** *vb* —**raid•er** *n*

¹**rail** \'rāl\ *n* 1 : bar serving as a guard or barrier 2 : bar forming a track for wheeled vehicles 3 : railroad

²**rail** *vb* : scold someone vehemently —**rail•er** *n*

rail•ing \'rāliŋ\ *n* : rail or a barrier of rails

rail•lery \'rālərē\ *n, pl* -**ler•ies** : good-natured ridicule

rail•road \'rāl,rōd\ *n* : road for a train laid with iron rails and wooden ties ~ *vb*

: force something hastily **—rail·road·er** *n* **—rail·road·ing** *n*

rail·way \-,wā\ *n* : railroad

rai·ment \'rāmənt\ *n* : clothing

rain \'rān\ *1* : water falling in drops from the clouds **2** : shower of objects ~ *vb* : fall as or like rain **—rain·coat** *n* **—rain·drop** *n* **—rain·fall** *n* **—rain·mak·er** *n* **—rain·mak·ing** *n* **—rain·storm** *n* **—rain·wa·ter** *n* **—rainy** *adj*

rain·bow \-,bō\ *n* : arc of colors formed by the sun shining through moisture

raise \'rāz\ *vb* **raised; rais·ing** 1 : lift **2** : arouse **3** : erect **4** : collect **5** : breed, grow, or bring up **6** : increase **7** : make light ~ *n* : increase esp. in pay **—rais·er** *n*

rai·sin \'rāzᵊn\ *n* : dried grape

ra·ja, ra·jah \'räjə\ *n* : Indian prince

¹**rake** \'rāk\ *n* : garden tool for smoothing or sweeping ~ *vb* **raked; rak·ing** 1 : gather, loosen, or smooth with or as if with a rake **2** : sweep with gunfire

²**rake** *n* : dissolute man

rak·ish \'rākish\ *adj* : smart or jaunty **—rak·ish·ly** *adv* **—rak·ish·ness** *n*

ral·ly \'ralē\ *vb* **-lied; -ly·ing** 1 : bring or come together **2** : revive or recover **3** : make a comeback ~ *n, pl* **-lies** 1 : act of rallying **2** : mass meeting

ram \'ram\ *n* 1 : male sheep **2** : beam used in battering down walls or doors ~ *vb* **-mm-** 1 : force or drive in or through **2** : strike against violently

RAM \'ram\ *n* : main internal storage area in a computer

ram·ble \'rambəl\ *vb* **-bled; -bling** : wander **—ramble** *n* **—ram·bler** \-blər\ *n*

ram·bunc·tious \ram'bəŋkshəs\ *adj* : unruly

ram·i·fi·ca·tion \,raməfə'kāshən\ *n* : consequence

ram·i·fy \'ramə,fī\ *vb* **-fied; -fy·ing** : branch out

ramp \'ramp\ *n* : sloping passage or connecting roadway

ram·page \'ram,pāj, ram'pāj\ *vb* **-paged; -pag·ing** : rush about wildly ~ \'ram,-\ *n* : violent or riotous action or behavior

ram·pant \'rampənt\ *adj* : widespread **—ram·pant·ly** *adv*

ram·part \'ram,pärt\ *n* : embankment of a fortification

ram·rod *n* : rod used to load or clean a gun ~ *adj* : strict or inflexible

ram·shack·le \'ram,shakəl\ *adj* : shaky

ran *past of* RUN

ranch \'ranch\ *n* 1 : establishment for the raising of cattle, sheep, or horses **2** : specialized farm ~ *vb* : operate a ranch **—ranch·er** *n*

ran·cid \'ransəd\ *adj* : smelling or tasting as if spoiled **—ran·cid·i·ty** \ran'sidətē\ *n*

ran·cor \'raŋkər\ *n* : bitter deep-seated ill will **—ran·cor·ous** *adj*

ran·dom \'randəm\ *adj* : occurring by chance **—ran·dom·ly** *adv* **—random·ness** *n* **—at random** : without definite aim or method

ran·dom·ize \'randə,mīz\ *vb* **-ized; -iz·ing** : select, assign, or arrange in a random way

rang *past of* RING

range \'rānj\ *n* 1 : series of things in a row **2** : open land for grazing **3** : cooking stove **4** : variation within limits **5** : place for target practice **6** : extent ~ *vb* **ranged; rang·ing** 1 : arrange **2** : roam at large, freely, or over **3** : vary within limits

rang·er \'rānjər\ *n* : officer who manages and protects public lands

rangy \'rānjē\ *adj* **rang·i·er; -est** : being slender with long limbs **—rang·i·ness** *n*

¹**rank** \'raŋk\ *adj* 1 : vigorous in growth **2** : unpleasantly strong-smelling **—rank·ly** *adv* **—rank·ness** *n*

²**rank** *n* 1 : line of soldiers **2** : orderly arrangement **3** : grade of official standing **4** : position within a group ~ *vb* 1 : arrange in formation or according to class **2** : take or have a relative position

rank and file *n* : general membership

ran·kle \'raŋkəl\ *vb* **-kled; -kling** : cause anger, irritation, or bitterness

ran·sack \'ran,sak\ *vb* : search through and rob

ran·som \'ransəm\ *n* : something demanded for the freedom of a captive ~ *vb* : gain the freedom of by paying a price **—ran·som·er** *n*

rant \'rant\ *vb* : talk or scold violently **—rant·er** *n* **—rant·ing·ly** *adv*

¹**rap** \'rap\ *n* : sharp blow or rebuke ~ *vb* **-pp-** : strike or criticize sharply

²**rap** *vb* **-pp-** : talk freely

ra·pa·cious \rə'pāshəs\ *adj* 1 : excessively greedy **2** : ravenous **—ra·pa·cious·ly** *adv* **—ra·pa·cious·ness** *n* **—ra·pac·i·ty** \-'pasətē\ *n*

¹**rape** \'rāp\ *n* : herb grown as a forage crop and for its seeds (**rape·seed**)

²**rape** *vb* **raped; rap·ing** : force to have sexual intercourse **—rape** *n* **—rap·er** *n* **—rap·ist** \'rāpist\ *n*

rap·id \'rapəd\ *adj* : very fast **—ra·pid·i·ty** \rə'pidətē\ *n* **—rap·id·ly** *adv*

rap·ids \-ədz\ *n pl* : place in a stream where the current is swift

ra·pi·er \'rāpēər\ *n* : narrow 2-edged sword

rap·ine \'rapən, -,īn\ *n* : plunder

rap·port \ra'pōr\ *n* : harmonious relationship

rapt \'rapt\ *adj* : engrossed **—rapt·ly** *adv* **—rapt·ness** *n*

rap·ture \'rapchər\ *n* : spiritual or emotional ecstasy **—rap·tur·ous** \-chərəs\ *adj* **—rap·tur·ous·ly** *adv*

¹**rare** \'rar\ *adj* **rar·er; rar·est** : having a portion relatively uncooked

²**rare** *adj* **rar·er; rar·est** 1 : not dense **2** : unusually fine **3** : seldom met with **—rare·ly** *adv* **—rare·ness** *n* **—rar·i·ty** \'rarətē\ *n*

rar·e·fy \'rarə,fī\ *vb* **-fied; -fy·ing** : make or become rare, thin, or less dense **—rar·e·fac·tion** \,rarə'fakshən\ *n*

rar·ing \'raran, -iŋ\ *adj* : full of enthusiasm

ras·cal \'raskəl\ *n* : mean, dishonest, or mischievous person **—ras·cal·i·ty** \ras-'kalətē\ *n* **—ras·cal·ly** \'raskəlē\ *adj*

¹**rash** \'rash\ *adj* : too hasty in decision or action **—rash·ly** *adv* **—rash·ness** *n*

²**rash** *n* : a breaking out of the skin with red spots

rasp \'rasp\ *vb* 1 : rub with or as if with a rough file **2** : to speak in a grating tone ~ *n* : coarse file

rasp·ber·ry \'raz,berē\ *n* : edible red or black berry

rat \'rat\ *n* : destructive rodent larger than the mouse ~ *vb* : betray or inform on

ratch·et \'rachət\ *n* : notched device for allowing motion in one direction

rate \'rāt\ *n* 1 : quantity, amount, or degree measured in relation to some other quantity **2** : rank ~ *vb* **rat·ed; rat·ing** 1 : estimate or determine the rank or quality of **2** : deserve

¹**rath·er** \'rathər, 'rɑth-, 'räth-\ *adv* 1 : preferably **2** : on the other hand **3** : more properly **4** : somewhat

rat·i·fy \'ratə,fī\ *vb* **-fied; -fy·ing** : approve and accept formally **—rat·i·fi·ca·tion** \,ratəfə'kāshən\ *n*

rat·ing \'rātiŋ\ *n* : classification according to grade

ra·tio \'rāshēō\ *n, pl* **-tios** : relation in number, quantity, or degree between things

ra·tion \'rashən, 'rāshən\ *n* : share or allotment (as of food) ~ *vb* : use or allot sparingly

ra·tio·nal \'rashənəl\ *adj* 1 : having reason or sanity **2** : relating to reason **—ra·tio·nal·ly** *adv*

ra·tio·nale \,rashə'nal\ *n* 1 : explanation of principles of belief or practice **2** : underlying reason

ra·tio·nal·ize \'rashənə,līz\ *vb* **-ized; -iz·ing** : justify (as one's behavior or weaknesses) esp. to oneself **—ra·tio·nal·i·za·tion** \,rashənələ'zāshən\ *n*

rat·tan \ra'tan, rə-\ *n* : palm with long stems used esp. for canes and wickerwork

rat·tle \'ratᵊl\ *vb* **-tled; -tling** 1 : make a series of clattering sounds **2** : say briskly **3** : confuse or upset ~ *n* 1 : series of clattering sounds **2** : something (as a toy) that rattles

rat·tler \'ratlər\ *n* : rattlesnake

rat·tle·snake *n* : American venomous snake with a rattle at the end of the tail

rat·ty \'ratē\ *adj* **rat·ti·er; -est** : shabby

rau·cous \'rókəs\ *adj* : harsh or boisterous **—rau·cous·ly** *adv* **—rau·cous·ness** *n*

rav·age \'ravij\ *n* : destructive effect ~ *vb* **-aged; -ag·ing** : lay waste **—rav·ag·er** *n*

rave \'rāv\ *vb* **raved; rav·ing** 1 : talk wildly in or as if in delirium **2** : talk with extreme enthusiasm ~ *n* 1 : act of raving **2** : enthusiastic praise

rav·el \'ravəl\ *vb* **-eled** *or* **-elled; -el·ing** *or* **-el·ling** 1 : unravel **2** : tangle ~ *n* 1 : something tangled **2** : loose thread

ra·ven \'rāvən\ *n* : large black bird ~ *adj* : black and shiny

rav·en·ous \'ravənəs\ *adj* : very hungry **—rav·en·ous·ly** *adv* **—rav·en·ous·ness** *n*

ra·vine \rə'vēn\ *n* : narrow steep-sided valley

rav·ish \'ravish\ *vb* 1 : seize and take away by violence **2** : overcome with joy or delight **3** : rape **—rav·ish·er** *n* **—rav·ish·ment** *n*

raw \'ró\ *adj* **raw·er** \'róər\; **raw·est** \'róəst\ 1 : not cooked **2** : not processed **3** : not trained **4** : having the surface rubbed off **5** : cold and damp **6** : vulgar **—raw·ness** *n*

raw·hide \'ró,hīd\ *n* : untanned skin of cattle

ray \'rā\ *n* 1 : thin beam of radiant energy (as light) **2** : tiny bit

ray·on \'rā,än\ *n* : fabric made from cellulose fiber

raze \'rāz\ *vb* **razed; raz·ing** : destroy or tear down

ra·zor \'rāzər\ *n* : sharp cutting instrument used to shave off hair

re- \rē, ,rē, 'rē\ *prefix* **1** : again or anew **2** : back or backward

reaccelerate	refocus
reaccept	refold
reacclimatize	reformulate
reaccredit	refreeze
reacquaint	refuel
reacquire	regain
reactivate	regrow
reactivation	regrowth
readdress	rehear
readjust	reheat
readjustment	rehire
readmit	rehospitalization
readopt	rehospitalize
reaffirm	reidentify
realign	reignite
realignment	reimplant
reallocate	reimpose
reanalysis	reincorporate
reanalyze	reindict
reappear	reinfection
reappearance	reinflate
reapply	reinject
reappoint	reinjection
reapportion	reinoculate
reappraisal	reinsert
reappraise	reinsertion
reapprove	reinspect
reargue	reinstall
rearrange	reinstitute
rearrest	reintegrate
reassemble	reintegration
reassert	reinter
reassess	reintroduce
reassessment	reinvent
reassign	reinvestigate
reassignment	reinvestigation
reattach	reinvigorate
reattain	rejudge
reawaken	rekindle
rebalance	reknit
rebaptize	relabel
rebid	relandscape
rebind	relaunch
reborn	relearn
rebroadcast	relight
rebuild	reline
rebury	reload
recalculate	remarriage
recapture	remarry
recast	rematch
recertification	remelt
recertify	remobilize
rechannel	remoisten
recharge	remold
rechargeable	remotivate
recheck	rename
rechristen	renegotiate
recirculate	reoccupy
recirculation	reoccur
reclassification	reoccurrence
reclassify	reoperate
recolonize	reorchestrate
recombine	reorganization
recompute	reorganize
reconceive	reorient
reconnect	repack
reconquer	repave
reconquest	rephotograph
reconsider	replan
reconsideration	replaster
reconsolidate	replay
reconstruct	replot
recontaminate	repolish
reconvene	repopulate
reconvict	repressurize
recopy	reprice
re-create	reprint
recross	reprocess
redecorate	reprogram
rededicate	reread
rededication	rereading
redefine	rerecord
redeposit	reregister
redesign	reroof
redevelop	reroute
rediscover	resalable
rediscovery	resale
redissolve	reschedule
redistribute	reseal
redraft	resegregate
redraw	resell
reemerge	resentence
reemergence	reset
reemphasize	resettle
reenergize	resew
reengage	reshoot
reenlist	reshow
reenlistment	resocialization
reenroll	resod
reenter	resolidify
reequip	restage
reestablish	restart
reestablishment	restate
reestimate	restatement
reevaluate	restimulate
reevaluation	restock
reexamination	restructure
reexamine	restudy
refinance	restyle
refire	resubmit
refloat	resupply

resurface	retune
resurvey	retype
resynthesis	reupholster
resynthesize	reusable
retarget	reuse
reteach	reutilize
retell	revaccinate
retest	revaccination
rethink	revisit
retighten	rewash
retrain	reweave
retranslate	rewind
retransmit	rewire
retry	rewrap

reach \'rēch\ *vb* 1 : stretch out **2** : touch or try to touch or grasp **3** : extend to or arrive at **4** : communicate with ~ *n* 1 : act of reaching **2** : distance one can reach **3** : ability to reach **—reach·able** *adj* **—reach·er** *n*

re·act \rē'akt\ *vb* 1 : act in response to some influence or stimulus **2** : undergo chemical change **—re·ac·tive** \-'aktiv\ *adj*

re·ac·tion \rē'akshən\ *n* 1 : action or emotion caused by and directly related or counter to another action **2** : chemical change

re·ac·tion·ary \-shə,nerē\ *adj* : relating to or favoring return to an earlier political order or policy **—reactionary** *n*

re·ac·tor \rē'aktər\ *n* 1 : one that reacts **2** : device for the controlled release of nuclear energy

read \'rēd\ *vb* **read** \'red\; **read·ing** \'rēdiŋ\ 1 : understand written language **2** : utter aloud printed words **3** : interpret **4** : study **5** : indicate ~ *adj* \'red\ : informed by reading **—read·a·bil·i·ty** \,rēdə'bilətē\ *n* **—read·able** *adj* **—read·ably** *adv* **—read·er** *n* **—read·er·ship** *n*

read·ing \'rēdiŋ\ *n* 1 : something read or for reading **2** : particular version, interpretation, or performance **3** : data indicated by an instrument

ready \'redē\ *adj* **read·i·er; -est** 1 : prepared or available for use or action **2** : willing to do something ~ *vb* **read·ied; ready·ing** : make ready ~ *n* : state of being ready **—read·i·ly** *adv* **—read·i·ness** *n*

re·al \'rēl\ *adj* 1 : relating to fixed or immovable things (as land) **2** : genuine **3** : not imaginary ~ *adv* : very **—re·al·ness** *n* **—for real** 1 : in earnest **2** : genuine

real estate *n* : property in houses and land

re·al·ism \'rēə,lizəm\ *n* 1 : disposition to deal with facts practically **2** : faithful portrayal of reality **—re·al·ist** \-list\ *adj or n* **—re·al·is·tic** \,rēə'listik\ *adj* **—re·al·is·ti·cal·ly** \-tiklē\ *adv*

re·al·i·ty \rē'alətē\ *n, pl* **-ties** 1 : quality or state of being real **2** : something real

re·al·ize \'rēə,līz\ *vb* **-ized; -iz·ing** 1 : make actual **2** : obtain **3** : be aware of **—re·al·iz·able** *adj* **—re·al·i·za·tion** \,rēələ'zā·shən\ *n*

re·al·ly \'rēlē, 'ril-\ *adv* : in truth

realm \'relm\ *n* 1 : kingdom **2** : sphere

¹**ream** \'rēm\ *n* : quantity of paper that is 480, 500, or 516 sheets

²**ream** *vb* : enlarge, shape, or clean with a specially shaped tool (**ream·er**)

reap \'rēp\ *vb* : cut or clear (as a crop) with a scythe or machine **—reap·er** *n*

¹**rear** \'rir\ *vb* 1 : raise upright **2** : breed or bring up **3** : rise on the hind legs

²**rear** *n* 1 : back **2** : position at the back of something **—** *adj* : being at the back **—rear·ward** \-wərd\ *adj or adv*

rear admiral *n* : commissioned officer in the navy or coast guard ranking next below a vice admiral

rea·son \'rēzᵊn\ *n* 1 : explanation or justification **2** : motive for action or belief **3** : power or process of thinking ~ *vb* 1 : use the faculty of reason **2** : try to persuade another **—rea·son·er** *n* **—rea·son·ing** \'rēzᵊniŋ\ *n*

rea·son·able \'rēzᵊnəbəl\ *adj* 1 : being within the bounds of reason **2** : inexpensive **—rea·son·able·ness** *n* **—rea·son·ably** \-blē\ *adv*

re·as·sure \,rēə'shùr\ *vb* : restore one's confidence **—re·as·sur·ance** \-'shùrəns\ *n* **—re·as·sur·ing·ly** *adv*

re·bate \'rē,bāt\ *n* : return of part of a payment **—rebate** *vb*

reb·el \'rebəl\ *n* : one that resists authority ~ \ri'bel\ *vb* **-belled; -bel·ling** 1 : resist authority **2** : feel or exhibit anger **—rebel** \'rebəl\ *adj*

re·bel·lion \ri'belyən\ *n* : resistance to authority and esp. to one's government

re·bel·lious \-yəs\ *adj* 1 : engaged in rebellion **2** : inclined to resist authority **—re·bel·lious·ly** *adv* **—re·bel·lious·ness** *n*

re·birth \rē'bərth\ *n* 1 : new or second birth **2** : revival

re·bound \'rē,baùnd, ri-\ *vb* 1 : spring back on striking something **2** : recover from a reverse ~ \'rē,-\ *n* 1 : action of rebounding **2** : reaction to a reverse

re•buff \ri'bəf\ *vb* : refuse or repulse rudely —**rebuff** *n*

re•buke \-'byük\ *vb* **-buked; -buk•ing** : reprimand sharply —**rebuke** *n*

re•bus \'rēbəs\ *n* : riddle representing syllables or words with pictures

re•but \ri'bət\ *vb* **-but•ted; -but•ting** : refute —**re•but•ter** *n*

re•but•tal \-'ətᵊl\ *n* : opposing argument

re•cal•ci•trant \ri'kalsətrənt\ *adj* 1 : stubbornly resisting authority 2 : resistant to handling or treatment —**re•cal•ci•trance** \-trəns\ *n*

re•call \ri'kȯl\ *vb* 1 : call back 2 : remember 3 : revoke ~ \ri'-, 'rē,-\ *n* 1 : a summons to return 2 : remembrance 3 : act of revoking

re•cant \ri'kant\ *vb* : take back (something said) publicly

re•ca•pit•u•late \rēkə'pichə,lāt\ *vb* **-lat•ed; -lat•ing** : summarize —**re•ca•pit•u•la•tion** \-,pichə'lāshən\ *n*

re•cede \ri'sēd\ *vb* **-ced•ed; -ced•ing** 1 : move back or away 2 : slant backward

re•ceipt \-'sēt\ *n* 1 : act of receiving 2 : something (as payment) received —usu. in pl. 3 : writing acknowledging something received

re•ceive \ri'sēv\ *vb* **-ceived; -ceiv•ing** 1 : take in or accept 2 : greet or entertain (visitors) 3 : pick up radio waves and convert into sounds or pictures —**re•ceiv•able** *adj*

re•ceiv•er \ri'sēvər\ *n* 1 : one that receives 2 : one having charge of property or money involved in a lawsuit 3 : apparatus for receiving radio waves —**re•ceiv•er•ship** *n*

re•cent \'rēsᵊnt\ *adj* 1 : having lately come into existence 2 : of the present time or time just past —**re•cent•ly** *adv* —**re•cent•ness** *n*

re•cep•ta•cle \ri'septikəl\ *n* : container

re•cep•tion \ri'sepshən\ *n* 1 : act of receiving 2 : social gathering at which guests are formally welcomed

re•cep•tion•ist \-shənist\ *n* : person employed to greet callers

re•cep•tive \ri'septiv\ *adj* : open and responsive to ideas, impressions, or suggestions —**re•cep•tive•ly** *adv* —**re•cep•tive•ness** *n* —**re•cep•tiv•i•ty** \,rē,sep'tivətē\ *n*

re•cess \'rē,ses, ri'ses\ *n* 1 : indentation in a line or surface 2 : suspension of a session for rest ~ *vb* 1 : make a recess in or put into a recess 2 : interrupt a session for a recess

re•ces•sion \ri'seshən\ *n* 1 : departing procession 2 : period of reduced economic activity

rec•i•pe \'resə,pē\ *n* : instructions for making something

re•cip•i•ent \ri'sipēənt\ *n* : one that receives

re•cip•ro•cal \ri'siprəkəl\ *adj* 1 : affecting each in the same way 2 : so related that one is equivalent to the other —**re•cip•ro•cal•ly** *adv* —**rec•i•proc•i•ty** \,resə'präsətē\ *n*

re•cip•ro•cate \-,kāt\ *vb* **-cat•ed; -cat•ing** : make a return for something done or given —**re•cip•ro•ca•tion** \-,siprə'kāshən\ *n*

re•cit•al \ri'sītᵊl\ *n* 1 : public reading or recitation 2 : music or dance concert or exhibition by pupils —**re•cit•al•ist** \-ᵊlist\ *n*

rec•i•ta•tion \,resə'tāshən\ *n* : a reciting or recital

re•cite \ri'sīt\ *vb* **-cit•ed; -cit•ing** 1 : repeat verbatim 2 : recount —**re•cit•er** *n*

reck•less \'rekləs\ *adj* : lacking caution —**reck•less•ly** *adv* —**reck•less•ness** *n*

reck•on \'rekən\ *vb* 1 : count or calculate 2 : consider

reck•on•ing *n* 1 : act or instance of reckoning 2 : settling of accounts

re•claim \ri'klām\ *vb* 1 : change to a desirable condition 2 : obtain from a waste product or by-product 3 : demand or obtain the return of —**re•claim•able** *adj* —**rec•la•ma•tion** \reklə'māshən\ *n*

re•cline \ri'klīn\ *vb* **-clined; -clin•ing** : lean backward or lie down

re•cluse \'rek,lüs, ri'klüs\ *n* : one who leads a secluded or solitary life

rec•og•ni•tion \,rekig'nishən\ *n* : act of recognizing or state of being recognized

re•cog•ni•zance \ri'känəzəns, -'käg-\ *n* : promise recorded before a court

rec•og•nize \'rekig,nīz\ *vb* **-nized; -niz•ing** 1 : identify as previously known 2 : take notice of 3 : acknowledge esp. with appreciation —**rec•og•niz•able** \rekəg,nī-zəbəl\ *adj* —**rec•og•niz•ably** \-blē\ *adv*

re•coil \ri'kȯil\ *vb* : draw or spring back ~ \'rē,-, ri'-\ *n* : action of recoiling

rec•ol•lect \,rekə'lekt\ *vb* : remember

rec•ol•lec•tion \,rekə'lekshən\ *n* 1 : act or power of recollecting 2 : something recollected

rec•om•mend \,rekə'mend\ *vb* 1 : present as deserving of acceptance or trial 2 : advise —**rec•om•mend•able** \-'mendəbəl\ *adj*

rec•om•men•da•tion \rekəmən'dāshən\ *n* 1 : act of recommending 2 : something recommended or that recommends

rec•om•pense \'rekəm,pens\ *n* : compensation —**recompense** *vb*

rec•on•cile \'rekən,sīl\ *vb* **-ciled; -cil•ing** 1 : cause to be friendly again 2 : adjust or settle 3 : bring to acceptance —**rec•on•cil•able** *adj* —**rec•on•cile•ment** *n* —**rec•on•cil•er** *n* —**rec•on•cil•i•a•tion** \rekən-,silē'āshən\ *n*

re•con•dite \'rekən,dīt, ri'kän-\ *adj* 1 : hard to understand 2 : little known

re•con•di•tion \,rekən,dishən\ *vb* : restore to good condition

re•con•nais•sance \ri'känəzəns, -səns\ *n* : exploratory survey of enemy territory

re•con•noi•ter, re•con•noi•tre \,rēkə'nȯitər, ,rekə-\ *vb* **-tered** *or* **-tred; -ter•ing** *or* **-tring** : make a reconnaissance of

re•cord \ri'kȯrd\ *vb* 1 : set down in writing 2 : register permanently 3 : indicate 4 : preserve (as sound or images) for later reproduction ~ \'rekərd\ *n* 1 : something recorded 2 : best performance

re•cord•er \ri'kȯrdər\ *n* 1 : person or device that records 2 : wind instrument with finger holes

¹re•count \ri'kaunt\ *vb* : relate in detail

²re•count \'rē'-\ *vb* : count again —**recount** \'rē,-, ,rē'-\ *n*

re•coup \ri'küp\ *vb* : make up for (an expense or loss)

re•course \'rē,kȯrs, ri'-\ *n* : source of aid or a turning to such a source

re•cov•er \ri'kəvər\ *vb* 1 : regain position, poise, or health 2 : recoup —**re•cov•er•able** *adj* —**re•cov•ery** \-'kəvərē\ *n*

rec•re•a•tion \,rekrē'āshən\ *n* : a refreshing of strength or spirits as a change from work or study —**rec•re•a•tion•al** \-shənəl\ *adj*

re•crim•i•na•tion \ri,krimə'nāshən\ *n* : retaliatory accusation —**re•crim•i•nate** *vb*

re•cruit \ri'krüt\ *n* : newly enlisted member ~ *vb* : enlist the membership or services of —**re•cruit•er** *n* —**re•cruit•ment** *n*

rect•an•gle \'rek,taŋgəl\ *n* : 4-sided figure with 4 right angles —**rect•an•gu•lar** \rek-'taŋgyələr\ *adj*

rec•ti•fy \'rektə,fī\ *vb* **-fied; -fy•ing** : make or set right —**rec•ti•fi•ca•tion** \,rektəfə-'kāshən\ *n*

rec•ti•tude \'rektə,tüd, -,tyüd\ *n* : moral integrity

rec•tor \'rektər\ *n* : pastor

rec•to•ry \'rektərē\ *n, pl* **-ries** : rector's residence

rec•tum \'rektəm\ *n, pl* **-tums** *or* **-ta** \-tə\ : last part of the intestine joining the colon and anus —**rec•tal** \-tᵊl\ *adj*

re•cum•bent \ri'kəmbənt\ *adj* : lying down

re•cu•per•ate \ri'küpə,rāt, -'kyü-\ *vb* **-at•ed; -at•ing** : recover (as from illness) —**re•cu•per•a•tion** \-,küpə'rāshən, -,kyü-\ *n* —**re•cu•per•a•tive** \-'küpərātiv, -,kyü-\ *adj*

re•cur \ri'kər\ *vb* **-rr-** 1 : return in thought or talk 2 : occur again —**re•cur•rence** \-'kərəns\ *n* —**re•cur•rent** \-ənt\ *adj*

re•cy•cle \rē'sīkəl\ *vb* : process (as glass or cans) in order to regain a material for human use —**re•cy•cla•ble** \-kələbəl\ *adj*

red \'red\ *n* 1 : color of blood or of the ruby 2 *cap* : communist —**red** *adj* —**red•dish** *adj* —**red•ness** *n*

red•den \'redᵊn\ *vb* 1 : make or become red or reddish

re•deem \ri'dēm\ *vb* 1 : regain, free, or rescue by paying a price 2 : atone for 3 : free from sin 4 : convert into something of value —**re•deem•able** *adj* —**re•deem•er** *n*

re•demp•tion \-'dempshən\ *n* : act of redeeming —**re•demp•tive** \-tiv\ *adj* —**re•demp•to•ry** \-tərē\ *adj*

red•head \-,hed\ *n* : one having red hair —**red•head•ed** \-'hedəd\ *adj*

red•o•lent \'redᵊlənt\ *adj* 1 : having a fragrance 2 : suggestive —**red•o•lence** \-əns\ *n* —**red•o•lent•ly** *adv*

re•dou•ble \rē'dəbəl\ *vb* : make twice as great in size or amount 2 : intensify

re•doubt \ri'daut\ *n* : small fortification

re•doubt•able \-əbəl\ *adj* : arousing dread

re•dound \ri'daund\ *vb* : have an effect

re•dress \ri'dres\ *vb* : set right ~ *n* 1 : relief or remedy 2 : compensation

red tape *n* : complex obstructive official routine

re•duce \ri'düs, -'dyüs\ *vb* **-duced; -duc•ing** 1 : lessen 2 : put in a lower rank 3 : lose weight —**re•duc•er** *n* —**re•duc•ible** \-'düsəbəl, -'dyü-\ *adj*

re•duc•tion \ri'dəkshən\ *n* 1 : act of reducing 2 : amount lost in reducing 3 : something made by reducing

re•dun•dant \ri'dəndənt\ *adj* : using more words than necessary —**re•dun•dan•cy** \-dənsē\ *n* —**re•dun•dant•ly** *adv*

red•wood *n* : tall coniferous timber tree

reed \'rēd\ *n* 1 : tall slender grass of wet areas 2 : elastic strip that vibrates to produce tones in certain wind instruments —**reedy** *adj*

reef \'rēf\ *n* : ridge of rocks or sand at or near the surface of the water

reek \'rēk\ *n* : strong or disagreeable fume or odor ~ *vb* : give off a reek

¹reel \'rēl\ *n* : revolvable device on which something flexible is wound or a quantity of something wound on it ~ *vb* 1 : wind on a reel 2 : pull in by reeling —**reel•able** *adj* —**reel•er** *n*

²reel *vb* 1 : whirl or waver as from a blow 2 : walk or move unsteadily ~ *n* : reeling motion

³reel *n* : lively dance

re•fer \ri'fər\ *vb* **-rr-** 1 : direct or send to some person or place 2 : submit for consideration or action 3 : have connection 4 : mention or allude to something —**re•fer•able** \'refərəbəl, ri'fərə-\ *adj* —**re•fer•ral** \ri'fərəl\ *n*

ref•er•ee \,refə'rē\ *n* 1 : one to whom an issue is referred for settlement 2 : sports official ~ *vb* **-eed; -ee•ing** : act as referee

ref•er•ence \'refərəns\ *n* 1 : act of referring 2 : a bearing on a matter 3 : consultation for information 4 : person who can speak for one's character or ability or a recommendation given by such a person

ref•er•en•dum \,refə'rendəm\ *n, pl* **-da** \-də\ *or* **-dums** : a submitting of legislative measures for voters' approval or rejection

re•fill \rē'fil\ *vb* : fill again —**re•fill** \'rē,-\ *n* —**re•fill•able** *adj*

re•fine \ri'fīn\ *vb* **-fined; -fin•ing** 1 : free from impurities or waste matter 2 : improve or perfect 3 : free or become free of what is coarse or uncouth —**re•fine•ment** \-mənt\ *n* —**re•fin•er** *n*

re•fin•ery \ri'fīnərē\ *n, pl* **-er•ies** : place for refining (as oil or sugar)

re•flect \ri'flekt\ *vb* 1 : bend or cast back (as light or heat) 2 : bring as a result 3 : cast reproach or blame 4 : ponder —**re•flec•tion** \-'flekshən\ *n* —**re•flec•tive** \-tiv\ *adj* —**re•flec•tor** \ri'flektər\ *n*

re•flex \'rē,fleks\ *n* : automatic response to a stimulus ~ *adj* 1 : bent back 2 : relating to a reflex —**re•flex•ly** *adv*

re•flex•ive \ri'fleksiv\ *adj* : of or relating to an action directed back upon the doer or the grammatical subject —**reflexive** *n* —**re•flex•ive•ly** *adv* —**re•flex•ive•ness** *n*

re•form \ri'fȯrm\ *vb* : make or become better esp. by correcting bad habits —**reform** *n* —**re•form•able** *adj* —**re•for•ma•tive** \-'fȯrmətiv\ *adj* —**re•form•er** *n*

re•for•ma•to•ry \ri'fȯrmə,tȯrē\ *n, pl* **-ries** : penal institution for reforming young offenders

re•fract \ri'frakt\ *vb* : subject to refraction

re•frac•tion \-'frakshən\ *n* : the bending of a ray (as of light) when it passes from one medium into another —**re•frac•tive** \-tiv\ *adj*

re•frac•to•ry \ri'fraktərē\ *adj* : obstinate or unmanageable

re•frain \ri'frān\ *vb* : hold oneself back ~ *n* : verse recurring regularly in a song —**re•frain•ment** *n*

re•fresh \ri'fresh\ *vb* 1 : make or become fresh or fresher 2 : supply or take refreshment —**re•fresh•er** *n* —**re•fresh•ing•ly** *adv*

re•fresh•ment \-mənt\ *n* 1 : act of refreshing 2 *pl* : light meal

re•frig•er•ate \ri'frija,rāt\ *vb* **-at•ed; -at•ing** : chill or freeze (food) for preservation —**re•frig•er•ant** \-ərənt\ *adj or n* —**re•frig•er•a•tion** \-,frijə'rāshən\ *n* —**re•frig•er•a•tor** \-'frijə,rātər\ *n*

ref•uge \'ref,yüj\ *n* 1 : protection from danger 2 : place that provides protection

ref•u•gee \,refyu'jē\ *n* : person who flees for safety

re•fund \ri'fənd, 'rē,fənd\ *vb* : give or put back (money) ~ \'rē,-\ *n* 1 : act of refunding 2 : sum refunded —**re•fund•able** *adj*

re•fur•bish \ri'fərbish\ *vb* : renovate

¹re•fuse \ri'fyüz\ *vb* **-fused; -fus•ing** : decline to accept, do, or give —**re•fus•al** \-'fyüzəl\ *n*

²ref•use \'ref,yüs, -,yüz\ *n* : worthless matter

re•fute \ri'fyüt\ *vb* **-fut•ed; -fut•ing** : prove to be false —**ref•u•ta•tion** \refyu'tāshən\ *n* —**re•fut•er** \ri'fyütər\ *n*

re•gal \'rēgəl\ *adj* 1 : befitting a king 2 : stately —**re•gal•ly** *adv*

re•gale \ri'gāl\ *vb* **-galed; -gal•ing** 1 : entertain richly or agreeably 2 : delight

re•ga•lia \ri'gālyə\ *n pl* 1 : symbols of royalty 2 : insignia of an office or order 3 : finery

re•gard \ri'gärd\ *n* 1 : consideration 2 : feeling of approval and liking 3 *pl* : friendly greetings 4 : relation ~ *vb* 1 : pay attention to 2 : show respect for 3 : have an opinion of 4 : look at 5 : relate to —**re•gard•ful** *adj* —**re•gard•less** *adj*

re•gard•ing *prep* : concerning

re•gard•less of \ri'gärdləs-\ *prep* : in spite of

re•gen•er•ate \ri'jenərət\ *adj* 1 : formed or created again 2 : spiritually reborn ~ \-'jenə,rāt\ *vb* 1 : reform completely 2

: replace (a lost body part) by new tissue growth 3 : give new life to —**re•gen•er•a•tion** \-,jenə'rāshən\ *n* —**re•gen•er•a•tive** \-'jenə,rātiv\ *adj* —**re•gen•er•a•tor** \-,rātər\ *n*

re•gent \'rējənt\ *n* 1 : person who rules during the childhood, absence, or incapacity of the sovereign 2 : member of a governing board —**re•gen•cy** \-jənsē\ *n*

re•gime \rā'zhēm, ri-\ *n* : government in power

reg•i•men \'rejəmən\ *n* : systematic course of treatment or training

reg•i•ment \'rejəmənt\ *n* : military unit ~ \-,ment\ *vb* 1 : organize rigidly for control 2 : make orderly —**reg•i•men•tal** \rejə'mentᵊl\ *adj* —**reg•i•men•ta•tion** \-mən'tāshən\ *n*

re•gion \'rējən\ *n* : indefinitely defined area —**re•gion•al** \'rējənəl\ *adj* —**re•gion•al•ly** *adv*

reg•is•ter \'rejəstər\ *n* 1 : record of items or details or a book for keeping such a record 2 : device to regulate ventilation 3 : counting or recording device 4 : range of a voice or instrument ~ *vb* 1 : enter in a register 2 : record automatically 3 : get special care for mail by paying more postage

reg•is•trar \-,strär\ *n* : official keeper of records

reg•is•tra•tion \,rejə'strāshən\ *n* 1 : act of registering 2 : entry in a register

reg•is•try \'rejəstrē\ *n, pl* **-tries** 1 : enrollment 2 : place of registration 3 : official record book

re•gress \ri'gres\ *vb* : go or cause to go back or to a lower level —**re•gres•sion** \-'greshən\ *n* —**re•gres•sive** *adj*

re•gret \ri'gret\ *vb* **-tt-** 1 : mourn the loss or death of 2 : be very sorry for ~ *n* 1 : sorrow or the expression of sorrow 2 *pl* : message declining an invitation —**re•gret•ful** \-fəl\ *adj* —**re•gret•ful•ly** *adv* —**re•gret•ta•ble** \-əbəl\ *adj* —**re•gret•ta•bly** \-blē\ *adv* —**re•gret•ter** *n*

reg•u•lar \'regyələr\ *adj* 1 : conforming to what is usual, normal, or average 2 : steady, uniform, or unvarying —**regular** *n* —**reg•u•lar•i•ty** \regyə'larətē\ *n* —**reg•u•lar•ize** \'regyələ,rīz\ *vb* —**reg•u•lar•ly** *adv*

reg•u•late \'regyə,lāt\ *vb* **-lat•ed; -lat•ing** 1 : govern according to rule 2 : adjust to a standard —**reg•u•la•tive** \-,lātiv\ *adj* —**reg•u•la•tor** \-,lātər\ *n* —**reg•u•la•to•ry** \-lə,tȯrē\ *adj*

reg•u•la•tion \regyə'lāshən\ *n* 1 : act of regulating 2 : rule dealing with details of procedure

re•gur•gi•tate \rē'gərjə,tāt\ *vb* **-tat•ed; -tat•ing** : vomit —**re•gur•gi•ta•tion** \-,gərjə'tāshən\ *n*

re•ha•bil•i•tate \,rēhə'bilə,tāt\ *vb* **-tat•ed; -tat•ing** 1 : reinstate 2 : make good or usable again —**re•ha•bil•i•ta•tion** \-,bilə'tāshən\ *n*

re•hears•al \ri'hərsəl\ *n* : practice session or performance

re•hearse \-'hərs\ *vb* **-hearsed; -hears•ing** 1 : repeat or recount 2 : engage in a rehearsal of —**re•hears•er** *n*

reign \'rān\ *n* : sovereign's authority or rule ~ *vb* : rule as a sovereign

re•im•burse \,rēəm'bərs\ *vb* **-bursed; -burs•ing** : repay —**re•im•burs•able** *adj* —**re•im•burse•ment** *n*

rein \'rān\ *n* 1 : strap fastened to a bit to control an animal 2 : restraining influence ~ *vb* : direct by reins

re•in•car•na•tion \,rē,in,kär'nāshən\ *n* : rebirth of the soul —**re•in•car•nate** \,rēin'kär,nāt\ *vb*

rein•deer \'rān,dir\ *n* : caribou

re•in•force \,rēən'fȯrs\ *vb* : strengthen or support —**re•in•force•ment** *n* —**re•in•forc•er** *n*

re•in•state \,rēən'stāt\ *vb* : restore to a former position —**re•in•state•ment** *n*

re•it•er•ate \rē'itə,rāt\ *vb* : say again —**re•it•er•a•tion** \-,itə'rāshən\ *n*

re•ject \ri'jekt\ *vb* 1 : refuse to grant or consider 2 : refuse to admit, believe, or receive 3 : throw out as useless or unsatisfactory ~ \'rē,-\ *n* : rejected person or thing —**re•jec•tion** \-'jekshən\ *n*

re•joice \ri'jȯis\ *vb* **-joiced; -joic•ing** : feel joy —**re•joic•er** *n*

re•join *vb* 1 \rē'jȯin\ : join again 2 \ri'-\ : say in answer

re•join•der \ri'jȯindər\ *n* : answer

re•ju•ve•nate \ri'jüvə,nāt\ *vb* **-nat•ed; -nat•ing** : make young again —**re•ju•ve•na•tion** \-,jüvə'nāshən\ *n*

re•lapse \ri'laps, 'rē,laps\ *n* : recurrence of illness after a period of improvement ~ \ri'-\ *vb* : suffer a relapse

re•late \ri'lāt\ *vb* **-lat•ed; -lat•ing** 1 : give a report of 2 : show a connection between 3 : have a relationship —**re•lat•able** *adj* —**re•lat•er, re•la•tor** *n*

re•la•tion \-'lāshən\ *n* 1 : account 2 : connection 3 : relationship 4 : reference 5 *pl* : dealings

re·la·tion·ship \-,ship\ n : the state of being related or interrelated

rel·a·tive \relətiv\ n : person connected with another by blood or marriage ~ adj : considered in comparison with something else —**rel·a·tive·ly** adv —**rel·a·tive·ness** n

re·lax \ri'laks\ vb 1 : make or become less tense or rigid 2 : make less severe 3 : seek rest or recreation —**re·lax·er** n

re·lax·a·tion \,rē,lak'sāshən\ n 1 : lessening of tension 2 : recreation

re·lay \'rē,lā\ n : fresh supply (as of horses or people) arranged to relieve others ~ \'rē,-, ri'-\ vb -layed; -lay·ing : pass along in stages

re·lease \ri'lēs\ vb -leased; -leas·ing 1 : free from confinement or oppression 2 : relinquish 3 : permit publication, performance, exhibition, or sale ~ n 1 : relief from trouble 2 : discharge from an obligation 3 : act of releasing or what is released

rel·e·gate \relə,gāt\ vb -gat·ed; -gat·ing 1 : remove to some less prominent position 2 : assign to a particular class or sphere —**rel·e·ga·tion** \,relə'gāshən\ n

re·lent \ri'lent\ vb : become less severe

re·lent·less \-ləs\ adj : mercilessly severe or persistent —**re·lent·less·ly** adv —**re·lent·less·ness** n

rel·e·vance \reləvəns\ n : relation to the matter at hand —**rel·e·vant** \-vənt\ adj —**rel·e·vant·ly** adv

re·li·able \ri'līəbəl\ adj : fit to be trusted —**re·li·abil·i·ty** \-,līə'bilətē\ n —**re·li·able·ness** n —**re·li·ably** \-'līəblē\ adv

re·li·ance \ri'līəns\ n : act or result of relying

re·li·ant \ri'līənt\ adj : dependent

rel·ic \relik\ n 1 : object venerated because of its association with a saint or martyr 2 : remaining trace

re·lief \ri'lēf\ n 1 : lightening of something oppressive 2 : welfare

re·lieve \ri'lēv\ vb -lieved; -liev·ing 1 : free from a burden or distress 2 : release from a post or duty 3 : break the monotony of —**re·liev·er** n

re·li·gion \ri'lijən\ n 1 : service and worship of God 2 : set or system of religious beliefs —**re·li·gion·ist** n

re·li·gious \-'lijəs\ adj 1 : relating to or devoted to an ultimate reality or deity 2 : relating to religious beliefs or observances 3 : faithful, fervent, or zealous —**re·li·gious·ly** adv

re·lin·quish \ri'liŋkwish, -'lin-\ vb 1 : renounce 2 : let go of —**re·lin·quish·ment** n

rel·ish \relish\ n 1 : keen enjoyment 2 : highly seasoned sauce (as of pickles) ~ vb : enjoy —**rel·ish·able** adj

re·live \rē'liv\ vb : live over again (as in the imagination)

re·lo·cate \rē'lō,kāt, ,rēlō'kāt\ vb : move to a new location —**re·lo·ca·tion** \,rēlō'kāshən\ n

re·luc·tant \ri'ləktənt\ adj : feeling or showing doubt or unwillingness —**re·luc·tance** \ri'ləktəns\ n —**re·luc·tant·ly** adv

re·ly \ri'lī\ vb -lied; -ly·ing : place faith or confidence—often with on

re·main \ri'mān\ vb 1 : be left after others have been removed 2 : be something yet to be done 3 : stay behind 4 : continue unchanged

re·main·der \-'māndər\ n : that which is left over

re·mains \-'mānz\ n pl 1 : remaining part or trace 2 : dead body

re·mark \ri'märk\ vb : express as an observation ~ n : passing comment

re·mark·able \ri'märkəbəl\ adj : extraordinary —**re·mark·able·ness** n —**re·mark·ably** \-blē\ adv

re·me·di·al \ri'mēdēəl\ adj : intended to remedy or improve

rem·e·dy \remədē\ n, pl -dies 1 : medicine that cures 2 : something that corrects an evil or compensates for a loss ~ vb -died; -dy·ing : provide or serve as a remedy for

re·mem·ber \ri'membər\ vb 1 : think of again 2 : keep from forgetting 3 : convey greetings from

re·mem·brance \-brəns\ n 1 : act of remembering 2 : something that serves to bring to mind

re·mind \ri'mīnd\ vb : cause to remember —**re·mind·er** n

rem·i·nisce \remə'nis\ vb -nisced; -nisc·ing : indulge in reminiscence

rem·i·nis·cence \-'nisəns\ n 1 : recalling of a past experience 2 : account of a memorable experience

rem·i·nis·cent \-³nt\ adj 1 : relating to reminiscence 2 : serving to remind —**rem·i·nis·cent·ly** adv

re·miss \ri'mis\ adj : negligent or careless in performance of duty —**re·miss·ly** adv —**re·miss·ness** n

re·mis·sion \ri'mishən\ n 1 : act of forgiving 2 : a period of relief from or easing of symptoms of a disease

re·mit \ri'mit\ vb -tt- 1 : pardon 2 : send money in payment

re·mit·tance \ri'mit³ns\ n : sum of money remitted

rem·nant \remnənt\ n : small part or trace remaining

re·mod·el \rē'mäd³l\ vb : alter the structure of

re·mon·strance \ri'mänstrəns\ n : act or instance of remonstrating

re·mon·strate \ri'män,strāt\ vb -strat·ed; -strat·ing : speak in protest, reproof, or opposition —**re·mon·stra·tion** \ri-,män'strāshən, remən-\

re·morse \ri'mórs\ n : distress arising from a sense of guilt —**re·morse·ful** adj —**re·morse·less** adj

re·mote \ri'mōt\ adj -mot·er; -est 1 : far off in place or time 2 : hard to reach or find 3 : acting, acted on, or controlled indirectly or from afar 4 : slight 5 : distant in manner —**re·mote·ly** adv —**re·mote·ness** n

re·move \ri'müv\ vb -moved; -mov·ing 1 : move by lifting or taking off or away 2 : get rid of —**re·mov·able** adj —**re·mov·al** \-vəl\ n —**re·mov·er** n

re·mu·ner·ate \ri'myünə,rāt\ vb -at·ed; -at·ing : pay —**re·mu·ner·a·tion** \-myünə'rāshən\ n —**re·mu·ner·a·tor** \-,rātər\ n

re·mu·ner·a·tive \ri'myünərətiv, -,rāt-\ adj : gainful

re·nais·sance \renə'säns, -'zäns\ n : rebirth or revival

re·nal \rēn³l\ adj : relating to the kidneys

rend \'rend\ vb rent \'rent\ rend·ing : tear apart forcibly

ren·der \rendər\ vb 1 : extract by heating 2 : hand over or give up 3 : do (a service) for another 4 : cause to be or become

ren·dez·vous \rändi,vü, -dā-\ n, pl ren·dez·vous \-,vüz\ 1 : place appointed for a meeting 2 : meeting at an appointed place ~ vb -voused; -vous·ing : meet at a rendezvous

ren·di·tion \ren'dishən\ n : version

ren·e·gade \reni,gād\ n : deserter of one faith or cause for another

re·nege \ri'nig, -'neg, -'nēg, -'nāg\ vb -neged; -neg·ing : go back on a promise —**re·neg·er** n

re·new \ri'nü, -'nyü\ vb 1 : make or become new, fresh, or strong again 2 : begin again 3 : grant or obtain an extension of —**re·new·able** adj —**re·new·al** n —**re·new·er** n

re·nounce \ri'nauns\ vb -nounced; -nounc·ing : give up, refuse, or resign —**re·nounce·ment** n

ren·o·vate \renə,vāt\ vb -vat·ed; -vat·ing : make like new again —**ren·o·va·tion** \renə'vāshən\ n —**ren·o·va·tor** \renə,vātər\ n

re·nown \ri'naun\ n : state of being widely known and honored —**re·nowned** \-naund\ adj

¹rent \'rent\ n : money paid or due periodically for the use of another's property ~ vb : hold or give possession and use of for rent —**rent·al** n or adj —**rent·er** n

²rent n : a tear in cloth

re·nun·ci·a·tion \ri,nənsē'āshən\ n : act of renouncing

¹re·pair \ri'par\ vb : go

²repair vb : restore to good condition ~ n 1 : act or instance of repairing 2 : condition —**re·pair·er** n —**re·pair·man** \-,man\ n

rep·a·ra·tion \repə'rāshən\ n : money paid for redress—usu. pl.

rep·ar·tee \repər'tē\ n : clever replies

re·past \ri'past, 'rē,past\ n : meal

re·pa·tri·ate \rē'pātrē,āt\ vb -at·ed; -at·ing : send back to one's own country —**re·pa·tri·ate** \-trēət, -trē,āt\ n —**re·pa·tri·a·tion** \-,pātrē'āshən\ n

re·pay \rē'pā\ vb -paid; -pay·ing : pay back —**re·pay·able** adj —**re·pay·ment** n

re·peal \ri'pēl\ vb : annul by legislative action —**repeal** n —**re·peal·er** n

re·peat \ri'pēt\ vb : say or do again ~ n 1 : act of repeating 2 : something repeated —**re·peat·able** adj —**re·peat·ed·ly** adv —**re·peat·er** n

re·pel \ri'pel\ vb -pelled; -pel·ling 1 : drive away 2 : disgust —**re·pel·lent** \-'pelənt\ adj or n

re·pent \ri'pent\ vb 1 : turn from sin 2 : regret —**re·pen·tance** \ri'pent³ns\ n —**re·pen·tant** \-³nt\ adj

re·per·cus·sion \,rēpər'kəshən, ,rep-\ n : effect of something done or said

rep·er·toire \repər,twär\ n : pieces a company or performer can present

rep·er·to·ry \repər,tórē\ n, pl -ries 1 : repertoire 2 : theater with a resident company doing several plays

rep·e·ti·tion \,repə'tishən\ n : act or instance of repeating

rep·e·ti·tious \-'tishəs\ adj : tediously repeating —**rep·e·ti·tious·ly** adv —**rep·e·ti·tious·ness** n

re·pet·i·tive \ri'petətiv\ adj : repetitious —**re·pet·i·tive·ly** adv —**re·pet·i·tive·ness** n

re·pine \ri'pīn\ vb re·pined; re·pin·ing 1 : feel or express discontent

re·place \ri'plās\ vb 1 : restore to a former position 2 : take the place of 3 : put something new in the place of —**re·place·able** adj —**re·place·ment** n —**re·plac·er** n

re·plen·ish \ri'plenish\ vb : stock or supply anew —**re·plen·ish·ment** n

re·plete \ri'plēt\ adj : full —**re·plete·ness** n —**re·ple·tion** \-'plēshən\ n

rep·li·ca \replikə\ n : exact copy

rep·li·cate \replə,kāt\ vb -cat·ed; -cat·ing 1 : duplicate or repeat —**rep·li·cate** \-likət\ n —**rep·li·ca·tion** \-lə'kāshən\ n

re·ply \ri'plī\ vb -plied; -ply·ing : say or do in answer ~ n, pl -plies : answer

re·port \ri'pōrt\ n 1 : rumor 2 : statement of information (as events or causes) 3 : explosive noise ~ vb 1 : give an account of 2 : present an account of (an event) as news 3 : present oneself 4 : make known to authorities —**re·port·age** \ri'pōrtij, ,repər'täzh, ,rep,ór'-\ n —**re·port·ed·ly** adv —**re·port·er** n —**re·por·to·ri·al** \,repər'tōrēəl\ adj

re·pose \ri'pōz\ vb -posed; -pos·ing : lay or lie at rest ~ n 1 : state of resting 2 : calm or peace —**re·pose·ful** adj

re·pos·i·to·ry \ri'päzə,tōrē\ n, pl -ries : place where something is stored

re·pos·sess \,rēpə'zes\ vb : regain possession and legal ownership of —**re·pos·ses·sion** \-'zeshən\ n

rep·re·hend \repri'hend\ vb : censure —**rep·re·hen·sion** \-'henchən\ n

rep·re·hen·si·ble \-'hensəbəl\ adj : deserving condemnation —**rep·re·hen·si·bly** adv

rep·re·sent \repri'zent\ vb 1 : serve as a sign or symbol of 2 : act or speak for 3 : describe as having a specified quality or character —**rep·re·sen·ta·tion** \repri-,zen'tāshən\ n

rep·re·sen·ta·tive \repri'zentətiv\ adj 1 : standing or acting for another 2 : carried on by elected representatives ~ n 1 : typical example 2 : one that represents another 3 : member of usu. the lower house of a legislature —**rep·re·sen·ta·tive·ly** adv —**rep·re·sen·ta·tive·ness** n

re·press \ri'pres\ vb : restrain or suppress —**re·pres·sion** \-'preshən\ n —**re·pres·sive** \-'presiv\ adj

re·prieve \ri'prēv\ n 1 : a delay in punishment 2 : temporary respite —**reprieve** vb

rep·ri·mand \reprə,mand\ n : formal or severe criticism —**reprimand** vb

re·pri·sal \ri'prīzəl\ n : act in retaliation

re·prise \ri'prēz\ n : musical repetition

re·proach \ri'prōch\ n 1 : disgrace 2 : rebuke ~ vb : express disapproval to —**re·proach·ful** adj —**re·proach·ful·ly** adv —**re·proach·ful·ness** n

rep·ro·bate \reprə,bāt\ n : scoundrel —**reprobate** adj

rep·ro·ba·tion \,reprə'bāshən\ n : strong disapproval

re·pro·duce \,rēprə'düs, -'dyüs\ vb 1 : produce again or anew 2 : produce offspring —**re·pro·duc·i·ble** \-'düsəbəl, -'dyü-\ adj —**re·pro·duc·tion** \-'dək-shən\ n —**re·pro·duc·tive** \-'dəktiv\ adj

re·proof \ri'prüf\ n : blame or censure for a fault

re·prove \ri'prüv\ vb -proved; -prov·ing : express disapproval to or of

rep·tile \rept³l, -,tīl\ n : air-breathing scaly vertebrate —**rep·til·ian** \rep'tilēən\ adj or n

re·pub·lic \ri'pəblik\ n : country with representative government

re·pub·li·can \-ən\ adj 1 : relating to or resembling a republic 2 : supporting a republic —**republican** n —**re·pub·li·can·ism** n

re·pu·di·ate \ri'pyüdē,āt\ vb -at·ed; -at·ing : refuse to have anything to do with —**re·pu·di·a·tion** \-,pyüdē'āshən\ n

re·pug·nant \ri'pəgnənt\ adj : contrary to one's tastes or principles —**re·pug·nance** \-nəns\ n —**re·pug·nant·ly** adv

re·pulse \ri'pəls\ vb -pulsed; -puls·ing 1 : drive or beat back 2 : rebuff 3 : be repugnant to —**repulse** n —**re·pul·sion** \-'pəlshən\ n

re·pul·sive \-siv\ adj : arousing aversion or disgust —**re·pul·sive·ly** adv —**re·pul·sive·ness** n

rep·u·ta·ble \repyətəbəl\ adj : having a good reputation —**rep·u·ta·bly** \-blē\ adv

rep·u·ta·tion \repyə'tāshən\ n : one's character or public esteem

re·pute \ri'pyüt\ vb -put·ed; -put·ing : think of as being ~ n : reputation —**re·put·ed** adj —**re·put·ed·ly** adv

re·quest \ri'kwest\ n : act or instance of asking for something or a thing asked for ~ vb 1 : make a request of 2 : ask for —**re·quest·er** n

re·qui·em \rekwēəm, 'rāk-\ n : Mass for a dead person or a musical setting for this

re·quire \ri'kwīr\ vb -quired; -quir·ing 1 : insist on 2 : call for as essential —**re·quire·ment** n

req·ui·site \rekwəzət\ adj : necessary —**requisite** n

req·ui·si·tion \,rekwə'zishən\ n : formal application or demand —**requisition** vb

re·quite \ri'kwīt\ vb -quit·ed; -quit·ing : make return for or to —**re·quit·al** \-'kwīt³l\ n

re·scind \ri'sind\ vb : repeal or cancel —**re·scis·sion** \-'sizhən\ n

res·cue \reskyü\ vb -cued; -cu·ing : set free from danger or confinement —**rescue** n —**res·cu·er** n

re·search \ri'sərch, 'rē,sərch\ n : careful or diligent search esp. for new knowledge —**research** vb —**re·search·er** n

re·sem·ble \ri'zembəl\ vb -sem·bled; -sem·bling : be like or similar to —**re·sem·blance** \-'zembləns\ n

re·sent \ri'zent\ vb : feel or show annoyance at —**re·sent·ful** adj —**re·sent·ful·ly** adv —**re·sent·ment** n

res·er·va·tion \,rezər'vāshən\ n 1 : act of reserving or something reserved 2 : limiting condition

re·serve \ri'zərv\ vb -served; -serv·ing 1 : store for future use 2 : set aside for special use ~ n 1 : something reserved 2 : restraint in words or bearing 3 : military forces withheld from action or not part of the regular services —**re·served** adj

res·er·voir \rezər,vwär, -,vwór, -,vór, -,vói\ n : place where something (as water) is kept in store

re·side \ri'zīd\ vb -sid·ed; -sid·ing 1 : make one's home 2 : be present

res·i·dence \rezədəns\ n 1 : act or fact of residing in a place 2 : place where one lives —**res·i·dent** \-ənt\ adj or n —**res·i·den·tial** \,rezə'denchəl\ adj

res·i·due \rezə,dü, -,dyü\ n : part remaining —**re·sid·u·al** \ri'zijəwəl\ adj

re·sign \ri'zīn\ vb 1 : give up deliberately 2 : give (oneself) over without resistance —**res·ig·na·tion** \,rezig'nāshən\ n —**re·sign·ed·ly** \-'zīnədlē\ adv

re·sil·ience \ri'zilyəns\ n : ability to recover or adjust easily

re·sil·ien·cy \-yənsē\ n : resilience

re·sil·ient \-yənt\ adj : elastic

res·in \rez³n\ n : substance from the gum or sap of trees —**res·in·ous** adj

re·sist \ri'zist\ vb 1 : withstand the force or effect of 2 : fight against —**re·sist·ible** \-'zistəbəl\ adj —**re·sist·less** adj

re·sis·tance \ri'zistəns\ n 1 : act of resisting 2 : ability of an organism to resist disease 3 : opposition to electric current

re·sis·tant \-tənt\ adj : giving resistance

res·o·lute \rezə,lüt\ adj : having a fixed purpose —**res·o·lute·ly** adv —**res·o·lute·ness** n

res·o·lu·tion \,rezə'lüshən\ n 1 : process of resolving 2 : firmness of purpose 3 : statement of the opinion, will, or intent of a body

re·solve \ri'zälv\ vb -solved; -solv·ing 1 : find an answer to 2 : make a formal resolution ~ n 1 : something resolved 2 : steadfast purpose —**re·solv·able** adj

res·o·nant \rez³nənt\ adj 1 : continuing to sound 2 : relating to intensification or prolongation of sound (as by a vibrating body) —**res·o·nance** \-əns\ n —**res·o·nant·ly** adv

re·sort \ri'zórt\ n 1 : source of help 2 : place to go for vacation ~ vb 1 : go often or habitually 2 : have recourse

re·sound \ri'zaund\ vb : become filled with sound

re·sound·ing \-iŋ\ adj : impressive —**re·sound·ing·ly** adv

re·source \rē,sórs, ri'sórs\ n 1 : new or reserve source 2 pl : available funds 3 : ability to handle situations —**re·source·ful** adj —**re·source·ful·ness** n

re·spect \ri'spekt\ n 1 : relation to something 2 : high or special regard 3 : detail ~ vb : consider deserving of high regard —**re·spect·er** n —**re·spect·ful** adj —**re·spect·ful·ly** adv —**re·spect·ful·ness** n

re·spect·able \ri'spektəbəl\ adj 1 : worthy of respect 2 : fair in size, quantity, or quality —**re·spect·abil·i·ty** \-,spektə'bilətē\ n —**re·spect·ably** \-'spektəblē\ adv

re·spec·tive \-tiv\ adj : individual and specific

re·spec·tive·ly \-lē\ adv 1 : as relating to each 2 : each in the order given

res·pi·ra·tion \,respə'rāshən\ n : act or process of breathing —**re·spi·ra·to·ry** \respərə,tōrē, ri'spīrə-\ adj —**re·spire** \ri'spīr\ vb

res·pi·ra·tor \respə,rātər\ n : device for artificial respiration

re·spite \respət\ n : temporary delay or rest

re·splen·dent \ri'splendənt\ adj : shining brilliantly —**re·splen·dence** \-dəns\ n —**re·splen·dent·ly** adv

re·spond \ri'spänd\ vb 1 : answer 2 : react —**re·spon·dent** \-'spändənt\ n or adj —**re·spond·er** n

re·sponse \ri'späns\ n 1 : act of responding 2 : answer

re·spon·si·ble \ri'spänsəbəl\ adj 1 : answerable for acts or decisions **2** : able to fulfill obligations **3** : having important duties —**re·spon·si·bil·i·ty** \ri,spänsə'bilətē\ n —**re·spon·si·ble·ness** n —**re·spon·si·bly** \-blē\ adv

re·spon·sive \-siv\ adj : quick to respond —**re·spon·sive·ly** adv —**re·spon·sive·ness** n

¹rest \'rest\ n **1** : sleep **2** : freedom from work or activity **3** : state of inactivity **4** : something used as a support ~ vb **1** : get rest **2** : cease action or motion **3** : give rest to **4** : sit or lie fixed or supported **5** : depend —**rest·ful** adj —**rest·ful·ly** adv

²rest n : remainder

res·tau·rant \'restərənt, -tə,ränt\ n : public eating place

res·ti·tu·tion \,restə'tüshən, -'tyü-\ n : act or fact of restoring something or repaying someone

res·tive \'restiv\ adj : uneasy or fidgety —**res·tive·ly** adv —**res·tive·ness** n

rest·less \'restləs\ adj **1** : lacking or giving no rest **2** : always moving **3** : uneasy —**rest·less·ly** adv —**rest·less·ness** n

re·store \ri'stōr\ vb -**stored**; -**stor·ing** **1** : give back **2** : put back into use or into a former state —**re·stor·able** adj —**res·to·ra·tion** \,restə'rāshən\ n —**re·stor·ative** \ri'stōrətiv\ n or adj —**re·stor·er** n

re·strain \ri'strān\ vb : limit or keep under control —**re·strain·able** adj —**re·strained** \-'strānd\ adj —**re·strain·ed·ly** \-'strānədlē\ adv —**re·strain·er** n

restraining order n : legal order directing one person to stay away from another

re·straint \-'strānt\ n **1** : act of restraining **2** : restraining force **3** : control over feelings

re·strict \ri'strikt\ vb **1** : confine within bounds **2** : limit use of —**re·stric·tion** \-'strikshən\ n —**re·stric·tive** adj —**re·stric·tive·ly** adv

re·sult \ri'zəlt\ vb : come about because of something else ~ n **1** : thing that results **2** : something obtained by calculation or investigation —**re·sul·tant** \-'zəlt⁼nt\ adj or n

re·sume \ri'züm\ vb -**sumed**; -**sum·ing** : return to or take up again after interruption —**re·sump·tion** \-'zəmp-shən\ n

ré·su·mé, re·su·me, re·su·mé \'rezə,mā, ,rezə'-\ n : summary of one's career and qualifications

re·sur·gence \ri'sərjəns\ n : a rising again —**re·sur·gent** \-jənt\ adj

res·ur·rect \,rezə'rekt\ vb **1** : raise from the dead **2** : bring to attention or use again —**res·ur·rec·tion** \-'rekshən\ n

re·sus·ci·tate \ri'səsə,tāt\ vb -**tat·ed**; -**tat·ing** : bring back from apparent death —**re·sus·ci·ta·tion** \ri,səsə'tāshən, ,rē-\ n —**re·sus·ci·ta·tor** \-,tātər\ n

re·tail \'rē,tāl\ vb : sell in small quantities directly to the consumer ~ n : business of selling to consumers —**retail** adj or adv —**re·tail·er** n

re·tain \ri'tān\ vb **1** : keep or hold onto **2** : engage the services of

re·tain·er n **1** : household servant **2** : retaining fee

re·tal·i·ate \ri'talē,āt\ vb -**at·ed**; -**at·ing** : return (as an injury) in kind —**re·tal·i·a·tion** \-,talē'āshən\ n —**re·tal·i·a·to·ry** \-'talyə,tōrē\ adj

re·tard \ri'tärd\ vb : hold back —**re·tar·da·tion** \,rē,tär'dāshən, ri-\ n

re·tard·ed \ri'tärdəd\ adj : slow or limited in intellectual development

retch \'rech\ vb : try to vomit

re·ten·tion \ri'tenchən\ n **1** : state of being retained **2** : ability to retain —**re·ten·tive** \-'tentiv\ adj

ret·i·cent \'retəsənt\ adj : tending not to talk —**ret·i·cence** \-səns\ n —**ret·i·cent·ly** adv

ret·i·na \'ret⁼nə\ n, pl -**nas** or -**nae** \-⁼n,ē\ : sensory membrane lining the eye —**ret·i·nal** \'ret⁼nəl\ adj

ret·i·nue \'ret⁼n,ü, -,yü\ n : attendants or followers of a distinguished person

re·tire \ri'tīr\ vb -**tired**; -**tir·ing** **1** : withdraw for privacy **2** : end a career **3** : go to bed —**re·tir·ee** \ri,tī'rē\ n —**re·tire·ment** n

re·tir·ing \ri'tīriŋ\ adj : shy

re·tort \ri'tȯrt\ vb : say in reply ~ n : quick, witty, or cutting answer

re·trace \,rē'trās\ vb **1** : draw back or in **2** : go over again or in reverse

re·tract \ri'trakt\ vb **1** : draw back or in **2** : withdraw a charge or promise —**re·tract·able** adj —**re·trac·tion** \-'trakshən\ n

re·treat \ri'trēt\ n **1** : act of withdrawing **2** : place of privacy or safety or meditation and study ~ vb : make a retreat

re·trench \ri'trench\ vb : cut down (as expenses) —**re·trench·ment** n

ret·ri·bu·tion \,retrə'byüshən\ n : retaliation —**re·trib·u·tive** \ri'tribyətiv\ adj —**re·trib·u·to·ry** \-yə,tōrē\ adj

re·trieve \ri'trēv\ vb -**trieved**; -**triev·ing** **1**

: search for and bring in game **2** : recover —**re·triev·able** adj —**re·triev·al** \-'trē-vəl\ n

re·triev·er \-'trēvər\ n : dog for retrieving game

ret·ro·ac·tive \,retrō'aktiv\ adj : made effective as of a prior date —**ret·ro·ac·tive·ly** adv

ret·ro·grade \'retrə,grād\ adj **1** : moving backward **2** : becoming worse

ret·ro·gress \,retrə'gres\ vb **1** : move backward —**ret·ro·gres·sion** \-'greshən\ n

ret·ro·spect \'retrə,spekt\ n : review of past events —**ret·ro·spec·tion** \,retrə'spek-shən\ n —**ret·ro·spec·tive** \-'spektiv\ adj —**ret·ro·spec·tive·ly** adv

re·turn \ri'tərn\ vb **1** : go or come back **2** : pass, give, or send back to an earlier possessor **3** : answer **4** : bring in as a profit **5** : give or do in return ~ n **1** : act of returning or something returned **2** pl : report of balloting results **3** : statement of taxable income **4** : profit —**return** adj —**re·turn·able** adj or n —**re·turn·er** n

re·union \rē'yünyən\ n **1** : act of reuniting **2** : a meeting of persons after a separation

re·vamp \rē'vamp\ vb : renovate or revise

re·veal \ri'vēl\ vb **1** : make known **2** : show plainly

re·veil·le \'revəlē\ n : military signal sounded about sunrise

rev·el \'revəl\ vb -**eled** or -**elled**; -**el·ing** or -**el·ling** **1** : take part in a revel **2** : take great pleasure ~ n : wild party or celebration —**rev·el·er, rev·el·ler** \-ər\ n —**rev·el·ry** \-rē\ n

rev·e·la·tion \,revə'lāshən\ n **1** : act of revealing **2** : something enlightening or astonishing

re·venge \ri'venj\ vb -**venged**; -**veng·ing** : avenge ~ n **1** : desire for retaliation **2** : act of retaliation —**re·venge·ful** adj —**re·veng·er** n

rev·e·nue \'revə,nü, -,nyü\ n : money collected by a government

re·vere \ri'vir\ vb -**vered**; -**ver·ing** : show honor and devotion to —**rev·er·ence** \'revərəns\ n —**rev·er·ent** \-rənt\ adj —**rev·er·ent·ly** adv

rev·er·end \'revərənd\ adj : worthy of reverence ~ n : clergy member

rev·er·ie \'revərē\ n, pl -**er·ies** : daydream

re·verse \ri'vərs\ adj **1** : opposite to a previous or normal condition **2** : acting in an opposite way ~ vb -**versed**; -**vers·ing** **1** : turn upside down or completely around **2** : change to the contrary or in the opposite direction ~ n **1** : something contrary **2** : change for the worse **3** : back of something —**re·ver·sal** \-səl\ n —**re·verse·ly** adv —**re·vers·ible** \-'vərsəbəl\ adj

re·vert \ri'vərt\ vb : return to an original type or condition —**re·ver·sion** \-'vər-zhⁿn\ n

re·view \ri'vyü\ n **1** : formal inspection **2** : general survey **3** : critical evaluation **4** : second or repeated study or examination ~ vb **1** : examine or study again **2** : reexamine judicially **3** : look back over **4** : examine critically **5** : inspect —**re·view·er** n

re·vile \ri'vīl\ vb -**viled**; -**vil·ing** : abuse verbally —**re·vile·ment** n —**re·vil·er** n

re·vise \-'vīz\ vb -**vised**; -**vis·ing** **1** : look over something written to correct or improve **2** : make a new version of —**re·vis·able** adj —**re·vis·er, re·vi·sor** \-'vīzər\ n —**re·vi·sion** \-'vizhən\ n

re·viv·al \-'vīvəl\ n **1** : act of reviving or state of being revived **2** : evangelistic meeting

re·vive \-'vīv\ vb -**vived**; -**viv·ing** : bring back to life or consciousness or into use —**re·viv·er** n

re·vo·ca·tion \,revə'kāshən\ n : act or instance of revoking

re·voke \-'vōk\ vb -**voked**; -**vok·ing** : annul by recalling —**re·vok·er** n

re·volt \-'vōlt\ vb **1** : throw off allegiance **2** : cause or experience disgust or shock ~ n : rebellion or revolution —**re·volt·er** n

re·volt·ing \-iŋ\ adj : extremely offensive —**re·volt·ing·ly** adv

rev·o·lu·tion \,revə'lüshən\ n **1** : rotation **2** : progress in an orbit **3** : sudden, radical, or complete change (as overthrow of a government) —**rev·o·lu·tion·ary** \-shə,narē\ adj or n

rev·o·lu·tion·ize \-shə,nīz\ vb -**ized**; -**iz·ing** : change radically —**rev·o·lu·tion·iz·er** n

re·volve \ri'välv\ vb -**volved**; -**volv·ing** **1** : ponder **2** : move in an orbit **3** : rotate —**re·volv·able** adj

re·volv·er \ri'välvər\ n : pistol with a revolving cylinder

re·vue \ri'vyü\ n : theatrical production of brief numbers

re·vul·sion \ri'vəlshən\ n : complete dislike or repugnance

re·ward \ri'wȯrd\ vb : give a reward to or

for ~ n : something offered for service or achievement

re·write \rē'rīt\ vb -**wrote**; -**writ·ten**; -**writ·ing** : revise —**rewrite** n

rhap·so·dy \'rapsədē\ n, pl -**dies** **1** : expression of extravagant praise **2** : flowing free-form musical composition —**rhap·sod·ic** \rap'sädik\ adj —**rhap·sod·i·cal·ly** \-iklē\ adv —**rhap·so·dize** \'rap-sə,dīz\ vb

rhet·o·ric \'retərik\ n : art of speaking or writing effectively —**rhe·tor·i·cal** \ri'tȯrikəl\ adj —**rhet·o·ri·cian** \,retə'ri-shən\ n

rheu·ma·tism \'rümə,tizəm, 'rùm-\ n : disorder marked by inflammation or pain in muscles or joints —**rheu·mat·ic** \rù-'matik\ adj

rhine·stone \'rīn,stōn\ n : a colorless imitation gem

rhi·no \'rīnō\ n, pl -**no** or -**nos** : rhinoceros

rhi·noc·er·os \rī'näsərəs\ n, pl -**noc·er·os·es** or -**noc·er·os** or -**noc·eri** \-'näsə,rī\ : large thick-skinned mammal with 1 or 2 horns on the snout

rho·do·den·dron \,rōdə'dendrən\ n : flowering evergreen shrub

rhom·bus \'rämbəs\ n, pl -**bus·es** or -**bi** \-,bī\ : parallelogram with equal sides

rhu·barb \'rü,bärb\ n : garden plant with edible stalks

rhyme \'rīm\ n **1** : correspondence in terminal sounds **2** : verse that rhymes ~ vb **rhymed**; **rhym·ing** : make or have rhymes

rhythm \'rithəm\ n : regular succession of sounds or motions —**rhyth·mic** \'rith-mik\, **rhyth·mi·cal** \-mikəl\ adj —**rhyth·mi·cal·ly** adv

rhythm and blues n : popular music based on blues and black folk music

rib \'rib\ n **1** : curved bone joined to the spine **2** : riblike thing ~ vb -**bb- 1** : furnish or mark with ribs **2** : tease —**rib·ber** n

rib·ald \'ribəld\ adj : coarse or vulgar —**rib·ald·ry** \-əldrē\ n

rib·bon \'ribən\ n **1** : narrow strip of fabric used esp. for decoration **2** : strip of inked cloth (as in a typewriter)

ri·bo·fla·vin \,rībō'flāvən, 'rībə,-\ n : growth-promoting vitamin

rice \'rīs\ n, pl **rice** : starchy edible seeds of an annual cereal grass

rich \'rich\ adj **1** : having a lot of money or possessions **2** : valuable **3** : containing much sugar, fat, or seasoning **4** : abundant **5** : deep and pleasing in color or tone **6** : fertile —**rich·ly** adv —**rich·ness** n

rich·es \'richəz\ n pl : wealth

rick·ets \'rikəts\ n : childhood bone disease

rick·ety \'rikətē\ adj : shaky

rick·sha, rick·shaw \'rik,shȯ\ n : small covered 2-wheeled carriage pulled by one person

ric·o·chet \'rikə,shā, Brit also -,shet\ vb -**cheted** \-,shād\ or -**chet·ted** \-,shetəd\; -**chet·ing** \-,shāiŋ\ or -**chet·ting** \-,shetiŋ\ : bounce off at an angle —**ricochet** n

rid \'rid\ vb **rid**; **rid·ding** : make free of something unwanted —**rid·dance** \'rid-ⁿs\ n

rid·den \'rid⁼n\ adj : overburdened with— used in combination

¹rid·dle \'rid⁼n\ n : puzzling question ~ vb -**dled**; -**dling** : speak in riddles

²riddle vb -**dled**; -**dling** : fill full of holes

ride \'rīd\ vb **rode** \'rōd\; **rid·den** \'rid⁼n\; **rid·ing** \'rīdiŋ\ **1** : be carried along **2** : sit on and cause to move **3** : travel over a surface **4** : tease or nag ~ n **1** : trip on an animal or in a vehicle **2** : mechanical device ridden for amusement

rid·er n **1** : one that rides **2** : attached clause or document —**rid·er·less** adj

ridge \'rij\ n **1** : range of hills **2** : raised line or strip **3** : line of intersection of 2 sloping surfaces —**ridgy** adj

rid·i·cule \'ridə,kyül\ vb -**culed**; -**cul·ing** : laugh at or make fun of —**ridicule** n

ri·dic·u·lous \rə'dikyələs\ adj : arousing ridicule —**ri·dic·u·lous·ly** adv —**ri·dic·u·lous·ness** n

rife \'rīf\ adj : abounding —**rife** adv

riff·raff \'rif,raf\ n : mob

¹ri·fle \'rīfəl\ vb -**fled**; -**fling** : ransack esp. with intent to steal —**ri·fler** \-flər\ n

²rifle n : long shoulder weapon with spiral grooves in the bore —**ri·fle·man** \-mən\ n —**ri·fling** n

rift \'rift\ n : separation —**rift** vb

¹rig \'rig\ vb -**gg- 1** : fit out with rigging **2** : set up esp. as a makeshift ~ n **1** : distinctive shape, number, and arrangement of sails and masts of a sailing ship **2** : equipment **3** : carriage with its horse

²rig vb -**gg- 1** : manipulate esp. by deceptive or dishonest means

rig·ging \'rigiŋ, -ən\ n : lines that hold and move the masts, sails, and spars of a sailing ship

right \'rīt\ adj **1** : meeting a standard of conduct **2** : correct **3** : genuine **4** : normal **5**

: opposite of left ~ n **1** : something that is correct, just, proper, or honorable **2** : something to which one has a just claim **3** : something that is on the right side ~ adv **1** : according to what is right **2** : immediately **3** : completely **4** : on or to the right ~ vb **1** : restore to a proper state **2** : bring or become upright again —**right·er** n —**right·ness** n —**right·ward** \-wərd\ adj

right angle n : angle whose sides are perpendicular to each other —**right-an·gled** \'rīt'aŋgəld\ or **right-an·gle** \-gəl\ adj

righ·teous \'rīchəs\ adj : acting or being in accordance with what is just or moral —**righ·teous·ly** adv —**righ·teous·ness** n

right·ful \'rītfəl\ adj : lawful —**right·ful·ly** \-ē\ adv —**right·ful·ness** n

right·ly \'rītlē\ adv **1** : justly **2** : properly **3** : correctly

rig·id \'rijəd\ adj : lacking flexibility —**ri·gid·i·ty** \rə'jidətē\ n —**rig·id·ly** adv

rig·ma·role \'rigmə,rōl, 'rigə-\ n **1** : meaningless talk **2** : complicated often unnecessary procedure

rig·or \'rigər\ n : severity —**rig·or·ous** adj —**rig·or·ous·ly** adv

rig·or mor·tis \,rigər'mȯrtəs\ n : temporary stiffness of muscles occurring after death

rile \'rīl\ vb **riled**; **ril·ing** : anger

rill \'ril\ n : small brook

¹rim \'rim\ n : edge esp. of something curved ~ vb -**mm-** : border

¹rime \'rīm\ n : frost —**rimy** \'rīmē\ adj

²rime var of RHYME

rind \'rīnd\ n : usu. hard or tough outer layer

¹ring \'riŋ\ n **1** : circular band used as an ornament or for holding or fastening **2** : something circular **3** : place for contest or display **4** : group with a selfish or dishonest aim ~ vb : surround —**ringed** \'riŋd\ adj —**ring·like** adj

²ring vb **rang** \'raŋ\; **rung** \'rəŋ\; **ring·ing** **1** : sound resonantly when struck **2** : cause to make a metallic sound by striking **3** : resound **4** : call esp. by a bell ~ n **1** : resonant sound or tone **2** : act or instance of ringing

ring·er \'riŋər\ n **1** : one that sounds by ringing **2** : illegal substitute **3** : one that closely resembles another

ring·lead·er \'riŋ,lēdər\ n : leader esp. of troublemakers

ring·let n : long curl

ring·worm n : contagious skin disease caused by fungi

rink \'riŋk\ n : enclosed place for skating

rinse \'rins\ vb **rinsed**; **rins·ing** **1** : cleanse usu. with water only **2** : treat (hair) with a rinse ~ n : liquid used for rinsing —**rins·er** n

ri·ot \'rīət\ n **1** : violent public disorder **2** : random or disorderly profusion —**riot** vb —**ri·ot·er** n —**ri·ot·ous** adj

rip \'rip\ vb -**pp-** : cut or tear open ~ n : rent made by ripping —**rip·per** n

ripe \'rīp\ adj **rip·er**; **rip·est** : fully grown, developed, or prepared —**ripe·ly** adv —**rip·en** \'rīpən\ vb —**ripe·ness** n

rip-off n : theft —**rip off** vb

rip·ple \'ripəl\ vb -**pled**; -**pling 1** : become lightly ruffled on the surface **2** : sound like rippling water —**ripple** n

rise \'rīz\ vb **rose** \'rōz\; **ris·en** \'riz⁼n\; **ris·ing** \'rīziŋ\ **1** : get up from sitting, kneeling, or lying **2** : take arms **3** : appear above the horizon **4** : ascend **5** : gain a higher position or rank **6** : increase ~ n **1** : act of rising **2** : origin **3** : elevation **4** : increase **5** : upward slope **6** : area of high ground —**ris·er** \'rīzər\ n

risk \'risk\ n : exposure to loss or injury —**risk** vb —**risk·i·ness** n —**risky** adj

ris·qué \ris'kā\ adj : nearly indecent

rite \'rīt\ n **1** : set form for conducting a ceremony **2** : liturgy of a church **3** : ceremonial action

rit·u·al \'richəwəl\ n : rite —**ritual** adj —**rit·u·al·ism** \-,izəm\ n —**rit·u·al·is·tic** \,richəwəl'istik\ adj —**rit·u·al·is·ti·cal·ly** \-tiklē\ adv —**rit·u·al·ly** \'richəwəlē\ adv

ri·val \'rīvəl\ n **1** : competitor **2** : peer ~ vb -**valed** or -**valled**; -**val·ing** or -**val·ling 1** : be in competition with **2** : equal —**rival** adj —**ri·val·ry** \-rē\ n

riv·er \'rivər\ n : large natural stream of water —**riv·er·bank** n —**riv·er·bed** n —**riv·er·boat** n —**riv·er·side** n

riv·et \'rivət\ n : headed metal bolt ~ vb : fasten with a rivet —**riv·et·er** n

riv·u·let \'rivyələt\ n : small stream

roach \'rōch\ n : cockroach

road \'rōd\ n : open way for vehicles, persons, and animals —**road·bed** n —**road·side** n or adj —**road·way** n

road·block n : obstruction on a road

road·run·ner n : large fast-running bird

roam \'rōm\ vb : wander

roan \'rōn\ adj : of a dark color sprinkled with white ~ n : animal with a roan coat

roar \'rȯr\ vb : utter a full loud prolonged sound —**roar** n —**roar·er** n

roast \rōst\ *vb* **1** : cook by dry heat **2** : criticize severely ~ *n* : piece of meat suitable for roasting —**roast** *adj* —**roast•er** *n*

rob \räb\ *vb* **-bb- 1** : steal from **2** : commit robbery —**rob•ber** *n*

rob•bery \räbərē\ *n, pl* **-ber•ies** : theft of something from a person by use of violence or threat

robe \rōb\ *n* **1** : long flowing outer garment **2** : covering for the lower body ~ *vb* **robed; rob•ing** : clothe with or as if with a robe

rob•in \räbən\ *n* : No. American thrush with a reddish breast

ro•bot \rō,bät, -bət\ *n* **1** : machine that looks and acts like a human being **2** : efficient but insensitive person —**ro•bot•ic** \rō'bätik\ *adj*

ro•bust \rō'bəst, 'rō,bəst\ *adj* : strong and vigorously healthy — **ro•bust•ly** *adv* —**ro•bust•ness** *n*

¹rock \räk\ *vb* : sway or cause to sway back and forth ~ *n* **1** : rocking movement **2** : popular music marked by repetition and a strong beat

²rock *n* : mass of hard mineral material —**rock** *adj* —**rocky** *adj*

rock•er *n* **1** : curved piece on which a chair rocks **2** : chair that rocks

rock•et \räkət\ *n* **1** : self-propelled firework or missile **2** : jet engine that carries its own oxygen ~ *vb* : rise abruptly and rapidly —**rock•et•ry** \-ətrē\ *n*

rod \räd\ *n* **1** : straight slender stick **2** : unit of length equal to 5 yards

rode *past of* RIDE

ro•dent \rōdᵊnt\ *n* : usu. small gnawing mammal

ro•deo \rōdē,ō, rō'dāō\ *n, pl* **-de•os** : contest of cowboy skills

roe \rō\ *n* : fish eggs

rogue \rōg\ *n* **1** : dishonest or mischievous person —**rogu•ery** \rōgərē\ *n* —**rogu•ish** \rōgish\ *adj* —**rogu•ish•ly** *adv* —**rogu•ish•ness** *n*

roil \roíl\ *vb* **1** : make cloudy or muddy by stirring up **2** : make angry

role \rōl\ *n* **1** : part to play **2** : function

roll \rōl\ *n* **1** : official record or list of names **2** : something rolled up or rounded **3** : bread baked in a small rounded mass **4** : sound of rapid drum strokes **5** : heavy reverberating sound **6** : rolling movement ~ *vb* **1** : move by turning over **2** : move on wheels **3** : flow in a continuous stream **4** : swing from side to side **5** : shape or be shaped in rounded form **6** : press with a roller

roll•er *n* **1** : revolving cylinder **2** : rod on which something is rolled up **3** : long heavy ocean wave

roller skate *n* : a skate with wheels instead of a runner —**roller–skate** *vb*

rol•lick•ing \rälikiŋ\ *adj* : full of good spirits

Ro•man Catholic \rōmən-\ *n* : member of a Christian church led by a pope —**Roman Catholic** *adj* —**Roman Catholicism** *n*

ro•mance \rō'mans, 'rō,mans\ *n* **1** : medieval tale of knightly adventure **2** : love story **3** : love affair ~ *vb* **-manced; -manc•ing 1** : have romantic fancies **2** : have a love affair with —**ro•manc•er** *n*

ro•man•tic \rō'mantik\ *adj* **1** : visionary or imaginative **2** : appealing to one's emotions —**ro•man•ti•cal•ly** \-iklē\ *adv*

romp \rämp\ *vb* : play actively and noisily —**romp** *n*

roof \rüf, 'rüf\ *n, pl* **roofs** \rüfs, 'rüfs; 'rüvz, 'rüvz\ : upper covering part of a building ~ *vb* : cover with a roof —**roofed** \rüft, 'rüft\ *adj* —**roof•ing** *n* —**roof•less** *adj* —**roof•top** *n*

¹rook \ruk\ *n* : crowlike bird

²rook *vb* : cheat

rook•ie \rukē\ *n* : novice

room \rüm, 'rum\ *n* **1** : sufficient space **2** : partitioned part of a building ~ *vb* : occupy lodgings —**room•er** *n* —**room•ful** *n* —**roomy** *adj*

room•mate *n* : one sharing the same lodgings

roost \rüst\ *n* : support on which birds perch ~ *vb* : settle on a roost

roost•er \rüstər, 'rüs-\ *n* : adult male domestic chicken

¹root \rüt, 'rut\ *n* **1** : leafless underground part of a seed plant **2** : rootlike thing or part **3** : source **4** : essential core ~ *vb* : form, fix, or become fixed by roots —**root•less** *adj* —**root•let** \-lət\ *n* —**root•like** *adj*

²root *vb* : turn up with the snout

³root \rüt, 'rut\ *vb* : applaud or encourage noisily —**root•er** *n*

rope \rōp\ *n* : large strong cord of strands of fiber ~ *vb* **roped; rop•ing 1** : tie with a rope **2** : lasso

ro•sa•ry \rōzərē\ *n, pl* **-ries 1** : string of beads used in praying **2** : Roman Catholic devotion

¹rose *past of* RISE

²rose \rōz\ *n* **1** : prickly shrub with bright flowers **2** : purplish red —**rose** *adj* —**rose•bud** *n* —**rose•bush** *n*

rose•mary \rōz,merē\ *n, pl* **-mar•ies** : fragrant shrubby mint

ro•sette \rō'zet\ *n* : rose-shaped ornament

Rosh Ha•sha•nah \,räshä'shänə, ,rōsh-\ *n* : Jewish New Year observed as a religious holiday in September or October

ros•in \räzᵊn\ *n* : brittle resin

ros•ter \rästər\ *n* : list of names

ros•trum \rästrəm\ *n, pl* **-trums** *or* **-tra** \-trə\ : speaker's platform

rosy \rōzē\ *adj* **ros•i•er; -est 1** : of the color rose **2** : hopeful —**ros•i•ly** *adv* —**ros•i•ness** *n*

rot \rät\ *vb* **-tt-** : undergo decomposition ~ *n* **1** : decay **2** : disease in which tissue breaks down

ro•ta•ry \rōtərē\ *adj* **1** : turning on an axis **2** : having a rotating part

ro•tate \rō,tāt\ *vb* **-tat•ed; -tat•ing 1** : turn about an axis or a center **2** : alternate in a series —**ro•ta•tion** \rō'tāshən\ *n* —**ro•ta•tor** \rō,tātər\ *n*

rote \rōt\ *n* : repetition from memory

ro•tor \rōtər\ *n* **1** : part that rotates **2** : system of rotating horizontal blades for supporting a helicopter

rot•ten \rätᵊn\ *adj* **1** : having rotted **2** : corrupt **3** : extremely unpleasant or inferior —**rot•ten•ness** *n*

ro•tund \rō'tənd\ *adj* : rounded —**ro•tun•di•ty** \-'təndətē\ *n*

ro•tun•da \rō'təndə\ *n* : building or room with a dome

roué \ru'ā\ *n* : man given to debauched living

rouge \rüzh, 'rüj\ *n* : cosmetic for the cheeks —**rouge** *vb*

rough \rəf\ *adj* **1** : not smooth **2** : not calm **3** : harsh, violent, or rugged **4** : crudely or hastily done ~ *n* : rough state or something in that state ~ *vb* **1** : roughen **2** : manhandle **3** : make roughly —**rough•ly** *adv* —**rough•ness** *n*

rough•age \rəfij\ *n* : coarse bulky food

rough•en \rəfən\ *vb* : make or become rough

rough•neck \rəf,nek\ *n* : rowdy

rou•lette \rü'let\ *n* : gambling game using a whirling numbered wheel

¹round \raund\ *adj* **1** : having every part the same distance from the center **2** : cylindrical **3** : complete **4** : approximate **5** : blunt **6** : moving in or forming a circle ~ *n* **1** : round or curved thing **2** : series of recurring actions or events **3** : period of time or a unit of action **4** : fired shot **5** : cut of beef ~ *vb* **1** : make or become round **2** : go around **3** : finish ~ *adv* or *prep* : around —**round•ish** *adj* —**round•ly** *adv* —**round•ness** *n*

²round *prep or adv* : around

round•about *adj* : indirect

round•up \raund,əp\ *n* **1** : gathering together of range cattle **2** : summary —**round up** *vb*

rouse \rauz\ *vb* **roused; rous•ing 1** : wake from sleep **2** : stir up

rout \raut\ *n* **1** : state of wild confusion **2** : disastrous defeat ~ *vb* : defeat decisively

route \rüt, 'raut\ *n* : line of travel ~ *vb* **rout•ed; rout•ing** : send by a selected route

rou•tine \rü'tēn\ *n* **1** : regular course of procedure **2** : an often repeated speech, formula, or part —**routine** *adj* —**rou•tine•ly** *adv*

rove \rōv\ *vb* **roved; rov•ing** : wander or roam —**rov•er** *n*

¹row \rō\ *vb* **1** : propel a boat with oars **2** : carry in a rowboat ~ *n* : act of rowing —**row•boat** *n* —**row•er** \rōər\ *n*

²row *n* : number of objects in a line

³row \rau\ *n* : noisy quarrel —**row** *vb*

row•dy \raudē\ *adj* **-di•er; -est** : coarse or boisterous in behavior —**row•di•ness** *n* —**rowdy** *n*

roy•al \roíəl\ *adj* : relating to or befitting a king ~ *n* : person of royal blood —**roy•al•ly** *adv*

roy•al•ty \roíəltē\ *n, pl* **-ties 1** : state of being royal **2** : royal persons **3** : payment for use of property

rub \rəb\ *vb* **-bb- 1** : use pressure and friction on a body **2** : scour, polish, erase, or smear by pressure and friction **3** : chafe with friction ~ *n* : difficulty

rub•ber \rəbər\ *n* **1** : one that rubs **2** : waterproof elastic substance or something made of it —**rubber** *adj* —**rub•ber•ize** \-,īz\ *vb* —**rub•bery** *adj*

rub•bish \rəbish\ *n* : waste or trash

rub•ble \rəbəl\ *n* : broken fragments esp. of a destroyed building

ru•ble \rübəl\ *n* : monetary unit of Russia

ru•by \rübē\ *n, pl* **-bies** : precious red stone or its color —**ruby** *adj*

rud•der \rədər\ *n* : steering device at the rear of a ship or aircraft

rud•dy \rədē\ *adj* **-di•er; -est** : reddish —**rud•di•ness** *n*

rude \rüd\ *adj* **rud•er; rud•est 1** : roughly made **2** : impolite —**rude•ly** *adv* —**rude•ness** *n*

ru•di•ment \rüdəmənt\ *n* **1** : something not fully developed **2** : elementary principle —**ru•di•men•ta•ry** \,rüdə'mentərē\ *adj*

rue \rü\ *vb* **rued; ru•ing** : feel regret for ~ *n* : regret —**rue•ful** \-fəl\ *adj* —**rue•ful•ly** *adv* —**rue•ful•ness** *n*

ruf•fi•an \rəfēən\ *n* : brutal person

ruf•fle \rəfəl\ *vb* **-fled; -fling 1** : draw into or provide with pleats **2** : roughen the surface of **3** : irritate ~ *n* : strip of fabric pleated on one edge —**ruf•fly** \rəfəlē, -flē\ *adj*

rug \rəg\ *n* : piece of heavy fabric used as a floor covering

rug•ged \rəgəd\ *adj* **1** : having a rough uneven surface **2** : severe **3** : strong —**rug•ged•ly** *adv* —**rug•ged•ness** *n*

ru•in \rüən\ *n* **1** : complete collapse or destruction **2** : remains of something destroyed —usu. in pl. **3** : cause of destruction ~ *vb* **1** : destroy **2** : damage beyond repair **3** : bankrupt

ru•in•ous \rüənəs\ *adj* : causing ruin —**ru•in•ous•ly** *adv*

rule \rül\ *n* **1** : guide or principle for governing action **2** : usual way of doing something **3** : government **4** : straight strip (as of wood or metal) marked off in units for measuring ~ *vb* **ruled; rul•ing 1** : govern **2** : give as a decision —**rul•er** *n*

rum \rəm\ *n* : liquor made from molasses or sugarcane

rum•ble \rəmbəl\ *vb* **-bled; -bling** : make a low heavy rolling sound —**rumble** *n*

ru•mi•nant \rümənənt\ *n* : hoofed mammal (as a cow or deer) that chews the cud —**ruminant** *adj*

ru•mi•nate \rümə,nāt\ *vb* **-nat•ed; -nat•ing** : contemplate —**ru•mi•na•tion** \,rümə'nāshən\ *n*

rum•mage \rəmij\ *vb* **-maged; -mag•ing** : search thoroughly

rum•my \rəmē\ *n* : card game

ru•mor \rümər\ *n* **1** : common talk **2** : widespread statement not authenticated —**rumor** *vb*

rump \rəmp\ *n* : rear part of an animal

rum•ple \rəmpəl\ *vb* **-pled; -pling** : tousle or wrinkle —**rumple** *n*

rum•pus \rəmpəs\ *n* : disturbance

run \rən\ *vb* **ran** \ran\; **run; run•ning 1** : go rapidly or hurriedly **2** : enter a race or election **3** : operate **4** : continue in force **5** : flow rapidly **6** : take a certain direction **7** : manage **8** : incur ~ *n* : act of running **2** : brook **3** : continuous series **4** : usual kind **5** : freedom of movement **6** : lengthwise ravel

run•around *n* : evasive or delaying action esp. in response to a request

run•away \rənə,wā\ *n* : fugitive ~ *adj* **1** : fugitive **2** : out of control

run–down *adj* : being in poor condition

¹rung *past part of* RING

²rung \rəŋ\ *n* : horizontal piece of a chair or ladder

run•ner \rənər\ *n* **1** : one that runs **2** : thin piece or part on which something slides **3** : slender creeping branch of a plant

run•ner–up *n, pl* **run•ners–up** : competitor who finishes second

run•ning \rəniŋ\ *adj* **1** : flowing **2** : continuous

runt \rənt\ *n* : small person or animal —**runty** *adj*

run•way \rən,wā\ *n* : strip on which aircraft land and take off

ru•pee \rü'pē, 'rü,-\ *n* : monetary unit (as of India)

rup•ture \rəpchər\ *n* **1** : breaking or tearing apart **2** : hernia ~ *vb* **-tured; -tur•ing** : cause or undergo rupture

ru•ral \rürəl\ *adj* : relating to the country or agriculture

ruse \rüs, 'rüz\ *n* : trick

¹rush \rəsh\ *n* : grasslike marsh plant

²rush *vb* **1** : move forward or act with too great haste **2** : perform in a short time ~ *n* : violent forward motion ~ *adj* : requiring speed —**rush•er** *n*

rus•set \rəsət\ *n* **1** : reddish brown color **2** : a baking potato —**russet** *adj*

rust \rəst\ *n* **1** : reddish coating on exposed iron **2** : reddish brown color —**rust** *vb* —**rusty** *adj*

rus•tic \rəstik\ *adj* : relating to or suitable for the country or country dwellers ~ *n* : rustic person —**rus•ti•cal•ly** *adv*

rus•tle \rəsəl\ *vb* **-tled; -tling 1** : make or cause a rustle **2** : forage food **3** : steal cattle from the range ~ *n* : series of small sounds —**rus•tler** \-lər\ *n*

rut \rət\ *n* **1** : track worn by wheels or feet **2** : set routine —**rut•ted** *adj*

-ry \rē\ *n suffix* : -ery

rud•dy \rədē\ *adj* **-di•er; -est** : reddish

rye \rī\ *n* **1** : cereal grass grown for grain **2** : whiskey from rye

S

s \es\ *n, pl* **s's** *or* **ss** \esəz\ : 19th letter of the alphabet

¹-s \s *after sounds* f, k, k̲, p, t, th; əz *after sounds* ch, j, s, sh, z, zh; z *after other sounds*\ —used to form the plural of most nouns

²-s *vb suffix* —used to form the 3d person singular present of most verbs

Sab•bath \sabəth\ *n* **1** : Saturday observed as a day of worship by Jews and some Christians **2** : Sunday observed as a day of worship by Christians

sa•ber, sa•bre \sābər\ *n* : curved cavalry sword

sa•ble \sābəl\ *n* **1** : black **2** : dark brown mammal or its fur

sab•o•tage \sabə,täzh\ *n* : deliberate destruction or hampering ~ *vb* **-taged; -tag•ing** : wreck through sabotage

sab•o•teur \,sabə'tər\ *n* : person who sabotages

sac \sak\ *n* : anatomical pouch

sac•cha•rin \sakərən\ *n* : low-calorie artificial sweetener

sac•cha•rine \-ərən\ *adj* : nauseatingly sweet

sa•chet \sa'shā\ *n* : small bag with perfumed powder (**sachet powder**)

¹sack \sak\ *n* : bag ~ *vb* : fire

²sack *vb* : plunder a captured place

sack•cloth *n* : rough garment worn as a sign of penitence

sac•ra•ment \sakrəmənt\ *n* : formal religious act or rite —**sac•ra•men•tal** \,sakrə'mentᵊl\ *adj*

sa•cred \sākrəd\ *adj* **1** : set apart for or worthy of worship **2** : worthy of reverence **3** : relating to religion —**sa•cred•ly** *adv* —**sa•cred•ness** *n*

sac•ri•fice \sakrə,fīs\ *n* **1** : the offering of something precious to a deity or the thing offered **2** : loss or deprivation ~ *vb* **-ficed; -fic•ing** : offer or give up as a sacrifice —**sac•ri•fi•cial** \,sakrə'fishəl\ *adj*

sac•ri•lege \sakrəlij\ *n* : violation of something sacred —**sac•ri•le•gious** \,sakrə'lijəs, -'lējəs\ *adj*

sac•ro•sanct \sakrō,saŋkt\ *adj* : sacred

sad \sad\ *adj* **-dd- 1** : affected with grief or sorrow **2** : causing sorrow —**sad•den** \sadᵊn\ *vb* —**sad•ly** *adv* —**sad•ness** *n*

sad•dle \sadᵊl\ *n* : seat for riding on horseback ~ *vb* **-dled; -dling** : put a saddle on

sa•dism \sā,dizəm, 'sad,iz-\ *n* : delight in cruelty —**sa•dist** \sādist, 'sad-\ *n* —**sa•dis•tic** \sə'distik\ *adj* —**sa•dis•ti•cal•ly** *adv*

sa•fa•ri \sə'färē, -'far-\ *n* : hunting expedition in Africa

safe \sāf\ *adj* **saf•er; saf•est 1** : free from harm **2** : providing safety ~ *n* : container to keep valuables safe —**safe•keep•ing** *n* —**safe•ly** *adv*

safe•guard *n* : measure or device for preventing accidents —**safeguard** *vb*

safe•ty \sāftē\ *n, pl* **-ties 1** : freedom from danger **2** : protective device

saf•flow•er \saf,lauər\ *n* : herb with seeds rich in edible oil

saf•fron \safrən\ *n* : orange powder from a crocus flower used in cooking

sag \sag\ *vb* **-gg-** : droop, sink, or settle —**sag** *n*

sa•ga \sägə\ *n* : story of heroic deeds

sa•ga•cious \sə'gāshəs\ *adj* : shrewd —**sa•gac•i•ty** \-'gasətē\ *n*

¹sage \sāj\ *adj* : wise or prudent ~ *n* : wise man —**sage•ly** *adv*

²sage *n* : mint used in flavoring

sage•brush *n* : low shrub of the western U.S.

said *past of* SAY

sail \sāl\ *n* **1** : fabric used to catch the wind and move a boat or ship **2** : trip on a sailboat ~ *vb* **1** : travel on a ship or sailboat **2** : move with ease or grace —**sail•boat** *n* —**sail•or** \sālər\ *n*

sail•fish *n* : large fish with a very large dorsal fin

saint \sānt, *before a name* ,sānt *or* sənt\ *n* **1** : holy or godly person —**saint•ed** \-əd\ *adj* —**saint•hood** \-,hud\ *n* —**saint•li•ness** *n* —**saint•ly** *adj*

¹**sake** \'sāk\ *n* **1** : purpose or reason **2** : one's good or benefit

²**sa•ke, sa•ki** \'säkē\ *n* : Japanese rice wine

sa•la•cious \sə'lāshəs\ *adj* : sexually suggestive —**sa•la•cious•ly** *adv*

sal•ad \'saləd\ *n* : dish usu. of raw lettuce, vegetables, or fruit

sal•a•man•der \'salə,mandər\ *n* : lizardlike amphibian

sa•la•mi \sə'lämē\ *n* : highly seasoned dried sausage

sal•a•ry \'salərē\ *n, pl* **-ries** : regular payment for services

sale \'sāl\ *n* **1** : transfer of ownership of property for money **2** : selling at bargain prices **3 sales** *pl* : activities involved in selling —**sal•able, sale•able** \'sāləbəl\ —**sales•man** \-mən\ *n* —**sales•per•son** *n* —**sales•wom•an** *n*

sa•lient \'sālyənt\ *adj* : standing out conspicuously

sa•line \'sā,lēn, -,līn\ *adj* : containing salt —**sa•lin•i•ty** \sā'linətē, sə-\ *n*

sa•li•va \sə'līvə\ *n* : liquid secreted into the mouth —**sal•i•vary** \'salə,verē\ *adj* —**sal•i•vate** \-,vāt\ *vb* —**sal•i•va•tion** \,salə-'vāshən\ *n*

sal•low \'salō\ *adj* : of a yellowish sickly color

sal•ly \'salē\ *n, pl* **-lies 1** : quick attack on besiegers **2** : witty remark —**sally** *vb*

salm•on \'samən\ *n, pl* **salmon 1** : food fish with pink or red flesh **2** : deep yellowish pink color

sa•lon \sə'län, 'sal,än, sa'lōⁿ\ *n* : elegant room or shop

sa•loon \sə'lün\ *n* **1** : public cabin on a passenger ship **2** : barroom

sal•sa \'sȯlsə, 'säl-\ *n* : spicy sauce of tomatoes, onions, and hot peppers

salt \'sȯlt\ *n* **1** : white crystalline substance that consists of sodium and chlorine **2** : compound formed usu. from acid and metal —**salt** *vb or adj* —**salt•i•ness** — **salty** *adj*

salt•wa•ter *adj* : relating to or living in salt water

sa•lu•bri•ous \sə'lübrēəs\ *adj* : good for health

sal•u•tary \'salyə,terē\ *adj* : health-giving or beneficial

sal•u•ta•tion \,salyə'tāshən\ *n* : greeting

sa•lute \sə'lüt\ *vb* **-lut•ed; -lut•ing** : honor by ceremony or formal movement —**sa•lute** *n*

sal•vage \'salvij\ *n* : something saved from destruction ~ *vb* **-vaged; -vag•ing** : rescue or save

sal•va•tion \sal'vāshən\ *n* : saving of a person from sin or danger

salve \'sav, 'säv\ *n* : medicinal ointment ~ *vb* **salved; salv•ing** : soothe

sal•ver \'salvər\ *n* : small tray

sal•vo \'salvō\ *n, pl* **-vos** *or* **-voes** : simultaneous discharge of guns

same \'sām\ *adj* : being the one referred to ~ *pron* : the same one or ones ~ *adv* : in the same manner —**same•ness** *n*

sam•ple \'sampəl\ *n* : piece or part that shows the quality of a whole ~ *vb* **-pled; -pling** : judge by a sample

sam•pler \'samplər\ *n* : piece of needlework testing skill in embroidering

san•a•to•ri•um \,sanə'tōrēəm\ *n, pl* **-riums** *or* **-ria** \-ēə\ : hospital for the chronically ill

sanc•ti•fy \'saŋktə,fī\ *vb* **-fied; -fy•ing** : make holy —**sanc•ti•fi•ca•tion** \,saŋk-təfə'kāshən\ *n*

sanc•ti•mo•nious \,saŋktə'mōnēəs\ *adj* : hypocritically pious —**sanc•ti•mo•nious•ly** *adv*

sanc•tion \'saŋkshən\ *n* **1** : authoritative approval **2** : coercive measure —usu. pl ~ *vb* : approve

sanc•ti•ty \'saŋktətē\ *n, pl* **-ties** : quality or state of being holy or sacred

sanc•tu•ary \'saŋkchə,werē\ *n, pl* **-ar•ies 1** : consecrated place **2** : place of refuge

sand \'sand\ *n* : loose granular particles of rock ~ *vb* : smooth with an abrasive —**sand•bank** *n* —**sand•er** *n* —**sand•storm** *n* —**sandy** *adj*

san•dal \'sand³l\ *n* : shoe consisting of a sole strapped to the foot

sand•pa•per *n* : abrasive paper —**sandpa•per** *vb*

sand•pip•er \-,pīpər\ *n* : long-billed shorebird

sand•stone *n* : rock made of naturally cemented sand

sand•wich \'sand,wich\ *n* : 2 or more slices of bread with a filling between them ~ *vb* : squeeze or crowd in

sane \'sān\ *adj* **san•er; san•est 1** : mentally healthy **2** : sensible —**sane•ly** *adv*

sang *past of* SING

san•gui•nary \'saŋgwə,nerē\ *adj* : bloody

san•guine \'saŋgwən\ *adj* **1** : reddish **2** : cheerful

san•i•tar•i•um \,sanə'terēəm\ *n, pl* **-i•ums** *or* **-ia** \-ēə\ : sanatorium

san•i•tary \'sanəterē\ *adj* **1** : relating to

health **2** : free from filth or infective matter

san•i•ta•tion \,sanə'tāshən\ *n* : protection of health by maintenance of sanitary conditions

san•i•ty \'sanətē\ *n* : soundness of mind

sank *past of* SINK

¹**sap** \'sap\ *n* **1** : fluid that circulates through a plant **2** : gullible person

²**sap** *vb* **-pp- 1** : undermine **2** : weaken or exhaust gradually

sa•pi•ent \'sāpēənt, 'sapē-\ *adj* : wise —**sa•pi•ence** \-əns\ *n*

sap•ling \'sapliŋ\ *n* : young tree

sap•phire \'saf,īr\ *n* : hard transparent blue gem

sap•py \'sapē\ *adj* **-pi•er; -est 1** : full of sap **2** : overly sentimental

sap•suck•er \'sap,səkər\ *n* : small No. American woodpecker

sar•casm \'sär,kazəm\ *n* **1** : cutting remark **2** : ironical criticism or reproach —**sar•cas•tic** \sär'kastik\ *adj* —**sar•cas•ti•cal•ly** *adv*

sar•coph•a•gus \sär'käfəgəs\ *n, pl* **-gi** \-,gī, -,jī\ : large stone coffin

sar•dine \sär'dēn\ *n* : small fish preserved for use as food

sar•don•ic \sär'dänik\ *adj* : disdainfully humorous —**sar•don•i•cal•ly** *adv*

sa•rong \sə'rȯŋ, -'räŋ\ *n* : loose garment worn esp. by Pacific islanders

sar•sa•pa•ril•la \,saspə'rilə, ,särs-\ *n* : dried roots of a tropical American plant used esp. for flavoring or a carbonated drink flavored with this

sar•to•ri•al \sär'tōrēəl\ *adj* : relating to a tailor or men's clothes

¹**sash** \'sash\ *n* : broad band worn around the waist or over the shoulder

²**sash** *n, pl* **sash 1** : frame for a pane of glass in a door or window **2** : movable part of a window

sas•sa•fras \'sasə,fras\ *n* **1** : No. American tree or its dried root bark

sassy \'sasē\ *adj* **sass•i•er; -est** : saucy

sat *past of* SIT

Sa•tan \'sāt³n\ *n* : devil —**sa•tan•ic** \sə'tanik, sā-\ *adj* —**sa•tan•i•cal•ly** *adv*

satch•el \'sachəl\ *n* : small bag

sate \'sāt\ *vb* **sat•ed; sat•ing** : satisfy fully

sat•el•lite \'sat³l,īt\ *n* **1** : toady **2** : body or object that revolves around a larger celestial body

sa•ti•ate \'sāshē,āt\ *vb* **-at•ed; -at•ing** : sate —**sa•ti•e•ty** \sə'tīətē\ *n*

sat•in \'sat³n\ *n* : glossy fabric —**sat•iny** *adj*

sat•ire \'sa,tīr\ *n* : literary ridicule done with humor —**sa•tir•ic** \sə'tirik\, **sa•tir•i•cal** \-ikəl\ *adj* —**sa•tir•i•cal•ly** *adv* —**sat•i•rist** \'satərist\ *n* —**sat•i•rize** \-ə,rīz\ *vb*

sat•is•fac•tion \,satəs'fakshən\ *n* : state of being satisfied —**sat•is•fac•to•ri•ly** \-'faktərəlē\ *adv* —**sat•is•fac•to•ry** \-'faktərē\ *adj*

sat•is•fy \'satəs,fī\ *vb* **-fied; -fy•ing 1** : make happy **2** : pay what is due to or on —**sat•is•fy•ing•ly** *adv*

sat•u•rate \'sachə,rāt\ *vb* **-rat•ed; -rat•ing** : soak or charge thoroughly —**sat•u•ra•tion** \,sachə'rāshən\ *n*

Sat•ur•day \'satərdā, -dē\ *n* : 7th day of the week

sat•ur•nine \'satər,nīn\ *adj* : sullen

sa•tyr \'sātər, 'sat-\ *n* : pleasure-loving forest god of ancient Greece

sauce \'sȯs\ *n* : fluid dressing or topping for food —**sauce•pan** *n*

sau•cer \'sȯsər\ *n* : small shallow dish under a cup

saucy \'sasē, 'sȯse\ *adj* **sauc•i•er; -est** : insolent —**sauc•i•ly** *adv* —**sauc•i•ness** *n*

sau•er•kraut \'saủər,kraủt\ *n* : finely cut and fermented cabbage

sau•na \'saủnə\ *n* : steam or dry heat bath or a room or cabinet used for such a bath

saun•ter \'sȯntər, 'sänt-\ *vb* : stroll

sau•sage \'sȯsij\ *n* : minced and highly seasoned meat

sau•té \sȯ'tā, sō-\ *vb* **-téed** *or* **-téd; -té•ing** : fry in a little fat —**sauté** *n*

sav•age \'savij\ *adj* **1** : wild **2** : cruel ~ *n* : person belonging to a primitive society —**sav•age•ly** *adv* —**sav•age•ness** *n* —**sav•age•ry** *n*

¹**save** \'sāv\ *vb* **saved; sav•ing 1** : rescue from danger **2** : guard from destruction **3** : redeem from sin **4** : put aside as a reserve —**sav•er** *n*

²**save** *prep* : except

sav•ior, sav•iour \'sāvyər\ *n* **1** : one who saves **2** *cap* : Jesus Christ

sa•vor \'sāvər\ *n* : special flavor ~ *vb* : taste with pleasure —**sa•vory** *adj*

¹**saw** *past of* SEE

²**saw** \'sȯ\ *n* : cutting tool with teeth ~ *vb* **sawed; sawed** *or* **sawn; saw•ing** : cut with a saw —**saw•dust** \-,dəst\ *n* —**saw•mill** *n* —**saw•yer** \-yər\ *n*

saw•horse *n* : support for wood being sawed

sax•o•phone \'saksə,fōn\ *n* : wind instrument with a reed mouthpiece and usu. a bent metal body

say \'sā\ *vb* **said** \'sed\; **say•ing** \'sāiŋ\; **says**

\'sez\ **1** : express in words **2** : state positively ~ *n, pl* **says** \'sāz\ **1** : expression of opinion **2** : power of decision

say•ing \'sāiŋ\ *n* : commonly repeated statement

scab \'skab\ *n* **1** : protective crust over a sore or wound **2** : worker taking a striker's place ~ *vb* **-bb- 1** : become covered with a scab **2** : work as a scab —**scab•by** *adj*

scab•bard \'skabərd\ *n* : sheath for the blade of a weapon

scaf•fold \'skafəld, -,ōld\ *n* **1** : raised platform for workmen **2** : platform on which a criminal is executed

scald \'skȯld\ *vb* **1** : burn with hot liquid or steam **2** : heat to the boiling point

¹**scale** \'skāl\ *n* : weighing device ~ *vb* **scaled; scal•ing** : weigh

²**scale** *n* : thin plate esp. on the body of a fish or reptile **2** : thin coating or layer — *vb* **scaled, scal•ing** : strip of scales — **scaled** \'skāld\ *adj* —**scale•less** *adj* — **scaly** *adj*

³**scale** *n* **1** : graduated series **2** : size of a sample (as a model) in proportion to the size of the actual thing **3** : standard of estimation or judgment **4** : series of musical tones ~ *vb* **scaled; scal•ing 1** : climb by a ladder **2** : arrange in a graded series

scal•lion \'skalyən\ *n* : bulbless onion

scal•lop \'skäləp, 'skal-\ *n* **1** : marine mollusk **2** : rounded projection on a border

scalp \'skalp\ *n* : skin and flesh of the head ~ *vb* **1** : remove the scalp from **2** : resell at a greatly increased price —**scalp•er** *n*

scal•pel \'skalpəl\ *n* : surgical knife

scamp \'skamp\ *n* : rascal

scam•per \'skampər\ *vb* : run nimbly — **scamper** *n*

scan \'skan\ *vb* **-nn- 1** : read (verses) so as to show meter **2** : examine closely or hastily **3** : examine with a sensing device — **scan** *n* —**scan•ner** *n*

scan•dal \'skand³l\ *n* **1** : disgraceful situation **2** : malicious gossip —**scan•dal•ous** *adj* —**scan•dal•ize** *vb*

scant \'skant\ *adj* : barely sufficient ~ *vb* : stint —**scant•i•ly** *adv* —**scanty** *adj*

scape•goat \'skāp,gōt\ *n* : one that bears the blame for others

scap•u•la \'skapyələ\ *n, pl* **-lae** \-,lē\ *or* **-las** : shoulder blade

scar \'skär\ *n* : mark where a wound has healed —**scar** *vb*

scar•ab \'skarəb\ *n* : large dark beetle or an ornament representing one

scarce \'skers\ *adj* **scarc•er; scarc•est** : lacking in quantity or number —**scar•ci•ty** \'skersətē\ *n*

scarce•ly \'skerslē\ *adv* **1** : barely **2** : almost not

scare \'sker\ *vb* **scared; scar•ing** : frighten ~ *n* : fright —**scary** *adj*

scare•crow \'sker,krō\ *n* : figure for scaring birds from crops

scarf \'skärf\ *n, pl* **scarves** \'skärvz\ *or* **scarfs** : cloth worn about the shoulders or the neck

scar•let \'skärlət\ *n* : bright red color — **scarlet** *adj*

scarlet fever *n* : acute contagious disease marked by fever, sore throat, and red rash

scath•ing \'skāthiŋ\ *adj* : bitterly severe

scat•ter \'skatər\ *vb* **1** : spread about irregularly **2** : disperse

scav•en•ger \'skavənjər\ *n* **1** : person that collects refuse or waste **2** : animal that feeds on decayed matter —**scav•enge** \'skavənj\ *vb*

sce•nar•io \sə'nare,ō, -'när-\ *n, pl* **-i•os 1** : plot of a play or movie **2** : possible sequence of events

scene \'sēn\ *n* **1** : single situation in a play or movie **2** : stage setting **3** : view **4** : display of emotion —**sce•nic** \'sēnik\ *adj*

scen•ery \'sēnərē\ *n, pl* **-er•ies 1** : painted setting for a stage **2** : picturesque view

scent \'sent\ *vb* **1** : smell **2** : fill with odor ~ *n* **1** : odor **2** : sense of smell **3** : perfume —**scent•ed** \'sentəd\ *adj*

scep•ter \'septər\ *n* : staff signifying authority

scep•tic \'skeptik\ *var of* SKEPTIC

sched•ule \'skejül, *esp Brit* 'shedyül\ *n* : list showing sequence of events ~ *vb* **-uled; -ul•ing** : make a schedule of

scheme \'skēm\ *n* **1** : crafty plot **2** : systematic design ~ *vb* **schemed; schem•ing** : form a plot —**sche•mat•ic** \ski'matik\ *adj* —**schem•er** *n*

schism \'sizəm, 'skiz-\ *n* : split —**schis•mat•ic** \siz'matik, skiz-\ *n or adj*

schizo•phre•nia \,skitsə'frēnēə\ *n* : severe mental illness —**schiz•oid** \'skit,sȯid\ *adj or n* —**schizo•phren•ic** \,skitsə'frenik\ *adj or n*

schol•ar \'skälər\ *n* : student or learned person —**schol•ar•ly** *adj*

schol•ar•ship \-,ship\ *n* **1** : qualities or learning of a scholar **2** : money given to a student to pay for education

scho•las•tic \skə'lastik\ *adj* : relating to schools, scholars, or scholarship

¹**school** \'skül\ *n* **1** : institution for learning

2 : pupils in a school **3** : group with shared beliefs ~ *vb* : teach —**school•boy** *n* —**school•girl** *n* —**school•house** *n* — **school•mate** *n* —**school•room** *n* — **school•teach•er** *n*

²**school** *n* : large number of fish swimming together

schoo•ner \'skünər\ *n* : sailing ship

sci•ence \'sīəns\ *n* : branch of systematic study esp. of the physical world —**sci•en•tif•ic** \,sīən'tifik\ *adj* —**sci•en•tif•i•cal•ly** *adv* —**sci•en•tist** \'sīəntist\ *n*

scin•til•late \'sint³l,āt\ *vb* **-lat•ed; -lat•ing** : flash —**scin•til•la•tion** \,sint³l'āshən\ *n*

scin•til•lat•ing *adj* : brilliantly lively or witty

sci•on \'sīən\ *n* : descendant

scis•sors \'sizərz\ *n pl* : small shears

scoff \'skäf\ *vb* : mock —**scoff•er** *n*

scold \'skōld\ *n* : person who scolds ~ *vb* : criticize severely

scoop \'sküp\ *n* : shovellike utensil ~ *vb* **1** : take out with a scoop **2** : dig out

scoot \'sküt\ *vb* : move swiftly

scoot•er \'skütər\ *n* : child's foot-propelled vehicle

¹**scope** \'skōp\ *n* **1** : extent **2** : room for development

²**scope** *n* : viewing device (as a microscope)

scorch \'skȯrch\ *vb* : burn the surface of

score \'skōr\ *n, pl* **scores 1** *or pl* **score** : twenty **2** : cut **3** : record of points made (as in a game) **4** : debt **5** : music of a composition ~ *vb* **scored; scor•ing 1** : record **2** : mark with lines **3** : gain in a game **4** : assign a grade to **5** : compose a score for —**score•less** *adj* —**scor•er** *n*

scorn \'skȯrn\ *n* : emotion involving both anger and disgust ~ *vb* : hold in contempt —**scorn•er** *n* —**scorn•ful** \-fəl\ *adj* — **scorn•ful•ly** *adv*

scor•pi•on \'skȯrpēən\ *n* : poisonous long-tailed animal

scoun•drel \'skaủndrəl\ *n* : villain

¹**scour** \'skaủər\ *vb* : examine thoroughly

²**scour** *vb* : rub in order to clean

scourge \'skərj\ *n* **1** : whip **2** : punishment ~ *vb* **scourged; scourg•ing 1** : lash **2** : punish severely

scout \'skaủt\ *vb* : inspect or observe to get information ~ *n* : person sent out to get information

scow \'skaủ\ *n* : large flat-bottomed boat with square ends

scowl \'skaủl\ *vb* : make a frowning expression of displeasure —**scowl** *n*

scrag•gly \'skraglē\ *adj* : irregular or unkempt

scram \'skram\ *vb* **-mm-** : go away at once

scram•ble \'skrambəl\ *vb* **-bled; -bling 1** : clamber clumsily around **2** : struggle for possession of something **3** : mix together **4** : cook (eggs) by stirring during frying —**scramble** *n*

¹**scrap** \'skrap\ *n* **1** : fragment **2** : discarded material ~ *vb* **-pp-** : get rid of as useless

²**scrap** *vb* **-pp-** : fight —**scrap** *n* —**scrap•per** *n*

scrap•book *n* : blank book in which mementos are kept

scrape \'skrāp\ *vb* **scraped; scrap•ing 1** : remove by drawing a knife over **2** : clean or smooth by rubbing **3** : draw across a surface with a grating sound **4** : damage by contact with a rough surface **5** : gather or proceed with difficulty ~ *n* **1** : act of scraping **2** : predicament — **scrap•er** *n*

scratch \'skrach\ *vb* **1** : scrape or dig with or as if with claws or nails **2** : cause to move gratingly **3** : delete by or as if by drawing a line through ~ *n* : mark or sound made in scratching —**scratchy** *adj*

scrawl \'skrȯl\ *vb* : write hastily and carelessly —**scrawl** *n*

scraw•ny \'skrȯnē\ *adj* **-ni•er; -est** : very thin

scream \'skrēm\ *vb* : cry out loudly and shrilly ~ *n* : loud shrill cry

screech \'skrēch\ *vb or n* : shriek

screen \'skrēn\ *n* : device or partition used to protect or decorate **2** : surface on which pictures appear (as in movies) ~ *vb* **1** : shield or separate with or as if with a screen

screw \'skrü\ *n* **1** : grooved fastening device **2** : propeller ~ *vb* **1** : fasten by means of a screw **2** : move spirally

screw•driv•er \-,drü,drīvər\ *n* : tool for turning screws

scrib•ble \'skribəl\ *vb* **-bled; -bling** : write hastily or carelessly —**scribble** *n* — **scrib•bler** \-ələr\ *n*

scribe \'skrīb\ *n* : one who writes or copies writing

scrimp \'skrimp\ *vb* : economize greatly

scrip \'skrip\ *n* **1** : paper money for less than a dollar **2** : certificate entitling one to something (as stock)

script \'skript\ *n* : text (as of a play)

scrip•ture \'skripchər\ *n* : sacred writings of a religion —**scrip•tur•al** \'skripchərəl\ *adj*

scroll \'skrōl\ *n* **1** : roll of paper for writing a document **2** : spiral or coiled design

scro•tum \'skrōtəm\ *n, pl* **-ta** \-ə\ *or* **-tums** : pouch containing the testes

scrounge \'skraúnj\ *vb* **scrounged; scroung•ing** : collect by or as if by foraging

¹scrub \'skrəb\ *n* : stunted tree or shrub or a growth of these —**scrub** *adj* —**scrub•by** *adj*

²scrub *vb* **-bb-** : clean or wash by rubbing —**scrub** *n*

scruff \'skrəf\ *n* : loose skin of the back of the neck

scrump•tious \'skrəmpshəs\ *adj* : delicious

scru•ple \'skrüpəl\ *n* : reluctance due to ethical considerations —**scruple** *vb* —**scru•pu•lous** \-pyələs\ *adj* —**scru•pu•lous•ly** *adv*

scru•ti•ny \'skrüt³nē\ *n, pl* **-nies** : careful inspection —**scru•ti•nize** \-³n₁īz\ *vb*

scud \'skəd\ *vb* **-dd-** : move speedily

scuff \'skəf\ *vb* : scratch, scrape, or wear away —**scuff** *n*

scuf•fle \'skəfəl\ *vb* **-fled; -fling 1** : struggle at close quarters **2** : shuffle one's feet —**scuffle** *n*

scull \'skəl\ *n* **1** : oar **2** : racing shell propelled with sculls ~ *vb* : propel a boat by an oar over the stern

scul•lery \'skələrē\ *n, pl* **-ler•ies** : room for cleaning dishes and cookware

sculpt \'skəlpt\ *vb* : sculpture

sculp•ture \'skəlpchər\ *n* : work of art carved or molded ~ *vb* **-tured; -tur•ing** : form as sculpture —**sculp•tor** \-tər\ *n* —**sculp•tur•al** \-chərəl\ *adj*

scum \'skəm\ *n* : slimy film on a liquid

scur•ri•lous \'skərələs\ *adj* : vulgar or abusive

scur•ry \'skərē\ *vb* **-ried; -ry•ing** : scamper

scur•vy \'skərvē\ *n* : vitamin-deficiency disease

¹scut•tle \'skət³l\ *n* : pail for coal

²scuttle *vb* **-tled; -tling** : sink (a ship) by cutting holes in its bottom

³scuttle *vb* **-tled; -tling** : scamper

scythe \'sīth\ *n* : tool for mowing by hand —**scythe** *vb*

sea \'sē\ *n* **1** : large body of salt water **2** : ocean **3** : rough water —**sea** *adj* —**sea•coast** *n* —**sea•food** *n* —**sea•port** *n* —**sea•shore** *n* —**sea•wa•ter** *n*

sea•bird *n* : bird frequenting the open ocean

sea•board *n* : country's seacoast

sea•far•er \-,farər\ *n* : seaman —**sea•far•ing** \-,farin\ *adj or n*

sea horse *n* : small fish with a horselike head

¹seal \'sēl\ *n* **1** : large sea mammal of cold regions —**seal•skin** *n*

²seal *n* **1** : device for stamping a design **2** : something that closes ~ *vb* **1** : affix a seal to **2** : close up securely **3** : determine finally —**seal•ant** \-ənt\ *n* —**seal•er** *n*

sea lion *n* : large Pacific seal with external ears

seam \'sēm\ *n* **1** : line of junction of 2 edges **2** : layer of a mineral ~ *vb* : join by sewing —**seam•less** *adj*

sea•man \'sēmən\ *n* **1** : one who helps to handle a ship **2** : naval enlisted man ranking next below a petty officer third class —**sea•man•ship** *n*

seaman apprentice *n* : naval enlisted man ranking next below a seaman

seaman recruit *n* : naval enlisted man of the lowest rank

seam•stress \'sēmstrəs\ *n* : woman who sews

seamy \'sēmē\ *adj* **seam•i•er; -est** : unpleasant or sordid

sé•ance \'sā,äns\ *n* : meeting for communicating with spirits

sea•plane *n* : airplane that can take off from and land on the water

sear \'sir\ *vb* : scorch —**sear** *n*

search \'sərch\ *vb* **1** : look through **2** : seek —**search** *n* —**search•er** *n* —**search•light** *n*

sea•sick *adj* : nauseated by the motion of a ship —**sea•sick•ness** *n*

¹sea•son \'sēz³n\ *n* **1** : division of the year **2** : customary time for something —**sea•son•al** \'sēz³nəl\ *adj* —**sea•son•al•ly** *adv*

²season *vb* **1** : add spice to (food) **2** : make strong or fit for use —**sea•son•ing** \-³niŋ\ *n*

sea•son•able \'sēznəbəl\ *adj* : occurring at a suitable time —**sea•son•ably** \-blē\ *adv*

seat \'sēt\ *n* **1** : place to sit **2** : chair, bench, or stool for sitting on **3** : place that serves as a capital or center ~ *vb* **1** : place in or on a seat **2** : provide seats for

sea•weed *n* : marine alga

sea•wor•thy *adj* : strong enough to hold up to a sea voyage

se•cede \si'sēd\ *vb* **-ced•ed; -ced•ing** : withdraw from a body (as a nation)

se•clude \si'klüd\ *vb* **-clud•ed; -clud•ing** : shut off alone —**se•clu•sion** \si'klüzhən\ *n*

¹sec•ond \'sekənd\ *adj* : next after the 1st ~

n **1** : one that is second **2** : one who assists (as in a duel) —**second, sec•ond•ly** *adv*

²second *n* **1** : 60th part of a minute **2** : moment

sec•ond•ary \'sekən,derē\ *adj* **1** : second in rank or importance **2** : coming after the primary or elementary

sec•ond•hand *adj* **1** : not original **2** : used before

second lieutenant *n* : lowest ranking commissioned officer of the army, air force, or marines

se•cret \'sēkrət\ *adj* **1** : hidden **2** : kept from general knowledge —**se•cre•cy** \-krəsē\ *n* —**secret** *n* —**se•cre•tive** \'sēkrətiv, si-'krēt-\ *adj* —**se•cret•ly** *adv*

sec•re•tar•i•at \,sekrə'terēət\ *n* : administrative department

sec•re•tary \'sekrə,terē\ *n, pl* **-tar•ies 1** : one hired to handle correspondence and other tasks for a superior **2** : official in charge of correspondence or records **3** : head of a government department —**sec•re•tari•al** \,sekrə'terēəl\ *adj*

¹se•crete \si'krēt\ *vb* **-cret•ed; -cret•ing** : produce as a secretion

²se•crete \si'krēt, 'sēkrēt\ *vb* **-cret•ed; -creting** : hide

se•cre•tion \si'krēshən\ *n* **1** : process of secreting **2** : product of glandular activity

sect \'sekt\ *n* : religious group

sec•tar•i•an \sek'terēən\ *adj* **1** : relating to a sect **2** : limited in character or scope ~ *n* : member of a sect

sec•tion \'sekshən\ *n* : distinct part —**sec•tion•al** \-shənəl\ *adj*

sec•tor \'sektər\ *n* **1** : part of a circle between 2 radii **2** : distinctive part

sec•u•lar \'sekyələr\ *adj* **1** : not sacred **2** : not monastic

se•cure \si'kyùr\ *adj* **-cur•er; -est** : free from danger or loss ~ *vb* **1** : fasten safely **2** : get —**se•cure•ly** *adv*

se•cu•ri•ty \si'kyúrətē\ *n, pl* **-ties 1** : safety **2** : something given to guarantee payment **3** *pl* : bond or stock certificates

se•dan \si'dan\ *n* **1** : chair carried by 2 men **2** : enclosed automobile

¹se•date \si'dāt\ *adj* : quiet and dignified —**se•date•ly** *adv*

²sedate *vb* **-dat•ed; -dat•ing** : dose with sedatives —**se•da•tion** \si'dāshən\ *n*

sed•a•tive \'sedətiv\ *adj* : serving to relieve tension ~ *n* : sedative drug

sed•en•tary \'sed³n,terē\ *adj* : characterized by much sitting

sedge \'sej\ *n* : grasslike marsh plant

sed•i•ment \'sedəmənt\ *n* : material that settles to the bottom of a liquid or is deposited by water or a glacier —**sed•i•men•ta•ry** \,sedə'mentərē\ *adj* —**sed•i•men•ta•tion** \-mən'tāshən, -,men-\ *n*

se•di•tion \si'dishən\ *n* : revolution against a government —**se•di•tious** \-əs\ *adj*

se•duce \si'düs, -'dyüs\ *vb* **-duced; -duc•ing 1** : lead astray **2** : entice to sexual intercourse —**se•duc•er** *n* —**se•duc•tion** \-'dəkshən\ *n* —**se•duc•tive** \-tiv\ *adj*

sed•u•lous \'sejələs\ *adj* : diligent

¹see \'sē\ *vb* **saw** \'só\; **seen** \'sēn\ **see•ing 1** : perceive by the eye **2** : have experience of **3** : understand **4** : make sure **5** : meet with or escort

²see *n* : jurisdiction of a bishop

seed \'sēd\ *n, pl* **seed** *or* **seeds 1** : part by which a plant is propagated **2** : source ~ *vb* **1** : sow **2** : remove seeds from —**seed•less** *adj*

seed•ling \-liŋ\ *n* : young plant grown from seed

seedy \-ē\ *adj* **seed•i•er; -est 1** : full of seeds **2** : shabby

seek \'sēk\ *vb* **sought** \'sót\; **seek•ing 1** : search for **2** : try to reach or obtain —**seek•er** *n*

seem \'sēm\ *vb* : give the impression of being —**seem•ing•ly** *adv*

seem•ly \-lē\ *adj* **seem•li•er; -est** : proper or fit

seep \'sēp\ *vb* : leak through fine pores or cracks —**seep•age** \'sēpij\ *n*

seer \'sēər\ *n* : one who foresees or predicts events

seer•suck•er \'sir,səkər\ *n* : light puckered fabric

see•saw \'sē,só\ *n* : board balanced in the middle —**seesaw** *vb*

seethe \'sēth\ *vb* **seethed; seeth•ing** : become violently agitated

seg•ment \'segmənt\ *n* : division of a thing —**seg•ment•ed** \-,mentəd\ *adj*

seg•re•gate \'segri,gāt\ *vb* **-gat•ed; -gat•ing 1** : cut off from others **2** : separate by races —**seg•re•ga•tion** \,segri'gāshən\ *n*

seine \'sān\ *n* : large weighted fishing net ~ *vb* : fish with a seine

seis•mic \'sīzmik, 'sīs-\ *adj* : relating to an earthquake

seis•mo•graph \-mə,graf\ *n* : apparatus for detecting earthquakes

seize \'sēz\ *vb* **seized; seiz•ing 1** : take by force —**sei•zure** \'sēzhər\ *n*

sel•dom \'seldəm\ *adv* : not often

se•lect \sə'lekt\ *adj* **1** : favored **2**

: discriminating ~ *vb* : take by preference —**se•lec•tive** \-'lektiv\ *adj*

se•lec•tion \sə'lekshən\ *n* : act of selecting or thing selected

se•lect•man \si'lekt,man, -mən\ *n* : New England town official

self \'self\ *n, pl* **selves** \'selvz\ : essential person distinct from others

self- *comb form* **1** : oneself or itself **2** : of oneself or itself **3** : by oneself or automatic **4** : to, for, or toward oneself

self-addressed	self-governing
self-administered	self-government
self-analysis	self-help
self-appointed	self-image
self-assertive	self-importance
self-assurance	self-important
self-assured	self-imposed
self-awareness	self-improvement
self-cleaning	self-indulgence
self-complacent	self-indulgent
self-conceit	self-inflicted
self-confessed	self-interest
self-confidence	self-love
self-confident	self-operating
self-contained	self-pity
self-contempt	self-portrait
self-contradiction	self-possessed
self-contradictory	self-possession
self-control	self-preservation
self-created	self-proclaimed
self-criticism	self-propelled
self-defeating	self-propelling
self-defense	self-protection
self-denial	self-reliance
self-denying	self-reliant
self-destruction	self-respect
self-destructive	self-respecting
self-determination	self-restraint
self-determined	self-sacrifice
self-discipline	self-satisfaction
self-doubt	self-satisfied
self-educated	self-service
self-employed	self-serving
self-employment	self-starting
self-esteem	self-styled
self-evident	self-sufficiency
self-explanatory	self-sufficient
self-expression	self-supporting
self-fulfilling	self-taught
self-fulfillment	self-winding

self-cen•tered *adj* : concerned only with one's own self

self-con•scious *adj* : uncomfortably aware of oneself as an object of observation —**self-con•scious•ly** *adv* —**self-con•scious•ness** *n*

self•ish \'selfish\ *adj* : excessively or exclusively concerned with one's own well-being —**self•ish•ly** *adv* —**self•ish•ness** *n*

self•less \'selfləs\ *adj* : unselfish —**self•less•ness** *n*

self-made *adj* : having succeeded by one's own efforts

self-righ•teous *adj* : strongly convinced of one's own righteousness

self•same \'self,sām\ *adj* : precisely the same

sell \'sel\ *vb* **sold** \'sōld\; **sell•ing 1** : transfer (property) esp. for money **2** : deal in as a business **3** : be sold —**sell•er** *n*

selves *pl of* SELF

se•man•tic \si'mantik\ *adj* : relating to meaning in language —**se•man•tics** \-iks\ *n sing or pl*

sem•a•phore \'semə,fōr\ *n* **1** : visual signaling apparatus **2** : signaling by flags

sem•blance \'semblans\ *n* : appearance

se•men \'sēmən\ *n* : male reproductive fluid

se•mes•ter \sə'mestər\ *n* : half a school year

semi- \'semi, 'sem-, -,ī\ *prefix* **1** : half **2** : partial

semi•co•lon \'semi,kōlən\ *n* : punctuation mark ;

semi•con•duc•tor *n* : substance between a conductor and a nonconductor in ability to conduct electricity —**semi•con•duct•ing** *adj*

semi•fi•nal *adj* : being next to the final —**semifinal** *n*

semi•for•mal *adj* : being or suitable for an occasion of moderate formality

sem•i•nal \'semən³l\ *adj* **1** : relating to seed or semen **2** : causing or influencing later development

sem•i•nar \'semə,när\ *n* : conference or conferencelike study

sem•i•nary \'semə,nerē\ *n, pl* **-nar•ies** : school esp. for a theological school —**sem•i•nar•i•an** \,semə'nerēən\ *n*

sen•ate \'senət\ *n* : upper branch of a legislature —**sen•a•tor** \-ər\ *n* —**sen•a•to•rial** \,senə'tōrēəl\ *adj*

send \'send\ *vb* **sent** \'sent\; **send•ing 1** : cause to go **2** : propel —**send•er** *n*

se•nile \'sēn,īl, 'sen-\ *adj* : mentally deficient through old age —**se•nil•i•ty** \si-'nilətē\ *n*

se•nior \'sēnyər\ *adj* : older or higher ranking —**senior** *n* —**se•nior•i•ty** \sēn-'yórətē\ *n*

senior chief petty officer *n* : petty officer in the navy or coast guard ranking next below a master chief petty officer

senior master sergeant *n* : noncommissioned officer in the air force ranking next below a chief master sergeant

sen•sa•tion \sen'sāshən\ *n* **1** : bodily feeling **2** : condition of excitement or the cause of it —**sen•sa•tion•al** \-shənəl\ *adj*

sense \'sens\ *n* **1** : meaning **2** : faculty of perceiving something physical **3** : sound mental capacity ~ *vb* **sensed; sens•ing 1** : perceive by the senses **2** : detect automatically —**sense•less** *adj* —**sense•less•ly** *adv*

sen•si•bil•i•ty \,sensə'bilətē\ *n, pl* **-ties** : delicacy of feeling

sen•si•ble \'sensəbəl\ *adj* **1** : capable of sensing or being sensed **2** : aware or conscious **3** : reasonable —**sen•si•bly** \-blē\ *adv*

sen•si•tive \'sensətiv\ *adj* **1** : subject to excitation by or responsive to stimuli **2** : having power of feeling **3** : easily affected —**sen•si•tive•ness** *n* —**sen•si•tiv•i•ty** \,sensə'tivətē\ *n*

sen•si•tize \'sensə,tīz\ *vb* **-tized; -tiz•ing** : make or become sensitive

sen•sor \'sen,sór, -sər\ *n* : device that responds to a physical stimulus

sen•so•ry \'sensərē\ *adj* : relating to sensation or the senses

sen•su•al \'senchəwəl, -shəwəl\ *adj* **1** : pleasing the senses **2** : devoted to the pleasures of the senses —**sen•su•al•ist** *n* —**sen•su•al•i•ty** \,senchə'walətē\ *n* —**sen•su•al•ly** *adv*

sen•su•ous \'senchəwəs\ *adj* : having strong appeal to the senses

sent *past of* SEND

sen•tence \'sent³ns, -³nz\ *n* **1** : judgment of a court **2** : grammatically self-contained speech unit ~ *vb* **-tenced; -tenc•ing** : impose a sentence on

sen•ten•tious \sen'tenchəs\ *adj* : using pompous language

sen•tient \'senchēənt\ *adj* : capable of feeling

sen•ti•ment \'sentəmənt\ *n* **1** : belief **2** : feeling

sen•ti•men•tal \,sentə'ment³l\ *adj* : influenced by tender feelings —**sen•ti•men•tal•ism** *n* —**sen•ti•men•tal•ist** *n* —**sen•ti•men•tal•i•ty** \-,men'talətē, -mən-\ *n* —**sen•ti•men•tal•ize** \-'ment³l,īz\ *vb* —**sen•ti•men•tal•ly** *adv*

sen•ti•nel \'sent³nəl\ *n* : sentry

sen•try \'sentrē\ *n, pl* **-tries** : one who stands guard

se•pal \'sēpəl, 'sep-\ *n* : modified leaf in a flower calyx

sep•a•rate \'sepə,rāt\ *vb* **-rat•ed; -rat•ing 1** : set or keep apart **2** : become divided or detached ~ \'seprət, 'sepə-\ *adj* **1** : not connected or shared **2** : distinct from each other —**sep•a•ra•ble** \'sepərəbəl\ *adj* —**sep•a•rate•ly** *adv* —**sep•a•ra•tion** \,sepə'rāshən\ *n* —**sep•a•ra•tor** \'sepə,rātər\ *n*

se•pia \'sēpēə\ *n* : brownish gray

Sep•tem•ber \sep'tembər\ *n* : 9th month of the year having 30 days

sep•ul•chre, sep•ul•cher \'sepəlkər\ *n* : burial vault —**se•pul•chral** \sə'pəlkrəl\ *adj*

se•quel \'sēkwəl\ *n* **1** : consequence or result **2** : continuation of a story

se•quence \'sēkwəns\ *n* : continuous or connected series —**se•quen•tial** \si'kwenchəl\ *adj* —**se•quen•tial•ly** *adv*

se•ques•ter \si'kwestər\ *vb* : segregate

se•quin \'sēkwən\ *n* : spangle

se•quoia \si'kwòiə\ *n* : huge California coniferous tree

sera *pl of* SERUM

ser•aph \'serəf\ *n, pl* **-a•phim** \-ə,fim\ *or* **-aphs** : angel —**se•raph•ic** \sə'rafik\ *adj*

sere \'sir\ *adj* : dried up or withered

ser•e•nade \,serə'nād\ *n* : music sung or played esp. to a woman being courted —**serenade** *vb*

ser•en•dip•i•ty \,serən'dipətē\ *n* : good luck in finding things not sought for —**ser•en•dip•i•tous** \-əs\ *adj*

se•rene \sə'rēn\ *adj* : tranquil —**se•rene•ly** *adv* —**se•ren•i•ty** \sə'renətē\ *n*

serf \'sərf\ *n* : peasant obligated to work the land —**serf•dom** \-dəm\ *n*

serge \'sərj\ *n* : twilled woolen cloth

ser•geant \'särjənt\ *n* : noncommissioned officer (as in the army) ranking next below a staff sergeant

sergeant first class *n* : noncommissioned officer in the army ranking next below a master sergeant

sergeant major *n, pl* **sergeants major** *or* **sergeant majors 1** : noncommissioned officer serving as an enlisted adviser in a headquarters **2** : noncommissioned officer in the marine corps ranking above a first sergeant

se•ri•al \'sirēəl\ *adj* : being or relating to a series or sequence ~ *n* : story appearing in parts —**se•ri•al•ly** *adv*

se•ries \'sirēz\ *n, pl* **series** : number of things in order

se•ri•ous \'sirēəs\ *adj* **1** : subdued in appearance or manner **2** : sincere **3** : of great importance —**se•ri•ous•ly** *adv* —**se•ri•ous•ness** *n*

ser•mon \'sərmən\ *n* : lecture on religion or behavior

ser•pent \'sərpənt\ *n* : snake —**ser•pen•tine** \-pən,tēn, -,tīn\ *adj*

ser•rat•ed \'ser,ātəd\ *adj* : saw-toothed

se•rum \'sirəm\ *n, pl* **-rums** *or* **-ra** \-ə\ : watery part of blood

ser•vant \'sərvənt\ *n* : person employed for domestic work

serve \'sərv\ *vb* **served; serv•ing 1** : work through or perform a term of service **2** : be of use **3** : prove adequate **4** : hand out (food or drink) **5** : be of service to — **serv•er** *n*

ser•vice \'sərvəs\ *n* **1** : act or means of serving **2** : meeting for worship **3** : branch of public employment or the persons in it **4** : set of dishes or silverware **5** : benefit ~ *vb* **-viced; -vic•ing** : repair —**ser•vice•able** *adj* —**ser•vice•man** \-,man, -mən\ *n* —**ser•vice•wom•an** *n*

ser•vile \'sərvəl, -,vīl\ *adj* : behaving like a slave —**ser•vil•i•ty** \sər'vilətē\ *n*

serv•ing \'sərviŋ\ *n* : helping

ser•vi•tude \'sərvə,tüd, -,tyüd\ *n* : slavery

ses•a•me \'sesəmē\ *n* : annual herb or its seeds that are used in flavoring

ses•sion \'seshən\ *n* : meeting

set \'set\ *vb* **set; set•ting 1** : cause to sit **2** : place **3** : settle, arrange, or adjust **4** : cause to be or do **5** : become fixed or solid **6** : sink below the horizon ~ *adj* : settled ~ *n* **1** : group classed together **2** : setting for the scene of a play or film **3** : electronic apparatus **4** : collection of mathematical elements —**set forth** : begin a trip —**set off** *vb* : set forth —**set out** *vb* : begin a trip or undertaking —**set up** *vb* **1** : assemble or erect **2** : cause

set•back *n* : reverse

set•tee \se'tē\ *n* : bench or sofa

set•ter \'setər\ *n* : large long-coated hunting dog

set•ting \'setiŋ\ *n* : the time, place, and circumstances in which something occurs

set•tle \'set³l\ *vb* **-tled; -tling 1** : come to rest **2** : sink gradually **3** : establish in residence **4** : adjust or arrange **5** : calm **6** : dispose of (as by paying) **7** : decide or agree on —**set•tle•ment** \-mənt\ *n* —**set•tler** \'set³lər\ *n*

sev•en \'sevən\ *n* : one more than 6 —**seven** *adj or pron* —**sev•enth** \-ənth\ *adj or adv or n*

sev•en•teen \,sevən'tēn\ *n* : one more than 16 —**seventeen** *adj or pron* —**sev•en•teenth** \-'tēnth\ *adj or n*

sev•en•ty \'sevəntē\ *n, pl* **-ties** : 7 times 10 —**sev•en•ti•eth** \-tēəth\ *adj or n* —**seventy** *adj or pron*

sev•er \'sevər\ *vb* **-ered; -er•ing** : cut off or apart —**sev•er•ance** \'sevrəns, -vərəns\ *n*

sev•er•al \'sevrəl, 'sevə-\ *adj* **1** : distinct **2** : consisting of an indefinite but not large number —**sev•er•al•ly** *adv*

se•vere \sə'vir\ *adj* **-ver•er; -est 1** : strict **2** : restrained or unadorned **3** : painful or distressing **4** : hard to endure —**se•vere•ly** *adv* —**se•ver•i•ty** \-'verətē\ *n*

sew \'sō\ *vb* **sewed; sewn** \'sōn\ *or* **sewed; sew•ing** : join or fasten by stitches —**sew•ing** *n*

sew•age \'süij\ *n* : liquid household waste

¹sew•er \'sōər\ *n* : one that sews

²sew•er \'süər\ *n* : pipe or channel to carry off waste matter

sex \'seks\ *n* **1** : either of 2 divisions into which organisms are grouped according to their reproductive roles or the qualities which differentiate them **2** : copulation —**sexed** \'sekst\ *adj* —**sex•less** —**sex•u•al** \'sekshəwəl\ *adj* —**sex•u•al•i•ty** \,sekshə'walətē\ *n* —**sex•u•al•ly** *adv* —**sexy** *adj*

sex•ism \'sek,sizəm\ *n* : discrimination based on sex and esp. against women —**sex•ist** \'seksist\ *adj or n*

sex•tant \'sekstənt\ *n* : instrument for navigation

sex•tet \sek'stet\ *n* : music for 6 performers **2** : group of 6

sex•ton \'sekstən\ *n* : church caretaker

shab•by \'shabē\ *adj* **-bi•er; -est 1** : worn and faded **2** : dressed in worn clothes **3** : not generous or fair —**shab•bi•ly** *adv* —**shab•bi•ness** *n*

shack \'shak\ *n* : hut

shack•le \'shakəl\ *n* : metal device to bind legs or arms ~ *vb* **-led; -ling** : bind or fasten with shackles

shad \'shad\ *n* : Atlantic food fish

shade \'shād\ *n* **1** : space sheltered from the light esp. of the sun **2** : gradation of color **3** : small difference **4** : something that shades ~ *vb* **shad•ed; shad•ing 1** : shelter from light and heat **2** : add shades of color to **3** : show slight differences esp. in color or meaning

shad•ow \'shadō\ *n* **1** : shade cast upon a surface by something blocking light **2** : trace **3** : gloomy influence ~ *vb* **1** : cast a shadow **2** : follow closely —**shad•owy** *adj*

shady \'shādē\ *adj* **shad•i•er; -est 1** : giving shade **2** : of dubious honesty

shaft \'shaft\ *n* **1** : long slender cylindrical part **2** : deep vertical opening (as of a mine)

shag \'shag\ *n* : shaggy tangled mat

shag•gy \'shagē\ *adj* **-gi•er; -est 1** : covered with long hair or wool **2** : not neat and combed

shake \'shāk\ *vb* **shook** \'shuk\; **shak•en** \'shākən\; **shak•ing 1** : move or cause to move quickly back and forth **2** : distress **3** : clasp (hands) as friendly gesture —**shake** *n* —**shak•er** \-ər\ *n*

shake-up *n* : reorganization

shaky \'shākē\ *adj* **shak•i•er; -est** : not sound, stable, or reliable —**shak•i•ly** *adv* —**shak•i•ness** *n*

shale \'shāl\ *n* : stratified rock

shall \'shal\ *vb, past* **should** \'shud\; *pres sing & pl* **shall** —used as an auxiliary to express a command, futurity, or determination

shal•low \'shalō\ *adj* **1** : not deep **2** : not intellectually profound

shal•lows \-ōz\ *n pl* : area of shallow water

sham \'sham\ *adj or n or vb* : fake

sham•ble \'shambəl\ *vb* **-bled; -bling** : shuffle along —**sham•ble** *n*

sham•bles \'shambəlz\ *n* : state of disorder

shame \'shām\ *n* **1** : distress over guilt or disgrace **2** : cause of shame or regret ~ *vb* **shamed; sham•ing 1** : make ashamed **2** : disgrace —**shame•ful** \-fəl\ *adj* —**shame•ful•ly** \-ē\ *adv* —**shame•less** *adj* —**shame•less•ly** *adv*

shame•faced \'shām'fāst\ *adj* : ashamed

sham•poo \sham'pü\ *vb* : wash one's hair ~ *n, pl* **-poos** : act of or preparation used in shampooing

sham•rock \'sham,räk\ *n* : plant of legend with 3-lobed leaves

shank \'shaŋk\ *n* : part of the leg between the knee and ankle

shan•ty \'shantē\ *n, pl* **-ties** : hut

shape \'shāp\ *vb* **shaped; shap•ing** : form esp. in a particular structure or appearance ~ *n* **1** : distinctive appearance or arrangement of parts **2** : condition —**shape•less** \-ləs\ *adj* —**shape•li•ness** *n* —**shape•ly** *adj*

shard \'shärd\ *n* : broken piece

share \'sher\ *n* **1** : portion belonging to one **2** : interest in a company's stock ~ *vb* **shared; shar•ing** : divide or use with others —**share•hold•er** *n* —**shar•er** *n*

share•crop•per \-,kräpər\ *n* : farmer who works another's land in return for a share of the crop —**share•crop** *vb*

shark \'shärk\ *n* : voracious sea fish

sharp \'shärp\ *adj* **1** : having a good point or cutting edge **2** : alert, clever, or sarcastic **3** : vigorous or fierce **4** : having prominent angles or a sudden change in direction **5** : distinct **6** : higher than the true pitch ~ *adv* : exactly ~ *n* : sharp note —**sharp•ly** *adv* —**sharp•ness** *n*

sharp•en \'shärpən\ *vb* : make sharp —**sharp•en•er** \-ənər\ *n*

sharp•shoot•er *n* : expert marksman —**sharp•shoot•ing** *n*

shat•ter \'shatər\ *vb* : smash or burst into fragments —**shat•ter•proof** \-,prüf\ *adj*

shave \'shāv\ *vb* **shaved; shaved** *or* **shaven** \'shāvən\; **shav•ing 1** : cut off with a razor **2** : make bare by cutting the hair from **3** : slice very thin ~ *n* : act or instance of shaving —**shav•er** *n*

shawl \'shol\ *n* : loose covering for the head or shoulders

she \'shē\ *pron* : that female one

sheaf \'shēf\ *n, pl* **sheaves** \'shēvz\ : bundle esp. of grain stalks

shear \'shir\ *vb* **sheared; sheared** *or* **shorn** \'shorn\; **shear•ing 1** : trim wool from **2** : cut off with scissorlike action

shears \'shirz\ *n pl* : cutting tool with 2 blades fastened so that the edges slide by each other

sheath \'shēth\ *n, pl* **sheaths** \'shēthz, 'shēths\ : covering (as for a blade)

sheathe \'shēth\ *vb* **sheathed; sheath•ing** : put into a sheath

shed \'shed\ *vb* **shed; shed•ding 1** : give off (as tears or hair) **2** : cause to flow or diffuse ~ *n* : small storage building

sheen \'shēn\ *n* : subdued luster

sheep \'shēp\ *n, pl* **sheep** : domesticated mammal covered with wool —**sheep•skin** *n*

sheep•ish \'shēpish\ *adj* : embarrassed by awareness of a fault

sheer \'shir\ *adj* **1** : pure **2** : very steep **3** : very thin or transparent —**sheer** *adv*

sheet \'shēt\ *n* : broad flat piece (as of cloth or paper)

sheikh, sheik \'shēk, 'shāk\ *n* : Arab chief —**sheikh•dom, sheik•dom** \-dəm\ *n*

shelf \'shelf\ *n, pl* **shelves** \'shelvz\ **1** : flat narrow structure used for storage or display **2** : sandbank or rock ledge

shell \'shel\ *n* **1** : hard or tough outer covering **2** : case holding explosive powder and projectile for a weapon **3** : light racing boat with oars ~ *vb* **1** : remove the shell of **2** : bombard —**shelled** \'sheld\ *adj* —**shell•er** *n*

shel•lac \shə'lak\ *n* : varnish ~ *vb* **-lacked; -lack•ing 1** : coat with shellac **2** : defeat —**shel•lack•ing** *n*

shell•fish *n* : water animal with a shell

shel•ter \'sheltər\ *n* : something that gives protection ~ *vb* : give refuge to

shelve \'shelv\ *vb* **shelved; shelv•ing 1** : place or store on shelves **2** : dismiss or put aside

she•nan•i•gans \shə'nanigənz\ *n pl* : mischievous or deceitful conduct

shep•herd \'shepərd\ *n* : one that tends sheep ~ *vb* : act as a shepherd or guardian —**shep•herd•ess** \'shepərdəs\ *n* : woman who tends sheep

sher•bet \'shərbət\, **sher•bert** \-,bərt\ *n* : fruit-flavored frozen dessert

sher•iff \'sherəf\ *n* : county law officer

sher•ry \'sherē\ *n, pl* **-ries** : type of wine

shield \'shēld\ *n* **1** : broad piece of armor carried on the arm **2** : something that protects —**shield** *vb*

shier *comparative of* SHY

shiest *superlative of* SHY

shift \'shift\ *vb* **1** : change place, position, or direction **2** : get by ~ *n* **1** : loose-fitting dress **2** : an act or instance of shifting **3** : scheduled work period

shift•less \-ləs\ *adj* : lazy

shifty \'shiftē\ *adj* **shift•i•er; -est** : tricky or untrustworthy

shil•le•lagh \shə'lālē\ *n* : club or stick

shil•ling \'shiliŋ\ *n* : former British coin

shil•ly-shal•ly \'shilē,shalē\ *vb* **-shall•ied; -shally•ing 1** : hesitate **2** : dawdle

shim•mer \'shimər\ *vb or n* : glimmer

shin \'shin\ *n* : front part of the leg below the knee ~ *vb* **-nn-** : climb by sliding the body close along

shine \'shīn\ *vb* **shone** \-shōn\ *or* **shined; shin•ing 1** : give off or cause to give off light **2** : be outstanding **3** : polish ~ *n* : brilliance

shin•gle \'shiŋgəl\ *n* : small thin piece used in covering roofs or exterior walls —**shingle** *vb*

shin•gles \-gəlz\ *n pl* : acute inflammation of spinal nerves

shin•ny \'shinē\ *vb* **-nied; -ny•ing** : shin

shiny \'shīnē\ *adj* **shin•i•er; -est** : bright or polished

ship \'ship\ *n* **1** : large oceangoing vessel **2** : aircraft or spacecraft ~ *vb* **-pp- 1** : put on a ship **2** : transport by carrier —**ship•board** *n* —**ship•build•er** *n* —**ship•per** *n* —**ship•wreck** *n or vb* —**ship•yard** *n*

-ship \,ship\ *n suffix* **1** : state, condition, or quality **2** : rank or profession **3** : skill **4** : something showing a state or quality

ship•ment \-mənt\ *n* : an act of shipping or the goods shipped

ship•ping \'shipiŋ\ *n* **1** : ships **2** : transportation of goods

ship•shape *adj* : tidy

shire \'shīr, *in place-name compounds* ,shir, shər\ *n* : British county

shirk \'shərk\ *vb* : evade —**shirk•er** *n*

shirr \'shər\ *vb* **1** : gather (cloth) by drawing up parallel lines of stitches **2** : bake (eggs) in a dish

shirt \'shərt\ *n* : garment for covering the torso —**shirt•less** *adj*

shiv•er \'shivər\ *vb* : tremble —**shiver** *n* —**shiv•ery** *adj*

shoal \'shōl\ *n* : shallow place (as in a river)

¹shock \'shäk\ *n* : pile of sheaves set up in a field

²shock *n* **1** : forceful impact **2** : violent mental or emotional disturbance **3** : effect of a charge of electricity **4** : depression of the vital bodily processes ~ *vb* **1** : strike with surprise, horror, or disgust **2** : subject to an electrical shock —**shock•proof** *adj*

³shock *n* : bushy mass (as of hair)

shod•dy \'shädē\ *adj* **-di•er; -est** : poorly made or done —**shod•di•ly** \'shäd³lē\ *adv* —**shod•di•ness** *n*

shoe \'shü\ *n* **1** : covering for the human foot **2** : horseshoe ~ *vb* **shod** \'shäd\; **shoe•ing** : put horseshoes on —**shoe•lace** *n* —**shoe•mak•er** *n*

shone *past of* SHINE

shook *past of* SHAKE

shoot \'shüt\ *vb* **shot** \'shät\; **shoot•ing 1** : propel (as an arrow or bullet) **2** : wound or kill with a missile **3** : discharge (a weapon) **4** : drive (as a ball) at a goal **5** : photograph **6** : move swiftly ~ *n* : new plant growth —**shoot•er** *n*

shop \'shäp\ *n* : place where things are made or sold ~ *vb* **-pp-** : visit stores —**shop•keep•er** *n* —**shop•per** *n*

shop•lift *vb* : steal goods from a store —**shop•lift•er** \-,liftər\ *n*

¹shore \'shōr\ *n* : land along the edge of water —**shore•line** *n*

²shore *vb* **shored; shor•ing** : prop up ~ *n* : something that props

shore•bird *n* : bird of the seashore

shorn *past part of* SHEAR

short \'short\ *adj* **1** : not long or tall or extending far **2** : brief in time **3** : curt **4** : not having or being enough ~ *adv* : curtly ~ *n* **1** *pl* : short drawers or trousers **2** : short circuit —**short•en** \-³n\ *vb* —**short•ly** *adv* —**short•ness** *n*

short•age \'shortij\ *n* : deficiency

short•cake *n* : dessert of biscuit with sweetened fruit

short•change *vb* : cheat esp. by giving too little change

short circuit *n* : abnormal electric connection —**short-circuit** *vb*

short•com•ing *n* : fault or failing

short•cut \-,kət\ *n* **1** : more direct route than that usu. taken **2** : quicker way of doing something

short•hand *n* : method of speed writing

short-lived \'short'līvd, -,līvd\ *adj* : of short life or duration

short•sight•ed \-'sītəd\ *adj* : lacking foresight

shot \'shät\ *n* **1** : act of shooting **2** : attempt (as at making a goal) **3** : small pellets forming a charge **4** : range or reach **5** : photograph **6** : injection of medicine **7** : small serving of liquor —**shot•gun** *n*

should \'shud\ *past of* SHALL —used as an auxiliary to express condition, obligation, or probability

shoul•der \'shōldər\ *n* **1** : part of the body where the arm joins the trunk **2** : part that projects or lies to the side ~ *vb* **1** : push with or bear on the shoulder

shoulder blade *n* : flat triangular bone at the back of the shoulder

shout \'shaut\ *vb* : give voice loudly —**shout** *n*

shove \'shəv\ *vb* **shoved; shov•ing** : push along or away —**shove** *n*

shov•el \'shəvəl\ *n* : broad tool for digging or lifting ~ *vb* **-eled** *or* **-elled; -el•ing** *or* **-el•ling** : take up or dig with a shovel

show \'shō\ *vb* **showed** \'shōd\; **shown** \'shōn\ *or* **showed; show•ing 1** : present to view **2** : reveal or demonstrate **3** : teach **4** : prove **5** : conduct or escort **6** : appear or be noticeable ~ *n* **1** : demonstrative display **2** : spectacle **3** : theatrical, radio, or television program —**show•case** *n* —**show off** *vb* **1** : display proudly **2** : act so as to attract attention —**show up** *vb* : arrive

show•down *n* : decisive confrontation

show•er \'shauər\ *n* **1** : brief fall of rain **2** : bath in which water sprinkles down on the person or a facility for such a bath **3** : party at which someone gets gifts ~ *vb* **1** : rain or fall in a shower **2** : bathe in a shower —**show•ery** *adj*

showy \'shōē\ *adj* **show•i•er; -est** : very noticeable or overly elaborate —**show•i•ly** *adv* —**show•i•ness** *n*

shrap•nel \'shrapn³l\ *n, pl* **shrapnel** : metal fragments of a bomb

shred \'shred\ *n* : narrow strip cut or torn off ~ *vb* **-dd-** : cut or tear into shreds

shrew \'shrü\ *n* **1** : scolding woman **2** : mouselike mammal —**shrew•ish** \-ish\ *adj*

shrewd \'shrüd\ *adj* : clever —**shrewd•ly** *adv* —**shrewd•ness** *n*

shriek \'shrēk\ *n* : shrill cry —**shriek** *vb*

shrill \'shril\ *adj* : piercing and high-pitched —**shril•ly** *adv*

shrimp \'shrimp\ *n* : small sea crustacean

shrine \'shrīn\ *n* **1** : tomb of a saint **2** : hallowed place

shrink \'shriŋk\ *vb* **shrank** \'shraŋk\; **shrunk** \'shrəŋk\ *or* **shrunk•en** \'shrəŋkən\; **shrink•ing 1** : draw back or away **2** : become smaller —**shrink•able** *adj*

shrink•age \'shriŋkij\ *n* : amount lost by shrinking

shriv•el \'shrivəl\ *vb* **-eled** *or* **-elled; -el•ing** *or* **-el•ling** : shrink or wither into wrinkles

shroud \'shraud\ *n* **1** : cloth put over a corpse **2** : cover or screen ~ *vb* : veil or screen from view

shrub \'shrəb\ *n* : low woody plant —**shrub•by** *adj*

shrub•bery \'shrəbərē\ *n, pl* **-ber•ies** : growth of shrubs

shrug \'shrəg\ *vb* **-gg-** : hunch the shoulders up in doubt, indifference, or uncertainty —**shrug** *n*

shuck \'shək\ *vb* : strip of a shell or husk —**shuck** *n*

shud•der \'shədər\ *vb* : tremble —**shudder** *n*

shuf•fle \'shəfəl\ *vb* **-fled; -fling 1** : mix together **2** : walk with a sliding movement —**shuffle** *n*

shuf•fle•board \'shəfəl,bōrd\ *n* : game of sliding disks into a scoring area

shun \'shən\ *vb* **-nn-** : keep away from

shunt \'shənt\ *vb* : turn off to one side

shut \'shət\ *vb* **shut; shut•ting 1** : bar passage into or through (as by moving a lid or door) **2** : suspend activity —**shut out** vb : exclude —**shut up** vb : stop or cause to stop talking

shut-in \'\ n : invalid

shut-ter \'shətər\ n **1** : movable cover for a window **2** : camera part that exposes film

shut-tle \'shət°l\ n **1** : part of a weaving machine that carries thread back and forth **2** : vehicle traveling back and forth over a short route ~ vb **-tled; -tling** : move back and forth frequently

shut-tle-cock \'shət°l,käk\ n : light conical object used in badminton

shy \'shī\ adj **shi-er** or **shy-er** \'shīər\; **shi-est** or **shy-est** \'shīəst\ **1** : sensitive and hesitant in dealing with others **2** : wary **3** : lacking ~ vb **shied; shy-ing** : draw back (as in fright) —**shy-ly** adv —**shy-ness** n

sib-i-lant \'sibələnt\ adj : having the sound of the s or the sh in sash —**sibilant** n

sib-ling \'siblin\ n : brother or sister

sick \'sik\ adj **1** : not in good health **2** : nauseated **3** : relating to or meant for the sick —**sick-bed** n —**sick-en** \-ən\ vb —**sick-ly** adv —**sick-ness** n

sic-kle \'sikəl\ n : curved short-handled blade

side \'sīd\ n **1** : part to left or right of an object or the torso **2** : edge or surface away from the center or at an angle to top and bottom or ends **3** : contrasting or opposing position or group —**sid-ed** adj

side-board n : piece of dining-room furniture for table service

side-burns \-,bərnz\ n pl : whiskers in front of the ears

side-long \'sīd,lȯn\ adv or adj : to or along the side

side-show n : minor show at a circus

side-step vb **1** : step aside **2** : avoid

side-swipe \-,swīp\ vb : strike with a glancing blow —**sideswipe** n

side-track vb : lead aside or astray

side-walk n : paved walk at the side of a road

side-ways \-,wāz\ adv or adj **1** : to or from the side **2** : with one side to the front

sid-ing \'sīdin\ n **1** : short railroad track **2** : material covering the outside of a building

si-dle \'sīd°l\ vb **-dled; -dling** : move sideways or unobtrusively

siege \'sēj\ n : persistent attack (as on a fortified place)

si-es-ta \sē'estə\ n : midday nap

sieve \'siv\ n : utensil with holes to separate particles

sift \'sift\ vb **1** : pass through a sieve **2** : examine carefully —**sift-er** n

sigh \'sī\ n : audible release of the breath (as to express weariness) —**sigh** vb

sight \'sīt\ n **1** : something seen or worth seeing **2** : process, power, or range of seeing **3** : device used in aiming **4** : view or glimpse ~ vb : get sight of —**sight-ed** adj —**sight-less** adj —**sight-see-ing** adj —**sight-seer** \-,sēər\ n

sign \'sīn\ n **1** : symbol **2** : gesture expressing a command or thought **3** : public notice to advertise or warn **4** : trace ~ vb **1** : mark with or make a sign **2** : write one's name on —**sign-er** n

sig-nal \'sign°l\ n **1** : sign of command or warning **2** : electronic transmission ~ vb **-naled** or **-nalled; -nal-ing** or **-nal-ling** : communicate or notify by signals ~ adj : distinguished

sig-na-to-ry \'signə,tōrē\ n, pl **-ries** : person or government that signs jointly with others

sig-na-ture \'signə,chùr\ n : one's name written by oneself

sig-net \'signət\ n : small seal

sig-nif-i-cance \sig'nifikəns\ n **1** : meaning **2** : importance —**sig-nif-i-cant** \-kənt\ adj —**sig-nif-i-cant-ly** adv

sig-ni-fy \'signə,fī\ vb **-fied; -fy-ing 1** : show by a sign **2** : mean —**sig-ni-fi-ca-tion** \,signəfə'kāshən\ n

si-lence \'sīləns\ n : state of being without sound ~ vb **-lenced; -lenc-ing** : keep from making noise or sound —**si-lenc-er** n

si-lent \'sīlənt\ adj : having or producing no sound —**si-lent-ly** adv

sil-hou-ette \,silə'wet\ n : outline filled in usu. with black ~ vb **-ett-ed; -ett-ing** : represent by a silhouette

sil-i-ca \'silikə\ n : mineral found as quartz and opal

sil-i-con \'silikən, -,kän\ n : nonmetallic chemical element

silk \'silk\ n **1** : fine strong lustrous protein fiber from moth larvae (**silk-worms** \-,wərmz\) **2** : thread or cloth made from silk —**silk-en** \'silkən\ adj —**silky** adj

sill \'sil\ n : bottom part of a window frame or a doorway

sil-ly \'silē\ adj **sil-li-er; -est** : foolish or stupid —**sil-li-ness** n

si-lo \'sīlō\ n, pl **-los** : tall building for storing animal feed

silt \'silt\ n : fine earth carried by rivers ~ vb : obstruct or cover with silt

sil-ver \'silvər\ n **1** : white ductile metallic chemical element **2** : silverware ~ adj : having the color of silver —**sil-very** adj

sil-ver-ware \-,war\ n : eating and serving utensils esp. of silver

sim-i-lar \'simələr\ adj : resembling each other in some ways —**sim-i-lar-i-ty** \,simə'larətē\ n —**sim-i-lar-ly** \'simələr-lē\ adv

sim-i-le \'simə,lē\ n : comparison of unlike things using like or as

sim-mer \'simər\ vb : stew gently

sim-per \'simpər\ vb : give a silly smile —**simper** n

sim-ple \'simpəl\ adj **-pler; -plest 1** : free from dishonesty, vanity, or pretense **2** : of humble origin or modest position **3** : not complex **4** : lacking education, experience, or intelligence —**sim-ple-ness** n —**sim-ply** \-plē\ adv

sim-ple-ton \'simpəltən\ n : fool

sim-plic-i-ty \sim'plisətē\ n : state or fact of being simple

sim-pli-fy \'simplə,fī\ vb **-fied; -fy-ing** : make easier —**sim-pli-fi-ca-tion** \,simpləfə'kāshən\ n

sim-u-late \'simyə,lāt\ vb **-lat-ed; -lat-ing** : create the effect or appearance of —**sim-u-la-tion** \,simyə'lāshən\ n —**sim-u-la-tor** \'simyə,lātər\ n

si-mul-ta-ne-ous \,sīməl'tānēəs\ adj : occurring or operating at the same time —**si-mul-ta-ne-ous-ly** adv —**si-mul-ta-ne-ous-ness** n

sin \'sin\ n **1** : offense against God ~ vb **-nn-** : commit a sin —**sin-ful** \-fəl\ adj —**sin-less** adj —**sin-ner** n

since \'sins\ adv **1** : from a past time until now **2** : backward in time ~ prep **1** : in the period after **2** : continuously from ~ conj **1** : from the time when **2** : because

sin-cere \sin'sir\ adj **-cer-er; -cer-est** : genuine or honest —**sin-cere-ly** adv —**sin-cer-i-ty** \-'serətē\ n

si-ne-cure \'sīni,kyúr, 'sini-\ n : well-paid job that requires little work

sin-ew \'sinyü\ n **1** : tendon **2** : physical strength —**sin-ewy** adj

sing \'sin\ vb **sang** \'san\ or **sung** \'sən\; **sung; sing-ing** : produce musical tones with the voice —**sing-er** n

singe \'sinj\ vb **singed; singe-ing** : scorch lightly

sin-gle \'singəl\ adj **1** : one only **2** : unmarried ~ n : separate one —**single-ness** n —**sin-gly** \-glē\ adv —**single out** : select or set aside

sin-gu-lar \'singyələr\ adj **1** : relating to a word form denoting one **2** : outstanding or superior **3** : queer —**singular** n —**sin-gu-lar-i-ty** \,singyə-'larətē\ n —**sin-gu-lar-ly** \'singyələrlē\ adv

sin-is-ter \'sinəstər\ adj : threatening evil

sink \'sink\ vb **sank** \'sank\ or **sunk** \'sənk\; **sunk; sink-ing 1** : submerge or descend **2** : grow worse **3** : make by digging or boring **4** : invest ~ n : basin with a drain

sink-er \'sinkər\ n : weight to sink a fishing line

sin-u-ous \'sinyəwəs\ adj : winding in and out —**sin-u-os-i-ty** \,sinyə'wäsətē\ n —**sin-u-ous-ly** adv

si-nus \'sīnəs\ n : skull cavity usu. connecting with the nostrils

sip \'sip\ vb **-pp-** : drink in small quantities —**sip** n

si-phon \'sīfən\ n : tube that draws liquid by suction —**siphon** vb

sir \'sər\ n **1** —used before the first name of a knight or baronet **2** —used as a respectful form of address

sire \'sīr\ n : father ~ vb **sired; sir-ing** : beget

si-ren \'sīrən\ n **1** : seductive woman **2** : wailing warning whistle

sir-loin \'sər,lȯin\ n : cut of beef

sirup var of SYRUP

si-sal \'sīsəl, -zəl\ n : strong rope fiber

sis-sy \'sisē\ n, pl **-sies** : timid or effeminate boy

sis-ter \'sistər\ n : female sharing one or both parents with another person —**sis-ter-hood** \-,hùd\ n —**sis-ter-ly** adj

sis-ter-in-law n, pl **sis-ters-in-law** : sister of one's spouse or wife of one's brother

sit \'sit\ vb **sat** \'sat\; **sit-ting 1** : rest on the buttocks or haunches **2** : roost **3** : hold a session **4** : pose for a portrait **5** : have a location **6** : rest or fix in place —**sit-ter** n

site \'sīt\ n : place

sit-u-at-ed \'sichə,wātəd\ adj : located

sit-u-a-tion \,sichə'wāshən\ n **1** : location **2** : condition **3** : job

six \'siks\ n : one more than 5 —**six** adj or pron —**sixth** \'siksth\ adj or n

six-teen \,siks'tēn\ n : one more than 15 —**sixteen** adj or pron —**six-teenth** \-'tēnth\ adj or n

six-ty \'sikstē\ n, pl **-ties** : 6 times 10 —**six-ti-eth** \-əth\ adj or n —**sixty** adj or pron

siz-able, size-able \'sīzəbəl\ adj : quite large —**siz-ably** \-blē\ adv

size \'sīz\ n : measurement of the amount of space something takes up ~ vb : grade according to size

siz-zle \'sizəl\ vb **-zled; -zling** : fry with a hissing sound —**sizzle** n

skate \'skāt\ n **1** : metal runner on a shoe for gliding over ice **2** : roller skate —**skate** vb —**skat-er** n

skein \'skān\ n : loosely twisted quantity of yarn or thread

skel-e-ton \'skelət°n\ n : bony framework —**skel-e-tal** \-ət°l\ adj

skep-tic \'skeptik\ n : one who is critical or doubting —**skep-ti-cal** \-tikəl\ adj —**skep-ti-cism** \-tə,sizəm\ n

sketch \'skech\ n **1** : rough drawing **2** : short story or essay —**sketch** vb —**sketchy** adj

skew-er \'skyüər\ n : long pin for holding roasting meat —**skewer** vb

ski \'skē\ n, pl **skis** : long strip for gliding over snow or water —**ski** vb —**ski-er** n

skid \'skid\ n **1** : plank for supporting something or on which it slides **2** : act of skidding ~ vb **-dd-** : slide sideways

skiff \'skif\ n : small boat

skill \'skil\ n : developed or learned ability —**skilled** \'skild\ adj —**skill-ful** \-fəl\ adj —**skill-ful-ly** adv

skil-let \'skilət\ n : pan for frying

skim \'skim\ vb **-mm- 1** : take off from the top of a liquid **2** : read or move over swiftly ~ adj : having the cream removed —**skim-mer** n

skimp \'skimp\ vb : give too little of something —**skimpy** adj

skin \'skin\ n **1** : outer layer of an animal body **2** : rind ~ vb **-nn-** : take the skin from —**skin-less** adj —**skinned** adj —**skin-tight** adj

skin diving n : sport of swimming under water with a face mask and flippers

skin-flint \'skin,flint\ n : stingy person

skin-ny \'skinē\ adj **-ni-er; -est** : very thin

skip \'skip\ vb **-pp- 1** : move with leaps **2** : read past or ignore —**skip** n

skip-per \'skipər\ n : ship's master —**skip-per** vb

skir-mish \'skərmish\ n : minor combat —**skirmish** vb

skirt \'skərt\ n : garment or part of a garment that hangs below the waist ~ vb : pass around the edge of

skit \'skit\ n : brief usu. humorous play

skit-tish \'skitish\ adj : easily frightened

skulk \'skəlk\ vb : move furtively

skull \'skəl\ n : bony case that protects the brain

skunk \'skənk\ n : mammal that can forcibly eject an ill-smelling fluid

sky \'skī\ n, pl **skies 1** : upper air **2** : heaven —**sky-line** n —**sky-ward** \-wərd\ adv or adj

sky-lark \'skī,lärk\ n : European lark noted for its song

sky-light n : window in a roof or ceiling

sky-rock-et n : shooting firework ~ vb : rise suddenly

sky-scrap-er \-,skrāpər\ n : very tall building

slab \'slab\ n : thick slice

slack \'slak\ adj **1** : careless **2** : not taut **3** : not busy ~ n **1** : part hanging loose **2** pl : casual trousers —**slack-en** —**slack-ly** adv —**slack-ness** n

slag \'slag\ n : waste from melting of ores

slain past of SLAY

slake \'slāk\ vb **slaked; slak-ing** : quench

slam \'slam\ n : heavy jarring impact ~ vb **-mm-** : shut, strike, or throw violently and loudly

slan-der \'slandər\ n : malicious gossip ~ vb : hurt (someone) with slander —**slan-der-er** n —**slan-der-ous** adj

slang \'slan\ n : informal nonstandard vocabulary —**slangy** adj

slant \'slant\ vb **1** : slope **2** : present with a special viewpoint ~ n : sloping direction, line, or plane

slap \'slap\ vb **-pp-** : strike sharply with the open hand —**slap** n

slash \'slash\ vb **1** : cut with sweeping strokes **2** : reduce sharply ~ n : gash

slat \'slat\ n : thin narrow flat strip

slate \'slāt\ n **1** : dense fine-grained layered rock **2** : roofing tile or writing tablet of slate **3** : list of candidates ~ vb **slat-ed; slat-ing** : designate

slat-tern \'slatərn\ n : untidy woman —**slat-tern-ly** adj

slaugh-ter \'slȯtər\ n **1** : butchering of livestock for market **2** : great and cruel destruction of lives ~ vb : commit slaughter upon —**slaugh-ter-house** n

slave \'slāv\ n : one owned and forced into service by another ~ vb **slaved; slav-ing** : work as or like a slave —**slave** adj —**slav-ery** \'slāvərē, 'slāv-\ n

sla-ver \'slavər, 'slāv-\ vb or n : slobber

slav-ish \'slāvish\ adj : of or like a slave —**slav-ish-ly** adv

slay \'slā\ vb **slew** \'slü\; **slain** \'slān\; **slay-ing** : kill —**slay-er** n

slea-zy \'slēzē, 'slā-\ adj **-zi-er; -est** : shabby or shoddy

sled \'sled\ n : vehicle on runners —**sled** vb

sledge \'slej\ n : sledgehammer

sledge n : heavy sled

sledge-ham-mer n : heavy long-handled hammer —**sledgehammer** adj or vb

sleek \'slēk\ adj : smooth or glossy —**sleek** vb

sleep \'slēp\ n : natural suspension of consciousness ~ vb **slept** \'slept\; **sleep-ing** : rest in a state of sleep —**sleep-er** n —**sleep-less** adj —**sleep-walk-er** n

sleepy \'slēpē\ adj **sleep-i-er; -est 1** : ready for sleep **2** : quietly inactive —**sleep-i-ly** \'slēpəlē\ adv —**sleep-i-ness** \-pēnəs\ n

sleet \'slēt\ n : frozen rain —**sleet** vb —**sleety** adj

sleeve \'slēv\ n : part of a garment for the arm —**sleeve-less** adj

sleigh \'slā\ n : horse-drawn sled with seats ~ vb : drive or ride in a sleigh

sleight of hand \'slīt-\ : skillful manual manipulation or a trick requiring it

slen-der \'slendər\ adj **1** : thin esp. in physique **2** : scanty

sleuth \'slüth\ n : detective

slew \'slü\ past of SLAY

slice \'slīs\ n : thin flat piece ~ vb **sliced; slic-ing** : cut a slice from

slick \'slik\ adj **1** : very smooth **2** : clever —**slick** vb

slick-er \'slikər\ n : raincoat

slide \'slīd\ vb **slid** \'slid\; **slid-ing** \'slīdin\ : move smoothly along a surface ~ n **1** : act of sliding **2** : surface on which something slides **3** : transparent picture for projection

slier comparative of SLY

sliest superlative of SLY

slight \'slīt\ adj **1** : slender **2** : frail **3** : small in degree ~ vb **1** : ignore or treat as unimportant —**slight** n —**slight-ly** adv

slim \'slim\ adj **-mm- 1** : slender **2** : scanty ~ vb **-mm-** : make or become more slender

slime \'slīm\ n : dirty slippery film (as on water) —**slimy** adj

sling \'slin\ vb **slung** \'slən\; **sling-ing** : hurl with or as if with a sling ~ n **1** : strap for swinging and hurling stones **2** : looped strap or bandage to lift or support

sling-shot n : forked stick with elastic bands for shooting pebbles

slink \'slink\ vb **slunk** \'slənk\; **slink-ing** : move stealthily or sinuously —**slinky** adj

slip \'slip\ vb **-pp- 1** : escape quietly or secretly **2** : slide along smoothly **3** : make a mistake **4** : to pass without being noticed or done **5** : fall off from a standard ~ n **1** : ship's berth **2** : sudden mishap **3** : mistake **4** : woman's undergarment

slip n **1** : plant shoot **2** : small strip (as of paper)

slip-per \'slipər\ n : shoe that slips on easily

slip-pery \'slipərē\ adj **-peri-er; -est 1** : slick enough to slide on **2** : tricky —**slip-peri-ness** n

slip-shod \'slip,shäd\ adj : careless

slit \'slit\ vb **slit; slit-ting** : make a slit in ~ n : long narrow cut

slith-er \'slithər\ vb : glide along like a snake —**slith-ery** adj

sliv-er \'slivər\ n : splinter

slob \'släb\ n : untidy person

slob-ber \'släbər\ vb : dribble saliva —**slob-ber** n

slo-gan \'slōgən\ n : word or phrase expressing the aim of a cause

sloop \'slüp\ n : one-masted sailboat

slop \'släp\ n : food waste for animal feed ~ vb **-pp-** : spill

slope \'slōp\ vb **sloped; slop-ing** : deviate from the vertical or horizontal ~ n **1** : upward or downward slant

slop-py \'släpē\ adj **-pi-er, -est 1** : muddy **2** : untidy

slot \'slät\ n : narrow opening

sloth \'slȯth, 'slōth\ n, pl **sloths** \with ths or thz\ **1** : laziness **2** : slow-moving mammal —**sloth-ful** adj

slouch \'slauch\ n **1** : drooping posture **2** : lazy or incompetent person ~ vb : walk or stand with a slouch

slough \'slü, 'slau\ n : swamp

slough \'sləf\ **sluff** vb : cast off (old skin)

slov-en-ly \'sləvənlē\ adj : untidy

slow \'slō\ adj **1** : sluggish or stupid **2** : moving, working, or happening at less than the usual speed ~ vb **1** : make slow **2** : go slower —**slow** adv —**slow-ly** adv —**slow-ness** n

sludge \'sləj\ n : slushy mass (as of treated sewage)

slug \'sləg\ n **1** : mollusk related to the snails **2** : bullet **3** : metal disk ~ vb **-gg-** : strike forcibly —**slug-ger** n

slug-gish \'sləgish\ adj : slow in movement or flow —**slug-gish-ly** adv —**slug-gish-ness** n

sluice \'slüs\ n : channel for water ~ vb **sluiced; sluic-ing** : wash in running water

slum \'sləm\ n : thickly populated area marked by poverty

slum-ber \'sləmbər\ vb or n : sleep

slump \'sləmp\ vb **1** : sink suddenly **2** : slouch —**slump** n

slung past of SLING

slunk past of SLINK

¹slur \'slər\ vb **-rr-** : run (words or notes) together **—slur** n

²slur n : malicious or insulting remark

slurp \'slərp\ vb : eat or drink noisily **—slurp** n

slush \'sləsh\ n : partly melted snow **—slushy** adj

slut \'slət\ n **1** : untidy woman **2** : lewd woman **—slut•tish** adj

sly \'slī\ adj **sli•er** \'slīər\; **sli•est** \'slīəst\ : given to or showing secrecy and deception **—sly•ly** adv **—sly•ness** n

¹smack \'smak\ n : characteristic flavor ~ vb : have a taste or hint

²smack vb **1** : move (the lips) so as to make a sharp noise **2** : kiss or slap with a loud noise ~ n **1** : sharp noise made by the lips **2** : noisy slap

³smack adv : squarely and sharply

⁴smack n : fishing boat

small \'smȯl\ adj **1** : little in size or amount **2** : few in number **3** : trivial **—small•ish** adj **—small•ness** n

small•pox \'smȯl,päks\ n : contagious virus disease

smart \'smärt\ vb **1** : cause or feel stinging pain **2** : endure distress ~ adj **1** : intelligent or resourceful **2** : stylish **—smart** n **—smart•ly** adv **—smart•ness** n

smash \'smash\ vb **1** : break or be broken into pieces ~ n **1** : smashing blow **2** : act or sound of smashing

smat•ter•ing \'smatəriŋ\ n **1** : superficial knowledge **2** : small scattered number or amount

smear \'smir\ n : greasy stain ~ vb **1** : spread (something sticky) **2** : smudge **3** : slander

smell \'smel\ vb **smelled** \'smeld\ or **smelt** \'smelt\; **smell•ing 1** : perceive the odor of **2** : have or give off an odor ~ n **1** : sense by which one perceives odor **2** : odor **—smelly** adj

¹smelt \'smelt\ n, pl **smelts** or **smelt** : small food fish

²smelt vb : melt or fuse (ore) in order to separate the metal **—smelt•er** n

smile \'smīl\ n : facial expression with the mouth turned up usu. to show pleasure **—smile** vb

smirk \'smərk\ vb : wear a conceited smile **—smirk** n

smite \'smīt\ vb **smote** \'smōt\; **smit•ten** \'smitᵊn\ or **smote**; **smit•ing** \'smītiŋ\ **1** : strike heavily or kill **2** : affect strongly

smith \'smith\ n : worker in metals and esp. a blacksmith

smithy \'smithē\ n, pl **smith•ies** : a smith's workshop

smock \'smäk\ n : loose dress or protective coat

smog \'smäg, 'smȯg\ n : fog and smoke **—smog•gy** adj

smoke \'smōk\ n : sooty gas from burning ~ vb **smoked; smok•ing 1** : give off smoke **2** : inhale the fumes of burning tobacco **3** : cure (as meat) with smoke **—smoke•less** adj **—smok•er** n **—smoky** adj

smoke•stack n : chimney through which smoke is discharged

smol•der, smoul•der \'smōldər\ vb **1** : burn and smoke without flame **2** : be suppressed but active **—smolder** n

smooth \'smüth\ adj **1** : having a surface without irregularities **2** : not jarring or jolting ~ vb : make smooth **—smooth•ly** adv **—smooth•ness** n

smor•gas•bord \'smȯrgəs,bȯrd\ n : buffet consisting of many foods

smoth•er \'sməthər\ vb **1** : kill by depriving of air **2** : cover thickly

smudge \'sməj\ vb **smudged; smudg•ing** : soil or blur by rubbing ~ n **1** : thick smoke **2** : dirty spot

smug \'sməg\ adj **-gg-** : content in one's own virtue or accomplishment **—smug•ly** adv **—smug•ness** n

smug•gle \'sməgəl\ vb **-gled; -gling** : import or export secretly or illegally **—smug•gler** \'sməglər\ n

smut \'smət\ n **1** : something that soils **2** : indecent language or matter **3** : disease of plants caused by fungi **—smut•ty** adj

snack \'snak\ n : light meal

snag \'snag\ n : unexpected difficulty ~ vb **-gg-** : become caught on something that sticks out

snail \'snāl\ n : small mollusk with a spiral shell

snake \'snāk\ n : long-bodied limbless reptile **—snake•bite** n

snap \'snap\ vb **-pp-** : bite at something **2** : utter angry words **3** : break suddenly with a sharp sound ~ n **1** : act or sound of snapping **2** : fastening that closes with a click **3** : something easy to do **—snap•per** n **—snap•pish** adj **—snap•py** adj

snap•drag•on n : garden plant with spikes of showy flowers

snap•shot \'snap,shät\ n : casual photograph

snare \'snar\ n : trap for catching game ~ vb : capture or hold with or as if with a snare

¹snarl \'snärl\ n : tangle ~ vb : cause to become knotted

²snarl vb or n : growl

snatch \'snach\ vb **1** : try to grab something suddenly **2** : seize or take away suddenly ~ n **1** : act of snatching **2** : something brief or fragmentary

sneak \'snēk\ vb : move or take in a furtive manner ~ n : one who acts in a furtive manner **—sneak•i•ly** \'snēkəlē\ adv **—sneak•ing•ly** adv **—sneaky** adj

sneak•er \'snēkər\ n : sports shoe

sneer \'snir\ vb : smile scornfully **—sneer** n

sneeze \'snēz\ vb **sneezed; sneez•ing** : force the breath out with sudden and involuntary violence **—sneeze** n

snick•er \'snikər\ n : partly suppressed laugh **—snicker** vb

snide \'snīd\ adj : subtly ridiculing

sniff \'snif\ vb **1** : draw air audibly up the nose **2** : detect by smelling **—sniff** n

snip \'snip\ n : fragment snipped off ~ vb **-pp-** : cut off by bits

¹snipe \'snīp\ n, pl **snipes** or **snipe** : game bird of marshy areas

²snipe vb **sniped; snip•ing** : shoot at an enemy from a concealed position **—snip•er** n

snips \'snips\ n pl : scissorslike tool

sniv•el \'snivəl\ vb **-eled** or **-elled; -el•ing** or **-el•ling 1** : have a running nose **2** : whine

snob \'snäb\ n : one who acts superior to others **—snob•bery** \-ərē\ n **—snob•bish** adj **—snob•bish•ly** adv **—snob•bish•ness** n

snoop \'snüp\ vb : pry in a furtive way ~ n : prying person

snooze \'snüz\ vb **snoozed; snooz•ing** : take a nap **—snooze** n

snore \'snȯr\ vb **snored; snor•ing** : breathe with a hoarse noise while sleeping **—snore** n

snort \'snȯrt\ vb : force air noisily through the nose **—snort** n

snout \'snaut\ n : long projecting muzzle (as of a swine)

snow \'snō\ n : crystals formed from water vapor ~ vb : fall as snow **—snow•ball** n **—snow•bank** n **—snow•drift** n **—snow•fall** n **—snow•plow** n **—snow•storm** n **—snowy** adj

snow•shoe n : frame of wood strung with thongs for walking on snow

snub \'snəb\ vb **-bb-** : ignore or avoid through disdain **—snub** n

¹snuff \'snəf\ vb : put out (a candle) **—snuff•er** n

²snuff vb : draw forcibly into the nose ~ n : pulverized tobacco

snug \'snəg\ adj **-gg-** **1** : warm, secure, and comfortable **2** : fitting closely **—snug•ly** adv **—snug•ness** n

snug•gle \'snəgəl\ vb **-gled; -gling** : curl up comfortably

so \'sō\ adv **1** : in the manner or to the extent indicated **2** : in the same way **3** : therefore **4** : finally **5** : thus ~ conj : for that reason

soak \'sōk\ vb **1** : lie in a liquid **2** : absorb ~ n : act of soaking

soap \'sōp\ n : cleaning substance **—soap** vb **—soapy** adj

soar \'sōr\ vb : fly upward on or as if on wings

sob \'säb\ vb **-bb-** : weep with convulsive heavings of the chest **—sob** n

so•ber \'sōbər\ adj **1** : not drunk **2** : serious or solemn **—so•ber•ly** adv

so•bri•ety \sə'brīətē, sō-\ n : quality or state of being sober

soc•cer \'säkər\ n : game played by kicking a ball

so•cia•ble \'sōshəbəl\ adj : friendly **—so•cia•bil•i•ty** \,sōshə'bilətē\ n **—so•cia•bly** \'sōshəblē\ adv

so•cial \'sōshəl\ adj **1** : relating to pleasant companionship **2** : naturally living or growing in groups **3** : relating to human society ~ n : social gathering **—so•cial•ly** adv

so•cial•ism \'sōshə,lizəm\ n : social system based on government control of the production and distribution of goods **—so•cial•ist** \'sōshəlist\ n or adj **—so•cial•is•tic** \,sōshə'listik\ adj

so•cial•ize \'sōshə,līz\ vb **-ized; -iz•ing 1** : regulate by socialism **2** : adapt to social needs **3** : participate in a social gathering **—so•cial•i•za•tion** \,sōshələ'zāshən\ n

social work n : services concerned with aiding the poor and socially maladjusted **—social worker** n

so•ci•ety \sə'sīətē\ n, pl **-et•ies 1** : companionship **2** : community life **3** : rich or fashionable class **4** : voluntary group

so•ci•ol•o•gy \,sōsē'äləjē\ n : study of social relationships **—so•ci•o•log•i•cal** \-sēə'läjikəl\ adj **—so•ci•ol•o•gist** \-'äləjist\ n

¹sock \'säk\ n, pl **socks** or **sox** : short stocking

²sock vb or n : punch

sock•et \'säkət\ n : hollow part that holds something

sod \'säd\ n : turf ~ vb **-dd-** : cover with sod

so•da \'sōdə\ n **1** : carbonated water or a soft drink **2** : ice cream drink made with soda

sod•den \'sädᵊn\ adj **1** : lacking spirit **2** : soaked or soggy

so•di•um \'sōdēəm\ n : soft waxy silver white metallic chemical element

so•fa \'sōfə\ n : wide padded chair

soft \'sȯft\ adj **1** : not hard, rough, or harsh **2** : nonalcoholic **—soft•en** \'sȯfən\ vb **—soft•en•er** \-ənər\ n **—soft•ly** adv **—soft•ness** n

soft•ball n : game like baseball

soft•ware \'sȯft,war\ n : computer programs

sog•gy \'sägē\ adj **-gi•er, -est** : heavy with moisture **—sog•gi•ness** \-ēnəs\ n

¹soil \'sȯil\ vb : make or become dirty ~ n : embedded dirt

²soil n : loose surface material of the earth

so•journ \'sō,jərn, sō'jərn\ n : temporary stay ~ vb : reside temporarily

so•lace \'säləs\ n or vb : comfort

so•lar \'sōlər\ adj : relating to the sun or the energy in sunlight

sold past of SELL

sol•der \'sädər, 'sȯd-\ n : metallic alloy melted to join metallic surfaces ~ vb : cement with solder

sol•dier \'sōljər\ n : person in military service ~ vb : serve as a soldier **—sol•dier•ly** adj or adv

¹sole \'sōl\ n : bottom of the foot or a shoe **—soled** adj

²sole n : flatfish caught for food

³sole adj : single or only **—sole•ly** adv

sol•emn \'säləm\ adj **1** : dignified and ceremonial **2** : highly serious **—so•lem•ni•ty** \sə'lemnətē\ n **—sol•emn•ly** adv

so•lic•it \sə'lisət\ vb : ask for **—so•lic•i•ta•tion** \-,lisə'tāshən\ n

so•lic•i•tor \sə'lisətər\ n **1** : one that solicits **2** : lawyer

so•lic•i•tous \sə'lisətəs\ adj : showing or expressing concern **—so•lic•i•tous•ly** adv **—so•lic•i•tude** \sə'lisə,tüd, -,tyüd\ n

sol•id \'säləd\ adj **1** : not hollow **2** : having 3 dimensions **3** : hard **4** : of good quality **5** : of one character ~ n **1** : 3-dimensional figure **2** : substance in solid form **—solid** adv **—so•lid•i•ty** \sə'lidətē\ n **—sol•id•ly** adv **—sol•id•ness** n

sol•i•dar•i•ty \,sälə'darətē\ n : unity of purpose

so•lid•i•fy \sə'lidə,fī\ vb **-fied; -fy•ing** : make or become solid **—so•lid•i•fi•ca•tion** \-,lidəfə'kāshən\ n

so•lil•o•quy \sə'liləkwē\ n, pl **-quies** : dramatic monologue **—so•lil•o•quize** \-,kwīz\ vb

sol•i•taire \'sälə,tar\ n **1** : solitary gem **2** : card game for one person

sol•i•tary \-,terē\ adj **1** : alone **2** : secluded **3** : single

sol•i•tude \-,tüd, -,tyüd\ n : state of being alone

so•lo \'sōlō\ n, pl **-los** : performance by only one person ~ adv : alone **—solo** adj or vb **—so•lo•ist** n

sol•stice \'sälstəs\ n : time of the year when the sun is farthest north or south of the equator

sol•u•ble \'sälyəbəl\ adj **1** : capable of being dissolved **2** : capable of being solved **—sol•u•bil•i•ty** \,sälyə'bilətē\ n

so•lu•tion \sə'lüshən\ n **1** : answer to a problem **2** : homogeneous liquid mixture

solve \'sälv\ vb **solved; solv•ing** : find a solution for **—solv•able** adj

sol•vent \'sälvənt\ adj **1** : able to pay all debts **2** : dissolving or able to dissolve ~ n : substance that dissolves or disperses another substance **—sol•ven•cy** \-vənsē\ n

som•ber, som•bre \'sämbər\ adj **1** : dark **2** : grave **—som•ber•ly** adv

som•bre•ro \səm'brerō\ n, pl **-ros** : broad-brimmed hat

some \'səm\ adj **1** : one unspecified **2** : unspecified or indefinite number of **3** : at least a few or a little ~ pron : a certain number or amount

-some \səm\ adj suffix : characterized by a thing, quality, state, or action

some•body \'səmbədē, -,bäd-\ pron : some person

some•day \'səm,dā\ adv : at some future time

some•how \-,hau\ adv : by some means

some•one \-,wən\ pron : some person

som•er•sault \'səmər,sȯlt\ n : body flip **—somersault** vb

some•thing \'səmthiŋ\ pron : some undetermined or unspecified thing

some•time \'səm,tīm\ adv **1** : at a future, unknown, or unnamed time

some•times \-,tīmz\ adv : occasionally

some•what \-,hwət, -,hwät\ adv : in some degree

some•where \-,hwer\ adv : in, at, or to an unknown or unnamed place

som•no•lent \'sämnələnt\ adj : sleepy **—som•no•lence** \-ləns\ n

son \'sən\ n : male offspring

so•nar \'sō,när\ n : device that detects and locates underwater objects using sound waves

so•na•ta \sə'nätə\ n : instrumental composition

song \'sȯŋ\ n : music and words to be sung

song•bird n : bird with musical tones

son•ic \'sänik\ adj : relating to sound waves or the speed of sound

son–in–law n, pl **sons–in–law** : husband of one's daughter

son•net \'sänət\ n : poem of 14 lines

so•no•rous \sə'nōrəs, 'sänərəs\ adj **1** : loud, deep, or rich in sound **2** : impressive **—so•nor•i•ty** \sə'nȯrətē\ n

soon \'sün\ adv **1** : before long **2** : promptly **3** : early

soot \'sut, 'sət, 'süt\ n : fine black substance formed by combustion **—sooty** adj

soothe \'süth\ vb **soothed; sooth•ing** : calm or comfort **—sooth•er** n

sooth•say•er \'süth,sāər\ n : prophet **—sooth•say•ing** \-iŋ\ n

sop \'säp\ n : conciliatory bribe, gift, or concession ~ vb **-pp-** **1** : dip in a liquid **2** : soak **3** : mop up

so•phis•ti•cat•ed \sə'fistə,kātəd\ adj **1** : complex **2** : wise, cultured, or shrewd in human affairs **—so•phis•ti•ca•tion** \-,fistə'kāshən\ n

soph•ist•ry \'säfəstrē\ n : subtly fallacious reasoning or argument **—soph•ist** \'säfist\ n

soph•o•more \'säfᵊm,ȯr, 'säf,mȯr\ n : 2d-year student

so•po•rif•ic \,säpə'rifik, ,sōp-\ adj : causing sleep or drowsiness

so•pra•no \sə'pranō\ n, pl **-nos** : highest singing voice

sor•cery \'sȯrsərē\ n : witchcraft **—sor•cer•er** \-rər\ n **—sor•cer•ess** \-rəs\ n

sor•did \'sȯrdəd\ adj : filthy or vile **—sor•did•ly** adv **—sor•did•ness** n

sore \'sōr\ adj **sor•er; sor•est 1** : causing pain or distress **2** : severe or intense **3** : angry ~ n : sore usu. infected spot on the body **—sore•ly** adv **—sore•ness** n

sor•ghum \'sȯrgəm\ n : forage grass

so•ror•i•ty \sə'rȯrətē\ n, pl **-ties** : women's student social group

¹sor•rel \'sȯrəl\ n : brownish orange to light brown color or an animal of this color

²sorrel n : herb with sour juice

sor•row \'särō\ n : deep distress, sadness, or regret or a cause of this **—sor•row•ful** \-fəl\ adj **—sor•row•ful•ly** adv

sor•ry \'särē\ adj **-ri•er, -est 1** : feeling sorrow, regret, or penitence **2** : dismal

sort \'sȯrt\ n **1** : kind **2** : nature ~ vb : classify **—out of sorts** : grouchy

sor•tie \'sȯrtē, sȯr'tē\ n : military attack esp. against besiegers

SOS \,es,ō'es\ n : call for help

so–so \'sō'sō\ adj or adv : barely acceptable

sot \'sät\ n : drunkard **—sot•tish** adj

souf•flé \sü'flā\ n : baked dish made light with beaten egg whites

sought past of SEEK

soul \'sōl\ n **1** : immaterial essence of an individual life **2** : essential part **3** : person

soul•ful \'sōlfəl\ adj : full of or expressing deep feeling **—soul•ful•ly** adv

¹sound \'saund\ adj **1** : free from fault, error, or illness **2** : firm or hard **3** : showing good judgment **—sound•ly** adv **—sound•ness** n

²sound n **1** : sensation of hearing **2** : energy of vibration sensed in hearing **3** : something heard ~ vb **1** : make or cause to make a sound **2** : seem **—sound•less** adj **—sound•less•ly** adv **—sound•proof** adj or vb

³sound n : wide strait ~ vb **1** : measure the depth of (water) **2** : investigate

soup \'süp\ n : broth usu. containing pieces of solid food **—soupy** adj

sour \'sauər\ adj **1** : having an acid or tart taste **2** : disagreeable ~ vb : become or make sour **—sour•ish** adj **—sour•ly** adv **—sour•ness** n

source \'sȯrs\ n **1** : point of origin **2** : one that provides something needed

souse \'saus\ vb **soused; sous•ing 1** : pickle **2** : immerse **3** : intoxicate ~ n **1** : something pickled **2** : drunkard

south \'sauth\ adv : to or toward the south ~ adj : situated toward, at, or coming from the south ~ n **1** : direction to the right of sunrise **2** cap : regions to the south **—south•er•ly** \'səthərlē\ adv or adj **—south•ern** \'səthərn\ adj **—South•ern•er** n **—south•ern•most** \-,mōst\ adj **—south•ward** \'sauthwərd\ adv or adj **—south•wards** \-wərdz\ adv

south•east \sauth'ēst, naut sau'ēst\ n **1** : direction between south and east **2** cap : regions to the southeast **—southeast** adj or adv **—south•east•er•ly** adv or adj **—south•east•ern** \-ərn\ adj

south pole n : the southernmost point of the earth

south•west \sauth'west, naut sau'west\ n **1** : direction between south and west **2** cap

: regions to the southwest —**southwest** *adj or adv* —**south•west•er•ly** *adv or adj* —**south•west•ern** \-ərn\ *adj*

sou•ve•nir \ˌsüvəˌnir\ *n* : something that is a reminder of a place or event

sov•er•eign \ˈsävərən\ *n* 1 : supreme ruler 2 : gold coin of the United Kingdom ~ *adj* 1 : supreme 2 : independent —**sov•er•eign•ty** \-tē\ *n*

¹**sow** \ˈsaü\ *n* : female swine

²**sow** \ˈsō\ *vb* **sowed; sown** \ˈsōn\ *or* **sowed, sow•ing** 1 : plant or strew with seed 2 : scatter abroad —**sow•er** \ˈsōər\ *n*

sox *pl of* SOCK

soy•bean \ˈsoiˌbēn\ *n* : legume with edible seeds

spa \ˈspä\ *n* : resort at a mineral spring

space \ˈspās\ *n* 1 : period of time 2 : area in, around, or between 3 : region beyond earth's atmosphere 4 : accommodations ~ *vb* **spaced; spac•ing** : place at intervals —**space•craft** *n* —**space•flight** *n* —**space•man** *n* —**space•ship** *n*

spa•cious \ˈspāshəs\ *adj* : large or roomy —**spa•cious•ly** *adv* —**spa•cious•ness** *n*

¹**spade** \ˈspād\ *n or vb* : shovel —**spade•ful** *n*

²**spade** *n* : playing card marked with a black figure like an inverted heart

spa•ghet•ti \spəˈgetē\ *n* : pasta strings

span \ˈspan\ *n* 1 : amount of time 2 : distance between supports ~ *vb* **-nn-** : extend across

span•gle \ˈspaŋgəl\ *n* : small disk of shining metal or plastic —**spangle** *vb*

span•iel \ˈspanyəl\ *n* : small or medium-sized dog with drooping ears and long wavy hair

spank \ˈspaŋk\ *vb* : hit on the buttocks with an open hand

¹**spar** \ˈspär\ *n* : pole or boom

²**spar** *vb* **-rr-** : practice boxing

spare \ˈspar\ *adj* 1 : held in reserve 2 : thin or scanty ~ *vb* **spared; spar•ing** 1 : reserve or avoid using 2 : avoid punishing or killing —**spare** *n*

spar•ing \ˈspariŋ\ *adj* : thrifty —**spar•ing•ly** *adv*

spark \ˈspärk\ *n* 1 : tiny hot and glowing particle 2 : smallest beginning or germ 3 : visible electrical discharge ~ *vb* 1 : emit or produce sparks 2 : stir to activity

spar•kle \ˈspärkəl\ *vb* **-kled; -kling** 1 : flash 2 : effervesce ~ *n* : gleam —**spar•kler** \-klər\ *n*

spar•row \ˈsparō\ *n* : small singing bird

sparse \ˈspärs\ *adj* **spars•er; spars•est** : thinly scattered —**sparse•ly** *adv*

spasm \ˈspazəm\ *n* 1 : involuntary muscular contraction 2 : sudden, violent, and temporary effort or feeling —**spas•mod•ic** \spazˈmädik\ *adj* —**spas•mod•i•cal•ly** *adv*

spas•tic \ˈspastik\ *adj* : relating to, marked by, or affected with muscular spasm —**spastic** *n*

¹**spat** \ˈspat\ *past of* SPIT

²**spat** *n* : petty dispute

spa•tial \ˈspāshəl\ *adj* : relating to space —**spa•tial•ly** *adv*

spat•ter \ˈspatər\ *vb* : splash with drops of liquid —**spatter** *n*

spat•u•la \ˈspachələ\ *n* : flexible knifelike utensil

spawn \ˈspȯn\ *vb* 1 : produce eggs or offspring 2 : bring forth ~ *n* : egg cluster —**spawn•er** *n*

spay \ˈspā\ *vb* : remove the ovaries of (a female)

speak \ˈspēk\ *vb* **spoke** \ˈspōk\; **spo•ken** \ˈspōkən\; **speak•ing** 1 : utter words 2 : express orally 3 : address an audience 4 : use (a language) in talking —**speak•er** *n*

spear \ˈspir\ *n* : long pointed weapon ~ *vb* : strike or pierce with a spear

spear•head *n* : leading force, element, or influence —**spearhead** *vb*

spear•mint *n* : aromatic garden mint

spe•cial \ˈspeshəl\ *adj* 1 : unusual or unique 2 : particularly favored 3 : set aside for a particular use —**special** *n* —**spe•cial•ly** *adv*

spe•cial•ist \ˈspeshəlist\ *n* : person who specializes in a particular branch of learning or activity 2 : any of four enlisted ranks in the army corresponding to the grades of corporal through sergeant first class

spe•cial•ize \ˈspeshəˌlīz\ *vb* **-ized; -iz•ing** : concentrate one's efforts —**spe•cial•i•za•tion** \ˌspeshələˈzāshən\ *n*

spe•cial•ty \ˈspeshəltē\ *n, pl* **-ties** : area or field in which one specializes

spe•cie \ˈspēshē, -sē\ *n* : money in coin

spe•cies \ˈspēshēz, -sēz\ *n, pl* **spe•cies** : biological grouping of closely related organisms

spe•cif•ic \spiˈsifik\ *adj* : definite or exact —**spe•cif•i•cal•ly** *adv*

spec•i•fi•ca•tion \ˌspesəfəˈkāshən\ *n* 1 : act or process of specifying 2 : detailed description of work to be done —usu. pl.

spec•i•fy \ˈspesəˌfī\ *vb* **-fied; -fy•ing** : mention precisely or by name

spec•i•men \-əmən\ *n* : typical example

spe•cious \ˈspēshəs\ *adj* : apparently but not really genuine or correct

speck \ˈspek\ *n* : tiny particle or blemish —**speck** *vb*

speck•led \ˈspekəld\ *adj* : marked with spots

spec•ta•cle \ˈspektikəl\ *n* 1 : impressive public display 2 *pl* : eyeglasses

spec•tac•u•lar \spekˈtakyələr\ *adj* : sensational or showy

spec•ta•tor \ˈspekˌtātər\ *n* : person who looks on

spec•ter, spec•tre \ˈspektər\ *n* 1 : ghost 2 : haunting vision

spec•tral \ˈspektrəl\ *adj* : relating to or resembling a specter or spectrum

spec•trum \ˈspektrəm\ *n, pl* **-tra** \-trə\ *or* **-trums** : series of colors formed when white light is dispersed into its components

spec•u•late \ˈspekyəˌlāt\ *vb* **-lat•ed; -lat•ing** 1 : think about things yet unknown 2 : risk money in a business deal in hope of high profit —**spec•u•la•tion** \ˌspekyəˈlāshən\ *n* —**spec•u•la•tive** \ˈspekyəˌlātiv\ *adj* —**spec•u•la•tor** \-ˌlātər\ *n*

speech \ˈspēch\ *n* 1 : power, act, or manner of speaking 2 : talk given to an audience —**speech•less** *adj*

speed \ˈspēd\ *n* 1 : quality of being fast 2 : rate of motion or performance ~ *vb* **sped** \ˈsped\ *or* **speed•ed; speed•ing** : go at a great or excessive rate of speed —**speed•boat** *n* —**speed•er** *n* —**speed•i•ly** \ˈspēdəlē\ *adv* —**speed•up** \-ˌəp\ *n* —**speedy** *adj*

speed•om•e•ter \spiˈdämətər\ *n* : instrument for indicating speed

¹**spell** \ˈspel\ *n* : influence of or like magic

²**spell** *vb* 1 : name, write, or print the letters of 2 : mean —**spell•er** *n*

³**spell** *vb* : substitute for or relieve (someone) ~ *n* 1 : turn at work 2 : period of time

spell•bound *adj* : held by a spell

spend \ˈspend\ *vb* **spent** \ˈspent\; **spend•ing** 1 : pay out 2 : cause or allow to pass —**spend•er** *n*

spend•thrift \ˈspend,thrift\ *n* : wasteful person

sperm \ˈspərm\ *n, pl* **sperm** *or* **sperms** : semen or a germ cell in it

spew \ˈspyü\ *vb* : gush out in a stream

sphere \ˈsfir\ *n* 1 : figure with every point on its surface at an equal distance from the center 2 : round body 3 : range of action or influence —**spher•i•cal** \ˈsfirikəl, ˈsfer-\ *adj*

spher•oid \ˈsfir-\ *n* : spherelike figure

spice \ˈspīs\ *n* 1 : aromatic plant product for seasoning food 2 : interesting quality —**spice** *vb* —**spicy** *adj*

spi•der \ˈspīdər\ *n* : small insectlike animal with 8 legs —**spi•dery** *adj*

spig•ot \ˈspigət, ˈspikət\ *n* : faucet

spike \ˈspīk\ *n* : very large nail ~ *vb* **spiked; spik•ing** : fasten or pierce with a spike —**spiked** \ˈspīkt\ *adj*

spill \ˈspil\ *vb* 1 : fall, flow, or run out unintentionally 2 : divulge ~ *n* 1 : act of spilling 2 : something spilled —**spill•able** *adj*

spill•way *n* : passage for surplus water

spin \ˈspin\ *vb* **spun** \ˈspən\; **spin•ning** 1 : draw out fiber and twist into thread 2 : form thread from a sticky body fluid 3 : revolve or cause to revolve extremely fast ~ *n* : rapid rotating motion —**spin•ner** *n*

spin•ach \ˈspinich\ *n* : garden herb with edible leaves

spi•nal \ˈspīnəl\ *adj* : relating to the backbone —**spi•nal•ly** *adv*

spinal cord *n* : thick strand of nervous tissue that extends from the brain along the back within the backbone

spin•dle \ˈspindəl\ *n* 1 : stick used for spinning thread 2 : shaft around which something turns

spin•dly \ˈspindlē\ *adj* : tall and slender

spine \ˈspīn\ *n* 1 : backbone 2 : stiff sharp projection on a plant or animal —**spine•less** *adj* —**spiny** *adj*

spin•et \ˈspinət\ *n* : small piano

spin•ster \ˈspinstər\ *n* : woman who has never married

spi•ral \ˈspīrəl\ *adj* : circling or winding around a single point or line —**spiral** *n or vb* —**spi•ral•ly** *adv*

spire \ˈspīr\ *n* : steeple —**spiry** *adj*

spir•it \ˈspirət\ *n* 1 : life-giving force 2 *cap* : presence of God 3 : ghost 4 : mood 5 : vivacity or enthusiasm 6 *pl* : alcoholic liquor ~ *vb* : carry off secretly —**spir•it•ed** *adj* —**spir•it•less** *adj*

spir•i•tu•al \ˈspirichəwəl\ *adj* 1 : relating to the spirit or sacred matters 2 : deeply religious ~ *n* : religious folk song —**spir•i•tu•al•i•ty** \ˌspirichəˈwalətē\ *n* —**spir•i•tu•al•ly** *adv*

spir•i•tu•al•ism \ˈspirichəwəˌlizəm\ *n* : belief that spirits communicate with the living —**spir•i•tu•al•ist** \-list\ *n or adj*

¹**spit** \ˈspit\ *n* 1 : rod for holding and turning meat over a fire 2 : point of land that runs into the water

²**spit** *vb* **spit** *or* **spat** \ˈspat\; **spit•ting** : eject saliva from the mouth ~ *n* 1 : saliva 2 : perfect likeness

spite \ˈspīt\ *n* : petty ill will ~ *vb* **spit•ed; spit•ing** : annoy or offend —**spite•ful** \-fəl\ *adj* —**spite•ful•ly** *adv* —**in spite of** : in defiance or contempt of

spit•tle \ˈspitəl\ *n* : saliva

spit•toon \spiˈtün\ *n* : receptacle for spit

splash \ˈsplash\ *vb* : scatter a liquid on —**splash** *n*

splat•ter \ˈsplatər\ *vb* : spatter —**splatter** *n*

splay \ˈsplā\ *vb* : spread out or apart —**splay** *n or adj*

spleen \ˈsplēn\ *n* 1 : organ for maintenance of the blood 2 : spite or anger

splen•did \ˈsplendəd\ *adj* 1 : impressive in beauty or brilliance 2 : outstanding —**splen•did•ly** *adv*

splen•dor \ˈsplendər\ *n* 1 : brilliance 2 : magnificence

splice \ˈsplīs\ *vb* **spliced; splic•ing** : join (2 things) end to end —**splice** *n*

splint \ˈsplint\ *n* 1 : thin strip of wood 2 : something that keeps an injured body part in place

splin•ter \ˈsplintər\ *n* : thin needlelike piece ~ *vb* : break into splinters

split \ˈsplit\ *vb* **split; split•ting** : divide lengthwise or along a grain —**split** *n*

splotch \ˈspläch\ *n* : blotch

splurge \ˈsplərj\ *vb* **splurged; splurg•ing** : indulge oneself —**splurge** *n*

splut•ter \ˈsplətər\ *vb* : sputter —**splutter** *vb*

spoil \ˈspȯil\ *n* : plunder ~ *vb* **spoiled** \ˈspȯild, ˈspȯilt\ *or* **spoilt** \ˈspȯilt\; **spoil•ing** 1 : pillage 2 : ruin 3 : rot —**spoil•age** \ˈspȯilij\ *n* —**spoil•er** *n*

¹**spoke** \ˈspōk\ *past of* SPEAK

²**spoke** *n* : rod from the hub to the rim of a wheel

spo•ken *past part of* SPEAK

spokes•man \ˈspōksmən\ *n* : person who speaks for others

spokes•wom•an \-ˌwumən\ *n* : woman who speaks for others

sponge \ˈspənj\ *n* 1 : porous water-absorbing mass that forms the skeleton of some marine animals 2 : spongelike material used for wiping ~ *vb* **sponged; spong•ing** 1 : wipe with a sponge 2 : live at another's expense —**spongy** \ˈspənjē\ *adj*

spon•sor \ˈspänsər\ *n* : one who assumes responsibility for another or who provides financial support —**sponsor** *vb* —**spon•sor•ship** *n*

spon•ta•ne•ous \spänˈtānēəs\ *adj* : done, produced, or occurring naturally or without planning —**spon•ta•ne•i•ty** \ˌspäntənˈēətē\ *n* —**spon•ta•ne•ous•ly** \spänˈtānēəslē\ *adv*

spoof \ˈspüf\ *vb* : make good-natured fun of —**spoof** *n*

spook \ˈspük\ *n* : ghost ~ *vb* : frighten —**spooky** *adj*

spool \ˈspül\ *n* : cylinder on which something is wound

spoon \ˈspün\ *n* : utensil consisting of a small shallow bowl with a handle —**spoon** *vb* —**spoon•ful** \-ˌfül\ *n*

spoor \ˈspür, ˈspȯr\ *n* : track or trail esp. of a wild animal

spo•rad•ic \spəˈradik\ *adj* : occasional —**spo•rad•i•cal•ly** *adv*

spore \ˈspȯr\ *n* : primitive usu. one-celled reproductive body

sport \ˈspȯrt\ *vb* 1 : frolic 2 : show off ~ *n* 1 : physical activity engaged in for pleasure 2 : jest 3 : person who shows good sportsmanship —**sport•ive** \-iv\ *adj* —**sporty** *adj*

sports•cast \ˈspȯrts,kast\ *n* : broadcast of a sports event —**sports•cast•er** \-ˌkastər\ *n*

sports•man \-mən\ *n* : one who enjoys hunting and fishing

sports•man•ship \-mən,ship\ *n* : ability to be gracious in winning or losing

spot \ˈspät\ *n* 1 : blemish 2 : distinctive small part 3 : location ~ *vb* **-tt-** 1 : mark with spots 2 : see or recognize ~ *adj* : made at random or in limited numbers —**spot•less** *adj* —**spot•less•ly** *adv*

spot•light *n* 1 : intense beam of light 2 : center of public interest —**spotlight** *vb*

spot•ty \ˈspätē\ *adj* **-ti•er; -est** : uneven in quality

spouse \ˈspaüs\ *n* : one's husband or wife

spout \ˈspaüt\ *vb* 1 : shoot forth in a stream 2 : say pompously ~ *n* 1 : opening through which liquid spouts 2 : jet of liquid

sprain \ˈsprān\ *n* : twisting injury to a joint ~ *vb* : injure with a sprain

sprat \ˈsprat\ *n* : small or young herring

sprawl \ˈsprȯl\ *vb* : lie or sit with limbs spread out —**sprawl** *n*

¹**spray** \ˈsprā\ *n* : branch or arrangement of flowers

²**spray** *n* 1 : mist 2 : device that discharges liquid as a mist —**spray** *vb* —**spray•er** *n*

spread \ˈspred\ *vb* **spread; spread•ing** 1 : open up or unfold 2 : scatter or smear over a surface 3 : cause to be known or to exist over a wide area ~ *n* 1 : extent to which something is spread 2 : cloth cover 3 : something intended to be spread —**spread•er** *n*

spread•sheet \ˈspred,shēt\ *n* : accounting program for a computer

spree \ˈsprē\ *n* : burst of indulging in something

sprig \ˈsprig\ *n* : small shoot or twig

spright•ly \ˈsprītlē\ *adj* **-li•er; -est** : lively —**spright•li•ness** *n*

spring \ˈspriŋ\ *vb* **sprang** \ˈspraŋ\ *or* **sprung** \ˈsprəŋ\; **sprung; spring•ing** 1 : move or grow quickly or by elastic force 2 : come from by descent 3 : make known suddenly ~ *n* 1 : source 2 : flow of water from underground 3 : season between winter and summer 4 : elastic body or device (as a coil of wire) 5 : leap 6 : elastic power —**springy** *adj*

sprin•kle \ˈspriŋkəl\ *vb* **-kled; -kling** : scatter in small drops or particles ~ *n* : light rainfall —**sprin•kler** *n*

sprint \ˈsprint\ *n* : short run at top speed —**sprint** *vb* —**sprint•er** *n*

sprite \ˈsprīt\ *n* : elf or elfish person

sprock•et \ˈspräkət\ *n* : toothed wheel whose teeth engage the links of a chain

sprout \ˈspraüt\ *vb* : send out new growth ~ *n* : plant shoot

¹**spruce** \ˈsprüs\ *n* : conical evergreen tree

²**spruce** *adj* **spruc•er; spruc•est** : neat and stylish in appearance ~ *vb* **spruced; spruc•ing** : make or become neat

spry \ˈsprī\ *adj* **spri•er** *or* **spry•er** \ˈsprīər\; **spri•est** *or* **spry•est** \ˈsprīəst\ : agile and active

spume \ˈspyüm\ *n* : froth

spun *past of* SPIN

spunk \ˈspəŋk\ *n* : courage —**spunky** *adj*

spur \ˈspər\ *n* 1 : pointed device used to urge on a horse 2 : something that urges to action 3 : projecting part ~ *vb* **-rr-** : urge on —**spurred** *adj*

spu•ri•ous \ˈspyürēəs\ *adj* : not genuine

spurn \ˈspərn\ *vb* : reject

¹**spurt** \ˈspərt\ *n* : burst of effort, speed, or activity ~ *vb* : make a spurt

²**spurt** *vb* : gush out ~ *n* : sudden gush

sput•ter \ˈspətər\ *vb* 1 : talk hastily and indistinctly in excitement 2 : make popping sounds —**sputter** *n*

spy \ˈspī\ *vb* **spied; spy•ing** : watch or try to gather information secretly —**spy** *n*

squab \ˈskwäb\ *n, pl* **squabs** *or* **squab** : young pigeon

squab•ble \ˈskwäbəl\ *n or vb* : dispute

squad \ˈskwäd\ *n* : small group

squad•ron \ˈskwädrən\ *n* : small military unit

squal•id \ˈskwäləd\ *adj* : filthy or wretched

squall \ˈskwȯl\ *n* : sudden violent brief storm —**squally** *adj*

squa•lor \ˈskwälər\ *n* : quality or state of being squalid

squan•der \ˈskwändər\ *vb* : waste

square \ˈskwar\ *n* 1 : instrument for measuring right angles 2 : flat figure that has 4 equal sides and 4 right angles 3 : open area in a city 4 : product of number multiplied by itself ~ *adj* **squar•er; squar•est** 1 : being a square in form 2 : having sides meet at right angles 3 : multiplied by itself 4 : being a square unit of area 5 : honest ~ *vb* **squared; squar•ing** 1 : form into a square 2 : multiply (a number) by itself 3 : conform 4 : settle —**square•ly** *adv*

¹**squash** \ˈskwäsh, ˈskwȯsh\ *vb* 1 : press flat 2 : suppress

²**squash** *n, pl* **squash•es** *or* **squash** : garden vegetable

squat \ˈskwät\ *vb* **-tt-** 1 : stoop or sit on one's heels 2 : settle on land one does not own ~ *n* : act or posture of squatting ~ *adj* **squat•ter; squat•test** : short and thick —**squat•ter** *n*

squaw \ˈskwȯ\ *n* : American Indian woman

squawk \ˈskwȯk\ *n* : harsh loud cry —**squawk** *vb*

squeak \ˈskwēk\ *vb* : make a thin high-pitched sound —**squeak** *n* —**squeaky** *adj*

squeal \ˈskwēl\ *vb* 1 : make a shrill sound or cry 2 : protest —**squeal** *n*

squea•mish \ˈskwēmish\ *adj* : easily nauseated or disgusted

squeeze \ˈskwēz\ *vb* **squeezed; squeez•ing** 1 : apply pressure to 2 : extract by pressure —**squeeze** *n* —**squeez•er** *n*

squelch \ˈskwelch\ *vb* : suppress (as with a retort) —**squelch** *n*

squid \ˈskwid\ *n, pl* **squid** *or* **squids** : 10-armed long-bodied sea mollusk

squint \ˈskwint\ *vb* : look with the eyes partly closed —**squint** *n or adj*

squire \ˈskwīr\ *n* 1 : knight's aide 2 : country landholder 3 : lady's devoted escort ~ *vb* **squired; squir•ing** : escort

squirm \ˈskwərm\ *vb* : wriggle

squir•rel \ˈskwərəl\ *n* : rodent with a long bushy tail

squirt \'skwərt\ *vb* : eject liquid in a spurt —**squirt** *n*

stab \'stab\ *n* **1** : wound made by a pointed weapon **2** : quick thrust **3** : attempt ~ *vb* **-bb-** : pierce or wound with or as if with a pointed weapon

¹sta•ble \'stābəl\ *n* : building for domestic animals ~ *vb* **-bled; -bling** : keep in a stable

²stable *adj* **sta•bler; sta•blest 1** : firmly established **2** : mentally and emotionally healthy **3** : steady —**sta•bil•i•ty** \stə'bilətē\ *n* —**sta•bil•iza•tion** \stābələ'zā-shən\ *n* —**sta•bi•lize** \'stābə,līz\ *vb* —**sta•bi•liz•er** *n*

stac•ca•to \stə'kätō\ *adj* : disconnected

stack \'stak\ *n* : large pile ~ *vb* : pile up

sta•di•um \'stādēəm\ *n* : outdoor sports arena

staff \'staf\ *n, pl* **staffs** \'stafs, stavz\ *or* **staves** \'stavz, 'stāvz\ **1** : rod or supporting cane **2** : people assisting a leader **3** : 5 horizontal lines on which music is written ~ *vb* : supply with workers —**staff•er** *n*

staff sergeant *n* : noncommissioned officer ranking next above a sergeant in the army, air force, or marine corps

stag \'stag\ *n, pl* **stags** *or* **stag** : male deer ~ *adj* : only for men ~ *adv* : without a date

stage \'stāj\ *n* **1** : raised platform for a speaker or performers **2** : theater **3** : step in a process ~ *vb* **staged; stag•ing** : produce (a play)

stage•coach *n* : passenger coach

stag•ger \'stagər\ *vb* **1** : reel or cause to reel from side to side **2** : overlap or alternate —**stagger** *n* —**stag•ger•ing•ly** *adv*

stag•nant \'stagnənt\ *adj* : not moving or active —**stag•nate** \-,nāt\ *vb* —**stag•na•tion** \stag'nāshən\ *n*

¹staid \'stād\ *adj* : sedate

²staid *past of* STAY

stain \'stān\ *vb* **1** : discolor **2** : dye (as wood) **3** : disgrace ~ *n* **1** : discolored area **2** : mark of guilt **3** : coloring preparation —**stain•less** *adj*

stair \'star\ *n* **1** : step in a series for going from one level to another **2** *pl* : flight of steps —**stair•way** *n*

stair•case *n* : series of steps with their framework

stake \'stāk\ *n* **1** : usu. small post driven into the ground **2** : bet **3** : prize in a contest ~ *vb* **staked; stak•ing 1** : mark or secure with a stake **2** : bet

sta•lac•tite \stə'lak,tīt\ *n* : icicle-shaped deposit hanging in a cavern

sta•lag•mite \stə'lag,mīt\ *n* : icicle-shaped deposit on a cavern floor

stale \'stāl\ *adj* **stal•er; stal•est 1** : having lost good taste and quality from age **2** : no longer new, strong, or effective —**stale•ness** *n*

stale•mate \'stāl,māt\ *n* : deadlock —**stale•mate** *vb*

¹stalk \'stók\ *vb* **1** : walk stiffly or proudly **2** : pursue stealthily

²stalk *n* : plant stem —**stalked** \'stókt\ *adj*

¹stall \'stól\ *n* **1** : compartment in a stable **2** : booth where articles are sold

²stall *vb* : bring or come to a standstill unintentionally

³stall *vb* : delay, evade, or keep a situation going to gain advantage or time

stal•lion \'stalyən\ *n* : male horse

stal•wart \'stólwərt\ *adj* : strong or brave

sta•men \'stāmən\ *n* : flower organ that produces pollen

stam•i•na \'stamənə\ *n* : endurance

stam•mer \'stamər\ *vb* : hesitate in speaking —**stammer** *n*

stamp \'stamp\ *vb* **1** : pound with the sole of the foot or a heavy implement **2** : impress or imprint **3** : cut out with a die **4** : attach a postage stamp to ~ *n* **1** : device for stamping **2** : act of stamping **3** : government seal showing a tax or fee has been paid

stam•pede \stam'pēd\ *n* : headlong rush of frightened animals ~ *vb* **-ped•ed; -ped•ing** : flee in panic

stance \'stans\ *n* : way of standing

¹stanch \'stónch, 'stänch\ *vb* : stop the flow of (as blood)

²stanch *var of* STAUNCH

stan•chion \'stanchən\ *n* : upright support

stand \'stand\ *vb* **stood** \'stu̇d\ **stand•ing 1** : be at rest or assume an upright position **2** : remain unchanged **3** : be steadfast **4** : maintain a relative position or rank **5** : set upright **6** : undergo or endure ~ *n* **1** : act or place of standing, staying, or resisting **2** : sales booth **3** : structure for holding something upright **4** : group of plants growing together **5** *pl* : tiered seats **6** : opinion or viewpoint

stan•dard \'standərd\ *n* **1** : symbolic figure or flag **2** : model, rule, or guide **3** : upright support —**standard** *adj* —**stan•dard•i•za•tion** \standərdə'zāshən\ *n* —**stan•dard•ize** \'standərd,īz\ *vb*

standard time *n* : time established over a region or country

stand•ing \'standin\ *n* **1** : relative position or rank **2** : duration

stand•still *n* : state of rest

stank *past of* STINK

stan•za \'stanzə\ *n* : division of a poem

¹sta•ple \'stāpəl\ *n* : U-shaped wire fastener —**staple** *vb* —**sta•pler** \-plər\ *n*

²staple *n* : chief commodity or item —**sta•ple** *adj*

star \'stär\ *n* **1** : celestial body visible as a point of light **2** : 5- or 6-pointed figure representing a star **3** : leading performer ~ *vb* **-rr- 1** : mark with a star **2** : play the leading role —**star•dom** \'stärdəm\ *n* —**star•less** *adj* —**star•light** *n* —**star•ry** *adj*

star•board \'stärbərd\ *n* : right side of a ship or airplane looking forward —**starboard** *adj*

starch \'stärch\ *n* : nourishing carbohydrate from plants also used in adhesives and laundering ~ *vb* : stiffen with starch —**starchy** *adj*

stare \'star\ *vb* **stared; star•ing** : look intently with wide-open eyes —**stare** *n* —**star•er** *n*

stark \'stärk\ *adj* **1** : absolute **2** : severe or bleak ~ *adv* : completely —**stark•ly** *adv*

star•ling \'stärlin\ *n* : bird related to the crows

start \'stärt\ *vb* **1** : twitch or jerk (as from surprise) **2** : perform or show performance of the first part of an action or process ~ *n* **1** : sudden involuntary motion **2** : beginning —**start•er** *n*

star•tle \'stärt°l\ *vb* **-tled; -tling** : frighten or surprise suddenly

starve \'stärv\ *vb* **starved; starv•ing 1** : suffer or die from hunger **2** : kill with hunger —**star•va•tion** \stär'vāshən\ *n*

stash \'stash\ *vb* : store in a secret place for future use —**stash** *n*

state \'stāt\ *n* **1** : condition of being **2** : condition of mind **3** : nation or a political unit within it ~ *vb* **stat•ed; stat•ing 1** : express in words **2** : establish —**state•hood** \-,hu̇d\ *n*

state•ly \'stātlē\ *adj* **-li•er; -est** : having impressive dignity —**state•li•ness** *n*

state•ment \'stātmənt\ *n* **1** : something stated **2** : financial summary

state•room *n* : private room on a ship

states•man \'stātsmən\ *n* : one skilled in government or diplomacy —**states•man•like** *adj* —**states•man•ship** *n*

stat•ic \'statik\ *adj* **1** : relating to bodies at rest or forces in equilibrium **2** : not moving **3** : relating to stationary charges of electricity ~ *n* : noise on radio or television from electrical disturbances

sta•tion \'stāshən\ *n* **1** : place of duty **2** : regular stop on a bus or train route **3** : social standing **4** : place where radio or television programs originate ~ *vb* : assign to a station

sta•tion•ary \'stāshə,nerē\ *adj* **1** : not moving or not movable **2** : not changing

sta•tio•nery \'stāshə,nerē\ *n* : letter paper with envelopes

sta•tis•tic \stə'tistik\ *n* : single item of statistics

sta•tis•tics \-tiks\ *n pl* : numerical facts collected for study —**sta•tis•ti•cal** \-tikəl\ *adj* —**sta•tis•ti•cal•ly** *adv* —**stat•is•ti•cian** \statə'stishən\ *n*

stat•u•ary \'stachə,werē\ *n, pl* **-ar•ies** : collection of statues

stat•ue \'stachü\ *n* : solid 3-dimensional likeness —**stat•u•ette** \stachə'wet\ *n*

stat•u•esque \,stachə'wesk\ *adj* : tall and shapely

stat•ure \'stachər\ *n* **1** : height **2** : status gained by achievement

sta•tus \'stātəs, 'stat-\ *n* : relative situation or condition

sta•tus quo \-'kwō\ *n* : existing state of affairs

stat•ute \'stachüt\ *n* : law —**stat•u•to•ry** \'stachə,tōrē\ *adj*

staunch \'stónch\ *adj* : steadfast —**staunch•ly** *adv*

¹stave \'stāv\ *n* : narrow strip of wood ~ *vb* **staved** *or* **stove** \'stōv\ **stav•ing 1** : break a hole in **2** : drive away

²stave *pl of* STAFF

¹stay \'stā\ *n* : support ~ *vb* **stayed; stay•ing** : prop up

²stay *vb* **stayed** \'stād\ *or* **staid** \'stād\ **stay•ing 1** : pause **2** : remain **3** : reside **4** : stop or postpone **5** : satisfy for a time ~ *n* : a staying

stead \'sted\ *n* : one's place, job, or function —**in good stead** : to advantage

stead•fast \-,fast\ *adj* : faithful or determined —**stead•fast•ly** *adv*

steady \'stedē\ *adj* **steadi•er; -est 1** : firm in position or sure in movement **2** : calm or reliable **3** : constant **4** : regular ~ *vb* **steadi•ed; steady•ing** : make or become steady —**steadi•ly** \'sted°lē\ *adv* —**steadi•ness** *n* —**steady** *adv*

steak \'stāk\ *n* : thick slice of meat

steal \'stēl\ *vb* **stole** \'stōl\ **sto•len** \'stōlən\ **steal•ing 1** : take and carry away wrong-

fully and with intent to keep **2** : move secretly or slowly

stealth \'stelth\ *n* : secret or unobtrusive procedure —**stealth•i•ly** \-thəlē\ *adv* —**stealthy** *adj*

steam \'stēm\ *n* : vapor of boiling water ~ *vb* : give off steam —**steam•boat** *n* —**steam•ship** *n* —**steamy** *adj*

steed \'stēd\ *n* : horse

steel \'stēl\ *n* : tough carbon-containing iron ~ *vb* : fill with courage —**steel** *adj* —**steely** *adj*

¹steep \'stēp\ *adj* : having a very sharp slope or great elevation —**steep•ly** *adv* —**steep•ness** *n*

²steep *vb* : soak in a liquid

stee•ple \'stēpəl\ *n* : usu. tapering church tower

stee•ple•chase *n* : race over hurdles

¹steer \'stir\ *n* : castrated ox

²steer *vb* **1** : direct the course of (as a ship or car) **2** : guide

steer•age \'stirij\ *n* : section in a ship for people paying the lowest fares

stein \'stīn\ *n* : mug

stel•lar \'stelər\ *adj* : relating to stars or resembling a star

¹stem \'stem\ *n* : main upright part of a plant ~ *vb* **-mm- 1** : derive **2** : make progress against —**stem•less** *adj* —**stemmed** *adj*

²stem *vb* **-mm-** : stop the flow of

stench \'stench\ *n* : stink

sten•cil \'stensəl\ *n* : printing sheet cut with letters to let ink pass through —**stencil** *vb*

ste•nog•ra•phy \stə'nägrəfē\ *n* : art or process of writing in shorthand —**ste•nog•ra•pher** \-fər\ *n* —**steno•graph•ic** \,stenə'grafik\ *adj*

sten•to•ri•an \sten'tōrēən\ *adj* : extremely loud and powerful

step \'step\ *n* **1** : single action of a leg in walking or running **2** : rest for the foot in going up or down **3** : degree, rank, or stage **4** : way of walking ~ *vb* **-pp- 1** : move by steps **2** : press with the foot

step- \'step-\ *comb form* : related by a remarriage and not by blood

step•lad•der *n* : light portable set of steps in a hinged frame

steppe \'step\ *n* : dry grassy treeless land esp. of Asia

-ster \stər\ *n suffix* **1** : one that does, makes, or uses **2** : one that is associated with or takes part in **3** : one that is

ste•reo \'sterē,ō, 'stir-\ *n, pl* **-reos** : stereophonic sound system —**stereo** *adj*

ste•reo•phon•ic \,sterēə'fänik, ,stir-\ *adj* : relating to a 3-dimensional effect of reproduced sound

ste•reo•type \'sterēə,tīp, 'stir-\ *n* : gross of item mistaken generalization —**stereotype** *vb* —**ste•reo•typ•i•cal** \,sterēə'tipikəl\ *adj* —**ste•reo•typ•i•cal•ly** *adv*

ste•reo•typed \'sterēə,tīpt, 'stir-\ *adj* : lacking originality or individuality

ster•ile \'sterəl\ *adj* **1** : unable to bear fruit, crops, or offspring **2** : free from disease germs —**ste•ril•i•ty** \stə'rilətē\ *n* —**ster•il•i•za•tion** \sterələ'zāshən\ *n* —**ster•il•ize** \,līz\ *vb* —**ster•il•iz•er** *n*

ster•ling \'stərlin\ *adj* **1** : being or made of an alloy of 925 parts of silver with 75 parts of copper **2** : excellent

¹stern \'stərn\ *adj* : severe —**stern•ly** *adv* —**stern•ness** *n*

²stern *n* : back end of a boat

ster•num \'stərnəm\ *n, pl* **-nums** *or* **-na** \-nə\ : long flat chest bone joining the 2 sets of ribs

stetho•scope \'stethə,skōp\ *n* : instrument used for listening to sounds in the chest

ste•ve•dore \'stēvə,dōr\ *n* : worker who loads and unloads ships

stew \'stü, 'styü\ *n* **1** : dish of boiled meat and vegetables **2** : state of worry or agitation —**stew** *vb*

stew•ard \'stüərd, 'styü-\ *n* **1** : manager of an estate or an organization **2** : person on a ship or airliner who looks after passenger comfort —**stew•ard•ship** *n*

stew•ard•ess \-əs\ *n* : woman who is a steward (as on an airplane)

¹stick \'stik\ *n* **1** : cut or broken branch **2** : long thin piece of wood or something resembling it

²stick *vb* **stuck** \'stək\ **stick•ing 1** : stab **2** : thrust or project **3** : hold fast to something **4** : attach **5** : become jammed or fixed

stick•er \'stikər\ *n* : adhesive label

stick•ler \'stiklər\ *n* : one who insists on exactness or completeness

sticky \'stikē\ *adj* **stick•i•er; -est 1** : adhesive or gluey **2** : muggy **3** : difficult

stiff \'stif\ *adj* **1** : not bending easily **2** : tense **3** : formal **4** : strong **5** : severe —**stiff•en** \'stifən\ *vb* —**stiff•en•er** \-ənər\ *n* —**stiff•ly** *adv* —**stiff•ness** *n*

sti•fle \'stīfəl\ *vb* **-fled; -fling 1** : smother or suffocate **2** : suppress

stig•ma \'stigmə\ *n, pl* **-ma•ta** \stig'mätə, 'stigmətə\ *or* **-mas** : mark of disgrace —**stig•ma•tize** \'stigmə,tīz\ *vb*

stile \'stīl\ *n* : steps for crossing a fence

sti•let•to \stə'letō\ *n, pl* **-tos** *or* **-toes** : slender dagger

¹still \'stil\ *adj* **1** : motionless **2** : silent ~ *vb* : make or become still ~ *adv* **1** : without motion **2** : up to and during this time **3** : in spite of that ~ *n* : silence —**still•ness** *n*

²still *n* : apparatus used in distillation

still•born *adj* : born dead —**still•birth** *n*

stilt \'stilt\ *n* : one of a pair of poles for walking

stilt•ed \'stiltəd\ *adj* : not easy and natural

stim•u•lant \'stimyələnt\ *n* : substance that temporarily increases the activity of an organism —**stimulant** *adj*

stim•u•late \-,lāt\ *vb* **-lat•ed; -lat•ing** : make active —**stim•u•la•tion** \stimyə'lāshən\ *n*

stim•u•lus \'stimyələs\ *n, pl* **-li** \-,lī\ : something that stimulates

sting \'stin\ *vb* **stung** \'stən\ **sting•ing 1** : prick painfully **2** : cause to suffer acutely ~ *n* : act of stinging or a resulting wound —**sting•er** *n*

stin•gy \'stinjē\ *adj* **stin•gi•er; -est** : not generous —**stin•gi•ness** *n*

stink \'stink\ *vb* **stank** \'stank\ *or* **stunk** \'stənk\ **stunk; stink•ing** : have a strong offensive odor —**stink** *n* —**stink•er** *n*

stint \'stint\ *vb* : be sparing or stingy ~ *n* **1** : restraint **2** : quantity or period of work

sti•pend \'stī,pend, -pənd\ *n* : money paid periodically

stip•ple \'stipəl\ *vb* **-pled; -pling** : engrave, paint, or draw with dots instead of lines —**stipple** *n*

stip•u•late \'stipyə,lāt\ *vb* **-lat•ed; -lat•ing** : demand as a condition —**stip•u•la•tion** \stipyə'lāshən\ *n*

stir \'stər\ *vb* **-rr- 1** : move slightly **2** : prod or push into activity **3** : mix by continued circular movement ~ *n* : act or result of stirring

stir•rup \'stərəp\ *n* : saddle loop for the foot

stitch \'stich\ *n* **1** : loop formed by a needle in sewing **2** : sudden sharp pain ~ *vb* **1** : fasten or decorate with stitches **2** : sew

stock \'stäk\ *n* **1** : block or part of wood **2** : original from which others derive **3** : farm animals **4** : supply of goods **5** : money invested in a large business **6** *pl* : instrument of punishment like a pillory with holes for the feet or feet and hands ~ *vb* : provide with stock

stock•ade \stä'kād\ *n* : defensive or confining enclosure

stock•ing \'stäkin\ *n* : close-fitting covering for the foot and leg

stock•pile *n* : reserve supply —**stockpile** *vb*

stocky \'stäkē\ *adj* **stock•i•er; -est** : short and relatively thick

stock•yard *n* : yard for livestock to be slaughtered or shipped

stodgy \'stäjē\ *adj* **stodg•i•er; -est 1** : dull **2** : old-fashioned

sto•ic \'stōik\ **sto•i•cal** \-ikəl\ *adj* : showing indifference to pain —**stoic** *n* —**sto•i•cal•ly** *adv* —**sto•i•cism** \stōə,sizəm\ *n*

stoke \'stōk\ *vb* **stoked; stok•ing** : stir up a fire or supply fuel to a furnace —**stok•er** *n*

¹stole \'stōl\ *past of* STEAL

²stole *n* : long wide scarf

stolen *past part of* STEAL

stol•id \'stäləd\ *adj* : having or showing little or no emotion —**stol•id•ly** \'stäledlē\ *adv*

stom•ach \'stəmək, -ik\ *n* **1** : saclike digestive organ **2** : abdomen **3** : appetite or desire ~ *vb* : put up with —**stom•ach•ache** *n*

stomp \'stämp, 'stómp\ *vb* : stamp

stone \'stōn\ *n* **1** : hardened earth or mineral matter **2** : small piece of rock **3** : seed that is hard or has a hard covering ~ *vb* **stoned; ston•ing** : pelt or kill with stones —**stony** *adj*

stood *past of* STAND

stool \'stül\ *n* **1** : seat usu. without back or arms **2** : footstool **3** : discharge of feces

¹stoop \'stüp\ *vb* **1** : bend over **2** : lower oneself ~ *n* **1** : act of bending over **2** : bent position of shoulders

²stoop *n* : small porch at a house door

stop \'stäp\ *vb* **-pp- 1** : block an opening **2** : end or cause to end **3** : pause for rest or a visit in a journey ~ *n* **1** : plug **2** : act or place of stopping **3** : delay in a journey —**stop•light** *n* —**stop•page** \-ij\ *n* —**stop•per** *n*

stop•gap *n* : temporary measure or thing

stor•age \'stōrij\ *n* : safekeeping of goods (as in a warehouse)

store \'stōr\ *vb* **stored; stor•ing** : put aside for future use ~ *n* **1** : something stored **2** : retail business establishment —**store•house** *n* —**store•keep•er** *n* —**store•room** *n*

stork \'stork\ *n* : large wading bird

storm \'storm\ *n* **1** : heavy fall of rain or snow **2** : violent outbreak ~ *vb* **1** : rain or snow heavily **2** : rage **3** : make an attack against —**stormy** *adj*

¹sto•ry \'stōrē\ *n, pl* **-ries 1** : narrative **2** : report —**sto•ry•tell•er** *n*

²**story** *n, pl* **-ries** : floor of a building

stout \'staút\ *adj* 1 : firm or strong 2 : thick or bulky —**stout·ly** *adv* —**stout·ness** *n*

¹**stove** \'stōv\ *n* : apparatus for providing heat (as for cooking or heating)

²**stove** *past of* STAVE

stow \'stō\ *vb* 1 : pack in a compact mass 2 : put or hide away

strad·dle \'strad°l\ *vb* **-dled; -dling** : stand over or sit on with legs on opposite sides —**straddle** *n*

strafe \'strāf\ *vb* **strafed; straf·ing** : fire upon with machine guns from a low-flying airplane

strag·gle \'stragəl\ *vb* **-gled; -gling** : wander or become separated from others —**strag·gler** \-ələr\ *n*

straight \'strāt\ *adj* 1 : having no bends, turns, or twists 2 : just, proper, or honest 3 : neat and orderly —*adv* 1 : in a straight manner —**straight·en** \'strāt°n\ *vb*

straight·for·ward \'strāt'fórwərd\ *adj* : frank or honest

straight·way *adv* : immediately

¹**strain** \'strān\ *n* 1 : lineage 2 : trace

²**strain** *vb* 1 : exert to the utmost 2 : filter or remove by filtering 3 : injure by improper use ~ *n* 1 : excessive tension or exertion 2 : bodily injury from excessive effort —**strain·er** *n*

strait \'strāt\ *n* 1 : narrow channel connecting 2 bodies of water 2 *pl* : distress

strait·en \'strāt°n\ *vb* 1 : hem in 2 : make distressing or difficult

¹**strand** \'strand\ *vb* 1 : drive or cast upon the shore 2 : leave helpless

²**strand** *n* 1 : twisted fiber of a rope 2 : length of something ropelike

strange \'strānj\ *adj* **strang·er; strang·est** 1 : unusual or queer 2 : new —**strange·ly** *adv* —**strange·ness** *n*

strang·er \'strānjər\ *n* : person with whom one is not acquainted

stran·gle \'stranggəl\ *vb* **-gled; -gling** : choke to death —**stran·gler** \-glər\ *n*

stran·gu·la·tion \stranggyə'lāshən\ *n* : act or process of strangling

strap \'strap\ *n* : narrow strip of flexible material used esp. for fastening —*vb* 1 : secure with a strap 2 : beat with a strap —**strap·less** *n*

strap·ping \'strapiŋ\ *adj* : robust

strat·a·gem \'stratəjəm, -,jem\ *n* : deceptive scheme or maneuver

strat·e·gy \'stratəjē\ *n, pl* **-gies** : carefully worked out plan of action —**stra·te·gic** \strə'tējik\ *adj* —**strat·e·gist** \'stratəjist\ *n*

strat·i·fy \'stratə,fī\ *vb* **-fied; -fy·ing** : form or arrange in layers —**strat·i·fi·ca·tion** \,stratəfə'kāshən\ *n*

strato·sphere \'stratə,sfir\ *n* : earth's atmosphere from about 7 to 31 miles above the surface

stra·tum \'strātəm, 'strat-\ *n, pl* **-ta** \'strātə, 'strat-\ : layer

straw \'strȯ\ *n* 1 : grass stems after grain is removed 2 : tube for drinking —*adj* : made of straw

straw·ber·ry \'strȯ,berē\ *n* : juicy red pulpy fruit

stray \'strā\ *vb* : wander or deviate ~ *n* : person or animal that strays ~ *adj* : separated from or not related to anyone close by

streak \'strēk\ *n* 1 : mark of a different color 2 : narrow band of light 3 : trace 4 : run (as of luck) or series ~ *vb* 1 : form streaks in or on 2 : move fast

stream \'strēm\ *n* 1 : flow of water on land 2 : steady flow (as of water or air) ~ *vb* 1 : flow in a stream 2 : pour out streams

stream·er \'strēmər\ *n* : long ribbon or ribbonlike flag

stream·lined \-,līnd, -'līnd\ *adj* 1 : made with contours to reduce air or water resistance 2 : simplified 3 : modernized —**streamline** *vb*

street \'strēt\ *n* : thoroughfare esp. in a city or town

street·car *n* : passenger vehicle running on rails in the streets

strength \'streŋth\ *n* 1 : quality of being strong 2 : toughness 3 : intensity

strength·en \'streŋthən\ *vb* : make, grow, or become stronger —**strength·en·er** \'streŋthənər\ *n*

stren·u·ous \'strenyəwəs\ *adj* 1 : vigorous 2 : requiring or showing energy —**stren·u·ous·ly** *adv*

stress \'stres\ *n* 1 : pressure or strain that tends to distort a body 2 : relative prominence given to one thing among others 3 : state of physical or mental tension or something inducing it ~ *vb* : put stress on —**stress·ful** \'stresfəl\ *adj*

stretch \'strech\ *vb* 1 : spread or reach out 2 : draw out in length or breadth 3 : make taut 4 : exaggerate 5 : become extended without breaking ~ *n* : act of extending beyond normal limits

stretch·er \'strechər\ *n* : device for carrying a sick or injured person

strew \'strü\ *vb* **strewed; strewed** *or* **strewn**

\'strün\; **strew·ing** 1 : scatter 2 : cover by scattering something over

strick·en \'strikən\ *adj* : afflicted with disease

strict \'strikt\ *adj* 1 : allowing no escape or evasion 2 : precise —**strict·ly** *adv* —**strict·ness** *n*

stric·ture \'strikchər\ *n* : hostile criticism

stride \'strīd\ *vb* **strode** \'strōd\; **strid·den** \'strid°n\; **strid·ing** : walk or run with long steps ~ *n* 1 : long step 2 : manner of striding

stri·dent \'strīd°nt\ *adj* : loud and harsh

strife \'strīf\ *n* : conflict

strike \'strīk\ *vb* **struck** \'strək\; **struck; strik·ing** \'strīkiŋ\ 1 : hit sharply 2 : delete 3 : produce by impressing 4 : cause to sound 5 : afflict 6 : occur to or impress 7 : cause (a match) to ignite by rubbing 8 : refrain from working 9 : find 10 : take on (as a pose) ~ *n* 1 : act or instance of striking 2 : work stoppage 3 : military attack —**strik·er** *n* —**strike out** *vb* : start out vigorously —**strike up** *vb* : start

strik·ing \'strīkiŋ\ *adj* : very noticeable —**strik·ing·ly** *adv*

string \'striŋ\ *n* 1 : line usu. of twisted threads 2 : series 3 *pl* : stringed instruments ~ *vb* **strung** \'strəŋ\; **string·ing** 1 : thread on or with a string 2 : hang or fasten by a string

stringed \'striŋd\ *adj* : having strings

strin·gent \'strinjənt\ *adj* : severe

stringy \'striŋē\ *adj* **string·i·er; -est** : tough or fibrous

¹**strip** \'strip\ *vb* **-pp-** 1 : take the covering or clothing from 2 : undress —**strip·per** *n*

²**strip** *n* : long narrow flat piece

stripe \'strīp\ *n* : distinctive line or long narrow section ~ *vb* **striped** \'strīpt\; **strip·ing** : make stripes on —**striped** \'strīpt, 'strīpəd\ *adj*

strive \'strīv\ *vb* **strove** \'strōv\; **striv·en** \'strivən\ *or* **strived; striv·ing** \'strīviŋ\ 1 : struggle 2 : try hard

strode *past of* STRIDE

stroke \'strōk\ *vb* **stroked; strok·ing** : rub gently ~ *n* 1 : act of swinging or striking 2 : sudden action

stroll \'strōl\ *vb* : walk leisurely —**stroll** *n* —**stroll·er** *n*

strong \'strȯŋ\ *adj* 1 : capable of exerting great force or of withstanding stress or violence 2 : healthy 3 : zealous —**strong·ly** *adv*

strong·hold *n* : fortified place

struck *past of* STRIKE

struc·ture \'strəkchər\ *n* 1 : building 2 : arrangement of elements ~ *vb* **-tured; -tur·ing** : make into a structure —**struc·tur·al** \-chərəl\ *adj*

strug·gle \'strəgəl\ *vb* **-gled; -gling** 1 : make strenuous efforts to overcome an adversary 2 : proceed with great effort ~ *n* 1 : strenuous effort 2 : intense competition for superiority

strum \'strəm\ *vb* **-mm-** : play (a musical instrument) by brushing the strings with the fingers

strum·pet \'strəmpət\ *n* : prostitute

strung *past of* STRING

strut \'strət\ *vb* **-tt-** : walk in a proud or showy manner ~ *n* 1 : proud walk 2 : supporting bar or rod

strych·nine \'strik,nīn, -nən, -,nēn\ *n* : bitter poisonous substance

stub \'stəb\ *n* : short end or section ~ *vb* **-bb-** : strike against something

stub·ble \'stəbəl\ *n* : short growth left after cutting —**stub·bly** *adj*

stub·born \'stəbərn\ *adj* 1 : determined not to yield 2 : hard to control —**stub·born·ly** *adv* —**stub·born·ness** *n*

stub·by \'stəbē\ *adj* : short, blunt, and thick

stuc·co \'stəkō\ *n, pl* **-cos** *or* **-coes** : plaster for coating outside walls —**stuc·coed** \'stəkōd\ *adj*

stuck *past of* STICK

stuck-up \'stək'əp\ *adj* : conceited

¹**stud** \'stəd\ *n* : male horse kept for breeding

²**stud** *n* 1 : upright beam for holding wall material 2 : projecting nail, pin, or rod ~ *vb* **-dd-** : supply or dot with studs

stu·dent \'stüd°nt, 'styü-\ *n* : one who studies

stud·ied \'stədēd\ *adj* : premeditated

stu·dio \'stüdē,ō, 'styü-\ *n, pl* **-dios** 1 : artist's workroom 2 : place where movies are made or television or radio shows are broadcast

stu·di·ous \'stüdēəs, 'styü-\ *adj* : devoted to study —**stu·di·ous·ly** *adv*

study \'stədē\ *n, pl* **stud·ies** 1 : act or process of learning about something 2 : branch of learning 3 : careful examination 4 : room for reading or studying ~ *vb* **stud·ied; study·ing** : apply the attention and mind to a subject

stuff \'stəf\ *n* 1 : personal property 2 : raw or fundamental material 3 : unspecified

material or things ~ *vb* : fill by packing things in —**stuff·ing** *n*

stuffy \'stəfē\ *adj* **stuff·i·er; -est** 1 : lacking fresh air 2 : unimaginative or pompous

stul·ti·fy \'stəltə,fī\ *vb* **-fied; -fy·ing** 1 : cause to appear foolish 2 : impair or make ineffective 3 : have a dulling effect on

stum·ble \'stəmbəl\ *vb* **-bled; -bling** 1 : lose one's balance or fall in walking or running 2 : speak or act clumsily 3 : happen by chance —**stumble** *n*

stump \'stəmp\ *n* : part left when something is cut off ~ *vb* : confuse —**stumpy** *adj*

stun \'stən\ *vb* **-nn-** 1 : make senseless or dizzy by or as if by a blow 2 : bewilder

stung *past of* STING

stunk *past of* STINK

stun·ning \'stəniŋ\ *adj* 1 : astonishing or incredible 2 : strikingly beautiful —**stun·ning·ly** *adv*

¹**stunt** \'stənt\ *vb* : hinder the normal growth or progress of

²**stunt** *n* : spectacular feat

stu·pe·fy \'stüpə,fī, 'styü-\ *vb* **-fied; -fy·ing** 1 : make insensible by or as if by drugs 2 : amaze

stu·pen·dous \stü'pendəs, styü-\ *adj* : very big or impressive —**stu·pen·dous·ly** *adv*

stu·pid \'stüpəd, 'styü-\ *adj* : not sensible or intelligent —**stu·pid·i·ty** \stü'pidətē, styü-\ *n* —**stu·pid·ly** *adv*

stu·por \'stüpər, 'styü-\ *n* : state of being conscious but not aware or sensible

stur·dy \'stərdē\ *adj* **-di·er; -est** : strong —**stur·di·ly** \'stərd°lē\ *adv* —**stur·di·ness** *n*

stur·geon \'stərjən\ *n* : fish whose roe is caviar

stut·ter \'stətər\ *vb or n* : stammer

¹**sty** \'stī\ *n, pl* **sties** : pig pen

²**sty, stye** \'stī\ *n, pl* **sties** *or* **styes** : inflamed swelling on the edge of an eyelid

style \'stīl\ *n* 1 : distinctive way of speaking, writing, or acting 2 : elegant or fashionable way of living ~ *vb* **styled; styl·ing** 1 : name 2 : give a particular design or style to —**styl·ish** \'stīlish\ *adj* —**styl·ish·ly** *adv* —**styl·ish·ness** *n* —**styl·ist** \-ist\ *n* —**styl·ize** \'stīl,īz\ *vb*

sty·lus \'stīləs\ *n, pl* **-li** \'stīl,ī\ 1 : pointed writing tool 2 : phonograph needle

sty·mie \'stīmē\ *vb* **-mied; -mie·ing** : block or frustrate

suave \'swäv\ *adj* : well-mannered and gracious —**suave·ly** *adv*

¹**sub** \'səb\ *n or vb* : substitute

²**sub** *n* : submarine

sub- \səb, 'səb\ *prefix* 1 : under or beneath 2 : subordinate or secondary 3 : subordinate portion of 4 : with repetition of a process so as to form, stress, or deal with subordinate parts or relations 5 : somewhat 6 : nearly

subacute	subindustry
subagency	sublease
subagent	sublethal
subarctic	sublevel
subarea	subliterate
subatmospheric	subnetwork
subaverage	suboceanic
subbase	suborder
subbasement	subpar
subbranch	subpart
subcabinet	subplot
subcategory	subpolar
subclass	subprincipal
subclassification	subprocess
subclassify	subprogram
subcommission	subproject
subcommittee	subregion
subcommunity	subsea
subcomponent	subsection
subcontract	subsense
subcontractor	subspecialty
subculture	subspecies
subdean	substage
subdepartment	subsurface
subdistrict	subsystem
subentry	subtemperate
subfamily	subtheme
subfreezing	subtopic
subgroup	subtotal
subhead	subtreasury
subheading	subtype
subhuman	subunit
subindex	subvariety

sub·con·scious \səb'känchəs\ *adj* : existing without conscious awareness ~ *n* : part of the mind concerned with subconscious activities —**sub·con·scious·ly** *adv*

sub·di·vide \,səbdə'vīd, 'səbdə,vīd\ *vb* 1 : divide into several parts 2 : divide (land) into building lots —**sub·di·vi·sion** \-'vizhən, -,vizh-\ *n*

sub·due \səb'dü, -'dyü\ *vb* **-dued; -du·ing** 1 : bring under control 2 : reduce the intensity of

sub·ject \'səbjikt\ *n* 1 : person under the authority of another 2 : something discussed or studied 3 : word or word group about which something is said in a sentence ~ *adj* 1 : being under one's au-

thority 2 : prone 3 : dependent on some condition or act ~ \səb'jekt\ *vb* 1 : bring under control 2 : cause to undergo —**sub·jec·tion** \-'jekshən\ *n*

sub·jec·tive \,səb'jektiv\ *adj* : deriving from an individual viewpoint or bias —**sub·jec·tive·ly** *adv* —**sub·jec·tiv·i·ty** \-,jek-'tivətē\ *n*

sub·ju·gate \'səbji,gāt\ *vb* **-gat·ed; -gat·ing** : bring under one's control —**sub·ju·ga·tion** \,səbji'gāshən\ *n*

sub·junc·tive \səb'jəŋktiv\ *adj* : relating to a verb form which expresses possibility or contingency —**subjunctive** *n*

sub·let \'səb,let\ *vb* **-let; -let·ting** : rent (a property) from a lessee

sub·lime \sə'blīm\ *adj* : splendid —**sub·lime·ly** *adv*

sub·ma·rine \'səbmə,rēn, ,səbmə'-\ *adj* : existing, acting, or growing under the sea ~ *n* : underwater boat

sub·merge \səb'mərj\ *vb* **-merged; -merg·ing** : put or plunge under the surface of water —**sub·mer·gence** \-'mərjəns\ *n* —**sub·mers·ible** \səb'mərsəbəl\ *adj or n* —**sub·mer·sion** \-'mərzhən\ *n*

sub·mit \səb'mit\ *vb* **-tt-** 1 : yield 2 : give or offer —**sub·mis·sion** \-'mishən\ *n* —**sub·mis·sive** \-'misiv\ *adj*

sub·nor·mal \,səb'nórməl\ *adj* : falling below what is normal

sub·or·di·nate \sə'bórd°nət\ *adj* : lower in rank ~ *n* : one that is subordinate ~ \sə'bórd°n,āt\ *vb* **-nat·ed; -nat·ing** : place in a lower rank or class —**sub·or·di·na·tion** \-,bórd°n'āshən\ *n*

sub·poe·na \sə'pēnə\ *n* : summons to appear in court ~ *vb* **-naed; -na·ing** : summon with a subpoena

sub·scribe \səb'skrīb\ *vb* **-scribed; -scrib·ing** 1 : give consent or approval 2 : agree to support or to receive and pay for —**sub·scrib·er** *n*

sub·scrip·tion \səb'skripshən\ *n* : order for regular receipt of a publication

sub·se·quent \'səbsikwənt, -sə,kwent\ *adj* : following after —**sub·se·quent·ly** \-,kwentlē, -kwənt-\ *adv*

sub·ser·vi·ence \səb'sərvēəns\ *n* : obsequious submission —**sub·ser·vi·en·cy** \-ənsē\ *n* —**sub·ser·vi·ent** \-ənt\ *adj*

sub·side \səb'sīd\ *vb* **-sid·ed; -sid·ing** : die down in intensity

sub·sid·iary \səb'sidē,erē\ *adj* 1 : furnishing support 2 : of secondary importance ~ *n* : company controlled by another company

sub·si·dize \'səbsə,dīz\ *vb* **-dized; -diz·ing** : aid with a subsidy

sub·si·dy \'səbsədē\ *n, pl* **-dies** : gift of supporting funds

sub·sist \səb'sist\ *vb* : acquire the necessities of life —**sub·sis·tence** \-'sistəns\ *n*

sub·stance \'səbstəns\ *n* 1 : essence or essential part 2 : physical material 3 : wealth

sub·stan·dard \,səb'standərd\ *adj* : falling short of a standard or norm

sub·stan·tial \səb'stanchəl\ *adj* 1 : plentiful 2 : considerable —**sub·stan·tial·ly** *adv*

sub·stan·ti·ate \səb'stanchē,āt\ *vb* **-at·ed; -at·ing** : verify —**sub·stan·ti·a·tion** \-,stanchē'āshən\ *n*

sub·sti·tute \'səbstə,tüt, -,tyüt\ *n* : replacement —*vb* **-tut·ed; -tut·ing** : put or serve in place of another —**substitute** *adj* —**sub·sti·tu·tion** \,səbstə'tüshən, -'tyü-\ *n*

sub·ter·fuge \'səbtər,fyüj\ *n* : deceptive trick

sub·ter·ra·nean \,səbtə'rānēən\ *adj* : lying or being underground

sub·ti·tle \'səb,tīt°l\ *n* : movie caption

sub·tle \'sət°l\ *adj* **-tler** \-ər\; **-tlest** \-ist\ 1 : hardly noticeable 2 : clever —**sub·tle·ty** \-tē\ *n* —**sub·tly** \-°lē\ *adv*

sub·tract \səb'trakt\ *vb* : take away (as one number from another) —**sub·trac·tion** \-'trakshən\ *n*

sub·urb \'səb,ərb\ *n* : residential area adjacent to a city —**sub·ur·ban** \sə'bərbən\ *adj or n* —**sub·ur·ban·ite** \-bə,nīt\ *n*

sub·vert \səb'vərt\ *vb* : overthrow or ruin —**sub·ver·sion** \-'vərzhən\ *n* —**sub·ver·sive** \-'vərsiv\ *adj*

sub·way \'səb,wā\ *n* : underground electric railway

suc·ceed \sək'sēd\ *vb* 1 : follow (someone) in a job, role, or title 2 : attain a desired object or end

suc·cess \-'ses\ *n* 1 : favorable outcome 2 : gaining of wealth and fame 3 : one that succeeds —**suc·cess·ful** \-fəl\ *adj* —**suc·cess·ful·ly** *adv*

suc·ces·sion \sək'seshən\ *n* 1 : order, act, or right of succeeding 2 : series

suc·ces·sive \-'sesiv\ *adj* : following in order —**suc·ces·sive·ly** *adv*

suc·ces·sor \-'sesər\ *n* : one that succeeds another

suc·cinct \sək'siŋkt, sə'siŋkt\ *adj* : brief —**suc·cinct·ly** *adv* —**suc·cinct·ness** *n*

suc·cor \'səkər\ *n or vb* : help

suc·co·tash \'səkə,tash\ *n* : beans and corn cooked together

suc·cu·lent \'səkyələnt\ *adj* : juicy —**suc·cu·lence** \-ləns\ *n* —**succulent** *n*

suc·cumb \sə'kəm\ *vb* 1 : yield 2 : die

such \'səch\ *adj* 1 : of this or that kind 2 : having a specified quality —**such** *pron or adv*

suck \'sək\ *vb* 1 : draw in liquid with the mouth 2 : draw liquid from by or as if by mouth —**suck** *n*

suck·er \'səkər\ *n* 1 : one that sucks or clings 2 : easily deceived person

suck·le \'səkəl\ *vb* -**led**; -**ling** : give or draw milk from the breast or udder

suck·ling \'səkliŋ\ *n* : young unweaned mammal

su·crose \'sü,krōs, -,krōz\ *n* : cane or beet sugar

suc·tion \'səkshən\ *n* 1 : act of sucking 2 : act or process of drawing in by partially exhausting the air

sud·den \'səd³n\ *adj* 1 : happening unexpectedly 2 : steep 3 : hasty —**sud·den·ly** *adv* —**sud·den·ness** *n*

suds \'sədz\ *n pl* : soapy water esp. when frothy —**sudsy** \'sədzē\ *adj*

sue \'sü\ *vb* **sued**; **su·ing** 1 : petition 2 : bring legal action against

suede, **suède** \'swād\ *n* : leather with a napped surface

su·et \'süət\ *n* : hard beef fat

suf·fer \'səfər\ *vb* 1 : experience pain, loss, or hardship 2 : permit —**suf·fer·er** *n*

suf·fer·ing \-əriŋ\ *n* : pain or hardship

suf·fice \sə'fīs\ *vb* -**ficed**; -**fic·ing** : be sufficient

suf·fi·cient \sə'fishənt\ *adj* : adequate —**suf·fi·cien·cy** \-ənsē\ *n* —**suf·fi·cient·ly** *adv*

suf·fix \'səf,iks\ *n* : letters added at the end of a word —**suffix** \sə'fiks\ *vb* —**suf·fix·a·tion** \,səf,ik'sāshən\ *n*

suf·fo·cate \'səfə,kāt\ *vb* -**cat·ed**; -**cat·ing** : suffer or die or cause to die from lack of air —**suf·fo·cat·ing·ly** *adv* —**suf·fo·ca·tion** \,səfə'kāshən\ *n*

suf·frage \'səfrij\ *n* : right to vote

suf·fuse \sə'fyüz\ *vb* -**fused**; -**fus·ing** : spread over or through

sug·ar \'shúgər\ *n* : sweet substance ~ *vb* : mix, cover, or sprinkle with sugar —**sug·ar·cane** *n* —**sug·ary** *adj*

sug·gest \sə'jest, səg-\ *vb* 1 : put into someone's mind 2 : remind one by association of ideas —**sug·gest·ible** \-'jestəbəl\ *adj* —**sug·ges·tion** \-'jeschən\ *n*

sug·ges·tive \-'jestiv\ *adj* : suggesting something improper —**sug·ges·tive·ly** *adv* —**sug·ges·tive·ness** *n*

sui·cide \'süə,sīd\ *n* 1 : act of killing oneself purposely 2 : one who commits suicide —**sui·cid·al** \,süə'sīd³l\ *adj*

suit \'süt\ *n* 1 : action in court to recover a right or claim 2 : number of things used or worn together 3 : one of the 4 sets of playing cards ~ *vb* 1 : be appropriate or becoming to 2 : meet the needs of —**suit·abil·i·ty** \,sütə'bilətē\ *n* —**suit·able** \'sütəbəl\ *adj* —**suit·ably** *adv*

suit·case *n* : case for a traveler's clothing

suite \'swēt, *for 2 also* 'süt\ *n* 1 : group of rooms 2 : set of matched furniture

suit·or \'sütər\ *n* : one who seeks to marry a woman

sul·fur \'səlfər\ *n* : nonmetallic yellow chemical element —**sul·fu·ric** \səl'fyúr-ik\ *adj* —**sul·fu·rous** \-'fyúrəs, 'səlfərəs, 'səlfyə-\ *adj*

sulk \'səlk\ *vb* : be moodily silent or irritable —**sulk** *n*

sulky \'səlkē\ *adj* : inclined to sulk ~ *n* : light 2-wheeled horse-drawn cart —**sulk·i·ly** \'səlkəlē\ *adv* —**sulk·i·ness** \-kēnəs\ *n*

sul·len \'sələn\ *adj* 1 : gloomily silent 2 : dismal —**sul·len·ly** *adv* —**sul·len·ness** *n*

sul·ly \'səlē\ *vb* -**lied**; -**ly·ing** : cast doubt or disgrace on

sul·tan \'səlt³n\ *n* : sovereign of a Muslim state —**sul·tan·ate** \-,āt\ *n*

sul·try \'səltrē\ *adj* -**tri·er**; -**est** 1 : very hot and moist 2 : sexually arousing

sum \'səm\ *n* 1 : amount 2 : gist 3 : result of addition ~ *vb* -**mm**- : find the sum of

su·mac \'shü,mak, 'sü-\ *n* : shrub with spikes of berries

sum·ma·ry \'səmərē\ *adj* 1 : concise 2 : done without delay or formality ~ *n, pl* -**ries** : concise statement —**sum·mar·i·ly** \sə'merəlē, 'səmərəlē\ *adv* —**sum·ma·rize** \'səmə,rīz\ *vb*

sum·ma·tion \sə'māshən\ *n* : a summing up esp. in court

sum·mer \'səmər\ *n* : season in which the sun shines most directly —**sum·mery** *adj*

sum·mit \'səmət\ *n* 1 : highest point 2 : high-level conference

sum·mon \'səmən\ *vb* 1 : send for or call together 2 : order to appear in court —**sum·mon·er** *n*

sum·mons \'səmənz\ *n, pl* **sum·mons·es** : an order to answer charges in court

sump·tu·ous \'səmpchəwəs\ *adj* : lavish

sun \'sən\ *n* 1 : shining celestial body around which the planets revolve 2 : light of the sun ~ *vb* -**nn**- : expose to the sun —**sun·beam** *n* —**sun·block** *n* —**sun·burn** *n or vb* —**sun·glass·es** *n pl* —**sun·light** *n* —**sun·ny** *adj* —**sun·rise** *n* —**sun·set** *n* —**sun·shine** *n* —**sun·tan** *n*

sun·dae \'səndē\ *n* : ice cream with topping

Sun·day \'səndā, -dē\ *n* : 1st day of the week

sun·di·al \-,dīəl\ *n* : device for showing time by the sun's shadow

sun·dries \'səndrēz\ *n, pl* : various small articles

sun·dry \-drē\ *adj* : several

sun·fish *n* : perchlike freshwater fish

sun·flow·er *n* : tall plant grown for its oil-rich seeds

sung *past of* SING

sunk *past of* SINK

sunk·en \'səŋkən\ *adj* 1 : submerged 2 : fallen in

sun·spot *n* : dark spot on the sun

sun·stroke *n* : heatstroke from the sun

sup \'səp\ *vb* -**pp**- : eat the evening meal

super \'süpər\ *adj* : very fine

super- \,süpər, 'sü-\ *prefix* 1 : higher in quantity, quality, or degree than 2 : in addition 3 : exceeding a norm 4 : in excessive degree or intensity 5 : surpassing others of its kind 6 : situated above, on, or at the top of 7 : more inclusive than 8 : superior in status or position

superabundance	superpolite
superabundant	superport
superambitious	superpowerful
superathlete	superrich
superbomb	supersalesman
superclean	superscout
supercolossal	supersecrecy
superconvenient	supersecret
supercop	supersensitive
superdense	supersize
supereffective	supersized
superefficiency	superslick
superefficient	supersmooth
superfast	supersoft
supergood	superspecial
supergovernment	superspecialist
supergroup	superspy
superhero	superstar
superheroine	superstate
superhuman	superstrength
superintellectual	superstrong
superintelligence	supersusive
superintelligent	supertanker
superman	superthick
supermodern	superthin
superpatriot	supertight
superpatriotic	superweapon
superpatriotism	superwoman
superplane	

su·perb \sù'pərb\ *adj* : outstanding —**su·perb·ly** *adv*

su·per·cil·ious \,süpər'silēəs\ *adj* : haughtily contemptuous

su·per·fi·cial \,süpər'fishəl\ *adj* : relating to what is only apparent —**su·per·fi·ci·al·i·ty** \-,fishē'alətē\ *n* —**su·per·fi·cial·ly** *adv*

su·per·flu·ous \sù'pərfləwəs\ *adj* : more than necessary —**su·per·flu·i·ty** \,süpər'flüətē\ *n*

su·per·im·pose \,süpərim'pōz\ *vb* : lay over or above something

su·per·in·tend \,süpərin'tend\ *vb* : have charge and oversight of —**su·per·in·ten·dence** \-'tendəns\ *n* —**su·per·in·ten·den·cy** \-dənsē\ *n* —**su·per·in·ten·dent** \-dənt\ *n*

su·pe·ri·or \sù'pirēər\ *adj* 1 : higher, better, or more important 2 : haughty —**superior** *n* —**su·pe·ri·or·i·ty** \-,pirē'órətē\ *n*

su·per·la·tive \sù'pərlətiv\ *adj* 1 : relating to or being an adjective or adverb form that denotes an extreme level 2 : surpassing others —**superlative** *n* —**su·per·la·tive·ly** *adv*

su·per·mar·ket \'süpər,märkət\ *n* : self-service grocery store

su·per·nat·u·ral \,süpər'nachərəl\ *adj* : beyond the observable physical world —**su·per·nat·u·ral·ly** *adv*

su·per·pow·er \'süpər,paúər\ *n* : politically and militarily dominant nation

su·per·sede \,süpər'sēd\ *vb* -**sed·ed**; -**sed·ing** : take the place of

su·per·son·ic \-'sänik\ *adj* : faster than the speed of sound

su·per·sti·tion \,süpər'stishən\ *n* : beliefs based on ignorance, fear of the unknown, or trust in magic —**su·per·sti·tious** \-əs\ *adj*

su·per·struc·ture \'süpər,strəkchər\ *n* : something built on a base or as a vertical extension

su·per·vise \'süpər,vīz\ *vb* -**vised**; -**vis·ing** : have charge of —**su·per·vi·sion** \,sü-pər'vizhən\ *n* —**su·per·vi·sor** \'süpər-,vīzər\ *n* —**su·per·vi·so·ry** \,süpər'vīzə-rē\ *adj*

su·pine \sù'pīn\ *adj* 1 : lying on the back 2 : indifferent or abject

sup·per \'səpər\ *n* : evening meal

sup·plant \sə'plant\ *vb* : take the place of

sup·ple \'səpəl\ *adj* -**pler**; -**plest** : able to bend easily

sup·ple·ment \'səpləmənt\ *n* : something that adds to or makes up for a lack —**supplement** *vb* —**sup·ple·men·tal** \,səplə'ment³l\ *adj* —**sup·ple·men·ta·ry** \-'mentərē\ *adj*

sup·pli·ant \'səplēənt\ *n* : one who supplicates

sup·pli·cate \'səplə,kāt\ *vb* -**cat·ed**; -**cat·ing** 1 : pray to God 2 : ask earnestly and humbly —**sup·pli·cant** \-likənt\ *n* —**sup·pli·ca·tion** \,səplə'kāshən\ *n*

sup·ply \sə'plī\ *vb* -**plied**; -**ply·ing** : furnish ~ *n, pl* -**plies** 1 : amount needed or available 2 *pl* : provisions —**sup·pli·er** \-'plīər\ *n*

sup·port \sə'pōrt\ *vb* 1 : take sides with 2 : provide with food, clothing, and shelter 3 : hold up or serve as a foundation for —**support** *n* —**sup·port·able** *adj* —**sup·port·er** *n*

sup·pose \sə'pōz\ *vb* -**posed**; -**pos·ing** 1 : assume to be true 2 : expect 3 : think probable —**sup·po·si·tion** \,səpə'zishən\ *n*

sup·pos·i·to·ry \sə'päzə,tōrē\ *n, pl* -**ries** : medicated material for insertion (as into the rectum)

sup·press \sə'pres\ *vb* 1 : put an end to by authority 2 : keep from being known 3 : hold back —**sup·pres·sant** \sə'pres³nt\ *n* —**sup·pres·sion** \-'preshən\ *n*

su·prem·a·cy \sù'preməsē\ *n, pl* -**cies** : supreme power or authority

su·preme \sù'prēm\ *adj* 1 : highest in rank or authority 2 : greatest possible —**su·preme·ly** *adv*

Supreme Being *n* : God

sur·charge \'sər,chärj\ *n* 1 : excessive load or burden 2 : extra fee or cost

sure \'shúr\ *adj* **sur·er**; **sur·est** 1 : confident 2 : reliable 3 : not to be disputed 4 : bound to happen ~ *adv* : surely —**sure·ness** *n*

sure·ly \'shúrlē\ *adv* 1 : in a sure manner 2 : without doubt 3 : indeed

sure·ty \'shúrətē\ *n, pl* -**ties** 1 : guarantee 2 : one who gives a guarantee for another person

surf \'sərf\ *n* : waves that break on the shore ~ *vb* : ride the surf —**surf·board** *n* —**surf·er** *n* —**surf·ing** *n*

sur·face \'sərfəs\ *n* 1 : the outside of an object 2 : outward aspect ~ *vb* -**faced**; -**fac·ing** : rise to the surface

sur·feit \'sərfət\ *n* 1 : excess 2 : excessive indulgence (as in food or drink) 3 : disgust caused by excess ~ *vb* : feed, supply, or indulge to the point of surfeit

surge \'sərj\ *vb* **surged**; **surg·ing** : rise and fall in or as if in waves ~ *n* : sudden increase

sur·geon \'sərjən\ *n* : physician who specializes in surgery

sur·gery \'sərjərē\ *n, pl* -**ger·ies** : medical treatment involving cutting open the body

sur·gi·cal \'sərjikəl\ *adj* : relating to surgeons or surgery —**sur·gi·cal·ly** *adv*

sur·ly \'sərlē\ *adj* -**li·er**; -**est** : having a rude nature —**sur·li·ness** *n*

sur·mise \sər'mīz\ *vb* -**mised**; -**mis·ing** : guess —**surmise** *n*

sur·mount \sər'maúnt\ *vb* 1 : prevail over 2 : get to or be the top of

sur·name \'sər,nām\ *n* 1 : family name

sur·pass \sər'pas\ *vb* : go beyond or exceed —**sur·pass·ing·ly** *adv*

sur·plice \'sərpləs\ *n* : loose white outer ecclesiastical vestment

sur·plus \'sər,pləs\ *n* : quantity left over

sur·prise \sə'prīz, sər-\ *vb* -**prised**; -**pris·ing** 1 : come upon or affect unexpectedly 2 : amaze —**surprise** *n* —**sur·pris·ing** *adj* —**sur·pris·ing·ly** *adv*

sur·ren·der \sə'rendər\ *vb* 1 : give up oneself or a possession to another ~ *n* : act of surrendering

sur·rep·ti·tious \,sərəp'tishəs\ *adj* : done, made, or acquired by stealth —**sur·rep·ti·tious·ly** *adv*

sur·rey \'sərē\ *n, pl* -**reys** : horse-drawn carriage

sur·ro·gate \'sərəgāt, -gət\ *n* : substitute

sur·round \sə'raúnd\ *vb* : enclose on all sides

sur·round·ings \sə'raúndiŋz\ *n pl* : objects, conditions, or area around something

sur·veil·lance \sər'vāləns, -'vālyəns, -'vā-əns\ *n* : careful watch

sur·vey \sər'vā\ *vb* -**veyed**; -**vey·ing** 1 : look over and examine closely 2 : make a survey of (as a tract of land) ~ \'sər,-\ *n, pl* -**veys** 1 : inspection 2 : process of measuring (as land) —**sur·vey·or** \-ər\ *n*

sur·vive \sər'vīv\ *vb* -**vived**; -**viv·ing** 1 : remain alive or in existence 2 : live longer or outlast —**sur·viv·al** *n* —**sur·vi·vor** \-'vīvər\ *n*

sus·cep·ti·ble \sə'septəbəl\ *adj* : likely to allow or be affected by something —**sus·cep·ti·bil·i·ty** \-,septə'bilətē\ *n*

sus·pect \'səs,pekt, sə'spekt\ *adj* 1 : regarded with suspicion 2 : questionable

~ \'səs,pekt\ *n* : one who is suspected (as of a crime) ~ \sə'spekt\ *vb* 1 : have doubts of 2 : believe guilty without proof 3 : guess

sus·pend \sə'spend\ *vb* 1 : temporarily stop or keep from a function or job 2 : withhold (judgment) temporarily 3 : hang

sus·pend·er *n* : one of 2 supporting straps holding up trousers and passing over the shoulders

sus·pense \sə'spens\ *n* : excitement and uncertainty as to outcome —**sus·pense·ful** *adj*

sus·pen·sion \sə'spenchən\ *n* : act of suspending or the state or period of being suspended

sus·pi·cion \sə'spishən\ *n* 1 : act of suspecting something 2 : trace

sus·pi·cious \-əs\ *adj* 1 : arousing suspicion 2 : inclined to suspect —**sus·pi·cious·ly** *adv*

sus·tain \sə'stān\ *vb* 1 : provide with nourishment 2 : keep going 3 : hold up 4 : suffer 5 : support or prove

sus·te·nance \'səstənəns\ *n* 1 : nourishment 2 : something that sustains or supports

svelte \'sfelt\ *adj* : slender and graceful

swab \'swäb\ *n* 1 : mop 2 : wad of absorbent material for applying medicine ~ *vb* -**bb**- : use a swab on

swad·dle \'swäd³l\ *vb* -**dled**; -**dling** \'swäd³liŋ\ : bind (an infant) in bands of cloth

swag·ger \'swagər\ *vb* -**gered**; -**ger·ing** 1 : walk with a conceited swing 2 : boast —**swagger** *n*

¹**swal·low** \'swälō\ *n* : small migratory bird

²**swallow** *vb* 1 : take into the stomach through the throat 2 : envelop or take in 3 : accept too easily —**swallow** *n*

swam *past of* SWIM

swamp \'swämp\ *n* : wet spongy land ~ *vb* : deluge (as with water) —**swampy** *adj*

swan \'swän\ *n* : white long-necked swimming bird

swap \'swäp\ *vb* -**pp**- : trade —**swap** *n*

swarm \'swórm\ *n* 1 : mass of honeybees leaving a hive to start a new colony 2 : large crowd ~ *vb* : gather in a swarm

swar·thy \'swórthē, -thē\ *adj* -**thi·er**; -**est** : dark in complexion

swash·buck·ler \'swäsh,bəklər\ *n* : swaggering or daring soldier or adventurer —**swash·buck·ling** \-,bəkliŋ\ *adj*

swat \'swät\ *vb* -**tt**- : hit sharply —**swat** *n* —**swat·ter** *n*

swatch \'swäch\ *n* : sample piece (as of fabric)

swath \'swäth, 'swóth\, **swathe** \'swäth, 'swóth, 'swäth\ *n* : row or path cut (as through grass)

swathe \'swäth, 'swóth, 'swäth\ *vb* **swathed**; **swath·ing** : wrap with or as if with a bandage

sway \'swā\ *vb* 1 : swing gently from side to side 2 : influence ~ *n* 1 : gentle swinging from side to side 2 : controlling power or influence

swear \'swar\ *vb* **swore** \'swōr\; **sworn** \'swōrn\; **swear·ing** 1 : make or cause to make a solemn statement under oath 2 : use profane language —**swear·er** *n* —**swear·ing** *n*

sweat \'swet\ *vb* **sweat** *or* **sweat·ed**; **sweat·ing** 1 : excrete salty moisture from skin glands 2 : form drops of moisture on the surface 3 : work or cause to work hard —**sweat** *n* —**sweaty** *adj*

sweat·er \'swetər\ *n* : knitted jacket or pullover

sweat·shirt \'swet,shərt\ *n* : loose collarless heavy cotton jersey pullover

sweep \'swēp\ *vb* **swept** \'swept\; **sweep·ing** 1 : remove or clean by a brush or a single forceful wipe (as of the hand) 2 : move over with speed and force (as of the hand) 3 : move or extend in a wide curve ~ *n* 1 : a clearing off or away 2 : single forceful wipe or swinging movement 3 : scope —**sweep·er** *n* —**sweep·ing** *adj*

sweep·stakes \'swēp,stāks\ *n, pl* **sweep·stakes** : contest in which the entire prize may go to the winner

sweet \'swēt\ *adj* 1 : being or causing the pleasing taste typical of sugar 2 : not stale or spoiled 3 : not salted 4 : pleasant 5 : much loved ~ *n* : something sweet —**sweet·en** \'swēt³n\ *vb* —**sweet·ly** *adv* —**sweet·ness** *n* —**sweet·en·er** \-³nər\ *n*

sweet·heart *n* : person one loves

sweet potato *n* : sweet yellow edible root of a tropical vine

swell \'swel\ *vb* **swelled**; **swelled** *or* **swol·len** \'swōlən\; **swell·ing** 1 : enlarge 2 : bulge 3 : fill or be filled with emotion ~ *n* 1 : long rolling ocean wave 2 : condition of bulging —**swell·ing** *n*

swel·ter \'sweltər\ *vb* : be uncomfortable from excessive heat

swept *past of* SWEEP

swerve \'swərv\ *vb* **swerved**; **swerv·ing** : move abruptly aside from a course —**swerve** *n*

¹swift \'swift\ *adj* **1** : moving with great speed **2** : occurring suddenly —**swift·ly** *adv* —**swift·ness** *n*

²swift *n* : small insect-eating bird

swig \'swig\ *vb* **-gg-** : drink in gulps —**swig** *n*

swill \'swil\ *vb* : swallow greedily ~ *n* **1** : animal food of refuse and liquid **2** : garbage

swim \'swim\ *vb* **swam** \'swam\; **swum** \'swəm\; **swim·ming 1** : propel oneself in water **2** : float in or be surrounded with a liquid **3** : be dizzy ~ *n* : act or period of swimming —**swim·mer** *n*

swin·dle \'swind⁰l\ *vb* **-dled; -dling** \-iŋ\ : cheat (someone) of money or property —**swindle** *n* —**swin·dler** \-ər\ *n*

swine \'swīn\ *n, pl* **swine** : short-legged hoofed mammal with a snout —**swin·ish** \'swīnish\ *adj*

swing \'swiŋ\ *vb* **swung** \'swəŋ\; **swing·ing 1** : move or cause to move rapidly in an arc **2** : sway or cause to sway back and forth **3** : hang so as to sway or sag **4** : turn on a hinge or pivot **5** : manage or handle successfully ~ *n* **1** : act or instance of swinging **2** : swinging movement (as in trying to hit something) **3** : suspended seat for swinging —**swing** *adj* —**swing·er** *n*

swipe \'swīp\ *n* : strong sweeping blow ~ *vb* **swiped; swip·ing 1** : strike or wipe with a sweeping motion **2** : steal esp. with a quick movement

swirl \'swərl\ *vb* : move or cause to move in a circle —**swirl** *n*

swish \'swish\ *n* : hissing, sweeping, or brushing sound —**swish** *vb*

switch \'swich\ *n* **1** : slender flexible whip or twig **2** : blow with a switch **3** : shift, change, or reversal **4** : device that opens or closes an electrical circuit ~ *vb* **1** : toilet or urge on with a switch **2** : change or reverse roles, positions, or subjects **3** : operate a switch of

switch·board *n* : panel of switches to make and break telephone connections

swiv·el \'swivəl\ *vb* **-eled** *or* **-elled; -el·ing** *or* **-el·ling** : swing or turn on a pivot —**swivel** *n*

swollen *past part of* SWELL

swoon \'swün\ *n* : faint —**swoon** *vb*

swoop \'swüp\ *vb* : make a swift diving attack —**swoop** *n*

sword \'sōrd\ *n* : thrusting or cutting weapon with a long blade

sword·fish *n* : large ocean fish with a long swordlike projection

swore *past of* SWEAR

sworn *past part of* SWEAR

swum *past part of* SWIM

swung *past of* SWING

syc·a·more \'sikə,mōr\ *n* : shade tree

syc·o·phant \'sikəfənt\ *n* : servile flatterer —**syc·o·phan·tic** \,sikə'fantik\ *adj*

syl·la·ble \'siləbəl\ *n* : unit of a spoken word —**syl·lab·ic** \sə'labik\ *adj*

syl·la·bus \'siləbəs\ *n, pl* **-bi** \-,bī\ *or* **-bus·es** : summary of main topics (as of a course of study)

syl·van \'silvən\ *adj* **1** : living or located in a wooded area **2** : abounding in woods

sym·bol \'simbəl\ *n* : something that represents or suggests another thing —**sym·bol·ic** \sim'bälik\ *adj* —**sym·bol·i·cal·ly** *adv*

sym·bol·ism \'simbə,lizəm\ *n* : representation of meanings with symbols

sym·bol·ize \'simbə,līz\ *vb* **-ized; -iz·ing** : serve as a symbol of —**sym·bol·i·za·tion** \,simbələ'zāshən\ *n*

sym·me·try \'simətrē\ *n, pl* **-tries** : regularity and balance in the arrangement of parts —**sym·met·ri·cal** \sə'metrikəl\ *adj* —**sym·met·ri·cal·ly** *adv*

sym·pa·thize \'simpə,thīz\ *vb* **-thized; -thiz·ing** : feel or show sympathy —**sym·pa·thiz·er** *n*

sym·pa·thy \'simpəthē\ *n, pl* **-thies 1** : ability to understand or share the feelings of another **2** : expression of sorrow for another's misfortune —**sym·pa·thet·ic** \,simpə'thetik\ *adj* —**sym·pa·thet·i·cal·ly** *adv*

sym·pho·ny \'simfənē\ *n, pl* **-nies** : composition for an orchestra or the orchestra itself —**sym·phon·ic** \sim'fänik\ *adj*

sym·po·sium \sim'pōzēəm\ *n, pl* **-sia** \-zēə\ *or* **-siums** : conference at which a topic is discussed

symp·tom \'simptəm\ *n* : unusual feeling or reaction that is a sign of disease —**symp·tom·at·ic** \,simptə'matik\ *adj*

syn·a·gogue, syn·a·gog \'sinə,gäg, -,gòg\ *n* : Jewish house of worship

syn·chro·nize \'siŋkrə,nīz, 'sin-\ *vb* **-nized; -niz·ing 1** : occur or cause to occur at the same instant **2** : cause to agree in time —**syn·chro·ni·za·tion** \,siŋkrənə'zāshən, ,sin-\ *n*

syn·co·pa·tion \,siŋkə'pāshən, ,sin-\ *n* : shifting of the regular musical accent to the weak beat —**syn·co·pate** \'siŋkə,pāt, 'sin-\ *vb*

syn·di·cate \'sindikət\ *n* : business association ~ \-də,kāt\ *vb* **-cat·ed; -cat·ing 1** : form a syndicate **2** : publish through a syndicate —**syn·di·ca·tion** \,sində'kāshən\ *n*

syn·drome \'sin,drōm\ *n* : particular group of symptoms

syn·onym \'sinə,nim\ *n* : word with the same meaning as another —**syn·on·y·mous** \sə'nänəməs\ *adj* —**syn·on·y·my** \-mē\ *n*

syn·op·sis \sə'näpsəs\ *n, pl* **-op·ses** \-,sēz\ : condensed statement or outline

syn·tax \'sin,taks\ *n* : way in which words are put together —**syn·tac·tic** \sin'taktik\ *or* **syn·tac·ti·cal** \-tikəl\ *adj*

syn·the·sis \'sinthəsəs\ *n, pl* **-the·ses** \-,sēz\ : combination of parts or elements into a whole —**syn·the·size** \-,sīz\ *vb*

syn·thet·ic \sin'thetik\ *adj* : artificially made —**synthetic** *n* —**syn·thet·i·cal·ly** *adv*

syph·i·lis \'sifələs\ *n* : venereal disease

sy·ringe \sə'rinj, 'sirinj\ *n* : plunger device for injecting or withdrawing liquids

syr·up \'sərəp, 'sirəp\ *n* : thick sticky sweet liquid —**syr·upy** *adj*

sys·tem \'sistəm\ *n* **1** : arrangement of units that function together **2** : regular order —**sys·tem·at·ic** \,sistə'matik\ *adj* —**sys·tem·at·i·cal·ly** *adv* —**sys·tem·a·tize** \'sistəmə,tīz\ *vb*

sys·tem·ic \sis'temik\ *adj* : relating to the whole body

T

t \'tē\ *n, pl* **t's** *or* **ts** \'tēz\ : 20th letter of the alphabet

tab \'tab\ *n* **1** : short projecting flap **2** *pl* : careful watch

tab·by \'tabē\ *n, pl* **-bies** : domestic cat

tab·er·na·cle \'tabər,nakəl\ *n* : house of worship

ta·ble \'tābəl\ *n* **1** : piece of furniture having a smooth slab fixed on legs **2** : supply of food **3** : arrangement of data in columns **4** : short list —**ta·ble·cloth** *n* —**ta·ble·top** *n* —**ta·ble·ware** *n* —**tab·u·lar** \'tabyələr\ *adj*

tab·leau \'tab,lō\ *n, pl* **-leaux** \-,lōz\ **1** : graphic description **2** : depiction of a scene by people in costume

ta·ble·spoon *n* **1** : large serving spoon **2** : measuring spoon holding ½ fluid ounce —**ta·ble·spoon·ful** \-,fùl\ *n*

tab·let \'tablət\ *n* **1** : flat slab suited for an inscription **2** : collection of sheets of paper glued together at one edge **3** : disk-shaped pill

tab·loid \'tab,lòid\ *n* : newspaper of small page size

ta·boo \tə'bü, ta-\ *adj* : banned esp. as immoral or dangerous —**taboo** *n or vb*

tab·u·late \'tabyə,lāt\ *vb* **-lat·ed; -lat·ing** : put in the form of a table —**tab·u·la·tion** \,tabyə'lāshən\ *n* —**tab·u·la·tor** \'tabyə,lātər\ *n*

tac·it \'tasət\ *adj* : implied but not expressed —**tac·it·ly** *adv* —**tac·it·ness** *n*

tac·i·turn \'tasə,tərn\ *adj* : not inclined to talk

tack \'tak\ *n* **1** : small sharp nail **2** : course of action ~ *vb* **1** : fasten with tacks **2** : add on

tack·le \'takəl, *naut often* 'tāk-\ *n* **1** : equipment **2** : arrangement of ropes and pulleys **3** : act of tackling ~ *vb* **-led; -ling 1** : seize or throw down **2** : start dealing with

¹tacky \'takē\ *adj* **tack·i·er; -est** : sticky to the touch

²tacky *adj* **tack·i·er; -est** : cheap or gaudy

tact \'takt\ *n* : sense of the proper thing to say or do —**tact·ful** \-fəl\ *adj* —**tact·ful·ly** *adv* —**tact·less** *adj* —**tact·less·ly** *adv*

tac·tic \'taktik\ *n* : action as part of a plan

tac·tics \'taktiks\ *n sing or pl* **1** : science of maneuvering forces in combat **2** : skill of using available means to reach an end —**tac·ti·cal** \-tikəl\ *adj* —**tac·ti·cian** \tak-'tishən\ *n*

tac·tile \'takt⁰l, -,tīl\ *adj* : relating to or perceptible through the sense of touch

tad·pole \'tad,pōl\ *n* : larval frog or toad with tail and gills

taf·fe·ta \'tafətə\ *n* : crisp lustrous fabric (as of silk)

taf·fy \'tafē\ *n, pl* **-fies** : candy stretched until porous

¹tag \'tag\ *n* : piece of hanging or attached material ~ *vb* **-gg- 1** : provide or mark with a tag **2** : follow closely

²tag *n* : children's game of trying to catch one another ~ *vb* : touch a person in tag

tail \'tāl\ *n* **1** : rear end of a growth extending from the rear end of an animal **2** : back or last part **3** : the reverse of a coin ~ *vb* : follow —**tailed** \'tāld\ *adj* —**tail·less** *adj*

tail·gate \-,gāt\ *n* : hinged gate on the back of a vehicle that can be lowered for loading ~ *vb* **-gat·ed; -gat·ing** : drive too close behind another vehicle

tail·light *n* : red warning light at the back of a vehicle

tai·lor \'tālər\ *n* : one who makes or alters garments ~ *vb* **1** : fashion or alter (clothes) **2** : make or adapt for a special purpose

tail·spin *n* : spiral dive by an airplane

taint \'tānt\ *vb* : affect or become affected with something bad and esp. decay ~ *n* : trace of decay or corruption

take \'tāk\ *vb* **took** \'tùk\; **tak·en** \'tākən\; **tak·ing 1** : get into one's possession **2** : become affected by **3** : receive into one's body (as by eating) **4** : pick out or remove **5** : use for transportation **6** : need or make use of **7** : lead, carry, or cause to go to another place **8** : undertake and do, make, or perform ~ *n* : amount taken —**take·over** *n* —**tak·er** *n* —**take advantage of** : profit by —**take exception** : object —**take off** *vb* **1** : remove **2** : go away **3** : mimic **4** : begin flight —**take over** *vb* : assume control or possession of or responsibility for —**take place** : happen

take·off *n* : act or instance of taking off

talc \'talk\ *n* : soft mineral used in making toilet powder (**tal·cum powder** \'tal-kəm-\)

tale \'tāl\ *n* **1** : story or anecdote **2** : falsehood

tal·ent \'talənt\ *n* : natural mental or creative ability —**tal·ent·ed** *adj*

tal·is·man \'taləsmən, -əz-\ *n, pl* **-mans** : object thought to act as a charm

talk \'tòk\ *vb* **1** : express one's thoughts in speech **2** : discuss **3** : influence to a position or course of action by talking ~ *n* **1** : act of talking **2** : formal discussion **3** : rumor **4** : informal lecture —**talk·a·tive** \-ətiv\ *adj* —**talk·er** *n*

tall \'tòl\ *adj* : extending to a great or specified height —**tall·ness** *n*

tal·low \'talō\ *n* : hard white animal fat used esp. in candles

tal·ly \'talē\ *n, pl* **-lies** : recorded amount ~ *vb* **-lied; -ly·ing 1** : add or count up **2** : match

tal·on \'talən\ *n* : bird's claw

tam \'tam\ *n* : tam-o'-shanter

tam·bou·rine \,tambə'rēn\ *n* : small drum with loose disks at the sides

tame \'tām\ *adj* **tam·er; tam·est 1** : changed from being wild to being controllable by man **2** : docile **3** : dull ~ *vb* **tamed; tam·ing** : make or become tame —**tam·able, tame·able** *adj* —**tame·ly** *adv* —**tam·er** *n*

tam-o'-shan·ter \'tamə,shantər\ *n* : Scottish woolen cap with a wide flat circular crown

tamp \'tamp\ *vb* : drive down or in by a series of light blows

tam·per \'tampər\ *vb* : interfere so as to change for the worse

tan \'tan\ *vb* **-nn- 1** : change (hide) into leather esp. by soaking in a liquid containing tannin **2** : make or become brown (as by exposure to the sun) ~ *n* **1** : brown skin color induced by the sun **2** : light yellowish brown —**tan·ner** *n* —**tan·nery** \'tanərē\ *n*

tan·dem \'tandəm\ *adv* : one behind another

tang \'taŋ\ *n* : sharp distinctive flavor —**tangy** *adj*

tan·gent \'tanjənt\ *adj* : touching a curve or surface at only one point ~ *n* **1** : tangent line, curve, or surface **2** : abrupt change of course —**tan·gen·tial** \tan'jenchəl\ *adj*

tan·ger·ine \'tanjə,rēn, ,tanjə'-\ *n* : deep orange citrus fruit

tan·gi·ble \'tanjəbəl\ *adj* **1** : able to be touched **2** : substantially real —**tan·gi·bly** *adv*

tan·gle \'taŋgəl\ *vb* **-gled; -gling** : unite in intricate confusion ~ *n* : tangled twisted mass

tan·go \'taŋgō\ *n, pl* **-gos** : dance of Latin-American origin —**tango** *vb*

tank \'taŋk\ *n* **1** : large artificial receptacle for liquids **2** : armored military vehicle —**tank·ful** *n*

tan·kard \'taŋkərd\ *n* : tall one-handled drinking vessel

tank·er \'taŋkər\ *n* : vehicle or vessel with tanks for transporting a liquid

tan·nin \'tanən\ *n* : substance of plant origin used in tanning and dyeing

tan·ta·lize \'tant⁰l,īz\ *vb* **-lized; -liz·ing** : tease or torment by keeping something

desirable just out of reach —**tan·ta·liz·er** *n* —**tan·ta·liz·ing·ly** *adv*

tan·ta·mount \'tantə,maùnt\ *adj* : equivalent in value or meaning

tan·trum \'tantrəm\ *n* : fit of bad temper

¹tap \'tap\ *n* **1** : faucet **2** : act of tapping ~ *vb* **-pp- 1** : pierce so as to draw off fluid **2** : connect into —**tap·per** *n*

²tap *vb* **-pp-** : rap lightly ~ *n* : light stroke or its sound

tape \'tāp\ *n* **1** : narrow flexible strip (as of cloth, plastic, or metal) **2** : tape measure ~ *vb* **taped; tap·ing 1** : fasten with tape **2** : record on tape

tape measure *n* : strip of tape marked in units for use in measuring

ta·per \'tāpər\ *n* **1** : slender wax candle **2** : gradual lessening of width in a long object ~ *vb* **1** : make or become smaller toward one end **2** : diminish gradually

tap·es·try \'tapəstrē\ *n, pl* **-tries** : heavy handwoven ruglike wall hanging

tape·worm *n* : long flat intestinal worm

tap·i·o·ca \,tapē'ōkə\ *n* : a granular starch used esp. in puddings

tar \'tär\ *n* : thick dark sticky liquid distilled (as from coal) ~ *vb* **-rr-** : treat or smear with tar

ta·ran·tu·la \tə'ranchələ, -'rant⁰lə\ *n* : large hairy usu. harmless spider

tar·dy \'tärdē\ *adj* **-di·er; -est** : late —**tar·di·ly** \'tärd⁰lē\ *adv* —**tar·di·ness** *n*

tar·get \'tärgət\ *n* **1** : mark to shoot at **2** : goal to be achieved ~ *vb* **1** : make a target of **2** : establish as a goal

tar·iff \'tarəf\ *n* **1** : duty or rate of duty imposed on imported goods **2** : schedule of tariffs, rates, or charges

tar·nish \'tärnish\ *vb* : make or become dull or discolored —**tarnish** *n*

tar·pau·lin \tär'pòlən, 'tärpə-\ *n* : waterproof protective covering

¹tar·ry \'tarē\ *vb* **-ried; -ry·ing** : be slow in leaving

²tar·ry \'tärē\ *adj* : resembling or covered with tar

¹tart \'tärt\ *adj* **1** : pleasantly sharp to the taste **2** : caustic —**tart·ly** *adv* —**tart·ness** *n*

²tart *n* : small pie

tar·tan \'tärt⁰n\ *n* : woolen fabric with a plaid design

tar·tar \'tärtər\ *n* : hard crust on the teeth

task \'task\ *n* : assigned work

task·mas·ter *n* : one that burdens another with labor

tas·sel \'tasəl, 'täs-\ *n* : hanging ornament made of a bunch of cords fastened at one end

taste \'tāst\ *vb* **tast·ed; tast·ing 1** : test or determine the flavor of **2** : eat or drink in small quantities **3** : have a specific flavor ~ *n* **1** : small amount tasted **2** : bit **3** : special sense that identifies sweet, sour, bitter, or salty qualities **4** : individual preference **5** : critical appreciation of quality —**taste·ful** \-fəl\ *adj* —**taste·ful·ly** *adv* —**taste·less** *adj* —**taste·less·ly** *adv* —**tast·er** *n*

tasty \'tāstē\ *adj* **tast·i·er; -est** : pleasing to the sense of taste —**tast·i·ness** *n*

tat·ter \'tatər\ *n* **1** : part torn and left hanging **2** *pl* : tattered clothing ~ *vb* : make or become ragged

tat·tle \'tat⁰l\ *vb* **-tled; -tling** : inform on someone —**tat·tler** *n*

tat·tle·tale *n* : one that tattles

tat·too \ta'tü\ *vb* : mark the skin with indelible designs or figures —**tattoo** *n*

taught *past of* TEACH

taunt \'tònt\ *n* : sarcastic challenge or insult —**taunt** *vb* —**taunt·er** *n*

taut \'tòt\ *adj* : tightly drawn —**taut·ly** *adv* —**taut·ness** *n*

tav·ern \'tavərn\ *n* : establishment where liquors are sold to be drunk on the premises

taw·dry \'tòdrē\ *adj* **-dri·er; -est** : cheap and gaudy —**taw·dri·ly** \'tòdrəlē\ *adv*

taw·ny \'tònē\ *adj* **-ni·er; -est** : brownish orange

tax \'taks\ *vb* **1** : impose a tax on **2** : charge **3** : put under stress ~ *n* **1** : charge by authority for public purposes **2** : strain —**tax·able** *adj* —**tax·a·tion** \tak'sāshən\ *n* —**tax·pay·er** *n* —**tax·pay·ing** *adj*

taxi \'taksē\ *n, pl* **tax·is** \-sēz\ : automobile transporting passengers for a fare ~ *vb* **tax·ied; taxi·ing** *or* **taxy·ing; tax·is** *or* **tax·ies 1** : transport or go by taxi **2** : move along the ground before takeoff or after landing

taxi·cab \'taksē,kab\ *n* : taxi

taxi·der·my \'taksə,dərmē\ *n* : skill or job of stuffing and mounting animal skins —**taxi·der·mist** \-mist\ *n*

tea \'tē\ *n* : cured leaves of an oriental shrub or a drink made from these —**tea·cup** *n* —**tea·pot** *n*

teach \'tēch\ *vb* **taught** \'tòt\; **teach·ing 1** : tell or show the fundamentals or skills of something **2** : cause to know the consequences **3** : impart knowledge of —

teach•able *adj* —**teach•er** *n* —**teaching**

teak \'tēk\ *n* : East Indian timber tree or its wood

tea•ket•tle \'tē,ket°l\ *n* : covered kettle with a handle and spout for boiling water

teal \'tēl\ *n, pl* **teal** *or* **teals** : small short-necked wild duck

team \'tēm\ *n* **1** : draft animals harnessed together **2** : number of people organized for a game or work ~ *vb* : form or work together as a team —**team** *adj* —**team•mate** *n* —**team•work** *n*

team•ster \'tēmstər\ *n* **1** : one that drives a team of animals **2** : one that drives a truck

¹tear \'tir\ *n* : drop of salty liquid that moistens the eye —**tear•ful** \-fəl\ *adj* —**tear•ful•ly** *adv*

²tear \'tar\ *vb* **tore** \'tōr\; **torn** \'tōrn\; **tear•ing 1** : separate or pull apart by force **2** : move or act with violence or haste ~ *n* : act or result of tearing

tease \'tēz\ *vb* **teased; teas•ing** : annoy by goading, coaxing, or tantalizing ~ *n* **1** : act of teasing or state of being teased **2** : one that teases

tea•spoon \'tē,spün\ *n* **1** : small spoon for stirring or sipping **2** : measuring spoon holding ⅙ fluid ounce —**tea•spoon•ful** \-,fùl\ *n*

teat \'tēt\ *n* : protuberance through which milk is drawn from an udder or breast

tech•ni•cal \'teknikəl\ *adj* **1** : having or relating to special mechanical or scientific knowledge **2** : by strict interpretation of rules —**tech•ni•cal•ly** *adv*

tech•ni•cal•i•ty \,teknə'kalətē\ *n, pl* **-ties** : detail meaningful only to a specialist

technical sergeant *n* : noncommissioned officer in the air force ranking next below a master sergeant

tech•ni•cian \tek'nishən\ *n* : person with the technique of a specialized skill

tech•nique \tek'nēk\ *n* : manner of accomplishing something

tech•nol•o•gy \tek'näləjē\ *n, pl* **-gies** : applied science —**tech•no•log•i•cal** \,teknə'läjikəl\ *adj*

te•dious \'tēdēəs\ *adj* : wearisome from length or dullness —**te•dious•ly** *adv* —**te•dious•ness** *n*

te•di•um \'tēdēəm\ *n* : tedious state or quality

tee \'tē\ *n* : mound or peg on which a golf ball is placed before beginning play —**tee** *vb*

teem \'tēm\ *vb* : become filled to overflowing

teen•age \'tēn,āj\, **teen•aged** \-,ājd\ *adj* : relating to people in their teens —**teen•ag•er** \-,ājər\ *n*

teens \'tēnz\ *n pl* : years 13 to 19 in a person's life

tee•pee *var of* TEPEE

tee•ter \'tētər\ *vb* **1** : move unsteadily **2** : seesaw —**teeter** *n*

teeth *pl of* TOOTH

teethe \'tēth\ *vb* **teethed; teeth•ing** : grow teeth

tele•cast \'teli,kast\ *vb* **-cast; -cast•ing** : broadcast by television —**telecast** *n* —**tele•cast•er** *n*

tele•com•mu•ni•ca•tion \'teləkəmyünə'kā-shən\ *n* : communication at a distance (as by radio or television)

tele•gram \'telə,gram\ *n* : message sent by telegraph

tele•graph \-,graf\ *n* : system for communication by electrical transmission of coded signals ~ *vb* : send by telegraph —**te•leg•ra•pher** \tə'legrəfər\ *n* —**tele•graph•ic** \,telə'grafik\ *adj*

te•lep•a•thy \tə'lepəthē\ *n* : apparent communication without known sensory means —**tele•path•ic** \,telə'pathik\ *adj* —**tele•path•i•cal•ly** *adv*

tele•phone \'telə,fōn\ *n* : instrument or system for electrical transmission of spoken words ~ *vb* **-phoned; -phon•ing** : communicate with by telephone —**tele•phon•er** *n*

tele•scope \-,skōp\ *n* : tube-shaped optical instrument for viewing distant objects ~ *vb* **-scoped; -scop•ing** : slide or cause to slide inside another similar section —**tele•scop•ic** \,telə'skäpik\ *adj*

tele•vise \'telə,vīz\ *vb* **-vised; -vis•ing** : broadcast by television

tele•vi•sion \-,vizhən\ *n* : transmission and reproduction of images by radio waves

tell \'tel\ *vb* **told** \'tōld\; **tell•ing 1** : count **2** : relate in detail **3** : reveal **4** : give information or an order to **5** : find out by observing

tell•er \'telər\ *n* **1** : one that relates or counts **2** : bank employee handling money

te•mer•i•ty \tə'merətē\ *n, pl* **-ties** : boldness

temp \'temp\ *n* **1** : temperature **2** : temporary worker

tem•per \'tempər\ *vb* **1** : dilute or soften **2** : toughen ~ *n* **1** : characteristic attitude or feeling **2** : toughness **3** : disposition or control over one's emotions

tem•per•a•ment \'tempərəmənt\ *n* : char-

acteristic frame of mind — **tem•per•a•men•tal** \,temprə'ment°l\ *adj*

tem•per•ance \'temprəns\ *n* : moderation in or abstinence from indulgence and esp. the use of intoxicating drink

tem•per•ate \'tempərət\ *adj* : moderate

tem•per•a•ture \'tempər,chùr, -prə,chùr, -chər\ *n* **1** : degree of hotness or coldness **2** : fever

tem•pest \'tempəst\ *n* : violent storm — **tem•pes•tu•ous** \tem'peschəwəs\ *adj*

¹tem•ple \'tempəl\ *n* : place of worship

²temple *n* : flattened space on each side of the forehead

tem•po \'tempō\ *n, pl* **-pi** \-,pē\ *or* **-pos** : rate of speed

tem•po•ral \'tempərəl\ *adj* : relating to time or to secular concerns

tem•po•rary \'tempə,rerē\ *adj* : lasting for a short time only —**tem•po•rar•i•ly** \,tempə'rerəlē\ *adv*

tempt \'tempt\ *vb* **1** : coax or persuade to do wrong **2** : attract or provoke —**tempt•er** *n* —**tempt•ing•ly** *adv* —**tempt•ress** \'temptrəs\ *n*

temp•ta•tion \temp'tāshən\ *n* **1** : act of tempting **2** : something that tempts

ten \'ten\ *n* **1** : one more than 9 **2** : 10th in a set or series **3** : thing having 10 units —**ten** *adj or pron* —**tenth** \'tenth\ *adj or adv or n*

ten•a•ble \'tenəbəl\ *adj* : capable of being held or defended —**ten•a•bil•i•ty** \,tenə'bilətē\ *n*

te•na•cious \tə'nāshəs\ *adj* **1** : holding fast **2** : retentive —**te•na•cious•ly** *adv* —**te•nac•i•ty** \tə'nasətē\ *n*

ten•ant \'tenənt\ *n* : one who occupies a rented dwelling —**ten•an•cy** \-ənsē\ *n*

¹tend \'tend\ *vb* : take care of or supervise something

²tend *vb* **1** : move in a particular direction **2** : show a tendency

ten•den•cy \'tendənsē\ *n, pl* **-cies** : likelihood to move, think, or act in a particular way

¹ten•der \'tendər\ *adj* **1** : soft or delicate **2** : expressing or responsive to love or sympathy **3** : sensitive (as to touch) —**ten•der•ly** *adv* —**ten•der•ness** *n*

²tend•er \'tendər\ *n* **1** : one that tends **2** : boat providing transport to a larger ship **3** : vehicle attached to a steam locomotive for carrying fuel and water

³ten•der *n* **1** : offer of a bid for a contract **2** : something that may be offered in payment —**tender** *vb*

ten•der•ize \'tendə,rīz\ *vb* **-ized; -iz•ing** : make (meat) tender —**ten•der•iz•er** \'tendə,rīzər\ *n*

ten•der•loin \'tendər,lòin\ *n* : tender beef or pork strip from near the backbone

ten•don \'tendən\ *n* : cord of tissue attaching muscle to bone —**ten•di•nous** \-dənəs\ *adj*

ten•dril \'tendrəl\ *n* : slender coiling growth of some climbing plants

ten•e•ment \'tenəmənt\ *n* **1** : house divided into apartments **2** : shabby dwelling

te•net \'tenət\ *n* : principle of belief

ten•nis \'tenəs\ *n* : racket-and-ball game played across a net

ten•or \'tenər\ *n* **1** : general drift or meaning **2** : highest natural adult male voice

ten•pin \'ten,pin\ *n* : bottle-shaped pin bowled at in a game (**tenpins**)

¹tense \'tens\ *n* : distinct verb form that indicates time

²tense *adj* **tens•er; tens•est 1** : stretched tight **2** : marked by nervous tension — **tense** *vb* —**tense•ly** *adv* —**tense•ness** — **ten•si•ty** \'tensətē\ *n*

ten•sile \'tensəl, -,sīl\ *adj* : relating to tension

ten•sion \'tenchən\ *n* **1** : tense condition **2** : state of mental unrest or of potential hostility or opposition

tent \'tent\ *n* : collapsible shelter

ten•ta•cle \'tentikəl\ *n* : long flexible projection of an insect or mollusk —**ten•ta•cled** \-kəld\ *adj* —**ten•tac•u•lar** \ten-'takyələr\ *adj*

ten•ta•tive \'tentətiv\ *adj* : subject to change or discussion —**ten•ta•tive•ly** *adv*

ten•u•ous \'tenyəwəs\ *adj* **1** : not dense or thick **2** : flimsy or weak —**ten•u•ous•ly** *adv* —**ten•u•ous•ness** *n*

ten•ure \'tenyər\ *n* : act, right, manner, or period of holding something —**ten•ured** \-yərd\ *adj*

te•pee \'tē,pē\ *n* : conical tent

tep•id \'tepəd\ *adj* : moderately warm

term \'tərm\ *n* **1** : period of time **2** : mathematical expression **3** : special word or phrase **4** : conditions **5** *pl* : relations ~ *vb* : name

ter•mi•nal \'tərmən°l\ *n* **1** : end **2** : device for making an electrical connection **3** : station at end of a transportation line — **terminal** *adj*

ter•mi•nate \'tərmə,nāt\ *vb* **-nat•ed; -nat•ing** : bring or come to an end —**ter•mi•na•ble** \-nəbəl\ *adj* —**ter•mi•na•tion** \,tərmə'nāshən\ *n*

ter•mi•nol•o•gy \,tərmə'näləjē\ *n* : terms used in a particular subject

ter•mi•nus \'tərmənəs\ *n, pl* **-ni** \-,nī\ *or* **-nus•es 1** : end **2** : end of a transportation line

ter•mite \'tər,mīt\ *n* : wood-eating insect

tern \'tərn\ *n* : small sea bird

ter•race \'terəs\ *n* **1** : balcony or patio **2** : bank with a flat top ~ *vb* **-raced; -rac•ing** : landscape in a series of banks

ter•ra-cot•ta \,terə'kätə\ *n* : reddish brown earthenware

ter•rain \tə'rān\ *n* : features of the land

ter•ra•pin \'terəpən\ *n* : No. American turtle

ter•rar•i•um \tə'rareəm\ *n, pl* **-ia** \-ēə\ *or* **-i•ums** : container for keeping plants or animals

ter•res•tri•al \tə'restrēəl\ *adj* **1** : relating to the earth or its inhabitants **2** : living or growing on land

ter•ri•ble \'terəbəl\ *adj* **1** : exciting terror **2** : distressing **3** : intense **4** : of very poor quality —**ter•ri•bly** \-blē\ *adv*

ter•ri•er \'terēər\ *n* : small dog

ter•rif•ic \tə'rifik\ *adj* **1** : exciting terror **2** : extraordinary

ter•ri•fy \'terə,fī\ *vb* **-fied; -fy•ing** : fill with terror —**ter•ri•fy•ing•ly** *adv*

ter•ri•to•ry \'terə,tōrē\ *n, pl* **-ries** : particular geographical region —**ter•ri•to•ri•al** \,terə'tōrēəl\ *adj*

ter•ror \'terər\ *n* : intense fear and panic or a cause of it

ter•ror•ism \-,izəm\ *n* : systematic covert warfare to produce terror for political coercion —**ter•ror•ist** \-ist\ *adj or n*

ter•ror•ize \-,īz\ *vb* **-ized; -iz•ing 1** : fill with terror **2** : coerce by threat or violence

ter•ry \'terē\ *n, pl* **-ries** : absorbent fabric with a loose pile

terse \'tərs\ *adj* **ters•er; ters•est** : concise —**terse•ly** *adv* —**terse•ness** *n*

ter•tia•ry \'tərshē,erē\ *adj* : of 3d rank, importance, or value

test \'test\ *n* : examination or evaluation ~ *vb* : examine by a test —**test•er** *n*

tes•ta•ment \'testəmənt\ *n* **1** *cap* : division of the Bible **2** : will —**tes•ta•men•ta•ry** \,testə'mentərē\ *adj*

tes•ti•cle \'testikəl\ *n* : testis

tes•ti•fy \'testə,fī\ *vb* **-fied; -fy•ing 1** : give testimony **2** : serve as evidence

tes•ti•mo•ni•al \,testə'mōnēəl\ *n* **1** : favorable recommendation **2** : tribute —**testimonial** *adj*

tes•ti•mo•ny \'testə,mōnē\ *n, pl* **-nies** : statement given as evidence in court

tes•tis \'testəs\ *n, pl* **-tes** \-,tēz\ : male reproductive gland

tes•ty \'testē\ *adj* **-ti•er; -est** : easily annoyed

tet•a•nus \'tet°nəs\ *n* : bacterial disease producing violent spasms

tête-à-tête \,tātə'tāt\ *adv* : privately ~ *n* : private conversation ~ *adj* : private

teth•er \'tethər\ *n* : leash ~ *vb* : restrain with a leash

text \'tekst\ *n* **1** : author's words **2** : main body of printed or written matter on a page **3** : textbook **4** : scriptural passage used as the theme of a sermon **5** : topic —**tex•tu•al** \'tekschəwəl\ *adj*

text•book \-,bùk\ *n* : book on a school subject

tex•tile \'tek,stīl, 'tekst°l\ *n* : fabric

tex•ture \'tekschər\ *n* **1** : feel and appearance of something **2** : structure

than \'than\ *conj or prep* —used in comparisons

thank \'thank\ *vb* : express gratitude to

thank•ful \-fəl\ *adj* : giving thanks — **thank•ful•ly** *adv* —**thank•ful•ness** *n*

thank•less *adj* : not appreciated

thanks \'thanks\ *n pl* : expression of gratitude

Thanks•giv•ing \thanks'givin\ *n* : 4th Thursday in November observed as a legal holiday for giving thanks for divine goodness

that \'that\ *pron, pl* **those** \'thōz\ **1** : something indicated or understood **2** : the one farther away ~ *adj, pl* **those** : being the one mentioned or understood or farther away ~ *conj or pron* —used to introduce a clause ~ *adv* : to such an extent

thatch \'thach\ *vb* : cover with thatch ~ *n* : covering of matted straw

thaw \'thò\ *vb* : melt or cause to melt — **thaw** *n*

the \thə, *before vowel sounds usu* thē\ *definite article* : that particular one ~ *adv* — used before a comparative or superlative

the•ater, the•atre \'thēətər\ *n* **1** : building or room for viewing a play or movie **2** : dramatic arts

the•at•ri•cal \thē'atrikəl\ *adj* **1** : relating to the theater **2** : involving exaggerated emotion

thee \'thē\ *pron, archaic objective case of* THOU

theft \'theft\ *n* : act of stealing

their \'ther\ *adj* : relating to them

theirs \'therz\ *pron* : their one or ones

the•ism \'thē,izəm\ *n* : belief in the exis-

tence of a god or gods —**the•ist** \-ist\ *n or adj* —**the•is•tic** \thē'istik\ *adj*

them \'them\ *pron, objective case of* THEY

theme \'thēm\ *n* **1** : subject matter **2** : essay **3** : melody developed in a piece of music —**the•mat•ic** \thi'matik\ *adj*

them•selves \them'selvz, them-\ *pron pl* : they, them —used reflexively or for emphasis

then \'then\ *adv* **1** : at that time **2** : soon after that **3** : in addition **4** : in that case **5** : consequently ~ *n* : that time ~ *adj* : existing at that time

thence \'thens, 'thens\ *adv* : from that place or fact

the•oc•ra•cy \thē'äkrəsē\ *n, pl* **-cies** : government by officials regarded as divinely inspired —**the•o•crat•ic** \thēə-'kratik\ *adj*

the•ol•o•gy \thē'äləjē\ *n, pl* **-gies** : study of religion —**the•o•lo•gian** \thēə'lōjən\ *n* —**the•o•log•i•cal** \-'läjikəl\ *adj*

the•o•rem \'thēərəm, 'thirəm\ *n* : provable statement of truth

the•o•ret•i•cal \,thēə'retikəl\ *adj* : relating to or being theory —**the•o•ret•i•cal•ly** *adv*

the•o•rize \'thēə,rīz\ *vb* **-rized; -riz•ing** : put forth theories —**the•o•rist** *n*

the•o•ry \'thēərē, 'thirē\ *n, pl* **-ries 1** : general principles of a subject **2** : plausible or scientifically acceptable explanation **3** : judgment, guess, or opinion

ther•a•peu•tic \,therə'pyütik\ *adj* : offering or relating to remedy —**ther•a•peu•ti•cal•ly** *adv*

ther•a•py \'therəpē\ *n, pl* **-pies** : treatment for mental or physical disorder —**ther•a•pist** \-pist\ *n*

there \'thar\ *adv* **1** : in, at, or to that place **2** : in that respect ~ *pron* —used to introduce a sentence or clause ~ *n* : that place or point

there•abouts, there•about \,tharə'baùts, 'tharə,-, -'baùt\ *adv* : near that place, time, number, or quantity

there•af•ter \thar'aftər\ *adv* : after that

there•by \thar'bī, 'thar,bī\ *adv* **1** : by that **2** : connected with or with reference to that

there•fore \'thar,fōr\ *adv* : for that reason

there•in \thar'in\ *adv* **1** : in or into that place, time, or thing **2** : in that respect

there•of \-'əv, -'äv\ *adv* **1** : of that or it **2** : from that

there•upon \'tharə,pòn, -,pän; ,tharə'pòn, -'pän\ *adv* **1** : on that matter **2** : therefore **3** : immediately after that

there•with \thar'with, -'with\ *adv* : with that

ther•mal \'thərməl\ *adj* : relating to, caused by, or conserving heat —**ther•mal•ly** *adv*

ther•mo•dy•nam•ics \,thərmōdī'namiks\ *n* : physics of heat

ther•mom•e•ter \thər'mämətər\ *n* : instrument for measuring temperature —**ther•mo•met•ric** \,thərmə'metrik\ *adj* —**ther•mo•met•ri•cal•ly** *adv*

ther•mos \'thərməs\ *n* : double-walled bottle used to keep liquids hot or cold

ther•mo•stat \'thərmə,stat\ *n* : automatic temperature control —**ther•mo•stat•ic** \,thərmə'statik\ *adj* —**ther•mo•stat•i•cal•ly** *adv*

the•sau•rus \thi'sòrəs\ *n, pl* **-sau•ri** \-'sòr,ī\ *or* **-sau•rus•es** \-'sòrəsəz\ : book of words and esp. synonyms

these *pl of* THIS

the•sis \'thēsəs\ *n, pl* **the•ses** \'thē,sēz\ **1** : proposition to be argued for **2** : essay embodying results of original research

thes•pi•an \'thespēən\ *adj* : dramatic ~ *n* : actor

they \'thā\ *pron* **1** : those ones **2** : people in general

thi•a•mine \'thīəmən, -,mēn\ *n* : essential vitamin

thick \'thik\ *adj* **1** : having relatively great mass from front to back or top to bottom **2** : viscous ~ *n* : most crowded or thickest part —**thick•ly** *adv* —**thick•ness** *n*

thick•en \'thikən\ *vb* : make or become thick —**thick•en•er** \-ənər\ *n*

thick•et \'thikət\ *n* : dense growth of bushes or small trees

thick-skinned \-'skind\ *adj* : insensitive to criticism

thief \'thēf\ *n, pl* **thieves** \'thēvz\ : one that steals

thieve \'thēv\ *vb* **thieved; thiev•ing** : steal —**thiev•ery** *n*

thigh \'thī\ *n* : upper part of the leg

thigh•bone \'thī,bōn\ *n* : femur

thim•ble \'thimbəl\ *n* : protective cap for the finger in sewing —**thim•ble•ful** *n*

thin \'thin\ *adj* **-nn- 1** : having relatively little mass from front to back or top to bottom **2** : not closely set or placed **3** : relatively free flowing **4** : lacking substance, fullness, or strength ~ *vb* **-nn-** : make or become thin —**thin•ly** *adv* — **thin•ness** *n*

thing \'thin\ *n* **1** : matter of concern **2** : event or act **3** : object **4** *pl* : possessions

think \'think\ *vb* **thought** \'thòt\; **think•ing 1** : form or have in the mind **2** : have as an opinion **3** : ponder **4** : devise by think-ing **5** : imagine **—think•er** n

thin–skinned adj : extremely sensitive to criticism

third \'thərd\ adj : being number 3 in a countable series ~ n **1** : one that is third **2** : one of 3 equal parts **—third, third•ly** adv

third dimension n : thickness or depth **—third–dimensional** adj

third world n : less developed nations of the world

thirst \'thərst\ n **1** : dryness in mouth and throat **2** : intense desire ~ vb : feel thirst **—thirsty** adj

thir•teen \thər'tēn\ n : one more than 12 **—thirteen** adj or pron **—thir•teenth** \-'tēnth\ adj or n

thir•ty \'thərtē\ n, pl **thirties** : 3 times 10 **—thir•ti•eth** \-ēath\ adj or n **—thirty** adj or pron

this \'this\ pron, pl **these** \'thēz\ : something close or under immediate discussion ~ adj, pl **these** : being the one near, present, just mentioned, or more immediately un-der observation ~ adv : to such an extent or degree

this•tle \'thisəl\ n : tall prickly herb

thith•er \'thithər\ adv : to that place

thong \'thòn\ n : strip of leather or hide

tho•rax \'thōr,aks\, n, pl **-rax•es** or **-ra•ces** \'thōrə,sēz\ **1** : part of the body between neck and abdomen **2** : middle of 3 divi-sions of an insect body **—tho•rac•ic** \thə'rasik\ adj

thorn \'thórn\ n : sharp spike on a plant or a plant bearing these **—thorny** adj

thor•ough \'thərō\ adj **1** : omitting or over-looking nothing **—thor•ough•ly** adv **—thor•ough•ness** n

thor•ough•bred \'thərə,bred\ n **1** cap : light speedy racing horse **2** : one of excellent quality **—thoroughbred** adj

thor•ough•fare \'thərə,far\ n : public road

those pl of THAT

thou \'thaù\ pron, archaic : you

though \'thō\ adv : however ~ conj **1** : despite the fact that **2** : granting that

thought \'thòt\ past of THINK ~ n **1** : process of thinking **2** : serious consid-eration **3** : idea

thought•ful \-fəl\ adj **1** : absorbed in or showing thought **2** : considerate of others **—thought•ful•ly** adv **—thought•ful•ness** n

thought•less \-ləs\ adj **1** : careless or reck-less **2** : lacking concern for others **—thought•less•ly** adv

thou•sand \'thaùzənd\ n, pl **-sands** or **-sand** : 10 times 100 **—thousand** adj **—thou-sandth** \-ənth\ adj or n

thrash \'thrash\ vb **1** : thresh **2** : beat **3** : move about violently **—thrash•er** n

thread \'thred\ n **1** : fine line of fibers **2** : train of thought **3** : ridge around a screw ~ vb **1** : pass thread through **2** : put to-gether on a thread **3** : make one's way through or between

thread•bare adj **1** : worn so that the thread shows **2** : trite

threat \'thret\ n **1** : expression of intention to harm **2** : thing that threatens

threat•en \'thretʲn\ vb **1** : utter threats **2** : show signs of being near or impending **—threat•en•ing•ly** adv

three \'thrē\ n **1** : one more than 2 **2** : 3d in a set or series **—three** adj or pron

three•fold \'thrē,fōld\ adj : triple **—three-fold** \-'fōld\ adv

three•score adj : being 3 times 20

thresh \'thresh, 'thrash\ vb : beat to separate grain **—thresh•er** n

thresh•old \'thresh,ōld\ n **1** : sill of a door **2** : beginning stage

threw past of THROW

thrice \'thrīs\ adv : 3 times

thrift \'thrift\ n : careful management or saving of money **—thrift•i•ly** \'thriftəlē\ adv **—thrift•less** adj **—thrifty** adj

thrill \'thril\ vb **1** : have or cause to have a sudden sharp feeling of excitement **2** : tremble **—thrill** n **—thrill•er** n **—thrill-ing•ly** adv

thrive \'thrīv\ vb **throve** \'thrōv\ or **thrived; thriv•en** \'thrivən\ **1** : grow vigorously **2** : prosper

throat \'thrōt\ n **1** : front part of the neck **2** : passage to the stomach **—throat•ed** adj **—throaty** adj

throb \'thräb\ vb **-bb-** : pulsate **—throb** n

throe \'thrō\ n **1** : pang or spasm **2** pl : hard or painful struggle

throne \'thrōn\ n : chair representing power or sovereignty

throng \'thròn\ n or vb : crowd

throt•tle \'thrätʲl\ vb **-tled; -tling** : choke ~ n : valve regulating volume of fuel and air delivered to engine cylinders

through \'thrü\ prep **1** : into at one side and out at the other side of **2** : by way of **3** : among, between, or all around **4** : because of **5** : throughout the time of ~ \'thrü\ adv **1** : from one end or side to the other **2** : from beginning to end **3** : to the

core **4** : into the open ~ adj **1** : going directly from origin to destination **2** : finished

through•out \thrü'aùt\ adv **1** : everywhere **2** : from beginning to end ~ prep **1** : in or to every part of **2** : during the whole of

throve past of THRIVE

throw \'thrō\ vb **threw** \'thrü\; **thrown** \'thrōn\; **throw•ing 1** : propel through the air **2** : cause to fall or fall off **3** : put sud-denly in a certain position or condition **4** : move quickly as if throwing **5** : put on or off hastily **—throw** n **—throw•er** \'thrōər\ n **—throw up** vb : vomit

thrush \'thrəsh\ n : songbird

thrust \'thrəst\ vb **thrust; thrust•ing 1** : shove forward **2** : stab or pierce **—thrust** n

thud \'thəd\ n : dull sound of something falling **—thud** vb

thug \'thəg\ n : ruffian or gangster

thumb \'thəm\ n **1** : short thick division of the hand opposing the fingers **2** : glove part for the thumb ~ vb : leaf through with the thumb **—thumb•nail** n

thump \'thəmp\ vb : strike with something thick or heavy causing a dull sound **—thump** n

thun•der \'thəndər\ n : sound following lightning **—thunder** vb **—thun•der•clap** n **—thun•der•ous** \'thəndərəs\ adj **—thun•der•ous•ly** adv

thun•der•bolt \-,bōlt\ n : discharge of light-ning with thunder

thun•der•show•er \'thəndər,shaùər\ n : shower with thunder and lightning

thun•der•storm n : storm with thunder and lightning

Thurs•day \'thərzdā, -dē\ n : 5th day of the week

thus \'thəs\ adv **1** : in this or that way **2** : to this degree or extent **3** : because of this or that

thwart \'thwórt\ vb : block or defeat

thy \'thī\ adj, archaic : your

thyme \'tīm, 'thīm\ n : cooking herb

thy•roid \'thī, róid\ adj : relating to a large endocrine gland (**thyroid gland**)

thy•self \thī'self\ pron, archaic : yourself

ti•ara \tē'arə, -'är-\ n : decorative formal headband

tib•ia \'tibēə\ n, pl **-i•ae** \-ē,ē\ : bone be-tween the knee and ankle

tic \'tik\ n : twitching of facial muscles

¹tick \'tik\ n : small 8-legged blood-sucking animal

²tick n **1** : light rhythmic tap or beat **2** : check mark ~ vb **1** : make ticks **2** : mark with a tick **3** : operate

tick•er \'tikər\ n **1** : something (as a watch) that ticks **2** : telegraph instrument that prints on paper tape

tick•et \'tikət\ n **1** : tag showing price, pay-ment of a fee or fare, or a traffic offense **2** : list of candidates ~ vb : put a ticket on

tick•ing \'tikin\ n : fabric covering of a mat-tress

tick•le \'tikəl\ vb **-led; -ling 1** : please or amuse **2** : touch lightly causing uneasi-ness, laughter, or spasmodic movements **—tickle** n

tick•lish \'tiklish\ adj **1** : sensitive to tickling **2** : requiring delicate handling **—tick-lish•ly** adv **—tick•lishness** n

tid•al wave \'tīdʲl-\ n : high sea wave fol-lowing an earthquake

tid•bit \'tid,bit\ n : choice morsel

tide \'tīd\ n : alternate rising and falling of the sea ~ vb **tid•ed; tid•ing** : be enough to allow (one) to get by for a time **—tid-al** \'tīdʲl\ adj **—tide•wa•ter** n

tid•ings \'tīdiŋz\ n pl : news or message

ti•dy \'tīdē\ adj **-di•er; -est 1** : well ordered and cared for **2** : large or substantial **—ti•di•ness** n **—tidy** vb

tie \'tī\ n **1** : line or ribbon for fastening, uniting, or closing **2** : cross support to which railroad rails are fastened **3** : uniting force **4** : equality in score or tally or a deadlocked contest **5** : necktie ~ vb **tied; ty•ing** or **tie•ing 1** : fasten or close by wrapping and knotting a tie **2** : form a knot in **3** : gain the same score or tally as an opponent

tier \'tir\ n : one of a steplike series of rows

tiff \'tif\ n : petty quarrel **—tiff** vb

ti•ger \'tīgər\ n : very large black-striped cat **—ti•ger•ish** \-gərish\ adj **—ti•gress** \-grəs\ n

tight \'tīt\ adj **1** : fitting close together esp. so as not to allow air or water in **2** : held very firmly **3** : taut **4** : fitting too snugly **5** : difficult **6** : stingy **7** : evenly contested **8** : low in supply **—tight** adv **—tight•en** \-ʲn\ vb **—tight•ly** adv **—tight•ness** n

tights \'tīts\ n pl : skintight garments

tight•wad \'tīt,wäd\ n : stingy person

tile \'tīl\ n : thin piece of stone or fired clay used on roofs, floors, or walls ~ vb : cover with tiles

¹till \'til\ prep or conj : until

²till vb : cultivate (soil) **—till•able** adj

³till n : money drawer

¹till•er \'tilər\ n : one that cultivates soil

²til•ler \'tilər\ n : lever for turning a boat's rudder

tilt \'tilt\ vb : cause to incline ~ n : slant

tim•ber \'timbər\ n **1** : cut wood for building **2** : large squared piece of wood **3** : wooded land or trees for timber ~ vb : cover, frame, or support with timbers **—tim•bered** **—tim•ber•land** \-,land\ n

tim•bre \'tambər, 'tim-\ n : sound quality

time \'tīm\ n **1** : period during which some-thing exists or continues or can be accom-plished **2** : point at which something hap-pens **3** : customary hour **4** : age **5** : tempo **6** : moment, hour, day, or year as indi-cated by a clock or calendar **7** : one's ex-perience during a particular period ~ vb **timed; tim•ing 1** : arrange or set the time of **2** : determine or record the time, du-ration, or rate of **—time•keep•er** n **—time•less** adj **—time•less•ness** n **—time-li•ness** n **—time•ly** adv **—tim•er** n

time•piece n : device to show time

times \'tīmz\ prep : multiplied by

time•ta•ble \'tīm,tābəl\ n : table of departure and arrival times

tim•id \'timəd\ adj : lacking in courage or self-confidence **—ti•mid•i•ty** \tə'midətē\ n **—tim•id•ly** adv

tim•o•rous \'timərəs\ adj : fearful **—tim•o-rous•ly** adv **—tim•o•rous•ness** n

tim•pa•ni \'timpənē\ n pl : set of kettle-drums **—tim•pa•nist** \-nist\ n

tin \'tin\ n **1** : soft white metallic chemical element **2** : metal food can

tinc•ture \'tiŋkchər\ n : alcoholic solution of a medicine

tin•der \'tindər\ n : substance used to kindle a fire

tine \'tīn\ n : one of the points of a fork

tin•foil \'tin,fóil\ n : thin metal sheeting

tinge \'tinj\ vb **tinged; tinge•ing** or **ting•ing** \'tinjin\ **1** : color slightly **2** : affect with a slight odor ~ n : slight coloring or flavor

tin•gle \'tiŋgəl\ vb **-gled; -gling** : feel a ring-ing, stinging, or thrilling sensation **—tin-gle** n

tin•ker \'tiŋkər\ vb : experiment in repairing something **—tin•ker•er** n

tin•kle \'tiŋkəl\ vb **-kled; -kling** : make or cause to make a high ringing sound **—tinkle** n

tin•sel \'tinsəl\ n : decorative thread or strip of glittering metal or paper

tint \'tint\ n **1** : slight or pale coloration **2** : color shade ~ vb : give a tint to

ti•ny \'tīnē\ adj **-ni•er; -est** : very small

¹tip \'tip\ vb **-pp- 1** : overturn **2** : lean ~ n : act or state of tipping

²tip n : pointed end of something ~ vb **-pp-1** : furnish with a tip **2** : cover the tip of

³tip n : small sum given for a service per-formed ~ vb : give a tip to

⁴tip n : piece of confidential information ~ vb **-pp-** : give confidential information to

tip–off \'tip,óf\ n : indication

tip•ple \'tipəl\ vb **-pled; -pling** : drink in-toxicating liquor esp. habitually or exces-sively **—tip•pler** n

tip•sy \'tipsē\ adj **-si•er; -est** : unsteady or foolish from alcohol

tip•toe \'tip,tō\ n : the toes of the feet ~ adv or adj : supported on tiptoe ~ vb **-toed; -toe•ing** : walk quietly or on tiptoe

tip–top n : highest point ~ adj : excellent

ti•rade \'tī,rād, 'tī,-\ n : prolonged speech of abuse

¹tire \'tīr\ vb **tired; tir•ing 1** : make or be-come weary **2** : wear out the patience of **—tire•less** adj **—tire•less•ly** adv **—tire-less•ness** n **—tire•some** \-səm\ adj **—tire•some•ly** adv **—tire•some•ness** n

²tire n : rubber cushion encircling a car wheel

tired \'tīrd\ adj : weary

tis•sue \'tishü\ n **1** : soft absorbent paper **2** : layer of cells forming a basic structural element of an animal or plant body

ti•tan•ic \tī'tanik, tə-\ adj : gigantic

ti•ta•ni•um \tī'tānēəm, tə-\ n : gray light strong metallic chemical element

tithe \'tīth\ n : tenth part paid or given esp. for the support of a church **—tithe** vb **—tith•er** n

tit•il•late \'titʲl,āt\ vb **-lat•ed; -lat•ing** : excite pleasurably **—tit•il•la•tion** \,titʲl'āshən\ n

ti•tle \'tītʲl\ n **1** : legal ownership **2** : distinguishing name **3** : designation of honor, rank, or office **4** : championship **—ti•tled** adj

tit•ter \'titər\ n : nervous or affected laugh **—titter** vb

tit•u•lar \'tichələr\ adj **1** : existing in title only **2** : relating to or bearing a title

tiz•zy \'tizē\ n, pl **tizzies** : state of agitation or worry

TNT \,tē,en'tē\ n : high explosive

to \'tü\ prep **1** : in the direction of **2** : at, on, or near **3** : resulting in **4** : before or until **5** —used to show a relationship or object of a verb **6** —used with an infinitive ~

adv **1** : forward **2** : to a state of conscious-ness

toad \'tōd\ n : tailless leaping amphibian

toad•stool \-,stül\ n : mushroom esp. when inedible or poisonous

toady \'tōdē\ n, pl **toad•ies** : one who flat-ters to gain favors **—toady** vb

toast \'tōst\ vb **1** : make (as a slice of bread) crisp and brown **2** : drink in honor of someone or something **3** : warm ~ n **1** : toasted sliced bread **2** : act of drinking in honor of someone **—toast•er** n

to•bac•co \tə'bakō\ n, pl **-cos** : broad-leaved herb or its leaves prepared for smoking or chewing

to•bog•gan \tə'bägən\ n : long flat-bot-tomed light sled ~ vb : coast on a tobog-gan

to•day \tə'dā\ adv **1** : on or for this day **2** : at the present time ~ n : present day or time

tod•dle \'tädʲl\ vb **-dled; -dling** : walk with tottering steps like a young child **—tod-dle** n **—tod•dler** \'tädʲlər\ n

to–do \tə'dü\ n, pl **to–dos** \-'düz\ : dis-turbance or fuss

toe \'tō\ n : one of the 5 end divisions of the foot **—toe•nail** n

tof•fee, tof•fy \'tófē, 'tä-\ n, pl **toffees** or **tof-fies** : candy made of boiled sugar and but-ter

to•ga \'tōgə\ n : loose outer garment of an-cient Rome

to•geth•er \tə'gethər\ adv **1** : in or into one place or group **2** : in or into contact or association **3** : at one time **4** : as a group **—to•geth•er•ness** n

togs \'tägz, 'tógz\ n pl : clothing

toil \'tóil\ vb : work hard and long **—toil** n **—toil•er** n **—toil•some** adj

toi•let \'tóilət\ n **1** : dressing and grooming oneself **2** : bathroom **3** : water basin to urinate and defecate in

to•ken \'tōkən\ n **1** : outward sign or ex-pression of something **2** : small part rep-resenting the whole **3** : piece resembling a coin

told past of TELL

tol•er•a•ble \'tälərəbəl\ adj **1** : capable of being endured **2** : moderately good **—tol-er•a•bly** \-blē\ adv

tol•er•ance \'tälərəns\ n **1** : lack of opposi-tion for beliefs or practices differing from one's own **2** : capacity for enduring **3** : allowable deviation **—tol•er•ant** adj **—tol•er•ant•ly** adv

tol•er•ate \'tälə,rāt\ vb **-at•ed; -at•ing 1** : allow to be or to be done without op-position **2** : endure or resist the action of **—tol•er•a•tion** \,tälə'rāshən\ n

¹toll \'tōl\ n **1** : fee paid for a privilege or service **2** : cost of achievement in loss or suffering **—toll•booth** n **—toll•gate** n

²toll vb **1** : cause the sounding of (a bell) **2** : sound with slow measured strokes ~ n : sound of a tolling bell

tom•a•hawk \'tämə,hók\ n : light ax used as a weapon by American Indians

to•ma•to \tə'mātō, -'mä-\ n, pl **-toes** : tropical American herb or its fruit

tomb \'tüm\ n : house, vault, or grave for burial

tom•boy \'täm,bói\ n : girl who behaves in a manner usu. considered boyish

tomb•stone n : stone marking a grave

tom•cat \'täm,kat\ n : male cat

tome \'tōm\ n : large or weighty book

to•mor•row \tə'märō\ adv : on or for the day after today **—tomorrow** n

tom–tom \'täm,täm\ n : small-headed drum beaten with the hands

ton \'tən\ n : unit of weight equal to 2000 pounds

tone \'tōn\ n **1** : vocal or musical sound **2** : sound of definite pitch **3** : manner of speaking that expresses an emotion or at-titude **4** : color quality **5** : healthy con-dition **6** : general character or quality ~ vb : soften or muffle —often used with down **—ton•al** \-ʲl\ adj **—to•nal•i•ty** \tō-'nalətē\ n

tongs \'täŋz, 'tòŋz\ n pl : grasping device of 2 joined or hinged pieces

tongue \'təŋ\ n **1** : fleshy movable organ of the mouth **2** : language **3** : something long and flat and fastened at one end **—tongued** \'təŋd\ adj **—tongue•less** adj

ton•ic \'tänik\ n : something (as a drug) that invigorates or restores health **—tonic** adj

to•night \tə'nīt\ adv : on this night ~ n : present or coming night

ton•sil \'tänsəl\ n : either of a pair of oval masses in the throat **—ton•sil•lec•to•my** \,tänsə'lektəmē\ n **—ton•sil•li•tis** \-'lītəs\ n

too \'tü\ adv **1** : in addition **2** : excessively

took past of TAKE

tool \'tül\ n : device worked by hand ~ vb : shape or finish with a tool

toot \'tüt\ vb : sound or cause to sound esp. in short blasts **—toot** n

tooth \'tüth\ n, pl **teeth** \'tēth\ **1** : one of the hard structures in the jaws for chewing **2** : one of the projections on the edge of a gear wheel —**tooth•ache** n —**tooth-brush** n —**toothed** \'tütht\ adj —**tooth-less** adj —**tooth•paste** n —**tooth•pick** n

tooth•some \'tüthsəm\ adj 1 : delicious 2 : attractive

¹**top** \'täp\ n 1 : highest part or level of something 2 : lid or covering ~ vb -**pp**-1 : cover with a top 2 : surpass 3 : go over the top of ~ adj : being at the top —**topped** adj

²**top** n : spinning toy

to•paz \'tō,paz\ n : hard gem

top•coat n : lightweight overcoat

top•ic \'täpik\ n : subject for discussion or study

top•i•cal \-ikəl\ adj 1 : relating to or arranged by topics 2 : relating to current or local events —**top•i•cal•ly** adv

top•most \'täp,mōst\ adj : highest of all

top-notch \-'näch\ adj : of the highest quality

to•pog•ra•phy \tə'pägrəfē\ n 1 : art of mapping the physical features of a place 2 : outline of the form of a place —**to•pog-ra•pher** \-fər\ n —**top•o•graph•ic** \tä-pə'grafik\, **top•o•graph•i•cal** \-ikəl\ adj

top•ple \'täpəl\ vb -**pled**; -**pling** : fall or cause to fall

top•sy-tur•vy \,täpsē'tərvē\ adv or adj 1 : upside down 2 : in utter confusion

torch \'tórch\ n : flaming light —**torch-bear•er** n —**torch•light** n

tore past of TEAR

tor•ment \'tór,ment\ n : extreme pain or anguish or a source of this ~ vb 1 : cause severe anguish to 2 : harass —**tor•men-tor** \-ər\ n

torn past part of TEAR

tor•na•do \tór'nādō\ n, pl -**does** or -**dos** : violent destructive whirling wind

tor•pe•do \tór'pēdō\ n, pl -**does** : self-propelled explosive submarine missile ~ vb : hit with a torpedo

tor•pid \'tórpəd\ adj 1 : having lost motion or the power of exertion 2 : lacking vigor —**tor•pid•i•ty** \tór'pidətē\ n

tor•por \'tórpər\ n : extreme sluggishness or lethargy

torque \'tórk\ n : turning force

tor•rent \'tórənt\ n 1 : rushing stream 2 : tumultuous outburst —**tor•ren•tial** \tó-'renchəl, tə-\ adj

tor•rid \'tórəd\ adj 1 : parched with heat 2 : impassioned

tor•sion \'tórshən\ n : a twisting or being twisted —**tor•sion•al** \'tórshənəl\ adj —**tor•sion•al•ly** adv

tor•so \'tórsō\ n, pl -**sos** or -**si** \-,sē\ : trunk of the human body

tor•til•la \tór'tēyə\ n : round flat cornmeal or wheat flour bread

tor•toise \'tórtəs\ n : land turtle

tor•tu•ous \'tórchəwəs\ adj 1 : winding 2 : tricky

tor•ture \'tórchər\ n 1 : use of pain to punish or force 2 : agony ~ vb -**tured**; -**tur•ing** : inflict torture on —**tor•tur•er** n

toss \'tós, 'täs\ vb 1 : move to and fro or up and down violently 2 : throw with a quick light motion 3 : move restlessly —**toss** n

toss-up n 1 : a deciding by flipping a coin 2 : even chance

tot \'tät\ n : small child

to•tal \'tōt³l\ n : entire amount ~ vb -**taled** or -**talled**; -**tal•ing** or -**tal•ling** 1 : add up 2 : amount to —**total** adj —**to•tal•ly** adv

to•tal•i•tar•i•an \tō,talə'terēən\ adj : relating to a political system in which the government has complete control over the people —**totalitarian** n —**to•tal•i•tar•i•an-ism** \-,ēə,nizəm\ n

to•tal•i•ty \tō'talətē\ n, pl -**ties** : whole amount or entirety

tote \'tōt\ vb **tot•ed**; **tot•ing** : carry

to•tem \'tōtəm\ n : often carved figure used as a family or tribe emblem

tot•ter \'tätər\ vb 1 : sway as if about to fall 2 : stagger

touch \'təch\ vb 1 : make contact with so as to feel 2 : be or cause to be in contact 3 : take into the hands or mouth 4 : treat or mention a subject 5 : relate or concern 6 : move to sympathetic feeling ~ n 1 : light stroke 2 : act or fact of touching or being touched 3 : sense of feeling 4 : trace 5 : state of being in contact —**touch up** vb : improve with minor changes

touch•down \'təch,daùn\ n : scoring of 6 points in football

touch•stone n : test or criterion of genuineness or quality

touchy \'təchē\ adj **touch•i•er**; -**est** 1 : easily offended 2 : requiring tact

tough \'təf\ adj 1 : strong but elastic 2 : not easily chewed 3 : severe or disciplined 4 : stubborn 5 : rowdy —**tough•ly** adv —**tough•ness** n

tough•en \'təfən\ vb : make or become tough

tou•pee \tü'pā\ n : small wig for a bald spot

tour \'tùr\ n 1 : period of time spent at work or on an assignment 2 : journey with a return to the starting point ~ vb : travel over to see the sights —**tour•ist** \'tùrist\ n

tour•na•ment \'tùrnəmənt, 'tər-\ n 1 : medieval jousting competition 2 : championship series of games

tour•ney \-nē\ n, pl -**neys** : tournament

tour•ni•quet \'tùrnikət, 'tər-\ n : tight bandage for stopping blood flow

tou•sle \'taùzəl\ vb -**sled**; -**sling** : dishevel (as someone's hair)

tout \'taùt, 'tüt\ vb : praise or publicize loudly

tow \'tō\ vb : pull along behind —**tow** n

to•ward, to•wards \'tōrd, tə'wórd, 'tórdz, tə'wórdz\ prep 1 : in the direction of 2 : with respect to 3 : in part payment on

tow•el \'taùəl\ n : absorbent cloth or paper for wiping or drying

tow•er \'taùər\ n 1 : tall structure ~ vb : rise to a great height —**tow•ered** \'taùərd\ adj —**tow•er•ing** adj

tow•head \'tō,hed\ n : person having whitish blond hair —**tow•head•ed** \-,hedəd\ adj

town \'taùn\ n 1 : small residential area 2 : city —**towns•peo•ple** \'taùnz,pēpəl\ n pl

town•ship \'taùn,ship\ n 1 : unit of local government 2 : 36 square miles of U.S. public land

tox•ic \'täksik\ adj : poisonous —**tox•ic•i•ty** \täk'sisətē\ n

tox•in \'täksən\ n : poison produced by an organism

toy \'tói\ n : something for a child to play with ~ vb 1 : amuse oneself or play with something ~ adj 1 : designed as a toy 2 : very small

¹**trace** \'trās\ vb **traced**; **trac•ing** 1 : mark over the lines of (a drawing) 2 : follow the trail or the development of ~ n 1 : track 2 : tiny amount or residue —**trace-able** adj —**trac•er** n

²**trace** n : line of a harness

tra•chea \'trākēə\ n, pl -**che•ae** \-kē,ē\ : windpipe —**tra•che•al** \-kēəl\ adj

track \'trak\ n 1 : trail left by wheels or footprints 2 : racing course 3 : train rails 4 : awareness of a progression 5 : looped belts propelling a vehicle ~ vb 1 : follow the trail of 2 : make tracks on —**track•er** n

track-and-field adj : relating to athletic contests of running, jumping, and throwing events

¹**tract** \'trakt\ n 1 : stretch of land 2 : system of body organs

²**tract** n : pamphlet of propaganda

trac•ta•ble \'traktəbəl\ adj : easily controlled

trac•tion \'trakshən\ n : gripping power to permit movement —**trac•tion•al** \-shə-nəl\ adj —**trac•tive** \traktiv\ adj

trac•tor \'traktər\ n 1 : farm vehicle used esp. for pulling 2 : truck for hauling a trailer

trade \'trād\ n 1 : one's regular business 2 : occupation requiring skill 3 : the buying and selling of goods 4 : act of trading ~ vb **trad•ed**; **trad•ing** 1 : give in exchange for something 2 : buy and sell goods 3 : be a regular customer —**trades•peo•ple** \'trādz,pēpəl\ n pl

trade-in \'trād,in\ n : an item traded to a merchant at the time of a purchase

trade•mark \'trād,märk\ n : word or mark identifying a manufacturer —**trademark** vb

trades•man \'trādzmən\ n : shopkeeper

tra•di•tion \trə'dishən\ n : belief or custom passed from generation to generation —**tra•di•tion•al** \-'dishənəl\ adj —**tra•di-tion•al•ly** adv

tra•duce \trə'düs, -'dyüs\ vb -**duced**; -**duc-ing** : lower the reputation of —**tra•duc-er** n

traf•fic \'trafik\ n 1 : business dealings 2 : movement along a route ~ vb : do business —**traf•fick•er** n —**traffic light** n

trag•e•dy \'trajədē\ n, pl -**dies** 1 : serious drama describing a conflict and having a sad end 2 : disastrous event

trag•ic \'trajik\ adj : being a tragedy —**trag-i•cal•ly** adv

trail \'trāl\ vb 1 : hang down and drag along the ground 2 : draw along behind 3 : follow the track of 4 : dwindle ~ n 1 : something that trails 2 : path or evidence left by something

trail•er \'trālər\ n 1 : vehicle intended to be hauled 2 : dwelling designed to be towed to a site

train \'trān\ n 1 : trailing part of a gown 2 : retinue or procession 3 : connected series 4 : group of linked railroad cars ~ vb 1 : cause to grow as desired 2 : make or become prepared or skilled 3 : point —**train•ee** n —**train•er** n —**train•load** n

traipse \'trāps\ vb **traipsed**; **traips•ing** : walk

trait \'trāt\ n : distinguishing quality

trai•tor \'trātər\ n : one who betrays a trust or commits treason —**trai•tor•ous** adj

tra•jec•to•ry \trə'jektərē\ n, pl -**ries** : path of something moving through air or space

tram•mel \'traməl\ vb -**meled** or -**melled**; -**mel•ing** or -**mel•ling** : impede —**tram-mel** n

tramp \'tramp\ vb 1 : walk or hike 2 : tread on ~ n 1 : beggar or vagrant

tram•ple \'trampəl\ vb -**pled**; -**pling** : walk or step on so as to bruise or crush —**trample** n —**tram•pler** \-plər\ n

tram•po•line \'trampə'lēn, 'trampə,-\ n : resilient sheet or web supported by springs and used for bouncing —**tram-po•lin•ist** \-ist\ n

trance \'trans\ n 1 : sleeplike condition 2 : state of mystical absorption

tran•quil \'traŋkwəl, 'tran-\ adj : quiet and undisturbed —**tran•quil•ize** \-kwə,līz\ vb —**tran•quil•iz•er** n —**tran•quil•li•ty** or **tran•quil•i•ty** \tran'kwilətē, traŋ-\ n —**tran•quil•ly** adv

trans•act \trans'akt, tranz-\ vb : conduct (business)

trans•ac•tion \-'akshən\ n 1 : business deal 2 pl : records of proceedings

tran•scend \trans'end\ vb : rise above or surpass —**tran•scen•dent** \-'endənt\ adj —**tran•scen•den•tal** \,trans,en'dent³l, -ən-\ adj

tran•scribe \trans'krīb\ vb -**scribed**; -**scrib-ing** : make a copy, arrangement, or recording of —**tran•scrip•tion** \trans-'kripshən\ n

tran•script \'trans,kript\ n : official copy

tran•sept \'trans,ept\ n : part of a church that crosses the nave at right angles

trans•fer \trans'fər, 'trans,fər\ vb -**rr**-1 : move from one person, place, or situation to another 2 : convey ownership of 3 : print or copy by contact 4 : change to another vehicle or transportation line ~ \'trans,fər\ n 1 : act or process of transferring 2 : one that transfers or is transferred 3 : ticket permitting one to transfer —**trans•fer•able** \trans'fərəbəl\ adj —**trans•fer•al** \-əl\ n —**trans•fer•ence** \-əns\ n

trans•fig•ure \trans'figyər\ vb -**ured**; -**ur-ing** 1 : change the form or appearance of 2 : glorify —**trans•fig•u•ra•tion** \trans-,figyə'rāshən\ n

trans•fix \trans'fiks\ vb 1 : pierce through 2 : hold motionless

trans•form \-'fórm\ vb 1 : change in structure, appearance, or character 2 : change (an electric current) in potential or type —**trans•for•ma•tion** \,transfər'māshən\ n —**trans•form•er** \trans'fórmər\ n

trans•fuse \trans'fyüz\ vb -**fused**; -**fus•ing** 1 : diffuse into or through 2 : transfer (as blood) into a vein —**trans•fu•sion** \-'fyüzhən\ n

trans•gress \trans'gres, tranz-\ vb : sin —**trans•gres•sion** \-'greshən\ n —**trans-gres•sor** \-'gresər\ n

tran•sient \'tranchənt\ adj : not lasting or staying long —**transient** n —**tran•sient-ly** adv

tran•sis•tor \tranz'istər, trans-\ n : small electronic device used in electronic equipment —**tran•sis•tor•ize** \-tə,rīz\ vb

tran•sit \'transət, 'tranz-\ n 1 : movement over, across, or through 2 : local and esp. public transportation 3 : surveyor's instrument

tran•si•tion \trans'ishən, tranz-\ n : passage from one state, stage, or subject to another —**tran•si•tion•al** \-'ishənəl\ adj

tran•si•to•ry \'transə,tōrē, 'tranz-\ adj : of brief duration

trans•late \trans'lāt, tranz-\ vb -**lat•ed**; -**lat-ing** : change into another language —**trans•lat•able** adj —**trans•la•tion** \-'lā-shən\ n —**trans•la•tor** \-'lātər\ n

trans•lu•cent \trans'lüsᵊnt, tranz-\ adj : not transparent but clear enough to allow light to pass through —**trans•lu•cence** \-ᵊns\ n —**trans•lu•cen•cy** \-ᵊnsē\ n —**trans•lu•cent•ly** adv

trans•mis•sion \-'mishən\ n 1 : act or process of transmitting 2 : system of gears between a car engine and drive wheels

trans•mit \-'mit\ vb -**tt**-1 : transfer from one person or place to another 2 : pass on by inheritance 3 : broadcast —**trans•mis•si-ble** \-'misəbəl\ adj —**trans•mit•ta•ble** \-'mitəbəl\ adj —**trans•mit•tal** \-'mitᵊl\ n —**trans•mit•ter** n

tran•som \'transəm\ n : often hinged window above a door

trans•par•ent \trans'parənt\ adj 1 : clear enough to see through 2 : obvious —**trans•par•en•cy** \-ənsē\ n —**trans•par-ent•ly** adv

tran•spire \trans'pīr\ vb -**spired**; -**spir•ing** : take place —**tran•spi•ra•tion** \,trans-pə'rāshən\ n

trans•plant \trans'plant\ vb 1 : dig up and move to another place 2 : transfer from one body part or person to another —**transplant** \'trans,-\ n —**trans•plan•ta-tion** \,trans,plan'tāshən\ n

trans•port \trans'pōrt\ vb 1 : carry or deliver to another place 2 : carry away by emotion ~ \'trans,-\ n 1 : act of transporting 2 : rapture 3 : ship or plane for carrying troops or supplies —**trans•por•ta•tion** \,transpər'tāshən\ n —**trans•port•er** n

trans•pose \trans'pōz\ vb -**posed**; -**pos•ing** : change the position, sequence, or key —**trans•po•si•tion** \,transpə'zishən\ n

trans•ship \tran'ship, trans-\ vb : transfer from one mode of transportation to another —**trans•ship•ment** n

trans•verse \trans'vərs, tranz-\ adj : lying across —**trans•verse** \'trans,vərs, 'tranz-\ n —**trans•verse•ly** adv

trap \'trap\ n 1 : device for catching animals 2 : something by which one is caught unawares 3 : device to allow one thing to pass through while keeping other things out ~ vb -**pp**- : catch in a trap —**trap-per** n

trap•door n : door in a floor or roof

tra•peze \tra'pēz\ n : suspended bar used by acrobats

trap•e•zoid \'trapə,zóid\ n : plane 4-sided figure with 2 parallel sides —**trap•e•zoi-dal** \,trapə'zóidᵊl\ adj

trap•pings \'trapiŋz\ n pl 1 : ornamental covering 2 : outward decoration or dress

trash \'trash\ n : something that is no good —**trashy** adj

trau•ma \'traùmə, 'tró-\ n : bodily or mental injury —**trau•mat•ic** \trə'matik, tró-, traù-\ adj

tra•vail \trə'vāl, 'trav,āl\ n : painful work or exertion ~ vb : labor hard

trav•el \'travəl\ vb -**eled** or -**elled**; -**el•ing** or -**el•ling** 1 : take a trip or tour 2 : move or be carried from point to point ~ n : journey —often pl. —**trav•el•er, trav-el•ler** n

tra•verse \trə'vərs, tra'vərs, 'travərs\ vb -**versed**; -**vers•ing** : go or extend across —**tra•verse** \'travers\ n

trav•es•ty \'travəstē\ n, pl -**ties** : imitation that makes crude fun of something —**travesty** vb

trawl \'tról\ vb : fish or catch with a trawl ~ n : large cone-shaped net —**trawl•er** n

tray \'trā\ n : shallow flat-bottomed receptacle for holding or carrying something

treach•er•ous \'trechərəs\ adj : disloyal or dangerous —**treach•er•ous•ly** adv

treach•ery \'trechərē\ n, pl -**er•ies** : betrayal of a trust

tread \'tred\ vb **trod** \'träd; **trod•den** \'trädᵊn\ or **trod**; **tread•ing** 1 : step on or over 2 : walk 3 : press or crush with the feet ~ n 1 : way of walking 2 : sound made in walking 3 : part on which a thing runs

trea•dle \'tredᵊl\ n : foot pedal operating a machine —**treadle** vb

tread•mill n 1 : mill worked by walking persons or animals 2 : wearisome routine

trea•son \'trēzᵊn\ n : attempt to overthrow the government —**trea•son•able** \'trēz-ᵊnəbəl\ adj —**trea•son•ous** \-ᵊnəs\ adj

trea•sure \'trezhər, 'trāzh-\ n 1 : wealth stored up 2 : something of great value ~ vb -**sured**; -**sur•ing** : keep as precious

trea•sur•er \'trezhərər, 'trāzh-\ n : officer who handles funds

trea•sury \'trezhərē, 'trāzh-\ n, pl -**sur•ies** : place or office for keeping and distributing funds

treat \'trēt\ vb 1 : have as a topic 2 : pay for the food or entertainment of 3 : act toward or regard in a certain way 4 : give medical care to ~ n 1 : food or entertainment paid for by another 2 : something special and enjoyable —**treat•ment** \-mənt\ n

trea•tise \'trētəs\ n : systematic written exposition or argument

trea•ty \'trētē\ n, pl -**ties** : agreement between governments

tre•ble \'trebəl\ n 1 : highest part in music 2 : upper half of the musical range ~ adj : triple in number or amount ~ vb -**bled**; -**bling** : make triple —**tre•bly** adv

tree \'trē\ n : tall woody plant ~ vb **treed**; **tree•ing** : force up a tree —**tree•less** adj

trek \'trek\ n : difficult trip ~ vb -**kk**- : make a trek

trel•lis \'treləs\ n : structure of crossed strips

trem•ble \'trembəl\ vb -**bled**; -**bling** 1 : shake from fear or cold 2 : move or sound as if shaken

tre•men•dous \tri'mendəs\ adj : amazingly large, powerful, or excellent —**tre•men-dous•ly** adv

trem•or \'tremər\ n : a trembling

trem•u•lous \'tremyələs\ adj : trembling or quaking

trench \'trench\ n : long narrow cut in land

tren•chant \'trenchənt\ adj : sharply perceptive

trend \'trend\ n : prevailing tendency, direction, or style ~ vb : move in a particular direction —**trendy** \'trendē\ adj

trep•i•da•tion \,trepə'dāshən\ n : nervous apprehension

tres•pass \'trespəs, -,pas\ n 1 : sin 2 : unauthorized entry onto someone's property ~ vb 1 : sin 2 : enter illegally —**tres•pass•er** n

tress \'tres\ n : long lock of hair

tres•tle \'tresᵊl\ n 1 : support with a horizontal piece and spreading legs **2** : framework bridge

tri•ad \'trī,ad, -əd\ *n* : union of 3

tri•age \trē'äzh, 'trē,äzh\ *n* : system of dealing with cases (as patients) according to priority guidelines intended to maximize success

tri•al \'trīəl\ *n* **1** : hearing and judgment of a matter in court **2** : source of great annoyance **3** : test use or experimental effort —**trial** *adj*

tri•an•gle \'trī,aŋgəl\ *n* : plane figure with 3 sides and 3 angles —**tri•an•gu•lar** \trī-'aŋgyələr\ *adj*

tribe \'trīb\ *n* : social group of numerous families —**trib•al** \'trībəl\ *adj* —**tribes•man** \'trībzmən\ *n*

trib•u•la•tion \,tribyə'lāshən\ *n* : suffering from oppression

tri•bu•nal \trī'byünəl, tri-\ *n* **1** : court **2** : something that decides

trib•u•tary \'tribyə,terē\ *n, pl* **-tar•ies** : stream that flows into a river or lake

trib•ute \'trib,yüt\ *n* **1** : payment to acknowledge submission **2** : tax **3** : gift or act showing respect

trick \'trik\ *n* **1** : scheme to deceive **2** : prank **3** : deceptive or ingenious feat **4** : mannerism **5** : knack **6** : tour of duty ~ *vb* : deceive by cunning —**trick•ery** \-ərē\ *n* —**trick•ster** \-stər\ *n*

trick•le \'trikəl\ *vb* **-led; -ling** : run in drops or a thin stream —**trickle** *n*

tricky \'trikē\ *adj* **trick•i•er; -est 1** : inclined to trickery **2** : requiring skill or caution

tri•cy•cle \'trī,sikəl\ *n* : 3-wheeled bicycle

tri•dent \'trīdənt\ *n* : 3-pronged spear

tri•en•ni•al \'trī'enēəl\ *adj* : lasting, occurring, or done every 3 years —**triennial** *n*

tri•fle \'trīfəl\ *n* : something of little value or importance ~ *vb* **-fled; -fling 1** : speak or act in a playful or flirting way **2** : toy —**tri•fler** *n*

tri•fling \'trīfliŋ\ *adj* : trivial

trig•ger \'trigər\ *n* : finger-piece of a firearm lock that fires the gun ~ *vb* : set into motion —**trigger** *adj* —**trig•gered** \-ərd\ *adj*

trig•o•nom•e•try \,trigə'nämətrē\ *n* : mathematics dealing with triangular measurement —**trig•o•no•met•ric** \-nə-'metrik\ *adj*

trill \'tril\ *n* **1** : rapid alternation between 2 adjacent tones **2** : rapid vibration in speaking ~ *vb* : utter in or with a trill

tril•lion \'trilyən\ *n* : 1000 billions —**trillion** *adj* —**tril•lionth** \-yənth\ *adj or n*

tril•o•gy \'triləjē\ *n, pl* **-gies** : 3-part literary or musical composition

trim \'trim\ *vb* **-mm- 1** : decorate **2** : make neat or reduce by cutting ~ *adj* **-mm-** : neat and compact ~ *n* **1** : state or condition **2** : ornaments —**trim•ly** *adv* —**trim•mer** *n*

trim•ming \'trimiŋ\ *n* : something that ornaments or completes

Trin•i•ty \'trinətē\ *n* : divine unity of Father, Son, and Holy Spirit

trin•ket \'triŋkət\ *n* : small ornament

trio \'trēō\ *n, pl* **tri•os 1** : music for 3 performers **2** : group of 3

trip \'trip\ *vb* **-pp- 1** : step lightly **2** : stumble or cause to stumble **3** : make or cause to make a mistake **4** : release (as a spring or switch) ~ *n* **1** : journey **2** : stumble **3** : drug-induced experience

tri•par•tite \trī'pär,tīt\ *adj* : having 3 parts or parties

tripe \'trīp\ *n* **1** : animal's stomach used as food **2** : trash

tri•ple \'tripəl\ *vb* **-pled; -pling** : make 3 times as great ~ *n* : group of 3 ~ *adj* **1** : having 3 units **2** : being 3 times as great or as many

trip•let \'triplət\ *n* **1** : group of 3 **2** : one of 3 offspring born together

trip•li•cate \'triplikət\ *adj* : made in 3 identical copies ~ *n* : one of 3 copies

tri•pod \'trī,päd\ *n* : a stand with 3 legs —**tripod, tri•po•dal** \'tripəd°l, 'trī,päd-\ *adj*

tri•sect \'trī,sekt, trī'-\ *vb* : divide into 3 usu. equal parts —**tri•sec•tion** \'trī,sekshən\ *n*

trite \'trīt\ *adj* **trit•er; trit•est** : commonplace

tri•umph \'trīəmf\ *n, pl* **-umphs** : victory or great success ~ *vb* : obtain or celebrate victory —**tri•um•phal** \trī'əmfəl\ *adj* —**tri•um•phant** \-fənt\ *adj* —**tri•um•phant•ly** *adv*

tri•um•vi•rate \trī'əmvərət\ *n* : ruling body of 3 persons

triv•et \'trivət\ *n* **1** : 3-legged stand **2** : stand to hold a hot dish

triv•ia \'trivēə\ *n sing or pl* : unimportant details

triv•i•al \'trivēəl\ *adj* : of little importance —**triv•i•al•i•ty** \,trivē'alətē\ *n*

trod *past of* TREAD

trodden *past part of* TREAD

troll \'trōl\ *n* : dwarf or giant of folklore inhabiting caves or hills

trol•ley \'trälē\ *n, pl* **-leys** : streetcar run by overhead electric wires

trol•lop \'träləp\ *n* : untidy or immoral woman

trom•bone \träm'bōn, 'träm,-\ *n* : musical instrument with a long sliding tube —**trom•bon•ist** \-'bōnist, -,bō-\ *n*

troop \'trüp\ *n* **1** : cavalry unit **2** *pl* : soldiers **3** : collection of people or things ~ *vb* : move or gather in crowds

troop•er \'trüpər\ *n* **1** : cavalry soldier **2** : police officer on horseback or state police officer

tro•phy \'trōfē\ *n, pl* **-phies** : prize gained by a victory

trop•ic \'träpik\ *n* **1** : either of the 2 parallels of latitude one 23½ degrees north of the equator (**tropic of Cancer** \-'kansər\) and one 23½ degrees south of the equator (**tropic of Cap•ri•corn** \-'kaprə,kórn\) **2** *pl* : region lying between the tropics —**tropic, trop•i•cal** \-ikəl\ *adj*

trot \'trät\ *n* : moderately fast gait esp. of a horse with diagonally paired legs moving together ~ *vb* **-tt-** : go at a trot —**trot•ter** *n*

troth \'träth, 'trōth, 'tróth\ *n* **1** : pledged faithfulness **2** : betrothal

trou•ba•dour \'trübə,dōr\ *n* : medieval lyric poet

trou•ble \'trəbəl\ *vb* **-bled; -bling 1** : disturb **2** : afflict **3** : make an effort ~ *n* **1** : cause of mental or physical distress **2** : effort —**trou•ble•mak•er** *n* —**trou•ble•some** *adj* —**trou•ble•some•ly** *adv*

trough \'tróf\ *n, pl* **troughs** \'tröfs, 'trövz\ **1** : narrow container for animal feed or water **2** : long channel or depression (as between waves)

trounce \'traúns\ *vb* **trounced; trounc•ing** : thrash, punish, or defeat severely

troupe \'trüp\ *n* : group of stage performers —**troup•er** *n*

trou•sers \'traúzərz\ *n pl* : long pants —**trouser** *adj*

trous•seau \'trü,sō, trü'sō\ *n, pl* **-seaux** \-sōz, -'sōz\ *or* **-seaus** : bride's collection of clothing and personal items

trout \'traút\ *n, pl* **trout** : freshwater food and game fish

trow•el \'traúəl\ *n* **1** : tool for spreading or smoothing **2** : garden scoop —**trowel** *vb*

troy \'trói\ *n* : system of weights based on a pound of 12 ounces

tru•ant \'trüənt\ *n* : student absent from school without permission —**tru•an•cy** \-ənsē\ *n* —**truant** *adj*

truce \'trüs\ *n* : agreement to halt fighting

truck \'trək\ *n* **1** : wheeled frame for moving heavy objects **2** : automotive vehicle for transporting heavy loads ~ *vb* : transport on a truck —**truck•er** *n* —**truck•load** *n*

truck•le \'trəkəl\ *vb* **-led; -ling** : yield slavishly to another

tru•cu•lent \'trəkyələnt\ *adj* : aggressively self-assertive —**tru•cu•lence** \-ləns\ *n* —**tru•cu•len•cy** \-lənsē\ *n* —**tru•cu•lent•ly** *adv*

trudge \'trəj\ *vb* **trudged; trudg•ing** : walk or march steadily and with difficulty

true \'trü\ *adj* **tru•er; tru•est 1** : loyal **2** : in agreement with fact or reality **3** : genuine ~ *adv* **1** : truthfully **2** : accurately ~ *vb* **trued; tru•ing** : make balanced or even —**tru•ly** *adv*

true–blue *adj* : loyal

truf•fle \'trəfəl\ *n* **1** : edible fruit of an underground fungus **2** : ball-shaped chocolate candy

tru•ism \'trü,izəm\ *n* : obvious truth

trump \'trəmp\ *n* : card of a designated suit any of whose cards will win over other cards ~ *vb* : take with a trump

trumped–up \'trəmpt'əp\ *adj* : made-up

trum•pet \'trəmpət\ *n* : tubular brass wind instrument with a flaring end ~ *vb* **1** : blow a trumpet **2** : proclaim loudly —**trum•pet•er** *n*

trun•cate \'trəŋ,kāt, 'trən-\ *vb* **-cat•ed; -cat•ing** : cut short —**trun•ca•tion** \,trəŋ-'kāshən\ *n*

trun•dle \'trəndᵊl\ *vb* **-dled; -dling** : roll along

trunk \'trəŋk\ *n* **1** : main part (as of a body or tree) **2** : long muscular nose of an elephant **3** : storage chest **4** : storage space in a car **5** *pl* : shorts

truss \'trəs\ *vb* : bind tightly ~ *n* **1** : set of structural parts forming a framework **2** : appliance worn to hold a hernia in place

trust \'trəst\ *n* **1** : reliance on another **2** : assured hope **3** : credit **4** : property held or managed in behalf of another **5** : combination of firms that reduces competition **6** : something entrusted to another's care **7** : custody ~ *vb* **1** : depend **2** : hope **3** : entrust **4** : have faith in —**trust•ful** \-fəl\ *adj* —**trust•ful•ly** *adv* —**trust•ful•ness** *n* —**trust•worth•i•ness** *n* —**trust•wor•thy** *adj*

trust•ee \,trəs'tē\ *n* : person holding property in trust —**trust•ee•ship** *n*

trusty \'trəstē\ *adj* **trust•i•er; -est** : dependable

truth \'trüth\ *n, pl* **truths** \'trüthz, 'trüths\ **1** : real state of things **2** : true or accepted statement **3** : agreement with fact or re-

ality —**truth•ful** \-fəl\ *adj* —**truth•ful•ly** *adv* —**truth•ful•ness** *n*

try \'trī\ *vb* **tried; try•ing 1** : conduct the trial of **2** : put to a test **3** : strain **4** : make an effort at ~ *n, pl* **tries** : act of trying

try•out *n* : competitive test of performance esp. for athletes or actors —**try out** *vb*

tryst \'trist, 'trīst\ *n* : secret rendezvous of lovers

tsar \'zär, 'tsär, 'sär\ *var of* CZAR

T–shirt \'tē,shərt\ *n* : collarless pullover shirt with short sleeves

tub \'təb\ *n* **1** : wide bucketlike vessel **2** : bathtub

tu•ba \'tübə, 'tyü-\ *n* : large low-pitched brass wind instument

tube \'tüb, 'tyüb\ *n* **1** : hollow cylinder **2** : round container from which a substance can be squeezed **3** : airtight circular tube of rubber inside a tire **4** : electronic device consisting of a sealed usu. glass container with electrodes inside —**tubed** \'tübd, 'tyübd\ *adj* —**tube•less** *adj*

tu•ber \'tübər, 'tyü-\ *n* : fleshy underground growth (as of a potato) —**tu•ber•ous** \-rəs\ *adj*

tu•ber•cu•lo•sis \tu̇,bərkyə'lōsəs, tyu̇-\ *n, pl* **-lo•ses** \-,sēz\ : bacterial disease esp. of the lungs —**tu•ber•cu•lar** \-'bərkyələr\ *adj* —**tu•ber•cu•lous** \-ləs\ *adj*

tub•ing \'tübiŋ, 'tyü-\ *n* : series or arrangement of tubes

tu•bu•lar \'tübyələr, 'tyü-\ *adj* : of or like a tube

tuck \'tək\ *vb* **1** : pull up into a fold **2** : put into a snug often concealing place **3** : make snug in bed —**with** *in* ~ *n* : fold in a cloth

tuck•er \'təkər\ *vb* : fatigue

Tues•day \'tüzdā, 'tyüz-, -dē\ *n* : 3d day of the week

tuft \'təft\ *n* : clump (as of hair or feathers) —**tuft•ed** \'təftəd\ *adj*

tug \'təg\ *vb* **-gg- 1** : pull hard **2** : move by pulling ~ *n* **1** : act of tugging **2** : tugboat

tug•boat *n* : boat for towing or pushing ships through a harbor

tug–of–war \,təgə'wör\ *n, pl* **tugs–of–war** : pulling contest between 2 teams

tu•ition \tu̇'ishən, tyü-\ *n* : cost of instruction

tu•lip \'tüləp, 'tyü-\ *n* : herb with cup-shaped flowers

tum•ble \'təmbəl\ *vb* **-bled; -bling 1** : perform gymnastic feats of rolling and turning **2** : fall or cause to fall suddenly **3** : toss ~ *n* : act of tumbling

tum•bler \'təmblər\ *n* **1** : acrobat **2** : drinking glass **3** : obstruction in a lock that can be moved (as by a key)

tu•mid \'tüməd, 'tyü-\ *adj* : turgid

tum•my \'təmē\ *n, pl* **-mies** : belly

tu•mor \'tümər 'tyü-\ *n* : abnormal and useless growth of tissue —**tu•mor•ous** *adj*

tu•mult \'tü,məlt 'tyü-\ *n* **1** : uproar **2** : violent agitation of mind or feelings —**tu•mul•tu•ous** \tu̇'məlchəwəs, tyü-\ *adj*

tun \'tən\ *n* : large cask

tu•na \'tünə 'tyü-\ *n, pl* **-na** *or* **-nas** : large sea food fish

tun•dra \'təndrə\ *n* : treeless arctic plain

tune \'tün, 'tyün\ *n* **1** : melody **2** : correct musical pitch **3** : harmonious relationship ~ *vb* **tuned; tun•ing 1** : bring or come into harmony **2** : adjust in musical pitch **3** : adjust a receiver so as to receive a broadcast **4** : put in first-class working order —**tun•able** *adj* —**tune•ful** \-fəl\ *adj* —**tun•er** *n*

tung•sten \'təŋstən\ *n* : metallic element used for electrical purposes and in hardening alloys (as steel)

tu•nic \'tünik, 'tyü-\ *n* **1** : ancient knee-length garment **2** : hip-length blouse or jacket

tun•nel \'tənᵊl\ *n* : underground passageway ~ *vb* **-neled** *or* **-nelled; -nel•ing** *or* **-nel•ling** : make a tunnel through or under something

tur•ban \'tərbən\ *n* : wound headdress worn esp. by Muslims

tur•bid \'tərbəd\ *adj* **1** : dark with stirred-up sediment **2** : confused —**tur•bid•i•ty** \,tər'bidətē\ *n*

tur•bine \'tərbən, -,bīn\ *n* : engine turned by the force of gas or water on fan blades

tur•bo•jet \'tərbō,jet\ *n* : airplane powered by a jet engine having a turbine-driven air compressor or the engine itself

tur•bo•prop \'tərbō,präp\ *n* : airplane powered by a propeller turned by a jet engine-driven turbine

tur•bu•lent \'tərbyələnt\ *adj* **1** : causing violence or disturbance **2** : marked by agitation or tumult —**tur•bu•lence** \-ləns\ *n* —**tur•bu•lent•ly** *adv*

tu•reen \tə'rēn, tyü-\ *n* : deep bowl for serving soup

turf \'tərf\ *n* : upper layer of soil bound by grass and roots

tur•gid \'tərjəd\ *adj* **1** : swollen **2** : too highly embellished in style —**tur•gid•i•ty** \,tər'jidətē\ *n*

tur•key \'tərkē\ *n, pl* **-keys** : large American bird raised for food

tur•moil \'tər,mói l\ *n* : extremely agitated condition

turn \'tərn\ *vb* **1** : move or cause to move around an axis **2** : twist (a mechanical part) to operate **3** : wrench **4** : cause to face or move in a different direction **5** : reverse the sides or surfaces of **6** : upset **7** : go around **8** : become or cause to become **9** : seek aid from a source ~ *n* **1** : act or instance of turning **2** : change **3** : place at which something turns **4** : place, time, or opportunity to do something in order —**turn•er** *n* —**turn down** *vb* : decline to accept —**turn in** *vb* **1** : deliver or report to authorities **2** : go to bed —**turn off** *vb* : stop the functioning of —**turn out** *vb* **1** : expel **2** : produce **3** : come together **4** : prove to be in the end —**turn over** *vb* : transfer —**turn up** *vb* **1** : discover or appear **2** : happen unexpectedly

turn•coat *n* : traitor

tur•nip \'tərnəp\ *n* : edible root of an herb

turn•out \'tərn,aút\ *n* **1** : gathering of people for a special purpose **2** : size of a gathering

turn•over *n* **1** : upset or reversal **2** : filled pastry **3** : volume of business **4** : movement (as of goods or people) into, through, and out of a place

turn•pike \'tərn,pīk\ *n* : expressway on which tolls are charged

turn•stile \-,stīl\ *n* : post with arms pivoted on the top that allows people to pass one by one

turn•ta•ble *n* : platform that turns a phonograph record

tur•pen•tine \'tərpən,tīn\ *n* : oil distilled from pine-tree resin and used as a solvent

tur•pi•tude \'tərpə,tüd, -,tyüd\ *n* : inherent baseness

tur•quoise \'tər,kóiz, -,kwóiz\ *n* : blue or greenish gray gemstone

tur•ret \'tərət\ *n* **1** : little tower on a building **2** : revolving tool holder or gun housing

tur•tle \'tərtᵊl\ *n* : reptile with the trunk enclosed in a bony shell

tur•tle•dove *n* : wild pigeon

tur•tle•neck *n* : high close-fitting collar that can be turned over or a sweater or shirt with this collar

tusk \'təsk\ *n* : long protruding tooth (as of an elephant) —**tusked** \'təskt\ *adj*

tus•sle \'təsəl\ *n or vb* : struggle

tu•te•lage \'tütᵊlij, 'tyüt-\ *n* **1** : act of protecting **2** : instruction esp. of an individual

tu•tor \'tütər, 'tyü-\ *n* : private teacher ~ *vb* : teach usu. individually

tux•e•do \,tək'sēdō\ *n, pl* **-dos** *or* **-does** : semiformal evening clothes for a man

TV \'tē'vē, 'tē,vē\ *n* : television

twain \'twān\ *n* : two

twang \'twaŋ\ *n* **1** : harsh sound like that of a plucked bowstring **2** : nasal speech or resonance ~ *vb* : sound or speak with a twang

tweak \'twēk\ *vb* : pinch and pull playfully —**tweak** *n*

tweed \'twēd\ *n* **1** : rough woolen fabric **2** *pl* : tweed clothing —**tweedy** *adj*

tweet \'twēt\ *n* : chirping note —**tweet** *vb*

twee•zers \'twēzərz\ *n pl* : small pincerlike tool

twelve \'twelv\ *n* **1** : one more than 11 **2** : 12th in a set or series **3** : something having 12 units —**twelfth** \'twelfth\ *adj or n* —**twelve** *adj or pron*

twen•ty \'twentē\ *n, pl* **-ties** : 2 times 10 —**twen•ti•eth** \-ēəth\ *adj or n* —**twenty** *adj or pron*

twen•ty–twen•ty, 20–20 *adj* : being vision of normal sharpness

twice \'twīs\ *adv* **1** : on 2 occasions **2** : 2 times

twig \'twig\ *n* : small branch —**twig•gy** *adj*

twi•light \'twī,līt\ *n* : light from the sky at dusk or dawn —**twilight** *adj*

twill \'twil\ *n* : fabric with a weave that gives an appearance of diagonal lines in the fabric

twilled \'twild\ *adj* : made with a twill weave

twin \'twin\ *n* : either of 2 offspring born together ~ *adj* **1** : born with one another or as a pair at one birth **2** : made up of 2 similar parts

twine \'twīn\ *n* : strong twisted thread ~ *vb* **twined; twin•ing 1** : twist together **2** : coil about a support —**twin•er** *n* —**twiny** *adj*

twinge \'twinj\ *vb* **twinged; twing•ing** *or* **twinge•ing** : affect with or feel a sudden sharp pain ~ *n* : sudden sharp stab (as of pain)

twin•kle \'twiŋkəl\ *vb* **-kled; -kling** : shine with a flickering light ~ *n* **1** : wink **2** : intermittent shining —**twin•kler** \-klər\ *n*

twirl \'twərl\ *vb* : whirl round ~ *n* **1** : act of twirling **2** : coil —**twirl•er** *n*

twist \'twist\ vb 1 : unite by winding (threads) together 2 : wrench 3 : move in or have a spiral shape 4 : follow a winding course ~ n 1 : act or result of twisting 2 : unexpected development

twist•er \'twistər\ n : tornado

¹**twit** \'twit\ n : fool

²**twit** vb **-tt-** : taunt

twitch \'twich\ vb : move or pull with a sudden motion ~ n : act of twitching

twit•ter \'twitər\ vb : make chirping noises ~ n : small intermittent noise

two \'tü\ n, pl **twos** 1 : one more than one 2 : the 2d in a set or series 3 : something having 2 units —**two** adj or pron

two•fold \'tü,fōld\ adj : double —**two•fold** \-'fōld\ adv

two•some \'tüsəm\ n : couple

-ty n suffix : quality, condition, or degree

ty•coon \tī'kün\ n : powerful and successful businessman

tying pres part of TIE

tyke \'tīk\ n : small child

tym•pa•num \'timpənəm\ n, pl **-na** \-nə\ : eardrum or the cavity which it closes externally —**tym•pan•ic** \tim'panik\ adj

type \'tīp\ n 1 : class, kind, or group set apart by common characteristics 2 : special design of printed letters ~ vb **typed; typ•ing** 1 : write with a typewriter 2 : identify or classify as a particular type

type•writ•er n : keyboard machine that produces printed material by striking a ribbon with raised letters —**type•write** vb

ty•phoid \'tī,fȯid, tī'-\ adj : relating to or being a communicable bacterial disease (**typhoid fever**)

ty•phoon \tī'fün\ n : hurricane of the western Pacific ocean

ty•phus \'tīfəs\ n : severe disease with fever, delirium, and rash

typ•i•cal \'tipikəl\ adj : having the essential characteristics of a group —**typ•i•cal•i•ty** \,tipə'kalətē\ n —**typ•i•cal•ly** adv —**typ•i•cal•ness** n

typ•i•fy \'tipə,fī\ vb **-fied; -fy•ing** : be typical of

typ•ist \'tīpist\ n : one who operates a typewriter

ty•pog•ra•phy \tī'pägrəfē\ n 1 : art of printing with type 2 : style, arrangement, or appearance of printed matter —**ty•po•graph•ic** \,tīpə'grafik\, **ty•po•graph•i•cal** \-ikəl\ adj —**ty•po•graph•i•cal•ly** adv

ty•ran•ni•cal \tə'ranikəl, tī-\ adj : relating to a tyrant —**ty•ran•ni•cal•ly** adv

tyr•an•nize \'tirə,nīz\ vb **-nized; -niz•ing** : rule or deal with in the manner of a tyrant —**tyr•an•niz•er** n

tyr•an•ny \'tirənē\ n, pl **-nies** : unjust use of absolute governmental power

ty•rant \'tīrənt\ n : harsh ruler having absolute power

ty•ro \'tīrō\ n, pl **-ros** : beginner

tzar \'zär, 'tsär, 'sär\ var of CZAR

U

u \'yü\ n, pl **u's** or **us** \'yüz\ : 21st letter of the alphabet

ubiq•ui•tous \yü'bikwətəs\ adj : omnipresent —**ubiq•ui•tous•ly** adv —**ubiq•ui•ty** \-wətē\ n

ud•der \'ədər\ n : animal sac containing milk glands and nipples

ug•ly \'əglē\ adj **ug•li•er; -est** 1 : offensive to look at 2 : mean or quarrelsome —**ug•li•ness** n

uku•le•le \,yükə'lālē\ n : small 4-string guitar

ul•cer \'əlsər\ n : eroded sore —**ul•cer•ous** adj

ul•cer•ate \'əlsə,rāt\ vb **-at•ed; -at•ing** : become affected with an ulcer —**ul•cer•a•tion** \,əlsə'rāshən\ n —**ul•cer•a•tive** \'əlsə,rātiv\ adj

ul•na \'əlnə\ n : bone of the forearm opposite the thumb

ul•te•ri•or \,əl'tirēər\ adj : not revealed

ul•ti•mate \'əltəmət\ adj 1 : final, maximum, or extreme —**ultimate** n —**ul•ti•mate•ly** adv

ul•ti•ma•tum \,əltə'mātəm, -'mät-\ n, pl **-tums** or **-ta** \-ə\ : final proposition or demand carrying or implying a threat

ul•tra•vi•o•let \,əltrə'vīələt\ adj : having a wavelength shorter than visible light

um•bi•li•cus \,əmbə'līkəs, ,əm'bili-\ n, pl

-li•ci \-bə'lī,kī, -,sī; -'bilə,kī, -,kē\ or **-li•cus•es** : small depression on the abdominal wall marking the site of the cord (**umbilical cord**) that joins the unborn fetus to its mother —**um•bil•i•cal** \,əm-'bilikəl\

um•brage \'əmbrij\ n : resentment

um•brel•la \,əm'brelə\ n : collapsible fabric device to protect from sun or rain

um•pire \'əm,pīr\ n 1 : arbitrator 2 : sport official —**umpire** vb

ump•teen \'əmp'tēn\ adj : very numerous —**ump•teenth** \-'tēnth\ adj

un- \,ən, 'ən\ prefix 1 : not 2 : opposite of

unable	**unfilled**
unabridged	**unfinished**
unacceptable	**unflattering**
unaccompanied	**unforeseeable**
unaccounted	**unforeseen**
unacquainted	**unforgivable**
unaddressed	**unforgiving**
unadorned	**unfulfilled**
unadulterated	**unfurnished**
unafraid	**ungenerous**
unaided	**ungentlemanly**
unalike	**ungraceful**
unambiguous	**ungrammatical**
unambitious	**unharmed**
unannounced	**unhealthful**
unanswered	**unheated**
unanticipated	**unhurt**
unappetizing	**unidentified**
unappreciated	**unimaginable**
unapproved	**unimaginative**
unarguable	**unimportant**
unarguably	**unimpressed**
unassisted	**uninformed**
unattended	**uninhabited**
unattractive	**uninjured**
unauthorized	**uninsured**
unavailable	**unintelligent**
unavoidable	**unintelligible**
unbearable	**unintelligibly**
unbiased	**unintended**
unbranded	**unintentional**
unbreakable	**unintentionally**
uncensored	**uninterested**
unchallenged	**uninteresting**
unchangeable	**uninterrupted**
unchanged	**uninvited**
unchanging	**unjust**
uncharacteristic	**unjustifiable**
uncharged	**unjustified**
unchaste	**unjustly**
uncivilized	**unknowing**
unclaimed	**unknowingly**
unclear	**unknown**
uncleared	**unleavened**
unclothed	**unlicensed**
uncluttered	**unlikable**
uncombed	**unlimited**
uncomfortable	**unlovable**
uncomfortably	**unmanageable**
uncomplimentary	**unmarked**
unconfirmed	**unmarried**
unconsummated	**unmerciful**
uncontested	**unmercifully**
uncontrolled	**unmerited**
uncontroversial	**unmolested**
unconventional	**unmotivated**
unconventionally	**unmoving**
unconverted	**unnamed**
uncooked	**unnecessarily**
uncooperative	**unnecessary**
uncoordinated	**unneeded**
uncovered	**unnoticeable**
uncultivated	**unnoticed**
undamaged	**unobjectionable**
undated	**unobservable**
undecided	**unobservant**
undeclared	**unobtainable**
undefeated	**unobtrusive**
undemocratic	**unobtrusively**
undependable	**unofficial**
undeserving	**unopened**
undesirable	**unopposed**
undetected	**unorganized**
undetermined	**unoriginal**
undeveloped	**unorthodox**
undeviating	**unorthodoxy**
undignified	**unpaid**
undisturbed	**unpardonable**
undivided	**unpatriotic**
undomesticated	**unpaved**
undrinkable	**unpleasant**
unearned	**unpleasantly**
uneducated	**unpleasantness**
unemotional	**unpopular**
unending	**unpopularity**
unendurable	**unposed**
unenforceable	**unpredictabil-ity**
unenlightened	
unethical	**unpredictable**
unexcitable	**unpredictably**
unexciting	**unprejudiced**
unexplainable	**unprepared**
unexplored	**unpretentious**
unfair	**unproductive**
unfairly	**unprofitable**
unfairness	**unprotected**
unfavorable	**unproved**
unfavorably	**unproven**
unfeigned	**unprovoked**

unpunished	**unsteadily**
unqualified	**unsteadiness**
unquenchable	**unsteady**
unquestioning	**unstructured**
unreachable	**unsubstantiated**
unreadable	**unsuccessful**
unready	**unsuitable**
unrealistic	**unsuitably**
unreasonable	**unsuited**
unreasonably	**unsupervised**
unrefined	**unsupported**
unrelated	**unsure**
unreliable	**unsurprising**
unremembered	**unsuspecting**
unrepentant	**unsweetened**
unrepresented	**unsympathetic**
unrequited	**untamed**
unresolved	**untanned**
unresponsive	**untidy**
unrestrained	**untouched**
unrestricted	**untrained**
unrewarding	**untreated**
unripe	**untrue**
unsafe	**untrustworthy**
unsalted	**untruthful**
unsanitary	**unusable**
unsatisfactory	**unusual**
unsatisfied	**unvarying**
unscented	**unverified**
unscheduled	**unwanted**
unseasoned	**unwarranted**
unseen	**unwary**
unselfish	**unwavering**
unselfishly	**unweaned**
unselfishness	**unwed**
unshaped	**unwelcome**
unshaven	**unwholesome**
unskillful	**unwilling**
unskillfully	**unwillingly**
unsolicited	**unwillingness**
unsolved	**unwise**
unsophisticated	**unwisely**
unsound	**unworkable**
unsoundly	**unworthily**
unsoundness	**unworthiness**
unspecified	**unworthy**
unspoiled	**unyielding**

un•ac•cus•tomed adj 1 : not customary 2 : not accustomed

un•af•fect•ed adj 1 : not influenced or changed by something 2 : natural and sincere —**un•af•fect•ed•ly** adv

unan•i•mous \yü'nanəməs\ adj 1 : showing no disagreement 2 : formed with the agreement of all —**una•nim•i•ty** \,yü-nə'nimətē\ n —**unan•i•mous•ly** adv

un•armed adj : not armed or armored

un•as•sum•ing adj : not bold or arrogant

un•at•tached adj 1 : not attached 2 : not married or engaged

un•aware adv : unawares ~ adj : not aware

un•awares \,ənə'warz\ adv 1 : without warning 2 : unintentionally

un•bal•anced adj 1 : not balanced 2 : mentally unstable

un•beat•en adj : not beaten

un•be•com•ing adj : not proper or suitable —**un•be•com•ing•ly** adv

un•be•liev•able adj 1 : improbable 2 : superlative —**un•be•liev•ably** adv

un•bend vb **-bent; -bend•ing** : make or become more relaxed and friendly

un•bend•ing adj : formal and inflexible

un•bind vb **-bound; -bind•ing** 1 : remove bindings from 2 : release

un•bolt vb : open or unfasten by withdrawing a bolt

un•born adj : not yet born

un•bo•som vb : disclose thoughts or feelings

un•bowed \,ən'baùd\ adj : not defeated or subdued

un•bri•dled \,ən'brīd³ld\ adj : unrestrained

un•bro•ken adj : not damaged 2 : not interrupted

un•buck•le vb : unfasten the buckle of

un•bur•den vb : relieve (oneself) of anxieties

un•but•ton vb : unfasten the buttons of

un•called-for adj : too harsh or rude for the occasion

un•can•ny \,ən'kanē\ adj 1 : weird 2 : suggesting superhuman powers —**un•can•ni•ly** \-'kan³lē\ adv

un•ceas•ing adj : never ceasing —**un•ceas•ing•ly** adv

un•cer•e•mo•ni•ous adj : acting without ordinary courtesy —**un•cer•e•mo•ni•ous•ly** adv

un•cer•tain adj 1 : not determined, sure, or definitely known 2 : subject to chance or change —**un•cer•tain•ly** adv —**un•cer•tain•ty** n

un•chris•tian adj : not consistent with Christian teachings

un•cle \'əŋkəl\ n 1 : brother of one's father or mother 2 : husband of one's aunt

un•clean adj : not clean or pure —**un•clean•ness** n

un•clog vb : remove an obstruction from

un•coil vb : release or become released from a coiled state

un•com•mit•ted adj : not pledged to a particular allegiance or course of action

un•com•mon adj 1 : rare 2 : superior —**un•com•mon•ly** adv

un•com•pro•mis•ing adj : not making or accepting a compromise

un•con•cerned adj 1 : disinterested 2 : not anxious or upset —**un•con•cerned•ly** adv

un•con•di•tion•al adj : not limited in any way —**un•con•di•tion•al•ly** adv

un•con•scio•na•ble adj : shockingly unjust or unscrupulous —**un•con•scio•na•bly** adv

un•con•scious adj 1 : not awake or aware of one's surroundings 2 : not consciously done ~ n : part of one's mental life that one is not aware of —**un•con•scious•ly** adv —**un•con•scious•ness** n

un•con•sti•tu•tion•al adj : not according to or consistent with a constitution

un•con•trol•la•ble adj : incapable of being controlled —**un•con•trol•la•bly** adv

un•count•ed adj : countless

un•couth \,ən'küth\ adj : rude and vulgar

un•cov•er vb 1 : reveal 2 : expose by removing a covering

unc•tion \'əŋkshən\ n 1 : rite of anointing 2 : exaggerated or insincere earnestness

unc•tu•ous \'əŋkchəwəs\ adj 1 : oily 2 : insincerely smooth in speech or manner —**unc•tu•ous•ly** adv

un•cut adj 1 : not cut down, into, off, or apart 2 : not shaped by cutting 3 : not abridged

un•daunt•ed adj : not discouraged —**un•daunt•ed•ly** adv

un•de•ni•able adj : plainly true —**un•de•ni•ably** adv

un•der \'əndər\ adv 1 : below or beneath something ~ prep 1 : lower than and sheltered by 2 : below the surface of 3 : covered or concealed by 4 : subject to the authority of 5 : less than ~ adj 1 : lying below or beneath 2 : subordinate 3 : less than usual, proper, or desired

un•der•age \,əndər'āj\ adj : of less than legal age

un•der•brush \'əndər,brəsh\ n : shrubs and small trees growing beneath large trees

un•der•clothes \'əndər,klōz, -,klōth_z\ n pl : underwear

un•der•cloth•ing \-,klōthiŋ\ n : underwear

un•der•cov•er \,əndər'kəvər\ adj : employed or engaged in secret investigation

un•der•cur•rent \'əndər,kərənt\ n : hidden tendency or opinion

un•der•cut \,əndər'kət\ vb **-cut; -cut•ting** : offer to sell or to work at a lower rate than

un•der•de•vel•oped \,əndərdi'veləpt\ adj : not normally or adequately developed esp. economically

un•der•dog \'əndər,dȯg\ n : contestant given least chance of winning

un•der•done \,əndər'dən\ adj : not thoroughly done or cooked

un•der•es•ti•mate \,əndər'estə,māt\ vb : estimate too low

un•der•ex•pose \,əndərik'spōz\ vb : give less than normal exposure to —**un•der•ex•po•sure** n

un•der•feed \,əndər'fēd\ vb **-fed; -feed•ing** : feed inadequately

un•der•foot \,əndər'fùt\ adv 1 : under the feet 2 : in the way of another

un•der•gar•ment \'əndər,gärmənt\ n : garment to be worn under another

un•der•go \,əndər'gō\ vb **-went** \-'went\; **-gone; -go•ing** 1 : endure 2 : go through (as an experience)

un•der•grad•u•ate \,əndər'grajəwət\ n : university or college student

un•der•ground \,əndər'graùnd\ adv 1 : beneath the surface of the earth 2 : in secret ~ \'əndər,-\ adj 1 : being or growing under the surface of the ground 2 : secret ~ \'əndər,-\ n : secret political movement or group

un•der•growth \'əndər,grōth\ n : low growth on the floor of a forest

un•der•hand \'əndər,hand\ adv or adj 1 : with secrecy and deception 2 : with the hand kept below the waist

un•der•hand•ed \,əndər'handəd\ adj or adv : underhand —**un•der•hand•ed•ly** adv —**un•der•hand•ed•ness** n

un•der•line \'əndər,līn\ vb 1 : draw a line under 2 : stress —**underline** n

un•der•ling \'əndərliŋ\ n : inferior

un•der•ly•ing \,əndər,līiŋ\ adj : basic

un•der•mine \,əndər'mīn\ vb 1 : excavate beneath 2 : weaken or wear away secretly or gradually

un•der•neath \,əndər'nēth\ prep : directly under ~ adv 1 : below a surface or object 2 : on the lower side

un•der•nour•ished \,əndər'nərisht\ adj : insufficiently nourished —**un•der•nour•ish•ment** n

un•der•pants \'əndər,pants\ n pl : short undergarment for the lower trunk

un•der•pass \-,pas\ n : passageway crossing underneath another

un•der•pin•ning \'əndər,piniŋ\ n : support

un•der•priv•i•leged adj : poor

un·der·rate \ˌəndərˈrāt\ vb : rate or value too low

un·der·score \ˈəndərˌskōr\ vb 1 : underline 2 : emphasize —**underscore** n

un·der·sea \ˌəndərˈsē\ adj : being, carried on, or used beneath the surface of the sea ~ \ˌəndərˈsē\ **un·der·seas** \-ˈsēz\ adv : beneath the surface of the sea

un·der·sec·re·tary n : deputy secretary

un·der·sell \ˌəndərˈsel\ vb -**sold**; -**sell·ing** : sell articles cheaper than

un·der·shirt \ˈəndərˌshərt\ n : shirt worn as underwear

un·der·shorts \ˈəndərˌshōrts\ n pl : short underpants

un·der·side \ˈəndərˌsīd, ˌəndərˈsīd\ n : side or surface lying underneath

un·der·sized \ˌəndərˈsīzd\ adj : unusually small

un·der·stand \ˌəndərˈstand\ vb -**stood** \-ˈstu̇d\ -**stand·ing** 1 : be aware of the meaning of 2 : deduce 3 : have a sympathetic attitude —**un·der·stand·able** \-ˈstandəbəl\ adj —**un·der·stand·ably** \-blē\ adv

un·der·stand·ing \ˌəndərˈstandiŋ\ n 1 : intelligence 2 : ability to comprehend and judge 3 : mutual agreement ~ adj : sympathetic

un·der·state \ˌəndərˈstāt\ vb 1 : represent as less than is the case 2 : state with restraint —**un·der·state·ment** n

un·der·stood \ˌəndərˈstu̇d\ adj 1 : agreed upon 2 : implicit

un·der·study \ˈəndərˌstədē, ˌəndərˈ-\ vb : study another actor's part in order to substitute —**understudy** \ˈəndərˌ-\ n

un·der·take \ˌəndərˈtāk\ vb -**took**; -**tak·en**; -**tak·ing** 1 : attempt (a task) or assume (a responsibility) 2 : guarantee

un·der·tak·er \ˈəndərˌtākər\ n : one in the funeral business

un·der·tak·ing \ˈəndərˌtākiŋ, ˌəndərˈ-\ n 1 : something (as work) that is undertaken 2 : promise

under–the–counter adj : illicit

un·der·tone \ˈəndərˌtōn\ n : low or subdued tone or utterance

un·der·tow \-ˌtō\ n : current beneath the waves that flows seaward

un·der·val·ue \ˌəndərˈvalyü\ vb : value too low

un·der·wa·ter \-ˈwȯtər, -ˈwät-\ adj : being or used below the surface of the water —**underwater** adv

under way : in motion or in progress

un·der·wear \ˈəndərˌwar\ n : clothing worn next to the skin and under ordinary clothes

un·der·world \ˈəndərˌwərld\ n 1 : place of departed souls 2 : world of organized crime

un·der·write \ˈəndərˌrīt, ˌəndərˈ-\ vb -**wrote**; -**writ·ten**; -**writ·ing** 1 : provide insurance for 2 : guarantee financial support of —**un·der·writ·er** n

un·dies \ˈəndēz\ n pl : underwear

un·do vb -**did**; -**done**; -**do·ing** 1 : unfasten 2 : reverse 3 : ruin —**un·do·ing** n

un·doubt·ed adj : certain —**un·doubt·ed·ly** adv

un·dress vb : remove one's clothes ~ n : state of being naked

un·due adj : excessive —**un·du·ly** adv

un·du·late \ˈənjəˌlāt\ vb -**lat·ed**; -**lat·ing** : rise and fall regularly —**un·du·la·tion** \ˌənjəˈlāshən\ n

un·dy·ing adj : immortal or perpetual

un·earth vb : dig up or discover

un·earth·ly adj : supernatural

un·easy adj 1 : awkward or embarrassed 2 : disturbed or worried —**un·eas·i·ly** adv —**un·eas·i·ness** n

un·em·ployed adj : not having a job —**un·em·ploy·ment** n

un·equal adj : not equal or uniform —**un·equal·ly** adv

un·equaled, un·equalled adj : having no equal

un·equiv·o·cal adj : leaving no doubt —**un·equiv·o·cal·ly** adv

un·err·ing adj : infallible —**un·err·ing·ly** adv

un·even adj 1 : not smooth 2 : not regular or consistent —**un·even·ly** adv —**un·even·ness** n

un·event·ful adj : lacking interesting or noteworthy incidents —**un·event·ful·ly** adv

un·ex·pect·ed \ˌənikˈspektəd\ adj : not expected —**un·ex·pect·ed·ly** adv

un·fail·ing adj : steadfast —**un·fail·ing·ly** adv

un·faith·ful adj : not loyal —**un·faith·ful·ly** adv —**un·faith·ful·ness** n

un·fa·mil·iar adj 1 : not well known 2 : not acquainted —**un·fa·mil·iar·i·ty** n

un·fas·ten vb : release a catch or lock

un·feel·ing adj : lacking feeling or compassion —**un·feel·ing·ly** adv

un·fit adj : not suitable —**un·fit·ness** n

un·flap·pa·ble \ˌənˈflapəbəl\ adj : not easily upset or panicked —**un·flap·pa·bly** adv

un·fold vb 1 : open the folds of 2 : reveal 3 : develop

un·for·get·ta·ble adj : memorable —**un·for·get·ta·bly** adv

un·for·tu·nate adj 1 : not lucky or successful 2 : deplorable —**unfortunate** n —**un·for·tu·nate·ly** adv

un·found·ed adj : lacking a sound basis

un·freeze vb -**froze**; -**fro·zen**; -**freez·ing** : thaw

un·friend·ly adj : not friendly or kind —**un·friend·li·ness** n

un·furl vb : unfold or unroll

un·gain·ly adj : clumsy —**un·gain·li·ness** n

un·god·ly adj : wicked —**un·god·li·ness** n

un·grate·ful adj : not thankful for favors —**un·grate·ful·ly** adv —**un·grate·ful·ness** n

un·guent \ˈəŋgwənt, ˈən-\ n : ointment

un·hand vb : let go

un·hap·py adj 1 : unfortunate 2 : sad —**un·hap·pi·ly** adv —**un·hap·pi·ness** n

un·healthy adj 1 : not wholesome 2 : not well

un·heard–of \ˌənˈhərdəv, -ˌäv\ adj : unprecedented

un·hinge \ˌənˈhinj\ vb 1 : take from the hinges 2 : make unstable esp. mentally

un·hitch vb : unfasten

un·ho·ly adj : sinister or shocking —**un·ho·li·ness** n

un·hook vb : release from a hook

uni·cel·lu·lar \ˌyüniˈselyələr\ adj : having or consisting of a single cell

uni·corn \ˈyüniˌkȯrn\ n : legendary animal with one horn in the middle of the forehead

uni·cy·cle \ˈyüniˌsīkəl\ n : pedal-powered vehicle with only a single wheel

uni·di·rec·tion·al \ˌyünidəˈrekshənəl, -dī-\ adj : working in only a single direction

uni·form \ˈyünəˌfȯrm\ adj : not changing or showing any variation ~ n : distinctive dress worn by members of a particular group —**uni·for·mi·ty** \ˌyünəˈfȯrmətē\ n —**uni·form·ly** adv

uni·fy \ˈyünəˌfī\ vb -**fied**; -**fy·ing** : make into a coherent whole —**uni·fi·ca·tion** \ˌyünəfəˈkāshən\ n

uni·lat·er·al \ˌyünəˈlatərəl\ adj : having, affecting, or done by one side only —**uni·lat·er·al·ly** adv

un·im·peach·able adj : blameless

un·in·hib·it·ed adj : free of restraint —**un·in·hib·it·ed·ly** adv

union \ˈyünyən\ n 1 : act or instance of joining 2 or more things into one or the state of being so joined 2 : confederation of nations or states 3 : organization of workers (**labor union, trade union**)

union·ize \ˈyünyəˌnīz\ vb -**ized**; -**iz·ing** : form into a labor union —**union·iza·tion** \ˌyünyənəˈzāshən\ n

unique \yu̇ˈnēk\ adj 1 : being the only one of its kind 2 : very unusual —**unique·ly** adv —**unique·ness** n

uni·son \ˈyünəsən, -nəzən\ n 1 : sameness in pitch 2 : exact agreement

unit \ˈyünət\ n 1 : smallest whole number 2 : definite amount or quantity used as a standard of measurement 3 : single part of a whole —**unit** adj

unite \yu̇ˈnīt\ vb -**nit·ed**; -**nit·ing** : put or join together

uni·ty \ˈyünətē\ n, pl -**ties** 1 : quality or state of being united or a unit 2 : harmony

uni·ver·sal \ˌyünəˈvərsəl\ adj 1 : relating to or affecting everyone or everything 2 : present or occurring everywhere —**uni·ver·sal·ly** adv

uni·verse \ˈyünəˌvərs\ n : the complete system of all things that exist

uni·ver·si·ty \ˌyünəˈvərsətē\ n, pl -**ties** : institution of higher learning

un·kempt \ˌənˈkempt\ adj : not neat or combed

un·kind adj : not kind or sympathetic —**un·kind·li·ness** n —**un·kind·ly** adv —**un·kind·ness** n

un·law·ful adj : illegal —**un·law·ful·ly** adv

un·leash vb : free from control or restraint

un·less \ˌənˈles\ conj : except on condition that

un·like \ˌənˈlīk, ˈənˌlīk\ adj 1 : not similar 2 : not equal ~ prep : different from —**un·like·ly** \ˈənˈlīklē\ adv —**un·like·ness** \-nəs\ n —**un·like·li·hood** \-lēˌhu̇d\ n

un·load vb 1 : take (cargo) from a vehicle, vessel, or plane 2 : take a load from 3 : discard

un·lock vb 1 : unfasten through release of a lock 2 : release or reveal

un·lucky adj 1 : experiencing bad luck 2 : likely to bring misfortune —**un·luck·i·ly** adv

un·mis·tak·able adj : not capable of being mistaken or misunderstood —**un·mis·tak·ably** adv

un·moved adj 1 : not emotionally affected 2 : remaining in the same place or position

un·nat·u·ral adj 1 : not natural or spontaneous 2 : abnormal —**un·nat·u·ral·ly** adv —**un·nat·u·ral·ness** n

un·nerve vb : deprive of courage, strength, or steadiness

un·oc·cu·pied adj 1 : not busy 2 : not occupied

un·pack vb 1 : remove (things packed) from a container 2 : remove the contents of (a package)

un·par·al·leled adj : having no equal

un·plug \ˌənˈpləg\ vb 1 : unclog 2 : disconnect from an electric circuit by removing a plug

un·prec·e·dent·ed adj : unlike or superior to anything known before

un·prin·ci·pled adj : unscrupulous

un·ques·tion·able adj : acknowledged as beyond doubt —**un·ques·tion·ably** adv

un·rav·el vb 1 : separate the threads of 2 : solve

un·re·al adj : not real or genuine —**un·re·al·i·ty** n

un·rea·son·ing adj : not using or being guided by reason

un·re·lent·ing adj : not yielding or easing —**un·re·lent·ing·ly** adv

un·rest n : turmoil

un·ri·valed, un·ri·valled adj : having no rival

un·roll vb 1 : unwind a roll of 2 : become unrolled

un·ruf·fled adj : not agitated or upset

un·ruly \ˌənˈrülē\ adj : not readily controlled or disciplined —**un·rul·i·ness** n

un·scathed \ˌənˈskāt͟hd\ adj : unharmed

un·sci·en·tif·ic adj : not in accord with the principles and methods of science

un·screw vb : loosen or remove by withdrawing screws or by turning

un·scru·pu·lous adj : being or acting in total disregard of conscience, ethical principles, or rights of others —**un·scru·pu·lous·ly** adv —**un·scru·pu·lous·ness** n

un·seal vb : break or remove the seal of

un·sea·son·able adj : not appropriate or usual for the season —**un·sea·son·ably** adv

un·seem·ly \ˌənˈsēmlē\ adj : not polite or in good taste —**un·seem·li·ness** n

un·set·tle vb : disturb —**un·set·tled** adj

un·sight·ly \ˌənˈsītlē\ adj : not attractive

un·skilled adj : not having or requiring a particular skill

un·snap vb : loosen by undoing a snap

un·speak·able \ˌənˈspēkəbəl\ adj : extremely bad —**un·speak·ably** \-blē\ adv

un·sta·ble adj 1 : not mentally or physically balanced 2 : tending to change

un·stop vb 1 : unclog 2 : remove a stopper from

un·stop·pa·ble \ˌənˈstäpəbəl\ adj : not capable of being stopped

un·strung \ˌənˈstrəŋ\ adj : nervously tired or anxious

un·sung \ˌənˈsəŋ\ adj : not celebrated in song or verse

un·tan·gle vb 1 : free from a state of being tangled 2 : find a solution to

un·think·able \ˌənˈthiŋkəbəl\ adj : not to be thought of or considered possible

un·think·ing adj : careless —**un·think·ing·ly** adv

un·tie vb -**tied**; -**ty·ing** or -**tie·ing** : open by releasing ties

un·til \ˌənˈtil\ prep : up to the time of ~ conj : to the time that

un·time·ly adj 1 : premature 2 : coming at an unfortunate time

un·to \ˈənˌtü, ˈən-ˌ\ prep : to

un·told adj 1 : not told 2 : too numerous to count

un·tow·ard \ˌənˈtōrd\ adj 1 : difficult to manage 2 : inconvenient

un·truth n 1 : lack of truthfulness 2 : lie

un·used adj 1 \ˌənˈyüst, -ˈyüzd\ : not accustomed 2 \-ˈyüzd\ : not used

un·well adj : sick

un·wieldy \ˌənˈwēldē\ adj : too big or awkward to manage easily

un·wind vb -**wound**; -**wind·ing** 1 : undo something that is wound 2 : become unwound 3 : relax

un·wit·ting adj 1 : not knowing 2 : not intended —**un·wit·ting·ly** adv

un·wont·ed adj 1 : unusual 2 : not accustomed by experience

un·wrap vb : remove the wrappings from

un·writ·ten adj : made or passed on only in speech or through tradition

un·zip vb : zip open

up \ˈəp\ adv 1 : in or to a higher position or level 2 : from beneath a surface or level 3 : in or into an upright position 4 : out of bed 5 : to or with greater intensity 6 : into existence, evidence, or knowledge 7 : away 8—used to indicate a degree of success, completion, or finality 9 : in or into parts ~ adj 1 : in the state of having risen 2 : raised to or at a higher level 3 : moving, inclining, or directed upward 4 : in a state of greater intensity 5 : at an end —vb **upped** or in 1 up; **upped**; up·**ping**; **ups** or in 1 up 1 : act abruptly 2 : move or cause to move upward ~ prep 1 : to, toward, or at a higher point of 2 : along or toward the beginning of

up·braid \ˌəpˈbrād\ vb : criticize or scold

up·bring·ing \ˈəpˌbriŋiŋ\ n : process of bringing up and training

up·com·ing \ˈəpˌkəmiŋ\ adj : approaching

up·date \ˌəpˈdāt\ vb : bring up to date —**update** \ˈəpˌdāt\ n

up·end \ˌəpˈend\ vb 1 : stand or rise on end 2 : overturn

up·grade \ˈəpˌgrād\ n 1 : upward slope 2 : increase ~ \ˈəpˌ-, ˌəpˈ-\ vb : raise to a higher position

up·heav·al \ˌəpˈhēvəl\ n 1 : a heaving up (as of part of the earth's crust) 2 : violent change

up·hill \ˈəpˈhil\ adv : upward on a hill or incline ~ \ˈəpˌ-\ adj 1 : going up 2 : difficult

up·hold \ˌəpˈhōld\ vb -**held**; -**hold·ing** : support or defend —**up·hold·er** n

up·hol·ster \ˌəpˈhōlstər\ vb : cover (furniture) with padding and fabric (**up·hol·stery** \-stərē\) —**up·hol·ster·er** n

up·keep \ˈəpˌkēp\ n : act or cost of keeping up or maintaining

up·land \ˈəplənd, -ˌland\ n : high land —**upland** adj

up·lift \ˌəpˈlift\ vb 1 : lift up 2 : improve the condition or spirits of —**uplift** \ˈəpˌ-\ n

up·on \əˈpȯn, -ˈpän\ prep : on

up·per \ˈəpər\ adj : higher in position, rank, or order ~ n : top part of a shoe

upper hand : advantage

up·per·most \ˈəpərˌmōst\ adv : in or into the highest or most prominent position —**uppermost** adj

up·pi·ty \ˈəpətē\ adj : acting with a manner of undue importance

up·right \ˈəpˌrīt\ adj 1 : vertical 2 : erect in posture 3 : morally correct ~ n : something that stands upright —**upright** adv —**up·right·ly** adv —**up·right·ness** n

up·ris·ing \ˈəpˌrīziŋ\ n : revolt

up·roar \ˈəpˌrōr\ n : state of commotion or violent disturbance

up·roar·i·ous \ˌəpˈrōrēəs\ adj 1 : marked by uproar 2 : extremely funny —**up·roar·i·ous·ly** adv

up·root \ˌəpˈrüt, -ˈru̇t\ vb : remove by or as if by pulling up by the roots

up·set \ˌəpˈset\ vb -**set**; -**set·ting** 1 : force or be forced out of the usual position 2 : disturb emotionally or physically ~ \ˈəpˌ-\ n 1 : act of throwing into disorder 2 : minor physical disorder ~ adj : emotionally disturbed or agitated

up·shot \ˈəpˌshät\ n : final result

up·side down \ˌəpˌsīdˈdau̇n\ adv 1 : turned so that the upper and lower parts are reversed 2 : in or into confusion or disorder —**upside–down** adj

up·stairs \ˈəpˌstarz, ˌəpˈ-\ adv : up the stairs or to the next floor ~ adj : situated on the floor above ~ n sing or pl : part of a building above the ground floor

up·stand·ing \ˌəpˈstandiŋ, ˈəpˌ-\ adj : honest

up·start \ˈəpˌstärt\ n : one who claims more personal importance than is warranted —**up·start** adj

up·swing \ˈəpˌswiŋ\ n : marked increase (as in activity)

up·tight \ˌəpˈtīt\ adj 1 : tense 2 : angry 3 : rigidly conventional

up–to–date adj : current —**up–to–date·ness** n

up·town \ˈəpˌtau̇n\ n : upper part of a town or city —**uptown** adj or adv

up·turn \ˈəpˌtərn\ n : improvement or increase

up·ward \ˈəpwərd\, **up·wards** \-wərdz\ adv 1 : in a direction from lower to higher 2 : toward a higher or greater state or number ~ adj : directed toward or situated in a higher place —**up·ward·ly** adv

up·wind \ˈəpˈwind\ adv or adj : in the direction from which the wind is blowing

ura·ni·um \yu̇ˈrānēəm\ n : metallic radioactive chemical element

ur·ban \ˈərbən\ adj : characteristic of a city

ur·bane \ˌərˈbān\ adj : polished in manner —**ur·ban·i·ty** \ərˈbanətē\ n

ur·ban·ite \ˈərbəˌnīt\ n : city dweller

ur·chin \ˈərchən\ n : mischievous youngster

-ure n suffix : act or process

ure·thra \yu̇ˈrēthrə\ n, pl -**thras** or -**thrae** \-ˌthrē\ : canal that carries off urine from the bladder —**ure·thral** \-thrəl\ adj

urge \ˈərj\ vb **urged**; **urg·ing** 1 : earnestly plead for or insist on (an action) 2 : try to persuade 3 : impel to a course of activity ~ n : force or impulse that moves one to action

ur·gent \ˈərjənt\ adj 1 : calling for immediate attention 2 : urging insistently —**ur·gen·cy** \-jənsē\ n —**ur·gent·ly** adv

uri·nal \ˈyu̇rənᵊl\ n : receptacle to urinate in

uri·nate \ˈyu̇rəˌnāt\ vb -**nat·ed**; -**nat·ing** : discharge urine —**uri·na·tion** \ˌyu̇rəˈnāshən\ n

urine \ˈyu̇rən\ n : liquid waste material from the kidneys —**uri·nary** \-ˌnerē\ adj

urn \ˈərn\ n 1 : vaselike or cuplike vessel on a pedestal 2 : large coffee pot

us \'əs\ *pron, objective case of* WE

us•able \'yüzəbəl\ *adj* : suitable or fit for use —**us•abil•i•ty** \yüzə'bilətē\ *n*

us•age \'yüsij, -zij\ *n* 1 : customary practice 2 : way of doing or of using something

use \'yüs\ *n* 1 : act or practice of putting something into action 2 : state of being used 3 : way of using 4 : privilege, ability, or power to use something 5 : utility or function 6 : occasion or need to use ~ \'yüz\ *vb* **used** \'yüzd\ ; *"used to"* usu \'yüstə\; **us•ing** \'yüziŋ\ 1 : put into action or service 2 : consume 3 : behave toward 4 : to make use of 5 —used in the past tense with *to* to indicate a former practice —**use•ful** \'yüsfəl\ *adj* —**use•ful•ly** *adv* —**use•ful•ness** *n* —**use•less** \'yüsləs\ *adj* —**use•less•ly** *adv* —**use•less•ness** *n* —**us•er** *n*

used \'yüzd\ *adj* : not new

ush•er \'əshər\ *n* 1 : one who escorts people to their seats ~ *vb* : conduct to a place —**ush•er•ette** \,əshə'ret\ *n* : woman or girl who is an usher

usu•al \'yüzhəwəl\ *adj* : being what is expected according to custom or habit —**usu•al•ly** \'yüzhəwəlē\ *adv*

usurp \yü'sərp, -'zərp\ *vb* : seize and hold by force or without right —**usur•pa•tion** \,yüsər'pāshən, -zər-\ *n* —**usurp•er** *n*

usu•ry \'yüzhərē\ *n, pl* -**ries** 1 : lending of money at excessive interest or the rate or amount of such interest —**usu•rer** \-zhərər\ *n* —**usu•ri•ous** \yü'zhürēəs\ *adj*

uten•sil \yü'tensəl\ *n* 1 : eating or cooking tool 2 : useful tool

uter•us \'yütərəs\ *n, pl* **uteri** \-,rī\ : organ for containing and nourishing an unborn offspring —**uter•ine** \-,rīn, -rən\ *adj*

util•i•tar•i•an \yü,tilə'terēən\ *adj* : being or meant to be useful rather than beautiful

util•i•ty \yü'tilətē\ *n, pl* -**ties** 1 : usefulness 2 : regulated business providing a public service (as electricity)

uti•lize \'yütəl,īz\ *vb* -**lized**; -**liz•ing** : make use of —**uti•li•za•tion** \,yütələ'zāshən\ *n*

ut•most \'ət,mōst\ *adj* 1 : most distant 2 : of the greatest or highest degree or amount —**utmost** *n*

uto•pia \yü'tōpēə\ *n* : place of ideal perfection —**uto•pi•an** \-pēən\ *adj or n*

ut•ter \'ətər\ *adj* 1 : absolute ~ *vb* : express with the voice —**ut•ter•er** \-ərər\ *n* —**ut•ter•ly** *adv*

ut•ter•ance \'ətərəns\ *n* : what one says

V

v \'vē\ *n, pl* **v's** *or* **vs** \'vēz\ : 22d letter of the alphabet

va•can•cy \'vākənsē\ *n, pl* -**cies** 1 : state of being vacant 2 : unused or unoccupied place or office

va•cant \-kənt\ *adj* 1 : not occupied, filled, or in use 2 : devoid of thought or expression —**va•cant•ly** *adv*

va•cate \,kāt\ *vb* -**cat•ed**; -**cat•ing** 1 : annul 2 : leave unfilled or unoccupied

va•ca•tion \vā'kāshən, və-\ *n* : period of rest from routine —**vacation** *vb* —**va•ca•tion•er** *n*

vac•ci•nate \'vaksə,nāt\ *vb* -**nat•ed**; -**nat•ing** : administer a vaccine usu. by injection

vac•ci•na•tion \,vaksə'nāshən\ *n* : act of or the scar left by vaccinating

vac•cine \vak'sēn, 'vak,-\ *n* : substance to induce immunity to a disease

vac•il•late \'vasə,lāt\ *vb* -**lat•ed**; -**lat•ing** : waver between courses or opinions —**vac•il•la•tion** \,vasə'lāshən\ *n*

vac•u•ous \'vakyəwəs\ *adj* 1 : empty 2 : dull or inane —**va•cu•i•ty** \va'kyüətē, və-\ *n* —**vac•u•ous•ly** *adv* —**vac•u•ous•ness** *n*

vac•u•um \'vak,yüm, -yəm\ *n, pl* **vac•u•ums** *or* **vac•ua** \-yəwə\ : empty space with no air ~ *vb* : clean with a vacuum cleaner

vacuum cleaner *n* : appliance that cleans by suction

vag•a•bond \'vagə,bänd\ *n* : wanderer with no home —**vagabond** *adj*

va•ga•ry \'vāgərē, və'gerē\ *n, pl* -**ries** : whim

va•gi•na \və'jīnə\ *n, pl* -**nae** \-,nē\ *or* -**nas** : canal that leads out from the uterus —**vag•i•nal** \'vajənəl\ *adj*

va•grant \'vāgrənt\ *n* : person with no home and no job —**va•gran•cy** \-grənsē\ *n* —**vagrant** *adj*

vague \'vāg\ *adj* **vagu•er**; **vagu•est** : not clear, definite, or distinct —**vague•ly** *adv* —**vague•ness** *n*

vain \'vān\ *adj* 1 : of no value 2 : unsuccessful 3 : conceited —**vain•ly** *adv*

va•lance \'valəns, 'vāl-\ *n* : border drapery

vale \'vāl\ *n* : valley

vale•dic•to•ri•an \,valə,dik'tōrēən\ *n* : student giving the farewell address at commencement

vale•dic•to•ry \-'diktərē\ *adj* : bidding farewell —**valedictory** *n*

va•lence \'vāləns\ *n* : degree of combining power of a chemical element

val•en•tine \'valən,tīn\ *n* : sweetheart or a card sent to a sweetheart or friend on St. Valentine's Day

va•let \'valət, 'val,ā, va'lā\ *n* : male personal servant

va•liant \'valyənt\ *adj* : brave or heroic —**val•iant•ly** *adv*

val•id \'valəd\ *adj* 1 : proper and legally binding 2 : founded on truth or fact —**va•lid•i•ty** \və'lidətē, va-\ *n* —**val•id•ly** *adv*

val•i•date \'valə,dāt\ *vb* -**dat•ed**; -**dat•ing** : establish as valid —**val•i•da•tion** \,valə'dāshən\ *n*

va•lise \və'lēs\ *n* : suitcase

val•ley \'valē\ *n, pl* -**leys** : long depression between ranges of hills

val•or \'valər\ *n* : bravery or heroism —**val•or•ous** \'valərəs\ *adj*

valu•able \'valyəwəbəl\ *adj* 1 : worth a lot of money 2 : being of great importance or use —**valuable** *n*

val•u•a•tion \,valyə'wāshən\ *n* 1 : act or process of valuing 2 : market value of a thing

val•ue \'valyü\ *n* 1 : fair return or equivalent for something exchanged 2 : how much something is worth 3 : distinctive quality (as of a color or sound) 4 : guiding principle or ideal—usu. pl. ~ *vb* **val•ued**; **val•u•ing** 1 : estimate the worth of 2 : appreciate the importance of —**val•ue•less** *adj* —**val•u•er** *n*

valve \'valv\ *n* : structure or device to control flow of a liquid or gas —**valved** \'valvd\ —**valve•less** *adj*

vam•pire \'vam,pīr\ *n* 1 : legendary nightwandering dead body that sucks human blood 2 : bat that feeds on the blood of animals

¹van \'van\ *n* : vanguard

²van *n* : enclosed truck

va•na•di•um \və'nādēəm\ *n* : soft ductile metallic chemical element

van•dal \'vandəl\ *n* : person who willfully defaces or destroys property —**van•dal•ism** \-,izəm\ *n* —**van•dal•ize** \-,īz\ *vb*

vane \'vān\ *n* : bladelike device designed to be moved by force of the air or water

van•guard \'van,gärd\ *n* 1 : troops moving at the front of an army 2 : forefront of an action or movement

va•nil•la \və'nilə\ *n* : a flavoring made from the pods of a tropical orchid or this orchid

van•ish \'vanish\ *vb* : disappear suddenly

van•i•ty \'vanətē\ *n, pl* -**ties** 1 : futility or something that is futile 2 : undue pride in oneself 3 : makeup case or table

van•quish \'vaŋkwish, 'van-\ *vb* 1 : overcome in battle or in a contest 2 : gain mastery over

van•tage \'vantij\ *n* : position of advantage or perspective

va•pid \'vapəd, 'vāpəd\ *adj* : lacking spirit, liveliness, or zest —**va•pid•i•ty** \va-'pidətē\ *n* —**vap•id•ly** \'vapədlē\ *adv* —**vap•id•ness** *n*

va•por \'vāpər\ *n* 1 : fine separated particles floating in and clouding the air 2 : gaseous form of an ordinarily liquid substance —**va•por•ous** \-pərəs\ *adj*

va•por•ize \'vāpə,rīz\ *vb* -**ized**; -**iz•ing** : convert into vapor —**va•por•i•za•tion** \,vāpərə'zāshən\ *n* —**va•por•iz•er** *n*

vari•able \'verēəbəl\ *adj* : apt to vary —**vari•abil•i•ty** \,verēə'bilətē\ *n* —**vari•able** *n* —**vari•ably** *adv*

vari•ance \'verēəns\ *n* 1 : instance or degree of variation 2 : disagreement or dispute 3 : legal permission to build contrary to a zoning law

vari•ant \-ənt\ *n* : something that differs from others of its kind —**variant** *adj*

vari•a•tion \,verē'āshən\ *n* : instance or extent of varying

var•ied \'verēd\ *adj* : showing variety —**var•ied•ly** *adv*

var•ie•gat•ed \'verēə,gātəd\ *adj* : having patches, stripes, or marks of different colors —**var•ie•gate** \-,gāt\ *vb* —**var•ie•ga•tion** \,verēə'gāshən\ *n*

va•ri•ety \və'rīətē\ *n, pl* -**et•ies** 1 : state of being different 2 : collection of different

things 3 : something that differs from others of its kind

var•i•ous \'verēəs\ *adj* : being many and unlike —**var•i•ous•ly** *adv*

var•nish \'värnish\ *n* : liquid that dries to a hard glossy protective coating ~ *vb* : cover with varnish

var•si•ty \'värsətē\ *n, pl* -**ties** : principal team representing a school

vary \'verē\ *vb* **var•ied**; **vary•ing** 1 : alter 2 : make or be of different kinds

vas•cu•lar \'vaskyələr\ *adj* : relating to a channel for the conveyance of a body fluid (as blood or sap)

vase \'vās, 'vāz\ *n* : tall usu. ornamental container to hold flowers

vas•sal \'vasəl\ *n* 1 : one acknowledging another as feudal lord 2 : one in a dependent position —**vas•sal•age** \-əlij\ *n*

vast \'vast\ *adj* : very great in size, extent, or amount —**vast•ly** *adv* —**vast•ness** *n*

vat \'vat\ *n* : large tub- or barrel-shaped container

vaude•ville \'vódvəl, 'väd-, 'vōd-, -,vil, -əvəl, -ə,vil\ *n* : stage entertainment of unrelated acts

¹vault \'vólt\ *n* 1 : masonry arch 2 : usu. underground storage or burial room ~ *vb* : form or cover with a vault —**vault•ed** *adj*

²vault *vb* : spring over esp. with the help of the hands or a pole ~ *n* : act of vaulting —**vault•er** *n*

vaunt \'vónt\ *vb* : boast —**vaunt** *n*

veal \'vēl\ *n* : flesh of a young calf

veer \'vir\ *vb* : change course esp. gradually —**veer** *n*

veg•e•ta•ble \'vejtəbəl, 'vejə-\ *adj* 1 : relating to or obtained from plants 2 : like that of a plant ~ *n* 1 : plant 2 : plant grown for food

veg•e•tar•i•an \,vejə'terēən\ *n* : person who eats no meat —**vegetarian** *adj* —**veg•e•tar•i•an•ism** \-ēə,nizəm\ *n*

veg•e•tate \'vejə,tāt\ *vb* -**tat•ed**; -**tat•ing** : lead a dull inert life

veg•e•ta•tion \,vejə'tāshən\ *n* : plant life —**veg•e•ta•tion•al** \-shənəl\ *adj* —**veg•e•ta•tive** \'vejə,tātiv\ *adj*

ve•he•ment \'vēəmənt\ *adj* : showing strong esp. violent feeling —**ve•he•mence** \-məns\ *n* —**ve•he•ment•ly** *adv*

ve•hi•cle \'vē,hikəl, 'vēəkəl\ *n* 1 : medium through which something is expressed, applied, or administered 2 : structure for transporting something esp. on wheels —**ve•hic•u•lar** \vē'hikyələr\ *adj*

veil \'vāl\ *n* 1 : sheer material to hide something or to cover the face and head 2 : something that hides ~ *vb* : cover with a veil

vein \'vān\ *n* 1 : rock fissure filled with deposited mineral matter 2 : vessel that carries blood toward the heart 3 : sap-carrying tube in a leaf 4 : distinctive element or style of expression —**veined** \'vānd\ *adj*

ve•loc•i•ty \və'läsətē\ *n, pl* -**ties** : speed

ve•lour, ve•lours \və'lúr\ *n, pl* **velours** \-'lúrz\ : fabric with a velvetlike pile

vel•vet \'velvət\ *n* : fabric with a short soft pile —**velvet** *adj* —**vel•vety** *adj*

ve•nal \'vēnəl\ *adj* : capable of being corrupted esp. by money —**ve•nal•i•ty** \vi-'nalətē\ *n* —**ve•nal•ly** *adv*

vend \'vend\ *vb* : sell —**vend•ible** *adj* —**ven•dor** \'vendər\ *n*

ven•det•ta \ven'detə\ *n* : feud marked by acts of revenge

ve•neer \və'nir\ *n* 1 : thin layer of fine wood glued over a cheaper wood 2 : superficial display ~ *vb* : overlay with a veneer

ven•er•a•ble \'venərəbəl\ *adj* : deserving of respect

ven•er•ate \'venə,rāt\ *vb* -**at•ed**; -**at•ing** : respect esp. with reverence —**ven•er•a•tion** \,venə'rāshən\ *n*

venereal disease \və'nirēəl-\ *n* : contagious disease spread through copulation

ven•geance \'venjəns\ *n* : punishment in retaliation for an injury or offense

venge•ful \'venjfəl\ *adj* : filled with a desire for revenge —**venge•ful•ly** *adv*

ve•nial \'vēnēəl\ *adj* : capable of being forgiven

ven•i•son \'venəsən, -əzən\ *n* : deer meat

ven•om \'venəm\ *n* 1 : poison secreted by certain animals 2 : ill will —**ven•om•ous** \-əmos\ *adj*

vent \'vent\ *vb* 1 : provide with or let out at a vent 2 : give expression to ~ *n* 1 : opening for passage or for relieving pressure

ven•ti•late \'vent³l,āt\ *vb* -**lat•ed**; -**lat•ing** : allow fresh air to circulate through —**ven•ti•la•tion** \,vent³l'āshən\ *n* —**ven•ti•la•tor** \'vent³l,ātər\ *n*

ven•tri•cle \'ventrikəl\ *n* : heart chamber that pumps blood into the arteries

ven•tril•o•quist \ven'trilə,kwist\ *n* : one who can make the voice appear to come from another source —**ven•tril•o•quism** \-,kwizəm\ *n* —**ven•tril•o•quy** \-kwē\ *n*

ven•ture \'venchər\ *vb* -**tured**; -**tur•ing** 1 : risk or take a chance on 2 : put forward (an opinion) ~ *n* : speculative business enterprise

ven•ture•some \-səm\ *adj* : brave or daring —**ven•ture•some•ly** *adv* —**ven•ture•some•ness** *n*

ven•ue \'venyü\ *n* : scene of an action or event

ve•rac•i•ty \və'rasətē\ *n, pl* -**ties** : truthfulness or accuracy —**ve•ra•cious** \və'rāshəs\ *adj*

ve•ran•da, ve•ran•dah \və'randə\ *n* : large open porch

verb \'vərb\ *n* : word that expresses action or existence

ver•bal \'vərbəl\ *adj* 1 : having to do with or expressed in words 2 : oral 3 : relating to or formed from a verb —**ver•bal•i•za•tion** \,vərbələ'zāshən\ *n* —**ver•bal•ize** \'vərbə,līz\ *vb* —**ver•bal•ly** \-ē\ *adv*

verbal auxiliary *n* : auxiliary verb

ver•ba•tim \vər'bātəm\ *adv or adj* : using the same words

ver•biage \'vərbēij\ *n* : excess of words

ver•bose \vər'bōs\ *adj* : using more words than are needed —**ver•bos•i•ty** \-'bäsətē\ *n*

ver•dant \'vərd³nt\ *adj* : green with growing plants —**ver•dant•ly** *adv*

ver•dict \'vərdikt\ *n* : decision of a jury

ver•dure \'vərjər\ *n* : green growing vegetation or its color

verge \'vərj\ *vb* **verged**; **verg•ing** : be almost on the point of happening or doing something ~ *n* 1 : edge 2 : threshold

ver•i•fy \'verə,fī\ *vb* -**fied**; -**fy•ing** : establish the truth, accuracy, or reality of —**ver•i•fi•able** *adj* —**ver•i•fi•ca•tion** \,verəfə-'kāshən\ *n*

ver•i•ly \'verəlē\ *adv* : truly or confidently

veri•si•mil•i•tude \,verəsə'milə,tüd\ *n* : appearance of being true

ver•i•ta•ble \'verətəbəl\ *adj* : actual or true —**ver•i•ta•bly** *adv*

ver•i•ty \'verətē\ *n, pl* -**ties** : truth

ver•mi•cel•li \,vərmə'chelē, -'sel-\ *n* : thin spaghetti

ver•min \'vərmən\ *n, pl* **vermin** : small animal pest

ver•mouth \vər'müth\ *n* : dry or sweet wine flavored with herbs

ver•nac•u•lar \vər'nakyələr\ *adj* : relating to a native language or dialect and esp. its normal spoken form ~ *n* : vernacular language

ver•nal \'vərn³l\ *adj* : relating to spring

ver•sa•tile \'vərsət³l\ *adj* : having many abilities or uses —**ver•sa•til•i•ty** \,vərsə-'tilətē\ *n*

¹verse \'vərs\ *n* 1 : line or stanza of poetry 2 : poetry 3 : short division of a chapter in the Bible

²verse *vb* **versed**; **vers•ing** : make familiar by experience, study, or practice

ver•sion \'vərzhən\ *n* 1 : translation of the Bible 2 : account or description from a particular point of view

ver•sus \'vərsəs\ *prep* : opposed to or against

ver•te•bra \'vərtəbrə\ *n, pl* -**brae** \-,brā, -,brē\ *or* -**bras** : segment of the backbone —**ver•te•bral** \vər'tēbrəl, 'vərtə-\ *adj*

ver•te•brate \'vərtəbrət, -,brāt\ *n* : animal with a backbone —**vertebrate** *adj*

ver•tex \'vər,teks\ *n, pl* **ver•ti•ces** \'vərtə-,sēz\ 1 : point of intersection of lines or surfaces 2 : highest point

ver•ti•cal \'vərtikəl\ *adj* : rising straight up from a level surface —**vertical** *n* —**ver•ti•cal•i•ty** \,vərtə'kalətē\ *n* —**ver•ti•cal•ly** *adv*

ver•ti•go \'vərti,gō\ *n, pl* -**goes** *or* -**gos** : dizziness

verve \'vərv\ *n* : liveliness or vividness

very \'verē\ *adj* **veri•er**; -**est** 1 : exact 2 : exactly suitable 3 : mere or bare 4 : precisely the same ~ *adv* 1 : to a high degree 2 : in actual fact

ves•i•cle \'vesikəl\ *n* : membranous cavity —**ve•sic•u•lar** \və'sikyələr\ *adj*

ves•pers \'vespərz\ *n pl* : late afternoon or evening worship service

ves•sel \'vesəl\ *n* 1 : a container (as a barrel, bottle, bowl, or cup) for a liquid 2 : craft for navigation esp. on water 3 : tube in which a body fluid is circulated

¹vest \'vest\ *vb* 1 : give a particular authority, right, or property to 2 : clothe with or as if with a garment

²vest *n* : sleeveless garment usu. worn under a suit coat

ves•ti•bule \'vestə,byül\ *n* : enclosed entrance —**ves•tib•u•lar** \ve'stibyələr\ *adj*

ves•tige \'vestij\ *n* : visible trace or remains —**ves•ti•gial** \ve'stijēəl\ *adj* —**ves•ti•gial•ly** *adv*

vest•ment \'vestmənt\ *n* : clergy member's garment

ves•try \'vestrē\ *n, pl* -**tries** : church storage room for garments and articles

vet•er•an \'vetərən\ *n* 1 : former member of the armed forces 2 : person with long experience —**veteran** *adj*

Veterans Day *n* : 4th Monday in October or formerly November 11 observed as a legal holiday in commemoration of the end of war in 1918 and 1945

vet·er·i·nar·i·an \vetərən'erēən\ *n* : doctor of animals —**vet·er·i·nary** \'vetərən,erē\ *adj*

ve·to \'vētō\ *n, pl* **-toes** 1 : power to forbid and esp. the power of a chief executive to prevent a bill from becoming law 2 : exercise of the veto ~ *vb* 1 : forbid 2 : reject a legislative bill

vex \'veks\ *vb* **vexed; vex·ing** : trouble, distress, or annoy —**vex·a·tion** \vek'sāshən\ *n* —**vex·a·tious** \-shəs\ *adj*

via \'vīə, 'vēə\ *prep* : by way of

vi·a·ble \'vīəbəl\ *adj* 1 : capable of surviving or growing 2 : practical or workable —**vi·a·bil·i·ty** \vīə'bilətē\ *n* —**vi·a·bly** \'vīəblē\ *adv*

via·duct \'vīə,dəkt\ *n* : elevated roadway or railway bridge

vi·al \'vīəl\ *n* : small bottle

vi·brant \'vībrənt\ *adj* 1 : vibrating 2 : pulsing with vigor or activity 3 : sounding from vibration —**vi·bran·cy** \-brənsē\ *n*

vi·brate \'vī,brāt\ *vb* **-brat·ed; -brat·ing** 1 : move or cause to move quickly back and forth or side to side 2 : respond sympathetically —**vi·bra·tion** \vī'brāshən\ *n* —**vi·bra·tor** \'vī,brātər\ *n* —**vi·bra·tory** \'vībrə,tórē\ *adj*

vic·ar \'vikər\ *n* : parish clergy member —**vic·ar·i·ate** \-ēət\ *n*

vi·car·i·ous \vī'karēəs\ *adj* : sharing in someone else's experience through imagination or sympathetic feelings —**vi·car·i·ous·ly** *adv* —**vi·car·i·ous·ness** *n*

vice \'vīs\ *n* 1 : immoral habit 2 : depravity

vice- \vīs\ *prefix* : one that takes the place of

vice-chancellor	vice president
vice-consul	vice presidential
vice presidency	vice-regent

vice admiral *n* : commissioned officer in the navy or coast guard ranking above a rear admiral

vice·roy \'vīs,roi\ *n* : provincial governor who represents the sovereign

vice ver·sa \vīsi'vərsə, ,vīs'vər-\ *adv* : with the order reversed

vi·cin·i·ty \və'sinətē\ *n, pl* **-ties** : surrounding area

vi·cious \'vishəs\ *adj* 1 : wicked 2 : savage 3 : malicious —**vi·cious·ly** *adv* —**vi·cious·ness** *n*

vi·cis·si·tude \və'sisə,tüd, vī-, -,tyüd\ *n* : irregular, unexpected, or surprising change —usu. used in pl.

vic·tim \'viktəm\ *n* : person killed, hurt, or abused

vic·tim·ize \'viktə,mīz\ *vb* **-ized; -iz·ing** : make a victim of —**vic·tim·i·za·tion** \,viktəmə'zāshən\ *n* —**vic·tim·iz·er** \'viktə,mīzər\ *n*

vic·tor \'viktər\ *n* : winner

Vic·to·ri·an \wik'tōrēən\ *adj* : relating to the reign of Queen Victoria of England or the art, taste, or standards of her time ~ *n* : one of the Victorian period

vic·to·ri·ous \wik'tōrēəs\ *adj* : having won a victory —**vic·to·ri·ous·ly** *adv*

vic·to·ry \'viktərē\ *n, pl* **-ries** : success in defeating an enemy or opponent or in overcoming difficulties

vict·uals \'vit°lz\ *n pl* : food

vid·eo \'vidē,ō\ *adj* : relating to the television image

vid·eo·cas·sette \,vidē,ōkə'set\ *n* : cassette containing videotape

vid·eo·tape \'vidē,ō,tāp\ *vb* : make a recording of (a television production) on special tape —**videotape** *n*

vie \'vī\ *vb* **vied; vy·ing** : contend —**vi·er** \'vīər\ *n*

view \'vyü\ *n* 1 : process of seeing or examining 2 : opinion 3 : area of landscape that can be seen 4 : range of vision 5 : purpose or object ~ *vb* 1 : look at 2 : think about or consider —**view·er** *n*

view·point *n* : position from which something is considered

vig·il \'vijəl\ *n* 1 : day of devotion before a religious feast 2 : act or time of keeping awake 3 : long period of keeping watch (as over a sick or dying person)

vig·i·lant \'vijələnt\ *adj* : alert esp. to avoid danger —**vig·i·lance** \-ləns\ *n* —**vig·i·lant·ly** *adv*

vig·i·lan·te \,vijə'lantē\ *n* : one of a group independent of the law working to suppress crime

vi·gnette \vin'yet\ *n* : short descriptive literary piece

vig·or \'vigər\ *n* 1 : energy or strength 2 : intensity or force —**vig·or·ous** \'vigərəs\ *adj* —**vig·or·ous·ly** *adv* —**vig·or·ous·ness** *n*

vile \'vīl\ *adj* **vil·er; vil·est** : thoroughly bad or contemptible —**vile·ly** *adv* —**vile·ness** *n*

vil·i·fy \'vilə,fī\ *vb* **-fied; -fy·ing** : speak evil of —**vil·i·fi·ca·tion** \,viləfə'kāshən\ *n* —**vil·i·fi·er** \'vilə,fīər\ *n*

vil·la \'vilə\ *n* : country estate

vil·lage \'vilij\ *n* : small country town —**vil·lag·er** *n*

vil·lain \'vilən\ *n* : bad person —**vil·lain·ess** \-ənəs\ *n* —**vil·lainy** *n*

vil·lain·ous \-ənəs\ *adj* : evil or corrupt —**vil·lain·ous·ly** *adv* —**vil·lain·ous·ness** *n*

vim \'vim\ *n* : energy

vin·di·cate \'vində,kāt\ *vb* **-cat·ed; -cat·ing** 1 : avenge 2 : exonerate 3 : justify —**vin·di·ca·tion** \,vində'kāshən\ *n* —**vin·di·ca·tor** \'vində,kātər\ *n*

vin·dic·tive \vin'diktiv\ *adj* : seeking or meant for revenge —**vin·dic·tive·ly** *adv* —**vin·dic·tive·ness** *n*

vine \'vīn\ *n* : climbing or trailing plant

vin·e·gar \'vinigər\ *n* : acidic liquid obtained by fermentation —**vin·e·gary** \-gərē\ *adj*

vine·yard \'vinyərd\ *n* : plantation of grapevines

vin·tage \'vintij\ *n* 1 : season's yield of grapes or wine 2 : period of origin ~ *adj* : of enduring interest

vi·nyl \'vīn°l\ *n* : strong plastic

vi·o·la \vē'ōlə\ *n* : instrument of the violin family tuned lower than the violin —**vi·o·list** \-list\ *n*

vi·o·late \'vīə,lāt\ *vb* **-lat·ed; -lat·ing** 1 : act with disrespect or disregard of 2 : rape 3 : desecrate —**vi·o·la·tion** \,vīə'lāshən\ *n* —**vi·o·la·tor** \'vīə,lātər\ *n*

vi·o·lence \'vīələns\ *n* : intense physical force that causes or is intended to cause injury or destruction —**vi·o·lent** \-lənt\ *adj* —**vi·o·lent·ly** *adv*

vi·o·let \'vīələt\ *n* 1 : small flowering plant 2 : reddish blue

vi·o·lin \,vīə'lin\ *n* : bowed stringed instrument —**vi·o·lin·ist** \-nist\ *n*

VIP \,vē,ī'pē\ *n, pl* **VIPs** \-'pēz\ : very important person

vi·per \'vīpər\ *n* 1 : venomous snake 2 : treacherous or malignant person

vi·ra·go \və'rägō, -'rä-; 'virə,gō\ *n, pl* **-goes** *or* **-gos** : shrew

vi·ral \'vīrəl\ *adj* : relating to or caused by a virus

vir·gin \'vərjən\ *n* 1 : unmarried woman 2 : a person who has never had sexual intercourse ~ *adj* 1 : chaste 2 : natural and unspoiled —**vir·gin·al** \-°l\ *adj* —**vir·gin·al·ly** *adv* —**vir·gin·i·ty** \vər'jinətē\ *n*

vir·gule \'vərgyül\ *n* : mark / used esp. to denote "or" or "per"

vir·ile \'virəl\ *adj* : masculine —**vi·ril·i·ty** \və'rilətē\ *n*

vir·tu·al \'vərchəwəl\ *adj* : being in effect but not in fact or name —**vir·tu·al·ly** *adv*

vir·tue \'vərchü\ *n* 1 : moral excellence 2 : effective or commendable quality 3 : chastity

vir·tu·os·i·ty \,vərchə'wäsətē\ *n, pl* **-ties** : great skill (as in music)

vir·tu·o·so \,vərchə'wōsō, -zō\ *n, pl* **-sos** *or* **-si** \-,sē, -,zē\ : highly skilled performer esp. of music —**virtuoso** *adj*

vir·tu·ous \'vərchəwəs\ *adj* 1 : morally good 2 : chaste —**vir·tu·ous·ly** *adv*

vir·u·lent \'virələnt, -yələnt\ *adj* 1 : extremely severe or infectious 2 : full of malice —**vir·u·lence** \-ləns\ *n* —**vir·u·lent·ly** *adv*

vi·rus \'vīrəs\ *n* 1 : tiny disease-causing agent 2 : a computer program that performs a malicious action (as destroying data)

vi·sa \'vēzə, -sə\ *n* : authorization to enter a foreign country

vis·age \'vizij\ *n* : face

vis·cera \'visərə\ *n pl* : internal bodily organs esp. of the trunk

vis·cer·al \'visərəl\ *adj* 1 : bodily 2 : instinctive 3 : deeply or crudely emotional —**vis·cer·al·ly** *adv*

vis·cid \'visəd\ *adj* : viscous —**vis·cid·i·ty** \vis'idətē\ *n*

vis·count \'vī,kaunt\ *n* : British nobleman ranking below an earl and above a baron

vis·count·ess \-əs\ *n* 1 : wife of a viscount 2 : woman with rank of a viscount

vis·cous \'viskəs\ *adj* : having a thick or sticky consistency —**vis·cos·i·ty** \vis·'käsətē\ *n*

vise \'vīs\ *n* : device for clamping something being worked on

vis·i·bil·i·ty \,vizə'bilətē\ *n, pl* **-ties** : degree or range to which something can be seen

vis·i·ble \'vizəbəl\ *adj* : capable of being seen 2 : manifest or apparent —**vis·i·bly** *adv*

vi·sion \'vizhən\ *n* 1 : vivid picture seen in a dream or trance or in the imagination 2 : foresight 3 : power of seeing ~ *vb* : imagine

vi·sion·ary \'vizhə,nerē\ *adj* 1 : given to dreaming or imagining 2 : illusory 3 : not practical ~ *n* : one with great dreams or projects

vis·it \'vizət\ *vb* 1 : go or come to see 2 : stay with for a time as a guest 3 : cause or be a reward, affliction, or punishment ~ *n* : short stay as a guest —**vis·it·able** *adj* —**vis·i·tor** \-ər\ *n*

vis·i·ta·tion \,vizə'tāshən\ *n* 1 : official visit 2 : divine punishment or favor 3 : severe trial

vi·sor \'vīzər\ *n* 1 : front piece of a helmet 2 : part (as on a cap or car windshield) that shades the eyes

vis·ta \'vistə\ *n* : distant view

vi·su·al \'vizhəwəl\ *adj* 1 : relating to sight 2 : visible —**vi·su·al·ly** *adv*

vi·su·al·ize \'vizhəwə,līz\ *vb* **-ized; -iz·ing** : form a mental image of —**vi·su·al·i·za·tion** \,vizhəwələ'zāshən\ *n* —**vi·su·al·iz·er** \'vizhəwə,līzər\ *n*

vi·tal \'vīt°l\ *adj* 1 : relating to, necessary for, or characteristic of life 2 : full of life and vigor 3 : fatal 4 : very important —**vi·tal·ly** *adv*

vi·tal·i·ty \vī'talətē\ *n, pl* **-ties** 1 : life force 2 : energy

vital signs *n pl* : body's pulse rate, respiration, temperature, and usu. blood pressure

vi·ta·min \'vītəmən\ *n* : natural organic substance essential to health

vi·ti·ate \'vishē,āt\ *vb* **-at·ed; -at·ing** 1 : spoil or impair 2 : invalidate —**vi·ti·a·tion** \vishē'āshən\ *n* —**vi·ti·a·tor** \'vishē,ātər\ *n*

vit·re·ous \'vitrēəs\ *adj* : relating to or resembling glass

vit·ri·ol \'vitrēəl\ *n* : something caustic, corrosive, or biting —**vit·ri·ol·ic** \,vitrē'älik\ *adj*

vi·tu·per·ate \vī'tüpə,rāt, və-, -'tyü-\ *vb* **-at·ed; -at·ing** : abuse in words —**vi·tu·per·a·tion** \-,tüpə'rāshən, -,tyü-\ *n* —**vi·tu·per·a·tive** \-'tüpərətiv, -'tyü-, -pə,rāt-\ *adj* —**vi·tu·per·a·tive·ly** *adv*

vi·va·cious \və'vāshəs, vī-\ *adj* : lively —**vi·va·cious·ly** *adv* —**vi·va·cious·ness** *n* —**vi·vac·i·ty** \-'vasətē\ *n*

viv·id \'vivəd\ *adj* 1 : lively 2 : brilliant 3 : intense or sharp —**viv·id·ly** *adv* —**viv·id·ness** *n*

viv·i·fy \'vivə,fī\ *vb* **-fied; -fy·ing** : give life or vividness to

vivi·sec·tion \,vivə'sekshən, 'vivə,-\ *n* : experimental operation on a living animal

vix·en \'viksən\ *n* 1 : scolding woman 2 : female fox

vo·cab·u·lary \vō'kabyə,lerē\ *n, pl* **-lar·ies** 1 : list or collection of words 2 : stock of words used by a person or about a subject

vo·cal \'vōkəl\ *adj* 1 : relating to or produced by or for the voice 2 : speaking out freely and usu. emphatically

vocal cords *n pl* : membranous folds in the larynx that are important in making vocal sounds

vo·cal·ist \'vōkəlist\ *n* : singer

vo·cal·ize \-,līz\ *vb* **-ized; -iz·ing** : give vocal expression to

vo·ca·tion \vō'kāshən\ *n* : regular employment —**vo·ca·tion·al** \-shənəl\ *adj*

vo·cif·er·ous \vō'sifərəs\ *adj* : noisy and insistent —**vo·cif·er·ous·ly** *adv*

vod·ka \'vädkə\ *n* : colorless distilled grain liquor

vogue \'vōg\ *n* : brief but intense popularity —**vogu·ish** \'vōgish\ *adj*

voice \'vóis\ *n* 1 : sound produced through the mouth by humans and many animals 2 : power of speaking 3 : right of choice or opinion ~ *vb* **voiced; voic·ing** : express in words —**voiced** \'vóist\ *adj*

void \'vóid\ *adj* 1 : containing nothing 2 : lacking —with *of* 3 : not legally binding ~ *n* 1 : empty space 2 : feeling of hollowness ~ *vb* 1 : discharge (as body waste) 2 : make (as a contract) void —**void·able** *adj* —**void·er** *n*

vol·a·tile \'välət°l\ *adj* 1 : readily vaporizing at a relatively low temperature 2 : likely to change suddenly —**vol·a·til·i·ty** \,välə'tilətē\ *n* —**vol·a·til·ize** \'välət°l,īz\ *vb*

vol·ca·no \väl'kānō\ *n, pl* **-noes** *or* **-nos** : opening in the earth's crust from which molten rock and steam come out —**vol·ca·nic** \-'kanik\ *adj*

vo·li·tion \vō'lishən\ *n* : free will —**vo·li·tion·al** \-'lishənəl\ *adj*

vol·ley \'välē\ *n, pl* **-leys** 1 : flight of missiles (as arrows) 2 : simultaneous shooting of many weapons

vol·ley·ball *n* : game of batting a large ball over a net

volt \'vōlt\ *n* : unit for measuring the force that moves an electric current

volt·age \'vōltij\ *n* : quantity of volts

vol·u·ble \'välyəbəl\ *adj* : fluent and smooth in speech —**vol·u·bil·i·ty** \,välyə'bilətē\ *n* —**vol·u·bly** \'välyəblē\ *adv*

vol·ume \'välyəm\ *n* 1 : book 2 : space occupied as measured by cubic units 3 : amount 4 : loudness of a sound

vo·lu·mi·nous \və'lümənəs\ *adj* : large or bulky

vol·un·tary \'välən,terē\ *adj* 1 : done, made, or given freely and without expecting compensation 2 : relating to or controlled by the will —**vol·un·tar·i·ly** *adv*

vol·un·teer \,välən'tir\ *n* : person who offers to help or work without expecting payment or reward ~ *vb* 1 : offer or give voluntarily 2 : offer oneself as a volunteer

vo·lup·tuous \və'ləpchəwəs\ *adj* 1 : luxurious 2 : having a full and sexually attractive figure —**vo·lup·tuous·ly** *adv* —**vo·lup·tuous·ness** *n*

vom·it \'vämət\ *vb* : throw up the contents of the stomach —**vomit** *n*

voo·doo \'vüdü\ *n, pl* **voodoos** 1 : religion derived from African polytheism and involving sorcery 2 : one who practices voodoo 3 : charm or fetish used in voodoo —**voodoo** *adj* —**voo·doo·ism** \-,izəm\ *n*

vo·ra·cious \vó'rāshəs, və-\ *adj* : greedy or exceedingly hungry —**vo·ra·cious·ly** *adv* —**vo·ra·cious·ness** *n* —**vo·rac·i·ty** \-'rasətē\ *n*

vor·tex \'vór,teks\ *n, pl* **vor·ti·ces** \'vórtə,sēz\ : whirling liquid

vo·ta·ry \'vōtərē\ *n, pl* **-ries** 1 : devoted participant, adherent, admirer, or worshiper

vote \'vōt\ *n* 1 : individual expression of preference in choosing or reaching a decision 2 : right to indicate one's preference or the preference expressed ~ *vb* **vot·ed; vot·ing** 1 : cast a vote 2 : choose or defeat by vote —**vote·less** *adj* —**vot·er** *n*

vo·tive \'vōtiv\ *adj* : consisting of or expressing a vow, wish, or desire

vouch \'vauch\ *vb* : give a guarantee or personal assurance

vouch·er \'vauchər\ *n* : written record or receipt that serves as proof of a transaction

vouch·safe \vauch'sāf\ *vb* **-safed; -saf·ing** : grant as a special favor

vow \'wau\ *n* : solemn promise to do something or to live or act a certain way —**vow** *vb*

vow·el \'vauəl\ *n* 1 : speech sound produced without obstruction or friction in the mouth 2 : letter representing such a sound

voy·age \'vóiij\ *n* : long journey esp. by water or through space ~ *vb* **-aged; -ag·ing** : make a voyage —**voy·ag·er** *n*

vul·ca·nize \'vəlkə,nīz\ *vb* **-nized; -niz·ing** : treat (as rubber) to make more elastic or stronger

vul·gar \'vəlgər\ *adj* 1 : relating to the common people 2 : lacking refinement 3 : offensive in manner or language —**vul·gar·ism** \-,rizəm\ *n* —**vul·gar·ize** \-,rīz\ *vb* —**vul·gar·ly** *adv*

vul·gar·i·ty \,vəl'garətē\ *n, pl* **-ties** 1 : state of being vulgar 2 : vulgar language or act

vul·ner·a·ble \'vəlnərəbəl\ *adj* : susceptible to attack or damage —**vul·ner·a·bil·i·ty** \,vəlnərə'bilətē\ *n* —**vul·ner·a·bly** *adv*

vul·ture \'vəlchər\ *n* : large flesh-eating bird

vul·va \'vəlvə\ *n, pl* **-vae** \-,vē, -,vī\ : external genital parts of the female

vying *pres part of* VIE

W

w \'dəbəl,yü\ *n, pl* **w's** *or* **ws** \-,yüz\ : 23d letter of the alphabet

wad \'wäd\ *n* 1 : little mass 2 : soft mass of fibrous material 3 : pliable plug to retain a powder charge 4 : considerable amount ~ *vb* 1 : form into a wad 2 : stuff with a wad

wad·dle \'wäd°l\ *vb* **-dled; -dling** : walk with short steps swaying from side to side —**waddle** *n*

wade \'wäd\ *vb* **wad·ed; wad·ing** 1 : step in or through (as water) 2 : move with difficulty —**wade** *n* —**wad·er** *n*

wa·fer \'wāfər\ *n* 1 : thin crisp cake or cracker 2 : waferlike thing

waf·fle \'wäfəl\ *n* : crisped cake of batter cooked in a hinged utensil (**waffle iron**) ~ *vb* : vacillate

waft \'wäft, 'waft\ *vb* : cause to move lightly by wind or waves —**waft** *n*

¹**wag** \'wag\ *vb* **-gg-** : sway or swing from side to side or to and fro —**wag** *n*

²**wag** *n* : wit —**wag·gish** *adj*

wage \'wāj\ *vb* **waged; wag·ing** : engage in ~ *n* 1 : payment for labor or services 2 : compensation

wa·ger \'wājər\ *n or vb* : bet

wag•gle \'wagəl\ vb -gled; -gling : wag — **waggle** n

wag•on \'wagən\ n 1 : 4-wheeled vehicle drawn by animals 2 : child's 4-wheeled cart

waif \'wāf\ n : homeless child

wail \'wāl\ vb 1 : mourn 2 : make a sound like a mournful cry —**wail** n

wain•scot \'wānskət, -,skōt, -,skät\ n : usu. paneled wooden lining of an interior wall —**wainscot** vb

waist \'wāst\ n 1 : narrowed part of the body between chest and hips 2 : waistlike part —**waist•line** n

wait \'wāt\ vb 1 : remain in readiness or expectation 2 : delay 3 : attend as a waiter ~ n 1 : concealment 2 : act or period of waiting

wait•er \'wātər\ n : person who serves others at tables

wait•per•son \'wāt,pərsən\ n : a waiter or waitress

wait•ress \'wātrəs\ n : woman who serves others at tables

waive \'wāv\ vb waived; waiv•ing : give up claim to

waiv•er \'wāvər\ n : act of waiving right, claim, or privilege

1wake \'wāk\ vb woke \'wōk\; wo•ken \'wōkən\; wak•ing 1 : keep watch 2 : bring or come back to consciousness after sleep ~ n 1 : state of being awake 2 : watch held over a dead body

2wake n : track left by a ship

wake•ful \'wākfəl\ adj : not sleeping or able to sleep —**wake•ful•ness** n

wak•en \'wākən\ vb : wake

wale \'wāl\ n : ridge on cloth

walk \'wók\ vb 1 : move or cause to move on foot 2 : pass over, through, or along by walking ~ n 1 : a going on foot 2 : place or path for walking 3 : distance to be walked 4 : way of living 5 : way of walking 6 : slow 4-beat gait of a horse —**walk•er** n

wall \'wól\ n 1 : structure for defense or for enclosing something 2 : upright enclosing part of a building or room 3 : something like a wall ~ vb : provide, separate, surround, or close with a wall —**walled** \'wóld\ adj

wal•la•by \'wäləbē\ n, pl -bies : small or medium-sized kangaroo

wal•let \'wälət\ n : pocketbook with compartments

wall•flow•er n 1 : mustardlike plant with showy fragrant flowers 2 : one who remains on the sidelines of social activity

wal•lop \'wäləp\ n 1 : powerful blow 2 : ability to hit hard ~ vb 1 : beat soundly 2 : hit hard

wal•low \'wälō\ vb 1 : roll about in deep mud 2 : indulge oneself excessively ~ n : place for wallowing

wall•pa•per n : decorative paper for walls —**wallpaper** vb

wal•nut \'wól,nət\ n 1 : nut with a furrowed shell and adherent husk 2 : tree on which this nut grows or its brown wood

wal•rus \'wólrəs, 'wäl-\ n, pl -rus or -rus•es : large seallike mammal of northern seas having ivory tusks

waltz \'wólts\ n : gliding dance to music having 3 beats to the measure or the music —**waltz** vb

wam•pum \'wämpəm\ n : strung shell beads used by No. American Indians as money

wan \'wän\ adj -nn- : sickly or pale —**wan•ly** adv —**wan•ness** n

wand \'wänd\ n : slender staff

wan•der \'wändər\ vb 1 : move about aimlessly 2 : stray 3 : become delirious —**wan•der•er** n

wan•der•lust \'wändər,ləst\ n : strong urge to wander

wane \'wān\ vb waned; wan•ing 1 : grow smaller or less 2 : lose power, prosperity, or influence —**wane** n

wan•gle \'waŋgəl\ vb -gled; -gling : obtain by sly or devious means

want \'wónt\ vb 1 : lack 2 : need 3 : desire earnestly ~ n 1 : deficiency 2 : dire need 3 : something wanted

want•ing \-iŋ\ adj 1 : not present or in evidence 2 : falling below standards 3 : lacking in ability ~ prep 1 : less or minus 2 : without

wan•ton \'wónt°n\ adj 1 : lewd 2 : having no regard for justice or for others' feelings, rights, or safety ~ n : lewd or immoral person ~ vb : be wanton —**wan•ton•ly** adv —**wan•ton•ness** n

wa•pi•ti \'wäpətē\ n, pl -ti or -tis : elk

war \'wór\ n 1 : armed fighting between nations 2 : state of hostility or conflict 3 : struggle between opposing forces or for a particular end ~ vb -rr- : engage in warfare —**war•less** \-ləs\ adj —**war•time** n

war•ble \'wórbəl\ n 1 : melodious succession of low pleasing sounds 2 : musical trill ~ vb -bled; -bling : sing or utter in a trilling way

war•bler \'wórblər\ n 1 : small thrushlike

singing bird 2 : small bright-colored insect-eating bird

ward \'wórd\ n 1 : a guarding or being under guard or guardianship 2 : division of a prison or hospital 3 : electoral or administrative division of a city 4 : person under protection of a guardian or a law court ~ vb : turn aside —**ward•ship** n

1-ward \wərd\ adj suffix 1 : that moves, tends, faces, or is directed toward 2 : that occurs or is situated in the direction of

2-ward, -wards adv suffix 1 : in a (specified) direction 2 : toward a (specified) point, position, or area

war•den \'wórd°n\ n 1 : guardian 2 : official charged with supervisory duties or enforcement of laws 3 : official in charge of a prison

ward•er \'wórdər\ n : watchman or warden

ward•robe \'wórd,rōb\ n 1 : clothes closet 2 : collection of wearing apparel

ware \'war\ n 1 : articles for sale —often pl. 2 : items of fired clay

ware•house \-,haús\ n : place for storage of merchandise —**warehouse•man** \-mən\ n —**ware•hous•er** \-,haúzər, -sər\ n

war•fare \'wór,far\ n 1 : military operations between enemies 2 : struggle

war•head \-,hed\ n : part of a missile holding the explosive material

war•like adj : fond of, relating to, or used in war

warm \'wórm\ adj 1 : having or giving out moderate or adequate heat 2 : serving to retain heat 3 : showing strong feeling 4 : giving a pleasant impression of warmth, cheerfulness, or friendliness ~ vb 1 : make or become warm 2 : give warmth or energy to 3 : experience feelings of affection 4 : become increasingly ardent, interested, or competent —**warm•er** n —**warm•ly** adv —**warm up** vb : make ready by preliminary activity

war•mon•ger \'wór,məŋgər, -,mäŋ-\ n : one who attempts to stir up war

warmth \'wórmth\ n 1 : quality or state of being warm 2 : enthusiasm

warn \'wórn\ vb 1 : put on guard 2 : notify in advance —**warn•ing** \-iŋ\ n or adj

warp \'wórp\ n 1 : lengthwise threads in a woven fabric 2 : twist ~ vb 1 : twist out of shape 2 : lead astray 3 : distort

war•rant \'wórənt, 'wär-\ n 1 : authorization 2 : legal writ authorizing action ~ vb 1 : declare or maintain positively 2 : guarantee 3 : approve 4 : justify

warrant officer n 1 : officer in the armed forces ranking next below a commissioned officer 2 : commissioned officer in the navy or coast guard ranking below an ensign

war•ran•ty \'wórəntē, 'wär-\ n, pl -ties : guarantee of the integrity of a product

war•ren \'wórən, 'wär-\ n : area where rabbits are bred and kept

war•rior \'wóryər, 'wórēər; 'wärē-, 'wäryər-\ n : man engaged or experienced in warfare

war•ship \'wór,ship\ n : naval vessel

wart \'wórt\ n 1 : small projection on the skin caused by a virus 2 : wartlike protuberance —**warty** adj

wary \'warē\ adj war•i•er; -est : careful in guarding against danger or deception

was past 1st & 3d sing of BE

wash \'wósh, 'wäsh\ vb 1 : cleanse with or as if with a liquid (as water) 2 : wet thoroughly with liquid 3 : flow along the border of 4 : flow in a stream 5 : move or remove by or as if by the action of water 6 : cover or daub lightly with a liquid 7 : undergo laundering ~ n 1 : act of washing or being washed 2 : articles to be washed 3 : surging action of water or disturbed air —**wash•able** \-əbəl\ adj

wash•board n : grooved board to scrub clothes on

wash•bowl n : large bowl for water for washing hands and face

wash•cloth n : cloth used for washing one's face and body

washed-up \'wósht'əp, 'wäsht-\ adj : no longer capable or usable

wash•er \'wóshər, 'wäsh-\ n 1 : machine for washing 2 : ring used around a bolt or screw to ensure tightness or relieve friction

wash•ing \'wóshiŋ, 'wäsh-\ n : articles to be washed

Washington's Birthday n : the 3d Monday in February or formerly February 22 observed as a legal holiday

wash•out n 1 : washing out or away of earth 2 : failure

wash•room n : bathroom

wasp \'wäsp, 'wósp\ n : slender-bodied winged insect related to the bees and having a formidable sting

wasp•ish \'wäspish, 'wós-\ adj : irritable

was•sail \'wäsəl, wä'säl\ n 1 : toast to someone's health 2 : liquor drunk on festive occasions 3 : riotous drinking —**was•sail** vb

waste \'wāst\ n 1 : sparsely settled or barren region 2 : act or an instance of wasting 3 : refuse (as garbage or rubbish) 4 : material (as feces) produced but not used by a living body ~ vb wast•ed; wast•ing 1 : ruin 2 : spend or use carelessly 3 : lose substance or energy ~ adj 1 : wild and uninhabited 2 : being of no further use —**wast•er** n —**waste•ful** \-fəl\ adj —**waste•ful•ly** adv —**waste•ful•ness** n

waste•bas•ket \-,baskət\ n : receptacle for refuse

waste•land \-,land, -lənd\ n : barren uncultivated land

wast•rel \'wāstrəl, 'wästrəl\ n : one who wastes

watch \'wäch, 'wóch\ vb 1 : be or stay awake intentionally 2 : be on the lookout for danger 3 : observe 4 : keep oneself informed about ~ n 1 : act of keeping awake to guard 2 : close observation 3 : one that watches 4 : period of duty on a ship or those on duty during this period 5 : timepiece carried on the person —**watch•er** n

watch•dog n 1 : dog kept to guard property 2 : one that protects

watch•ful \-fəl\ adj : steadily attentive —**watch•ful•ly** adv —**watch•ful•ness** n

watch•man \-mən\ n : person assigned to watch

watch•word n 1 : secret word used as a signal 2 : slogan

wa•ter \'wótər, 'wät-\ n 1 : liquid that descends as rain and forms rivers, lakes, and seas 2 : liquid containing or resembling water ~ vb 1 : supply with or get water 2 : dilute with or as if with water 3 : form or secrete watery matter

water buffalo n : common oxlike often domesticated Asian buffalo

wa•ter•col•or n 1 : paint whose liquid part is water 2 : picture made with watercolors

wa•ter•course n : stream of water

wa•ter•cress \-,kres\ n : perennial salad plant with white flowers

wa•ter•fall n : steep descent of the water of a stream

wa•ter•fowl n 1 : bird that frequents the water 2 **waterfowl** pl : swimming game birds

wa•ter•front n : land fronting a body of water

water lily n : aquatic plant with floating leaves and showy flowers

wa•ter•logged \-,lógd, -,lägd\ adj : filled or soaked with water

wa•ter•mark n 1 : mark showing how high water has risen 2 : a marking in paper visible under light ~ vb : mark (paper) with a watermark

wa•ter•mel•on n : large fruit with sweet juicy usu. red pulp

water moccasin n : venomous snake of the southeastern U.S.

wa•ter•pow•er n : power of moving water used to run machinery

wa•ter•proof n : not letting water through ~ vb : make waterproof —**wa•ter•proof•ing** n

wa•ter•shed \-,shed\ n : dividing ridge between two drainage areas or one of these areas

water ski n : ski used on water when the wearer is towed —**wa•ter-ski** vb —**wa•ter-ski•er** n

wa•ter•spout n 1 : pipe from which water is spouted 2 : tornado over a body of water

wa•ter•tight adj 1 : so tight as not to let water in 2 : allowing no possibility for doubt or uncertainty

wa•ter•way n : navigable body of water

wa•ter•works n pl : system by which water is supplied (as to a city)

wa•tery \'wótərē, 'wät-\ adj 1 : containing, full of, or giving out water 2 : being like water 3 : soft and soggy

watt \'wät\ n : unit of electric power —**watt•age** \'wätij\ n

wat•tle \'wät°l\ n 1 : framework of flexible branches used in building 2 : fleshy process hanging usu. about the head or neck (as of a bird) —**wat•tled** \-°ld\ adj

wave \'wāv\ vb waved; wav•ing 1 : flutter 2 : signal with the hands 3 : wave to and fro with the hand 4 : curve up and down like a wave ~ n 1 : moving swell on the surface of water 2 : wave-like shape 3 : waving motion 4 : surge 5 : disturbance that transfers energy from point to point —**wave•let** \-lət\ n —**wave•like** adj —**wavy** adj

wave•length \'wāv,leŋth\ n 1 : distance from crest to crest in the line of advance of a wave 2 : line of thought that reveals a common understanding

wa•ver \'wāvər\ vb 1 : fluctuate in opinion, allegiance, or direction 2 : flicker 3 : falter —**waver** n —**wa•ver•er** n —**wa•ver•ing•ly** adv

1wax \'waks\ n 1 : yellowish plastic substance secreted by bees 2 : substance like beeswax ~ vb : treat or rub with wax esp. for polishing

2wax vb 1 : grow larger 2 : become

wax•en \'waksən\ adj : made of or resembling wax

waxy \'waksē\ adj wax•i•er; -est : made of, full of, or resembling wax

way \'wā\ n 1 : thoroughfare for travel or passage 2 : route 3 : course of action 4 : method 5 : detail 6 : usual or characteristic state of affairs 7 : condition 8 : distance 9 : progress along a course —**by the way** : in a digression —**by way of** 1 : for the purpose of 2 : by the route through —**out of the way** : remote

way•bill n : paper that accompanies a shipment and gives details of goods, route, and charges

way•far•er \'wā,farər\ n : traveler esp. on foot —**way•far•ing** \-,fariŋ\ adj

way•lay \-,lā\ vb -laid \-,lād\ -lay•ing : lie in wait for

way•side n : side of a road

way•ward \'wāwərd\ adj 1 : following one's own capricious inclinations 2 : unpredictable

we \'wē\ pron —used of a group that includes the speaker or writer

weak \'wēk\ adj 1 : lacking strength or vigor 2 : deficient in vigor of mind or character 3 : of less than usual strength 4 : not having or exerting authority —**weak•en** \'wēkən\ vb —**weak•ly** adv

weak•ling \-liŋ\ n : person who is physically, mentally, or morally weak

weak•ly \'wēklē\ adj : feeble

weak•ness \-nəs\ n 1 : quality or state of being weak 2 : fault 3 : object of special liking

wealth \'welth\ n 1 : abundant possessions or resources 2 : profusion

wealthy \'welthē\ adj wealth•i•er; -est : having wealth

wean \'wēn\ vb 1 : accustom (a young mammal) to take food by means other than nursing 2 : free from dependence

weap•on \'wepən\ n 1 : something (as a gun) that may be used to fight with 2 : means by which one contends against another —**weap•on•less** adj

wear \'war\ vb wore \'wōr\; worn \'wōrn\; wear•ing 1 : use as an article of clothing or adornment 2 : carry on the person 3 : show an appearance of 4 : decay by use or by scraping 5 : lessen the strength of 6 : endure use ~ n 1 : act of wearing 2 : clothing 3 : lasting quality 4 : result of use —**wear•able** \'warəbəl\ adj —**wear•er** n —**wear out** vb 1 : make or become useless by wear 2 : tire

wea•ri•some \'wirēsəm\ adj : causing weariness —**wea•ri•some•ly** adv —**wea•ri•some•ness** n

wea•ry \'wirē\ adj -ri•er; -est 1 : worn out in strength, freshness, or patience 2 : expressing or characteristic of weariness ~ vb -ried; -ry•ing : make or become weary —**wea•ri•ly** adv —**wea•ri•ness** n

wea•sel \'wēzəl\ n : small slender flesh-eating mammal

weath•er \'wethər\ n 1 : state of the atmosphere ~ vb 1 : expose to or endure the action of weather 2 : endure

weath•er-beat•en adj : worn or damaged by exposure to the weather

weath•er•man \-,man\ n : one who forecasts and reports the weather

weath•er•proof adj : able to withstand exposure to weather —**weatherproof** vb

weather vane n : movable device that shows the way the wind blows

weave \'wēv\ vb wove \'wōv\ or weaved; wo•ven \'wōvən\ or weaved; weav•ing 1 : form by interlacing strands of material 2 : to make as if by weaving together parts 3 : follow a winding course ~ n : pattern or method of weaving —**weav•er** n

web \'web\ n 1 : cobweb 2 : animal or plant membrane 3 : network ~ vb -bb- : cover or provide with a web —**webbed** \'webd\ adj

web•bing \'webiŋ\ n : strong closely woven tape

wed \'wed\ vb -dd- 1 : marry 2 : unite

wed•ding \'wediŋ\ n : marriage ceremony and celebration

wedge \'wej\ n : V-shaped object used for splitting, raising, forcing open, or tightening ~ vb wedged; wedg•ing 1 : tighten or split with a wedge 2 : force into a narrow space

wed•lock \'wed,läk\ n : marriage

Wednes•day \'wenzdā, -dē\ n : 4th day of the week

wee \'wē\ adj : very small

weed \'wēd\ n : unwanted plant ~ vb 1 : remove weeds 2 : get rid of —**weed•er** n —**weedy** adj

weeds n pl : mourning clothes

week \'wēk\ n 1 : 7 successive days 2 : calendar period of 7 days beginning with Sunday and ending with Saturday 3 : the working or school days of the calendar week

week·day \'wēk,dā\ n : any day except Sunday and often Saturday

week·end \-,end\ n : Saturday and Sunday ~ vb : spend the weekend

week·ly \'wēklē\ adj : occurring, appearing, or done every week ~ n, pl **-lies** : weekly publication —**weekly** adv

weep \'wēp\ vb **wept** \'wept\; **weep·ing** : shed tears —**weep·er** n —**weepy** adj

wee·vil \'wēvəl\ n : small injurious beetle with a long head usu. curved into a snout —**wee·vily, wee·vil·ly** \'wēvəlē\ adj

weft \'weft\ n : crosswise threads or yarn in weaving

weigh \'wā\ vb 1 : determine the heaviness of 2 : have a specified weight 3 : consider carefully 4 : raise (an anchor) off the sea floor 5 : press down or burden

weight \'wāt\ n 1 : amount that something weighs 2 : relative heaviness 3 : heavy object 4 : burden or pressure 5 : importance ~ vb 1 : load with a weight 2 : oppress —**weight·less** \-ləs\ adj —**weight·less·ness** n —**weighty** \'wātē\ adj

weird \'wird\ adj 1 : unearthly or mysterious 2 : strange —**weird·ly** adv —**weird·ness** n

wel·come \'welkəm\ vb **-comed; -com·ing** : accept or greet cordially ~ adj : received or permitted gladly ~ n : cordial greeting or reception

weld \'weld\ vb : unite by heating, hammering, or pressing ~ n : union by welding —**weld·er** n

wel·fare \'wel,far\ n 1 : prosperity 2 : government aid for those in need

1well \'wel\ n 1 : spring 2 : hole sunk in the earth to obtain a natural deposit (as of oil) 3 : source of supply 4 : open space extending vertically through floors ~ vb : flow forth

2well adv **better** \'betər\; **best** \'best\ 1 : in a good or proper manner 2 : satisfactorily 3 : fully 4 : intimately 5 : considerably ~ adj 1 : satisfactory 2 : prosperous 3 : desirable 4 : healthy

well-adjusted \,welə'jəstəd\ adj : well-balanced

well-ad·vised \,weləd'vīzd\ adj : prudent

well-balanced \'wel'balənst\ adj 1 : evenly balanced 2 : emotionally or psychologically sound

well-be·ing \'wel'bēiŋ\ n : state of being happy, healthy, or prosperous

well-bred \-'bred\ adj : having good manners

well-done adj 1 : properly performed 2 : cooked thoroughly

well-heeled \-'hēld\ adj : financially well-off

well-mean·ing adj : having good intentions

well-nigh adv : nearly

well-off adj : being in good condition esp. financially

well-read \-'red\ adj : well informed through reading

well-round·ed \-'raundəd\ adj : broadly developed

well·spring n : source

well-to-do \,weltə'dü\ adj : prosperous

welsh \'welsh, 'welch\ vb 1 : avoid payment 2 : break one's word

Welsh rabbit n : melted then seasoned cheese poured over toast or crackers

Welsh rare·bit \-'rarbət\ n : Welsh rabbit

welt \'welt\ n 1 : narrow strip of leather between a shoe upper and sole 2 : ridge raised on the skin usu. by a blow ~ vb : hit hard

wel·ter \'weltər\ vb 1 : toss about 2 : wallow ~ n : confused jumble

wen \'wen\ n : abnormal growth or cyst

wench \'wench\ n : young woman

wend \'wend\ vb : direct one's course

went past of GO

wept past of WEEP

were past 2d sing, past pl, or past subjunctive of BE

were·wolf \'wer,wulf, 'wir-, 'wər-\ n, pl **-wolves** \-,wulvz\ : person held to be able to change into a wolf

west \'west\ adv : to or toward the west ~ adj : situated toward or at or coming from the west ~ n 1 : direction of sunset 2 cap : regions to the west —**west·er·ly** \'westərlē\ adv or adj —**west·ward** \-wərd\ adv or adj —**west·wards** \-wərdz\ adv

west·ern \'westərn\ adj 1 cap : of a region designated West 2 : lying toward or coming from the west —**West·ern·er** n

wet \'wet\ adj **-tt-** 1 : consisting of or covered or soaked with liquid 2 : not dry ~ n : moisture ~ vb **-tt-** : make or become moist —**wet·ly** adv —**wet·ness** n

whack \'hwak\ vb : strike sharply ~ n 1 : sharp blow 2 : proper working order 3 : chance 4 : try

1whale \'hwāl\ n, pl **whales** or **whale** : large marine mammal ~ vb **whaled; whal·ing** : hunt for whales —**whaleboat** n —**whal·er** n

2whale vb **whaled; whal·ing** : strike or hit vigorously

whale·bone n : horny substance attached to the upper jaw of some large whales (**whalebone whales**)

wharf \'hworf\ n, pl **wharves** \'hworvz\ : structure alongside which boats lie to load or unload

what \'hwät\ pron 1 —used to inquire the identity or nature of something 2 : that which 3 : whatever ~ adv : in what respect ~ adj 1 —used to inquire about the identity or nature of something 2 : how remarkable or surprising 3 : whatever

what·ev·er \hwät'evər\ pron 1 : anything or everything that 2 : no matter what ~ adj : of any kind at all

what·not \'hwät,nät\ pron : any of various other things that might be mentioned

what·so·ev·er \,hwätsō'evər\ pron or adj : whatever

wheal \'hwēl\ n : a welt on the skin

wheat \'hwēt\ n : cereal grain that yields flour —**wheat·en** adj

whee·dle \'hwēdəl\ vb **-dled; -dling** : coax or tempt by flattery

wheel \'hwēl\ n 1 : disk or circular frame capable of turning on a central axis 2 : device of which the main part is a wheel ~ vb 1 : convey or move on wheels or a wheeled vehicle 2 : rotate 3 : turn so as to change direction —**wheeled** adj —**wheel·er** n —**wheel·less** adj

wheel·bar·row \-,barō\ n : one-wheeled vehicle for carrying small loads

wheel·base n : distance in inches between the front and rear axles of an automotive vehicle

wheel·chair n : chair mounted on wheels esp. for the use of disabled persons

wheeze \'hwēz\ vb **wheezed; wheez·ing** : breathe with difficulty and with a whistling sound —**wheeze** n —**wheezy** adj

whelk \'hwelk\ n : large sea snail

whelp \'hwelp\ n : one of the young of various carnivorous mammals (as a dog) ~ vb : bring forth whelps

when \'hwen\ adv —used to inquire about or designate a particular time ~ conj 1 : at or during the time that 2 : every time that 3 : if 4 : although ~ pron : what time

whence \'hwens\ adv or conj : from what place, source, or cause

when·ev·er \hwen'evər\ conj or adv : at whatever time

where \'hwer\ adv 1 : at, in, or to what place 2 : at, in, or to what situation, position, direction, circumstances, or respect ~ conj 1 : at, in, or to what place, position, or circumstance 2 : at, in, or to which place ~ n : place

where·abouts \-ə,bauts\ adv : about where ~ n sing or pl : place where a person or thing is

where·as \hwer'az\ conj 1 : while on the contrary 2 : since

where·by conj : by, through, or in accordance with which

where·fore \'hwer,fōr\ adv 1 : why 2 : therefore ~ n : reason

where·in \hwer'in\ adv : in what respect

where·of \-'əv, -äv\ conj : of what, which, or whom

where·up·on \'hwerə,pón, -,pän\ conj 1 : on which 2 : and then

wher·ev·er \hwer'evər\ adv : where ~ conj : at, in, or to whatever place or circumstance

where·with·al \'hwerwith,ól, -with-\ n : resources and esp. money

whet \'hwet\ vb **-tt-** 1 : sharpen by rubbing (as with a stone) 2 : stimulate —**whet·stone** n

whether \'hwethər\ conj 1 : if it is or was true that 2 : if it is or was better 3 : whichever is the case

whey \'hwā\ n : watery part of sour milk

which \'hwich\ adj 1 : being what one or ones out of a group 2 : whichever ~ pron 1 : which one or ones 2 : whichever

which·ev·er \hwich'evər\ pron or adj : no matter what one

whiff \'hwif\ n 1 : slight gust 2 : inhalation of odor, gas, or smoke 3 : slight trace ~ vb : inhale an odor

while \'hwīl\ n 1 : period of time 2 : time and effort used ~ conj 1 : during the time that 2 : as long as 3 : although ~ vb **whiled; whil·ing** : cause to pass esp. pleasantly

whim \'hwim\ n : sudden wish, desire, or change of mind

whim·per \'hwimpər\ vb : cry softly —**whimper** n

whim·si·cal \'hwimzikəl\ adj 1 : full of whims 2 : erratic —**whim·si·cal·i·ty** \,hwimzə'kalətē\ n —**whim·si·cal·ly** adv

whim·sy, whim·sey \'hwimzē\ n, pl **-sies** or **-seys** 1 : whim 2 : fanciful creation

whine \'hwīn\ vb **whined; whin·ing** 1 : utter a usu. high-pitched plaintive cry 2 : complain —**whine** n —**whin·er** n —**whiny** adj

whin·ny \'hwinē\ vb **-nied; -ny·ing** : neigh —**whinny** n

whip \'hwip\ vb **-pp-** 1 : move quickly 2 : strike with something slender and flexible 3 : defeat 4 : incite 5 : beat into a froth ~ n 1 : flexible device used for whipping 2 : party leader responsible for discipline 3 : thrashing motion —**whip·per** n

whip·cord n 1 : thin tough cord 2 : cloth made of hard-twisted yarns

whip·lash n : injury from a sudden sharp movement of the neck and head

whip·per·snap·per \'hwipər,snapər\ n : small, insignificant, or presumptuous person

whip·pet \'hwipət\ n : small swift dog often used for racing

whip·poor·will \'hwipər,wil\ n : American nocturnal bird

whir \'hwər\ vb **-rr-** : move, fly, or revolve with a whir ~ n : continuous fluttering or vibratory sound

whirl \'hwərl\ vb 1 : move or drive in a circle 2 : spin 3 : move or turn quickly 4 : reel ~ n 1 : rapid circular movement 2 : state of commotion or confusion 3 : try

whirl·pool n : whirling mass of water having a depression in the center

whirl·wind n : whirling wind storm

whisk \'hwisk\ n 1 : quick light sweeping or brushing motion 2 : usu. wire kitchen implement for beating ~ vb 1 : move or convey briskly 2 : beat 3 : brush lightly

whisk broom n : small broom

whis·ker \'hwiskər\ n 1 pl : beard 2 : long bristle or hair near an animal's mouth —**whis·kered** \-kərd\ adj

whis·key, whis·ky \'hwiskē\ n, pl **-keys** or **-kies** : liquor distilled from a fermented mash of grain

whis·per \'hwispər\ vb 1 : speak softly 2 : tell by whispering ~ n 1 : soft low sound 2 : rumor

whist \'hwist\ n : card game

whis·tle \'hwisəl\ n 1 : device by which a shrill sound is produced 2 : shrill clear sound made by a whistle or through the lips ~ vb **-tled; -tling** 1 : make or utter a whistle 2 : signal or call by a whistle 3 : produce by whistling —**whis·tler** n

whis·tle-blow·er \'hwisəl,blōər\ n : informer

whis·tle-stop n : brief political appearance

whit \'hwit\ n : bit

white \'hwīt\ adj **whit·er; -est** 1 : free from color 2 : of the color of new snow or milk 3 : having light skin ~ n 1 : color of maximum lightness 2 : white part or thing 3 : person who is light-skinned —**white·ness** n —**whit·ish** adj

white blood cell n : blood cell that does not contain hemoglobin

white·cap \'hwīt,kap\ n : wave crest breaking into white foam

white-col·lar adj : relating to salaried employees with duties not requiring protective or work clothing

white elephant n : something costly but of little use or value

white·fish \'hwīt,fish\ n : freshwater food fish

whit·en \'hwītən\ vb : make or become white —**whit·en·er** \'hwītənər\ n

white slave n : woman or girl held unwillingly for purposes of prostitution —**white slavery** n

white·tail \'hwīt,tāl\ n : No. American deer

white·wash vb 1 : whiten with a composition (as of lime and water) 2 : gloss over or cover up faults or wrongdoing —**whitewash** n

whith·er \'hwithər\ adv 1 : to what place 2 : to what situation, position, degree, or end

1whit·ing \'hwītiŋ\ n : usu. light or silvery food fish

2whiting n : pulverized chalk or limestone

whit·tle \'hwitəl\ vb **-tled; -tling** 1 : pare 2 : shape by paring 3 : reduce gradually

whiz, whizz \'hwiz\ vb **-zz-** : make a sound like a speeding object —**whiz, whizz** n

who \'hü\ pron 1 : what or which person or persons 2 : person or persons that 3 : —used to introduce a relative clause

who·dun·it \hü'dənət\ n : detective or mystery story

who·ev·er \hü'evər\ pron : no matter who

whole \'hōl\ adj 1 : being in healthy or sound condition 2 : having all its parts or elements 3 : constituting the total sum of ~ n 1 : complete amount or sum 2 : something whole or entire —**on the whole** 1 : considering all circumstances 2 : in general —**whole·ness** n

whole·heart·ed \'hōl'härtəd\ adj : sincere

whole number n : integer

whole·sale n : sale of goods in quantity usu. for resale by a retail merchant ~ adj 1 : of or relating to wholesaling 2 : performed on a large scale ~ vb **-saled; -sal·ing** : sell at wholesale —**wholesale** adv —**wholesaler** n

whole·some \-səm\ adj 1 : promoting mental, spiritual, or bodily health 2 : healthy —**whole·some·ness** n

whole wheat adj : made of ground entire wheat kernels

whol·ly \'hōlē\ adv 1 : totally 2 : solely

whom \'hüm\ pron, objective case of WHO

whom·ev·er \hüm'evər\ pron, objective case of WHOEVER

whoop \'hwüp, 'hwup, 'hüp, 'hup\ vb : shout loudly ~ n : shout

whooping cough n : infectious disease marked by convulsive coughing fits

whop·per \'hwäpər\ n 1 : something unusually large or extreme of its kind 2 : monstrous lie

whop·ping \'hwäpiŋ\ adj : extremely large

whore \'hōr\ n : prostitute

whorl \'hwórl, 'hwərl\ n : spiral —**whorled** adj

whose \'hüz\ adj : of or relating to whom or which ~ pron : whose one or ones

who·so·ev·er \,hüsō'evər\ pron : whoever

why \'hwī\ adv 1 : for what reason, cause, or purpose ~ conj 1 : reason for which 2 : for which ~ n, pl **whys** : reason ~ interj —used esp. to express surprise

wick \'wik\ n : cord that draws up oil, tallow, or wax to be burned

wick·ed \'wikəd\ adj 1 : morally bad 2 : harmful or troublesome 3 : very unpleasant 4 : very impressive —**wick·ed·ly** adv —**wick·ed·ness** n

wick·er \'wikər\ n 1 : small pliant branch 2 : wickerwork —**wicker** adj

wick·er·work n : work made of wickers

wick·et \'wikət\ n 1 : small gate, door, or window 2 : frame in cricket or arch in croquet

wide \'wīd\ adj **wid·er; wid·est** 1 : covering a vast area 2 : measured at right angles to the length 3 : having a great measure across 4 : opened fully 5 : far from the thing in question ~ adv **wid·er; wid·est** 1 : over a great distance 2 : so as to leave considerable space between 3 : fully —**wide·ly** adv —**wid·en** \'wīdən\ vb

wide-awake adj : alert

wide-eyed adj 1 : having the eyes wide open 2 : amazed 3 : naive

wide·spread adj : widely extended

wid·ow \'widō\ n : woman who has lost her husband by death and has not married again ~ vb 1 : cause to become a widow —**wid·ow·hood** n

wid·ow·er \'widōər\ n : man who has lost his wife by death and has not married again

width \'width\ n 1 : distance from side to side 2 : largeness of extent 3 : measured and cut piece of material

wield \'wēld\ vb 1 : use or handle esp. effectively 2 : exert —**wield·er** n

wie·ner \'wēnər\ n : frankfurter

wife \'wīf\ n, pl **wives** \'wīvz\ : married woman —**wife·hood** n —**wife·less** adj —**wife·ly** adj

wig \'wig\ n : manufactured covering of hair for the head

wig·gle \'wigəl\ vb **-gled; -gling** 1 : move with quick jerky or shaking movements 2 : wriggle —**wiggle** n —**wig·gler** n

wig·gly \-əlē\ adj 1 : tending to wiggle 2 : wavy

wig·wag \'wig,wag\ vb : signal by a flag or light waved according to a code

wig·wam \'wig,wäm\ n : American Indian hut consisting of a framework of poles overlaid with bark, rush mats, or hides

wild \'wīld\ adj 1 : living or being in a state of nature and not domesticated or cultivated 2 : unrestrained 3 : turbulent 4 : crazy 5 : uncivilized 6 : erratic ~ n 1 : wilderness 2 : undomesticated state ~ adv : without control —**wild·ly** adv —**wild·ness** n

wild·cat \-,kat\ n : any of various undomesticated cats (as a lynx) ~ adj 1 : not sound or safe 2 : unauthorized

wil·der·ness \'wildərnəs\ n : uncultivated and uninhabited region

wild·fire \'wīld,fir\ n : sweeping and destructive fire

wild·fowl n : game waterfowl

wild·life \'wīld,līf\ n : undomesticated animals

wile \'wīl\ n : trick to snare or deceive ~ vb **wiled; wil·ing** : lure

will \'wil\ vb, past **would** \'wůd\ pres sing & pl **will** 1 : wish 2 —used as an auxiliary verb to express (1) desire or willingness (2) customary action (3) simple future time (4) capability (5) determination (6) probability (7) inevitability or (8) a command 3 : dispose of by a will ~ n 1 : often determined wish 2 : act, process, or experience of willing 3 : power of controlling one's actions or emotions 4 : legal document disposing of property after death

will·ful, wil·ful \'wilfəl\ adj 1 : governed by will without regard to reason 2 : intentional —**will·ful·ly** adv

will·ing \'wiliŋ\ adj 1 : inclined or favorably disposed in mind 2 : prompt to act 3 : done, borne, or accepted voluntarily or without reluctance —**will·ing·ly** adv — **will·ing·ness** n

will-o'-the-wisp \wiləthə'wisp\ n 1 : light that appears at night over marshy grounds 2 : misleading or elusive goal or hope

wil·low \'wilō\ n : quick-growing shrub or tree with flexible shoots

wil·lowy \'wiləwē\ adj : gracefully tall and slender

will·pow·er \'wil,pauॅr\ n : energetic determination

wil·ly–nil·ly \,wilē'nilē\ adv or adj : without regard for one's choice

wilt \'wilt\ vb 1 : lose or cause to lose freshness and become limp esp. from lack of water 2 : grow weak

wily \'wīlē\ adj **wil·i·er; -est** : full of craftiness —**wil·i·ness** n

win \'win\ vb **won** \'wən\, **win·ning 1** : get possession of esp. by effort 2 : gain victory in battle or a contest 3 : make friendly or favorable ~ n 1 : victory

wince \'wins\ vb **winced; winc·ing** : shrink back involuntarily —**wince** n

winch \'winch\ n : machine for hoisting or pulling with a drum around which rope is wound —**winch** vb

¹wind \'wind\ n 1 : movement of the air 2 : breath 3 : gas in the stomach or intestines 4 : air carrying a scent 5 : intimation ~ vb 1 : get a scent of 2 : cause to be out of breath

²wind \'wīnd\ vb **wound** \'waund\; **wind·ing 1** : have or follow a curving course 2 : move or lie to encircle 3 : encircle or cover with something pliable 4 : tighten the spring of ~ n : turn or coil —**wind·er** n

wind·break \-,brāk\ n : trees and shrubs to break the force of the wind

wind·break·er \-,brākər\ n : light wind-resistant jacket

wind·fall \'wind,fol\ n 1 : thing blown down by wind 2 : unexpected benefit

wind instrument n : musical instrument (as a flute or horn) sounded by wind esp. by the breath

wind·lass \'windləs\ n : winch esp. for hoisting anchor

wind·mill \'wind,mil\ n : machine worked by the wind turning vanes

win·dow \'windō\ n 1 : opening in the wall of a building to let in light and air 2 : pane in a window 3 : span of time for something 4 : area of a computer display —**win·dow·less** adj

win·dow–shop vb : look at the displays in store windows —**win·dow–shop·per** n

wind·pipe \'wind,pīp\ n : passage for the breath from the larynx to the lungs

wind·shield \-,shēld\ n : transparent screen in front of the occupants of a vehicle

wind·up \'wīnd,əp\ n : end —**wind up** vb

wind·ward \'windwərd\ adj : being in or facing the direction from which the wind is blowing ~ n : direction from which the wind is blowing

windy \'windē\ adj **wind·i·er; -est 1** : having wind 2 : indulging in useless talk

wine \'wīn\ n 1 : fermented grape juice 2 : usu. fermented juice of a plant product (as fruit) used as a beverage ~ vb : treat to or drink wine

wing \'wiŋ\ n 1 : movable paired appendage for flying 2 : winglike thing 3 pl : area at the side of the stage out of sight 4 : faction ~ vb 1 : fly 2 : propel through the air —**winged** adj —**wing·less** adj —**on the wing** : in flight —**under one's wing** : in one's charge or care

wink \'wiŋk\ vb 1 : close and open the eyes quickly 2 : avoid seeing or noticing something 3 : twinkle 4 : close and open one eye quickly as a signal or hint ~ n 1 : brief sleep 2 : act of winking 3 : instant —**wink·er** n

win·ner \'winər\ n : one that wins

win·ning \-iŋ\ n 1 : victory 2 : money won at gambling ~ adj 1 : victorious 2 : charming

win·now \'winō\ vb 1 : remove (as chaff) by a current of air 2 : sort or separate something

win·some \'winsəm\ adj 1 : causing joy 2 : cheerful or gay —**win·some·ly** adv —**win·some·ness** n

win·ter \'wintər\ n : season between autumn and spring ~ adj : sown in autumn for harvest the next spring or summer —**win·ter·time** n

win·ter·green \'wintər,grēn\ n : low heath-like evergreen plant with red berries

win·try \'wintrē\ adj **win·tri·er; -est 1** : characteristic of winter 2 : cold in feeling

wipe \'wīp\ vb **wiped; wip·ing 1** : clean or dry by rubbing 2 : remove by rubbing 3 : erase completely 4 : destroy 5 : pass over a surface ~ n : act or instance of wiping —**wip·er** n

wire \'wīr\ n 1 : thread of metal 2 : work made of wire 3 : telegram or cablegram ~ vb 1 : provide with wire 2 : bind or

mount with wire 3 : telegraph —**wire·less** adj

wire·less \-ləs\ n, chiefly Brit : radio

wire·tap vb : connect into a telephone or telegraph wire to get information —**wire·tap** n —**wire·tap·per** n

wir·ing \'wīriŋ\ n : system of wires

wiry \'wīrē\ adj **wir·i·er; -est 1** : resembling wire 2 : slender yet strong and sinewy —**wir·i·ness** n

wis·dom \'wizdəm\ n 1 : accumulated learning 2 : good sense

wisdom tooth n : last tooth on each half of each human jaw

¹wise \'wīz\ n : manner

²wise adj **wis·er; wis·est 1** : having or showing wisdom, good sense, or good judgment 2 : aware of what is going on —**wise·ly** adv

wise·crack n : clever, smart, or flippant remark ~ vb : make a wisecrack

wish \'wish\ vb 1 : have a desire 2 : express a wish concerning 3 : request ~ n 1 : a wishing or desire 2 : expressed will or desire

wish·bone n : forked bone in front of the breastbone in most birds

wish·ful \-fəl\ adj 1 : expressive of a wish 2 : according with wishes rather than fact

wishy–washy \'wishē,wóshē, -,wäsh-\ adj : weak or insipid

wisp \'wisp\ n 1 : small bunch of hay or straw 2 : thin strand, strip, fragment, or streak 3 : something frail, slight, or fleeting —**wispy** adj

wis·te·ria \wis'tirēə\ n : pealike woody vine with long clusters of flowers

wist·ful \'wistfəl\ adj : full of longing —**wist·ful·ly** adv —**wist·ful·ness** n

wit \'wit\ n 1 : reasoning power 2 : mental soundness —usu. pl. 3 : quickness and cleverness in handling words and ideas 4 : talent for clever remarks or one noted for witty remarks —**wit·less** adj —**wit·less·ly** adv —**wit·less·ness** n —**wit·ted** adj

witch \'wich\ n 1 : person believed to have magic power 2 : ugly old woman ~ vb : bewitch

witch·craft \'wich,kraft\ n : power or practices of a witch

witch·ery \'wichərē\ n, pl **-er·ies 1** : witchcraft 2 : charm

witch ha·zel \'wich,hāzəl\ n 1 : shrub having small yellow flowers in fall 2 : alcoholic lotion made from witch hazel bark

witch–hunt n 1 : searching out and persecution of supposed witches 2 : harassment esp. of political opponents

with \'with, 'with\ prep 1 : against, to, or toward 2 : in support of 3 : because of 4 : in the company of 5 : having 6 : despite 7 : containing 8 : by means of

with·draw \with'dro, with-\ vb **-drew** \-'drü\, **-drawn** \-'dron\; **-draw·ing** \-'droiŋ\ 1 : take back or away 2 : call back or retract 3 : go away 4 : terminate one's participation in or use of —**with·draw·al** \-'droəl\ n

with·drawn \with'dron\ adj : socially detached and unresponsive

with·er \'withər\ vb 1 : shrivel 2 : lose or cause to lose energy, force, or freshness

with·ers \'withərz\ n pl : ridge between the shoulder bones of a horse

with·hold \with'hōld, with-\ vb **-held** \-'held\; **-hold·ing 1** : hold back 2 : refrain from giving

with·in \with'in, with-\ adv 1 : in or into the interior 2 : inside oneself ~ prep 1 : in or to the inner part of 2 : in the limits or compass of

with·out \with'aút, with-\ prep 1 : outside 2 : lacking 3 : unaccompanied or unmarked by —**without** adv

with·stand \with'stand, with-\ vb **-stood** \-'stúd\; **-stand·ing** : oppose successfully

wit·ness \'witnəs\ n 1 : testimony 2 : one who testifies 3 : one present at a transaction to testify that it has taken place 4 : one who has personal knowledge or experience 5 : something serving as proof ~ vb 1 : bear witness 2 : act as legal witness of 3 : furnish proof of 4 : be a witness of 5 : be the scene of

wit·ti·cism \'witə,sizəm\ n : witty saying or phrase

wit·ting \'witiŋ\ adj : intentional —**witting·ly** adv

wit·ty \'witē\ adj **-ti·er; -est** : marked by or full of wit —**wit·ti·ly** \'witᵊlē\ adv —**wit·ti·ness** n

wives pl of WIFE

wiz·ard \'wizərd\ n 1 : magician 2 : very clever person —**wiz·ard·ry** \-ərdrē\ n

wiz·ened \'wizᵊnd\ adj : dried up

wob·ble \'wäbəl\ vb **-bled; -bling 1** : move or cause to move with an irregular rocking motion 2 : tremble 3 : waver —**wob·ble** n —**wob·bly** \'wäbəlē\ adj

woe \'wō\ n 1 : deep suffering 2 : misfortune

woe·be·gone \'wōbi,gòn\ adj : exhibiting woe, sorrow, or misery

woe·ful \'wōfəl\ adj 1 : full of woe 2 : bringing woe —**woe·ful·ly** adv

woke past of WAKE

woken past part of WAKE

wolf \'wúlf\ n, pl **wolves** \'wúlvz\ : large doglike predatory mammal ~ vb : eat greedily —**wolf·ish** adj

wol·fram \'wúlfrəm\ n : tungsten

wol·ver·ine \,wúlvə'rēn\ n, pl **-ines** : flesh-eating mammal related to the weasels

wom·an \'wúmən\ n, pl **wom·en** \'wimən\ 1 : adult female person 2 : womankind 3 : feminine nature —**wom·an·hood** \-,húd\ n —**wom·an·ish** adj

wom·an·kind \-,kīnd\ n : females of the human race

wom·an·ly \-lē\ adj : having qualities characteristic of a woman —**wom·an·li·ness** \-lēnəs\ n

womb \'wüm\ n : uterus

won past of WIN

won·der \'wəndər\ n 1 : cause of astonishment or surprise 2 : feeling (as of astonishment) aroused by something extraordinary ~ vb 1 : feel surprise 2 : feel curiosity or doubt

won·der·ful \'wəndərfəl\ adj 1 : exciting wonder 2 : unusually good —**won·der·ful·ly** adv —**won·der·ful·ness** n

won·der·land \-,land, -lənd\ n 1 : fairylike imaginary realm 2 : place that excites admiration or wonder

won·der·ment \-mənt\ n : wonder

won·drous \'wəndrəs\ adj : wonderful —**won·drous·ly** adv —**won·drous·ness** n

wont \'wont, 'wōnt\ adj : accustomed ~ n : habit —**wont·ed** adj

woo \'wü\ vb : try to gain the love or favor of —**woo·er** n

wood \'wúd\ n 1 : dense growth of trees usu. smaller than a forest —often pl. 2 : hard fibrous substance of trees and shrubs beneath the bark 3 : wood prepared for some use (as burning) ~ adj 1 : wooden 2 : suitable for working with wood 3 or **woods** \'wúdz\ : living or growing in woods —**wood·chop·per** n —**wood·pile** n —**wood·shed** n

wood·bine \'wúd,bīn\ n : climbing vine

wood·chuck \-,chək\ n : thick-bodied grizzled animal of No. America

wood·craft n 1 : skill and practice in matters relating to the woods 2 : skill in making articles from wood

wood·cut \-,kət\ n 1 : relief printing surface engraved on wood 2 : print from a woodcut

wood·ed \'wúdəd\ adj : covered with woods

wood·en \'wúdᵊn\ adj 1 : made of wood 2 : lacking resilience 3 : lacking ease, liveliness or interest —**wood·en·ly** adv —**wood·en·ness** n

wood·land \-lənd, -,land\ n : land covered with trees

wood·peck·er \'wúd,pekər\ n : brightly marked bird with a hard bill for drilling into trees

woods·man \'wúdzmən\ n : person who works in the woods

wood·wind \'wúd,wind\ n : one of a group of wind instruments (as a flute or oboe)

wood·work n : work (as interior house fittings) made of wood

woody \'wúdē\ adj **wood·i·er; -est 1** : abounding with woods 2 : of, containing, or like wood fibers —**wood·i·ness** n

woof \'wúf\ n : weft

wool \'wúl\ n 1 : soft hair of some mammals and esp. the sheep 2 : something (as a textile) made of wool —**wooled** \'wúld\ adj

wool·en, wool·len \'wúlən\ adj 1 : made of wool 2 : relating to the manufacture of woolen products ~ n 1 : woolen fabric 2 : woolen garments —usu. pl.

wool·gath·er·ing n : idle daydreaming

wool·ly \'wúlē\ adj **-li·er; -est 1** : of, relating to, or bearing wool 2 : consisting of or resembling wool 3 : confused or turbulent

woo·zy \'wüzē\ adj **-zi·er; -est 1** : confused 2 : somewhat dizzy, nauseated, or weak —**woo·zi·ness** n

word \'wərd\ n 1 : brief remark 2 : speech sound or series of speech sounds that communicates a meaning 3 : written representation of a word 4 : order 5 : news 6 : promise 7 pl : dispute ~ vb : express in words —**word·less** adj

word·ing \'wərdiŋ\ n : verbal expression

word processing n : production of structured and printed documents through a computer program (**word processor**) —**word process** vb

wordy \'wərdē\ adj **word·i·er; -est** : using many words —**word·i·ness** n

wore past of WEAR

work \'wərk\ n 1 : labor 2 : employment 3 : task 4 : something (as an artistic production) produced by mental effort or physical labor 5 pl : place where industrial labor is done 6 pl : moving parts of a mechanism 7 : workmanship ~ adj 1 : suitable for wear while working 2 : used for work ~ vb **worked** \'wərkt\ or

wrought \'rot\, **work·ing 1** : bring to pass 2 : create by expending labor upon 3 : bring or get into a form or condition 4 : set or keep in operation 5 : solve 6 : cause to labor 7 : arrange 8 : excite 9 : labor 10 : perform work regularly for wages 11 : function according to plan or design 12 : produce a desired effect —**work·bench** n —**work·man** \-mən\ n —**work·room** n —**in the works** : in preparation

work·able \'wərkəbəl\ adj 1 : capable of being worked 2 : feasible —**work·able·ness** n

work·a·day \'wərkə,dā\ adj 1 : relating to or suited for working days 2 : ordinary

work·a·hol·ic \,wərkə'holik, -'häl-\ n : compulsive worker

work·day \'wərk,dā\ n 1 : day on which work is done 2 : period of time during which one is working

work·er \'wərkər\ n : person who works esp. for wages

work·horse n 1 : horse used for hard work 2 : person who does most of the work of a group task

work·house n : place of confinement for persons who have committed minor offenses

work·ing \'wərkiŋ\ adj 1 : adequate to allow work to be done 2 : adopted or assumed to help further work or activity ~ n : operation —usu. used in pl.

work·ing·man \'wərkiŋ,man\ n : worker

work·man·like \-,līk\ adj : worthy of a good workman

work·man·ship \-,ship\ n 1 : art or skill of a workman 2 : quality of a piece of work

work·out \'wərk,aút\ n : exercise to improve one's fitness

work out vb 1 : bring about by effort 2 : solve 3 : develop 4 : to be successful 5 : perform exercises

work·shop n 1 : small establishment for manufacturing or handicrafts 2 : seminar emphasizing exchange of ideas and practical methods

world \'wərld\ n 1 : universe 2 : earth with its inhabitants and all things upon it 3 : people in general 4 : great number or quantity 5 : class of persons or their sphere of interest

world·ly \'wərldlē\ adj 1 : devoted to this world and its pursuits rather than to religion 2 : sophisticated —**world·li·ness** n

world·ly–wise adj : possessing understanding of human affairs

world·wide adj : extended throughout the entire world —**worldwide** adv

worm \'wərm\ n 1 : earthworm or a similar animal 2 pl : disorder caused by parasitic worms ~ vb 1 : move or cause to move in a slow and indirect way 2 : to free from worms —**wormy** adj

worm·wood \'wərm,wúd\ n 1 : aromatic woody herb (as sagebrush) 2 : something bitter or grievous

worn past part of WEAR

worn–out \'worn'aút\ adj : exhausted or used up by or as by wear

wor·ri·some \'wərēsəm\ adj 1 : causing worry 2 : inclined to worry

wor·ry \'wərē\ vb **-ried; -ry·ing 1** : shake and mangle with the teeth 2 : disturb 3 : feel or express anxiety ~ n, pl **-ries 1** : anxiety 2 : cause of anxiety —**wor·ri·er** n

worse \'wərs\ adj, comparative of BAD or of ILL 1 : bad or evil in a greater degree 2 : more unwell ~ n 1 : one that is worse 2 : greater degree of badness ~ adv, comparative of BAD or of ILL 1 : in a worse manner

wors·en \'wərsᵊn\ vb : make or become worse

wor·ship \'wərshəp\ n 1 : reverence toward a divine being or supernatural power 2 : expression of reverence 3 : extravagant respect or devotion ~ vb -**shiped** or -**shipped**; -**ship·ing** or -**ship·ping 1** : honor or reverence 2 : perform or take part in worship —**wor·ship·er, wor·ship·per** n

worst \'wərst\ adj, superlative of BAD or of ILL 1 : most bad, evil, ill, or corrupt 2 : most unfavorable, unpleasant, or painful ~ n : one that is worst ~ adv, superlative of ILL or of BAD or BADLY 1 : to the extreme degree of badness ~ vb : defeat

wor·sted \'wústəd, 'wərstəd\ n : smooth compact wool yarn or fabric made from such yarn

worth \'wərth\ prep 1 : equal in value to 2 : deserving of ~ n 1 : monetary value 2 : value of something measured by its qualities 3 : moral or personal merit

worth·less \-ləs\ adj 1 : lacking worth 2 : useless —**worth·less·ness** n

worth·while \-'hwīl\ adj : being worth the time or effort spent

wor·thy \'wərthē\ adj **-thi·er; -est 1** : having worth or value 2 : having sufficient worth ~ n, pl **-thies** : worthy person —**wor·thi·ly** adv —**wor·thi·ness** n

would \\'wu̇d\\ *past of* WILL —used to express (1) preference (2) intent (3) habitual action (4) contingency (5) probability or (6) a request

would–be \\'wu̇d'bē\\ *adj* : desiring or pretending to be

¹wound \\'wünd\\ *n* **1** : injury in which the skin is broken **2** : mental hurt ~ *vb* : inflict a wound to or in

²wound \\'au̇nd\\ *past of* WIND

wove *past of* WEAVE

woven *past part of* WEAVE

wrack \\'rak\\ *n* : ruin

wraith \\'rāth\\ *n, pl* **wraiths** \\'rāths, 'rāthz\\ **1** : ghost **2** : insubstantial appearance

wran•gle \\'raŋgəl\\ *vb or n* : quarrel —**wrang•ler** *n*

wrap \\'rap\\ *vb* **-pp- 1** : cover esp. by winding or folding **2** : envelop and secure for transportation or storage **3** : enclose, surround, or conceal wholly **4** : coil, fold, draw, or twine about something ~ *n* **1** : wrapper or wrapping **2** : outer garment (as a shawl)

wrap•per \\'rapər\\ *n* **1** : that in which something is wrapped **2** : one that wraps

wrap•ping *n* : something used to wrap an object

wrath \\'rath\\ *n* : violent anger —**wrath•ful** \\-fəl\\ *adj*

wreak \\'rēk\\ *vb* **1** : inflict **2** : bring about

wreath \\'rēth\\ *n, pl* **wreaths** \\'rēthz, 'rēths\\ : something (as boughs) intertwined into a circular shape

wreathe \\'rēth\\ *vb* **wreathed; wreathing** **1** : shape into or take on the shape of a wreath **2** : decorate or cover with a wreath

wreck \\'rek\\ *n* **1** : broken remains (as of a ship or vehicle) after heavy damage **2** : something disabled or in a state of ruin **3** : an individual who has become weak or infirm **4** : action of breaking up or destroying something ~ *vb* : ruin or damage by breaking up

wreck•age \\'rekij\\ *n* **1** : act of wrecking **2** : remains of a wreck

wreck•er \\-ər\\ *n* **1** : automotive vehicle for removing disabled cars **2** : one that wrecks or tears down and removes buildings

wren \\'ren\\ *n* : small mostly brown singing bird

wrench \\'rench\\ *vb* **1** : pull with violent twisting or force **2** : injure or disable by a violent twisting or straining ~ *n* **1** : forcible twisting **2** : tool for exerting a twisting force

wrest \\'rest\\ *vb* **1** : pull or move by a forcible twisting movement **2** : gain with difficulty ~ *n* : forcible twist

wres•tle \\'resəl, 'ras-\\ *vb* **-tled; -tling 1** : scuffle with and attempt to throw and pin an opponent **2** : compete against in wrestling **3** : struggle (as with a problem) ~ *n* : action or an instance of wrestling —**wres•tler** \\'reslər, 'ras-\\ *n*

wres•tling \\'resliŋ\\ *n* : sport in which 2 opponents try to throw and pin each other

wretch \\'rech\\ *n* **1** : miserable unhappy person **2** : vile person

wretch•ed \\'rechəd\\ *adj* **1** : deeply afflicted, dejected, or distressed **2** : grievous **3** : inferior —**wretch•ed•ly** *adv* —**wretch•ed•ness** *n*

wrig•gle \\'rigəl\\ *vb* **-gled; -gling 1** : twist and turn restlessly **2** : move along by twisting and turning —**wriggle** *n* —**wrig•gler** \\'rigələr\\ *n*

wring \\'riŋ\\ *vb* **wrung** \\'rəŋ\\; **wring•ing 1** : squeeze or twist out moisture **2** : get by or as if by twisting or pressing **3** : twist together in anguish **4** : pain —**wring•er** *n*

wrin•kle \\'riŋkəl\\ *n* : crease or small fold on a surface (as in the skin or in cloth) ~ *vb* **-kled; -kling** : develop or cause to develop wrinkles —**wrin•kly** \\-kəlē\\ *adj*

wrist \\'rist\\ *n* : joint or region between the hand and the arm

writ \\'rit\\ *n* **1** : something written **2** : legal order in writing

write \\'rīt\\ *vb* **wrote** \\'rōt\\; **writ•ten** \\'rit°n\\; **writ•ing** \\'rītiŋ\\ **1** : form letters or words on a surface **2** : form the letters or the words of (as on paper) **3** : make up and set down for others to read **4** : write a letter to —**write off** *vb* : cancel

writ•er \\'rītər\\ *n* : one that writes esp. as a business or occupation

writhe \\'rīth\\ *vb* **writhed; writh•ing** : twist and turn this way and that

writ•ing \\'rītiŋ\\ *n* **1** : act of one that writes **2** : handwriting **3** : something written or printed

wrong \\'róŋ\\ *n* **1** : unfair or unjust act **2** : something that is contrary to justice **3** : state of being or doing wrong ~ *adj* : **wronger** \\'róŋər\\; **wrong•est** \\'róŋəst\\ **1** : sinful **2** : not right according to a standard **3** : unsuitable **4** : incorrect ~ *adj* **1** : in a wrong direction or manner **2** : incorrectly ~ *vb* **wronged; wrong•ing 1** : do wrong to **2** : treat unjustly —**wrong•ly** *adv*

wrong•do•er \\-'düər\\ *n* : one who does wrong —**wrong•do•ing** \\-'düiŋ\\ *n*

wrong•ful \\-fəl\\ *adj* **1** : wrong **2** : illegal —**wrong•ful•ly** *adv* —**wrong•ful•ness** *n*

wrong•head•ed \\'róŋ'hedəd\\ *adj* : stubborn in clinging to wrong opinion or principles —**wrong•head•ed•ly** *adv* —**wrong•head•ed•ness** *n*

wrote *past of* WRITE

wrought \\'rót\\ *adj* **1** : formed **2** : hammered into shape **3** : deeply stirred

wrung *past of* WRING

wry \\'rī\\ *adj* **wri•er** \\'rīər\\; **wri•est** \\'rīəst\\ **1** : turned abnormally to one side **2** : twisted **3** : cleverly and often ironically humorous —**wry•ly** *adv* —**wry•ness** *n*

X

x \\'eks\\ *n, pl* **x's** *or* **xs** \\'eksəz\\ **1** : 24th letter of the alphabet **2** : unknown quantity ~ *vb* **x-ed; x-ing** *or* **x'ing 1** : cancel with a series of x's—usu. with *out*

xe•non \\'zē,nän,'zen,än\\ *n* : heavy gaseous chemical element

xe•no•pho•bia \\,zenə'fōbēə, ,zēn-\\ *n* : fear and hatred of foreign people and things —**xe•no•phobe** \\'zenə,fōb, 'zēn-\\ *n*

Xmas \\'krisməs\\ *n* : Christmas

x–ra•di•a•tion *n* **1** : exposure to X rays **2** : radiation consisting of X rays

x–ray \\'eks,rā\\ *vb* : examine, treat, or photograph with X rays

X ray *n* **1** : radiation of short wavelength that is able to penetrate solids **2** : photograph taken with X rays —**X-ray** *adj*

xy•lo•phone \\'zīlə,fōn\\ *n* : musical instrument with wooden bars that are struck —**xy•lo•phon•ist** \\-,fōnist\\ *n*

Y

y \\'wī\\ *n, pl* **y's** *or* **ys** \\'wīz\\ **:** 25th letter of the alphabet

¹-y \\ē\\ *adj suffix* **1** : composed or full of **2** : like **3** : performing or apt to perform an action

²-y \\ē\\ *n suffix, pl* **-ies 1** : state, condition, or quality **2** : activity, place of business, or goods dealt with **3** : whole group

yacht \\'yät\\ *n* : luxurious pleasure boat ~ *vb* : race or cruise in a yacht

ya•hoo \\'yähü, 'yā-\\ *n* : uncouth or stupid person

yak \\'yak\\ *n* : big hairy Asian ox

yam \\'yam\\ *n* **1** : edible root of a tropical vine **2** : deep orange sweet potato

yam•mer \\'yamər\\ *vb* **1** : whimper **2** : chatter —**yammer** *n*

yank \\'yaŋk\\ *n* : strong sudden pull —**yank** *vb*

Yank \\'yaŋk\\ *n* : Yankee

Yan•kee \\'yaŋkē\\ *n* : native or inhabitant of New England, the northern U.S., or the U.S.

yap \\'yap\\ *vb* **-pp- 1** : yelp **2** : chatter —**yap** *n*

¹yard \\'yärd\\ *n* **1** : 3 feet **2** : long spar for supporting and spreading a sail —**yard•age** \\-ij\\ *n*

²yard *n* **1** : enclosed roofless area **2** : grounds of a building **3** : work area

yard•arm \\'yärd,ärm\\ *n* : end of the yard of a square-rigged ship

yard•stick *n* **1** : measuring stick 3 feet long **2** : standard for judging

yar•mul•ke \\'yäməkə, 'yär-, -məl-\\ *n* : a small brimless cap worn by Jewish males in a synagogue

yarn \\'yärn\\ *n* **1** : spun fiber for weaving or knitting **2** : tale

yaw \\'yö\\ *vb* : deviate erratically from a course —**yaw** *n*

yawl \\'yól\\ *n* : sailboat with 2 masts

yawn \\'yón\\ *vb* : open the mouth wide ~ *n* : deep breath through a wide-open mouth —**yawn•er** *n*

ye \\'yē\\ *pron* : you

yea \\'yā\\ *adv* **1** : yes **2** : truly ~ *n* : affirmative vote

year \\'yir\\ *n* **1** : period of about 365 days **2** *pl* : age

year•book *n* : annual report of the year's events

year•ling \\'yirliŋ, 'yərlən\\ *n* : one that is or is rated as a year old

year•ly \\'yirlē\\ *adj* : annual —**yearly** *adv*

yearn \\'yərn\\ *vb* **1** : feel desire esp. for what one cannot have **2** : feel tenderness or compassion

yearn•ing \\-iŋ\\ *n* : tender or urgent desire

yeast \\'yēst\\ *n* : froth or sediment in sugary liquids containing a tiny fungus and used in making alcoholic liquors and as a leaven in baking —**yeasty** *adj*

yell \\'yel\\ *vb* : utter a loud cry —**yell** *n*

yel•low \\'yelō\\ *adj* **1** : of the color yellow **2** : sensational **3** : cowardly ~ *vb* : make or turn yellow ~ *n* **1** : color of lemons **2** : yolk of an egg —**yel•low•ish** \\'yeləwish\\ *adj*

yellow fever *n* : virus disease marked by prostration, jaundice, fever, and often hemorrhage

yellow jacket *n* : wasp with yellow stripes

yelp \\'yelp\\ *vb* : utter a sharp quick shrill cry —**yelp** *n*

yen \\'yen\\ *n* : strong desire

yeo•man \\'yōmən\\ *n* **1** : attendant or officer in a royal or noble household **2** : small farmer **3** : naval petty officer with clerical duties —**yeo•man•ry** \\-rē\\ *n*

-yer —see -ER

yes \\'yes\\ *adv* : —used to express consent or agreement ~ *n* : affirmative answer

ye•shi•va, ye•shi•vah \\yə'shēvə\\ *n, pl* **ye•shivas** *or* **ye•shi•voth** \\-,shē'vōt, -'vóth\\ : Jewish school

yes–man \\'yes,man\\ *n* : person who agrees with every opinion or suggestion of a boss

yes•ter•day \\'yestərdē\\ *adv* **1** : on the day preceding today **2** : only a short time ago ~ *n* **1** : day last past **2** : time not long past

yet \\'yet\\ *adv* **1** : in addition **2** : up to now **3** : so soon as now **4** : nevertheless ~ *conj* : but

yew \\'yü\\ *n* : evergreen tree or shrubs with dark stiff poisonous needles

yield \\'yēld\\ *vb* **1** : surrender **2** : grant **3** : bear as a crop **4** : produce **5** : cease opposition or resistance ~ *n* : quantity produced or returned

yo•del \\'yōd°l\\ *vb* **-deled** *or* **-delled; -deling** *or* **-del•ling** : sing by abruptly alternating between chest voice and falsetto —**yodel** —**yo•del•er** \\'yōd°lər\\ *n*

yo•ga \\'yōgə\\ *n* : system of exercises for attaining bodily or mental control and well-being

yo•gi \\'yōgē\\ *n* : person who practices yoga

yo•gurt \\'yōgərt\\ *n* : fermented slightly acid soft food made from milk

yoke \\'yōk\\ *n* **1** : neck frame for coupling draft animals or for carrying loads **2** : clamp **3** : slavery **4** : tie or link **5** : piece of a garment esp. at the shoulder ~ *vb* **yoked; yok•ing 1** : couple with a yoke **2** : join

yo•kel \\'yōkəl\\ *n* : naive and gullible country person

yolk \\'yōk\\ *n* : yellow part of an egg —**yolked** \\'yōkt\\ *adj*

Yom Kip•pur \\,yōmki'pu̇r, ,yäm-, -'kipər\\ *n* : Jewish holiday observed in September or October with fasting and prayer as a day of atonement

yon \\'yän\\ *adj or adv* : YONDER

yon•der \\'yändər\\ *adv* : at or to that place ~ *adj* : distant

yore \\'yōr\\ *n* : time long past

you \\'yü\\ *pron* **1** : person or persons addressed **2** : person in general

young \\'yəŋ\\ *adj* **young•er** \\'yəŋgər\\; **young•est** \\'yəŋgəst\\ **1** : being in the first or an early stage of life, growth, or development **2** : recently come into being **3** : youthful ~ *n, pl* **young** : persons or animals that are young —**young•ish** \\-ish\\ *adj*

young•ster \\-stər\\ *n* **1** : young person **2** : child

your \\yər, 'yu̇r, 'yōr\\ *adj* : relating to you or yourself

yours \\'yu̇rz, 'yórz\\ *pron* : the ones belonging to you

your•self \\yər'self\\ *pron, pl* **your•selves** \\-'selvz\\ **:** you —used reflexively or for emphasis

youth \\'yüth\\ *n, pl* **youths** \\'yüthz, 'yüths\\ **1** : period between childhood and maturity **2** : young man **3** : young persons **4** : state or quality of being young, fresh, or vigorous

youth•ful \\'yüthfəl\\ *adj* **1** : relating to or appropriate to youth **2** : young **3** : vigorous

and fresh —**youth•ful•ly** *adv* —**youth•ful•ness** *n*

yowl \\'yau̇l\\ *vb* : utter a loud long mournful cry —**yowl** *n*

yo–yo \\'yō,yō\\ *n, pl* **-yos** : toy that falls from or rises to the hand as it unwinds and rewinds on a string

yuc•ca \\'yəkə\\ *n* : any of several plants related to the lilies that grow in dry regions

yule \\'yül\\ *n* : Christmas —**yule•tide** \\-,tīd\\ *n*

yum•my \\'yəmē\\ *adj* **-mi•er; -est** : highly attractive or pleasing

Z

z \\'zē\\ *n, pl* **z's** *or* **zs** : 26th letter of the alphabet

za•ny \\'zānē\\ *n, pl* **-nies 1** : clown **2** : silly person ~ *adj* **-ni•er; -est** : crazy or foolish —**za•ni•ly** *adv* —**za•ni•ness** *n*

zeal \\'zēl\\ *n* : enthusiasm

zeal•ot \\'zelət\\ *n* : fanatical partisan

zeal•ous \\'zeləs\\ *adj* : filled with zeal —**zeal•ous•ly** *adv* —**zeal•ous•ness** *n*

ze•bra \\'zēbrə\\ *n* : horselike African mammal marked with light and dark stripes

zeit•geist \\'tsīt,gīst, 'zīt-\\ *n* : general spirit of an era

ze•nith \\'zēnəth\\ *n* : highest point

zeph•yr \\'zefər\\ *n* : gentle breeze

zep•pe•lin \\'zepələn\\ *n* : rigid airship like a blimp

ze•ro \\'zērō\\ *n, pl* **-ros 1** : number represented by the symbol 0 or the symbol itself **2** : starting point **3** : lowest point ~ *adj* : having no size or quantity

zest \\'zest\\ *n* **1** : quality of enhancing enjoyment **2** : keen enjoyment —**zest•ful** \\-fəl\\ *adj* —**zest•ful•ly** *adv* —**zest•ful•ness** *n*

zig•zag \\'zig,zag\\ *n* : one of a series of short sharp turns or angles ~ *adj* : having zigzags ~ *adv* : in or by a zigzag path ~ *vb* **-gg-** : proceed along a zigzag path

zil•lion \\'zilyən\\ *n* : large indeterminate number

zinc \\'ziŋk\\ *n* : bluish white crystaline metallic chemical element

zing \\'ziŋ\\ *n* **1** : shrill humming noise **2** : energy —**zing** *vb*

zin•nia \\'zinēə, 'zēnyə\\ *n* : American herb widely grown for its showy flowers

¹zip \\'zip\\ *vb* **-pp-** : move or act with speed ~ *n* : energy

²zip *vb* **-pp-** : close or open with a zipper

zip code *n* : number that identifies a U.S. postal delivery area

zip•per \\'zipər\\ *n* : fastener consisting of 2 rows of interlocking teeth

zip•py \\'zipē\\ *adj* **-pi•er; -est** : brisk

zir•con \\'zər,kän\\ *n* : zirconium-containing mineral sometimes used in jewelry

zir•co•ni•um \\,zər'kōnēəm\\ *n* : corrosion-resistant gray metallic element

zith•er \\'zithər, 'zith-\\ *n* : stringed musical instrument played by plucking

zi•ti \\'zētē\\ *n, pl* **ziti** : short tubular pasta

zo•di•ac \\'zōdē,ak\\ *n* : imaginary belt in the heavens encompassing the paths of the planets and divided into 12 signs used in astrology —**zo•di•a•cal** \\zō'dīəkəl\\ *adj*

zom•bie \\'zämbē\\ *n* : person thought to have died and been brought back to life without free will

zon•al \\'zōn°l\\ *adj* : of, relating to, or having the form of a zone —**zon•al•ly** *adv*

zone \\'zōn\\ *n* **1** : division of the earth's surface based on latitude and climate **2** : distinctive area ~ *vb* **zoned; zon•ing 1** : mark off into zones **2** : reserve for special purposes —**zo•na•tion** \\zō'nāshən\\ *n*

zoo \\'zü\\ *n, pl* **zoos** : collection of living animals usu. for public display —**zoo•keep•er** *n*

zo•ol•o•gy \\zō'äləjē\\ *n* : science of animals —**zo•o•log•i•cal** \\,zōə'läjikəl\\ *adj* —**zo•ol•o•gist** \\zō'äləjist\\ *n*

zoom \\'züm\\ *vb* **1** : move with a loud hum or buzz **2** : move or increase with great speed —**zoom** *n*

zuc•chi•ni \\zu̇'kēnē\\ *n, pl* **-ni** *or* **-nis** : summer squash with smooth cylindrical dark green fruits

zwie•back \\'swēbak, 'swī-, 'zwē-, 'zwī-\\ *n* : biscuit of baked, sliced, and toasted bread

zy•gote \\'zī,gōt\\ *n* : cell formed by the union of 2 sexual cells —**zy•got•ic** \\zī'gätik\\ *adj*

Abbreviations

Most of these abbreviations have been given in one form. Variation in use of periods, in type, and in capitalization is frequent and widespread (as *mph, MPH, m.p.h., Mph*).

abbr abbreviation
AC alternating current
acad academic, academy
AD in the year of our Lord
adj adjective
adv adverb, advertisement
advt advertisement
AF air force, audio frequency
agric agricultural, agriculture
AK Alaska
aka also known as
AL, Ala Alabama
alg algebra
Alta Alberta
a.m., AM before noon
Am, Amer America, American
amp ampere
amt amount
anc ancient
anon anonymous
ans answer
ant antonym
APO army post office
approx approximate, approximately
Apr April
apt apartment, aptitude
AR Arkansas
arith arithmetic
Ariz Arizona
Ark Arkansas
art article, artificial
assn association
assoc associate, associated, association
asst assistant
ATM automated teller machine
att attached, attention, attorney
attn attention
atty attorney
Aug August
auth authentic, author, authorized
aux, auxil auxiliary
av avoirdupois
AV audiovisual
ave avenue
avg average
AZ Arizona
BA bachelor of arts
bal balance
bar barometer, barrel
bbl barrel, barrels
BC before Christ, British Columbia
BCE before the Christian Era, before the Common Era
bet between
biog biographer, biographical, biography
biol biologic, biological, biologist, biology
bldg building
blvd boulevard
BO backorder, best offer, body odor, box office, branch office
Brit Britain, British
bro brother, brothers
bros brothers
BS bachelor of science
Btu British thermal unit
bu bureau, bushel
c carat, cent, centimeter, century, chapter, circa, cup
C Celsius, centigrade
ca circa
CA, Cal, Calif California
cal calendar, caliber, calorie
Can, Canad Canada, Canadian
cap capacity, capital, capitalize, capitalized
Capt captain
CB citizens band
CDT central daylight time
cen central
cert certificate, certification, certified, certify
cf compare
chap chapter
chem chemistry
cir circle, circuit, circular, circumference
civ civil, civilian
cm centimeter
co company, county
CO Colorado
c/o care of
COD cash on delivery, collect on delivery
col colonial, colony, color, colored, column, counsel
Col colonel, Colorado
Colo Colorado

comp comparative, compensation, compiled, compiler, composition, compound, comprehensive, comptroller
cong congress, congressional
conj conjunction
Conn Connecticut
cont continued
contr contract, contraction
corp corporal, corporation
corr corrected, correction
cp compare, coupon
CPR cardiopulmonary resuscitation
cr credit, creditor
CSA Confederate States of America
CST Central standard time
ct carat, cent, count, court
CT central time, certified teacher, Connecticut
cu cubic
cur currency, current
CZ Canal Zone
d penny
DA district attorney
dag dekagram
dal dekaliter
dam dekameter
dbl double
DC direct current, District of Columbia
DDS doctor of dental science, doctor of dental surgery
DE Delaware
dec deceased, decrease
Dec December
deg degree
Del Delaware
Dem Democrat, Democratic
dept department
det detached, detachment, detail, determine
dg decigram
dia, diam diameter
diag diagonal, diagram
dict dictionary
dif, diff difference
dim dimension, diminished
dir director
disc discount
dist distance, district
div divided, dividend, division, divorced
dl deciliter
dm decimeter
DMD doctor of dental medicine
DOB date of birth
doz dozen
DP data processing
dr dram, drive, drum
Dr doctor
DST daylight saving time
DUI driving under the influence
DWI driving while intoxicated
dz dozen
e east, eastern, excellent
ea each
ecol ecological, ecology
econ economics, economist, economy
EDT Eastern daylight time
e.g. for example
EKG electrocardiogram, electrocardiograph
elec electric, electrical, electricity
elem elementary
eng engineer, engineering
Eng England, English
esp especially
EST Eastern standard time
ET eastern time
et al and others
etc et cetera
ex example, express, extra
exec executive
f false, female, feminine
F, Fah, Fahr Fahrenheit
Feb February
fed federal, federation
fem female, feminine
FL, Fla Florida
fl oz fluid ounce
FPO fleet post office
fr father, friar, from
Fri Friday
ft feet, foot, fort
fut future
FYI for your information
g gram

Ga, GA Georgia
gal gallery, gallon
gen general
geog geographic, geographical, geography
geol geologic, geological, geology
geom geometric, geometrical, geometry
gm gram
GMT Greenwich mean time
GOP Grand Old Party (Republican)
gov government, governor
govt government
GP general practice, general practitioner
gr grade, grain, gram
gram grammar, grammatical
gt great
GU Guam
hd head
hf half
hgt height
hgwy highway
HI Hawaii
hist historian, historical, history
hon honor, honorable, honorary
hr here, hour
HS high school
ht height
HT Hawaiian time
hwy highway
i intransitive, island, isle
Ia, IA Iowa
ICU intensive care unit
ID Idaho, identification
i.e. that is
IL, Ill Illinois
imp imperative, imperfect
in inch
IN Indiana
inc incomplete, incorporated
ind independent
Ind Indian, Indiana
inf infinitive
int interest
interj interjection
intl, intnl international
ital italic, italicized
Jan January
JD juvenile delinquent
jour journal, journeyman
JP justice of the peace
jr, jun junior
JV junior varsity
Kans Kansas
kg kilogram
km kilometer
KS Kansas
kW kilowatt
Ky, KY Kentucky
l late, left, liter, long
L large
La Louisiana
LA Los Angeles, Louisiana
lat latitude
lb pound
lg large, long
lib liberal, librarian, library
long longitude
m male, masculine, meter, mile
M medium
MA Massachusetts
Man Manitoba
Mar March
masc masculine
Mass Massachusetts
math mathematical, mathematician
max maximum
Md Maryland
MD doctor of medicine, Maryland
MDT mountain daylight time
Me, ME Maine
med medium
mg milligram
mgr manager
MI, Mich Michigan
mid middle
min minimum, minor, minute
Minn Minnesota
misc miscellaneous
Miss Mississippi
ml milliliter
mm millimeter
MN Minnesota
mo month
Mo, MO Missouri
Mon Monday
Mont Montana
mpg miles per gallon

mph miles per hour
MRI magnetic resonance imaging
MS Mississippi
MST Mountain standard time
mt mount, mountain
MT Montana, Mountain time
n neuter, noun
N north, northern
NA North America, not applicable
nat national, native, natural
natl national
naut nautical
NB New Brunswick
NC North Carolina
ND, N Dak North Dakota
NE, Neb, Nebr Nebraska
neg negative
neut neuter
Nev Nevada
Nfld Newfoundland
NH New Hampshire
NJ New Jersey
NM, N Mex New Mexico
no north, number
Nov November
NR not rated
NS Nova Scotia
NV Nevada
NWT Northwest Territories
NY New York
NYC New York City
O Ohio
obj object, objective
occas occasionally
Oct October
off office, officer, official
OH Ohio
OJ orange juice
OK, Okla Oklahoma
Ont Ontario
opp opposite
OR, Ore, Oreg Oregon
orig original, originally
oz ounce, ounces
p page
Pa Pennsylvania
PA Pennsylvania, public address
PAC political action committee
par paragraph, parallel
part participle, particular
pass passenger, passive
pat patent
PC percent, politically correct, postcard
pd paid
PD police department
PDT Pacific daylight time
PE physical education
PEI Prince Edward Island
Penn, Penna Pennsylvania
pg page
PIN personal identification number
pk park, peak, peck
pkg package
pl place, plural
p.m., PM afternoon
PMS premenstrual syndrome
PO post office
Port Portugal, Portuguese
pos position, positive
poss possessive
pp pages
PQ Province of Quebec
pr pair, price, printed
PR public relations, Puerto Rico
prep preposition
pres present, president
prob probable, probably, problem
prof professor
pron pronoun
prov province
PS postscript, public school
PST Pacific standard time
psych psychology
pt part, payment, pint, point
PT Pacific time, physical therapy
pvt private
qr quarter
qt quantity, quart
Que Quebec
quot quotation
r right, river
rd road, rod, round
RDA recommended daily allowance, recommended dietary allowance

recd received
reg region, register, registered, regular
rel relating, relative, religion
rep report, reporter, representative, republic
Rep Republican
res residence
rev reverse, review, revised, revision, revolution
Rev reverend
RFD rural free delivery
RI Rhode Island
rm room
rpm revolutions per minute
RR railroad, rural route
RSVP please reply
rt right
rte route
s small, south, southern
SA South America
SASE self-addressed stamped envelope
Sask Saskatchewan
Sat Saturday
SC South Carolina
sci science, scientific
SD, S Dak South Dakota
secy secretary
sen senate, senator, senior
Sept, Sep September
sing singular
sm small
so south, southern
soph sophomore
sp spelling
spec special, specifically
specif specific, specifically
SPF sun protection factor
sq square
sr senior
Sr sister
SSN Social Security number
SSR Soviet Socialist Republic
st street
St saint
std standard
subj subject
Sun Sunday
supt superintendent
SWAT Special Weapons and Tactics
syn synonym
t teaspoon, temperature, ton, transitive, troy, true
T tablespoon
tbs, tbsp tablespoon
TD touchdown
tech technical, technician, technology
Tenn Tennessee
terr territory
Tex Texas
Th, Thu, Thur, Thurs Thursday
TN Tennessee
trans translated, translation, translator
tsp teaspoon
Tu, Tue, Tues Tuesday
TX Texas
UK United Kingdom
UN United Nations
univ universal, university
US United States
USA United States of America
USSR Union of Soviet Socialist Republics
usu usual, usually
UT Utah
UV ultraviolet
v verb, versus
Va, VA Virginia
var variant, variety
vb verb
VG very good
VI Virgin Islands
vol volume, volunteer
VP vice-president
vs versus
Vt, VT Vermont
W west, western
WA, Wash Washington
Wed Wednesday
WI, Wis, Wisc Wisconsin
wk week, work
wt weight
WV, W Va West Virginia
WY, Wyo Wyoming
XL extra large, extra long
yd yard
yr year, younger, your
YT Yukon Territory

A Brief Guide to Punctuation

APOSTROPHE '

1. **indicates the possessive case of nouns and indefinite pronouns** ⟨the boy's mother⟩ ⟨the boys' mothers⟩ ⟨It is anyone's guess.⟩
2. **marks omissions in contracted words** ⟨didn't⟩ ⟨o'clock⟩
3. **often forms plurals of letters, figures, and words referred to as words** ⟨You should dot your *i*'s and cross your *t*'s.⟩ ⟨several 8's⟩ ⟨She has trouble pronouncing her *the*'s.⟩

BRACKETS [ ]

1. **set off extraneous data such as editorial additions esp. within quoted material** ⟨wrote that the author was "trying to dazzle his readers with phrases like *jeu de mots* [play on words]"⟩
2. **function as parentheses within parentheses** ⟨Bowman Act (22 Stat., ch. 4, § [or sec.] 4, p. 50)⟩

COLON :

1. **introduces word, clause, or phrase that explains, illustrates, amplifies, or restates what has gone before** ⟨The sentence was poorly constructed: it lacked both unity and coherence.⟩
2. **introduces a series** ⟨Three countries were represented: England, France, and Belgium.⟩
3. **introduces lengthy quoted material set off from the rest of a text by indentation but not by quotation marks** ⟨I quote from the text of Chapter One:⟩
4. **separates data in time-telling and data in bibliographic and biblical references** ⟨8:30 a.m.⟩ ⟨New York: Smith Publishing Co.⟩ ⟨John 4:10⟩
5. **separates titles and subtitles (as of books)** ⟨*The Tragic Dynasty: A History of the Romanovs*⟩
6. **follows the salutation in formal correspondence** ⟨Dear Sir:⟩ ⟨Gentlemen:⟩

COMMA ,

1. **separates main clauses joined by a coordinating conjunction (as *and, but, or, nor,* or *for*) and very short clauses not so joined** ⟨She knew very little about him, and he volunteered nothing.⟩ ⟨I came, I saw, I conquered.⟩
2. **sets off an adverbial clause (or a long phrase) that precedes the main clause** ⟨When she found that her friends had deserted her, she sat down and cried.⟩
3. **sets off from the rest of the sentence transitional words and expressions (as *on the contrary, on the other hand*), conjunctive adverbs (as *consequently, furthermore, however*), and expressions that introduce an illustration or example (as *namely, for example*)** ⟨Your second question, on the other hand, remains open.⟩ ⟨The mystery, however, remains unsolved.⟩ ⟨She expects to travel through two countries, namely, France and England.⟩
4. **separates words, phrases, or clauses in series and coordinate adjectives modifying a noun** ⟨Men, women, and children crowded into the square.⟩ ⟨The harsh, cold wind was strong.⟩
5. **sets off from the rest of the sentence parenthetic elements (as nonrestrictive modifiers)** ⟨Our guide, who wore a blue beret, was an experienced traveler.⟩ ⟨We visited Gettysburg, the site of a famous battle.⟩
6. **introduces a direct quotation, terminates a direct quotation that is neither a question nor an exclamation, and encloses split quotations** ⟨John said, "I am leaving."⟩ ⟨"I am leaving," John said.⟩ ⟨"I am leaving," John said with determination, "even if you want me to stay."⟩
7. **sets off words in direct address, absolute phrases, and mild interjections** ⟨You may go, Mary, if you wish.⟩ ⟨I fear the encounter, his temper being what it is.⟩ ⟨Ah, that's my idea of an excellent dinner.⟩
8. **separates a question from the rest of the sentence which it ends** ⟨It's a fine day, isn't it?⟩
9. **indicates the omission of a word or words, and esp. a word or words used earlier in the sentence** ⟨Common stocks are preferred by some investors; bonds, by others.⟩
10. **is used to avoid ambiguity** ⟨To Mary, Jane was someone special.⟩
11. **sets off geographical names (as state or country from city), items in dates, and addresses from the rest of a text** ⟨Shreveport, Louisiana, is the site of a large air base.⟩ ⟨On Sunday, June 23, 1940, he was wounded.⟩ ⟨Number 10 Downing Street, London, is a famous address.⟩
12. **follows the salutation in informal correspondence and follows the closing line of a formal or informal letter** ⟨Dear Mary,⟩ ⟨Affectionately,⟩ ⟨Very truly yours,⟩

DASH —

1. **usu. marks an abrupt change or break in the continuity of a sentence** ⟨When in 1960 the stockpile was sold off—indeed, dumped as surplus—natural-rubber sales were hard hit.—Barry Commoner⟩
2. **introduces a summary statement after a series** ⟨Oil, steel, and wheat—these are the sinews of industrialization.⟩
3. **often precedes the attribution of a quotation** ⟨My foot is on my native heath . . . . —Sir Walter Scott⟩

ELLIPSIS . . .   .

1. **indicates the omission of one or more words within a quoted passage** ⟨The head is not more native to the heart . . . than is the throne of Denmark to thy father.—Shakespeare⟩ **four dots indicates the omission of one or more sentences within the passage or the omission of words at the end of a sentence** ⟨Avoiding danger is no safer in the long run than outright exposure. . . . Life is either a daring adventure or nothing.—Helen Keller⟩
2. **indicates halting speech or an unfinished sentence in dialogue** ⟨"I'd like to . . . that is . . . if you don't mind. . . ." He faltered and then stopped speaking.⟩

EXCLAMATION POINT !

1. **terminates an emphatic phrase or sentence** ⟨Get out of here!⟩
2. **terminates an emphatic interjection** ⟨Encore!⟩

HYPHEN -

1. **marks separation or division of a word at the end of a line** ⟨mill-[end of line]stone⟩
2. **is used between some prefix and word combinations, as prefix + proper name;** ⟨pre-Renaissance⟩ **prefix ending with a vowel + word beginning often with the same vowel** ⟨co-opted⟩ ⟨re-ink⟩; **stressed prefix + word, esp. when this combination is similar to a different one** ⟨recover a sofa⟩ *but* ⟨recover from an illness⟩
3. **is used in some compounds, esp. those containing prepositions** ⟨president-elect⟩ ⟨sister-in-law⟩
4. **is often used between elements of a unit modifier in attributive position in order to avoid ambiguity** ⟨He is a small-business man.⟩ ⟨She has gray-green eyes.⟩
5. **suspends the first part of a hyphenated compound when used with another hyphenated compound** ⟨a six- or eight-cylinder engine⟩
6. **is used in writing out compound numbers between 21 and 99** ⟨thirty-four⟩ ⟨one hundred twenty-eight⟩
7. **is used between the numerator and the denominator in writing out fractions esp. when they are used as modifiers** ⟨a two-thirds majority of the vote⟩
8. **serves instead of the phrase "(up) to and including" between numbers and dates** ⟨pages 40-98⟩ ⟨the decade 1960-69⟩

HYPHEN, DOUBLE =

is used in the end-of-line division of a hyphenated compound to indicate that the compound is hyphenated and not closed ⟨self-[end of line]seeker⟩ *but* ⟨self-[end of line]same⟩

PARENTHESES ( )

1. **set off supplementary, parenthetic, or explanatory material when the interruption is more marked than that usu. indicated by commas** ⟨Three old destroyers (all now out of commission) will be scrapped.⟩ ⟨He is hoping (as we all are) that this time he will succeed.⟩
2. **enclose numerals which confirm a written number in a text** ⟨Delivery will be made in thirty (30) days.⟩
3. **enclose numbers or letters in a series** ⟨We must set forth (1) our long-term goals, (2) our immediate objectives, and (3) the means at our disposal.⟩

PERIOD .

1. **terminates sentences or sentence fragments that are neither interrogatory nor exclamatory** ⟨Obey the law.⟩ ⟨He obeyed the law.⟩
2. **follows some abbreviations and contractions** ⟨Dr.⟩ ⟨Jr.⟩ ⟨etc.⟩ ⟨cont.⟩

QUESTION MARK ?

1. **terminates a direct question** ⟨Who threw the bomb?⟩ ⟨"Who threw the bomb?" he asked.⟩ ⟨To ask the question Who threw the bomb? is unnecessary.⟩
2. **indicates the writer's ignorance or uncertainty** ⟨Omar Khayyám, Persian poet (1048?-1122)⟩

QUOTATION MARKS, DOUBLE " "

1. **enclose direct quotations in conventional usage** ⟨He said, "I am leaving."⟩
2. **enclose words or phrases borrowed from others, words used in a special way, and often slang when it is introduced into formal writing** ⟨He called himself "emperor," but he was really just a dictator.⟩ ⟨He was arrested for smuggling "smack."⟩
3. **enclose titles of short poems, short stories, articles, lectures, chapters of books, songs, short musical compositions, and radio and TV programs** ⟨Robert Frost's "Dust of Snow"⟩ ⟨Pushkin's "Queen of Spades"⟩ ⟨The third chapter of *Treasure Island* is entitled "The Black Spot."⟩ ⟨Ravel's "Bolero"⟩ ⟨NBC's "Today Show"⟩
4. **are used with other punctuation marks in the following ways: the period and the comma fall *within* the quotation marks** ⟨"I am leaving," he said.⟩ ⟨His camera was described as "waterproof," but "moisture-resistant" would have been a better description.⟩ **the semicolon falls *outside* the quotation marks** ⟨He spoke of his "little cottage in the country"; he might have called it a mansion.⟩ **the dash, the question mark, and the exclamation point fall *within* the quotation marks when they refer to the quoted matter only; they fall *outside* when they refer to the whole sentence** ⟨He asked, "When did you leave?"⟩ ⟨What is the meaning of "the open door"?⟩ ⟨The sergeant shouted, "Halt!"⟩ ⟨Save us from his "mercy"!⟩

QUOTATION MARKS, SINGLE ' '

enclose a quotation within a quotation in conventional usage ⟨The witness said, "I distinctly heard him say, 'Don't be late,' and then I heard the door close."⟩

SEMICOLON ;

1. **links main clauses not joined by coordinating conjunctions** ⟨Some people have the ability to write well; others do not.⟩
2. **links main clauses joined by conjunctive adverbs (as *consequently, furthermore, however*)** ⟨Speeding is illegal; furthermore, it is very dangerous.⟩
3. **links clauses which themselves contain commas even when such clauses are joined by coordinating conjunctions** ⟨Mr. King, whom you met yesterday, will represent us on the committee; but you should follow the proceedings yourself, because they are vitally important to us.⟩

SLASH /

1. **separates alternatives** ⟨. . . designs intended for high-heat and/or high-speed applications—F. S. Badger, Jr.⟩
2. **separates successive divisions (as months or years) of an extended period of time** ⟨the fiscal year 1972/73⟩
3. **serves as a dividing line between run-in lines of poetry** ⟨Say, sages, what's the charm on earth/Can turn death's dart aside?—Robert Burns⟩
4. **often represents *per* in abbreviations** ⟨9 ft/sec⟩ ⟨20 km/hr⟩

Webster's
Atlas
of the World

Contents

Preface

Webster's Atlas of the World provides a concise and up-to-date picture of the political and physical forces that shape our world today. It enables readers to locate features of the earth's surface, measure distances, plan trips, and trace routes, but most importantly visualize a world in transition.

In today's political environment, transitions are characterized by the formation of new countries, changes in borders between countries, and the adoption of new place names within countries. Today's maps are changed by many other forces as well. Advances in technology, for instance, are reshaping the way we measure the world, the way we see the world, and, consequently, the way we think about creating the maps that represent the world. Simply applying computer technology, of course, does not guarantee that an atlas will be accurate or current. That is the mapmaker's responsibility. New technology can, however, provide the tools to create an atlas of much improved clarity, legibility, and design.

With features such as these, an atlas becomes a unique tool for discovering the political and physical patterns, distributions, and relationships that are an inherent part of any regional or global landscape. The information within it graphically defines the world and helps the reader to comprehend the complexity of the changing world in which we live.

© 1999, Encyclopædia Britannica, Inc.

OCEAN

SVALBARD (Norway)

NORWEGIAN
SEA

FRANZ JOSEF
LAND

NOVAYA
ZEMLYA

KARA SEA

NEW SIBERIAN
IS.

EAST
SIBERIAN
SEA

NORTH
SEA

NORWAY

SWEDEN

FINLAND

Arkhangelsk

Helsinki

St. Petersburg

WEST
SIBERIAN
PLAIN

R U S S I A

Lower Tunguska

VERKHOYANSK MTS.

Kolyma

Arctic Circle

KOLYMA MTS.

Lena

Yakutsk

60° N

DENMARK

Oslo
Stockholm

EST.
LAT.
LITH.

Moscow

Perm

Yekaterinburg
Chelyabinsk

Omsk

Ob

Novosibirsk

Krasnoyarsk

Yenisey

Lake
Baikal

Irkutsk

Chita

SEA OF
OKHOTSK

KAMCHATKA
PEN.

BERING
SEA

NETH.
Copenhagen
Berlin

BELARUS

Minsk

Nizhniy
Novgorod

Kazan

Ufa

Samara

Barnaul

Novokuznetsk

Ulaanbaatar

Amur

Khabarovsk

Sakhalin

BEL.
Paris

GER.
CZ. REP.

POL.

Warsaw

Kiev

UKRAINE

Volgograd

KAZAKSTAN

L. Balkhash

MONGOLIA

GOBI DESERT

Shenyang

NORTH
KOREA

Harbin

Vladivostok

Hokkaido

SWITZ.
ITALY

AUS. HUN.
SLK.

MOL.

ROM.

GEORGIA

Astana

Almaty

Bishkek

TIAN SHAN

Beijing

Tianjin

P'yongyang
Seoul

SOUTH
KOREA

Pusan

JAPAN

Honshu
Tokyo

PACIFIC
OCEAN

Rome
ALB.

YUGO.
MAC.

BUL.

Bucharest

BLACK SEA

ARMENIA

ARAL
SEA

UZBEKISTAN

Tashkent

KYRGYZSTAN

KUNLUN MTS.

C H I N A

Huang

Xi'an

Lanzhou

Chongqing

YELLOW
SEA

Osaka
Shikoku

Kyushu

Wulu

Shanghai

MIDWAY IS.
(U.S.)

30° N

Algiers
Tunis
MEDITERRANEAN

MTS.

GREECE

Athens

TURKEY

Ankara

CYPRUS

AZERBAIJAN

Tbilisi

Ashkhabad

TURKMENISTAN

ZAGROS
MOUNTAINS

Tehran

TAJIKISTAN

AFGHANISTAN

Kabul

PLATEAU OF
TIBET

Lhasa

Yangtze

Nanjing

Guangzhou

TAIWAN

Taipei

Kaohsiung

Tropic of Cancer

TUNISIA

Tripoli

LEBANON
ISRAEL
Jerusalem

SYRIA
Damascus

IRAQ
Baghdad

CASPIAN SEA

Islamabad

PAKISTAN

Delhi

NEPAL

Kathmandu

Mount
Everest

BHUTAN

Thimphu

BANGLADESH

Dhaka

Xi

HONG
KONG

SOUTH
CHINA
SEA

Luzon

PHILIPPINE
SEA

Guam
(U.S.)

NORTHERN
MARIANA
IS. (U.S.)

MARSHALL IS.

ALGERIA

LIBYA

EGYPT

JORDAN KUWAIT

Kuwait

BAHRAIN

QATAR U.A.E.

Muscat

Ahmadabad

New Delhi

Lahore

Karachi

Nagpur

Calcutta

MYANMAR

Yangon

Hanoi

LAOS

Vientiane

VIETNAM

Manila

PHILIPPINES

Mindanao

Koror

PALAU

FEDERATED STATES OF MICRONESIA

Palikir

Majuro

SAHARA

AHAGGAR
MTS.

HOGGAR
MTS.

Alexandria

Cairo

Nile

L. Nasser

RED SEA

Riyadh

SAUDI
ARABIA

Jiddah

RUB' AL KHALI
DESERT

OMAN

ARABIAN
SEA

Bombay

Hyderabad

Madras

ANDAMAN IS.
(India)

Bangkok

THAILAND

Phnom Penh

CAMBODIA

Ho Chi Minh City

Bandar Seri Begawan

BRUNEI

Bairiki

KIRIBATI

NIGER

CHAD

L. Chad

THE
SUDAN

Khartoum

ERITREA

Asmara

Sanaa

YEMEN

DJIBOUTI
Djibouti

Gulf of Aden

Socotra
(Yemen)

Cape
Gwardafuy

Bay of
Bengal

Bangalore

Colombo

SRI
LANKA

NICOBAR IS.
(India)

Kuala
Lumpur

MALAYSIA

SINGAPORE

Medan

Equator

NIGERIA

BENIN
TOGO

Niamey

Abuja

N'Djamena

CAMEROON

Yaoundé

C.A.R.

Bangui

ETHIOPIA

ETHIOPIAN
PLATEAU

Addis
Ababa

White Nile

SOMALIA

Mogadishu

MALDIVES

Male

Sumatra

Palembang

Borneo

I N D O N E S I A

New Guinea

PAPUA
NEW GUINEA

SOLOMON
ISLANDS

Honiara

TUVALU

Funafuti

VANUATU

EQ.
GUINEA

Malabo

Libreville

UGANDA

Kampala

KENYA

Nairobi

Jakarta

Semarang

Java

Celebes

Bandung

Surabaya

Port Moresby

ARAFURA
SEA

CORAL
SEA

Port-Vila

Efate

FIJI

Suva

Brazzaville

RWANDA

BURUNDI

Bujumbura

Kigali

Lake
Victoria

DEM. REP.
OF THE
CONGO

Kinshasa

Congo

TANZANIA

Lake
Tanganyika

Kilimanjaro

Dar es Salaam

Victoria

SEYCHELLES

BRITISH
INDIAN
OCEAN
TERRITORY
(U.K.)

INDIAN
OCEAN

KEELING IS.
(Austl.)

Timor

New Caledonia
(Fr.)

Tropic of Capricorn

Luanda

Kasai

ANGOLA

ZAMBIA

Lusaka

MALAWI

Lake
Malawi

Lilongwe

Moroni

COMOROS

Great Barrier Reef

ARNHEM
LAND

NAMIBIA

NAMIB
DESERT

Windhoek

BOTSWANA

Gaborone

Kalahari

ZIMBABWE

Harare

MOZAMBIQUE

Mozambique Channel

Antananarivo

MADAGASCAR

MAURITIUS
Port Louis

Réunion (Fr.)

GREAT SANDY
DESERT

GREAT
ARTESIAN
BASIN

GREAT DIVIDING RANGE

Brisbane

SOUTH
AFRICA

Pretoria

Johannesburg

Maputo

Mbabane

SWAZILAND

LESOTHO

Orange

Maseru

Cape Town

Cape of Good Hope

Saint Paul I. (Fr.)

Amsterdam I. (Fr.)

A U S T R A L I A

GREAT VICTORIA
DESERT

Perth

Darling

Adelaide

Sydney

Canberra

30° S

Great Australian
Bight

Melbourne

Auckland

NEW
ZEALAND

Wellington

PRINCE EDWARD IS.
(South Africa)

CROZET IS.
(Fr.)

Kerguelen I.
(Fr.)

Tasmania

TASMAN
SEA

Hobart

AUCKLAND IS.
(N.Z.)

60° S

Antarctic Circle

ENDERBY
LAND

QUEEN MAUD LAND

W I L K E S L A N D

VICTORIA
LAND

ROSS SEA

A N T A R C T I C A

30° E

60° E

90° E

© 1999, Encyclopædia Britannica, Inc.

30° E 60° E 90° E 120° E 150° E

ATLANTIC OCEAN

BERMUDA (U.K.)
Hamilton

Tropic of Cancer

TURKS AND CAICOS

Nassau
THE BAHAMAS

Equator

LESSER ANTILLES

VIRGIN ISLANDS (U.K.)
BRITISH VIRGIN ISLANDS (U.K.)
ANGUILLA (U.K.)
ST. KITTS AND NEVIS
ANTIGUA AND BARBUDA
MONTSERRAT (U.K.)
GUADELOUPE (Fr.)
DOMINICA
MARTINIQUE (Fr.)
ST. LUCIA
ST. VINCENT AND THE GRENADINES
BARBADOS
GRENADA
Port-of-Spain
TRINIDAD AND TOBAGO

VIRGIN ISLANDS (U.S.)
PUERTO RICO (U.S.)
San Juan
DOMINICAN REPUBLIC
SANTO DOMINGO

ARUBA (Neth.)
NETHERLANDS ANTILLES (Neth.)

Port-au-Prince
HAITI

G R E A T E R   A N T I L L E S

CUBA
HAVANA

Yucatan Channel

Cockburn Town

Port-au-Prince

George Town
CAYMAN ISLANDS (U.K.)

Kingston
JAMAICA

CARIBBEAN SEA

MOSQUITO COAST

Panama City
PANAMA
San José
COSTA RICA
Mount Chirripó 3819 m
NICARAGUA
Lake Nicaragua
Managua
Gulf of Fonseca
Tegucigalpa
HONDURAS
BELIZE
Belmopan
Guatemala City
GUATEMALA
San Salvador
EL SALVADOR

YUCATAN PENINSULA

Laguna de Terminos

Bay of Campeche

Gulf of Mexico

Jacksonville
Savannah
Chattahoochee
Tombigbee

Chesapeake Bay
WASHINGTON, D.C.
BALTIMORE
PHILADELPHIA
NEW YORK CITY
CLEVELAND
DETROIT
Lake Erie
Ohio
COLUMBUS
A P P A L A C H I A N   M O U N T A I N S
Mount Mitchell 2037 m
CHICAGO
INDIANAPOLIS
NASHVILLE
Kentucky Lake
MEMPHIS
Tennessee
Lake of the Ozarks
OZARK PLATEAU
Mississippi
Missouri
Platte
N. Platte
Arkansas
Red
Colorado
Pecos
Conchos
Rio Grande

U N I T E D   S T A T E S

HOUSTON
SAN ANTONIO
DALLAS
Brazos
MONTERREY
Rio Grande
Ciudad Juárez
El Paso
PHOENIX
Gila
Salton Sea
Salt
California Aqueduct
LOS ANGELES
SAN DIEGO
SAN JOSE
SAN FRANCISCO
SIERRA NEVADA
DEATH VALLEY
MOHAVE DESERT
PAINTED DESERT
Hoover Dam
Lake Powell
Lake Mead
GRAND CANYON
G R E A T   B A S I N
Pikes Peak 4301 m
ROCKY MOUNTAINS

SONORAN DESERT
SIERRA MADRE OCCIDENTAL
MEXICAN PLATEAU
BOLSON DE MAPIMI
MAPIMI BASIN
MESA DEL NORTE
CHIHUAHUAN DESERT
Fuerte
Nazas
GUADALAJARA
Lake Chapala
Colima Volcano 3820 m
MEXICO CITY
Pico de Orizaba 5700 m
SIERRA MADRE DEL SUR
Balsas
MEXICO

MARIAS ISLANDS
REVILLAGIGEDO ISLANDS
Sebastián Vizcaíno Bay
BAJA CALIFORNIA
Gulf of California

SIERRA MADRE ORIENTAL
COSTERA DEL GOLFO PLAIN
Laguna de Tamiahua
Catemaco Volcano 1610 m
Pánuco
ISTHMUS OF TEHUANTEPEC
Gulf of Tehuantepec

Scale 1:33,296,000
Chamberlin Trimetric
0   50   100   150   200   250   300   350   400   450   500   550 mi
0   200   400   600   800 km

BERING SEA
PRIBILOF ISLANDS
St. Matthew Island
Nunivak Island
Bristol Bay
Pavlof Volcano 2714 m
Shishaldin Volcano 2857 m
A L E U T I A N   I S L A N D S
Atu Island

MEXICO CITY   Cities over 1,000,000
Washington, D.C.   Cities 500,000 to 1,000,000
Ottawa   Cities 100,000 to 500,000
Port-of-Spain   Cities 50,000 to 100,000
Belmopan   Cities under 50,000

⊛ Capital symbols
■ • City symbols
—— Canals
↦ Aqueducts
⊃ Dams
⌇ Intermittent rivers
〜 Waterfalls
〰 Reefs
◉ Glaciers
▨ Salt lakes
▨ Swamps
▨ Sand areas

PUEBLA Cities over 1,000,000
Acapulco Cities 500,000 to 1,000,000
La Paz Cities 100,000 to 500,000
Guaymas Cities 50,000 to 100,000
Taxco Cities under 50,000

✹ Capital symbols
■ City symbols
¤ Points of interest
⌐ Dams
Intermittent rivers
Salt lakes
National Parks
Aboriginal lands
Swamps
Sand areas

*1 AGUASCALIENTES
2 DISTRITO FEDERAL
3 MORELOS
4 QUERÉTARO
5 TLAXCALA

Scale 1:13,573,000
0   50   100   150   200 mi
0   80 160 240 320 km
Lambert Conformal Conic

N

PACIFIC OCEAN

Gulf of Mexico

Bay of Campeche

Gulf of California

Tropic of Cancer

REVILLAGIGEDO ISLANDS

© 1999, Encyclopædia Britannica, Inc.

© 1999, Encyclopaedia Britannica, Inc.

CARIBBEAN SEA

PACIFIC OCEAN

JAMAICA

COLOMBIA

MEXICO

BELIZE

GUATEMALA

HONDURAS

Tegucigalpa

EL SALVADOR

NICARAGUA

Managua

COSTA RICA

PANAMA

Panama City

San José

San Miguel

N

Scale 1: 7,857,000

Lambert Conformal Conic

0   25   50   75   100 mi
0 40 80 120 160 km

GUATEMALA CITY   Cities over 1,000,000
Tegucigalpa   Cities 500,000 to 1,000,000
San José   Cities 100,000 to 500,000
Estelí   Cities 50,000 to 100,000
Belmopan   Cities under 50,000

⊛   Capital symbols
■   City symbols
¤   Points of interest
∷   Canals
⚓   Dams
〰   Reefs
▲   National Parks
     Swamps

BOGOTÁ Cities over 1,000,000
Asunción Cities 500,000 to 1,000,000
Brasília Cities 100,000 to 500,000
Paramaribo Cities 50,000 to 100,000
Stanley Cities under 50,000

⊛ Capital symbols
▪ City symbols
Canals
Dams
Intermittent rivers
Waterfalls
Rapids
Glaciers
Swamps
Salt flats
Sand areas

Scale 1:23,628,000
0 100 200 300 400 mi
0 150 300 450 600 km
Lambert Azimuthal Equal-Area

PACIFIC OCEAN

ATLANTIC OCEAN

SOUTH GEORGIA (U.K.)

FALKLAND ISLANDS
(ISLAS MALVINAS)
(Administered by U.K.,
claimed by Arg.)
⊛ Stanley

Bandeira Peak 2890 m
Sugar Loaf 395 m
Guanabara Bay
RIO DE JANEIRO ▪ Santo André
SÃO PAULO
▪ Curitiba
SERRA DA MANTIQUEIRA
Furnas Reservoir
Tietê
Paraná (Alto)
Paranapanema
Grand Falls
Iguaçu
Itaipu Reservoir
Itaipu Dam
SERRA DE AMAMBAI
Apa
GRAN CHACO
CHACO BOREAL
CHACO CENTRAL
PARAGUAY
⊛ Asunción
Paraguay
Pilcomayo
Bermejo
CHACO AUSTRAL
Salado
Paraná
MISIONES
SERRA DE MISIONES
Ijuí
Uruguay
Salto Grande Reservoir
Cuareim
URUGUAY
Mount Catedral 513 m
GRANDE RANGE
MONTEVIDEO
Rio de la Plata
Point Sur del Cabo San Antonio
PORTO ALEGRE
Patos Lagoon
Mirim Lagoon
Este Point
▪ Rosario
La Plata
BUENOS AIRES
PAMPAS
ARGENTINA
Mount Champaqui 2790 m
▪ CÓRDOBA
SIERRA DE CÓRDOBA
SIERRAS PAMPEAN
Salado
Salado
Colorado
Negro
San Matías Gulf
VALDÉS PENINSULA
Cape Tres Puntas
San Jorge Gulf
Chubut
Senguerr
Chico
Lake Buenos Aires
Lake General Carrera
Lake Cochrane
Lake Argentino
Lake Viedma
Mount Fitz Roy 3375 m
Santa Cruz
Grande Bay
PATAGONIA
Neuquén
Limay
Lake Nahuel Huapi
Damayo Volcano 3709 m
Colorado
Bío-Bío
Mount Tronador 3491 m
Gulf of Ancud
Chiloé Island
Corcovado Volcano 2300 m
Gulf of Penas
Strait of Magellan
Tierra del Fuego
Estados Island
Beagle Channel
Cape Horn
Drake Passage
DIEGO RAMÍREZ ISLANDS
Mount Darwin 2438 m
CHILE
DESERT
ATACAMA PLATEAU
Llullaillaco Volcano 6739 m
Mount Ojos del Salado 6893 m
ATACAMA Salt Flat
Mount Bonete 6872 m
Mount Mercedario 6770 m
Mount Aconcagua 6959 m
Mount Tupungato 6570 m
Mount Barroso
Desaguadero
SANTIAGO ⊛
ANDES
Tropic of Capricorn
20° S
30° S
40° S
50° S
60° W
50° W
40° W
70° W
80° W
90° W
30° W

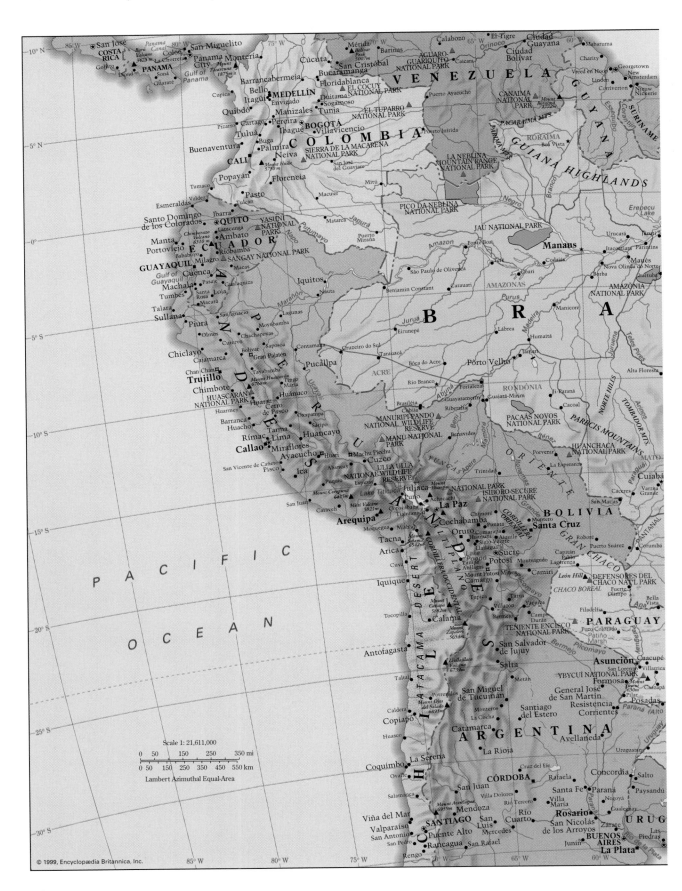

PACIFIC

OCEAN

Scale 1: 21,611,000

0   50   150   250   350 mi

0 50 150 250 350 450 550 km

Lambert Azimuthal Equal-Area

© 1999, Encyclopædia Britannica, Inc.

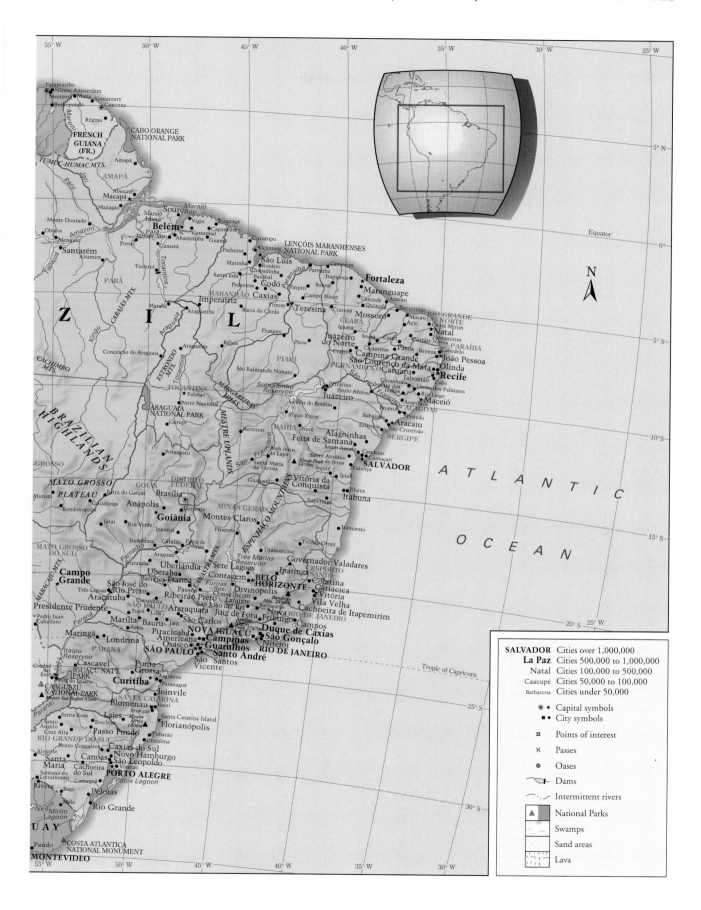

Paramaribo
Nieuw Amsterdam
Meerzorg Maria Sinnamary
Brokopondo Cayenne
Régina

FRENCH GUIANA (FR.)

TUMUC-HUMAC MTS.

CABO ORANGE NATIONAL PARK

Amapá

AMAPÁ

Monte Dourado Abecate
Macapá
Mazagão

Óbidos Monte Alegre
Alenquer
Santarém
Altamira

Marajó Island
Souré
Marajó Bay
Belém
Vigia Bragança
Castanhal Capanema
Abaetetuba Guamá
Portel
Pará Igarapé-Miri Cururupu
Tracuateua
Cametá
Pinheiro

LENÇÓIS MARANHENSES NATIONAL PARK

Matinha Alcântara Parnaíba Camocim
São Luís Rosário
Santa Inês Chapadinha Itapipoca
Bacabal Aracati
Pedreiras Piripiri
Codó Sobral
Campo Maior **Fortaleza**
Maranguape
Caxias Crateús **Mossoró**
Timon Macau Ceará Mirim
Teresina Quixadá Açu **RIO GRANDE**
Iguatú **DO NORTE**
Currais Novos **Natal**
Pedro II Parnamirim
Floriano **Juàzeiro** Caicó **PARAÍBA**
do Norte Sousa Bayeux Cabedelo
Picos Crato **Campina Grande** **João Pessoa**
São Lourenço da Mata **Olinda**
São Raimundo Nonato **Caruaru** **Recife**
Garanhuns Jaboatão
Petrolina Palmares União dos Palmares
Paulo Afonso Rio Largo
Juàzeiro Penedo **Maceió**
Senhor do Bonfim Propriá **ALAGOAS**
Xique-Xique Irecê **Aracaju**
Itabaiana Estância São Cristóvão
Feira de Santana **SERGIPE**
Bom Jesus da Lapa Sapé-Açu Candeias
Santa Maria da Vitória Santo Antônio Camaçari
Almas Peak Jequié de Jesus
Valença
Barreiras **SALVADOR**
Ipiaú
Guanambi **Vitória da Conquista**
Itabuna
Itapetinga **Ilhéus**

ATLANTIC
OCEAN

Scale 1: 20,286,000

0 100 200 300 mi
0 50 150 250 350 450 km
Bipolar Oblique Conic Conformal

PERU

BOLIVIA

PARAGUAY

BRAZIL

CHILE

ARGENTINA

URUGUAY

PACIFIC OCEAN

ATLANTIC OCEAN

FALKLAND ISLANDS
(Administered by U.K.;
claimed by Argentina)
Stanley

N

© 1999, Encyclopædia Britannica, Inc.

Legend:

CÓRDOBA	Cities over 1,000,000
La Plata	Cities 500,000 to 1,000,000
Temuco	Cities 100,000 to 500,000
Las Piedras	Cities 50,000 to 100,000
Porvenir	Cities under 50,000

⊛ ★ Capital symbols
■ • City symbols
▫ Points of interest
≈ Bridges
)(Passes
------ Canals
-·-· Intermittent rivers
∿ Waterfalls
Glaciers
National Parks
Swamps
Salt flats

2° W   Unst
Yell   Fetlar
Mainland
Aith   60° N
Lerwick
Foula
ATLANTIC
OCEAN   SHETLAND
ISLANDS
Fair Isle

Map Legend

LONDON	Cities over 1,000,000
Glasgow	Cities 500,000 to 1,000,000
Oxford	Cities 100,000 to 500,000
Limerick	Cities 50,000 to 100,000
Cheddar	Cities under 50,000

★ ⊛ Capital symbols
■ ● City symbols
----- Canals
⌐⊏ Dams
〜 Waterfalls
▓ National Parks

Scale 1: 5,546,000
0   20   40   60   80 mi
0   30   60   90   120 km
Polyconic

© 1999, Encyclopædia Britannica, Inc.

ATLANTIC OCEAN

NORTH SEA

IRISH SEA

CELTIC SEA

English Channel

SCOTLAND

NORTHERN IRELAND

IRELAND

WALES

ENGLAND

NORMANDY

BRITTANY

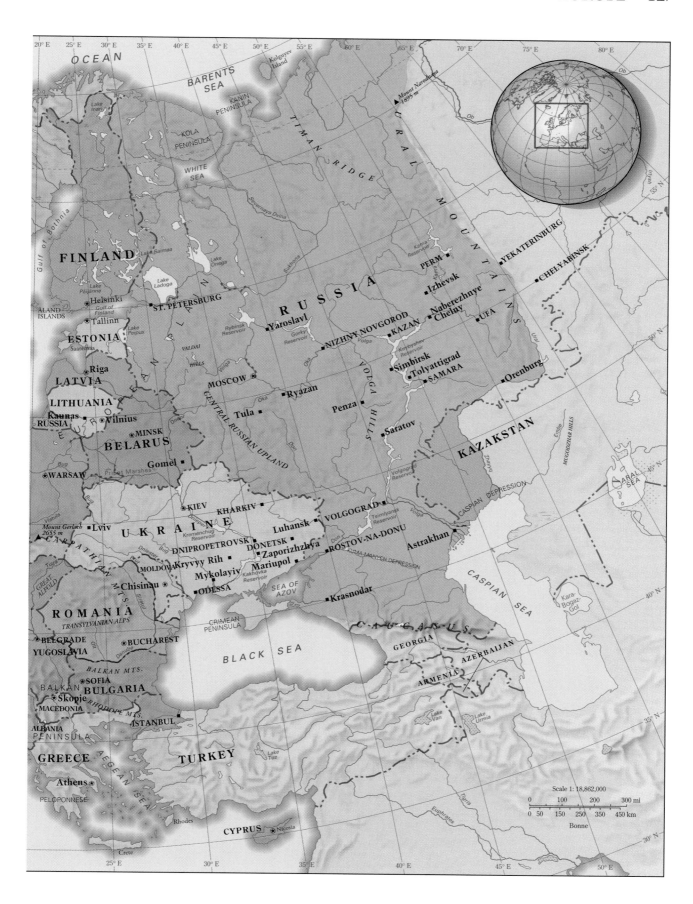

OCEAN
BARENTS SEA
Kolguyev Island
KANIN PENINSULA
KOLA PENINSULA
WHITE SEA
TIMAN RIDGE
Mount Narodnaya 1895 m
Ob
Ob
URAL MOUNTAINS

FINLAND
Lake Inari
Lake Saimaa
Lake Onega
Lake Ladoga
Severnaya Dvina
Sukhona
YEKATERINBURG
CHELYABINSK
Helsinki
Gulf of Finland
ST. PETERSBURG
Tallinn
ESTONIA
Saaremaa
Lake Peipus
RUSSIA
PERM
Izhevsk
Naberezhnye Chelny
UFA
Kama Reservoir
Yaroslavl
Rybinsk Reservoir
Gorky Reservoir
NIZHNY NOVGOROD
KAZAN
Volga
Kuybyshev Reservoir
Simbirsk
Tolyattigrad
SAMARA
Orenburg
Ural
Gulf of Bothnia
VALDAI HILLS
Riga
LATVIA
MOSCOW
Oka
Ryazan
Volga
VOLGA HILLS
LITHUANIA
Kaunas
RUSSIA
Vilnius
Tula
Penza
Saratov
KAZAKSTAN
Zhayyq
MUGODZHAR HILLS
Emba
MINSK
BELARUS
Don
Volgograd Reservoir
CASPIAN DEPRESSION
ARAL SEA
Gomel
Pripet Marshes
Bug
WARSAW
Vistula
KIEV
KHARKIV
VOLGOGRAD
Tsimlyansk Reservoir
Volga
Mount Gerlach 2655 m
Lviv
CARPATHIAN MTS.
UKRAINE
Dnieper
Kremenchug Reservoir
Luhansk
ROSTOV-NA-DONU
Astrakhan
DNIPROPETROVSK
DONETSK
Zaporizhzhya
Don
KUMA-MANYCH DEPRESSION
Tisza
MOLDOVA
Kryvyy Rih
Bug
Mykolayiv
Mariupol
Kakhovka Reservoir
CASPIAN SEA
GREAT ALFÖLD
Chisinau
Dniester
ODESSA
SEA OF AZOV
Krasnodar
Kara-Bogaz-Gol
Prut
ROMANIA
TRANSYLVANIAN ALPS
CRIMEAN PENINSULA
CAUCASUS
Siret
BELGRADE
BUCHAREST
Olt
Danube
GEORGIA
YUGOSLAVIA
BLACK SEA
AZERBAIJAN
BALKAN MTS.
BALKAN
SOFIA
BULGARIA
ARMENIA
Skopje
RHODOPE MTS.
MACEDONIA
ALBANIA
PENINSULA
ISTANBUL
Lake Van
Lake Urmia
GREECE
AEGEAN SEA
TURKEY
Lake Tuz
Athens
PELOPONNESE
CYPRUS
Nicosia
Tigris
Euphrates
Crete
Rhodes

CENTRAL RUSSIAN UPLAND
E A S T   E U R O P E A N   P L A I N

ÅLAND ISLANDS

Scale 1: 18,862,000
0   100   200   300 mi
0   50   150   250   350   450 km
Bonne

Scale 1:6,123,000

Albers Conical Equal-Area

PARIS   Cities over 1,000,000
Marseille   Cities 500,000 to 1,000,000
Orléans   Cities 100,000 to 500,000
Créteil   Cities 50,000 to 100,000
Évry   Cities under 50,000

⊛ ★   Capital symbols
● ■   City symbols

              Canals
              Glaciers
              National parks

ROME Cities over 1,000,000
Venice Cities 500,000 to 1,000,000
Verona Cities 100,000 to 500,000
Pisa Cities 50,000 to 100,000
Assiso Cities under 50,000

✳ ★ Capital symbols
• ▪ City symbols

⊡ Points of interest

⋊ Passes

------- Canals

⊐ Dams

⌐·- Intermittent rivers

🌀 Glaciers

National parks

Swamps

Salt flats

Scale 1: 6,208,000

0   25   50   75   100 mi

0   40   80   120   160 km

Secant Conic

© 1999, Encyclopædia Britannica, Inc.

BERLIN Cities over 1,000,000
Poznan Cities 500,000 to 1,000,000
Innsbruck Cities 100,000 to 500,000
Arnsberg Cities 50,000 to 100,000
Pápa Cities under 50,000

⊛ ★ Capital symbols
■ • City symbols

Scale 1: 4,390,000
0　20　40　60 mi
0　20　40　60　100　120 km
Lambert Conformal Conic

⊡ Points of interest
✕ Passes
Canals
Dams
Glaciers
National Parks
Swamps
Sand areas

14° E   Ronne •   16° E   18° E   20° E   22° E   24° E   ▽ Neris

• Bornholm (Dm.)

BALTIC SEA   Władysławowo   Kazly Ruda •   Birstonas •
                Łeba • Puck   Kaliningrad   • Marijampole
        • Ustka   Weihersberg   Baltiysk   • Alytus
Rügen   Gdynia   Hel   Gulf of   LITHUANIA
        • Słupsk   Sopot   Gdansk   RUSSIA   • Lazdijai
    • Darłowo   Gdansk   Druskininkai   54° N
Peenemünde   • Kolobrzeg   Braniewo   Bartoszyce • Węgorzewo   • Goldap
• Greifswald   Trzebiatów   • Orneta   • Kętrzyn   Suwałki ★   • Olecko   • Grodno
    Zatoka   • Białogard   • Elbląg   Lidzbark   Mragowo •   • Augustów
Pomorska   Koszalin   Malbork   Warmiński   Mragowo   POJEZIERZE   Sokółka •   • Mosty
• Kamień Pomorski Bytów •   Morąg •   • Pisz   MAZURSKIE   Grajewo •
Swinoujście   Gryfice •   Koszczyzna   Kwidzyn   Iława •   Szczytno   Kolno •   Bielsk •   • Bialystok   Volkovysk •
• Nowogard   Świdwin   Czersk   Tczew   Nidzica   Łomża   Zambrów •
Torgelow   Szczecinek •   Chojnice • Tuchola   Ostróda •   Przasnysz •   Łapy •   • Hajnówka   • Pruzhany
★ Szczecin   • Złocieniec   • Grudziądz   Chełmno   Brodnica •   Mława •   Ciechanów •   Ostrów   Bielsk
    Stargard   Wałcz •   Świecie •   Wąbrzeźno   • Rypin   Maz.   Siemiatycze • Podlaski   Vysokoye • Kamenets
Szczeciński   • Gryfino   Piła •   Bydgoszcz   Toruń   Lipno •   Sierpc •   Wyszków   Sokołów   • Zhabinka
Pyrzyce •   Choszczno •   Naklo nad   • Czarnków   Aleksandrów   • Płońsk   Pułtusk   Podlaski   Brest
    Schwedt   Chodzież   Notecią   Kujawski   Włocławek   NIZINA   Węgrów •   Biala
Eberswalde-   Debno •   Gorzów   Wronki •   Wągrowiec •   Inowrocław   • Gostynin   MAZOWIECKA   Sokołów   Podlaska
Finow   Wielkopolski   Wełna •   Szamotuły •   Mogilno •   Włocławek   Płock   Wołomin •   • Malorita
BERLIN ★   Strausberg   Kostrzyn •   • Skwierzyna   Gniezno •   Poznań   Płock   WARSAW ★   Minsk Mazowiecki   • Brest
• Frankfurt   Międzyrzecz •   Nowy Tomyśl •   POJEZIERZE WIELKOPOLSKIE   Kutno •   Pruszków   Siedlce •   Pripet   BELARUS
    Świebodzin •   Śrem •   Sroda   Konin   Brzeziny   Łowicz   Żyrardów •   Radzyń   Parczew •   52° N
Zielona   Wolsztyn •   Śrem   Jarocin   Turek   Leczyca   Skierniewice   Grójec •   Garwolin   Podlaski
Góra   Guben   Nowa Sól •   • Jarocin   Zgierz   • Dęblin   Łukowo
• Cottbus   Forst   Leszno   Kalisz   ★   Łódź   Tomaszów   Lubartów •   • Chelm
Spremberg   Żary •   Głogów •   Rawicz •   Ostrów   Sieradz •   Pabianice   Mazowiecki   Radom   Puławy   Lublin   Krasnystaw •
Senftenberg   Bobr   • NIZINA   Wielkopolski   Piotrków   Zwoleń •   Opole   • Chelm   50° N
• Hoyerswerda   Boleslawiec   Trzebnica •   Kępno •   Trybunalski   Bełchatów   Starachowice   Ostrowiec   Lubelskie   WYZYNA
    Lubin •   • Oleśnica   Namysłów •   Wieluń   Radomsko   Skarzysko-   Świętokrzyski   Kraśnik •   LUBELSKA   • Zamość
Dresden •   Görlitz   Legnica   Kluczbork •   • Kielce   GÓRY   Sandomierz   Janów   Hrubieszów •
Freital   Zawiercie •   Jawor   Strzegom •   Brzeg   Częstochowa ★   WYŻYNA   ŚWIĘTOKRZYSKIE   • Opatów   Lubelski   Szczebrzeszyn •
ERZGEBIRGE   Świdnica   Strzelin   ŚLĄSKA   Tarnowskie   Opole •   Staszów •   Stalowa
Děčín   Jelenia   Wałbrzych   Nysa •   Góry   Opole   Pińczów •   Tarnobrzeg •   Wola   Tomaszów
• Ústí   Góra   ▲ Mount Śnieżka   Kędzierzyn-   Dabrowa   Miechów •   Mielec •   Lubelski
nad Labem   Jablonec   1602 m   Kłodzko   Kozle   Bytom   Górnicza   Olkusz •   Lezajsk •   • Lubaczów
• Most   Nová Ruda   Zabrze   Sosnowiec   Kazimierza Wielka •   Rzeszów
Chomutov •   Melník •   Kłodzko   Zabkowice   Gliwice   Katowice   Tychy   Kraków   Tarnów   Przemyśl •   Lviv •
Teplice •   Boleslav •   Śląskie   Wodzisław   Oświęcim   Bochnia •   • Jarosław
Litoměřice   Nymburk •   Hradec   Pradnik •   Raciborz •   Rybnik   Śląski   Concentration Camp   • Rzeszów   Sambir •
Slaný •   Kralové   Glubczyce •   Krnov   Havirov   Cieszyn   Ustron   • Krosno   Drohobych •
Kladno •   Pardubice   • VYCHODNÍ ČECHY   Ostrava   Orlová   Český Těšín   Gorlice •   Sanok •   Boryslav •
PRAGUE   Kolín •   Litomyšl •   Zábřeh •   Opava •   Karvina   Bielsko-Biała   Jasło •   Truskavets •   Stry •
• Plzeň   Čáslav •   STREDNÍ ČECHY   Moravská   Žywiec •   Rabka   CARPATHIAN MTS.
Pribram •   Zevlika •   Brod •   Třebová   Nový   BESKID MTS.   Nowy Sącz ★   UKRAINE
Zevlika   Jihlava •   Prostějov •   Jičín   Frýdek   Mistek   Nowy Targ   Poprad •   • Uzhhorod
Tábor •   Reservoir   BOHEMIAN-MORAVIAN   Přerov •   Valašské   Ryby ▲   Gerlachovský Peak 2655 m
• Plzeň   HIGHLANDS   Meziříčí   Zilina   ▲ 2499 m   Lintovský •   VYCHODNÉ SLOVENSKO
CZECH   REPUBLIC   Olomouc   Kroměříž •   Považská   Mikuláš   Spišská   Humenné •
JIŽNÍ ČECHY   Zlín •   Bystrica   Martin   Nízke Tatry Mts.   Nová Ves •   ŠIANSKE   • Michalovce
České •   Brno   Uherské   Ružomberok •   HRON   Prešov •   MOUNTAINS
Budějovice   Znojmo •   JIŽNÍ MORAVA   Hradiště   JAVORNÍKY MTS.   Spišská   Košice
Krumlov •   Schrems •   Hodonín •   BIELE KARPATY MTS.   Trenčín •   STREDNÉ SLOVENSKO   SLOVENSKÉ RUDOHORIE
Passau   Břeclav •   Senica •   Partizánske •   Banská Bystrica •   Mukacheve •
BOHEMIAN FOREST   Piešťany •   Prievidza •   Zvolen •   SLOVAKIA   Uzhhorod
Mistelbach •   Topoľčany •   BÖRZÖ BÜK MTS.
NIEDERÖSTERREICH   Dürnkrut •   ZÁPADNÉ SLOVENSKO   Zlaté Moravce •   Lučenec •   Ózd •   Rozsava-borcica   48° N
Linz   Krems •   Klosterneuburg   Nitra •   Levice •   Salgotarian •   NORTHERN MTS.   Miskolc
• Wels   Sankt Pölten   VIENNA   WIEN   BRATISLAVA   Galanta •   Nové   ▲ Mount Kékes 1015 m   Eger •   Nyíregyháza ★   • Satu Mare
Traun •   Perchtoldsdorf •   Hainburg   Trnava •   Zámky •   MATRA MTS.   Ujfeherto •   HAJDÚSÁG   • Carei
Vorchdorf   Steyr •   Mödling •   Bratislava   Komárno •   Hajduboszormeny •
Grünburg •   Baden •   Brunn •   Vác •   HEVES   Debrecen ★
Steyr   Ebensee   Berndorf •   Sopron •   Györ   Váci   Danube   Dunakeszi •   Budapest   Nyírbátor •
AUSTRIA   Wiener Neustadt   Neunkirchen   Neusiedler   Tatabánya   Danube   BUDAPEST •   JÁSZSÁG   • Zalau
• Ternitz   See   LITTLE ALFOLD   Vecsés •   Szolnok •
STEIERMARK   Kapfenberg •   BURGENLAND   Pápa   HUNGARY   Cegléd •   Szolnok   TRANSTISZA   Oradea •
Leoben •   Bruck   Szombathely •   Veszprém •   Székesfehérvár ★   Kecskemét •   ROMANIA
NIEDERE TAUERN   Graz   Hartberg   VAS   Veszprém   • Mezöberény   Salonta •
▲ Mount Rosennock   Judenburg   Zeltweg •   Sárvár •   Zalaegerszeg •   Lake   Dunaújváros •   Kiskunság •   Szolnok •   Békéscsaba •   Gyula •
2440 m   Zalaegerszeg   Keszthely •   Balaton   Sárbogárd •   Hódmezővásárhely •   ▲ Mount Biher 1849 m
Wolfsberg •   Deutschlandsberg •   TRANSDANUBIA   Nagykanizsa •   ▲ Mount Gaina 1486 m
KARNTEN   Sankt Veit •   ZALA   Kaposvár •   MECSEK MTS.   Kalocsa •   Szeged ★   Arad •
Villach   Klagenfurt   Maribor •   Nagyatad •   Szekszárd •   GIRELA   • Subotica   POIANA RUSCAL MOUNTAINS
JULIAN ALPS   Ptuj •   Velenje •   Pécs •   MECSEK MTS.   Nagyszőlős •   CARPATII
▲ Mount   Kranj •   Celje •   Koprivnica •   Kikinda •   Timișoara •   Lugoj •   Deva •   46° N
Triglav 2864 m   SLOVENIA   Trbovlje •   CROATIA   Kotoriba •   Sombor •   YUGOSLAVIA   Hunedoara •   Orastu •
Gorizia   Ljubljana •   Novo Mesto •   Krško •   Bjelovar •   Drava   • Zrenjanin
Postojna   Idrija •   Ssvete •   Zagreb ★   Virovitica •   © 1999, Encyclopædia Britannica, Inc.
14° E   16° E   18° E   20° E

N

MEDITERRANEAN SEA

AEGEAN SEA

SEA OF CRETE

IONIAN SEA

TYRRHENIAN SEA

TURKEY

GREECE

ITALY

LIBYA

Athens

IZMIR

Bursa

Thessaloníki

Iráklion

Crete

Sicily

DODECANESE

CYCLADES

Scale 1:5,913,000
Albers

© 1999, Encyclopædia Britannica, Inc.

SOFIA Cities over 1,000,000
Sarajevo Cities 500,000 to 1,000,000
Tiranë Cities 100,000 to 500,000
Nikea Cities 50,000 to 100,000
Tecuci Cities under 50,000

⊛ Capital symbols
■ • City symbols
⌑ Points of interest
Bridges
Canals
Dams
Intermittent rivers
National parks
Swamps
Sand areas

ARCTIC OCEAN

SEVERNAYA ZEMLYA
Komsomolets Island
Rabocheostrovsk Island
Bolshevik Island
Cape Chelyuskin

NEW SIBERIAN ISLANDS
New Siberia Island
Kotelny Island
LYAKHOVSKY ISLANDS
Dmitriya Lapteva Strait

LAPTEV SEA

EAST SIBERIAN SEA

WRANGEL ISLAND NATURE RESERVE
Wrangel Island
Long Strait

CHUKCHI SEA

CHUKCHI PENINSULA
Cape Dezhnev
UNITED STATES
Saint Lawrence Island (U.S.)

TAYMYR PENINSULA
BYRRANGA MTS.
Lake Taymyr
TAYMYR NATURE RESERVE
SIBERIAN LOWLAND

Bolshoy Begichev Island
Khatanga
Olenyok

Yansky Gulf
Yana
Indigirka

CHERSKY MOUNTAINS
Verkhoyansk
Adycha
Indigirka
Mount Pobeda 3147 m

KOLYMA LOWLAND
Ayon Island
Omolon
Kolyma

CHUKCHI MOUNTAINS
Pevek
Anadyr

KOLYMA MOUNTAINS
Magadan
MAGADAN NATURE RESERVE
Cape Yuzhny

KORYAK MOUNTAINS
Cape Olyutorsky
Velikaya
Karagin Island

SREDINNY
KOMANDOR ISLANDS

KAMCHATKA PENINSULA
KRONOTSKY NATURE RESERVE
Petropavlovsk-Kamchatsky
Kamchatka

PUTORAN MTS.
Mount Kamen 1664 m
CENTRAL SIBERIAN PLATEAU
ANABARSKOYE PLATEAU
EVENK AUTONOMOUS OKRUG
Tura
Lower Tunguska
Stony Tunguska
Chunya

ANABARSKOYE OKRUG AUTONOMOUS

SAKHA (YAKUTIA) REPUBLIC
Mount Mus-Khaya 2959 m
SUNTAR-KHAYATA MOUNTAINS

CENTRAL YAKUT LOWLAND
Vilyuy
VILYUY MOUNTAINS
Vilyuy Reservoir
Mirny
Udachny
Markha

VERKHOYANSKA MOUNTAINS

Kotuy
Muna
Lena
Anabar

Yakutsk
Aldan
Anga

Maya
DZHUGDZHUR RANGE

SEA OF OKHOTSK
N
Cape Yelizavety
Sakhalin Island
SHANTAR ISLANDS
Cape Patience
Yuzhno-Sakhalinsk
WESTERN SAKHALIN MTS.
EASTERN SAKHALIN MTS.

Paramushir Island
KURIL ISLANDS

SIBERIA
PLATEAU
PRILENSKOYE PLATEAU
Lensk
PATOM PLATEAU

ALDAN PLATEAU
Aldan

STANOVOY MOUNTAINS
Uda

Olyokma
Vitim
Uchur

RIDGE
Angara
Ust-Ilimsk
PRIANGARSKOYE PLATEAU
Bratsk
Bratsk Reservoir
EASTERN
Krasnoyarsk
Krasnoyarsk Reservoir
Kansk

SAYAN MTS.
SAYAN MOUNTAINS
TVA REPUBLIC
Kyzyl
Yenisey
OLA MTS.
Lake Uvs
Lake Hyargas

Usolye-Sibirskoye
Angarsk
Irkutsk
Ulan-Ude
BAIKAL LENA NATURE RESERVE
BARGUZIN NATURE RESERVE
VITIM PLATEAU
STANOVOY PLATEAU
Lake Baikal
Olkhon Island
Lake BAIKAL NATURE RESERVE
BURYATIA REPUBLIC
Chita
YABLONOVY RANGE

NATURE RESERVE
ZEYA
Zeya Reservoir
Zeya

HUZHONG NATURE RESERVE
HANMA NATURE RESERVE
Mount Fenshui 1398 m
Mount Feushui

Blagoveshchensk
KHINGANSK NATURE RESERVE
Amur
Komsomolsk na-Amure
KOMSOMOLSK NATURE RESERVE
Mount Tardoki-Yani 2077 m
Khabarovsk
SIKHOTE-ALIN MTS.
SIKHOTE-ALIN NATURE RESERVE

Hokkaido
KUSHIRO-SHITSUGEN NATIONAL PARK
Asahikawa
Otaru
SAPPORO
Muroran
Hachinohe
Morioka

China
Manzhouli
Hailar
DA HINGGAN RANGE
XIAO HINGGAN RANGE
Nen
Butha Qi
Bei'an
Zhaodong
Suihua
QIQIHAR
Daqing
Anda
HARBIN

Yichun
Hegang
Jiamusi
Qitaihe
Jixi
Mudanjiang
CHANGCHUN
JILIN

Vladivostok
LAZOVSKY NATURE RESERVE
Ussuriysk
Nakhodka
Peter the Great Bay
Lake Khanka

Ussuri
Sungari

SEA OF JAPAN

JAPAN
Honshu
Aomori
Akita
Sendai
Niigata
Fukushima
Kanazawa
NOTO PENINSULA
Mount Fuji 3776 m
Gifu
Yamagata
Tokomachi
Obihiro
Kushiro

Tatar Strait

La Perouse Strait
KITAMI MTS.

MONGOLIA
Ulaanbaatar
HANGAYN MTS.
Tsetserleg
Mount Otgontenger 3905 m
Lake Hovsgol
Möron
Erdenet
Darhan
Sühbaatar
Selenge
Bulgan
Orhon
Nalayh
Choybalsan
Kerulen
Baruun-Urt
Tümentsogt

ALTAI MTS.
Dzhavan
Altay
Lake Dörgön
Hami
Lake Uvs
Tes
Kyzyl
Uliastay
Bayanhongor
Arvayheer
Mount Suvraga Havirhan 3179 m
Mount Tergün-Bogd 3957 m
GOBI ALTAI MTS.
GURVAN SAYHAN MTS.
EDRENGIYN MTS.

GOBI DESERT

Tongliao
Tiefa
Tieling
Horqin Youyi Qianqi
Baicheng
Lake Qagan
Songhua Reservoir
MANCHURIAN PLAIN
Yanji
Tumen
Hunjiang
Ch'ŏngjin
NORTH KOREA
Kanggye
Hyesan
Tanch'ŏn

100°E 120°E 140°E   160°E   170°E   180°   170°W   70°N
110°E   100°E   120°E   130°E   50°N

Key to Political subdivision names (shown by number on map):

1 ADYGEA REPUBLIC
2 KARACHAY-CHERKESSIA REPUBLIC
3 KABARDINO-BALKARIA REPUBLIC
4 NORTH OSSETIA (ALANIA) REPUBLIC
5 CHECHNIA REPUBLIC
6 DAGESTAN REPUBLIC
7 INGUSHETIA REPUBLIC
8 MORDVINIA REPUBLIC
9 CHUVASHIA REPUBLIC
10 MARI EL REPUBLIC
11 TATARSTAN REPUBLIC
12 UDMURTIA REPUBLIC
13 BASHKORTOSTAN REPUBLIC
14 KOMI-PERMYAK AUTONOMOUS OKRUG
15 UST-ORDA BURYAT AUTONOMOUS OKRUG
16 AGA-BURYAT AUTONOMOUS OKRUG

Scale 1: 42,683,000

0   100   300   500   700 mi

0 200 400 600 800 1000 km

Bonne

ARCTIC OCEAN

FRANZ JOSEF
LAND ISLANDS

SEVERNAYA
ZEMLYA
ISLANDS

Cape Chelyuskin

NOVAYA ZEMLYA
ISLANDS

KARA
SEA

TAIMYR
PENINSULA

LAPTEV
SEA

YAMAL
PENINSULA

NORTH SIBERIAN LOWLAND

CENTRAL

Lower Tunguska

SIBERIAN

WEST

Mount
Narodnaya
1895 m

R U S S I A

PLATEAU

MOSCOW

SIBERIAN

Angara

Lake
Baikal

YEKATERINBURG

Tomsk   Krasnoyarsk

CHELYABINSK   NOVOSIBIRSK

Kemerovo

SAYAN
MTS.

OMSK

Novokuznetsk

Irkutsk

PLAIN

Barnaul

Yenisey

SEA OF
AZOV

KUMA-MANYCH
DEPRESSION

CASPIAN
DEPRESSION

Astana

Qaraghandy

ALTAI
MOUNTAINS

MONGOLIA

BLACK SEA

Mount Elbrus
5642 m

K A Z A K S T A N

Mount Yenya
4374 m

Bursa   ISTANBUL

GEORGIA

T'BILISI

ARAL
SEA

Lake
Balkhash

IZMIR   TURKEY   ANKARA   YEREVAN

Syr Darya

ALMATY

ÜRÜMQI

Konya   Adana

TAURUS MTS

ARMENIA

AZERBAIJAN

Gaziantep

Kara-
Bogaz

UZBEKISTAN

Bishkek
Victory Peak
439 m

T I A N   S H A N

GOBI
DESERT

MEDITERRANEAN
SEA

LEBANON

ALEPPO

Mosul

Tabriz

BAKU

TURKMENISTAN

KARA-KUM
DEPRESSION

TASHKENT

KYRGYZSTAN

Lop
Nor

SYRIA   Kirkuk

Hims

Ashgabat

Kara-Kum Canal

TAJIKISTAN
Communism Peak
495 m

TAKLA MAKAN DESERT

Xining

BEIRUT   DAMASCUS   Bakhtaran

TEHRAN

ELBURZ MTS.

PAMIRS

Dushanbe

ISRAEL   Qom

Mount Damavand 567 m

HINDU KUSH MTS.

K2
8611 m

KUNLUN MOUNTAINS

Jerusalem   AMMAN   IRAQ   BAGHDAD

MASHHAD

Srinagar
Nanga Parbat
8126 m

JORDAN

ZAGROS MTS.

KABUL

Peshawar

KARAKORAM RANGE

KASHMIR

AN-NAFUD
DESERT

Basra

Ahvaz

Esfahan

AFGHANISTAN

Islamabad

PLATEAU   OF   TIBET

Kuwait

IRAN

FAISALABAD

LAHORE   Amritsar

SAUDI
ARABIA

Kuwait

LUDHIANA

Mount Manaslu
163 m
Mount Everest
848 m

Shiraz

Multan

Chandigarh

NEPAL

RIYADH

Manama

Meerut

Kathmandu

BHUTAN

ARABIAN

BAHRAIN

MAKRAN MTS.

DELHI

Agra

LUCKNOW

Brahmaputra

JIDDAH

QATAR

LOMAN

Jodhpur   JAIPUR   New Delhi   KANPUR   Patna

Guwahati

PENINSULA

Abu
Dhabi

Gulf of Oman

THAR DESERT

Gwalior

Kota

Ganges

RED SEA

Mecca

UNITED ARAB
EMIRATES

Muscat

Hyderabad

Allahabad

Varanasi

BANGLADESH

DHAKA

KARACHI

PAKISTAN

Indus

Sutlej

Yamuna

BHOPAL

I N D I A

Ranchi

Mandalay

RUB' AL-KHALI DESERT

OMAN

AHMADABAD

Jabalpur

Howrah

CHITTAGONG

Rajkot

Narmada

INDORE

CALCUTTA

MYANMAR

ARABIAN

SURAT

VADODARA

NAGPUR

Mount Inthanon
2588 m

Sanaa
Mount an-Nabi Shu'ayb
3660 m

SEA

Nashik

DECCAN PLATEAU

Mount Inthanon
2588 m

YEMEN

BOMBAY

PUNE

Vishakhapatnam

Bay
of
Bengal

YANGON

Gulf of Aden

Sholapur

Godavari

HYDERABAD

Krishna

Vijayawada

Socotra Island
(YEMEN)

Hubli-Dharwad

WESTERN GHATS

EASTERN GHATS

LAKSHADWEEP
ISLANDS
(INDIA)

BANGALORE

MADRAS

ANDAMAN
ISLANDS
(INDIA)

ANDAMAN
SEA

Coimbatore
Anai Peak
2695 m

Cochin   Madurai

NICOBAR
ISLANDS
(INDIA)

Trivandrum

SRI LANKA

Colombo

Male

INDIAN OCEAN

MALDIVES

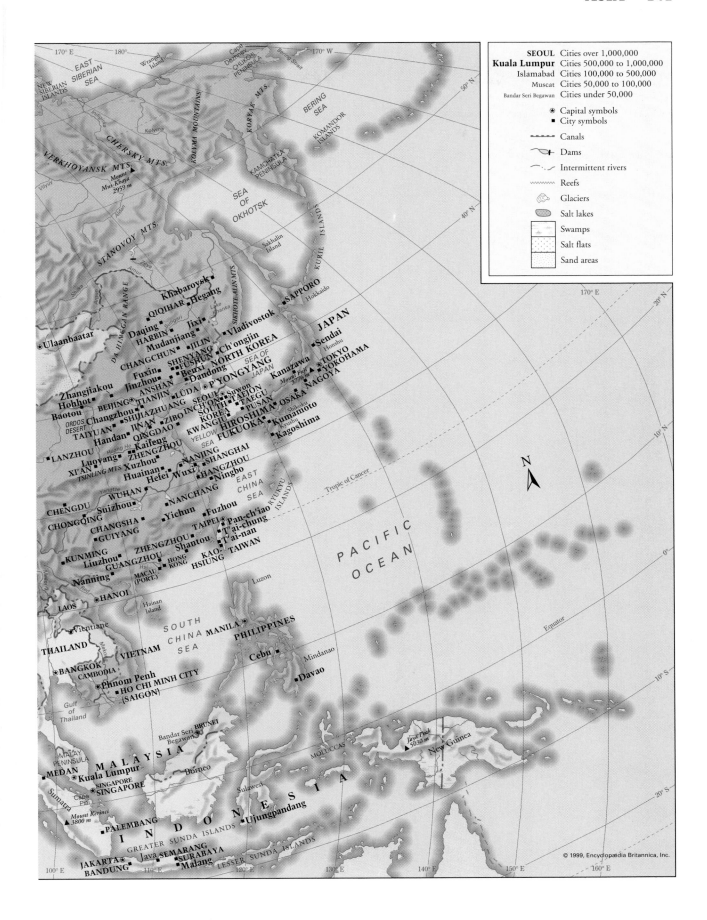

Legend:

SEOUL — Cities over 1,000,000
Kuala Lumpur — Cities 500,000 to 1,000,000
Islamabad — Cities 100,000 to 500,000
Muscat — Cities 50,000 to 100,000
Bandar Seri Begawan — Cities under 50,000

⊛ Capital symbols
■ City symbols
---- Canals
⌐ Dams
⌐ Intermittent rivers
∿ Reefs
🝆 Glaciers
🝆 Salt lakes
Swamps
Salt flats
Sand areas

Scale 1: 18,257,000

0	100	200	300 mi

0	50	150	250	350	450 km

Conical Equal-Area

SEOUL	Cities over 1,000,000
Jinzhou	Cities 500,000 to 1,000,000
Hitachi	Cities 100,000 to 500,000
Tunxi	Cities 50,000 to 100,000
Hondo	Cities under 50,000
✸ ★	Capital symbols
■ ·	City symbols
▫	Points of interest
⌒⌒⌒	Great Wall
)(	Passes
------	Canals
⌒⌒	Dams
-·-	Intermittent rivers
🌀	Glaciers
⬭	Salt lakes
▲	National parks
	Swamps
	Sand areas

N

Scale 1: 21,022,000

0 50 150 250 350 mi
0 50 150 250 350 450 550 km

Oblique Mercator

Huangshi
HANGZHOU Shaoxing
Jiujiang **Ningbo**
Jingdezhen Jinhua
NANCHANG Quzhou Haimen
CHANGSHA Fuzhou Shangrao Wenzhou
Yichun Xinyu Nanping
Ji'an
Zixing **Fuzhou**
Ganzhou Quanzhou **TAIPEI**
Shaoguan Longyan Hsin-chu **Pan-ch'iao**
ZHENGZHOU Xiamen **T'ai-chung**
Chao'an **TAIWAN**
GUANGZHOU Chia-i ▲ Yü Shan 3997 m
Zhuhai Huzhou **Shantou** **T'ai-nan**
Shenzhen
HONG KONG **KAO-HSIUNG**
MACAU
(Port.)

Lake
Poyang

Xin'anjiang Res.
Min

WUYI MOUNTAINS

Bei

Taiwan Strait

Luzon BATAN
ISLANDS

Strait BABUYAN
ISLANDS

Cape Bojeador
Mount Sicapoo ▲ Escarpada Point
2361 m Aparri
Banguea
Candon Luzon
Baguio ▲ Mount Pulog 2934 m
Mangaldan **PHILIPPINES**
Dagupan
San Carlos Cabanatuan **PHILIPPINE**
Angeles
Olongapo **Caloocan** **SEA**
MANILA **QUEZON CITY**
Tagig San Pablo
Lipa **Lucena** MOUNT ISAROG
Batangas Santa **Naga** NATIONAL PARK
Cruz Mayon Volcano 2462 m
LAKE NAUJAN **Legazpi**
NATIONAL PARK Irosin Laoang
Mindoro San Odiongan
CALAMIAN José Dimasalang Samar Dolores
GROUP Puray Catbalogan **Calbayog**
Roxas VISAYAN
San José ISLANDS Leyte **Tacloban**
Dumaran **Iloilo City** Cebu **Ormoc**
Island **Bacolod** Carigara
Puerto Princesa San Carlos **Mandaue**
Palawan Negros **Cebu** **Lapu-Lapu**
Narra Tagbilaran General Luna
Dumaguete **BOHOL** **Surigao**
Dapitan **SEA**
Balabac Island Balabac **Butuan**
SULU Gingoog **Bislig**
SEA **Iligan** **Cagayan de Oro**
Balabac Strait ZAMBOANGA Marawi Valencia
PENINSULA **Pagadian** **Mindanao** MAINIT HOT SPRING
Zamboanga **Cotabato** NATIONAL PARK
KINABALU
NATIONAL PARK Moro **Davao**
Kota Kinabalu Jolo Gulf Isulan Mount Apo 2954 m
BRUNEI ▲ Mount **Zamboanga** Davao Gulf
Bandar Seri Kinabalu 4101 m Tawitawi **General Santos**
Begawan Victoria Sandakan Polomolok
Miri SABAH Bongaaw SARANGANI
MOUNT MULU Tawau SULU ARCHIPELAGO ISLANDS Cape San Agustin
NATIONAL PARK
SARAWAK Mount Murud ▲
Bintulu 2422 m Tarakan
Batu Hill ▲ Island
2011 m Kayan TALAUD
ISLANDS

CHINA SEA

Mindoro Strait

Palawan Passage

Balabac

CROCKER RANGE

MULLER MOUNTAINS

MERATUS MOUNTAINS

Borneo

KALIMANTAN

Samarinda
Balikpapan

Mahakam

Banjarmasin Banjarbaru
Palangkaraya

PACIFIC

OCEAN

PALAU ISLANDS

Mount Awu ▲
1320 m

CELEBES SEA SANGIHE
ISLANDS

Morotai

MINAHASA
PENINSULA **Manado** Bitung
Mount Soputan Tondano MOLUCCA Halmahera
1784 m Gorontalo Ternate Island Island
SEA Tidore Island

Gulf of
Tomini Luwuk Peleng Island
Samarinda Palu OBI
Sulawesi SULA ISLANDS ISLANDS
Lake Poso BANGGAI
Mount Kambuno ▲ ISLANDS
2950 m Mount Balease Gulf
▲ 3016 m of **Moluccas** **CERAM SEA**
Rantepao Tolo
Lake Towuti Buru Ceram Fakfak
Mount Rantekombola ▲
3450 m Kendari **Ambon**
Pinrang Kolaka Ambon
Parepare Gulf Muna Island Banda
Watampone of Buton Island Besar
Bone Island
ISLANDS Kabaena
Ujungpandang Island TUKANGBESI **KAI**
SEA Selayar ISLANDS ISLANDS
Bawean Island
Island Madura **INDONESIA** **BANDA SEA**
Gresik Kangean ARU
SURABAYA ISLANDS ISLANDS
Jombang Madura Strait
Probolinggo Mount Tambora ▲ Damar Island
Jember 2851 m Pantar TANIMBAR
Singaraja Lomblen Alor Wetar Island Romang Island ISLANDS
Malang Bali Lombok Island Island
Denpasar **Mataram** Sumbawa **Dili** Babar
WESTERN BALI KOMODO ISLAND Komodo Flores Island
NATIONAL PARK NATIONAL PARK Island Alambuti Mount Tata Mailau
Sumba 2965 m
FLORES SEA SOLOR ISLANDS **Timor**
Savu Kefamenanu
BALI SEA Island Soe
Kupang
LESSER SUNDA ISLANDS Roti Island **SAVU SEA**

ARAFURA SEA

Mamberamo

Jayapura
Vanimo

SCHOUTEN
Waigeo Island ISLANDS
Sorong Biak Manokwari
Gag
Island Yapen Island
Dampier Strait
Misool
Island

MAPIA ISLANDS

Equator

Wewak
Sepik

MAOKE MOUNTAINS STERREN
Jaya Peak ▲ JAYAWIJAYA MOUNTAINS
5030 m MOUNTAINS Mount Capela
3932 m

New Guinea

Kiunga Mount Hagen
Digul **PAPUA**
NEW GUINEA
Balimo

Yos Sudarso Daru
Island Merauke

Torres Strait

TIMOR SEA

CAIRO Cities over 1,000,000
Tripoli Cities 500,000 to 1,000,000
Batman Cities 100,000 to 500,000
Zugdidi Cities 50,000 to 100,000
al-Faydah Cities under 50,000
⊛★ Capital symbols
■● City symbols
‧‧‧‧ Canals
—— Intermittent rivers
⌢ Intermittent lakes
▬ Salt lakes
▲ National Parks
Swamps
Salt flats
Sand areas
Lava

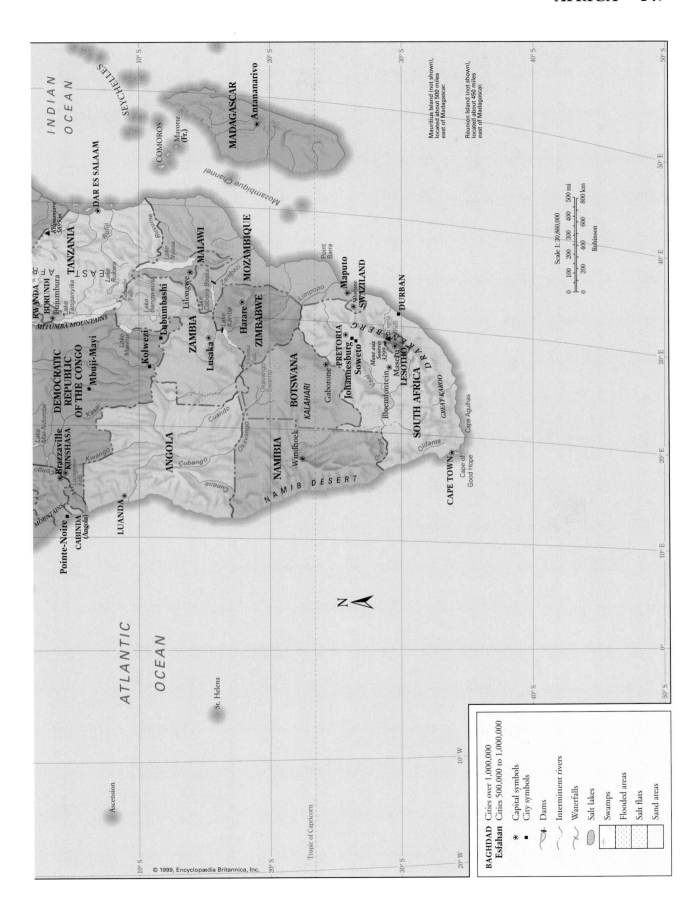

INDIAN

OCEAN

SEYCHELLES

DAR ES SALAAM

COMOROS

Mayotte (Fr.)

MADAGASCAR

⊛ Antananarivo

Mozambique Channel

Mauritius Island (not shown), located about 500 miles east of Madagascar.

Reunion Island (not shown), located about 450 miles east of Madagascar.

Kilimanjaro 5895 m

TANZANIA

RWANDA
BURUNDI
Bujumbura

Lake Rukwa

Lake Nyasa

MALAWI

Lilongwe ⊛

MOZAMBIQUE

Point Barra

Ruvuma

Rufiji

EAST

Lake Tanganyika

MITUMBA MOUNTAINS

Lake Mweru

Kolwezi

Lubumbashi

ZAMBIA

Lusaka ⊛

Lake Kariba

Harare ⊛

ZIMBABWE

Lake Cabora Bassa

Zambezi

Limpopo

Maputo ⊛

Mbabane

SWAZILAND

DURBAN

DEMOCRATIC
REPUBLIC
OF THE CONGO

Mbuji-Mayi

Lake Bangweulu

Boyoma Falls

Lake Mai-Ndombe

Brazzaville
KINSHASA ⊛

Kasai

Kwango

BOTSWANA

KALAHARI

Gaborone ⊛

Okavango Swamp

Cuando

PRETORIA
Johannesburg
Soweto

Mont aux Sources 3299

Vaal

Maseru

LESOTHO

Bloemfontein ⊛

SOUTH AFRICA

DRAKENSBERG

Tugela Falls

GREAT KAROO

Olifants

Cape Agulhas

ANGOLA

LUANDA

Pointe-Noire
CABINDA (Angola)

MOUNTAINS

Congo

Cubango

Cunene

Okavango

NAMIBIA

Windhoek ⊛

NAMIB DESERT

Orange

CAPE TOWN ⊛

Cape of Good Hope

ATLANTIC

OCEAN

St. Helena

Ascension

Tropic of Capricorn

N

© 1999, Encyclopædia Britannica, Inc.

Scale 1:30,860,000

0   100   200   300   400   500 mi

0   200   400   600   800 km

Robinson

BAGHDAD Cities over 1,000,000
Esfahan Cities 500,000 to 1,000,000

⊛ Capital symbols
▪ City symbols
Dams
Intermittent rivers
Waterfalls
Salt lakes
Swamps
Flooded areas
Salt flats
Sand areas

CAIRO	Cities over 1,000,000
Rabat	Cities 500,000 to 1,000,000
Monrovia	Cities 100,000 to 500,000
Bambari	Cities 50,000 to 100,000
Timbuktu	Cities under 50,000
⊛	Capital symbols
▪	City symbols
⊡	Points of interest
	Canals
	Aqueducts
	Dams
	Intermittent rivers
	Salt lakes
▲	National parks
	Swamps
	Flooded areas
	Salt flats
	Sand areas
	Lava
	Oases

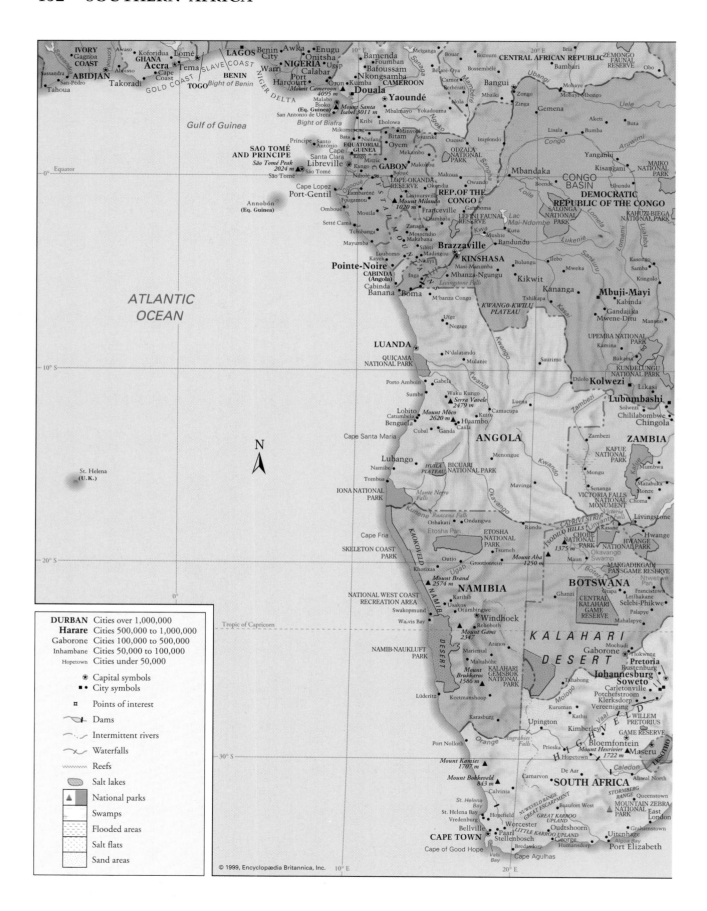

ATLANTIC
OCEAN

IVORY
COAST
Gagnoa
GHANA
Sassandra   Abisso   Accra
San-Pédro   Cape
Tahoua   Takoradi   Coast
GOLD COAST
Komoé

Awaso   Koforidua Lomé
Kpandu
Accra   Tema
TOGO
BENIN
Bight of Benin
NIGER DELTA

LAGOS   Benin Awka **Enugu**
City   •Onitsha
NIGERIA   Ugep •Enugu
Warri   Calabar
Port
Harcourt Oron Kumba **CAMEROON**
Bonny
Mount Cameroon
4095 m
Malabo
(Eq. Guinea)
Bioko   Mount Santa
San Antonio de Ureca Isabel 3011 m

Gulf of Guinea

Bight of Biafra

SAO TOMÉ
AND PRINCIPE
São Tomé Peak
2024 m
São Tomé

Annobón
(Eq. Guinea)

Príncipe Santo
Antonio
Bata   **EQUATORIAL**
GUINEA
Cape
Santa Clara
Libreville Ndjolé
São Tomé

Cape Lopez
Port-Gentil

Setté Cama

Bamenda
Foumban
Bafoussam
Nkongsamba
Douala
•**Yaoundé**

Mbalmayo Yokadouma
Kribi Ebolowa
Mikomeseng
Minvoul
Bitam
Oyem
Mekambo
Makokou
Booué
GABON
Lastoursville
Mount Milondo
1020 m
Franceville
Zanaga
Djambala
Mouila
Omb_oue
Mayumba
Makabana
Sibiti
Madingou
Loubomo
Kayes
Nkayi
Pointe-Noire
CABINDA
(Angola)
Cabinda
Banana **Boma**

Nola
Mbalmayo
Souanke

Ouesso
Impfondo

ODZALA
NATIONAL
PARK
Owando
Makoua

LOPE-OKANDA
RESERVE
Okonja

REP. OF THE
CONGO
Gamboma
LEFINI FAUNAL
RESERVE
Kwe
Mushie
Brazzaville
Masi-Manimba
KINSHASA
Mbanza-Ngungu
Inga Livingstone Falls
M'banza Congo

Ufge
Negage

LUANDA
N'dalatando
QUIÇAMA
NATIONAL PARK
Mulanie

Porto Amboim
Sumbe   Gabela
Waku Kungo
Serra Vavele
2479 m
Lobito   Mount Môco
Catumbela 2620 m
Benguela **Huambo**
Cubal Ganda Caála
Cape Santa Maria
ANGOLA

Lubango
Namibe **HUÍLA**
PLATEAU
Tombua
IONA NATIONAL
PARK
Monte Negro
Falls
Cape Fria
Ruacana Falls
SKELETON COAST
PARK
Oshakati Ondangwa
Etosha Pan
Cape Frio

Khorixas
Mount Brand
2574 m
NATIONAL WEST COAST
RECREATION AREA
Karibib
Usakos
Swakopmund Otjimbingwe
Walvis Bay

NAMIB-NAUKLUFT
PARK
Mariental
Maltahöhe
Mount
Brukkaros
1586 m
Lüderitz
Keetmanshoop
Karasburg

Port Nolloth
Mount Kamies
1707 m
Mount Bokkeveld
843 m
Calvinia

St. Helena
Bay
St. Helena Bay
Vredenburg
Hopefield
Bellville
CAPE TOWN
Paarl Stellenbosch
Bredasdorp
Cape of Good Hope

Menongue
BICUARI
NATIONAL PARK
Mavinga

CAPRIVI STRIP
KAOKOVELD
Outio
Grootfontein Tsumeb
ETOSHA
NATIONAL
PARK
Mount Aha
1250 m
Maun
Rundu

Mount Gani
2347

Aranos

KALAHARI
GEMSBOK
NATIONAL PARK
Upington

Kuruman
Kathu
Kimberley
Prieska
Hopetown
De Aar
Carnarvon

Beaufort West
GREAT KAROO
UPLAND
Worcester
Oudtshoorn
George

Bria
Bozoum
CENTRAL AFRICAN REPUBLIC **ZEMONGO**
FAUNAL
RESERVE
Obo
Bétaré-Oya Bossembélé Bambari
Bangui
Mbaiki
Congo

Mohaye
Zongo Mobayi-Mbongo
Uele
Gemena Aketi
Lisala Bumba Buta
Yanganbi Kisangani
Mbandaka Boende
CONGO BASIN
Tshuapa

DEMOCRATIC
REPUBLIC OF THE CONGO
SALONGA
NATIONAL
PARK
Ilebo Kutu
Bandundu
Kikwit
Kananga
Tshikapa
Gandajika
Mwene-Ditu
Mbuji-Mayi
Kabinda

KWANGO-KWILU
PLATEAU

Dilolo **Kolwezi**
Likasi
Lubumbashi
Solwezi
Chingola
Chililabombwe

MAIKO
NATIONAL
PARK
KAHUZI-BIEGA
NATIONAL PARK
Kasongo
Samba
Kongolo

UPEMBA NATIONAL
PARK
Kamina
Bukama
KUNDELUNGU
NATIONAL PARK

Kabwe
ZAMBIA
KAFUE
NATIONAL
PARK
Mumbwa
Mongu Mazabuka
Senanga Monze Choma
VICTORIA FALLS
NATIONAL
MONUMENT
Livingstone
Hwange
HWANGE
NATIONAL PARK

CHOBE
NATIONAL
PARK
Kasane
MAKGADIKGADI
PANS GAME RESERVE
Ntwetwe
Pan
Orapa Francistown
Letlhakane Selebi-Phikwe
CENTRAL
KALAHARI
GAME
RESERVE
Palapye
Mahalapye
KALAHARI
DESERT
Mochudi Tlokweng
Gaborone
Pretoria
Rustenburg
Ghanzi
Thabong
Tshabong

Johannesburg **Soweto**
Carletonville
Potchefstroom
Klerksdorp
Vereeniging
WILLEM
PRETORIUS
GAME RESERVE
Bloemfontein
Mount Hexrivier
1722 m
Maseru
Caledon
Aliwal North
SOUTH AFRICA
STORMBERG
RANGE Queenstown
MOUNTAIN ZEBRA
NATIONAL
PARK East
London
Grahamstown
Uitenhage
Algoa Bay
Port Elizabeth
Cape Agulhas

N

St. Helena
(U.K.)

Equator 0°

10° S

20° S

Tropic of Capricorn

30° S

0° E

10° E

20° E

DURBAN   Cities over 1,000,000
Harare   Cities 500,000 to 1,000,000
Gaborone   Cities 100,000 to 500,000
Inhambane   Cities 50,000 to 100,000
Hopetown   Cities under 50,000

⊛   Capital symbols
■ •   City symbols

⌑   Points of interest

⌐⊔   Dams

‿·‿   Intermittent rivers

‿⌄‿   Waterfalls

⌄⌄⌄⌄   Reefs

⬮   Salt lakes

▲   National parks

Swamps

Flooded areas

Salt flats

Sand areas

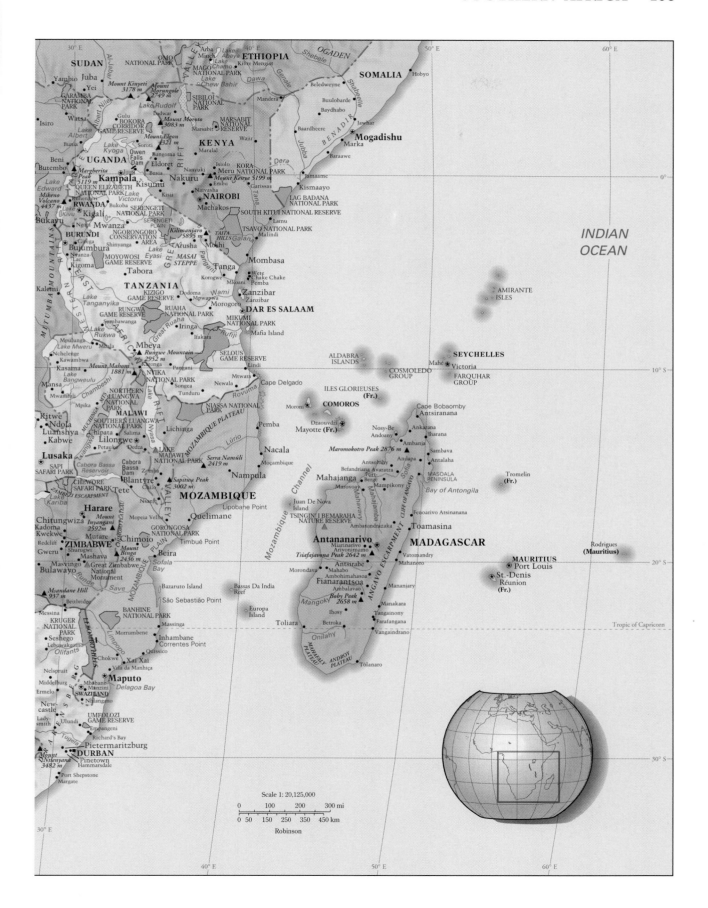

SUDAN

OMO
NATIONAL PARK

• Yambio • Juba

GARAMBA
NATIONAL
PARK

• Isiro • Watsa

Mount Kinyeti
3178 m

Mount
Morungole
2749 m

SIBILOI
NATIONAL
PARK

ETHIOPIA

Arba
Minch

Lake
Abaya

Kibre Mengist

OGADEN

Shebele

SOMALIA

• Hobyo

Lake
Chamo

MAGO
NATIONAL PARK

Lake
Chew Bahir

Dawa

Genale

Beledweyne

Buulobarde

• Yei

• Gulu
BOKORA
CORRIDOR
GAME RESERVE

Ludwar

Mount Moroto
3083 m

MARSABIT
NATIONAL
RESERVE

Baardheere

Baydhabo

• Jawhar

Mogadishu

Marka

Bunia

• Beni
Butembo

Margherita
Peak
5119 m

Mount Elgon
4321 m

Marsabit

Maralal

Wajir

Dera

Baraawe

BENADIR

UGANDA

Lake
Albert

Lake
Kyoga

Soroti

Bungoma

KENYA

KORA
NATIONAL PARK

Jamaame

Kampala

Owen
Falls
Dam

Jinja

Eldoret

Nanyuki

Isiolo

Meru

Mount Kenya 5199 m

Kismaayo

Kisumu

Busia

Embu

LAG BADANA
NATIONAL PARK

Mbarara

Margherita

Lake
Edward

QUEEN ELIZABETH
NATIONAL PARK

Mikeno
Volcano
4437 m

RWANDA

Ruhengeri

Lake
Victoria

Bukoba

Nakuru

Kisii

Naivasha

NAIROBI

Machakos

Tana

Garissa

SOUTH KITUI NATIONAL RESERVE

Lamu

**INDIAN
OCEAN**

Bukavu

Lake
Kivu

Kigali

Mwanza

SERENGETI
NATIONAL PARK

SERENGETI
PLAIN

Kilimanjaro
5895 m

TSAVO NATIONAL PARK

Malindi

Bujumbura

BURUNDI

Gitega

Ngozi

Shinyanga

NGORONGORO
CONSERVATION
AREA

Lake
Eyasi

Arusha

TAITA
HILLS

Galan

• Nyanza
Lac

MOYOWOSI
GAME RESERVE

Dodoma

Moshi

MASAI
STEPPE

Kigoma

Tabora

Mpwapwa

Morogoro

Pangani

Tanga

Mombasa

Korogwe

Wete

Chake Chake

Mkoani

Pemba

TANZANIA

KIZIGO
GAME
RESERVE

Wami

DAR ES SALAAM

Zanzibar

Zanzibar

Kalemi

Lake
Tanganyika

RUNGWA
GAME RESERVE

RUAHA
NATIONAL PARK

MIKUMI
NATIONAL PARK

Sumbawanga

Iringa

Great Ruaha

Mafia Island

Mpulungu

Lake
Mweru

Nchelenge

Kawambwa

Mbala

Rungwe Mountain
2952 m

Karonga

Mount Mahosi
1881 m

NYIKA
NATIONAL
PARK

Rufiji

SELOUS
GAME RESERVE

Ifakara

Kasama

Paguli

Mtwara

ALDABRA
ISLANDS

AMIRANTE
ISLES

Lake
Bangweulu

Mansa

Chambeshi

Songea

Newala

Lindi

Cape Delgado

COSMOLEDO
GROUP

SEYCHELLES

Mahé
Victoria

Mwamfuli

Mpika

NORTHERN
LUANGWA
NATIONAL
PARK

Tunduru

Rovuma

NIASSA NATIONAL
PARK

ILES GLORIEUSES
(Fr.)

FARQUHAR
GROUP

• Kitwe

SOUTHERN LUANGWA
NATIONAL PARK

Lichinga

MOZAMBIQUE PLATEAU

Pemba

COMOROS

Moroni

Cape Bobaomby
Antsiranana

Tromelin
(Fr.)

Ndola

Luanshya

MALAWI

Chipata

LAKE
MALAWI
NATIONAL PARK

Dzaoudzi
Mayotte (Fr.)

Nosy-Be
Andoany

Ankarana

Ambanja

tharana

Kabwe

Petauke

Salima

Dedza

Lürio

Nacala

Maromokotro Peak 2876 m

Sambava

Antalaha

Lilongwe

Serra Namúli
2419 m

Moçambique

Antsohihy

Andapa

MASOALA
PENINSULA

Lusaka

SAPI
SAFARI PARK

Cabora Bassa
Reservoir

Cabora
Bassa
Dam

Zomba

Sapitwa Peak
3002 m

Nampula

Mahajanga

Befandriana Avaratra

Port
Bergé

Mampikony

Bay of Antongila

CHEWORE
SAFARI PARK

Tete

Nsanje

Marovoay

Blantyre

Chiromo

Zambezi Escarpment

Lake
Kariba

Harare

Mount
Inyangani
2592 m

GORONGOSA
NATIONAL PARK

Lipobane Point

Juan De Nova
Island

Fenoarivo Atsinanana

Chitungwiza

Kadoma

Mutare

Chinoio

Timbué Point

TSINGIN'I BEMARAHA
NATURE RESERVE

Ambatondrazaka

Toamasina

Kwekwe

Mount
Binga
2436 m

Beira

Rodrigues
(Mauritius)

Redcliff

ZIMBABWE

Shurugwi

Mashava

Antananarivo

Miarinarivo

Arivonimamo

MADAGASCAR

Vatomandry

Gweru

Masvingo

Great Zimbabwe
National
Monument

Sofala
Bay

Tsiafajavona Peak 2642 m

Antsirabe

Mahanoro

MAURITIUS
Port Louis

Bulawayo

Runde

MOZAMBIQUE
PLAIN

Morondava

Mahabo

Ambohimahasoa

St.-Denis
Réunion
(Fr.)

Msandane Hill
937 m

Beitbridge

Bazaruto Island

Fianarantsoa

Ambalavao

Mananjary

Messina

São Sebastião Point

Europa
Island

Boby Peak
2658 m

Manakara

KRUGER
NATIONAL
PARK

BANHINE
NATIONAL PARK

Bassas Da India
Reef

Mangoky

Ihosy

Manambondro

Tanganinony

• Seshego

Lebowakgomo

Massinga

Massinga

Betroka

Farafangana

Olifants

Morrumbene

Inhambane

Toliara

Onilahy

Vangaindrano

MAHAFALY PLATEAU

Chokwe

Correntes Point

Qissico

Nelspruit

Xai Xai

Vila da Manhiça

ANDROY
PLATEAU

Tôlanaro

Middelburg

Mbabane

Manzini

Maputo

Delagoa Bay

Ermelo

SWAZILAND

Namaacha

New-
castle

Lady-
smith

UMFOLOZI
GAME RESERVE

Ulundi

Empangeni

Mount
Ntlenyana
3482 m

DURBAN

Pietermaritzburg

Pinetown

Hammarsdale

Port Shepstone

Margate

Scale 1: 20,125,000

0   100   200   300 mi

0 50 150 250 350 450 km

Robinson

QATAR

Al-Muharraq Island

Al-Hadd

Al-Muharraq

Manbat Isa

Sitrah

Manama

Madinat Hamad

Awali

Ad-Diraz

Hill 134 m

HAWAR ISLANDS (Bahrain)

Ar-Rumaythah

SAUDI ARABIA

King Fahd Causeway

Umm an Na'san

Ar-Rifa ash-Sharqi

Ar-Rifa' al-Gharbi

BAHRAIN

Gulf of Bahrain

Scale 1: 1,689,000

20 mi

30 km

Lambert Conformal Conic

Points of interest

Bridges

Oases

Intermittent rivers

Intermittent lakes

Salt lakes

National Parks

Swamps

Flooded areas

Salt flats

Sand areas

Lava

N

ARABIAN SEA

Tropic of Cancer

Khalij-e Gavater

Cape al-Hadd

Gulf of Oman

Masandam Peninsula

OMAN

JIDDAT AL-HARASIS PLAIN

Sawqirah Bay

KHURIYA MURIYA ISLANDS

Socotra (Yemen)

Scale 1: 13,699,000

200 mi

300 km

Lambert Conformal Conic

RIYADH Cities over 1,000,000
Dubayy Cities 500,000 to 1,000,000
San'a' Cities 100,000 to 500,000
Muscat Cities 50,000 to 100,000
Layla Cities under 50,000

* Capital symbols
▪ City symbols

I R A N

ZAGROS MTS

Zard Kūh 4222 m

Shiraz

Ahvaz

Dezful

Basra

IRAQ

MESOPOTAMIA

KUWAIT

Kuwait

Hawalli

Persian Gulf

Bandar-e 'Abbas

Strait of Hormuz

UNITED ARAB EMIRATES

Abu Dhabi

Ash-Shariqah

Dubayy

Al-'Ayn

QATAR

Doha

BAHRAIN

Ad-Dammam

Al-Hufuf

AL-HASA

AS-SUMMAN PLATEAU

AD-DAHNA' DESERT

AL-'ARAMAH PLATEAU

AL-JAFURAH DESERT

ARABIAN PENINSULA

RUB' AL-KHALI DESERT

RAMLAT AS-SAB'ATAYN DESERT

HADHRAMAUT

Ash-Shihr

Al-Mukalla

Gulf of Aden

SYRIAN DESERT

JORDAN

AMMAN

Az-Zarqa'

WEST BANK

ISRAEL

Jerusalem

GAZA STRIP

SINAI PEN

AL-'AJMAH MTS

EGYPT

Gulf of Aqaba

Gulf of Suez

AN-NAFUD DESERT

Medina

Mecca

At-Ta'if

JIDDAH

RED SEA

RED SEA HILLS

SUDAN

Port Sudan

NUBIAN DESERT

ERITREA

Kassala

Keren

DANAKIL

DAHLAK ARCHIPELAGO

FARASAN ISLANDS

Al-Hudaydah

TIHAMAH PLAIN

YEMEN

Sanaa

Ta'izz

Aden

Bab al-Mandeb Strait

DJIBOUTI

NAJD

SAUDI ARABIA

RIYADH

TUWAYQ MOUNTAINS

NAJRAN

Layla

Al-Kharj Oasis

Buraydah

Hail

HIJAZ MOUNTAINS

ASIR

AL-QARA MTS

MAHRAT MOUNTAINS

© 1999, Encyclopædia Britannica, Inc.

BRISBANE Cities over 1,000,000
Canberra Cities 500,000 to 1,000,000
Port Moresby Cities 100,000 to 500,000
Suva Cities 50,000 to 100,000
Majuro Cities under 50,000

⊛ Capital symbols
■ • City symbols

Scale 1: 50,660,000

750 mi
250   500   750   1000 km
Miller

NORTH PACIFIC OCEAN

SOUTH PACIFIC OCEAN

Philippine Sea

PITCAIRN (U.K.)
Pitcairn I.

MARQUESAS IS.

TUAMOTU ARCHIPELAGO

FRENCH POLYNESIA (FR.)

Papeete
Tahiti

SOCIETY IS.

Îles Maria

AUSTRAL ISLANDS

Rapa

Rarotonga
Mangaia

COOK ISLANDS (N.Z.)

LINE IS.

Kiritimati (Christmas I.)

Teraina
Tabuaeran

KIRIBATI

TOKELAU (N.Z.)

AMERICAN SAMOA (U.S.)
Pago Pago

NIUE (N.Z.)

SAMOA
Apia

PHOENIX ISLANDS

Kanton Atoll

TONGA
Nukuʻalofa ⊛

WALLIS AND FUTUNA (FR.)

Rotuma

FIJI
Suva
Vanua Levu
Viti Levu
Lautoka

KERMADEC IS. (N.Z.)

HAWAIIAN ISLANDS (U.S.)

Hawaii
Oahu
Maui
Kauai
Honolulu

Johnston Atoll (U.S.)

Midway Is.

Wake I. (U.S.)

MARSHALL ISLANDS
Majuro ⊛

Kwajalein

Enewetak

GILBERT IS.

Tarawa (Bairiki) ⊛

Banaba

Kosrae I.

TUVALU
Funafuti ⊛

NAURU ⊛

SOLOMON ISLANDS
Honiara

SANTA CRUZ IS.

Luganville

VANUATU
Port Vila
Éfaté
Espiritu Santo I.

Dumbéa
Nouméa

NEW CALEDONIA (FR.)

Norfolk I. (N.Z.)

Lord Howe I. (N.Z.)

NORTHERN MARIANA ISLANDS (U.S.)
Saipan
Rota
Tinian
Guam (U.S.)

FEDERATED STATES OF MICRONESIA

CAROLINE ISLANDS

Yap

PALAU
Babelthuap
Koror

TRUK IS.
Pohnpei
SENYAVIN IS.
Palikir

NEW ZEALAND
Wellington ⊛
Auckland
Manukau
North I.
Whangarei
Hamilton
Tauranga
Gisborne
Napier
Hastings
Wanganui
Palmerston North
Nelson
Te Kao
Kaikohe
East Coast Bays
New Plymouth
South I. (N.Z.)

Tasman Sea

PAPUA NEW GUINEA
Port Moresby ⊛
Lae
Madang
Goroka
Mt. Hagen
Wewak
Rabaul
New Ireland
New Britain
Bougainville
Popondetta
Hula
Daru

New Guinea
Wabag
Kundiawa
Maprik
Telefomin
Bulolo
Mendi

INDONESIA
Jayapura
Manokwari
Mamberamo
Biak
Arafura Sea

Solomon Sea

Coral Sea

Gulf of Carpentaria

CAPE YORK PENINSULA

GREAT DIVIDING RANGE

GREAT ARTESIAN BASIN

CARNARVON RANGE

GREY RANGE

FLINDERS RANGES

AUSTRALIA

BRISBANE
Gold Coast
SYDNEY
Canberra ⊛
MELBOURNE
ADELAIDE

Cairns
Townsville
Mackay
Rockhampton
Gladstone
Bundaberg
Maryborough
Gympie
Lismore
Coffs Harbour
Port Macquarie
Newcastle
Gosford
Wollongong
Queanbeyan
Toowoomba
Warwick
Tamworth
Armidale
Grafton
Moree
Dubbo
Orange
Bathurst
Mudgee
Cobar
Bourke
Broken Hill
Wagga Wagga
Albury
Wodonga
Shepparton
Bendigo
Ballarat
Geelong
Warrnambool
Mount Gambier
Millicent
Naracoorte

Cloncurry
Mount Isa
Winton
Longreach
Quilpie
Charleville
Tennant Creek
Daly Waters
Alice Springs
Coober Pedy
Ceduna
Port Augusta
Whyalla
Kangaroo Island

Darling
Murray
Murrumbidgee

Tropic of Capricorn

Equator

Bass Strait
King I.
Flinders Island
Devonport
Burnie
Smithton
Queenstown

Eden

Portland

Name	Lat./Long.

AFGHANISTAN ....pg. 139

Capital: ....Kabul
Area: ....652,225 sq km; 251,825 sq mi
Highest Elev.: ...Mt. Nowshak 7,490 m; 24,580 ft
Longest River: ...Amu 2,540 km; 1,580 mi
Avg. Temperature: .Jan = -3°C; Jul = 25°C
Currency: ....Afghani
Official Language: .Pashto, Dari (Persian)

Name	Lat./Long.
Adraskan	33°39' N, 062°16' E
Ajrestan	33°31' N, 067°11' E
Almar	35°50' N, 064°32' E
Anar Darreh	32°46' N, 061°39' E
Andkhvoy	36°56' N, 065°08' E
Aqchah	36°56' N, 066°11' E
Asadabad	34°52' N, 071°09' E
Baghlan	36°13' N, 068°46' E
Baghran	33°04' N, 065°05' E
Balkh (Bactra)	36°46' N, 066°54' E
Bala Boluk	32°38' N, 062°28' E
Bamian (Bamyan)	34°50' N, 067°50' E
Banow	35°38' N, 069°15' E
Baraki	33°58' N, 068°58' E
Bazar-e Panjva'i	31°32' N, 065°28' E
Chahar Borjak	30°17' N, 062°03' E
Chaghcharan	34°31' N, 065°15' E
Chakhansur	31°10' N, 062°04' E
Deh Rawod	32°37' N, 065°27' E
Deh Shu	30°26' N, 063°19' E
Delaram	32°11' N, 063°25' E
Do Qal'eh	32°08' N, 061°27' E
Dowlatabad	36°26' N, 064°55' E
Duraj	37°56' N, 070°43' E
Eshkashem	36°42' N, 071°34' E
Eslam Qal'eh	34°40' N, 061°04' E
Farah (Farrah, Ferah)	32°22' N, 062°07' E
Feyzabad (Faizabad)	37°06' N, 070°34' E
Gardeyz (Gardez)	33°37' N, 069°07' E
Gereshk	31°48' N, 064°34' E
Ghazni	33°33' N, 068°26' E
Ghowrmach	35°44' N, 063°47' E
Ghurian	34°21' N, 061°30' E
Gizab	33°23' N, 066°16' E
Golestan	32°37' N, 063°39' E
Golran	35°06' N, 061°41' E
Gowmal Kalay	32°31' N, 068°51' E
Herat (Harat)	34°20' N, 062°12' E
Jalalabad	34°26' N, 070°28' E
Jaldak	31°58' N, 066°43' E
Jawand	35°04' N, 064°09' E
Kabul	34°31' N, 069°12' E
Kajaki	32°16' N, 065°03' E
Keshendeh (Aq Kopruk)	36°05' N, 066°51' E
Khadir	33°55' N, 065°56' E
Khanabad	36°41' N, 069°07' E
Kholm	36°42' N, 067°41' E
Khowst	33°22' N, 069°57' E
Konduz (Qonduz)	36°45' N, 068°51' E
Koshk	34°57' N, 062°15' E
Kowt-e 'Ashrow (Maidanshar)	34°27' N, 068°48' E
Kuhestanat	35°49' N, 065°52' E
Khwazagak	34°53' N, 065°18' E
Lash-e Joveyn	31°43' N, 061°37' E
Lashkar Gah (Bust)	31°35' N, 064°21' E
Mahmud-e Raqi	35°01' N, 069°20' E
Mazar-e Sharif	36°42' N, 067°06' E
Meymaneh (Maimana)	35°55' N, 064°47' E
Mundul	35°17' N, 070°10' E
Navor	33°53' N, 067°57' E
Owbeh	34°22' N, 063°10' E
Palalak	30°14' N, 062°54' E
Panjab	34°22' N, 067°01' E
Pasaband	33°41' N, 064°51' E
Qades	34°48' N, 063°26' E
Qal'eh-ye Now	34°59' N, 063°08' E
Qalat	32°07' N, 066°54' E
Qandahar (Kandahar)	31°35' N, 065°45' E
Samangan (Aybak)	36°16' N, 068°01' E
Sar-e Pol	36°14' N, 065°55' E
Sayghan	35°11' N, 067°42' E
Shah Juy	32°31' N, 067°25' E
Shahr-e Safa	31°50' N, 066°22' E
Shahrak	34°06' N, 064°18' E
Shahrestan	33°41'N, 066°33' E
Sheberghan (Shebirghan, Shibarghan)	36°41' N, 065°45' E
Shindand (Sabzevar)	33°18' N, 062°08' E
Shir Khan	37°11' N, 068°36' E
Tarin Kowt	32°38' N, 065°52' E
Teywarah	33°21' N, 064°25' E
Tokzar	35°52' N, 066°26' E
Tulak	33°58' N, 063°44' E
Warsaj	36°12' N, 070°02' E
Yangi Qal'eh	37°28' N, 069°36' E
Zareh Sharan	33°08' N, 068°47' E
Zarghun Shahr	32°51' N, 068°25' E

ALBANIA ....pg. 134

Capital: ....Tiranë
Area: ....28,748 sq km; 11,100 sq mi
Highest Elev.: .....Mt. Korab 2,750 m; 9,030 ft
Longest River: .....Drin 280 km; 170 mi
Avg. Temperature: .Jan = 7°C; Jul = 25°C
Currency: ....lek
Official Language: .Albanian

Name	Lat./Long.
Berat	40°42' N, 019°57' E
Cerrik	41°02' N, 019°59' E
Çorovodë	40°30' N, 020°13' E
Durres	41°19' N, 019°27' E
Elbasan	41°06' N, 020°05' E
Fier	40°43' N, 019°34' E
Himare	40°07' N, 019°44' E
Kavajë	41°11' N, 019°33' E
Korce (Koritsa)	40°37' N, 020°46' E
Laç	41°38' N, 019°43' E
Patos	40°38' N, 019°39' E
Pogradec	40°54' N, 020°00' E
Puke	42°03' N, 019°54' E
Sarandë	39°52' N, 020°00' E
Shkoder (Scutari)	42°05' N, 019°30' E
Tiranë (Tirana)	41°20' N, 019°50' E

Name	Lat./Long.
Vlore	40°27' N, 019°30' E
Vorë	41°23' N, 019°40' E

ALGERIA ....pg. 150

Capital: ....Algiers
Area: ....2,381,741 sq km; 919,595 sq mi
Highest Elev.: .....Mt. Tahat 2,920 m; 9,570 ft
Longest River: .....Chelif 730 km; 450 mi
Avg. Temperature: .Jan = 12°C; Jul = 24°C
Currency: ....Algerian dinar
Official Language: .Arabic

Name	Lat./Long.
Aïn Beïda (Daoud)	35°48' N, 007°24' E
Algiers (or Al-Jaza'ir)	36°47' N, 003°03' E
Annaba (Bone)	36°54' N, 007°46' E
Batna	35°34' N, 006°11' E
Béchar (Colomb-Bechar)	31°37' N, 002°13' W
Bejaïa (Bougie)	36°45' N, 005°05' E
Biskra (Beskra)	34°51' N, 005°44' E
Bordj Bou Arréridj	36°04' N, 004°47' E
Chlef (El-Asnam or Orleansville)	36°10' N, 001°20' E
Constantine (Qacentina)	36°22' N, 006°37' E
Ghardaïa	32°29' N, 003°40' E
Mostaganem (Mestghanem)	35°56' N, 000°05' E
Orleansville, see Chlef	
Oran (Wahran)	35°42' N, 000°38' W
Ouargla (Warqla)	31°57' N, 005°20' E
Qacentina, see Constantine	
Saïda	34°50' N, 000°09' E
Sétif (Stif)	36°12' N, 005°24' E
Sidi Bel Abbes	35°12' N, 000°38' W
Skikda (Philippeville)	36°52' N, 006°54' E
Souk-Ahras	36°17' N, 007°57' E
Stif, see Sétif	
Tébessa (Tbessa or Theveste)	35°24' N, 008°07' E
Tiaret (Tihert or Tagdempt)	35°22' N, 001°19' E
Tlemcen (Tlemsen)	34°52' N, 001°19' W
Wahran, see Oran	
Wargla, see Ouargla	

ANDORRA ....pg. 128

Capital: ....Andorra la Vella
Area: ....468 sq km; 181 sq mi
Highest Elev.: .....Coma Pedrosa 2,950 m; 9,680 ft
Longest River: .....Valira d'Orient 20 km; 10 mi
Avg. Temperature: .Jan = 2.3°C; Jul = 19.3°C
Currency: ....French franc, Spanish Peseta
Official Language: .Catalan

Name	Lat./Long.
Andorra la Vella	42°30' N, 001°30' E

ANGOLA ....pg. 152

Capital: ....Luanda
Area: ....1,246,700 sq km; 481,354 sq mi
Highest Elev.: .....Mt. Moca 2,620 m; 8,600 ft
Longest River: .....Kwanza 960 km; 600 mi
Avg. Temperature: .Jan = 26°C; Jul = 20°C
Currency: ....new kwanza
Official Language: .Portuguese

Name	Lat./Long.
Benguela (São Félipe de Benguela)	12°35' S, 013°24' E
Cabinda	05°33' S, 012°12' E
Caála (Robert Williams)	12°51' S, 015°34' E
Camacupa (General Machado)	12°01' S, 017°29' E
Catumbela	12°26' S, 013°33' E
Cubal	13°02' S, 014°15' E
Dalatando, see N'dalatando	
Gabela	10°51' S, 014°22' E
Ganda (Mariano Machado)	13°01' S, 014°38' E
General Machado, see Camacupa	
Henrique de Carvalho, see Saurimo	
Huambo (Nova Lisboa)	12°46' S, 015°44' E
Kuito (Silva Porto)	12°23' S, 016°56' E
Lobito	12°21' S, 013°33' E
Luanda (São Paulo de Luanda)	08°49' S, 013°15' E
Lubango (Sá da Bandeira)	14°55' S, 013°30' E
Luena (Vila Luso)	11°47' S, 019°55' E
Mariano Machado, see Ganda	
Mavinga	15°48' S, 020°21' E
M'banza Congo (São Salvador)	06°16' S, 014°15' E
Menongue (Serpa Pinto)	14°40' S, 017°42' E
Moçâmedes, see Namibe	
Mossamedes, see Namibe	
Namibe (Moçâmedes, or Mossamedes)	15°10' S, 012°09' E
N'dalatando (Dalatando, or Salazar)	09°18' S, 014°55' E
Negage	07°46' S, 015°16' E
Nova Lisboa, see Huambo	
Novo Redondo, see Sumbe	
Porto Alexandre, see Tombua	
Porto Amboim	10°44' S, 013°45' E
Robert Williams, see Caála	
Sá da Bandeira, see Lubango	
Salazar, see N'dalatando	
Santa Comba, see Waku Kungo	
São Félipe de Benguela, see Benguela	
São Paulo de Luanda, see Luanda	
São Salvador, see M'banza Congo	
Saurimo (Henrique de Carvalho)	09°39' S, 020°24' E
Serpa Pinto, see Menongue	
Silva Porto, see Kuito	
Soyo	06°08' S, 012°22' E
Sumbe (Novo Redondo)	11°12' S, 013°50' E
Tombua (Porto Alexandre)	15°48' S, 011°51' E
Uíge (Carmona)	07°37' S, 015°03' E
Vila Luso, see Luena	
Waku Kungo (Santa Comba)	11°21' S, 015°07' E

ANTIGUA & BARBUDA pg. 116

Capital: ....Saint John's
Area: ....441.6 sq km; 170.5 sq mi
Highest Elev.: .....Boggy Pk. 410 m; 1,330 ft
Avg. Temperature: .Jan = 25.5°C; Jul = 25.5°C
Currency: ....East Caribbean dollar
Official Language: .English

Name	Lat./Long.
Codrington	17°38' N, 061°50' W
St. John's	17°06' N, 061°51' W

ARGENTINA ....pg. 122

Capital: ....Buenos Aires
Area: ....2,780,400 sq km; 1,073,518 sq mi
Highest Elev.: .....Mt. Aconcagua 6,960 m; 22,830 ft
Longest River: .....Parana 4,880 km; 3,030 mi
Avg. Temperature: .Jan = 24°C; Jul = 10°C
Currency: ....peso
Official Language: .Spanish

Name	Lat./Long.
Aguilares	27°26' N, 065°37' E
Avellaneda	29°07' S, 059°40' W
Ayacucho	37°09' S, 058°29' W
Azul	36°47' S, 059°51' W
Bahía Blanca	38°43' S, 062°17' W
Balcarce	37°50' S, 058°15' W
Baradero	33°48' S, 059°30' W
Belén	27°39' S, 067°02' W
Bell Ville	32°37' S, 062°42' W
Bolívar	36°15' S, 061°06' W
Bragado	35°08' S, 060°30' W
Buenos Aires	34°36' S, 058°27' W
Caleta Olivia	46°26' S, 067°32' W
Campo del Cielo	27°35' S, 062°00' W
Campo Durán	22°14' S, 063°42' W
Carmen de Patagones	40°48' S, 062°59' W
Casilda	33°03' S, 061°10' W
Castelli	35°37' S, 060°37' W
Catamarca	28°28' S, 065°47' W
Caucete	31°39' S, 068°17' W
Chacabuco	34°38' S, 060°29' W
Chascomus	35°34' S, 058°01' W
Chilecito	29°10' S, 067°30' W
Cipolletti	38°56' S, 067°59' W
Clorinda	25°17' S, 057°43' W
Comodoro Rivadavia	45°52' S, 067°30' W
Concepción	27°20' S, 065°35' W
Concordia	31°24' S, 058°02' W
Cordoba	31°24' S, 064°11' W
Coronel Dorrego	38°42' S, 061°17' W
Coronel Pringles	37°58' S, 061°22' W
Corrientes	27°28' S, 058°50' W
Cruz Del Eje	30°44' S, 064°48' W
Curuzú Cuatiá	29°47' S, 058°03' W
Daireaux	36°36' S, 061°45' W
Dean Funes	30°26' S, 064°21' W
Dolores	36°20' S, 057°40' W
Eduardo Castex	35°54' S, 064°18' W
El Colorado	26°18' S, 059°22' W
Esquel	42°54' S, 071°19' W
Formosa	26°11' S, 058°11' W
Frías	28°38' S, 065°09' W
General Alvear	34°58' S, 067°42' W
General José de San Martín	26°33' S, 059°21' W
General Juan Madariaga	37°00' S, 057°09' W
General Martín Miguel de Güemes	24°40' S, 065°03' W
General Roca	39°02' S, 067°35' W
General Villegas	35°02' S, 063°01' W
Gualeguay	33°09' S, 059°20' W
Gualeguaychu	33°01' S, 058°31' W
Ibarreta	25°13' S, 059°51' W
Juárez	37°40' S, 059°48' W
Junín	34°35' S, 060°57' W
La Cocha	27°47' S, 065°34' W
La Paz	30°45' S, 059°39' W
La Plata	34°55' S, 057°57' W
La Rioja	29°26' S, 066°51' W
Las Flores	36°01' S, 059°07' W
Libertador General San Martín	23°48' S, 064°48' W
Lobos	35°11' S, 059°06' W
Mar del Plata	38°00' S, 057°33' W
Marcos Juárez	32°42' S, 062°06' W
Mendoza	32°53' S, 068°49' W
Mercedes	33°40' S, 065°28' W
Metán	25°29' S, 064°57' W
Miramar	38°16' S, 057°51' W
Monteros	27°10' S, 065°30' W
Necochea	38°33' S, 058°45' W
Neuquén	38°57' S, 068°04' W
Nogoyá	32°24' S, 059°49' W
Olavarria	36°54' S, 060°17' W
Paraná	31°44' S, 060°32' W
Paso de los Libres	29°43' S, 057°05' W
Pehuajó	35°48' S, 061°53' W
Pergamino	33°53' S, 060°35' W
Pigüe	37°37' S, 062°25' W
Pirané	25°43' S, 059°06' W
Posadas	27°23' S, 055°53' W
Presidencia Roque Saenz Pena	26°47' S, 060°27' W
Puerto Madryn	42°46' S, 065°03' W
Rafaela	31°16' S, 061°29' W
Rauch	36°46' S, 059°06' W
Rawson	43°18' S, 065°06' W
Reconquista	29°09' S, 059°39' W
Resistencia	27°27' S, 058°59' W
Río Cuarto	33°08' S, 064°21' W
Río Gallegos	51°38' S, 069°13' W
Río Grande	53°47' S, 067°42' W
Río Tercero	32°11' S, 064°06' W
Río Turbio	51°32' S, 072°18' W
Rosario	32°57' S, 060°40' W
Salta	24°47' S, 065°25' W
San Carlos de Bariloche	41°09' S, 071°18' W
San Francisco	31°26' S, 062°05' W
San Juan	31°32' S, 068°31' W
San Luis	33°18' S, 066°21' W
San Martín	33°04' S, 068°28' W
San Miguel de Tucumán	26°49' S, 065°13' W
San Nicolás de los Arroyos	33°20' S, 060°13' W
San Pedro de Jujuy	24°14' S, 064°52' W
San Rafael	34°36' S, 068°20' W
San Ramón de la Nueva Orán	23°08' S, 064°20' W
San Salvador de Jujuy	24°11' S, 065°18' W
Santa Rosa	36°37' S, 064°17' W
Santiago del Estero	27°47' S, 064°16' W
Santo Tomé	28°33' S, 056°03' W
Tafí Viejo	26°44' S, 065°16' W
Tandil	37°19' S, 059°09' W
Tartagal	22°32' S, 063°49' W
Tigre	34°25' S, 058°34' W
Tinogasta	28°04' S, 067°34' W
Trelew	43°15' S, 065°18' W
Trenque Lauquen	35°58' S, 062°42' W
Tres Arroyos	38°23' S, 060°17' W
Ushuaia	54°48' S, 068°18' W

Name	Lat./Long.
Venado Tuerto	33°45' S, 061°58' W
Viedma	40°48' S, 063°00' W
Villa Angela	27°35' S, 060°43' W
Villa Carlos Paz	31°24' S, 064°30' W
Villa Dolores	31°56' S, 065°12' W
Villa María	32°25' S, 063°15' W
Zapala	38°54' S, 070°04' W
Zárate	34°06' S, 059°02' W

ARMENIA ....pg. 147

Capital: ....Yerevan
Area: ....29,800 sq km; 11,500 sq mi
Highest Elev.: .....Mt. Aragats 4,090 m; 13,420 ft
Longest River: .....Aras 1,070 km; 670 mi
Avg. Temperature: .Jan = -5°C; Jul = 25°C
Currency: ....dram
Official Language: .Armenian

Name	Lat./Long.
Ejmiadzin (Echmiadzin)	40°10' N, 044°18' E
Gyumri (Kumayri, Alexandropol, or Leninakan)	40°48' N, 043°50' E
Hoktemberyan (Oktemberyan)	40°09' N, 044°02' E
Hrazdan (Razdan)	40°29' N, 044°46' E
Sevan	40°32' N, 044°56' E
Vanadzor	40°48' N, 044°30' E

AUSTRALIA ....pg. 155

Capital: ....Canberra
Area: ....7,682,300 sq km; 2,966,200 sq mi
Highest Elev.: .....Mt. Kosciusko 2,330 m; 7,310 ft
Longest River: .....Murray 2,590 km; 1,610 mi
Avg. Temperature: .Jan = 22°C; Jul = 12°C
Currency: ....Australian dollar
Official Language: .English

Name	Lat./Long.
Adelaide	34°56' S, 138°36' E
Albany	35°02' S, 117°53' E
Albury-Wodonga	36°05' S, 146°55' E
Alice Springs	23°42' S, 133°53' E
Armidale	30°31' S, 151°39' E
Ayr	19°35' S, 147°24' E
Ballarat	37°33' S, 143°51' E
Balranald	34°38' S, 143°34' E
Bathurst	33°25' S, 149°34' E
Bendigo	36°46' S, 144°16' E
Bourke	30°06' S, 145°56' E
Bowen	20°01' S, 148°14' E
Bowral	34°28' S, 150°25' E
Brisbane	27°30' S, 153°01' E
Broken Hill	31°57' S, 141°26' E
Broome	17°58' S, 122°14' E
Bunbury	33°20' S, 115°38' E
Bundaberg	24°51' S, 152°21' E
Burnie	41°04' S, 145°55' E
Busselton	33°39' S, 115°20' E
Caboolture	27°05' S, 152°57' E
Cairns	16°55' S, 145°46' E
Canberra	35°20' S, 149°10' E
Carnarvon	24°52' S, 113°38' E
Casino	28°52' S, 153°03' E
Ceduna	32°07' S, 133°40' E
Charleville	26°24' S, 146°15' E
Cloncurry	20°42' S, 140°30' E
Cobar	31°30' S, 145°49' E
Coffs Harbour	30°18' S, 153°08' E
Colac	38°20' S, 143°35' E
Coober Pedy	29°01' S, 134°43' E
Cooma	36°14' S, 149°08' E
Coonabarabran	31°16' S, 149°17' E
Copley, see Leigh Creek	
Darwin	12°28' S, 130°50' E
Denham	25°55' S, 113°32' E
Derby	17°18' S, 123°38' E
Devonport	41°10' S, 146°21' E
Dubbo	32°15' S, 148°37' E
Eden	37°04' S, 149°54' E
Esperance	33°51' S, 121°53' E
Gawler	34°36' S, 138°44' E
Geelong	38°09' S, 144°21' E
Geraldton	28°46' S, 114°36' E
Gladstone	23°51' S, 151°15' E
Glen Innes	29°44' S, 151°44' E
Gold Coast	28°06' S, 153°27' E
Goondiwindi	28°33' S, 150°19' E
Gosford	33°26' S, 151°21' E
Goulburn	34°45' S, 149°43' E
Grafton	29°41' S, 152°56' E
Gympie	26°11' S, 152°40' E
Hay	34°30' S, 144°51' E
Hobart	42°53' S, 147°20' E
Ingham	18°39' S, 146°10' E
Innisfail	17°32' S, 146°02' E
Kalgoorlie-Boulder	30°45' S, 121°28' E
Kambalda	31°12' S, 121°40' E
Karratha	20°53' S, 116°40' E
Katanning	33°42' S, 117°33' E
Katherine	14°28' S, 132°16' E
Kempsey	31°05' S, 152°50' E
Kiama	34°41' S, 150°52' E
Launceston	41°25' S, 147°08' E
Leigh Creek (Copley)	30°32' S, 138°26' E
Lismore	28°48' S, 153°16' E
Mackay	21°09' S, 149°12' E
Maitland	32°44' S, 151°33' E
Mandurah	32°33' S, 115°42' E
Manjimup	34°14' S, 116°09' E
Maroochydore	26°39' S, 153°06' E
Maryborough	25°32' S, 152°42' E
Meekatharra	26°36' S, 118°29' E
Melbourne	37°50' S, 145°00' E
Melton	37°41' S, 144°35' E
Merredin	31°29' S, 118°16' E
Mildura	34°12' S, 142°09' E
Millicent	37°36' S, 140°21' E
Moe	38°10' S, 146°16' E
Moree	29°28' S, 149°51' E
Mount Gambier	37°50' S, 140°46' E
Mount Isa	20°44' S, 139°30' E
Mudgee	32°36' S, 149°35' E
Naracoorte	36°58' S, 140°44' E
Narrabri	30°19' S, 149°47' E
Narrogin	32°56' S, 117°10' E
New Norfolk	42°47' S, 147°04' E
Newcastle	32°55' S, 151°45' E

Name	Lat./Long.
Northam	31°40' S, 116°40' E
Orange	33°17' S, 149°06' E
Parkes	33°08' S, 148°11' E
Perth	31°56' S, 115°50' E
Port Augusta	32°30' S, 137°46' E
Port Hedland	20°19' S, 118°34' E
Port Macquarie	31°26' S, 152°55' E
Port Pirie	33°11' S, 138°01' E
Queanbeyan	35°21' S, 149°14' E
Queenscliff (Shortland Bluff,	
Whale Head)	38°16' S, 144°39' E
Queenstown	42°05' S, 145°33' E
Renmark	34°10' S, 140°45' E
Rockhampton	23°23' S, 150°30' E
Rockingham	32°17' S, 115°43' E
Roma	26°35' S, 148°47' E
Sale	38°06' S, 147°04' E
Shepparton	36°23' S, 145°24' E
Shortland Bluff, see Queenscliff	
Smithton	40°50' S, 145°07' E
Stanthorpe	28°40' S, 151°57' E
Swan Hill	35°21' S, 143°34' E
Sydney	33°53' S, 151°12' E
Tamworth	31°05' S, 150°56' E
Taree	31°54' S, 152°28' E
Tennant Creek	19°39' S, 134°12' E
Tenterfield	29°03' S, 152°01' E
Toowoomba	27°33' S, 151°58' E
Townsville	19°15' S, 146°48' E
Tumut	35°18' S, 148°13' E
Victor Harbour	35°34' S, 138°37' E
Wagga Wagga	35°07' S, 147°22' E
Warrnambool	38°23' S, 142°29' E
Warwick	28°14' S, 152°01' E
Wauchope	31°27' S, 152°44' E
West Wyalong	33°55' S, 147°13' E
Whale Head, see Queenscliff	
Whyalla	33°02' S, 137°35' E
Wilcannia	31°34' S, 143°23' E
Winton	22°24' S, 143°02' E
Wollongong	34°25' S, 150°54' E
Wonthaggi	38°37' S, 145°42' E
Wyndham	15°28' S, 128°06' E
Wynyard	41°00' S, 145°43' E
Young	34°19' S, 148°18' E

AUSTRIA ....pg. 133
Capital: ....Vienna
Area: ....83,859 sq km; 32,378 sq mi
Highest Elev.: ...Grossglockner 3,800 m; 12,460 ft
Longest River: ....Danube 2,850 km; 1770 mi
Avg. Temperature: .Jan = -2°C; Jul = 20°C
Currency: ....Austrian schilling
Official Language: .German

Bruck	47°25' N, 015°17' E
Graz	47°04' N, 015°27' E
Innsbruck	47°16' N, 011°24' E
Klagenfurt	46°38' N, 014°18' E
Leoben (Donawitz)	47°23' N, 015°06' E
Linz	48°18' N, 014°18' E
Neunkirchen	47°43' N, 016°05' E
Trofaiach	47°25' N, 015°00' E
Salzburg	47°48' N, 013°02' E
Sankt Pölten	48°12' N, 015°38' E
Steyr	48°03' N, 014°25' E
Villach	46°36' N, 013°50' E
Vienna (Bécs, Viden, Wien))	48°12' N, 016°22' E
Wien, see Vienna	

AZERBAIJAN ....pg. 147
Capital: ....Baku
Area: ......86,600 sq km; 33,400 sq mi
Highest Elev.: ...Mt. Bazardyuzyu 4,470m;
14,650 ft
Longest River: ...Kura 1,360 km; 850 mi
Avg. Temperature: ..Jan = -4°C; Jul = 26°C
Currency: ....manat
Official Language: .Azerbaijani

Äli-Bayramli	39°55' N, 048°56' E
Baku (Baky)	40°23' N, 049°51' E
Gäncä (Gyandzha, Gandzha,	
Kirovabad,or Yelizavetpol)	40°41' N, 046°22' E
Mingäçevir (Mingechaur)	40°45' N, 047°03' E
Naxcivan (Nakhichevan)	39°12' N, 045°24' E
Säki (Sheki, Nukha)	41°12' N, 047°12' E
Xankändi (Stepanakert)	39°50' N, 046°46' E
Sumqait (Sumgait)	40°36' N, 049°38' E
Yelizavetpol, see Gäncä	

BAHAMAS, THE ....pg. 116
Capital: ....Nassau
Area: ......13,939 sq km; 5,382 sq mi
Highest Elev.: ...Mt. Alvernia 60 m; 210 ft
Avg. Temperature: ..Jan = 22.1°C; Jul = 20.9°C
Currency: ....Bahamian dollar
Official Language: .English

Dunmore Town	25°30' N, 076°39' W
Freeport	26°32' N, 078°42' W
Matthew Town	20°57' N, 073°40' W
Nassau	25°05' N, 077°21' W
West End	26°41' N, 078°58' W

BAHRAIN ....pg. 154
Capital: ....Manama
Area: ......694.2 sq km; 268.0 sq mi
Highest Elev.: ...ad-Dukhan Hill 130 m; 440 ft
Avg. Temperature: ..Jan = 17.4°C; Jul = 33.8°C
Currency: ....Bahrain dinar
Official Language: .Arabic

Manama	26°13' N, 050°35' E
Muharraq, al-	26°16' N, 050°37' E
Rifa'a ash-Sharqi, ar-	26°07' N, 050°34' E
Rumaythah, ar-	25°55' N, 050°33' E

BANGLADESH ....pg. 146
Capital: ....Dhaka
Area: ......148,393 sq km; 57,295 sq mi
Highest Elev.: ...Keokradong 930 m; 3,040 ft
Longest River: ...Brahmaputra 2,900 km; 1,800 mi
Avg. Temperature: .Jan = 19°C; Jul = 29°C
Currency: ....Bangladesh taka
Official Language: .Bengali

Azmiriganj	24°33' N, 091°14' E
Bagerhat (Bagherhat)	22°40' N, 089°48' E
Bajitpur	24°13' N, 090°57' E
Barisal	22°42' N, 090°22' E
Bhairab Bazar	24°04' N, 090°58' E
Bogra	24°51' N, 089°22' E
Brahmanbaria	23°59' N, 091°07' E
Chandpur	23°13' N, 090°39' E
Chittagong	22°20' N, 091°50' E
Chuadanga	23°38' N, 088°51' E
Comilla (Kumilla)	23°27' N, 091°12' E
Dhaka (Dacca or Dhakal)	23°43' N, 090°25' E
Dinajpur	25°38' N, 088°38' E
Faridpur	23°36' N, 089°50' E
Gopalpur	24°50' N, 090°06' E
Jamalpur	24°55' N, 089°56' E
Jessore	23°10' N, 089°13' E
Jhenida	23°33' N, 089°10' E
Khulna	22°48' N, 089°33' E
Kishorganj	24°26' N, 090°46' E
Kurigram	25°49' N, 089°39' E
Kushtia	23°55' N, 089°07' E
Laksham	23°14' N, 091°08' E
Lakshmipur	22°57' N, 090°50' E
Lalmanir Hat (Lalmonirhat)	25°54' N, 089°27' E
Madaripur	23°10' N, 090°12' E
Mymensingh (Nasirabad)	24°45' N, 090°24' E
Naogaon	24°47' N, 088°56' E
Narayanganj	23°37' N, 090°30' E
Narsinghdi (Narsingdi)	23°55' N, 090°43' E
Noakhali (Sudharam)	22°49' N, 091°06' E
Pabna (Pubna)	24°00' N, 089°15' E
Patuakhali	22°21' N, 090°21' E
Rajshahi	24°22' N, 088°36' E
Rangpur	25°45' N, 089°15' E
Saidpur	25°47' N, 088°54' E
Satkhira	22°43' N, 089°06' E
Sherpur	24°41' N, 089°25' E
Sherpur	25°01' N, 090°01' E
Siraganj (Seraganj)	24°27' N, 089°43' E
Sylhet	24°54' N, 091°52' E
Tangail	24°15' N, 089°55' E

BARBADOS ....pg. 116
Capital: ....Bridgetown
Area: ......430 sq km; 166 sq mi
Highest Elev.: ...Mt. Hillaby 340 m; 1,110 ft
Avg. Temperature: ..Jan = 24.5°C; Jul = 27.0°C
Currency: ....Barbados dollar
Official Language: .English

Bridgetown	13°06' N, 059°37' W

BELARUS ....pg. 138
Capital: ....Minsk
Area: ......207,600 sq km; 80,200 sq mi
Highest Elev.: ...Dzerzhinskaya Mtn. 350 m;
1,140 ft
Longest River: ...Dnieper 2,200 km; 1,370 mi
Avg. Temperature: ..Jan = -6°C; Jul = 17°C
Currency: ....Belarusian rubel
Official Language: .Belarusian

Baranovichi	53°08' N, 026°02' E
Bereza (Beryoza)	52°32' N, 024°59' E
Berezovka (Beryozovka)	53°43' N, 025°30' E
Bobruysk	53°09' N, 029°14' E
Borisov	54°15' N, 028°30' E
Brest (Brest-Litovsk)	52°06' N, 023°42' E
Bykhov	53°31' N, 030°15' E
Chashniki	54°52' N, 029°10' E
Chausy	53°48' N, 030°58' E
Chechersk (Chechyorsk)	52°55' N, 030°55' E
Cherikov	53°34' N, 031°23' E
Dokshitsy	54°54' N, 027°46' E
Dobrush	52°25' N, 031°19' E
Drogichin	52°11' N, 025°09' E
Dzerzhinsk	53°41' N, 027°08' E
Glubokoye	55°08' N, 027°41' E
Gorki	54°17' N, 030°59' E
Gomel	52°25' N, 031°00' E
Grodno (Hrodna)	53°41' N, 023°50' E
Ivanovo	52°09' N, 025°32' E
Kalinkovichi	52°08' N, 029°19' E
Kamenets	52°24' N, 023°49' E
Kletsk	53°04' N, 026°38' E
Kobrin	52°13' N, 024°21' E
Kossovo	52°45' N, 025°09' E
Kostyukovichi	53°20' N, 032°03' E
Lepel	54°53' N, 028°42' E
Lida	53°53' N, 025°18' E
Luninets	52°15' N, 026°48' E
Malorita	51°47' N, 024°05' E
Maryina Gorka	53°31' N, 028°09' E
Minsk (Mensk)	53°54' N, 027°34' E
Miory	55°37' N, 027°38' E
Mogilyov (Mogilev or Mahilyou)	53°54' N, 030°21' E
Molodechno	54°19' N, 026°51' E
Mosty	53°25' N, 024°32' E
Mozyr (Mazyr)	52°03' S, 029°16' E
Novolukoml	54°39' N, 029°13' E
Novopolotsk (Navapolatsk)	55°32' N, 028°39' E
Orsha	54°31' N, 030°26' E
Osipovichi	53°18' N, 028°38' E
Petrikov	52°08' N, 028°30' E
Pinsk	52°07' N, 026°07' E
Polotsk (Polatsk)	55°29' N, 028°47' E
Postavy	55°07' N, 026°50' E
Pruzhany	52°33' N, 024°28' E
Rechitsa (Rechytsa)	52°22' N, 030°23' E

Rogachev (Rogachyov)	53°05' N, 030°03' E
Slonim	53°06' N, 025°19' E
Slutsk	53°01' N, 027°33' E
Stolbtsy	53°29' N, 026°44' E
Soligorsk (Salihorsk)	52°48' N, 027°32' E
Stolin	51°53' N, 026°51' E
Svetlogorsk (Svetlahorsk)	52°38' N, 029°46' E
Tolochin	54°25' N, 029°42' E
Vasilevichi	52°15' N, 029°50' E
Vileyka	54°30' N, 026°55' E
Vitebsk	55°12' N, 030°11' E
Volkovysk	53°10' N, 024°28' E
Vysokoye	52°22' N, 023°22' E
Zaslavl	54°00' N, 027°17' E
Zhabinka	52°12' N, 024°01' E
Zhitkovichi	52°14' N, 027°52' E
Zhlobin	52°54' N, 030°03' E
Zhodino	54°06' N, 028°21' E

BELGIUM ....pg. 132
Capital: ....Brussels
Area: ......30,518 sq km; 11,783 sq mi
Highest Elev.: ...Botrange 690 m; 2,280 ft
Longest River: ...Meuse (Maas) 950 km; 590 mi
Avg. Temperature: ..Jan = 2°C; Jul = 17°C
Currency: ....Belgian franc
Official Language: .Dutch, French, German

Aalst (Alost)	50°56' N, 004°02' E
Anderlecht	50°50' N, 004°18' E
Antwerp (Antwerpen, Anvers)	51°13' N, 004°25' E
Bastogne	50°00' N, 005°43' E
Brugge (Bruges)	51°13' N, 003°14' E
Brussels (Brussel, Bruxelles)	50°50' N, 004°20' E
Charleroi	50°25' N, 004°26' E
Doornik, see Tournai	
Etterbeek	50°50' N, 004°23' E
Forest (Vorst)	50°48' N, 004°19' E
Genk (Genck)	50°58' N, 005°30' E
Ghent (Gand, Gent)	51°03' N, 003°43' E
Hasselt	50°56' N, 005°20' E
Ixelles (Elsene)	50°50' N, 004°22' E
Jemappes	50°27' N, 003°53' E
Kapellen	51°19' N, 004°26' E
Kortrijk (Courtrai)	50°50' N, 003°16' E
La Louvière	50°28' N, 004°11' E
Liege (Luttich)	50°38' N, 005°34' E
Louvain (Leuven)	50°53' N, 004°42' E
Mechelen (Malines)	51°02' N, 004°28' E
Mons (Bergen)	50°27' N, 003°56' E
Mouscron (Moeskroen)	50°44' N, 003°13' E
Namur (Namen)	50°28' N, 004°52' E
Ostend (Oostende)	51°13' N, 002°55' E
Roeselare (Roulers)	50°57' N, 003°08' E
Schaerbeek (Schaarbeek)	50°51' N, 004°23' E
Seraing	50°36' N, 005°29' E
Sint-Gillis-Waas	51°13' N, 004°08' E
Sint-Niklaas	51°10' N, 004°08' E
Spa	50°30' N, 005°52' E
Tournai (Doornik)	50°36' N, 003°23' E
Uccle (Ukkel)	50°48' N, 004°19' E
Waterloo	50°43' N, 004°23' E

BELIZE ....pg. 117
Capital: ....Belmopan
Area: ......22,965 sq km; 8,867 sq mi
Highest Elev.: ...Victoria Pk. 1,120 m; 3,680 ft
Longest River: ...Belize 290 km; 180 mi
Avg. Temperature: ..Jan = 24°C; Jul = 28°C
Currency: ....Belize dollar
Official Language: .English

Belize City (Belice)	17°30' N, 088°12' W
Belmopan	17°15' N, 088°46' W
Corozal	18°24' N, 088°24' W
Dangriga (Stann Creek)	16°58' N, 088°13' W
Monkey River	16°22' N, 088°29' W
Orange Walk	18°06' N, 088°33' W
Pembroke Hall	18°17' N, 088°27' W

BENIN ....pg. 150
Capital: ....Porto-Novo
Area: ......112,680 sq km; 43,500 sq mi
Highest Elev.: ...Atakora Mts. 640 m; 2,100 ft
Longest River: ...Ouémé 450 km; 280 mi
Avg. Temperature: ..Jan = 28°C; Jul = 26°C
Currency: ....CFA franc
Official Language: ..French

Cotonou	06°21' N, 002°26' E
Parakou	09°21' N, 002°37' E
Porto-Novo	06°29' N, 002°37' E

BHUTAN ....pg. 146
Capital: ....Thimphu
Area: ......47,000 sq km; 18,150 sq mi
Highest Elev.: ...Mt. Kula 7,550 m; 24,780 ft
Longest River: ...Wong 370 km; 230 mi
Avg. Temperature: ..Jan = 0°C; Jul = 15°C
Currency: ....ngultrum
Official Language: .Dzongkha

Thimphu	27°28' N 089°38' E

BOLIVIA ....pg. 120
Capital: ....La Paz
Area: ......1,098,581 sq km; 424,164 sq mi
Highest Elev.: ...Mt. Sajama 6,540 m; 21,460 ft
Longest River: ...Mamoré 1,900 km; 1,200 mi
Avg. Temperature: ..Jan = 18°C; Jul = 10°C
Currency: ....boliviano
Official Language: .Spanish, Aymara, Quechua

Cochabamba	17°24' S, 066°09' W
La Paz	16°30' S, 068°09' W

Monteagudo	19°49' S, 063°59' W
Montero	17°20' S, 063°15' W
Oruro	17°59' S, 067°09' W
Porvenir	11°15' S, 068°41' W
Potosí	19°35' S, 065°45' W
Sucre	19°02' S, 065°17' W
Tarija	21°31' S, 064°45' W
Tiahuanaco (Tiwanacu)	16°33' S, 068°42' W
Trinidad	14°47' S, 064°47' W

BOSNIA & HERZEGOVINA pg. 134
Capital: ....Sarajevo
Area: ......51,129 sq km; 19,741 sq mi
Highest Elev.: ...Mt. Maglic 2,390 m; 7,830 ft
Longest River: ...Sava 940 km; 580 mi
Avg. Temperature: ..Jan = -1.4°C; Jul = 19.6°C
Currency: ....Bosnian dinar
Official Language: .Serbo-Croatian

Brcko	44°52' N, 018°49' E
Gorazde	43°40' N, 018°59' E
Jablanica	43°39' N, 017°45' E
Jajce	44°21' N, 017°17' E
Kladanj	44°14' N, 018°42' E
Kljuc	44°32' N, 016°47' E
Konjic	43°39' N, 017°58' E
Prijedor	44°59' N, 016°42' E
Sanski Most	44°46' N, 016°40' E
Sarajevo	43°50' N, 018°25' E
Srebrenica	44°06' N, 019°18' E
Titov Vrbas, see Vrbas	
Travnik	44°14' N, 017°40' E
Tuzla	44°33' N, 018°41' E
Vares	44°10' N, 018°20' E
Vrbas (Titov Vrbas)	45°34' N, 019°39' E
Zenica	44°13' N, 017°55' E

BOTSWANA ....pg. 152
Capital: ....Gaborone
Area: ......581,730 sq km; 224,607 sq mi
Highest Elev.: ...Otse Mtn. 1,490 m; 4,890 ft
Longest River: ...Limpopo 1,610 km; 1,000 mi
Avg. Temperature: ..Jan = 25°C; Jul = 15°C
Currency: ....pula
Official Language: .English

Francistown	21°13' S, 027°31' E
Gaborone	24°40' S, 025°57' E
Ghanzi	21°34' S, 021°47' E
Kasane	17°49' S, 025°09' E
Letlhakane	21°25' S, 025°35' E
Mahalapye	23°04' S, 026°50' E
Maun	19°59' S, 023°25' E
Mochudi	24°25' S, 026°09' E
Orapa	21°17' S, 025°22' E
Palapye (Palapye Road)	22°33' S, 027°08' E
Selebi-Phikwe	22°01' S, 027°50' E
Shashe	21°26' S, 027°27' E
Tlokweng	24°32' S, 025°58' E
Tshabong	26°03' S, 022°27' E

BRAZIL ....pg. 121
Capital: ....Brasília
Area: ......8,547,404 sq km; 3,300,171 sq mi
Highest Elev.: ...Neblina Pk. 3,010 m; 9,890 ft
Longest River: ...Amazon 6,570 km; 4,080 mi
Avg. Temperature: ..Jan = 25°C; Jul = 20°C
Currency: ....real
Official Language: .Portuguese

Abacate	00°19' N, 050°53' W
Abaetetuba	01°42' S, 048°54' W
Alagoinhas	12°07' S, 038°26' W
Alcântara	02°24' S, 044°24' W
Alegrete	29°46' S, 055°46' W
Altamira	03°12' S, 052°12' W
Americana	22°45' S, 047°20' W
Amapá	02°03' N, 050°48' W
Anápolis	16°20' S, 048°58' W
Aracaju	10°55' S, 037°04' W
Araçatuba	21°12' S, 050°25' W
Araguaína	07°12' S, 048°12' W
Araguari	18°38' S, 048°11' W
Arapiraca	09°45' S, 036°39' W
Araraquara	21°47' S, 048°10' W
Assis	22°40' S, 050°25' W
Bacabal	04°14' S, 044°47' W
Bagé	31°20' S, 054°06' W
Balsas	07°31' S, 046°02' W
Barreiras	12°08' S, 045°00' W
Barretos	20°33' S, 048°33' W
Bauru	22°19' S, 049°04' W
Bayeux	07°08' S, 034°56' W
Belém (Para)	01°27' S, 048°29' W
Belo Horizonte	19°55' S, 043°56' W
Blumenau	26°56' S, 049°03' W
Boa Vista	02°49' N, 060°30' W
Bom Jesus da Lapa	13°15' S, 043°25' W
Braganca	01°03' S, 046°46' W
Brasília	15°47' S, 047°55' W
Brusque	27°06' S, 048°56' W
Cabo	08°17' S, 035°02' W
Caceres	16°04' S, 057°41' W
Cachoeira do Sul	30°02' S, 052°54' W
Cachoeiro de Itapemirim	20°51' S, 041°06' W
Camaçari	12°41' S, 038°18' W
Campina Grande	07°13' S, 035°53' W
Campinas	22°54' S, 047°05' W
Campo Grande	20°27' S, 054°37' W
Campos	21°45' S, 041°18' W
Candeias	12°40' S, 038°33' W
Canoas	29°56' S, 051°11' W
Cariacica	20°16' S, 040°25' W
Caruaru	08°17' S, 035°58' W
Cascavel	24°57' S, 053°28' W
Castanhal	01°18' S, 047°55' W
Catanduva	21°08' S, 048°58' W
Caxias	04°50' S, 043°21' W
Caxias do Sul	29°10' S, 051°11' W
Coari	04°05' S, 063°08' W
Codo	04°29' S, 043°53' W

Name	Lat./Long.
Colatina	19°32' S, 040°37' W
Conselheiro Lafaiete	20°40' S, 043°48' W
Contagem	19°55' S, 044°06' W
Corumbá	19°01' S, 057°39' W
Crato	07°14' S, 039°23' W
Criciúma	28°40' S, 049°23' W
Cruz Alta	28°39' S, 053°36' W
Cruzeiro do Sul	07°38' S, 072°36' W
Cuiaba	15°35' S, 056°05' W
Curitibá	25°25' S, 049°15' W
Diamantina	18°15' S, 043°36' W
Divinópolis	20°09' S, 044°54' W
Duque de Caxias	22°47' S, 043°18' W
Erechim	27°38' S, 052°17' W
Feira de Santana	12°15' S, 038°57' W
Florianópolis	27°35' S, 048°34' W
Fonte Boa	02°32' S, 066°01' W
Fortaleza	03°43' S, 038°30' W
Foz do Iguacu	25°33' S, 054°35' W
Franca	20°32' S, 047°24' W
Garanhuns	08°54' S, 036°29' W
Goiânia	16°40' S, 049°16' W
Governador Valadares	18°51' S, 041°56' W
Guarulhos	23°28' S, 046°32' W
Gurupi	11°43' S, 049°04' W
Ilhéus	14°49' S, 039°02' W
Imperatriz	05°32' S, 047°29' W
Itabuna	14°48' S, 039°16' W
Itaituba	04°17' S, 055°59' W
Itajaí	26°53' S, 048°39' W
Itamaraju	17°04' S, 039°32' W
Itapetinga	15°15' S, 040°15' W
Itapipoca	03°30' S, 039°35' W
Ituiutaba	18°58' S, 049°28' W
Itumbiara	18°25' S, 049°13' W
Jaboatão	08°07' S, 035°01' W
Jataí	17°53' S, 051°43' W
Jau	22°18' S, 048°33' W
Jequié	13°51' S, 040°05' W
Ji-Paraná	10°55' S, 061°59' W
João Pessoa	07°07' S, 034°52' W
Joinville	26°18' S, 048°50' W
Juazeiro	09°25' S, 040°30' W
Juàzeiro do Norte	07°12' S, 039°20' W
Juiz de Fora	21°45' S, 043°20' W
Lajes	27°48' S, 050°19' W
Limeira	22°34' S, 047°24' W
Lins	21°40' S, 049°45' W
Londrina	23°18' S, 051°09' W
Luziânia	16°15' S, 047°56' W
Macapà	00°02' N, 051°03' W
Maceió	09°40' S, 035°43' W
Manaus	03°08' S, 060°01' W
Marabá	05°21' S, 049°07' W
Maranguape	03°53' S, 038°40' W
Marilia	22°13' S, 049°56' W
Maringá	23°25' S, 051°55' W
Maues	03°24' S, 057°42' W
Monte Dourado	00°52' S, 052°31' W
Montes Claros	16°43' S, 043°52' W
Mossoró	05°11' S, 037°20' W
Natal	05°47' S, 035°13' W
Niteroi	22°53' S, 043°07' W
Nova Friburgo	22°16' S, 042°32' W
Nova Iguaçu	22°45' S, 043°27' W
Novo Hamburgo	29°41' S, 051°08' W
Olinda	08°01' S, 034°51' W
Osasco	23°32' S, 046°46' W
Paranaguá	25°31' S, 048°30' W
Parnaiba	02°54' S, 041°47' W
Parnamirim	05°55' S, 035°15' W
Passo Fundo	28°15' S, 052°24' W
Passos	20°43' S, 046°37' W
Patos	07°01' S, 037°16' W
Patos de Minas	18°35' S, 046°32' W
Paulo Afonso	09°21' S, 038°14' W
Pelotas	31°46' S, 052°20' W
Petrolina	09°24' S, 040°30' W
Piracicaba	22°43' S, 047°38' W
Pocos de Caldas	21°48' S, 046°34' W
Ponta Grossa	25°05' S, 050°09' W
Pôrto Alegre	30°04' S, 051°11' W
Pôrto Velho	08°46' S, 063°54' W
Presidente Prudente	22°07' S, 051°22' W
Recife	08°03' S, 034°54' W
Ribeirão Prêto	21°10' N, 047°48' W
Rio Branco	09°58' S, 067°48' W
Rio de Janeiro	22°54' S, 043°14' W
Rio Grande	32°02' S, 052°05' W
Rio Largo	09°29' S, 035°51' W
Rio Verde	17°43' S, 050°56' W
Rondonópolis	16°28' S, 054°38' W
Salvador	12°59' S, 038°31' W
Santa Inês	03°39' S, 045°22' W
Santa Maria	29°41' S, 053°48' W
Santa Maria da Vitoria	13°24' S, 044°12' W
Santa Rosa	27°52' S, 054°29' W
Santana do Livramento	30°53' S, 055°31' W
Santarém	02°26' S, 054°42' W
Santo Andre	23°40' S, 046°31' W
Santo Antônio de Jesus	12°58' S, 039°16' W
Santos	23°57' S, 046°20' W
São Carlos	22°01' S, 047°54' W
São Cristóvão	11°01' S, 037°12' W
São Gonçalo	22°51' S, 043°04' W
São Joao del Rei	21°09' S, 044°16' W
São José do Rio Prêto	20°48' S, 049°23' W
São Leopoldo	29°46' S, 051°09' W
São Lourenço da Mata	08°00' S, 035°03' W
São Luís	02°31' S, 044°16' W
São Paulo	23°32' S, 046°37' W
São Raimundo Nonato	09°01' S, 042°42' W
São Vicente	23°58' S, 046°23' W
Sete Lagoas	19°27' S, 044°14' W
Sobral	03°42' S, 040°21' W
Tefé	03°22' S, 064°42' W
Teófilo Otoni	17°51' S, 041°30' W
Teresina	05°05' S, 042°49' W
Timon	05°06' S, 042°49' W
Três Lagoas	20°48' S, 051°43' W
Tubarão	28°30' S, 049°01' W
Tucurui	03°42' S, 049°27' W
Tupã	21°56' S, 050°30' W
Uberaba	19°45' S, 047°55' W
Uruguaiana	29°45' S, 057°05' W
Varzea Grande	15°39' S, 056°08' W
Viamao	30°05' S, 051°02' W
Vila Velha (Espirito Santo)	20°20' S, 040°17' W

Name	Lat./Long.
Vitoria	20°19' S, 040°21' W
Vitória da Conquista	14°51' S, 040°51' W

BRUNEI .... pg. 145

Capital: ....Bandar Seri Begawan
Area: ....5,765 sq km; 2,226 sq mi
Highest Elev.: ...Pagon Pk. 1,850 m; 6,070 ft
Avg. Temperature: .Jan = 26.7°C; Jul = 27.8°C
Currency: ....Brunei dollar
Official Language: ..Malay

Bandar Seri Begawan (Brunei)	04°53' N, 114°56' E
Seria	04°37' N, 114°19' E

BULGARIA .... pg. 134

Capital: ....Sofia
Area: ....110,994 sq km; 42,855 sq mi
Highest Elev.: ...Musala Pk. 2,930 m; 9,600 ft
Longest River: ....Danube 2,850 km; 1770 mi
Avg. Temperature: .Jan = -2°C; Jul = 21°C
Currency: ....lev
Official Language: ..Bulgarian

Balchik	43°25' N, 028°10' E
Berkovitsa	43°14' N, 023°07' E
Blagoevgrad	42°01' N, 023°06' E
Burgas	42°30' N, 027°28' E
Gabrovo	42°52' N, 025°19' E
Kazanluk	42°37' N, 025°24' E
Khaskovo	41°56' N, 025°33' E
Kurdzhali	41°39' N, 025°22' E
Kyustendil	42°17' N, 022°41' E
Lovech	43°08' N, 024°43' E
Montana	43°25' N, 023°13' E
Nikopol	43°42' N, 024°54' E
Pazardzhik	42°12' N, 024°20' E
Pernik (Dimitrovo)	42°36' N, 023°02' E
Petrich	41°24' N, 023°13' E
Pleven	43°25' N, 024°37' E
Plovdiv	42°09' N, 024°45' E
Razgrad	43°32' N, 026°31' E
Ruse	43°50' N, 025°57' E
Silistra	44°07' N, 027°16' E
Sliven	42°40' N, 026°19' E
Sofia	42°41' N, 023°19' E
Stara Zagora	42°25' N, 025°38' E
Troyan	42°53' N, 024°43' E
Varna	43°13' N, 027°55' E
Veliko Turnovo	43°04' N, 025°39' E
Velingrad	42°01' N, 024°00' E
Vidin	43°59' N, 022°52' E
Vratsa (Vraca)	43°12' N, 023°33' E
Yambol	42°29' N, 026°30' E

BURKINA FASO .... pg. 150

Capital: ....Ouagadougou
Area: ....274,400 sq km; 105,946 sq mi
Highest Elev.: ...Tena Kourou 750 m; 2,460 ft
Longest River: ....Black Volta 1,160 km; 720 mi
Avg. Temperature: .Jan = 25°C; Jul = 28°C
Currency: ....CFA franc
Official Language: ..French

Bobo Dioulasso	11°12' N, 004°18' W
Koudougou	12°15' N, 002°22' W
Ouagadougou	12°22' N, 001°31' W

BURUNDI .... pg. 153

Capital: ....Bujumbura
Area: ....27,816 sq km; 10,740 sq mi
Highest Elev.: ...Mt. Heha 2,670 m; 8,760 ft
Longest River: ....Ruvubu 480 km; 300 mi
Avg. Temperature: .Jan = 23°C; Jul = 23°C
Currency: ....Burundi franc
Official Language: ..Rundi; French

Bujumbura	03°23' S, 029°22' E
Gitega	03°26' S, 029°56' E
Ngozi	02°54' S, 029°50' E
Nyanza-Lac	04°21' S, 029°36' E

CAMBODIA .... pg. 144

Capital: ....Phnom Penh
Area: ....181,916 sq km; 70,238 sq mi
Highest Elev.: ...Mt. Aôral 1,810 m; 5,950 ft
Longest River: ....Mekong 4,350 km; 2,700 mi
Avg. Temperature: .Jan = 26°C; Jul = 28°C
Currency: ....riel
Official Language: ..Khmer

Batdambang (Battambang)	13°06' N, 103°12' E
Chong Kal	13°57' N, 103°35' E
Kâmpóng Saôm (Sihanoukville)	10°38' N, 103°30' E
Kâmpôt	10°37' N, 104°11' E
Krong Kaôh Kong	11°37' N, 102°59' E
Phnom Penh (Phnum Penh or Pnom Penh)	11°33' N, 104°55' E
Phnum Tbeng Meanchey	13°49' N, 104°58' E
Pouthisat (Pursat)	12°32' N, 103°55' E
Prey Veng	11°29' N, 105°19' E
Siempang	14°07' N, 106°23' E
Siemreab	13°22' N, 103°51' E

CAMEROON .... pg. 150

Capital: ....Yaoundé
Area: ....475,442 sq km; 183,569 sq mi
Highest Elev.: ...Mt. Cameroon 4,100 m; 13,440 ft
Longest River: ....Sanaga 530 km; 330 mi
Avg. Temperature: .Jan = 24°C; Jul = 23°C
Currency: ....CFA franc
Official Language: ..French, English

Bafoussam	05°28' N, 010°25' E
Bamenda	05°56' N, 010°10' E

Name	Lat./Long.
Douala	04°03' N, 009°42' E
Fomban	05°43' N, 010°55' E
Kumba	04°38' N, 009°25' E
Nkongsamba	04°57' N, 009°56' E
Yaoundé	03°52' N, 011°31' E

CANADA .... pg. 114

Capital: ....Ottawa
Area: ....9,970,610 sq km; 3,849,674 sq mi
Highest Elev.: ...Mt. Logan 5,950 m; 19,520 ft
Longest River: ...Mackenzie 4,240 km; 2,640 mi
Avg. Temperature: Jan = -11°C; Jul = 21°C
Currency: ....Canadian dollar
Official Language: English, French

Amos	48°35' N, 078°07' W
Arctic Bay	73°02' N, 085°11' W
Baie-Comeau	49°13' N, 068°09' W
Baker Lake	64°15' N, 096°00' W
Banff	51°10' N, 115°34' W
Barrie	44°24' N, 079°40' W
Battleford	52°44' N, 108°19' W
Beauport	46°52' N, 071°11' W
Bonavista	48°39' N, 053°07' W
Brandon	49°50' N, 099°57' W
Bridgewater	44°23' N, 064°31' W
Brooks	50°35' N, 111°53' W
Buchans	48°49' N, 056°52' W
Burlington	43°19' N, 079°47' W
Burnaby	49°16' N, 122°57' W
Calgary	51°03' N, 114°05' W
Cambridge Bay	69°03' N, 105°05' W
Camrose	53°01' N, 112°50' W
Carbonear	47°44' N, 053°13' W
Carmacks	62°05' N, 136°17' W
Charlesbourg	46°51' N, 071°16' W
Charlottetown	46°14' N, 063°08' W
Chatham	47°02' N, 082°11' W
Chibougamau	49°55' N, 074°22' W
Chicoutimi	48°26' N, 071°04' W
Churchill	58°46' N, 094°10' W
Churchill Falls	53°33' N, 064°01' W
Cranbrook	49°30' N, 115°46' W
Dartmouth	44°40' N, 063°34' W
Dauphin	51°09' N, 100°03' W
Dawson	64°04' N, 139°26' W
Dawson Creek	55°46' N, 120°14' W
Duck Lake	52°49' N, 106°14' W
Edmonton	53°33' N, 113°28' W
Elliot Lake	46°23' N, 082°42' W
Enderby	50°33' N, 119°09' W
Eskimo Point	61°07' N, 094°03' W
Esterhazy	50°39' N, 102°05' W
Estevan	49°08' N, 102°59' W
Faro	62°14' N, 133°20' W
Fernie	49°30' N, 115°04' W
Flin Flon	54°46' N, 101°53' W
Fogo	49°43' N, 054°17' W
Fort Liard	60°15' N, 123°28' W
Fort MacLeod	49°43' N, 113°25' W
Fort McMurray	56°44' N, 111°23' W
Fort McPherson	67°27' N, 134°53' W
Fort Qu'Appelle	50°46' N, 103°48' W
Fort Smith	60°00' N, 111°53' W
Fort St. John	56°15' N, 120°51' W
Fredericton	45°58' N, 066°39' W
Gagnon	51°53' N, 068°10' W
Gander	48°57' N, 054°37' W
Gaspe	48°50' N, 064°29' W
Glace Bay	46°12' N, 059°57' W
Granby	45°24' N, 072°43' W
Grand Bank	47°06' N, 055°46' W
Grand Falls	48°56' N, 055°40' W
Grande Prairie	55°10' N, 118°48' W
Grimshaw	56°11' N, 117°36' W
Grise Fiord	76°25' N, 082°55' W
Haines Junction	60°45' N, 137°30' W
Halifax	44°39' N, 063°36' W
Hamilton	43°15' N, 079°51' W
Happy Valley-Goose Bay	53°19' N, 060°20' W
Harbour Grace	47°42' N, 053°13' W
Hay River	60°49' N, 115°47' W
Inuvik	68°21' N, 133°43' W
Iqaluit (Frobisher Bay)	63°45' N, 068°31' W
Iroquois Falls	48°46' N, 080°41' W
Jasper	52°53' N, 118°05' W
Joliette	46°01' N, 073°27' W
Jonquiere	48°25' N, 071°13' W
Kamloops	50°40' N, 120°19' W
Kapuskasing	49°25' N, 082°26' W
Kelowna	49°53' N, 119°29' W
Kenora	49°47' N, 094°29' W
Kindersley	51°28' N, 109°10' W
Kirkland Lake	48°09' N, 080°02' W
Kitchener	43°27' N, 080°29' W
La Baie	48°20' N, 070°52' W
La Tuque	47°26' N, 072°47' W
Labrador City	52°57' N, 066°55' W
Lethbridge	49°42' N, 112°49' W
Lewisporte	49°14' N, 055°03' W
Liverpool	44°02' N, 064°43' W
Lloydminster	53°17' N, 110°00' W
London	42°59' N, 081°14' W
Longueuil	45°32' N, 073°30' W
Lynn Lake	56°51' N, 101°03' W
Maple Creek	49°55' N, 109°29' W
Marystown	47°10' N, 055°09' W
Mayo	63°36' N, 135°54' W
Medicine Hat	50°03' N, 110°40' W
Mississauga	43°35' N, 079°39' W
Moncton	46°07' N, 064°48' W
Montagny	46°59' N, 070°33' W
Montreal	45°31' N, 073°34' W
Moose Jaw	50°24' N, 105°32' W
Mount Pearl	47°31' N, 052°47' W
Nanaimo	49°10' N, 123°56' W
Nelson	49°30' N, 117°17' W
Nepean	45°16' N, 075°46' W
New Liskeard	47°30' N, 079°40' W
Niagara Falls	43°06' N, 079°04' W
Nickel Centre	46°35' N, 080°57' W
Nipawin	53°22' N, 104°00' W
North Battleford	52°47' N, 108°17' W
North Bay	46°19' N, 079°28' W
North West River	53°32' N, 060°08' W
Old Crow	67°34' N, 139°50' W
Oshawa	43°54' N, 078°51' W

Name	Lat./Long.
Ottawa	45°25' N, 075°42' W
Pangnirtung	66°08' N, 065°43' W
Parry Sound	45°21' N, 080°02' W
Peace River	56°14' N, 117°17' W
Perce	48°32' N, 064°13' W
Peterborough	44°18' N, 078°19' W
Pine Point	60°50' N, 114°28' W
Port Alberni	49°14' N, 124°48' W
Port Hawkesbury	45°37' N, 061°21' W
Portage la Prairie	49°59' N, 098°18' W
Prince Albert	53°12' N, 105°46' W
Prince George	53°55' N, 122°45' W
Prince Rupert	54°19' N, 130°19' W
Quebec	46°49' N, 071°14' W
Quesnel	53°00' N, 122°30' W
Rae-Edzo	62°50' N, 116°03' W
Rankin Inlet	62°49' N, 092°05' W
Red Deer	52°16' N, 113°48' W
Regina	50°27' N, 104°37' W
Resolute Bay	74°41' N, 094°54' W
Revelstoke	50°59' N, 118°12' W
Rimouski	48°26' N, 068°33' W
Roberval	48°31' N, 072°13' W
Ross River	61°59' N, 132°26' W
Sachs Harbour	72°00' N, 125°13' W
Saint Albert	53°38' N, 113°38' W
Saint John	45°16' N, 066°03' W
Saint John's	47°34' N, 052°43' W
Sainte-Foy	46°47' N, 071°17' W
Saskatoon	52°07' N, 106°38' W
Sault Ste. Marie	46°31' N, 084°20' W
Scarborough	43°47' N, 079°15' W
Schefferville	54°48' N, 066°50' W
Selkirk	50°09' N, 096°52' W
Senneterre	48°23' N, 077°14' W
Sept-Iles	50°12' N, 066°23' W
Shawinigan	46°33' N, 072°45' W
Shelburne	43°46' N, 065°19' W
Sherbrooke	45°25' N, 071°54' W
Snow Lake	54°53' N, 100°02' W
Springdale	49°30' N, 056°04' W
Sturgeon Falls	46°22' N, 079°55' W
Sudbury	46°30' N, 081°00' W
Surrey	49°06' N, 122°47' W
Swan River	52°07' N, 101°16' W
Sydney	46°09' N, 060°11' W
Teslin	60°10' N, 132°43' W
The Pas	53°50' N, 101°15' W
Thompson	55°45' N, 097°52' W
Thunder Bay	48°24' N, 089°19' W
Timmins	48°28' N, 081°20' W
Toronto	43°39' N, 079°23' W
Trois-Rivières	46°21' N, 072°33' W
Truro	45°22' N, 063°16' W
Tuktoyaktuk	69°27' N, 133°02' W
Val-d'Or	48°06' N, 077°47' W
Vancouver	49°15' N, 123°07' W
Vernon	50°16' N, 119°16' W
Wabush	52°55' N, 066°52' W
Watson Lake	60°04' N, 128°42' W
Weyburn	49°40' N, 103°51' W
Whitehorse	60°43' N, 135°03' W
Williams Lake	52°08' N, 122°09' W
Windsor	42°18' N, 083°01' W
Windsor	54°59' N, 064°08' W
Winnipeg	49°53' N, 097°09' W
Yarmouth	43°50' N, 066°07' W
Yellowknife	62°27' N, 114°22' W
Yorkton	51°13' N, 102°28' W

CAPE VERDE .... pg. 148

Capital: ....Praia
Area: ....4,033 sq km; 1,557 sq mi
Highest Elev.: ...Mt. Cano 2,830 m; 9,280 ft
Avg. Temperature: .Jan = 22°C; Jul = 27°C
Currency: ....escudo
Official Language: ..Portuguese

Mindelo	16°53' N, 025°00' W
Praia	14°55' N, 023°31' W

CENTRAL AFRICAN REP. pg. 151

Capital: ....Bangui
Area: ....622,436 sq km; 240,324 sq mi
Highest Elev.: ...Mt. Gaou 1,420 m; 4,660 ft
Longest River: ...Ubangi-Uele 2,250 km; 1,400 mi
Avg. Temperature: .Jan = 26°C; Jul = 25°C
Currency: ....CFA franc
Official Language: .French, Sango

Bangui	04°22' N 018°35' E

CHAD .... pg. 151

Capital: ....N'Djamena
Area: ....1,284,000 sq km; 495,755 sq mi
Highest Elev.: ...Mt. Koussi 3,410 m; 11,200 ft
Longest River: ...Chari 1,400 km; 870 mi
Avg. Temperature: .Jan = 24°C; Jul = 28°C
Currency: ....CFA franc
Official Language: .Arabic, French

Abéché	13°49' N, 020°49' E
Moundou	08°34' N, 016°05' E
N'Djamena (Fort Lamy)	12°07' N, 015°03' E
Sarh (Fort-Archambault)	09°09' N, 018°23' E

CHILE .... pg. 122

Capital: ....Santiago
Area: ....756,626 sq km; 292,135 sq mi
Highest Elev.: ...Ojos del Salado 6,890 m; 22,610 ft
Longest River: ...Loa 440 km; 280 mi
Avg. Temperature: .Jan = 21°C; Jul = 9°C
Currency: ....peso
Official Language: .Spanish

Achao	42°28' S, 073°30' W
Ancud	41°52' S, 073°50' W

CHILE (cont.)

Name	Lat./Long.
Andacollo	30°14' S, 071°06' W
Antofagasta	23°39' S, 070°24' W
Arica	18°29' S, 070°20' W
Baquedano	23°20' S, 069°51' W
Calama	22°28' S, 068°56' W
Caldera	27°04' S, 070°50' W
Cañete	37°48' S, 073°24' W
Castro	42°29' S, 073°46' W
Catalina	25°13' S, 069°43' W
Cauquenes	35°58' S, 072°21' W
Chaitén	42°55' S, 072°43' W
Chile Chico	46°33' S, 071°44' W
Chillán	36°36' S, 072°07' W
Chonchi	42°38' S, 073°47' W
Chuquicamata	22°19' S, 068°56' W
Coihaique	45°34' S, 072°04' W
Concepción	36°50' S, 073°03' W
Constitución	35°20' S, 072°25' W
Copiapo	27°22' S, 070°20' W
Coquimbo	29°58' S, 071°21' W
Coronel	37°01' S, 073°08' W
Curacautín	38°26' S, 071°53' W
Curico	34°59' S, 071°14' W
Cuya	19°07' S, 070°08' W
El Salvador	26°14' S, 069°37' W
El Toro	37°17' S, 071°24' W
Huara	19°59' S, 069°47' W
Huasco	28°28' S, 071°14' W
Iquique	20°13' S, 070°10' W
La Serena	29°54' S, 071°16' W
La Tirana	20°21' S, 069°40' W
La Unión	40°17' S, 073°05' W
Lebu	37°37' S, 073°39' W
Linares	35°51' S, 071°36' W
Los Andes	32°50' S, 070°37' W
Los Angeles	37°28' S, 072°21' W
Los Canchones	20°27' S, 069°37' W
Los Lagos	39°51' S, 072°50' W
Los Vilos	31°55' S, 071°31' W
Mejillones	23°06' S, 070°27' W
Molina	35°07' S, 071°17' W
Monte Patria	30°42' S, 070°58' W
Nueva Imperial	38°44' S, 072°57' W
Osorno	40°34' S, 073°09' W
Ovalle	30°36' S, 071°12' W
Oyahue	21°14' S, 068°16' W
Parral	36°09' S, 071°50' W
Pica	20°30' S, 069°21' W
Pitrufquén	38°59' S, 072°39' W
Porvenir	53°18' S, 070°22' W
Potrerillos	26°26' S, 069°29' W
Puente Alto	33°37' S, 070°35' W
Puerto Aisén	45°24' S, 072°42' W
Puerto Cisnes	44°45' S, 072°42' W
Puerto Montt	41°28' S, 072°57' W
Puerto Natales	51°44' S, 072°31' W
Puerto Quellon	43°07' S, 073°37' W
Puerto Varas	41°19' S, 072°59' W
Punta Arenas	53°09' S, 070°55' W
Purranque	40°55' S, 073°10' W
Quirihue	36°17' S, 072°32' W
Rancagua	34°10' S, 070°45' W
Rengo	34°25' S, 070°52' W
Río Blanco	40°50' S, 073°32' W
Salamanca	31°47' S, 070°58' W
San Antonio	33°35' S, 071°38' W
San Bernardo	33°36' S, 070°43' W
San Fernando	34°35' S, 071°00' W
San Pedro	33°54' S, 071°28' W
Santiago	33°27' S, 070°40' W
Sauzal	35°45' S, 072°07' W
Talca	35°26' S, 071°40' W
Talcahuano	36°43' S, 073°07' W
Taltal	25°24' S, 070°29' W
Temuco	38°44' S, 072°36' W
Tierra Amarilla	27°29' S, 070°17' W
Tiltil	33°05' S, 070°56' W
Tocopilla	22°05' S, 070°12' W
Tome	36°37' S, 072°57' W
Valdivia	39°48' S, 073°14' W
Vallenar	28°35' S, 070°46' W
Valparaíso	33°02' S, 071°38' W
Victoria	38°13' S, 072°20' W
Vicuna	30°02' S, 070°44' W
Villarrica	39°16' S, 072°13' W
Viña del Mar	33°02' S, 071°34' W
Yungay	37°07' S, 072°01' W

CHINA .... pg. 142

Capital: ...... Peking
Area: ......9,572,900 sq km; 3,696,100 sq mi
Highest Elev.: ....Mt. Everest 8,850 m; 29,020 ft
Longest River: ..Yangtze 6,300 km; 3,920 mi
Avg. Temperature: .Jan = -5°C; Jul = 26°C
Currency: ......Renminbi
Official Language: .Mandarin Chinese

Name	Lat./Long.
Aksu	41°09' N, 080°15' E
Altay	47°52' N, 088°07' E
Anda (locally Sartu)	46°24' N, 125°19' E
Anqing	30°31' N, 117°02' E
Anshan	41°07' N, 122°57' E
Anshun	26°15' N, 105°56' E
Anyang (locally Zhangde)	36°05' N, 114°21' E
Baicheng	45°37' N, 122°49' E
Baiyin	36°32' N, 104°12' E
Baoding	38°52' N, 115°29' E
Baoji	34°23' N, 107°09' E
Baoshan	25°07' N, 099°09' E
Baotou	40°36' N, 109°59' E
Bei'an	48°16' N, 126°36' E
Beihai	21°29' N, 109°06' E
Beijing	39°56' N, 116°24' E
Beipiao	41°48' N, 120°44' E
Bengbu	32°57' N, 117°20' E
Benxi	41°20' N, 123°45' E
Bose	23°54' N, 106°37' E
Bozhou	33°52' N, 109°18' E
Butha Qi (locally Zalantun)	48°00' N, 123°43' E
Cangzhou	38°19' N, 116°52' E
Changchun	43°52' N, 125°21' E
Changde	29°02' N, 111°14' E
Changji	44°01' N, 087°19' E
Changsha	28°12' N, 112°58' E
Changzhi	36°11' N, 113°06' E
Changzhou	38°19' N, 116°52' E
Chaoyang	41°33' N, 122°25' E
Chengde	40°58' N, 117°53' E
Chengdu	30°40' N, 104°04' E
Chenzhou	25°48' N, 113°02' E
Chifeng	42°17' N, 118°53' E
Chongqing (locally Yuzhou)	29°34' N, 106°35' E
Dandong	40°08' N, 124°24' E
Daqing	46°36' N, 125°00' E
Daxian	31°16' N, 107°31' E
Denyang	31°08' N, 104°24' E
Dezhou	37°27' N, 116°18' E
Dongsheng	39°49' N, 109°59' E
Dongying	37°30' N, 118°31' E
Dukou	26°33' N, 101°44' E
Dunhua	43°21' N, 128°13' E
Duyun	26°16' N, 107°31' E
Enshi	30°18' N, 109°29' E
Fengcheng	28°12' N, 115°46' E
Fuling	29°43' N, 107°24' E
Fushun	41°52' N, 123°53' E
Fuxian (locally Wafangdian)	39°38' N, 122°00' E
Fuxin	42°06' N, 121°46' E
Fuyang	32°54' N, 115°49' E
Fuzhou	26°05' N, 119°18' E
Fuzhou	28°01' N, 116°20' E
Ganzhou	25°51' N, 114°56' E
Gejiu	23°23' N, 103°09' E
Golmud	36°22' N, 094°55' E
Guanghua (locally Laohekou)	32°22' N, 111°40' E
Guangzhou	23°07' N, 113°15' E
Guilin	25°17' N, 110°17' E
Guiyang	26°35' N, 106°43' E
Haicheng	40°52' N, 122°00' E
Haikou	20°03' N, 110°19' E
Hailar	49°12' N, 119°42' E
Hailong (locally Meichekou)	42°32' N, 125°38' E
Hami	42°48' N, 093°27' E
Handan	36°35' N, 114°29' E
Hanzhong	33°08' N, 107°02' E
Harbin	45°45' N, 126°39' E
Hebi	35°57' N, 114°13' E
Hechi (locally Jinchengjiang)	24°42' N, 108°02' E
Hefei	31°51' N, 117°17' E
Hegang	47°24' N, 130°22' E
Hengshui	37°43' N, 115°42' E
Hengyang	26°54' N, 112°36' E
Heshan	23°42' N, 108°48' E
Heze (locally Caozhou)	35°14' N, 115°27' E
Hohhot	40°51' N, 111°37' E
Horqin Youyi Qianqi (locally Ulan Hot)	46°05' N, 122°05' E
Houma	35°36' N, 111°21' E
Huaibei	33°57' N, 116°45' E
Huaide (locally Gongzhuling)	43°30' N, 124°49' E
Huaihua (locally Yushuwan)	27°33' N, 109°57' E
Huainan	32°40' N, 117°00' E
Huaiyin (locally Wangying)	33°35' N, 119°02' E
Huangshi	30°13' N, 115°06' E
Huizhou	23°05' N, 114°24' E
Hunjiang (locally Badaojiang)	41°54' N, 126°26' E
Huzhou (locally Wuxing)	30°52' N, 120°06' E
Jiamusi	46°50' N, 130°21' E
Jiangmen	22°35' N, 113°05' E
Jiaozuo	35°15' N, 113°13' E
Jiaxing	30°46' N, 120°45' E
Jiayuguan	39°49' N, 098°18' E
Jilin	43°51' N, 126°33' E
Jinan	36°40' N, 117°00' E
Jinchang	38°24' N, 102°06' E
Jincheng	35°30' N, 112°50' E
Jingdezhen	29°16' N, 117°11' E
Jinggangshan	26°37' N, 114°05' E
Jinhua	29°07' N, 119°39' E
Jining	35°24' N, 116°33' E
Jinshi	29°40' N, 111°45' E
Jinxi	40°45' N, 120°50' E
Jinzhou	41°07' N, 121°06' E
Jishou	28°19' N, 109°43' E
Jiujiang	29°44' N, 115°59' E
Jiuquan (locally Suzhou)	39°46' N, 098°34' E
Jixi	45°18' N, 130°58' E
Kaifeng	34°51' N, 114°21' E
Kaili	26°35' N, 107°55' E
Kaiyuan	23°42' N, 103°14' E
Karamay	45°30' N, 084°55' E
Kashi	39°29' N, 075°58' E
Korla	41°44' N, 086°09' E
Kunming	25°04' N, 102°41' E
Kuytun	44°25' N, 085°00' E
Laiwu	36°41' N, 118°28' E
Lanxi	29°13' N, 119°28' E
Lanzhou	36°03' N, 103°41' E
Lengshuitan	26°27' N, 111°35' E
Leshan	29°34' N, 103°44' E
Lhasa	29°39' N, 091°06' E
Lianyungang (locally Xinpu)	34°36' N, 119°13' E
Liaocheng	36°26' N, 115°58' E
Liaoyang	41°17' N, 123°11' E
Liaoyuan	42°55' N, 125°09' E
Linfen	36°05' N, 111°31' E
Linhe	40°50' N, 107°30' E
Linxia	35°28' N, 102°55' E
Linyi	37°05' N, 118°20' E
Liuzhou	24°19' N, 109°24' E
Longyan	25°11' N, 117°00' E
Loudi	27°45' N, 111°59' E
Lu'an	31°45' N, 116°29' E
Luoyang	34°41' N, 112°28' E
Luzhou	28°53' N, 105°23' E
Maoming	21°39' N, 110°54' E
Mianyang	31°28' N, 104°46' E
Mudanjiang	44°35' N, 129°36' E
Nanchang	28°41' N, 115°53' E
Nanchong	30°48' N, 106°04' E
Nanjing	32°03' N, 118°47' E
Nanning	22°49' N, 108°19' E
Nanping	26°38' N, 118°10' E
Nantong	32°02' N, 120°53' E
Nanyang	33°00' N, 112°32' E
Ningbo	29°53' N, 121°33' E
Pingdingshan	33°44' N, 113°18' E
Pingliang	35°32' N, 106°41' E
Pingxiang	22°06' N, 106°44' E
Puqi	29°43' N, 113°53' E
Putian	25°26' N, 119°01' E
Puyang	35°42' N, 114°59' E
Qingdao	36°04' N, 120°19' E
Qingyuan	21°57' N, 108°37' E
Qiqihar	47°22' N, 123°57' E
Qitaihe	45°48' N, 130°53' E
Quanzhou	24°54' N, 118°35' E
Qujing	25°36' N, 103°49' E
Sanming	26°14' N, 117°35' E
Shanghai	31°14' N, 121°28' E
Shangqiu (locally Zhuji)	34°27' N, 115°39' E
Shangrao	28°26' N, 117°58' E
Shantou	23°22' N, 116°40' E
Shaoguan	24°48' N, 113°35' E
Shaowu	27°18' N, 117°30' E
Shaoxing	30°00' N, 120°35' E
Shashi	30°19' N, 112°14' E
Shenyang	41°48' N, 123°27' E
Shenzhen	22°32' N, 114°08' E
Shihezi	44°18' N, 086°02' E
Shijiazhuang	38°03' N, 114°29' E
Shiyan	32°34' N, 110°47' E
Shuangyashan	46°40' N, 131°21' E
Shuicheng	26°36' N, 104°51' E
Siping	43°10' N, 124°20' E
Suining	30°32' N, 105°32' E
Suizhou	31°36' N, 113°03' E
Tacheng	46°45' N, 082°57' E
Tai'an	36°12' N, 117°07' E
Taiyuan	37°52' N, 112°33' E
Taizhou	32°29' N, 119°55' E
Tianshui	34°35' N, 105°43' E
Tiefa	42°30' N, 123°25' E
Tieling	42°18' N, 123°49' E
Tongchuan	35°05' N, 109°05' E
Tonghua	41°41' N, 125°55' E
Tongliao	43°37' N, 122°16' E
Tunxi	29°43' N, 118°19' E
Turpan	42°56' N, 089°10' E
Urumqi	43°48' N, 087°35' E
Wanxian	30°49' N, 108°24' E
Weifang	36°43' N, 119°06' E
Weihai	37°30' N, 122°06' E
Weinan	34°30' N, 109°30' E
Wenzhou	28°01' N, 120°39' E
Wuhai	39°47' N, 106°52' E
Wuhan	30°35' N, 114°16' E
Wuhu	31°21' N, 118°22' E
Wuwei (locally Liangzhou)	37°58' N, 102°48' E
Wuxi	31°35' N, 120°18' E
Wuzhong	38°00' N, 106°10' E
Wuzhou	23°29' N, 111°19' E
Xi'an	34°16' N, 108°54' E
Xiangfan	32°03' N, 112°05' E
Xiangtan	27°51' N, 112°54' E
Xianyang	34°22' N, 108°42' E
Xichang	27°53' N, 102°18' E
Xingtai	37°03' N, 114°30' E
Xining	36°37' N, 101°46' E
Xintai	35°54' N, 117°44' E
Xinyang (locally Pingqiao)	32°03' N, 114°05' E
Xinyu	27°48' N, 114°56' E
Yan'an	36°36' N, 109°28' E
Yancheng	33°23' N, 120°08' E
Yangquan	37°54' N, 113°36' E
Yangzhou	32°24' N, 119°26' E
Yanji	42°53' N, 129°31' E
Yantai	37°32' N, 121°24' E
Yibin	28°46' N, 104°34' E
Yichang	30°42' N, 111°17' E
Yichun	27°50' N, 114°24' E
Yichun	47°42' N, 128°54' E
Yinchuan	38°28' N, 106°19' E
Yingkou	40°40' N, 122°17' E
Yingtan	28°14' N, 117°00' E
Yining	43°54' N, 081°21' E
Yiyang	28°36' N, 112°20' E
Yongzhou	26°14' N, 111°37' E
Yuci	37°42' N, 112°44' E
Yueyang	29°23' N, 113°06' E
Yulin	22°38' N, 110°09' E
Yumen (locally Laojunmiao)	39°50' N, 097°44' E
Yuncheng	35°01' N, 110°59' E
Yuyao	30°03' N, 121°09' E
Zaozhuang	34°53' N, 117°34' E
Zhangjiakou	40°50' N, 114°56' E
Zhangye	38°56' N, 100°27' E
Zhaoqing	23°03' N, 112°27' E
Zhaotong	27°19' N, 103°43' E
Zhumadian	32°58' N, 114°03' E
Zhuozhou	39°30' N, 115°58' E
Zibo (locally Zhangdian)	36°48' N, 118°03' E
Zixing	25°58' N, 113°24' E
Zunyi	27°42' N, 106°55' E

COLOMBIA .... pg. 124

Capital: ....Bogotá
Area: ....1,141,748 sq km; 440,831 sq mi
Highest Elev.: ..Sierra Nevada de Santa Marta 5,780 m; 18,950 ft
Longest River: ..Magdalena 1,500 km; 930 mi
Avg. Temperature: .Jan = 14°C; Jul = 13°C
Currency: ......peso
Official Language: ..Spanish

Name	Lat./Long.
Acandí	08°32' N, 077°14' W
Aguachica	08°19' N, 073°38' W
Andes	05°40' N, 075°53' W
Anserma	05°13' N, 075°48' W
Apartadó	07°54' N, 076°39' W
Arauca	07°05' N, 070°45' W
Arica	02°08' S, 071°47' W
Armenia	04°31' N, 075°41' W
Barrancabermeja	07°03' N, 073°52' W
Barranquilla	10°59' N, 074°48' W
Bello	06°20' N, 075°33' W
Bisinaca	04°30' N, 069°40' W
Bogotá	04°36' N, 074°05' W
Bolívar	01°50' N, 076°58' W
Bucaramanga	07°08' N, 073°09' W
Buenaventura	03°53' N, 077°04' W
Buga	03°54' N, 076°19' W
Caldas	06°05' N, 075°38' W
Cali	03°27' N, 076°31' W
Campo de la Cruz	10°23' N, 074°53' W
Caranacoa	02°25' N, 068°57' W
Cartagena	10°25' N, 075°32' W
Cartago	04°45' N, 075°55' W
Caucasia	08°00' N, 075°12' W
Cereté	08°53' N, 075°48' W
Cerrejón	11°02' N, 072°39' W
Chigorodó	07°41' N, 076°42' W
Chiquinquirá	05°37' N, 073°50' W
Ciénaga	11°01' N, 074°15' W
Codazzi	10°02' N, 073°14' W
Copacabana	06°21' N, 075°30' W
Corozal	09°19' N, 075°18' W
Cravo Norte	06°18' N, 070°12' W
Cúcuta	07°54' N, 072°31' W
Cupica	06°41' N, 077°30' W
Duitama	05°50' N, 073°02' W
El Banco	09°00' N, 073°58' W
El Carmen	09°43' N, 075°08' W
El Dorado	01°11' N, 071°52' W
El Yopal	05°21' N, 072°23' W
Envigado	06°10' N, 075°35' W
Facatativá	04°49' N, 074°22' W
Florencia	01°36' N, 075°36' W
Florida	03°21' N, 076°15' W
Floridablanca	07°04' N, 073°06' W
Garzón	02°12' N, 075°38' W
Girardot	04°18' N, 074°48' W
Granada	03°34' N, 073°45' W
Honda	05°12' N, 074°45' W
Ibagué	04°27' N, 075°14' W
Ipiales	00°50' N, 077°37' W
Itagüí	06°10' N, 075°36' W
La Ceja	06°02' N, 075°26' W
La Dorada	05°27' N, 074°40' W
Leticia	04°09' S, 069°57' W
Loreto	03°48' N, 070°15' W
Lorica	09°14' N, 075°49' W
Macujer	00°24' N, 073°07' W
Magangué	09°14' N, 074°45' W
Maicao	11°23' N, 072°13' W
Malambo	10°52' N, 074°47' W
Matarca	00°30' S, 072°38' W
Macanal	02°45' N, 067°58' W
Manizales	05°05' N, 075°32' W
Medellín	06°15' N, 075°35' W
Mitú	01°08' N, 070°03' W
Mocoa	01°09' N, 076°37' W
Mompós	09°14' N, 074°26' W
Montería	08°46' N, 075°53' W
Mosquera	02°30' N, 078°29' W
Mulatos	08°39' N, 076°44' W
Nazareth	12°11' N, 071°17' W
Neiva	02°56' N, 075°18' W
Ocaña	08°15' N, 073°20' W
Palmira	03°32' N, 076°16' W
Pamplona	07°23' N, 072°39' W
Pasto	01°13' N, 077°17' W
Paz de Río	05°59' N, 072°47' W
Pereira	04°49' N, 075°43' W
Pitalito	01°51' N, 076°02' W
Pizarro	04°58' N, 077°22' W
Planeta Rica	08°25' N, 075°36' W
Plato	09°47' N, 074°47' W
Popayán	02°27' N, 076°36' W
Puerto Alfonso	02°11' S, 070°59' W
Puerto Berrío	06°29' N, 074°24' W
Puerto Carreño	06°12' N, 067°22' W
Puerto Inírida	03°51' N, 067°55' W
Puerto Leguízamo	00°12' S, 074°46' W
Puerto Miraña	01°20' S, 070°19' W
Puerto Tejada	03°14' N, 076°24' W
Quibdó	05°42' N, 076°40' W
Ráquira	05°33' N, 073°38' W
Ríohacha	11°33' N, 072°55' W
Sahagún	08°57' N, 075°27' W
San Felipe	01°52' N, 067°06' W
San Jacinto	09°50' N, 075°08' W
San José	03°15' N, 067°20' W
San José de Guaviare	02°35' N, 072°38' W
San Juan Nepomuceno	09°57' N, 075°05' W
San Martín	03°42' N, 073°42' W
San Pedro de Arimena	04°37' N, 071°42' W
Santa Marta	11°15' N, 074°13' W
Santa Rosa	03°32' N, 069°48' W
Santander	03°01' N, 076°28' W
Sincelejo	09°18' N, 075°24' W
Soacha	04°35' N, 074°13' W
Socorro	06°29' N, 073°16' W
Sogamoso	05°43' N, 072°56' W
Soledad	10°55' N, 074°46' W
Sonsón	05°42' N, 075°18' W
Tame	06°28' N, 071°44' W
Tuluá	04°06' N, 076°11' W
Turbaco	10°20' N, 075°25' W
Turbo	08°06' N, 076°43' W
Tumaco	01°49' N, 078°46' W
Tunja	05°31' N, 073°22' W
Uribia	11°43' N, 072°16' W
Urrao	06°20' N, 076°11' W
Valledupar	10°29' N, 073°15' W
Villa Rosario	07°50' N, 072°28' W
Villavicencio	04°09' N, 073°37' W
Yarumal	06°58' N, 075°24' W
Zipaquirá	05°02' N, 074°00' W

COMOROS .... pg. 153

Capital: ....Moroni
Area: ....1,862 sq km; 719 sq mi
Highest Elev.: ....Mt. Karthala 2,360 m; 7,750 ft
Avg. Temperature: .Jan = 19°C; Jul = 30°C
Currency: ......Comorian franc
Official Language: ..Comorian, Arabic, French

Name	Lat./Long.
Moroni	11°41' S, 043°16' E

CONGO, DEMOCRATIC REPUBLIC OF THE ....pg. 152

Capital: ....Kinshasa
Area: ....2,344,858 sq km; 905,354 sq mi
Highest Elev.: ...Margherita Pk. 5,120 m; 16,800 ft
Longest River: ..Congo 4,630 km; 2,880 mi
Avg. Temperature: .Jan = 27°C; Jul = 22°C
Currency: ......new zaïre
Official Language: .French

Name	Lat./Long.
Aketi	02°44' N, 023°46' E
Banana	06°01' S, 012°24' E
Bandundu	03°19' S, 017°22' E
Beni	00°30' N, 029°28' E
Boende	00°13' S, 020°52' E
Boma	05°51' S, 013°03' E

Name	Lat./Long.
Bukama	09°12' S, 025°51' E
Bukavu	02°30' S, 028°52' E
Bulungu	04°33' S, 018°36' E
Bumba	02°11' N, 022°28' E
Bunia	01°34' N, 030°15' E
Buta	02°48' N, 024°44' E
Butembo	00°09' N, 029°17' E
Dilolo	10°42' S, 022°20' E
Gandajika	06°45' S, 023°57' E
Gemena	03°15' N, 019°46' E
Ilebo	04°19' S, 020°35' E
Inga	05°39' S, 013°39' E
Isiro	02°46' N, 027°37' E
Kabinda	06°08' S, 024°29' E
Kalemi (Albertville)	05°56' S, 029°12' E
Kamina	08°44' S, 025°00' E
Kananga (Luluabourg)	05°54' S, 022°25' E
Kasongo	04°27' S, 026°40' E
Kikwit	05°02' S, 018°49' E
Kinshasa (Leopoldville)	04°18' S, 015°18' E
Kisangani (Stanleyville)	00°30' N, 025°12' E
Kolwezi	10°43' S, 025°28' E
Kongolo	05°23' S, 027°00' E
Kutu	02°44' S, 018°09' E
Likasi	10°59' S, 026°44' E
Lisala	02°09' N, 021°31' E
Lubumbashi (Elisabethville)	11°40' N, 027°28' E
Manono	07°18' S, 027°25' E
Masi-Manimba	04°46' S, 017°55' E
Mbandaka	00°04' N, 018°16' E
Mbanza-Ngungu	05°15' S, 014°52' E
Mbuji-Mayi	06°09' S, 023°36' E
Mobayi-Mbongo	04°18' N, 021°11' E
Mushie	03°01' S, 016°54' E
Mweka	04°51' S, 021°34' E
Mwene-Ditu	07°03' S, 023°27' E
Samba	04°38' S, 026°22' E
Tshikapa	06°25' S, 020°48' E
Ubundu	00°21' S, 025°29' E
Watsa	03°03' N, 029°32' E
Yangambi	00°47' N, 024°28' E
Zongo	04°21' N, 018°36' E

CONGO, REPUBLIC OF THE pg. 152

Capital: . . . . .Brazzaville
Area: . . . . . .342,000 sq km; 132,047 sq mi
Longest River: . . . .Congo 4,700 km; 2,900 mi
Avg. Temperature: . .Jan = 25°C; Jul = 25°C
Currency: . . . . .CFA franc
Official Language: . .French

Name	Lat./Long.
Brazzaville	04°16' S, 015°17' E
Djambala	02°33' S, 014°45' E
Gamboma	01°53' S, 015°51' E
Impfondo	01°37' N, 018°04' E
Kayes	04°25' S, 011°41' E
Loubomo	04°12' N, 012°41' E
Madingou	04°09' S, 013°34' E
Makabana	02°48' S, 012°29' E
Makoua	00°01' N, 015°39' E
Mossendjo	02°57' S, 012°44' E
Nkayi	04°11' S, 013°18' E
Ouesso	01°37' N, 016°04' E
Owando	00°29' S, 015°55' E
Pointe-Noire	04°48' S, 011°51' E
Sibiti	03°41' S, 013°21' E
Souanke	02°05' N, 014°03' E
Zanaga	02°15' S, 013°50' E

COSTA RICA . . . . .pg. 117

Capital: . . . . .San José
Area: . . . .51,100 sq km; 19,730 sq mi
Highest Elev.: . .Mt. Chirripó 3,820 m; 12,530 ft
Longest River: . . .San Juan 200 km; 120 mi
Avg. Temperature: . .Jan = 19°C; Jul = 21°C
Currency: . . . . . . .Costa Rican colón
Official Language: . .Spanish

Name	Lat./Long.
Alajuela	10°01' N, 084°13' W
Desamparados	09°54' N, 084°05' W
Puerto Limón (Limón)	10°00' N, 083°02' W
Puntarenas	09°58' N, 084°50' W
San José	09°56' N, 084°05' W

CÔTE D'IVOIRE . . . . . . .pg. 150

Capital: . . . . .Abidjan
Area: . .320,763 sq km; 123,847 sq mi
Highest Elev.: . . . .Mt. Nimba 1,750 m; 5,750 ft
Longest River: . . .Bandama 800 km; 500 mi
Avg. Temperature: . .Jan = 27°C; Jul = 26°C
Currency: . . . . . . .CFA franc
Official Language: . .French

Name	Lat./Long.
Abidjan	05°19' N, 004°02' W
Bouaké	07°41' N, 005°02' W
Daloa	06°53' N, 006°27' W
Gagnoa	06°08' N, 005°56' W
Man	07°24' N, 007°33' W
San-Pédro	04°44' N, 006°37' W
Yamoussoukro	06°49' N, 005°17' W

CROATIA . . . . .pg. 130

Capital: . . . . .Zagreb
Area: . . . .56,538 sq km; 21,829 sq mi
Highest Elev.: . . . .Mt. Troglav 1,910 m; 6,280 ft
Longest River: . . .Sava 940 km; 580 mi
Avg. Temperature: . .Jan = 0°C; Jul = 22°C
Currency: . . . . . . .kuna
Official Language: . .Croatian

Name	Lat./Long.
Karlovac	45°29' N, 015°33' E
Knin	44°02' N, 016°12' E
Nin	44°14' N, 015°11' E
Opatija	45°20' N, 014°19' E
Osijek	45°33' N, 018°42' E
Ploce	43°04' N, 017°26' E
Pozega (Slavonska Pozega)	45°20' N, 017°41' E
Pula	44°52' N, 013°50' E

Name	Lat./Long.
Rijeka	45°21' N, 014°24' E
Sisak	45°29' N, 016°22' E
Slavonski Brod	45°09' N, 018°02' E
Split	43°31' N, 016°26' E
Trogir	43°32' N, 016°15' E
Vukovar	45°21' N, 019°00' E
Zadar	44°07' N 015°15' E
Zagreb	45°48' S, 016°00' E

CUBA . . . . .pg. 116

Capital: . . . . .Havana
Area: . . . . . . .110,861 sq km; 42,804 sq mi
Highest Elev.: . . .Turquino Pk. 1,970 m; 6,480 ft
Longest River: . . . .Cauto 370 km; 230 mi
Avg. Temperature: . .Jan = 22°C; Jul = 28°C
Currency: . . . . . . .Cuban peso
Official Language: . .Spanish

Name	Lat./Long.
Banes	20°58' N, 075°43' W
Bayamo	20°23' N, 076°39' W
Camaguey	21°23' N, 077°55' W
Cárdenas	23°02' N, 081°12' W
Ciego de Avila	21°51' N, 078°46' W
Cienfuegos	22°09' N, 080°27' W
Colón	22°43' N, 080°54' W
Florida	21°32' N, 078°14' W
Güantánamo	20°08' N, 075°12' W
Guines	22°50' N, 082°02' W
Havana (La Habana)	23°08' N, 082°22' W
Holguín	20°53' N, 076°15' W
Jovellanos	22°48' N, 081°12' W
Las Tunas	20°58' N, 076°57' W
Manzanillo	20°21' N, 077°07' W
Matanzas	23°03' N, 081°35' W
Morón	22°06' N, 078°38' W
Palma Soriano	20°13' N, 076°00' W
Pinar del Rio	22°25' N, 083°42' W
Placetas	22°19' N, 079°40' W
Sagua la Grande	22°49' N, 080°05' W
San Antonio de los Baños	22°53' N, 082°30' W
Sancti Spíritus	21°56' N, 079°27' W
Santa Clara	22°24' N, 079°58' W
Santiago de Cuba	20°01' N, 075°49' W

CYPRUS . . . . .pg. 147

Capital: . . . . .Nicosia
Area: . . . . . . .9,251 sq km; 3,572 sq mi
Highest Elev.: . . . .Mt. Olympus 1,950 m; 6,400 ft
Longest River: . . . .Pedieos 100 km; 60 mi
Avg. Temperature: . .Jan = 10°C; Jul = 28°C
Currency: . . . . . . .Cyprus pound
Official Language: . .Greek, Turkish

Name	Lat./Long.
Larnaca	34°55' N, 033°38' E
Limassol	34°40' N, 033°02' E
Nicosia	35°10' N, 033°22' E

CZECH REPUBLIC . . . . .pg. 133

Capital: . . . . .Prague
Area: . . . . . . .78,864 sq km; 30,450 sq mi
Highest Elev.: . . . .Mt. Snezka 1,600 m; 5,260 ft
Longest River: . . . .Elbe 1,160 km; 720 mi
Avg. Temperature: . .Jan = -1.5°C; Jul = 19.4°C
Currency: . . . . . . .Czech koruna
Official Language: . .Czech

Name	Lat./Long.
Brno	49°12' N, 016°38' E
Ceská Lípa	50°41' N, 014°33' E
Ceské Budejovice	48°59' N, 014°28' E
Cesky Tesin	49°45' N, 018°37' E
Cheb	50°04' N, 012°22' E
Chomutov	50°27' N, 013°26' E
Decin	50°47' N, 014°13' E
Frydek-Mistek	49°41' N, 018°21' E
Havírov	49°47' N, 018°22' E
Hodonín	48°52' N, 017°08' E
Hradec Králové	50°13' N, 015°50' E
Jablonec	50°43' N, 015°11' E
Jihlava	49°24' N, 015°35' E
Karlovy Vary	50°13' N, 012°54' E
Karvina	49°52' N, 018°33' E
Kladno	50°09' N, 014°06' E
Kolín	50°02' N, 015°12' E
Kromeríz	49°18' N, 017°24' E
Liberec	50°47' N, 015°03' E
Litvinov	50°36' N, 013°37' E
Mladá Boleslav	50°25' N, 014°54' E
Most	50°32' N, 013°39' E
Novy Jicín	49°36' N, 018°01' E
Olomouc	49°35' N, 017°15' E
Opava	49°57' N, 017°55' E
Orlova	49°51' N, 018°25' E
Ostrava	49°50' N, 018°17' E
Písek	49°18' N, 014°09' E
Plzen	49°45' N, 013°22' E
Prague (Praha)	50°05' N, 014°28' E
Pribram	49°42' N, 014°01' E
Prostejov	49°28' N, 017°07' E
Sumperk	49°58' N, 016°58' E
Tábor	49°25' N, 014°40' E
Teplice	50°38' N, 013°50' E
Trebic	49°13' N, 015°53' E
Trinec	49°41' N, 018°39' E
Trutnov	50°34' N, 015°54' E
Ústí nad Labem	50°40' N, 014°02' E
Valasské Mezirící	49°28' N, 017°58' E
Vsetín	49°20' N, 018°00' E
Znojmo	48°51' N, 016°03' E

DENMARK . . . . .pg. 131

Capital: . . . . .Copenhagen
Area: . . . . . . .43,094 sq km; 16,639 sq mi
Highest Elev.: . . . .Yding Forest Hill 170 m; 570 ft
Longest River: . . . .Gudena 160 km; 100 mi
Avg. Temperature: . .Jan = 0°C; Jul = 18°C
Currency: . . . . . . .Danish krone
Official Language: . .Danish

Name	Lat./Long.
Alborg (Aalborg)	57°03' N, 009°56' E
Arhus (Aarhus)	56°09' N, 010°13' E

Name	Lat./Long.
Copenhagen (Kobenhavn)	55°40' N, 012°35' E
Esbjerg	55°28' N, 008°27' E
Fredericia	55°35' N, 009°46' E
Frederiksberg	55°41' N, 012°32' E
Helsingor	56°02' N, 012°37' E
Horsens	55°52' N, 009°52' E
Kolding	55°29' N, 009°29' E
Odense	55°24' N, 010°23' E
Randers	56°28' N, 010°03' E
Ronne	55°06' N, 014°42' E
Roskilde	55°39' N, 012°05' E
Vejle	55°42' N, 009°32' E

DJIBOUTI . . . . .pg. 151

Capital: . . . . .Djibouti
Area: . . . . .23,200 sq km; 8,950 sq mi
Highest Elev.: . . . .Mt. Mousa 2,060 m; 6,770 ft
Avg. Temperature: . .Jan = 25°C; Jul = 36°C
Currency: . . . . . . .Djibouti franc
Official Language: . .Arabic, French

Name	Lat./Long.
Djibouti	11°36' N, 043°09' E

DOMINICA . . . . .pg. 116

Capital: . . . . .Roseau
Area: . . . . . .750 sq km; 290 sq mi
Highest Elev.: . . .Mt. Diablotin 1,450 m; 4,750 ft
Avg. Temperature: . .Jan = 27°C; Jul = 32°C
Currency: . . . . . . .East Caribbean dollar
Official Language: . .English

Name	Lat./Long.
Marigot	15°32' N, 061°18' W
Portsmouth	15°35' N, 061°28' W
Roseau	15°18' N, 061°24' W

DOMINICAN REP. . . . . . .pg. 116

Capital: . . . . .Santo Domingo
Area: . . . .48,443sq km; 18,704 sq mi
Highest Elev.: . . . .Duarta Pk. 3,180 m; 10,420 ft
Longest River: . . .Yaque del Norte 390 km; 240 mi
Avg. Temperature: . .Jan = 24°C; Jul = 27°C
Currency: . . . . . . .Dominican peso
Official Language: . .Spanish

Name	Lat./Long.
Barahona	18°12' N, 071°06' W
La Romana	18°25' N, 068°58' W
La Vega	19°13' N, 070°31' W
Mao	19°34' N, 071°05' W
Puerto Plata	19°48' N, 070°41' W
San Cristóbal	18°25' N, 070°06' W
San Francisco De Macorís	19°18' N, 070°15' W
San Juan	18°48' N, 071°14' W
San Pedro De Macoris	18°27' N, 069°18' W
Santiago	19°27' N, 070°42' W
Santo Domingo	18°28' N, 069°54' W

ECUADOR . . . . .pg. 123

Capital: . . . . .Quito
Area: . . .272,045 sq km; 105,037 sq mi
Highest Elev.: . . . .Chimborazo 6,310 m; 20,700 ft
Longest River: . . . .Napo 890 km; 550 mi
Avg. Temperature: . .Jan = 13°C; Jul = 13°C
Currency: . . . . . . .Sucre
Official Language: . .Spanish

Name	Lat./Long.
Ambato	01°15' S, 078°37' W
Babahoyo	01°49' S, 079°31' W
Bahia de Caraquez	00°36' S, 080°25' W
Catacocha	04°04' S, 079°38' W
Celica	04°07' S, 079°57' W
Chone	00°41' S, 080°06' W
Cuenca	02°53' S, 078°59' W
Daule	01°52' S, 079°58' W
Esmeraldas	00°59' N, 079°42' W
General Leonidas Plaza Gutierrez	02°58' S, 078°25' W
Gualaquiza	03°24' S, 078°33' W
Guaranda	01°36' S, 079°00' W
Guayaquil	02°10' S, 079°54' W
Ibarra	00°21' N, 078°07' W
Jipijapa	01°20' S, 080°35' W
Lago Agrio (Nueva Loja)	00°06' N, 076°52' W
Latacunga	00°56' S, 078°37' W
Loja	04°00' S, 079°13' W
Macas	02°19' S, 078°07' W
Machala	03°16' S, 079°58' W
Manta	00°57' S, 080°44' W
Milagro	02°07' S, 079°36' W
Montecristi	01°03' S, 080°40' W
Naranjal	02°40' S, 079°37' W
Pasaje	03°20' S, 079°49' W
Portoviejo	01°03' S, 080°27' W
Puerto Francisco de Orellana (Coca)	00°28' S, 076°58' W
Puyo	01°28' S, 077°59' W
Quevedo	01°02' S, 079°29' W
Quito	00°13' S, 078°30' W
Riobamba	01°40' S, 078°38' W
Rosa Zarate	00°20' N, 079°28' W
Samborondon	01°57' S, 079°44' W
San Gabriel	00°36' N, 077°49' W
San Lorenzo	01°17' N, 078°50' W
Sangolqui	00°19' S, 078°27' W
San Miguel de Salcedo (San Miguel)	01°02' S, 078°34' W
Santa Elena	02°14' S, 080°51' W
Santa Isabel	03°16' S, 079°19' W
Santa Rosa	03°27' S, 079°58' W
Santo Domingo de los Colorados (Santo Domingo)	00°15' S, 079°09' W
Sucre	01°16' S, 080°26' W
Sucua	02°28' S, 078°10' W
Tena	00°59' S, 077°49' W
Tulcan	00°48' N, 077°43' W
Valdez	01°15' N, 079°00' W
Yantanza	03°51' S, 078°45' W
Zamora	04°04' S, 078°58' W
Zaruma	03°41' S, 079°37' W

EGYPT . . . . .pg. 151

Capital: . . . . .Cairo
Area: . . . . .997,739 sq km; 385,229 sq mi
Highest Elev.: . . .Mt. Catherine 2,640 m; 8,670 ft
Longest River: . . . .Nile 6,650 km; 4,130 mi
Avg. Temperature: . .Jan = 13°C; Jul = 28°C
Currency: . . . . . . .Egyptian pound
Official Language: . .Arabic

Name	Lat./Long.
Al-Fayyum	29°19' N, 030°50' E
Al-Jizah	30°01' N, 031°13' E
Al-Minya	28°06' N, 030°45' E
Akhmim	26°34' N, 031°44' E
Alexandria (al-Iskandariyah)	31°12' N, 029°54' E
Aswan	24°05' N, 032°53' E
Asyut	27°11' N, 031°11' E
Az-Zaqaziq	30°35' N, 031°31' E
Banha	30°28' N, 031°11' E
Bani Suwayf	29°05' N, 031°05' E
Bur Sa'id, see Port Said	
Cairo (Al-Qahirah)	30°03' N, 031°15' E
Damanhur	31°02' N, 030°28' E
Jirja	26°20' N, 031°53' E
Luxor (al-Uqsur)	25°41' N, 032°39' E
Mallawi	27°44' N, 030°50' E
Marsa Matruh	31°21' N, 027°14' E
Port Said (Bur Sa'id)	31°16' N, 032°18' E
Qina	26°10' N, 032°43' E
Sawhaj	26°33' N, 031°42' E
Shibin al-Kawm	30°33' N, 031°01' E
Suez (as-Suways)	29°58' N, 032°33' E
Tanta	30°47' N, 031°00' E

EL SALVADOR . . . . .pg. 117

Capital: . . . . .San Salvador
Area: . . . .21,041 sq km; 8,124 sq mi
Highest Elev.: . . .Santa Ana Volc. 2,360 m; 7,750 ft
Longest River: . . .Lempa 320 km; 200 mi
Avg. Temperature: . .Jan = 22°C; Jul = 23°C
Currency: . . . . . . .colón
Official Language: . .Spanish

Name	Lat./Long.
San Miguel	13°29' N, 088°11' W
San Salvador	13°42' N, 089°12' W

EQUATORIAL GUINEA .pg. 152

Capital: . . . . .Malabo
Area: . . . .28,051 sq km; 10,831 sq mi
Highest Elev.: . . .Mt. Santa Isabel 3,010 m; 9,880 ft
Longest River: . . .Benito 3200 km; 200 mi
Avg. Temperature: . .Jan = 25°C; Jul = 24°C
Currency: . . . . . . .CFA franc
Official Language: . .Spanish

Name	Lat./Long.
Malabo (Santa Isabel)	03°21' N, 008°40' E

ERITREA . . . . .pg. 151

Capital: . . . . .Asmara
Area: . . . .117,400 sq km; 45,300 sq mi
Highest Elev.: . . . .Mt. Soira 3,010 m; 9,890 ft
Avg. Temperature: . .Jan = 21.1°C; Jul = 25.6°C
Currency: . . . . . . .Ethiopian birr
Official Language: . .Tigrinya, Arabic

Name	Lat./Long.
Asmara	15°20' N, 038°56' E
Mitsiwa (Massawa)	15°36' N, 039°28' E

ESTONIA . . . . .pg. 138

Capital: . . . . .Tallinn
Area: . . . .45,227 sq km; 17,462 sq mi
Highest Elev.: . . . .Suur Munamägi 320 m; 1,040 ft
Longest River: . . . .Pärnu 140 km; 90 mi
Avg. Temperature: . .Jan = -6°C; Jul = 17°C
Currency: . . . . . . .kroon
Official Language: . .Estonian

Name	Lat./Long.
Jõgeva	58°45' N, 026°24' E
Kehra	59°20' N, 025°20' E
Kilingi-Nõmme	58°09' N, 024°58' E
Kohtla-Järve	59°24' N, 027°15' E
Kuressaare (Kingisepa)	58°15' N, 022°28' E
Lihula (Lihula)	58°41' N, 023°50' E
Marjamaa	58°54' N, 024°26' E
Mustla	58°14' N, 025°52' E
Narva	59°23' N, 028°12' E
Nuia	58°06' N, 025°33' E
Otepaa	58°03' N, 026°30' E
Paldiski	59°20' N, 024°06' E
Paide	58°54' N, 025°33' E
Pärnu	58°24' N, 024°32' E
Parnu-Jaagupi	58°37' N, 024°30' E
Rapla	59°01' N, 024°47' E
Rapina	58°06' N, 027°27' E
Saue	59°18' N, 024°34' E
Tallinn	59°25' N, 024°45' E
Tamsalu	59°10' N, 026°06' E
Tapa	59°16' N, 025°58' E
Tartu	58°23' N, 026°43' E
Voru	57°50' N, 027°03' E

ETHIOPIA . . . . .pg. 151

Capital: . . . . .Addis Ababa
Area: . . . . . . .1,133,882 sq km; 437,794 sq mi
Highest Elev.: . . .Mt. Ras Dejen 4,620 m; 15,160 ft
Avg. Temperature: . .Jan = 16°C; Jul = 15°C
Currency: . . . . . . .Ethiopian birr
Official Language: . .Amharic

Name	Lat./Long.
Addis Ababa (Adis Abeba)	09°02' N, 038°42' E
Bahir Dar	11°36' N, 037°23' E
Debre Zeyit	08°45' N, 038°59' E
Dese (Dase)	11°08' N, 039°38' E

Name	Lat./Long.
Dire Dawa	09°35' N, 041°52' E
Gonder	12°36' N, 037°28' E
Harer (Harar)	09°19' N, 042°07' E
Jima (Jimma)	07°40' N, 036°50' E
Mekele	13°30' N, 039°28' E
Nazret	08°33' N, 039°16' E

FIJI ... pg. 156

Capital: Suva
Area: 18,274 sq km; 7,056 sq mi
Highest Elev.: Mt. Tomaniivi 1,320 m; 4,340 ft
Longest River: Rewa 150 km; 95 mi
Avg. Temperature: Jan = 27°C; Jul = 24°C
Currency: Fiji dollar
Official Language: English

Name	Lat./Long.
Lautoka	17°37' S, 177°28' E
Suva	18°08' S, 178°25' E

FINLAND ... pg. 131

Capital: Helsinki
Area: 338,145 sq km; 130,559 sq mi
Highest Elev.: Mt. Haltia 1,330 m; 4,360 ft
Longest River: Kemi 550 km; 340 mi
Avg. Temperature: Jan = -6°C; Jul = 17°C
Currency: markka
Official Language: Finnish, Swedish

Name	Lat./Long.
Espoo (Esbo)	60°13' N, 024°40' E
Forssa	60°49' N, 023°38' E
Hameenlinna (Tavastehus)	61°00' N, 024°27' E
Hanko	59°50' N, 022°57' E
Heinola	61°13' N, 026°02' E
Helsinki	60°10' N, 024°58' E
Ivalo	68°39' N, 027°36' E
Joensuu	62°36' N, 029°46' E
Jyväskylä	62°14' N, 025°44' E
Kangasala	61°28' N, 024°05' E
Kotka	60°28' N, 026°55' E
Kouvola	60°52' N, 026°42' E
Kuhmo	64°08' N, 029°31' E
Kuopio	62°54' N, 027°41' E
Lahti	60°58' N, 025°40' E
Lappeenranta (Villmanstrand)	61°04' N, 028°11' E
Lapua	62°57' N, 023°00' E
Lohja	60°15' N, 024°05' E
Mikkeli (Sankt Michel)	61°41' N, 027°15' E
Nivala	63°55' N, 024°58' E
Nurmes	63°33' N, 029°07' E
Oulu (Uleåborg)	65°01' N, 025°28' E
Pello	66°47' N, 023°55' E
Pori (Björneborg)	61°29' N, 021°47' E
Posio	66°06' N, 028°09' E
Raahe	64°41' N, 024°29' E
Rauma	61°08' N, 021°30' E
Salla	66°50' N, 028°40' E
Salo	60°23' N, 023°08' E
Sotkamo	64°08' N, 028°25' E
Tampere (Tammerfors)	61°30' N, 023°45' E
Turku (Åbo)	60°27' N, 022°17' E
Vaasa (Vasa)	63°06' N, 021°36' E
Vantaa (Vanda)	60°18' N, 024°51' E

FRANCE ... pg. 129

Capital: Paris
Area: 543,965 sq km; 210,026 sq mi
Highest Elev.: Mont Blanc 4,810 m; 15,770 ft
Longest River: Loire 1,020 km; 630 mi
Avg. Temperature: Jan = 19°C; Jul = 27°C
Currency: franc
Official Language: French

Name	Lat./Long.
Abbeville	50°06' N, 001°50' E
Agde	43°19' N, 003°28' E
Agen	44°12' N, 000°38' E
Aigues-Mortes	43°34' N, 004°11' E
Aire-sur-la-Lys	50°38' N, 002°24' E
Aix-en-Provence	43°32' N, 005°26' E
Aix-les-Bains	45°42' N, 005°55' E
Ajaccio	41°55' N, 008°44' E
Albi	43°56' N, 002°09' E
Alençon	48°26' N, 000°05' E
Aleria	42°06' N, 009°31' E
Alès	44°08' N, 004°05' E
Amboise	47°25' N, 000°59' E
Amiens	49°54' N, 002°18' E
Angers	47°28' N, 000°33' W
Angoulême	45°39' N, 000°09' E
Annecy	45°54' N, 006°07' E
Annemasse	46°12' N, 006°15' E
Antibes	43°35' N, 007°07' E
Arles	43°40' N, 004°38' E
Armentières	50°41' N, 002°53' E
Arras	50°17' N, 002°47' E
Aubagne	43°17' N, 005°34' E
Aubusson	45°57' N, 002°10' E
Auch	43°39' N, 000°35' E
Auray	47°40' N, 002°59' W
Aurillac	44°55' N, 002°27' E
Autun	46°57' N, 004°18' E
Auxerre	47°48' N, 003°34' E
Avignon	43°57' N, 004°49' E
Avranches	48°41' N, 001°22' W
Azay-le-Rideau	47°16' N, 000°28' E
Bar-le-Duc	48°47' N, 005°10' E
Bastia	42°42' N, 009°27' E
Bayeux	49°16' N, 000°42' W
Bayonne	43°29' N, 001°29' W
Beaucaire	43°48' N, 004°38' E
Beaugency	47°47' N, 001°38' E
Beaune	47°02' N, 004°50' E
Beauvais	49°26' N, 002°05' E
Belfort	47°38' N, 006°52' E
Bergerac	44°51' N, 000°29' E
Besançon	47°15' N, 006°02' E
Béthune	50°32' N, 002°38' E
Béziers	43°21' N, 003°15' E
Biarritz	43°29' N, 001°34' W
Blanzy	46°42' N, 004°23' E
Blois	47°35' N, 001°20' E
Bobigny	48°54' N, 002°27' E
Bonifacio	41°23' N, 009°09' E
Bonneville	46°05' N, 006°25' E
Bordeaux	44°50' N, 000°34' W
Boulogne-Billancourt	48°50' N, 002°15' E
Boulogne-sur-Mer	50°43' N, 001°37' E
Bourg-en-Bresse	46°12' N, 005°13' E
Bourges	47°05' N, 002°24' E
Bourgoin	45°35' N, 005°17' E
Brest	48°24' N, 004°29' W
Briançon	44°54' N, 006°39' E
Brive-la-Gaillarde	45°09' N, 001°32' E
Caen	49°11' N, 000°21' W
Cahors	44°26' N, 001°26' E
Calais	50°57' N, 001°50' E
Calvi	42°34' N, 008°45' E
Cambrai	50°10' N, 003°14' E
Cannes	43°33' N, 007°01' E
Carcassonne	43°13' N, 002°21' E
Carnac	47°35' N, 003°05' W
Carpentras	44°03' N, 005°03' E
Castres	43°36' N, 002°15' E
Cenon	44°51' N, 000°32' W
Chalon-sur-Saône	46°47' N, 004°51' E
Châlons-Sur-Marne	48°57' N, 004°22' E
Chambéry	45°34' N, 005°56' E
Chambord	47°37' N, 001°31' E
Chamonix-Mont-Blanc	45°55' N, 006°52' E
Chantilly	49°12' N, 002°28' E
Charleville-Mézières	49°46' N, 004°43' E
Chartres	48°27' N, 001°30' E
Châteauroux	46°49' N, 001°42' E
Châteaux-Thierry	49°03' N, 003°24' E
Châtellerault	46°48' N, 000°32' E
Chaumont	48°07' N, 005°08' E
Chenonceaux	47°20' N, 001°04' E
Cherbourg	49°39' N, 001°39' W
Chinon	47°10' N, 000°15' E
Cholet	47°04' N, 000°53' W
Clairvaux	48°09' N, 004°47' E
Clermont-Ferrand	45°47' N, 003°05' E
Cluny	46°26' N, 004°39' E
Cognac	45°42' N, 000°20' W
Colmar	48°05' N, 007°22' E
Colomiers	43°37' N, 001°21' E
Compiègne	49°25' N, 002°50' E
Concarneau	47°52' N, 003°55' W
Corbeil-Essonnes	48°36' N, 002°29' E
Corte	42°18' N, 009°09' E
Coucy-Auffrique	49°31' N, 003°19' E
Coutances	49°03' N, 001°26' W
Creil	49°16' N, 002°29' E
Crèteil	48°47' N, 002°28' E
Croix	50°40' N, 003°09' E
Dax	43°43' N, 001°03' W
Decazeville	44°33' N, 002°15' E
Dieppe	49°56' N, 001°05' E
Digne	44°06' N, 006°14' E
Dijon	47°19' N, 005°01' E
Dinan	48°27' N, 002°02' W
Dole	47°06' N, 005°30' E
Douai	50°22' N, 003°04' E
Douarnenez	48°06' N, 004°20' W
Draguignan	43°32' N, 006°28' E
Dreux	48°44' N, 001°22' E
Dunkirk (Dunkerque)	51°03' N, 002°22' E
Eauze	43°52' N, 000°06' E
Falaise	48°54' N, 000°12' W
Fécamp	49°45' N, 000°22' E
Firminy	45°23' N, 004°18' E
Foix	42°58' N, 001°36' E
Fontaine	45°11' N, 005°40' E
Fontainebleau	48°24' N, 002°42' E
Fontenay-le-Comte	46°28' N, 000°49' W
Fontevrault	47°11' N, 000°03' E
Forbach	49°11' N, 006°54' E
Fougères	48°21' N, 001°12' W
Fréjus	43°26' N, 006°44' E
Gap	44°34' N, 006°05' E
Gavarnie	42°44' N, 000°00' E
Gisors	49°17' N, 001°47' E
Granville	48°50' N, 001°36' W
Grasse	43°40' N, 006°55' E
Gravelines	50°59' N, 002°07' E
Grenoble	45°10' N, 005°43' E
Guéret	46°10' N, 001°52' E
Guingamp	48°33' N, 003°09' W
Haguenau	48°49' N, 007°47' E
Herouville	49°12' N, 000°19' W
Hesdin	50°22' N, 002°02' E
Honfleur	49°25' N, 000°14' E
Hyères	43°07' N, 006°07' E
Istres	43°31' N, 004°59' E
Joué-lès-Tours	47°21' N, 000°40' E
Kaysersberg	48°08' N, 007°15' E
La Baule-Escoublac	47°17' N, 002°24' W
La Ciotat	43°10' N, 005°36' E
La Roche-sur-Yon	46°40' N, 001°26' W
La Rochelle	46°10' N, 001°09' W
La Seyne-sur-Mer	43°06' N, 005°53' E
Lacq	43°25' N, 000°38' W
Lanester	47°45' N, 003°21' W
Langres	47°52' N, 005°20' E
Laon	49°34' N, 003°37' E
Laval	48°04' N, 000°46' W
Le Cannet	43°34' N, 007°01' E
Le Creusot	46°48' N, 004°26' E
Le Croisic	47°18' N, 002°31' W
Le Havre	49°30' N, 000°08' E
Le Mans	48°00' N, 000°12' E
Le Petit Quevilly	49°26' N, 001°02' E
Le Puy	45°02' N, 003°53' E
Lens	50°26' N, 002°50' E
Les Baux-de-Provence	43°45' N, 004°48' E
Lescar	43°20' N, 000°25' W
Libourne	44°55' N, 000°14' W
Liévin	50°25' N, 002°46' E
Lille	50°38' N, 003°04' E
Lillebonne	49°31' N, 000°33' E
Lillers	50°34' N, 002°29' E
Limoges	45°45' N, 001°20' E
Lisieux	49°09' N, 000°14' E
Loches	47°08' N, 001°00' E
Locmariaquer	47°34' N, 002°57' W
Longwy	49°31' N, 005°46' E
Lons-le-Saunier	46°40' N, 005°33' E
Lorient	47°45' N, 003°22' W
Loudun	47°00' N, 000°04' E
Lourdes	43°06' N, 000°03' W
Luçon	46°27' N, 001°10' W
Lunéville	48°36' N, 006°30' E
Lyon	45°45' N, 004°51' E
Mâcon	46°18' N, 004°50' E
Maillezais	46°22' N, 000°44' W
Marignane	43°25' N, 005°13' E
Marseille	43°18' N, 005°24' E
Martigues	43°24' N, 005°03' E
Maubeuge	50°17' N, 003°58' E
Meaux	48°57' N, 002°52' E
Melun	48°32' N, 002°40' E
Mende	44°31' N, 003°30' E
Menton	43°47' N, 007°30' E
Metz	49°08' N, 006°10' E
Millau	44°06' N, 003°05' E
Mirebeau	46°47' N, 000°11' E
Mont-de-Marsan	43°53' N, 000°30' W
Montauban	44°01' N, 001°21' E
Montbéliard	47°31' N, 006°48' E
Montceau	46°40' N, 004°22' E
Montdidier	49°39' N, 002°34' E
Montélimar	44°34' N, 004°45' E
Montigny	49°06' N, 006°09' E
Montluçon	46°20' N, 002°36' E
Montpellier	43°36' N, 003°53' E
Morlaix	48°35' N, 003°50' W
Moulins	46°34' N, 003°20' E
Mulhouse	47°45' N, 007°20' E
Munster	48°03' N, 007°08' E
Nancy	48°41' N, 006°12' E
Nanterre	48°54' N, 002°12' E
Nantes	47°13' N, 001°33' W
Narbonne	43°11' N, 003°00' E
Nemours	48°16' N, 002°42' E
Nevers	46°59' N, 003°10' E
Nice	43°42' N, 007°15' E
Nîmes	43°50' N, 004°21' E
Niort	46°19' N, 000°28' W
Noirmoutier	47°00' N, 002°15' W
Noyon	49°35' N, 003°00' E
Obernai	48°28' N, 007°29' E
Oradour-sur-Glane	45°56' N, 001°02' E
Orange	44°08' N, 004°48' E
Orléans	47°55' N, 001°54' E
Oyonnax	46°15' N, 005°40' E
Paimpol	48°46' N, 003°03' W
Paris	48°52' N, 002°20' E
Parthenay	46°39' N, 000°15' W
Pau	43°18' N, 000°22' W
Périgueux	45°11' N, 000°43' E
Péronne	49°56' N, 002°56' E
Perpignan	42°41' N, 002°53' E
Pessac	44°48' N, 000°37' W
Poitiers	46°35' N, 000°20' E
Pontoise	49°03' N, 002°06' E
Porto-Vecchio	41°35' N, 009°17' E
Privas	44°44' N, 004°36' E
Provins	48°33' N, 003°18' E
Quimper	48°00' N, 004°06' W
Rambouillet	48°39' N, 001°50' E
Reims	49°15' N, 004°02' E
Remiremont	48°01' N, 006°35' E
Rennes	48°05' N, 001°41' W
Rezé	47°12' N, 001°34' W
Ribeauvillé	48°12' N, 007°19' E
Richelieu	47°01' N, 000°19' E
Riom	45°54' N, 003°07' E
Roanne	46°02' N, 004°04' E
Rochefort	45°56' N, 000°59' W
Rocroi	49°55' N, 004°31' E
Rodez	44°20' N, 002°34' E
Romans-sur-Isère	45°03' N, 005°03' E
Rosheim	48°30' N, 007°28' E
Roubaix	50°42' N, 003°10' E
Rouen	49°26' N, 001°05' E
Saint-Affrique	43°57' N, 002°53' E
Saint-Amand-les-Eaux	50°26' N, 003°26' E
Saint-Amand-Montrond	46°43' N, 002°31' E
Saint-Benoît-sur-Loire	47°49' N, 002°18' E
Saint-Brieuc	48°31' N, 002°47' W
Saint-Chamond	45°28' N, 004°30' E
Saint-Denis	48°56' N, 002°22' E
Saint-Dié	48°17' N, 006°57' E
Saint-Étienne	45°26' N, 004°24' E
Saint-Jean-de-Luz	43°23' N, 001°40' W
Saint-Lô	49°07' N, 001°05' W
Saint-Malo	48°39' N, 002°01' W
Saint-Maur-des-Fossés	48°48' N, 002°30' E
Saint-Mihiel	48°54' N, 005°33' E
Saint-Nazaire	47°17' N, 002°12' W
Saint-Omer	50°45' N, 002°15' E
Saint-Pol	51°02' N, 002°21' E
Saint-Priest	45°42' N, 004°57' E
Saint-Quentin	49°51' N, 003°17' E
Saint-Raphaël	43°25' N, 006°46' E
Saint-Tropez	43°16' N, 006°38' E
Saintes	45°45' N, 000°38' W
Saintes-Maries-de-la-Mer	43°27' N, 004°26' E
Salon-de-Provence	43°38' N, 005°06' E
Sancerre	47°20' N, 002°50' E
Sarreguemines	49°06' N, 007°03' E
Sartène	41°37' N, 008°59' E
Saumur	47°16' N, 000°05' W
Sedan	49°42' N, 004°57' E
Sélestat	48°16' N, 007°27' E
Senlis	49°12' N, 002°35' E
Sens	48°12' N, 003°17' E
Sète	43°24' N, 003°41' E
Soissons	49°22' N, 003°20' E
Strasbourg	48°35' N, 007°45' E
Talence	44°49' N, 000°36' W
Tarascon	43°48' N, 004°40' E
Tarbes	43°14' N, 000°05' E
Thionville	49°22' N, 006°10' E
Thonon-les-Bains	46°22' N, 006°29' E
Thouars	46°58' N, 000°13' W
Tignes	45°30' N, 006°55' E
Toul	48°41' N, 005°54' E
Toulon	43°07' N, 005°56' E
Toulouse	43°36' N, 001°26' E
Tourcoing	50°43' N, 003°09' E
Tours	47°23' N, 000°41' E
Trouville	49°22' N, 000°05' E
Troyes	48°18' N, 004°05' E
Tulle	45°16' N, 001°46' E
Valence	44°56' N, 004°54' E
Valenciennes	50°21' N, 003°32' E
Vandoeuvre	48°39' N, 006°11' E
Vannes	47°40' N, 002°45' W
Vaulx-en-Velin	45°47' N, 004°56' E
Vendôme	47°48' N, 001°04' E
Vénissieux	45°41' N, 004°53' E
Verdun	49°10' N, 005°23' E
Vernon	49°05' N, 001°29' E
Versailles	48°48' N, 002°08' E
Vesoul	47°38' N, 006°10' E
Vézelay	47°28' N, 003°44' E
Vichy	46°07' N, 003°25' E
Vienne	45°31' N, 004°52' E
Vierzon	47°13' N, 002°05' E
Villefranche-sur-Mer	43°42' N, 007°19' E
Villefranche-sur-Saône	45°59' N, 004°43' E
Villeneuve-sur-Lot	44°24' N, 000°42' E
Villeurbanne	45°46' N, 004°53' E
Vouillé	46°38' N, 000°10' E
Wattrelos	50°42' N, 003°13' E
Wissembourg	49°02' N, 007°57' E

GABON ... pg. 152

Capital: Libreville
Area: 267,667 sq km; 103,347 sq mi
Highest Elev.: Mt. Iboundji 980 m; 3,220 ft
Longest River: Ogooué 1,200 km; 750 mi
Avg. Temperature: Jan = 27°C; Jul = 24°C
Currency: CFA franc
Official Language: French

Name	Lat./Long.
Bitam	02°05' N, 011°29' E
Booué	00°06' S, 011°56' E
Fougamou	01°13' S, 010°36' E
Franceville	01°38' N, 013°35' E
Kango	00°09' S, 010°08' E
Lambaréné	00°42' S, 010°13' E
Lastoursville	00°49' S, 012°42' E
Libreville	00°23' S, 009°27' E
Makokou	00°34' N, 012°52' E
Mayumba	03°25' S, 010°39' E
Mekambo	01°01' N, 013°56' E
Minvoul	02°09' S, 012°08' E
Mitzic	00°47' N, 011°34' E
Mouila	01°52' S, 011°01' E
Ndjolé	00°11' S, 010°45' E
Okondja	00°41' S, 013°47' E
Omboue	01°34' S, 009°15' E
Oyem	01°37' N, 011°35' E
Port-Gentil	00°43' S, 008°47' E
Setté Cama	02°32' S, 009°45' E
Tchibanga	02°51' S, 011°02' E

GAMBIA, THE ... pg. 150

Capital: Banjul
Area: 10,689sq km; 4,127 sq mi
Longest River: Gambia 1,130 km; 700 mi
Avg. Temperature: Jan = 23°C; Jul = 28°C
Currency: dalasi
Official Language: English

Name	Lat./Long.
Banjul	13°27' N, 016°35' W

GEORGIA ... pg. 147

Capital: Tbilisi
Area: 69,700 sq km; 26,900 sq mi
Highest Elev.: Mt. Shkhara 5,070 m; 16,630 ft
Longest River: Kura 1,360 km; 850 mi
Avg. Temperature: Jan = 0°C; Jul = 39°C
Currency: Georgian coupon
Official Language: Georgian

Name	Lat./Long.
Batumi	41°38' N, 041°38' E
Gori	41°58' N, 044°07' E
Kutaisi	42°15' N, 042°40' E
Poti	42°09' N, 041°40' E
Sokhumi	43°00' N, 041°02' E
Tbilisi (Tiflis)	41°42' N, 044°45' E
Zugdidi	42°30' N, 041°53' E

GERMANY ... pg. 132

Capital: Berlin
Area: 356,733 sq km; 137,735sq mi
Highest Elev.: Zugspitze 2,960 m; 9,720 ft
Longest River: Rhine 1,390 km; 870 mi
Avg. Temperature: Jan = -0.5°C; Jul = 17.4°C
Currency: Deutsche mark
Official Language: German

Name	Lat./Long.
Aachen	50°46' N, 006°06' E
Aalen	48°50' N, 010°06' E
Ahlen	51°45' N, 007°55' E
Altenburg	50°59' N, 012°27' E
Amberg	49°27' N, 011°52' E
Amorbach	49°39' N, 009°14' E
Andernach	50°26' N, 007°24' E
Ansbach	49°18' N, 010°35' E
Apolda	51°01' N, 011°30' E
Arnsberg	51°23' N, 008°05' E
Arnstadt	50°50' N, 010°57' E
Aschaffenburg	49°59' N, 009°09' E
Aschersleben	51°45' N, 011°28' E
Aue	50°35' N, 012°42' E
Augsburg	48°22' N, 010°53' E
Aurich	53°28' N, 007°29' E
Bad Harzburg	51°53' N, 010°34' E
Bad Hersfeld	50°52' N, 009°42' E
Bad Homburg	50°13' N, 008°37' E
Bad Kissingen	50°12' N, 010°05' E
Bad Kreuznach	49°50' N, 007°52' E

Name	Lat./Long.
Bad Mergentheim	49°29' N, 009°46' E
Bad Salzuflen	52°05' N, 008°46' E
Baden-Baden	48°45' N, 008°15' E
Bamberg	49°52' N, 010°52' E
Bautzen	51°11' N, 014°26' E
Bayreuth	49°57' N, 011°35' E
Berchtesgaden	47°38' N, 013°00' E
Bergheim	50°58' N, 006°39' E
Bergisch Gladbach	50°59' N, 007°08' E
Berlin	52°30' N, 013°22' E
Bernburg	51°48' N, 011°44' E
Bernkastel-Kues	49°55' N, 007°04' E
Bielefeld	52°02' N, 008°32' E
Blankenburg	51°47' N, 010°57' E
Bocholt	51°50' N, 006°36' E
Bonn	50°44' N, 007°06' E
Borna	51°07' N, 012°30' E
Brandenburg	52°25' N, 012°33' E
Braunschweig (Brunswick)	52°16' N, 010°32' E
Breisach	48°02' N, 007°35' E
Bremen	53°05' N, 008°48' E
Bremerhaven	53°33' N, 008°35' E
Brilon	51°24' N, 008°35' E
Bruchsal	49°08' N, 008°36' E
Brühl	50°50' N, 006°54' E
Brunswick, see Braunschweig	
Burg	52°16' N, 011°51' E
Buxtehude	53°27' N, 009°42' E
Calw	48°43' N, 008°44' E
Celle	52°37' N, 010°05' E
Chemnitz (Karl-Marx-Stadt)	50°50' N, 012°55' E
Cloppenburg	52°51' N, 008°02' E
Coburg	50°15' N, 010°58' E
Cochem	50°08' N, 007°09' E
Cologne (Köln)	50°56' N, 006°57' E
Coswig	51°08' N, 013°35' E
Cottbus	51°46' N, 014°20' E
Crailsheim	49°09' N, 010°05' E
Crimmitschau	50°49' N, 012°23' E
Cuxhaven	53°53' N, 008°42' E
Dachau	48°16' N, 011°26' E
Darmstadt	49°52' N, 008°39' E
Deggendorf	48°50' N, 012°58' E
Delmenhorst	53°03' N, 008°37' E
Dessau	51°50' N, 012°15' E
Detmold	51°56' N, 008°53' E
Dinkelsbühl	49°04' N, 010°19' E
Donauwörth	48°42' N, 010°48' E
Dormagen	51°06' N, 006°50' E
Dorsten	51°40' N, 006°58' E
Dortmund	51°31' N, 007°27' E
Dresden	51°03' N, 013°45' E
Duisburg	51°26' N, 006°45' E
Düren	50°48' N, 006°29' E
Düsseldorf	51°13' N, 006°46' E
Eberswalde-Finow	52°50' N, 013°47' E
Eichstätt	48°53' N, 011°11' E
Eisenach	50°59' N, 010°19' E
Eisenberg	50°58' N, 011°54' E
Eisenhüttenstadt	52°09' N, 014°39' E
Eisleben	51°32' N, 011°33' E
Ellwangen	48°57' N, 010°08' E
Elmshorn	53°45' N, 009°39' E
Emden	53°22' N, 007°13' E
Erding	48°18' N, 011°56' E
Erfurt	50°59' N, 011°02' E
Erlangen	49°36' N, 011°01' E
Eschwege	51°11' N, 010°04' E
Eschweiler	50°49' N, 006°17' E
Essen	51°27' N, 007°01' E
Esslingen	48°45' N, 009°18' E
Ettlingen	48°57' N, 008°24' E
Falkensee	52°34' N, 013°05' E
Flensburg	54°47' N, 009°26' E
Forchheim	49°43' N, 011°04' E
Forst	51°44' N, 014°38' E
Frankenthal	49°32' N, 008°21' E
Frankfurt	52°21' N, 014°33' E
Frankfurt am Main	50°07' N, 008°41' E
Freiberg	50°55' N, 013°22' E
Freiburg	48°00' N, 007°51' E
Freising	48°24' N, 011°44' E
Freital	51°01' N, 013°39' E
Freudenstadt	48°26' N, 008°25' E
Friedberg	48°21' N, 010°59' E
Friedrichshafen	47°39' N, 009°29' E
Fulda	50°33' N, 009°40' E
Fürstenfeldbruck	48°11' N, 011°15' E
Fürth	49°28' N, 011°00' E
Furtwangen	48°03' N, 008°12' E
Füssen	47°34' N, 010°42' E
Ganderkesee	53°02' N, 008°32' E
Garbsen	52°25' N, 009°36' E
Garmisch-Partenkirchen	47°30' N, 011°06' E
Gelsenkirchen	51°31' N, 007°06' E
Genthin	52°24' N, 012°10' E
Gera	50°52' N, 012°05' E
Germering	48°08' N, 011°22' E
Giessen	50°35' N, 008°39' E
Glückstadt	53°47' N, 009°25' E
Göppingen	48°42' N, 009°40' E
Görlitz	51°10' N, 015°00' E
Goslar	51°54' N, 010°26' E
Gotha	50°57' N, 010°43' E
Göttingen	51°32' N, 009°56' E
Greifswald	54°06' N, 013°23' E
Greiz	50°39' N, 012°12' E
Grevesmühlen	53°52' N, 011°11' E
Grossenhain	51°17' N, 013°33' E
Guben (Wilhelm-Pieck Stadt Guben)	51°57' N, 014°43' E
Güstrow	53°48' N, 012°10' E
Gütersloh	51°54' N, 008°23' E
Hagen	51°21' N, 007°28' E
Hagenow	53°26' N, 011°11' E
Halberstadt	51°54' N, 011°03' E
Haldensleben	52°18' N, 011°25' E
Halle	51°30' N, 012°00' E
Halle-Neustadt	51°29' N, 011°56' E
Hamburg	53°33' N, 010°00' E
Hameln	52°06' N, 009°21' E
Hamm	51°41' N, 007°48' E
Hannover	52°22' N, 009°43' E
Harzgerode	51°38' N, 011°09' E
Havelburg	52°51' N, 012°05' E
Hechingen	48°21' N, 008°59' E
Heidelberg	49°25' N, 008°42' E
Heidenheim	48°41' N, 010°09' E
Heilbronn	49°08' N, 009°13' E
Herford	52°08' N, 008°41' E

Name	Lat./Long.
Herne	51°33' N, 007°13' E
Hildesheim	52°09' N, 009°58' E
Hof	50°19' N, 011°55' E
Homburg	49°19' N, 007°20' E
Höxter	51°46' N, 009°23' E
Hoyerswerda	51°26' N, 014°15' E
Hürth	50°52' N, 006°52' E
Ingolstadt	48°46' N, 011°26' E
Jena	50°56' N, 011°35' E
Jülich	50°56' N, 006°22' E
Kaiserslautern	49°27' N, 007°45' E
Karl-Marx-Stadt, see Chemnitz	
Karlsruhe	49°01' N, 008°24' E
Kassel	51°19' N, 009°30' E
Kaufbeuren	47°53' N, 010°37' E
Kelheim	48°55' N, 011°52' E
Kempten	47°43' N, 010°19' E
Kerpen	50°52' N, 006°41' E
Kiel	54°20' N, 010°08' E
Kleve	51°47' N, 006°09' E
Koblenz	50°21' N, 007°36' E
Köln, see Cologne	
Königswinter	50°41' N, 007°11' E
Konstanz	47°40' N, 009°11' E
Korbach	51°17' N, 008°52' E
Köthen	51°45' N, 011°58' E
Krefeld	51°20' N, 006°34' E
Kulmbach	50°06' N, 011°27' E
Landshut	48°32' N, 012°09' E
Leinefelde	51°23' N, 010°20' E
Leipzig	51°18' N, 012°20' E
Lemgo	52°02' N, 008°54' E
Leuna	51°19' N, 012°01' E
Leverkusen	51°01' N, 006°59' E
Limburg	50°23' N, 008°03' E
Lingen	52°31' N, 007°19' E
Lippstadt	51°40' N, 008°21' E
Löbau	51°06' N, 014°40' E
Lörrach	47°37' N, 007°40' E
Lorsch	49°39' N, 008°34' E
Lübeck	53°52' N, 010°42' E
Ludwigsburg	48°54' N, 009°11' E
Ludwigshafen	49°29' N, 008°27' E
Lüneburg	53°15' N, 010°24' E
Lünen	51°37' N, 007°31' E
Lutter	51°59' N, 010°16' E
Maasholm	54°41' N, 009°59' E
Magdeburg	52°10' N, 011°40' E
Mainz	50°00' N, 008°15' E
Mannheim	49°29' N, 008°28' E
Mansfeld	51°35' N, 011°28' E
Marburg	50°49' N, 008°46' E
Marl	51°39' N, 007°05' E
Meerane	50°51' N, 012°28' E
Meiningen	50°33' N, 010°25' E
Memmingen	47°59' N, 010°10' E
Menden	51°26' N, 007°48' E
Merseburg	51°22' N, 012°00' E
Minden	52°17' N, 008°55' E
Mittenwald	47°26' N, 011°15' E
Moers	51°27' N, 006°39' E
Molln	53°38' N, 010°41' E
Monchengladbach	51°12' N, 006°26' E
Mühlhausen	51°13' N, 010°27' E
Mülheim	51°26' N, 006°53' E
München	50°54' N, 011°02' E
Munich	48°09' N, 011°35' E
Münster	51°58' N, 007°38' E
Naumburg	51°09' N, 011°49' E
Neubrandenburg	53°34' N, 013°16' E
Neumarkt	49°17' N, 011°28' E
Neumünster	54°04' N, 009°59' E
Neunkirchen	49°21' N, 007°11' E
Neuruppin	52°56' N, 012°48' E
Neuss	51°12' N, 006°42' E
Neustrelitz	53°22' N, 013°05' E
Neuwied	50°26' N, 007°28' E
Norden	53°36' N, 007°12' E
Nordenham	53°30' N, 008°29' E
Norderstedt	53°42' N, 010°01' E
Nordhausen	51°31' N, 010°48' E
Nordhorn	52°26' N, 007°05' E
Nördlingen	48°51' N, 010°30' E
Northeim	51°42' N, 010°00' E
Nürnberg (Nuremberg)	49°27' N, 011°05' E
Offenbach	50°06' N, 008°46' E
Offenburg	48°29' N, 007°56' E
Oldenburg	54°18' N, 010°53' E
Oldenburg	53°10' N, 008°12' E
Osnabrück	52°16' N, 008°03' E
Osterode	51°44' N, 010°11' E
Ottobrunn	48°04' N, 011°41' E
Paderborn	51°43' N, 008°46' E
Parchim	53°26' N, 011°51' E
Passau	48°35' N, 013°29' E
Peenemünde	54°08' N, 013°47' E
Peine	52°19' N, 010°14' E
Petersdorf	52°29' N, 011°04' E
Pforzheim	48°53' N, 008°42' E
Pirmasens	49°12' N, 007°36' E
Pirna	50°58' N, 013°56' E
Plauen	50°30' N, 012°08' E
Potsdam	52°24' N, 013°04' E
Prenzlau	53°19' N, 013°52' E
Quedlinburg	51°47' N, 011°09' E
Rathenow	52°36' N, 012°20' E
Ravensburg	47°47' N, 009°37' E
Recklinghausen	51°37' N, 007°12' E
Regensburg	49°01' N, 012°06' E
Reichenbach	50°37' N, 012°18' E
Remagen	50°34' N, 007°14' E
Remscheid	51°11' N, 007°12' E
Rendsburg	54°18' N, 009°40' E
Reutlingen	48°29' N, 009°13' E
Rheine	52°17' N, 007°27' E
Riesa	51°18' N, 013°18' E
Rosenheim	47°51' N, 012°08' E
Rostock	54°05' N, 012°08' E
Rothenburg	49°23' N, 010°11' E
Rottweil	48°10' N, 008°37' E
Rudolstadt	50°43' N, 011°20' E
Rüsselsheim	50°00' N, 008°25' E
Saalfeld	50°39' N, 011°22' E
Saarbrücken	49°14' N, 007°00' E
Saarlouis	49°19' N, 006°45' E
Salzgitter	52°05' N, 010°20' E
Salzwedel	52°51' N, 011°09' E
Sankt Augustin	50°46' N, 007°11' E
Schleswig	54°31' N, 009°33' E

Name	Lat./Long.
Schönebeck	52°01' N, 011°45' E
Schwäbisch Gmünd	48°48' N, 009°47' E
Schwäbisch Hall	49°06' N, 009°44' E
Schwedt	53°04' N, 014°18' E
Schweinfurt	50°03' N, 010°14' E
Schwerin	53°38' N, 011°23' E
Seevetal	53°24' N, 009°58' E
Senftenberg	51°31' N, 014°01' E
Siegen	50°52' N, 008°02' E
Sikéai (Sikies)	37°31' N, 021°53' E
Sindelfingen	48°42' N, 009°01' E
Singen	47°46' N, 008°50' E
Solingen	51°11' N, 007°05' E
Sömmerda	51°09' N, 011°06' E
Sondershausen	51°22' N, 010°52' E
Sonneberg	50°21' N, 011°10' E
Speyer	49°19' N, 008°26' E
Spremberg	51°33' N, 014°22' E
Stassfurt	51°52' N, 011°35' E
Stendal	52°36' N, 011°51' E
Stolberg	50°46' N, 006°14' E
Stralsund	54°18' N, 013°06' E
Straubing	48°53' N, 012°34' E
Strausberg	52°35' N, 013°53' E
Stuttgart	48°46' N, 009°11' E
Suhl	50°36' N, 010°42' E
Torgau	51°34' N, 013°00' E
Torgelow	53°38' N, 014°01' E
Triberg	48°08' N, 008°14' E
Trier	49°45' N, 006°38' E
Tübingen	48°32' N, 009°03' E
Tuttlingen	47°59' N, 008°49' E
Uelzen	52°58' N, 010°34' E
Ulm	48°24' N, 010°00' E
Vechta	52°43' N, 008°17' E
Velzen	52°58' N, 010°34' E
Verden	52°55' N, 009°14' E
Villingen-Schwenningen	48°04' N, 008°27' E
Völklingen	49°15' N, 006°51' E
Walsrode	52°54' N, 009°40' E
Waren	53°31' N, 012°41' E
Warnemünde	54°10' N, 012°05' E
Weiden	49°41' N, 012°10' E
Weimar	50°59' N, 011°19' E
Weinheim	49°33' N, 008°40' E
Weissenfels	51°12' N, 011°58' E
Wernigerode	51°50' N, 010°47' E
Wesel	51°40' N, 006°37' E
Wetzlar	50°33' N, 008°30' E
Weyhe	52°58' N, 008°48' E
Wiesbaden	50°05' N, 008°15' E
Wilhelm-Pieck-Stadt Guben, see Guben	
Wilhelmshaven	53°31' N, 008°08' E
Wismar	53°54' N, 011°28' E
Wittenberg	51°52' N, 012°39' E
Wittenberge	53°00' N, 011°45' E
Wolfen	51°40' N, 012°17' E
Wolfenbüttel	52°10' N, 010°33' E
Wolfsburg	52°26' N, 010°48' E
Worms	49°38' N, 008°21' E
Wuppertal	51°16' N, 007°11' E
Würzburg	49°48' N, 009°56' E
Zeitz	51°03' N, 012°09' E
Zell	50°02' N, 007°11' E
Zerbst	51°58' N, 012°05' E
Zittau	50°54' N, 014°50' E
Zweibrucken	49°15' N, 007°22' E
Zwickau	50°44' N, 012°30' E

GHANA . . . . .pg. 150

Capital: . . . . .Accra
Area: . . . . .238,533 sq km; 92,098 sq mi
Highest Elev.: . . . .Mt. Afadjato 890 m; 2,900 ft
Longest River: . . . .Black Volta 1,160 km; 720 mi
Avg. Temperature: . .Jan = 28°C; Jul = 25°C
Currency: . . . . . . .cedi
Official Language: . .English

Accra	05°33' N, 000°13' W
Cape Coast	05°06' N, 001°15' W
Koforidua	05°14' N, 001°20' W
Kumasi	06°41' N, 001°37' W
Obuasi	06°12' N, 001°40' W
Sekondi	04°56' N, 001°42' W
Takoradi	04°53' N, 001°45' W
Tamale	09°24' N, 000°50' W
Tema	05°37' N, 000°01' W

GREECE . . . . .pg. 135

Capital: . . . . .Athens
Area: . . . . .131,957 sq km; 50,949 sq mi
Highest Elev.: . . . .Mt. Olympus 2,920 m; 9,570 ft
Longest River: . . . .Aliákmon 300 km; 190 mi
Avg. Temperature: . .Jan = 9°C; Jul = 28°C
Currency: . . . . . . .drachma
Official Language: . .Greek

Alexandroúpolis (Alexandhroupolis)	40°51' N, 025°52' E
Almirós	39°11' N, 022°46' E
Amphissa (Amfissa)	38°32' N, 022°23' E
Ándros	37°50' N, 024°56' E
Athens (Athinai)	37°59' N, 023°44' E
Árgos	37°38' N, 022°44' E
Agostólion	38°11' N, 020°29' E
Argos Orestikón	40°28' N, 021°16' E
Arkhángelos	36°12' N, 028°08' E
Áyios Kírikos	37°35' N, 026°14' E
Corinth (Korinthos)	37°56' N, 022°56' E
Dráma	41°09' N, 024°09' E
Elassón	39°54' N, 022°11' E
Ermoupolis, see Hermoupolis	
Flórina	40°47' N, 021°24' E
Glifadha (Glyphada)	37°52' N, 023°45' E
Idhra	37°21' N, 023°28' E
Igoumenitsa	39°30' N, 020°16' E
Ioannina (Yannina)	39°40' N, 020°50' E
Ios	36°44' N, 025°17' E
Iraklion (Candia or Herakleion)	35°20' N, 025°08' E
Kalabáka	39°42' N, 021°38' E
Kalamai (Kalamata)	37°02' N, 022°07' E
Kalamaria	40°35' N, 022°58' E
Kallithea	37°57' N, 023°42' E
Kardhitsa	39°22' N, 021°55' E
Karpenísion	38°55' N, 021°47' E

Katerini	40°16' N, 022°30' E
Kavala (Kavalla or Neapolis)	40°56' N, 024°25' E
Kariaí	40°15' N, 024°15' E
Kérkira	39°36' N, 019°55' E
Khalkidhón (Nea Khalkidhon)	40°44' N, 022°36' E
Kilkís	41°00' N, 022°52' E
Kími	38°38' N, 024°06' E
Kíthira	36°09' N, 022°59' E
Khalkis (Chalcis)	38°28' N, 023°36' E
Khania (Canea)	35°31' N, 024°02' E
Khios (Chios)	38°22' N, 026°08' E
Komotiní	41°07' N, 025°24' E
Korinthos, see Corinth	
Kos	36°53' N, 027°18' E
Kozáni	40°18' N, 021°47' E
Kranídhion	37°23' N, 023°09' E
Lágos	41°01' N, 025°07' E
Larisa (Larissa)	39°38' N, 022°25' E
Lávrion (Laurium)	37°43' N, 024°03' E
Leondárion	39°11' N, 022°08' E
Leonídhion	37°10' N, 022°52' E
Levkás	38°50' N, 020°42' E
Lindhos (Lindos)	36°06' N, 028°04' E
Mestá	38°16' N, 025°55' E
Monemvasía	36°41' N, 023°03' E
Navplion (Nauplia)	37°34' N, 022°48' E
Nea Ionia	38°02' N, 023°45' E
Neapolis	40°19' N, 021°23' E
Nikea (Nikaia)	37°58' N, 023°39' E
Orestiás	41°30' N, 026°31' E
Párga	39°17' N, 020°24' E
Patrai	38°15' N, 021°44' E
Páros	37°05' N, 025°09' E
Pérama	39°42' N, 020°51' E
Peristerion	38°01' N, 023°42' E
Pílos	36°55' N, 021°42' E
Piraeus (Piraievs)	37°57' N, 028°38' E
Políyiros	40°23' N, 023°27' E
Pyrgos (Pirgos)	37°41' N, 021°27' E
Rodhos (Rhodes)	36°26' N, 028°13' E
Sámos	37°45' N, 026°58' E
Serrai	41°05' N, 023°33' E
Siátista	40°16' N, 021°33' E
Souflion	41°12' N, 026°18' E
Sparta (Sparti)	37°05' N, 022°26' E
Thásos	40°47' N, 024°43' E
Thebes (Thivai)	38°19' N, 023°19' E
Thessaloniki (Salonika)	40°38' N, 022°56' E
Thíra	36°25' N, 025°26' E
Tinos	37°32' N, 025°10' E
Trikala	39°33' N, 021°46' E
Tripolis	37°31' N, 022°22' E
Valestínon	39°23' N, 022°45' E
Veroia	40°31' N, 022°12' E
Xánthi	41°08' N, 024°53' E

GRENADA . . . . .pg. 116

Capital: . . . . .St. George's
Area: . . . . .344 sq km; 133 sq mi
Highest Elev.: . . . .Mt. St. Catherine 840 m; 2,7600 ft
Avg. Temperature: . .Jan = 28°C; Jul = 28°C
Currency: . . . . . . .East Caribbean dollar
Official Language: . .English

St. George's	12°03' N, 061°45' W

GUATEMALA . . . . .pg. 117

Capital: . . . . .Guatemala City
Area: . . . . .108,889 sq km; 42,042 sq mi
Highest Elev.: . . . .Tajumulco Volc. 4,220 m; 13,850 ft
Longest River: . . . .Motagua 400 km; 250 mi
Avg. Temperature: . .Jan = 16°C; Jul = 19°C
Currency: . . . . . . .Guatemalan quetzal
Official Language: . .Spanish

Escuintla	14°18' N, 090°47' W
Guatemala City (Guatemala)	14°38' N, 090°31' W
Puerto San Jose (San Jose)	13°55' N, 090°49' W
Quezaltenango	14°50' N, 091°31' W

GUINEA . . . . .pg. 150

Capital: . . . . .Conakry
Area: . . . . .245,857 sq km; 94,926 sq mi
Highest Elev.: . . . .Mt. Nimba 1,750 m; 5,750 ft
Longest River: . . . .Niger 4,200 km; 2,600 mi
Avg. Temperature: . .Jan = 26°C; Jul = 26°C
Currency: . . . . . . .Guinean franc
Official Language: . .French

Conakry	09°31' N, 013°43' W
Kankan	10°23' N, 009°18' W
Kindia	10°04' N, 012°51' W
Labé	11°19' N, 012°17' W
Nzérékoré	07°45' N, 008°49' W

GUINEA-BISSAU . . . . .pg. 150

Capital: . . . . .Bissau
Area: . . . . .36,125 sq km; 13,948 sq mi
Avg. Temperature: . .Jan = 25°C; Jul = 27°C
Currency: . . . . . . .Guinea-Bissau peso
Official Language: . .Portuguese

Bissau	11°51' N, 015°35' W

GUYANA . . . . .pg. 120

Capital: . . . . .Georgetown
Area: . . . . .215,083 sq km; 83,044 sq mi
Highest Elev.: . . . .Mt. Roraima 2,770 m; 9,090 ft
Longest River: . . . .Essequibo 1,010 km; 630 mi
Avg. Temperature: . .Jan = 26°C; Jul = 27°C
Currency: . . . . . . .Guyana dollar
Official Language: . .English

Charity	07°24' N, 058°36' W
Corriverton	05°52' N, 057°10' W
Georgetown	06°48' N, 058°10' W

Name	Lat./Long.
Mabaruma	08°12' N, 059°47' W
New Amsterdam	06°15' N, 057°31' W
Vreed en Hoop	06°48' N, 058°11' W

HAITI . . . . .pg. 116

Capital: . . . . .Port-au-Prince
Area: . . . . .27,700 sq km; 10,695 sq mi
Highest Elev.: . . . . .Mt. la Selle 2,700 m; 8,770 ft
Longest River: . . . .Artibonite 280 km; 170 mi
Avg. Temperature: . .Jan = 31°C; Jul = 35°C
Currency: . . . . .gourde
Official Language: .Haitian Creole, French

Cap-Haïtien	19°45' N, 072°12' W
Gonaives	19°27' N, 072°41' W
Port-au-Prince	18°32' N, 072°20' W

HONDURAS . . . . .pg. 117

Capital: . . . . .Tegucigalpa
Area: . . . . . . .112,088 sq km; 43,277 sq mi
Highest Elev.: . . . .Mt. Celaque 2,850 m; 9,350 ft
Longest River: . . . .Coco 780 km; 4900 mi
Avg. Temperature: . .Jan = 19°C; Jul = 23°C
Currency: . . . . .Honduran lempira
Official Language: .Spanish

Choluteca	13°18' N, 087°12' W
El Progreso	15°24' N, 087°48' W
La Ceiba	15°47' N, 086°48' W
San Marcos de Colón	13°26' N, 086°48' W
San Pedro Sula	15°30' N, 088°02' W
Tegucigalpa	14°06' N, 087°13' W

HUNGARY . . . . pg. 134

Capital: . . . . .Budapest
Area: . . . . .93,033 sq km; 35,920 sq mi
Highest Elev.: . . . .Mt. Kekes 1,010 m; 3,330 ft
Longest River: . . . .Danube 2,850 km; 1,770 mi
Avg. Temperature: . .Jan = -1°C; Jul = 22°C
Currency: . . . . .forint
Official Language: .Hungarian

Békéscsaba	46°41' N, 021°06' E
Budapest	47°30' N, 019°05' E
Debrecen	47°32' N, 021°38' E
Dunakeszi	47°38' N, 019°08' E
Dunaújváros (Sztálinváros)	46°59' N, 018°56' E
Eger	47°54' N, 020°23' E
Gyor	47°41' N, 017°38' E
Hódmezővásárhely	46°25' N, 020°20' E
Kaposvár	46°22' N, 017°48' E
Kecskemét	46°54' N, 019°42' E
Miskolc	48°06' N, 020°47' E
Nagyatád	46°13' N, 017°22' E
Nagykanizsa	46°27' N, 016°59' E
Nyíregyháza	47°57' N, 021°43' E
Ózd	48°13' N, 020°18' E
Pécs	46°05' N, 018°14' E
Salgótarján	48°07' N, 019°49' E
Sopron	47°41' N, 016°36' E
Szeged	46°15' N, 020°10' E
Székesfehérvár	47°12' N, 018°25' E
Szolnok	47°11' N, 020°12' E
Szombathely	47°14' N, 016°37' E
Tatabánya	47°34' N, 018°25' E
Vác	47°47' N, 019°08' E
Veszprém	47°06' N, 017°55' E
Zalaegerszeg	46°50' N, 016°51' E

ICELAND . . . . .pg. 131

Capital: . . . . .Reykjavík
Area: . . . . .102,819 sq km; 39,699 sq mi
Highest Elev.: . . . .Mt. Hvannadals 2,120 m; 6,950 ft
Longest River: . . . .Thjorsa 230 km; 140 mi
Avg. Temperature: . .Jan = 1°C; Jul = 11°C
Currency: . . . . .króna
Official Language: .Icelandic

Akureyri	65°40' N, 018°06' W
Reykjavík	64°09' N, 021°57' W

INDIA . . . . .pg. 146

Capital: . . . . .New Delhi
Area: . . . . . . .3,165,596 sq km; 1,222,243sq mi
Highest Elev.: . . . .KanchenjungaPk. 8,590 m;
. . . . .28,210 ft
Longest River: . . . .Ganges 2,510 km; 1,560 mi
Avg. Temperature: . .Jan = 13.9°C; Jul = 31.1°C
Currency: . . . . .Indian rupee
Official Language: .Hindi, English

Adoni	15°38' N, 077°17' E
Agartala	23°49' N, 091°16' E
Agra	27°11' N, 078°01' E
Ahmadabad (Ahmedabad)	23°02' N, 072°37' E
Ahmadnagar (Ahmednagar)	19°05' N, 074°44' E
Ajmer	26°27' N, 074°38' E
Akola	20°44' N, 077°00' E
Aligarh	27°53' N, 078°05' E
Allahabad	25°27' N, 081°51' E
Alleppey	09°29' N, 076°19' E
Alwar	27°34' N, 076°36' E
Amaravati (Amaravathi)	16°35' N, 080°22' E
Amritsar	31°35' N, 074°53' E
Anantapur	14°41' N, 077°36' E
Ara (Arrah)	25°34' N, 084°40' E
Aurangabad	19°53' N, 075°20' E
Baharampur (Berhampore)	24°06' N, 088°15' E
Bahraich	27°35' N, 081°36' E
Ballia	25°45' N, 084°10' E
Balurghat	25°13' N, 088°46' E
Bangalore	12°59' N, 077°35' E
Barddhaman (Burdwan)	23°15' N, 087°51' E
Bareilly	28°21' N, 079°25' E
Barmer	25°45' N, 071°23' E
Batala	31°48' N, 075°12' E

Name	Lat./Long.
Bathinda (Bhatinda)	30°12' N, 074°57' E
Beawar	26°06' N, 074°19' E
Belgaum	15°52' N, 074°30' E
Bellary	15°09' N, 076°56' E
Bettiah	26°48' N, 084°30' E
Bhadravati	13°52' N, 075°43' E
Bharatpur	27°13' N, 077°29' E
Bharuch (Broach)	21°42' N, 072°58' E
Bhatpara	22°52' N, 088°24' E
Bhavnagar (Bhaunagar)	21°46' N, 072°09' E
Bhilainagar	21°13' N, 081°26' E
Bhilwara	25°21' N, 074°38' E
Bhimavaram	16°32' N, 081°32' E
Bhind	26°34' N, 078°48' E
Bhiwandi	19°18' N, 073°04' E
Bhopal	23°16' N, 077°24' E
Bhubaneshwar	20°14' N, 085°50' E
Bhuj	23°16' N, 069°40' E
Bhusawal	21°03' N, 075°46' E
Bid (Bhir)	18°59' N, 075°46' E
Bidar	17°54' N, 077°33' E
Bihar Sharif	25°11' N, 085°31' E
Bijapur	16°50' N, 075°42' E
Bikaner	28°01' N, 073°18' E
Bilaspur	31°20' N, 076°45' E
Bilaspur	22°05' N, 082°09' E
Bombay (Mumbai)	18°58' N, 072°50' E
Brahmapur (Berhampur)	19°19' N, 084°47' E
Burhanpur	21°18' N, 076°14' E
Calcutta	22°32' N, 088°22' E
Calicut (Kozhikode)	11°15' N, 075°46' E
Chandigarh	30°44' N, 076°55' E
Chandrapur (Chanda)	19°57' N, 079°18' E
Chatrapur, see Chhatrapur	
Chengalpattu (Chingleput)	12°42' N, 079°59' E
Chhapra	25°46' N, 084°45' E
Chhatrapur (Chatrapur)	19°21' N, 084°54' E
Chhindwara	22°04' N, 078°56' E
Chikmagalur	13°19' N, 075°47' E
Chitradurga (Chitaldrug)	14°14' N, 076°24' E
Chittoor	13°12' N, 079°07' E
Churu	28°18' N, 074°57' E
Cochin	09°58' N, 076°14' E
Coimbatore	11°00' N, 076°58' E
Cuddalore	11°45' N, 079°45' E
Cuddapah	14°28' N, 078°49' E
Cuttack	20°30' N, 085°50' E
Darbhanga	26°10' N, 085°54' E
Datia	25°40' N, 078°28' E
Davangere	14°28' N, 075°55' E
Dehra Dun	30°19' N, 078°02' E
Delhi	28°40' N, 077°13' E
Devghar (Deoghar)	24°29' N, 086°42' E
Dewas	22°58' N, 076°04' E
Dhanbad	23°48' N, 086°27' E
Dhule (Dhulia)	20°54' N, 074°47' E
Dibrugarh	27°29' N, 094°54' E
Dimapur	25°54' N, 093°44' E
Dindigul	10°21' N, 077°57' E
Durg	21°11' N, 081°17' E
Eluru (Ellore)	16°42' N, 081°06' E
Erode	11°21' N, 077°44' E
Etawah	26°46' N, 079°02' E
Faizabad (Fyzabad)	26°47' N, 082°08' E
Faridabad	28°26' N, 077°19' E
Fatehpur	25°56' N, 080°48' E
Firozabad	27°09' N, 078°25' E
Firozpur (Ferozepore)	30°55' N, 074°36' E
Gadag-Betigeri	15°25' N, 075°37' E
Gandhinagar	23°12' N, 072°40' E
Gangtok	27°20' N, 088°37' E
Gauhati, see Guwahati	
Gaya	24°47' N, 085°00' E
Ghaziabad	28°40' N, 077°26' E
Gorakhpur	26°45' N, 083°22' E
Gulbarga	17°20' N, 076°50' E
Guna	24°39' N, 077°19' E
Guntur	16°18' N, 080°27' E
Gurgaon	28°28' N, 077°02' E
Guwahati (Gauhati)	26°11' N, 091°44' E
Gwalior	26°13' N, 078°10' E
Hanumangarh (Sadulgarh)	29°35' N, 074°19' E
Haridwar (Hardwar)	29°58' N, 078°10' E
Hassan	13°00' N, 076°05' E
Hisar (Hissar)	29°10' N, 075°43' E
Hoshangabad	22°45' N, 077°43' E
Hoshiarpur	31°32' N, 075°54' E
Howrah (Haora)	22°35' N, 088°20' E
Hubli-Dharwad	15°21' N, 075°10' E
Hugli-Chunchura	22°54' N, 088°24' E
Hyderabad	17°23' N, 078°28' E
Ichalkaranji	16°42' N, 074°28' E
Imphal	24°49' N, 093°57' E
Indore	22°43' N, 075°50' E
Itanagar	27°09' N, 093°33' E
Jabalpur (Jubbulpore)	23°10' N, 079°57' E
Jaipur	26°55' N, 075°49' E
Jalandhar (Jullundur)	31°19' N, 075°34' E
Jalgaon	21°01' N, 075°34' E
Jalna	19°50' N, 075°53' E
Jamalpur	25°18' N, 086°30' E
Jammu	32°44' N, 074°52' E
Jamnagar	22°28' N, 070°04' E
Jamshedpur	22°48' N, 086°11' E
Jhansi	25°26' N, 078°35' E
Jodhpur	26°17' N, 073°02' E
Kakinada (Cocanada)	16°56' N, 082°13' E
Kanchipuram (Conjeeveram)	12°50' N, 079°43' E
Kanpur (Cawnpore)	26°28' N, 080°21' E
Karimnagar	18°26' N, 079°09' E
Karnal	29°41' N, 076°59' E
Katihar	25°32' N, 087°35' E
Khammam (Khammamett)	17°15' N, 080°09' E
Khandwa	21°50' N, 076°20' E
Kharagpur	22°20' N, 087°20' E
Kohima	25°40' N, 094°07' E
Kolar	13°08' N, 078°08' E
Kolhapur	16°42' N, 074°14' E
Kota (Kotah)	25°11' N, 075°50' E
Kottayam	09°35' N, 076°31' E
Krishnanagar	23°24' N, 088°30' E
Kumbakonam	10°58' N, 079°23' E
Lalitpur	24°41' N, 078°25' E
Latur	18°24' N, 076°35' E
Lucknow	26°51' N, 080°55' E
Ludhiana	30°54' N, 075°51' E
Machilipatnam (Bandar, Masulipatam)	16°10' N, 081°08' E
Madgaon (Margao)	15°18' N, 073°57' E
Madras	13°05' N, 080°17' E

Name	Lat./Long.
Madurai (Madura)	09°56' N, 078°07' E
Mahbubnagar	16°44' N, 077°59' E
Malegaon	20°33' N, 074°32' E
Mandsaur (Mandasor)	24°04' N, 075°04' E
Mandya	12°33' N, 076°54' E
Mangalore	12°52' N, 074°53' E
Marmagao (Mormugao)	15°24' N, 073°48' E
Mathura (Muttra)	27°30' N, 077°41' E
Meerut	28°59' N, 077°42' E
Mhow	22°33' N, 075°46' E
Miraj	16°50' N, 074°38' E
Morena (Pech Morena)	26°29' N, 078°01' E
Munger (Monghyr)	25°23' N, 086°28' E
Murwara	23°51' N, 080°24' E
Muzaffarpur	26°07' N, 085°24' E
Mysore	12°18' N, 076°39' E
Nadiad	22°42' N, 072°52' E
Nagaon (Nowgong)	26°21' N, 092°40' E
Nagercoil	08°10' N, 077°26' E
Nagpur	21°09' N, 079°06' E
Naihati	22°54' N, 088°25' E
Nanded (Nander)	19°09' N, 077°20' E
Nashik (Nasik)	19°59' N, 073°48' E
Nathdwara	24°56' N, 073°49' E
Navadwip (Nabadwip)	23°25' N, 088°22' E
Navsari	20°51' N, 072°55' E
Nellore	14°26' N, 079°58' E
New Delhi	28°36' N, 077°12' E
Nizamabad	18°40' N, 078°07' E
Palghat	10°47' N, 076°39' E
Pali	25°46' N, 073°20' E
Pandharpur	17°40' N, 075°20' E
Parbhani	19°16' N, 076°47' E
Pathankot	32°17' N, 075°39' E
Patna	25°36' N, 085°07' E
Pilibhit	28°38' N, 079°48' E
Pimpri-Chinchwad	18°36' N, 073°43' E
Pondicherry (Pondichery, Puduchcheri)	11°56' N, 079°53' E
Porbandar	21°38' N, 069°36' E
Port Blair	11°40' N, 092°45' E
Proddatur	14°44' N, 078°33' E
Pune (Poona)	18°32' N, 073°52' E
Quilon	08°53' N, 076°36' E
Rae Bareli	26°13' N, 081°14' E
Raichur	16°12' N, 077°22' E
Raiganj	25°37' N, 088°07' E
Raipur	21°14' N, 081°38' E
Rajapalaiyam	09°27' N, 077°34' E
Rajkot	22°18' N, 070°47' E
Ranchi	23°21' N, 085°20' E
Ratlam	23°19' N, 075°04' E
Ratnagiri	16°59' N, 073°18' E
Rewa (Rewah)	24°32' N, 081°18' E
Sagar (Saugor)	23°50' N, 078°43' E
Saharanpur	29°58' N, 077°33' E
Salem	11°39' N, 078°10' E
Sambalpur	21°27' N, 083°58' E
Sangli	16°52' N, 074°34' E
Sasaram	24°57' N, 084°02' E
Satara	17°41' N, 073°59' E
Satna	24°35' N, 080°50' E
Shahdol (Sahdol)	23°17' N, 081°21' E
Shahjahanpur	27°53' N, 079°55' E
Shiliguri (Siliguri)	26°42' N, 088°26' E
Shillong	25°34' N, 091°53' E
Shimla (Simla)	31°06' N, 077°10' E
Shimoga	13°55' N, 075°34' E
Shivpuri	25°26' N, 077°39' E
Sholapur (Solapur)	17°41' N, 075°55' E
Sikar	27°37' N, 075°09' E
Silchar	24°49' N, 092°48' E
Silvassa	20°15' N, 073°00' E
Simla, see Shimla	
Sirsa	29°32' N, 075°01' E
Sitapur	27°34' N, 080°41' E
Sonipat (Sonepat)	28°59' N, 077°01' E
South Dum Dum	22°34' N, 088°23' E
Srikakulam (Chicacole)	18°18' N, 083°54' E
Srinagar	34°05' N, 074°49' E
Surat	21°10' N, 072°50' E
Surendranagar (Wadhwan)	22°42' N, 071°41' E
Tenali	16°15' N, 080°35' E
Thanjavur (Tanjore)	10°48' N, 079°09' E
Tiruchchirappalli (Tiruchirappalli, Trichinopoly)	10°49' N, 078°41' E
Tirunelveli (Tinnevelly)	08°44' N, 077°42' E
Tirupati	13°39' N, 079°25' E
Tirupper (Tiruppur)	11°06' N, 077°21' E
Tiruvottiyur	13°09' N, 080°18' E
Tonk	26°10' N, 075°47' E
Trichur	10°31' N, 076°13' E
Trivandrum	08°29' N, 076°55' E
Tumkur	13°21' N, 077°05' E
Tuticorin	08°47' N, 078°08' E
Udaipur	24°35' N, 073°41' E
Ujjain	23°11' N, 075°46' E
Ulhasnagar	19°12' N, 072°58' E
Vasai (Bassein)	19°21' N, 072°48' E
Valsad (Bulsar)	20°38' N, 072°56' E
Vellore	12°56' N, 079°08' E
Vijayawada (Vijayavada, Bezwada)	16°31' N, 080°37' E
Vizianagaram (Vizianagram)	18°07' N, 083°25' E
Wadhwan, see Surendranagar	
Wardha	20°45' N, 078°37' E
Yavatmal (Yeotmal)	20°24' N, 078°08' E

INDONESIA . . . . .pg. 144

Capital: . . . . .Jakarta
Area: . . . . .1,919,317 sq km; 741,052 sq mi
Highest Elev.: . . . .Jaya Pk. 5,030 m; 16,500 ft
Longest River: . . . .Kapuas 1,140 km; 710 mi
Avg. Temperature: . .Jan = 26°C; Jul = 27°C
Currency: . . . . .Indonesian rupiah
Official Language: .Bahasa Indonesia

Ambon	03°43' S, 126°12' E
Atambua	09°07' S, 124°54' E
Balikpapan	01°17' S, 116°50' E
Banda Aceh (Kuta Raja)	05°34' N, 095°20' E
Bandung	06°54' S, 107°36' E
Bagansiapiapi	02°09' N, 100°49' E
Banjarbaru	03°25' S, 114°50' E
Banjarmasin	03°20' S, 114°35' E
Bantul	07°54' S, 110°20' E
Batang	06°55' S, 109°45' E
Bekasi	06°14' S, 106°59' E

Name	Lat./Long.
Belinyu	01°38' S, 105°46' E
Binjai	03°36' N, 098°30' E
Bitung	01°27' N, 125°11' E
Blitar	08°06' S, 112°09' E
Bogor	06°35' S, 106°47' E
Brebes	06°53' S, 109°03' E
Bukittinggi	00°19' S, 100°22' E
Cianjur	06°49' S, 107°08' E
Cikampek	06°24' S, 107°27' E
Cilacap	07°44' S, 109°00' E
Cimahi	06°53' S, 107°32' E
Cirebon	06°44' S, 108°34' E
Denpasar	08°39' S, 115°13' E
Depok	06°24' S, 106°50' E
Dili	08°33' S, 125°34' E
Dumai	01°41' N, 101°27' E
Garut	07°13' S, 107°54' E
Gresik	07°09' S, 112°38' E
Indramayu	06°20' S, 108°19' E
Jakarta	06°10' S, 106°48' E
Jambi	01°36' S, 103°37' E
Jayapura	02°32' S, 140°42' E
Jember	08°10' S, 113°42' E
Jepara (Japara)	06°35' S, 110°39' E
Jombang	07°33' S, 112°14' E
Karawang	06°19' S, 107°17' E
Kediri	07°49' S, 112°01' E
Kefamenanu	09°27' S, 124°29' E
Kendari	03°57' S, 122°35' E
Ketapang	01°52' S, 109°59' E
Klaten	07°42' S, 110°35' E
Kolaka	04°03' S, 121°36' E
Kotabumi	04°50' S, 104°54' E
Kudus	06°48' S, 110°50' E
Kuningan	06°59' S, 108°29' E
Kupang	10°10' S, 123°35' E
Langsa	04°28' N, 097°58' E
Lubuklinggau	03°10' S, 102°52' E
Lumajang	08°08' S, 113°13' E
Madiun	07°37' S, 111°31' E
Magelang	07°28' S, 110°13' E
Malang	07°59' S, 112°37' E
Mampawah, see Mempawah	
Manado	01°29' N, 124°51' E
Manokwari	00°52' S, 134°05' E
Mataram	08°35' S, 116°07' E
Medan	03°35' N, 098°40' E
Mempawah (Mampawah)	00°22' N, 108°58' E
Metro	05°05' S, 105°20' E
Mojokerto	07°28' S, 112°26' E
Muncar	08°26' S, 114°20' E
Padang	00°57' S, 100°21' E
Padangpanjang	00°27' S, 100°25' E
Padangsidempuan	01°22' N, 099°16' E
Palangkaraya	02°16' S, 113°56' E
Palembang	02°55' S, 104°45' E
Palu	00°53' S, 119°53' E
Pangkalpinang	02°08' S, 106°08' E
Pare	07°46' S, 112°11' E
Parepare	04°01' S, 119°38' E
Pasuruan	07°38' S, 112°54' E
Pati	06°45' S, 111°02' E
Payakumbuh	00°14' S, 100°38' E
Pekalongan	06°53' S, 109°40' E
Pekanbaru (Pakanbaru)	00°32' N, 101°27' E
Pemalang	06°54' S, 109°22' E
Pematangsiantar	02°57' N, 099°03' E
Perabumulih	03°27' S, 104°15' E
Pinrang	03°48' S, 119°38' E
Ponorogo	07°52' S, 111°27' E
Pontianak	00°02' S, 109°20' E
Probolinggo	07°45' S, 113°13' E
Purwakarta	06°34' S, 107°26' E
Purwokerto	07°25' S, 109°14' E
Purworejo	07°43' S, 110°01' E
Rantepao	02°59' S, 119°54' E
Salatiga	07°19' S, 110°30' E
Samarinda	00°30' S, 117°09' E
Semarang	06°58' S, 110°25' E
Serang	06°07' S, 106°09' E
Sibolga	01°45' N, 098°48' E
Sidoarjo	07°27' S, 112°43' E
Singaraja	08°07' S, 115°06' E
Singkawang	00°54' N, 109°00' E
Situbondo	07°42' S, 114°00' E
Soe	09°52' S, 124°17' E
Sorong	00°53' S, 131°15' E
Subang	06°34' S, 107°45' E
Sukabumi	06°55' S, 106°37' E
Sumedang	06°51' S, 107°55' E
Sumenep	07°01' S, 113°52' E
Sungailiat	01°51' S, 106°08' E
Surabaya	07°15' S, 112°45' E
Surakarta	07°35' S, 110°50' E
Tangerang	06°11' S, 106°37' E
Tanggul	08°10' S, 113°26' E
Tanjungbalai	02°58' N, 099°48' E
Tanjungpandan	02°45' S, 107°39' E
Tanjungkarang-Telukbetung	05°27' S, 105°16' E
Tasikmalaya	07°20' S, 108°12' E
Tebingtinggi	03°20' N, 099°09' E
Tegal	06°52' S, 109°08' E
Tembilahan	00°19' S, 103°09' E
Tondano	01°19' N, 124°54' E
Tuban	06°54' S, 112°03' E
Tulungagung	08°04' S, 111°54' E
Ujungpandang	05°07' S, 119°24' E
Watampone	04°32' S, 120°20' E
Yogyakarta	07°48' S, 110°22' E

IRAN . . . . .pg. 139

Capital: . . . . .Tehran
Area: . . . . .1,638,057 sq km; 632,457 sq mi
Highest Elev.: . . . .Mt. Demavend 5,610 m; 18,400 ft
Longest River: . . . .Karun 830 km; 520 mi
Avg. Temperature: .Jan = 2°C; Jul = 30°C
Currency: . . . . .rial
Official Language: .Farsi

Abadan	30°20' N, 048°16' E
Ahar	38°28' N, 047°04' E
Ahvaz	31°19' N, 048°42' E
Amol	36°28' N, 052°21' E
Arak	34°05' N, 049°41' E
Ardabil	38°15' N, 048°18' E
Bafq	31°36' N, 055°24' E

Name	Lat./Long.
Bajestan	34°31' N, 058°10' E
Bakhtaran	34°19' N, 047°04' E
Bam	29°06' N, 058°21' E
Bampur	27°12' N, 060°27' E
Bandar Beheshti	25°18' N, 060°37' E
Bandar-e 'Abbas	27°11' N, 056°17' E
Bandar-e Anzali	37°28' N, 049°27' E
Bandar-e Bushehr	28°59' N, 050°50' E
Bandar-e Khomeyni	30°25' N, 049°05' E
Bandar-e Lengeh	26°33' N, 054°53' E
Bastam	36°29' N, 055°00' E
Behbahan	30°35' N, 050°14' E
Behshahr	36°43' N, 053°34' E
Birjand	32°53' N, 059°13' E
Bojnurd	37°28' N, 057°19' E
Borujerd	33°54' N, 048°46' E
Darab	28°45' N, 054°34' E
Delijan	33°59' N, 050°40' E
Dezful	32°23' N, 048°24' E
Esfahan	32°40' N, 051°38' E
Ferdows	34°00' N, 058°09' E
Firuzabad	28°50' N, 052°36' E
Gachsaran	30°12' N, 050°47' E
Gonabad	34°20' N, 058°42' E
Gonbad-e Qabus	37°15' N, 055°09' E
Gorgan	36°50' N, 054°29' E
Haft Gel	31°27' N, 049°32' E
Hamadan	34°48' N, 048°30' E
Ilam	33°38' N, 046°26' E
Jahrom	28°31' N, 053°33' E
Jask	25°38' N, 057°46' E
Jolfa	38°57' N, 045°38' E
Karaj	35°48' N, 050°59' E
Kashan	33°59' N, 051°29' E
Kazerun	29°37' N, 051°38' E
Kerman	30°17' N, 057°05' E
Khomeynishahr	32°41' N, 051°31' E
Khorramabad	33°30' N, 048°20' E
Khorramshahr	30°25' N, 048°11' E
Khvoy	38°33' N, 044°58' E
Ladiz	28°56' N, 061°19' E
Lar	27°41' N, 054°17' E
Mahabad	36°45' N, 045°43' E
Malayer	34°18' N, 048°50' E
Manjil	36°44' N, 049°24' E
Maragheh	37°23' N, 046°14' E
Marv Dasht	29°52' N, 052°48' E
Mashhad	36°18' N, 059°36' E
Masjed-e Soleyman	31°58' N, 049°18' E
Mianeh	37°26' N, 047°42' E
Najafabad	32°37' N, 051°21' E
Nehbandan	31°32' N, 060°02' E
Neyshabur	36°12' N, 058°50' E
Orumiyeh	37°33' N, 045°04' E
Qa'en	33°44' N, 059°11' E
Qazvin	36°16' N, 050°00' E
Qom	34°39' N, 050°54' E
Quchan	37°06' N, 058°30' E
Rafsanjan	30°24' N, 056°00' E
Rasht	37°16' N, 049°36' E
Sabzevar	36°13' N, 057°42' E
Sakht Sar	36°53' N, 050°41' E
Sanandaj	35°19' N, 047°00' E
Saqqez	36°14' N, 046°16' E
Sarab	37°56' N, 047°32' E
Sari	36°34' N, 053°04' E
Semnan	35°33' N, 053°24' E
Shahr-e Kord	32°19' N, 050°50' E
Shahr-e Rey	35°35' N, 051°25' E
Shahrud	36°25' N, 054°58' E
Shiraz	29°36' N, 052°32' E
Surmaq	31°03' N, 052°48' E
Tabriz	38°05' N, 046°18' E
Tehran	35°40' N, 051°26' E
Torbat-e Heydariyeh	35°16' N, 059°13' E
Torbat-e Jam	35°14' N, 060°36' E
Yasuj	30°40' N, 051°36' E
Yazd	31°53' N, 054°22' E
Zabol	31°02' N, 061°30' E
Zahedan	29°30' N, 060°52' E
Zanjan	36°40' N, 048°29' E

IRAQ ....pg. 147

Capital: ....Baghdad
Area: ....435,052 sq km; 167,975 sq mi
Longest River: .... Tigris 1,900 km; 1,180 mi
Avg. Temperature: Jan ≈ 10°C; Jul ≈ 34°C
Currency: ....Iraqi dinar
Official Language: .Arabic

Ad-Diwaniyah	31°59' N, 044°56' E
Al-'Amarah	31°50' N, 047°09' E
Al-Basrah, see Basra	
Al-Hillah	32°29' N, 044°25' E
Al-Kut	32°30' N, 045°49' E
Al-Mawsil, see Mosul	
An-Najaf	31°59' N, 044°20' E
An-Nasiriyah	31°02' N, 046°16' E
Ar-Ramadi	33°25' N, 043°17' E
As-Samawah	31°18' N, 045°17' E
As-Sulaymaniyah	35°33' N, 045°26' E
Ba'qubah	33°45' N, 044°38' E
Baghdad	33°21' N, 044°25' E
Basra (Al-Basrah)	30°30' N, 047°47' E
Irbil (Arbela, Arbil, or Erbil)	36°11' N, 044°01' E
Karbala'	32°36' N, 044°02' E
Kirkuk	35°28' N, 044°23' E
Mosul (Al-Mawsil)	36°20' N, 043°08' E

IRELAND ....pg. 125

Capital: .... Dublin
Area: ....70,285 sq km; 27,137 sq mi
Highest Elev.: .....Carrantuohill 1,040 m; 3,410 ft
Longest River: .....Shannon 260 km; 160 mi
Avg. Temperature: .Jan ≈ 5°C; Jul ≈ 15°C
Currency: ....Irish pound
Official Language: .Irish, English

Abbeyfeale	52°23' N, 009°18' W
Abbeyleix	52°54' N, 007°21' W
Athenry	53°18' N, 008°45' W
Ardee	53°51' N, 006°32' W
Ballinasloe	53°20' N, 008°13' W
Ballinrobe	53°38' N, 009°14' W
Ballycotton	51°50' N, 008°01' W

Name	Lat./Long.
Ballymote	54°05' N, 008°31' W
Ballyvaghan	53°07' N, 009°09' W
Bantry	51°41' N, 009°27' W
Boyle	53°58' N, 008°18' W
Blackrock (Carraig Dubh)	53°18' N, 006°10' W
Bray (Bre)	53°12' N, 006°06' W
Cahersiveen	51°58' N, 010°13' W
Carrick on Shannon	53°57' N, 008°05' W
Castlebar	53°50' N, 009°18' W
Castleblayney	54°07' N, 006°44' W
Cavan (Cabhan, An)	54°00' N, 007°22' W
Celbridge	53°20' N, 006°33' W
Clara	53°20' N, 007°37' W
Claremorris	53°43' N, 009°00' W
Clonakilty	51°37' N, 008°53' W
Clonmel (Cluain Meala)	52°21' N, 007°42' W
Cobh	51°51' N, 008°17' W
Cork (Corcaigh)	51°54' N, 008°28' W
Crosshaven	51°48' N, 008°18' W
Dingle	52°08' N, 010°15' W
Drogheda (Droichead Atha)	53°43' N, 006°21' W
Dublin	53°20' N, 006°15' W
Dundalk (Dun Dealgan)	54°00' N, 006°25' W
Dun Laoghaire	53°17' N, 006°07' W
Ennis (Inis)	52°51' N, 008°59' W
Enniscorthy	52°30' N, 006°34' W
Fermoy	52°08' N, 008°17' W
Galway (Gaillimh)	53°17' N, 009°03' W
Gorey	52°40' N, 006°18' W
Greystones	53°09' N, 006°04' W
Kanturk	52°10' N, 008°54' W
Kilkenny (Cill Chainnigh)	52°39' N, 007°15' W
Killarney (Cill Airne)	52°03' N, 009°31' W
Kilrush	52°38' N, 009°29' W
Limerick (Luimneach)	52°40' N, 008°37' W
Lismore (Lios Mor)	52°08' N, 007°55' W
Longford	53°44' N, 007°48' W
Louth (Lu)	53°57' N, 006°32' W
Lucan	53°21' N, 006°27' W
Malahide	53°27' N, 006°09' W
Midleton	51°55' N, 008°10' W
Monaghan	54°15' N, 006°58' W
Mullingar	53°32' N, 007°21' W
Naas (Nas, An)	53°13' N, 006°40' W
Nenagh	52°52' N, 008°12' W
Portlaoise (Maryborough, Portlaoighise)	53°02' N, 007°18' W
Portumna	53°05' N, 008°13' W
Roscommon	53°38' N, 008°11' W
Roscrea	52°57' N, 007°48' W
Shannon	52°42' N, 008°52' W
Skerries	53°35' N, 006°07' W
Skibbereen	51°33' N, 009°16' W
Sligo	54°16' N, 008°29' W
Swinford	53°57' N, 008°57' W
Swords	53°27' N, 006°13' W
Templemore	52°47' N, 007°50' W
Thomastown	52°31' N, 007°08' W
Tralee	52°16' N, 009°43' W
Tramore	52°09' N, 007°09' W
Trim	53°33' N, 006°48' W
Tullamore	53°16' N, 007°29' W
Waterford (Port Lairge)	52°15' N, 007°06' W
Westport	53°48' N, 009°31' W
Wexford (Loch Garman)	52°20' N, 006°28' W
Wicklow (Cill Mhantain)	52°59' N, 006°03' W

ISRAEL ....pg. 147

Capital: ....Jerusalem
Area: ....20,700 sq km; 7,992 sq mi
Highest Elev.: ...Mt. Meron 1,210 m; 3,960 ft
Longest River: ...Jordan 360 km; 220 mi
Avg. Temperature: .Jan ≈ 9°C; Jul ≈ 24°C
Currency: ......New (Israeli) sheqel
Official Language: ..Hebrew, Arabic

Beersheba (Be'er Sheva')	31°14' N, 034°47' E
Haifa (Hefa)	32°50' N, 035°00' E
Jerusalem (Yerushalayim)	31°46' N, 035°14' E
Nazareth (Nazerat)	32°42' N, 035°18' E
Tel Aviv-Jaffa	32°04' N, 034°46' E

ITALY ....pg. 130

Capital: ....Rome
Area: ....301,277 sq km; 116,324 sq mi
Highest Elev.: ....Mont Blanc 4,810 m; 15,770 ft
Longest River: ....Po 650 km; 400 mi
Avg. Temperature: .Jan ≈ 7°C; Jul ≈ 25°C
Currency: ....lira
Official Language: ..Italian

Acireale	37°37' N, 015°10' E
Adrano (Aderno)	37°40' N, 014°50' E
Adria	45°03' N, 012°03' E
Agrigento (Girgenti)	37°19' N, 013°34' E
Alba	44°42' N, 008°02' E
Alcamo	37°59' N, 012°58' E
Alessandria	44°54' N, 008°37' E
Alghero	40°33' N, 008°19' E
Altamura	40°49' N, 016°33' E
Ancona	43°38' N, 013°30' E
Andria	41°13' N, 016°17' E
Anzio (Antium)	41°27' N, 012°37' E
Aosta	45°44' N, 007°20' E
Aquileia	45°46' N, 013°22' E
Arezzo	43°25' N, 011°53' E
Argenta	44°37' N, 011°50' E
Ascoli Piceno	42°51' N, 013°34' E
Assisi	43°04' N, 012°37' E
Asti	44°54' N, 008°12' E
Atri	42°35' N, 013°58' E
Augusta	37°13' N, 015°13' E
Avellino	40°54' N, 014°47' E
Aversa	40°58' N, 014°12' E
Avezzano	42°02' N, 013°25' E
Avola	36°54' N, 015°08' E
Bardonecchia	45°05' N, 006°42' E
Bari	41°08' N, 016°51' E
Barletta	41°19' N, 016°17' E
Belluno	46°09' N, 012°13' E
Benevento	41°08' N, 014°45' E
Bergamo	45°41' N, 009°43' E
Biella	45°34' N, 008°03' E
Bitonto	41°06' N, 016°41' E
Bobbio	44°46' N, 009°23' E

Name	Lat./Long.
Bologna	44°29' N, 011°20' E
Bolzano	46°31' N, 011°22' E
Bordighera	43°46' N, 007°39' E
Brescia	45°33' N, 010°15' E
Bressanone (Brixen)	46°43' N, 011°39' E
Brindisi	40°38' N, 017°56' E
Bronte	37°47' N, 014°50' E
Busto Arsizio	45°37' N, 008°51' E
Cagliari	39°13' N, 009°07' E
Caltanissetta	37°29' N, 014°04' E
Campobasso	41°34' N, 014°39' E
Canosa di Puglia	41°13' N, 016°04' E
Cantù	45°44' N, 009°08' E
Carbonia	39°10' N, 008°31' E
Carpi	44°47' N, 010°53' E
Carrara	44°05' N, 010°06' E
Cascina	43°41' N, 010°33' E
Caserta	41°04' N, 014°20' E
Castellammare di Stabia	40°42' N, 014°29' E
Castelvetrano	37°41' N, 012°47' E
Catania	37°30' N, 015°06' E
Catanzaro	38°54' N, 016°35' E
Cerignola	41°16' N, 015°54' E
Cesena	44°08' N, 012°15' E
Chianciano Terme	43°02' N, 011°49' E
Chiavari	44°19' N, 009°19' E
Chieti	42°21' N, 014°10' E
Chioggia	45°13' N, 012°17' E
Civitavecchia	42°06' N, 011°48' E
Como	45°47' N, 009°05' E
Coni, see Cuneo	
Corleone	37°49' N, 013°18' E
Corneto, see Tarquinia	
Cosenza	39°18' N, 016°15' E
Cremona	45°07' N, 010°02' E
Crotone	39°05' N, 017°08' E
Cuneo (Coni)	44°23' N, 007°32' E
Eboli	40°36' N, 015°04' E
Empoli	43°43' N, 010°57' E
Enna	37°34' N, 014°16' E
Erice (Monte San Giuliano)	38°02' N, 012°35' E
Este	45°14' N, 011°39' E
Fabriano	43°20' N, 012°54' E
Fano	43°50' N, 013°01' E
Feltre	46°01' N, 011°54' E
Fermo	43°09' N, 013°43' E
Ferrara	44°50' N, 011°35' E
Florence (Firenze or Florentia)	43°46' N, 011°15' E
Foggia	41°27' N, 015°34' E
Foligno	42°57' N, 012°42' E
Fondi	41°21' N, 013°25' E
Forli	44°13' N, 012°03' E
Formia	41°15' N, 013°37' E
Fossano	44°33' N, 007°43' E
Frascati	41°48' N, 012°41' E
Frosinone	41°38' N, 013°19' E
Gela	37°04' N, 014°15' E
Genoa (Genova)	44°25' N, 008°57' E
Gorizia (Gorz)	45°57' N, 013°38' E
Grosseto	42°46' N, 011°08' E
Guastalla	44°55' N, 010°39' E
Iesi, see Jesi	
Iglesias	39°19' N, 008°32' E
Imola	44°21' N, 011°42' E
Imperia	43°53' N, 008°03' E
Jesi (Iesi)	43°31' N, 013°14' E
L'Aquila	42°22' N, 013°22' E
La Spezia	44°07' N, 009°50' E
Lanciano	42°14' N, 014°23' E
Larderello	43°14' N, 010°53' E
Latina	41°28' N, 012°52' E
Lecce	40°23' N, 018°11' E
Lecco	45°51' N, 009°23' E
Leghorn (Livorno)	43°33' N, 010°19' E
Legnano	45°36' N, 008°54' E
Lucca	43°50' N, 010°29' E
Lucera	41°30' N, 015°20' E
Lugo	44°25' N, 011°54' E
Macerata	43°18' N, 013°27' E
Manfredonia	41°38' N, 015°55' E
Mantua (Mantova)	45°09' N, 010°48' E
Marsala	37°48' N, 012°26' E
Martina Franca	40°42' N, 017°20' E
Massa	44°01' N, 010°09' E
Matera	40°40' N, 016°36' E
Mazara del Vallo	37°39' N, 012°35' E
Melfi	40°60' N, 015°39' E
Merano	46°40' N, 011°09' E
Messina (Messana)	38°11' N, 015°34' E
Mestre	45°29' N, 012°15' E
Milan (Milano)	45°28' N, 009°12' E
Modena	44°40' N, 010°55' E
Mola di Bari	41°04' N, 017°05' E
Molfetta	41°12' N, 016°36' E
Moncalieri	45°00' N, 007°41' E
Monreale	38°05' N, 013°17' E
Monte San Giuliano, see Erice	
Monza	45°35' N, 009°16' E
Naples (Napoli or Neapolis)	40°50' N, 014°15' E
Nardò	40°11' N, 018°02' E
Nola	40°55' N, 014°33' E
Novara	45°28' N, 008°38' E
Nuoro	40°19' N, 009°20' E
Olbia	40°55' N, 009°31' E
Oristano	39°54' N, 008°36' E
Orosei	40°23' N, 009°42' E
Ortona	42°21' N, 014°24' E
Orvieto	42°43' N, 012°07' E
Otranto	40°09' N, 018°30' E
Padua (Padova)	45°25' N, 011°53' E
Palazzolo Acreide	37°04' N, 014°54' E
Palermo	38°07' N, 013°22' E
Parma	44°48' N, 010°20' E
Pavia	45°10' N, 009°10' E
Perugia (Perusia)	43°08' N, 012°22' E
Pesaro (Pisaurum)	43°54' N, 012°55' E
Pescara	42°28' N, 014°13' E
Peschiera del Garda	45°26' N, 010°42' E
Piacenza	45°01' N, 009°40' E
Piombino	42°55' N, 010°32' E
Pisa	43°43' N, 010°23' E
Pisaurum, see Pesaro	
Pistoia	43°55' N, 010°54' E
Pordenone	45°57' N, 012°39' E
Portici	40°49' N, 014°20' E
Porto Torres	40°50' N, 008°24' E
Potenza	40°38' N, 015°48' E
Pozzuoli	40°49' N, 014°07' E
Prato	43°53' N, 011°06' E
Ragusa	36°55' N, 014°44' E
Ravenna	44°25' N, 012°12' E
Recanati	43°24' N, 013°32' E

Name	Lat./Long.
Reggio di Calabria	38°06' N, 015°39' E
Reggio nell'Emilia	44°43' N, 010°36' E
Rimini	44°04' N, 012°34' E
Rivoli	45°04' N, 007°31' E
Rome (Roma)	41°54' N, 012°29' E
Rovereto	45°53' N, 011°02' E
Rovigo	45°04' N, 011°47' E
Ruvo di Puglia	41°07' N, 016°29' E
Salerno	40°41' N, 014°47' E
San Giovanni Rotondo	41°42' N, 015°44' E
San Remo	43°49' N, 007°46' E
San Severo	41°41' N, 015°23' E
Sansepolcro	43°34' N, 012°08' E
Sarroch	39°04' N, 009°00' E
Sassari	40°43' N, 008°34' E
Savona	44°17' N, 008°30' E
Schio	45°43' N, 011°21' E
Sciacca	37°31' N, 013°03' E
Scicli	36°47' N, 014°42' E
Sesto San Giovanni	45°32' N, 009°14' E
Siena	43°19' N, 011°21' E
Siracusa, see Syracuse	
Sondrio	46°10' N, 009°52' E
Sora	41°43' N, 013°37' E
Spezia, see La Spezia	
Spoleto	42°44' N, 012°44' E
Sulmona	42°03' N, 013°55' E
Syracuse (Siracusa)	37°04' N, 015°18' E
Taormina	37°51' N, 015°17' E
Taranto (Taras or Tarentum)	40°28' N, 017°14' E
Tarquinia (Corneto)	42°15' N, 011°45' E
Tempio Pausania	40°54' N, 009°06' E
Teramo	42°39' N, 013°42' E
Terni	42°34' N, 012°37' E
Terracina	41°17' N, 013°15' E
Tivoli (Tibur)	41°58' N, 012°48' E
Todi	42°47' N, 012°24' E
Torino, see Turin	
Torre Annunziata	40°45' N, 014°27' E
Torre del Greco	40°47' N, 014°22' E
Tortona	44°54' N, 008°52' E
Trapani	38°01' N, 012°29' E
Trento	46°04' N, 011°08' E
Treviso	45°40' N, 012°15' E
Trieste	45°40' N, 013°46' E
Turin (Torino)	45°03' N, 007°40' E
Udine	46°03' N, 013°14' E
Umbertide	43°18' N, 012°20' E
Urbino	43°43' N, 012°38' E
Varese	45°48' N, 008°50' E
Vasto	42°07' N, 014°42' E
Venice (Venezia)	45°27' N, 012°21' E
Vercelli	45°19' N, 008°25' E
Verona	45°27' N, 011°00' E
Viareggio	43°52' N, 010°14' E
Vibo Valentia	38°40' N, 016°06' E
Vicenza	45°33' N, 011°33' E
Vigevano	45°19' N, 008°51' E
Viterbo	42°25' N, 012°06' E
Vittoria	36°57' N, 014°32' E
Volterra	43°24' N, 010°51' E

JAMAICA ....pg. 116

Capital: ....Kingston
Area: ....10,991 sq km; 4,244 sq mi
Highest Elev.: ...Blue Mountain Pk. 2,260 m; 7,400 ft
Longest River: ...Black 70 km; 40 mi
Avg. Temperature: .Jan ≈ 25°C; Jul ≈ 28°C
Currency: ....Jamaica dollar
Official Language: .English

Kingston	17°58' N, 076°48' W
Montego Bay	18°28' N, 077°55' W

JAPAN ....pg. 143

Capital: ....Tokyo
Area: ....337,835 sq km; 145,883 sq mi
Highest Elev.: ...Mt. Fuji 3,780 m; 12,390 ft
Longest River: ...Shinano 370 km; 230 mi
Avg. Temperature: .Jan ≈ 4°C; Jul ≈ 25°C
Currency: ....yen
Official Language: ..Japanese

Akita	39°43' N, 140°07' E
Aomori	40°49' N, 140°45' E
Asahikawa	43°46' N, 142°22' E
Chiba	35°36' N, 140°07' E
Fukuoka	33°35' N, 130°24' E
Fukushima	37°45' N, 140°28' E
Funabashi	35°42' N, 139°59' E
Gifu	35°25' N, 136°45' E
Hachinohe	40°30' N, 141°29' E
Hakodate	41°45' N, 140°43' E
Hiroshima	34°24' N, 132°27' E
Hofu	34°03' N, 131°34' E
Iwaki	37°05' N, 140°50' E
Kagoshima	31°36' N, 130°33' E
Kanazawa	36°34' N, 136°39' E
Kawasaki	35°32' N, 139°43' E
Kita-Kyushu	33°50' N, 130°50' E
Kobe	34°41' N, 135°10' E
Kochi	33°33' N, 133°33' E
Kumamoto	32°48' N, 130°43' E
Kushiro	42°58' N, 144°23' E
Kutchan	42°54' N, 140°45' E
Matsue	35°28' N, 133°04' E
Matsuyama	33°50' N, 132°45' E
Mito	36°22' N, 140°28' E
Miyazaki	31°52' N, 131°25' E
Morioka	39°42' N, 141°09' E
Muroran	42°18' N, 140°59' E
Nagasaki	32°48' N, 129°55' E
Nagoya	35°10' N, 136°55' E
Niigata	37°55' N, 139°03' E
Obihiro	42°55' N, 143°12' E
Okayama	34°39' N, 133°55' E
Osaka	34°40' N, 135°30' E
Otaru	43°13' N, 141°00' E
Sakai	34°35' N, 135°28' E
Sapporo	43°03' N, 141°21' E
Sendai	38°15' N, 140°53' E
Shizuoka	34°58' N, 138°23' E
Tokyo	35°42' N, 139°46' E
Tomakomai	42°38' N, 141°36' E
Tottori	35°30' N, 134°14' E

Name	Lat./Long.
Wakayama	34°13' N, 135°11' E
Wakkanai	45°25' N, 141°40' E
Yaizu	34°52' N, 138°20' E
Yamagata	38°15' N, 140°20' E
Yokohama	35°27' N, 139°39' E

JORDAN ....pg. 147

Capital: . . . . .Amman
Area: . . . . . . .88,946 sq km; 34,342 sq mi
Highest Elev.: . . . .Mt. Ramm 1,750 m; 5,760 ft
Longest River: . . . .Jordan 360 km; 220 mi
Avg. Temperature: . .Jan = 8°C; Jul = 25°C
Currency: . . . . . . .Jordan dinar
Official Language: . .Arabic

Name	Lat./Long.
Amman ('Amman)	31°57' N, 035°56' E
As Salt	32°03' N, 035°44' E
Az Zarqa'	32°05' N, 036°06' E
Irbid	32°33' N, 035°51' E

KAZAKSTAN ....pg. 136

Capital: . . . . . . .Astana
Area: . . . . . . .2,717,300 sq km; 1,049,200 sq mi
Highest Elev.: . . . .Mt. Khan-Tengri 7,000 m;
22,950 ft
Longest River: . . . .Irtysh 4,250 km; 2,640 mi
Avg. Temperature: . .Jan = -10°C; Jul = 24°C
Currency: . . . . . . .tenge
Official Language: . .Kazakh

Name	Lat./Long.
Almaty (Alma-Ata)	43°15' N, 076°57' E
Atyrau (Atenau, Gurjev, or Guryev)	47°07' N, 051°53' E
Aqtau (Aktau, or Shevchenko)	43°39' N, 051°12' E
Aqtöbe (Aktyubinsk)	50°17' N, 057°10' E
Astana	51°10' N, 071°30' E
Balqhas (Balkhash or Balchas)	46°49' N, 075°00' E
Celinograd, see Aqmola	
Dzhezkazgan	47°47' N, 067°46' E
Kökshetau (Kokchetav)	53°17' N, 069°30' E
Leningor (Leninogorsk or Ridder)	50°22' N, 083°32' E
Leninsk, see Tyrutam	
Oral (Uralsk)	51°14' N, 051°22' E
Öskemen (Ust-Kamenogorsk)	49°58' N, 082°40' E
Pavlodar	52°18' N, 076°57' E
Petropavl (Petropavlovsk)	54°52' N, 069°06' E
Qaraghandy (Karaganda)	49°50' N, 073°10' E
Qostanay (Kustanay)	53°10' N, 063°35' E
Qyzylorda (Kyzl-Orda)	44°48' N, 065°28' E
Rudnyy (Rudny)	52°57' N, 063°07' E
Semey (Semipalatinsk)	50°28' N, 080°13' E
Shchuchinsk (Scucinsk)	52°56' N, 070°12' E
Shymkent (Chimkent or Cimkent)	42°18' N, 069°36' E
Taldyqorghan (Taldy-Kurgan)	45°00' N, 078°24' E
Termirtau (Samarkand)	50°05' N, 072°56' E
Tyrutam (Turaram or Leninsk)	45°40' N, 063°20' E
Zhezqazghan (Ekibastuz)	51°40' N, 075°22' E
Zhmbyl (Dzhambul)	42°54' N, 071°22' E

KENYA ....pg. 153

Capital: . . . . .Nairobi
Area: . . . . . . .582,646 sq km; 224,961 sq mi
Highest Elev.: . . . .Mt. Kenya 5,200 m; 17,0600 ft
Longest River: . . . .Tana 710 km; 440 mi
Avg. Temperature: . .Jan = 18°C; Jul = 15°C
Currency: . . . . . . .Kenya shilling
Official Language: . .Swahili, English

Name	Lat./Long.
Bungoma	00°34' N, 034°34' E
Busia	00°28' N, 034°06' E
Eldoret	00°31' N, 035°17' E
Embu	00°32' S, 037°27' E
Garissa	00°28' S, 039°38' E
Isiolo	00°21' N, 037°35' E
Kisii	00°41' S, 034°46' E
Kisumu	00°06' S, 034°45' E
Lamu	02°16' S, 040°54' E
Lodwar	03°07' N, 035°36' E
Machakos	01°31' S, 037°16' E
Malindi	03°13' S, 040°07' E
Mandera	03°56' N, 041°52' E
Maralal	01°06' N, 036°42' E
Marsabit	02°20' N, 037°59' E
Meru	00°03' N, 037°39' E
Nairobi	01°17' S, 036°49' E
Nakuru	00°17' S, 036°04' E
Nanyuki	00°01' N, 037°04' E
Wajir	01°45' N, 040°04' E

KIRIBATI ....pg. 156

Capital: . . . . .Bairiki
Area: . . . . . . .811 sq km; 313 sq mi
Highest Elev.: . . . .Banaba 80 m; 270 ft
Avg. Temperature: . .Jan = 28°C; Jul = 28°C
Currency: . . . . . . .Australian dollar
Official Language: . .English

Name	Lat./Long.
Bairiki	01°20' N, 173°01' E

KOREA, NORTH ....pg. 143

Capital: . . . . .P'yongyang
Area: . . . . . . .122,762 sq km; 47,399 sq mi
Highest Elev.: . . . .Mt. Paektu 2,740 m; 9,000 ft
Longest River: . . . .Yalu 810 km; 500 mi
Avg. Temperature: . .Jan = -8°C; Jul = 24°C
Currency: . . . . . . .won
Official Language: . .Korean

Name	Lat./Long.
Ch'ongjin	41°46' N, 129°49' E
Haeju	38°02' N, 125°42' E
Kanggye	40°58' N, 126°36' E
Kimch'aek (Songjin)	40°41' N, 129°12' E
Namp'o	38°44' N, 125°24' E
Pyongyang	39°01' N, 125°45' E
Sinuiju	40°06' N, 124°24' E
Wonsan	39°10' N, 127°26' E

KOREA, SOUTH ....pg. 143

Capital: . . . . .Seoul
Area: . . . . . . .99,274 sq km; 38,330 sq mi
Highest Elev.: . . . .Mt. Halla 1,950 m; 6,400 ft
Longest River: . . . .Naktong 520 km; 330 mi
Avg. Temperature: . .Jan = 2°C; Jul = 24°C
Currency: . . . . . . .won
Official Language: . .Korean

Name	Lat./Long.
Inch'on	37°28' N, 126°38' E
Kwangju	35°09' N, 126°55' E
Masan	35°11' N, 128°34' E
Pusan	35°06' N, 129°03' E
Seoul (Soul)	37°34' N, 127°00' E
Suwon	37°16' N, 127°01' E
Taegu (Daegu or Taiku)	35°52' N, 128°36' E
Taejon	36°20' N, 127°26' E

KUWAIT ....pg. 154

Capital: . . . . .Kuwait
Area: . . . . . . .17,818 sq km; 6,880 sq mi
Highest Elev.: . . . .Ash-Shaqaya Pk. 290 m; 950 ft
Avg. Temperature: . .Jan = 13°C; Jul = 35°C
Currency: . . . . . . .Kuwaiti dinar
Official Language: . .Arabic

Name	Lat./Long.
Ahmadi, al-	29°05' N, 048°04' E
Hawalli	29°19' N, 048°02' E
Jahrah, al-	29°20' N, 047°40' E
Kuwait	29°20' N, 047°59' E
Shu'aybah, ash-	29°03' N, 048°08' E

KYRGYZSTAN ....pg. 139

Capital: . . . . .Bishkek
Area: . . . . . . .198,500 sq km; 76,600 sq mi
Highest Elev.: . . . .Victory Pk. 7,440 m; 24,410 ft
Longest River: . . . .Naryn 700 km; 430 mi
Avg. Temperature: . .Jan = -13°C; Jul = 21°C
Currency: . . . . . . .som
Official Language: . .Kyrgyz, Russian

Name	Lat./Long.
Bishkek (Frunze)	42°54' N, 074°36' E
Kara-Balta	42°50' N, 073°52' E
Karakol (Przhevalsk)	42°33' N, 078°18' E
Osh	40°32' N, 072°48' E
Tokmok	42°52' N, 075°18' E
Ysyk-Köl (Rybachye)	42°26' N, 076°12' E

LAOS ....pg. 144

Capital: . . . . .Vientiane
Area: . . . . . . .236,800 sq km; 91,429 sq mi
Highest Elev.: . . . .Mt. Bia 2,820 m; 9,250 ft
Longest River: . . . .Mekong 4,350 km; 2,700 mi
Avg. Temperature: . .Jan = 21°C; Jul = 27°C
Currency: . . . . . . .kip
Official Language: . .Lao

Name	Lat./Long.
Savannakhet	16°33' N, 104°45' E
Vientiane (Viangchan)	17°58' N, 102°36' E

LATVIA ....pg. 138

Capital: . . . . .Riga
Area: . . . . . . .64,610 sq km; 24,946 sq mi
Highest Elev.: . . . .Mt. Gaizins 310 m; 1,020 ft
Longest River: . . . .Daugava 1,020 km; 630 mi
Avg. Temperature: . .Jan = -4°C; Jul = 17°C
Currency: . . . . . . .lats
Official Language: . .Latvian

Name	Lat./Long.
Aluksne	57°25' N, 027°03' E
Aizpute	56°43' N, 021°36' E
Auce	56°28' N, 022°53' E
Balvi	57°08' N, 027°15' E
Cesis	57°18' N, 025°15' E
Daugavpils	55°53' N, 026°32' E
Dobele	56°37' N, 023°16' E
Gulbene	57°11' N, 026°45' E
Ilukste	55°58' N, 026°18' E
Jekabpils	56°29' N, 025°51' E
Jelgava	56°39' N, 023°42' E
Jurmala	56°58' N, 023°34' E
Karsava	56°47' N, 027°40' E
Limbazi	56°31' N, 021°01' E
Ludza	57°31' N, 024°42' E
Mazsalace	56°33' N, 027°43' E
Ogre	57°52' N, 025°03' E
Piltene	56°49' N, 024°36' E
Preili	57°13' N, 021°40' E
Riga (Riga)	56°18' N, 026°43' E
Rujiena	56°57' N, 024°06' E
Sabile	57°54' N, 025°19' E
Salacgriva	57°03' N, 022°35' E
Saldus	57°45' N, 024°21' E
Sigulda	56°40' N, 022°30' E
Valmiera	57°09' N, 024°51' E
Ventspils	57°33' N, 025°24' E
Viesite	57°24' N, 021°31' E
Vilani	56°21' N, 025°33' E
Zilupe	56°23' N, 028°07' E

LEBANON ....pg. 147

Capital: . . . . .Beirut
Area: . . . . . . .10,230 sq km; 3,950 sq mi
Highest Elev.: . . . .Qurnet as-Sawda 3,090 m;
10,140 ft
Longest River: . . . .Litani 150 km; 90 mi
Avg. Temperature: . .Jan = 14°C; Jul = 26°C
Currency: . . . . . . .Lebanese pound
Official Language: . .Arabic

Name	Lat./Long.
Beirut (Bayrut)	33°53' N, 035°30' E
Sayda, see Sidon	

Name	Lat./Long.
Sidon (Sayda)	33°33' N, 035°22' E
Tripoli (Tarabulus)	34°26' N, 035°51' E

LESOTHO ....pg. 152

Capital: . . . . .Maseru
Area: . . . . . . .30,355 sq km; 11,720 sq mi
Highest Elev.: . . . .Mt. Ntlenyana 3,480 m; 11,420 ft
Longest River: . . . .Orange 2,100 km; 1,300 mi
Avg. Temperature: . .Jan = 21.1°C; Jul = 7.7°C
Currency: . . . . . . .loti
Official Language: . .Sotho, English

Name	Lat./Long.
Maseru	29°19' S, 027°29' E

LIBERIA ....pg. 150

Capital: . . . . .Monrovia
Area: . . . . . . .99,067 sq km; 38,250 sq mi
Highest Elev.: . . . .Mt. Nimba 1,750 m; 5,750 ft
Longest River: . . . .Cavalla 510 km; 320 mi
Avg. Temperature: . .Jan = 26°C; Jul = 24°C
Currency: . . . . . . .Liberian dollar
Official Language: . .English

Name	Lat./Long.
Monrovia	06°19' N, 010°48' E

LIBYA ....pg. 150

Capital: . . . . .Tripoli
Area: . . . . . . .1,757,000 sq km; 678,400 sq mi
Highest Elev.: . . . .Bikku Bitti. 2,290 m; 7,500 ft
Avg. Temperature: . .Jan = 12°C; Jul = 26°C
Currency: . . . . . . .Libyan dinar
Official Language: . .Arabic

Name	Lat./Long.
Banghazi (Bengasi or Benghazi)	32°07' N, 020°04' E
Darnah (Derna)	32°46' N, 022°39' E
Misratah (Misurata)	32°23' N, 015°06' E
Tarabulus, see Tripoli	
Taziru	25°45' N, 021°00' E
Tobruk (Tubruq)	32°05' N, 023°59' E
Tripoli (Tarabulus)	32°54' N, 013°11' E

LIECHTENSTEIN ....pg. 132

Capital: . . . . .Vaduz
Area: . . . . . . .160 sq km; 618 sq mi
Highest Elev.: . . . .Grauspitz 2,600 m; 8,530 ft
Longest River: . . . .Rhine 1,390 km; 870 mi
Avg. Temperature: . .Jan = -1°C; Jul = 17°C
Currency: . . . . . . .Swiss franc
Official Language: . .German

Name	Lat./Long.
Vaduz	47°09' N, 009°31' E

LITHUANIA ....pg. 138

Capital: . . . . .Vilnius
Area: . . . . . . .65,301 sq km; 25,213 sq mi
Highest Elev.: . . . .Mt. Juozapine 290 m; 960 ft
Longest River: . . . .Neman 940 km; 580 mi
Avg. Temperature: . .Jan = -5°C; Jul = 17°C
Currency: . . . . . . .litas
Official Language: . .Lithuanian

Name	Lat./Long.
Alytus	54°24' N, 024°03' E
Birstonas	54°37' N, 024°02' E
Birzai	56°12' N, 024°45' E
Druskininkai	54°01' N, 023°58' E
Gargzdai	55°43' N, 021°24' E
Joniskis	56°14' N, 023°37' E
Jurbarkas	55°04' N, 022°46' E
Kaunas	54°54' N, 023°54' E
Kazly Ruda	54°46' N, 023°30' E
Kedainiai	55°17' N, 023°58' E
Klaipeda	55°43' N, 021°07' E
Kursenai	56°00' N, 022°56' E
Lazdijai	54°14' N, 023°31' E
Marijampole (Kapsukas)	54°34' N, 023°21' E
Mazeikiai	56°19' N, 022°20' E
Naujoji Akmene	56°19' N, 022°54' E
Neringa	55°22' N, 021°04' E
Pagegiai	55°09' N, 021°54' E
Pakruojis	58°58' N, 023°52' E
Palanga	55°55' N, 021°03' E
Pandelys	56°01' N, 025°13' E
Panevezys	55°44' N, 024°21' E
Ramygala	55°31' N, 024°18' E
Salcininkai	54°18' N, 025°23' E
Siauliai	55°56' N, 023°19' E
Silale	55°28' N, 022°12' E
Silute	55°21' N, 021°29' E
Sirvintos	55°03' N, 024°57' E
Taurage	55°15' N, 022°17' E
Utena	55°30' N, 025°36' E
Vilkija	55°03' N, 023°35' E
Vilnius	54°41' N, 025°19' E

LUXEMBOURG ....pg. 132

Capital: . . . . .Luxembourg
Area: . . . . . . .2,586 sq km; 999 sq mi
Highest Elev.: . . . .Buurgplaatz 560 m; 1,840 ft
Longest River: . . . .Sûre 170 km; 110 mi
Temperature: . . . . .Jan = 0°C; Jul = 17°C
Currency: . . . . . . .Luxembourg franc
Official Language: . .none

Name	Lat./Long.
Esch-sur-Alzette	49°30' N, 005°59' E
Luxembourg	49°36' N, 006°08' E

MACEDONIA ....pg. 135

Capital: . . . . .Skopje
Area: . . . . . . .25,713 sq km; 9,928 sq mi
Highest Elev.: . . . .Mt. Korab 2,750 m; 9,030 ft
Longest River: . . . .Vardar 420 km; 260 mi
Avg. Temperature: . .Jan = 4°C; Jul = 31°C
Currency: . . . . . . .denar
Official Language: . .Macedonian

Name	Lat./Long.
Gostivar	41°48' N, 020°54' E
Krusevo	41°22' N, 021°15' E
Kumanovo	42°08' N, 021°43' E
Ohrid	41°07' N, 020°48' E
Prilep	41°21' N, 021°34' E
Skopje (Skoplje)	42°00' N, 021°29' E
Stip	41°44' N, 022°12' E
Strumica	41°26' N, 022°39' E
Tetovo	42°01' N, 020°59' E

MADAGASCAR ....pg. 153

Capital: . . . . .Antananarivo
Area: . . . . . . .587,041 sq km; 226,658 sq mi
Highest Elev.: . . . .Maromokotro Pk. 2,880 m;
9,440 ft
Longest River: . . . .Mangoky 560 km; 350 mi
Avg. Temperature: . .Jan = 20°C; Jul = 13°C
Currency: . . . . . . .Malagasy franc
Official Language: . .Malagasy, French

Name	Lat./Long.
Ambalavao	21°50' S, 046°56' E
Ambanja	13°41' S, 048°27' E
Ambatondrazaka	17°50' S, 048°25' E
Ambohimahasoa	21°07' S, 047°13' E
Andapa	14°39' S, 049°39' E
Andoany (Hell-Ville, Helville, or Nosy-Be)	13°24' S, 048°16' E
Ankarana (Sosumav)	13°05' S, 046°58' E
Antananarivo (Tananarive)	18°55' S, 047°31' E
Antsirabe	19°51' S, 047°02' E
Antsiranana (Diego-Suarez)	12°16' S, 049°17' E
Antsohihy	14°52' S, 047°59' E
Arivonimamo	19°01' S, 047°11' E
Befandriana Avaratra (Befandriana-Nord)	15°16' S, 048°32' E
Betroka	23°16' S, 046°05' E
Diego-Suarez, see Antsiranana	
Farafangana	22°49' S, 047°50' E
Fianarantsoa	21°26' S, 047°05' E
Hell-Ville, see Andoany	
Iharana (Vohemar or Vohimarina)	13°21' S, 050°00' E
Ihosy	22°24' S, 046°07' E
Mahabo	20°23' S, 044°40' E
Mahajanga (Majunga)	15°43' S, 046°19' E
Mahanoro	19°54' S, 048°48' E
Mampikony	16°06' S, 047°38' E
Manakara	22°08' S, 048°01' E
Mananjary	21°13' S, 048°20' E
Marovoay	16°06' S, 046°38' E
Miarinarivo	18°57' S, 046°55' E
Morondava	20°17' S, 044°17' E
Nosy-Be, see Andoany	
Port-Bergé (Boriziny)	15°33' S, 047°40' E
Sosumav, see Ankarana	
Tangainony	22°42' S, 047°45' E
Taolanaro, see Tolanaro	
Toamasina (Tamatave)	18°10' S, 049°23' E
Tôlanaro (Faradofay, Fort-Dauphin or Taolanaro)	25°02' S, 047°00' E
Toliara (Toliary or Tulear)	23°21' S, 043°40' E
Vangaindrano	23°21' S, 047°36' E
Vatomandry	19°20' S, 048°59' E
Vohemar, see Iharana	
Vohimarina, see Iharana	

MALAWI ....pg. 153

Capital: . . . . .Lilongwe
Area: . . . . . . .118,484 sq km; 45,747 sq mi
Highest Elev.: . . . .Mlanje 3,000 m; 9,850 ft
Longest River: . . . .Shire 400 km; 250 mi
Avg. Temperature: . .Jan = 22°C; Jul = 16°C
Currency: . . . . . . .Malawi kwacha
Official Language: . .English

Name	Lat./Long.
Blantyre	15°47' S, 035°00' E
Dedza	14°22' S, 034°20' E
Karonga	09°56' S, 033°56' E
Lilongwe	13°59' S, 033°47' E
Mzuzu	11°27' S, 033°55' E
Nsanje (Port Herald)	16°55' S, 035°16' E
Port Herald, see Nsanje	
Salima	13°47' S, 034°26' E
Zomba	15°23' S, 035°20' E

MALAYSIA ....pg. 144

Capital: . . . . .Kuala Lumpur
Area: . . . . . . .330,442 sq km; 127,584 sq mi
Highest Elev.: . . . .Mt. Kinabalu 4,100 m; 13,450 ft
Longest River: . . . .Pahang 430 km; 270 mi
Avg. Temperature: . .Jan = 28°C; Jul = 28°C
Currency: . . . . . . .ringgit
Official Language: . .Malay

Name	Lat./Long.
Alor Setar	06°07' N, 100°22' E
Batu Pahat	01°51' N, 102°56' E
Bintulu	03°10' N, 113°02' E
Butterworth	05°25' N, 100°24' E
George Town (Pinang)	05°25' N, 100°20' E
Ipoh	04°35' N, 101°05' E
Johor Baharu	01°28' N, 103°45' E
Kangar	06°26' N, 100°12' E
Kelang (Klang)	03°02' N, 101°27' E
Keluang	02°02' N, 103°19' E
Kota Baharu	06°08' N, 102°15' E
Kota Kinabalu (Jesselton)	05°59' N, 116°04' E
Kuala Lumpur	03°10' N, 101°42' E
Kuala Terengganu	05°20' N, 103°08' E

Name	Lat./Long.
Kuantan	03°48' N, 103°20' E
Kuching	01°33' N, 110°20' E
Melaka (Malacca)	02°12' N, 102°15' E
Miri	04°23' N, 113°59' E
Muar (Bandar Maharani)	02°02' N, 102°34' E
Petaling Jaya	03°05' N, 101°39' E
Sandakan	05°50' N, 118°07' E
Seremban	02°43' N, 101°56' E
Song	02°01' N, 112°33' E
Sibu	02°18' N, 111°49' E
Taiping	04°51' N, 100°44' E
Teluk Intan (Telok Anson)	04°02' N, 101°01' E
Victoria (Labuan)	05°17' N, 115°15' E

MALDIVES ....pg. 146

Capital: ....Male
Area: ......298 sq km; 115 sq mi
Temperature: .....Jan = 30°C; Jul = 30°C
Currency: ......Maldivian rufiyaa
Official Language: ..Divehi

Male	04°10' N, 073°30' E

MALI ....pg. 150

Capital: ....Bamako
Area: ....1,248,574 sq km; 482,077 sq mi
Highest Elev.: ..Hombori Tondo 1,160 m; 3,770 ft
Longest River: ..Niger 4,200 km; 2,600 mi
Avg. Temperature: .Jan =23°C; Jul = 29°C
Currency: ......CFA franc
Official Language: French

Bamako	12°39' N, 008°00' W
Gao	16°16' N, 000°03' W
Kayes	14°27' N, 011°26' W
Mopti	14°30' N, 004°12' W
Ségou	13°27' N, 006°16' W
Sikasso	11°19' N, 005°40' W
Timbuktu	16°46' N, 003°01' W

MALTA ....pg. 133

Capital: ....Valletta
Area: ......316 sq km; 122 sq mi
Highest Elev.: ..Ta' Zuta 250 m; 830 ft
Avg. Temperature: .Jan = 13°C; Jul = 26°C
Currency: ......Maltese lira
Official Language: ..Maltese, English

Valletta (Valetta)	35°54' N, 014°31' E

MARSHALL ISLANDS ..pg. 156

Capital: ....Majuro
Area: ......181.5 sq km; 70.1 sq mi
Avg. Temperature: .Jan = 28°C; Jul = 28°C
Currency: ......U.S. dollar
Official Language: ..Marshallese, English

Majuro	07°09' N,171°12' E

MAURITANIA ....pg. 150

Capital: ....Nouakchott
Area: ....1,030,700 sq km; 398,000 sq mi
Highest Elev.: ..Ijill 910 m; 3,000 ft
Longest River: ..Senegal 1,080 km; 670 mi
Avg. Temperature: .Jan = 21°C; Jul = 28°C
Currency: ......ouguiya
Official Language: ..Arabic

Nouakchott	18°06' N, 015°57' W

MAURITIUS ....pg. 153

Capital: ....Port Louis
Area: ....2,040 sq km; 788 sq mi
Highest Elev.: ..Petite Rivière-Noire Pk 830 m; 2,710 ft
Longest River: ..Grand River South East 40 km; 25 mi
Avg. Temperature: .Jan = 23°C; Jul = 23°C
Currency: ......Mauritian rupee
Official Language: ..English

Port Louis	20°10' S, 057°30' E

MEXICO ....pg. 115

Capital: ....Mexico City
Area: ....1,958,201 sq km; 756,066 sq mi
Highest Elev.: ..Citlaltepetl 5,700 m; 18,700 ft
Longest River: ..Rio Grande 2.830 km; 1,760 mi
Avg. Temperature: .Jan = 12°C; Jul = 17°C
Currency: ......new peso
Official Language: ..Spanish

Acámbaro	20°02' N, 100°44' W
Acapulco	16°51' N, 099°56' W
Aguascalientes	21°53' N, 102°18' W
Apatzingán	19°05' N, 102°21' W
Arriaga	16°14' N, 093°54' W
Autlán	19°46' N, 104°22' W
Caborca	30°37' N, 112°06' W
Campeche	19°51' N, 090°32' W
Cananea	30°57' N, 110°18' W
Cancún	21°05' N, 086°46' W
Casas Grandes	30°22' N, 107°57' W
Celaya	20°31' N, 100°49' W
Cerro Azul	21°12' N, 097°44' W
Chetumal	18°30' N, 088°18' W
Chihuahua	28°38' N, 106°05' W
Chilpancingo	17°33' N, 099°30' W
Ciudad Acuña (Las Vacas)	29°18' N, 100°55' W
Ciudad de Mexico, see Mexico City	
Ciudad Delicias	28°13' N, 105°28' W
Ciudad Guzmán	19°41' N, 103°29' W

Name	Lat./Long.
Ciudad Hidalgo	19°41' N, 100°34' W
Ciudad Juárez	31°44' N, 106°29' W
Ciudad Mante	22°44' N, 098°57' W
Ciudad Obregón	27°29' N, 109°56' W
Ciudad Pemex	17°54' N, 092°30' W
Ciudad Victoria	23°44' N, 099°08' W
Coatzacoalcos	18°09' N, 094°25' W
Colima	19°14' N, 103°43' W
Comitán	16°15' N, 092°08' W
Cozumel	20°31' N, 086°55' W
Cuauhtémoc	28°25' N, 106°52' W
Cuernavaca	18°55' N, 099°15' W
Culiacán	24°48' N, 107°24' W
Díaz Gutiérrez	22°12' N, 100°57' W
Durango	24°02' N, 104°40' W
El Dorado	24°17' N, 107°21' W
Ensenada	31°52' N, 116°37' W
Escuinapa	22°51' N, 105°48' W
Fresnillo	23°10' N, 102°53' W
Gómez Palacio	25°34' N, 103°30' W
Guadalajara	20°40' N, 103°20' W
Guadalupe	25°41' N, 100°15' W
Guadalupe Victoria	24°27' N, 104°07' W
Guanajuato	21°01' N, 101°15' W
Guasave	25°34' N, 108°27' W
Guaymas	27°56' N, 110°54' W
Hermosillo	29°04' N, 110°58' W
Heroica Nogales	31°20' N, 110°56' W
Hidalgo del Parral (Parral)	26°56' N, 105°40' W
Iguala de la Independencia	18°21' N, 099°32' W
Irapuato	20°41' N, 101°21' W
Jalapa	19°32' N, 096°55' W
Jerez de Garcia Salinas	22°39' N, 103°00' W
Jiménez	27°08' N, 104°55' W
Juchitan	16°26' N, 095°01' W
La Paz	24°10' N, 110°18' W
La Piedad Cavadas	20°21' N, 102°00' W
Las Penas, see Puerto Vallarta	
Las Vacas, see Ciudad Acuña	
León	21°07' N, 101°40' W
Linares	24°52' N, 099°34' W
Los Mochis	25°45' N, 108°57' W
Los Tuxtlas, see San Andres Tuxtla	
Macuspana	17°46' N, 092°36' W
Manzanillo	19°03' N, 104°20' W
Matamoros	18°36' N, 098°28' W
Matamoros	25°53' N, 097°30' W
Matehuala	23°39' N, 100°39' W
Mazatlán	23°13' N, 106°25' W
Mérida	20°58' N, 089°37' W
Mexicali	32°40' N, 115°29' W
Mexico City (Ciudad de Mexico)	19°24' N, 099°09' W
Minatitlán	17°59' N, 094°31' W
Monclova	26°54' N, 101°25' W
Monterrey	25°40' N, 100°19' W
Morelia	19°42' N, 101°07' W
Muleje	26°53' N, 112°01' W
Navojoa	27°06' N, 109°26' W
Nueva Rosita	27°57' N, 101°13' W
Nuevo Laredo	27°30' N, 099°31' W
Oaxaca	17°03' N, 096°43' W
Orizaba	18°51' N, 097°06' W
Pachuca	20°07' N, 098°44' W
Papantla	20°27' N, 097°19' W
Parral, see Hidalgo del Parral	
Piedras Negras	28°42' N, 100°31' W
Poza Rica	20°33' N, 097°27' W
Progreso	21°17' N, 089°40' W
Puebla	19°03' N, 098°12' W
Puerto Escondido	25°48' N, 111°20' W
Puerto Vallarta (Las Penas)	20°37' N, 105°15' W
Querétaro	20°36' N, 100°23' W
Reynosa	26°07' N, 098°18' W
Río Bravo	25°59' N, 098°06' W
Sabinas	27°51' N, 101°07' W
Salamanca	20°34' N, 101°12' W
Saltillo	25°25' N, 101°00' W
San Andrés Tuxtla (Los Tuxtlas)	18°27' N, 095°13' W
San Cristóbal de las Casas	16°45' N, 092°38' W
San Felipe	31°00' N, 114°52' W
San Francisco del Rincon	21°01' N, 101°51' W
San Ignacio	27°27' N, 112°51' W
San Lucas	22°53' N, 109°54' W
San Luis	32°29' N, 114°48' W
San Luis Potosi	22°09' N, 100°59' W
San Miguel de Allende	20°55' N, 100°45' W
San Pedro	25°45' N, 102°59' W
Sánta Barbara	26°48' N, 105°49' W
Santa Catarina	25°41' N, 100°28' W
Santiago Papasquiaro	25°03' N, 105°25' W
Silao	20°56' N, 101°26' W
Tampico	22°13' N, 097°51' W
Tapachula	14°54' N, 092°17' W
Taxco	18°33' N, 099°36' W
Tecoman	18°55' N, 103°53' W
Tecpan	17°15' N, 100°41' W
Tehuacán	18°27' N, 097°23' W
Tepic	21°30' N, 104°54' W
Tequila	20°54' N, 103°47' W
Tierra Blanca	18°27' N, 096°21' W
Tijuana	32°32' N, 117°01' W
Tizimin	21°09' N, 088°09' W
Tlaquepaque	20°39' N, 103°19' W
Tlaxcala	19°19' N, 098°14' W
Toluca	19°17' N, 099°40' W
Torreón	25°33' N, 103°26' W
Tula	23°00' N, 099°43' W
Tuxpan	20°57' N, 097°24' W
Tuxpan	21°57' N, 105°18' W
Tuxtla	16°45' N, 093°07' W
Uruapan	19°25' N, 102°04' W
Valles	21°59' N, 099°01' W
Veracruz	19°12' N, 096°08' W
Villahermosa	17°59' N, 092°55' W
Zacapu	19°50' N, 101°43' W
Zacatecas	22°47' N, 102°35' W
Zamora de Hidalgo	19°59' N, 102°16' W
Zapopan	20°43' N, 103°24' W

MICRONESIA ....pg. 156

Capital: ....Palikir, on Pohnpei
Area: ......701.4 sq km; 270.8 sq mi
Highest Elev.: ..Mt. Totolom 790 m; 2,590 ft
Avg. Temperature: .Jan = 27°C; Jul = 26°C
Currency: ......U.S. dollar
Official Language: ..none

Palikir	06°59' N, 158°08' E

Name	Lat./Long.

MOLDOVA ....pg. 134

Capital: ....Chisinau
Area: ......33,700 sq km; 13,000 sq mi
Highest Elev.: ..Mt. Balanesti 430 m; 1,410 ft
Longest River: ..Dniester 1,350 km; 840 mi
Avg. Temperature: .Jan = -4°C; Jul = 20°C
Currency: ......Moldovan leu
Official Language: ..Romanian

Calaras	47°16' N, 028°19' E
Causeni	46°38' N, 029°25' E
Comrat (Komrat)	46°18' N, 028°39' E
Chisinau	47°00' N, 028°50' E
Drochia	48°02' N, 027°48' E
Dubasari	47°07' N, 029°10' E
Falesti (Faleshty)	47°34' N, 027°42' E
Jura (Kagul)	45°54' N, 028°11' E
Leova (Leovo)	46°28' N, 028°15' E
Orhei (Orgeyev)	47°22' N, 028°49' E
Rabnita	47°45' N, 029°00' E
Rezina	47°45' N, 028°58' E
Soroca (Soroki)	48°09' N, 028°18' E
Tiraspol	46°50' N, 029°37' E
Ungheni	47°12' N, 027°48' E

MONGOLIA ....pg. 142

Capital: ....Ulaanbaatar
Area: ....1,566,500 sq km; 604,800 sq mi
Highest Elev.: ..Nayramadlin Pk. 4,370 m; 14,350 ft
Longest River: ..Selenga 1,480 km; 920 mi
Temperature: ....Jan = -26°C; Jul = 16°C
Currency: ......tugrik
Official Language: Khalkha Mongolian

Darhan	49°29' N, 105°55' E
Ulaanbaatar	47°55' N, 106°53' E

MOROCCO ....pg. 150

Capital: ....Rabat
Area: ......458,730 sq km; 177,117 sq mi
Highest Elev.: ..Mt. Toubkal 4,170 m, 13,670 ft
Longest River: ..Oum er-Rbia 560 km; 350 mi
Avg. Temperature: .Jan =13°C; Jul = 33°C
Currency: ......Moroccan dirham
Official Language: ..Arabic

Agadir	30°24' N, 009°36' W
Beni Mellal	32°20' N, 006°21' W
Casablanca (Ad-Dar al-Bayda' or Dar el-Beida)	33°37' N, 007°35' W
El-Jadida (Mazagan)	33°15' N, 008°30' W
Fès (Fez)	34°02' N, 004°59' W
Kenitra (Mina Hassan Tani or Port-Lyautey)	34°16' N, 006°36' W
Khouribga	32°53' N, 006°54' W
Marrakech	31°38' N, 008°00' W
Meknès	33°54' N, 005°33' W
Mohammedia (Fedala)	33°42' N, 007°24' W
Oujda	34°40' N, 001°54' W
Rabat (Ribat)	34°02' N, 006°50' W
Safi (Asfi)	32°18' N, 009°14' W
Salé (Sla)	34°04' N, 006°48' W
Tan-Tan	28°26' N, 011°06' W
Tangier (Tanger)	35°48' N, 005°48' W
Tétouan (Tetuan)	35°34' N, 005°22' W

MOZAMBIQUE ....pg. 153

Capital: ....Maputo
Area: ......812,379 sq km; 313,661 sq mi
Highest Elev.: ..Mt. Binga 2,440 m; 7,990 ft
Longest River: ..Zambezi 3,500 km; 2,200 mi
Avg. Temperature: .Jan = 25°C; Jul = 18°C
Currency: ......metical
Official Language: ..Portuguese

Beira	19°50' S, 034°52' E
Chimoio (Vila Pery)	19°08' S, 033°29' E
Chokwe	24°32' S, 032°59' E
Inhambane	23°52' S, 035°23' E
Lichinga	13°18' S, 035°14' E
Maputo (Lourenco Marques)	25°58' S, 032°34' E
Massinga	23°20' S, 035°22' E
Moçambique (Mozambique)	15°03' S, 040°45' E
Mopeia Velha	17°59' S, 035°43' E
Morrumbene	23°39' S, 035°20' E
Nacala	14°33' S, 040°40' E
Nampula	15°09' S, 039°18' E
Pemba	12°57' S, 040°30' E
Quelimane	17°51' S, 036°52' E
Quissico	24°43' S, 034°45' E
Tete	16°10' S, 033°36' E
Vila da Manhiça	25°24' S, 032°48' E
Xai Xai (Joao Belo)	25°04' S, 033°39' E

MYANMAR ....pg. 144

Capital: ....Yangôn
Area: ......676,577 sq km; 261,228 sq mi
Highest Elev.: ..Mt. Hkakabo 5,880 m, 19,300 ft
Longest River: ..Irrawaddy 2,170 km; 1,350 mi
Avg. Temperature: .Jan = 25°C; Jul = 27°C
Currency: ......Myanmar kyat
Official Language: ..Burmese

Bassein (Pathein)	16°47' N, 094°44' E
Chauk	20°53' N, 094°49' E
Gangaw	22°10' N, 094°08' E
Henzada	17°38' N, 095°28' E
Kale	16°05' N, 097°54' E
Kyaukme	22°32' N, 097°02' E
Lashio	22°56' N, 097°45' E
Lewe	19°38' N, 096°07' E
Magwe (Magway)	20°09' N, 094°55' E

Name	Lat./Long.
Mandalay	22°00' N, 096°05' E
Maungdaw	20°49' N, 092°22' E
Mawlamyine, see Moulmein	
Maymyo	22°02' N, 096°28' E
Meiktila	20°52' N, 095°52' E
Mergui	12°26' N, 098°36' E
Mogok	22°55' N, 096°30' E
Mohnyin	24°47' N, 096°22' E
Monywa	22°07' N, 095°08' E
Moulmein (Mawlamyine)	16°30' N, 097°38' E
Myaungmya	16°36' N, 094°56' E
Myingyan	21°28' N, 095°23' E
Myitkyina	25°23' N, 097°24' E
Nyaunglebin	17°57' N, 096°44' E
Pakokku	21°20' N, 095°06' E
Palaw	12°58' N, 098°39' E
Pegu (Bago)	17°20' N, 096°29' E
Prome (Pye)	18°49' N, 095°13' E
Pyapon	16°17' N, 095°41' E
Pyinmana	19°44' N, 096°13' E
Rangoon, see Yangôn	
Sagaing	21°52' N, 095°59' E
Shwebo	22°34' N, 095°42' E
Sittwe (Akyab)	20°09' N, 092°54' E
Tangyan	22°29' N, 098°24' E
Tatkon	20°07' N, 096°13' E
Tamu	24°13' N, 094°19' E
Taunggyi	20°47' N, 097°02' E
Tavoy (Dawei)	14°05' N, 098°12' E
Tenasserim	12°05' N, 099°01' E
Thaton	16°55' N, 097°22' E
Thanbyuzayat	15°58' N, 097°44' E
Toungoo	18°56' N, 096°26' E
Yangôn (Rangoon)	16°47' N, 096°10' E

NAMIBIA ....pg. 152

Capital: ....Windhoek
Area: ......825,118 sq km; 318,580 sq mi
Highest Elev.: ..Mt. Brand 2,570 m; 8,440 ft
Longest River: ..Orange 2,100 km; 1,300 mi
Avg. Temperature: .Jan = 23.3°C; Jul = 12.9°C
Currency: ......Namibian dollar
Official Language: ..English

Aranos	24°08' S, 019°07' E
Grootfontein	19°34' S, 018°07' E
Karasburg	28°01' S, 018°45' E
Karibib	21°56' S, 015°50' E
Keetmanshoop	26°35' S, 018°08' E
Khorixas	20°22' S, 014°58' E
Lüderitz	26°38' S, 015°09' E
Maltahöhe	24°50' S, 016°59' E
Mariental	24°38' S, 017°58' E
Ondangwa (Ondangua)	17°55' S, 015°57' E
Oshakati	17°47' S, 015°41' E
Otjimbingwe	22°21' S, 016°08' E
Outjo	20°07' S, 016°09' E
Rehoboth	23°19' S, 017°05' E
Rundu	17°56' S, 019°46' E
Swakopmund	22°41' S, 014°32' E
Tsumeb	19°14' S, 017°43' E
Usakos	22°00' S, 015°36' E
Walvis Bay	22°57' S, 014°30' E
Windhoek	22°35' S, 017°05' E

NEPAL ....pg. 146

Capital: ....Kathmandu
Area: ......147,181 sq km; 56,827 sq mi
Highest Elev.: ..Mt. Everest 8,850 m; 29,020 ft
Longest River: ..Karnali 510 km; 320 mi
Avg. Temperature: .Jan = 10°C; Jul = 24°C
Currency: ......Nepalese rupee
Official Language: ..Nepali

Bhaktpur (Bhadgaon)	27°41' N, 085°25' E
Kathmandu	27°43' N, 085°19' E
Lalitpur, see Patan	
Patan (Lalitpur)	27°40' N, 085°20' E

NETHERLANDS, THE ..pg. 132

Capital: ....Amsterdam
Area: ......41,526 sq km; 16,033 sq mi
Highest Elev.: ..Vaalser Hill 320 m; 1,050 ft
Longest River: ..Rhine 1,390 km; 870 mi
Avg. Temperature: .Jan = 2.3°C; Jul = 16.5°C
Currency: ......Netherlands guilder
Official Language: ..Dutch

Alkmaar	52°38' N, 004°45' E
Almelo	52°21' N, 006°40' E
Amersfoort	52°09' N, 005°23' E
Amstelveen	52°18' N, 004°52' E
Amsterdam	52°21' N, 004°55' E
Apeldoorn	52°13' N, 005°58' E
Arnhem	51°59' N, 005°55' E
Assen	53°00' N, 006°33' E
Bergen op Zoom	51°30' N, 004°18' E
Breda	51°34' N, 004°48' E
Delft	52°00' N, 004°22' E
Den Helder	52°58' N, 004°46' E
Deventer	52°15' N, 006°12' E
Dordrecht (Dort or Dordt)	51°48' N, 004°40' E
Ede	52°02' N, 005°40' E
Eindhoven	51°27' N, 005°28' E
Emmen	52°47' N, 006°54' E
Enschede	52°13' N, 006°54' E
Geleen	50°58' N, 005°50' E
Groningen	53°13' N, 006°33' E
Haarlem	52°22' N, 004°39' E
Haarlemmermeer, see Hoofddorp	
Heerlen	50°54' N, 005°59' E
Helmond	51°29' N, 005°40' E
Hengelo	52°16' N, 006°48' E
Hilversum	52°14' N, 005°11' E
Hoofddorp (Haarlemmermeer)	52°18' N, 004°41' E
Hoorn	52°39' N, 005°04' E
Ijmuiden	52°28' N, 004°36' E
Lelystad	52°31' N, 005°28' E
Leeuwarden (Ljouwert)	53°12' N, 005°47' E
Leiden (Leyden)	52°09' N, 004°30' E

Name	Lat./Long.
Maastricht	50°51' N, 005°41' E
Middelburg	51°30' N, 003°37' E
Nieuwegein	52°02' N, 005°06' E
Nijmegen (Nimwegen)	51°50' N, 005°52' E
Oss	51°46' N, 005°32' E
Purmerend	52°31' N, 004°57' E
Ridderkerk	51°52' N, 004°36' E
Roosendaal	51°32' N, 004°28' E
Rosmalen	51°43' N, 005°22' E
Rotterdam	51°55' N, 004°30' E
's-Gravenhage, *see* The Hague	
's-Hertogenbosch (Den Bosch or Bois-le-Duc)	51°42' N, 005°19' E
Schiedam	51°55' N, 004°24' E
Soest	52°11' N, 005°18' E
The Hague ('s-Gravenhage, Den Haag, or La Haye)	52°05' N, 004°18' E
Tilburg	51°33' N, 005°07' E
Utrecht	52°05' N, 005°08' E
Veenendaal	52°02' N, 005°33' E
Vlaardingen	51°55' N, 004°21' E
Vlissingen (Flushing)	51°27' N, 003°35' E
Zaanstad	52°27' N, 004°50' E
Zoetermeer	52°03' N, 004°30' E
Zwolle	52°30' N, 006°05' E

NEW ZEALAND ......pg. 155

Capital: ....Wellington
Area: ....270,534 sq km; 104,454 sq mi
Highest Elev.: ...Mt. Cook 3,760 m; 12,350 ft
Longest River: ...Waikato 420 km; 260 mi
Avg. Temperature: ..Jan = 16°C; Jul = 8°C
Currency: ......New Zealand dollar
Official Language: ..English, Maori

Auckland	36°52' S, 174°46' E
Cheviot	42°49' S, 173°16' E
Christchurch	43°32' S, 172°39' E
Dunedin	45°53' S, 170°29' E
Hamilton	37°47' S, 175°16' E
Invercargill	46°25' S, 168°22' E
Lower Hutt	41°13' S, 174°56' E
Manukau	36°57' S, 174°56' E
Napier	39°31' S, 176°54' E
Palmerston North	40°21' S, 175°37' E
Rotorua	38°10' S, 176°14' E
Takapuna	36°47' S, 174°45' E
Tauranga	37°42' S, 176°08' E
Waihi Beach	37°24' S, 175°56' E
Wellington	41°18' S, 174°47' E
Whangarei	35°43' S, 174°20' E

NICARAGUA ......pg. 117

Capital: ....Managua
Area: ....131,670 sq km; 50,838 sq mi
Highest Elev.: ...Mogoton Pk. 2,100 m; 6,900 ft
Longest River: ...Coco 780 km; 490 mi
Avg. Temperature: ..Jan = 26°C; Jul = 27°C
Currency: ......córdoba oro
Official Language: ..Spanish

Esteli	13°05' N, 086°21' W
Granada	11°56' N, 085°57' W
León	12°26' N, 086°53' W
Managua	12°09' N, 086°17' W
Masaya	11°58' N, 086°06' W
Matagalpa	12°55' N, 085°55' W

NIGER ......pg. 150

Capital: ....Niamey
Area: ....1,186,408 sq km; 458,075 sq mi
Highest Elev.: ...Mt. Gréboun 1,940 m; 6,380 ft
Longest River: ...Niger 4,200 km; 2,600 mi
Temperature: ....Jan = 24°C; Jul = 29°C
Currency: ......CFA franc
Official Language: ..French

Agadez	16°58' N, 007°59' E
Maradi	13°29' N, 007°06' E
Niamey	13°31' N, 002°07' E
Tahoua	14°54' N, 005°16' E
Zinder	13°48' N, 008°59' E

NIGERIA ......pg. 150

Capital: ....Abuja
Area: ....923,768 sq km; 356,669 sq mi
Longest River: ...Niger 4,200 km; 2,600 mi
Avg. Temperature: ..Jan =27°C; Jul = 25°C
Currency: ......Nigerian naira
Official Language: ..English

Abuja	09°15' N, 006°56' E
Azare	11°41' N, 010°12' E
Bauchi	10°19' N, 009°50' E
Benin City	06°20' N, 005°38' E
Bida	09°05' N, 006°01' E
Calabar	04°57' N, 008°19' E
Deba Habe	10°13' N, 011°23' E
Dukku	10°49' N, 010°46' E
Enugu	06°26' N, 007°29' E
Gboko	07°19' N, 009°00' E
Gombe	10°17' N, 011°10' E
Gusau	12°10' N, 006°40' E
Ife	07°28' N, 004°34' E
Ihiala	05°51' N, 006°51' E
Ikerre	07°30' N, 005°14' E
Ilorin	08°30' N, 004°33' E
Iwo	07°38' N, 004°11' E
Jega	12°13' N, 004°23' E
Jimeta	09°17' N, 012°28' E
Jos	09°55' N, 008°54' E
Kaduna	10°31' N, 007°26' E
Kano	12°00' N, 008°31' E
Katsina	13°00' N, 007°36' E
Kaura Namoda	12°36' N, 006°35' E
Keffi	08°51' N, 007°52' E

Name	Lat./Long.
Kishi	09°05' N, 003°51' E
Kumo	10°03' N, 011°13' E
Lafia	08°29' N, 008°31' E
Lafiagi	08°52' N, 005°25' E
Lagos	06°27' N, 003°23' E
Lere	09°43' N, 009°21' E
Maiduguri	11°51' N, 013°09' E
Makurdi	07°44' N, 008°32' E
Minna	09°37' N, 006°33' E
Mubi	10°16' N, 013°16' E
Mushin	06°32' N, 003°22' E
Nguru	12°53' N, 010°28' E
Nkuka	06°52' N, 007°23' E
Nsukka	06°52' N, 007°23' E
Ogbomosho	08°08' N, 004°16' E
Ondo	07°06' N, 004°50' E
Onitsha	06°10' N, 006°47' E
Opobo Town	04°31' N, 007°32' E
Oron	04°50' N, 008°14' E
Oshogbo	07°46' N, 004°34' E
Oyo	07°51' N, 003°56' E
Pindiga	09°59' N, 010°54' E
Port Harcourt	04°46' N, 007°01' E
Potiskum	11°43' N, 011°04' E
Sapele	05°55' N, 005°42' E
Shaki	08°40' N, 003°23' E
Sokoto	13°04' N, 005°15' E
Ugep	05°48' N, 008°05' E
Uyo	05°03' N, 007°56' E
Warri	05°31' N, 005°45' E
Zaria	11°04' N, 007°42' E

NORWAY ......pg. 131

Capital: ....Oslo
Area: ....323,878 sq km; 125,050 sq mi
Highest Elev.: ...Galdho Pk. 2,470 m; 8,100 ft
Longest River: ...Glomma 600 km; 370 mi
Avg. Temperature: ..Jan = 5°C; Jul = 17°C
Currency: ......Norwegian krone
Official Language: ..Norwegian

Alta	69°58' N, 023°15' E
Arendal	58°27' N, 008°48' E
Ärnes	60°09' N, 011°28' E
Batsfjord	70°38' N, 029°44' E
Bergen	60°23' N, 005°20' E
Berkåk	62°50' N, 010°00' E
Bodø	67°17' N, 014°23' E
Brumunddal	60°53' N, 010°56' E
Drammen	59°44' N, 010°15' E
Dombås	62°05' N, 009°08' E
Eidsvoll	60°19' N, 011°14' E
Elverum	60°53' N, 011°34' E
Fauske	67°15' N, 015°24' E
Fredrikstad	59°13' N, 010°57' E
Gjøvik	60°48' N, 010°42' E
Gol	60°42' N, 008°57' E
Hamar	60°48' N, 011°06' E
Hammerfest	70°40' N, 023°42' E
Hermansverk	61°11' N, 006°51' E
Hønefoss	60°10' N, 010°18' E
Honningsvag	70°59' N, 025°59' E
Kautokeino	68°59' N, 023°08' E
Kjøllefjord	70°56' N, 027°21' E
Kolsås	59°55' N, 010°31' E
Kongsberg	59°39' N, 009°39' E
Kongsvinger	60°12' N, 012°00' E
Kristiansand	58°10' N, 008°00' E
Lakselv	70°03' N, 024°56' E
Levanger	63°45' N, 011°18' E
Lillehammer	61°08' N, 010°30' E
Mandal	58°02' N, 007°27' E
Mo	66°19' N, 014°10' E
Molde	62°44' N, 007°11' E
Mosjøen	65°50' N, 013°12' E
Namsos	64°29' N, 011°30' E
Narvik	68°26' N, 017°25' E
Notodden	59°34' N, 009°17' E
Oslo (Christiania, Kristiania)	59°55' N, 010°45' E
Skien	59°12' N, 009°36' E
Stavanger	58°58' N, 005°45' E
Steinkjer	64°01' N, 011°30' E
Tønsberg	59°17' N, 010°25' E
Tromsø	69°40' N, 018°58' E
Trondheim	63°25' N, 010°25' E
Vadsø	70°05' N, 029°46' E
Vardø	70°22' N, 031°06' E

OMAN ......pg. 154

Capital: ....Muscat
Area: ....306,000 sq km; 118,150 sq mi
Highest Elev.: ...Mt. Al-Jabal al-Akhdar 3000 m; 14,350 ft
Avg. Temperature: ..Jan = 22°C; Jul = 34°C
Currency: ......rial Omani
Official Language: ..Arabic

Bahla' (Bahlah)	22°58' N, 057°18' E
Barka'	23°43' N, 057°53' E
Dank	23°33' N, 056°16' E
Duqm	19°39' N, 057°42' E
Hayma'	19°56' N, 056°19' E
Izki	22°56' N, 057°46' E
Ibra'	22°43' N, 058°32' E
Khaburah, al-	23°59' N, 057°08' E
Khasab	26°12' N, 056°15' E
Khawr Rawri (Khor Rori)	17°02' N, 054°27' E
Masna'ah, al-	23°47' N, 057°38' E
Masqat, *see* Muscat	
Matrah	23°37' N, 058°34' E
Mirbat	17°00' N, 054°41' E
Muscat (Masqat)	23°37' N, 058°35' E
Nizwa (Nazwah)	22°56' N, 057°32' E
Qurayyat	23°15' N, 058°54' E
Rakhyut	16°44' N, 053°20' E
Rustaq, ar-	23°24' N, 057°26' E
Salalah	17°00' N, 054°06' E
Shinas	24°46' N, 056°28' E
Suhar	24°22' N, 056°45' E
Sur	22°34' N, 059°32' E
Taqah	17°02' N, 054°24' E
Thamarit	17°39' N, 054°02' E

PAKISTAN ......pg. 139

Capital: ....Islamabad
Area: ....796,095 sq km; 307,374 sq mi
Highest Elev.: ...K2 8,610 m; 28,250 ft
Longest River: ...Indus 2,900 km; 1,800 mi
Avg. Temperature: ..Jan = 13°C; Jul = 32°C
Currency: ......Pakistan rupee
Official Language: ..Urdu

Ahmadpur East	29°09' N, 071°16' E
Badin	24°39' N, 068°50' E
Bahawalnagar	29°59' N, 073°16' E
Bahawalpur	29°24' N, 071°41' E
Bela	26°14' N, 066°19' E
Bhakkar	31°38' N, 071°04' E
Chakwal	32°56' N, 072°52' E
Chaman	30°55' N, 066°27' E
Charsadda	34°09' N, 071°44' E
Chiniot	31°43' N, 072°59' E
Chishtian Mandi	29°48' N, 072°52' E
Chitral	35°51' N, 071°47' E
Dadu	26°44' N, 067°47' E
Dera Ghazi Khan	30°03' N, 070°38' E
Dera Ismail Khan	31°50' N, 070°54' E
Dir	35°12' N, 071°53' E
Faisalabad (Lyallpur)	31°25' N, 073°05' E
Gojra	31°09' N, 072°41' E
Gujranwala	32°09' N, 074°11' E
Gujrat	32°34' N, 074°05' E
Gwadar	25°07' N, 062°19' E
Hab Chauki	25°01' N, 066°53' E
Haripur	33°59' N, 072°56' E
Hasilpur	29°43' N, 072°33' E
Hyderabad	25°22' N, 068°22' E
Islamabad	33°42' N, 073°10' E
Jacobabad	28°17' N, 068°26' E
Jampur	29°39' N, 070°36' E
Jhang Sadar (Jhang-Maghiana)	31°16' N, 072°19' E
Jhelum	32°56' N, 073°44' E
Kamalia	30°44' N, 072°39' E
Kambar	27°36' N, 068°00' E
Kandhkot	28°14' N, 069°11' E
Karachi	24°52' N, 067°03' E
Kasur	31°07' N, 074°27' E
Khairpur	29°35' N, 072°14' E
Khushab	32°18' N, 072°21' E
Khuzdar	27°48' N, 066°37' E
Kohat	33°35' N, 071°26' E
Kot Addu	30°28' N, 070°58' E
Kundian	32°27' N, 071°28' E
Lahore	31°35' N, 074°18' E
Larkana	27°33' N, 068°13' E
Leiah	30°58' N, 070°56' E
Mailsi	29°48' N, 072°11' E
Mansehra	34°20' N, 073°12' E
Mardan	34°12' N, 072°02' E
Mianwali	32°35' N, 071°33' E
Mingaora	34°47' N, 072°22' E
Mirpur Khas	25°32' N, 069°00' E
Mithankot	28°57' N, 070°22' E
Moro	26°40' N, 068°00' E
Multan	30°11' N, 071°29' E
Nawabshah	26°15' N, 068°25' E
Nushki	29°33' N, 066°01' E
Okara	30°49' N, 073°27' E
Ormara	25°12' N, 064°38' E
Panjgur	26°58' N, 064°06' E
Pasni	25°16' N, 063°28' E
Peshawar	34°01' N, 071°33' E
Pipri	24°52' N, 067°23' E
Pishin	30°35' N, 067°00' E
Port Muhammad Bin Qasim	24°46' N, 067°20' E
Quetta	30°12' N, 067°00' E
Rahimyar Khan	28°25' N, 070°18' E
Rawalpindi	33°36' N, 073°04' E
Sadiqabad	28°18' N, 070°08' E
Sahiwal (Montgomery)	30°40' N, 073°06' E
Sanghar	26°02' N, 068°57' E
Sangla (Sangla Hill)	31°43' N, 073°23' E
Sargodha	32°05' N, 072°40' E
Shahdadkot	27°51' N, 067°54' E
Shahdadpur	25°56' N, 068°37' E
Shekhupura	31°42' N, 073°59' E
Shikarpur	27°57' N, 068°38' E
Sialkot	32°30' N, 074°31' E
Sui	28°37' N, 069°19' E
Sukkur	27°42' N, 068°52' E
Tando Adam	25°46' N, 068°40' E
Tando Allahyar	25°28' N, 068°43' E
Tando Muhammad Khan	25°08' N, 068°32' E
Thatta	24°45' N, 067°55' E
Turbat	25°59' N, 063°04' E
Uthal	25°48' N, 066°37' E
Vihari	30°02' N, 072°21' E
Wah	33°48' N, 072°42' E
Wazirabad	32°27' N, 074°07' E
Zhob (Fort Sandeman)	31°20' N, 069°27' E

PALAU ......pg. 156

Capital: ....Koror
Area: ....487 sq km; 181 sq mi
Highest Elev.: ...Koror 630 m; 2,060 ft
Avg. Temperature: ..Jan =27°C; Jul = 28°C
Currency: ......U. S. dollar
Official Language: ..Palauan, English

Koror	07°20' N, 134°29' E

PANAMA ......pg. 117

Capital: ....Panama City
Area: ....75,517 sq km; 29,157 sq mi
Highest Elev.: ...Baru Volc. 3,480 m; 11,400 ft
Longest River: ...Tuira 170 km; 110 mi
Avg. Temperature: ..Jan = 27°C; Jul = 27°C
Currency: ......balboa
Official Language: ..Spanish

Aguadulce	08°15' N, 080°33' W
Almirante	09°18' N, 082°24' W
Antón	08°24' N, 080°16' W

Name	Lat./Long.
Boquete	08°47' N, 082°26' W
Cañazas	09°06' N, 078°10' W
Capira	08°45' N, 079°53' W
Changuinola	09°26' N, 082°31' W
Chepo	09°10' N, 079°06' W
Chitré	07°58' N, 080°26' W
Colón	09°22' N, 079°54' W
David	08°26' N, 082°26' W
Guararé	07°49' N, 080°17' W
La Chorrera	08°53' N, 079°47' W
La Concepción	08°31' N, 082°37' W
La Palma	08°25' N, 078°09' W
Las Cumbres	09°05' N, 079°32' W
Las Lajas	08°15' N, 081°52' W
Las Tablas	07°46' N, 080°17' W
Ocú	07°57' N, 080°47' W
Panama City (Panama)	08°58' N, 079°32' W
Penonomé	08°31' N, 080°22' W
Portobelo (Puerto Bello)	09°33' N, 079°39' W
Puerto Armuelles	08°17' N, 082°52' W
Puerto Bello, *see* Portobelo	
San Miguelito	09°02' N, 079°30' E
Santiago	08°06' N, 080°59' W
Soná	08°01' N, 081°19' W
Yaviza (Yavisa)	08°11' N, 077°41' W

PAPUA NEW GUINEA ...pg. 156

Capital: ....Port Moresby
Area: ....462,840 sq km; 104,454 sq mi
Highest Elev.: ...Mt. Whilhem 4,510 m; 14,790 ft
Longest River: ...Sepic 1,100 km; 78 mi
Avg. Temperature: ..Jan = 28°C; Jul = 27°C
Currency: ......Papua New Guinea kina
Official Language: ..English, Maori

Alotau	10°20' S, 150°25' E
Goroka	06°05' S, 145°23' E
Lae	06°44' S, 147°00' E
Madang	05°13' S, 145°48' E
Mt. Hagen	05°52' S, 144°13' E
Port Moresby	09°29' S, 147°11' E
Rabaul	04°12' S, 152°11' E
Telefomin	05°08' S, 141°35' E
Wewak	03°33' S, 143°38' E

PARAGUAY ......pg. 122

Capital: ....Asunción
Area: ....406,752 sq km; 157,048 sq mi
Highest Elev.: ...Mt. San Rafael 850 m; 2,790 ft
Longest River: ...Paraguay 2,550 km; 1,580 mi
Avg. Temperature: ..Jan = 29°C; Jul = 18°C
Currency: ......Paraguayan Guaraní
Official Language: ..Spanish, Guaraní

Asunción	25°16' S, 057°40' W
Caaguazu	25°26' S, 056°02' W
Ciudad del Este (Puerto Presidente Stroessner)	25°31' S, 054°37' W
Encarnacion	27°20' S, 055°54' W
Pedro Juan Caballero	22°34' S, 055°37' W
San Lazaro	22°10' S, 057°58' W

PERU ......pg. 123

Capital: ....Lima
Area: ....1,285,216 sq km; 496,225 sq mi
Highest Elev.: ...Mt. Huascarán 6,770 m; 22,210 ft
Longest River: ...Ucayali 1,470 km; 910 mi
Avg. Temperature: ..Jan = 22°C; Jul = 15°C
Currency: ......nuevo sol
Official Language: ..Spanish, Quechua, Aymara

Ancon	11°47' S, 077°11' W
Acomayo	13°55' S, 071°41' W
Andahuaylas	13°39' S, 073°23' W
Ascope	07°43' S, 079°07' W
Arequipa	16°24' S, 071°33' W
Ayacucho	13°07' S, 074°13' W
Ayabaca	04°38' S, 079°43' W
Ayaviri	14°52' S, 070°35' W
Bolivar	07°18' S, 077°48' W
Barranca	10°45' S, 077°46' W
Cajabamba	07°37' S, 078°03' W
Cajamarca	07°10' S, 078°31' W
Callao	12°04' S, 077°09' W
Camana	16°37' S, 072°42' W
Canta	11°25' S, 076°38' W
Caraveli	15°46' S, 073°22' W
Casma	09°28' S, 078°19' W
Castilla	05°12' S, 080°38' W
Cerro de Pasco	10°41' S, 076°16' W
Chiclayo	06°46' S, 079°51' W
Chicla	11°45' S, 076°18' W
Chimbote	09°05' S, 078°36' W
Chachapoyas	06°12' S, 077°51' W
Chaupimarca	10°26' S, 076°32' W
Chincha Alta	13°27' S, 076°08' W
Chulucanas	05°06' S, 080°10' W
Contamana	07°15' S, 074°54' W
Coracora	15°02' S, 073°47' W
Cotahuasi	15°12' S, 072°06' W
Cuzco	13°31' S, 071°59' W
Ferreñafe	06°38' S, 079°48' W
Espinar	14°47' S, 071°29' W
Huacho	11°07' S, 077°37' W
Huallanca	09°51' S, 076°56' W
Huamachuco	07°48' S, 078°04' W
Huancavelica	12°46' S, 075°02' W
Huancayo	12°04' S, 075°14' W
Huanta	12°56' S, 074°15' W
Huánuco	09°55' S, 076°14' W
Huari	09°20' S, 077°14' W
Huarmey	10°04' S, 078°10' W
Ica	14°04' S, 075°42' W
Ilave	16°05' S, 069°40' W
Ilo	17°38' S, 071°20' W
Imperial	13°04' S, 076°21' W
Iquitos	03°46' S, 073°15' W
Jaén	05°42' S, 078°47' W
Juli	16°13' S, 069°27' W
Juliaca	15°30' S, 070°08' W
Junín	11°10' S, 076°00' W
La Oroya	11°32' S, 075°54' W
Lagunas	05°14' S, 075°38' W

Name	Lat./Long.
Lambayeque	06°42' S, 079°55' W
Lampa	15°21' S, 070°22' W
Lima	12°03' S, 077°03' W
Macusani	14°05' S, 070°26' W
Miraflores	12°07' S, 077°02' W
Moquegua	17°12' S, 070°56' W
Moyobamba	06°03' S, 076°58' W
Mollendo	17°02' S, 072°01' W
Nauta	04°32' S, 073°33' W
Nazca	14°50' S, 074°57' W
Olmos	05°59' S, 079°46' W
Otuzco	07°54' S, 078°35' W
Oxapampa	10°34' S, 075°24' W
Pampas	12°24' S, 074°54' W
Paita	05°06' S, 081°07' W
Paucara	12°42' S, 074°41' W
Paucartambo	13°18' S, 071°40' W
Pisco	13°42' S, 076°13' W
Piura	05°12' S, 080°38' W
Pucallpa	08°23' S, 074°32' W
Puerto Chicama	07°42' S, 079°27' W
Puno	15°50' S, 070°02' W
Rioja	06°05' S, 077°09' W
Requena	04°58' S, 073°50' W
Rímac	12°03' S, 077°03' W
San Ignacio	05°08' S, 078°59' W
San Juan	15°21' S, 075°10' W
San Pedro de Lloc	07°26' S, 079°31' W
San Ramón	11°08' S, 075°20' W
San Vicente de Canete	13°05' S, 076°24' W
Saña	06°55' S, 079°35' W
Santo Tomás	14°29' S, 072°06' W
Sicuani	14°16' S, 071°13' W
Socabaya	16°25' S, 071°31' W
Sullana	04°53' S, 080°41' W
Tacna	18°01' S, 070°15' W
Talara	04°34' S, 081°17' W
Tarapoto	06°30' S, 076°25' W
Tarata	17°28' S, 070°02' W
Tayabamba	08°17' S, 077°18' W
Tingo Maria	09°09' S, 075°56' W
Trujillo	08°07' S, 079°02' W
Tumbes	03°34' S, 080°28' W
Urcos	13°42' S, 071°38' W
Viru	08°25' S, 078°45' W
Yurimaguas	05°54' S, 076°05' W

PHILIPPINES ... pg. 145

Capital: Manila
Area: 300,076 sq km; 115,860 sq mi
Highest Elev.: Mt. Apo 2,950 m; 9,690 ft
Longest River: Agusan 390 km; 240 mi
Avg. Temperature: Jan = 25°C; Jul = 27°C
Currency: Philippine peso
Official Language: Filipino, English

Name	Lat./Long.
Angeles	15°09' N, 120°35' E
Antipolo	14°35' N, 121°10' E
Bacolod	10°40' N, 122°56' E
Baguio	16°25' N, 120°36' E
Balabac	07°59' N, 117°04' E
Baliuag	14°57' N, 120°54' E
Bangued	17°36' N, 120°37' E
Bislig	08°13' N, 126°19' E
Butuan	08°54' N, 125°35' E
Cabanatuan	15°29' N, 120°58' E
Cagayan de Oro	08°29' N, 124°39' E
Caloocan	14°39' N, 120°58' E
Candon	17°12' N, 120°27' E
Cavite	14°29' N, 120°54' E
Cebu	10°18' N, 123°54' E
Cotabato	07°13' N, 124°15' E
Dagupan	16°03' N, 120°20' E
Dapitan	08°39' N, 123°25' E
Davao	07°04' N, 125°36' E
Dumaguete	09°18' N, 123°18' E
General Luna	09°47' N, 126°09' E
General Santos	06°07' N, 125°07' E
Gingoog	08°50' N, 125°07' E
Iligan	08°14' N, 124°14' E
Iloilo City	10°42' N, 122°33' E
Isabela	06°42' N, 121°58' E
Isulan	06°37' N, 124°40' E
Jolo	06°03' N, 121°00' E
Lapu-Lapu (Opon)	10°19' N, 123°57' E
Laoang	12°34' N, 125°00' E
Lazi	09°08' N, 123°38' E
Legazpi	13°08' N, 121°37' E
Lucena	13°56' N, 121°37' E
Malolos	14°51' N, 120°49' E
Mandaue	10°20' N, 123°56' E
Mangaldan	16°04' N, 120°24' E
Manila	14°35' N, 121°00' E
Marawi (Dansalan)	08°01' N, 124°18' E
Naga (Nueva Caceres)	13°37' N, 123°11' E
Narra	09°16' N, 118°25' E
Olongapo	14°50' N, 120°16' E
Ormoc	11°00' N, 124°37' E
Pagadian	07°49' N, 123°25' E
Polomolok	06°13' N, 125°04' E
Puerto Princesa	09°44' N, 118°44' E
Quezon City	14°38' N, 121°00' E
San Fernando	16°37' N, 120°19' E
San Jose	12°21' N, 121°04' E
San Pablo	14°04' N, 121°19' E
Santa Cruz	13°29' N, 122°02' E
Tacloban	11°15' N, 125°00' E
Tagbilaran	09°39' N, 123°51' E
Tagig	14°32' N, 121°04' E
Tanjay	09°31' N, 123°09' E
Valencia	07°57' N, 125°03' E
Zamboanga	06°54' N, 122°04' E

POLAND ... pg. 133

Capital: Warsaw
Area: 312,685 sq km; 120,728 sq mi
Highest Elev.: Rysy 2,500 m; 8,200 ft
Longest River: Vistula 1,050 km; 650 mi
Avg. Temperature: Jan = -4°C; Jul = 19°C
Currency: zloty
Official Language: Polish

Name	Lat./Long.
Belchatów	51°22' N, 019°23' E
Biala Podlaska	52°02' N, 023°08' E
Bialystok	53°08' N, 023°09' E
Bielsko-Biala	49°49' N, 019°02' E
Bydgoszcz	53°09' N, 018°00' E
Bytom	50°21' N, 018°58' E
Chelm	51°08' N, 023°30' E
Czestochowa	50°48' N, 019°07' E
Dabrowa Górnicza	50°20' N, 019°12' E
Elblag	54°10' N, 019°23' E
Gdansk (Danzig)	54°21' N, 018°40' E
Gdynia	54°30' N, 018°33' E
Gliwice	50°17' N, 018°40' E
Glogów	51°40' N, 016°06' E
Gniezno	52°33' N, 017°36' E
Gorzów Wielkopolski	52°44' N, 015°14' E
Grudziadz	53°29' N, 018°46' E
Inowroclaw	52°48' N, 018°16' E
Jelenia Góra	50°54' N, 015°44' E
Kalisz	51°45' N, 018°05' E
Katowice	50°16' N, 019°01' E
Kedzierzyn-Kozle	50°21' N, 018°12' E
Kielce	50°50' N, 020°40' E
Konin	52°13' N, 018°16' E
Koszalin	54°12' N, 016°11' E
Kraków	50°05' N, 019°55' E
Krosno	49°41' N, 021°47' E
Kutno	52°14' N, 019°22' E
Legnica	51°12' N, 016°12' E
Leszno	51°51' N, 016°35' E
Lódz	51°45' N, 019°28' E
Lomza	53°11' N, 022°05' E
Lubin	51°24' N, 016°12' E
Lublin	51°15' N, 022°34' E
Mielec	50°17' N, 021°25' E
Nowy Sacz	49°38' N, 020°43' E
Olsztyn	53°47' N, 020°29' E
Opole	50°40' N, 017°57' E
Ostroleka	53°05' N, 021°34' E
Ostrow Wielkopolski	51°39' N, 017°49' E
Ostrowiec Shwietokrzyski	50°56' N, 021°24' E
Pabianice	51°40' N, 019°22' E
Pila	53°09' N, 016°45' E
Piotrków Trybunalski	51°24' N, 019°41' E
Plock	52°33' N, 019°42' E
Poznan	52°25' N, 016°58' E
Pruszków	52°10' N, 020°50' E
Przemysl	49°47' N, 022°47' E
Pulawy	51°25' N, 021°58' E
Racibórz	50°05' N, 018°12' E
Radom	51°25' N, 021°09' E
Radomsko	51°04' N, 019°27' E
Rybnik	50°07' N, 018°32' E
Rzeszów	50°03' N, 022°00' E
Siedlce	52°10' N, 022°18' E
Skarzysko-Kamienna	51°07' N, 020°54' E
Slupsk	54°27' N, 017°02' E
Sopot	54°27' N, 018°34' E
Sosnowiec	50°18' N, 019°10' E
Stalowa Wola	50°34' N, 022°03' E
Starachowice	51°04' N, 021°04' E
Stargard Szczecinski	53°20' N, 015°03' E
Suwalki	54°06' N, 022°56' E
Szczecin (Stettin)	53°25' N, 014°35' E
Tarnów	50°01' N, 020°59' E
Tarnowskie Góry	50°27' N, 018°52' E
Tczew	54°06' N, 018°48' E
Tomaszow Mazowiecki	51°32' N, 020°01' E
Torun	53°02' N, 018°36' E
Tychy	50°08' N, 018°59' E
Walbrzych	50°46' N, 016°17' E
Warsaw (Warszawa)	52°15' N, 021°00' E
Wloclawek	52°39' N, 019°05' E
Wodzislaw Slaski	50°00' N, 018°28' E
Wroclaw (Breslau)	51°06' N, 017°02' E
Zabrze	50°19' N, 018°47' E
Zamosc	50°43' N, 023°15' E
Zawiercie	50°30' N, 019°26' E
Zgierz	51°51' N, 019°25' E
Zielona Góra	51°56' N, 015°30' E

PORTUGAL ... pg. 128

Capital: Lisbon
Area: 91,831 sq km; 35,456 sq mi
Highest Elev.: Serra da Estrela 1,990 m; 6,530 ft
Longest River: Douro 900 km; 560 mi
Avg. Temperature: Jan = 11°C; Jul = 22°C
Currency: escudo
Official Language: Portuguese

Name	Lat./Long.
Amadora	38°45' N, 009°14' W
Barreiro	38°40' N, 009°04' W
Braga	41°33' N, 008°26' W
Coimbra	40°12' N, 008°25' W
Lisbon (Lisboa)	38°43' N, 009°08' W
Ponta Delgada	37°44' N, 025°40' W
Porto (Oporto)	41°09' N, 008°37' W
Setúbal	38°32' N, 008°54' W
Vila Franca de Xira	38°57' N, 008°59' W

QATAR ... pg. 154

Capital: Doha
Area: 11,427 sq km; 4,412 sq mi
Avg. Temperature: Jan = 21°C; Jul = 40°C
Currency: riyal
Official Language: Arabic

Name	Lat./Long.
Doha (ad-Dawhah)	25°17' N, 051°32' E
Dukhan	25°25' N, 050°47' E
Musay'id	25°00' N, 051°33' E
Ruways, ar-	26°08' N, 051°13' E
Wakrah, al-	25°10' N, 051°36' E

ROMANIA ... pg. 134

Capital: Bucharest
Area: 237,500 sq km; 91,699 sq mi
Highest Elev.: Mt. Moldoveanu 2,540 m; 8,350 ft
Longest River: Danube 2,850 km; 1,770 mi
Avg. Temperature: Jan = -3°C; Jul = 23°C
Currency: Romanian leu
Official Language: Romanian

Name	Lat./Long.
Alba Iulia (Gyulafehervar)	46°04' N, 023°35' E
Alexandria	43°59' N, 025°20' E
Arad	46°11' N, 021°19' E
Bacau	46°34' N, 026°54' E
Baia Mare	47°40' N, 023°35' E
Bârlad	46°14' N, 027°40' E
Bistrita	47°08' N, 024°29' E
Botosani	47°45' N, 026°40' E
Braila	45°16' N, 027°59' E
Brasov (Orasul Stalin)	45°38' N, 025°35' E
Bucharest	44°26' N, 026°06' E
Buzau	45°09' N, 026°50' E
Calafat	43°59' N, 022°56' E
Calarasi	44°12' N, 027°20' E
Campia Turzii	46°33' N, 023°53' E
Câmpulung	45°16' N, 025°03' E
Câmpulung Moldovenesc	47°32' N, 025°34' E
Cluj-Napoca	46°46' N, 023°36' E
Constanta	44°11' N, 028°39' E
Costesti	44°40' N, 024°53' E
Craiova	44°19' N, 023°48' E
Curtea De Arges	45°08' N, 024°41' E
Dej	47°09' N, 023°52' E
Deva	45°53' N, 022°54' E
Drobeta-Turnu Severin	44°38' N, 022°40' E
Eforie (Eforia)	44°06' N, 028°38' E
Faurei	45°04' N, 027°14' E
Fetesti	44°23' N, 027°50' E
Focsani	45°42' N, 027°11' E
Gaesti	44°43' N, 025°19' E
Galati (Galatz)	45°27' N, 028°03' E
Gheorghe Gheorghiu Dej, see Onesti	
Giurgiu	43°53' N, 025°58' E
Hunedoara	45°45' N, 022°54' E
Iasi (Jassy)	47°10' N, 027°36' E
Lugoj	45°41' N, 021°55' E
Mangalia	43°48' N, 028°35' E
Medgidia	44°15' N, 028°17' E
Medias	46°10' N, 024°21' E
Miercurea-Ciuc	46°21' N, 025°48' E
Mizil	45°01' N, 026°27' E
Odorheiul Secuiesc	46°18' N, 025°18' E
Onesti (Gheorghe Gheorghiu Dej)	46°15' N, 026°45' E
Oradea (Nagyvarad)	47°04' N, 021°56' E
Pascani	47°15' N, 026°44' E
Petrosani	45°25' N, 023°22' E
Piatra-Neamt	46°55' N, 026°20' E
Pitesti	44°51' N, 024°52' E
Ploiesti (Ploesti)	44°57' N, 026°01' E
Râmnicu Sarat	45°23' N, 027°03' E
Reghin	46°46' N, 024°42' E
Resita	45°18' N, 021°55' E
Roman	46°55' N, 026°55' E
Satu Mare	47°48' N, 022°53' E
Sebes	45°58' N, 023°34' E
Sfantu Gheorghe	45°52' N, 025°47' E
Sibiu (Nagyszeben)	45°48' N, 024°09' E
Sighisoara	46°13' N, 024°48' E
Sinaia	45°21' N, 025°33' E
Slatina	44°26' N, 024°22' E
Slobozia	44°34' N, 027°22' E
Suceava	47°38' N, 026°15' E
Tandarei	44°39' N, 027°40' E
Târgoviste	44°56' N, 025°27' E
Târgu Secuesc	46°00' N, 026°08' E
Targu Jiu	45°03' N, 023°17' E
Targu Mures	46°33' N, 024°34' E
Tecuci	45°52' N, 027°25' E
Techirghiol	44°03' N, 028°36' E
Timisoara	45°45' N, 021°13' E
Titu-Targ	44°39' N, 025°32' E
Topoloveni	44°49' N, 025°05' E
Tulcea	45°10' N, 028°48' E
Turda	46°34' N, 023°47' E
Urziceni	44°43' N, 026°38' E
Vaslui	46°38' N, 027°44' E
Videle	44°17' N, 025°31' E
Zalau	47°12' N, 023°03' E

RUSSIA ... pg. 136

Capital: Moscow
Area: 17,075,400 sq km; 6,592,800 sq mi
Highest Elev.: Mt. Elbrus 5,640 m; 18,510 ft
Longest River: Lena 4,400 km; 2,730 mi
Avg. Temperature: Jan = -10°C; Jul = 18°C
Currency: ruble
Official Language: Russian

Name	Lat./Long.
Abakan	53°43' N, 091°26' E
Achinsk	56°17' N, 090°30' E
Aginskoye	51°06' N, 114°32' E
Akademgorodok	54°49' N, 083°09' E
Aldan	58°37' N, 125°24' E
Aleksandrovsk-Grushevsky, see Shakhty	
Aleksandrovsk-Sakhalinsky	50°54' N, 142°10' E
Aleksin	54°31' N, 037°05' E
Almetyevsk	54°53' N, 052°20' E
Anadyr (Novo-Mariinsk)	64°45' N, 177°29' E
Andropov, see Rybinsk	
Angarsk	52°34' N, 103°54' E
Anzhero-Sudzhensk	56°07' N, 086°00' E
Arkhangelsk (Archangel)	64°34' N, 040°32' E
Armavir	45°00' N, 041°08' E
Arzamas	55°23' N, 043°50' E
Astrakhan	46°21' N, 048°03' E
Balakovo	52°02' N, 047°47' E
Barnaul	53°22' N, 083°45' E
Belgorod	50°36' N, 036°34' E
Berezniki	59°24' N, 056°46' E
Birobidzhan	48°48' N, 132°57' E
Biysk (Biisk)	52°34' N, 085°15' E
Blagoveshchensk	50°16' N, 127°32' E
Bobriki, see Novomoskovsk	
Bratsk	56°21' N, 101°55' E
Brezhnev, see Naberezhnye Chelny	
Bryansk	53°15' N, 034°22' E
Cheboksary	56°09' N, 047°15' E
Chelyabinsk	55°10' N, 061°24' E
Cherepovets	59°08' N, 037°54' E
Cherkessk	44°14' N, 042°03' E
Chita	52°03' N, 113°30' E
Chkalov, see Orenburg	
Dimitrovgrad (Melekess)	54°15' N, 049°33' E
Dudinka	69°25' N, 086°15' E
Dzaudzhikau, see Vladikavkaz	
Dzerzhinsk	56°15' N, 043°24' E
Ekaterinodar, see Krasnodar	
Elektrostal	55°47' N, 038°28' E
Elista	46°16' N, 044°14' E
Engels	51°30' N, 046°07' E
Gatchina (Krasnogvardeysk)	59°34' N, 030°08' E
Glazov	58°09' N, 052°40' E
Gorky, see Nizhny Novgorod	
Gorno-Altaysk (Ulala, or Oyrot-Tura)	51°58' N, 085°58' E
Grozny	43°20' N, 045°42' E
Ioshkar-Ola, see Yoshkar-Ola	
Irkutsk	52°16' N, 104°20' E
Ivanovo	57°00' N, 040°59' E
Izhevsk (Ustinov)	56°51' N, 053°14' E
Kalinin, see Tver	
Kaliningrad (Königsberg)	54°43' N, 020°30' E
Kaluga	54°31' N, 036°16' E
Kamensk-Uralsky	56°25' N, 061°54' E
Kamyshin	50°06' N, 045°24' E
Kansk	56°13' N, 095°41' E
Kazan	55°45' N, 049°08' E
Kemerovo	55°20' N, 086°05' E
Khabarovsk	48°30' N, 135°06' E
Khanty-Mansiysk (Ostyako-Vogulsk)	61°00' N, 069°06' E
Kineshma	57°28' N, 042°07' E
Kirov, see Vyatka	
Kiselevsk (Kiselyovsk)	54°00' N, 086°39' E
Kislovodsk	43°55' N, 042°43' E
Kolchugino, see Leninsk-Kuznetsky	
Kolomna	55°05' N, 038°47' E
Kolpino	59°45' N, 030°36' E
Komsomolsk-na-Amure	50°35' N, 137°02' E
Königsberg, see Kaliningrad	
Kostroma	57°46' N, 040°55' E
Kovrov	56°25' N, 041°18' E
Kozlov, see Michurinsk	
Krasnodar (Ekaterinodar, or Yekaterinodar)	45°02' N, 039°00' E
Krasnogvardeysk, see Gatchina	
Krasnoyarsk	56°01' N, 092°50' E
Kudymkar	59°01' N, 054°39' E
Kurgan	55°26' N, 065°18' E
Kursk	51°42' N, 036°12' E
Kuybyshev, see Samara	
Kuznetsk, see Novokuznetsk	
Kyzyl (Khem-Beldyr)	51°42' N, 094°27' E
Leningrad, see St. Petersburg	
Leninsk-Kuznetsky (Kolchugino)	54°38' N, 086°10' E
Lensk	60°43' N, 114°55' E
Lipetsk	52°37' N, 039°35' E
Lyubertsy	55°41' N, 037°53' E
Magadan	59°34' N, 150°48' E
Magnitogorsk	53°27' N, 059°04' E
Makhachkala	42°58' N, 047°30' E
Maykop (Maikop)	44°35' N, 040°10' E
Melekess, see Dimitrovgrad	
Mezhdurechensk	53°42' N, 088°03' E
Miass	54°59' N, 060°06' E
Michurinsk (Kozlov)	52°54' N, 040°30' E
Mikhaylovka (Mikhailovka)	50°04' N, 043°15' E
Mirny	62°33' N, 113°53' E
Molotov, see Perm	
Molotovsk, see Severodvinsk	
Moscow (Moskva)	55°45' N, 037°35' E
Murmansk	68°58' N, 033°05' E
Naberezhnye Chelny (Brezhnev)	55°42' N, 052°19' E
Nadezhdinsk, see Serov	
Nakhodka	42°47' N, 132°52' E
Nalchik	43°29' N, 043°37' E
Naryan-Mar	67°39' N, 053°00' E
Nizhnekamsk	55°36' N, 051°47' E
Nizhnevartovsk	60°56' N, 076°38' E
Nizhniy Novgorod (Gorky)	56°20' N, 044°00' E
Nizhniy Tagil	57°55' N, 059°57' E
Norilsk	69°20' N, 088°06' E
Novgorod	58°31' N, 031°17' E
Novo-Mariinsk, see Anadyr	
Novocherkassk	47°25' N, 040°06' E
Novokuybyshevsk	53°07' N, 049°58' E
Novokuznetsk (Kuznetsk, or Stalinsk)	53°45' N, 087°06' E
Novomoskovsk (Bobriki, or Stalinogorsk)	54°05' N, 038°13' E
Novorossiysk	44°43' N, 037°47' E
Novoshakhtinsk	47°47' N, 039°56' E
Novosibirsk	55°02' N, 082°55' E
Novotroitsk	51°12' N, 058°20' E
Omsk	55°00' N, 073°24' E
Ordzhonikidze, see Vladikavkaz	
Orenburg (Chkalov)	51°45' N, 055°06' E
Orsk	51°12' N, 058°34' E
Oryol	52°55' N, 036°05' E
Ostyako-Vogulsk, see Khanty-Mansiysk	
Oyrot-Tura, see Gorno-Altaysk	
Palana	59°07' N, 159°58' E
Penza	53°13' N, 045°00' E
Perm (Molotov)	58°00' N, 056°15' E
Pervouralsk	56°54' N, 059°58' E
Petropavlovsk-Kamchatsky	53°01' N, 158°39' E
Petrozavodsk	61°49' N, 034°20' E
Pevek	69°42' N, 170°17' E
Podolsk	55°26' N, 037°33' E
Prokopyevsk	53°53' N, 086°45' E
Pskov	57°50' N, 028°20' E
Pyatigorsk	44°01' N, 043°05' E
Rostov-na-Donu (Rostov-on-Don)	47°14' N, 039°42' E
Rubtsovsk	51°30' N, 081°15' E
Ryazan (Riazan)	54°38' N, 039°44' E
Rybinsk (Andropov, or Shcherbakov)	58°03' N, 038°50' E
Salavat	53°21' N, 055°55' E
Salekhard	66°33' N, 066°42' E
Samara (Kuybyshev)	53°12' N, 050°09' E
Sankt Peterburg, see St. Petersburg	
Saransk	54°11' N, 045°11' E
Sarapul	56°28' N, 053°48' E
Saratov	51°34' N, 046°02' E
Serov (Nadezhdinsk)	59°36' N, 060°35' E
Serpukhov	54°55' N, 037°25' E
Severodvinsk (Molotovsk)	64°34' N, 039°50' E
Shakhty (Aleksandrovsk-Grushevsky)	47°42' N, 040°13' E
Shcherbakov, see Rybinsk	
Simbirsk, see Ulyanovsk	
Smolensk	54°47' N, 032°03' E
Sochi	43°35' N, 039°45' E

Name	Lat./Long.
Solikamsk	59°39' N, 056°47' E
Srednekolymsk	67°27' N, 153°41' E
St. Petersburg (Leningrad, or Sankt Peterburg)	59°55' N, 030°15' E
Stalingrad, *see* Volgograd	
Stalinogorsk, *see* Novomoskovsk	
Stalinsk, *see* Novokuznetsk	
Stary Oskol	51°17' N, 037°51' E
Stavropol (Voroshilovsk)	45°03' N, 041°58' E
Sterlitamak	53°37' N, 055°58' E
Surgut	61°14' N, 073°20' E
Susuman	62°47' N, 148°10' E
Sverdlovsk, *see* Yekaterinburg	
Syktyvkar	61°40' N, 050°48' E
Syzran	53°11' N, 048°27' E
Taganrog	47°12' N, 038°56' E
Tambov	52°43' N, 041°27' E
Tolyatti (Stavropal, or Tolyattigrad)	53°31' N, 049°26' E
Tomsk	56°30' N, 084°58' E
Tsaritsyn, *see* Volgograd	
Tula	54°12' N, 037°37' E
Tura	64°17' N, 100°14' E
Tver (Kalinin)	56°52' N, 035°55' E
Tyumen	57°09' N, 065°26' E
Udachny	62°33' N, 113°53' E
Ufa	55°45' N, 055°56' E
Ukhta	63°33' N, 053°40' E
Ulala, *see* Gorno-Altaysk	
Ulan-Ude	51°50' N, 107°37' E
Ulyanovsk (Simbirsk)	54°20' N, 048°24' E
Usolye-Sibirskoye	52°45' N, 103°41' E
Ussuriysk	43°48' N, 131°59' E
Ust-Ordinsky	52°48' N, 104°45' E
Ustinov, *see* Izhevsk	
Velikiye Luki	56°20' N, 030°32' E
Verkhoyansk	67°35' N, 133°27' E
Viipuri, *see* Vyborg	
Vladikavkaz (Dzaudzhikau, or Ordzhonikidze)	43°40' N, 044°40' E
Vladimir	56°10' N, 040°25' E
Vladivostok	43°08' N, 131°54' E
Volgodonsk	47°32' N, 042°09' E
Volgograd (Stalingrad, or Tsaritsyn)	48°45' N, 044°25' E
Vologda	59°13' N, 039°54' E
Volzhsky	48°49' N, 044°44' E
Vorkuta	67°30' N, 064°00' E
Voronezh	51°38' N, 039°12' E
Voroshilovsk, *see* Stavropol	
Votkinsk	57°03' N, 053°39' E
Vyatka (Viatka, or Kirov)	58°33' N, 049°42' E
Vyborg (Viipuri)	60°42' N, 028°45' E
Yakutsk	62°00' N, 129°40' E
Yaroslavl	57°37' N, 039°52' E
Yekaterinburg (Sverdlovsk)	56°51' N, 060°36' E
Yekaterinodar, *see* Krasnodar	
Yelets	52°37' N, 038°30' E
Yoshkar-Ola (Ioshkar-Ola)	56°40' N, 047°55' E
Yuzhno-Sakhalinsk	46°57' N, 142°44' E
Zlatoust	55°10' N, 059°40' E

RWANDA ....pg. 153
Capital: Kigali
Area: 25,271 sq km; 9,757 sq mi
Highest Elev.: Karisimbi 4,510 m; 14,790 ft
Longest River: Kagura 400 km; 250 mi
Avg. Temperature: Jan = 20.8°C; Jul = 20.2°C
Currency: Rwanda franc
Official Language: Rwanda, French

Kigali	01°57' S, 030°04' E
Ruhengeri	01°30' S, 029°38' E

SAINT KITTS AND NEVIS pg. 116
Capital: Basseterre
Area: 269.4 sq km; 104 sq mi
Highest Elev.: Mt. Liamuiga 1,160 m; 3,790 ft
Avg. Temperature: Jan = 27°C; Jul = 27°C
Currency: East Caribbean dollar
Official Language: English

Basseterre	17°18' N, 062°43' W
Charlestown	17°08' N, 062°37' W

SAINT LUCIA ....pg. 116
Capital: Castries
Area: 617 sq km; 238 sq mi
Highest Elev.: Mt. Gimie 960 m; 3,150 ft
Avg. Temperature: Jan = 24.2°C; Jul = 27.0°C
Currency: East Caribbean dollar
Official Language: English

Castries	14°01' N, 061°00' W

SAINT VINCENT AND THE GRENADINES ....pg. 116
Capital: Kingstown
Area: 389.3 sq km; 150.3 sq mi
Highest Elev.: Soufrière 1,230 m; 4,080 ft
Avg. Temperature: Jan = 25°C; Jul = 27°C
Currency: East Caribbean dollar
Official Language: English

Kingstown	13°09' N, 061°14' W

SAMOA ....pg. 156
Capital: Apia
Area: 2,831 sq km; 1,093 sq mi
Highest Elev.: Mt. Silisili 1,860 m; 6,100 ft
Avg. Temperature: Jan = 26.3°C; Jul = 25.1°C
Currency: tala
Official Language: Samoan, English

Apia	13°50' S, 171°44' W

SAN MARINO ....pg. 130
Capital: San Marino
Area: 61.2 sq km; 23.6 sq mi
Highest Elev.: Mt. Titano 740 m; 2,420 ft
Avg. Temperature: Jan = 26°C; Jul = -7°C
Currency: Italian lira
Official Language: Italian

San Marino	43°56' N, 012°25' E

SÃO TOMÉ AND PRÍNCIPE ...pg. 150
Capital: São Tomé
Area: 1,001 sq km; 386 sq mi
Highest Elev.: São Tomé Peak 2,020 m; 6,640 ft
Avg. Temperature: Jan = 26°C; Jul = 26°C
Currency: dobra
Official Language: Portuguese

São Tomé	00°20' N, 006°44' E

SAUDI ARABIA ....pg. 154
Capital: Riyadh
Area: 2,240,000 sq km; 865,000 sq mi
Avg. Temperature: Jan = 15°C; Jul = 34°C
Currency: Saudi riyal
Official Language: Arabic

Abha	18°13' N, 042°30' E
Abqaiq (Buqayq)	25°56' N, 049°40' E
Afif	23°55' N, 042°56' E
Ar'ar	30°59' N, 041°02' E
Badanah	30°59' N, 040°58' E
Bahah, al-	20°01' N, 041°28' E
Badi', al-	22°02' N, 046°34' E
Bi'ar, al-	22°39' N, 039°40' E
Birkah	23°48' N, 038°50' E
Buraydah	26°20' N, 043°59' E
Buraykah	22°21' N, 039°20' E
Dammam, ad-	26°26' N, 050°07' E
Hafar al-Batin	28°27' N, 045°58' E
Ha'il	27°33' N, 041°42' E
Halaban	23°29' N, 044°23' E
Harajah	17°56' N, 043°21' E
Ha'ir, al-	24°23' N, 046°50' E
Hufuf, al-	25°22' N, 049°34' E
Ju'aydah, al-	19°40' N, 041°34' E
Jubayl, al-	27°01' N, 049°40' E
Jiddah	21°29' N, 039°12' E
Khamis Mushayt	18°18' N, 042°44' E
Khawsh	18°59' N, 041°53' E
Khubar, al-	26°17' N, 050°12' E
Layla	22°17' N, 046°45' E
Mada'in Salih	26°48' N, 037°57' E
Madinah, al-, *see* Medina	
Mecca (Makkah)	21°27' N, 039°49' E
Medina (al-Madinah; Yathrib)	24°28' N, 039°36' E
Mish'ab, al-	28°12' N, 048°36' E
Miskah	24°49' N, 042°56' E
Mubarraz, al-	25°25' N, 049°35' E
Musabih	18°42' N, 042°01' E
Na'jan	24°05' N, 047°10' E
Najran	17°26' N, 044°15' E
Qana	27°47' N, 041°25' E
Qatif, al-	26°33' N, 050°00' E
Qunfudhah, al-	19°08' N, 041°05' E
Rabigh	22°48' N, 039°02' E
Rafha'	29°38' N, 043°30' E
Ras Tanura	26°42' N, 050°06' E
Riyadh (ar-Riyad)	24°38' N, 046°43' E
Tabuk	28°23' N, 036°35' E
Safra', as-	24°02' N, 038°56' E
Sahwah	19°19' N, 042°06' E
Sakakah	29°59' N, 040°07' E
Shidad	21°19' N, 040°03' E
Ta'if, at-	21°16' N, 040°25' E
Tayma'	27°38' N, 038°29' E
Turayf	31°41' N, 038°39' E
Ula, al-	26°38' N, 037°52' E
'Usfan	21°55' N, 039°22' E
Yathrib, *see* Medina	
Zalim	22°43' N, 042°10' E
Zahran	17°40' N, 043°30' E
Zilfi, az-	26°18' N, 044°48' E

SENEGAL ....pg. 150
Capital: Dakar
Area: 196,712 sq km; 75,951 sq mi
Highest Elev.: Fouta Djallon 500 m; 1,640 ft
Longest River: Senegal 1,080 km; 670 mi
Avg. Temperature: Jan =21°C; Jul = 28°C
Currency: CFA franc
Official Language: French

Dakar	14°40' N, 017°26' W
Diourbel	14°40' N, 016°15' W
Kaolack	14°09' N, 016°04' W
Louga	15°37' N, 016°13' W
Thiès	14°48' N, 016°56' W
Saint Louis	16°02' N, 016°30' W
Ziguinchor	12°35' N, 016°16' W

SEYCHELLES ....pg. 153
Capital: Victoria
Area: 455 sq km; 176 sq mi
Highest Elev.: Morne Seychelles 910 m; 2,970 ft
Avg. Temperature: Jan = 30°C; Jul = 24°C
Currency: Seychelles rupee
Official Language: Seselwa

Victoria	04°37' S, 055°27' E

SIERRA LEONE ....pg. 150
Capital: Freetown
Area: 71,740 sq km; 27,699 sq mi
Highest Elev.: Mt. Loma Mansa 1,940 m; 6,390 ft
Longest River: Rokel 400 km; 250 mi
Avg. Temperature: Jan = 27°C; Jul = 26°C
Currency: leone
Official Language: English

Freetown	08°30' N, 013°15' W
Koidu	08°38' N, 010°59' W

SINGAPORE ....pg. 144
Capital: Singapore
Area: 641.0 sq km; 247.5 sq mi
Highest Elev.: Timah Hill 160 m; 530 ft
Avg. Temperature: Jan = 25.6°C; Jul = 27.1°C
Currency: Singapore dollar
Official Language: Chinese, Malay, Tamil, English

Singapore	01°16' N, 103°50' E

SLOVAKIA ....pg. 134
Capital: Bratislava
Area: 49,036 sq km; 18,933 sq mi
Highest Elev.: Gerlachovsky Pk. 2,660 m; 8,710 ft
Longest River: Vah 390 km; 240 mi
Avg. Temperature: Jan = 0.7°C; Jul = 19.1°C
Currency: Slovak koruna
Official Language: Slovak

Banská Bystrica	48°44' N, 019°09' E
Bratislava	48°09' N, 017°07' E
Komárno	47°46' N, 018°08' E
Kosice	48°42' N, 021°15' E
Martin	49°04' N, 018°56' E
Michalovce	48°45' N, 021°56' E
Nitra	48°19' N, 018°05' E
Nové Zámky	47°59' N, 018°10' E
Poprad	49°03' N, 020°18' E
Povazska Bystrica	49°07' N, 018°27' E
Presov	49°00' N, 021°15' E
Spisska Nová Ves	48°57' N, 020°34' E
Trencin	48°54' N, 018°02' E
Trnava	48°22' N, 017°36' E
Zilina	49°13' N, 018°44' E
Zvolen	48°35' N, 019°08' E

SLOVENIA ....pg. 134
Capital: Ljubljana
Area: 20,256 sq km; 7,821 sq mi
Highest Elev.: Mt. Triglav 2,860 m; 9,400 ft
Longest River: Sava 580 km; 940 mi
Avg. Temperature: Jan = 0°C; Jul = 21°C
Currency: Yugoslav dinar
Official Language: Slovene

Idrija	46°00' N, 014°02' E
Kocevje	45°39' N, 014°51' E
Kranj	46°14' N, 014°22' E
Ljubljana	46°02' N, 014°30' E
Novo Mesto	45°48' N, 015°10' E
Postojna	45°47' N, 014°14' E
Ptuj	46°25' N, 015°52' E
Trbovlje	46°10' N, 015°03' E
Velenje	46°22' N, 015°07' E

SOLOMON ISLANDS ...pg. 156
Capital: Honiara
Area: 28,370 sq km; 10,954 sq mi
Highest Elev.: Makarakombou 2,450 m; 8,030 ft
Avg. Temperature: Jan = 28.9°C; Jul = 27.8°C
Currency: Soloman Islands dollar
Official Language: English

Honiara	09°26' S, 159°57' E

SOMALIA ....pg. 151
Capital: Mogadishu
Area: 637,00 sq km; 246,00 sq mi
Highest Elev.: Mt. Surud Cad 2,410 m; 7,900 ft
Longest River: Shabeelle 1,820 km; 1,130 mi
Avg. Temperature: Jan = 26°C; Jul = 26°C
Currency: Somali shilling
Official Language: Somali, Arabic

Berbera	10°25' N, 045°02' E
Hargeysa	09°35' N, 044°04' E
Kismaayo (Chisimayu)	00°22' S, 042°32' E
Marka (Merca)	01°43' N, 044°53' E
Merca, *see* Marka	
Mogadishu (Mogadiscio or Muqdisho)	02°04' N, 045°22' E

SOUTH AFRICA ....pg. 153
Capital: Pretoria, Bloemfontein, Cape Town
Area: 1,223,201 sq km; 472,281 sq mi
Highest Elev.: Mt. Aux Sources 3,300 m; 10,820 ft
Avg. Temperature: Jan = 21°C; Jul = 13°C
Currency: rand
Official Language: Afrikaans, English, Ndebele, Pedi, Sotho, Swazi, Tsonga, Tswana, Venda, Xhosa, Zulu,

Aliwal North	30°42' S, 026°42' E
Beaufort West	32°21' S, 022°35' E
Bellville	33°54' S, 018°38' E
Bloemfontein	29°08' S, 026°10' E
Boksburg	26°13' S, 028°15' E
Bredasdorp	34°32' S, 020°02' E
Calvinia	31°28' S, 019°47' E
Cape Town (Kaapstad)	33°55' S, 018°25' E
Carletonville	26°22' S, 027°24' E
Carnarvon	30°57' S, 022°08' E
De Aar	30°39' S, 024°01' E
Durban (Port Natal)	29°51' S, 031°01' E
East London	33°02' S, 027°55' E
Empangeni	28°45' S, 031°54' E
Ermelo	26°32' S, 029°59' E
George	33°58' S, 022°27' E
Germiston	26°13' S, 028°11' E
Grahamstown	33°18' S, 026°32' E
Hammarsdale	29°48' S, 030°39' E
Hopefield	33°04' S, 018°21' E
Hopetown	29°37' S, 024°05' E
Humansdorp	34°02' S, 024°46' E
Johannesburg	26°12' S, 028°05' E
Kaapstad, *see* Cape Town	
Kathu (Sishen)	27°40' S, 023°01' E
Kimberley	28°45' S, 024°46' E
Klerksdorp	26°52' S, 026°40' E
Krugersdorp	26°06' S, 027°46' E
Kuruman	27°28' S, 023°26' E
Ladysmith	28°33' S, 029°47' E
Lebowakgomo	24°12' S, 029°30' E
Margate	30°51' S, 030°22' E
Messina	22°21' S, 030°03' E
Middelburg	25°28' S, 029°28' E
Nelspruit	25°28' S, 030°58' E
Newcastle	27°45' S, 029°56' E
Oudtshoorn	33°35' S, 022°12' E
Paarl	33°44' S, 018°58' E
Pietermaritzburg	29°37' S, 030°23' E
Pinetown	29°49' S, 030°51' E
Port Elizabeth	33°58' S, 025°35' E
Port Shepstone	30°45' S, 030°27' E
Potchefstroom	26°43' S, 027°06' E
Pretoria	25°45' S, 028°10' E
Prieska	29°40' S, 022°45' E
Queenstown	31°54' S, 026°53' E
Richard's Bay	28°48' S, 032°05' E
Rustenburg	25°40' S, 027°15' E
Seshego	23°51' S, 029°23' E
Soweto	26°16' S, 027°52' E
Stellenbosch	33°56' S, 018°51' E
Tembisa	25°59' S, 028°13' E
Uitenhage	33°45' S, 025°24' E
Ulundi	28°17' S, 031°25' E
Umlazi	29°59' S, 030°52' E
Upington	28°27' S, 021°15' E
Vanderbijlpark	26°40' S, 027°49' E
Vereeniging	26°40' S, 027°56' E
Vredenburg	32°54' S, 017°59' E
Welkom	27°59' S, 026°42' E
Worcester	33°39' S, 019°26' E

SPAIN ....pg. 128
Capital: Madrid
Area: 504,783 sq km; 194,898 sq mi
Highest Elev.: Mulhacén Pk. 3,480 m; 11,420 ft
Longest River: Ebro 920 km; 570 mi
Avg. Temperature: Jan = 5°C; Jul = 24°C
Currency: peseta
Official Language: Castilian Spanish

Albacete	38°59' N, 001°51' W
Alcalá de Guadaira	37°20' N, 005°50' W
Alcalá de Henares	40°29' N, 003°22' W
Alcoy	38°42' N, 000°28' W
Algeciras	36°08' N, 005°30' W
Almería	36°50' N, 002°27' W
Avilés	43°33' N, 005°55' W
Badajoz	38°53' N, 006°58' W
Badalona	41°27' N, 002°15' E
Barcelona	41°23' N, 002°11' E
Bilbao	43°15' N, 002°58' W
Burgos	42°21' N, 003°42' W
Cáceres	39°29' N, 006°22' W
Cádiz (Cadiz)	36°32' N, 006°18' W
Cartagena	37°36' N, 000°59' W
Castellón de la Plana	39°59' N, 000°02' W
Ciudad Real	38°59' N, 003°56' W
Cornella de Llobregat	41°21' N, 002°05' E
Coslada	40°26' N, 003°34' W
Donostia (San Sebastian)	43°19' N, 001°59' W
Dos Hermanas	37°17' N, 005°55' W
El Prat de Llobregat	41°20' N, 002°06' E
El Puerto de Santa Maria	36°36' N, 006°13' W
Elda	38°29' N, 000°47' W
Elx, *see* Elche	
Gernika-Lumo (Guernica y Luno)	43°19' N, 002°41' W
Getafe	40°18' N, 003°43' W
Gijón	43°32' N, 005°40' W
Granada	37°11' N, 003°36' W
Granollers	41°37' N, 002°18' E
Guadalajara	37°16' N, 006°57' W
Huelva	37°16' N, 006°57' W
Irun	43°21' N, 001°47' W
Jaén	37°46' N, 003°47' W
Jerez de la Frontera	36°41' N, 006°08' W
La Coruña (A Coruna)	43°22' N, 008°23' W
Las Palmas de Gran Canaria	28°06' N, 015°24' W
Leganés	40°19' N, 003°45' W
León	42°36' N, 005°34' W
Linares	38°05' N, 003°38' W
Lleida (Lerida)	41°37' N, 000°37' E
Logroño	42°28' N, 002°27' W
Lugo	43°00' N, 007°34' W
Madrid	40°24' N, 003°41' W
Málaga	36°43' N, 004°25' W
Manresa	41°44' N, 001°50' E
Mataró	41°32' N, 002°27' E
Mérida	38°55' N, 006°20' W
Móstoles	40°19' N, 003°51' W
Murcia	37°59' N, 001°07' W
Oviedo	43°22' N, 005°50' W
Palencia	42°01' N, 004°32' W
Pamplona (Iruna)	42°49' N, 001°38' W
Parla	40°14' N, 003°46' W

Name	Lat./Long.
Portugalete	43°19' N, 003°01' W
Puertollano	38°41' N, 004°07' W
Reus	41°09' N, 001°07' E
Sabadell	41°33' N, 002°06' E
Salamanca	40°58' N, 005°39' W
San Fernando	36°28' N, 006°12' W
San Sebastian, *see* Donostia	
Santa Coloma de Gramanet	41°27' N, 002°13' E
Santa Cruz de Tenerife	28°27' N, 016°14' W
Santander	43°28' N, 003°48' W
Santiago de Compostela	42°53' N, 008°33' W
Saragossa (Zaragoza)	41°38' N, 000°53' W
Segovia	40°57' N, 004°07' W
Seville (Sevilla)	37°23' N, 005°59' W
Talavera de la Reina	39°57' N, 004°50' W
Tarragona	41°07' N, 001°15' E
Toledo	39°52' N, 004°01' W
Torrent	39°26' N, 000°28' W
Valencia	39°28' N, 000°22' W
Valladolid	41°39' N, 004°43' W
Vigo	42°14' N, 008°43' W
Vitoria (Gasteiz)	42°51' N, 002°40' W
Zamora	41°30' N, 005°45' W
Zaragossa, *see* Saragossa	

SRI LANKA ....pg. 146

Capital: ....Colombo
Area: .....65,610 sq km; 25,332 sq mi
Highest Elev.: ...Mt. Pidurutalagala 2,520 m;
         8,280 ft
Longest River: ....Mahaweli 330 km; 210 mi
Avg. Temperature: .Jan = 26°C; Jul = 27°C
Currency: ....Sri Lankan rupee
Official Language: .Sinhala, Timil

Batticaloa	07°43' N, 081°42' E
Colombo	06°56' N, 079°51' E
Dehiwala-Mount Lavinia	06°51' N, 079°52' E
Galle	06°02' N, 080°13' E
Jaffna	09°40' N, 080°00' E
Kandy	07°18' N, 080°38' E
Kotte (Sri Jayewardenepura Kotte)	06°54' N, 079°54' E
Moratuwa	06°46' N, 079°53' E
Negombo	07°13' N, 079°50' E
Trincomalee	08°34' N, 081°14' E

SUDAN ....pg. 151

Capital: ......Khartoum
Area: ...2,503,890 sq km; 966,757 sq mi
Highest Elev.: ..Mt. Kinyeti 3,190 m; 10,460 ft
Longest River: ....Nile 6,650 km; 4,130 mi
Avg. Temperature: .Jan =23°C; Jul = 31°C
Currency: ......Sudanese dinar
Official Language: .Arabic

Al-Fashir	13°38' N, 025°21' E
Al-Khartum Bahri, *see* Khartoum North	
Al-Qadarif (Gedaref)	14°02' N, 035°24' E
Al-Ubbayid (El-Obeid)	13°11' N, 030°13' E
Bur Sudan, *see* Port Sudan	
Juba	04°51' N, 031°37' E
Kassala	15°28' N, 036°24' E
Khartoum (Al-Khartum)	15°36' N, 032°32' E
Khartoum North (Al-Khartum Bahri)	15°38' N, 032°33' E
Kusti	13°10' N, 032°40' E
Nyala	12°03' N, 024°53' E
Omdurman (Umm Durman)	15°38' N, 032°30' E
Port Sudan (Bur Sudan)	19°37' N, 037°14' E
Umm Durman, *see* Omdurman	
Wad Madani	14°24' N, 033°32' E
Waw	07°42' N, 028°00' E

SURINAME ....pg. 121

Capital: ......Paramaribo
Area: ...163,820 sq km; 63,251sq mi
Highest Elev.: ...Juliana Top 1,230 m; 4,040 ft
Longest River: ....Courantyne 700 km; 450 mi
Avg. Temperature: .Jan = 26°C; Jul = 27°C
Currency: ......Suriname guilder
Official Language: .Dutch

Brownsweg	05°01' N, 055°10' W
Paramaribo	05°50' N, 055°10' W
Zanderij	05°27' N, 055°12' W

SWAZILAND ....pg. 153

Capital: ......Mbabane
Area: ...17,364 sq km; 6,704 sq mi
Highest Elev.: ...Mt. Emlembe 1,860 m; 6,110 ft
Avg. Temperature: .Jan = 20.0°C; Jul = 12.2°C
Currency: ......lilangeni
Official Language: .Swazi, English

Manzini (Bremersdorp)	26°29' S, 031°22' E
Mbabane	26°19' S, 031°08' E
Nhlangano	27°07' S, 031°12' E

SWEDEN ....pg. 131

Capital: ......Stockholm
Area: ...449,964 sq km; 173,732 sq mi
Highest Elev.: ...Mt. Kebne 2,110 m; 6,930 ft
Longest River: ....Klar 720 km; 450 mi
Avg. Temperature: .Jan = -3°C; Jul = 18°C
Currency: ......Swedish krona
Official Language: .Swedish

Alingsås	57°56' N, 012°31' E
Ålmhult	56°33' N, 014°08' E
Alvesta	56°54' N, 014°33' E
Älvsbyn	65°40' N, 021°00' E
Ånge	62°31' N, 015°37' E
Ängelholm	56°15' N, 012°51' E
Arboga	59°24' N, 015°50' E
Arvika	59°40' N, 012°34' E

Avesta	60°09' N, 016°12' E
Bengtsfors	59°02' N, 012°13' E
Bjästa	63°12' N, 018°30' E
Boden	65°50' N, 021°42' E
Bollnäs	61°21' N, 016°22' E
Borås	57°43' N, 012°55' E
Borlänge	60°29' N, 015°25' E
Bräcke	62°45' N, 015°25' E
Brunflo	63°05' N, 014°49' E
Eksjö	57°40' N, 014°57' E
Eskilstuna	59°22' N, 016°30' E
Eslöv	55°50' N, 013°20' E
Falkenberg	56°54' N, 012°28' E
Falköping	58°10' N, 013°31' E
Falun	60°36' N, 015°38' E
Filipstad	59°43' N, 014°10' E
Forshaga	59°32' N, 013°28' E
Gammelstaden	65°38' N, 022°01' E
Gävle	60°40' N, 017°10' E
Göteborg	57°43' N, 011°58' E
Gullspång	58°59' N, 014°06' E
Habo	57°55' N, 014°04' E
Hagfors	60°02' N, 013°39' E
Halmstad	56°39' N, 012°50' E
Haparanda	65°50' N, 024°10' E
Härnösand	62°38' N, 017°56' E
Hässleholm	56°09' N, 013°46' E
Helsingborg	56°03' N, 012°42' E
Hofors	60°33' N, 016°17' E
Höganas	56°12' N, 012°33' E
Holmsund	63°42' N, 020°21' E
Hudiksvall	61°44' N, 017°07' E
Hultsfred	57°29' N, 015°50' E
Jönköping	57°47' N, 014°11' E
Kalix	65°51' N, 023°08' E
Kalmar	56°40' N, 016°22' E
Karlshamn	56°10' N, 014°51' E
Karlskoga	59°20' N, 014°31' E
Karlskrona	56°10' N, 015°35' E
Karlstad	59°22' N, 013°30' E
Katrineholm	59°00' N, 016°12' E
Kinna	57°30' N, 012°41' E
Kiruna	67°51' N, 020°13' E
Köping	59°31' N, 016°00' E
Kramfors	62°56' N, 017°47' E
Kristianstad	56°02' N, 014°08' E
Kumla	59°08' N, 015°08' E
Kungälv	57°52' N, 011°58' E
Kungsbacka	57°29' N, 012°04' E
Laholm	56°31' N, 013°02' E
Landskrona	55°52' N, 012°50' E
Laxå	58°59' N, 014°37' E
Lerum	57°46' N, 012°16' E
Lidingö	59°22' N, 018°08' E
Linköping	58°25' N, 015°37' E
Ljungby	56°50' N, 013°56' E
Ljusdal	61°50' N, 016°06' E
Ludvika	60°09' N, 015°11' E
Luleå	65°34' N, 022°10' E
Lund	55°42' N, 013°11' E
Lycksele	64°36' N, 018°40' E
Malmberget	67°10' N, 020°40' E
Malmö	55°36' N, 013°00' E
Malung	60°40' N, 013°42' E
Mariestad	58°43' N, 013°51' E
Märsta	59°37' N, 017°51' E
Mjölby	58°19' N, 015°08' E
Mölnlycke	57°39' N, 012°09' E
Mora	61°00' N, 014°33' E
Motala	58°33' N, 015°03' E
Nassjö	57°39' N, 014°41' E
Norrköping	58°36' N, 016°11' E
Norrtälje	59°46' N, 018°42' E
Nybro	56°45' N, 015°54' E
Nyköping	58°45' N, 017°00' E
Nynäshamn	58°54' N, 017°57' E
Ockelbo	60°53' N, 016°43' E
Örebro	59°17' N, 015°13' E
Örnsköldsvik	63°18' N, 018°43' E
Øskarshamn	57°16' N, 016°26' E
Östersund	63°11' N, 014°39' E
Östhammar	60°16' N, 018°22' E
Oxelösund	58°40' N, 017°06' E
Piteå	65°20' N, 021°30' E
Rättvik	60°53' N, 015°06' E
Robertsfors	64°11' N, 020°51' E
Ronneby	56°12' N, 015°18' E
Säffle	59°08' N, 012°54' E
Sala	59°55' N, 016°36' E
Sandviken	60°37' N, 016°46' E
Skara	58°22' N, 013°25' E
Skellefteå	64°46' N, 020°57' E
Skövde	58°24' N, 013°50' E
Soderhamn	61°18' N, 017°03' E
Sodertalje	59°12' N, 017°37' E
Sollefteå	63°10' N, 017°16' E
Sollentuna	59°25' N, 017°57' E
Staffanstorp	55°38' N, 013°13' E
Stenungsund	58°05' N, 011°49' E
Stockholm	59°20' N, 018°03' E
Strömstad	58°56' N, 011°10' E
Strömsund	63°51' N, 015°35' E
Sundsvall	62°23' N, 017°18' E
Svenljunga	57°30' N, 013°07' E
Täby	59°30' N, 018°03' E
Tierp	60°20' N, 017°30' E
Timrå	62°29' N, 017°18' E
Tranås	58°03' N, 014°59' E
Trelleborg	55°22' N, 013°10' E
Trollhättan	58°16' N, 012°18' E
Uddevalla	58°21' N, 011°55' E
Umeå	63°50' N, 020°15' E
Uppsala	59°52' N, 017°38' E
Vänersborg	58°22' N, 012°19' E
Varberg	57°06' N, 012°15' E
Värnamo	57°11' N, 014°02' E
Västerås	59°37' N, 016°33' E
Västerhaninge	59°07' N, 018°06' E
Västervik	57°45' N, 016°38' E
Växjö	56°53' N, 014°49' E
Vetlanda	57°26' N, 015°04' E
Vimmerby	57°40' N, 015°51' E
Visby	57°38' N, 018°18' E
Ystad	55°25' N, 013°49' E

SWITZERLAND ....pg. 132

Capital: ....Bern
Area: .....41,284 sq km; 15,940 sq mi
Highest Elev.: ...Dufourspitze 4,630 m; 15,200 ft
Longest River: ...Rhine 1,390 km; 870 mi
Avg. Temperature: .Jan = -1°C; Jul = 18°C
Currency: .....Swiss franc
Official Language: ..French, German, Italian

Aarau	47°23' N, 008°03' E
Arbon	47°31' N, 009°26' E
Baden	47°28' N, 008°18' E
Basel (Bale)	47°35' N, 007°32' E
Bern	46°55' N, 007°28' E
Biel (Bienne)	47°10' N, 007°15' E
Chur (Coire)	46°51' N, 009°30' E
Frauenfeld	47°33' N, 008°54' E
Fribourg (Freiburg)	46°48' N, 007°09' E
Geneva (Geneve, Genf, Ginevra)	46°12' N, 006°10' E
Lausanne	46°32' N, 006°40' E
Lucerne (Luzern)	47°05' N, 008°18' E
Lugano (Lauis)	46°00' N, 008°58' E
Neuchâtel (Neuenburg)	47°00' N, 006°58' E
Saint Gall (Sankt Gallen)	47°28' N, 009°24' E
Schaffhausen	47°42' N, 008°38' E
Thun (Thoune)	46°45' N, 007°37' E
Vevey	46°27' N, 006°51' E
Winterthur	47°30' N, 008°45' E
Zug	47°10' N, 008°31' E
Zürich	47°22' N, 008°33' E

SYRIA ....pg. 154

Capital: ....Damascus
Area: .....185,180 sq km; 71,498 sq mi
Highest Elev.: ...Mt. Hermon 2,810 m; 9,230 ft
Longest River: ....Euphrates 2,700 km; 1,700 mi
Avg. Temperature: .Jan = 7°C; Jul = 27°C
Currency: ....Syrian pound
Official Language: ..Arabic

Al-Hasakah	36°29' N, 040°45' E
Al-Ladhiqiyah, *see* Latakia	
Al-Qamishli (Al-Kamishly)	37°02' N, 041°14' E
Ar-Raqqah (Rakka)	35°57' N, 039°01' E
As-Suwayda'	32°42' N, 036°34' E
Damascus	33°30' N, 036°18' E
Dar'a	32°37' N, 036°06' E
Dayr az-Zawr	35°20' N, 040°09' E
Halab, *see* Aleppo	
Hamah (Hama)	35°08' N, 036°45' E
Hims (Homs)	34°44' N, 036°43' E
Idlib	35°55' N, 036°38' E
Latakia (Al-Ladhiqiyah)	35°31' N, 035°47' E
Tartus	34°53' N, 035°53' E

TAIWAN ....pg. 143

Capital: ....Taipei
Area: .....36,179 sq km; 13,969 sq mi
Highest Elev.: ...Yü Shan 4,000 m; 13,110 ft
Longest River: ...Choshui 190 km; 120 mi
Avg. Temperature: .Jan = 15°C; Jul = 28°C
Currency: ....New Taiwan dollar
Official Language: ..Mandarin Chinese

Chang-hua	24°05' N, 120°32' E
Chi-lung	25°08' N, 121°44' E
Chia-i	23°29' N, 120°27' E
Chu-tung	24°44' N, 121°05' E
Feng-shan	22°38' N, 120°21' E
Feng-yuan	24°15' N, 120°43' E
Hsin-chu	24°48' N, 120°58' E
Hua-lien	23°59' N, 121°36' E
I-lan	24°46' N, 121°45' E
Kang-shan	22°48' N, 120°17' E
Kao-hsiung	22°38' N, 120°17' E
Lo-tung	24°41' N, 121°46' E
Lu-kang	24°03' N, 120°25' E
Miao-li	24°34' N, 120°49' E
Nan-t'ou	23°55' N, 120°41' E
San-ch'ung	25°04' N, 121°30' E
T'ai-chung	24°09' N, 120°41' E
T'ai-nan	23°00' N, 120°12' E
T'ai-tung	22°45' N, 121°09' E
T'ao-yuan	25°00' N, 121°18' E
Taipei (T'ai-pei)	25°03' N, 121°30' E
Yuan-lin	23°58' N, 120°34' E
Yung-k'ang	23°02' N, 120°15' E

TAJIKISTAN ....pg. 139

Capital: .....Dushanbe
Area: .....143,100 sq km; 55,300 sq mi
Highest Elev: ...Communism Pk. 7,500 m; 24,590 ft
Longest River: ...Pyandzh 1,130 km; 700 mi
Avg. Temperature: .Jan = 1°C; Jul = 28°C
Currency: .....Russian ruble
Official Language: Tajik

Dushanbe	38°33' N, 068°48' E
Khujand (Leninabad, or Khojand)	40°17' N, 069°37' E
Qurghonteppa	37°50' N, 068°47' E

TANZANIA ....pg. 153

Capital: .....Dodoma
Area: .....942,799 sq km; 364,017 sq mi
Highest Elev.: ..Kilimanjaro 5,890 m; 19,340 ft
Longest River: ...Rufiji 280 km; 175 mi
Avg. Temperature: .Jan = 28°C; Jul = 24°C
Currency: .....Tanzanian shilling
Official Language: ..Swahili, English

Arusha	03°22' S, 036°41' E
Bukoba	01°20' S, 031°49' E
Chake Chake	05°15' S, 039°46' E
Dar es Salaam	06°48' S, 039°17' E
Dodoma	06°11' S, 035°45' E

Ifakara	08°08' S, 036°41' E
Iringa	07°46' S, 035°42' E
Kigoma	04°52' S, 029°38' E
Korogwe	05°09' S, 038°29' E
Lindi	10°00' S, 039°43' E
Mbeya	08°54' S, 033°27' E
Mkoani	05°22' S, 039°39' E
Morogoro	06°49' S, 037°40' E
Moshi	03°21' S, 037°20' E
Mpwapwa	06°21' S, 036°29' E
Mtwara	10°16' S, 040°11' E
Mwanza	02°31' S, 032°54' E
Pangani	09°32' S, 035°31' E
Songea	10°41' S, 035°39' E
Sumbawanga	07°58' S, 031°37' E
Tabora	05°01' S, 032°48' E
Tanga	05°04' S, 039°06' E
Tunduru	11°07' S, 037°21' E
Wete	05°04' S, 039°43' E
Zanzibar	06°10' S, 039°11' E

THAILAND ....pg. 144

Capital: ....Bangkok
Area: .....513,115 sq km; 198,115 sq mi
Highest Elev.: ...Mt. Inthanon 2,590 m; 8,480 ft
Longest River: ...Chao Phraya 370 km; 230 mi
Avg. Temperature: .Jan = 26°C; Jul = 29°C
Currency: ....Thai baht
Official Language: ..Thai

Bangkok (Krung Thep)	13°45' N, 100°31' E
Chiang Mai (Chiengmai)	18°47' N, 098°59' E
Chon Buri	13°22' N, 100°59' E
Hat Yai (Haad Yai)	07°01' N, 100°28' E
Khon Kaen	16°26' N, 102°50' E
Krung Thep, *see* Bangkok	
Nakhon Ratchasima (Khorat)	14°58' N, 102°07' E
Nakhon Sawan	15°41' N, 100°07' E
Nakhon Si Thammarat	08°26' N, 099°58' E
Nong Khai	17°52' N, 102°44' E
Nonthaburi	13°50' N, 100°29' E
Pattaya	12°54' N, 100°51' E
Phra Nakhon Si Ayutthaya (Ayutthaya)	14°21' N, 100°33' E
Phichit	16°26' N, 100°22' E
Phitsanulok	16°50' N, 100°15' E
Phuket	07°53' N, 098°24' E
Sakon Nakhon	17°10' N, 104°09' E
Samut Prakan	13°36' N, 100°36' E
Samut Sakhon (Samut Sakorn)	13°32' N, 100°17' E
Sara Buri	14°32' N, 100°55' E
Trang	07°33' N, 099°36' E
Ubon Ratchathani	15°14' N, 104°54' E
Udon Thani	17°26' N, 102°46' E
Uthai Thani	15°22' N, 100°03' E
Yala	06°33' N, 101°18' E

TOGO ....pg. 150

Capital: ....Lomé
Area: .....56,785 sq km; 21,925 sq mi
Highest Elev.: ...Mt. Baumann 990 m; 3,240 ft
Longest River: ...Oti 520 km; 320 mi
Avg. Temperature: .Jan =28°C; Jul = 27°C
Currency: ....CFA franc
Official Language: ..French

Lomé	06°08' N, 001°13' E

TONGA ....pg. 156

Capital: ....Nuku'alofa
Area: .....749.9 sq km; 289.5 sq mi
Highest Elev.: ...Kao 1,030 m; 3,380 ft
Avg. Temperature: .Jan = 30°C; Jul = 25°C
Currency: ....pa'anga
Official Language: ..Tongan, English

Nuku'alofa	21°08' N, 175°12' E

TRINIDAD & TOBAGO pg. 116

Capital: ....Port of Spain
Area: .....5,128 sq km; 1,980 sq mi
Highest Elev.: ...Aripo Mtn. 940 m; 3,080 ft
Longest River: ...Ortoire 50 km; 30 mi
Avg. Temperature: .Jan = 24°C; Jul = 26°C
Currency: ....Trinidad & Tobago dollar
Official Language: ..English

Port of Spain	10°39' N, 061°31' W
San Fernando	10°17' N, 061°28' W

TUNISIA ....pg. 150

Capital: ....Tunis
Area: .....164,150 sq km; 63,378 sq mi
Highest Elev.: ...Mt. ash-Sha'nabi 1,540 m; 5,070 ft
Longest River: ...Marjardah 460 km; 290 mi
Avg. Temperature: .Jan = 10°C; Jul = 26°C
Currency: .....dinar
Official Language: Arabic

Bizerte (Banzart)	37°17' N, 009°52' E
Gabes, *see* Qabis	
Gafsa, *see* Qafsah	
Jarjis (Zarzis)	33°30' N, 011°07' E
Safaqis (Sfax)	34°44' N, 010°46' E
Susah (Sousa or Sousse)	35°49' N, 010°38' E
Tunis (Tunis)	36°48' N, 010°11' E
Qabis (Gabes or Tacape)	33°53' N, 010°07' E
Qafsah (Gafsa)	34°25' N, 008°48' E
Zarzis, *see* Jarjis	

Name	Lat./Long.

TURKEY . . . . pg. 147

Capital: . . . . Ankara
Area: . . . . .779,452 sq km; 300,948 sq mi
Highest Elev.: . . . .Mt. Ararat 5,140 m; 16,850 ft
Longest River: . . . . Kizil 1,180 km; 730 mi
Avg. Temperature: . Jan = 0°C; Jul = 23°C
Currency: . . . . .Turkish lira
Official Language: . .Turkish

Name	Lat./Long.
Adana	37°01' N, 035°18' E
Adapazari	40°46' N, 030°24' E
Adiyaman (Husnumansur)	37°46' N, 038°17' E
Afyon	38°45' N, 030°33' E
Agri (Karakose)	39°44' N, 043°03' E
Akhisar (Thyatira)	38°55' N, 027°51' E
Aksaray	38°23' N, 034°03' E
Aksehir	38°21' N, 031°25' E
Amasya	40°39' N, 035°51' E
Ankara (Angora)	39°56' N, 032°52' E
Antalya (Attalia or Hatay)	36°53' N, 030°42' E
Antioch (Antakya)	36°14' N, 036°07' E
Aydin	37°51' N, 027°51' E
Bafra	41°34' N, 035°56' E
Balikesir	39°39' N, 027°53' E
Bandirma (Panderma)	40°20' N, 027°58' E
Batman	37°52' N, 041°07' E
Bilecik	40°09' N, 029°59' E
Bolu	40°44' N, 031°37' E
Burdur (Buldur)	37°43' N, 030°17' E
Bursa (Brusa)	40°11' N, 029°04' E
Çanakkale	40°09' N, 026°24' E
Ceyhan	37°04' N, 035°47' E
Çorlu	41°09' N, 027°48' E
Çorum	40°33' N, 034°58' E
Denizli	37°46' N, 029°06' E
Diyarbakir (Amida)	37°55' N, 040°14' E
Düzce	40°50' N, 031°10' E
Edirne (Adrianople or Hadrianople)	41°40' N, 026°34' E
Elazig	38°41' N, 039°14' E
Elbistan	38°13' N, 037°12' E
Eregli	37°31' N, 034°04' E
Eregli (Bender-Eregli or Karadenizereglisi)	41°17' N, 031°25' E
Erzincan	39°44' N, 039°29' E
Erzurum	39°55' N, 041°17' E
Eskisehir	39°46' N, 030°32' E
Gaziantep	37°05' N, 037°22' E
Gebze	40°48' N, 029°25' E
Giresun	40°55' N, 038°24' E
Gümüshane	40°27' N, 039°29' E
Hakkâri (Colemerik)	37°34' N, 043°44' E
Igdir	39°56' N, 044°02' E
Inegöl	40°05' N, 029°31' E
Iskenderun (Alexandretta)	36°35' N, 036°10' E
Isparta (Hamid-Abad)	37°46' N, 030°33' E
Istanbul (Constantinople)	41°01' N, 028°58' E
Izmir (Smyrna)	38°25' N, 027°09' E
Izmit	40°46' N, 029°55' E
Kadirli	37°23' N, 036°05' E
Kahramanmaras (Maras)	37°36' N, 036°55' E
Karabük	41°12' N, 032°37' E
Karaman	37°11' N, 033°14' E
Kars	40°37' N, 043°05' E
Kastamonu (Castamoni)	41°22' N, 033°47' E
Kayseri (Caesarea)	38°43' N, 035°30' E
Kherson	46°38' N, 032°36' E
Kirikkale	39°50' N, 033°31' E
Kirsehir	39°09' N, 034°10' E
Kiziltepe	37°12' N, 040°36' E
Konya (Iconium)	37°52' N, 032°31' E
Körfez	40°46' N, 029°45' E
Kozan	37°27' N, 035°49' E
Kütahya	39°25' N, 029°59' E
Malatya	38°21' N, 038°19' E
Manisa	38°36' N, 027°26' E
Mardin	37°18' N, 040°44' E
Mersin	36°48' N, 034°38' E
Nazilli	37°55' N, 028°21' E
Nevsehir	38°38' N, 034°43' E
Nigde	37°59' N, 034°42' E
Ödemis	38°13' N, 027°59' E
Oleksandriya	48°40' N, 033°07' E
Ordu	41°00' N, 037°53' E
Osmaniye	37°05' N, 036°14' E
Polatli	39°36' N, 032°09' E
Rize	41°02' N, 040°31' E
Salihli	38°29' N, 028°09' E
Samsun (Amisus)	41°17' N, 036°20' E
Siirt	37°56' N, 041°57' E
Silvan	38°08' N, 041°01' E
Sinop	42°01' N, 035°09' E
Sivas (Sebastia)	39°45' N, 037°02' E
Siverek	37°45' N, 039°19' E
Söke	37°45' N, 027°24' E
Soma	39°10' N, 027°36' E
Tarsus	36°55' N, 034°53' E
Tatvan	38°30' N, 042°16' E
Tekirdag (Rodosto)	40°59' N, 027°31' E
Tokat	40°19' N, 036°34' E
Trabzon (Trapezus or Trebizond)	41°00' N, 039°43' E
Tunceli (Kalan)	39°07' N, 039°32' E
Turhal	40°24' N, 036°06' E
Urfa	37°08' N, 038°46' E
Usak (Ushak)	38°41' N, 029°25' E
Van	38°30' N, 043°23' E
Yalova	40°39' N, 029°15' E
Yozgat	39°50' N, 034°48' E
Zonguldak	41°27' N, 031°49' E

TURKMENISTAN . . . . . . pg. 139

Capital: . . . . Ashgabat
Area: . . . . .488,100 sq km; 188,500 sq mi
Longest River: . .Amu Darya 2.540 km; 1,580 mi
Avg. Temperature: . .Jan = -1°C; Jul = 29°C
Currency: . . . . .manat
Official Language: . .Turkmen

Name	Lat./Long.
Ashgabat (Ashgabat, or Poltoratsk)	37°57' N, 058°23' E
Cheleken	39°26' N, 053°07' E
Chirchiq	41°50' N, 059°58' E
Mary (Merv)	37°36' N, 061°50' E
Nebitdag	39°30' N, 054°22' E
Turkmenbashi (Krasnovodsk)	40°00' N, 053°00' E

TUVALU . . . . pg. 156

Capital: . . . . .Fangafale on Funafuti atoll
Area: . . . . .23.9 sq km; 9.3 sq mi
Avg. Temperature: . Jan = 26°C; Jul = 26°C
Currency: . . . . .Tuvalu dollar
Official Language: . .none

Name	Lat./Long.
Funafuti	22°14' N, 138°45' E

UGANDA . . . . pg. 153

Capital: . . . . .Kampala
Area: . . . . .241,040 sq km; 93.070 sq mi
Highest Elev.: . .Margherita Pk. 5,110 m; 16,760 ft
Longest River: . .Victoria Nile 420 km; 260 mi
Avg. Temperature: . Jan = 22°C; Jul = 21°C
Currency: . . . . .Uganda shilling
Official Language: .English, Swahili

Name	Lat./Long.
Gulu	02°47' N, 032°18' E
Kampala	00°19' N, 032°35' E
Soroti	01°43' N, 033°37' E

UKRAINE . . . . pg. 138

Capital: . . . . .Kiev
Area: . . . . .603,700 sq km; 233,100 sq mi
Highest Elev.: . .Mt. Hoverlya 2,060 m; 6,760 ft
Longest River: . .Dnieper 2,200 km; 1,370 mi
Avg. Temperature: . Jan = -6.1°C; Jul = 20.4°C
Currency: . . . . .karbovanets
Official Language: . .Ukrainian

Name	Lat./Long.
Alchevsk	48°30' N, 038°47' E
Berdyansk	46°45' N, 036°47' E
Berdychiv	49°54' N, 028°35' E
Bila Tserkva	49°47' N, 030°07' E
Bilhorod-Dnistrovsky	46°12' N, 030°22' E
Boryspil	50°21' N, 030°57' E
Brody	50°05' N, 025°09' E
Bryanka	48°30' N, 038°40' E
Cherkasy	49°26' N, 032°04' E
Chernihiv	51°30' N, 031°18' E
Chernivtsi	48°18' N, 025°56' E
Chervonohrad	50°23' N, 024°14' E
Chornobyl (Chernobyl)	51°16' N, 030°14' E
Chortkiv	49°01' N, 025°48' E
Dniprodzerzhynsk	48°30' N, 034°37' E
Dnipropetrovsk	48°27' N, 034°59' E
Donetsk	48°00' N, 037°48' E
Drohobych	49°21' N, 023°30' E
Dymytrov	48°16' N, 037°17' E
Dzerzhynsk	48°26' N, 037°50' E
Dzhankoy	45°43' N, 034°24' E
Enerhodar	47°29' N, 034°47' E
Fastiv	50°05' N, 029°55' E
Feodosiya	45°02' N, 035°23' E
Illichivsk	46°18' N, 030°40' E
Inhulets	47°44' N, 033°15' E
Ivano-Frankivsk	48°56' N, 024°43' E
Izmayil	45°21' N, 028°50' E
Izyum	49°12' N, 037°19' E
Kalush	49°01' N, 024°22' E
Kamyanets	48°40' N, 026°34' E
Kerch	45°21' N, 036°28' E
Kharkiv	50°00' N, 036°15' E
Kiev (Kyyiv)	50°26' N, 030°31' E
Kirovohrad	48°30' N, 032°18' E
Kolomyya	48°32' N, 025°02' E
Komsomolsk	49°02' N, 033°40' E
Konotop	51°14' N, 033°12' E
Korosten	50°57' N, 028°39' E
Kostyantynivka	48°32' N, 037°43' E
Kotovsk	47°45' N, 029°32' E
Kovel	51°13' N, 024°43' E
Kramatorsk	48°43' N, 037°32' E
Krasnoarmiysk	48°17' N, 037°11' E
Krasnyy Luch	48°08' N, 038°56' E
Kremenchuk	49°04' N, 033°25' E
Kryvyy Rih	47°55' N, 033°21' E
Lozova	48°54' N, 036°20' E
Lubny	50°01' N, 033°00' E
Luhansk	48°34' N, 039°20' E
Lutsk	50°45' N, 025°20' E
Lviv	49°50' N, 024°00' E
Lysychansk	48°55' N, 038°26' E
Makiyivka	48°02' N, 037°58' E
Marhanets	47°38' N, 034°38' E
Mariupol	47°06' N, 037°33' E
Melitopol	46°50' N, 035°22' E
Merefa	49°48' N, 036°03' E
Mukacheve	48°27' N, 022°43' E
Mykolayiv	46°58' N, 032°00' E
Nikopol	47°34' N, 034°24' E
Nizhyn	51°03' N, 031°53' E
Nova Kakhovka	46°46' N, 033°22' E
Novohrad-Volynskyy	50°36' N, 027°37' E
Novovolynsk	50°44' N, 024°10' E
Odessa	46°28' N, 030°44' E
Pavlohrad	48°31' N, 035°52' E
Pervomaysk	48°03' N, 030°52' E
Poltava	49°35' N, 034°34' E
Pryluky	50°36' N, 032°24' E
Rivne	50°37' N, 026°15' E
Romny	50°45' N, 033°28' E
Sevastopol	44°36' N, 033°32' E
Shepetivka	50°11' N, 027°04' E
Shostka	51°52' N, 033°29' E
Simferopol	44°57' N, 034°06' E
Smila	49°14' N, 031°53' E
Snizhne	48°01' N, 038°46' E
Stakhanov	48°34' N, 038°40' E
Stryy	49°15' N, 023°51' E
Sumy	50°54' N, 034°48' E
Sverdlovsk	48°04' N, 039°40' E
Svitlovodsk	49°05' N, 033°15' E
Ternopil	49°33' N, 025°35' E
Torez	48°02' N, 038°35' E
Uman	48°45' N, 030°13' E
Uzhhorod	48°37' N, 022°18' E
Vinnytsya	49°14' N, 028°29' E

Name	Lat./Long.
Zaporizhzhya	47°49' N, 035°11' E
Zhovti Vody	48°21' N, 033°32' E
Zhytomyr	50°15' N, 028°40' E

UNITED ARAB EMIRATES pg. 154

Capital: . . . . .Abu Dhabi
Area: . . . . .83,600 sq km; 32,280 sq mi
Avg. Temperature: . .Jan = 18°C; Jul = 34°C
Currency: . . . . .U.A.E. dirham
Official Language: .Arabic

Name	Lat./Long.
Abu Dhabi	24°28' N, 054°22' E
'Ajman	25°25' N, 055°27' E
'Aradah, al-	22°59' N, 053°26' E
'Ayn, al-	24°13' N, 055°46' E
Diqdaqah	25°40' N, 055°58' E
Dubayy	25°16' N, 055°18' E
Fujayrah, al-	25°08' N, 056°21' E
Khawr Fakkan	25°21' N, 056°22' E
Khis, al-	23°00' N, 054°12' E
Ra's al-Khaymah	25°47' N, 055°57' E
Shariqah, ash-	25°22' N, 055°23' E
Tarif	24°03' N, 053°46' E
Wadhil	23°03' N, 054°08' E

UNITED KINGDOM . . . .pg. 125

Capital: . . . . .London
Area: . . . . .244,110 sq km; 94,251 sq mi
Highest Elev.: . .Ben Nevis 1,340 m; 4,410 ft
Longest River: . . . .Severn 290 km; 180 mi
Avg. Temperature: . .Jan = 4°C; Jul = 18°C
Currency: . . . . .pound sterling
Official Language: . .English

Name	Lat./Long.
Aberdare (Aberdar)	51°43' N, 003°27' W
Aberdeen	57°09' N, 002°08' W
Aberystwyth	52°25' N, 004°05' W
Aith	60°17' N, 001°23' W
Alness	57°42' N, 004°15' W
Amesbury	51°10' N, 001°47' W
Armagh	54°21' N, 006°40' W
Aylesbury	51°49' N, 000°49' W
Ayr	55°28' N, 004°38' W
Ballymoney	55°05' N, 006°31' W
Bangor	53°13' N, 004°08' W
Bangor	54°39' N, 005°42' W
Barrow-in-Furness	54°07' N, 003°14' W
Barry	51°25' N, 003°16' W
Basingstoke	51°16' N, 001°05' W
Bath	51°23' N, 002°22' W
Battle	50°55' N, 000°29' E
Bedford	52°08' N, 000°28' W
Belfast	54°35' N, 005°56' W
Bideford	51°01' N, 004°12' W
Birmingham	52°29' N, 001°51' W
Blackburn	53°45' N, 002°29' W
Blackpool	53°49' N, 003°03' W
Blandford Forum	50°51' N, 002°10' W
Bolton	53°34' N, 002°26' W
Bournemouth	50°43' N, 001°53' W
Bracknell	51°25' N, 000°45' W
Bradford	53°47' N, 001°45' W
Brentwood	51°37' N, 000°19' E
Brighton	50°51' N, 000°08' W
Bristol	51°26' N, 002°35' W
Buckhaven	56°11' N, 003°02' W
Buckie	57°41' N, 002°59' W
Burton upon Trent	52°48' N, 001°38' W
Bury	53°35' N, 002°19' W
Bury St. Edmunds	52°15' N, 000°43' E
Caernarfon	53°08' N, 004°16' W
Cambridge	52°12' N, 000°08' E
Campbeltown	55°26' N, 005°37' W
Cardiff	51°29' N, 003°11' W
Cardigan	52°05' N, 004°40' W
Carlisle	54°53' N, 002°57' W
Carrickfergus	54°43' N, 005°44' W
Castle Douglas	54°57' N, 003°56' W
Chatham	51°22' N, 000°32' E
Cheddar	51°17' N, 002°47' W
Chelmsford	51°44' N, 000°28' E
Cheltenham	51°54' N, 002°05' W
Chester	53°12' N, 002°54' W
Chesterfield	53°14' N, 001°25' W
Colchester	51°54' N, 000°54' E
Comber	54°33' N, 005°42' W
Coventry	52°24' N, 001°31' W
Crawley	51°07' N, 000°11' W
Crewe	53°06' N, 002°27' W
Cromer	52°56' N, 001°18' E
Crowland	52°41' N, 000°10' W
Cwmbran	51°39' N, 003°01' W
Darlington	54°32' N, 001°34' W
Dartmouth	50°21' N, 003°35' W
Deal	51°13' N, 001°24' E
Derby	52°55' N, 001°28' W
Devizes	51°21' N, 002°00' W
Doncaster	53°31' N, 001°08' W
Douglas	54°09' N, 004°28' W
Dover	51°08' N, 001°19' E
Downpatrick	54°19' N, 005°42' W
Droitwich	52°16' N, 002°09' W
Dudley	52°31' N, 002°06' W
Dumfries	55°04' N, 003°36' W
Dunbar	56°00' N, 002°31' W
Dundee	56°29' N, 003°02' W
Dunfermline	56°04' N, 003°26' W
Dunoon	55°57' N, 004°55' W
East Kilbride	55°46' N, 004°11' W
Eastleigh	50°58' N, 001°21' W
Edinburgh	55°57' N, 003°10' W
Enniskillen	54°22' N, 007°38' W
Evesham	52°05' N, 001°57' W
Exeter	50°43' N, 003°31' W
Exmouth	50°37' N, 003°24' W
Falmouth	50°09' N, 005°04' W
Felixstowe	51°58' N, 001°21' E
Fishguard	52°00' N, 004°59' W
Flint	53°15' N, 003°08' W
Forfar	56°39' N, 002°54' W
Fowey	50°20' N, 004°38' W
Gateshead	54°56' N, 001°37' W
Gillingham	51°23' N, 000°33' E
Glasgow	55°52' N, 004°15' W

Name	Lat./Long.
Gloucester	51°52' N, 002°14' W
Gosport	50°48' N, 001°09' W
Gravesend	51°27' N, 000°23' E
Great Walsingham	52°54' N, 000°54' E
Great Yarmouth	52°36' N, 001°44' E
Greenock	55°57' N, 004°46' W
Grimsby	53°34' N, 000°05' W
Guildford	51°14' N, 000°35' W
Halifax	53°44' N, 001°51' W
Hamilton	55°47' N, 004°02' W
Harlech	52°52' N, 004°06' W
Harlow	51°46' N, 000°07' E
Harrogate	54°00' N, 001°32' W
Hartlepool	54°41' N, 001°13' W
Hastings	50°52' N, 000°35' E
Havant	50°51' N, 000°59' W
Haverfordwest	51°48' N, 004°58' W
Hemel Hempstead	51°45' N, 000°28' W
Hereford	52°04' N, 002°43' W
High Wycombe	51°38' N, 000°45' W
Hove	50°50' N, 000°11' W
Huddersfield	53°39' N, 001°47' W
Huntly	57°27' N, 002°48' W
Inverness	57°29' N, 004°14' W
Ipswich	52°03' N, 001°09' E
Jedburgh	55°28' N, 002°33' W
John o'Groats	58°38' N, 003°04' W
Kelso	55°36' N, 002°26' W
Kilmarnock	55°36' N, 004°30' W
King's Lynn	52°45' N, 000°24' E
Kingston upon Hull	53°45' N, 000°20' W
Kinross	56°12' N, 003°25' W
Kirkwall	58°59' N, 002°57' W
Lampeter	52°07' N, 004°05' W
Lanark	55°40' N, 003°46' W
Launceston	50°38' N, 004°21' W
Leamington	52°15' N, 001°32' W
Leeds	53°48' N, 001°32' W
Leicester	52°38' N, 001°08' W
Lincoln	53°14' N, 000°32' W
Liverpool	53°25' N, 002°57' W
Llandudno	53°19' N, 003°50' W
Llangollen	52°58' N, 003°10' W
Lochmaddy	57°36' N, 007°10' W
London	51°30' N, 000°07' W
Lossiemouth	57°43' N, 003°17' W
Lowestoft	52°28' N, 001°45' E
Lurgan	54°28' N, 006°20' W
Luton	51°53' N, 000°25' W
Lydd	50°57' N, 000°55' E
Maidstone	51°16' N, 000°32' E
Manchester	53°29' N, 002°15' W
Mansfield	53°09' N, 001°12' W
Margate	51°23' N, 001°23' E
Middlesbrough	54°34' N, 001°12' W
Montrose	56°43' N, 002°28' W
Morpeth	55°10' N, 001°41' W
Nairn	57°35' N, 003°52' W
Newcastle upon Tyne	54°58' N, 001°36' W
Newport	51°35' N, 002°59' W
Newquay	50°25' N, 005°05' W
Newtownabbey	54°40' N, 005°57' W
Northampton	52°15' N, 000°54' W
Norwich	52°38' N, 001°18' E
Nottingham	52°58' N, 001°10' W
Oldham	53°32' N, 002°07' W
Omagh	54°36' N, 007°18' W
Oswestry	52°52' N, 003°03' W
Oxford	51°45' N, 001°15' W
Paisley	55°50' N, 004°25' W
Peterborough	52°35' N, 000°14' W
Peterhead	57°31' N, 001°47' W
Peterlee	54°45' N, 001°20' W
Plymouth	50°23' N, 004°09' W
Poole	50°43' N, 001°59' W
Port Talbot	51°35' N, 003°48' W
Portadown	54°26' N, 006°27' W
Portree	57°25' N, 006°11' W
Portsmouth	50°49' N, 001°04' W
Preston	53°46' N, 002°42' W
Ramsey	54°19' N, 004°23' W
Ramsgate	51°20' N, 001°25' E
Reading	51°27' N, 000°58' W
Redditch	52°18' N, 001°56' W
Rhondda	51°39' N, 003°29' W
Ripon	54°08' N, 001°31' W
Ross-on-Wye	51°55' N, 002°35' W
Rotherham	53°26' N, 001°21' W
Royal Tunbridge Wells	51°08' N, 000°16' E
Ryde	50°44' N, 001°10' W
St. Albans	51°45' N, 000°20' W
St. Helens	53°27' N, 002°45' W
Scunthorpe	53°35' N, 000°39' W
Selkirk	55°33' N, 002°50' W
Sheffield	53°23' N, 001°28' W
Shrewsbury	52°42' N, 002°45' W
Sicugh	51°30' N, 000°34' W
South Shields	54°59' N, 001°26' W
Southampton	50°55' N, 001°24' W
Southend-on-Sea	51°33' N, 000°42' E
Southport	53°39' N, 003°00' W
Stafford	52°49' N, 002°07' W
Stockport	53°25' N, 002°10' W
Stockton-on-Tees	54°35' N, 001°20' W
Stoke-on-Trent	53°01' N, 002°11' W
Stonehaven	56°58' N, 002°12' W
Stornoway	58°12' N, 006°23' W
Sudbury	52°02' N, 000°44' E
Sunderland	54°55' N, 001°23' W
Sutton Coldfield	52°33' N, 001°48' W
Swansea	51°38' N, 003°58' W
Swindon	51°34' N, 001°46' W
Tain	57°48' N, 004°03' W
Tamworth	52°38' N, 001°40' W
Tarbert	57°54' N, 006°48' W
Telford	52°41' N, 002°28' W
Thurso	58°36' N, 003°31' W
Torquay	50°29' N, 003°32' W
Troon	55°32' N, 004°39' W
Truro	50°16' N, 005°03' W
Wakefield	53°41' N, 001°30' W
Walsall	52°35' N, 001°59' W
Watford	51°40' N, 000°24' W
Wells	51°12' N, 002°39' W
West Bromwich	52°32' N, 002°01' W
Weston-super-Mare	51°21' N, 002°58' W
Weymouth	50°37' N, 002°28' W
Whitehaven	54°33' N, 003°35' W

Name	Lat./Long.
Wick	58°26' N, 003°06' W
Widnes	53°22' N, 002°44' W
Wigan	53°33' N, 002°38' W
Wilton	51°05' N, 001°52' W
Winchester	51°04' N, 001°19' W
Wolverhampton	52°35' N, 002°08' W
Worcester	52°12' N, 002°13' W
Worthing	50°49' N, 000°23' W
York	53°57' N, 001°06' W

UNITED STATES ......pg. 109

Capital: ....Washington, D.C.
Area: ....9,529,063 sq km; 3,679,192 sq mi
Highest Elev.:....Mt. McKinley 6,190 m; 20,320 ft
Longest River:...Missouri 3,730 km; 2,320 mi
Avg. Temperature: Jan = 3°C; Jul = 26°C
Currency: ....dollar
Official Language: .none

Name	Lat./Long.
Aberdeen, S.D.	45°28' N, 098°29' W
Aberdeen, Wash.	46°59' N, 123°50' W
Abilene, Kan.	38°55' N, 097°13' W
Abilene, Tex.	32°28' N, 099°43' W
Ada, Okla.	34°46' N, 096°41' W
Akron, Ohio	41°05' N, 081°31' W
Alamogordo, N.M.	32°54' N, 105°57' W
Alamosa, Colo.	37°28' N, 105°52' W
Albany, Ga.	31°35' N, 084°10' W
Albany, N.Y.	42°39' N, 073°45' W
Albuquerque, N.M.	35°05' N, 106°39' W
Alexandria, La.	31°18' N, 092°27' W
Alexandria, Va.	38°48' N, 077°03' W
Alliance, Neb.	42°06' N, 102°52' W
Alpena, Mich.	45°04' N, 083°27' W
Alton, Ill.	38°53' N, 090°11' W
Alturas, Calif.	41°29' N, 120°32' W
Altus, Okla.	34°38' N, 099°20' W
Amarillo, Tex.	35°13' N, 101°50' W
Americus, Ga.	32°04' N, 084°14' W
Anaconda, Mont.	46°08' N, 112°57' W
Anchorage, Alaska	61°13' N, 149°54' W
Andalusia, Ala.	31°18' N, 086°29' W
Ann Arbor, Mich.	42°17' N, 083°45' W
Annapolis, Md.	38°59' N, 076°30' W
Appleton, Wis.	44°16' N, 088°25' W
Arcata, Calif.	40°52' N, 124°05' W
Arlington, Tex.	32°44' N, 097°07' W
Arlington, Va.	38°53' N, 077°07' W
Asheville, N.C.	35°36' N, 082°33' W
Ashland, Ky.	38°28' N, 082°38' W
Ashland, Wis.	46°35' N, 090°53' W
Aspen, Colo.	39°11' N, 106°49' W
Astoria, Ore.	46°11' N, 123°50' W
Athens, Ga.	33°57' N, 083°23' W
Atlanta, Ga.	33°45' N, 084°23' W
Atlantic City, N.J.	39°21' N, 074°27' W
Augusta, Ga.	33°28' N, 081°58' W
Augusta, Me.	44°19' N, 069°47' W
Aurora, Colo.	39°43' N, 104°49' W
Austin, Minn.	43°40' N, 092°58' W
Austin, Tex.	30°17' N, 097°45' W
Baker, Mont.	46°22' N, 104°17' W
Baker, Ore.	44°47' N, 117°50' W
Bakersfield, Calif.	35°23' N, 119°01' W
Baltimore, Md.	39°17' N, 076°37' W
Bangor, Me.	44°48' N, 068°46' W
Bar Harbor, Me.	44°23' N, 068°13' W
Barrow, Alaska	71°18' N, 156°47' W
Bartlesville, Okla.	36°45' N, 095°59' W
Baton Rouge, La.	30°27' N, 091°11' W
Bay City, Mich.	43°36' N, 083°54' W
Beaumont, Tex.	30°05' N, 094°06' W
Bellingham, Wash.	48°46' N, 122°29' W
Beloit, Wis.	42°31' N, 089°01' W
Bemidji, Minn.	47°28' N, 094°52' W
Bend, Ore.	44°04' N, 121°19' W
Berlin, N.H.	44°28' N, 071°11' W
Bethel, Alaska	60°48' N, 161°45' W
Beulah, N.D.	47°15' N, 101°46' W
Billings, Mont.	45°47' N, 108°30' W
Biloxi, Miss.	30°24' N, 088°53' W
Birmingham, Ala.	33°31' N, 086°48' W
Bismarck, N.D.	46°48' N, 100°47' W
Bloomington, Ind.	39°10' N, 086°32' W
Blythe, Calif.	33°37' N, 114°36' W
Boca Raton, Fla.	26°21' N, 080°05' W
Bogalusa, La.	30°47' N, 089°52' W
Boise, Idaho	43°37' N, 116°13' W
Boston, Mass.	42°22' N, 071°04' W
Boulder, Colo.	40°01' N, 105°17' W
Bowling Green, Ky.	36°59' N, 086°27' W
Bozeman, Mont.	45°41' N, 111°02' W
Bradenton, Fla.	27°30' N, 082°34' W
Brady, Tex.	31°09' N, 099°20' W
Brainerd, Minn.	46°22' N, 094°12' W
Bremerton, Wash.	47°34' N, 122°38' W
Brigham City, Utah	41°31' N, 112°01' W
Brookings, S.D.	44°19' N, 096°48' W
Brownsville, Tex.	25°54' N, 097°30' W
Brunswick, Ga.	31°10' N, 081°30' W
Bryan, Tex.	30°40' N, 096°22' W
Buffalo, N.Y.	42°53' N, 078°53' W
Buffalo, Wyo.	31°28' N, 096°04' W
Burlington, Ia.	40°48' N, 091°06' W
Burlington, Vt.	44°29' N, 073°12' W
Burns, Ore.	43°35' N, 119°03' W
Butte, Mont.	46°00' N, 112°32' W
Cairo, Ill.	37°00' N, 089°11' W
Caldwell, Idaho	43°40' N, 116°41' W
Canton, Ohio	40°48' N, 081°23' W
Cape Girardeau, Mo.	37°19' N, 089°43' W
Carbondale, Ill.	37°44' N, 089°13' W
Carlsbad, N.M.	32°25' N, 104°14' W
Carson City, Nev.	39°10' N, 119°46' W
Casa Grande, Ariz.	32°53' N, 111°45' W
Casper, Wyo.	42°51' N, 106°19' W
Cedar City, Utah	37°41' N, 113°04' W
Chadron, Neb.	42°50' N, 103°00' W
Champaign, Ill.	40°07' N, 088°15' W
Charleston, S.C.	32°46' N, 079°56' W
Charleston, W.Va.	38°21' N, 081°39' W
Charlotte, N.C.	35°13' N, 080°50' W
Chattanooga, Tenn.	35°03' N, 085°19' W
Chesapeake, Va.	36°50' N, 076°17' W
Cheyenne, Wyo.	41°08' N, 104°49' W
Chicago, Ill.	41°53' N, 087°38' W
Chico, Calif.	39°44' N, 121°50' W

Name	Lat./Long.
Chula Vista, Calif.	32°38' N, 117°05' W
Cincinnati, Ohio	39°06' N, 084°31' W
Clarksdale, Miss.	34°12' N, 090°35' W
Clayton, N.M.	36°27' N, 103°11' W
Clearwater, Fla.	27°58' N, 082°48' W
Cleveland, Ohio	41°30' N, 081°42' W
Clinton, Okla.	35°31' N, 098°58' W
Clovis, N.M.	34°24' N, 103°12' W
Cody, Wyo.	44°32' N, 109°03' W
Coeur d'Alene, Idaho	47°41' N, 116°46' W
College Station, Tex.	30°37' N, 096°21' W
Colorado Springs, Colo.	38°50' N, 104°49' W
Columbia, S.C.	34°00' N, 081°03' W
Columbus, Ga.	32°29' N, 084°59' W
Columbus, Miss.	33°30' N, 088°25' W
Columbus, Ohio	39°58' N, 083°00' W
Concord, N.H.	43°12' N, 071°32' W
Coos Bay, Ore.	43°22' N, 124°12' W
Coral Gables, Fla.	25°45' N, 080°16' W
Cordele, Ga.	31°58' N, 083°47' W
Cordova, Alaska	60°33' N, 145°45' W
Corinth, Miss.	34°56' N, 088°31' W
Corpus Christi, Tex.	27°47' N, 097°24' W
Corsicana, Tex.	32°06' N, 096°28' W
Corvallis, Ore.	44°34' N, 123°16' W
Council Bluffs, Ia.	41°16' N, 095°52' W
Covington, Ky.	39°05' N, 084°31' W
Crescent City, Calif.	41°45' N, 124°12' W
Crystal City, Tex.	28°41' N, 099°50' W
Dalhart, Tex.	36°04' N, 102°31' W
Dallas, Tex.	32°47' N, 096°49' W
Dalton, Ga.	34°46' N, 084°58' W
Danville, Va.	36°36' N, 079°23' W
Davenport, Ia.	41°32' N, 090°35' W
Davis, Calif.	38°33' N, 121°44' W
Dayton, Ohio	39°45' N, 084°12' W
Daytona Beach, Fla.	29°13' N, 081°01' W
Decorah, Ia.	43°18' N, 091°48' W
Denver, Colo.	39°44' N, 104°59' W
Des Moines, Ia.	41°35' N, 093°37' W
Detroit, Mich.	42°20' N, 083°03' W
Dickinson, N.D.	46°53' N, 102°47' W
Dillingham, Alaska	59°03' N, 158°28' W
Dillon, Mont.	45°13' N, 112°38' W
Dodge City, Kan.	37°45' N, 100°00' W
Dothan, Ala.	31°13' N, 085°24' W
Dover, Del.	39°10' N, 075°32' W
Dover, N.H.	43°12' N, 070°53' W
Dubuque, Ia.	42°30' N, 090°41' W
Duluth, Minn.	46°47' N, 092°07' W
Duncan, Okla.	34°30' N, 097°57' W
Durango, Colo.	37°17' N, 107°53' W
Durham, N.C.	36°00' N, 078°54' W
Dutch Harbor, Alaska	53°53' N, 166°32' W
East St. Louis, Ill.	38°37' N, 090°09' W
Eau Claire, Wis.	44°49' N, 091°30' W
El Cajon, Calif.	32°48' N, 116°58' W
El Dorado, Ark.	33°12' N, 092°40' W
El Paso, Tex.	31°45' N, 106°29' W
Elko, Nev.	40°50' N, 115°46' W
Ely, Minn.	47°55' N, 091°51' W
Ely, Nev.	39°15' N, 114°54' W
Emporia, Kan.	38°25' N, 096°11' W
Enid, Okla.	36°24' N, 097°53' W
Erie, Pa.	42°08' N, 080°05' W
Escanaba, Mich.	45°45' N, 087°04' W
Escondido, Calif.	33°07' N, 117°05' W
Eugene, Ore.	44°05' N, 123°04' W
Eunice, La.	30°30' N, 092°25' W
Eureka, Calif.	40°47' N, 124°09' W
Eustis, Fla.	28°51' N, 081°41' W
Evanston, Wyo.	41°16' N, 110°58' W
Everett, Wash.	47°59' N, 122°12' W
Fairbanks, Alaska	64°51' N, 147°45' W
Falls City, Neb.	40°03' N, 095°36' W
Fargo, N.D.	46°53' N, 096°48' W
Farmington, N.M.	36°44' N, 108°12' W
Fayetteville, Ark.	36°03' N, 094°09' W
Fayetteville, N.C.	35°03' N, 078°53' W
Fergus Falls, Minn.	46°17' N, 096°04' W
Flagstaff, Ariz.	35°12' N, 111°39' W
Flint, Mich.	43°01' N, 083°41' W
Florence, S.C.	34°12' N, 079°46' W
Fort Bragg, Calif.	39°26' N, 123°48' W
Fort Collins, Colo.	40°35' N, 105°05' W
Fort Dodge, Ia.	42°30' N, 094°11' W
Fort Lauderdale, Fla.	26°07' N, 080°08' W
Fort Madison, Ia.	40°38' N, 091°27' W
Fort Myers, Fla.	26°39' N, 081°52' W
Fort Pierce, Fla.	27°26' N, 080°19' W
Fort Smith, Ark.	35°23' N, 094°25' W
Fort Wayne, Ind.	41°04' N, 085°09' W
Fort Worth, Tex.	32°45' N, 097°18' W
Frankfort, Ky.	38°12' N, 084°52' W
Freeport, Ill.	42°17' N, 089°36' W
Freeport, Tex.	28°57' N, 095°21' W
Fremont, Neb.	41°26' N, 096°30' W
Fresno, Calif.	36°44' N, 119°47' W
Gadsden, Ala.	34°01' N, 086°01' W
Gainesville, Fla.	29°40' N, 082°20' W
Gainesville, Ga.	34°17' N, 083°49' W
Galena, Alaska	64°44' N, 156°56' W
Gallup, N.M.	35°31' N, 108°45' W
Galveston, Tex.	29°18' N, 094°48' W
Garden City, Kan.	37°58' N, 100°52' W
Garland, Tex.	32°54' N, 096°38' W
Gary, Ind.	41°36' N, 087°20' W
Georgetown, S.C.	33°23' N, 079°17' W
Gillette, Wyo.	44°18' N, 105°30' W
Glasgow, Ky.	37°00' N, 085°55' W
Glasgow, Mont.	48°12' N, 106°38' W
Glendive, Mont.	47°07' N, 104°43' W
Glenwood Springs, Colo.	39°33' N, 107°19' W
Goliad, Tex.	28°40' N, 097°23' W
Goodland, Kan.	39°21' N, 101°43' W
Grand Forks, N.D.	47°55' N, 097°03' W
Grand Island, Neb.	40°55' N, 098°21' W
Grand Junction, Colo.	39°04' N, 108°33' W
Grand Rapids, Mich.	42°58' N, 085°40' W
Granite Falls, Minn.	44°49' N, 095°33' W
Great Falls, Mont.	47°30' N, 111°17' W
Greeley, Colo.	40°25' N, 104°42' W
Green Bay, Wis.	44°31' N, 088°00' W
Greensboro, N.C.	36°04' N, 079°48' W
Greenville, Ala.	31°50' N, 086°38' W
Greenville, Miss.	33°24' N, 091°04' W
Greenwood, S.C.	34°12' N, 082°10' W
Griffin, Ga.	33°15' N, 084°16' W
Gulfport, Miss.	30°22' N, 089°06' W

Name	Lat./Long.
Guymon, Okla.	36°41' N, 101°29' W
Hampton, Va.	37°02' N, 076°21' W
Hannibal, Mo.	39°42' N, 091°22' W
Harlingen, Tex.	26°12' N, 097°42' W
Harrisburg, Pa.	40°16' N, 076°53' W
Hartford, Conn.	41°46' N, 072°41' W
Hattiesburg, Miss.	31°20' N, 089°17' W
Helena, Mont.	46°36' N, 112°02' W
Henderson, Nev.	36°02' N, 114°59' W
Hialeah, Fla.	25°51' N, 080°16' W
Hilo, Hawaii	19°44' N, 155°05' W
Hobbs, N.M.	32°42' N, 103°08' W
Hollywood, Fla.	26°01' N, 080°09' W
Honokaa, Hawaii	20°05' N, 155°28' W
Honolulu, Hawaii	21°19' N, 157°52' W
Hope, Ark.	33°40' N, 093°36' W
Hot Springs, Ark.	34°31' N, 093°03' W
Houghton, Mich.	47°07' N, 088°34' W
Houston, Tex.	29°46' N, 095°22' W
Hugo, Okla.	34°01' N, 095°31' W
Huntsville, Ala.	34°44' N, 086°35' W
Hutchinson, Kan.	38°05' N, 097°56' W
Idaho Falls, Idaho	43°30' N, 112°02' W
Independence, Mo.	39°05' N, 094°24' W
Indianapolis, Ind.	39°46' N, 086°09' W
International Falls, Minn.	48°36' N, 093°25' W
Iron Mountain, Mich.	45°49' N, 088°04' W
Ironwood, Mich.	46°27' N, 090°09' W
Ithaca, N.Y.	42°26' N, 076°30' W
Jackson, Miss.	32°18' N, 090°12' W
Jackson, Tenn.	35°37' N, 088°49' W
Jacksonville, Fla.	30°20' N, 081°39' W
Jacksonville, N.C.	34°45' N, 077°26' W
Jamestown, N.Y.	42°06' N, 079°14' W
Jefferson City, Mo.	38°34' N, 092°10' W
Jersey City, N.J.	40°44' N, 074°04' W
Joliet, Ill.	41°32' N, 088°05' W
Jonesboro, Ark.	35°50' N, 090°42' W
Jonesboro, Ga.	33°31' N, 084°22' W
Juneau, Alaska	58°20' N, 134°27' W
Kaktovik, Alaska	70°08' N, 143°38' W
Kalamazoo, Mich.	42°17' N, 085°35' W
Kalispell, Mont.	48°12' N, 114°19' W
Kansas City, Kan.	39°07' N, 094°38' W
Kansas City, Mo.	39°06' N, 094°35' W
Kapaa, Hawaii	22°05' N, 159°19' W
Kearney, Neb.	40°42' N, 099°05' W
Kenai, Alaska	60°33' N, 151°16' W
Ketchikan, Alaska	55°21' N, 131°39' W
Key Largo, Fla.	25°06' N, 080°27' W
Key West, Fla.	24°33' N, 081°49' W
King City, Calif.	36°13' N, 121°08' W
Kingman, Ariz.	35°12' N, 114°04' W
Kingsville, Tex.	27°31' N, 097°52' W
Kirksville, Mo.	40°12' N, 092°35' W
Klamath Falls, Ore.	42°12' N, 121°46' W
Knoxville, Tenn.	35°58' N, 083°55' W
Kodiak, Alaska	57°47' N, 152°24' W
Kokomo, Ind.	40°30' N, 086°08' W
La Crosse, Wis.	43°48' N, 091°15' W
La Junta, Colo.	37°59' N, 103°33' W
Lafayette, La.	30°14' N, 092°01' W
Lake Charles, La.	30°14' N, 093°13' W
Lake Havasu City, Ariz.	34°29' N, 114°19' W
Lakeland, Fla.	28°03' N, 081°57' W
Lansing, Mich.	42°44' N, 084°33' W
Laramie, Wyo.	41°19' N, 105°35' W
Laredo, Tex.	27°30' N, 099°30' W
Las Cruces, N.M.	32°19' N, 106°47' W
Las Vegas, N.M.	35°36' N, 105°13' W
Las Vegas, Nev.	36°01' N, 115°09' W
Laurel, Miss.	31°41' N, 089°08' W
Lawton, Okla.	34°37' N, 098°25' W
Lebanon, N.H.	43°39' N, 072°15' W
Lewiston, Idaho	46°25' N, 117°01' W
Lewiston, Me.	44°06' N, 070°13' W
Lewiston, Mont.	47°03' N, 109°25' W
Lexington, Ky.	38°01' N, 084°30' W
Liberal, Kan.	37°02' N, 100°55' W
Lihue, Hawaii	21°59' N, 159°23' W
Lima, Ohio	40°44' N, 084°06' W
Lincoln, Me.	45°22' N, 068°30' W
Lincoln, Neb.	40°50' N, 096°41' W
Little Rock, Ark.	34°45' N, 092°17' W
Logan, Utah	41°44' N, 111°50' W
Long Beach, Calif.	33°47' N, 118°11' W
Los Alamos, N.M.	35°53' N, 106°19' W
Los Angeles, Calif.	34°04' N, 118°15' W
Louisville, Ky.	38°15' N, 085°46' W
Lowell, Mass.	42°38' N, 071°19' W
Lubbock, Tex.	33°35' N, 101°51' W
Lynchburg, Va.	37°25' N, 079°09' W
Macomb, Ill.	40°27' N, 090°40' W
Macon, Ga.	32°51' N, 083°38' W
Madison, Wis.	43°04' N, 089°24' W
Manchester, N.H.	43°00' N, 071°28' W
Mandan, N.D.	46°50' N, 100°54' W
Mankato, Minn.	44°10' N, 094°00' W
Marietta, Ohio	39°25' N, 081°27' W
Marinette, Wis.	45°06' N, 087°38' W
Marion, Ind.	40°32' N, 085°40' W
Marquette, Mich.	46°33' N, 087°24' W
Massillon, Ohio	40°48' N, 081°32' W
McAllen, Tex.	26°12' N, 098°14' W
McCall, Idaho	44°55' N, 116°06' W
McCook, Neb.	40°12' N, 100°38' W
Medford, Ore.	42°19' N, 122°52' W
Meeker, Colo.	40°02' N, 107°55' W
Melbourne, Fla.	28°05' N, 080°37' W
Memphis, Tenn.	35°08' N, 090°03' W
Meridian, Miss.	32°22' N, 088°42' W
Mesa, Ariz.	33°25' N, 111°49' W
Miami, Fla.	25°47' N, 080°11' W
Midland, Mich.	43°36' N, 084°14' W
Midland, Tex.	32°00' N, 102°05' W
Miles City, Mont.	46°25' N, 105°51' W
Milledgeville, Ga.	33°05' N, 083°14' W
Milwaukee, Wis.	43°02' N, 087°55' W
Minneapolis, Minn.	44°59' N, 093°16' W
Minot, N.D.	48°14' N, 101°18' W
Missoula, Mont.	46°52' N, 114°01' W
Mitchell, S.D.	43°43' N, 098°02' W
Moab, Utah	38°35' N, 109°33' W
Mobile, Ala.	30°41' N, 088°03' W
Moline, Ill.	41°30' N, 090°31' W
Monterey, Calif.	36°37' N, 121°55' W
Montgomery, Ala.	32°23' N, 086°19' W
Montpelier, Vt.	44°16' N, 072°35' W
Montrose, Colo.	38°29' N, 107°53' W

Name	Lat./Long.
Morehead City, N.C.	34°43' N, 076°43' W
Morgan City, La.	29°42' N, 091°12' W
Morgantown, W.Va.	39°38' N, 079°57' W
Moscow, Idaho	46°44' N, 117°00' W
Mount Vernon, Ill.	38°19' N, 088°55' W
Murfreesboro, Ark.	34°04' N, 093°41' W
Murfreesboro, Tenn.	35°50' N, 086°23' W
Muskogee, Okla.	35°45' N, 095°22' W
Myrtle Beach, S.C.	33°42' N, 078°53' W
Naples, Fla.	26°08' N, 081°48' W
Nashville-Davidson, Tenn.	36°10' N, 086°47' W
Natchez, Miss.	31°34' N, 091°24' W
Needles, Calif.	34°51' N, 114°37' W
Nevada, Mo.	37°51' N, 094°22' W
New Albany, Ind.	38°18' N, 085°49' W
New Bedford, Mass.	41°38' N, 070°56' W
New Bern, N.C.	35°07' N, 077°03' W
New Haven, Conn.	41°18' N, 072°55' W
New Madrid, Mo.	36°36' N, 089°32' W
New Orleans, La.	29°58' N, 090°04' W
New York City, N.Y.	40°43' N, 074°00' W
Newark, N.J.	40°44' N, 074°10' W
Newcastle, Wyo.	43°50' N, 104°11' W
Newport News, Va.	36°59' N, 076°25' W
Newport, Ore.	44°39' N, 124°03' W
Newport, R.I.	41°29' N, 071°18' W
Niagara Falls, N.Y.	43°06' N, 079°03' W
Nogales, Ariz.	31°20' N, 110°56' W
Nome, Alaska	64°30' N, 165°25' W
Norfolk, Va.	36°51' N, 076°17' W
Norman, Okla.	35°13' N, 097°26' W
North Augusta, S.C.	33°30' N, 081°59' W
North Platte, Neb.	41°08' N, 100°46' W
O'neill, Neb.	42°27' N, 098°39' W
Oakland, Calif.	37°49' N, 122°16' W
Ocala, Fla.	29°11' N, 082°08' W
Oceanside, Calif.	33°12' N, 117°23' W
Odessa, Tex.	31°52' N, 102°23' W
Ogallala, Neb.	41°08' N, 101°43' W
Ogden, Utah	41°13' N, 111°58' W
Oklahoma City, Okla.	35°30' N, 097°30' W
Omaha, Neb.	41°17' N, 096°01' W
Orem, Utah	40°18' N, 111°42' W
Orlando, Fla.	28°33' N, 081°23' W
Oshkosh, Wis.	44°01' N, 088°33' W
Ottawa, Ill.	41°20' N, 088°50' W
Ottumwa, Ia.	41°01' N, 092°25' W
Overton, Nev.	36°33' N, 114°27' W
Owensboro, Ky.	37°46' N, 087°07' W
Paducah, Ky.	37°05' N, 088°37' W
Pahala, Hawaii	19°12' N, 155°29' W
Palm Springs, Calif.	33°50' N, 116°33' W
Palo Alto, Calif.	37°27' N, 122°10' W
Panama City, Fla.	30°10' N, 085°40' W
Paris, Tex.	33°40' N, 095°33' W
Parsons, Kan.	37°20' N, 095°16' W
Pasadena, Calif.	34°09' N, 118°09' W
Pasadena, Tex.	29°43' N, 095°13' W
Pascagoula, Miss.	30°21' N, 088°33' W
Paterson, N.J.	40°55' N, 074°11' W
Pecos, Tex.	31°26' N, 103°30' W
Pendleton, Ore.	45°40' N, 118°47' W
Pensacola, Fla.	30°25' N, 087°13' W
Peoria, Ill.	40°42' N, 089°36' W
Petoskey, Mich.	45°22' N, 084°57' W
Philadelphia, Pa.	39°57' N, 075°10' W
Phoenix, Ariz.	33°27' N, 112°04' W
Pierre, S.D.	44°22' N, 100°21' W
Pine Bluff, Ark.	34°13' N, 092°01' W
Pittsburgh, Pa.	40°26' N, 080°01' W
Plano, Tex.	33°01' N, 096°41' W
Plattsburgh, N.Y.	44°42' N, 073°27' W
Pocatello, Idaho	42°52' N, 112°27' W
Point Hope, Alaska	68°21' N, 166°41' W
Port Gibson, Miss.	31°58' N, 090°59' W
Port Lavaca, Tex.	28°37' N, 096°38' W
Port Royal, S.C.	32°23' N, 080°42' W
Portland, Me.	43°39' N, 070°16' W
Portland, Ore.	45°32' N, 122°37' W
Prescott, Ariz.	34°33' N, 112°28' W
Presque Isle, Me.	46°41' N, 068°01' W
Providence, R.I.	41°49' N, 071°24' W
Provo, Utah	40°14' N, 111°39' W
Pueblo, Colo.	38°15' N, 104°36' W
Pullman, Wash.	46°44' N, 117°10' W
Racine, Wis.	42°44' N, 087°48' W
Raleigh, N.C.	35°46' N, 078°38' W
Rapid City, S.D.	44°05' N, 103°14' W
Red Bluff, Calif.	40°11' N, 122°15' W
Redding, Calif.	40°35' N, 122°24' W
Redfield, S.D.	44°53' N, 098°31' W
Reno, Nev.	39°31' N, 119°48' W
Rice Lake, Wis.	45°30' N, 091°44' W
Richfield, Utah	38°46' N, 112°05' W
Richmond, Ind.	39°50' N, 084°54' W
Richmond, Va.	37°33' N, 077°27' W
Riverside, Calif.	33°59' N, 117°22' W
Riverton, Wyo.	43°02' N, 108°23' W
Roanoke, Va.	37°16' N, 079°56' W
Rochester, Minn.	44°01' N, 092°28' W
Rochester, N.Y.	43°10' N, 077°37' W
Rock Hill, S.C.	34°56' N, 081°01' W
Rock Island, Ill.	41°30' N, 090°34' W
Rock Springs, Wyo.	41°35' N, 109°12' W
Rockford, Ill.	42°16' N, 089°06' W
Rolla, Mo.	37°57' N, 091°46' W
Rome, Ga.	34°15' N, 085°09' W
Roseburg, Ore.	43°13' N, 123°20' W
Roswell, N.M.	33°24' N, 104°32' W
Sacramento, Calif.	38°35' N, 121°29' W
Saginaw, Mich.	43°26' N, 083°56' W
Salem, Ore.	44°56' N, 123°02' W
Salina, Kan.	38°50' N, 097°37' W
Salinas, Calif.	36°40' N, 121°39' W
Salmon, Idaho	45°11' N, 113°54' W
Salt Lake City, Utah	40°45' N, 111°53' W
San Angelo, Tex.	31°28' N, 100°26' W
San Antonio, Tex.	29°25' N, 098°30' W
San Bernardino, Calif.	34°07' N, 117°19' W
San Diego, Calif.	32°43' N, 117°09' W
San Francisco, Calif.	37°47' N, 122°25' W
San Jose, Calif.	37°20' N, 121°53' W
San Luis Obispo, Calif.	35°17' N, 120°40' W
Sanderson, Tex.	30°09' N, 102°24' W
Santa Ana, Calif.	33°46' N, 117°52' W
Santa Barbara, Calif.	34°25' N, 119°42' W
Santa Maria, Calif.	34°57' N, 120°26' W
Sarasota, Fla.	27°20' N, 082°32' W

Name	Lat./Long.
Sault Ste. Marie, Mich.	46°30' N, 084°21' W
Savannah, Ga.	32°05' N, 081°06' W
Scott City, Kan.	38°29' N, 100°54' W
Scottsbluff, Neb.	41°52' N, 103°40' W
Scottsdale, Ariz.	33°29' N, 111°56' W
Searcy, Ark.	35°15' N, 091°44' W
Seattle, Wash.	47°36' N, 122°20' W
Sebring, Fla.	27°30' N, 081°27' W
Seguin, Tex.	29°34' N, 097°58' W
Selawik, Alaska	66°36' N, 160°00' W
Seldovia, Alaska	59°26' N, 151°43' W
Selma, Ala.	32°25' N, 087°01' W
Sharpsburg, Md.	39°28' N, 077°45' W
Sheboygan, Wis.	43°45' N, 087°42' W
Sheridan, Wyo.	44°48' N, 106°58' W
Show Low, Ariz.	34°15' N, 110°02' W
Shreveport, La.	32°31' N, 093°45' W
Sierra Vista, Ariz.	31°33' N, 110°18' W
Silver City, N.M.	32°46' N, 108°17' W
Sioux City, Ia.	42°30' N, 096°24' W
Sioux Falls, S.D.	43°33' N, 096°44' W
Skagway, Alaska	59°28' N, 135°19' W
Snyder, Tex.	32°44' N, 100°55' W
Socorro, N.M.	34°04' N, 106°54' W
Somerset, Ky.	37°05' N, 084°36' W
South Bend, Ind.	41°41' N, 086°15' W
Sparks, Nev.	39°32' N, 119°45' W
Spencer, Ia.	43°09' N, 095°10' W
Spokane, Wash.	47°40' N, 117°24' W
Springfield, Ill.	39°48' N, 089°38' W
Springfield, Mo.	37°13' N, 093°17' W
St. Augustine, Fla.	29°54' N, 081°19' W
St. Cloud, Minn.	45°34' N, 094°10' W
St. George, Utah	37°06' N, 113°35' W
St. Joseph, Mo.	39°46' N, 094°50' W
St. Louis, Mo.	38°37' N, 090°11' W
St. Maries, Idaho	47°19' N, 116°35' W
St. Paul, Minn.	44°57' N, 093°06' W
St. Petersburg, Fla.	27°46' N, 082°39' W
State College, Pa.	40°48' N, 077°52' W
Ste. Genevieve, Mo.	37°59' N, 090°03' W
Steamboat Springs, Colo.	40°29' N, 106°50' W
Stillwater, Minn.	45°03' N, 092°49' W
Sumter, S.C.	33°55' N, 080°21' W
Sun Valley, Idaho	43°42' N, 114°21' W
Superior, Wis.	46°44' N, 092°06' W
Syracuse, N.Y.	43°03' N, 076°09' W
Tacoma, Wash.	47°14' N, 122°26' W
Tallahassee, Fla.	30°27' N, 084°17' W
Tampa, Fla.	27°57' N, 082°27' W
Tempe, Ariz.	33°25' N, 111°56' W
Temple, Tex.	31°06' N, 097°21' W
Terre Haute, Ind.	39°28' N, 087°25' W
Texarkana, Ark.	33°26' N, 094°03' W
Thief River Falls, Minn.	48°07' N, 096°10' W
Tifton, Ga.	31°27' N, 083°31' W
Titusville, Fla.	28°37' N, 080°49' W
Toledo, Ohio	41°39' N, 083°33' W
Tonopah, Nev.	38°04' N, 117°14' W
Topeka, Kan.	39°03' N, 095°40' W
Traverse City, Mich.	44°46' N, 085°38' W
Trenton, N.J.	40°14' N, 074°46' W
Trinidad, Colo.	37°10' N, 104°31' W
Troy, Ala.	31°48' N, 085°58' W
Troy, N.Y.	42°44' N, 073°41' W
Tucson, Ariz.	32°13' N, 110°58' W
Tulsa, Okla.	36°10' N, 095°55' W
Tupelo, Miss.	34°16' N, 088°43' W
Tuscaloosa, Ala.	33°12' N, 087°34' W
Twin Falls, Idaho	42°34' N, 114°28' W
Tyler, Tex.	32°21' N, 095°18' W
Ukiah, Calif.	39°09' N, 123°12' W
Utica, N.Y.	43°06' N, 075°14' W
Uvalde, Tex.	29°13' N, 099°47' W
Valdez, Alaska	61°07' N, 146°16' W
Valdosta, Ga.	30°50' N, 083°17' W
Valentine, Neb.	42°52' N, 100°33' W
Vero Beach, Fla.	27°38' N, 080°24' W
Vicksburg, Miss.	32°21' N, 090°53' W
Victoria, Tex.	28°48' N, 097°00' W
Vincennes, Ind.	38°41' N, 087°32' W
Virginia Beach, Va.	36°51' N, 075°59' W
Waco, Tex.	31°33' N, 097°09' W
Wahpeton, N.D.	46°15' N, 096°36' W
Wailuku, Hawaii	20°53' N, 156°30' W
Walla Walla, Wash.	46°04' N, 118°20' W
Warren, Pa.	41°51' N, 079°08' W
Washington, D.C.	38°54' N, 077°02' W
Waterloo, Ia.	42°30' N, 092°21' W
Watertown, N.Y.	43°59' N, 075°55' W
Waycross, Ga.	31°13' N, 082°21' W
Wayne, Neb.	42°14' N, 097°01' W
Weiser, Idaho	44°45' N, 116°58' W
West Palm Beach, Fla.	26°43' N, 080°03' W
Wheeling, W.Va.	40°04' N, 080°43' W
Wichita Falls, Tex.	33°54' N, 098°30' W
Wichita, Kan.	37°42' N, 097°20' W
Williamsport, Pa.	41°15' N, 077°00' W
Wilmington, N.C.	34°14' N, 077°55' W
Winfield, Kan.	37°15' N, 096°59' W
Winnemucca, Nev.	40°58' N, 117°44' W
Winslow, Ariz.	35°02' N, 110°42' W
Winston-Salem, N.C.	36°06' N, 080°14' W
Worcester, Mass.	42°16' N, 071°48' W
Worthington, Minn.	43°37' N, 095°36' W
Wrangell, Alaska	56°28' N, 132°23' W
Yakima, Wash.	46°36' N, 120°31' W
Yankton, S.D.	42°53' N, 097°23' W
Yazoo City, Miss.	32°51' N, 090°25' W
Youngstown, Ohio	41°06' N, 080°39' W
Yuba City, Calif.	39°08' N, 121°37' W
Yuma, Ariz.	32°43' N, 114°37' W
Zanesville, Ohio	39°56' N, 082°01' W

URUGUAY ....pg. 122

Capital: ....Montevideo
Area: ......176,215 sq km; 68,037 sq mi
Highest Elev.: ..Mt. Mirador 500 m; 1,640 ft
Longest River: ...Negro 800 km; 500 mi
Avg. Temperature: .Jan = 23°C; Jul = 11°C
Currency: ......peso uruguayo
Official Language: .Spanish

Las Piedras	34°44' S, 056°13' W
Melo	32°22' S, 054°11' W
Mercedes	33°16' S, 058°01' W
Minas	34°23' S, 055°14' W

Montevideo	34°53' S, 056°11' W
Paysandu	32°19' S, 058°05' W
Rivera	30°54' S, 055°31' W
Salto	31°23' S, 057°58' W

UZBEKISTAN ....pg. 139

Capital: ....Tashkent
Area: ......447,400 sq km; 172,700 sq mi
Highest Elev.: .. Beshtor Pk. 4,300 m; 14,400 ft
Longest River: ..Amu Darya 2,540 km; 1,580 mi
Avg. Temperature: .. Jan = 0°C; Jul = 29°C
Currency: ....sum
Official Language: .Uzbek

Andijon	40°45' N, 072°22' E
Angren	41°01' N, 070°12' E
Bekobod	40°13' N, 069°14' E
Beruniy(Biruni)	41°42' N, 060°44' E
Bukhara (Bokhara)	39°48' N, 064°25' E
Denow	38°16' N, 067°54' E
Fergana (Skobelev)	40°23' N, 071°46' E
Guliston(Mirzachul)	40°29' N, 068°46' E
Jizzakh	40°06' N, 067°50' E
Kattaqurghan	39°55' N, 066°15' E
Kogon	39°43' N, 064°33' E
Marghilon	40°27' N, 071°42' E
Namangan	41°00' N, 071°40' E
Nawoiy	40°09' N, 065°22' E
Nukus	42°29' N, 059°38' E
Olmaliq	40°50' N, 069°35' E
Qarshi	38°53' N, 065°48' E
Quqon	40°30' N, 070°57' E
Samarkand	39°40' N, 066°58' E
Tashkent (Toshkent)	41°20' N, 069°18' E
Turmiz	37°14' N, 067°16' E
Urganch	41°33' N, 060°38' E

VANUATU ....pg. 156

Capital: ....Vila
Area: ......12,190 sq km; 4,707 sq mi
Highest Elev.: ..Mt. Tabwémasana 1,880 m; 6,170 ft
Avg. Temperature: .. Jan = 22.6°C; Jul = 27.6°C
Currency: ......vatu
Official Language: .Bislama, French, English

Port-Vila, *see* Vila
Vila (Port-Vila) .... 17°44' S, 168°18' E

VENEZUELA ....pg. 124

Capital: ....Caracas
Area: ......912,050 sq km; 352,144 sq mi
Highest Elev.: ..Mt. Bolívar 5,010 m; 16,430 ft
Longest River: ....Orinoco 2,740 km; 1,700 mi
Avg. Temperature: .. Jan = 19°C; Jul = 21°C
Currency: ......bolívar
Official Language: .Spanish

Acarigua	09°33' N, 069°12' W
Achaguas	07°46' N, 068°14' W
Altagracia	10°07' N, 071°14' W
Altagracia de Orituco	09°52' N, 066°23' W
Anaco	09°27' N, 064°28' W
Aragua de Barcelona	09°28' N, 064°49' W
Araya	10°34' N, 064°15' W
Barcelona	10°08' N, 064°42' W
Barinas	08°38' N, 070°12' W
Barinitas	08°45' N, 070°25' W
Barquisimeto	10°04' N, 069°19' W
Barrancas	08°46' N, 070°06' W
Betijoque	09°23' N, 070°44' W
Biscucuy	09°22' N, 069°59' W
Bobures	09°15' N, 071°11' W
Boca de Pozo	11°00' N, 064°23' W
Cabimas	10°23' N, 071°28' W
Caicara (Caicara de Orinoco)	07°37' N, 066°10' W
Caicara	09°49' N, 063°36' W
Caja Seca	09°09' N, 071°05' W
Calabozo	08°56' N, 067°26' W
Camaguán	08°06' N, 067°36' W
Cantaura	09°19' N, 064°21' W
Caracas	10°30' N, 066°55' W
Cariaco	10°29' N, 063°33' W
Caripito	10°08' N, 063°06' W
Carora	10°11' N, 070°05' W
Carúpano	10°40' N, 063°14' W
Casigua	08°46' N, 072°30' W
Catia la Mar	10°36' N, 067°02' W
Ciudad Bolívar	08°08' N, 063°33' W
Ciudad Guayana (San Felix)	08°23' N, 062°40' W
Ciudad Ojeda	10°12' N, 071°19' W
Clarines	09°56' N, 065°10' W
Coro	11°25' N, 069°41' W
Cumana	10°28' N, 064°10' W
Duaca	10°18' N, 069°10' W
El Callao	07°21' N, 061°49' W
El Pao	08°01' N, 062°38' W
El Samán de Apure	07°55' N, 068°44' W
El Socorro	08°59' N, 065°44' W
El Sombrero	09°23' N, 067°03' W
El Tigre	08°55' N, 064°15' W
El Tocuyo	09°47' N, 069°48' W
Guacara	10°14' N, 067°53' W
Guanare	09°03' N, 069°45' W
Guanarito	08°42' N, 069°12' W
Guasdualito	07°15' N, 070°44' W
Guasipati	07°28' N, 061°54' W
Güiria	10°34' N, 062°18' W
Irapa	10°34' N, 062°35' W
Juangriego	11°05' N, 063°57' W
La Asunción	11°02' N, 063°53' W
La Fría	08°13' N, 072°15' W
La Grita	08°08' N, 071°59' W
La Vela de Coro	11°27' N, 069°34' W
La Victoria	10°14' N, 067°20' W
Las Mercedes	09°07' N, 066°24' W
Los Teques	10°21' N, 067°02' W
Machiques	10°04' N, 072°34' W
Maiquetia	10°36' N, 066°57' W
Maracaibo	10°40' N, 071°37' W
Maracay	10°15' N, 067°36' W

Maturín	09°45' N, 063°11' W
Mene Grande	09°49' N, 070°56' W
Mérida	08°36' N, 071°08' W
Morón	10°29' N, 068°11' W
Pariaguán	08°51' N, 064°43' W
Petare	10°29' N, 066°49' W
Píritu	09°23' N, 069°12' W
Porlamar	10°57' N, 063°51' W
Pozuelos	10°11' N, 064°39' W
Pueblo Nuevo	11°07' N, 069°28' W
Puerto Ayacucho	05°40' N, 067°35' W
Puerto Cabello	10°28' N, 068°01' W
Puerto Cumarebo	11°29' N, 069°21' W
Punta Cardón	11°38' N, 070°14' W
Punta de Mata	09°43' N, 063°38' W
Punto Fijo	11°42' N, 070°13' W
San Carlos	09°40' N, 068°36' W
San Carlos	09°01' N, 071°55' W
San Carlos de Río Negro	01°55' N, 067°04' W
San Cristóbal	07°46' N, 072°14' W
San Felipe	10°20' N, 068°44' W
San Felix, *see* Ciudad Guayana	
San Fernando de Apure	07°54' N, 067°28' W
San Fernando de Atabapo	04°03' N, 067°42' W
San José	10°01' N, 072°23' W
San José de Guanipa (El Tigrito)	08°54' N, 064°09' W
San Juan de los Morros	09°55' N, 067°21' W
Santa Bárbara	07°47' N, 071°10' W
Santa Elena	04°37' N, 061°08' W
Santa María de Ipire	08°49' N, 065°19' W
Santa Rita	10°32' N, 071°32' W
Siquisique	10°34' N, 069°42' W
Soledad	08°10' N, 063°34' W
Temblador	08°59' N, 062°44' W
Tía Juana	10°16' N, 071°22' W
Tinaco	09°42' N, 068°26' W
Tinaquillo	09°55' N, 068°18' W
Tovar	08°20' N, 071°46' W
Trujillo	09°22' N, 070°26' W
Tucacas	10°48' N, 068°19' W
Tucupido	09°17' N, 065°47' W
Tucupita	09°04' N, 062°03' W
Tumeremo	07°18' N, 061°30' W
Turmero	10°14' N, 067°29' W
Upata	08°01' N, 062°24' W
Valencia	10°11' N, 068°00' W
Valera	09°19' N, 070°37' W
Valle de la Pascua	09°13' N, 066°00' W
Villa Bruzual	09°20' N, 069°06' W
Villa de Cura	10°02' N, 067°29' W
Zaraza	09°21' N, 065°19' W

VIETNAM ....pg. 144

Capital: ....Hanoi
Area: ......331,041 sq km; 127,816 sq mi
Highest Elev.: ..Fan Si Pk. 3,140 m; 10,310 ft
Longest River: ....Red 1,200 km; 750 mi
Avg. Temperature: .. Jan = 17°C; Jul = 29°C
Currency: ......dong
Official Language: .Vietnamese

Bac Giang	21°16' N, 106°12' E
Bac Can	22°08' N, 105°50' E
Bac Lieu	09°17' N, 105°43' E
Bien Hoa	10°57' N, 106°49' E
Buon Me Thuot (Lac Giao)	12°40' N, 108°03' E
Ca Mau	09°11' N, 105°08' E
Cam Pha	21°01' N, 107°19' E
Cam Ranh	11°54' N, 109°13' E
Can Tho	10°02' N, 105°47' E
Chau Doc	10°42' N, 105°07' E
Da Lat	11°56' N, 108°25' E
Da Nang (Tourane)	16°04' N, 108°13' E
Dong Ha	16°49' N, 107°08' E
Dong Hoi	17°29' N, 106°36' E
Ha Giang	22°50' N, 104°59' E
Hai Duong	20°56' N, 106°19' E
Haiphong (Hai Phong)	20°52' N, 106°41' E
Hanoi (Ha Noi)	21°02' N, 105°51' E
Ho Chi Minh City (Saigon)	10°45' N, 106°40' E
Hoa Binh	20°50' N, 105°20' E
Hoi An	15°52' N, 108°19' E
Hong Gai (Hon Gai)	20°57' N, 107°05' E
Hue	16°28' N, 107°36' E
Kon Tum (Cong Tum or Kontun)	14°21' N, 108°00' E
Lai Chau	22°04' N, 103°10' E
Long Xuyen	10°23' N, 105°25' E
Minh Hoa	17°47' N, 106°01' E
My Tho	10°21' N, 106°21' E
Nam Dinh	20°25' N, 106°10' E
Nha Trang	12°15' N, 109°11' E
Phan Rang	11°34' N, 108°59' E
Phan Thiet	10°56' N, 108°06' E
Pleiku (Play Cu)	13°59' N, 108°00' E
Qui Nhon	13°46' N, 109°14' E
Rach Gia	10°01' N, 105°05' E
Sa Dec	10°18' N, 105°46' E
Soc Trang	09°36' N, 105°58' E
Son La	21°19' N, 103°54' E
Tam Ky	15°34' N, 108°29' E
Tan An	10°32' N, 106°25' E
Thai Binh	20°27' N, 106°20' E
Thai Nguyen	21°36' N, 105°50' E
Thanh Hoa	19°48' N, 105°46' E
Tuy Hoa	13°05' N, 109°18' E
Viet Tri	21°18' N, 105°26' E
Vinh	18°40' N, 105°40' E
Vung Tau	10°21' N, 107°04' E
Yen Bai	21°42' N, 104°52' E

YEMEN ....pg. 154

Capital: ....Sanaa
Area: ......472,099 sq km; 182,278 sq mi
Highest Elev.: ....Mt. An-Nabi Shu'ayb 3,660 m; 12,010 ft
Avg. Temperature: .. Jan = 25°C; Jul = 32°C
Currency: ......Yemen rial
Official Language: .Arabic

Aden ('Adan)	12°46' N, 045°02' E
'Amran	15°41' N, 043°55' E
Balhaf	13°58' N, 048°11' E
Dhamar	14°33' N, 044°24' E
Ghaydah, al-	16°13' N, 052°11' E

Habban	14°21' N, 047°05' E
Hayjan	16°40' N, 044°05' E
Hays	13°56' N, 043°29' E
Hudaydah, al-	14°48' N, 042°57' E
Ibb	13°58' N, 044°11' E
Madinat ash-Sha'b	12°50' N, 044°56' E
Ma'rib	15°25' N, 045°21' E
Maydi	16°19' N, 042°48' E
Min'ar	16°43' N, 051°18' E
Mocha (al-Mukha)	13°19' N, 043°15' E
Mukalla, al-	14°32' N, 049°08' E
Qana	14°00' N, 048°20' E
Raydah	15°50' N, 044°03' E
Rida'	14°25' N, 044°50' E
Sa'dah	16°57' N, 043°46' E
Sanaa	15°21' N, 044°12' E
Sayhut	15°12' N, 051°14' E
Shaharah	16°11' N, 043°42' E
Sirwah	15°27' N, 045°01' E
Ta'izz	13°34' N, 044°02' E
Yarim	14°18' N, 044°23' E
Zabid	14°12' N, 043°19' E

YUGOSLAVIA ....pg. 134

Capital: ....Belgrade
Area: ......102,173 sq km; 39,449 sq mi
Highest Elev.: ....Titov Vrb 2,750 m; 9,010 ft
Longest River: ....Danube 2,850 km; 1,770 mi
Avg. Temperature: .. Jan = 0°C; Jul = 23°C
Currency: ......new dinar
Official Language: .Serbo-Croatian

Belgrade	44°50' N, 020°30' E
Cacak	43°54' N, 020°21' E
Kragujevac	44°01' N, 020°55' E
Kraljevo	43°44' N, 020°43' E
Krusevac	43°35' N, 021°20' E
Leskovac	42°59' N, 021°57' E
Nis	43°19' N, 021°54' E
Novi Pazar	43°08' N, 020°31' E
Novi Sad	45°15' N, 019°50' E
Pancevo	44°52' N, 020°39' E
Podgorica (Titograd)	42°26' N, 019°16' E
Pristina	42°21' N, 021°10' E
Sabac	44°45' N, 019°43' E
Smederevo	44°39' N, 020°56' E
Sombor	45°46' N, 019°07' E
Subotica	46°06' N, 019°40' E
Uzice (Titovo Uzice)	43°52' N, 019°51' E
Valjevo	44°16' N, 019°53' E
Vranje	42°33' N, 021°54' E
Zrenjanin	45°23' N, 020°23' E

ZAMBIA ....pg. 153

Capital: ....Lusaka
Area: ......752,614 sq km; 290,586 sq mi
Highest Elev.: ....Mt. Mahoni 2,150 m; 7,100 ft
Longest River: ....Zambezi 3,500 km; 2,200 mi
Avg. Temperature: .. Jan = 21°C; Jul = 16°C
Currency: ......Zambian kwacha
Official Language: .English

Chililabombwe (Bancroft)	12°22' S, 027°50' E
Chingola	12°32' S, 027°52' E
Chipata (Fort Jameson)	13°39' S, 032°40' E
Choma	16°49' S, 026°59' E
Fort Jameson, *see* Chipata	
Kabwe (Broken Hill)	14°27' S, 028°27' E
Kasama	10°13' S, 031°12' E
Kawambwa	09°47' S, 029°05' E
Kitwe	12°49' S, 028°13' E
Livingstone (Maramba)	17°51' S, 025°52' E
Luanshya	13°08' S, 028°25' E
Lusaka	15°25' S, 028°17' E
Mansa (Fort Rosebery)	11°12' S, 028°53' E
Mazabuka	15°51' S, 027°46' E
Mbala	08°50' S, 031°22' E
Mongu	15°17' S, 023°08' E
Monze	16°16' S, 027°29' E
Mpika	11°50' S, 031°27' E
Mpulungu	08°46' S, 031°07' E
Mumbwa	14°59' S, 027°04' E
Mwamfuli (Samfya)	11°21' S, 029°33' E
Nchelenge	09°21' S, 029°44' E
Ndola	12°58' S, 028°38' E
Petauke	14°15' S, 031°20' E
Samfya, *see* Mwamfuli	
Senanga	16°07' S, 023°16' E
Solwezi	12°11' S, 026°24' E
Zambezi	13°33' S, 023°07' E

ZIMBABWE ....pg. 153

Capital: ....Harare
Area: ......390,757 sq km; 150,872 sq mi
Highest Elev.: ....Mt. Inyangani 2,590 m; 8,500 ft
Longest River: ....Zambezi 3,500 km; 2,200 mi
Avg. Temperature: .. Jan = 21°C; Jul = 14°C
Currency: ......Zimbabwe dollar
Official Language: .English

Beitbridge	22°13' S, 030°00' E
Bulawayo	20°09' S, 028°35' E
Chitungwiza	18°47' S, 032°37' E
Fort Victoria, *see* Masvingo	
Gatooma, *see* Kadoma	
Gweru (Gwelo)	19°27' S, 029°49' E
Harare (Salisbury)	17°50' S, 031°03' E
Hwange (Wankie)	18°22' S, 026°29' E
Kadoma (Gatooma)	18°21' S, 029°55' E
Kwekwe (Que Que)	18°55' S, 029°49' E
Mashava	20°03' S, 030°29' E
Masvingo (Fort Victoria, or Nyanda)	20°05' S, 030°50' E
Mutare (Umtali)	18°58' S, 032°40' E
Nyanda, *see* Masvingo	
Que Que, *see* Kwekwe	
Redcliff	19°02' S, 029°47' E
Salisbury, *see* Harare	
Selulwe, *see* Shurugwi	
Shurugwi (Selukwe)	19°40' S, 030°00' E
Umtali, *see* Mutare	
Wankie, *see* Hwange	

Webster's
Guide to
Punctuation
and Style

Contents

1 Punctuation

Punctuation marks are used to help clarify the structure and meaning of sentences. They separate groups of words for meaning and emphasis; they convey an idea of the variations in pitch, volume, pauses, and intonation of the spoken language; and they help avoid ambiguity. The choice of what punctuation to use, if any, will often be clear and unambiguous. In other cases, a sentence may allow for several punctuation patterns. In cases like these, varying notions of correctness have developed, and two writers might, with equal correctness, punctuate the same sentence quite differently, relying on their individual judgment and taste.

Apostrophe

The apostrophe is used to form most possessives and contractions as well as some plurals and inflections.

1. The apostrophe is used to indicate the possessive of nouns and indefinite pronouns. (For details, see the section beginning on page 203.)

   the girl's shoe
   the boys' fathers
   Simmons's role
   children's laughter
   anyone's guess
   the Browns' house
   Arkansas's capital

2. Apostrophes are sometimes used to form plurals of letters, numerals, abbreviations, symbols, and words referred to as words. (For details, see the section beginning on page 201.)

   cross your *t*'s
   three 8's *or* three 8s
   two L.H.D.'s *or* two L.H.D.s
   used &'s instead of *and*'s

3. Apostrophes mark omissions in contractions made of two or more words and in contractions of single words.

   wasn't
   they're

she'd rather not
Jake's had it
ass'n
dep't

4. The apostrophe is used to indicate that letters have been intentionally omitted from a word in order to imitate informal speech.

   "Singin' in the Rain," the popular song and movie
   "Snap 'em up" was his response.

   Sometimes such words are so consistently spelled with an apostrophe that the spelling becomes an accepted variant.

   rock 'n' roll [*for* rock and roll]
   ma'am [*for* madam]
   sou'wester [*for* southwester]

5. Apostrophes mark the omission of digits in numerals.

   class of '98
   fashion in the '90s

   If the apostrophe is used when writing the plurals of numerals, either the apostrophe that stands for the missing figures is omitted or the word is spelled out.

   90's *or* nineties *but not* '90's

6. In informal writing, apostrophes are used to produce forms of verbs that are made of individually pronounced letters. An apostrophe or a hyphen is also sometimes used to add an -*er* ending to an abbreviation; if no confusion would result, the apostrophe is usually omitted.

   OK'd the budget
   X'ing out the mistakes
   4-H'er
   49er

Brackets

Outside of mathematics and chemistry texts, brackets are primarily used for insertions into carefully handled quoted matter. They are rarely seen in general writing but are common in historical and scholarly contexts.

1. Brackets enclose editorial comments, corrections, and clarifications inserted into quoted matter.

   Surely that should have peaked [sic] the curiosity of a serious researcher.
   Here they much favour the tiorba [theorbo], the arclute [archlute], and the cittarone [chitarrone], while we at home must content ourselves with the lute alone.
   In Blaine's words, "All the vocal aristocracy showed up—Nat [Cole], Billy [Eckstine], Ella [Fitzgerald], Mabel Mercer— 'cause nobody wanted to miss that date."

2. Brackets enclose insertions that take the place of words or phrases.

   And on the next page: "Their assumption is plainly that [Durocher] would be the agent in any such negotiation."

3. Brackets enclose insertions that supply missing letters.

   A postscript to a December 17 letter to Waugh notes, "If D[eutsch] won't take the manuscript, perhaps someone at Faber will."

4. Brackets enclose insertions that alter the form of a word used in an original text.

> He dryly observes (p. 78) that the Gravely investors had bought stocks because "they want[ed] to see themselves getting richer."

5. Brackets are used to indicate that capitalization has been altered. This is generally optional; it is standard practice only where meticulous handling of original source material is crucial (particularly legal and scholarly contexts).

> As Chief Justice Warren held for the Court, "[T]he Attorney General may bring an injunctive action . . ."
> *or in general contexts*
> "The Attorney General may bring . . ."

Brackets also enclose editorial notes when text has been italicized for emphasis.

> But tucked away on page 11 we find this fascinating note: "In addition, we anticipate that *siting these new plants in marginal neighborhoods will decrease the risk of organized community opposition*" [italics added].

6. Brackets function as parentheses within parentheses, especially where two sets of parentheses could be confusing.

> Posner's recent essays (including the earlier *Law and Literature* [1988]) bear this out.

7. In mathematical copy, brackets are used with parentheses to indicate units contained within larger units. They are also used with various meanings in chemical names and formulas.

> $x + 5[(x + y)(2x - y)]$
> $Ag[Pt(NO_2)_4]$

With Other Punctuation

8. Punctuation that marks the end of a phrase, clause, item in a series, or sentence follows any bracketed material appended to that passage.

> The report stated, "if we fail to find additional sources of supply [of oil and gas], our long-term growth will be limited."

When brackets enclose a complete sentence, closing punctuation is placed within the brackets.

> [Since this article was written, new archival evidence of document falsification has come to light.]

Colon

The colon is usually a mark of introduction, indicating that what follows it—generally a clause, a phrase, or a list—has been pointed to or described in what precedes it. (For the use of capitals following a colon, see paragraphs 7–8 on page 192.)

With Phrases and Clauses

1. A colon introduces a clause or phrase that explains, illustrates, amplifies, or restates what has gone before.

> An umbrella is a foolish extravagance: if you don't leave it in the first restaurant, a gust of wind will destroy it on the way home.
> Dawn was breaking: the distant peaks were already glowing with the sun's first rays.

2. A colon introduces an appositive.

> The issue comes down to this: Will we offer a reduced curriculum, or will we simply cancel the program?
> That year Handley's old obsession was replaced with a new one: jazz.

3. A colon introduces a list or series, often following a phrase such as *the following* or *as follows*.

> She has trial experience on three judicial levels: county, state, and federal.
> Anyone planning to participate should be prepared to do the following: hike five miles with a backpack, sleep on the ground without a tent, and paddle a canoe through rough water.

It is occasionally used like a dash to introduce a summary statement following a series.

> Baseball, soccer, skiing, track: he excelled in every sport he took up.

4. Although the colon usually follows a full independent clause, it also often interrupts a sentence before the clause is complete.

> The nine proposed program topics are: offshore supply, vessel traffic, ferry services, ship repair, . . .
> Information on each participant includes: name, date of birth, mailing address, . . .
> For example: 58 percent of union members voted, but only 44 percent of blue-collar workers as a whole.
> The association will:
>> Act with trust, integrity, and professionalism.
>> Operate in an open and effective manner.
>> Take the initiative in seeking diversity.

With Quotations

5. A colon usually introduces lengthy quoted material that is set off from the rest of a text by indentation but not by quotation marks.

> The *Rumpole* series has been nicely encapsulated as follows: Rumpled, disreputable, curmudgeonly barrister Horace Rumpole often wins cases despite the disdain of his more aristocratic colleagues. Fond of cheap wine ("Château Thames Embankment") and Keats's poetry, he refers to his wife as "She Who Must Be Obeyed" (an allusion to the title character of H. Rider Haggard's *She*).

6. A colon is often used before a quotation in running text, especially when (1) the quotation is lengthy, (2) the quotation is a formal statement or is being given special emphasis, or (3) a full independent clause precedes the colon.

> Said Murdoch: "The key to the success of this project is good planning. We need to know precisely what steps we will need to take, what kind of staff we will require, what the project will cost, and when we can expect completion."
> The inscription reads: "Here lies one whose name was writ in water."
> This was his verbatim response: "At this time Mr. Wilentz is still in the company's employ, and no change in his status is anticipated imminently."

Other Uses

7. A colon separates elements in bibliographic publication data and page references, in biblical citations, and in formulas used to express time and ratios. No space precedes or follows a colon between numerals.

Stendhal, *Love* (New York: Penguin, 1975)
Paleobiology 3:121
John 4:10
8:30 a.m.
a winning time of 3:43:02
a ration of 3:5

8. A colon separates titles and subtitles.

Southwest Stories: Tales from the Desert

9. A colon follows the salutation in formal correspondence.

Dear Judge Wright:
Dear Laurence:
Dear Product Manager:
Ladies and Gentlemen:

10. A colon follows headings in memorandums, government correspondence, and general business letters.

TO:
SUBJECT:
VIA:
REFERENCE:

11. An unspaced colon separates the writer's and typist's initials in the identification lines of business letters.

WAL:jml

A colon also separates copy abbreviations from the initials of copy recipients. (The abbreviation *cc* stands for *carbon* or *courtesy copy; bcc* stands for *blind carbon* or *courtesy copy.*) A space follows a colon used with the fuller name of a recipient.

cc:RSP
 JES
bcc:MWK
bcc: Mr. Jones

With Other Punctuation

12. A colon is placed outside quotation marks and parentheses that punctuate the larger sentence.

The problem becomes most acute in "Black Rose and Destroying Angel": plot simply ceases to exist.
Wilson and Hölldobler remark on the same phenomenon in *The Ants* (1990):

Comma

The comma is the most frequently used punctuation mark in English and the one that provides the most difficulties to writers. Its most common uses are to separate items in a series and to set off or distinguish grammatical elements within sentences.

Between Main Clauses

1. A comma separates main clauses joined by a coordinating conjunction, such as *and, but, or, nor,* or *so.*

She knew very little about the new system, and he volunteered nothing.
The trial lasted for nine months, but the jury took only four hours to reach its verdict.
We will not respond to any more questions on that topic this afternoon, nor will we respond to similar questions in the future.

All the first-floor windows were barred, so he had clambered up onto the fire escape.

2. When one or both of the clauses are short or closely related in meaning, the comma is often omitted.

They said good-bye and everyone hugged.

If commas set off another phrase that modifies the whole sentence, the comma between main clauses is often omitted.

Six thousand years ago, the top of the volcano blew off in a series of powerful eruptions and the sides collapsed into the middle.

3. Commas are sometimes used to separate short and obviously parallel main clauses that are not joined by conjunctions.

One day you're a successful corporate lawyer, the next day you're out of work.

Use of a comma to join clauses that are neither short nor obviously parallel, called *comma fault* or *comma splice,* is avoided. Clauses not joined by conjunctions are normally separated by semicolons. For details, see paragraph 1 on page 190.

4. If a sentence is composed of three or more clauses that are short and free of commas, the clauses are occasionally all separated by commas even if the last two are not joined by a conjunction. If the clauses are long or punctuated, they are separated with semicolons; the last two clauses are sometimes separated by a comma if they are joined by a conjunction. (For more details, see paragraph 5 on page 191.)

Small fish fed among the marsh weed, ducks paddled along the surface, an occasional muskrat ate greens along the bank.
The kids were tired and whiny; Napoleon, usually so calm, was edgy; Tabitha seemed to be going into heat, and even the guinea pigs were agitated.

With Compound Predicates

5. Commas are not normally used to separate the parts of a compound predicate.

The firefighter tried to enter the burning building but was turned back by the thick smoke.

However, they are often used if the predicate is long and complicated, if one part is being stressed, or if the absence of a comma could cause a momentary misreading.

The board helps to develop the financing and marketing strategies for new corporate divisions, and issues periodic reports on expenditures, revenues, and personnel appointments.
This is an unworkable plan, and has been from the start.
I try to explain to him what I want him to do, and get nowhere.

With Subordinate Clauses and Phrases

6. Adverbial clauses and phrases that begin a sentence are usually set off with commas.

Having made that decision, we turned our attention to other matters.
In order to receive a high school diploma, a student must earn 16 credits from public or private secondary schools.

In addition, staff members respond to queries, take new orders, and initiate billing.

If the sentence can be easily read without a comma, the comma may be omitted. The phrase will usually be short—four words or less—but even after a longer phrase the comma is often omitted.

> As cars age, they depreciate. *or* As cars age they depreciate.
> In January the firm will introduce a new line of investigative services.
> On the map the town appeared as a small dot in the midst of vast emptiness.
> If nobody comes forward by Friday I will have to take further steps.

7. Adverbial clauses and phrases that introduce a main clause other than the first main clause are usually set off with commas. If the clause or phrase follows a conjunction, one comma often precedes the conjunction and one follows the clause or phrase. Alternatively, one comma precedes the conjunction and two more enclose the clause or phrase, or a single comma precedes the conjunction. Short phrases, and phrases in short sentences, tend not to be enclosed in commas.

> They have redecorated the entire store, but[,] to the delight of their customers, it retains much of its original flavor.
> We haven't left Springfield yet, but when we get to Boston we'll call you.

8. A comma is not used after an introductory phrase if the phrase immediately precedes the main verb.

> From the next room came a loud expletive.

9. A subordinate clause or phrase that modifies a noun is not set off by commas if it is *restrictive* (or *essential*)—that is, if its removal would alter the noun's meaning.

> The man who wrote this obviously had no firsthand knowledge of the situation.
> They entered through the first door that wasn't locked.

If the meaning would not be altered by its removal, the clause or phrase is considered *nonrestrictive* (or *nonessential*) and usually is set off by commas.

> The new approach, which was based on team teaching, was well received.
> Wechsler, who has done solid reporting from other battlefronts, is simply out of his depth here.
> They tried the first door, which led nowhere.

10. Commas set off an adverbial clause or phrase that falls between the subject and the verb.

> The Clapsaddle sisters, to keep up appearances, rode to the park every Sunday in their rented carriage.

11. Commas set off modifying phrases that do not immediately precede the word or phrase they modify.

> Scarbo, intent as usual on his next meal, was snuffling around the butcher's bins.
> The negotiators, tired and discouraged, headed back to the hotel.
> We could see the importance, both long-term and short-term, of her proposal.

12. An absolute phrase (a participial phrase with its own subject that is grammatically independent of the rest of the sentence) is set off with commas.

Our business being concluded, we adjourned for refreshments.
We headed southward, the wind freshening behind us, to meet the rest of the fleet in the morning.
I'm afraid of his reaction, his temper being what it is.

With Appositives

13. Commas set off a word, phrase, or clause that is in apposition to (that is, equivalent to) a preceding or following noun and that is nonrestrictive.

> It sat nursing its front paw, the injured one.
> Aleister Crowley, Britain's most infamous satanist, is the subject of a remarkable new biography.
> A cherished landmark in the city, the Hotel Sandburg has managed once again to escape the wrecking ball.
> The committee cochairs were a lawyer, John Larson, and an educator, Mary Conway.

14. Restrictive appositives are not set off by commas.

> He next had a walk-on role in the movie *The Firm.*
> Longfellow's poem *Evangeline* was a favorite of my grandmother's.
> The committee cochairs were the lawyer John Larson and the educator Mary Conway.
> Lord Castlereagh was that strange anomaly[,] a Labor-voting peer.

With Introductory and Interrupting Elements

15. Commas set off transitional words and phrases.

> Indeed, close coordination will be essential.
> Defeat may be inevitable; however, disgrace is not.
> The second report, on the other hand, shows a strong bias.

When such words and phrases fall in the middle of a clause, commas are sometimes unnecessary.

> They thus have no chips left to bargain with.
> The materials had indeed arrived.
> She would in fact see them that afternoon.

16. Commas set off parenthetic elements, such as authorial asides.

> All of us, to tell the truth, were completely amazed.
> It was, I should add, not the first time I'd seen him in this condition.

17. Commas are often used to set off words or phrases that introduce examples or explanations, such as *namely, for example,* and *that is.*

> He expects to visit three countries, namely, France, Spain, and Germany.
> I would like to develop a good, workable plan, that is, one that would outline our goals and set a timetable for accomplishing them.

Such introductory words and phrases may also often be preceded by a dash, parenthesis, or semicolon. Regardless of the punctuation that precedes the word or phrase, a comma usually follows it.

> Sports develop two valuable traits—namely, self-control and the ability to make quick decisions.
> In writing to the manufacturer, be as specific as possible (i.e., list the missing or defective parts, describe the malfunction, and identify the store where the unit was purchased).
> Most had traveled great distances to participate; for example, three had come from Australia, one from Japan, and two from China.

18. Commas set off words in direct address.

> This is our third and final notice, Mr. Sutton.
> The facts, my fellow Americans, are very different.

19. Commas set off mild interjections or exclamations.

> Ah, the mosaics in Ravenna are matchless.
> Uh-oh, His Eminence seems to be on the warpath this morning.

With Contrasting Expressions

20. A comma is sometimes used to set off contrasting expressions within a sentence.

> This project will take six months, not six weeks.

21. When two or more contrasting modifiers or prepositions, one of which is introduced by a conjunction or adverb, apply to a noun that follows immediately, the second is set off by two commas or a single comma, or not set off at all.

> A solid, if overly wordy, assessment
> *or* a solid, if overly wordy assessment
> *or* a solid if overly wordy assessment
> This street takes you away from, not toward, the capitol.
> *or* This street takes you away from, not toward the capitol.
> grounds for a civil, and maybe a criminal, case
> *or* grounds for a civil, and maybe a criminal case
> *or* grounds for a civil and maybe a criminal case

Dashes or parentheses are often used instead of commas in such sentences.

> grounds for a civil (and maybe a criminal) case

22. A comma does not usually separate elements that are contrasted through the use of a pair of correlative conjunctions such as *either . . . or, neither . . . nor,* and *not only . . . but also.*

> Neither my brother nor I noticed the error.
> He was given the post not only because of his diplomatic connections but also because of his great tact and charm.

When correlative conjunctions join main clauses, a comma usually separates the clauses unless they are short.

> Not only did she have to see three salesmen and a visiting reporter, but she also had to prepare for next day's meeting.
> Either you do it my way or we don't do it at all.

23. Long parallel contrasting and comparing clauses are separated by commas; short parallel phrases are not.

> The more that comes to light about him, the less savory he seems.
> The less said the better.

With Items in a Series

24. Words, phrases, and clauses joined in a series are separated by commas.

> Men, women, and children crowded aboard the train.
> Her job required her to pack quickly, to travel often, and to have no personal life.
> He responded patiently while reporters shouted questions, flashbulbs popped, and the crowd pushed closer.

When the last two items in a series are joined by a conjunction, the final comma is often omitted, especially where this would not result in ambiguity. In individual publications, the final comma is usually consistently used, consistently omitted, or used only where a given sentence would otherwise be ambiguous or hard to read. It is consistently used in most nonfiction books; elsewhere it tends to be used or generally omitted equally often.

> We are looking for a house with a big yard, a view of the harbor[,] and beach and docking privileges.

25. A comma is not generally used to separate items in a series all of which are joined with conjunctions.

> I don't understand what this policy covers or doesn't cover or only partially covers.
> They left behind the fogs and the wood storks and the lonesome soughing of the wind.

26. When the elements in a series are long or complex or consist of clauses that themselves contain commas, the elements are usually separated by semicolons, not commas. See paragraph 7 on page 191.

With Coordinate Modifiers

27. A comma is generally used to separate two or more adjectives, adverbs, or phrases that modify the same word or phrase.

> She spoke in a calm, reflective manner.
> They set to their work again grimly, intently.

The comma is often omitted when the adjectives are short.

> one long thin strand
> a small white stone
> little nervous giggles
> skinny young waiters
> in this harsh new light

The comma is generally omitted where it is ambiguous whether the last modifier and the noun—or two of the modifiers—constitute a unit.

> the story's stark dramatic power
> a pink stucco nightclub

In some writing, especially works of fiction, commas may be omitted from most series of coordinate modifiers as a matter of style.

28. A comma is not used between two adjectives when the first modifies the combination of the second plus the noun it modifies.

> the last good man
> a good used car
> his protruding lower lip
> the only fresh water
> the only freshwater lake
> their black pickup truck

A comma is also not used to separate an adverb from the adjective or adverb that it modifies.

> this formidably difficult task

In Quotations

29. A comma usually separates a direct quotation from a phrase identifying its source or speaker. If the quotation is a question or an exclamation and the identifying phrase follows the quotation, the comma is replaced by a question mark or an exclamation point.

She answered, "I'm afraid it's all we've got."

"The comedy is over," he muttered.

"How about another round?" Elaine piped up.

"I suspect," said Mrs. Horowitz, "we haven't seen the last of her."

"You can sink the lousy thing for all I care!" Trumbull shouted back.

"And yet . . . ," she mused.

"We can't get the door op—" Captain Hunt is heard shouting before the tape goes dead.

In some cases, a colon can replace a comma preceding a quotation; see paragraph 6 on page 178.

30. When short or fragmentary quotations are used in a sentence that is not primarily dialogue, they are usually not set off by commas.

He glad-handed his way through the small crowd with a "Looking good, Joe" or "How's the wife" for every beaming face.

Just because he said he was "about to leave this minute" doesn't mean he actually left.

Sentences that fall within sentences and do not constitute actual dialogue are not usually set off with commas. These may be mottoes or maxims, unspoken or imaginary dialogue, or sentences referred to as sentences; and they may or may not be enclosed in quotation marks. Where quotation marks are not used, a comma is often inserted to mark the beginning of the shorter sentence clearly. (For the use of quotation marks with such sentences, see paragraph 6 on page 189.)

"The computer is down" was the response she dreaded.

He spoke with a candor that seemed to insist, This actually happened to me and in just this way.

The first rule is, When in doubt, spell it out.

When the shorter sentence functions as an appositive (the equivalent to an adjacent noun), it is set off with commas when nonrestrictive and not when restrictive.

We had the association's motto, "We make waves," printed on our T-shirts.

He was fond of the slogan "Every man a king, but no man wears a crown."

31. A comma introduces a directly stated question, regardless of whether it is enclosed in quotation marks or if its first word is capitalized. It is not used to set off indirect discourse or indirect questions introduced by a conjunction (such as *that* or *what*).

I wondered, what is going on here?

The question is, How do we get out of this situation?

but

Margot replied quietly that she'd never been happier.

I wondered what was going on here.

The question is how do we get out of this situation.

32. The comma is usually omitted before quotations that are very short exclamations or representations of sounds.

He jumped up suddenly and cried "I've got it!"

Replacing Omitted Words

33. A comma may indicate the omission of a word or phrase in parallel constructions where the omitted word or phrase appears earlier in the sentence. In short sentences, the comma is usually omitted.

The larger towns were peopled primarily by shopkeepers, artisans, and traders; the small villages, by peasant farmers.

Seven voted for the proposal, three against.

He critiqued my presentation and I his.

34. A comma sometimes replaces the conjunction *that*.

The smoke was so thick, they were forced to crawl.

Chances are, there are still some tickets left.

With Addresses, Dates, and Numbers

35. Commas set off the elements of an address except for zip codes.

Write to Bureau of the Census, Washington, DC 20233.

In Needles, California, their luck ran out.

When a city name and state (province, country, etc.) name are used together to modify a noun that follows, the second comma may be omitted but is more often retained.

We visited their Enid, Oklahoma plant.

but more commonly

We visited their Enid, Oklahoma, plant.

36. Commas set off the year in a full date.

On July 26, 1992, the court issued its opinion.

Construction for the project began on April 30, 1995.

When only the month and year are given, the first comma is usually omitted.

In December 1903, the Wright brothers finally succeeded in keeping an airplane aloft for a few seconds.

October 1929 brought an end to all that.

37. A comma groups numerals into units of three to separate thousands, millions, and so on.

2,000 case histories

15,000 units

a population of 3,450,000

a fee of $12,500

Certain types of numbers do not contain commas, including decimal fractions, street addresses, and page numbers. (For more on the use of the comma with numbers, see paragraphs 1–3 on page 216.)

2.5544

12537 Wilshire Blvd.

page 1415

With Names, Degrees, and Titles

38. A comma separates a surname from a following professional, academic, honorary, or religious degree or title, or an abbreviation for a branch of the armed forces.

Amelia P. Artandi, M.D.

Robert Hynes Menard, Ph.D., L.H.D.

John L. Farber, Esq.

Sister Mary Catherine, S.C.

Admiral Herman Washington, USN

39. A comma is often used between a surname and the abbreviations *Jr.* and *Sr.*

Douglas Fairbanks, Sr.   *or*   Douglas Fairbanks Sr.

Dr. Martin Luther King, Jr.   *or*   Dr. Martin Luther King Jr.

40. A comma is often used to set off corporate identifiers such as *Incorporated, Inc., Ltd., P.C.,* and *L.P.* However, many company names omit this comma.

> StarStage Productions, Incorporated
> Hart International Inc.
> Walsh, Brandon & Kaiser, P.C.
> The sales manager from Doyle Southern, Inc., spoke at Tuesday's meeting.

Other Uses

41. A comma follows the salutation in informal correspondence and usually follows the complimentary close in both informal and formal correspondence.

> Dear Rachel,
> Affectionately,
> Very truly yours,

42. The comma is used to avoid ambiguity when the juxtaposition of two words or expressions could cause confusion.

> Under Mr. Thomas, Jefferson High School has flourished.
> He scanned the landscape that opened out before him, and guided the horse gently down.

43. When normal sentence order is inverted, a comma often precedes the subject and verb. If the structure is clear without it, it is often omitted.

> That we would succeed, no one doubted.
> And a splendid occasion it was.

With Other Punctuation

44. Commas are used next to brackets, ellipsis points, parentheses, and quotation marks. Commas are not used next to colons, dashes, exclamation points, question marks, or semicolons. If one of the latter falls at the same point where a comma would fall, the comma is dropped. (For more on the use of commas with other punctuation, see the sections for each individual mark.)

> "If they find new sources [of oil and gas], their earnings will obviously rebound. . . ."
> "This book takes its place among the most serious, . . . comprehensive, and enlightened treatments of its great subject."
> There are only six small files (at least in this format), which take up very little disk space.
> According to Hartmann, the people are "savage," their dwellings are "squalid," and the landscape is "a pestilential swamp."

Dash

The dash can function like a comma, a colon, or a parenthesis. Like commas and parentheses, dashes set off parenthetic material such as examples, supplemental facts, and explanatory or descriptive phrases. Like a colon, a dash introduces clauses that explain or expand upon something that precedes them. Though sometimes considered a less formal equivalent of the colon and parenthesis, the dash may be found in all kinds of writing, including the most formal, and the choice of which mark to use is often a matter of personal preference.

The common dash (also called the *em dash,* since it is approximately the width of a capital M in typeset material) is usually represented by two hyphens in typed and keyboarded material. (Word-processing programs make it available as a special character.)

Spacing around the dash varies. Most newspapers insert a space before and after the dash; many popular magazines do the same; but most books and journals omit spacing.

The *en dash* and the *two-* and *three-em dashes* have more limited uses, which are explained in paragraphs 13–15 on page 184.

Abrupt Change or Suspension

1. The dash marks an abrupt change or break in the structure of a sentence.

> The students seemed happy enough with the new plan, but the alumni—there was the problem.

2. A dash is used to indicate interrupted speech or a speaker's confusion or hesitation.

> "The next point I'd like to bring up—" the speaker started to say.
> "Yes," he went on, "yes—that is—I guess I agree."

Parenthetic and Amplifying Elements

3. Dashes are used in place of commas or parentheses to emphasize or draw attention to parenthetic or amplifying material.

> With three expert witnesses in agreement, the defense can be expected to modify its strategy—somewhat.
> This amendment will finally prevent corporations—large and small—from buying influence through exorbitant campaign contributions.

When dashes are used to set off parenthetic elements, they often indicate that the material is more digressive than elements set off with commas but less digressive than elements set off by parentheses. For examples, see paragraph 16 on page 180 and paragraph 1 on page 186.

4. Dashes set off or introduce defining phrases and lists.

> The fund sought to acquire controlling positions—a minimum of 25% of outstanding voting securities—in other companies.
> Davis was a leading innovator in at least three styles—bebop, cool jazz, and jazz-rock fusion.

5. A dash is often used in place of a colon or semicolon to link clauses, especially when the clause that follows the dash explains, summarizes, or expands upon the preceding clause in a somewhat dramatic way.

> The results were in—it had been a triumphant success.

6. A dash or a pair of dashes often sets off illustrative or amplifying material introduced by such phrases as *for example, namely,* and *that is,* when the break in continuity is greater than that shown by a comma, or when the dash would clarify the sentence structure better than a comma. (For more details, see paragraph 17 on page 180.)

> After some discussion the motion was tabled—that is, it was removed indefinitely from the board's consideration.
> Lawyers should generally—in pleadings, for example—attempt to be as specific as possible.

7. A dash may introduce a summary statement that follows a series of words or phrases.

> Crafts, food booths, children's activities, cider-making demonstrations—there was something for everyone.
> Once into bankruptcy, the company would have to pay cash for its supplies, defer maintenance, and lay off workers—moves that could threaten its future.

8. A dash often precedes the name of an author or source at the end of a quoted passage—such as an epigraph, extract, or book or film blurb—that is not part of the main text. The attribution may appear immediately after the quotation or on the next line.

> Only the sign is for sale.
> —Søren Kierkegaard
> "I return to her stories with more pleasure, and await them with more anticipation, than those of any of her contemporaries."—William Logan, *Chicago Tribune*

With Other Punctuation

9. If a dash appears at a point where a comma could also appear, the comma is omitted.

> Our lawyer has read the transcript—all 1,200 pages of it—and he has decided that an appeal would not be useful.
> If we don't succeed—and the critics say we won't—then the whole project is in jeopardy.

In a series, dashes that would force a comma to be dropped are often replaced by parentheses.

> The holiday movie crowds were being entertained by street performers: break dancers, a juggler (who doubled as a sword swallower), a steel-drummer, even a three-card-monte dealer.

10. If the second of a pair of dashes would fall where a period should also appear, the dash is omitted.

> Instead, he hired his mother—an odd choice by any standard.

Much less frequently, the second dash will be dropped in favor of a colon or semicolon.

> Valley Health announced general improvements to its practice—two to start this week: evening office hours and a voice-mail message system.
> His conduct has always been exemplary—near-perfect attendance, excellent productivity, a good attitude; nevertheless, his termination cannot be avoided.

11. When a pair of dashes sets off material ending with an exclamation point or a question mark, the mark is placed inside the dashes.

> His hobby was getting on people's nerves—especially mine!—and he was extremely good at it.
> There would be a "distinguished guest speaker"—was there ever any other kind?—and plenty of wine afterwards.

12. Dashes are used inside parentheses, and vice versa, to indicate parenthetic material within parenthetic material. The second dash is omitted if it would immediately precede the closing parenthesis; a closing parenthesis is never omitted.

> We were looking for a narrator (or narrators—sometimes a script call for more than one) who could handle a variety of assignments.

> The wall of the Old City contains several gates—particularly Herod's Gate, the Golden Gate, and Zion Gate (or "David's Gate")—with rich histories.

En Dash and Long Dashes

13. The *en dash* generally appears only in typeset material; in typed or keyboarded material the simple hyphen is usually used instead. (Word-processing programs provide the en dash as a special character.) Newspapers similarly use the hyphen in place of the en dash. The en dash is shorter than the em dash but longer than the hyphen. It is most frequently used between numbers, dates, or other notations to signify "(up) to and including."

> pages 128–34
> 1995–97
> September 24–October 5
> 8:30 a.m.–4:30 p.m.

The en dash replaces a hyphen in compound adjectives when at least one of the elements is a two-word compound. It replaces the word *to* between capitalized names, and is used to indicate linkages such as boundaries, treaties, and oppositions.

> post–Cold War era
> Boston–Washington train
> New Jersey–Pennsylvania border
> male–female differences *or* male-female differences

14. A *two-em dash* is used to indicate missing letters in a word and, less frequently, to indicate a missing word.

> The nearly illegible letter is addressed to a Mr. P——— of Baltimore.

15. A *three-em dash* indicates that a word has been left out or that an unknown word or figure is to be supplied.

> The study was carried out in ———, a fast-growing Sunbelt city.

Ellipsis Points

Ellipsis points (also known as *ellipses, points of ellipsis,* and *suspension points*) are periods, usually in groups of three, that signal an omission from quoted material or indicate a pause or trailing off of speech. A space usually precedes and follows each ellipsis point. (In newspaper style, spaces are usually omitted.)

1. Ellipsis points indicate the omission of one or more words within a quoted sentence.

> We the People of the United States . . . do ordain and establish this Constitution for the United States of America.

2. Ellipsis points are usually not used to indicate the omission of words that precede the quoted portion. However, in some formal contexts, especially when the quotation is introduced by a colon, ellipsis points are used.

> He ends with a stirring call for national resolve that "government of the people, by the people, for the people shall not perish from the earth."
> Its final words define the war's purpose in democratic terms: ". . . that government of the people, by the people, for the people shall not perish from the earth."

Ellipsis points following quoted material are omitted when it forms an integral part of a larger sentence.

> She maintained that it was inconsistent with "government of the people, by the people, for the people."

3. Punctuation used in the original that falls on either side of the ellipsis points is often omitted; however, it may be retained, especially if this helps clarify the sentence.

> Now we are engaged in a great civil war testing whether that nation . . . can long endure.
>
> But, in a larger sense, we can not dedicate, . . . we can not hallow this ground.
>
> We the People of the United States, in Order to . . . promote the general Welfare, and secure the Blessings of Liberty . . . , do ordain and establish this Constitution for the United States of America.

4. If an omission includes an entire sentence within a passage, the last part of a sentence within a passage, or the first part of a sentence other than the first quoted sentence, the period preceding or following the omission is retained (with no space preceding it) and is followed by three ellipsis points. When the first part of a sentence is omitted but the quoted portion acts as a sentence, the first quoted word is usually capitalized.

> We have come to dedicate a portion of that field, as a final resting place for those who here gave their lives that this nation might live. . . . But, in a larger sense, we can not dedicate—we can not consecrate—we can not hallow—this ground.
>
> Now we are engaged in a great civil war. . . . We are met on a great battlefield of that war.
>
> The brave men, living and dead, who struggled here, have consecrated it, far above our poor power to add or detract. . . . From these honored dead we take increased devotion to that cause for which they gave the last full measure of devotion. . . .

Alternatively, the period may be dropped and all omissions may be indicated simply by three ellipsis points.

5. If the last words of a quoted sentence are omitted and the original sentence ends with punctuation other than a period, the end punctuation often follows the ellipsis points, especially if it helps clarify the quotation.

> He always ends his harangues with some variation on the question, "What could you have been thinking when you . . . ?"

6. When ellipsis points are used to indicate that a quotation has been intentionally left unfinished, the terminal period is omitted.

> The paragraph beginning "Recent developments suggest . . . " should be deleted.

7. A line of ellipsis points indicates that one or more lines have been omitted from a poem.

> When I heard the learned astronomer,
> . . . .
> How soon unaccountable I became tired and sick,
> Til rising and gliding out I wandered off by myself,
> In the mystical moist night-air, and from time to time,
> Looked up in perfect silence at the stars.

8. Ellipsis points are used to indicate faltering speech, especially if the faltering involves a long pause or a sentence that trails off or is intentionally left unfinished. Generally no other terminal punctuation is used.

> The speaker seemed uncertain. "Well, that's true . . . but even so . . . I think we can do better."
>
> "Despite these uncertainties, we believe we can do it, but . . ."
>
> "I mean . . ." he said, "like . . . How?"

9. Ellipsis points are sometimes used informally as a stylistic device to catch a reader's attention, often replacing a dash or colon.

> They think that nothing can go wrong . . . but it does.

10. In newspaper and magazine columns consisting of social notes, local events listings, or short items of celebrity news, ellipsis points often take the place of paragraphing to separate the items. (Ellipsis points are also often used in informal personal correspondence in place of periods or paragraphing.)

> Congratulations to Debra Morricone, our up-and-coming singing star, for her full scholarship to the Juilliard School this fall! . . . And kudos to Paul Chartier for his winning All-State trumpet performance last Friday in Baltimore! . . . Look for wit and sparkling melody when the Lions mount their annual Gilbert & Sullivan show at Syms Auditorium. This year it's . . .

Exclamation Point

The exclamation point is used to mark a forceful comment or exclamation.

1. An exclamation point can punctuate a sentence, phrase, or interjection.

> There is no alternative!
> Without a trace!
> My God! It's monstrous!

2. The exclamation point may replace the question mark when an ironic, angry, or emphatic tone is more important than the actual question.

> Aren't you finished yet!
> Do you realize what you've done!
> Why me!

Occasionally it is used *with* the question mark to indicate a very forceful question.

> How much did you say?!
> You did what!?

3. The exclamation point falls within brackets, dashes, parentheses, and quotation marks when it punctuates only the enclosed material. It is placed outside them when it punctuates the entire sentence.

> All of this proves—at long last!—that we were right from the start.
>
> Somehow the dog got the gate open (for the third time!) and ran into the street.
>
> He sprang to his feet and shouted "Point of order!"
>
> At this rate the national anthem will soon be replaced by "You Are My Sunshine"!

4. If an exclamation point falls where a comma could also go, the comma is dropped.

> "Absolutely not!" he snapped.
> They wouldn't dare! she told herself over and over.

If the exclamation point is part of a title, it may be followed by a comma. If the title falls at the end of a sentence, no period follows it.

> *Hello Dolly!*, which opened in 1964, would become one of the ten longest-running shows in Broadway history.
> His favorite management book is still *Up the Organization!*

Hyphen

Hyphens have a variety of uses, the most significant of which is to join the elements of compound nouns and modifiers.

1. Hyphens are used to link elements in compound words. (For more on compound words, see the section beginning on page 204.)

> secretary-treasurer
> cost-effective
> fund-raiser
> spin-off

2. In some words, a hyphen separates a prefix, suffix, or medial element from the rest of the word. Consult a dictionary in doubtful cases. (For details on using a hyphen with a prefix or a suffix, see the section beginning on page 208.)

> anti-inflation
> umbrella-like
> jack-o'-lantern

3. In typed and keyboarded material, a hyphen is generally used between numbers and dates with the meaning "(up) to and including." In typeset material it is replaced by an en dash. (For details on the en dash, see paragraph 13 on page 184.)

> pages 128–34
> the years 1995–97

4. A hyphen marks an end-of-line division of a word.

> In 1975 smallpox, formerly a great scourge, was declared totally eradicated by the World Health Organization.

5. A hyphen divides letters or syllables to give the effect of stuttering, sobbing, or halting speech.

> "S-s-sammy, it's my t-toy!"

6. Hyphens indicate a word spelled out letter by letter.

> l-i-a-i-s-o-n

7. Hyphens are sometimes used to produce inflected forms of verbs made of individually pronounced letters or to add an *-er* ending to an abbreviation. However, apostrophes are more commonly used for these purposes. (For details on these uses of the apostrophe, see paragraph 6 on page 177.)

> DH-ing for the White Sox   *or*   DH'ing for the White Sox
> a dedicated UFO-er   *or*   a dedicated UFO'er

Parentheses

Parentheses generally enclose material that is inserted into a main statement but is not intended to be an essential part of it. For some of the cases described below, commas or dashes are frequently used instead. (For examples, see paragraph 16 on page 180 and paragraph 3 on page 183.) Parentheses are particularly used when the inserted material is only incidental. Unlike commas and dashes, an opening parenthesis is always followed by a closing one. Because parentheses are almost always used in pairs, and their shapes indicate their relative functions, they often clarify a sentence's structure better than commas or dashes.

Parenthetic Elements

1. Parentheses enclose phrases and clauses that provide examples, explanations, or supplementary facts or numerical data.

> Nominations for principal officers (president, vice president, treasurer, and secretary) were heard and approved.
> Four computers (all outdated models) will be replaced.
> First-quarter sales figures were good (up 8%), but total revenues showed a slight decline (down 1%).

2. Parentheses sometimes enclose phrases and clauses introduced by expressions such as *namely, that is, e.g.,* and *i.e.,* particularly where parentheses would clarify the sentence's structure better than commas. (For more details, see paragraph 17 on page 180.)

> In writing to the manufacturer, be as specific as possible (i.e., list the defective parts, describe the malfunction, and identify the store where the unit was purchased), but also as concise.

3. Parentheses enclose definitions or translations in the main part of a sentence.

> The company announced plans to sell off its housewares (small-appliances) business.
> The *grand monde* (literally, "great world") of prewar Parisian society consisted largely of titled aristocracy.

4. Parentheses enclose abbreviations that follow their spelled-out forms, or spelled-out forms that follow abbreviations.

> She cited a study by the Food and Drug Administration (FDA).
> They attended last year's convention of the ABA (American Booksellers Association).

5. Parentheses often enclose cross-references and bibliographic references.

> Specialized services are also available (see list of stores at end of brochure).
> The diagram (Fig. 3) illustrates the action of the pump.
> Subsequent studies (Braxton 1990; Roh and Weinglass 1993) have confirmed these findings.

6. Parentheses enclose numerals that confirm a spelled-out number in a business or legal context.

> Delivery will be made in thirty (30) days.
> The fee is Four Thousand Dollars ($4,000), payable to UNCO, Inc.

7. Parentheses enclose the name of a state that is inserted into a proper name for identification.

the Kalispell (Mont.) Regional Hospital
the *Sacramento* (Calif.) *Bee*

8. Parentheses may be used to enclose personal asides.

> Claims were made of its proven efficacy (some of us were skeptical).
>
> *or*
>
> Claims were made of its proven efficacy. (Some of us were skeptical.)

9. Parentheses are used to enclose quotations that illustrate or support a statement made in the main text.

> After he had a few brushes with the police, his stepfather had him sent to jail as an incorrigible ("It will do him good").

Other Uses

10. Parentheses enclose unpunctuated numbers or letters indicating individual elements or items in a series within a sentence.

> Sentences can be classified as (1) simple, (2) multiple or compound, and (3) complex.

11. Parentheses indicate alternative terms.

> Please sign and return the enclosed form(s).

12. Parentheses may be used to indicate losses in accounting.

> Operating Profits
> (in millions)
>
> Cosmetics 26.2
> Food products 47.7
> Food services 54.3
> Transportation . . . . (17.7)
> Sporting goods . . . . (11.2)
> _____
> Total 99.3

With Other Punctuation

13. When an independent sentence is enclosed in parentheses, its first word is capitalized and a period (or other closing punctuation) is placed inside the parentheses.

> The discussion was held in the boardroom. (The results are still confidential.)

A parenthetic expression that occurs within a sentence—even if it could stand alone as a separate sentence—does not end with a period but may end with an exclamation point, a question mark, or quotation marks.

> Although several trade organizations opposed the legislation (there were at least three paid lobbyists working on Capitol Hill), the bill passed easily.
> The conference was held in Portland (Me., not Ore.).
> After waiting in line for an hour (why do we do these things?), we finally left.

A parenthetic expression within a sentence does not require capitalization unless it is a quoted sentence.

> He was totally confused ("What can we do?") and refused to see anyone.

14. If a parenthetic expression within a sentence is composed of two independent clauses, a semicolon rather than a period usually separates them. Independent sentences enclosed together in parentheses employ normal sentence capitalization and punctuation.

> We visited several showrooms, looked at the prices (it wasn't a pleasant experience; prices in this area have not gone down), and asked all the questions we could think of.
> We visited several showrooms and looked at the prices. (It wasn't a pleasant experience. Prices in this area have not gone down.)

Entire paragraphs are rarely enclosed in parentheses; instead, paragraphs of incidental material often appear as footnotes or endnotes.

15. No punctuation (other than a period after an abbreviation) is placed immediately before an opening parenthesis within a sentence; if punctuation is required, it follows the final parenthesis.

> I'll get back to you tomorrow (Friday), when I have more details.
> Tickets cost $14 in advance ($12 for seniors); the price at the door is $18.
> The relevant figures are shown below (in millions of dollars):

16. Parentheses sometimes appear within parentheses when no confusion would result; alternatively, the inner parentheses are replaced with brackets.

> Checks must be drawn in U.S. dollars. (*Please note:* We cannot accept checks drawn on Canadian banks for amounts less than four U.S. dollars ($4.00). The same regulation applies to Canadian money orders.)

17. Dashes and parentheses may be used together to set off parenthetic material. (For details, see paragraph 12 on page 184.)

> The orchestra is spirited, and the cast—an expert and enthusiastic crew of Savoyards (some of them British imports)—comes through famously.

Period

Periods almost always serve to mark the end of a sentence or abbreviation.

1. A period ends a sentence or a sentence fragment that is neither a question nor an exclamation.

> From the Format menu, choose Style.
> Robert decided to bring champagne.
> Unlikely. In fact, inconceivable.

Only one period ends a sentence.

> The jellied gasoline was traced to the Trenton-based Quality Products, Inc.
> Miss Toklas states categorically that "This is the best way to cook frogs' legs."

2. A period punctuates some abbreviations. No space follows an internal period within an abbreviation. (For details on punctuating abbreviations, see the section beginning on page 210.)

> Assn.   e.g.
> Ph.D.   p.m.
> Dr.   etc.

3. Periods are used with a person's initials, each followed by a space. (Newspaper style omits the space.) If the initials replace the name, they are unspaced and may also be written without periods.

J. B. S. Haldane
L.B.J.   *or*   LBJ

4. A period follows numerals and letters when they are used without parentheses in outlines and vertical lists.

> I. Objectives
>   A. Economy
>   1. Low initial cost
>   2. Low maintenance cost
>   B. Ease of operation
> Required skills are:
>   1. Shorthand
>   2. Typing
>   3. Transcription

5. A period is placed within quotation marks, even when it did not punctuate the original quoted material. (In British practice, the period goes outside the quotation marks whenever it does not belong to the original quoted material.)

> The founder was known to his employees as "the old man."
> "I said I wanted to fire him," Henry went on, "but she said, 'I don't think you have the contractual privilege to do that.'"

6. When brackets or parentheses enclose an independent sentence, the period is placed inside them. When brackets or parentheses enclose a sentence that is part of a larger sentence, the period for the enclosed sentence is omitted.

> Arturo finally arrived on the 23rd with the terrible news that Katrina had been detained by the police. [This later proved to be false; see letter 255.]
> I took a good look at her (she was standing quite close to me).

Question Mark

The question mark always indicates a question or doubt.

1. A question mark ends a direct question.

> What went wrong?
> "When do they arrive?" she asked.

A question mark follows a period only when the period punctuates an abbreviation. No period follows a question mark.

> Is he even an M.D.?
> "Will you arrive by 10 p.m.?"
> A local professor would be giving a paper with the title "Economic Stagnation or Equilibrium?"

2. Polite requests that are worded as questions usually take periods, because they are not really questions. Conversely, a sentence that is intended as a question but whose word order is that of a statement is punctuated with a question mark.

> Could you please send the necessary forms.
> They flew in yesterday?

3. The question mark ends a question that forms part of a sentence. An indirect question is not followed by a question mark.

> What was her motive? you may be asking.
> I naturally wondered, Will it really work?
> I naturally wondered whether it would really work.
> He asked when the report was due.

4. The question mark punctuates each element of a series of questions that share a single beginning and are neither numbered nor lettered. When the series is numbered or lettered, only one question mark is generally used.

> Can you give us a reasonable forecast? Back up your predictions? Compare them with last year's earnings?
> Can you (1) give us a reasonable forecast, (2) back up your predictions, and (3) compare them with last year's earnings?

5. The question mark indicates uncertainty about a fact or the accuracy of a transcription.

> Homer, Greek epic poet (9th–8th? cent. B.C.)
> He would have it that Farjeon[?] is the onlie man for us.

6. The question mark is placed inside brackets, dashes, parentheses, or quotation marks when it punctuates only the material enclosed by them and not the sentence as a whole. It is placed outside them when it punctuates the entire sentence.

> I took a vacation in 1992 (was it really that long ago?), but I haven't had time for one since.
> What did Andrew mean when he called the project "a fiasco from the start"?
> Williams then asks, "Do you realize the extent of the problem [the housing shortage]?"

Quotation Marks

The following paragraphs describe the use of quotation marks to enclose quoted matter in regular text, and for other, less frequent uses. For the use of quotation marks to enclose titles, see paragraph 70 on page 199.

Basic Uses

1. Quotation marks enclose direct quotations but not indirect quotations or paraphrases.

> Dr. Mee added, "We'd be grateful for anything you could do."
> "We just got the lab results," he crowed, "and the blood types match!"
> "I'm leaving," she whispered. "This meeting could go on forever."
> "Mom, we *tried* that already!" they whined in unison.
> "Ssshh!" she hissed.
> She said she was leaving.
> Algren once said something like, Don't ever play poker with anyone named Doc, and never eat at a diner called Mom's.

2. Quotation marks enclose fragments of quoted matter.

> The agreement makes it clear that he "will be paid only upon receipt of an acceptable manuscript."
> As late as 1754, documents refer to him as "yeoman" and "husbandman."

3. Quotation marks enclose words or phrases borrowed from others, and words of obvious informality introduced into formal writing. Words introduced as specialized terminology are sometimes enclosed in quotation marks but more often italicized.

> Be sure to send a copy of your résumé—or as some folks would say, your "biodata summary."
> They were afraid the patient had "stroked out"—had had a cerebrovascular accident.

referred to as "closed" or "privately held" corporations
but more frequently
referred to as *closed* or *privately held* corporations
New Hampshire's only "green" B&B

4. Quotation marks are sometimes used to enclose words referred to as words. Italics are also frequently used for this purpose.

> changed every "he" to "she"
> *or*
> changed every *he* to *she*

5. Quotation marks may enclose representations of sounds, though these are also frequently italicized.

> If it sounds like "quank, quank" [*or* like *quank, quank*], it may be the green treefrog.

6. Quotation marks often enclose short sentences that fall within longer sentences, especially when the shorter sentence is meant to suggest spoken dialogue. Mottoes and maxims, unspoken or imaginary dialogue, and sentences referred to as sentences may all be treated in this way.

> On the gate was the inscription "Arbeit macht frei" [*or Arbeit macht frei*]—"Work will make you free."
> The fact was, the poor kid didn't know "C'mere" from "Sic 'em."
> In effect, the voters were saying "You blew it, and you don't get another chance."
> Their reaction could only be described as "Kill the messenger."
> She never got used to their "That's the way it goes" attitude.
> *or*
> She never got used to their that's-the-way-it-goes attitude.

Quotation marks are often omitted in sentences of this kind when the structure is clear without them. (For the use of commas in such sentences, see paragraphs 29–30 on page 181.)

> The first rule is, When in doubt, spell it out.

7. Direct questions are enclosed in quotation marks when they represent quoted dialogue, but usually not otherwise.

> She asked, "What went wrong?"
> The question is, What went wrong?
> We couldn't help wondering, Where's the plan?
> *or*
> We couldn't help wondering, "Where's the plan?"

8. Quotation marks enclose translations of foreign or borrowed terms.

> This is followed by the Dies Irae ("Day of Wrath"), a climactic movement in many settings of the Requiem.
> The term comes from the Latin *sesquipedalis,* meaning "a foot and a half long."

They also frequently enclose definitions.

> *Concupiscent* simply means "lustful."
> *or*
> *Concupiscent* simply means lustful.

9. Quotation marks sometimes enclose letters referred to as letters.

> The letter "m" is wider than the letter "i."
> Put an "x" in the right spot.

However, such letters are more frequently italicized (or underlined), or left undifferentiated from the surrounding text where no confusion would result.

> How many *e*'s are in her name?
> a V-shaped blade
> He was happy to get a B in the course.

With Longer Quotations

10. Quotation marks are not used with longer passages of prose or poetry that are indented as separate paragraphs, called *extracts* or *block quotations*. Quoted text is usually set as an extract when it is longer than a sentence or runs to at least four lines, but individual requirements of consistency, clarity, or emphasis may alter these limits. Extracts are set off from the normal text by (1) indenting the passage on the left, and often on the right as well, and (2) usually setting it in smaller type. Extracts are usually preceded by a sentence ending with a colon, and they usually begin with a capitalized first word. The first line of an extract has no added indention; however, if the extract consists of more than one paragraph, the subsequent paragraphs are indented. (For the use of ellipsis points to show omissions within extracts, see the section beginning on page 184.)

> The chapter begins with a general description of memos:
>> The interoffice memorandum or memo is a means of informal communication within a firm or organization. It replaces the salutation, complimentary close, and written signature of the letter with identifying headings.

If the extract continues the flow of an incomplete sentence, no punctuation is required and the extract begins with a lowercase letter.

> They describe the memo as
>> a means of informal communication within a firm or organization. It replaces the salutation, complimentary close, and written signature of the letter with identifying headings.

If the sentence preceding the extract does not refer directly to it, the sentence usually ends with a period, though a colon is also common.

> As of the end of April she believed that the product stood a good chance of success.
>> Unit sales are strong, revenues are better than forecast, shipments are being made on schedule, and inventory levels are stable.

11. When an extract itself includes quoted material, double quotation marks enclose the material.

> The authors recommend the following procedure:
>> The presiding officer will call for the appropriate report from an officer, board member, standing committee, or special committee by saying, "Will the chairperson of the Ways and Means Committee please present the committee's report?"

12. When poetry is set as an extract, the lines are divided exactly as in the original. A spaced slash separates lines of run-in poetry.

> The experience reminded them of Pope's observation:
>> A little learning is a dang'rous thing;
>> Drink deep, or taste not the Pierian spring:
>> There shallow draughts intoxicate the brain,
>> And drinking largely sobers us again.
>
> When Gerard Manley Hopkins wrote that "Nothing is so beautiful as spring— / When weeds, in wheels, shoot long and lovely and lush," he probably had my yard in mind.

13. Quotation marks are not used with epigraphs. However, they are generally used with advertising blurbs.

> The whole of science is nothing more than a refinement of everyday thinking.
> —Albert Einstein
>
> "A brutal irony, a slam-bang humor and a style of writing as balefully direct as a death sentence."—*Time*

With Other Punctuation

14. When a period or comma follows text enclosed in quotation marks, it is placed within the quotation marks, even if the original language quoted was not followed by a period or comma.

> He smiled and said, "I'm happy for you."
> But perhaps Pound's most perfect poem was "The Return."
> The cameras were described as "waterproof," but "moisture-resistant" would have been a better description.

In British usage, the period or comma goes outside the quoted matter whenever the original text did not include the punctuation.

15. When a colon or semicolon follows text enclosed in quotation marks, the colon or semicolon is placed outside the quotation marks.

> But they all chimed in on "O Sole Mio": raw adolescents, stately matrons, decrepit old pensioners, their voices soaring in passion together.
> She spoke of her "little cottage in the country"; she might better have called it a mansion.

16. The dash, question mark, and exclamation point are placed inside quotation marks when they punctuate the quoted matter only, but outside the quotation marks when they punctuate the whole sentence.

> "I can't see how—" he started to say.
> He thought he knew where he was going—he remembered her saying, "Take two lefts, then stay to the right"—but the streets didn't look familiar.
> He asked, "When did they leave?"
> What is the meaning of "the open door"?
> She collapsed in her seat with a stunned "Good God!"
> Save us from his "mercy"!

Single Quotation Marks

17. Single quotation marks replace double quotation marks when the quoted material occurs within quoted material.

> The witness said, "I distinctly heard him say, 'Don't be late,' and then I heard the door close."
> "We'd like to close tonight with that great Harold Arlen wee-hours standard, 'One for My Baby.'"
> This analysis is indebted to Del Banco's "Elizabeth Bishop's 'Insomnia': An Inverted View."

When both single and double quotation marks occur at the end of a sentence, the period falls within both sets of marks.

> The witness said, "I distinctly heard him say, 'Don't be late.'"

British usage often reverses American usage, enclosing quoted material in single quotation marks, and enclosing quotations within quotations in double quotation marks. In British usage, commas and periods following quoted material go inside only those quotation marks that enclose material that originally included the period or comma.

18. A quotation within a quotation within a quotation is usually enclosed in double quotation marks. (Such constructions are usually avoided by rewriting.)

> As the *Post* reported it, "Van Houten's voice can be clearly heard saying, 'She said "You wouldn't dare" and I said "I just did."'"
> *or*
> The *Post* reported that Van Houten's voice was clearly heard saying, "She said 'You wouldn't dare' and I said 'I just did.'"

Semicolon

The semicolon may be used much like the comma, period, or colon, depending on the context. Like a comma, it may separate elements in a series. Like a period or colon, it frequently marks the end of a complete clause, and like a colon it signals that the remainder of the sentence is closely related to the first part. However, in each case the semicolon is normally used in a distinctive way. It serves as a higher-level comma; it connects clauses, as a period does not; and it does not imply any following exemplification, amplification, or description, as a colon generally does.

Between Clauses

1. A semicolon separates related independent clauses joined without a coordinating conjunction.

> Cream the shortening and sugar; add the eggs and beat well.
> The river rose and overflowed its banks; roads became flooded and impassable; freshly plowed fields disappeared from sight.

2. A semicolon often replaces a comma between two clauses joined by a coordinating conjunction if the sentence might otherwise be confusing—for example, because of particularly long clauses or the presence of other commas.

> In a society that seeks to promote social goals, government will play a powerful role; and taxation, once simply a means of raising money, becomes, in addition, a way of furthering those goals.

3. A semicolon joins two clauses when the second includes a conjunctive adverb such as *accordingly, however, indeed,* or *thus,* or a phrase that acts like a conjunctive adverb such as *in that case, as a result,* or *on the other hand.*

> Most people are covered by insurance of some kind; indeed, many don't even see their medical bills.
> It won't be easy to sort out the facts; a decision must be made, however.
> The case could take years to work its way through the courts; as a result, many plaintiffs will accept settlements.

When *so* and *yet* are treated as conjunctive adverbs, they are often preceded by a semicolon and followed by a comma. When treated as coordinating conjunctions, as they usually are, they are generally only preceded by a comma.

> The new recruits were bright, diligent, and even enthusiastic; yet[,] the same problems persisted.
> His grades improved sharply, yet the high honor roll still eluded him.

4. A semicolon may join two statements when the second clause is elliptical, omitting essential words that are supplied by the first. In short sentences, a comma often replaces the semicolon.

> The conference sessions, designed to allow for full discussions, were much too long; the breaks between them, much too short.
> The aged Scotch was haunting, the Asiago piquant.

5. When a series of clauses are separated by semicolons and a coordinating conjunction precedes the final clause, the final semicolon is sometimes replaced with a comma.

> The bars had all closed hours ago; a couple of coffee shops were open but deserted[; *or ,*] and only a few lighted upper-story windows gave evidence of other victims of insomnia.

6. A semicolon is often used before introductory expressions such as *for example, that is,* and *namely,* in place of a colon, comma, dash, or parenthesis. (For more details, see paragraph 17 on page 180.)

> On one point only did everyone agree; namely, too much money had been spent already.
> We were fairly successful on that project; that is, we made our deadlines and met our budget.

In a Series

7. A semicolon is used in place of a comma to separate phrases or items in a series when the phrases or items themselves contain commas. A comma may replace the semicolon before a conjunction that precedes the last item in a series.

> The assets in question include $22 million in land, buildings, and equipment; $34 million in cash, investments, and accounts receivable; and $8 million in inventory.
> The votes against were: Precinct 1, 418; Precinct 2, 332; Precinct 3, 256.
> The debate about the nature of syntactic variation continues to this day (Labov 1991; Dines 1991, 1993; Romaine 1995).
> The Pissarro exhibition will travel to Washington, D.C.; Manchester, N.H.; Portland, Ore., and Oakland, Calif.

When the items in a series are long or are sentences themselves, they are usually separated by semicolons even if they lack internal commas.

> Among the committee's recommendations were the following: more hospital beds in urban areas where there are waiting lines for elective surgery; smaller staff size in half-empty rural hospitals; and review procedures for all major purchases.

With Other Punctuation

8. A semicolon that punctuates the larger sentence is placed outside quotation marks and parentheses.

> I heard the senator on yesterday's "All Things Considered"; his views on Medicare are encouraging.
> She found him urbane and entertaining (if somewhat overbearing); he found her charmingly ingenuous.

Slash

The slash (also known as the *virgule, diagonal, solidus, oblique, and slant*) is most commonly used in place of a short word or a hyphen or en dash, or to separate numbers or text elements. There is generally no space on either side of the slash.

1. A slash represents the words *per* or *to* when used between units of measure or the terms of a ratio.

> 40,000 tons/year
> 29 mi/gal
> price/earnings ratio *or* price–earnings ratio
> cost/benefit analysis *or* cost–benefit analysis
> a 50/50 split *or* a 50-50 split
> 20/20 vision

2. A slash separates alternatives, usually representing the words *or* or *and/or.*

> alumni/ae
> his/her
> the *affect/effect* problem *or* the *affect-effect* problem

3. A slash replaces the word *and* in some compound terms.

> air/sea cruise *or* air-sea cruise
> the May/June issue *or* the May-June issue
> 1996/97 *or* 1996–97
> travel/study trip *or* travel-study trip

4. A slash is sometimes used to replace certain prepositions such as *at, versus,* and *for.*

> U.C./Berkeley *or* U.C.–Berkeley
> parent/child issues *or* parent–child issues
> Vice President/Editorial *or* Vice President, Editorial

5. A slash punctuates a few abbreviations.

> w/o [*for* without]
> c/o [*for* care of]
> I/O [*for* input/output]
> d/b/a [*for* doing business as]
> w/w [*for* wall-to-wall]
> o/a [*for* on or about]

6. The slash separates the elements in a numerical date, and numerators and denominators in fractions.

> 11/29/95
> 2 3/16 inches wide *or* $2\frac{3}{16}$ inches wide
> a 7/8-mile course *or* a $\frac{7}{8}$-mile course

7. The slash separates lines of poetry that are run in with the text around them. A space is usually inserted before and after the slash.

> Alexander Pope once observed: "'Tis with our judgments as our watches, none / Go just alike, yet each believes his own."

2 Capitals and Italics

Words and phrases are capitalized or italicized (underlining takes the place of italics in typed or handwritten text) to indicate that they have a special significance in particular contexts. (Quotation marks sometimes perform the same functions; see paragraphs 69–71 on page 199 and the section on quotation marks beginning on page 188.)

Beginnings

1. The first word of a sentence or sentence fragment is capitalized.

   > They make a desert and call it peace.
   > So many men, so many opinions.
   > O times! O customs!

2. The first word of a sentence contained within parentheses is capitalized. However, a parenthetical sentence occurring inside another sentence is not capitalized unless it is a complete quoted sentence.

   > No one answered the telephone. (They were probably on vacation.)
   > The road remains almost impassable (the locals don't seem to care), and the journey is only for the intrepid.
   > After waiting in line for an hour (what else could we do?), we finally left.
   > In the primary election Evans placed third ("My campaign started late").

3. The first word of a direct quotation is capitalized. However, if the quotation is interrupted in mid-sentence, the second part does not begin with a capital.

   > The department manager explained, "We have no budget for new computers."
   > "We have no budget for new computers," explained the department manager, "but we may next year."

4. When a quotation, whether a sentence fragment or a complete sentence, is syntactically dependent on the sentence in which it occurs, the quotation does not begin with a capital.

   > The brochure promised a tour of "the most exotic ancient sites."
   > His first response was that "there is absolutely no truth to the reports."

5. The first word of a sentence within a sentence that is not a direct quotation is usually capitalized. Examples include mottoes and rules, unspoken or imaginary dialogue, sentences referred to as sentences, and direct questions. (For the use of commas and quotation marks with such sentences, see paragraphs 30–31 on page 182 and paragraphs 6–7 on page 189.)

   > You know the saying "Fools rush in where angels fear to tread."
   > The first rule is, When in doubt, spell it out.

   > One ballot proposition sought to enforce the sentencing rule of "Three strikes and you're out."
   > My question is, When can we go?

6. The first word of a line of poetry is traditionally capitalized. However, in the poetry of this century line beginnings are often lowercased. The poem's original capitalization is always reproduced.

   > Death is the mother of beauty, mystical,
   > Within whose burning bosom we devise
   > Our earthly mothers waiting, sleeplessly.
   > —Wallace Stevens

   >   If tributes cannot
   > be implicit,
   > give me diatribes and the fragrance of iodine,
   > the cork oak acorn grown in Spain . . .
   > —Marianne Moore

7. The first word following a colon is lowercased when it begins a list and usually lowercased when it begins a complete sentence. However, when the sentence introduced is lengthy and distinctly separate from the preceding clause, it is often capitalized.

   > In the early morning they broadcast an urgent call for three necessities: bandages, antibiotics, and blood.
   > The advantage of this system is clear: it's inexpensive.
   > The situation is critical: This company cannot hope to recoup the fourth-quarter losses that were sustained in five operating divisions.

8. If a colon introduces a series of sentences, the first word of each sentence is capitalized.

   > Consider the steps we have taken: A subcommittee has been formed to evaluate past performance. New sources of revenue are being explored. Several candidates have been interviewed for the new post of executive director.

9. The first words of items that form complete sentences in run-in lists are usually capitalized, as are the first words of items in vertical lists. However, numbered phrases within a sentence are lowercased. For details, see the section beginning on page 219.

10. The first word in an outline heading is capitalized.

    > I. Editorial tasks
    > II. Production responsibilities
    >   A. Cost estimates
    >   B. Bids

11. In minutes and legislation, the introductory words *Whereas* and *Resolved* are capitalized (and *Resolved* is also italicized). The word immediately following is also capitalized.

    > Whereas, Substantial benefits . . .
    > *Resolved*, That . . .

12. The first word and certain other words of the salutation of a letter and the first word of a complimentary close are capitalized.

    > Dear Sir or Madam:
    > Ladies and Gentlemen:
    > To whom it may concern:
    > Sincerely yours,
    > Very truly yours,

13. The first word and each subsequent major word following a SUBJECT or TO heading in a memorandum are capitalized.

> SUBJECT: Pension Plans
> TO: All Department Heads and Editors

Proper Nouns and Adjectives

The following paragraphs describe the ways in which a broad range of proper nouns and adjectives are styled. Capitals are always employed, sometimes in conjunction with italics or quotation marks.

Abbreviations

1. Abbreviated forms of proper nouns and adjectives are capitalized, just as the spelled-out forms would be. (For details on capitalizing abbreviations, see the section beginning on page 210.)

> Jan. [*for* January]
> NATO [*for* North Atlantic Treaty Organization]

Abstractions and Personifications

2. Abstract concepts and qualities are sometimes capitalized when the concept or quality is being personified. If the term is simply used in conjunction with other words that allude to human characteristics or qualities, it is not capitalized.

> as Autumn paints each leaf in fiery colors
> the statue of Justice with her scales
> hoping that fate would lend a hand

Academic Degrees

3. The names of academic degrees are capitalized when they follow a person's name. The names of specific degrees used without a person's name are usually lowercased. More general names for degrees are lowercased.

> Lawton I. Byrne, Doctor of Laws
> earned his associate in science degree
>   *or* earned his Associate in Science degree
> completed course work for his doctorate
> working for a master's degree

Abbreviations for academic degrees are always capitalized. (For details, see paragraphs 11–12 on page 212.)

> Susan L. Wycliff, M.S.W.
> received her Ph.D. in clinical psychology

Animals and Plants

4. The common names of animals and plants are not capitalized unless they contain a proper noun, in which case the proper noun is usually capitalized and any name element preceding (but not following) it is often capitalized. When in doubt, consult a dictionary. (For scientific names, see the section on page 198.)

> the springer spaniel   Queen Anne's lace
> Holstein cows   black-eyed Susan
> California condor   mayflower
> a Great Dane   jack-in-the-pulpit

Awards and Prizes

5. Names of awards and prizes are capitalized. Words and phrases that are not actually part of the award's name are lowercased.

> Academy Award
> Emmy
> Rhodes Scholarship
> Rhodes scholar
> Pulitzer Prize–winning novelist
> Nobel Prize winner
> Nobel Prize in medicine
>   *but*
> Nobel Peace Prize

Derivatives of Proper Names

6. Derivatives of proper names are capitalized when used in their primary sense. If the derived term has taken on a specialized meaning, it is often lowercased. Consult a dictionary when in doubt.

> Roman sculpture
> Viennese culture
> Victorian prudery
> a Britishism
> Hodgkins disease
> chinaware
> pasteurized milk
> french fries
>   *but*
> American cheese
> Dutch door

Geographical and Topographical References

7. Terms that identify divisions of the earth's surface and distinct areas, regions, places, or districts are capitalized, as are derivative nouns and adjectives.

> the Pacific Rim   Burgundy
> the Great Lakes   Burgundians
> Arnhem Land   the Highlands
> the Golan Heights   Highland attitudes

8. Popular names of localities are capitalized.

> Little Italy   the Sunbelt
> the Left Bank   the Big Easy

9. Compass points are capitalized when they refer to a geographical region or form part of a street name. They are lowercased when they refer to a simple direction.

> the Southwest   North Pole
> West Coast   north of the Rio Grande
> North Atlantic   born in the East
> East Pleasant Street   driving east on I-90

10. Nouns and adjectives that are derived from compass points and that designate or refer to a specific geographical region are usually capitalized.

> Southern hospitality
> Easterners
> Southwestern recipes
> Northern Europeans

11. Words designating global, national, regional, and local political divisions are capitalized when they are essential elements of specific names. They are usually lowercased when they precede a proper name or are not part of a specific name.

> the Roman Empire
> British Commonwealth nations
> New York State
> the state of New York
> the Third Precinct
> voters in three precincts

In legal documents, such words are often capitalized regardless of position.

> the State of New York

12. Common geographical terms (such as *lake, mountain, river,* or *valley*) are capitalized if they are part of a proper name.

> Lake Tanganyika   Cape of Good Hope
> Great Salt Lake   Massachusetts Bay
> Atlas Mountains   Cayman Islands
> Mount Everest   Yosemite Valley

13. Common geographical terms preceding names are usually capitalized.

> Lakes Huron and Erie
> Mounts McKinley and Whitney

When *the* precedes the common term, the term is lowercased.

> the river Nile

14. Common geographical terms that are not used as part of a single proper name are not capitalized. These include plural terms that follow two or more proper names, and terms that are used descriptively or alone.

> the Indian and South Pacific oceans
> the Mississippi and Missouri rivers
> the Pacific coast of Mexico
> Caribbean islands
> the river delta

15. The names of streets, monuments, parks, landmarks, well-known buildings, and other public places are capitalized. However, common terms that are part of these names (such as *street, park,* or *bridge*) are lowercased when they occur after multiple names or are used alone.

> State Street   Golden Gate Bridge
> the Lincoln Memorial   Empire State Building
> Statue of Liberty   Beverly Hills Hotel
> the Pyramids   back to the hotel
> Grant Park   Main and Oak streets

Well-known shortened forms of place-names are capitalized.

> the Hill [*for* Capitol Hill]
> the Channel [*for* English Channel]
> the Street [*for* Wall Street]

Governmental, Judicial, and Political Bodies

16. Full names of legislative, deliberative, executive, and administrative bodies are capitalized, as are easily recognizable short forms of these names. However, nonspe-

cific noun and adjective references to them are usually lowercased.

> United States Congress
> Congress
> the House
> the Fed
> congressional hearings
> a federal agency

When words such as *department, committee,* or *agency* are used in place of a full name, they are most often capitalized when the department or agency is referring to itself, but otherwise usually lowercased.

> This Department welcomes constructive criticism . . .
> The department claimed to welcome such criticism . . .

When such a word is used in the plural to describe more than one specific body, it is usually capitalized when it precedes the names and lowercased when it follows them.

> involving the Departments of State and Justice
> a briefing from the State and Justice departments

17. Full names of high courts are capitalized. Short forms of such names are often capitalized in legal documents but lowercased otherwise.

> . . . in the U.S. Court of Appeals for the Ninth Circuit
> International Court of Justice
> The court of appeals [*or* Court of Appeals] held . . .
> the Virginia Supreme Court
> a federal district court
> the state supreme court

However, both the full and short names of the U.S. Supreme Court are capitalized.

> the Supreme Court of the United States
> the Supreme Court
> the Court

18. Names of city and county courts are usually lowercased.

> the Springfield municipal court
> small-claims court
> the county court
> juvenile court

19. The noun *court,* when it applies to a specific judge or presiding officer, is capitalized in legal documents.

> It is the opinion of this Court that . . .
> The Court found that . . .

20. The terms *federal* and *national* are capitalized only when they are essential elements of a name or title. (*Federal* is also capitalized when it refers to a historical architectural style, to members of the original Federalist party, or to adherents of the Union in the Civil War.)

> Federal Election Commission
> a federal commission
> Federalist principles
> National Security Council
> national security

21. The word *administration* is sometimes capitalized when it refers to the administration of a specific U.S. president, but is more commonly lowercased. Otherwise, it is

lowercased except when it is a part of the official name of a government agency.

> the Reagan administration *or* the Reagan Administration
> the administration *or* the Administration
> from one administration to the next
> the Social Security Administration

22. Names of political organizations and their adherents are capitalized, but the word *party* is often lowercased.

> the Democratic National Committee
> the Republican platform
> the Christian Coalition
> most Republicans
> the Democratic party *or* the Democratic Party
> party politics

Names of less-distinct political groupings are usually lowercased, as are their derivative forms.

> the right wing
> the liberals
> the conservative agenda
> *but often*
> the Left
> the Right

23. Terms describing political and economic philosophies are usually lowercased; if derived from proper names, they are usually capitalized. Consult a dictionary for doubtful cases.

> authoritarianism   nationalism
> democracy   social Darwinist
> fascism *or* Fascism   Marxist

Historical Periods and Events

24. The names of some historical and cultural periods and movements are capitalized. When in doubt, consult a dictionary or encyclopedia.

> Bronze Age   Third Reich
> Middle Ages   the atomic age
> Prohibition   Victorian era
> the Renaissance   age of Pericles
> New Deal   the baby boom
> Fifth Republic

25. Century and decade designations are normally lowercased.

> the nineteenth century
> the twenties
> the turn of the century
> a 12th-century manuscript
> *but*
> Gay Nineties
> Roaring Twenties

26. The names of conferences, councils, expositions, and specific sporting, cultural, and historical events are capitalized.

> Fourth World Conference on Women
> Council of Trent
> New York World's Fair
> Super Bowl
> Cannes Film Festival

> Miss America Contest
> San Francisco Earthquake
> Johnstown Flood

27. Full names of specific treaties, laws, and acts are capitalized.

> Treaty of Versailles
> the Nineteenth Amendment
> the Bill of Rights
> Clean Air Act of 1990
> *but*
> gun-control laws
> an equal-rights amendment

28. The words *war, revolution,* and *battle* are capitalized when they are part of a full name. Official names of actions are capitalized. Descriptive terms such as *assault* and *siege* are usually lowercased even when used in conjunction with a place-name.

> War of the Roses
> World War II
> the French Revolution
> Battle of Gettysburg
> Operation Desert Storm
> between the two world wars
> the American and French revolutions
> the siege of Leningrad
> Washington's winter campaign

Hyphenated Compounds

29. The second (third, etc.) element of a hyphenated compound is generally capitalized only if it is itself a proper noun or adjective.

> Arab-Israeli negotiations
> East-West trade agreements
> French-speaking peoples
> Forty-second street
> twentieth-century architecture

30. When joined to a proper noun or adjective, common prefixes (such as *pre-* or *anti-*) are usually lowercased, but geographical and ethnic combining forms (such as *Anglo-* or *Sino-*) are capitalized. (For details, see paragraphs 45 and 52 on pages 208–209.)

> anti-Soviet forces
> Sino-Japanese relations

Legal Material

31. The names of the plaintiff and defendant in legal case titles are italicized. The *v.* (for *versus*) may be roman or italic. Cases that do not involve two opposing parties are also italicized. When the party involved rather than the case itself is being discussed, the reference is not italicized. In running text, a case name involving two opposing parties may be shortened.

> *Jones* v. *Massachusetts*
> *Smith et al. v. Jones*
> *In re Jones*
> She covered the *Jones* trial for the newspaper.
> The judge based his ruling on a precedent set in the *Jones* decision.

Medical Terms

32. Proper names that are elements in terms designating diseases, symptoms, syndromes, and tests are capitalized. Common nouns are lowercased; however, abbreviations of such nouns are all-capitalized.

Alzheimer's disease   black lung disease
Tourette's syndrome   mumps
Schick test   AIDS

33. Scientific names of disease-causing organisms follow the rules discussed in paragraph 58 on page 198. The names of diseases or conditions derived from scientific names of organisms are lowercased and not italicized.

a neurotoxin produced by *Clostridium botulinum*
nearly died of botulism

34. Generic names of drugs are lowercased; trade names should be capitalized.

retinoic acid
Retin-A

Military Terms

35. The full titles of branches of the U.S. armed forces are capitalized, as are standard short forms.

U.S. Marine Corps   the Marines
the Marine Corps   the Corps

Those of other countries are capitalized when the precise title is used; otherwise they are usually lowercased. The plurals of *army, navy, air force,* and *coast guard* are lowercased.

Royal Air Force
the Guatemalan army
the tiny armies of both countries

The modifiers *army, navy, marine, coast guard,* and *air force* are usually lowercased; *naval* is lowercased unless it is part of an official name. The noun *marine* is usually lowercased.

an army helicopter   the first naval engagement
a career navy man   the Naval Reserves
the marine barracks   a former marine

Full or shortened names of specific units of a branch are usually capitalized.

U.S. Army Corps of Engineers
the Third Army
the Eighty-second [*or* 82nd] Airborne
the U.S. Special Forces, or Green Berets
. . . of the First Battalion. The battalion commander . . .

36. Military ranks are capitalized when they precede the names of their holders, or replace the name in direct address. Otherwise they are lowercased.

Major General Smedley Butler
Please be seated, Admiral.
The major arrived precisely on time.

37. The names of decorations, citations, and medals are capitalized.

Medal of Honor
Purple Heart

Numerical Designations

38. A noun introducing a reference number is usually capitalized. The abbreviation *No.* is usually omitted.

Order 704   Form 2E
Flight 409   Policy 118-4-Y

39. Nouns used with numbers or letters to refer to major reference entities or actual captions in books or periodicals are usually capitalized. Nouns that designate minor reference entities and do not appear in captions are lowercased.

Book II   Figure D.4
Volume 5   page 101
Chapter 2   line 8
Table 3   paragraph 6.1
Example 16.2   question 21

Organizations

40. Names of organizations, corporations, and institutions, and terms derived from those names to designate their members, are capitalized.

the League of Women Voters
General Motors Corporation
the Smithsonian Institution
the University of the South
the Rotary Club
all Rotarians

Common nouns used descriptively or occurring after the names of two or more organizations are lowercased.

enrolled at the university
Yale and Harvard universities
    but
the Universities of Utah and Nevada

41. Words such as *agency, department, division, group,* or *office* that designate corporate and organizational units are capitalized only when used as part of a specific proper name. (For governmental units, see paragraph 16 on page 194.)

head of the Sales Division of K2 Outfitters
a memo to the sales divisions of both companies

42. Nicknames for organizations are capitalized.

the Big Six accounting firms
referred to IBM as Big Blue
trading on the Big Board

People

43. The names and initials of persons are capitalized. If a name is hyphenated, both elements are capitalized. Particles forming the initial elements of surnames (such as *de, della, der, du, l', la, le, ten, ter, van,* and *von*) may or may not be capitalized, depending on the practice of the family or individual. However, the particle is always capitalized at the beginning of a sentence. The prefixes *Mac, Mc,* and *O'* are always capitalized.

Cecil Day-Lewis
Agnes de Mille
Cecil B. DeMille
Walter de la Mare

Mark deW. Howe
Martin Van Buren
. . . of van Gogh's life. Van Gogh's technique is . . .

44. A nickname or epithet that either is added to or replaces the name of a person or thing is capitalized.

Babe Ruth   the Sun King
Stonewall Jackson   Deep Throat
Billy the Kid   Big Mama Thornton

A nickname or epithet placed between a person's first and last name is enclosed in quotation marks or parentheses or both. If it precedes the first name, it is sometimes enclosed in quotation marks but more often not.

Charlie "Bird" [*or* ("Bird") *or* (Bird)] Parker
Mother Maybelle Carter

45. Words of family relationship preceding or used in place of a person's name are capitalized; otherwise, they are lowercased.

Uncle Fred   her uncle's book
Mother's birthday   my mother's legacy

46. Words designating languages, nationalities, peoples, races, religious groups, and tribes are capitalized. Designations based on color are usually lowercased.

Spanish   Muslims
Spaniards   Assiniboin
Chinese   both blacks and whites
Asians   white, black, and Hispanic
                         jurors

47. Corporate, professional, and governmental titles are capitalized when they immediately precede a person's name, unless the name is being used as an appositive.

President John Tyler
Professor Wendy Doniger of the University of Chicago
Senator William Fulbright of Arkansas
Arkansas's late former senator, William Fulbright

48. When corporate or governmental titles are used as part of a descriptive phrase to identify a person rather than as part of the name itself, the title is lowercased.

Marcia Ramirez, president of Logex Corp.
the president of Logex Corp., Marcia Ramirez
    but
Logex Corp.'s prospects for the coming year were outlined by President Marcia Ramirez.

49. High governmental titles may be capitalized when used in place of individuals' names. In minutes and official records of proceedings, corporate or organizational titles are capitalized when used in place of individuals' names.

The Secretary of State objected.
The Judge will respond to questions in her chambers.
The Treasurer then stated his misgivings about the project.
    but
The report reached the senator's desk yesterday.
The judge's rulings were widely criticized.
The co-op's treasurer, it turned out, had twice been convicted of embezzlement.

50. The word *president* may be capitalized whenever it refers to the U.S. presidency, but more commonly is capitalized only when it refers to a specific U.S. president.

It is the duty of the president [*or* President] to submit a budget to Congress.
The President's budget, due out on Wednesday, is being eagerly awaited.

51. Titles are capitalized when they are used in direct address.

Is it very contagious, Doctor?
You may call your next witness, Counselor.

Religious Terms

52. Words designating the supreme being are capitalized. Plural forms such as *gods, goddesses,* and *deities* are not.

Allah   the Almighty
Brahma   the Trinity
Jehovah   in the eyes of God
Yahweh   the angry gods

53. Personal pronouns referring to the supreme being are often capitalized, especially in religious writing. Relative pronouns (such as *who, whom,* and *whose*) usually are not.

God gave His [*or* his] Son
Allah, whose Prophet, Muhammad . . .

54. Traditional designations of apostles, prophets, and saints are capitalized.

the Madonna   the Twelve
the Prophet   St. John of the Cross
Moses the Lawgiver   John the Baptist

55. Names of religions, denominations, creeds and confessions, and religious orders are capitalized, as are adjectives and nouns derived from these names.

Judaism   Eastern Orthodox
Church of England   Islamic
Apostles' Creed   Jesuit teachers
Society of Jesus   a Buddhist

Full names of specific places of worship are capitalized, but terms such as *church, synagogue,* and *mosque* are lowercased when used alone. The word *church* is sometimes capitalized when it refers to the worldwide Catholic Church.

Hunt Memorial Church
the local Baptist church
Beth Israel Synagogue
services at the synagogue

56. Names of the Bible and other sacred works, their books and parts, and versions or editions of them are capitalized but not italicized. Adjectives derived from the names of sacred books are capitalized, except for the words *biblical* and *scriptural.*

Bible   biblical
the Scriptures   Talmud
Revised Standard Version   Talmudic
Old Testament   Koran *or* Qur'an
Book of Revelation   Koranic *or* Qur'anic

57. The names of prayers and well-known passages of the Bible are capitalized.

the Ave Maria	Ten Commandments
Lord's Prayer	Sermon on the Mount
the Our Father	the Beatitudes

Scientific Terms

58. Genus names in biological binomial nomenclature are capitalized; species names are lowercased, even when derived from a proper name. Both names are italicized.

> Both the wolf and the domestic dog are included in the genus *Canis.*
>
> The California condor *(Gymnogyps californianus)* is facing extinction.

The names of races, varieties, or subspecies are lowercased and italicized.

> *Hyla versicolor chrysoscelis*
> *Otis asio naevius*

59. The New Latin names of classes, families, and all groups above the genus level in zoology and botany are capitalized but not italicized. Their derivative nouns and adjectives are lowercased.

Gastropoda	gastropod
Thallophyta	thallophytic

60. The names, both scientific and informal, of planets and their satellites, stars, constellations, and other specific celestial objects are capitalized. However, except in technical writing, the words *sun, earth,* and *moon* are usually lowercased unless they occur with other astronomical names. A generic term that follows the name of a celestial object is usually lowercased.

Jupiter	Mars, Venus, and Earth
the North Star	life on earth
Andromeda	a voyage to the moon
Ursa Major	Halley's comet
the Little Dipper	

Names of meteorological phenomena are lowercased.

> aurora australis
> northern lights
> parhelic circle

61. Terms that identify geological eons, eras, periods, systems, epochs, and strata are capitalized. The generic terms that follow them are lowercased.

> Mesozoic era
> Upper Cretaceous epoch
> Quaternary period
> in the Middle Ordovician
> the Age of Reptiles

62. Proper names that are elements of the names of scientific laws, theorems, and principles are capitalized, but the common nouns *law, theorem, theory,* and the like are lowercased. In the names of popular or fanciful theories or observations, such words are usually capitalized as well.

> Mendel's law
> the Pythagorean theorem
> Occam's razor

Einstein's theory of relativity
Murphy's Law
the Peter Principle

63. The names of computer services and databases are capitalized. Some names of computer languages are written with an initial capital letter, some with all letters capitalized, and some commonly both ways. When in doubt, consult a dictionary.

> America Online
> World Wide Web
> CompuServe
> Microsoft Word
> Pascal *or* PASCAL
> BASIC
> Internet *or* internet

Time Periods and Dates

64. The names of the days of the week, months of the year, and holidays and holy days are capitalized. Names of the seasons are lowercased.

Tuesday	Ramadan
June	Holy Week
Yom Kippur	last winter's storm
Veterans Day	

Titles of Works

65. Words in titles of books, magazines, newspapers, plays, movies, long poems, and works of art such as paintings and sculpture are capitalized except for internal articles, coordinating conjunctions, prepositions, and the *to* of infinitives. Prepositions of four or more letters are often capitalized. The entire title is italicized. For sacred works, see paragraph 56 on page 197.

> *Far from* [or *From*] *the Madding Crowd*
> Wolfe's *Of Time and the River*
> *Publishers Weekly*
> *USA Today*
> the original play *A Streetcar Named Desire*
> *All about* [or *About*] *Eve,* with Bette Davis
> Monet's *Water-Lily Pool,* in the Louvre
> Rodin's *Thinker*

The elements of hyphenated compounds in titles are usually capitalized, but articles, coordinating conjunctions, and prepositions are lowercased.

> *The Post-Physician Era: Medicine in the Twenty-First Century*
> *Politics in Early Seventeenth-Century England*

66. The first word following a colon in a title is capitalized.

> *Jane Austen: A Literary Life*

67. An initial article that is part of a title is capitalized and italicized. It is often omitted if it would be awkward in context.

> *The Oxford English Dictionary*
> the 20-volume *Oxford English Dictionary*

68. In the titles of newspapers, the city or local name is usually italicized, but the preceding *the* is usually not italicized or capitalized.

> reported in the *New York Times*
> last Thursday's *Atlanta Constitution*

69. Many periodicals, especially newspapers, do not use italics for titles, but instead either simply capitalize the important words of the title or, more commonly, capitalize the words and enclose the title in quotation marks.

> the NB. column in the Times Literary Supplement
> The Nobel committee singled out Walcott's book-length epic "Omeros."

70. The titles of articles in periodicals, short poems, short stories, essays, lectures, dissertations, chapters of books, radio and television programs, and novellas published in a collection are capitalized and enclosed in quotation marks. The capitalization of articles, conjunctions, and prepositions follows the rules explained in paragraph 65 above.

> an article on Rwanda, "After the Genocide," in the *New Yorker*
> Robert Frost's "Death of the Hired Man"
> O'Connor's story "Good Country People"
> "The Literature of Exhaustion," John Barth's seminal essay
> last Friday's lecture, "Labor's Task: A View for the Nineties"
> *The Jungle Book*'s ninth chapter is the well-known "Rikki-tikki-tavi."
> listening to "All Things Considered"
> watched "Good Morning America"

71. The titles of long musical compositions are generally capitalized and italicized; the titles of songs and other short compositions are capitalized and enclosed in quotation marks, as are the popular names of longer works. The titles of compositions identified primarily by their musical forms (such as *quartet, sonata,* or *mass*) are capitalized only, as are movements identified by their tempo markings.

> Mozart's *The Magic Flute*
> Frank Loesser's *Guys and Dolls*
> "The Lady Is a Tramp"
> Beethoven's "Für Elise"
> the Piano Sonata in C-sharp minor, Op. 27, No. 2, or "Moonlight" Sonata
> Symphony No. 104 in D major
> Brahms's Violin Concerto in D
> the Adagietto movement from Mahler's Fifth Symphony

72. Common titles of book sections (such as *preface, introduction,* or *index*) are usually capitalized when they refer to a section of the same book in which the reference is made. Otherwise, they are usually lowercased. (For numbered sections of books, see paragraph 39 on page 196.)

> See the Appendix for further information.
> In the introduction to her book, the author explains her goals.

Trademarks

73. Registered trademarks, service marks, collective marks, and brand names are capitalized. They do not normally require any further acknowledgment of their special status.

Frisbee	Jacuzzi	Levi's
Coke	Kleenex	Vaseline
College Board	Velcro	Dumpster
Realtor	Xerox	Scotch tape
Walkman	Band-Aid	Teflon

Transportation

74. The names of individual ships, submarines, airplanes, satellites, and space vehicles are capitalized and italicized. The designations *U.S.S., S.S., M.V.,* and *H.M.S.* are not italicized.

> *Challenger*
> *Enola Gay*
> H.M.S. *Bounty*

Other Styling Conventions

1. Foreign words and phrases that have not been fully adopted into English are italicized. In general, any word that appears in the main section of *Merriam-Webster's Collegiate Dictionary* does not need to be italicized.

> These accomplishments will serve as a monument, *aere perennius,* to the group's skill and dedication.
> "The cooking here is *wunderbar!*"
> The prix fixe lunch was $20.
> The committee meets on an ad hoc basis.

A complete foreign-language sentence (such as a motto) can also be italicized. However, long sentences are usually treated as quotations; that is, they are set in roman type and enclosed in quotation marks. (For details, see paragraph 6 on page 189.)

> The inscription *Honi soit qui mal y pense* encircles the seal.

2. In nonfiction writing, unfamiliar words or words that have a specialized meaning are set in italics on their first appearance, especially when accompanied by a short definition. Once these words have been introduced and defined, they are not italicized in subsequent references.

> *Vitiligo* is a condition in which skin pigment cells stop making pigment. Vitiligo usually affects . . .
> Another method is the *direct-to-consumer* transaction, in which the publisher markets directly to the individual by mail or door-to-door.

3. Italics are often used to indicate words referred to as words. However, if the word was actually spoken, it is usually enclosed in quotation marks instead.

> Purists still insist that *data* is a plural noun.
> *Only* can also be an adverb, as in "I *only* tried to help."
> We heard his warning, but we weren't sure what "repercussions" meant in that context.

4. Italics are often used for letters referred to as letters, particularly when they are shown in lowercase.

> You should dot your *i*'s and cross your *t*'s.

If the letter is being used to refer to its sound and not its printed form, slashes or brackets are used instead of italics in technical contexts.

> The pure /p/ sound is rarely heard in the mountain dialect.

A letter used to indicate a shape is capitalized but not italicized. Such letters are often set in sans-serif type.

> an A-frame house
> the I beam
> Churchill's famous V sign
> forming a giant X

5. Italics are often used to show numerals referred to as numerals. However, if there is no chance of confusion, they are usually not italicized.

> The first *2* and the last *1* are barely legible.
> Anyone whose ticket number ends in 4 or 6 will win a door prize.

6. Italics are used to emphasize or draw attention to words in a sentence.

> Students must notify the dean's office *in writing* of any added or dropped courses.
> It was not *the* model for the project, but merely *a* model.

7. Italics are used to indicate a word created to suggest a sound.

> Its call is a harsh, drawn-out *kreee-awww.*

8. Individual letters are sometimes italicized when used for lists within sentences or for identifying elements in an illustration.

> providing information about *(a)* typing, *(b)* transcribing, *(c)* formatting, and *(d)* graphics
> located at point A on the diagram

9. Commas, colons, and semicolons that follow italicized words are usually italicized.

> the Rabbit tetralogy (*Rabbit Run, Rabbit Redux, Rabbit is Rich,* and *Rabbit at Rest*)*; Bech: A Book; S;* and others

However, question marks, exclamation points, quotation marks, and apostrophes are not italicized unless they are part of an italicized title.

> Did you see the latest issue of *Newsweek*?
> Despite the greater success of *Oklahoma!* and *South Pacific,* Rodgers was fondest of *Carousel.*
> "Over Christmas vacation he finished *War and Peace.*"
> Students always mistake the old script *s*'s for *f*'s.

Parentheses and brackets may be italicized if most of the words they enclose are also italicized, or if both the first and last words are italicized.

> *(see also Limited Partnership)*
> [German, *wunderbar*]
> *(and* is replaced throughout by *&)*

10. Full capitalization is occasionally used for emphasis or to indicate that a speaker is talking very loudly. It is avoided in formal writing, where italics are far more often used for emphasis.

> Term papers received after Friday, May 18, WILL BE RETURNED UNREAD.
> Scalpers mingled in the noisy crowd yelling "SIXTY DOLLARS!"

11. The text of signs, labels, and inscriptions may be reproduced in various ways.

> a poster reading SPECIAL THRILLS COMING SOON
> a gate bearing the infamous motto "Arbeit macht frei"
> a Do Not Disturb sign
> a barn with an old CHEW MAIL POUCH ad on the side
> the stop sign

12. *Small capitals,* identical to large capitals but usually about the height of a lowercase *x,* are commonly used for era designations and computer commands. They may also be used for cross-references, for headings in constitutions and bylaws, and for speakers in a dramatic dialogue.

> The dwellings date from A.D. 200 or earlier.
> Press ALT+CTRL+PLUS SIGN on the numeric keyboard.
> (See LETTERS AS LETTERS, page 162.)
> SECTION IV. The authority for parliamentary procedure in meetings of the Board . . .
> LADY WISHFORT. O dear, has my Nephew made his Addresses to Millamant? I order'd him.
> FOIBLE. Sir Wilfull is set in to drinking, Madam, in the Parlour.

13. *Underlining* indicates italics in typed material. It is almost never seen in typeset text.

14. *Boldface* type has traditionally been used primarily for headings and captions. It is sometimes also used in place of italics for terminology introduced in the text, especially for terms that are accompanied by definitions; for cross-references; for headwords in listings such as glossaries, gazetteers, and bibliographies; and for page references in indexes that locate a specific kind of material, such as illustrations, tables, or the main discussions of a given topic. (In mathematical texts, arrays, tensors, vectors, and matrix notation are standardly set bold as well.)

> **Application Forms and Tests**   Many offices require applicants to fill out an employment form. Bring a copy . . .
> **Figure 4.2: The Electromagnetic Spectrum**
> The two axes intersect at a point called the **origin.**
> See **Medical Records**, page 123.
> **antecedent:** the noun to which a pronoun refers
> **appositive:** a word, phrase, or clause that is equivalent to a preceding noun
> Records, medical, **123–37**, 178, 243
> Referrals, **38–40**, 139

Punctuation that follows boldface type is set bold when it is part of a heading or heading-like text; otherwise it is generally set roman.

> **Table 9:** Metric Conversion
> **Warning:** This and similar medications . . .
> Excellent fourth-quarter earnings were reported by the pharmaceutical giants **Abbott Laboratories, Burroughs Wellcome,** and **Merck.**

3 Plurals, Possessives, and Compounds

This chapter describes the ways in which plurals, possessives, and compounds are most commonly formed.

In regard to plurals and compounds, consulting a dictionary will solve many of the problems discussed in this chapter. A good college dictionary, such as *Merriam-Webster's Collegiate Dictionary,* will provide plural forms for any common word, as well as a large number of permanent compounds. Any dictionary much smaller than the *Collegiate* will often be more frustrating in what it fails to show than helpful in what it shows.

Plurals

The basic rules for writing plurals of English words, stated in paragraph 1, apply in the vast majority of cases. The succeeding paragraphs treat the categories of words whose plurals are most apt to raise questions.

Most good dictionaries give thorough coverage to irregular and variant plurals, and many of the rules provided here are reflected in the dictionary entries.

The symbol → is used here to link the singular and plural forms.

1. The plurals of most English words are formed by adding *-s* to the singular. If the noun ends in *-s, -x, -z, -ch,* or *-sh,* so that an extra syllable must be added in order to pronounce the plural, *-es* is added. If the noun ends in a *-y* preceded by a consonant, the *-y* is changed to *-i* and *-es* is added.

   voter → voters
   anticlimax → anticlimaxes
   blitz → blitzes
   blowtorch → blowtorches
   calabash → calabashes
   allegory → allegories

Abbreviations

2. The plurals of abbreviations are commonly formed by adding *-s* or *-'s;* however, there are some significant exceptions. (For details, see paragraphs 1–5 on page 211.)

   yr. → yrs.   M.B.A. → M.B.A.'s
   TV → TVs   p. → pp.

Animals

3. The names of many fishes, birds, and mammals have both a plural formed with a suffix and one that is identical with the singular. Some have only one or the other.

   bass → bass   *or*   basses
   partridge → partridge   *or*   partridges
   sable → sables   *or*   sable
   lion → lions
   sheep → sheep

Many of the animals that have both plural forms are ones that are hunted, fished, or trapped; those who hunt, fish for, and trap them are most likely to use the unchanged form. The *-s* form is often used to emphasize diversity of kinds.

   caught three bass
     but
   basses of the Atlantic Ocean
   a place where antelope feed
     but
   antelopes of Africa and southwest Asia

Compounds and Phrases

4. Most compounds made up of two nouns—whether they appear as one word, two words, or a hyphenated word—form their plurals by pluralizing the final element only.

   courthouse → courthouses
   judge advocate → judge advocates
   player-manager → player-managers

5. The plural form of a compound consisting of an *-er* noun and an adverb is made by pluralizing the noun element only.

   runner-up → runners-up
   onlooker → onlookers
   diner-out → diners-out
   passerby → passersby

6. Nouns made up of words that are not nouns form their plurals on the last element.

   show-off → show-offs
   pushover → pushovers
   tie-in → tie-ins
   lineup → lineups

7. Plurals of compounds that consist of two nouns separated by a preposition are normally formed by pluralizing the first noun.

   sister-in-law → sisters-in-law
   attorney-at-law → attorneys-at-law
   power of attorney → powers of attorney
   chief of staff → chiefs of staff
   grant-in-aid → grants-in-aid

8. Compounds that consist of two nouns separated by a preposition and a modifier form their plurals in various ways.

   snake in the grass → snakes in the grass
   justice of the peace → justices of the peace
   jack-in-the-box → jack-in-the-boxes   *or*   jacks-in-the-box
   will-o'-the wisp → will-o'-the-wisps

9. Compounds consisting of a noun followed by an adjective are usually pluralized by adding *-s* to the noun. If the adjective tends to be understood as a noun, the compound may have more than one plural form.

   attorney general → attorneys general   *or*   attorney generals
   sergeant major → sergeants major   *or*   sergeant majors
   poet laureate → poets laureate   *or*   poet laureates
   heir apparent → heirs apparent
   knight-errant → knights-errant

Foreign Words and Phrases

10. Many nouns of foreign origin retain the foreign plural. However, most also have a regular English plural.

> alumnus → alumni
> genus → genera
> crisis → crises
> criterion → criteria
> appendix → appendixes *or* appendices
> concerto → concerti *or* concertos
> symposium → symposia *or* symposiums

11. Phrases of foreign origin may have a foreign plural, an English plural, or both.

> pièces de résistance → pièces de résistance
> hors d'oeuvre → hors d'oeuvres
> beau monde → beau mondes *or* beaux mondes

Irregular Plurals

12. A few English nouns form their plurals by changing one or more of their vowels, or by adding *-en* or *-ren*.

> foot → feet   woman → women
> goose → geese   tooth → teeth
> louse → lice   ox → oxen
> man → men   child → children
> mouse → mice

13. Some nouns do not change form in the plural. (See also paragraph 3 above.)

> series → series   corps → corps
> politics → politics   species → species

14. Some nouns ending in *-f, -fe,* and *-ff* have plurals that end in *-ves.* Some of these also have regularly formed plurals.

> elf → elves
> loaf → loaves
> scarf → scarves *or* scarfs
> wife → wives
> staff → staffs *or* staves

Italic Elements

15. Italicized words, phrases, abbreviations, and letters are usually pluralized by adding *-s* or *-'s* in roman type. (See also paragraphs 16, 21, and 26 below.)

> three *Fortune*s missing from the stack
> a couple of *Gravity's Rainbow*s in stock
> used too many *etc.*'s in the report
> a row of *x*'s

Letters

16. The plurals of letters are usually formed by adding *-'s,* although capital letters are often pluralized by adding *-s* alone.

> p's and q's
> V's of migrating geese *or* Vs of migrating geese
> dot your *i*'s
> straight As *or* straight A's

Numbers

17. Numerals are pluralized by adding *-s* or, less commonly, *-'s.*

> two par 5s *or* two par 5's
> 1990s *or* 1990's
> in the 80s *or* in the 80's *or* in the '80s
> the mid-$20,000s *or* the mid-$20,000's

18. Written-out numbers are pluralized by adding *-s.*

> all the fours and eights
> scored three tens

Proper Nouns

19. The plurals of proper nouns are usually formed with *-s* or *-es.*

> Clarence → Clarences
> Jones → Joneses
> Fernandez → Fernandezes

20. Plurals of proper nouns ending in *-y* usually retain the *-y* and add *-s.*

> Sunday → Sundays
> Timothy → Timothys
> Camry → Camrys

Words ending in *-y* that were originally proper nouns are usually pluralized by changing *-y* to *-i* and adding *-es,* but a few retain the *-y.*

> bobby → bobbies
> johnny → johnnies
> Tommy → Tommies
> Bloody Mary → Bloody Marys

Quoted Elements

21. The plural of words in quotation marks are formed by adding *-s* or *-'s* within the quotation marks, or *-s* outside the quotation marks.

> too many "probably's" [*or* "probablys"] in the statement
> one "you" among millions of "you"s
> a record number of "I can't recall"s

Symbols

22. When symbols are referred to as physical characters, the plural is formed by adding either *-s* or *-'s.*

> printed three *s
> used &'s instead of *and*'s
> his π's are hard to read

Words Ending in *-ay, -ey,* and *-oy*

23. Words that end in *-ay, -ey,* or *-oy,* unlike other words ending in *-y,* are pluralized by simply adding *-s.*

> castaways
> donkeys
> envoys

Words Ending in *-ful*

24. Any noun ending in *-ful* can be pluralized by adding *-s,* but most also have an alternative plural with *-s* preceding the suffix.

> handful → handfuls
> teaspoonful → teaspoonfuls
> armful → armfuls *or* armsful
> bucketful → bucketfuls *or* bucketsful

Words Ending in *-o*

25. Most words ending in *-o* are normally pluralized by adding *-s*. However, some words ending in *-o* preceded by a consonant take *-es* plurals.

> solo → solos
> photo → photos
> tomato → tomatoes
> potato → potatoes
> hobo → hoboes
> hero → heroes
> cargo → cargoes *or* cargos
> proviso → provisos *or* provisoes
> halo → haloes *or* halos
> echo → echoes
> motto → mottoes

Words Used as Words

26. Words referred to as words and italicized usually form their plurals by adding *-'s* in roman type. (See also paragraph 21 above.)

> five *and*'s in one sentence
> all those *wherefore*'s and *howsoever*'s

When a word referred to as a word has become part of a fixed phrase, the plural is usually formed by adding *-s* without the apostrophe.

> oohs and aahs
> dos and don'ts *or* do's and don'ts

Possessives

Common Nouns

1. The possessive of singular and plural common nouns that do not end in an *s* or *z* sound is formed by adding *-'s* to the end of the word.

> the child's skates
> women's voices
> the cat's dish
> this patois's range
> people's opinions
> the criteria's common theme

2. The possessive of singular nouns ending in an *s* or *z* sound is usually formed by adding *-'s*. A less common alternative is to add *-'s* only when it is easily pronounced; if it would create a word that is difficult to pronounce, only an apostrophe is added.

> the witness's testimony
> the disease's course
> the race's sponsors
> the prize's recipient
> rickets's symptoms *or* rickets' symptoms

A multisyllabic singular noun that ends in an *s* or *z* sound drops the *-s* if it is followed by a word beginning with an *s* or *z* sound.

> for appearance' sake
> for goodness' sake

3. The possessive of plural nouns ending in an *s* or *z* sound is formed by adding only an apostrophe. However, the possessive of one-syllable irregular plurals is usually formed by adding *-'s*.

> dogs' leashes   buyers' guarantees
> birds' migrations   lice's lifespans

Proper Names

4. The possessives of proper names are generally formed in the same way as those of common nouns. The possessive of singular proper names is formed by adding *-'s*.

> Jane's rules of behavior
> three books of Carla's
> Tom White's presentation
> Paris's cafes

The possessive of plural proper names, and of some singular proper names ending in an *s* or *z* sound, is made by adding just an apostrophe.

> the Stevenses' reception
> the Browns' driveway
> Massachusetts' capital
> New Orleans' annual festival
> the United States' trade deficit
> Protosystems' president

5. The possessive of singular proper names ending in an *s* or *z* sound may be formed by adding either *-'s* or just an apostrophe. Adding *-'s* to all such names, without regard for the pronunciation of the resulting word, is more common than adding just the apostrophe. (For exceptions see paragraph 6 below.)

> Jones's car *or* Jones' car
> Bliss's statue *or* Bliss' statue
> Dickens's novels *or* Dickens' novels

6. The possessive form of classical and biblical names of two or more syllables ending in *-s* or *-es* is usually made by adding just an apostrophe. If the name has only one syllable, the possessive form is made by adding *-'s*.

> Socrates' students   Elias' prophecy
> Claudius' reign   Zeus's warnings
> Ramses' kingdom   Cis's sons

The possessives of the names *Jesus* and *Moses* are always formed with just an apostrophe.

> Jesus' disciples
> Moses' law

7. The possessive of names ending in a silent *-s*, *-z*, or *-x* are usually formed with *-'s*.

> Des Moines's recreation department
> Josquin des Prez's music
> Delacroix's painting

8. When the possessive ending is added to an italicized name, it is not italicized.

> *East of Eden*'s main characters
> the *Spirit of St. Louis*'s historic flight
> *Brief Encounter*'s memorable ending

Pronouns

9. The possessive of indefinite pronouns is formed by adding *-'s*.

anyone's rights
everybody's money
someone's coat
somebody's wedding
one's own
either's preference

Some indefinite pronouns usually require an *of* phrase to indicate possession.

the rights of each
the inclination of many
the satisfaction of all

10. Possessive pronouns do not include apostrophes.

mine	hers
ours	his
yours	theirs
its	

Miscellaneous Styling Conventions

11. No apostrophe is generally used today with plural nouns that are more descriptive than possessive.

weapons systems
managers meeting
singles bar
steelworkers union
awards banquet

12. The possessive form of a phrase is made by adding an apostrophe or *-'s* to the last word in the phrase.

his father-in-law's assistance
board of directors' meeting
from the student of politics' point of view
after a moment or so's thought

Constructions such as these are often rephrased.

from the point of view of the student of politics
after thinking for a moment or so

13. The possessive form of words in quotation marks can be formed in two ways, with *-'s* placed either inside the quotation marks or outside them.

the "Marseillaise"'s [*or* "Marseillaise's"] stirring melody

Since both arrangements look awkward, this construction is usually avoided.

the stirring melody of the "Marseillaise"

14. Possessives of abbreviations are formed like those of nouns that are spelled out. The singular possessive is formed by adding *-'s;* the plural possessive, by adding an apostrophe only.

the IRS's ruling
AT&T's long-distance service
IBM Corp.'s annual report
Eli Lilly & Co.'s chairman
the HMOs' lobbyists

15. The possessive of nouns composed of numerals is formed in the same way as for other nouns. The possessive of singular nouns is formed by adding *-'s;* the possessive of plural nouns is formed by adding an apostrophe only.

1996's commencement speaker
the 1920s' greatest jazz musicians

16. Individual possession is indicated by adding *-'s* to each noun in a sequence. Joint possession may be indicated in the same way, but is most commonly indicated by adding an apostrophe or *-'s* to the last noun in the sequence.

Joan's and Emily's friends
Jim's, Ed's, and Susan's reports
her mother and father's anniversary
Peter and Jan's trip   *or*   Peter's and Jan's trip

Compounds

A compound is a word or word group that consists of two or more parts that work together as a unit to express a specific concept. Compounds can be formed by combining two or more words (as in *double-check, cost-effective, farmhouse, graphic equalizer, park bench, around-the-clock,* or *son of a gun*), by combining prefixes or suffixes with words (as in *ex-president, shoeless, presorted,* or *uninterruptedly*), or by combining two or more word elements (as in *macrophage* or *photochromism*). Compounds are written in one of three ways: solid (as in *cottonmouth*), hyphenated (*screenwriter-director*), or open (*health care*). Because of the variety of standard practice, the choice among these styles for a given compound represents one of the most common and vexing of all style issues that writers encounter.

A good dictionary will list many *permanent compounds,* compounds so commonly used that they have become permanent parts of the language. It will not list *temporary compounds,* those created to meet a writer's need at a particular moment. Most compounds whose meanings are self-evident from the meanings of their component words will not be listed, even if they are permanent and quite widely used. Writers thus cannot rely wholly on dictionaries to guide them in writing compounds.

One approach is to hyphenate all compounds not in the dictionary, since hyphenation immediately identifies them as compounds. But hyphenating all such compounds runs counter to some well-established American practice and can therefore call too much attention to the compound and momentarily distract the reader. Another approach (which applies only to compounds whose elements are complete words) is to leave open any compound not in the dictionary. Though this is widely done, it can result in the reader's failing to recognize a compound for what it is. A third approach is to pattern the compound after other similar ones. Though this approach is likely to be more complicated, it can make the compound look more familiar and thus less distracting or confusing. The paragraphs that follow are intended to help you use this approach.

As a general rule, writing meant for readers in specialized fields usually does not hyphenate compounds, especially technical terminology.

Compound Nouns

Compound nouns are combinations of words that function in a sentence as nouns. They may consist of two or more nouns, a noun and a modifier, or two or more elements that are not nouns.

Short compounds consisting of two nouns often begin as open compounds but tend to close up as they become familiar.

1. **noun + noun**   Compounds composed of two nouns that are short and commonly used, of which the first is accented, are usually written solid.

farmhouse	paycheck
hairbrush	football
lifeboat	workplace

2. When a noun + noun compound is short and common but pronounced with nearly equal stress on both nouns, it is more likely to be open.

fuel oil	health care
park bench	desk lamp

3. Noun + noun compounds that consist of longer nouns and are self-evident or temporary are usually written open.

costume designer
computer terminal
billiard table

4. When a noun + noun compound describes a double title or double function, the compound is hyphenated.

hunter-gatherer
secretary-treasurer
bar-restaurant

   Sometimes a slash is used in place of the hyphen.

bar/restaurant

5. Compounds formed from a noun or adjective followed by *man, woman, person,* or *people* and denoting an occupation are normally solid.

anchorman	spokesperson
congresswoman	salespeople

6. Compounds that are units of measurement are hyphenated.

foot-pound	column-inch
kilowatt-hour	light-year

7. **adjective + noun**   Most adjective + noun compounds are written open.

municipal court	minor league
genetic code	nuclear medicine
hazardous waste	basic training

8. Adjective + noun compounds consisting of two short words are often written solid when the first word is accented. However, some are usually written open, and a few are hyphenated.

notebook	dry cleaner
bluebird	steel mill
shortcut	two-step

9. **participle + noun**   Most participle + noun compounds are written open.

landing craft	barbed wire
frying pan	preferred stock
sounding board	informal consent

10. **noun's + noun**   Compounds consisting of a possessive noun followed by another noun are usually written open; a few are hyphenated. Compounds of this type that have become solid have lost the apostrophe.

fool's gold	cat's-paw
hornet's nest	bull's-eye
seller's market	foolscap
Queen Anne's lace	menswear

11. **noun + verb + -*er* or -*ing***   Compounds in which the first noun is the object of the verb or gerund to which the suffix has been added are most often written open but sometimes hyphenated. Permanent compounds like these are sometimes written solid.

problem solver	fund-raiser
deal making	gene-splicing
ticket-taker	air conditioner
street-sweeping	lifesaving

12. **object + verb**   Noun compounds consisting of a verb preceded by a noun that is its object are written in various ways.

fish fry	bodyguard
eye-opener	roadblock

13. **verb + object**   A few, mostly older compounds are formed from a verb followed by a noun that is its object; they are written solid.

cutthroat	carryall
breakwater	pickpocket

14. **noun + adjective**   Compounds composed of a noun followed by an adjective are written open or hyphenated.

sum total	president-elect
consul general	secretary-general

15. **particle + noun**   Compounds consisting of a particle (usually a preposition or adverb) and a noun are usually written solid, especially when they are short and the first syllable is accented.

downturn	undertone
outfield	upswing
input	afterthought
outpatient	onrush

   A few particle + noun compounds, especially when composed of longer elements or having equal stress on both elements, are hyphenated or open.

on-ramp	off year
cross-reference	cross fire

16. **verb + particle; verb + adverb**   These compounds may be hyphenated or solid. Compounds with particles such as *to, in,* and *on* are often hyphenated. Compounds with particles such as *up, off,* and *out* are hyphenated or solid with about equal frequency. Those with longer particles or adverbs are usually solid.

lean-to	spin-off
trade-in	payoff
add-on	time-out
start-up	turnout
backup	hideaway

17. **verb + -*er* + particle; verb + -*ing* + particle**   Except for *passerby,* these compounds are hyphenated.

runner-up	carrying-on
diners-out	talking-to
listener-in	falling-out

18. **letter + noun** Compounds formed from a single letter (or sometimes a combination of them) followed by a noun are either open or hyphenated.

T square	T-shirt
B vitamin	f-stop
V neck	H-bomb
Rh factor	A-frame
D major	E-mail *or* e-mail

19. **Compounds of three or four elements** Compounds of three or four words may be either hyphenated or open. Those incorporating prepositional phrases are more often open; others are usually hyphenated.

editor in chief	right-of-way
power of attorney	jack-of-all-trades
flash in the pan	give-and-take
base on balls	rough-and-tumble

20. **Reduplication compounds** Compounds that are formed by reduplication and so consist of two similar-sounding elements are hyphenated if each element has more than one syllable. If each element has only one syllable, the compound is often written solid. Very short words and newly coined words are more often hyphenated.

namby-pamby	singsong
razzle-dazzle	sci-fi
crisscross	hip-hop

Compound Adjectives

Compound adjectives are combinations of words that work together to modify a noun—that is, they work as *unit modifiers*. As unit modifiers they can be distinguished from other strings of adjectives that may also precede a noun.

For instance, in "a low, level tract of land" the two adjectives each modify the noun separately; the tract is both low and level. These are *coordinate* (i.e., equal) *modifiers*. In "a low monthly fee" the first adjective modifies the noun plus the second adjective; the phrase denotes a monthly fee that is low. It could not be revised to "a monthly and low fee" without altering or confusing its meaning. Thus, these are *noncoordinate modifiers*. However, "low-level radiation" does not mean radiation that is low and level or level radiation that is low, but rather radiation that is at a low level. Both words work as a unit to modify the noun.

Unit modifiers are usually hyphenated, in order to help readers grasp the relationship of the words and to avoid confusion. The hyphen in "a call for more-specialized controls" removes any ambiguity as to which word *more* modifies. By contrast, the lack of a hyphen in a phrase like "graphic arts exhibition" may give it an undesirable ambiguity.

21. **Before the noun (attributive position)** Most two-word compound adjectives are hyphenated when placed before the noun.

the fresh-cut grass
its longer-lasting effects
her lace-trimmed dress

a made-up excuse
his best-selling novel
projected health-care costs

22. Compounds whose first word is an adverb ending in *-ly* are usually left open.

a privately chartered boat
politically correct opinions
its weirdly skewed perspective
a tumultuously cascading torrent

23. Compounds formed of an adverb not ending in *-ly* followed by a participle (or sometimes an adjective) are usually hyphenated when placed before a noun.

the well-worded statement
more-stringent measures
his less-exciting prospects
their still-awaited assignments
her once-famous uncle

24. The combination of *very* + adjective is not a unit modifier. (See also paragraph 33 below.)

a very happy baby

25. When a compound adjective is formed by using a compound noun to modify another noun, it is usually hyphenated.

a hazardous-waste site
the basic-training period
a minor-league pitcher
a roll-call vote
their problem-solving abilities

Some familiar open compound nouns are frequently left open when used as adjectives.

a high school diploma *or* a high-school diploma
a real estate license *or* a real-estate license
an income tax refund *or* an income-tax refund

26. A proper name used as a modifier is not hyphenated. A word that modifies the proper name is attached by a hyphen (or an en dash in typeset material).

the Civil War era
a New England tradition
a *New York Times* article
the Supreme Court decision
the splendid *Gone with the Wind* premiere
a Los Angeles–based company
a Pulitzer Prize–winning author
pre–Bull Run skirmishes

27. Compound adjectives composed of foreign words are not hyphenated when placed before a noun unless they are hyphenated in the foreign language itself.

per diem expenses
an ad hoc committee
her *faux-naïf* style
a comme il faut arrangement
the a cappella chorus
a ci-devant professor

28. Compounds that are quoted, capitalized, or italicized are not hyphenated.

a "Springtime in Paris" theme
the book's "I'm OK, you're OK" tone
his AMERICA FIRST sign
the *No smoking* notice

29. Chemical names and most medical names used as modifiers are not hyphenated.

> a sodium hypochlorite bleach
> the amino acid sequence
> a new Parkinson's disease medication

30. Compound adjectives of three or more words are hyphenated when they precede the noun.

> step-by-step instructions
> state-of-the-art equipment
> a wait-and-see attitude
> a longer-than-expected list
> turn-of-the-century medicine

31. **Following the noun** When a compound adjective follows the noun it modifies, it usually ceases to be a unit modifier and is therefore no longer hyphenated.

> instructions that guide you step by step
> a list that was longer than expected

However, a compound that follows the noun it modifies often keeps its hyphen if it continues to function as a unit modifier, especially if its first element is a noun.

> hikers who were ill-advised to cross the glacier
> an actor too high-strung to relax
> industries that could be called low-tech
> metals that are corrosion-resistant
> tends to be accident-prone

32. Permanent compound adjectives are usually written as they appear in the dictionary even when they follow the noun they modify.

> for reasons that are well-known
> a plan we regarded as half-baked
> The problems are mind-boggling.

However, compound adjectives of three or more words are normally not hyphenated when they follow the noun they modify, since they usually cease to function as adjectives.

> These remarks are off the record.
> medical practice of the turn of the century

When compounds of three or more words appear as hyphenated adjectives in dictionaries, the hyphens are retained as long as the phrase is being used as a unit modifier.

> The candidate's position was middle-of-the-road.

33. When an adverb modifies another adverb that is the first element of a compound modifier, the compound may lose its hyphen. If the first adverb modifies the whole compound, however, the hyphen is retained.

> a very well developed idea
> *but*
> a delightfully well-written book
> a most ill-timed event

34. Adjective compounds that are color names in which each element can function as a noun are almost always hyphenated.

> red-orange fabric
> The fabric was red-orange.

Color names in which the first element can only be an adjective are often unhyphenated before a noun and usually unhyphenated after.

> a bright red tie
> the pale yellow-green chair
> reddish orange fabric *or* reddish-orange fabric
> The fabric was reddish orange.

35. Compound modifiers that include a number followed by a noun (except for the noun *percent*) are hyphenated when they precede the noun they modify, but usually not when they follow it. (For details on measurement, see paragraph 42 on page 221.)

> the four-color press
> a 12-foot-high fence
> a fence 12 feet high
> a 300-square-mile area
> an area of 300 square miles
> *but*
> a 10 percent raise

If a currency symbol precedes the number, the hyphen is omitted.

> an $8.5 million deficit

36. An adjective composed of a number followed by a noun in the possessive is not hyphenated.

> a nine days' wonder
> a two weeks' wait
> *but*
> a two-week wait

Compound Adverbs

37. Adverb compounds consisting of preposition + noun are almost always written solid. However, there are a few important exceptions.

> downstairs
> uphill
> offshore
> overnight
> *but*
> in-house
> off-key
> on-line

38. Compound adverbs of more than two words are usually written open, and they usually follow the words they modify.

> here and there
> more or less
> head and shoulders
> hand in hand
> every which way
> once and for all
> *but*
> a more-or-less certain result

A few three-word adverbs are usually hyphenated, but many are written open even if the corresponding adjective is hyphenated.

> placed back-to-back
> met face-to-face
> *but*

a word-for-word quotation
quoted word for word
software bought off the shelf

Compound Verbs

39. Two-word verbs consisting of a verb followed by an adverb or a preposition are written open.

follow up	take on
roll back	run across
strike out	set back

40. A compound composed of a particle followed by a verb is written solid.

overlook	undercut
outfit	download

41. A verb derived from an open or hyphenated compound noun is hyphenated.

double-space	water-ski
rubber-stamp	field-test

42. A verb derived from a solid noun is written solid.

mastermind	brainstorm
highlight	sideline

Compounds Formed with Word Elements

Many new and temporary compounds are formed by adding word elements to existing words or by combining word elements. There are three basic kinds of word elements: prefixes (such as *anti-, non-, pre-, post-, re-, super-*), suffixes (such as *-er, -fold, -ism, -ist, -less, -ness*), and combining forms (such as *mini-, macro-, pseudo-, -graphy, -logy*). Prefixes and suffixes are usually attached to existing words; combining forms are usually combined to form new words.

43. prefix + word   Except as specified in the paragraphs below, compounds formed from a prefix and a word are usually written solid.

anticrime	subzero
nonaligned	superheroine
premedical	transnational
reorchestration	postdoctoral

44. If the prefix ends with a vowel and the word it is attached to begins with the same vowel, the compound is usually hyphenated.

anti-incumbent	semi-independent
de-escalate	intra-arterial
co-organizer	pre-engineered

However, there are many exceptions.

reelect
preestablished
cooperate

45. If the base word or compound to which a prefix is added is capitalized, the resulting compound is almost always hyphenated.

pre-Victorian
anti-Western
post-Darwinian
non-English-speaking
   but

transatlantic
transalpine

If the prefix and the base word together form a new proper name, the compound may be solid with the prefix capitalized.

Postimpressionists
Precambrian
   but
Pre-Raphaelite

46. Compounds made with *ex-*, in its "former" sense, and *self-* are hyphenated.

ex-mayor	self-control
ex-husband	self-sustaining

Compounds formed from *vice-* are usually hyphenated. Some permanent compounds are open.

vice-chair	vice president
vice-consul	vice admiral

A temporary compound with *quasi(-)* or *pseudo(-)* may be written open (if *quasi* or *pseudo* is being treated as a modifier) or hyphenated (if it is being treated as a combining form).

quasi intellectual   *or*   quasi-intellectual
pseudo liberal   *or*   pseudo-liberal

47. If a prefix is added to a hyphenated compound, it may be either followed by a hyphen or closed up solid to the next element. Permanent compounds of this kind should be checked in a dictionary.

unair-conditioned
ultra-up-to-date
non-self-governing
unself-confident

48. If a prefix is added to an open compound, the hyphen is often replaced by an en dash in typeset material.

ex–campaign treasurer
post–World War I era

49. A compound that would be identical with another word if written solid is usually hyphenated to prevent misreading.

a re-creation of the setting
shopped at the co-op
multi-ply fabric

50. Compounds that might otherwise be solid are often hyphenated in order to clarify their formation, meaning, or pronunciation.

tri-city	non-news
de-iced	anti-fur
re-oil	pro-choice

51. When prefixes are attached to numerals, the compounds are hyphenated.

pre-1995 models
post-1945 economy
non-19th-century architecture

52. Compounds created from proper ethnic or national combining forms are hyphenated when the second element is an independent word, but solid when it is a combining form.

Anglo-Saxon	Anglophile
Judeo-Christian	Francophone
Sino-Japanese	Sinophobe

53. Prefixes that are repeated in the same compound are separated by a hyphen.

re-refried

post-postmodern

54. Compounds consisting of different prefixes or adjectives with the same base word which are joined by *and* or *or* are shortened by pruning the first compound back to a hyphenated prefix.

pre- and postoperative care

anti- or pro-Revolutionary sympathies

over- and underachievers

early- and mid-20th-century painters

4-, 6-, and 8-foot lengths

55. word + suffix Except as noted in the paragraphs below, compounds formed by adding a suffix to a word are written solid.

Fourierism	characterless
benightedness	custodianship
yellowish	easternmost

56. Compounds made with a suffix or a terminal combining form are often hyphenated if the base word is more than two syllables long, if it ends with the same letter the suffix begins with, or if it is a proper name.

industry-wide	jewel-like
recession-proof	Hollywood-ish
American-ness	Europe-wide

57. Compounds made from a number + *-odd* are hyphenated. A number + *-fold* is written solid if the number is spelled out but hyphenated if it is in numerals.

fifty-odd	tenfold
50-odd	10-fold

58. Most compounds formed from an open or hyphenated compound + a suffix do not separate the suffix with a hyphen. But combining forms that also exist as independent words, such as *-like, -wide, -worthy,* and *-proof,* are attached by a hyphen.

self-righteousness

middle-of-the-roadism

bobby-soxer

a Red Cross-like approach

a New York-wide policy

Open compounds often become hyphenated when a suffix is added unless they are proper nouns.

flat-taxer

Ivy Leaguer

World Federalist

59. combining form + combining form New terms in technical fields created with one or more combining forms are normally written solid.

cyberworld

macrographic

4 Abbreviations

Abbreviations may be used to save space and time, to avoid repetition of long words and phrases, or simply to conform to conventional usage.

The contemporary styling of abbreviations is inconsistent and arbitrary, and no set of rules can hope to cover all the possible variations, exceptions, and peculiarities encountered in print. The form abbreviations take—capitalized vs. lowercased, punctuated vs. unpunctuated—often depends on a writer's preference or a publisher's or organization's policy. However, the following paragraphs provide a number of useful guidelines to contemporary practice. In doubtful cases, a good general dictionary or a dictionary of abbreviations will usually show standard forms for common abbreviations.

The present discussion deals largely with general, nontechnical writing. In scientific writing, abbreviations are almost never punctuated.

An abbreviation is not divided at the end of a line.

Abbreviations are almost never italicized. An abbreviation consisting of single initial letters, whether punctuated or not, never standardly has spacing between the letters. (Initials of personal names, however, normally are separated by spaces.)

The first reference to any frequently abbreviated term or name that could be confusing or unfamiliar is commonly spelled out, often followed immediately by its abbreviation in parentheses. Later references employ the abbreviation alone.

Punctuation

1. A period follows most abbreviations that are formed by omitting all but the first few letters of a word.

   cont. [*for* continued]
   enc. [*for* enclosure]
   Oct. [*for* October]
   univ. [*for* university]

   Former abbreviations that are now considered words do not need a period.

   | lab | photo |
   | gym | ad |

2. A period follows most abbreviations that are formed by omitting letters from the middle of a word.

   govt. [*for* government]
   atty. [*for* attorney]
   bros. [*for* brothers]
   Dr. [*for* Doctor]

   Some abbreviations, usually called *contractions,* replace the omitted letters with an apostrophe. Such contractions do not end with a period. (In American usage, very few contractions other than two-word contractions involving verbs are in standard use.)

   ass'n   *or*   assn. [*for* association]
   dep't   *or*   dept. [*for* department]
   nat'l   *or*   natl. [*for* national]
   can't [*for* cannot]

3. Periods are usually omitted from abbreviations made up of single initial letters. However, for some of these abbreviations, especially uncapitalized ones, the periods are usually retained. No space follows an internal period.

   GOP [*for* Grand Old Party]
   PR [*for* public relations]
   CEO   *or*   C.E.O. [*for* chief executive officer]
   a.m. [*for* ante meridiem]

4. A few abbreviations are punctuated with one or more slashes in place of periods. (For details on the slash, see the section beginning on page 191.)

   c/o [*for* care of]
   d/b/a   *or*   d.b.a. [*for* doing business as]
   w/o [*for* without]
   w/w [*for* wall-to-wall]

5. Terms in which a suffix is added to a numeral are not genuine abbreviations and do not require a period. (For details on ordinal numbers, see the section on page 216.)

   | 1st | 3d |
   | 2nd | 8vo |

6. Isolated letters of the alphabet used to designate a shape or position in a sequence are not abbreviations and are not punctuated.

   T square
   A1
   F minor

7. When a punctuated abbreviation ends a sentence, its period becomes the terminal period.

   For years she claimed she was "the oldest living fossil at Briggs & Co."

Capitalization

1. Abbreviations are capitalized if the words they represent are proper nouns or adjectives.

   F [*for* Fahrenheit]
   IMF [*for* International Monetary Fund]
   Jan. [*for* January]
   Amer. [*for* American]
   LWV [*for* League of Women Voters]

2. Abbreviations are usually all-capitalized when they represent initial letters of lowercased words. However, some common abbreviations formed in this way are often lowercased.

   IQ [*for* intelligence quotient]
   U.S. [*for* United States]
   COLA [*for* cost-of-living allowance]
   FYI [*for* for your information]
   f.o.b.   *or*   FOB [*for* free on board]
   c/o [*for* care of]

3. Most abbreviations formed from single initial letters that are pronounced as words, rather than as a series of letters, are capitalized. Those that are not proper nouns and have been assimilated into the language as words in their own right are most often lowercased.

OSHA	snafu
NATO	laser
CARE	sonar
NAFTA	scuba

4. Abbreviations that are ordinarily capitalized are commonly used to begin sentences, but abbreviations that are ordinarily uncapitalized are not.

> Dr. Smith strongly disagrees.
> OSHA regulations require these new measures.
> Page 22 [*not* P. 22] was missing.

Plurals, Possessives, and Compounds

1. Punctuated abbreviations of single words are pluralized by adding -*s* before the period.

> yrs. [*for* years]
> hwys. [*for* highways]
> figs. [*for* figures]

2. Punctuated abbreviations that stand for phrases or compounds are usually pluralized by adding - *'s* after the last period.

> M.D.'s *or* M.D.s
> Ph.D.'s *or* Ph.D.s
> LL.B.'s *or* LL.B.s
> v.p.'s

3. All-capitalized, unpunctuated abbreviations are usually pluralized by adding a lowercase -*s*.

IRAs	CPAs
PCs	SATs

4. The plural form of a few lowercase one-letter abbreviations is made by repeating the letter.

> ll. [*for* lines]
> pp. [*for* pages]
> nn. [*for* notes]
> vv. [*for* verses]
> ff. *or* ff [*for* and the following ones *or* folios]

5. The plural form of abbreviations of units of measurement (including one-letter abbreviations) is the same as the singular form. (For more on units of measurement, see the section on page 221.)

> 10 cc *or* cc. [*for* cubic centimeters]
> 30 m *or* m. [*for* meters]
> 15 mm *or* mm. [*for* millimeters]
> 24 h. [*for* hours]
> 10 min. [*for* minutes]
> 45 mi. [*for* miles]

However, in informal nontechnical text several such abbreviations are pluralized like other single-word abbreviations.

lbs.	qts.
gals.	hrs.

6. Possessives of abbreviations are formed like those of spelled-out nouns: the singular possessive is formed by adding - *'s*, the plural possessive simply by adding an apostrophe.

> the CEO's speech
> Apex Co.'s profits
> the PACs' influence
> Brown Bros.' ads

7. Compounds that consist of an abbreviation added to another word are formed in the same way as compounds that consist of spelled-out nouns.

> an FDA-approved drug
> an R&D-driven company
> the Eau Claire, Wisc.–based publisher

Compounds formed by adding a prefix or suffix to an abbreviation are usually hyphenated.

> pre-CD recordings
> non-IRA deductions
> a CIA-like operation
> a PCB-free product

Specific Styling Conventions

A and *An*

1. The choice of the article *a* or *an* before abbreviations depends on the sound, rather than the actual letter, with which the abbreviation begins. If it begins with a consonant sound, *a* is normally used; if with a vowel sound, *an* is used.

> a CD-ROM version
> a YAF member
> a U.S. Senator
> an FDA-approved drug
> an M.D. degree
> an ABA convention

A.D. and *B.C.*

2. The abbreviations A.D. and B.C. and other abbreviated era designations usually appear in books and journals as small capitals; in newspapers and in typed or keyboarded material, they usually appear as full capitals. The abbreviation B.C. follows the date; A.D. usually precedes the date, though in many publications A.D. follows the date as well. In references to whole centuries, A.D. follows the century. (For more on era designations, see paragraph 12 on page 218.)

> A.D. 185 *but also* 185 A.D.
> 41 B.C.
> the fourth century A.D.

Agencies, Associations, Organizations, and Companies

3. The names of agencies, associations, and organizations are usually abbreviated after being spelled out on their first occurrence in a text. If a company is easily recognizable from its initials, the abbreviation is likewise usually employed after the first mention. The abbreviations are usually all-capitalized and unpunctuated. (In contexts

where the abbreviation will be recognized, it often replaces the full name throughout.)

> Next, the president of the Pioneer Valley Transit Authority presented the annual PVTA award.
> ... at the American Bar Association (ABA) meeting in June. The ABA's new officers ...
> International Business Machines released its first-quarter earnings figures today. An IBM spokesperson ...

4. The words *Company, Corporation, Incorporated,* and *Limited* in company names are commonly abbreviated even at their first appearance, except in quite formal writing.

> Procter & Gamble Company   *or*   Procter & Gamble Co.
> Brandywine Corporation   *or*   Brandywine Corp.

Ampersand

5. The ampersand (&), representing the word *and,* is often used in the names of companies.

> H&R Block
> Standard & Poor's
> Ogilvy & Mather

It is not used in the names of federal agencies.

> U.S. Fish and Wildlife Service
> Office of Management and Budget

Even when a spelled-out *and* appears in a company's official name, it is often replaced by an ampersand in writing referring to the company, whether for the sake of consistency or because of the writer's inability to verify the official styling.

6. When an ampersand is used in an abbreviation, there is usually no space on either side of the ampersand.

> The Barkers welcome all guests to their B&B at 54 West Street.
> The S&P 500 showed gains in technology stocks.
> The Texas A&M Aggies prevailed again on Sunday.

7. When an ampersand is used between the last two elements in a series, the comma is omitted.

> Jones, Kuhn & Malloy, Attorneys at Law

Books of the Bible

8. Books of the Bible are spelled out in running text but generally abbreviated in references to chapter and verse.

> The minister based his first Advent sermon on Matthew.
> Ye cannot serve God and mammon.—Matt. 6:24

Compass Points

9. Compass points are normally abbreviated when they follow street names; these abbreviations may be punctuated and are usually preceded by a comma.

> 1600 Pennsylvania Avenue[,] NW [N.W.]

When a compass point precedes the word *Street, Avenue,* etc., or when it follows the word but forms an integral part of the street name, it is usually spelled out.

> 230 West 43rd Street
> 50 Park Avenue South

Dates

10. The names of days and months are spelled out in running text.

> at the Monday editorial meeting
> the December issue of *Scientific American*
> a meeting held on August 1, 1995

The names of months usually are not abbreviated in datelines of business letters, but they are often abbreviated in government and military correspondence.

> *business dateline:*   November 1, 1995
> *military dateline:*   1 Nov 95

Degrees and Professional Ratings

11. Abbreviations of academic degrees are usually punctuated; abbreviations of professional ratings are slightly more commonly unpunctuated.

> Ph.D.
> B.Sc.
> M.B.A.
> PLS   *or*   P.L.S. [*for* Professional Legal Secretary]
> CMA   *or*   C.M.A. [*for* Certified Medical Assistant]
> FACP   *or*   F.A.C.P. [*for* Fellow of the American College of Physicians]

12. Only the first letter of each element in abbreviations of degrees and professional ratings is generally capitalized.

> D.Ch.E. [*for* Doctor of Chemical Engineering]
> Litt.D. [*for* Doctor of Letters]
> D.Th. [*for* Doctor of Theology]
> *but*
> LL.B. [*for* Bachelor of Laws]
> LL.M. [*for* Master of Laws]
> LL.D. [*for* Doctor of Laws]

Geographical Names

13. When abbreviations of state names are used in running text immediately following the name of a city or county, the traditional state abbreviations are often used.

> Ellen White of 49 Lyman St., Saginaw, Mich., has been chosen ...
> the Dade County, Fla., public schools
> *but*
> Grand Rapids, in western Michigan, ...

Official postal service abbreviations for states are used in mailing addresses.

> 6 Bay Rd.
> Gibson Island, MD 21056

14. Terms such as *Street, Road,* and *Boulevard* are often written as punctuated abbreviations in running text when they form part of a proper name.

> an accident on Windward Road [*or* Rd.]
> our office at 1234 Cross Blvd. [*or* Boulevard]

15. Names of countries are usually spelled in full in running text.

> South Africa's president urged the United States to impose meaningful sanctions.

Abbreviations for country names (in tables, for example), are usually punctuated. When formed from the single initial letters of two or more individual words, they are sometimes unpunctuated.

Mex.	Scot.
Can.	U.K. *or* UK
Ger.	U.S. *or* US

16. *United States* is normally abbreviated when used as an adjective or attributive. When used as a noun, it is generally spelled out.

> the U.S. Department of Justice
> U.S. foreign policy
> The United States has declined to participate.

17. *Saint* is usually abbreviated when it is part of a geographical or topographical name. *Mount, Point,* and *Fort* may be either spelled out or abbreviated. (For the abbreviation of *Saint* with personal names, see paragraph 25 below.)

> St. Paul, Minnesota   *or*   Saint Paul, Minnesota
> St. Thomas, U.S.V.I.   *or*   Saint Thomas
> Mount Vernon   *or*   Mt. Vernon
> Point Reyes   *or*   Pt. Reyes
> Fort Worth   *or*   Ft. Worth
> Mt. Kilimanjaro   *or*   Mount Kilimanjaro

Latin Words and Phrases

18. Several Latin words and phrases are almost always abbreviated. They are punctuated, lowercased, and usually not italicized.

etc.	ibid.
i.e.	op. cit.
e.g.	q.v.
cf.	c. *or* ca.
viz.	fl.
et al.	et seq.

Versus is usually abbreviated *v.* in legal writing, *vs.* otherwise.

> *Da Costa* v. *United States*
> good vs. evil
>   *or*   good versus evil

Latitude and *Longitude*

19. The words *latitude* and *longitude* are abbreviated in tables and in technical contexts but often written out in running text.

> *in a table:* lat. 10°20′N   *or*   lat. 10-20N
> *in text:*   from 10°20′ north latitude to 10°30′ south latitude
>   *or*   from lat. 10°20′N to lat. 10°30′S

Military Ranks and Units

20. Official abbreviations for military ranks follow specific unpunctuated styles for each branch of the armed forces. Nonmilitary writing usually employs a punctuated and less concise style.

> *in the military:*   BG Carter R. Stokes, USA
>   LCDR Dawn Wills-Craig, USN
>   Col S. J. Smith, USMC
>   LTJG Carlos Ramos, USCG
>   Sgt Bernard P. Brodkey, USAF

> *outside the military:*   Brig. Gen. Carter R. Stokes
>   Lt. Comdr. Dawn Wills-Craig
>   Col. S. J. Smith
>   Lt. (j.g.) Carlos Ramos
>   Sgt. Bernard P. Brodkey

21. Outside the military, military ranks are usually given in full when used with a surname only but abbreviated when used with a full name.

> Major Mosby
> Maj. John S. Mosby

Number

22. The word *number,* when followed by a numeral, is usually abbreviated to *No.* or *no.*

> The No. 1 priority is to promote profitability.
> We recommend no. 6 thread.
> Policy No. 123-5-X
> Publ. Nos. 12 and 13

Personal Names

23. When initials are used with a surname, they are spaced and punctuated. Unspaced initials of a few famous persons, which may or may not be punctuated, are sometimes used in place of their full names.

> E. M. Forster
> C. P. E. Bach
> JFK   *or*   J.F.K.

24. The abbreviations *Jr.* and *Sr.* may or may not be preceded by a comma.

> Martin Luther King Jr.
>   *or*   Martin Luther King, Jr.

Saint

25. The word *Saint* is often abbreviated when used before the name of a saint. When it forms part of a surname or an institution's name, it follows the style used by the person or institution. (For the styling of *Saint* in geographical names, see paragraph 17 above.)

> St. [*or* Saint] Teresa of Avila
> Augustus Saint-Gaudens
> Ruth St. Denis
> St. Martin's Press
> St. John's College

Scientific Terms

26. In binomial nomenclature, a genus name may be abbreviated to its initial letter after the first reference. The abbreviation is always capitalized, punctuated, and italicized.

> . . . its better-known relative *Atropa belladonna* (deadly nightshade).
> Only *A. belladonna* is commonly found in . . .

27. Abbreviations for the names of chemical compounds and the symbols for chemical elements and formulas are unpunctuated.

MSG	O
PCB	NaCl
Pb	FeS

28. Abbreviations in computer terms are usually unpunctuated.

PC	Esc
RAM	Alt
CD-ROM	Ctrl
I/O	ASCII
DOS	EBCDIC

Time

29. When time is expressed in figures, the abbreviations *a.m. (ante meridiem)* and *p.m. (post meridiem)* are most often written as punctuated lowercase letters, sometimes as punctuated small capital letters. In newspapers, they usually appear in full-size capitals. (For more on *a.m.* and *p.m.,* see paragraph 39 on page 221.)

8:30 a.m.   *or*   8:30 A.M.   *or*   8:30 A.M.
10:00 p.m.   *or*   10:00 P.M.   *or*   10:00 P.M.

Time-zone designations are usually capitalized and unpunctuated.

9:22 a.m. EST [*for* eastern standard time]
4:45 p.m. CDT [*for* central daylight time]

Titles and Degrees

30. The courtesy titles *Mr., Ms., Mrs.,* and *Messrs.* occur only as abbreviations today. The professional titles *Doctor, Professor, Representative,* and *Senator* are often abbreviated.

Ms. Lee A. Downs
Messrs. Lake, Mason, and Nambeth
Doctor Howe   *or*   Dr. Howe

31. Despite some traditional objections, the honorific titles *Honorable* and *Reverend* are often abbreviated, with and without *the* preceding the titles.

the Honorable Samuel I. O'Leary
or   [the] Hon. Samuel I. O'Leary

the Revered Samuel I. O'Leary
or   [the] Rev. Samuel I. O'Leary

32. When an abbreviation for an academic degree, professional certification, or association membership follows a name, no courtesy or professional title precedes it.

Dr. Jesse Smith   *or*   Jesse Smith, M.D.
but not   Dr. Jesse Smith, M.D.
Katherine Fox Derwinski, CLU
Carol W. Manning, M.D., FACPS
Michael B. Jones II, J.D.
Peter D. Cohn, Jr., CPA

33. The abbreviation *Esq.* (for *Esquire*) often follows attorneys' names in correspondence and in formal listings, and less often follows the names of certain other professionals, including architects, consuls, clerks of court, and justices of the peace. It is not used if a degree or professional rating follows the name, or if a courtesy title or honorific (*Mr., Ms., Hon., Dr.,* etc.) precedes the name.

Carolyn B. West, Esq.
not   Ms. Carolyn B. West, Esq.
and not   Carolyn B. West, J.D., Esq.

Units of Measurement

34. A unit of measurement that follows a figure is often abbreviated, especially in technical writing. The figure and abbreviation are separated by a space. If the numeral is written out, the unit should also be written out.

15 cu. ft.   *but*   fifteen cubic feet
What is its capacity in cubic feet?

35. Abbreviations for metric units are usually unpunctuated; those for traditional units are usually punctuated in nonscientific writing. (For more on units of measurement, see the section on page 221.)

14 ml	8 ft.
12 km	4 sec.
50 m	20 min.

5 Numbers

The treatment of numbers presents special difficulties because there are so many conventions to follow, some of which may conflict in a particular passage. The major issue is whether to spell out numbers or to express them in figures, and usage varies considerably on this point.

Numbers as Words or Figures

At one style extreme—usually limited to proclamations, legal documents, and some other types of very formal writing—all numbers (sometimes even including dates) are written out. At the other extreme, some types of technical writing may contain no written-out numbers. Figures are generally easier to read than spelled-out numbers; however, the spelled-out forms are helpful in certain circumstances, and are often felt to be less jarring than figures in nontechnical writing.

Basic Conventions

1. Two alternative basic conventions are in common use. The first and more widely used system requires that numbers up through nine be spelled out, and that figures be used for exact numbers greater than nine. (In a variation of this system, the number ten is spelled out.) Round numbers that consist of a whole number between one and nine followed by *hundred, thousand, million,* etc., may either be spelled out or expressed in figures.

   > The museum includes four rooms of early American tools and implements, 345 pieces in all.
   > He spoke for almost three hours, inspiring his audience of 19,000 devoted followers.
   > They sold more than 700 [*or* seven hundred] TVs during the 10-day sale.
   > She'd told him so a thousand times.

2. The second system requires that numbers from one through ninety-nine be spelled out, and that figures be used for all exact numbers above ninety-nine. (In a variation of this system, the number one hundred is spelled out.) Numbers that consist of a whole number between one and ninety-nine followed by *hundred, thousand, million,* etc., are also spelled out.

   > Audubon's engraver spent nearly twelve years completing these four volumes, which comprise 435 hand-colored plates.
   > In the course of four hours, she signed twenty-five hundred copies of her book.

3. Written-out numbers only use hyphens following words ending in *-ty.* The word *and* before such words is usually omitted.

   > twenty-two
   > five hundred ninety-seven
   > two thousand one hundred forty-nine

Sentence Beginnings

4. Numbers that begin a sentence are written out. An exception is occasionally made for dates. Spelled-out numbers that are lengthy and awkward are usually avoided by restructuring the sentence.

   > Sixty-two new bills will be brought before the committee.
   > *or* There will be 62 new bills brought before the committee.
   > Nineteen ninety-five was our best earnings year so far.
   > *or occasionally* 1995 was our best earnings year so far.
   > One hundred fifty-seven illustrations, including 86 color plates, are contained in the book.
   > *or* The book contains 157 illustrations, including 86 color plates.

Adjacent Numbers and Numbers in Series

5. Two separate figures are generally not written adjacent to one another in running text unless they form a series. Instead, either the sentence is rephrased or one of the figures is spelled out—usually the figure with the shorter written form.

   > sixteen ½-inch dowels
   > worked five 9-hour days in a row
   > won twenty 100-point games
   > lost 15 fifty-point matches
   > By 1997, thirty schools . . .

6. Numbers paired at the beginning of a sentence are usually written alike. If the first word of the sentence is a spelled-out number, the second number is also spelled out. However, each number may instead be styled independently, even if that results in an inconsistent pairing.

   > Sixty to seventy-five copies will be required.
   > *or* Sixty to 75 copies will be required.

7. Numbers that form a pair or a series within a sentence or a paragraph are often treated identically even when they would otherwise be styled differently. The style of the largest number usually determines that of the others. If one number is a mixed or simple fraction, figures are used for all the numbers in the series.

   > She wrote one composition for English and translated twelve [*or* 12] pages for French that night.
   > His total record sales came to a meager 8 [*or* eight] million; Bing Crosby's, he mused, may have surpassed 250 million.
   > The three jobs took 5, 12, and 4½ hours, respectively.

Round Numbers

8. Approximate or round numbers, particularly those that can be expressed in one or two words, are often spelled out in general writing. In technical and scientific writing, they are expressed as numerals.

   > seven hundred people   *or*   700 people
   > five thousand years   *or*   5,000 years
   > four hundred thousand volumes   *or*   400,000 volumes
   > *but not*   400 thousand volumes
   > *but in technical writing*
   > 200 species of fish
   > 50,000 people per year
   > 300,000 years

9. Round (and round-appearing) numbers of one million and above are often expressed as figures followed by the word *million, billion,* and so forth. The figure may in-

clude a one- or two-digit decimal fraction; more exact numbers are written entirely in figures.

the last 600 million years
about 4.6 billion years old
1.2 million metric tons of grain
$7.25 million
$3,456,000,000

Ordinal Numbers

10. Ordinal numbers generally follow the styling rules for cardinal numbers. In technical writing, ordinal numbers are usually written as figure-plus-suffix combinations. Certain ordinal numbers—for example, those for percentiles and latitudes—are usually set as figures even in nontechnical contexts.

entered the seventh grade
wrote the 9th [*or* ninth] and 12th [*or* twelfth] chapters
in the 21st [*or* twenty-first] century
the 7th percentile
the 38th parallel

11. In figure-plus-suffix combinations where the figure ends in 2 or 3, either a one- or a two-letter suffix may be used. A period does not follow the suffix.

2d *or* 2nd
33d *or* 33rd
102d *or* 102nd

Roman Numerals

12. Roman numerals are traditionally used to differentiate rulers and popes with identical names.

King George III
Henri IV
Innocent X

13. When Roman numerals are used to differentiate related males with the same name, they are used only with the full name. Ordinals are sometimes used instead of Roman numerals. The possessive is formed in the usual way. (For the use of *Jr.* and *Sr.,* see paragraph 24 on page 213.)

James R. Watson II
James R. Watson 2nd *or* 2d
James R. Watson II's [*or* 2nd's *or* 2d's] alumni gift

14. Lowercase Roman numerals are generally used to number book pages that precede the regular Arabic sequence (often including a table of contents, acknowledgments, foreword, or other material).

on page iv of the preface
See Introduction, pp. ix–xiii.

15. Roman numerals are used in outlines; see paragraph 23 on page 220.

16. Roman numerals are found as part of a few established scientific and technical terms. Chords in the study of music harmony are designated by capital and lowercase Roman numerals (often followed by small Arabic numbers). Most technical terms that include numbers, however, express them in Arabic form.

blood-clotting factor VII
quadrant III

the cranial nerves II and IX
HIV-III virus
Population II stars
type I error
vii$_6$ chord
   but
adenosine 3′,5′-monophosphate
cesium 137
PL/1 programming language

17. Miscellaneous uses of Roman numerals include the Articles, and often the Amendments, of the Constitution. Roman numerals are still sometimes used for references to the acts and scenes of plays and occasionally for volume numbers in bibliographic references.

Article IX
Act III, Scene ii   *or*   Act 3, Scene 2
(III, ii)   *or*   (3, 2)
Vol. XXIII, No. 4   *but usually*   Vol. 23, No. 4

Punctuation

These paragraphs provide general rules for the use of commas, hyphens, and en dashes with compound and large numbers. For specific categories of numbers, such as dates, money, and decimal fractions, see Specific Styling Conventions, beginning on page 217.

Commas in Large Numbers

1. In general writing, figures of four digits may be written with or without a comma; including the comma is more common. If the numerals form part of a tabulation, commas are necessary so that four-digit numerals can align with numerals of five or more digits.

2,000 cases   *or less commonly*   2000 cases

2. Whole numbers of five digits or more (but not decimal fractions) use a comma to separate three-digit groups, counting from the right.

a fee of $12,500
15,000 units
a population of 1,500,000

3. Certain types of numbers of four digits or more do not contain commas. These include decimal fractions and the numbers of policies and contracts, checks, street addresses, rooms and suites, telephones, pages, military hours, and years.

2.5544	Room 1206
Policy 33442	page 145
check 34567	1650 hours
12537 Wilshire Blvd.	in 1929

4. In technical writing, the comma is frequently replaced by a thin space in numerals of five or more digits. Digits to the right of the decimal point are also separated in this way, counting from the decimal point.

28 666 203
209.775 42

Hyphens

5. Hyphens are used with written-out numbers between 21 and 99.

> forty-one years old
> his forty-first birthday
> Four hundred twenty-two visitors were counted.

6. A hyphen is used in a written-out fraction employed as a modifier. A nonmodifying fraction consisting of two words only is usually left open, although it may also be hyphenated. (For details on fractions, see the section beginning on page 219.)

> a one-half share
> three fifths of her paycheck   *or*   three-fifths of her paycheck
> *but*
> four five-hundredths

7. Numbers that form the first part of a modifier expressing measurement are followed by a hyphen. (For units of measurement, see the section on page 221.)

> a 5-foot board
> a 28-mile trip
> an eight-pound baby
> *but*
> a $6 million profit

8. Serial numbers, Social Security numbers, telephone numbers, and extended zip codes often contain hyphens that make lengthy numerals more readable or separate coded information.

> 020-42-1691
> 413-734-3134   *or*   (413) 734-3134
> 01102-2812

9. Numbers are almost never divided at the end of a line. If division is unavoidable, the break occurs only after a comma.

Inclusive Numbers

10. Inclusive numbers—those that express a range—are usually separated either by the word *to* or by a hyphen or en dash, meaning "(up) to and including."

> spanning the years 1915 to 1941
> the fiscal year 1994–95
> the decade 1920–1929
> pages 40 to 98
> pp. 40–98

Inclusive numbers separated by a hyphen or en dash are not used after the words *from* or *between*.

> from page 385 to page 419   *not*   from page 385–419
> from 9:30 to 5:30   *not*   from 9:30–5:30
> between 1997 and 2000   *not*   between 1997–2000
> between 80 and 90 percent   *not*   between 80–90 percent

11. Inclusive page numbers and dates may be either written in full or elided (i.e., shortened) to save space or for ease of reading.

> pages 523–526   *or*   pages 523–26
> 1955–1969   *or*   1955–69

However, inclusive dates that appear in titles and other headings are almost never elided. Dates that appear with era designations are also not elided.

> *England and the French Revolution 1789–1797*
> 1900–1901   *not*   1900–01   *and not*   1900–1
> 872–863 B.C.   *not*   872–63 B.C.

12. The most common style for the elision of inclusive numbers is based on the following rules: Never elide inclusive numbers that have only two digits.

> 24–28   *not*   24–8
> 86–87   *not*   86–7

Never elide inclusive numbers when the first number ends in 00.

> 100–103   *not*   100–03   *and not*   100–3
> 300–329   *not*   300–29

In other numbers, do not omit the tens digit from the higher number. *Exception:* Where the tens digit of both numbers is zero, write only one digit for the higher number.

> 234–37   *not*   234–7
> 3,824–29   *not*   3,824–9
> 605–7   *not*   605–07

13. Units of measurement expressed in words or abbreviations are usually used only after the second element of an inclusive number. Symbols, however, are repeated.

> ten to fifteen dollars
> 30 to 35 degrees Celsius
> an increase in dosage from 200 to 500 mg
> *but*
> 45° to 48° F
> $50–$60 million
> *or* $50 million to $60 million

14. Numbers that are part of an inclusive set or range are usually styled alike: figures with figures, spelled-out words with other spelled-out words.

> from 8 to 108 absences
> five to twenty guests
> 300,000,000 to 305,000,000
> *not*   300 million to 305,000,000

Specific Styling Conventions

The following paragraphs, arranged alphabetically, describe styling practices commonly followed for specific situations involving numbers.

Addresses

1. Numerals are used for all building, house, apartment, room, and suite numbers except for *one,* which is usually written out.

> 6 Lincoln Road   Room 982
> 1436 Fremont Street   Suite 2000
> Apartment 609   One Bayside Drive

When the address of a building is used as its name, the number in the address is often written out.

> the sophisticated elegance of Ten Park Avenue

2. Numbered streets have their numbers written as ordinals. Street names from First through Tenth are usually written out, and numerals are used for all higher-numbered streets. Less commonly, all numbered street names up to and including One Hundredth are spelled out.

> 167 Second Avenue
> 19 South 22nd Street
> *or less commonly*   19 South Twenty-second Street
> 145 East 145th Street
> in the 60s   *or*   in the Sixties [streets from 60th to 69th]
> in the 120s [streets from 120th to 129th]

When a house or building number immediately precedes the number of a street, a spaced hyphen may be inserted between the two numbers, or the street number may be written out, for the sake of clarity.

> 2018 - 14th Street
> 2018 Fourteenth Street

3. Arabic numerals are used to designate highways and, in some states, county roads.

> Interstate 90   *or*   I-90
> U.S. Route 1   *or*   U.S. 1
> Texas 23
> County 213

Dates

4. Year numbers are written as figures. If a year number begins a sentence, it may be left as a figure but more often is spelled out; the sentence may also be rewritten to avoid beginning it with a figure.

> the 1997 edition
> Nineteen thirty-seven marked the opening of the Golden Gate Bridge.
> *or*   The year 1937 marked the opening of the Golden Gate Bridge.
> *or*   The Golden Gate Bridge opened in 1937.

5. A year number may be abbreviated to its last two digits when an event is so well known that it needs no century designation. In these cases an apostrophe precedes the numerals.

> the blizzard of '88
> class of '91   *or*   class of 1991
> the Spirit of '76

6. Full dates are traditionally written in the sequence month-day-year, with the year set off by commas that precede and follow it. An alternative style, used in the military and in U.S. government publications, is the inverted sequence day-month-year, which does not require commas.

> *traditional:*   July 8, 1976, was a warm, sunny day in Philadelphia.
> the explosion on July 16, 1945, at Alamogordo
> *military:*   the explosion on 16 July 1945 at Alamogordo
> the amendment ratified on 18 August 1920

7. Ordinal numbers are not used in full dates. Ordinals are sometimes used, however, for a date without an accom-

panying year, and they are always used when preceded in a date by the word *the.*

> December 4, 1829
> on December 4th   *or*   on December 4
> on the 4th of December

8. All-figure dating, such as 6-8-95 or 6/8/95, is usually avoided except in informal writing. For some readers, such dates are ambiguous; the examples above generally mean June 8, 1995, in the United States, but in almost all other countries mean August 6, 1995.

9. Commas are usually omitted from dates that include the month and year but not the day. The word *of* is sometimes inserted between the month and year.

> in October 1997
> back in January of 1981

10. References to specific centuries may be either written out or expressed in figures.

> in the nineteenth century   *or*   in the 19th century
> a sixteenth-century painting   *or*   a 16th-century painting

11. The name of a specific decade often takes a short form, usually with no apostrophe and uncapitalized. When the short form is part of a set phrase, it is capitalized.

> a song from the sixties
> *occasionally*   a song from the 'sixties   *or*   a song from the Sixties
> tunes of the Gay Nineties

The name of a decade is often expressed in numerals, in plural form. The figure may be shortened, with an apostrophe to indicate the missing numerals; however, apostrophes enclosing the figure are generally avoided. Any sequence of such numbers is generally styled consistently.

> the 1950s and 1960s   *or*   the '50s and '60s
> *but not*
> the '50's and '60's
> the 1950s and '60s
> the 1950s and sixties

12. Era designations precede or follow words that specify centuries or numerals that specify years. Era designations are unspaced abbreviations, punctuated with periods. They are usually typed or keyboarded as regular capitals, and typeset in books as small capitals and in newspapers as full-size capitals. The abbreviation B.C. (before Christ) is placed after the date, while A.D. (*anno Domini,* "in the year of our Lord") is usually placed before the date but after a century designation. Any date given without an era designation or context is understood to mean A.D.

> 1792–1750 B.C.
> between 600 and 400 B.C.
> from the fifth or fourth millennium to c. 250 B.C.
> between 7 B.C. and A.D. 22
> c. A.D. 100 to 300
> the second century A.D.
> the 17th century

13. Less common era designations include A.H. (*anno Hegirae,* "in the year of [Muhammad's] Hegira," or *anno Hebraico,* "in the Hebrew year"); B.C.E. (before the com-

mon era; a synonym for B.C.); C.E. (of the common era; a synonym for A.D.); and B.P. (before the present; often used by geologists and archeologists, with or without the word *year*). The abbreviation A.H. is usually placed before a specific date but after a century designation, while B.C.E., C.E., and B.P., are placed after both a date and a century.

> the tenth of Muharram, A.H. 61 (October 10, A.D. 680)
> the first century A.H.
> from the 1st century B.C.E. to the 4th century C.E.
> 63 B.C.E.
> the year 200 C.E.
> 5,000 years B.P.
> two million years B.P.

Degrees of Temperature and Arc

14. In technical writing, a quantity expressed in degrees is generally written as a numeral followed by the degree symbol (°). In the Kelvin scale, neither the word *degree* nor the symbol is used with the figure.

> a 45° angle
> 6°40′10″N
> 32° F
> 0° C
> Absolute zero is zero kelvins or 0 K.

15. In general writing, the quantity expressed in degrees may or may not be written out. A figure may be followed by either the degree symbol or the word *degree;* a spelled-out number is always followed by the word *degree.*

> latitude 43°19″N
> latitude 43 degrees N
> a difference of 43 degrees latitude
> The temperature has risen about thirty degrees.

Fractions and Decimal Fractions

16. In nontechnical prose, fractions standing alone are usually written out. Common fractions used as nouns are usually unhyphenated, although the hyphenated form is also common. When fractions are used as modifiers, they are hyphenated.

> lost three quarters of its value   *or*   lost three-quarters of its value
> had a two-thirds chance of winning

Multiword numerators and denominators are usually hyphenated, or written as figures.

> one one-hundredth of an inch   *or*   1/100 of an inch

17. Mixed fractions (fractions with a whole number, such as 3½) and fractions that form part of a modifier are usually expressed in figures in running text.

> waiting 2½ hours
> a ⅞-mile course
> 2½-pound weights

Fractions that are not on the keyboard or available as special characters on a computer may be typed in full-sized digits; in mixed fractions, a space is left between the whole number and the fraction.

> a 7/8-mile course
> waiting 2 3/4 hours

18. Fractions used with units of measurement are usually expressed in figures, but common short words are often written out.

> ⅒ km   half a mile
> ⅓ oz.   a half-mile walk
> ⅞ inch   a sixteenth-inch gap

19. Decimal fractions are always set as figures. In technical writing, a zero is placed to the left of the decimal point when the fraction is less than a whole number; in general writing, the zero is usually omitted. Commas are not used in numbers following a decimal point.

> An example of a pure decimal fraction is 0.375, while 1.402 is classified as a mixed decimal fraction.
> a .22-caliber rifle
> 0.142857

20. Fractions and decimal fractions are usually not mixed in a text.

> weights of 5½ lbs., 3¼ lbs., and ½ oz.
> *or*   weights of 5.5 lbs., 3.25 lbs., and .5 oz.
> *not* weights of 5.5 lbs., 3¼ lbs., and ½ oz.

Lists and Outlines

21. Both run-in and vertical lists are often numbered. In run-in numbered lists—that is, numbered lists that form part of a normal-looking sentence—each item is preceded by a number (or, less often, an italicized letter) enclosed in parentheses. The items are separated by commas if they are brief and unpunctuated; if they are complex or punctuated, they are separated by semicolons. The entire list is introduced by a colon if it is preceded by a full clause, and often when it is not.

> Among the fastest animals with measured maximum speeds are (1) the cheetah, clocked at 70 mph; (2) the pronghorn antelope, at 61 mph; (3) the lion, at 50 mph; (4) the quarter horse, at 47 mph; and (5) the elk, at 45 mph.
> The new medical dictionary has several special features: *(a)* common variant spellings; *(b)* examples of words used in context; *(c)* abbreviations, combining forms, prefixes, and suffixes; and *(d)* brand names for drugs and their generic equivalents.

22. In vertical lists, each number is followed by a period; the periods align vertically. Run-over lines usually align under the item's first word. Each item may be capitalized, especially if the items are syntactically independent of the words that introduce them.

> The English peerage consists of five ranks, listed here in descending order:
>   1. Duke (duchess)
>   2. Marquess (marchioness)
>   3. Earl (countess)
>   4. Viscount (viscountess)
>   5. Baron (baroness)

The listed items end with periods (or question marks) when they are complete sentences, and also often when they are not.

> We require answers to the following questions:
>   1. Does the club intend to engage heavy-metal bands to perform in the future?
>   2. Will any such bands be permitted to play past midnight on weekends?
>   3. Are there plans to install proper acoustic insulation?

Items that are syntactically dependent on the words that introduce them often begin with a lowercase letter and end with a comma or semicolon just as in a run-in series in an ordinary sentence.

> Among the courts that are limited to special kinds of cases are
> 1. probate courts, for the estates of deceased persons;
> 2. commercial courts, for business cases;
> 3. juvenile courts, for cases involving children under 18; and
> 4. traffic courts, for minor cases involving highway and motor vehicle violations.

A vertical list may also be unnumbered, or may use bullets (•) in place of numerals, especially where the order of the items is not important.

> Chief among the important advances in communication were these 19th-century inventions:
> Morse's telegraph
> Daguerre's camera
> Bell's telephone
> Edison's phonograph

> This book covers in detail:
> • Punctuation
> • Capitalization and italicization
> • Numbers
> • Abbreviations
> • Grammar and composition

23. Outlines standardly use Roman numerals, capitalized letters, Arabic numerals, and lowercase letters, in that order. Each numeral or letter is followed by a period, and each item is capitalized.

> III. The United States from 1816 to 1850
>   A. Era of mixed feelings
>   1. Effects of the War of 1812
>   2. National disunity
>   B. The economy
>   1. Transportation revolution
>   a. Waterways
>   b. Railroads
>   2. Beginnings of industrialization
> IV. The Civil War and Reconstruction, 1850–77

Money

24. A sum of money that can be expressed in one or two words is usually written out in running text, as is the unit of currency. But if several sums are mentioned in the sentence or paragraph, all are usually expressed as figures and are used with the unspaced currency symbol.

> The scalpers were asking eighty dollars.
> Grandfather remembered the days of the five-cent cigar.
> The shoes on sale are priced at $69 and $89.
> Jill wanted to sell the lemonade for 25¢, 35¢, and 45¢.

25. Monetary units of mixed dollars-and-cents amounts are expressed in figures.

> $16.75
> $307.02

26. Even-dollar amounts are often expressed in figures without a decimal point and zeros. But when even-dollar amounts appear near amounts that include cents, the decimal point and zeros are usually added for consis-

tency. The dollar sign is repeated before each amount in a series or inclusive range.

> They paid $500 for the watercolor.
> The price had risen from $8.00 to $9.95.
> bids of $80, $90, and $100
> in the $80–$100 range

27. Sums of money in the millions or above rounded to no more than one decimal place are usually expressed in a combination of figures and words.

> a $10-million building program
> $4.5 billion

28. In legal documents a sum of money is usually written out fully, often capitalized, with the corresponding figures in parentheses immediately following.

> Twenty-five Thousand Dollars ($25,000)

Organizations and Governmental Entities

29. Ordinal numbers in the names of religious organizations and churches are usually written out.

> Seventh-Day Adventists
> Third Congregational Church

30. Local branches of labor unions and fraternal organizations are generally identified by a numeral, usually placed after the name.

> Motion Picture Studio Mechanics Local 476
> Loyal Order of Moose No. 220
> Local 4277 Communications Workers of America

31. In names of governmental bodies and electoral, judicial, and military units, ordinal numbers of one hundred or below are usually written out but often not.

> Second Continental Congress
> Fifth Republic
> First Congressional District
> Court of Appeals for the Third Circuit
> U.S. Eighth Army
> Twelfth Precinct *or* 12th Precinct
> Ninety-eighth Congress *or* 98th Congress

Percentages

32. In technical writing, and often in business and financial writing, percentages are written as a figure followed by an unspaced % symbol. In general writing, the word *percent* normally replaces the symbol, and the number may either be written out (if it does not include a decimal) or expressed as a figure.

> *technical:*   15%
>   13.5%
> *general:*   15 percent
>   87.2 percent
>   Fifteen percent of the applicants were accepted.
>   a four percent increase *or* a 4% increase

33. In a series or range, the percent sign is usually included with all numbers, even if one of the numbers is zero.

> rates of 8.3%, 8.8%, and 9.1%
> a variation of 0% to 10% *or* a 0%–10% variation

Plurals

34. The plurals of written-out numbers, including fractions, are formed by adding *-s* or *-es.*

> at sixes and sevens
> divided into eighths
> ever since the thirties
> still in her thirties

35. The plurals of figures are formed by adding *-s* or less commonly *-'s,* especially where the apostrophe can prevent a confusing typographic appearance.

> in the '80s
> since the 1980s [*or less commonly* 1980's]
> temperatures in the 80s and 90s [*or* 80's and 90's]
> the *1*'s looked like *l*'s

Ratios

36. Ratios are generally expressed in figures, usually with the word *to;* in technical writing the figures may be joined by a colon or a slash instead. Ratios expressed in words use a hyphen (or en dash) or the word *to.*

> odds of 10 to 1
> a proportion of 1 to 4
> a 3:1 ratio
> 29 mi/gal
> a fifty-fifty chance
> a ratio of ten to four

Time of Day

37. In running text, the time of day is usually spelled out when expressed in even, half, or quarter hours or when it is followed by *o'clock.*

> around four-thirty
> arriving by ten
> planned to leave at half past five
> now almost a quarter to two
> arrived at nine o'clock

38. Figures are generally used when specifying a precise time.

> an appointment at 9:30 tomorrow morning
> buses at 8:42, 9:12, and 10:03 a.m.

39. Figures are also used when the time of day is followed by *a.m.* and *p.m.* These are usually written as punctuated lowercase letters, sometimes as small capital letters. They are not used with *o'clock* or with other words that specify the time of day.

> 8:30 a.m. *or* 8:30 A.M.
> 10:30 p.m. *or* 10:30 P.M.
> 8 a.m. *or* 8 A.M.
> home by nine o'clock
> 9:15 in the morning
> eleven in the evening

With *twelve o'clock* or 12:00, it is helpful to specify *midnight* or *noon* rather than the ambiguous *a.m.* or *p.m.*

> The third shift begins at 12:00 (midnight).

40. Even-hour times are generally written with a colon and two zeros when used in a series or pairing with any times not ending in two zeros.

> started at 9:15 a.m. and finished at 2:00 p.m.
> worked from 8:30 to 5:00

41. The 24-hour clock system—also called *military time*—uses no punctuation and omits *o'clock, a.m., p.m.,* or any other additional indication of the time of day. The word *hours* sometimes replaces them.

> from 0930 to 1100
> at 1600 hours

Units of Measurement

42. In technical writing, all numbers used with units of measurement are written as numerals. In nontechnical writing, such numbers often simply follow the basic conventions explained on page 215; alternatively, even in nontechnical contexts all such numbers often appear as numerals.

> In the control group, only 8 of the 90 plants were affected.
> picked nine quarts of berries
> chugging along at 9 [*or* nine] miles an hour
> a pumpkin 5 [*or* five] feet in diameter
> weighing 7 pounds 9 ounces
> a journey of 3 hours and 45 minutes

The singular form of units of measurement is used in a modifier before a noun, the plural form in a modifier that follows a noun.

> a 2- by 9-inch board *or* a two-inch by nine-inch board *or* a two- by nine-inch board
> measured 2 inches by 9 inches *or* measured two inches by nine inches
> a 6-foot 2-inch man
> is 6 feet 2 inches tall *or* is six feet two inches tall
> is six feet two *or* is 6 feet 2

43. When units of measurement are written as abbreviations or symbols, the adjacent numbers are always figures. (For abbreviations with numerals, see the section on page 214.)

> | | |
> |---|---|
> | 6 cm | 67.6 fl. oz. |
> | 1 mm | 4' |
> | $4.25 | 98.6° |

44. When two or more quantities are expressed, as in ranges or dimensions or series, an accompanying symbol is usually repeated with each figure.

> 4" × 6" cards
> temperatures of 30°, 55°, 43°, and 58°
> $450–$500 suits

Other Uses

45. Figures are generally used for precise ages in newspapers and magazines, and often in books as well.

> Taking the helm is Colin Corman, 51, a risk-taking high roller.
> At 9 [*or* nine] she mastered the Mendelssohn Violin Concerto.
> the champion 3[*or* three]-year-old filly
> for anyone aged 62 and over

46. Figures are used to refer to parts of a book, such as volume, chapter, illustration, and table numbers.

vol. 5, p. 202
Chapter 8   *or*   Chapter Eight
Fig. 4

47. Serial, policy, and contract numbers use figures. (For punctuation of these numbers, see paragraph 3 on page 216.)

Serial No. 5274
Permit No. 63709

48. Figures are used to express stock-market quotations, mathematical calculations, scores, and tabulations.

Industrials were up 4.23.
$3 \times 15 = 45$
a score of 8 to 2   *or*   a score of 8–2
the tally: 322 ayes, 80 nays

6 Notes and Bibliographies

Writers and editors use various methods to indicate the source of a quotation or piece of information borrowed from another work.

In high-school papers and in popular writing, sources are usually identified only by casual mentions within the text itself.

In college term papers, in serious nonfiction books published for the general public, and traditionally in scholarly books and articles in the humanities, footnotes or endnotes are preferred. In this system, sequential numbers within the text refer the reader to notes at the bottom of the page or at the end of the article, chapter, or book; these notes contain full bibliographic information on the works cited.

In scholarly works in the natural sciences, and increasingly in the social sciences and humanities as well, parenthetical references within the text refer the reader to an alphabetically arranged list of references at the end of the article, chapter, or book.

The system of footnotes or endnotes is the more flexible, since it allows for commentary on the work or subject and can also be used for brief discussions not tied to any specific work. However, style manuals tend to encourage the use of parenthetical references in addition to or instead of footnotes or endnotes, since for most kinds of material they are efficient and convenient for both writer and reader.

In a carefully documented work, an alphabetically ordered bibliography or list of references normally follows the entire text (including any endnotes), regardless of which system is used.

Though different publishers and journals have adopted slightly varying styles, the following examples illustrate standard styles for footnotes and endnotes, parenthetical references, and bibliographic entries. For more extensive treatment than can be provided here, consult *Merriam-Webster's Standard American Style Manual; The Chicago Manual of Style; The MLA Handbook for Writers of Research Papers; A Manual for Writers of Term Papers, Theses and Dissertations;* or *Scientific Style and Format.*

Footnotes and Endnotes

Footnotes and endnotes are usually indicated by superscript numbers placed immediately after the material to be documented, whether it is an actual quotation or a paraphrase of the language used in the source. The number is placed at the end of a paragraph, sentence or clause, or at some other natural break in the sentence; it follows all marks of punctuation except the dash.

As one observer noted, "There was, moreover, a degree of logic in the new LDP-SDPJ axis, in that the inner cores of both parties felt threatened by the recent electoral reform legislation,"[7] and . . .

The numbering is consecutive throughout a paper, article, or monograph; in a book, it usually starts over with each new chapter.

The note itself begins with the corresponding number. Footnotes appear at the bottom of the page; endnotes, which take exactly the same form as footnotes, are gathered at the end of the article, chapter, or book.

Endnotes are generally preferred over footnotes by writers and publishers because they are easier to handle when preparing both manuscript and printed pages, though they can be less convenient for the reader.

Both footnotes and endnotes provide full bibliographic information for a source the first time it is cited. In subsequent references, this information is shortened to the author's last name and the page number. If more than one book by an author is cited, a shortened form of the title is also included. The Latin abbreviation *ibid.* is sometimes used to refer to the book cited in the immediately preceding note.

The following examples describe specific elements of first references and reflect humanities citation style; notes 12–14 show examples of subsequent references. All of the cited works appear again in the Bibliographies and Lists of References section beginning on page 224.

Books

The basic elements for book citations are (1) the author's name; (2) the book's title; (3) the place of publication, publisher, and date of publication; and (4) the page(s) where the information appears.

One author:
1. Elizabeth Bishop, *The Complete Poems: 1927–1979* (New York: Farrar, Straus & Giroux, 1983), 46.

Two or three authors:
2. Bert Hölldobler and Edward O. Wilson, *The Ants* (Cambridge, Mass.: Belknap–Harvard Univ. Press, 1990), 119.

3. Charles T. Brusaw, Gerald J. Alred, and Walter E. Oliu, *The Business Writer's Handbook,* 4th rev. ed. (New York: St. Martin's, 1993), 182–84.

Four or more authors:
4. Randolph Quirk et al., *A Comprehensive Grammar of the English Language* (London: Longman, 1985), 135.

Corporate author:
5. Commission on the Humanities, *The Humanities in American Life* (Berkeley: Univ. of California Press, 1980), 58.

No author:
6. *Information Please Almanac: 1996* (Boston: Houghton Mifflin, 1995), 324.

Editor and/or translator:
7. Arthur S. Banks, ed., *Political Handbook of the World: 1994–1995* (Binghamton, N.Y.: CSA Publications, 1995), 293–95.

8. Simone de Beauvoir, *The Second Sex,* trans. and ed. H. M. Parshley (New York: Knopf, 1953; Vintage, 1989), 446.

Part of a book:
9. Ernst Mayr, "Processes of Speciation in Animals," *Mechanisms of Speciation,* ed. C. Barigozzi (New York: Alan R. Liss, 1982), 1–3.

Second or later edition:
10. Albert C. Baugh and Thomas Cable, *A History of the English Language,* 4th ed. (Englewood Cliffs, N.J.: Prentice Hall, 1992), 14.

Two or more volumes:

11. Ronald M. Nowak, *Walker's Mammals of the World,* 5th ed., 2 vols. (Baltimore: Johns Hopkins Univ. Press, 1991), 2: 661.

In subsequent references:

12. Nowak, 662.

13. Baugh and Cable, *History,* 18–19.

14. Ibid., 23.

Articles

The basic elements for citations of articles are (1) the author's name, (2) the article's title, (3) the name of the periodical, with information identifying the issue (following the form the periodical itself uses), and (4) the page(s) referred to.

Weekly magazine:

15. Richard Preston, "A Reporter at Large: Crisis in the Hot Zone," *New Yorker,* Oct. 26, 1992: 58.

Monthly magazine:

16. John Lukacs, "The End of the Twentieth Century," *Harper's,* Jan. 1993: 40.

Journal paginated by issue:

17. Roseann Duenas Gonzalez, "Teaching Mexican American Students to Write: Capitalizing on the Culture," *English Journal* 71, no. 7 (Nov. 1982): 22–24.

Journal paginated by volume:

18. Stephen Jay Gould and Niles Eldredge, "Punctuated Equilibria: The Tempo and Mode of Evolution Reconsidered," *Paleobiology* 3 (1977): 121.

Newspaper:

19. William J. Broad, "Big Science Squeezes Small-Scale Researchers," *New York Times,* Dec. 29, 1992: C1.

Signed review:

20. Gordon Craig, review of *The Wages of Guilt: Memories of War in Germany and Japan,* by Ian Buruma, *New York Review of Books,* July 14, 1994: 43–45.

In subsequent reference:

21. Gonzalez, 23.

Parenthetical References

Parenthetical references are highly abbreviated bibliographic citations that appear within the text itself, enclosed in parentheses. These direct the reader to a detailed bibliography or list of references at the end of the work, often removing the need for footnotes or endnotes.

A parenthetical reference, like a footnote or endnote number, is placed immediately after the quotation or piece of information whose source it refers to; punctuation not associated with a quotation follows the reference.

> As one observer noted, "There was, moreover, a degree of logic in the new LDP-SDPJ axis, in that the inner cores of both parties felt threatened by the recent electoral reform legislation" (Banks, 448), and . . .

Any element of a reference that is clear from the context of the running text may be omitted.

> As noted in Banks, "There was, moreover, a degree of logic in the new LDP-SDPJ axis, in that the inner cores of both parties

> felt threatened by the recent electoral reform legislation" (448), and . . .

Parenthetical references in the humanities usually include only the author's (or editor's) last name and a page reference (see extract above). This style is known as the *author-page system.*

In the sciences, the year of publication is included after the author's name with no intervening punctuation, and the page number is usually omitted. This scientific style is commonly called the *author-date system.*

> As some researchers noted, "New morphological, biochemical, and karyological studies suggest that *P. boylii* actually comprises several distinct species" (Nowak 1991), and . . .

To distinguish among cited works by the same author, the author's name may be followed by the specific work's title, which is usually shortened. (If the author-date system is being used, a lowercase letter can be added after the year—e.g., 1992a, 1992b—to distinguish between works published in the same year.)

Each of the following references is keyed to an entry in the bibliographic listings in the following section.

Humanities style:

(Banks, 448)
(Quirk et al., 135)
(Baugh and Cable, *History,* 14)
(Comm. on the Humanities, 58)

Sciences style:

(Gould and Eldredge 1977)
(Nowak 1991a)

Bibliographies and Lists of References

A *bibliography* lists all of the works that a writer has found relevant in writing the text. A *list of references* includes only works specifically mentioned in the text or from which a particular quotation or piece of information was taken. In all other respects, the two listings are identical.

Bibliographies and lists of references both differ from bibliographic endnotes in that their entries are unnumbered, are arranged in alphabetical order by author, and use different patterns of indention and punctuation. Entries for periodical articles also list their inclusive page numbers. The following lists illustrate standard styles employed in, respectively, the humanities and social sciences and the natural sciences.

The principal differences between the two styles are these: In the sciences, (1) an initial is generally used instead of the author's first name, (2) the date is placed directly after the author's name, (3) all words in titles are lowercased except the first word, the first word of any subtitle, and proper nouns and adjectives, and (4) article titles are not enclosed in quotation marks. Increasingly in scientific publications, (5) the author's first and middle initials are closed up without any punctuation, and (6) book and journal titles are not italicized. The following bibliographic lists include both books and periodical articles.

Humanities style

Banks, Arthur S., ed. *Political Handbook of the World: 1994–1995.* Binghamton, N.Y.: CSA Publications, 1995.

Baugh, Albert C., and Thomas Cable. *A History of the English Language.* 4th ed. Englewood Cliffs, N.J.: Prentice Hall, 1992.

Beauvoir, Simone de. *The Second Sex.* Trans. and ed. H. M. Parshley. New York: Alfred A. Knopf, 1953; Vintage, 1989.

Bishop, Elizabeth. *The Complete Poems: 1927–1979.* New York: Farrar, Straus & Giroux, 1983.

Brusaw, Charles T., Gerald J. Alred, and Walter E. Oliu. *The Business Writer's Handbook.* 4th rev. ed. New York: St. Martin's, 1993.

Commission on the Humanities. *The Humanities in American Life.* Berkeley: University of California Press, 1980.

Craig, Gordon. Review of *The Wages of Guilt: Memories of War in Germany and Japan,* by Ian Buruma. *New York Review of Books,* July 14, 1994: 43–45.

Gonzalez, Roseann Duenas. "Teaching Mexican American Students to Write: Capitalizing on the Culture." *English Journal* 71, no. 7 (November 1982): 22–24.

Information Please Almanac: 1996. Boston: Houghton Mifflin, 1995.

Lukacs, John. "The End of the Twentieth Century." *Harper's,* January 1993: 39–58.

Quirk, Randolph, Sidney Greenbaum, Geoffrey Leech, and Jan Svartvik. *A Comprehensive Grammar of the English Language.* London: Longman, 1985.

Sciences style

Broad, W. J. 1992. Big science squeezes small-scale researchers. *New York Times,* 29 Dec.:C1.

Gould, S. J., and N. Eldredge. 1977. Punctuated equilibria: The tempo and mode of evolution reconsidered. *Paleobiology* 3:115–51.

Hölldobler, B., and E. O. Wilson. 1990. *The ants.* Cambridge, Mass.: Belknap–Harvard Univ. Press.

Mayr, E. 1982. Processes of speciation in animals. *Mechanisms of speciation.* Ed. C. Barigozzi. New York: Alan R. Liss.

Nowak, R. M. 1991. *Walker's mammals of the world.* 5th ed. 2 vols. Baltimore: Johns Hopkins Univ. Press.

Preston, R. 1992. A reporter at large: Crisis in the hot zone. *New Yorker,* 26 Oct.:58–81.

Special Cases

Lists of references frequently contain items that do not fit neatly into any of the categories described above. Some are printed items such as government publications, others are nonprint items. These special references are styled in formats similar to those used for books and articles.

Television and radio programs

Burns, Ken. *Baseball.* PBS. WGBY-TV, Springfield, Mass. 28 Sept. 1994.

Computer software

World Atlas. CD-ROM. Novato, Calif.: Software Toolworks, 1990.

Microform

"Marine Mammals; Permit Modification: Naval Facilities Engineering Commission (P8D)." *Federal Register* 55.1:90. Washington: CIS, 1990. Microfiche.

Government publications

United States. Department of Labor. Employment and Training Administration. *Dictionary of Occupational Titles.* Rev. 4th ed. Washington: GPO, 1991.

U.S. Congress. Senate. Subcommittee on Administrative Law and Government Relations of the Committee on the Judiciary. *Hearings on Post-Employment Restrictions for Federal Officers and Employees.* 101st Cong., 1st sess. 27 Apr. 1989. H.R. 2267.

Congressional Record. 29 June 1993: S8269–70.

Personal interview

Norris, Nancy Preston. Conversation with author. Wilkes-Barre, Pa., 10 October 1995.

Christian, Dr. Lionel. Telephone conversation with author, 2 January 1996.

Webster's
Quick
Homework
Help

Contents

Presidents of the U.S.

No.	Name (pronunciation)	Life dates	Birthplace	Term dates
1	George Washington \'wȯsh-ing-tən, 'wäsh-\	1732–1799	Va.	1789–1797
2	John Adams \'ad-əmz\	1735–1826	Mass.	1797–1801
3	Thomas Jefferson\'jef-ər-sən\	1743–1826	Va.	1801–1809
4	James Madison \'mad-ə-sən\	1751–1836	Va.	1809–1817
5	James Monroe \mən-'rō\	1758–1831	Va.	1817–1825
6	John Quincy Adams \'ad-əmz\	1767–1848	Mass.	1825–1829
7	Andrew Jackson \'jak-sən\	1767–1845	S.C.	1829–1837
8	Martin Van Buren \van-'byur-ən\	1782–1862	N.Y.	1837–1841
9	William Henry Harrison \'har-ə-sən\	1773–1841	Va.	1841
10	John Tyler \'tī-lər\	1790–1862	Va.	1841–1845
11	James Knox Polk \'pōk\	1795–1849	N.C.	1845–1849
12	Zachary Taylor \'tā-lər\	1784–1850	Va.	1849–1850
13	Millard Fillmore \'fil-ˌmōr\	1800–1874	N.Y.	1850–1853
14	Franklin Pierce \'piərs\	1804–1869	N.H.	1853–1857
15	James Buchanan \byü-'kan-ən\	1791–1868	Penn.	1857–1861
16	Abraham Lincoln \'ling-kən\	1809–1865	Ky.	1861–1865
17	Andrew Johnson \'jän-sən\	1808–1875	N.C.	1865–1869
18	Ulysses S. Grant \'grant\	1822–1885	Ohio	1869–1877
19	Rutherford B. Hayes \'hāz\	1822–1893	Ohio	1877–1881
20	James A. Garfield \'gär-ˌfēld\	1831–1881	Ohio	1881
21	Chester A. Arthur \'är-thər\	1830–1886	Vt.	1881–1885
22	Grover Cleveland \'klēv-lənd\	1837–1908	N.J.	1885–1889
23	Benjamin Harrison \'har-ə-sən\	1833–1901	Ohio	1889–1893
24	Grover Cleveland \'klēv-lənd\	1837–1908	N.J.	1893–1897
25	William McKinley \mə-'kin-lē\	1843–1901	Ohio	1897–1901
26	Theodore Roosevelt \'rō-zə-ˌvelt\	1858–1919	N.Y.	1901–1909
27	William Howard Taft \'taft\	1857–1930	Ohio	1909–1913
28	Woodrow Wilson \'wil-sən\	1856–1924	Va.	1913–1921
29	Warren G. Harding \'härd-ing\	1865–1923	Ohio	1921–1923
30	Calvin Coolidge \'kü-lij\	1872–1933	Vt.	1923–1929
31	Herbert C. Hoover \'hü-vər\	1874–1964	Iowa	1929–1933
32	Franklin D. Roosevelt \'rō-zə-ˌvelt\	1882–1945	N.Y.	1933–1945
33	Harry S Truman \'trü-mən\	1884–1972	Miss.	1945–1953
34	Dwight D. Eisenhower \'īz-n-ˌhau̇-ər\	1890–1969	Texas	1953–1961
35	John F. Kennedy \'ken-ə-dē\	1917–1963	Mass.	1961–1963
36	Lyndon B. Johnson \'jän-sən\	1908–1973	Texas	1963–1969
37	Richard M. Nixon \'nik-sən\	1913–1994	Calif.	1969–1974
38	Gerald R. Ford \'fōrd\	1913–	Neb.	1974–1977
39	Jimmy Carter \'kärt-ər\	1924–	Ga.	1977–1981
40	Ronald W. Reagan \'rā-gən\	1911–	Ill.	1981–1989
41	George H. W. Bush \'bush\	1924–	Mass.	1989–1993
42	William J. Clinton \'klin-tən\	1946–	Ark.	1993–

Prime Ministers of Canada

No.	Name (pronunciation)	Life dates	Term dates
1	John A. Macdonald \mək-'dän-əld\	1815–1891	1867–1873
2	Alexander Mackenzie \mə-'ken-zē\	1822–1892	1873–1878
3	John A. Macdonald \mək-'dän-əld\	1815–1891	1878–1891
4	John J. C. Abbott \'ab-ət\	1821–1893	1891–1892
5	John S. D. Thompson \'täm(p)-sən\	1844–1894	1892–1894
6	Mackenzie Bowell \'bō(-ə)l\	1823–1917	1894–1896
7	Charles Tupper \'təp-ər\	1821–1915	1896
8	Wilfrid Laurier \lȯr-yā, lȯr-ē-ˌā\	1841–1919	1896–1911
9	Robert L. Borden \'bȯrd-ᵊn\	1854–1937	1911–1920
10	Arthur Meighen \'mē-ən\	1874–1960	1920–1921
11	W. L. Mackenzie King \'kiŋ\	1874–1950	1921–1926
12	Arthur Meighen \'mē-ən\	1874–1960	1926
13	W. L. Mackenzie King \'kiŋ\	1874–1950	1926–1930
14	Richard B. Bennett \'ben-ət\	1870–1947	1930–1935
15	W. L. Mackenzie King \'kiŋ\	1874–1950	1935–1948
16	Louis Stephen St. Laurent \saⁿ-lȯ-räⁿ\	1882–1973	1948–1957
17	John George Diefenbaker \'dē-fən-ˌbā-kər\	1895–1979	1957–1963
18	Lester B. Pearson \'pi(ə)rs-ᵊn\	1897–1972	1963–1968
19	Pierre Elliott Trudeau \'trü(ˌ)dō, trü-'\	1919–	1968–1979
20	Joe Clark \'klärk\	1939–	1979–1980
21	Pierre Elliott Trudeau \'trü(ˌ)dō, trü-'\	1919–	1980–1984
22	John Turner \'tərn-ər\	1929–	1984
23	Brian Mulroney \məl-'rü-nē\	1939–	1984–1993
24	Kim Campbell \'kam-bəl\	1947–	1993
25	Jean Chrétien \krā-tyaⁿ\	1934–	1993–

Place Names and Capitals

STATES OF THE U.S.

NAME, U.S. P.O. ABBR., and NICKNAME	AREA[1] sq. mi. (sq. km.)	rank	POPULATION 1990 census	rank	ADMITTED TO UNION[2] date rank		CAPITAL	MOTTO
Alabama (AL) *Heart of Dixie*	51,705 (133,916)	29th	4,040,587	22d	1819	22d	Montgomery	We Dare Defend Our Rights
Alaska[3] (AK) *The Last Frontier*	591,004 (1,530,700)	1st	550,043	49th	1959	49th	Juneau	North to the Future
Arizona (AZ) *Grand Canyon State*	114,000 (295,260)	6th	3,665,228	24th	1912	48th	Phoenix	*Ditat Deus* (God Enriches)
Arkansas (AR) *Land of Opportunity*	53,187 (137,754)	27th	2,350,725	33d	1836	25th	Little Rock	*Regnat Populus* (The People Rule)
California (CA) *Golden State*	158,706 (411,048)	3d	29,760,020	1st	1850	31st	Sacramento	*Eureka* (I Have Found It)
Colorado (CO) *Centennial State*	104,247 (270,000)	8th	3,294,394	26th	1876	38th	Denver	*Nil Sine Numine* (Nothing Without the Divine Will)
Connecticut[2] (CT) *Constitution State, Nutmeg State*	5,018 (12,997)	48th	3,287,116	27th	1788	5th	Hartford	*Qui Transtulit Sustinet* (He Who Transplanted Sustains)
Delaware[2] (DE) *First State, Diamond State*	2,057 (5,328)	49th	666,168	46th	1787	1st	Dover	Liberty and Independence
Florida (FL) *Sunshine State*	58,664 (151,940)	22d	12,937,926	4th	1845	27th	Tallahassee	In God We Trust
Georgia[2] (GA) *Empire State of the South, Peach State*	58,910 (152,577)	21st	6,478,216	11th	1788	4th	Atlanta	Wisdom, Justice, Moderation
Hawaii[3] (HI) *Aloha State*	6,471 (16,760)	47th	1,108,229	41st	1959	50th	Honolulu	*Ua Mau Ke Ea O Ka Aina I Ka Pono* (The Life of the Land Is Established in Righteousness)
Idaho (ID) *Gem State*	83,557 (216,413)	13th	1,006,749	42d	1890	43d	Boise	*Esto Perpetua* (May She Endure Forever)
Illinois (IL) *Prairie State*	56,400 (146,076)	24th	11,430,602	6th	1818	21st	Springfield	State Sovereignty—National Union
Indiana (IN) *Hoosier State*	36,291 (93,994)	38th	5,544,159	14th	1816	19th	Indianapolis	The Crossroads of America
Iowa (IA) *Hawkeye State*	56,275 (145,752)	25th	2,776,755	30th	1846	29th	Des Moines	Our Liberties We Prize and Our Rights We Will Maintain
Kansas (KS) *Sunflower State*	82,277 (213,097)	14th	2,477,574	32d	1861	34th	Topeka	*Ad Astra per Aspera* (To the Stars by Hard Ways)
Kentucky (KY) *Bluegrass State*	40,395 (104,623)	37th	3,685,296	23d	1792	15th	Frankfort	United We Stand, Divided We Fall
Louisiana (LA) *Pelican State*	48,523 (125,674)	31st	4,219,973	21st	1812	18th	Baton Rouge	Union, Justice, Confidence
Maine (ME) *Pine Tree State*	33,265 (86,156)	39th	1,227,928	38th	1820	23d	Augusta	*Dirigo* (I Direct)
Maryland[2] (MD) *Old Line State*	10,460 (27,091)	42d	4,781,468	19th	1788	7th	Annapolis	*Fatti Maschii, Parole Femine* (Manly Deeds, Womanly Words)

230

NAME, U.S. P.O. ABBR., and NICKNAME	AREA[1] sq. mi. (sq. km.)	rank	POPULATION 1990 census	rank	ADMITTED TO UNION[2] date rank		CAPITAL	MOTTO
Massachusetts[2] (MA) Bay State	8,284 (21,456)	45th	6,016,425	13th	1788	6th	Boston	*Ense Petit Placidam Sub Libertate Quietem* (By the Sword We Seek Peace, but Peace Only Under Liberty)
Michigan (MI) Wolverine State, Great Lakes State	58,216 (150,779)	23d	9,295,297	8th	1837	26th	Lansing	*Si Quaeris Peninsulam Amoenam Circumspice* (If You Seek a Beautiful Peninsula, Look Around)
Minnesota (MN) Gopher State, North Star State	84,068 (217,736)	12th	4,375,099	20th	1858	32d	St. Paul	*L'étoile du Nord* (Star of the North)
Mississippi (MS) Magnolia State	47,689 (123,514)	32d	2,573,216	31st	1817	20th	Jackson	*Virtute et Armis* (By Valor and Arms)
Missouri (MO) Show Me State	69,697 (180,515)	19th	5,117,073	15th	1821	24th	Jefferson City	*Salus Populi Suprema Lex Esto* (Let the Welfare of the People Be the Supreme Law)
Montana (MT) Treasure State	147,046 (380,849)	4th	799,065	44th	1889	41st	Helena	*Oro y Plata* (Gold and Silver)
Nebraska (NE) Cornhusker State	77,355 (200,349)	15th	1,578,385	36th	1867	37th	Lincoln	Equality Before the Law
Nevada (NV) Silver State	110,561 (286,353)	7th	1,201,833	39th	1864	36th	Carson City	All for Our Country
New Hampshire[2] (NH) Granite State	9,279 (24,033)	44th	1,109,252	40th	1788	9th	Concord	Live Free or Die
New Jersey[2] (NJ) Garden State	7,787 (20,168)	46th	7,730,188	9th	1787	3d	Trenton	Liberty and Prosperity
New Mexico (NM) Land of Enchantment	121,593 (314,926)	5th	1,515,069	37th	1912	47th	Santa Fe	*Crescit Eundo* (It Grows as It Goes)
New York[2] (NY) Empire State	49,576 (128,402)	30th	17,990,456	2d	1788	11th	Albany	*Excelsior* (Still Higher)
North Carolina[2] (NC) Tar Heel State, Old North State	52,669 (136,413)	28th	6,628,637	10th	1789	12th	Raleigh	To Be Rather Than to Seem
North Dakota (ND) Flickertail State	70,665 (183,022)	17th	638,800	47th	1889	39th	Bismarck	Liberty and Union, Now and Forever, One and Inseparable
Ohio (OH) Buckeye State	41,222 (106,765)	35th	10,847,115	7th	1803	17th	Columbus	no motto
Oklahoma (OK) Sooner State	69,956 (181,186)	18th	3,145,585	28th	1907	46th	Oklahoma City	*Labor Omnia Vincit* (Labor Conquers All Things)
Oregon (OR) Beaver State	97,073 (251,419)	10th	2,842,321	29th	1859	33d	Salem	*Alis Volat Propriis* (She Flies with Her Own Wings)
Pennsylvania[2] (PA) Keystone State	45,333 (117,412)	33d	11,881,643	5th	1787	2d	Harrisburg	Virtue, Liberty, and Independence
Rhode Island[2] (RI) Ocean State, Little Rhody	1,212 (3,139)	50th	1,003,464	43d	1790	13th	Providence	Hope
South Carolina[2] (SC) Palmetto State	31,113 (80,583)	40th	3,486,703	25th	1788	8th	Columbia	*Dum Spiro, Spero* (While I Breathe, I Hope)

NAME, U.S. P.O. ABBR., and NICKNAME	AREA[1]		POPULATION		ADMITTED TO UNION[2]		CAPITAL	MOTTO
	sq. mi. (sq. km.)	rank	1990 census	rank	date	rank		
South Dakota (SD) *Mount Rushmore State*	77,116 (199,730)	16th	696,004	45th	1889	40th	Pierre	Under God the People Rule
Tennessee (TN) *Volunteer State*	42,144 (109,153)	34th	4,877,185	17th	1796	16th	Nashville	Agriculture and Commerce
Texas (TX) *Lone Star State*	266,807 (691,030)	2d	16,986,510	3d	1845	28th	Austin	Friendship
Utah (UT) *Beehive State*	84,899 (219,888)	11th	1,722,850	35th	1896	45th	Salt Lake City	Industry
Vermont (VT) *Green Mountain State*	9,609 (24,887)	43d	562,758	48th	1791	14th	Montpelier	Freedom and Unity
Virginia[2] (VA) *Old Dominion*	40,767 (105,586)	36th	6,187,358	12th	1788	10th	Richmond	*Sic Semper Tyrannis* (Thus Ever to Tyrants)
Washington (WA) *Evergreen State*	68,192 (176,617)	20th	4,866,692	18th	1889	42d	Olympia	*Alki* (By and By)
West Virginia (WV) *Mountain State*	24,181 (62,629)	41st	1,793,477	34th	1863	35th	Charleston	*Montani Semper Liberi* (Mountaineers Are Always Free)
Wisconsin (WI) *Badger State*	56,154 (145,439)	26th	4,891,769	16th	1848	30th	Madison	Forward
Wyoming (WY) *Equality State, Cowboy State*	97,914 (253,597)	9th	453,588	50th	1890	44th	Cheyenne	Equal Rights
District of Columbia[4] (DC)	69 (179)		609,909				Washington	*E Pluribus Unum* (One Out of Many)

1 Total land and inland water.
2 Date of admission of the 13 original colonies is that of ratification of the Constitution.
3 The Alaska Statehood Act was signed by the president on July 7, 1958; the Hawaii Statehood Act, Mar. 18, 1959.
4 Coextensive with the city of Washington.

PROVINCES AND TERRITORIES OF CANADA

NAME and P.O. ABBR.	AREA		POPULATION		DATE ADMITTED TO CONFED-ERATION**	CAPITAL	MOTTO
	sq. km. (sq. mi.)	rank	1996 census*	rank			
Alberta (AB)	661,190 sq. km. (255,285 sq. mi.)	6th	2,696,826	4th	1905	Edmonton	*Fortis et Liber* (Strong and Free)
British Columbia (BC)	947,800 sq. km. (365,946 sq. mi.)	5th	3,724,500	3d	1871	Victoria	*Splendor Sine Occasu* (Splendor Without Diminishment)
Manitoba (MB)	649,950 sq. km. (250,946 sq. mi.)	8th	1,113,898	5th	1870	Winnipeg	Glorious and Free
New Brunswick (NB)	73,440 sq. km. (28,355 sq. mi.)	11th	738,133	8th	1867	Fredericton	*Spem Reduxit* (Hope Was Restored)
Newfoundland (NF)	405,720 sq. km. (156,648 sq. mi.)	10th	551,792	9th	1949	St. John's	*Quaerite Prime Regnum Dei* (Seek Ye First the Kingdom of God)
Northwest Territories (NT)	1,432,320 sq. km. (553,019 sq. mi.)	3d	41,668	11th	1870	Yellowknife	no motto
Nova Scotia (NS)	55,490 sq. km. (21,425 sq. mi.)	12th	909,282	7th	1867	Halifax	*Munit Haec et Altera Vincit* (One Defends and the Other Conquers)
Nunavut (NU)	1,994,000 sq. km. (769,883 sq. mi.)	1st	27,219	13th	1999	Iqaluit	no motto
Ontario (ON)	1,068,580 sq. km. (412,579 sq. mi.)	4th	10,753,573	1st	1867	Toronto	*Ut Incepit Fidelis Sic Permanet* (Loyal She Began, Loyal She Remains)
Prince Edward Island (PE)	5,660 sq. km. (2,185 sq. mi.)	13th	134,557	10th	1873	Charlottetown	*Parva Sub Ingenti* (The Small Under the Protection of the Great)
Quebec (PQ)	1,540,680 sq. km. (594,857 sq. mi.)	2d	7,138,795	2d	1867	Quebec	*Je me souviens* (I Remember)
Saskatchewan (SK)	652,330 sq. km. (251,864 sq. mi.)	7th	990,237	6th	1905	Regina	*Multis E Gentibus Vires* (From Many Peoples Strength)
Yukon Territory (YT)	483,450 sq. km. (186,660 sq. mi.)	9th	30,766	12th	1898	Whitehorse	no motto

*All population figures are from the 1996 census, except those for the Northwest Territories and Nunavut, which are estimates from 1999.
**Four provinces—New Brunswick, Nova Scotia, Ontario, and Quebec—were first united in 1867 in a confederation as the Dominion of Canada.

Important Events in American History

1565 • First permanent European settlement in what is now the United States established by the Spanish at St. Augustine (Fla.).

1598 • Spanish begin settlements in what is now New Mexico.

1607 • First permanent English settlement established at Jamestown (Va.).

1620 • Pilgrims land *Mayflower* and establish a colony at Plymouth (Mass.).

1626 • Dutch establish a settlement on what is now Manhattan Island (N.Y.), naming it New Amsterdam.

1629-36 • Colonies established in Massachusetts, Maryland, Connecticut, and Rhode Island.

1643 • New England Confederation, a union of colonies, is governed by the first written constitution in America.

1660 • Parliament introduces Navigation Acts that restrict the shipment of goods to and from the colonies.

1663 • Carolina colony established.

1664 • Duke of York acquires land between the Connecticut and Delaware rivers, naming it New York; later separates a portion for New Jersey colony.

1679-81 • New Hampshire and Pennsylvania colonies established.

1682 • French from Canada explore Mississippi River, claiming entire valley for France and naming the area Louisiana.

1692-93 • Salem witchcraft trials held in Massachusetts.

1704 • Delaware becomes a colony.

1729 • North and South Carolina become colonies.

1732 • Charter granted for Georgia colony.

1749 • Ohio Company organized for colonizing Ohio River Valley, west of the Appalachian Mountains, challenging French dominance in the area.

1754 • Georgia becomes a royal colony.

1763 • After a seven-year war in Europe, France gives to Great Britain all of Canada and Louisiana east of the Mississippi River.

1764 • Parliament passes Sugar Act to raise money in the colonies to pay off war debt; limits much of colonies' independent trade.

1765 • Parliament passes Stamp Act, which is first direct tax on the colonies.

1767 • Townshend Acts: duties imposed on imports to colonies from Britain; colonies resist by boycotting British goods.

1769 • Spanish begin settlements in California.

1770 • Boston Massacre: several colonists shot in clash with British troops at the Customs House.

1773 • Tea Act gives British East India Company a virtual monopoly on tea sales to colonies; Bostonians rebel with Boston Tea Party.

1774 • First Continental Congress meets in Philadelphia to outline grievances with Britain.

1775 • Parliament declares Massachusetts in rebellion; troops sent to restore order. • Minutemen repel British troops at Concord (Mass.); the clash begins the American Revolution. • Second Continental Congress meets in Philadelphia, and serves as the first federal government. • George Washington assumes command of Continental Army. • Kentucky settlements established.

1776 • Continental Congress adopts Declaration of Independence (on July 4).

1777 • Continental Congress adopts Articles of Confederation; ratified by the states by 1781.

1781 • Continental Army, with help from French fleet, defeats British at Yorktown (Va.).

1783 • Revolutionary War ends with Treaty of Paris; America given unlimited independence.

1784 • Russians establish settlements in Alaska.

1787 • Constitutional Convention in Philadelphia drafts a federal Constitution. • Delaware becomes first of the original 13 states to ratify new Constitution.

1789 • George Washington unanimously elected first President. • Congress submits to the states 12 Amendments to the Constitution for ratification; 10 of the 12 are ratified and become the Bill of Rights in 1791.

1790 • First United States census taken.

1791 • Vermont becomes 14th state.

1792 • Kentucky becomes 15th state.

1796 • Tennessee becomes 16th state.

1798 • Mississippi organized as a Territory.

1800 • Washington (D.C.) becomes the seat of government.

1803 • Ohio becomes 17th state. • Louisiana Purchase: President Thomas Jefferson purchases from France all of Louisiana Territory (most of the land between the Mississippi River and Rocky Mountains) for $11,250,000 plus the payment of debts of U.S. citizens to France; U.S. claims western part of Florida as part of purchase.

1804-6 • Lewis and Clark expedition explores Louisiana Territory.

1805 • Michigan organized as a Territory.

1808 • Congress outlaws African slave trade.

1809 • Illinois organized as a Territory.

1812 • Louisiana becomes 18th state.

1814 • "Star-Spangled Banner" written by Francis Scott Key during War of 1812.

1816 • Indiana becomes 19th state.

1817 • Alabama organized as a Territory. • Mississippi becomes 20th state. • Work begins on Erie Canal, 584 km waterway from Hudson River (in N.Y.) to Lake Erie.

1818 • Illinois becomes 21st state.

1819 • U.S. purchases eastern part of Florida from Spain for $5 million. • Arkansas organized as a Territory. • Alabama becomes 22nd state.

1820 • Missouri Compromise: congressional compromise between the forces for and against slavery to balance the number of free and slave states admitted to the Union. • Maine (a free state) and Missouri (a slave state) become 23rd and 24th states.

1821-80 • Santa Fe Trail, from Missouri to New Mexico, becomes a major route to the Southwest.

1822 • U.S. colony established in Texas (part of Mexico).

1823 • Monroe Doctrine advanced by President James Monroe to set out a policy of discouraging further European colonization in the New World.

1830s • Underground Railroad begins and operates for some 30 years as a clandestine route by which fugitive slaves escape from the South.

1836 • Texas declares independence from Mexico after battles, including siege of the Alamo; recognized by U.S. as an independent nation. • Wisconsin organized as a Territory. • Arkansas becomes 25th state.

1837 • Michigan becomes 26th state.

1838 • Trail of Tears: Government removes Indians from homelands in Georgia, Tennessee, Arkansas, and Missouri, and forces them to march overland to reservations in Oklahoma and Kansas. • Iowa organized as a Territory.

1842-60 • Oregon Trail, a 2000-mile trail from Missouri to Oregon, becomes a major route to the West.

1845 • Florida becomes 27th state. • Texas annexed by U.S. and becomes 28th state.

1846 • Iowa becomes 29th state. • Treaty establishes the northwestern border between U.S. and Canada.

1846-8 • War with Mexico, over annexation of Texas; Treaty of Guadalupe Hidalgo in 1848 gives U.S. rights to New Mexico Territory and California; Mexico gives up all claim to Texas in exchange for $15 million.

1847 • Mormons migrate from Iowa to Utah, arriving at the Great Salt Lake Valley.

1848 • Wisconsin becomes 30th state. • Oregon organized as a Territory. • Gold discovered in California. • Women's Rights Convention in Seneca Falls (N.Y.).

1849 • California gold rush. • Minnesota organized as a Territory.

1850 • Compromise of 1850 between forces for and against slavery, admits California as a free state (31st state), establishes Texas boundaries, establishes New Mexico and Utah as Territories, and abolishes slave trade in District of Columbia.

1853 • Gadsden Purchase: U.S. pays Mexico $10 million for 300,000 square miles, now part of Arizona and New Mexico. • Washington organized as a Territory.

1854 • Kansas and Nebraska organized as Territories. • Chinese immigrants begin arriving in large numbers on the West Coast.

1858 • Minnesota becomes 32nd state.

1859 • Oregon becomes 33rd state. • Abolitionist John Brown attacks government arsenal at Harper's Ferry (Va.); becomes symbol for antislavery cause.

1860 • South Carolina secedes from Union after Abraham Lincoln is elected president. • Pony Express begins overland mail service from Missouri to California.

1861 • Transcontinental telegraph line completed. • Mississippi, Florida, Alabama, Georgia, Louisiana, and Texas secede from Union and with South Carolina form Confederate States of America. • Kansas becomes 34th state. • Civil War begins. Virginia, Arkansas, Tennessee, and North Carolina secede and join Confederacy. • Western counties of Virginia separate from Virginia and form West Virginia, the 35th state, loyal to the Union. • Dakota, Colorado, and Nevada organized as Territories.

1863 • Emancipation Proclamation grants freedom to all slaves in the states joining the Confederacy. • Arizona organized as a Territory. • Battle of Gettysburg; casualties for both sides numbered more than 40,000 in three days; Abraham Lincoln's Gettysburg Address given later at the dedication of a cemetery at the battlefield.

1864 • Montana organized as a Territory. • Nevada becomes 36th state.

1865 • Confederate General Lee surrenders to General Grant, ending Civil War. • President Abraham Lincoln is assassinated. • Thirteenth Amendment ratified, abolishing slavery.

1867 • Reconstruction of the former Confederate states begins. • Nebraska becomes 37th state. • Alaska bought from Russia for $7.2 million.

1868 • Wyoming organized as a Territory; grants women the right to vote.

1869 • Union Pacific and Central Pacific Railroad lines join at Promontory (Utah), establishing first transcontinental railroad.

1872 • Yellowstone established as first national park.

1876 • Colorado becomes 38th state. • Alexander Graham Bell demonstrates the telephone.

1878 • Congress establishes local government for the District of Columbia.

1879 • Thomas Edison introduces the modern electric lightbulb.

1881 • President James Garfield is assassinated.

1883 • Four standard time zones adopted by U.S. and Canadian railroads.

1886 • Statue of Liberty dedicated.

1889 • North Dakota, South Dakota, Montana, and Washington become 39th, 40th, 41st, and 42nd states. • Johnstown (Pa.) and four other towns destroyed by flood after dam breaks. • Oklahoma land rush.

1890 • Oklahoma organized as a Territory. • Idaho and Wyoming become 43rd and 44th states. • Wounded Knee (S. Dak.): Some 200 Sioux Indians are massacred by U.S. cavalry forces; this site later becomes a focal point of Native American protests against the government.

1893 • Colorado gives women the right to vote.

1893 • Hawaii Republic established when Queen Liliuokalani is overthrown with American intervention.

1896 • Utah becomes 45th state.

1897 • First subway in North America opens in Boston (Mass.).

1898 • Annexation of Hawaii by U.S. • Spanish-American War: U.S. invades Cuba to ensure Cuban independence from Spain; U.S. declares war on Spain, conquers Puerto Rico, Guam, Philippines; by Treaty of Paris, Spain abandons Cuba, gives Puerto Rico and Guam to U.S.; U.S. gives Spain $20 million for Philippines.

1900 • Orville and Wilbur Wright fly glider at Kitty Hawk (N.C.).

1901 • Oil found in Texas • President William McKinley is assassinated.

1903 • Panama revolts, seeking independence from Colombia; U.S. supports Panama and in treaty gives Panama $10 million plus $250,000 annually for a 10-mile-wide strip for a canal zone. • Orville Wright flies powered airplane.

1904 • Work begins on Panama Canal.

1906 • Earthquake destroys most of San Francisco (Calif.).

1907 • Oklahoma becomes 46th state.

1908 • Henry Ford introduces the Model T automobile.

1909 • NAACP formed.

1912 • New Mexico and Arizona become 47th and 48th states. • Alaska organized as a Territory.

1913 • Sixteenth Amendment ratified, establishing a federal income tax.

1914 • In treaty, U.S. agrees to give Colombia $25 million compensation for taking Panama; treaty not ratified until 1921. • Panama Canal opens.

1917 • U.S. declares war on Germany and enters World War I. • Puerto Rico established as a U.S. Territory. • U.S. buys Virgin Islands (Danish West Indies) from Denmark for $25 million.

1918 • Daylight savings time goes into effect. • Armistice signed, ending World War I.

1920 • Nineteenth Amendment ratified, giving women the right to vote. • Eighteenth Amendment, prohibition, goes into effect.

1925 • Nellie Tayloe Ross becomes governor of Wyoming: first woman governor. • "Monkey trial": John Scopes convicted of teaching the theory of evolution in Tennessee in defiance of state law. • Demonstration of television.

1926 • Robert Goddard successfully tests a liquid-fuel rocket.

1929 • Stock market crash leads to an economic depression.

1931 • "Star-Spangled Banner" officially made the national anthem.

1933 • Prohibition ends with ratification of the 21st Amendment.

1934 • U.S. grants independence to Cuba.

1935 • Social Security is established. • Philippines begins United States Commonwealth status.

1941 • U.S. enters World War II after Japan attacks Pearl Harbor naval base in Hawaii.

1942-45 • Federal government moves more than 100,000 Japanese immigrants and American citizens of Japanese ancestry from the West Coast into inland relocation camps for the duration of the war. • First American jet airplane test flown.

1945 • Germany surrenders. • First use of atomic bombs; bombs dropped by U.S. on Japanese cities of Hiroshima and Nagasaki. • Japan surrenders.

1946 • Philippines granted independence. • First general-purpose electronic digital computer introduced.

1947 • Marshall Plan: Secretary of State George Marshall proposes a plan by which the U.S. contributes to the economic recovery of European countries after World War II. • Transistor is invented.

1948-49 • U.S. and Britain airlift supplies into West Berlin (East Germany) after the Soviet Union blockades surface transport.

1949 • North Atlantic Treaty Organization (NATO) established.

1950-53 • Korean War: U.S. troops are sent to support South Korea after North Korea invades; fighting ends with an armistice. • Guam becomes a U.S. Territory.

1954 • McCarthy hearings: Senate Permanent Subcommittee on Investigations, chaired by Senator Joseph McCarthy, holds televised hearings after McCarthy makes unsubstantiated charges of Communist activity in the U.S. Army and accuses the Democratic Party of treason. • Brown v. Board of Education of Topeka (Kan.): Supreme Court holds that racial segregation violates the Constitution.

1954-59 • St. Lawrence Seaway is constructed.

1956 • Interstate highway system begins.

1958 • U.S. launches first space satellites; begins "space race" with Soviet Union.

1959 • Alaska and Hawaii become 49th and 50th states.

1961 • Astronaut Alan Shepard becomes first American in space.

1962 • Astronaut John Glenn is first American to orbit the earth.

1963 • President John Kennedy is assassinated.

1965-73 • Vietnam War: U.S. troops become directly involved in fighting between North and South Vietnam.

1967 • Thurgood Marshall becomes first African-American Supreme Court justice.

1968 • Civil Rights leader Rev. Martin Luther King, Jr., and presidential candidate Robert Kennedy (brother of John) are assassinated.

1969 • U.S. mission lands on the moon; American astronaut Neil Armstrong becomes first person to walk on the Moon.

1971 • Twenty-sixth Amendment ratified, giving 18-year-olds the right to vote in national elections.

1974 • President Richard Nixon resigns from office after Watergate scandal.

1977 • Treaty (approved by Senate in 1978) gives complete control of Panama Canal to Panama by the year 2000.

1979 • Iranian militants seize the U.S. embassy in Tehran and hold 90 hostages (63 Americans) for more than a year. • Nuclear reactor at Three Mile Island (Pa.) undergoes a partial meltdown.

1981 • Sandra Day O'Connor becomes first woman Supreme Court justice. • Space shuttle *Columbia* completes maiden voyage, becoming the first reusable spacecraft.

1986 • Space shuttle *Challenger* explodes after liftoff, killing all seven astronauts aboard, including Christa McAuliffe, a schoolteacher, who was to be the first private citizen in space.

1991 • Persian Gulf War: U.S. armed forces, supported by a coalition of nations, help liberate Kuwait after earlier invasion by Iraq.

Important Events in Canadian History

1497 • John Cabot reaches North America, possibly at Newfoundland or Cape Breton Island.

1535 • Jacques Cartier visits and names Mount Royal.

1541 • Jacques Cartier and the Sieur de Roberval establish the first French settlement in North America at Charlesbourg-Royal.

1576 • Martin Frobisher reaches Frobisher Bay.

1587 • John Davis reaches the entrance to Baffin Bay.

1608 • Samuel de Champlain founds Quebec.

1610 • Henry Hudson sails into Hudson Bay and reaches James Bay.

1611 • The Jesuits form a mission in Acadia.

1627 • The French form the Company of One Hundred Associates.

1666 • Canada's first official census reports 3,215 non-native inhabitants in New France.

1670 • The Hudson's Bay Company is founded.

1697 • The French and English sign the Treaty of Ryswick.

1713 • English and French colony boundaries established by the Treaty of Utrecht.

1745 • The governor of Massachusetts captures Louisbourg from the French.

1748 • Treaty of Aix-la-Chapelle is signed, returning Louisbourg to the French.

1752 • The first issue of the Halifax *Gazette*, Canada's first newspaper, is released.

1755 • The British exile the Acadians from Nova Scotia after the Acadians refuse to swear allegiance to Britain.

1756 • The Seven Years' War begins between Britain and France.

1759 • English general Wolfe defeats French general Montcalm on the Plains of Abraham.

1763 • The Treaty of Paris is signed, giving Britain control of French colonies in North America.

1774 • The Quebec Act provides for the practice of Catholicism and the use of French civil law in Quebec.

1775 • Americans attack Quebec.

1778 • Captain James Cook sails into Nootka Sound on Vancouver Island.

1780 • The Loyalists begin to arrive in Canada.

1783 • The boundary between Canada and the United States is established.

1784 • New Brunswick is formed • The North West Company is established, in competition with the Hudson's Bay Company.

1789 • Alexander Mackenzie discovers the Mackenzie River and reaches the Beaufort Sea.

1791 • Constitutional Act establishes Upper and Lower Canada.

1792 • Captain George Vancouver explores the west coast.

1793 • Alexander Mackenzie reaches the Pacific Ocean via an overland route.

1808 • Simon Fraser follows the Fraser River to the Pacific.

1811 • David Thompson follows the Columbia River to the Pacific • John McIntosh discovers the McIntosh apple.

1812 • The War of 1812 begins, when the U.S. declares war on Britain.

1814 • The Treaty of Ghent is signed, ending the War of 1812.

1821 • The Hudson's Bay Company and the North West Company unite.

1827 • Nancy Shanawdithit, the last of the Beothuk people, dies in St. John's.

1834 • Emancipation Act abolishes slavery in the British empire, including Canada.

1839 • Lord Durham's report recommends that Upper and Lower Canada be joined and that a responsible government be established.

1841 • The Act of Union unites Upper and Lower Canada and establishes an appointed legislative council and an elected House of Assembly.

1843 • Fort Victoria is established on Vancouver Island.

1845 • Sir John Franklin sets out in search of the Northwest Passage.

1848 • A responsible government is established.

1855 • The first recorded game of hockey is played in Kingston, Ontario.

1857 • Queen Victoria names Ottawa capital of Canada.

1858 • The Fraser River gold rush begins.

1864 • The Charlottetown Conference lays the groundwork for confederation.

1866 • The London Conference establishes the basis for the British North America Act.

1867 • Dominion of Canada created with the proclamation of the British North America Act • Sir John A. Macdonald becomes Canada's first prime minister.

1869 • The Red River Rebellion begins, and Louis Riel forms a provisional government.

1870 • British government cedes control of the North-Western Territory to Canada • Hudson's Bay Company sells Rupert's Land to the Canadian government • The province of Manitoba is created • Louis Riel leads a Métis rebellion.

1871 • British Columbia enters confederation.

1873 • Prince Edward Island joins Canada • Alexander Mackenzie becomes prime minister.

1878 • Sir John A. Macdonald becomes prime minister.

1881 • The Canadian Pacific Railway is established • Chinese immigrants arrive to work on the railway.

1885 • The transcontinental railway is completed with the driving of the last spike in Eagle Pass, British Columbia • Louis Riel is hanged after the North West Rebellion • The government imposes a head tax on Chinese immigrants.

1891 • Sir John Abbott becomes prime minister.

1892 • Sir John Thompson becomes prime minister.

1894 • Sir Mackenzie Bowell becomes prime minister.

1896 • Sir Charles Tupper becomes prime minister • Sir Wilfrid Laurier becomes prime minister.

1897 • The Klondike gold rush begins.

1898 • The Yukon Territory is established • Several thousand Doukhobors immigrate to Canada.

1899 • Canadian troops fight in the Boer War.

1901 • Anna Elson Taylor becomes the first person to be carried over Niagara Falls in a barrel.

1903 • The Alaska Boundary Dispute is resolved in favor of the U.S., after British representative Lord Alverstone votes for the American viewpoint.

1905 • The provinces of Alberta and Saskatchewan are created.

1911 • Robert Borden becomes prime minister.

1914 • Canada is at war with Germany when Britain declares war • Parliament passes the War Measures Act.

1915 • Canadian troops fight in the Battle of Ypres, where they face poison gas.

1916 • Manitoba grants women the right to vote, after the movement led by Nellie McClung.

1917 • Conscription leads to the Conscription Crisis in Quebec • Munitions ship explodes in the Halifax harbor, killing almost 2,000 people • Louise McKinney is elected to the Alberta legislature, becoming the first woman in the British Empire to be elected to a legislative assembly • Canadian troops capture Vimy Ridge. Eleven thousand are killed.

1918 • First World War ends.

1920 • Canada becomes member of the League of Nations • Arthur Meighen becomes prime minister.

1921 • Mackenzie King becomes prime minister • Frederick Banting and Charles H. Best discover insulin at the University of Toronto.

1922 • Joseph-Armand Bombardier invents the snowmobile.

1923 • Canadian National Railways is established.

1926 • Arthur Meighen becomes prime minister • Mackenzie King becomes prime minister.

1929 • Great Depression begins • Due to the efforts of women such as Emily Murphy and Nellie McClung, the Privy Council rules that women are persons.

1930 • Richard B. Bennett becomes prime minister.

1931 • Statute of Westminster allows Canada authority over domestic and foreign affairs.

1934 • The Bank of Canada is established • The Dionne quintuplets are born.

1935 • "On to Ottawa Trek" by unemployed men leads to a riot in Regina • Mackenzie King becomes prime minister.

1937 • The first Governor General's Awards are announced.

1939 • Canada declares war on Germany • Parliament founds the National Film Board of Canada.

1941 • Canada declares war on Japan, and the government interns Japanese citizens.

1945 • War in Europe ends • Canada becomes a member of the United Nations.

1947 • Chinese immigrants gain the right to vote.

1948 • Louis St. Laurent becomes prime minister.

1949 • Newfoundland joins Canada.

1950 • Canadian troops fight in the Korean War.

1953 • The National Library is established.

1955 • Marilyn Bell swims the English Channel.

1957 • John Diefenbaker becomes prime minister • Paliament establishes the Canada Council for the Arts • Lester B. Pearson wins the Nobel Peace Prize.

1962 • The New Democratic Party introduces Medicare in Saskatchewan • The Trans-Canada Highway is officially opened.

1963 • Lester B. Pearson becomes prime minister.

1967 • Montreal hosts Expo '67.

1968 • Pierre Elliott Trudeau becomes prime minister.

1969 • English and French are named Canada's official languages.

1971 • Greenpeace is formed in Vancouver.

1975 • CN Tower is completed.

1979 • Joe Clark becomes prime minister.

1980 • Terry Fox begins his "Marathon of Hope" • Pierre Elliott Trudeau becomes prime minister • Quebec votes against sovereignty-association in a referendum.

1981 • The Canadarm is used for the first time in space on the shuttle *Columbia*.

1983 • Jeanne Sauvé becomes the first female governor general.

1984 • John Turner becomes prime minister • Brian Mulroney becomes prime minister.

1986 • Vancouver hosts Expo '86.

1989 • Free Trade between Canada and the U.S. begins • Goods and Services Tax introduced.

1990 • The Meech Lake Accord fails.

1991 • Rita Johnston becomes premier of British Columbia and Canada's first female premier.

Math Refresher

Fractions

Simple or common fractions are those having a **numerator**, or top number, that is smaller than the **denominator**, or bottom number. The fraction $\frac{3}{4}$ is a simple fraction. An **improper fraction** is one in which the numerator is larger than the denominator. The fraction $\frac{14}{12}$ is an improper fraction.

Fractions can often be **reduced** to a smaller fraction with the same value but with a smaller numerator and denominator. The fraction $\frac{2}{4}$ can be reduced to $\frac{1}{2}$, which has the same value, and $\frac{6}{8}$ can be reduced to $\frac{3}{4}$. Any improper fraction can be reduced to a **mixed number**, that is, one that is the sum of a whole number and a simple fraction (such as $\frac{3}{2}$, which can be reduced to $1\frac{1}{2}$).

To reduce a simple fraction, it is necessary to discover a common **factor** of the numerator and denominator. (Factors are two numbers that can be multiplied together to produce a given number. The number 6, for example, has 2 and 3 as factors.) When the numerator and denominator have a common factor, they can both be divided by that common factor. (This is the same as canceling out these common factors.)

$$\frac{12}{16} = \frac{4 \times 3}{4 \times 4} = \frac{3}{4}$$

$$\frac{10}{15} = \frac{2 \times 5}{3 \times 5} = \frac{2}{3}$$

To reduce an improper fraction to a mixed number, divide the numerator by the denominator. This gives a whole number and possibly a remainder. Any remainder can be expressed in the numerator of a simple fraction over the original denominator. This simple fraction may be further reduced, if necessary.

$$\frac{14}{12} = 14 \div 12 = 1\frac{2}{12} = 1\frac{1}{6}$$

$$\frac{13}{5} = 13 \div 5 = 2\frac{3}{5}$$

Changing a mixed number to an improper fraction involves addition of fractions, and this will be covered after the discussion of adding and subtracting fractions.

Multiplying and Dividing Fractions

In multiplying two fractions, the numerators are multiplied and the denominators are multiplied, regardless of whether or not they are the same.

$$\frac{2}{5} \times \frac{7}{6} = \frac{2 \times 7}{5 \times 6} = \frac{14}{30} = \frac{7}{15}$$

Dividing fractions is a matter of multiplying one fraction, the **dividend,** by the **reciprocal** of the other, the **divisor.** (The reciprocal of a fraction is the result of reversing the positions of the numerator and denominator—turning the fraction upside down.)

$$\frac{7}{9} \div \frac{1}{5} = \frac{7}{9} \times \frac{5}{1} = \frac{7 \times 5}{9 \times 1} = \frac{35}{9} = 3\frac{8}{9}$$

Adding and Subtracting Fractions

In order to add or subtract two fractions, they need to have the same denominator. If they already have the same denominator, simply add or subtract the numerators and put the result over the common denominator. If the denominators are not the same, one or more of the fractions has to be converted so that both have a common denominator. Find the lowest number for the denominator that is common to both (the **lowest common denominator**, or **LCD**), that is, the lowest number that has both denominators as factors. One way is to multiply each denominator successively by 1, 2, 3, etc., until you find a multiple that the denominators have in common. This lowest common multiple is the lowest common denominator.

To find the LCD of the fractions $\frac{3}{4}$ and $\frac{1}{6}$, list the multiples of each denominator:

multiples of 4: 4, 8, 12, 16, 20...
multiples of 6: 6, 12, 18, 24...

The lowest common multiple is 12, which is the lowest common denominator.

Once the LCD is found, the fractions have to be converted to equivalent fractions with the common denominators. To do this, find the factors of the LCD that include the first denominator and the factors of the LCD that include the second denominator. In the example above, the factors of 12 that include the denominator 4 are 3 and 4; the factors of 12 that include the denominator 6 are 2 and 6.

To keep the same value in the new fraction, it is necessary to multiply both the numerator and the denominator by the same number—which is the same as multiplying the fraction by another fraction equal to 1—and this same number is the factor that will result in the LCD—12 in this example. For the fraction $\frac{3}{4}$, that would be $\frac{3}{3}$; for $\frac{1}{6}$, it would be $\frac{2}{2}$.

$$\frac{3}{4} + \frac{1}{6} = \frac{3 \times 3}{4 \times 3} + \frac{1 \times 2}{6 \times 2} = \frac{9}{12} + \frac{2}{12} = \frac{11}{12}$$

To find the LCD of the fractions $\frac{2}{3}$ and $\frac{4}{5}$, write out the multiples or multiply the denominators together: 3 x 5 = 15

$$\frac{2}{3} + \frac{4}{5} = \frac{2 \times 5}{3 \times 5} + \frac{4 \times 3}{5 \times 3} = \frac{10}{15} + \frac{12}{15} = \frac{22}{15} = 1\frac{7}{15}$$

To subtract, create fractions with the LCD and then perform subtraction:

$$\frac{9}{14} - \frac{1}{7} = \frac{9}{14} - \frac{1 \times 2}{7 \times 2} = \frac{9}{14} - \frac{2}{14} = \frac{7}{14} = \frac{1}{2}$$

To change a mixed number to an improper fraction, convert the whole number to a fraction having the same denominator as the fractional part and then add the two fractions together. A whole number is the same as a fraction with that number over "1," and any fraction equal to "1" will have the same number in the numerator and the denominator. Thus, the conversion involves putting the whole number over "1" and multiplying it by a fraction consisting of the value of the original denominator over itself.

$$2\frac{2}{3} = \left(\frac{2 \times 3}{1 \times 3}\right) + \frac{2}{3} = \frac{6}{3} + \frac{2}{3} = \frac{8}{3}$$

Decimal Numbers

Numbers that include a decimal point are considered fractions in which the numerator is the part to the right of the decimal and the denominator is always 10 or a multiple of 10, depending on the number of decimal places. The number 5.3 is a **decimal number** that is the equivalent of a mixed number with 5 as the whole number and $\frac{3}{10}$ as the fraction, and the number 16.348 is equivalent to a mixed number with 16 as the whole number and $\frac{348}{1000}$ as the fraction.

Each position to the right of any given decimal position is one-tenth the value of the position before. Thus, the first position to the right of the decimal point represents tenths; the next position to the right, hundredths; the third position, thousandths; and so on.

To convert a decimal number into a fraction, the whole number is unchanged and the decimal portion is placed over the appropriate power of 10 (depending on the number of digits).

$$1.3 = 1\frac{3}{10}$$

$$3.25 = 3\frac{25}{100}$$

$$2.325 = 2\frac{325}{1000}$$

To convert a fraction into a decimal number, divide the numerator by the denominator.

$$\frac{1}{2} = 1 \div 2 = .5$$

$$\frac{3}{16} = 3 \div 16 = .1875$$

Percent

The word **percent** means "per hundred" or "in a hundred" or "of one hundred parts." In other words, a number expressed as a percent is the number of parts out of 100 possible parts. Percents are often written with a percent sign (%). Thus, 10 percent, or 10%, means "10 parts in 100." A U.S. dollar can be divided into 100 cents, so a quarter (25 cents) can be said to have a value that is 25% of a dollar (a quarter-dollar).

To convert a decimal to a percent, multiply the decimal number by 100 (or move the decimal point two places to the right) and add the percent sign.

$$.35 = \frac{35}{100} \times \frac{100}{1} = 35\%$$

$$3.14 = 314\%$$

To convert percent to a decimal number, remove the percent sign and divide by 100 (or move the decimal point two places to the left).

$$1.6\% = \frac{1.6}{100} = .016$$

$$30.25\% = .3025$$

Exponents and Powers

When a number is multiplied by itself, the result is the **square** of the number. When 2 is multiplied by 2 (2 x 2) the result is 4; thus, 4 is the square of 2. When 5 is multiplied by 5, the result is 25; thus, 25 is the square of 5.

This operation can also be expressed by the use of a small, raised number to the right of the factor, called an **exponent**, as 2^2 or 5^2. The exponent tells the number of times the number is taken as a factor in multiplication. Thus, 2^2 and 5^2 can be read as "two squared" and "five squared." The exponent also indicates the **power** of the number. Power indicates the number of times a number is used as a factor (2^2 is read "two to the second power," and 5^2, "five to the second power").

$$3^3 = 3 \times 3 \times 3$$

$$5^4 = 5 \times 5 \times 5 \times 5$$

Exponents can also be negative as well as positive. Where positive exponents indicate the number of times the number itself is used as a factor in multiplication, negative exponents indicate the number of times the reciprocal of the number is used in multiplication. The reciprocal of a whole number is a fraction consisting of "1" over the number.

$$2^{-2} = \frac{1}{2} \times \frac{1}{2} = \frac{1}{4}$$

$$5^{-4} = \frac{1}{5} \times \frac{1}{5} \times \frac{1}{5} \times \frac{1}{5} = \frac{1}{625}$$

Scientific Notation

Just as exponents are a form of shorthand for indicating operations, **scientific notation** is a form of shorthand for representing large numbers. In scientific notation, a large number is shown as a whole number having a value between 1 and 9 and having a decimal part. This is multiplied by a specified power of 10 (indicated by the exponent).

$$225 = 2.25 \times 10^2$$

The scientific notation has little value in such a small number as 225, but for large numbers, it is quite useful. Take the distance light travels in one year, called a light-year. This is estimated to be about 9,460,000,000,000 kilometers—that's "trillion" kilometers. To write it out takes 10 zeros, but in scientific notation, it can be represented in a much more compact form.

$$9.46 \times 10^{12} \text{ } kilometers$$

On electronic calculators that do not indicate the exponent as a small, raised number, scientific notation is normally indicated by a capital "E," which stands in place of the "x 10" in the previous example and indicates what follows is the exponent of the "10."

The positive exponent shows the number of times 10 is multiplied by itself. It has the effect of moving the decimal point the indicated number of places to the right (to make the number larger). A negative exponent indicates the number of times the reciprocal of 10 ("1" over "10") is multiplied by itself. It has the effect of moving the decimal point the indicated number of places to the left (to make the number smaller). Thus, while something like 1.23×10^8 is a very large number (123,000,000)—the multiplication moves the decimal point 8 places to the right, the number 1.23×10^{-8} is a very small number (.0000000123)—the multiplication moves the decimal point 8 places to the left.

Area Measurements

(The examples given here are arbitrary; they can be in any linear measurements, feet, centimeters, inches, meters, etc.

Regardless of the measurement used or the type of plane figure, the area is expressed in "square" measurement, that is, square feet, square centimeters, etc.)

A flat, closed figure—that is, one in which all sides come together—is named according to the number of sides it has. A three-sided figure is a **triangle**, a four-sided figure is a **quadrilateral**, a five-sided figure is a **pentagon**, and so forth.

The most common quadrilateral figures are the **square**, which is a four-sided figure with all sides the same length and all angles the same, and the **rectangle**, a four-sided figure with all angles the same, but only opposite sides the same size. Whether one is talking about a square or a rectangle, one side is considered the length, and an adjacent side is considered the width. To find the area of a square or rectangle, simply multiply the length by the width.

$$A = l \times w$$

$A(1) = 4 \times 4 = 16 \; square \; feet$ (1)

4'
4'

$A(2) = 5 \times 4.2 = 21 \; square \; meters$ (2)

4.2m
5m

To find the area of a figure that can be viewed as a combination of rectangles, simply find the areas of each component rectangle and add the areas together:

$$A = A(1) + A(2)$$

$$A(1) = 12 \times 3 = 36$$

$$A(2) = 5 \times 4 = 20$$

$$A = 36 + 20 = 56 \; square \; meters$$

3m
8m
12m (1)
5m
(2) 4m
8m

There are other kinds of four-sided figures: A **parallelogram** is like a rectangle in that opposite sides are parallel, but all four angles are not the same.

$$A = b \times h$$

h = 1.5m
b = 3m

$$A = 3 \times 1.5 = 4.5 \; square \; meters$$

A **trapezoid** is another four-sided figure that is not a rectangle. It is a figure with one set of opposite sides parallel to each other but with the other set not parallel to each other.

$$A = \frac{1}{2}(a + b) \times h$$

a = 3"
h = 2.5"
b = 4.5"

$$A = \frac{1}{2}(3 + 4.5) \times 2.5 = 8.625 \; square \; inches$$

A triangle, which has three sides, has many forms. The **right triangle** is one in which one side is perpendicular to another. An **isosceles triangle** has two sides of equal length. An **equi-**

lateral triangle is one in which all three sides are equal in length.

To find the area of a triangle, it is necessary to determine the base and the height. Any side can serve as the base, but in a right triangle, the base is usually one of the sides adjacent to the right angle. The height is the distance from the base to the opposite angle. For a right triangle, the height is the side that is perpendicular to the base.

$$A = \frac{1}{2}b \times h$$

h = .4"
b = 3"

$$A = \frac{1}{2}(3) \times .4 = 1.5 \times .4 = .6 \; square \; inches$$

The area of any other plane **polygon**, that is, any other plane figure with three or more sides, would be a combination of all of the enclosed, non-overlapping quadrilateral and triangle areas.

$$A = Aa + Ab + Ac$$

a b c

A **circle** is a closed plane figure with no angles. The formula for finding the area of a circle is:

$$A = \pi r^2$$

d = 4 cm
r = 2 cm

The character π represents the ratio of the circumference to the diameter and has the rounded-off value of 3.1416; r is the radius, or one-half the diameter.

$$A = 3.1416 \times 2^2 = 3.1416 \times (2 \times 2)$$

$$= 12.5664 \; square \; centimeters$$

Conversion from Fahrenheit to Celsius and from Celsius to Fahrenheit

For converting from Fahrenheit to Celsius, subtract 32 from the starting temperature and multiply by $\frac{5}{9}$. To convert a temperature of 72° Fahrenheit to Celsius:

$$(72 - 32) \times \frac{5}{9} = 40 \times \frac{5}{9} = 22.2°C$$

To convert from Celsius to Fahrenheit, multiply the starting temperature by $\frac{9}{5}$ and add 32. To convert 40° Celsius to Fahrenheit:

$$(40 \times \frac{9}{5}) + 32 = 72 + 32 = 104°F$$

Weights and Measures

Length

UNIT (abbreviation)	EQUIVALENTS (same system)	METRIC EQUIVALENT
mile (mi)	5280 feet, 1760 yards	1.609 kilometers
rod (rd)	5.50 yards, 16.5 feet	5.029 meters
yard (yd)	3 feet, 36 inches	0.9144 meter
foot (ft or ')	12 inches, 1/3 yard	30.48 centimeters
inch (in or ")		2.54 centimeters

Area

UNIT (abbreviation)	EQUIVALENTS (same system)	METRIC EQUIVALENT
square mile (sq mi, mi²)	640 acres	2.590 square kilometers
acre	4840 square yards, 43,560 square feet	4047 square meters
square rod (sq rd, rd²)	30.25 square yards	25.293 square meters
square yard (sq yd, yd²)	1296 square inches, 9 square feet	0.836 square meter
square foot (sq ft, ft²)	144 square inches	0.093 square meter
square inch (sq in, in²)		6.452 square centimeters

Volume

UNIT (abbreviation)	EQUIVALENTS (same system)	METRIC EQUIVALENT
cubic yard (cu yd, yd³)	27 cubic feet, 46,656 cubic inches	0.765 cubic meter
cubic foot (cu ft, ft³)	1728 cubic inches	0.028 cubic meter
cubic inch (cu in, in³)		16.387 cubic centimeters

Weight

UNIT (abbreviation)	EQUIVALENTS (same system)	METRIC EQUIVALENT
avoirdupois		
ton		
short ton	20 short cwt, 2000 pounds	0.907 metric ton
long ton	20 long cwt, 2240 pounds	1.016 metric tons
hundredweight (cwt)		
short cwt	100 pounds	45.359 kilograms
long cwt	112 pounds	50.802 kilograms
pound (lb, #)	16 ounces, 7000 grains	0.454 kilogram
ounce (oz)	16 drams, 437.5 grains	28.350 grams
dram (dr)	27.344 grains	1.772 grams
grain (gr)		0.0648 gram
troy		
pound (lb t)	12 ounces, 5760 grains	0.373 kilogram
ounce (oz t)	20 pennyweight, 480 grains	31.103 grams
pennyweight (dwt, pwt)	24 grains, 1/20 ounce	1.555 grams
grain (gr)		0.0648 gram
apothecaries'		
pound (lb ap)	12 ounces, 5760 grains	0.373 kilogram
ounce (oz ap)	8 drams, 480 grains	31.103 grams
dram (dr ap)	3 scruples, 60 grains	3.888 grams
scruple (s ap)	20 grains, 1/3 dram	1.296 grams
grain (gr)		0.0648 gram

Capacity

UNIT (abbreviation)	EQUIVALENTS (same system)	METRIC EQUIVALENT
U.S. liquid measure		
gallon (gal)	4 quarts	3.785 liters
quart (qt)	2 pints	0.946 liter
pint (pt)	4 gills	0.473 liter
gill (gi)	4 fluidounces	118.294 milliliters
fluidounce (fl oz)	8 fluidrams	29.573 milliliters
fluidram (fl dr)	60 minims	3.697 milliliters
minim (min)	1/60 fluidram	0.061 milliliter
U.S. dry measure		
bushel (bu)	4 pecks	35.239 liters
peck (pk)	8 quarts	8.810 liters
quart (qt)	2 pints	1.101 liters
pint (pt)	1/2 quart	0.551 liter

METRIC SYSTEM

Length

UNIT (abbreviation)	METERS	U.S. EQUIVALENT
kilometer (km)	1,000	0.62 mile
hectometer (hm)	100	109.36 yards
dekameter (dam)	10	32.81 feet
meter (m)	1	39.37 inches
decimeter (dm)	1/10	3.94 inches
centimeter (cm)	1/100	0.39 inch
millimeter (mm)	1/1000	0.039 inch

Area

UNIT (abbreviation)	SQUARE METERS	U.S. EQUIVALENT
square kilometer (sq km, km^2)	1,000,000	0.3861 square mile
hectare (ha)	10,000	2.47 acres
are (a)	100	119.60 square yards
square centimeter (sq cm, cm^2)	1/10000	0.155 square inch

Volume

UNIT (abbreviation)	CUBIC CENTIMETERS	U.S. EQUIVALENT
cubic meter (m^3)	1,000,000	1.307 cubic yards
cubic decimeter (dm^3)	1,000	61.023 cubic inches
cubic centimeter (cm^3, cc)	1	0.061 cubic inch

Capacity

UNIT (abbreviation)	LITERS	U.S. EQUIVALENT	
		dry	liquid
kiloliter (kl)	1,000		
hectoliter (hl)	100	2.84 bushels	
dekaliter (dal)	10	1.14 pecks	2.64 gallons
liter (l)	1	0.908 quart	1.057 quarts
deciliter (dl)	1/10	0.18 pint	0.21 pint
centiliter (cl)	1/100	0.338 fluidounce	
milliliter (ml)	1/1000		0.27 fluidram

Mass and Weight

UNIT (abbreviation)	GRAMS	U.S. EQUIVALENT	
metric ton (t)	1,000,000	1.102	short tons
kilogram (kg)	1,000	2.2046	pounds
hectogram (hg)	100	3.527	ounces
dekagram (dag)	10	0.353	ounce
gram (g)	1	0.035	ounce
decigram (dg)	1/10	1.543	grains
centigram (cg)	1/100	0.154	grain
milligram (mg)	1/1000	0.015	grain

PLANETS OF THE SOLAR SYSTEM

SYMBOL	NAME	MEAN DISTANCE FROM THE SUN (million miles)	PERIOD OF REVOLUTION	EQUATORIAL DIAMETER (in miles)
☿	Mercury	36.0	87.97 days	3,032
♀	Venus	67.2	224.70 days	7,523
☉	Earth	92.9	365.26 days	7,928
♂	Mars	141.5	686.98 days	4,218
♃	Jupiter	483.4	11.86 years	88,900
♄	Saturn	884.6	29.46 years	74,900
♅	Uranus	1783.8	84.01 years	31,800
♆	Neptune	2793.9	164.79 years	30,800
♇	Pluto	3690.5	247.69 years	1,400